SOTHEBY'S
INTERNATIONAL PRICE GUIDE

SOTHEBY'S
INTERNATIONAL PRICE GUIDE

1985-86 EDITION

(including 1984 prices)

General Editor: John L. Marion

THE VENDOME PRESS
NEW YORK   PARIS

Produced and designed by Philip Wilson Publishers Ltd
Russell Chambers, Covent Garden, London WC2E 8AA

Designers: Theo Hodges and Christopher Matthews

Photographs copyright © Sotheby's, 1985
Text copyright © Sotheby's, Hachette, Philip Wilson Publishers Ltd, 1985

First published in Great Britain by Penguin Books Ltd
Harmondsworth, Middlesex

First published in the United States of America by
The Vendome Press, 515 Madison Avenue, N.Y., N.Y. 10022
Distributed in the United States of America by
Rizzoli International Publications, 597 Fifth Avenue, N.Y., N.Y. 10017
Distributed in Canada by Methuen Publications

Library of Congress Cataloging-in-Publication Data
Main entry under title:
Sotheby's international price guide.
1. Sotheby's (Firm) — Prices. 2. Antiques —
Prices. I. Marion, John. II. Sotheby's (Firm)
NK1133.S68 1985 707'.5 8515730

ISBN 0-86565-055-1
ISBN 0-86565-060-8 (pbk.)

Printed and bound in France by Offset-Aubin a Poitiers

Contents

Bold headings indicate main sections; inset italic headings indicate articles within these sections.

Sotheby's Expert Departments

American Furniture & Folk Art
Leslie Keno (New York)
Nancy Druckman (New York)

Antiquities
Felicity Nicholson (London)
Richard M Keresey (New York)

Arms and Armour
Michael Baldwin (London)
J David Wille (New York)

Asian Art
Brendan Lynch (London)

Ceramics
David Battie (London)
Letitia Roberts (New York)

Chinese Works of Art
Colin Mackay (London)
Timothy S Sammons (New York)

Clocks and Watches
Tina Millar (London)
John Vaughan (London)
Kevin Tierney (New York)
Daryn Schnipper (New York)

Collectors' Items
Hilary Kay (London)
Jon Baddeley (London)
Dana Hawkes (New York)

Decorative Arts
Philippe Garner (London)
Nicola Redway (London)
Barbara E Deisroth (New York)
Sarah Hill (New York)

English Furniture
Graham Child (London)
George Read (New York)

European Furniture
Jonathan Bourne (London)
Thierry Millerand (New York)

European Works of Art
George Hughes-Hartman (London)
Elizabeth Wilson (London)
J David Wille (New York)

19th Century Furniture and Works of Art including Bronzes
Robert Bowman (London)
Christopher Payne (London)
Elaine Whitmire (New York)

Glass and Paperweights
Perran Wood (London)
Debe Cuevas (New York)

Islamic Art
Jack Franses (London)
Richard M Keresey (New York)

Japanese Works of Art
Neil Davey (London)
Jane Oliver (New York)

Jewellery
David Bennett (London)
Jacqueline Fay (New York)

Judaica
Camilla Previte (London)
Harry Charteris (London)
Jay Weinstein (New York)

Medals
Michael Naxton (London)

Musical Instruments
Graham Wells (London)
Charles Rudig (New York)

Objects of Vertu
Richard Allen (London)
Julia Clarke (London)
Gerard Hill (New York)

Pre-Columbian Art
Fatma Turkkan-Wille (New York)

Rugs and Carpets
Jack Franses (London)
William Ruprecht (New York)

Russian Works of Art
Heinrich Graf von Spreti (London)
Gerard Hill (New York)

Silver
Eleanor Thompson (London)
Peter Waldron (London)
Kevin Tierney (New York)
Ian Irving (New York)

Sporting Guns
James Booth (Sussex & London)

Tribal Art
Roberto Fainello (London)
Ellen Napiura (New York)

> Departments not included in this guide can be found listed in catalogues.

Sotheby's Principal Auction Locations

United Kingdom
34-35 New Bond Street,
London W1A 2AA.
Telephone (01) 493 8080.

Booth Mansion,
28 Watergate Street,
Chester,
Cheshire CH1 2NA.
Telephone (0244) 315531.

Summers Place,
Billinghurst,
Sussex RH14 9AD.
Telephone (040 381) 3933

United States
1334 York Avenue,
New York,
N.Y. 10021.
Telephone (212) 606 7000.

Holland
102 Rokin,
1012 KZ Amsterdam.
Telephone (20) 246 215.

Hong Kong
PO Box 83,
705 Lane Crawford House,
64-70 Queen's Road Central,
Hong Kong.
Telephone (5) 248 121.

Italy
Palazzo Capponi,
Via Gino Capponi 26,
50121 Florence.
Telephone (55) 2479021.

Monaco
Le Sporting d'Hiver,
Place du Casino,
MC 98001 Monaco Cedex.
Telephone (93) 30 88 80.

South Africa
4th Floor,
Total House,
Smit Street,
Cnr. Rissik Street,
Braamfontein,
Johannesburg.
Telephone (11) 339 3726/7.

Spain
Plaza de la Independencia 8,
Madrid 28001.
Telephone (1) 232 6488 & 6572.

Switzerland
24 Rue de la Cité,
CH 1204 Geneva.
Telephone (22) 21 3377.

20 Bleicherweg, CH-8022,
Zurich.
Telephone (1) 202 0011.

Preface

It is a distinct pleasure to introduce this new guide, the first of an annual series designed to illustrate the wealth of decorative works of art available at auction and to serve as a ready reference to the value of individual works of art.

Compiled in collaboration with Sotheby's staff of experts worldwide, this is the first price guide for collectors that is fully international. Some 8,000 objects are included, representing the decorative arts—rugs and carpets, furniture, silver, porcelain—as well as Western antiquities and Oriental art, medals, and jewels for the collector. All of these passed through Sotheby's salerooms during 1984, the majority in London and New York, but with examples also drawn from Amsterdam, Florence, Hong Kong, Geneva, Johannesburg, Monte Carlo and many other venues.

During every auction season, there are dramatic moments and high, even record, prices for the rarest and most beautiful works of art. This guide, however, is not intended as a record of these outstanding highlights of the year. Rather, most of the pieces included were selected because they are representative of the various types of object handled by each department at Sotheby's and because they are accessible to most collectors. Generally, these works of art were in good condition and realized a price close to our pre-sale estimate.

The guide is organized by collecting area, corresponding with the various departments at Sotheby's. For each section, the London and New York experts in charge have prepared an introductory text that provides an overview of the field and describes its particular characteristics. Most sections also include one or more articles featuring a particular topic. Throughout, the objects illustrated are fully described, with medium and dimensions as well as sale date and price.

The 1970s and 1980s have witnessed a period of tremendous growth in the art market with many new collectors participating in our auctions around the world. Because of this expansion, we are broadening our services to clients and developing new ways of keeping them informed of developments in a vast and ever-changing market. The publication of this guide is one example.

In every field, the development of an educated eye and a knowledge of current values are essential to success in collecting. Study of the illustrations and text of the guide will give an idea of the range of objects that make up the various areas of collecting and a basic introduction to the field and the factors that influence each market. Through this and subsequent editions of the guide, collectors will be able to build a substantial body of reference material that is updated annually and so maintain an illustrated record of each year at auction and the international prices for works of art.

JULIAN THOMPSON
Chairman Sotheby's London and
Sotheby's International

JOHN L. MARION
Chairman Sotheby's
North America

A Guide to Collecting

There are probably few people — certainly few readers of this book — who have never collected, whether it be shells from a beach holiday, cards from cereal packets, stamps or badges. For some, these early beginnings develop into a lifelong passion. Collecting is great fun. People buy for many different reasons — to decorate and furnish a house, to form a collection in a particular field of interest, or to speculate in the hope of making money by buying and selling, as with any other commodity.

Collecting need not be as expensive a pursuit as many would imagine. Some of the objects that pass through the art market are, indeed, immensely valuable. These marvellous things often make headline news and perhaps foster the glamorous image of the art market as a realm of activity reserved exclusively for the very rich. It is not. Works of art and collectors' items are available for everyone to enjoy and the majority of items offered on the art market sell at relatively low prices.

But, regardless of price range, every collector should be knowledgeable about the approximate market value of the objects he or she has collected or intends to collect, since price variations can be confusingly wide, depending on the place and/or manner of purchase. Collectors principally buy at auction, from dealers or from one another. An auction house, like any commercial exchange, is a place where willing sellers and knowledgeable buyers come together for reasons of mutual interest. Consequently, an object sold at auction generally reflects its current fair-market value. A Greek shipping magnate and an international tycoon, bidding against each other, may create an inordinately high world record price or a blizzard may keep a competing dealer and a private collector at home so that a treasure is knocked down below its market worth. And sometimes, of course, a Renaissance masterpiece lurks beneath a 19th century landscape. Such exceptions to the rule, however exciting, are not the subject of the present book.

To create this collector's guide, the publishers asked Sotheby's, the world's largest and most international auction house, to select 8,000 objects representative of all areas of collecting (except, naturally, those of painting, drawings and graphics, which would warrant a similar volume all their own). Each object in the book has been chosen and carefully described as indicative of the price a collector should be prepared to pay or accept. But an encyclopaedic knowledge of art prices is useless without that degree of connoisseurship which is every collector's joy to develop.

The best way of learning about works of art is to handle them. Many budding collectors are intimidated by walking in 'cold' to survey a dealer's wares, although good dealers welcome their interest and can provide truly priceless information. The more public and thus more comfortable venue is the sale-room in an auction house, which may, for that very reason, offer an ideal place to learn, a place where anyone can examine pieces awaiting sale, no matter how valuable. Moreover, the pieces change every week. Knowledge gained in this way must be worked up by reading, by visiting museums and by meeting other collectors with similar interests. Books have been written on almost every conceivable subject, but no amount of reading is a substitute for first hand knowledge. There are also study courses, run by many different organizations, which can assist enormously in developing an appreciation of the fine and decorative arts, as well as many other related subjects, such as interior design and conservation. Once your eye and taste develop, you are well on the way to becoming a collector.

Serious collectors consider numerous factors when buying or selling a work of art. Some like to study a field that interests them before buying into it; others prefer to launch straight into acquisition, gaining knowledge as they collect. Many people feel the need for advice, since only with time can one gain a thorough knowledge of the market. Thus, it is important to create a good relationship with specialists willing to share their love of and enthusiasm for beautiful and interesting objects. Generous-spirited professionals can advise on the quality and condition of any object and the price it is likely to fetch. So much depends today on fashion, the availability of similar pieces and the vagaries of world economics that even the most sophisticated art collectors seek advice. Museum curators spend a good deal of time counselling major collectors, since inheritance taxes inexorably propel important works of art toward public institutions. Enlightened self-interest encourages dealers to help collectors, for this develops their trade. And, finally, the major auction houses are ever ready to service their clients' needs. Collector, dealer, and auctioneer are interdependent entities, all relying on one another to create the conditions in which the art market can thrive and prosper. Modern communication and travel make an auction house accessible to everybody, either through catalogues or by personal visits. The art market is international, and the globe is a collector's oyster. The great auction houses such as Sotheby's, without whom this book would not exist, will inevitably become the habitat of anybody involved in the exciting world of collecting. Thus, a few words on how Sotheby's operate are appropriate here.

The sections into which this book has been divided correspond, for the most part, to the system developed by Sotheby's for handling the decorative arts and collectors' items. Other auction houses may categorise property in a slightly different way. Within Sotheby's each department has its own team of experts, some of whom may specialise in a particular field within that department. The departmental director is often also an auctioneer, so that the same person who accepts an object for sale may well write its catalogue description and 'bring down the hammer' when the item is sold. This continuity is desirable, to the degree that it is important for the person sitting on the rostrum to know the pieces he or she is selling and also know the principal dealers and collectors who may wish to buy.

Sotheby's hold few general sales. In principle, each of their catalogues is restricted to a particular collecting field, such as those categorised in the various sections of this guide. However, most of the catalogues are even more specialized than the categories given here. There may, for instance, be different sales for English and Continental ceramics or for American or 19th-century furniture. The calendar of sales is compiled so that important sales likely to appeal to the same buyers are held at the same time. The timing of dealers' fairs and seminars also plays an important part in deciding when to hold a sale. In this way dealers and collectors from all over the world are certain to be attracted to the event.

It is not necessary to attend an auction in order to make a purchase, though there is no substitute for viewing a prospective purchase before a sale. Regardless of whether you may or may not be able to attend a sale preview, the relevant expert can advise you about matters of quality, condition, etc. He or she will also be happy to discuss the level of bid you should leave, but the final decision on this point must always be yours. Commission bids (those that are operated on your behalf by the staff) can be given by post or telephone. It is also possible to arrange to bid direct by telephone while the sale is in progress. Sales are open to the public free, and it is only for the occasional highly important sale that the auction house issues tickets.

If you wish to buy regularly at auction you should subscribe to catalogues for those sales that interest you. Alternatively, it is possible to buy catalogues individually, beginning about three weeks prior to the sale. Catalogues vary greatly in price, depending on the type of sale.

The catalogue gives a description of the object, shows the price it is estimated to reach and often, but not always, provides some indication of condition. In this regard, many of the entries in the present book give no indication of condition, and readers are asked to bear that in mind when comparing similar pieces. Although only one of the factors that must be considered when making an assessment, condition is often crucial to the value of an object. An understanding of the language used in catalogues is also desirable. Each department has its own terminology, and the most important terms are usually explained at the front of the catalogue, such as those that distinguish between a painting considered to be *by* an artist and one *attributed* to him. Equally, it is important to understand the difference between a 'George III' table and a 'George III *style*' table. A staff member will always explain anything in a catalogue that you do not understand. Most catalogues are profusely illustrated but descriptions or unillustrated items are sufficiently detailed to permit the informed reader unable to view the sale to gain some idea of the piece.

Conditions of sale are printed in every catalogue and should be read by every new buyer. In some countries a sales tax is payable, and there is also a buyer's premium, usually of 10 percent, on top of the hammer price. This should be borne in mind when you are deciding how much to bid. And if, on occasion, the competitive atmosphere of the sale-room impels you to pay more than you had budgeted, think back on the words of the late Nicolas Landau, one of France's greatest dealers in works of art. Landau said that the purchase of any work is the cause of a moment of pain and a lifetime of pleasure.

Collectors' tastes often change, and mortality — alas — assures that we are merely temporary custodians of the beautiful things under our roof. When the moment to sell arrives, therefore, a few details must be kept in mind.

The first step in selling at auction is to obtain a valuation, which is generally given free of charge. If you are unable to bring your property personally, arrange for it to be sent, and you will receive a written valuation. If you have a large collection, or pieces that are not readily transportable, you can ask that a valuator visit your home.

When consigning an object for sale you will need to decide with the expert about the following points:

1. The reserve: This is the price below which the piece cannot be sold. The expert will advise you on the basis of recent auction experience. The reserve is not disclosed to the public and is known only to the client and the auctioneer.

2. The commission rates will be explained together with any other charges, such as local taxes, which may be payable.

3. The property should be insured, unless covered by your own policy, and this can be arranged for you.

4. The type of sale and place of sale must be discussed. Much will depend on the quality of the object.

5. Illustrations in the catalogue and possible advertising must be discussed if the object is of sufficient importance.

Approximately two weeks before the sale the owner will receive a copy of the catalogue. Sales are on view to the public for at least three days immediately preceding the sale. Many owners' like to see their property in Sotheby's galleries and to attend the sale, although this is not necessary. It is not advisable to bid on your own property in an attempt to raise the bidding, since the reserve is fixed to safeguard your interests.

A check for the proceeds of the sale, less any expenses already agreed between you and the expert, will be sent a few weeks after the sale. If an item fails to sell because bidding did not reach the reserve, you will be advised whether to attempt a second sale immediately or to wait for a later date.

The great advantages of selling at auction come from the wide circulation of catalogues, a process that ensures international competition for objects being sold, and the exposure of your piece to the largest and most knowledgeable audience.

Whether buying, selling or merely dreaming about beautiful things, *Sotheby's International Price Guide* will prove to be a priceless companion. Look up your areas of interest, compare the objects, study the prices and articles written by acknowledged international experts, and keep the book in a safe place. This is an annual, and the next edition will implement and update the enormous amount of information the 1985-86 edition presently contains.

The Publishers
New York City, July 6, 1985

An Economic Review of the Art Market

SOTHEBY'S RESEARCH DEPARTMENT

The recovery within the international art market, which has been taking place over the last few years, has revealed the market to be much more responsive to economic and financial stimuli than was previously the case. This may be partly attributed to increasing widespread sophistication among buyers and sellers and their willingness to look beyond their home markets.

As far as financial influences are concerned, volatile exchange rates undoubtedly played the most important role in determining market activity. In particular, the strengthening of the US dollar against the major European currencies, such as Sterling, the Deutschmark, and the Swiss Franc, had a profound impact on the pattern of buying in the art market during 1984. This can be fully understood given that the dollar appreciated by 23 per cent against Sterling (from $1.41 to $1.15), by 12 per cent against the Deutschmark (from DM2.82 to DM3.17) and by 17 per cent against the Swiss Franc (from SF2.24 to SF2.62).

This buoyancy of the US dollar led to a significant penetration into European markets; the potential purchasing power of American buyers overseas being much enhanced. Furthermore, even within the United States the strong currency contributed to a general feeling of confidence, which, in turn, encouraged especially active participation in the domestic market. In addition, the near 7 per cent growth in the United States economy in 1984, together with special opportunities on the stock market, contributed to the level of disposable funds available to Americans.

The combination of exchange rate fluctuations and a healthy United States economy has been a major factor in the variation between the performances of different sectors of the art market. Those with a broadly-based international appeal, such as English furniture and English silver among the decorative arts, tended to perform significantly better than European fields with more domestic attractions, such as Continental ceramics and silver, which did not benefit as much from increased American interest. The following examples illustrate this point. According to figures calculated by Sotheby's, English furniture was one of the most outstanding performers with prices overall rising approximately 16 per cent (in dollar terms), while English silver increased by approximately 19 per cent. On the other hand, Continental ceramics showed no increase at all and Continental silver appreciated by around 12 per cent, with most of this growth occurring towards the end of 1984 as a result of a series of successful sales held in Geneva.

However, it is worth noting that there are cases where domestic demand can be sufficient to sustain a specific market. American furniture and paintings are one example: a high level of demand from the home market has not only assisted in maintaining but has also boosted interest and subsequent price movements. For example, overall prices for American furniture during the period from January 1984 to early 1985 rose by about one third.

Another important influence on the art market is inflation. This is because in the recent past works of art were often purchased with a view to yielding a real rate of return; in other words in the belief that prices would appreciate by more than the prevailing level of inflation. This is the usual pattern over the long-term for any market in which demand follows a rising trend, while supply remains more or less fixed. This relationship was temporarily disturbed during periods of high inflation. In 1984, however, with inflation in North America and most of Europe well below 10 per cent and art market prices rising substantially more than 10 per cent across the board, the traditional relationship between the art market's performance and inflation appears to have been re-established. Furthermore, even though interest rates were relatively high (for example, base lending rate in the United Kingdom reached a peak of 12 per cent, while inflation was well below half of that figure) and so offered a seemingly attractive return on money held on deposit, the flow of funds coming into the art market did not seem to be diminished.

To date 1985 has been characterized by stability and steady progress in the market, which could be expected to continue for the rest of the year.

All prices given are inclusive of buyer's premium

The condition of an object is crucial to its value. Although condition is mentioned in some sections of this guide, the description may not be detailed. Many entries give no indication of condition, but in the majority of cases it can be assumed that the entry is in reasonably good condition, bearing in mind the date of the piece and the nature of its material. Readers are asked to remember this when comparing similar pieces and to take into consideration fluctuations in the market.

The currency exchange rates for the entries in this book from January to April are taken from the *Financial Times* for the beginning of each month. In May 1984 Sotheby's price lists began to show the daily rate and these are the figures used from May to December.

Abbreviations used in the captions

A	Amsterdam	HH	Hopetoun House	NY	New York
C	Chester	HK	Hong Kong	P	Pulborough, Sussex
CT	Capetown	HS	House Sale	St M	St Moritz
F	Florence	JHB	Johannesburg		
G	Geneva	L	London		
Glen	Gleneagles	LA	Los Angeles	h	height
H	Houston	M	Monaco	w	width

Rugs and Carpets

JACK FRANSES • WILLIAM RUPRECHT

Oriental rugs have been popular in Europe ever since the Renaissance period. Historically they were considered luxury items available only to the very wealthy, but today this is not entirely so and there are excellent opportunities for the buyer of relatively modest means, nor is the choice so limited. While it remains true that the majority of rugs and carpets sold at auction do come from the Middle East, many originate in other parts of the world — Europe, China and the Indian sub-continent in particular.

Some of the finest rugs ever produced were made in the 16th and 17th centuries and these are of the greatest interest to the serious academic collector. But the rugs most likely to appear on the market were made in the 19th century. They can be of exceptional quality and incorporate both vigorous and traditional designs.

Since the turn of this century, a considerable amount of scholarship has been devoted to the study of rugs. As a result there are now a number of books on the subject. These, together with the advice of an expert and a careful examination of the carpets themselves, should give a buyer a good start. For the collector, however, it becomes essential to have a clear understanding of the basic differences between the various knots, weaves, dyes and patterns used in rug manufacture. Only then is it really possible to distinguish between one type of rug and another.

Oriental rugs and carpets fall broadly into three groups: i) those made in court manufactories for a royal household or diplomatic presentation; ii) those woven in urban centres; iii) those produced in villages and tribal settlements. Rugs of the first group, which includes the most splendid — and expensive — of all carpets, are characterized by a tight weave and well balanced court designs. So, also, to a lesser extent are the second. They are classified by the name of the town or city in which they were made and include the familiar Tabriz, Sarough, Kerman and Kashan. The third group encompasses the Caucasian and Turkman rugs. Geometric forms in bold colours epitomize the former and include Kazakhs, Shirvans and many others.

In recent years tastes and trends in western interior design have had a marked influence on aspects of the antique rug and carpet market. There has been a noticeable tendency for designers to favour large and decorative rugs in pale colours; types of European rug are particularly sought after in this regard. The soft pastel colours of French late 19th century Aubusson rugs, as well as the paler Persian rugs, are in demand.

Tribal rugs still remain within the reach of most collectors. Rugs from Turkestan, the Caucasus and Turkey, with their traditional designs, can still be acquired relatively cheaply and look well with modern contemporary furnishings or English oak. Also, with their close knots, vegetable dyes and hand-spun wools, they last far longer than the modern equivalent. The latter's mill-spun, chemically treated, blended wool is much less resilient. Furthermore, antique rugs can be repaired when necessary without injury to their value provided that the repairs are well done. They are, therefore, a practical and sound investment as well as being beautiful in themselves.

1
A **Bidjar rug**, 19th cent,
the red field with a
central indigo medallion,
the wide borders with an
indigo field decorated in
red, blue and ivory,
670 x 380cm
(21ft 11¾in x 12ft 5½in),
M 28 June,
**FF 99,900 (£8,575;
$11,684)**

2
An **Abadeh rug**, the
madder field with two
camel medallions, sur-
rounded by botehs, two
borders, 178 x 133cm
(5ft 10in x 4ft 4in), *L 10 Dec,*
£385 ($485)

3
A **Beluchistan rug**, last
quarter 19th cent, approx
191 x 117cm
(6ft 3in x 3ft 10in),
NY 19 May,
$2,090 (£1,441)

4
An **Afshar runner**, the
indigo field with a dense
overall design of madder
floral botehs within a
madder border of star
guls, single guard
stripes, 236 x 104cm
(7ft 9in x 3ft 5in), *L 18 July,*
£2,860 ($3,818)

5
A **Beluchistan prayer rug**,
the camel mehrab with a
central Tree-of-Life,
madder chevron spandrels,
seven borders, 171 x 86cm
(5ft 7in x 2ft 10in), *L 10 Dec,*
£550 ($693)

6
An **Afshar rug**, *c*1875, the
blue field with ivory,
pale blue, mustard and
brick angular medallions,
approx 132 x 102cm
(4ft 4in x 3ft 4in),
NY 19 May,
$2,200 (£1,517)

7
A **Bidjar panel rug**, the
field with connecting
diamond motifs in various
colours, saffron, madder,
ivory, indigo, the indigo
palmette and trailing
leaf border with single
guard stripes,
203 x 137cm
(6ft 8in x 4ft 6in),
P 20 Nov,
£484 ($649)

8
A **Bactiari rug**, the dark-
indigo field with three
rows of connecting
hexagonal motifs, inner
and outer guard stripe,
201 x 146cm
(6ft 7in x 4ft 9½in),
P 20-22 Mar,
£297 ($443)

1

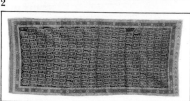
2

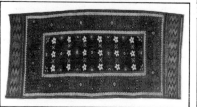
3

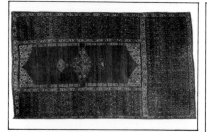
4

5

6

7

8

1
An Esfahan pictorial rug, the field depicting courtiers and musicians in a forest clearing, the ivory border with palmettes and exotic birds, 112 x 150cm (3ft 8in x 4ft 11in), *L 31 July,* £1,320 ($1,795)

2
An Esfahan Sanaye carpet, woven on silk, decorated on an ivory ground with a central madder lobed floral medallion, a madder border, twin guard stripes, 411 x 310cm (13ft 6in x 10ft 2in), *G 15 May,* SF 71,500 (£22,756; $32,541)

3
An Esfahan prayer rug, the ivory mehrab with a central flowering Tree-of-Life surrounded by animals and birds, ivory border with trees, birds and animals, 208 x 137cm (6ft 10in x 4ft 6in), *HS 28 Mar,* £1,650 ($2,459)

4
An Esfahan rug, decorated on an indigo ground with a stylised vase and flowers, vines, trees, palmettes, birds and animals, the beige border with palmettes and leaves, 156 x 105cm (5ft 2in x 3ft 5in), *G 15 May,* SF 4,950 (£1,575; $2,252)

5
An Esfahan carpet, the ivory field with an overall design of trees, rocks, animals and birds, beige border, twin guard stripes, water damage, 235 x 150cm (7ft 8in x 4ft 11in), *L 1 Feb,* £1,430 ($2,004)

6
An Esfahan rug, the ivory field with a duck pond and a pictorial representation of a rug above, madder border, twin guard stripes, 236 x 150cm (7ft 9in x 4ft 11in), *L 3 Apr,* £1,500 ($2,165)

7
An Esfahan Emadzadeh carpet, the ivory ground decorated with a slate and ivory lobed medallion, all within a beige palmette, vine and leaf border, signature panel at one end, 353 x 214cm (11ft 7in x 7ft), *G 13 Nov,* SF 20,900 (£6,451; $8,515)

8
An Esfahan part silk Tree-of-Life rug, the ivory field with flowering Trees-of-Life, a duck pond in the foreground, madder border, twin guard stripes, 226 x 152cm (7ft 5in x 5ft), *L 17 Oct,* £3,740 ($4,675)

9
An Esfahan prayer rug, the ivory mehrab with a central vase flanked by flowering Trees-of-Life, pale indigo border with animals and birds, single guard stripes, 185 x 109cm (6ft 1in x 3ft 7in), *C 12 Jan,* £1,265 ($1,834)

10
An Esfahan prayer rug, the ivory mehrab with a vase, palmettes, trees, birds and animals, pale indigo bird and flower spandrels, beige border, water damage, 176 x 104cm (5ft 9in x 3ft 5in), *L 18 July,* £418 ($558)

11
An Esfahan carpet, the ivory ground decorated with a pale indigo medallion, with radiating and scrolling vines ending in arabesques, within an indigo border of palmettes, vines and arabesques, 310 x 209cm (10ft 2in x 6ft 10in), *G 15 May,* SF 5,500 (£1,751; $2,503)

12
An Esfahan rug, the ivory field with an overall design of vines, palmettes and leaves, madder border, single guard stripes, 211 x 150cm (6ft 11in x 4ft 11in), *L 21 Feb,* £900 ($1,261)

1
An Esfahan Ghafarian rug,
the madder field with a
central indigo lobed
medallion, ivory floral
spandrels, a pale indigo
vine and palmette border,
a signature panel at one
end, 239 x 150cm
(7ft 10in x 4ft 11in),
L 21 Feb,
£3,520 ($4,935)

2
An Esfahan carpet, signed
in a cartouche 'Iran-
Isphahan Khord-Azad
workshop', silk warp,
318 x 213cm (10ft 5in x 7ft)
NY 11 Feb,
$31,900 (£22,786)

3
An Esfahan Seirafian rug,
with a design of
palmettes, flowers and
vines, 228 x 148cm
(7ft 5in x 4ft 9in), *L 1 Feb,*
£3,300 ($4,627)

4
An Esfahan rug, the ivory
field with an overall
design of scrolling vines,
the madder border with
palmettes interlaced by
flowering vines on a
green surround, 229 x
142cm (7ft 6in x 4ft 8in),
L 18 Sept,
£2,640 ($3,406)

5
An Esfahan Seirafian rug,
the ivory field with an
indigo pole medallion
and spandrels, a signature
panel at one end,
167 x 99cm (5ft 6in x
3ft 3in), *L 10 Dec,*
£1,320 ($1,663)

6
A Faraghan carpet, with
ivory field, the terracotta
border with rosettes interlaced by vines, five inner
and outer guard stripes,
533 x 305cm (17ft 6in x
10ft), *L 18 Apr,*
£4,950 ($7,143)

7
A Faraghan carpet, 19th
cent, the indigo field
with an overall design of
feathered guls, three inner
and two outer guard
stripes, 455 x 236cm
(14ft 11in x 7ft 9in),
L 18 Apr,
£660 ($952)

8
A Faraghan rug, decorated
on an ivory ground with
a madder medallion and
spandrels with an
overall design of the
herati pattern, single guard
stripes, 196 x 124cm
(6ft 5in x 4ft 1in),
G 13 Nov,
SF 11,000 (£3,610; $4,765)

9
A Faraghan rug, the
dark-indigo field with a
central madder medallion
and spandrels, within a
madder bracket and
cartouche border,
201 x 130cm (6ft 5in x
4ft 3in), *P 15-18 May,*
£968 ($1,346)

10
A Ghashghai rug, last
quarter 19th cent, 218 x
132cm (7ft 2in x 4ft 4in),
NY 1 Dec,
$4,950 (£4,159)

11
A Ghashghai carpet, the
madder field with two
vases of flowers on a
millefleurs background,
the walnut border with
stylised vines, single
guard stripes, 244 x 150cm
(8ft x 4ft 11in), *L 18 Apr,*
£7,700 ($11,111)

12
A Gashghai carpet, the
indigo ground decorated
with madder spandrels,
triple guard stripes,
247 x 172cm (8ft 1in x
5ft 8in), *G 15 May,*
SF 15,400 (£4,899; $6,851)

1   2
3   4
5   6
7   8
9   10
11   12

1
A **Ghashghai carpet**, late
19th cent, 318 x 170cm
(10ft 5in x 5ft 7in), *NY 1 Dec*,
$17,600 (£14,679)

2
A **Ghashghai saddle rug**,
late 19th cent, rewoven
cantle crescent and
pommel opening,
104 x 84cm (3ft 5in x
2ft 9in), *NY 19 May*,
$9,900 (£7,122)

3
A **Gabeh rug**, the field
with an overall design of
polychrome chevron
bands, within a
chequerboard surround,
six outer borders,
198 x 124cm (6ft 6in x
4ft 1in), *L 1 Feb*,
£1,375 ($1,928)

4
A **Ghom silk rug**, the
ivory field with a central
medallion with vines and
palmettes, ochre floral
spandrels, an indigo floral
border, triple guard stripes,
75 x 107cm (5ft 9in x
3ft 6in), *L 10 Jan*,
£1,100 ($1,595)

5
A **Ghom silk rug**, the
ivory field with an all-
over cartouche design,
each panel containing a
bouquet of flowers, the
black border with leaves
and flowerheads,
219 x 139cm (7ft 2in x
4ft 6½in), *P 18-25 Sept*,
£1,980 ($2,554)

6
A **Ghom silk rug**, the
indigo ground decorated
with a saffron lobed
medallion and
spandrels, all within a
madder border of
flowerheads and trees,
213 x 136cm (7ft x 4ft 5in),
G 15 May,
SF 9,900 (£3,150; $4,505)

7
A **Ghom carpet**, the pale
indigo field with an
ivory medallion and panels
enclosing floral sprays
and palmettes, ivory
floral spandrels, the indigo
border with willow trees
and floral sprays,
452 x 323cm (14ft 10in x
10ft 7in), *L 31 July*,
£1,320 ($1,795)

8
A **Ghom rug**, the madder
field with an ivory
flowerhead medallion and
spandrels, the indigo
border with willow trees
and palmettes, one inner
and two outer guard
stripes, 221 x 140cm
(7ft 3in x 4ft 7in),
L 21 Feb,
£770 ($1,080)

9
A **Ghom carpet**, the
saffron and indigo field
with an ivory and indigo
pole medallion and
spandrels, all with a
honeycomb design, a
similar pale indigo border,
333 x 221cm (10ft 11in x
7ft 3in), *L 21 Feb*,
£1,430 ($2,005)

10
A **Ghom rug**, the ivory
field with an overall
design of stylised
medallions, the ivory
border with rosettes and
stylised flowerheads, single
guard stripes, 213 x 140cm
(7ft x 4ft 7in), *L 21 Feb*,
£880 ($1,234)

11
A **Ghom rug**, the ivory
field with sprays of
flowers with birds and
leaves, the madder border
with floral roundels and
vines, one inner and two
outer guard stripes,
208 x 140cm (6ft 10in x
4ft 7in), *L 21 Feb*,
£935 ($1,311)

1

2

3

4

5

6

7

8

9

10

11

1
A **Hamadan rug,** the ivory field with a central medallion surrounded by flowers, saffron border, 240 x 152cm (7ft 10in x 5ft), *M 28 June,*
FF 5,550 (£476; $649)

2
A **Heriz carpet,** last quarter 19th cent, 538 x 348cm (17ft 8in x 11ft 5in), *NY 19 May,*
$28,600 (£19,724)

3
A **Heriz carpet,** last quarter 19th cent, the pale salmon field with a brick red medallion with cream and midnight-blue smaller medallions with brick and salmon spandrels, 358 x 244cm (11ft 9in x 8ft), *NY 19 May,*
$7,975 (£11,564)

4
A **Heriz carpet,** the madder field with a lobed indigo pole medallion, ivory serrated leaf spandrels, the indigo border with turtle palmettes, rosettes and flowering vines, 378 x 297cm (12ft 5in x 9ft 9in), *L 17 Oct,*
£3,300 ($4,125)

5
A **Heriz carpet,** last quarter 19th cent, 393 x 287cm (12ft 10in x 9ft 5in), *NY 11 Feb,*
$13,750 (£9,821)

6
A **Heriz carpet,** *c.*1900, 760 x 447cm (24ft 11in x 14ft 8in), *NY 11 Feb,*
$30,800 (£22,000)

7
A **Heriz silk rug,** 19th cent, the ivory field with an overall design of large stylised palmettes, flower-heads and rhombs, the madder border with turtle palmettes, vines and serrated leaves, 180 x 122cm (5ft 11in x 4ft), *L 1 Feb,*
£7,700 ($10,795)

8
A **Heriz carpet,** the madder field with an indigo and ivory medallion and ivory spandrels, a madder turtle palmette and vine border, 444 x 353cm (14ft 7in x 11ft 7in), *L 1 Feb,*
£5,060 ($7,094)

1

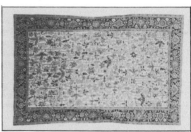

2

3

4

5

6

7

8

1
A Kashan silk prayer rug, the madder mehrab with a central tree supporting a slate palmette, flanked by vases of flowers, madder spandrels, a slate border of palmettes and meandering vines, 206 x 132cm (6ft 9in x 4ft 4in), *G 15 May,* **SF 71,500 (£22,749; $32,531)**

2
A Kashan rug, the indigo ground with a madder cusped medallion and spandrels, an indigo border of palmettes, flowerheads and vines, twin guard stripes, 204 x 133cm (6ft 8in x 4ft 4in), *G 13 Nov,* **SF 6,050 (£1,867; $2,465)**

3
A Kashan raised silk prayer carpet, the flat woven beige mehrab with a small vase of flowers, flanked by twin entwining trees with leaves, flowers, palmettes and birds, 316 x 214cm (10ft 4in x 7ft), *G 13 Nov,* **SF 38,500 (£11,883; $15,685)**

4
A Kashan Mohtasham carpet, the indigo ground decorated with a large brilliant madder medallion enclosing a smaller indigo quatrefoil medallion, with an overall design of diamond guls, vines and trees within an indigo border, 520 x 370cm (17ft 1in x 12ft 2in), *G 13 Nov,* **SF 176,000 (£54,321; $71,704)**

5
A Kashan Mohtasham rug, the indigo field with a central madder panel enclosing an indigo and ivory medallion, indigo border, triple guard stripes, 198 x 137cm (6ft 6in x 4ft 6in), *L 29 May,* **£2,090 ($3,010)**

6
A Kashan Kurk prayer rug, the walnut mehrab with a vase of flowers and trees, pale indigo spandrels, the indigo border with scrolling vines and flowers, 198 x 135cm (6ft 6in x 4ft 5in), *L 1 Feb,* **£2,860 ($4,010)**

7
A Kerman embroidered velvet ground panel, late 19th cent, the madder field decorated in gold- and silver-coloured threads, with a central cartouche bearing inscription, in mahogany frame, 137 x 86cm (4ft 6in x 2ft 9in), *P 24-26 Jan,* **£473 ($686)**

8
A Kerman rug, the madder field with an ivory floral medallion with wild animals and trees at either end, the border with cartouches enclosing verse, 185 x 137cm (6ft 1in x 4ft 6in), *L 17 Oct,* **£2,860 ($3,575)**

9
A Kerman rug, the plain madder field with a central ivory floral pole medallion, polychrome floral vase spandrels and surround, the indigo border with palmettes and arabesques, 221 x 140cm (7ft 3in x 4ft 7in), *L 17 Oct,* **£990 ($1,238)**

10
A Kerman rug, with a pictorial central medallion, surrounded by mille-fleurs, 214 x 137cm (7ft x 4ft 6in), *M 10 Dec,* **FF 33,300 (£2,934; $3,543)**

11
A Kerman pictorial rug, depicting Nur Ali Shah with kashkul and mace before a pond, green spandrels, an indigo border with portrait roundels, trees, animals and birds, 213 x 132cm (7ft x 4ft 4in), *G 13 Nov,* **SF 9,350 (£2,886; $3,809)**

12
A Kerman pictorial rug, the floral panelled field depicting Nur Ali Shah, seated with kashkul and mace, pictorial spandrels, ivory mille-fleurs border, 198 x 135cm (6ft 6in x 4ft 5in), *L 31 July,* **£935 ($1,272)**

1

2

3

4

5

6

7

8

9

10

11

12

1
A Khorrassan silk rug, the dark-madder field with a profusely flowering Tree-of-Life, within an indigo border depicting deer and trees, twin guard stripes, perishing, 145 x 125cm (4ft 9in x 4ft 1in), *P 15-18 May,* **£3,300 ($4,587)**

2
A Khorrassan rug, the indigo field with a madder floral medallion surrounded by animals, floral madder border, 200 x 300cm (6ft 7in x 9ft 10in), *M 10 Dec,* **FF 5,550 (£489, $590)**

3
A West Persian carpet, possibly Kurdish, 3rd quarter 19th cent, 285 x 155cm (9ft 4in x 5ft 1in), *NY 1 Dec,* **$4,675 (£3,929)**

4
A Malayer rug, the indigo field decorated overall with flowers and leaves in ivory, red and indigo, the ivory border with flowers and leaves, 198 x 138cm (6ft 6in x 4ft 6in), *M 28 June,* **FF 6,600 (£566; $772)**

5
A Teheran part silk rug, decorated with a dense overall design of madder floral *botehs,* 210 x 135cm (6ft 11in x 4ft 5in), *G 15 May,* **SF 17,600 (£5,600; $8,008)**

6
A Mashhad prayer rug, the saffron mehrab with a central vase of flowers flanked by trees, pale indigo spandrels, the indigo border with vines an palmettes, 180 x 122cm (5ft 11in x 4ft), *L 10 Jan,* **£825 ($1,196)**

7
A Mashhad Amoghli carpet, the indigo ground decorated with an overall design of scrolling vines, within an indigo border, five inner and outer guard stripes in shades of madder, indigo, green and ivory, 342 x 235cm (11ft 3in x 7ft 8in), *G 13 Nov,* **SF 110,000 (£33,951; $44,815)**

8
A Nain carpet, silk highlights, silk warp, inscription cartouche reading 'Habibian Nain', 328 x 213cm (10ft 9in x 7ft), *NY 1 Dec,* **$27,500 (£23,110)**

9
A Nain carpet, the madder field with an ivory lobed medallion and beige floral spandrels, the beige border with palmettes, flowers and leaves, 272 x 168cm (8ft 11in x 5ft 6in), *L 18 Sept,* **£1,980 ($2,554)**

10
A Nain part silk hunting rug, the ivory field with a design of mounted huntsmen pursuing wild animals, beige border with trees, birds and animals, 259 x 155cm (8ft 6in x 5ft 1in), *L 1 Feb,* **£3,300 ($4,627)**

11
A Nain part silk rug, the indigo field with two entwining Trees-of-Life, with exotic birds and wild animals, the pale indigo border with trees and shrubs flanked by wild animals, 257 x 155cm (8ft 5in x 5ft 1in), *L 1 Feb,* **£2,640 ($3,701)**

1   2   3

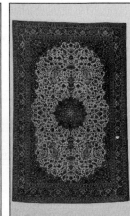

4   5

6   7   8

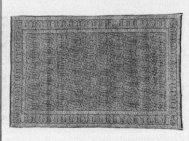
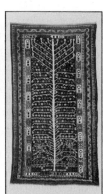

9   10   11

1

A Neriz rug, the ivory field with an overall design of large botehs, all with guls and stylised flowerheads, five borders, 251 x 155cm (8ft 3in x 5ft 1in), *L 10 Jan,* **£825 ($1,196)**

2

A Senneh rug, last quarter 19th cent, multicolour silk warp, 203 x 145cm (6ft 8in x 4ft 9in), *NY 19 May,* **$14,850 (£10,241)**

3

A Senneh rug, the ivory field with an overall design of floral vases, stylised birds and people, the madder border with palmettes and vines, single guard stripes, 206 x 135cm (6ft 9in x 4ft 5in), *L 18 Sept,* **£858 ($1,107)**

4

A Senneh rug, the saffron field with madder medallion and spandrels, the madder border with flowers and leaves, triple guard stripes, 188 x 122cm (6ft 2in x 4ft), *M 28 June,* **FF 29,970 (£2,573; $3,505)**

5

A Rasht hanging, the black felt ground with a central floral medallion, all with profusely flowering leafy vines, an inner vine border, a plain black outer border with large floral botehs, 381 x 277cm (12ft 6in x 9ft 1in), *L 1 Feb,* **£880 ($1,234)**

6

A Sarough rug, the ivory field with a bold madder fluted diamond pole medallion with indigo centre madder spandrels, dark-indigo border, twin guard stripes, 188 x 130cm (6ft 2in x 4ft 3in), *P 18 Sept,* **£825 ($1,064)**

7

A Sarough rug, the ivory field decorated with an indigo medallion and spandrels, the madder border with flowers, leaves and palmettes, 204 x 133cm (6ft 9in x 4ft 4in), *M 10 Dec,* **FF 22,200 (£1,956; $2,362)**

8

A Sarough rug, the black field with a pale-indigo shaped medallion containing a madder rosette, madder and indigo spandrels, within a black and madder waved border, 211 x 142cm (6ft 11in x 4ft 8in), *P 10-13 July,* **£528 ($718)**

9

A Sarough Faraghan rug, last quarter 19th cent, 193 x 132cm (6ft 4in x 4ft 4in), *NY 1 Dec,* **$10,450 (£8,782)**

10

A Sarough Faraghan rug, c 1875, minor stain along one side, 201 x 132cm (6ft 7in x 4ft 4in), *NY 1 Dec,* **$23,100 (£19,412)**

11

A Sarough Faraghan carpet, last quarter 19th cent, 292 x 221cm (9ft 7in x 7ft 3in), *NY 1 Dec,* **$8,800 (£7,395)**

1   2   3

4   5   6

7   8   9

10   11

1
A **Tabriz carpet,** the madder field with a central ivory and indigo pole medallion and spandrels, all with the herati pattern, the indigo border with turtle palmettes, 358 x 249cm (11ft 9in x 8ft 2in), *L 21 Feb,* **£1,870 ($2,622)**

2
A **Tabriz carpet,** the ivory field with floral palmettes and vines in shades of blue, rose and green, two inner and one outer guard stripes, 382 x 293cm (12ft 6in x 9ft 7in), *M 28 June,* **FF 8,320 (£714; $973)**

3
A **Tabriz carpet,** the ivory field with willow trees, vases of flowers, palmettes and flowerheads, a similar border, single guard stripes, 312 x 246cm (10ft 3in x 8ft 1in), *L 10 Jan,* **£682 ($988)**

4
A **Tabriz carpet,** the saffron field with a madder lobed medallion and ivory spandrels, with an overall design of palmettes, leaves, vines and flowers, a madder border, signed, 323 x 254cm (10ft 7in x 8ft 4in), *L 10 Jan,* **£935 ($1,356)**

5
A **Tabriz carpet,** 554 x 371cm (18ft 2in x 12ft 2in), *NY 11 Feb,* **$10,450 (£7,464)**

6
A **Tabriz carpet,** possibly Hajiyalil, 3rd quarter 19th cent, 447 x 333cm (14ft 8in x 10ft 11in), *NY 11 Feb,* **$8,800 (£6,286)**

7
A **Tabriz pictorial rug,** depicting Napoleon in his study, after a painting by David, within a slate floral border, 117 x 74cm (3ft 10in x 2ft 5in), *L 31 July,* **£880 ($1,197)**

8
A **Tabriz rug,** the ivory field with a central Tree-of-Life bearing curving branches with animal heads, birds, fish and fantastic masks, the indigo border with lions and stylised script, 201 x 129cm (6ft 7in x 4ft 3in), *L 17 Oct,* **£1,045 ($1,306)**

9
A **Tabriz carpet,** the madder field decorated with a cusped indigo medallion and spandrels, with an overall design of the herati pattern, within an indigo border of palmettes 335 x 208cm (11ft x 6ft 10in), *G 13 Nov,* **SF 30,800 (£9,506; $12,548)**

10
A **Tabriz Narvani carpet,** the beige field with a rose madder medallion, the pale walnut border with flowers and acanthus leaves, with a gelim and pile deer surround, 258 x 168cm (8ft 6in x 5ft 6in), *L 1 Feb,* **£6,050 ($8,482)**

11
A **Tabriz Narvani carpet,** the beige field with a rose madder and pale green medallion, the pale walnut border with flowerheads and acanthus leaves, deer gelim ends, 285 x 182cm (9ft 4in x 6ft), *L 1 Feb,* **£27,500 ($38,555)**

12
A **Zel-ol-Soltan Teheran rug,** the ivory field with the nightingale and rose design, all with vases of flowers and birds, the ivory border with flowerheads and botehs, 213 x 140cm (7ft x 4ft 7in), *L 1 Feb,* **£3,850 ($5,398)**

13
A **Teheran rug,** the saffron field with a central flowering Tree-of-Life, with animals, monkeys and exotic birds, the indigo border with animals and birds, 231 x 142cm (7ft 7in x 4ft 8in), *L 17 Oct,* **£1,210 ($1,513)**

1   2   3

4   5

6   7   8

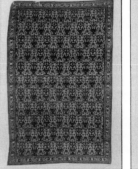

9   10

11   12   13

Kum Kapour Rugs

JACK FRANSES

During the reign of the Ottoman sultan, Abdulhamid I (1774-84), a workshop for fine carpets was set up in the town of Hereke under the supervision of the weaver Fezhane. It became known as the Fezhane workshop. The weavers came from the Kerman province of Persia, famous for its 16th century Kerman designs. They used silk and metal thread and an asymmetrical knot. The Salting group (known after the carpet in the Victoria and Albert Museum, originally thought to be 16th century) may have come from this workshop.

Fezhane died in about 1840 and the workshop went into decline until Sultan Abdulmecid (1839-61) became its new patron in 1844. It came to be known as the Hereke factory and the Turkish weavers, using Turkish symmetrical knots, started to incorporate the famous Hereke mark in their work.

It was an Ottoman tradition for the sultan to present fine rugs to visitors and diplomats. These rugs were brought to the Topkapi palace for the ceremony—a much less expensive process than importing them from Persia. Under Abdulhamid II (1876-1909), an atelier was opened within the palace precinct at the Kum Kapour gates (Gates to the Sands). It was to house the leading weaver from Hereke, an Armenian called Hagop Kapuchjian. Kapuchjian was exceptionally skilled—possibly the finest weaver in the Middle East—and remained the sultan's master weaver from 1880 to 1900. Because the work was so fine, master weavers could only work for a maximum of about ten years. All the apprentices were carefully selected to follow in their footsteps. Kapuchjian's successor as master weaver was Kanata (1900-03); he was followed by Sara (Zara), who was officially master weaver from 1903 to 1906. Nemzur succeeded him (1906-18),

although Sara stayed on with the workshop for many years in the role of overseer and adviser. He died in 1930.

From 1918 to 1922 the master weaver was a woman—the first time a woman had been chosen. Mme Takouchi, as she was called, was an excellent weaver and skilled copyist. In 1922, after the fall of the Ottoman empire, a Paris dealer persuaded her to go and work for him in Paris. There she produced superb copies of the so-called 'polonaise' carpets. Attaturk's revolution effectively removed any incentive to weave or sell fine rugs and little was produced between 1922 and the mid 1930s when the factories were re-established and began producing rugs much the same as those we see today.

True Kum Kapours are the world's finest modern carpets. There is nothing to match them in Persia or elsewhere and they are equal to anything made in earlier times. These exceptionally lush prayer rugs are woven entirely of silk and metal thread at over 1,000 knots per square inch. They are all legibly signed by the master weaver and the metal thread is worked throughout to highlight cloud bands, palmettes, inscriptions and the outer edge with its reciprocal design of epaulettes or flowerheads. The other basic elements include curvilinear vines, vases, flowers and birds among the architectural features and the central mehrab itself. Pale green, yellow and red are the predominant colours.

Many rugs are wrongly called Kum Kapour. They are not legibly signed and were made in Istanbul by fine Armenian weavers, such as Tosounian, Cassian and Kantalian. All were weavers of exceptional skill, but the dye selection is usually poor and they did not use metalwork highlighted in silks. Some writers have tried to establish that there was a Kum Kapour Armenian quarter in Istanbul. This is unfounded.

1
A Kum Kapour Zare silk and metal thread prayer rug, the madder mehrab with a central palmette with an inscription palmette above, the spandrels with vases containing foliage, vines and birds, within a saffron border, signed, 195 x 128cm (6ft 5in x 4ft 2in), *G 13 Nov,* **SF 187,000 (£57,716; $76,185)**

2
A Kum Kapour silk and metal thread prayer rug, the madder mehrab with radiating palmettes and flowering scrolling vines, with an indigo inscription cartouche, slate spandrels, saffron border, 172 x 111cm (5ft 8in x 3ft 8in), *G 15 May,* **SF 165,000 (£52,498; $75,072)**

1

2

1
A Bergamo rug, 3rd
quarter 19th cent, minor
splits, 178 x 163cm
(5ft 10in x 5ft 4in),
NY 1 Dec,
$11,000 (£9,244)

2
An Afyon Gelim, the ivory
field with three stepped
medallions enclosing guls,
within an ivory, madder
and indigo serrated
surround, polychrome
banded ends, 353 x 190cm
(11ft 7in x 6ft 3in),
L 17 Oct,
£1,760 ($2,200)

3
A Melas rug, mid-19th
cent, the red ground
containing two aubergine
and red latchhook-framed
floral reserves, a saffron
border of floral palmettes,
minor restorations, re-
selvaged, 165 x 117cm
(5ft 5in x 3ft 10in),
NY 11 Feb,
$3,080 (£2,200)

4
**A Hereke silk and metal
thread rug,** the madder
ground with a small
central flowerhead radiating palmettes, vines,
birds and cloudbanks,
the indigo border with
flowerheads and palmettes,
100 x 79cm (3ft 3in x
2ft 7in), *G 13 Nov,*
**SF 55,000 (£16,975;
$22,407**

5
An Ushak Lotto rug, 16th
cent, the madder field
with an overall design of
angular vines flanked by
arabesques, 160 x 114cm
(5ft 3in x 3ft 9in), *L 17 Oct,*
£11,000 ($13,750)

6
An Ushak prayer rug,
18th cent, the madder
mehrab with a central
floral medallion, pale
indigo, pistachio and
madder spandrels, with
an overall design of guls
and stylised flowerheads,
244 x 190cm (8ft x
6ft 3in), *L 17 Oct,*
£7,150 ($8,937)

7
A Ladik prayer rug,
inscribed and dated 1203
(1786), restorations to
borders and ends,
175 x 119cm (5ft 9in x
3ft 11in), *NY 19 May,*
$3,410 (£2,352)

8
A Ladik prayer rug, 18th
cent, the madder mehrab
with three rosettes flanked
by ewers, pale indigo
spandrels, with a pale
madder panel below, the
indigo border with car-
nations and vines, 168 x
112cm (5ft 6in x
3ft 8in), *L 17 Oct,*
£3,520 ($4,400)

9
A Mudjar prayer rug,
*c*1875, 142 x 99cm
(4ft 8in x 3ft 3in),
NY 19 May,
$4,400 (£3,034)

7   1   2

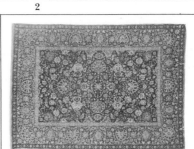

3   4

5   6

7   8   9

1
An Akstafa rug, 3rd quarter 19th cent, 340 x 127cm (10ft 6in x 4ft 2in), *NY 19 May,* $4,950 (£7,177)

2
A Baku rug, the indigo field with three feathered medallions, all with guls, stylised birds and animals, a saffron and ivory barber's pole border, 168 x 109cm (5ft 6in x 3ft 7in), *L 18 July,* £1,375 ($1,836)

3
A Chichi rug, last quarter 19th cent, the pale blue field with a rectangular central reserve with three octagonal medallions and an oxidized brown slant-leaf and floral rosette border, 158 x 119cm (5ft 2in x 3ft 11in), *NY 19 May,* $2,420 (£3,509)

4
A Chichi rug, the madder ground with an overall design of akcha guls, the indigo border with the rosette and band design, triple guard stripes, 282 x 155cm (9ft 3in x 5ft 1in), *L 1 Feb,* £1,650 ($2,313)

5
A Daghestan prayer rug, last quarter 19th cent, 158 x 104cm (5ft 2in x 3ft 5in), *NY 11 Feb,* $4,400 (£3,143)

6
A Garabagh carpet, the black floral field with four floral medallions, three narrow borders, 571 x 218cm (18ft 9in x 7ft 2in), *L 18 July,* £1,375 ($1,836)

7
A Daghestan rug, the polychrome barberpole field within an ivory border of rows of inverted arrowheads, two inner and three outer guard stripes, 206 x 107cm (6ft 9in x 3ft 6in), *L 18 July,* £418 ($558)

8
A Garagashli rug, *c* 1875, 147 x 102cm (4ft 10in x 3ft 4in), *NY 19 May,* $11,000 (£7,586)

9
A Garabagh runner, the madder field with six connecting stepped diamond indigo medallions, supported each side by columns of halved medallions of similar design, a horse in each spandrel, within a sage serrated border, madder guard stripes, 368 x 117cm (12ft 1in x 3ft 10in), *P 18-25 Sept,* £297 ($383)

10
A Gullu-Chichi rug, dated 1320 AH, 1903 AD, the ivory field with three cruciform medallions, the walnut border with rosettes interlaced with vines, one inner and one outer guard stripe, *C 12 Jan,* £935 ($1,355)

11
A Kazakh tree rug, mid-19th cent, the brick field with ivory and blue tree motifs centring octagaonal ivory medallions within a blue floral rosette border, fold cut and reweaves, 229 x 165cm (7ft 6in x 5ft 5in), *NY 11 Feb,* $6,600 (£4,714)

1

3

9

2

5

6

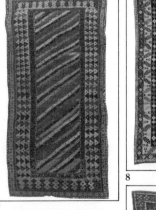

4

7

9

10   11

1
A Kazakh tree rug, dated 1303 AH, 1886 AD, the red ground with three octagonal medallions flanked by tree motifs, minor reweaves, 218 x 196cm (7ft 2in x 6ft 5in), *NY 1 Dec,*
$4,400 (£3,697)

2
A Kazakh rug, the narrow sage field with nine gul medallions, the ivory border with flower-heads in madder, indigo, sage, saffron and camel, 199 x 97cm (6ft 6in x 3ft 2in), *P 20 Nov,*
£1,100 ($1,474)

3
A Kazakh rug, the madder ground decorated with diagonal rows of stylised flowerheads and botehs, within an ivory border of guls and stylised vines, 248 x 123cm (8ft 2in x 4ft 1in), *G 15 May,*
SF 3,300 (£1,050; $1,501)

4
A Kazakh Sewan rug, the madder field with a green and madder bird medallion with stylised tree spandrels, an ivory double 'E' border, triple guard stripes, 231 x 162cm (7ft 7in x 5ft 4in), *L 18 July,*
£3,850 ($5,140)

5
A Kazakh Sewan rug, the madder field with an ivory bird medallion enclosing a smaller green and red medallion, the indigo border with guls, triple guard stripes, 231 x 168cm (7ft 7in x 5ft 6in), *L 3 Apr,*
£2,860 ($4,118)

6
A Kazakh Loripambak rug, the madder field with an ivory hooked medallion with two smaller hooked star medallions, the ivory border with a meandering hooked vine, 239 x 160cm (7ft 10in x 5ft 3in), *L 1 Feb,*
£2,200 ($3,084)

7
A Kuba rug, the indigo field with two madder stepped guls with bold ivory angular vines, rosettes and combs, the ivory border with guls and brackets, 175 x 124cm (5ft 9in x 4ft 1in), *L 18 July,*
£715 ($955)

8
A double-ended Kazakh Frachlo prayer rug, the dark-indigo mehrab with five central squared medallions in madder, ivory and sage, within an ivory border of tarantula and cross design, 217 x 148cm (7ft 1in x 4ft 10in), *P 10-13 July,*
£1,815 ($2,468)

9
A Kazakh Sewan rug, the madder field with an ivory, green and madder bird medallion, all with stylised Trees-of-Life, the walnut border with stepped guls, 216 x 188cm (7ft 1in x 6ft 2in), *L 17 Oct,*
£6,050 ($7,563)

10
A Kazakh rug, the indigo field with a trellis work containing botehs, the ivory border with hooked guls, within triple guard stripes, 211 x 107cm (6ft 11in x 3ft 6in), *L 10 Jan,*
£880 ($1,276)

11
A Kazakh double-ended prayer carpet, *c*1910, the madder field with a central ivory hooked medallion, the ivory spandrels with star guls, the pale indigo border with stylised tulips and stepped leaves, 292 x 152cm (9ft 7in x 5ft), *L 10 Jan,*
£704 ($1,021)

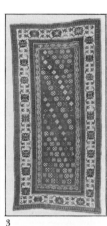
1   2   3

4   5

6   7

8   9

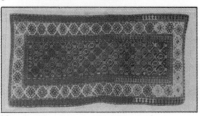

10   11

1
A Lenkoran runner, last quarter 19th cent, the oxidised brown-black field with magenta Lenkoran medallions flanked by red and green octagons and yellow poled reserves, an ivory stepped flower-head border, 330 x 109cm (10ft 10in x 3ft 7in), *NY 19 May,* **$3,300 (£2,276)**

2
A Shirvan prayer rug, the ivory mehrab with a trellis containing flowering plants, 175 x 107cm (5ft 9in x 3ft 6in), *P 20-22 Mar,* **£935 ($1,393)**

3
A Mereze prayer rug, the indigo mehrab with a diagonal design of polychrome serrated botehs with similar spandrels, ivory border with stepped guls and brackets, 181 x 122cm (5ft 11in x 4ft), *G 13 Nov,* **SF 52,800 (£16,296; $21,511)**

4
A Shirvan prayer rug, 3rd quarter 19th cent, 163 x 91cm (5ft 4in x 3ft), *NY 11 Feb,* **$6.050 (£4,321)**

5
A Shirvan rug, the ivory field with three medallions surrounded by flowerheads, an ivory star border, 145 x 109cm (4ft 9in x 3ft 7in), *M 10 Dec,* **FF 11,655 (£1,027; $1,240)**

6
A Shirvan prayer rug, the blue mehrab with a mustard trellis containing latchhook and star-formed medallions and an ivory prayer arch, ivory latch-hooked border, partially restored selvage, 213 x 89cm (7ft 2in x 2ft 11in), *NY 1 Dec,* **$4,125 (£3,466)**

7
A Shirvan rug, the shaped indigo field with a madder surround, centred by three ivory gul medallions containing birds, within an ivory star border, 193 x 122cm (6ft 4in x 4ft), *P 10-13 July,* **£1,595 ($2,169)**

8
A Kuba prayer rug, the pale indigo mehrab with an overall design of star guls, similar spandrels, an ivory hooked vine border, 162 x 109cm (5ft 4in x 3ft 7in), *L 18 July,* **£1,045 ($1,395)**

9
A Shirvan runner, the indigo field with six medallions enclosing guls within a saffron frame, an ivory star and bracket border, 292 x 109cm (9ft 7in x 3ft 7in), *C 12 Jan,* **£1,540 ($2,233)**

10
A Shirvan carpet, the indigo field with ten madder cruciform medallions, with smaller stepped guls and star guls, five borders, restored, 414 x 216cm (13ft 7in x 7ft 1in), *L 18 July,* **£1,320 ($1,762)**

11
A Shirvan rug, dated 1213 AH, 1895 AD, the indigo field with three diamond connecting medallions, a madder serrated bar at each end, the ivory border with pairs of polychrome birds, 180 x 127cm (5ft 11in x 4ft 2in), *P 20 Nov,* **£1,210 ($1,621)**

1

2

3

4

5

6

7

8

9

10

11

1
A Shirvan Gelim carpet, the indigo field with five stepped medallions, all with hooked panels and guls, a madder gul border, single guard stripes, 338 x 190cm (11ft 1in x 6ft 3in), *L 1 Feb,* £1,650 ($2,313)

2
A Shirvan Gelim carpet, the madder field with eight guls, and a madder vine border, 310 x 169cm (10ft 2in x 5ft 7in), *L 10 Dec,* £385 ($485)

3
A Shirvan prayer rug, the ivory trellis mehrab with guls and a comb, the walnut border with a lovebird design, triple guard stripes, 188 x 89cm (6ft 2in x 2ft 11in), *L 1 Feb,* £1,045 ($1,465)

4
A Soumakh rug, last quarter 19th cent, the brick red ground with three latchhook-framed reserves flanking floral rosettes and palmette motifs, with a brown sawtooth border, ivory guard borders and a running-dog outer border 178 x 155cm (5ft 10in x 5ft 1in), *NY 11 Feb,* $3,520 (£2,514)

5
A Soumakh carpet, *c*.1875, the abrashed brick field with three lobed pale blue medallions with flanking straw-coloured octagons, with a pale blue ascending floral border, 259 x 239cm (8ft 6in x 7ft 10in), *NY 19 May,* $5,500 (£3,793)

6
A Kuba Soumakh runner, 3rd quarter 19th cent, the blue ground with green, straw, ivory and apricot floral motifs, with red brick and ivory floral borders, oxidised brown, 292 x 119cm (9ft 7in x 3ft 11in), *NY 1 Dec,,* $3,850 (£3,234)

7
A Talysh runner, the indigo field with ten hooked medallions, all with hooked guls and combs, the ivory border with rosettes and dice, triple guard stripes, 274 x 107cm (9ft x 3ft 6in), *L 17 Oct,* £2,200 ($2,750)

8
A Soumakh rug, the madder field with three indigo medallions enclosing guls, a black wave border, one inner and two outer guard stripes, 193 x 150cm (6ft 4in x 4ft 11in), *L 18 July,* £1,650 ($2,203)

9
A Caucasian Kelim, last quarter 19th cent, woven with ivory, brick, and midnight blue and abrashed blue horizontally banded panels of stepped medallions, 211 x 99cm (6ft 11in x 3ft 3in), *NY 1 Dec,* $1,320 (£1,109)

10
A Soumakh bagface, last quarter 19th cent, 63 x 58cm (2ft 1in x 1ft 11in), *NY 1 Dec,* $2,750 (£2,311)

1

2

3

4

6

7

9

8

10

1
A Khotan silk and metal thread carpet, the saffron star tile pattern field with a central circular thread medallion and spandrels with flowers and vines, within a saffron border, an inner pearl guard stripe, 290 x 196cm (9ft 6in x 6ft 5in), *L 18 July,* £1,540 ($2,056)

2
A Khotan carpet, mid-19th cent, the deep salmon field with a blue, mustard and pink central ovoid medallion, with flanking polychrome floral rosettes and urns, wave motif and floral cluster borders, ragged side borders, 348 x 196cm (11ft 5in x 6ft 5in), *NY 19 May,* $4,400 (£3,034)

3
A Khotan rug, 1st half 19th cent, the pale brick field with a central flattened ovoid star-filled blue medallion, blue spandrels with a creamy yellow trefoil-filled border, 236 x 112cm (7ft 6in x 3ft 8in), *NY 11 Feb,* $3,300 (£2,357)

4
A Khotan rug, the madder field with three indigo medallions enclosing flowerheads and guls, fretwork spandrels, a madder flowerhead border, 244 x 117cm (8ft x 3ft 10in), *L 17 Oct,* £2,750 ($3,437)

5
A Khotan carpet, the beige field with three indigo medallions and scattered floral sprays, Greek key spandrels, a beige wave border, one inner and three outer guard stripes, 376 x 183cm (12ft 4in x 6ft), *L 18 July,* £4,620 ($6,167)

6
A Khotan rug, the saffron field with an aubergine medallion, Greek key spandrels, an aubergine rosette border, one inner and three outer guard stripes, 221 x 152cm (7ft 3in x 5ft), *L 18 July,* £4,620 ($6,168)

7
A Samarkand carpet, the indigo field with three medallions with floral sprays, aubergine floral spandrels, an inner aubergine rosette border, an outer aubergine wave border on a plain aubergine ground, 277 x 140cm (9ft 1in x 4ft 7in), *L 18 July,* £3,520 ($4,699)

8
A Suzani embroidery, Uzbekistan, 3rd quarter 19th cent, the ivory field with a variety of floral clusters with a central ewer motif with a slant-leaf and bouquet border, 254 x 198cm (8ft 4in x 6ft 6in), *NY 19 May,* $2,750 (£1,897)

9
A Tekke carpet, the madder ground with four-teen rows of five guls, with secondary guls, within a madder border of sun-burst guls and chevrons, serrated leaf skirts, 315 x 230cm (10ft 4in x 7ft 6in), *G 13 Nov,* SF 7,700 (£2,377; $3,137)

10
A Kashgar rug, last quarter 19th cent, the ivory ground with blue pomegranates and angular vinery with a deep red floral bouquet border, 259 x 107cm (8ft 6in x 3ft 6in), *NY 1 Dec,* $8,250 (£6,932)

11
A Tekke carpet, the madder field with twelve rows of four guls, a madder sunburst gul border, diamond elems, 277 x 221cm (9ft 1in x 7ft 5in), *L 18 July,* £1,210 ($1,615)

1   2   3

4   5

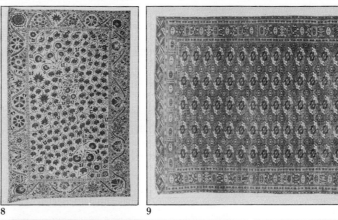
6   7

8   9

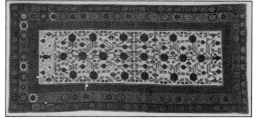

10   11

1
An Aubusson carpet, the ivory trellis-work field with an indigo medallion enclosing three fleur-de-lys, pale indigo spandrels and surround, the indigo border with cabochon panels, 546 x 508cm (17ft 11in x 16ft 8in), *L 17 Oct,* **£8,250 ($10,312)**

2
A Swedish cushion cover, Skåne, late 18th cent, with a central indigo octagonal medallion with ivory diamond medallions at each corner, a reciprocal indigo and madder border, rölakan weave, rosengång backing, 56 x 56cm (1ft 10in x 1ft 10in), *L 1 Feb,* **£275 ($386)**

3
A Swedish woven cushion cover, Skåne, late 18th cent, the central indigo medallion enclosing a red horse and initials, within a red border of star medallions, rölakan weave, 53 x 48cm (1ft 9in x 1ft 7in), *L 17 Oct,* **£440 ($550)**

4
A Swedish cushion cover, Skåne, 19th cent, the walnut field with a floral design with a large parrot, a unicorn and a girl, flamskav weave, 99 x 51cm (3ft 3in x 1ft 8in), *L 1 Feb,* **£440 ($617)**

5
A needlepoint carpet, 3rd quarter 19th cent, composed of six ivory and two black panels containing a floral bouquet in red, cornflower blue, and moss green, all within a floral border, holes, 315 x 201cm (10ft 4in x 6ft 7in), *NY 20 Oct,* **$7,700 (£6,471)**

6
A Swedish cushion cover, Skåne, late 18th cent, the red field with a trellis design with stepped guls, rölakan weave, rosengång backing, 89 x 57cm (2ft 11in x 1ft 10in), *L 1 Feb,* **£770 ($1,079)**

7
A Swedish woven cushion cover, Skåne, late 18th cent, the red field with a design of stepped medallions within a polychrome blixt border, rölakan weave, 109 x 48cm (3ft 7in x 1ft 7in), *L 17 Oct,* **£1,320 ($1,650)**

8
A Savonnerie tufted carpet, the indigo field with a central floral spray enclosed within a floral garland, the broad indigo border with scrolling floral cartouches; this appears to be a loosely interpreted copy of a 17th cent Royal Savonnerie carpet, 427 x 290cm (14ft x 9ft 6in), *L 1 Feb,* **£4,620 ($6,477)**

9
A needlework carpet, *c* 1925, in the Egyptian style, the red centre with a quatrefoil medallion enclosing a portrait of Tutankhamen with a beige surround, walnut border of stylised flowerheads, 282 x 287cm (9ft 3in x 9ft 5in), *L 21 Feb,* **£302 ($423)**

10
An Aubusson carpet, last quarter 19th cent, the pearl-grey field with an ivory cartouche medallion and an ivory floral surround within a swirling vine border, 369 x 259cm (12ft 1in x 8ft 6in), *NY 11 Feb,* **$6,325 (£4,517)**

11
An Aubusson carpet, mid 19th cent, the central circular medallion on a mocha field with scrolling arabesques and floral motifs, a floral border, 574 x 544cm (18ft 10in x 17ft 10in), *NY 20 Oct,* **$3,850 (£3,235)**

1

2

4

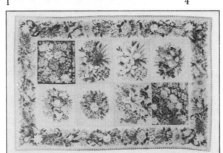
5

6

7

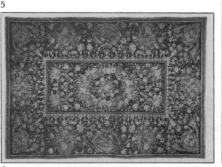
8

9

10

11

1
An Aubusson carpet, mid-
19th cent, 480 x 358cm
(15ft 9in x 11ft 9in),
NY 4 May,
$34,100 (£24,357)

2
An Aubusson carpet, 19th
cent, 571 x 500cm
(18ft 9in x 16ft 5in),
NY 4 May,
$29,600 (£21,143)

3
**An Aubusson throne
carpet,** woven for the
coronation of the first
King of Romania in
1881, 597 x 467cm
(19ft 7in x 15ft 4in),
NY 4 May,
$11,550 (£8,250)

4
An Aubusson rug, the field
with an ivory floral spray
medallion within an
acanthus leaf surround,
within a madder surround,
a strapwork cartouche
border, 175 x 168cm
(5ft 9in x 5ft 6in), *L 1 Feb,*
£1,870 ($2,622)

5
An Aubusson carpet, mid-
19th cent, 462 x 417cm
(15ft 2in x 13ft 8in),
NY 17 Nov,
$5,500 (£4,400)

6
An Aubusson carpet, the
two-tone madder field
with flowerheads and
vines, an ivory gul
medallion and spandrels
with acanthus leaves,
470 x 351cm (15ft 5in x
11ft 6in), *L 17 Oct,*
£6,050 ($7,562)

7
An Aubusson carpet, 3rd
quarter 19th cent,
638 x 574cm
(20ft 11in x 18ft 10in),
NY 17 Nov,
$23,100 (£18,480)

8
An Aubusson carpet, 2nd
quarter 19th cent,
757 x 465cm
(24ft 10in x 15ft 3in),
NY 17 Nov,
$25,300 (£20,240)

1

2

3

4

5

6

7

8

1

A **Chinese rug**, late 19th cent, the saffron field with a central circular floral medallion supported by floral sprays, within an ochre border, 253 x 161cm (8ft 3½in x 5ft 3½in), *P 15-18 May*, **£1,100 ($1,529)**

2

A **Chinese carpet**, the indigo field with a trellis pattern of flowerheads and madder spandrels, the surrounding border of flowerheads and other motifs, 261 x 270cm (8ft 7in x 8ft 10½in), *P 24-26 Jan*, **£286 ($415)**

3

A **Kansu rug**, 1st half 19th cent, the abrashed blue ground with an ivory and peach ovoid floral medallion, the field with tangerine and cream spots, 201 x 114cm (6ft 7in x 3ft 9in), *NY 1 Dec*, **$1,870 (£1,571)**

4

An **Indian Dhurry**, the beige field with a triple pole medallion, all with stylised vines and flower-heads, the border with rosettes within single guard stripes, 371 x 335cm (12ft 2in x 11ft), *L 1 Feb*, **£1,100 ($1,542)**

5

An **Agra rug**, the ochre field with a madder pole medallion and spandrels, all with the herati pattern, saffron border with pal-mettes and vines, triple guard stripes, 229 x 132cm (7ft 6in x 4ft 4in), *L 18 July*, **£3,300 ($4,406)**

6

An **Indian Dhurry**, the beige field with a diamond trelliswork design enclos-ing stepped guls, all in shades of pale indigo and madder, 358 x 206cm (11ft 9in x 6ft 9in), *L 1 Feb*, **£2,640 ($3,701)**

7

An **Indian Dhurry**, the field with an overall design of lozenges enclos-ing stepped guls, in shades of madder, green, beige and indigo, the ivory border with a stepped gul design, 470 x 409cm (15ft x 13ft 5in), *L 1 Feb*, **£1,870 ($2,622)**

8

An **Indian Dhurry**, the indigo field with stepped guls all in two shades of pale indigo, 196 x 124cm (6ft 5in x 4ft 1in), *L 1 Feb*, **£198 ($278)**

9

A **Srinagar rug**, the ivory field with a Tree-of-Life, with flowers and birds, an ivory floral border, triple guard stripes, 210 x 142cm (6ft 7in x 4ft 8in), *L 31 July*, **£495 ($673)**

10

An **Indian prayer rug**, the pale-indigo mehrab centred by a hanging lantern surmounted by a darker indigo arch, indigo flowerhead border, 241 x 159cm (7ft 11in x 5ft 2½in), *P 24-26 Jan*, **£605 ($877)**

1

2

3

4

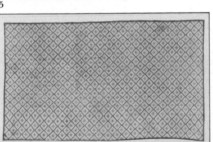
5

6
7

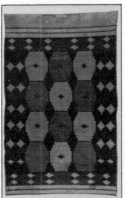
8

9

10

1
A Tabriz carpet, last quarter 19th cent, 467 x 342cm (15ft 4in x 11ft 3in), *NY 19 May,* **$14,300 (£9,862)**

2
A Kazakh rug, 19th cent, the indigo field with an ivory medallion enclosing guls and stylised flowerheads, the madder border with brackets and 'S' motifs, 221 x 183cm (7ft 3in x 6ft), *L 17 Oct,* **£1,980 ($2,475)**

3
A Heriz carpet, *c* 1875, minor losses to end borders, 330 x 236cm (10ft 10in x 7ft 9in), *NY 1 Dec,* **$11,000 (£9,244)**

4
A Veramin silk carpet, the madder ground decorated with a small indigo medallion outlined in pale indigo and enclosing a flowerhead and palmettes, similar spandrels, all within an indigo border, 315 x 186cm (10ft 4in x 6ft 1in), *G 15 May,* **SF 33,000 (£10,500; $15,014)**

1

2

3

4

1

A Savonnerie carpet, 17th cent, the indigo field with a central scallopshell rosette surrounded by concentric bands of acanthus leaves forming a double 'L' monogram, within an oak leaf and acorn frame bearing the Bourbon crown, indigo border with Fleurs-de-Lyse within frame guard stripes, woven *c.*1667-89, the central medallion from a larger carpet, thought to be a Royal Commission for the Palais du Louvre, 340 x 323cm (11ft 2in x 10ft 7in), *L 23-30 Nov,* **£104,500 ($126,445)**

2

A Bessarabian Gelim carpet, 18th cent, the field with a central circular medallion enclosing a walnut floral medallion surrounded by ivory and green panels, walnut spandrels, a saffron acanthus leaf border, 513 x 498cm (16ft 10in x 16ft 4in), *L 17 Oct,* **£30,800 ($38,500)**

1

2

Furniture

GRAHAM CHILD • THIERRY MILLERAND • GEORGE READ • LESLIE KENO

Sotheby's holds sales of fine furniture all over the world. French and Continental furniture is sold regularly in London, New York and Monaco and also in Florence and Amsterdam. English furniture is auctioned in New York and London. American furniture is sold in New York; Cape furniture in South Africa.

Buying furniture at auction can be a complicated process and potential buyers should always seek the advice of the expert staff in each location. The way furniture is described is the best indication of what the Sotheby's expert feels about the authenticity of the piece. For example, the inclusion of the word 'style' in a description means that the piece is a reproduction and not of the original period. If a particular historical or stylistic period (e.g., Biedermeier, Federal or Empire), or a particular reign (e.g., George III, Louis XV or Queen Anne), is listed with a date (e.g., circa 1750 or late 18th century), this indicates that the piece is genuine in the opinion of the expert in charge.

Although every effort is made to describe the condition of the furniture being offered, a piece may be described as 'restored' or 'repaired' without going into a great deal of detail. Therefore, all buyers should consult with Sotheby's expert staff to obtain all the information that is known. This knowledge will help buyers determine the cost of any repairs which may be necessary. Restoration can be very costly and the value of the piece may not justify the expense. However, period furniture is subject to wear over time and may appear at first sight to be in a much worse state than is, in fact, the case. A certain amount of restoration is almost always inevitable: legs may be spliced or renewed; broken mouldings and missing veneers may be restored and worn-out hinges may be replaced. Whilst none of these features is likely to worry the purchaser who wishes to use a piece of furniture, the specialist collector will often only buy pieces in their original state. In fact, many collectors will pay a premium price if the finish or patina of the piece of furniture is original.

Due to the extensive scholarly research that has been taking place over the past few decades, a great deal is now known about where fine furniture was made. It is now often possible to attribute the manufacture of furniture to particular craftsmen and to know for whom the furniture was made and, perhaps, even where it was placed. Due to guild regulations French furniture is often stamped by the maker. An article on signed French furniture of the 19th century appears on page 96. The attribution of American furniture is becoming much more precise, as is discussed on page 84.

This desire for knowledge is closely linked to the current widespread interest in historic houses and interior decoration, as borne out by the large number of new books and magazines published each year on these subjects. This in turn leads to the need for buyers to be aware of current ideas in fashion and taste as these directly influence the prices realized in today's market. The popularity of all styles of furniture fluctuates over time. At the moment, however, most periods of furniture production are widely sought after, with the possible exception of Renaissance and 17th century oak and walnut furniture.

1
A Charles I oak tester bedstead, c1640, the carved cornice and valence flanking a plain panelled tester, the headboard with carved panels and framework with four caryatid figures, 213 x 141cm (84 x 55½in), *HS 28 Mar,* **£8,250 ($12,293)**

2
A George III mahogany tester bed, c1790, the canopy with three arched sides painted with acanthus on slender leaf-carved gadrooned baluster supports, 239 x 159 x 203cm (94 x 62½ x 80in), *L 10 Feb,* **£3,740 ($5,243)**

3
A Louis XV walnut daybed, mid-18th cent, with scrolled ends carved with flowerheads and trailing vines, 208cm (82in), *NY 13 Oct,* **$7,425 (£6,086)**

4
A George IV mahogany tester bed, 2nd quarter 19th cent, the front posts with cluster pillars on acanthus-carved balusters, 321 x 229 x 171cm (91 x 90 x 67in), *C 10 Jan,* **£3,630 ($5,263)**

5
A Louis XVI mahogany bed, c1785, stamped G Jacob, with simple panelled ends, each flanked by a pair of stop-fluted pillars surmounted by pomegranate finials, 196 x 114cm (77 x 45in), *L 6 July,* **£2,200 ($3,036)**

6
A lacquered and gilt bedroom suite, early 20th cent, comprising a pair of single beds, a gentleman's wardrobe, a dressing table, a dressing stool, a pair of pedestal cupboards, a centre table, a pair of bergères and a side chair, a cheval mirror, and a metal wall appliqué, *C 29 Mar,* **£4,180 ($6,228)**

7
An Italian daybed, c1800, possibly Naples, in inlaid wood, lacquered and gilded, upholstered in velvet, 148cm (58¼in), *F 3/4 Oct,* **L 3,000,000 (£1,284; $1,604)**

8
An Empire ormolu-mounted mahogany bed, early 19th cent, with slightly scrolled headboard and footboard, the front rail fitted with ormolu mounts, 122 x 202 x 134cm (48 x 79½ x 53in), *NY 17 Nov,* **$8,800 (£7,040)**

9
A porcelain and ormolu-mounted kingwood bedroom suite, c1880, comprising a dressing table, a bedside table, a small armoire, and a double bed, dressing table w 84cm (33in), *L 9 Nov,* **£6,380 ($8,485)**

Condition is not stated in captions to furniture. Measurements are given height x width x depth.

1

2

3

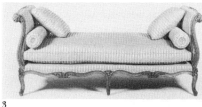
4

5

6

7

8

9

1
A George III mahogany tray-top bedside commode, c.1790, inlaid with satinwood stringing, the pair of crossbanded doors with foliate medallions, w 56cm (22in), *P 13 Nov*, £396 ($531)

2
A George III mahogany tray-top bedside commode, c.1790, the commode drawer with ceramic liner and cover, w 56cm (22in), *P 13 Nov*, £374 ($501)

3
A George III mahogany bedside table, 3rd quarter 18th cent, with shaped wooden gallery pierced with lifting handles, 81 x 48 x 43cm (32 x 19 x 17in), *NY 9 June*, $1,210 (£871)

4
A George III mahogany dressing or washing table, early 19th cent, the slightly raised back fitted with a shelf above an ebony strung top, 97 x 77cm (38 x 30½in), *C 10 Jan*, £660 ($957)

5
A Regency mahogany bow-front dressing table, c.1810, with ebonised strung borders and spiral reeded pillar terminals, 81 x 130cm (32 x 51in), *P 16 Oct*, £2,035 ($2,544)

6
A Regency mahogany dressing table, 1st quarter 19th cent, the galleried top carved with scrolling foliage and centred by a shell, 96.5 x 105cm (38 x 41½in), *C 4 Oct*, £1,540 ($1,987)

7
A Victorian mahogany dressing table, mid-19th cent, with an arched swing plate flanked by pierced spandrel supports, 163 x 120cm (64 x 47in), *C 27 Mar*, £594 ($885)

8
An Edwardian mahogany and marquetry bedroom suite, late 19th/early 20th cent, including a bedside cupboard, a dressing table, a gentleman's wardrobe and a double bed, wardrobe 214.6 x 208cm (84½ x 82in), *C 15 Aug*, £1,540 ($2,002)

9
A Victorian carved walnut dressing table, c.1860, 160 x 122cm (63 x 48in), *NY 18 July*, $1,100 (£840)

10
An Edwardian mahogany bedroom suite, c.1910, stamped Maple & Co, including a breakfront wardrobe, a pedestal dressing table and a pedestal bedside cupboard, wardrobe 241.3 x 208cm (95 x 82in), *C 27-30 Nov*, £1,210 ($1,464)

11
A mahogany, kingwood and thuya wood bedroom suite, late 19th cent, including a five-foot bed, a wardrobe, a kidney-shaped dressing table, a bedside cupboard and a pair of side chairs, wardrobe 213 x 173cm (84 x 68in), *C 27 Mar*, £1,100 ($1,639)

1   2   3   4

5   6   7

8   9

10   11

1

A Louis XVI-style marquetry and parquetry poudreuse, last quarter 19th cent, inspired by J H Riesener, the central lid lifting to reveal a mirror, the side sections opening to reveal wells, 75 x 94cm (29½ x 37in), *NY 15 Dec,* $4,950 (£4,160)

2

A Louis XV rosewood marquetry dressing table, 75 x 84 x 56cm (29½ x 33 x 22in), *M 25/26 June,* FF 13,320 (£1,143; $1,558)

3

An Empire mahogany dressing table, stamped Chapuis, early 19th cent, 147 x 66cm (58 x 26in), *L 18 May,* £1,155 ($1,615)

4

A German mahogany dressing chest, 2nd quarter 19th cent, with shaped swing mirror above a serpentine marble-topped drawer, the lower part with four graduated drawers, 203 x 104cm (80 x 41in), *C 4 Oct,* £638 ($823)

5

An American carved cherrywood tray-top dressing table, Connecticut, 1780-95, with one long and three short drawers, the centre drawer fan-carved, 76 x 72 x 50cm (30 x 28¼ x 19¾in), *NY 28 June,* $29,700 (£22,000)

6

A Federal bird's-eye maple inlaid mahogany corner basin stand, probably Salem, Massachusetts, 1800-1815, h 98cm (38½in), *NY 26 Jan,* $4,950 (£3,413)

7

A Federal inlaid mahogany corner basin stand, New England, *c*1815, the top fitted for receptacles, a line-inlaid single drawer below, 99 x 57 x 38cm (39 x 22½ x 15in), *NY 26 Jan,* $2,090 (£1,441)

8

An American rosewood dressing table, *c*1860, John Henry Belter, New York, 214 x 122cm (87 x 48in), *NY 24/25 Feb,* $16,500 (£11,379)

9

A rare Venetian carved giltwood and painted cradle, mid-18th cent, boat-shaped, the shell-shaped ends carved with rococo scrollwork and foliage, 122 x 150cm (48 x 59in), *L 18 May,* £4,400 ($6,153)

10

An oak cradle, 18th cent, with a shaped canopy above panelled sides on rockers, 84 x 96cm (33 x 37¾in), *C 10 Jan,* £495 ($718)

11

An Italian neoclassical walnut cradle, 1st quarter 19th cent, with slatted sides supported on circular supports with a lion's head finial, 164 x 125cm (64½ x 49in), *NY 13 Oct,* $1,430 (£1,172)

12

A Dutch marquetry cradle, 19th cent, the sides filled with turned spindles and with a domed head, inlaid with fruit and floral marquetry, 82 x 104cm (32½ x 41in), *L 9 Mar,* £1,485 ($2,214)

13

An English mahogany cradle, mid-19th cent, with gothic-shaped canopy and caned sides, 104cm (41in), *L 14 Dec,* £396 ($495)

1
A Jacobean oak
marquetry cupboard, with
later marquetry, 123 x
125 x 45cm (48½ x 49 x
17½in), *NY 9 June*,
$2,420 (£1,741)

2
A carved and inlaid oak
press cupboard, 2nd
quarter 17th cent, the
blind strapwork frieze on
a pair of leaf-curved cup
and cover balusters, 166
x 139cm (65½ x 54½in),
L 21 Sept,
£1,430 ($1,816)

3
A Welsh oak cwpwrdd
deuddarn, probably Den-
bighshire, early 18th cent,
the projecting frieze
initialled SW and dated
1728, 155 x 144cm (61 x
56in), *L 21 Sept*,
£1,925 ($2,445)

4
A Queen Anne oak press
cupboard, *c*1710, the
projecting cornice with
turned pendants above
triple fielded panelled
doors, three frieze
drawers and a pair of
fielded panelled doors
below, 183 x 135cm (72
x 53in), *P 11 Dec*,
£1,100 ($1,318)

5
A Charles I oak press
cupboard, early 17th cent,
with star-inlaid panelled
cupboards and a similar
panel fluted on baluster
supports, 168 x 145cm
(66 x 57in), *L 21 Sept*,
£1,870 ($2,375)

6
A Cape yellow-wood
server, late 19th cent, the
shaped backrail with a
platform supported by
two turned columns, the
lower section with two
drawers above two
doors, 136 x 120cm (53½
x 47¼in), *JHB 22 Nov*,
R 900 (£405; $495)

7
A James I oak and
marquetry food cupboard,
early 17th cent, the
cornice centred by a lion's
mask above a pair of
doors each with two
panels of four balusters,
86.5 x 91.5cm (34 x 36in),
L 24 Feb,
£572 ($801)

8
A Charles II oak mural
spice cupboard, *c*1680,
the top surmounted by a
moulding over a shallow
'cushion' drawer, the
door enclosing four
further drawers, 40 x
30cm (16 x 11½in),
L 12 Oct,
£770 ($986)

9
A Victorian rosewood
buffet, mid-19th cent,
with a galleried platform,
above two panelled doors
131 x 122cm (51 x 38in),
C 27 Mar,
£506 ($574)

10
A Victorian mahogany
three-tier buffet, 3rd
quarter 19th cent, the
moulded back surmounted
by fruiting foliage, 127 x
91cm (50 x 36in),
C 15 Aug,
£484 ($629)

1

2

3

4

5

6

7   8   9   10

1
**An Henri II walnut
cupboard,** mid-16th cent,
in two parts, with a pair
of fielded doors centred
by a carved female half-
figure, 160 x 117cm (63 x
46in), *L 18 May,*
£2,640 ($3,692)

2
**A French Burgundy
Renaissance oak armoire,**
16th cent, the doors with
pierced and scrolled
lockplates and hinges
and panels of portrait
roundels, 217 x 175 x
68cm (85½ x 69 x 27in),
NY 23/24 Nov,
$19,800 (£16,363)

3
**An Henri IV carved
walnut cupboard,** late
16th cent, the leaf-carved
frieze set with corbels,
the doors with carved
panels, 153 x 135cm (60 x
53in), *L 18 May,*
£2,200 ($3,190)

4
**A French walnut and oak
armoire,** *c*.1780, the
moulded cavetto cornice
above a leaf-and-berry
carved frieze, the doors
and drawers with shaped
panels, 256 x 152cm (100
x 60in), *CT 21 Mar,*
R 2,800 (£1,547; $2,307)

5
**An Henri II walnut
cupboard,** mid-16th cent,
the upper part with a
moulded cornice and a
frieze set with floral
corbels, the field panelled
doors flanked by columns,
formerly with a cresting,
181 x 118cm (63 x 46in),
L 18 May,
£3,520 ($5,104)

6
**A Louis XVI provincial
carved oak armoire,**
c.1780, with carved
cornice and a vine-
carved frieze, 229 x
175cm (90 x 69in), *L 25 May,*
£2,640 ($3,775)

7
**A Louis XVI provincial
oak armoire,** *c*.1780, the
rectangular cornice carved
with leaves and egg and
dart moulding, the
moulded panelled doors
with baskets of flowers,
229 x 175cm (90 x 69in),
L 3 Feb,
£3,080 ($4,318)

8
**A Louis XV provincial
oak buffet à deux corps,**
mid-18th cent, in two
parts, 236 x 155 x 56cm
(93 x 61 x 22in),
NY 16 June,
$2,200 (£1,606)

9
**A Louis XV provincial
oak buffet à deux corps,**
3rd quarter 18th cent,
with three grille-work
doors, the lower part
with three panelled
cupboard doors, 229 x
158 x 47cm (90 x 62 x
18½in), *NY 13 Oct,*
$6,600 (£5,410)

1

2

5

3

4

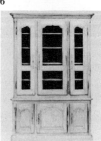

6

7

8

9

1

A Louis XV provincial
oak buffet à deux corps,
mid-18th cent, in two
parts, the upper with two
shelves with balustrated
fronts, the lower part
with panelled long drawer
and doors, 216 x 135 x
70cm (85 x 52 x 17½in),
NY 16 June,
$3,025 (£2,208)

2

A Louis XV/XVI pro-
vincial oak buffet à deux
corps, 3rd quarter 18th
cent, the upper part with
moulded rectangular
cornice, 253 x 150 x
58cm, (99½ x 59 x 23in),
NY 16 June,
$2,200 (£1,606)

3

A Louis XVI provincial
oak buffet à deux corps,
late 18th cent, in two
parts, with carving
overall, 249 x 166 x 71cm
(99 x 65½ x 28in),
NY 16 June,
$7,975 (£5,821)

4

A Louis XV marquetry
small armoire, *c.*1770, the
brown veined moulded
marble top above a pair
of inlaid doors, short
cabriole legs with gilt-
bronze sabots, 131 x 98cm
(51½ x 38½in), *L 6 July,*
£5,280 ($7,286)

5

A Dutch oak display
cabinet, mid-18th cent,
the moulded gable top
applied with a central
cartouche above a pair
of glazed doors enclosing
shelves, similarly glazed
canted sides, 210 x
135cm (112½ x 53in),
JHB 23 Aug,
R 3,100 (£1,649; $2,156)

6

A Dutch miniature
applewood cupboard,
mid-18th cent, the shaped
arched cornice above a
pair of panelled doors,
the bombé lower part
with drawers with ebonised
banded borders 92 x 67
x 30cm (36¼ x 26¼ x
11¾in), *NY 13 Oct,*
$2,475 (£2,029)

7

A Dutch burr-walnut
display cabinet, *c.*1750,
the upper part with a
shaped serpentine cornice
above a pair of glazed
doors, 244 x 178 x 43cm
(96 x 70 x 17in), *NY 13 Oct,*
$7,700 (£6,311)

8

A Louis XVI-style gilt-
bronze-mounted mahogany
armoire, early 20th cent,
of breakfront form sur-
mounted by two gilt-
bronze putti, decorated
overall with cast mounts,
h 309cm (125in), *NY 3 Nov,*
$20,900 (£16,720)

1

2

3

4

5

6

7

8

1

A Flemish carved oak cupboard, mid-17th cent, with gadrooned cornice faced by three masks above a pair of panelled doors incorporating carved strapwork panels, 210 x 152cm (82½ x 60in), *L 3 Feb,* **£2,090 ($2,930)**

2

A Dutch rosewood and marquetry armoire, *c*.1700, the marquetry 19th cent, with moulded cornice above a pair of panelled doors each outlined with a cavetto moulding, 203 x 185cm (80 x 73in), *L 3 Feb,* **£2,750 ($3,856)**

3

A Frankfurt walnut armoire, early 18th cent, with moulded cornice above a pair of arched moulded panelled inlaid doors, 207 x 194cm (81½ x 76½in), *L 18 May,* **£10,450 ($14,614)**

4

A Lombard walnut armoire, 2nd half 17th cent, the pair of doors with inlaid panels, 225 x 185cm (88½ x 73in), *F 10 May,* **L 9,605,000 (£3,912; $5,633)**

5

A German fruitwood armoire, *c*.1780, in two parts, with a serpentine moulded cornice and a pair of doors each with two fielded panels, 191 x 181cm (75 x 71in), *L 3 Feb,* **£3,080 ($4,318)**

6

A Dutch mahogany armoire, *c*.1770, with a pair of serpentine-topped doors and three drawers in the ogee front, 226 x 150cm (89 x 59in), *L 3 Feb,* **£858 ($1,203)**

7

A Dutch marquetry armoire, *c*.1770, the marquetry 19th cent, with a pair of panelled doors and three drawers inlaid throughout with birds and flowers, 231 x 155cm (91 x 61in), *L 3 Feb,* **£3,410 ($4,781)**

8

A Cape stinkwood and beefwood armoire, late 18th cent, the moulded arched cornice centred by a leaf-carved keyblock, a pair of shaped panelled doors and three linen-fold drawers below, 260 x 171cm (102 x 67in), *JHB 2 May,* **R 8,500 (£4,293; $6,004)**

9

A Dutch Colonial armoire, late 18th cent, 184 x 125 x 51.5cm (84 x 49 x 20¼in), *A 13-16 Mar,* **Dfl 2,088 (£477; $711)**

10

A Dutch oak armoire, *c*.1790, the arched cornice with an appliqué of leaves and harvest trophies above a pair of panelled doors, 262 x 190cm (103 x 75in), *L 3 Feb,* **£1,012 ($1,419)**

11

A Dutch mahogany and marquetry armoire, late 18th cent, the broken architectural cornice centred by an urn, 282 x 163cm (111 x 64in), *L 25 May,* **£3,520 ($4,923)**

12

A Biedermeier mahogany armoire, 2nd quarter 19th cent, the cupboard door panelled to resemble a secretaire, 211 x 115 x 53cm (83½ x 45¼ x 21in), *NY 16 June,* **$2,750 (£2,007)**

1   2   3

4   5   6

7   8   9

10   11   12

1

A Dutch rococo ormolu-mounted walnut marquetry cabinet on chest, mid-18th cent, inlaid in stained and natural fruitwoods, 192 x 83 x 53cm (75 x 32½ x 21in), *NY 16 June*, $3,850 (£2,810)

2

A Dutch walnut and marquetry display cabinet on chest, mid-18th cent, the marquetry 19th cent, the serpentine upper part with carved cresting and glazed door, 188 x 94cm (74 x 37in), *L 3 Feb*, £2,200 ($3,084)

3

A Dutch walnut and marquetry cabinet, late 18th cent, possibly inlaid in the 19th cent, with an arched moulded pediment, inlaid throughout with vases, flowers and foliage, 228 x 163cm (89½ x 64in), *C 10 Jan*, £2,530 ($3,669)

4

A mahogany corner cabinet, 18th cent, with shaped top and four doors, 228 x 120 x 62cm (89¾ x 47¼ x 24½in), *A 1 Oct*, Dfl 10,440 (£2,456; $3,168)

5

A German parquetry cabinet on chest, early 18th cent, in stained maple with walnut bandings and crossbandings, the doors inlaid with a crown monogram, 206 x 108cm (81 x 42½in), *L 18 May*, £2,860 ($4,147)

6

A French carved oak cabinet, c.1900, with profile portraits, linenfold and foliate motifs, the pair of doors with steel hinges and escutcheons, 148 x 104cm (58 x 41in), *P 16 Oct*, £330 ($413)

7

An Islamic bone and mother-of-pearl inlaid wood cabinet, probably Damascus or Cairo, c.1900, the canted form with shaped cresting and an arrangement of open shelves, 178 x 106cm (70 x 41½in), *L 9 Nov*, £1,705 ($2,268)

8

A Dutch marquetry press, mid-18th cent, the whole now inlaid with floral marquetry on a walnut ground, 246 x 170cm (97 x 67in), *L 30 Nov*, £7,700 ($9,317)

9

A maplewood wardrobe, c.1880, with a pyramidal top, a mirror door and drawer applied with mouldings carved as bamboo, 224 x 102cm (88 x 40in), *L 9 Nov*, £715 ($951)

10

An Indian carved ebony double cabinet, c.1860, of breakfront form, carved throughout with exotic fruits and flowers of India and elephant heads, the interior with 'secret' drawers, 229 x 157cm (90 x 62in), *L 9 Mar*, £5,060 ($7,539)

11

A French Renaissance revival walnut cabinet, c.1875, the upper part with doors flanked by Ionic columns, the lower part with carved female terms, 174 x 130cm (68½ x 51in), *L 9 Mar*, £440 ($656)

1   2   3

4   5

6   7   8

9   10   11

English Furniture

GRAHAM CHILD

English furniture prior to 1800 can be divided roughly according to the timbers used. It is desirable for a collector to have some knowledge of the various woods, together with an understanding of the styles which were fashionable at the period when a particular timber was most popular.

Until the closing years of the 17th century, Britain's traditional timber, oak, was predominantly in use. Oak does not blend easily with furniture from later periods and requires the right setting to be shown to greatest advantage. Today, oak furniture is comparatively rare and fine examples command high prices. However, pieces of cottage furniture, such as coffers, chairs and gateleg tables, are well within the scope of the collector with a relatively modest budget.

The age of walnut, from the end of the 17th century until the 1730s, is much loved today. The change of lifestyle at this time to smaller, more intimate, rooms, with a greater degree of comfort, required similar furniture. The reigns of William and Mary, Queen Anne and George I saw great changes not only in the type of object made, but also in their style. The pattern books that began to be circulated amongst cabinet makers at this time showed designs that were strongly influenced by France and the Low Countries. Tables and cabinet furniture, particularly small dressing tables and desks, withstand regular use better than the upholstered wing chairs and dining chairs which first appeared at this time. The finest pieces of walnut have become very expensive, but many provincial examples are available more reasonably.

The full range of domestic furniture from the age of mahogany provides a rich area for the collector. Mahogany began to be imported to Europe from the West Indies in quantity from the early 18th century and its popularity lasted from about 1730 until well into the 19th century. Furniture for the dining room, drawing room and bedroom can be found easily today at prices that vary enormously depending on the quality and condition of the object. This is the first period from which it is still not unusual to find sets of furniture—pairs of tables or mirrors, six to twelve (or more) dining chairs—though the collector must always be aware of 'harlequin' sets (those made up from not entirely matching pieces).

The age of satinwood, covering the last quarter of the 18th century, is by no means a time when satinwood was used exclusively, but was the period during which many rare and exotic timbers were used individually or together. There is considerable variety at this time between large cabinet furniture intended for architectural schemes and smaller pieces such as work tables and chairs, which have great delicacy and lightness of style. Robert Adam, Hepplewhite and Sheraton are amongst the most notable makers and designers of this period.

The 19th century witnessed the widespread use of all types of wood, walnut being particularly popular. Many ingenious inventions, for example patented furniture (p. 109, fig. 6), were produced, as well as much furniture copying or reviving earlier styles. These vary widely in quality and, although the best examples are inevitably fetching high prices, the majority is less expensive than 18th century furniture. The 19th century is a relatively new field for academic research and can prove a fascinating subject for the collector.

1
A Charles II oak panel-back armchair, South Yorkshire, late 17th cent, the scrolled cresting centred with a human mask, *L 21 Sept*, £1,375 ($1,746)

2
A pair of George II needlepoint upholstered carved walnut side chairs, *c*1740, each with an elongated rectangular backrest, the seat on leaf and scroll-carved cabriole legs ending in claw and ball feet, *NY 21 Jan*, $34,100 (£23,517)

3
A George III carved mahogany tilt-top tripod table, *c*1760, 71 x 76cm (28 x 30in), *NY 20 Oct*, $6,050 (£5,084)

4
A Regency octagonal inlaid satinwood work table, 1st quarter 19th cent, 76 x 48 x 36cm (30 x 18½ x 14in), *NY 12-14 Apr*, $3,080 (£2,154)

5
A William IV rosewood writing table, *c*1830, 73 x 107cm (28½ x 42in), *L 26 Oct*, £1,980 ($2,534)

1

A pair of **Regency inlaid rosewood side cabinets,** 19th cent, each with a moulded grey porphyry rectangular top, 88 x 163 x 47cm (34¼ x 64 x 18½in), *NY 21 Jan,* $13,200 (£9,428)

2

A pair of **Regency brass-inlaid rosewood side cabinets,** *c*.1815, each with a pair of grille-fronted doors within borders of scrolling foliage, 86.5 x 131cm (34 x 51½in), *L 16 Nov,* £9,900 ($13,068)

3

A pair of **Regency rosewood breakfront side cabinets,** *c*.1815, the red and grey-veined marble tops above a cupboard door applied with brass trellis flanked by open shelves, 90 x 140 x 33cm (35½ x 55 x 13in), *L 16 Nov,* £28,600 ($37,752)

4

A pair of **Regency mahogany side cabinets,** 1st quarter 19th cent, the slightly recessed front with a pair of grille-work doors, 91 x 133 x 35cm (36 x 52½ x 13¾in), *NY 20 Oct,* $4,950 (£4,160)

5

A **walnut and gilt-bronze side cabinet,** mid-19th cent, with a reddish marble top above an open section fitted with shelves, and flanked by outset parcel-gilt and fluted columns, 103 x 71cm (40½ x 28in), *C 4 Oct,* £462 ($596)

6

A **Victorian walnut and tulipwood banded display cabinet,** *c*.1850, with ormolu mounts and floral inlay, the glazed door enclosing a velvet-lined and shelved interior, 107 x 74cm (42 x 29in), *P 12-15 June,* £440 ($634)

7

A **walnut credenza,** mid-19th cent, the shaped moulded top with a cross-banded and glazed central door flanked by ogee glazed sides, applied with gilt-bronze mounts, 107 x 122cm (42 x 48in), *C 10 Jan,* £825 ($1,196)

8

A **Victorian walnut vitrine,** *c*.1860, with rectangular moulded top and concave cornice above glazed panel doors enclosing shelves, raised on a moulded plinth, 122 x 180cm (48 x 71in), *L 28 Sept,* £825 ($1,073)

9

A **Victorian burr-walnut small side cabinet,** *c*.1860, the rectangular amboyna crossbanded top outset with Corinthian columns with a pair of arched glazed doors enclosing shelves, 102 x 115.5cm (40 x 45½in), *L 28 Sept,* £748 ($972)

10

A **Victorian ebonised and walnut credenza,** *c*.1880, with two convex glazed doors, flanking a panelled door applied with a painted 'Sèvres' panel, 105 x 151cm (41½ x 59½in), *C 30 Oct-2 Nov,* £306 ($392)

11

A **Victorian walnut and kingwood side cabinet,** one door inlaid with flowers, birds and figures on an ebony ground and flanked by shaped glazed doors, 114 x 204cm (45 x 80in), *L 28 Sept,* £2,970 ($3,861)

1

2

3

4

5

6

7

8

9

10

11

1
A George III satinwood collector's cabinet, c.1790, the base with a pair of brass grille-filled doors enclosing twenty graduated specimen drawers, top and base associated, 153 x 93cm (60¼ x 36½in), *L 16 Mar,*
£2,970 ($4,425)

2
A Regency rosewood chiffonier, by Gillow's, Lancaster, early 19th cent, the top enclosed by a gallery above a mirrored panel, the lower part with a pair of silk panel doors on gadrooned feet, 137 x 92cm (54 x 36in), *C 4 Oct,*
£1,430 ($1,845)

3
A Regency concave-fronted rosewood chiffonier, c.1815, the galleried shelf on a pair of brass pillars and with a pair of conforming glazed doors, 122 x 99cm (48 x 39in), *L 5 Oct,*
£3,410 ($4,433)

4
A Regency mahogany cabinet, c.1810, with a raised two-tier open back, below are a pair of panelled doors enclosing an adjustable shelf, on sabre feet, 156 x 91.5cm (61½ x 36in), *P 20-22 Mar,*
£1,650 ($2,459)

5
A George IV rosewood chiffonier, c.1815, the raised mirror back with an open tier, pierced brass gallery and turned pillar supports, the frieze drawer with a brass-strung border above a pair of brass grille doors, 117 x 86cm (46 x 34in), *P 24 July,*
£1,265 ($1,689)

6
A late Victorian mahogany display cabinet, late 19th cent, with two tall slender glazed doors, flanking a bevelled mirror and a bow-front centre section with two glazed doors, 155 x 119cm (61 x 47in), *C 16 Oct,*
£352 ($451)

7
A rosewood display cabinet, c.1900, the back with broken-arched pediment above shelves and bevelled mirrors, the base with a galleried recess and panelled cupboard, 249 x 152.5cm (98 x 60in), *C 30 Oct-2 Nov,*
£858 ($1,098)

8
A rosewood and marquetry corner display cabinet, late 19th cent, the upper part with three galleried shelves interposed by bevelled mirrored plates, 205cm (91in), *C 5 July,*
£660 ($896)

9
An Edwardian mahogany and satinwood banded display cabinet, c.1910, inlaid with arabesques and swags, the arched back above a pair of glazed panelled doors enclosing velvet-lined shelves, 196 x 118cm (77½ x 46½in), *P 10-13 July,*
£616 ($838)

10
An Edwardian small mahogany display cabinet on stand, c.1910, with satinwood banding and stringing, the moulded cornice above a bow-fronted glazed panel flanked by a pair of doors with applied astragals, 121 x 61cm (47½ x 24in), *P 18-25 Sept,*
£550 ($710)

1

2

3

4

5

6

7

8

9

10

1
A French walnut meuble d'appui, c.1900, with ormolu mounts, the frieze drawer above a pair of glazed doors, the interior with shelves, 121 x 109cm (47½ x 43in), *P 21-24 Feb,*
£880 ($1,234)

2
A French kingwood and gilt-bronze-mounted serpentine vitrine, c.1880, the glazed door with concave and convex sides enclosing a mirror-backed interior, 152.5 x 90cm (60 x 35½in), *L 9 Mar,*
£2,530 ($3,770)

3
A French gilt-bronze-mounted kingwood veneered display cabinet, c.1890, the shaped serpentine front with glazed door, mounted throughout with foliate rococo mounts, 181 x 117cm (71 x 46in), *L 9 Nov,*
£4,180 ($5,559)

4
A gilt-bronze-mounted kingwood display cabinet, late 19th cent, the lower part of the door incorporating a Vernis Martin panel, 175 x 84cm (63 x 33in), *L 8 June,*
£1,485 ($2,153)

5
A Belgian marquetry cabinet, late 19th cent, 239 x 137cm (94 x 54in), *L 9 Mar,*
£1,100 ($1,640)

6
A French painted kingwood veneered vitrine, c.1900, the lower panels painted in the Vernis Martin style, 184 x 85cm (72½ x 33½in), *L 9 Mar,*
£1,155 ($1,722)

7
A gilt-bronze-mounted kingwood veneered display cabinet, c.1900, with galleried top, the mirror-lined interior with a door, 135 x 68cm (53 x 27in), *L 8 June,*
£1,705 ($2,472)

8
A gilt-bronze-mounted kingwood display cabinet, early 20th cent, in Louis XV style, the front with door and set with three glazed panels, with glazed serpentine sides and mirrored back, 168 x 132cm (66 x 52in), *L 8 June,*
£3,410 ($4,945)

9
A French gilt-bronze kingwood and Vernis Martin vitrine, c.1900, the bombé lower part painted by Albertini, with concave side sections and serpentine ends, 197 x 122cm (77 x 48in), *L 8 June,*
£2,750 ($3,988)

1

2

3

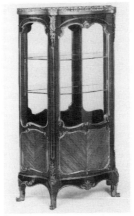

4

5

6

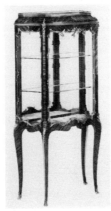

7

8

9

1
A George II carved mahogany breakfront cabinet, 2nd quarter 18th cent, with a moulded broken pediment, the front with an arched mirror flanked by classical female heads, and by a glass at each side, 240 x 137 x 56cm (94½ x 54 x 22in), *NY 20 Oct,*
$28,600 (£24,034)

2
A mahogany cabinet, early 19th cent, the central section with an arched pediment above a pair of fielded doors opening to later sliding shelves, flanked by a pair of subsidiary cabinets, 226 x 239 x 64cm (89 x 94 x 25in), *NY 9 June,*
$2,200 (£1,583)

3
A George III mahogany breakfront library bookcase, c.1770, the lancet-moulded cornice with a swan's-neck cresting and four diamond-glazed doors, slightly projecting lower part, 272 x 279cm (107 x 109½in), *L 16 Nov,*
£8,250 ($10,890)

4
A George III mahogany breakfront bookcase, last quarter 18th cent, with a moulded dentil cornice above four glazed doors, the projecting lower part with cupboard doors and drawers, 214 x 253 x 58cm (83½ x 99½ x 23in), *NY 9 June,*
$4,675 (£3,363)

5
A Regency mahogany display cabinet, c.1810, the pair of glazed doors with delicate glazing bars, the projecting lower part with a pair of doors enclosing drawers, 249 x 122cm (98 x 48in), *L 10 Feb,*
£1,100 ($1,542)

6
A George III carved mahogany bookcase cabinet, c.1770, a pair of glazed doors enclosing later glass shelves, the lower part enclosing shelves, 257 x 148 x 51cm (101 x 58 x 20in), *NY 21 Jan,*
$4,400 (£3,142)

7
A pair of George III inlaid and carved mahogany bookcase cabinets, last quarter 18th cent, 263 x 125 x 43cm (103½ x 49 x 17in), *NY 12-14 Apr,*
$81,400 (£56,923)

8
A George III inlaid mahogany breakfront secrétaire cabinet, c.1790, 244 x 256 x 58cm (96 x 100½ x 23in), *NY 21 Jan,*
$11,550 (£7,966)

9
A late George III mahogany breakfront bookcase, first quarter 19th cent, with a moulded frieze above four glazed doors enclosing shelves, 221 x 214 x 59cm (87 x 84 x 23in), *NY 12-14 Apr,*
$6,600 (£4,615)

1

2

3

4

5

6

7

8

9

1
**A George IV mahogany
breakfront bookcase,**
c.1825, the reeded
pilasters surmounted by
brass inlaid medallions
above open shelves, four
panelled doors below,
254 x 254cm (100 x
100in), *P 18-25 Sept,*
£3,740 ($4,825)

2
**A Victorian mahogany
breakfront library bookcase,**
c.1840, the glazed doors
with horizontal scroll-
and-paterae-carved bars,
the projecting lower part
with panelled doors, 267
x 221cm (105 x 87in),
L 6 Apr,
£2,530 ($3,643)

3
**A Victorian mahogany
breakfront secrétaire bookcase,** c.1840, the moulded
cornice above two pairs
of glazed doors, the
lower part with fitted
writing drawer, 249 x
226 x 43cm (86 x 89 x
17in), *L 14 Dec,*
£2,530 ($3,163)

4
**A George III style
breakfront bookcase,** 19th
cent, four astragal-glazed
doors above seven
panelled doors, 282 x
337cm (111 x 132½in),
C 4 Oct,
£3,300 ($4,257)

5
**A Victorian mahogany
and pitched pine bookcase,**
2nd quarter 19th cent,
with two glazed doors,
drawers and two panelled
doors below, 234 x
129.5cm (92 x 51in),
C 30 Oct-2 Nov,
£572 ($732)

6
**A George III style inlaid
mahogany breakfront
secrétaire bookcase,**
stamped Edwards &
Roberts, c.1870, with
four glazed doors, the
lower section with a
secrétaire drawer enclosing
compartments, 246 x 246cm
(97 x 97in), *NY 24/25 Feb,*
$9,075 (£6,259)

7
**A George III style mahogany
breakfront bookcase,** 20th
cent, with a moulded
dentil cornice above four
doors, drawers and
panelled doors below,
222 x 173cm (87½ x 68in),
C 4-6 Sept,
£1,430 ($1,859)

8
**A Biedermeier maple
bookcase,** early 19th cent,
with a stepped moulded
cornice above a pair of
glazed doors raised on
bracket feet, 181 x 117 x
51cm (71 x 46 x 20in),
NY 7 Apr,
$2,640 (£1,846)

9
**A Biedermeier maple
bookcase,** early 19th cent,
with a stepped moulded
cornice above a pair of
partially glazed doors
raised on block feet, 181
x 112 x 37cm (72 x 44 x
14¼in), *NY 7 Apr,*
$2,750 (£1,923)

1

2

3

4

5

6

7

8

9

1
A George III mahogany canterbury, c.1790, with latticework sides, the frieze drawer outlined with boxwood stringing, 48cm (18¾in), P 24-26 Jan, £792 ($1,148)

2
A Regency mahogany canterbury, c.1810, 47cm (18½in), P 20-22 Mar, £715 ($1,065)

3
A George III mahogany canterbury, c.1800, with single frieze drawer, 45 x 68.5cm (21½ x 27in), C 10 Jan, £374 ($542)

4
A Regency rosewood canterbury, c.1810, inlaid with cut brass, the legs ending in brass cappings and castors, 53cm (21in), P 18-25 Sept, £902 ($1,163)

5
A George IV rosewood canterbury, c.1820, 53cm (21in), P 10-13 July, £484 ($658)

6
A Victorian rosewood canterbury, c.1840, 61cm (24in), L 28 Sept, £495 ($643)

7
A Victorian walnut music canterbury, c.1850, the open tier with pierced fret gallery, h 100cm (39½in), P 24-27 July, £726 ($966)

8
A William IV carved and turned rosewood seven tier étagère, c.1830, 173 x 156 x 43cm (68 x 61½ x 17in), NY 21 Jan, $16,500 (£11,785)

9
A William IV rosewood whatnot, c.1835, each tier supported by turned spindles, h 147.5cm (58in), L 14 Dec, £990 ($1,237)

10
A Victorian walnut whatnot, c.1850, inlaid with boxwood designs, on turned fluted supports, h 134.6cm (53in), C 11-14 Dec, £440 ($550)

11
An Edwardian mahogany revolving bookcase, late 19th cent, with two tiers joined by rails on a central column, 86.5 x 49.5cm (34 x 19½in), C 4-6 Sept, £550 ($715)

12
A French rosewood marquetry étagère, early 19th cent, with galleried top and three shelves, the frieze with a pull-out writing surface, grille sides, 100 x 82 x 32cm (39½ x 32 x 12½in), M 24/25 June, FF 55,500 (£4,764; $6,491)

13
A gilt-bronze and lacquer étagère, late 19th cent, the three rectangular shelves formed of chinoiserie lacquer panels decorated with figures, the top one with a gallery, 76 x 41cm (30 x 16in), L 6 July, £990 ($1,366)

14
A pair of French brass-mounted mahogany étagère tables, c.1900, with three galleried lozenge-shaped tiers and trestle supports, with splayed legs, 68 x 54cm (27 x 21½in), L 8 June, £825 ($1,196)

15
A French kingwood and ormolu mounted étagère, c.1910, the quarter-veneered removable tray top on scrolling supports, the lower part with a sunburst veneer with a crossbanded border, 92.5 x 76cm (36½ x 30in), L 9 Nov, £682 ($907)

1   2   3

4   5   6

7   8   9

10   11   12

13   14   15

1
A William and Mary walnut cabinet on chest, c.1695, with a pair of feather-banded doors enclosing drawers, handles and feet replaced, 179 x 110cm (70½ x 43in), *L 15 June*, £3,300 ($4,653)

2
A Queen Anne walnut chest on chest, with oak sides, on later turned legs joined by stretchers, 155 x 102cm (61 x 42in), *L 5 Oct*, £1,495 ($1,943)

3
A George I walnut chest on chest, c.1720, inlaid with featherbanding, 175 x 107cm (69 x 42in), *P 15-18 May*, £3,520 ($4,893)

4
A George III carved mahogany chest on chest, c.1770, with a fret-carved and dentil moulded swan's-neck cresting above a blind fret-carved frieze, the drawers flanked by fluted canted corners, 212 x 109 x 66cm (83½ x 43 x 22in), *NY 21 Jan*, $4,400 (£3,034)

5
A Queen Anne walnut chest on chest, c.1710, in well-figured burr-wood, with oak sides, 169 x 104cm (66½ x 41in), *L 10 Feb*, £2,860 ($4,004)

6
A George I walnut chest on chest, c.1730, with canted reeded corners, 179 x 104cm (70½ x 41in), *L 14 Dec*, £1,430 ($1,787)

7
A George III inlaid mahogany chest on chest, last quarter 18th cent, the canted corners inlaid with geometric stringing, later bracket feet, 191 x 115 x 59cm (75 x 45 x 23¼in), *NY 9 June*, $2,420 (£1,741)

8
A George III mahogany tallboy, c.1780, with blind scrollwork frieze, the drawers flanked by canted blind gothic fret corners, pierced bracket feet, 183 x 107cm (72 x 42in), *L 10 Feb*, £2,420 ($3,388)

9
A George III mahogany chest on chest, 3rd quarter 18th cent, flanked by canted fluted pilasters, 186 x 121 x 60cm (73 x 47½ x 23½in), *NY 12-14 Apr*, $4,400 (£3,677)

10
A George III plum pudding mahogany inlaid clothes press, last quarter 18th cent, the lower part with two short above two long graduated drawers, 207 x 127 x 59cm (81½ x 50 x 23½in), *NY 20 Oct*, $3,740 (£3,142)

1

2

5

3

6

9

7

8

4

10

1
A Commonwealth oak chest of drawers, c.1650, the rectangular top above a saw-edged banding above two short and three graduated panelled drawers, 94 x 114cm (37 x 45in), *L 21 Sept,* £605 ($768)

2
A Charles II walnut chest of drawers, c.1675, a frieze drawer and two long drawers each applied with geometric mouldings divided by a bead moulding, w 94cm (37in), *L 21 Sept,* £1,430 ($1,816)

3
A William and Mary walnut and marquetry chest of drawers, c.1690, with panels of floral marquetry on ebonised reserves, partly on an oyster-veneered ground, 90 x 102cm (35½ x 40in), *L 16 Mar,* £4,070 ($6,064)

4
A William and Mary burr-walnut and crossbanded chest, c.1690, inlaid with satinwood stringing, on later turned feet, 91.5 x 99cm (36 x 39in), *HS 25 June,* £1,265 ($1,783)

5
A Queen Anne walnut chest, early 18th cent, handles replaced, 95 x 99cm (37½ x 39in), *L 27 Jan,* £726 ($1,053)

6
A George I walnut chest of drawers, c.1720, with moulded quarter-veneered top, 89 x 94cm (35 x 37in), *L 12 Oct,* £1,540 ($1,971)

7
A George II walnut chest, c.1730, 84cm (33in), *L 16 Mar,* £4,400 ($6,556)

8
A late George II mahogany small chest, c.1755, with baize-lined slide, above two short and three graduated drawers, 89.5cm (35¼in), *L 16 Nov,* £1,430 ($1,888)

9
A George III mahogany small chest of drawers, c.1770, 76 x 81 x 19½cm (30 x 32 x 19½in), *NY 21 Jan,* $2,310 (£1,650)

10
An early George III mahogany small chest, c.1760, w 76cm (30in), *L 5 Oct,* £2,640 ($3,432)

11
A George II mahogany dressing chest, with a brushing slide above four drawers, 76 x 81cm (30 x 32in), *L 15 June,* £1,760 ($2,482)

12
A small George III mahogany chest of drawers, 3rd quarter 18th cent, 79 x 62 x 49cm (31 x 24½ x 19½in), *NY 12-14 Apr,* $3,740 (£2,615)

13
An early George III mahogany serpentine chest, c.1770, w 112cm (44in), *L 6 April,* £825 ($1,188)

1
A late George III inlaid mahogany bow-fronted chest of drawers, early 19th cent, with a kingwood crossbanded top, 95 x 85 x 49cm (37½ x 33½ x 19½in), *NY 21 Jan*, $2,750 (£1,964)

2
A George III mahogany serpentine chest, c.1790, the top and sides outlined with 'barber's pole' stringing leading to slender splayed feet, w 86.6cm (34¾in), *L 5 Oct*, £2,750 ($3,575)

3
A George III mahogany chest, early 19th cent, of bow-front outline, 94 x 112cm (37 x 44in), *C 5 July*, £825 ($1,119)

4
A George III mahogany and satinwood serpentine chest of drawers, c.1790, crossbanded in kingwood and inlaid with chequered lines, 99 x 125cm (39 x 49in), *L 15 June*, £3,850 ($5,428)

5
A George III inlaid satinwood and rosewood serpentine-fronted chest of drawers, last quarter 18th cent, top inlaid with an oval satinwood panel, the sides inlaid to match, 81 x 117 x 57cm (32 x 46½ x 22½in), *NY 20 Oct*, $16,500 (£13,865)

6
A William IV rosewood Wellington fall-front secretary chest of drawers, 2nd quarter 19th cent, the slightly recessed front with two false drawers opening to form a writing surface, 122 x 61 x 36cm (48 x 24 x 14¼in), *NY 20 Oct*, $3,300 (£2,773)

7
A Victorian bird's-eye maple Wellington chest, c.1860, the six drawers with a locking pilaster, on a plinth base, 122 x 58.5cm (48 x 23in), *P 11 Dec*, £968 ($1,152)

8
A George III marquetry inlaid harewood serpentine-fronted commode, with a gilt-metal banded top centring an oval marquetry reserve, the panelled doors enclosing a shelf, sold with a later matching copy, 90 x 100 x 54cm (35½ x 39½ x 21½in), *NY 21 Jan*, $24,200 (£17,285)

9
A Victorian rosewood and crossbanded Wellington chest, c.1870, inlaid with satinwood arabesques, the six drawers flanked by locking pilasters with foliate carving, 113 x 64cm (44½ x 25in), *P 17-19 Apr*, £1,320 ($1,887)

10
A George III mahogany linen press or side cabinet, c.1770, of serpentine shape with a pair of panelled doors with rosettes at the corners, 94 x 119cm (37 x 47in), *L 15 June*, £6,820 ($9,616)

11
A George III inlaid burr-walnut and burr-yew-wood demi-lune commode, c.1790, with a pair of doors enclosing a shelf, 86 x 137 x 66cm (34 x 54 x 22in), *NY 21 Jan*, $9,900 (£6,828)

12
An Irish harewood and burr-elm commode, late 18th cent, veneered in segments and crossbanded in kingwood, dummy frieze drawer, 82 x 144cm (32½ x 56in), *L 15 June*, £5,500 ($7,755)

13
A satinwood and marquetry demi-lune side cabinet, c.1880, in George III style, crossbanded in rosewood, inlaid throughout with ovals and swags partly in green-stained wood, 93 x 150cm (37½ x 59in), *L 28 Sept*, £2,420 ($3,146)

1

An American carved cherrywood flat-top highboy, New England, 1750-75, in two parts, the upper with moulded cornice above five drawers, the lower with one long and three short moulded drawers, 185 x 100 x 47cm (73 x 39¼ x 18½in), *NY 30 June,* **$6,600 (£4,889)**

2

An American carved mahogany flat-top highboy, Salem, Massachusetts, 1755-75, in two parts, 175 x 92 x 53cm (69 x 36 x 21in), *NY 28 Jan,* **$9,900 (£6,828)**

3

An American carved cherrywood bonnet-top highboy, Connecticut, 1760-80, in two parts, the upper with moulded swan's-neck crest with three finials, two drawers with fan moulding, 224 x 99 x 49cm (88 x 39 x 19½in), *NY 30 June,* **$23,100 (£17,111)**

4

An American carved cherrywood lowboy, Connecticut, c.1760, with one long and three short moulded drawers, the shaped skirt centred by a carved fan, 74 x 90 x 58cm (29¼ x 35½ x 22¾in), *NY 8 Dec,* **$16,500 (£13,750)**

5

A carved curly maple tall chest of drawers, New England, c.1770-90, with five graduated moulded long drawers, 120 x 100 x 52cm (47 x 39 x 20½in), *NY 8 Dec,* **$3,300 (£2,750)**

6

An American carved walnut tall chest of drawers, Pennsylvania, c.1780, the projecting moulded cornice over five short and four long moulded graduated drawers, 163 x 109 x 59cm (64 x 43 x 23in), *NY 8 Dec,* **$5,225 (£4,354)**

7

An American carved cherrywood tall chest of drawers, Connecticut, c.1785, five short drawers and five graduated long drawers below, 143 x 102 x 53cm (56½ x 40 x 21in), *NY 8 Dec,* **$7,425 (£6,188)**

8

A Federal carved walnut tall chest of drawers, Chester County, Pennsylvania, c.1800, the moulded cornice with punch-work motifs above graduated drawers, 175 x 100 x 53cm (69½ x 39½ x 21in), *NY 28 Jan,* **$4,400 (£3,034)**

9

A Federal inlaid walnut tall chest of drawers, Pennsylvania, c.1800, the moulded cornice with line-inlaid edge above six graduated long drawers with cockbeaded surrounds, 170 x 105 x 56cm (67 x 42½ x 22in), *NY 28 Jan,* **$6,600 (£4,552)**

10

An American carved maple chest on chest, Northern New England, c.1760, in two parts, 188 x 102 x 52cm (74 x 40 x 20½in), *NY 8 Dec,* **$5,775 (£4,813)**

11

A carved walnut tall chest of drawers, Chester County, Pennsylvania, c.1770, with five short and four long graduated drawers, 147 x 105 x 57cm (58 x 41½ x 22½in), *NY 26 Jan,* **$9,900 (£6,827)**

12

An American carved maple bonnet-top chest on chest, Massachusetts, c.1775, in two parts, the upper with moulded swan's-neck crest with three turned finials, 213 x 98 x 47cm (84 x 38½ x 18½in), *NY 30 June,* **$14,850 (£11,000)**

1

2

3

4

5

6

7

8

9

10

11

12

1
An American carved
mahogany block-front
chest of drawers,
Massachusetts, c.1760,
80 x 98.5 x 54.5cm (31½ x
38¾ x 21½in), *NY 8 Dec,*
$46,750 (£38,958)

2
An American carved
mahogany block-front
chest of drawers,
Massachusetts, c.1765,
77 x 85 x 51cm (30½ x 33½
x 20in), *NY 28 Jan,*
$15,950 (£11,000)

3
A carved maple chest of
drawers, New England,
1780-1800, 85 x 109 x
51cm (33½ x 43 x 20in),
NY 28 June,
$2,750 (£2,037)

4
A curved curly maple
chest of drawers, New
England, c.1785, four
graduated long drawers,
the upper faced to
simulate two short
drawers, 101 x 99 x 53cm
(39¾ x 39 x 21in),
NY 28 June,
$7,150 (£5,296)

5
An inlaid mahogany bow-
front chest of drawers,
Massachusetts, 1780-1800,
80 x 105 x 56cm (31½ x
41½ x 22in), *NY 26 Jan,*
$5,500 (£3,793)

6
A Federal inlaid cherry-
wood bow-front chest of
drawers, Connecticut,
c.1800, with four cock-
beaded graduated long
drawers, 86 x 100 x 53cm
(34 x 39½ x 20¾in),
NY 26 Jan,
$7,150 (£4,931)

7
A Federal inlaid cherry-
wood bow-front chest of
drawers, probably
Connecticut, c.1805, the
oblong top above four
cockbeaded graduated
long drawers, 96 x 105 x
57cm (38 x 41½ x 22½in),
NY 28 Jan,
$2,750 (£1,897)

8
A Federal inlaid
mahogany bow-front chest
of drawers, New England,
1800-15, the oblong top
over four cockbeaded
long drawers, 96 x 102 x
56cm (38 x 40 x 22in),
NY 28 Jan,
$1,320 (£910)

9
A Federal painted and
decorated chest of drawers,
New England, c.1810,
painted and grained
overall in shades of
brown with simulated
line-inlay, 101 x 99 x
49cm (40 x 39 x 19in),
NY 8 Dec,
$2,420 (£2,017)

10
A Federal inlaid walnut
bow-front chest of drawers,
Middle Atlantic States,
c.1815, with ivory
keyholes, 99 x 102 x
61cm (39 x 40 x 24in),
NY 28 June,
$880 (£651)

11
An American painted pine
blanket chest, New
England, 1750-70, the
rectangular moulded
hinged lid opening to a
well, the case with two
long drawers, painted
red, 107 x 94 x 49.5cm
(42 x 37 x 19½in), *NY 8 Dec,*
$660 (£550)

12
An American painted and
decorated blanket chest,
New England, 1750-80,
painted and grained
overall in red and black
during the 19th cent, 94
x 99 x 46cm (37 x 39 x
18in), *NY 8 Dec,*
$1,100 (£917)

13
A Federal painted and
decorated blanket chest,
possibly Thomas Matteson,
Vermont, c.1820, the
rectangular hinged lid
opening to a well with
till, the case with simu-
lated drawers, painted
and grained overall in
shades of brown, 98 x 97
x 47cm (38½ x 38 x
18½in), *NY 8 Dec,*
$8,800 (£7,333)

1

2

3

4

5

6

7

8

9

10

11

12

13

1
An early Louis XV king-wood parquetry commode, c.1730, with mottled rust and grey marble top above two short and two long drawers, 84 x 129.5cm (33 x 51in), *L 30 Nov,* **£4,620 ($5,590)**

2
A Louis XV commode, with a grey and white marble top, the drawers veneered with marquetry, gilt-bronze mounts, 86 x 126 x 66cm (33⅞ x 59½ x 26in), *M 25/26 June,* **FF 44,400 (£3,811; $5,193)**

3
A Louis XV ormolu-mounted provincial walnut commode, mid-18th cent, with a marble top above three long drawers, 99 x 124 x 58.6cm (39 x 49 x 23in), *NY 13 Oct,* **$3,300 (£2,705)**

4
A Louis XV provincial walnut commode, 2nd quarter 18th cent, with a serpentine-fronted wooden top, the drawers fitted with wrought-iron handles, 87 x 133 x 65.5cm (34¼ x 52½ x 25¾in), *NY 7 Apr,* **$5,775 (£4,038)**

5
A Louis XV provincial walnut commode, c.1750, the serpentine front with drawers with simple recessed panels, 87 x 125cm (34 x 49in), *L 18 May,* **£5,060 ($7,337)**

6
A Louis XV provincial ormolu-mounted fruitwood commode, mid-18th cent, 88 x 137 x 67cm (34½ x 55¾ x 26½in), *NY 16 June,* **$3,300 (£2,409)**

7
A Louis XV provincial serpentine-fronted marble-topped commode in oak and walnut, mid-18th cent, with mottled white-veined black marble top, 85 x 120cm (33½ x 47in), *L 30 Nov,* **£2,310 ($2,795)**

8
A Louis XV provincial ormolu-mounted fruitwood commode, mid-18th cent, with a serpentine-fronted wooden top, 90 x 127 x 59cm (35½ x 50 x 23¼in), *NY 13 Oct,* **$3,575 (£2,930)**

9
A Louis XV black lacquer commode, stamped 'I Dubois JME', mid-18th cent, with moulded white-streaked mottled red marble top, the drawers veneered with a panel of Chinese lacquer painted in red and gilt, 88 x 114cm (34½ x 45in), *L 6 July,* **£26,400 ($36,432)**

1

2

3

4

6

7

8

9

1
Two Louis XV commodes, stamped F Rubestuck, Jurande, with marble tops, the drawers inlaid with flowers on a sycamore ground, h 85 and 85.5cm (33⅜ and 33⅝in), w 93 and 95cm (36½ and 37½in), d 48cm (18⅞in), *M 24/25 June*, **FF 721,500 (£61,931; $84,386)**

2
A Louis XV marquetry serpentine commode, mid-18th cent, with a grey and white marble top, the drawers veneered with floral marquetry within geometric strapwork borders, 130cm (51in), *L 6 July*, **£3,740 ($5,161)**

3
A Louis XV/XVI ormolu-mounted tulipwood and fruitwood parquetry and marquetry commode, 3rd quarter 18th cent, signed I P Dusautoy, *NY 17 Nov*, **$30,800 (£24,640)**

4
A Louis XVI kingwood commode, c 1780, stamped A Gosselin, 84 x 97cm (33 x 38in), *L 6 July*, **£4,620 ($6,376)**

5
A Louis XVI brass-mounted tulipwood and purplewood parquetry commode, last quarter 18th cent, signed J B Henry, with a rouge Languedoc marble top, 87 x 131 x 61.5cm (34¼ x 51½ x 24¼in), *NY 7 Apr*, **$4,400 (£3,077)**

6
A Louis XVI ormolu-mounted commode, last quarter 18th cent, signed J Demoulin, with shaped rectangular grey mottled marble top, 84 x 81 x 42cm (33 x 32 x 16½in), *NY 16 Nov*, **$2,970 (£2,376)**

7
A Louis XVI ormolu-mounted purplewood and tulipwood parquetry chiffonnier, last quarter 18th cent, signed G Dester, with a rectangular rouge Languedoc marble top above eight drawers, 165 x 67 x 34cm (65 x 26½ x 13½in), *NY 17 Nov*, **$13,200 (£10,560)**

8
An Empire brass-mounted mahogany commode, early 19th cent, with a black marble top, the drawers flanked by free-standing columns, 91 x 130 x 63cm (35¾ x 51¼ x 24¾in), *NY 7 Apr*, **$3,575 (£2,500)**

9
A Louis XV-style gilt-bronze marquetry commode, late 19th cent, with serpentine rouge de Flandres marble top, 86.5 x 70cm (34 x 27½in), *L 9 Nov*, **£770 ($1,024)**

10
A Louis-XV style gilt-bronze-mounted tulipwood marquetry commode, late 19th cent, after Charles Cressent, with a shaped marble top, mounted overall with gilt-bronze trees, acorns, leaves, birds and putti, 91 x 141cm (36 x 56in), *NY 3 Nov*, **$16,500 (£13,200)**

11
A bois de citron marquetry commode, c 1900, in Louis XV style, the moulded serpentine breche violette marble top above two drawers, 65 x 130cm (33½ x 51¼in), *L 8 June*, **£2,585 ($3,748)**

1

2

3

4

5

6

7

8

9

10

11

1
A Tuscan walnut side cabinet, mid-16th cent, with three drawers in the frieze, above a pair of panelled doors centred by fluted bosses, 118 x 140cm (46½ x 55in), *HS 28 Mar,* **£6,050 ($9,015)**

2
A North Italian walnut side cabinet, possibly Genoese, late 16th cent, the panelled front faced with moulded strapwork and containing three drawers above a pair of cupboards, 124.5 x 156cm (49 x 61½in), *HS 28 Mar,* **£4,620 ($6,884)**

3
A Bolognese walnut side cabinet, 1st half 17th cent, with panelled front and sides, the frieze with three drawers, the front with applied metal bosses, the top 164 x 64cm (64½ x 25in), *F 5 June,* **L 10,500,000 (£4,357; $6,318)**

4
A pair of small Venetian walnut veneered side cabinets, mid-18th cent, with walnut and briarwood inlay, the top 55 x 35cm (21½ x 13¾in), *F 19 Dec,* **L 12,000,000 (£5,070; $6,338)**

5
A Sicilian painted and parcel-gilt side cabinet, mid-18th cent, the top decorated to simulate *verde antico* marble, the front and sides with gilt scrolling foliage on a stamped green ground centred by a mirror panel, 89 x 97cm (35 x 38in), *L 30 Nov,* **£880 ($1,065)**

6
An Italian walnut commode, Emilia, mid-17th cent, the three drawers with framed panelling, bracket feet, the top 62 x 162cm (24½ x 63¾in), *F 10 May,* **L 7,345,000 (£3,128; $4,376)**

7
A Flemish walnut chest, c.1700, with four drawers, all applied with ripple mouldings, the top drawer concealed in the frieze, on bun feet, 91.4 x 96.5cm (36 x 38in), *C 11-14 Dec,* **£506 ($633)**

8
Two similar Lombard bone-inlaid ebonised secrétaire commodes, c.1700, with hinged divided rectangular tops above three long drawers, the top one with a fall-front, extensively altered, 86.5 x 138.5cm (34 x 54½in), *L 30 Nov,* **£3,850 ($4,659)**

9
A German walnut commode, 1st half 18th cent, with four drawers, the top inlaid with a rosette, 88 x 117.5 x 55cm (34½ x 46¼ x 21½in), *A 1 Oct,* **Dfl 9,048 (£2,129; $2,746)**

10
A Dutch burr-walnut and parquetry chest of drawers, early 18th cent, the rectangular top inlaid with bird and foliate motifs, the drawers similarly inlaid, 91 x 97cm (36 x 38in), *JHB 23 Aug,* **R 2,500 (£1,220; $1,595)**

11
A German serpentine walnut commode, c.1740, with a broad crossbanding and moulded top, the three drawers outlined with simple ebony strapwork, 82 x 123cm (32½ x 48½in), *L 30 Nov,* **£2,750 ($3,327)**

12
A German walnut marquetry and parquetry tall chest, mid-18th cent, the top inlaid with an eagle holding a cherry branch, 109 x 118cm (43 x 46½in), *L 18 May,* **£1,650 ($2,393)**

1   2
3   4
5   6   7
8   9

10   11   12

1
A Lombard walnut parquetry chest, mid-18th cent, the serpentine front with three long drawers raised on cabriole feet, 98 x 147.5cm (38 x 58in), *L 3 Feb,* **£2,090 ($2,930)**

2
A Venetian commode, mid-18th cent, inlaid in olive- and carob wood, with three drawers, the handles in bronze, the top 144 x 70cm (58½ x 27½in), *F 5 June,* **L 6,800,000 (£2,822; $4,092)**

3
A small Danish parcel-gilt and walnut-veneered commode, attributed to Matthias Ortmann, *c.*1750, with moulded *verde antico* marble top, 81 x 69cm (32 x 27in), *L 18 May,* **£5,720 ($7,999)**

4
A Sicilian painted commode, mid-18th cent, the serpentine front containing three drawers, painted with flowers on white reserves within gilt borders on a sealing-wax red ground, 102 x 137cm (40 x 54in), *L 30 Nov,* **£2,310 ($2,795)**

5
A Genoese painted bombé commode, mid-18th cent, the moulded top painted to resemble peach and beige marble, the sides and drawers painted on a pale blue ground with blue and buff scrolls and pink roses, 142cm (56in), *L 30 Nov,* **£8,250 ($9,983)**

6
A small Italian commode, probably Sicilian, *c.*1760, the sides and drawers with reserves of sprays of flowers, the top 40 x 62cm (15¾ x 24½in), *F 19 Dec,* **L 1,200,000 (£507; $634)**

7
A French commode with Austrian decoration, 18th cent, in giltwood and white lacquer, the top painted with imitation marble, 101 x 166 x 57cm (40 x 65½ x 22½in), *M 24/25 June,* **FF 66,600 (£5,717; $7,789)**

8
A Lombard bone-inlaid walnut commode, *c.*1760, of serpentine bombé shape, the whole inlaid with scrolling foliage and flowers, incorporating animals' heads in ivory and pewter, 93 x 137cm (37 x 54in), *L 18 May,* **£6,050 ($8,461)**

9
A small Sicilian walnut and marquetry commode, mid-18th cent, the top inlaid with an armorial cartouche, the front and sides with panels of birds, legs replaced, 84 x 63cm (33 x 25in), *L 25 May,* **£770 ($1,077)**

10
A pair of German fruitwood marquetry small commodes, *c.*1770, each with a russett and grey mottled marble top above a frieze drawer and two drawers veneered and inlaid with tulips, 86.5 x 53cm (34 x 21in), *L 18 May,* **£2,640 ($3,828)**

11
An Italian commode, Piedmont, 3rd quarter 18th cent, inlaid with walnut and rosewood, the top 125 x 59cm (49 x 23in), *F 5 June,* **L 7,000,000 (£2,905; $4,212)**

12
A Dutch marquetry commode, *c.*1760, of bombé form with four long drawers and splayed feet, now inlaid with floral marquetry on a mahogany ground, 79 x 92cm (31 x 36in), *L 30 Nov,* **£3,960 ($4,792)**

1

2

3

4

5

6

7

8

9

10

11

12

1
A Neapolitan commode,
mid-18th cent, of bombé
form, the top with
yellow marble, inlaid
with various woods and
crossbanding, the legs
with gilt bronze, the top
147 x 67cm (58 x 26½in),
F 10 May,
L 11,865,000 (£5,053;
$7,024)

2
A North Italian rosewood
commode, probably
Genoese, *c.*1770, the later
mottled marble top
above two long drawers
inlaid with scrolls, 84 x
102cm (33 x 37in), *L 30 Nov,*
£4,180 ($5,058)

3
An Italian walnut inlaid
commode, Savona, late
18th cent, the top inlaid
with a central medallion,
the whole inlaid with
festoons and foliage in
various woods, top 120 x
58cm (47¾ x 23in),
F 10 May,
L 6,780,000 (£2,888; $4,014)

4
A Lombard walnut inlaid
commode, workshops of
Giuseppe Maggiolini,
late 18th cent, the two
drawers decorated with a
classical scene surrounded
by floral garlands, the
top in mottled marble,
135 x 69cm (53 x 27in),
F 10 May,
L 56,500,000 (£24,063;
$33,448)

5
A Lombard commode,
late 18th cent, the two
drawers and sides inlaid
with fruit woods with
geometric motifs and
warriors' profiles, top
122 x 58.5cm (48 x 23in),
F 3/4 Oct,
L 6,800,000 (£2,685; $3,491)

6
A Milanese rosewood and
marquetry commode, late
18th cent, the rectangular
top above a frieze
drawer formed of two
inlaid panels, above two
further drawers, 89 x
124.5cm (35 x 49in),
L 30 Nov,
£6,600 ($7,986)

7
An Italian neoclassical
inlaid walnut parquetry
chest of drawers, last
quarter 18th cent, the
front with a frieze
drawer above two
drawers *sans traverse,* 90
x 121 x 61cm (35½ x 47½
x 24in), *NY 16 June,*
$3,410 (£2,489)

8
A North Italian
neoclassical burr-walnut
parquetry chest of drawers,
late 18th cent, the whole
veneered with walnut
outlined with chevron
banding, 90 x 132 x 60cm
(35½ x 52 x 23½in),
NY 13 Oct,
$4,070 (£3,336)

9
A North Italian neo-
classical fruitwood
parquetry commode, late
18th cent, with a rec-
tangular banded wooden
top, the front with two
long drawers, 80 x 121 x
56cm (32 x 48 x 22in),
NY 13 Oct,
$1,100 (£902)

10
A Cape stinkwood
opflaptafel, late 18th cent,
the serpentine hinged
top with folding shelves
on the underside, fitted
with a zinc basin, 95 x
105cm (37½ x 41½in),
CT 21 Mar,
R 11,200 (£6,188; $9,226)

11
A Swedish kingwood and
burr-walnut serpentine
commode, *c.*1880, with
black fossilised moulded
marble top, the drawers
inlaid with diamond
trellis, gilt-bronze mounts,
w 96.5cm (38in), *L 3 Feb,*
£1,210 ($1,696)

12
A Swedish walnut
parquetry commode,
*c.*1900, of serpentine
bombé form inlaid with
diamonds within cross-
banding, 80 x 92cm (32½
x 36in), *L 9 Mar,*
£682 ($1,016)

1
A Liégois carved oak marble-topped side cabinet, c.1730, the moulded marble top with four central flower-carved drawers flanked by panelled cupboard doors, w 212cm (83½in), *L 23 Nov,* £4,070 ($4,925)

2
A Louis XV provincial cherrywood side cabinet, c.1760, frieze drawers above a pair of doors with serpentine-topped fielded panels, 112 x 139cm (44 x 54½in), *L 30 Nov,* £2,200 ($2,662)

3
A Louis XV provincial walnut side cabinet, c.1750, with moulded pink and russet top, with panelled sides and serpentine front with panelled and carved doors, 101 x 190cm (39½ x 75in), *L 18 May,* £2,200 ($3,190)

4
A French provincial oak buffet, c.1900, the bowed centre with two frieze drawers above a pair of fielded panel doors, the concave wings with two frieze drawers and similar doors, 97 x 190cm (38 x 75in), *P 13 Nov,* £715 ($872)

5
A Louis XV-style ormolu-mounted marquetry tulip-wood and purpleheart bombé side cabinet, last quarter 19th cent, with a mottled white and pale red marble top, 112 x 137cm (44½ x 54in), *NY 15 Dec,* $5,500 (£4,622)

6
An early Louis XVI par-quetry side cabinet, stamped P H Mewesen JME, c.1775, with a grey and white marble top, inlaid with cube parquetry, the guilloche-mounted frieze containing a drawer, 98 x 81.5cm (38½ x 32in), *L 6 July,* £3,960 ($5,465)

7
A small parquetry side cabinet, Southern French or Genoese, c.1770, with later grey marble top, veneered with horizontal bands of Greek-key fret above a roundel, 85 x 69cm (33½ x 27in), *L 18 May,* £1,760 ($2,461)

8
An Empire mahogany side cabinet, c.1820, with Ste Anne marble top, a frieze drawer and a pair of grille-fronted doors flanked by applied pilasters, 90 x 130cm (35½ x 51in), *L 3 Feb,* £935 ($1,311)

9
A boulle side cabinet, c.1850, after an original by André-Charles Boulle, with inset red serpentine marble top, inlaid with delicate cut pewter and brass and tortoiseshell ground, 102 x 79cm (40 x 31in), *L 9 Nov,* £6,600 ($8,778)

10
A pair of boulle side cabinets, c.1870, each with a glazed door within a border of boulle marquetry in red shell and engraved brass, with gilt metal cherub term and mask mounts, 112 x 84cm (36 x 33in), *L 9 Nov,* £1,012 ($1,346)

11
A kingwood and tulipwood side cabinet, English, mid-19th cent, with gilt-metal mounts, the mirror-backed super-structure with shelves above small drawers, the door with a porcelain plaque painted with flowers, 166 x 65cm (65½ x 25½in), *L 9 Nov,* £1,430 ($1,902)

1   2

3   4

5   6   7

8   9

10

11

1
An English oak plank coffer, 16th cent, the rectangular hinged top with two bands of incised decoration, plain stile feet, 119cm (59in), *L 21 Sept,* £880 ($1,118)

2
An English oak coffer, 17th cent, with a three-panelled top and front, on stump feet, 72.5 x 112cm (28½ x 44in), *C 10 Jan,* £330 ($479)

3
A James I oak coffer, the four-panelled moulded lid above a leaf and scroll-carved frieze, the front centred by the initials IF and the date 1613, 70 x 138cm (27¼ x 54¼in), *L 12 Oct,* £1,408 ($1,802)

4
A James I oak chest, *c.*1620, with hinged plank lid and moulded frieze, the three front panels applied with diamond mouldings and two carved with roses, 66 x 106cm (26 x 41½in), *L 12 Oct,* £1,100 ($1,408)

5
A Charles I oak chest, *c.*1630, the front formed of four panels filled with flowers, caryatids between, w 155cm (61in), *L 21 Sept,* £2,310 ($2,933)

6
An English oak chest, mid-17th cent, carved with S-scrolls, fruit and flowers, 137cm (54in), *L 21 Sept,* £1,045 ($1,327)

7
A large Central Italian cassone, late 15th cent, 192cm (75½in), *F 19 Dec,* L 16,000,000 (£6,760; $8,450)

8
A Westphalian oak chest, 16th cent, of simple pegged construction with ironwork lock and clasps, 84 x 177cm (33 x 69½in), *L 24 Feb,* £4,180 ($5,852)

9
A Westphalian iron-bound oak coffer, 16th cent, the hinged lid, sides and front with iron strapwork with simple six-petalled rosettes, 94 x 196cm (37 x 77in), *L 30 Nov,* £5,280 ($6,389)

10
A Florentine walnut cassapanca, early 16th cent, with double hinged top, the frieze carved with triglyphs and flowerheads, 318cm (125½in), *L 18 May,* £2,420 ($3,385)

11
A Tuscan walnut cassone, early 16th cent, with hinged lid, the front panel flanked by an eagle and a wolf, 126cm (49¾in), *L 18 May,* £1,375 ($1,923)

12
A Renaissance carved walnut cassone, late 16th/early 17th cent, the frieze with strapwork and four winged cherub heads above a carved panel, 81 x 126cm (32 x 49½in), *L 18 May,* £1,980 ($2,871)

13
An Italian walnut cassone, late 16th cent, the frieze with stop-fluted pilasters and winged female terms at the corners, wrought-iron handles, 74 x 189 x 61.5cm (29 x 74¼ x 24¼in), *NY 23/24 Nov,* $2,200 (£1,818)

14
An Italian walnut and fruitwood marquetry cassone, early 17th cent, a central cartouche flanked by marquetry panels of boar hunting, raised on later paw feet, 65 x 180 x 60cm (25½ x 71 x 23½in), *NY 23/24 Nov,* $2,860 (£2,363)

1

2

3

4

5

6

7

8

9

10

11

12

13

14

1
A Spanish painted and parcel-gilt walnut vargueno on chest, the vargueno 16th cent, the fall-front with giltwood and brasswork on a velvet ground and the interior with an arrangement of drawers, the later base similarly decorated, 107 x 148cm (58 x 42in),
L 18 May,
£6,600 ($9,230)

2
A Spanish walnut vargueno, 17th cent, the front and sides outlined with brass mouldings and cut brass against a velvet ground, the interior with engraved ivory panels and bone columns, later carved stand, 147 x 108cm (58 x 42in), *L 30 Nov,*
£4,400 ($5,324)

3
A Flemish ebony-veneered and needlework cabinet, *c*1660, the lid enclosing a mirror flanked by finely worked vases of flowers, the interior with numerous drawers applied with stumpwork, on a stand with baluster legs, 114 x 52cm (45 x 20½in), *L 18 May,*
£11,000 ($15,384)

4
A Flemish cabinet, mid-17th cent, the front with tortoiseshell panels within ivory and ebony borders, on an ebonised stand, 193 x 135cm (73 x 53in), *L 18 May,*
£14,300 ($19,999)

5
A Flemish carved ebony and ebonised cabinet, mid-17th cent, the stand 19th cent, the frieze carved with sportive mer-folk above doors each carved with a Roman triumph, 198 x 174cm (78 x 44½in), *L 18 May,*
£5,500 ($7,975)

6
A Swiss cabinet on stand, *c*1670, with a central cupboard surrounded by small drawers inlaid in pewter and walnut in première and contra-partie, the stand altered, 159 x 120cm (62½ x 47in), *L 30 Nov,*
£4,400 ($5,324)

7
A Spanish ivory-inlaid ebony cabinet, mid-17th cent, the exterior with gilt-metal mounts and geometric designs in ivory stringing, the interior with ivory and ebony inlay, later ebonised stand, 127 x 66cm (50 x 20in), *L 30 Nov,*
£2,420 ($2,928)

8
An Indo-Portuguese ivory-inlaid cabinet on stand, late 17th cent, the cabinet with six drawers, the stand with three drawers and raised on female term figures standing on lions, 79 x 41cm (31 x 16in), *L 18 May,*
£4,400 ($6,153)

9
A pique-posé and mother-of-pearl inlaid tortoiseshell table cabinet, *c*1838, the doors mirrored on the inside with small drawers, one fitted with sewing accessories, the lower drawer with a writing slope, 128 x 58.5 x 57cm (50½ x 23 x 18½in), *L 9 Nov,*
£7,150 ($9,510)

10
A Roman ebony, mother-of-pearl and ivory exhibition cabinet on stand, by Giovanni Battista Gatti, signed Roma and dated 1870, set with semi-precious stones, 165 x 107cm (65 x 42in), *L 8 June,*
£55,000 ($79,750)

11
An Italian ivory-inlaid hardstone and pietra-paesina side cabinet, by Ferdinando Pogliani of Milan, *c*1860, the arched cresting with a figure of Minerva, two alberese panels inlaid with Florentine scenes, 290 x 165 x 64cm (114 x 65 x 25in), *L 8 June,*
£55,000 ($79,750)

1   2   3

4   5   6

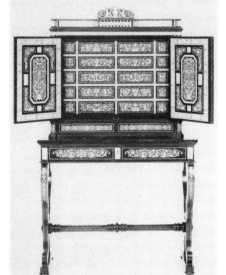

7   8   9

10   11

1
A William and Mary japanned cabinet on a silvered wood stand, c.1690, the green-black exterior painted with chinoiserie figures and landscapes and gilt, 176 x 110cm (69½ x 43in), *L 1 June,* £4,070 ($5,617)

2
A pair of Japanese lacquer cabinets on Charles II giltwood stands, 3rd quarter 17th cent, 141 x 82 x 49cm (54 x 32½ x 19in), *NY 12-14 Apr,* $44,000 (£30,769)

3
A George II black lacquered bow-front corner cupboard, 2nd quarter 18th cent, two convex doors painted with garden scenes, 91.5 x 55cm (36 x 21¾in), *C 29 Mar,* £330 ($492)

4
A George III mahogany hanging corner cupboard, c.1770, the panelled door flanked by fluted canted corners, 123 x 89cm (48½ x 35in), *NY 21 Jan,* $1,210 (£834)

5
A late George III mahogany standing corner cupboard, early 19th cent, the upper part enclosing shaped shelves, 216 x 112cm (85 x 44in), *C 29 Mar,* £682 ($1,016)

6
A George III oak bow-front hanging corner cupboard, early 19th cent, with a pair of crossbanded doors enclosing three shelves, 107 x 72cm (42 x 28½in), *C 10 Jan,* £484 ($702)

7
A George III mahogany hanging wall cupboard, late 18th cent, the door with hourglass-shaped astragals, enclosing three shelves, inlaid with box-wood lines throughout, 112 x 79cm (44 x 31in), *C 5 July,* £748 ($1,015)

8
A Louis XV lacquered corner cupboard, the curved front decorated with a Chinese landscape on a camomile ground, 92 x 65 x 48cm (36 x 25½ x 18¾in), *M 25/26 June,* FF 7,770 (£661; $901)

9
A pair of Louis XVI ormolu-mounted bois satiné and purplewood marquetry encoignures, signed N Petit JME, last quarter 18th cent, each with a veined grey and pink marble top, 89 x 79 x 48cm (35 x 31 x 19in), *NY 4 May,* $52,250 (£37,321)

10
A gilt-bronze and boulle corner standing cupboard, mid-19th cent, the door applied with an oval cut brass and tortoiseshell panel, flanked by styles, above a shaped plinth, 109 x 79cm (43 x 31in), *C 4 Oct,* £638 ($823)

1

2

5 6 7

8 9 10

1
A George II oak dresser, mid-18th cent, the front with six drawers and two pairs of arched panelled doors, on bun feet, 85 x 217 x 59cm (33½ x 85½ x 23in), *NY 21 Jan,* $6,875 (£4,741)

2
A George II oak dresser base, *c*1730, the frieze with three drawers, above columnar turned supports united by a platform base, w 185cm (72½in), *P 11 Dec,* £1,980 ($2,372)

3
An English oak dresser base, mid-18th cent, with three frieze drawers and a pair of doors each with an octagonal fielded panel, later brasses, 88 x 178cm (34½ x 70in), *L 21 Sept,* £1,760 ($2,235)

4
A George II inlaid oak dresser, with associated superstructure, 189 x 191 x 49cm (74 x 75 x 19½in), *NY 21 Jan,* $1,980 (£1,366)

5
An oak dresser, possibly Welsh, 1st half 18th cent, the superstructure with moulded cornice and three open shelves, the base with rectangular top above two drawers, 187 x 130 x 39cm (73½ x 51 x 15½in), *NY 20 Oct,* $2,420 (£2,034)

6
A George II oak dresser, mid-18th cent, the upper part with three plate rails, the lower part with two short and three long drawers flanked by a pair of cupboards, 203 x 186cm (80 x 73in), *C 10 Jan,* £1,430 ($2,074)

7
A George III oak breakfront dresser, *c*1770, the raised open shelf back with small apron drawers, the base with four centre drawers flanked by a pair of drawers and panelled doors, 203 x 183cm (80 x 72in), *P 20-22 Mar,* £1,925 ($2,868)

8
A George III oak dresser, *c*1770, with raised open-shelved back, the base with three frieze drawers and a pair of panelled doors flanking two drawers, 185 x 162cm (73 x 64in), *P 20-22 Mar,* £1,540 ($2,295)

9
A George III oak dresser, *c*1800, the elm super-structure with three plate rails, the lower part with three drawers above three cupboards, 196 x 163cm (77 x 64in), *C 29 Nov,* £968 ($1,171)

10
A George III oak dresser, late 18th cent, the lower part crossbanded in oak and with chevron stringing, 206 x 211cm (81 x 35in), *L 24 Feb,* £4,510 ($6,314)

11
An English stripped pine and deal dresser, early 19th cent, with three plate rails, the lower part with three drawers above a pair of cupboard doors flanking three central drawers, 206 x 174cm (81 x 68½in), *C 29 Mar,* £858 ($1,278)

1

2 3

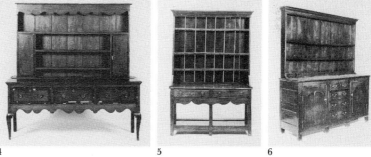

4 5 6

7 8

9 10 11

1
A walnut armchair,
French or Flemish, c.1680,
with stuffed rectangular
back and seat, the leaf-
carved shaped arms and
baluster supports raised
on turned legs, and H-
stretchers, L 18 May,
£1,760 ($2,552)

2
A pair of late Louis XIV
walnut wing armchairs,
c.1700, the stuffed seats
with squab cushions,
upholstered in point
d'Hongrie, L 18 May,
£5,500 ($7,975)

3
A suite of Régence
beechwood seat furniture,
c.1725, comprising a
canapé and four
fauteuils à la reine,
upholstered in contem-
porary needlepoint,
188cm (74in), NY 4 May,
$33,000 (£23,571)

4
A Régence moulded and
carved wood canapé,
decorated with shellwork,
acanthus leaves and
scrollwork, supported by
eight cabriole legs,
197cm (77½in),
M 24/25 June,
FF 22,200 (£1,906; $2,596)

5
A Régence caned flat-back
fauteuil, in natural
carved wood with shells
and cross of Lorraine
motifs, M 25/26 June,
FF 49,950 (£4,288; $5,842)

6
A pair of Louis XV walnut
side chairs, stamped B
Meunier, c.1750, with
leaf-carved frames and
caned backs and seats,
L 23 Nov,
£880 ($1,065)

7
A set of six Louis XV caned
fruitwood fauteuils à la
reine, mid-18th cent,
each with a loose cushion,
NY 13 Oct,
$20,900 (£17,131)

8
A set of four Louis XV
cane-backed chairs, in
moulded natural wood
carved with floral motifs,
with fawn leather loose
cushions, M 24/25 June,
FF 49,950 (£4,288; $5,842)

9
A Louis XV walnut caned
fauteuil de cabinet, mid-
18th cent, with a
moulded frame, the top-
rail centred by a flower-
head, the padded
armrests raised on voluted
supports, NY 13 Oct,
$4,400 (£3,607)

10
A Louis XV provincial
fruitwood fauteuil à la
reine, mid-18th cent, with
loose seat cushion,
NY 16 June,
$2,200 (£1,606)

11
A set of three Louis XV
gilt-wood fauteuils, c.1760,
with moulded flower-
carved frames, stuffed
cartouche-shaped backs,
padded arms, stuffed
serpentine-fronted seats
and cabriole legs, L 6 July,
£1,045 ($1,442)

12
A pair of Louis XV stained
beechwood fauteuils à la
reine, mid-18th cent,
each with an upholstered
backrest with arched
moulded frame, NY 7 Apr,
$9,075 (£6,346)

13
A pair of Louis XV
painted fauteuils en
cabriolet, mid-18th cent,
each with a cartouche-
shaped upholstered
backrest carved at the
cresting with flowerheads
and foliage, NY 4 May,
$8,250 (£5,893)

14
A pair of Louis XV gilt-
wood fauteuils en cabriolet,
signed L Delanois, 3rd
quarter 18th cent, each
with a cartouche-shaped
upholstered backrest,
upholstered in pale blue
silk, NY 4 May,
$8,250 (£5,893)

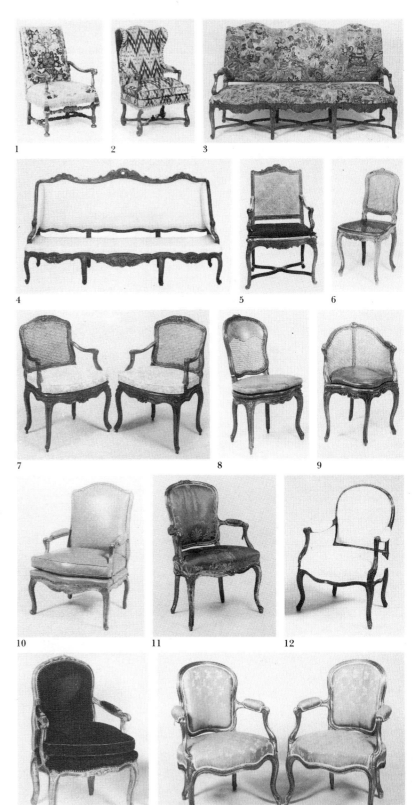

1
A pair of Louis XV giltwood fauteuils à la reine, signed N Heurtaut, mid-18th cent, each with a cartouche-shaped backrest carved with scrolls and flower-heads, upholstered à chassis in beige velvet; *NY 17 Nov,* **$48,400 (£38,720)**

2
An early Louis XVI kingwood and tulipwood small bureau plat, stamped J F Leleu JME, *c*.1775, the top inset with a panel of leather with a moulded gilt-bronze border, 79 x 123cm (31 x 48½in), *L 6 July,* **£25,300 ($34,914)**

3
A Louis XV/XVI ormolu-mounted holly and tulipwood parquetry table à écrire, signed R Lacroix, (Roger van der Cruse), 3rd quarter 18th cent, the oval top with a pierced three-quarter ormolu gallery and ormolu tasselled swags, the frieze with a drawer fitted for writing, 72.5 x 49 x 36cm (28½ x 19¼ x 14¼in), *NY 17 Nov,* **$104,500 (£83,600)**

4
A Louis XV/XVI ormolu-mounted bois satiné tulipwood and purplewood marquetry commode, 3rd quarter 18th cent, signed P A Foullet, 88 x 146 x 62cm (34¾ x 57½ x 24½in), *NY 4 May,* **$159,500 (£113,929)**

1

2

3

4

1
A pair of Louis XV ormolu two-branch wall-lights, mid-18th cent, the voluted branches decorated with acanthus leaves and berries, the voluted backplates also entwined with acanthus leaves, 53cm (21in), *NY 4 May,* **$28,600 (£20,429)**

2
An ebony and lacquer bonheur du jour, by P-G Durand, *c*1860, in the manner of Adam Weisweiler, the galleried super-structure above three Japanese lacquer panels, the lower part fitted with a secrétaire drawer, 117 x 79cm (46 x 31in), *L 9 Nov,* **£20,900 ($27,797)**

3
A Louis XV provincial fruitwood cupboard, *c*1760, with carved panelled doors and drawers, the apron centred by a shallow vase, 231 x 142cm (91in x 56in), *L 30 Nov,* **£6,180 ($7,478)**

4
An Empire gilt-bronze and marble guéridon, early 19th cent, with circular rouge-royale marble top raised on three reeded in-scrolled supports, h 87.5cm(34½in), d 48.5cm (19in), *L 6 July,* **£5,720 ($7,894)**

1

3

2

4

1
A pair of Louis XV cabriolet chairs, in simply moulded wood lacquered in blue and white, upholstered in blue silk, *M 24/25 June,* **FF 8,880 (£762; $1,039)**

2
A Louis XV beechwood bergère, stamped C-L Burgat, with simple moulded frame, upholstered in contemporary silk brocade, *M 25/26 June,* **FF 17,760 (£1,524; $2,077)**

3
A Louis XV beechwood bergère à la reine, mid-18th cent, with a shaped rectangular upholstered backrest and serpentine foliate carved top rail, traces of paint, *NY 13 Oct,* **$4,125 (£3,381)**

4
A set of six Louis XV caned beechwood chairs, mid-18th cent, each with a cartouche-shaped back-rest with foliate carved top rail and serpentine-fronted seat, with loose cushion, *NY 16 June,* **$4,180 (£3,051)**

5
A Louis XV provincial fruitwood fauteuil à la reine, mid-18th cent, the upholstered backrest with serpentine moulded frame, padded armrests raised on voluted supports, *NY 13 Oct,* **$3,850 (£3,156)**

6
A pair of Louis XVI voyeuses à genoux, stamped C Séné, dated 1787, *M 24/25 June,* **FF 466,200 (£40,017; $54,526)**

7
A Louis XVI painted chauffeuse, last quarter 18th cent, the cartouche-shaped upholstered back-rest above padded arms and bow-fronted uphol-stered seat, painted grey, *NY 7 Apr,* **$3,190 (£2,231)**

1　　　　　2　　　　　3

4　　　　　5

6　　　　　7

1
A Louis XV flat-backed bergère, with simple moulded frame, upholstered in green velour, *M 24/25 June*, **FF 37,740 (£3,239; $4,414)**

2
A Louis XV walnut duchesse brisée, mid-18th cent, with moulded flower-carved frame, the arched ends of differing heights, each with three padded sections, with loose-cushioned seats, *L 6 July* **£1,980 ($2,732)**

3
A large Louis XV canapé à confidents, stamped L Cresson, upholstered in yellow velour, 107 x 330 x 85cm (42 x 130 x 34in), *M 25/26 June*, **FF 88,800 (£7,622; $10,386)**

4
A Louis XV/XVI reclining wing armchair, with an arched upholstered backrest and wings with steel ratchet movement, now painted pale green highlighted with dark green, *NY 13 Oct*, **$1,100 (£902)**

5
A Louis XVI painted fauteuil à la reine, last quarter 18th cent, the rectangular upholstered backrest with chapeau de gendarme toprail continuing down to form padded arms, painted green, *NY 7 Apr*, **$2,420 (£1,692)**

6
A pair of Louis XVI painted fauteuils à la reine, last quarter 18th cent, each with a square upholstered backrest with arched toprail, painted off-white highlighted with yellow, *NY 4 May*, **$16,500 (£11,786)**

7
A pair of Louis XVI painted fauteuils à la reine, last quarter 18th cent, each with an arched toprail flanked by plumed finials above the upholstered backrest, *NY 16 Nov*, **$8,250 (£6,600)**

8
A pair of Louis XVI beechwood fauteuils en cabriolet, late 18th cent, each with an oval upholstered backrest, serpentine-fronted upholstered seat raised on tapering stop-fluted legs headed by paterae, *NY 16 June*, **$2,860 (£2,088)**

9
A Louis XVI canapé, stamped St Georges, in grey and beige lacquered wood, 160cm (63in), *M 24/25 June*, **FF 8,880 (£762; $1,039)**

10
A set of six Louis XVI mahogany dining chairs, last quarter 18th cent, signed B Molitor, each with a shield-shaped open backrest with pierced palmette-shaped splat, upholstered in brown leather, *NY 17 Nov*, **$22,000 (£17,600)**

11
A pair of late Louis XVI mahogany chairs, one stamped J Louis, the other stamped Sefert and Palais de Tuileries, *c.1789*, *L 6 July*, **£1,155 ($1,594)**

12
A set of four Louis XVI painted lyre-back chairs, *c.1780*, each with fluted uprights and lyre splat, *L 30 Nov*, **£1,760 ($2,130)**

13
An Empire ormolu-mounted mahogany bergère, 1st quarter 19th cent, with carved upholstered backrest and straight toprail continuing to form the wooden armrests, *NY 13 Oct*, **$1,540 (£1,262)**

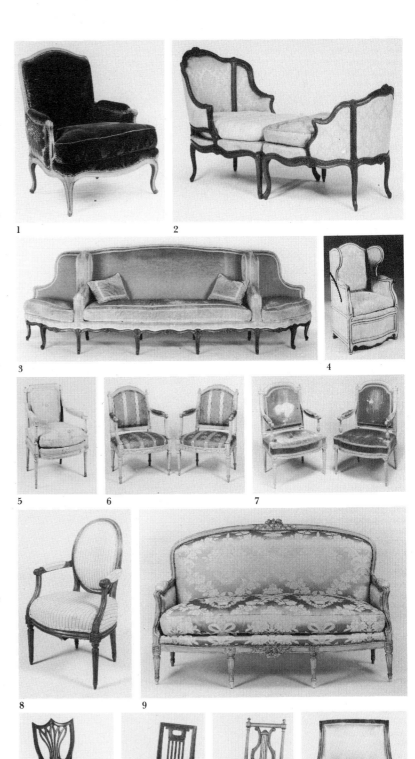

1

2

3

4

5

6

7

8

9

10

11

12

13

1
A set of six Empire bleached mahogany dining chairs, early 19th cent, each with a slightly curved toprail, raised on tapering legs headed by paterae and terminating in animal paw feet, *NY 16 June,*
$3,190 (£2,328)

2
A pair of Charles X chairs, in maple, with tapestry loose-cushions, *M 24/25 June,*
FF 15,450 (£1,334; $1,818)

3
A set of six Charles X neoclassical fruitwood dining chairs, early 19th cent, each with a scrolled rectangular toprail, lattice-work splat, *NY 13 Oct,*
$3,850 (£3,156)

4
A Charles X inlaid mahogany side chair, *c.*1825, stamped FON and with inventory marks, *NY 7 Apr,*
$990 (£692)

5
A set of six French provincial ashwood dining chairs, early 19th cent, the shaped cresting rails over a simple moulded slat back, with plank seats, raised turned front legs and chamfered rear legs, *HS 28 Mar,*
£1,440 ($2,145)

6
A Louis XV-style gilt-bronze and procelain-mounted mahogany armchair, late 19th cent, with an upholstered back, seat and arms continuing to richly mounted lion-pelt supports, the back mounted with a jasper panel depicting a classical figure, *NY 3 Nov,*
$8,800 (£7,040)

7
A suite of carved beechwood seat furniture, in Louis XIV style, the rectangular upholstered backs and seats covered in early 18th cent tapestry, the seat of the sofa woven later, *L 30 Nov,*
£10,450 ($12,645)

8
A pair of French gilt wood salon armchairs, *c.*1860, covered in original red-ground Aubusson tapestry, *L 9 Nov,*
£572 ($761)

9
A three-piece Aubusson-covered giltwood salon suite, *c.*1880, comprising a pair of bergères and a sofa, sofa 190cm (75in), *L 8 June,*
£1,430 ($2,074)

10
A set of four Louis XV-style carved giltwood fauteuils, last quarter 19th cent, each cartouche-shaped backrest carved with shells, scrolling foliage and flowerheads, *NY 15 Dec,*
$7,150 (£6,008)

11
A large Louis XIV gilt-wood tabouret, *M 25/26 June,*
FF 12,210 (£1,048; $1,428)

12
A pair of Régence walnut tabourets, *c.*1720, *NY 17 Nov,*
$6,875 (£5,500)

13
A pair of Louis XV benches, with arched backs, painted in grey carved with floral motifs, supported on five cabriole legs, 83cm (32¾in), *M 25/26 June,*
FF 55,500 (£4,764; $6,491)

14
A pair of Louis XV walnut stools, *c.*1750, upholstered in contemporary Aubusson tapestry with scenes from Aesop's fables, on cabriole legs joined by turned stretchers, 63.5cm (25in), *L 18 May,*
£2,750 ($3,988)

15
A Napoleon III giltwood stool, attributed to A M E Fournier, *c.*1860, the domed upholstered top with buttoned border, the seat-rail and legs formed of knotted rope with tassels forming the feet, *L 9 Nov,*
£5,060 ($6,730)

1   2   3

4   5   6

7   8   9   10

11   12

13   14   15

1

A pair of Tuscan walnut armchairs, part late 16th cent, the panelled box seats with a cupboard door, the whole inlaid with geometric flowerheads and bandings, *L 3 Feb,* £1,012 ($1,419)

2

A Franco-Flemish walnut armchair, mid-17th cent, with rectangular stuffed back and seat and bobbin-turned frame, *HS 28 Mar,* £1,045 ($1,557)

3

A Central Italian walnut armchair, 17th cent, with carved extended back supports, *F 19 Dec,* L 900,000 (£380; $475)

4

Two Italian walnut armchairs, 2nd half 17th cent, the back finials carved and gilded, *F 19 Dec,* L 1,900,000 (£803; $1,004)

5

A set of four Genoese walnut armchairs, c.1650, the seats and backs upholstered in embossed leather and painted with floral motifs, *F 10 May,* L 10,000,000 (£4,073; $5,866)

6

A set of seven walnut armchairs, late 17th cent, inlaid in boxwood, upholstered in the original leather, *F 10 May,* L 32,000,000 (£13,035; $18,770)

7

A set of four Dutch marquetry, walnut and elm chairs, c.1725, *P 24 July,* £3,850 ($5,140)

8

A North Italian kingwood parqeutry tub chair, mid-18th cent, the shaped seatrail and scrolling cabriole legs inlaid with flowerheads, *L 18 May,* £4,620 ($6,461)

9

A set of eight Italian painted and gilt chairs, c.1740, with shaped splat decorated with a cartouche beneath a coronet, *L 30 Nov,* £6,050 ($7,321)

10

A pair of Italian rococo walnut armchairs, mid-18th cent, each with cartouche-shaped padded backrest and slightly serpentine upholstered seat, *NY 13 Oct,* $3,080 (£2,525)

11

A set of four Venetian rococo painted armchairs, mid-18th cent, each with a cartouche-shaped backrest upholstered à chassis, with moulded frame, now painted red highlighted with gilding, *NY 13 Oct,* $5,225 (£4,283)

12

A set of six Italian rococo painted dining chairs, mid-18th cent, each with cartouche-shaped upholstered backrest and serpentine-fronted upholstered seat raised on cabriole legs, *NY 16 June,* $4,125 (£3,011)

13

A set of six Piedmontese painted and parcel-gilt armchairs, c.1770, each with an oval padded back, the cresting carved with a basket of flowers, the backs and seats covered in the original cream silk painted with chinoiserie birds, insects and pavilions, *L 30 Nov,* £28,600 ($34,606)

14

A set of eight parcel-gilt side chairs, possibly Swedish, c.1770, the moulded frames each carved with a rose at the toprail flanked by trailing foliage, *L 18 May,* £3,520 ($5,104)

15

A set of six Dutch rococo mahogany dining chairs, 3rd quarter 18th cent, each with a cartouche-shaped upholstered backrest with moulded frame, *NY 13 Oct,* $2,090 (£1,713)

16

A Portuguese rosewood armchair, mid-18th cent, the moulded cartouche back with triple-tier pierced gothic splat headed by a flower, *L 23 Nov,* £550 ($666)

1   2   3   4

5

6

7   8   9   10

11   12

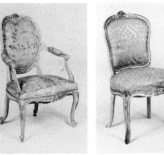

13   14   15   16

1
A pair of Piedmontese giltwood sofas, c.1770, the frames carved with guilloche and the padded backs headed by ribboned oval medallions with a pair of swans, 220cm (89in), *L 18 May*, £4,180 ($5,846)

2
A set of eight Dutch walnut dining chairs, late 18th cent, including two armchairs, the shaped moulded toprails above five fluted splats united by carved drapery, *JHB 3 July*, R 6,000 (£3,191; $4,329)

3
A Cape stinkwood armchair, c.1800, with stepped toprail, pierced splat, the drop-in seat now caned, *CT 21 Mar*, R 1,025 (£566; $844)

4
A Cape stinkwood side chair, c.1780, the moulded solid toprail above a pierced waisted splat, caned seat, on fluted tapering square-section legs, wavy H-stretcher, *CT 21 Mar*, R 380 (£210; $313)

5
A Cape stinkwood tub chair, c.1780, with caned back and seat, on cabriole legs, *CT 21 Mar*, R 1,020 (£564; $841)

6
A Cape stinkwood tub chair, c.1810, with rounded back rail, the splat pierced with circle and crosses, caned seat, *CT 21 Mar*, R 700 (£387; $577)

7
A set of seven Cape stinkwood dining chairs, late 18th cent, with stepped toprail, riempie seat, *CT 21 Mar*, R 2,600 (£1,436; $2,141)

8
A pair of Cape stinkwood side chairs, c.1800, the set-back moulded toprails above a pierced splat, now with caned seats, *CT 21 Mar*, R 1,750 (£967; $1,442)

9
A set of eight Italian neoclassical painted and parcel-gilt dining chairs, late 18th/early 19th cent, each with a rectangular guilloche carved backrest centred by a lyre-form splat, upholstered in beige leather, *NY 13 Oct*, $4,620 (£3,787)

10
A set of four Italian neoclassical painted armchairs, late 18th cent, each open backrest with concave crest-rail continuing down to form armrests terminating in lions' heads, highlighted with gilding, *NY 16 June*, $7,700 (£5,620)

11
A suite of Italian neoclassical brass-mounted mahogany dining chairs, 1st quarter 19th cent, comprising two armchairs and five side chairs, *NY 7 Apr*, $3,300 (£2,308)

12
A set of seven Italian neoclassical fruitwood dining chairs, early 19th cent, comprising one armchair and six side chairs, *NY 13 Oct*, $3,300 (£2,705)

13
A pair of Italian neoclassical ormolu-mounted mahogany and parcel-gilt armchairs, early 19th cent, each with a lyre-form splat, *NY 13 Oct*, $3,575 (£2,930)

1 2

3 4 5 6

7 8

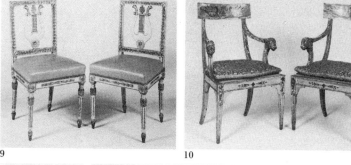

9 10

11 12 13

1
A set of six carved chairs, early 19th cent, the pierced curved backs with interlacing segments, upholstered in green satin, *F 19 Dec,*
L 6,500,000 (£2,746; $3,433)

2
A set of eight Baltic Empire-influence mahogany dining chairs, including a pair of arm-chairs, possibly Riga, *c.*1830, the slightly curved wide backs carved with acanthus, *L 9 Nov,*
£2,035 ($2,730)

3
A mahogany armchair, Empire/Biedermeier, with straight backrail with downswept scrolled arms, *A 1 Oct,*
Dfl 1,972 (£464; $599)

4
A set of six Biedermeier mahogany chairs, Swedish or Danish, *c.*1825, the curved arched toprails with lotus scrolls at each end and with carved anthemion crossbars, *L 3 Feb,*
£1,045 ($1,465)

5
A set of four Biedermeier fruitwood side chairs, 2nd quarter 19th cent, each with serpentine toprail and tripartite ebonised splat, *NY 16 June,*
$1,760 (£1,285)

6
A pair of Biedermeier gilt-mounted mahogany side chairs, early 19th cent, *NY 7 Apr,*
$1,980 (£1,385)

7
An Italian walnut and marquetry Savonarola armchair, *c.*1880, the hinged shaped back inlaid with a Medici crest flanked by a pair of chimera, *L 8 June,*
£715 ($1,037)

8
A German fruitwood child's chair, mid-19th cent, the back with concave toprail above a vase-shaped splat, downswept siderails, rush seat on splayed supports, *C 5 July,*
£165 ($224)

9
A Florentine walnut sgabello, *c.*1870, the tall back with an armorial device held by putti, lion mask solid carved seats, above pierced eagle supports, the feet carved as fabulous animals, *L 8 June,*
£550 ($798)

10
A German antler and ivory armchair, attributed to Rampendahl of Hamburg, mid-19th cent, with button-upholstered back and seat, *L 9 Mar,*
£1,595 ($2,378)

11
A painted and parcel-gilt suite, possibly German, *c.*1860, in Louis XVI style, the sofa and four armchairs with oval backs, within moulded frames with rose-carved crestings, *L 9 Mar,*
£638 ($951)

12
A pair of Italian baroque walnut stools, 17th cent, each with a shaped rectangular top, raised on curved foliate carved supports, 52.5 x 37cm (20¾ x 14¾in), *NY 23/24 Nov,*
$6,050 (£5,000)

13
An Italian rococo giltwood stool, mid-18th cent, with a cartouche-shaped upholstered seat above moulded and leaf-carved cabriole legs ending in scrolled toes and joined by foliate rails, *NY 16 June,*
$1,045 (£763)

14
An Italian neoclassical parcel-gilt mahogany tabouret, with a rectangular upholstered seat above a pair of X-form legs joined by a stretcher, with impressed marks and inventory marks, *NY 7 Apr,*
$1,485 (£1,038)

15
A Colonial hardwood window seat, 19th cent, the padded seat flanked by scroll sides, on sabre supports, 81 x 137cm (32 x 54in), *C 27-30 Nov,*
£528 ($639)

1
A James I oak joint stool, c.1610, with moulded top, a frieze with flower-filled lunettes, on turned reeded and pelleted legs joined by moulded stretchers, 58 x 46cm (23 x 18in), *L 12 Oct*, £2,200 ($2,816)

2
A Charles II oak joint stool, c.1685, with moulded top and moulded frieze, on ball-and elongated baluster legs joined by moulded stretchers, 56 x 42cm (22 x 16½in), *L 12 Oct*, £605 ($774)

3
A pair of Charles I-style oak joint stools, with a lightly moulded over-hanging top and outset ring-turned legs joined by stretchers, constructed from old timber, w 48cm (19in), *L 21 Sept*, £748 ($950)

4
A Queen Anne walnut stool, c.1710, the rectangular stuffed needlework seat above cabriole legs and pad feet, w 53cm (21in), *P 20-22 Mar*, £385 ($574)

5
A pair of Queen Anne carved walnut stools, 1st quarter 18th cent, with upholstered drop-in seat, the legs finely carved with shells and pendent bellflowers, *NY 12-14 Apr*, $9,900 (£6,923)

6
A Charles II carved walnut armchair, c.1680, with cane seat and back, on spiral twist supports with stretcher, *HS 24/25 Oct*, £495 ($629)

7
A Queen Anne oak armchair, Welsh, c.1710, 110.5 x 51cm (43½ x 20in), *HS 28 Mar*, £1,320 ($1,967)

8
A carved oak settee, last quarter 17th cent, w 139cm (54½in), *NY 9 June*, $935 (£673)

9
A Queen Anne walnut wing armchair, c.1710, the rectangular back with scrolled wings, arms and loose cushion seat covered in late 17th cent Flemish tapestry, *L 16 Nov*, £5,720 ($7,550)

10
A George II carved walnut armchair, 2nd quarter 18th cent, on cabriole legs carved with a well-carved scallop shell above acanthus foliage, *NY 20 Oct*, $15,400 (£12,941)

11
A late George II mahogany library armchair, c.1750, with boldly outswept animal-head terminals on square-cut acanthus-carved supports, the serpentine seat on carved cabriole legs, *L 16 Mar*, £4,180 ($6,228)

12
A set of six late George II mahogany chairs, c.1755, each with stuffed serpentine-topped back, the square chambered legs with blind Chinese fret, *L 5 Oct*, £4,400 ($5,720)

13
A pair of George I walnut-veneered side chairs, c.1720, each with a solid vase splat and 'mushroom' top rail, the drop-in seats upholstered in gros and petit point, on acanthus-carved cabriole legs ending in claw and ball feet, *L 16 Nov*, £17,050 ($22,506)

14
A pair of George I carved walnut side chairs, 1st quarter 18th cent, the cresting rail carved with a shell above a solid baluster-form splat, raised on cabriole legs carved with fan motifs, *NY 12-14 Apr*, $7,425 (£5,192)

15
A set of six George II oak chairs, c.1730, with solid vase splats and shaped uprights and toprails, the drop-in rush seats on turned front legs with pad feet, *L 24 Feb*, £3,410 ($4,774)

1
A George II plum pudding mahogany 'Shepherd's Crook' writing armchair, mid-18th cent, with a moulded cartouche-shaped back, an ovoid drop-in seat, raised on cabriole legs ending in claw and ball feet, *NY 20 Oct,* $8,800 (£7,395)

2
A George II red walnut armchair, *c*1740, of generous proportions, the solid vase splat with outswept arms, cabriole legs carved with acanthus ending in pad feet, *L 1 June,* £1,320 ($1,822)

3
A pair of George II carved mahogany armchairs, in the manner of Thomas Manwaring, each with a bellflower carved pierced radiating backrest, *NY 21 Jan,* $5,225 (£3,603)

4
A mid-Georgian mahogany corner armchair, 3rd quarter 18th cent, with a U-shaped rail, solid vase splat, on square supports joined by a rail, *C 5 July,* £286 ($388)

5
A George III mahogany corner armchair, mid-18th cent, with fan-shaped splats, a drop-in seat, a shaped apron and cabriole legs ending in pad feet, *NY 9 June,* $2,090 (£1,504)

6
A harlequin set of six George III oak and elm spindle-back chairs, *c*1800, with fan carved cresting rails and rush seats, the circular tapering legs with turned stretchers and pad feet, *P 13 Nov,* £1,155 ($1,548)

7
A George III mahogany child's highchair, early 19th cent, with a concave rail, stick-filled back, open arms, drop-in seat, 92cm (36in), *C 5 July,* £418 ($567)

8
A set of eight oak dining chairs, 1st half 19th cent, of country manufacture in George III style, including two armchairs *NY 9 June,* $1,100 (£791)

9
An ash and elm comb back armchair, 18th cent, the high railed back with curved arms, dished solid seat, on turned supports joined by a crinoline stretcher, *C 29 Mar,* £209 ($311)

10
A yew wood Windsor armchair, early 19th cent, *C 29 Mar,* £242 ($361)

11
A pair of yew wood and elmwood Windsor armchairs, early 19th cent, sold with a beechwood armchair, *NY 21 Jan,* $1,870 (£1,290)

12
A yew wood Windsor armchair, early 19th cent, with a high arched back with central pierced splat, on ring-turned tapering supports joined by a crinoline stretcher, *C 4 Oct,* £605 ($780)

13
A matched set of eight ash and elm Windsor armchairs, with stick backs and solid seats, the turned splayed legs joined by H-shaped stretchers, *HS 25 June,* £1,485 ($2,094)

14
A harlequin set of eight George IV ash and elm ladder-back chairs, *c*1825, with rush seats, the turned legs joined by stretchers, *P 11-18 Dec,* £1,430 ($1,713)

15
A pair of yew and beechwood Windsor chairs, *c*1800, *L 12 Oct,* £880 ($1,126)

16
A pair of Windsor armchairs, mid-19th cent, in yewwood and elm, *L 21 Sept,* £1,375 ($1,746)

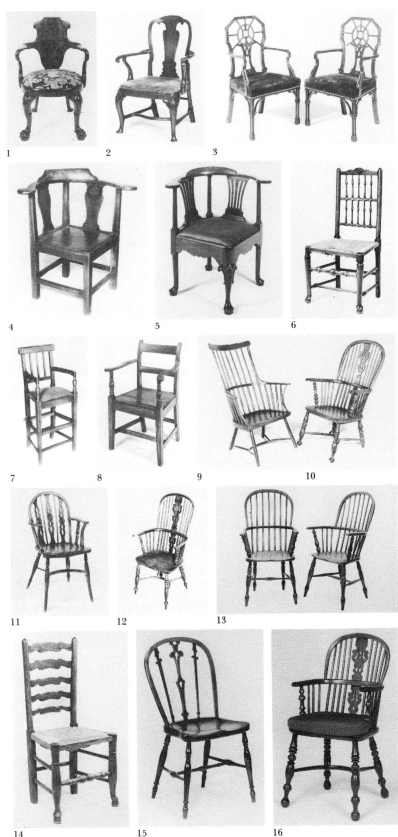

1
**A pair of George III
carved yew wood hall
chairs,** after a design by
Ince and Mayhew, 3rd
quarter 18th cent, with a
solid cartouche-shaped
backrest pierced with lobed
arches, with a dipped
seat, *NY 20 Oct,*
$8,525 (£7,164)

2
**A pair of George II
mahogany hall chairs,**
*c*1750, each with heart-
shaped back, dished
solid seat and shaped
trestle front supports,
L 1 June,
£825 ($1,139)

3
**An early George III
mahogany library armchair,**
*c*1770, now with a
sprung seat, the down-
swept arm supports and
legs carved with
interlaced Chinese fret-
work, *L 14 Dec,*
£1,980 ($2,475)

4
**A George III giltwood
armchair,** *c*1765, with
gadrooned frame,
padded cartouche-
shaped back, stuffed
serpentine-fronted seat
and moulded cabriole
legs, covered in mid-19th
cent Aubusson tapestry,
L 16 Nov,
£3,190 ($4,211)

5
**A set of six George III
painted armchairs,** *c*1780,
each fluted oval back
headed by a patera, with
padded arms, fluted
serpentine-fronted seat-
rails and inverted baluster
legs, painted gilt and
pale eau-de-nil, *L 15 June,*
£7,150 ($10,082)

6
**A set of four George III
mahogany armchairs,**
*c*1780, *L 15 June,*
£8,360 ($11,788)

7
**A pair of George III
mahogany armchairs,** 1st
quarter 18th cent, each
cartouche-shaped
backrest with a moulded
gadrooned frame, the
legs and rails gadrooned
to match the backrest,
NY 20 Oct,
$17,600 (£14,790)

8
**A set of six George III
carved mahogany dining
chairs,** last quarter 18th
cent, including two arm-
chairs with padded
arms, each moulded oval
backrest with a trefoil
open splat centred by a
patera, *NY 20 Oct,*
$7,150 (£6,008)

9
**A pair of George III
mahogany armchairs,**
*c*1780, with carved oval
backs centred by
paterae, the arms with
voluted supports, the
fluted seatrails faced
with paterae and raised
on fluted tapering legs,
L 27 Jan,
£2,970 ($4,307)

10
**A pair of early George III
carved mahogany 'Gothic'
side chairs,** *c*1765, each
with arched and pierced
backrest, upholstered seat
and cluster column legs
joined by a turned
stretcher, *NY 21 Jan,*
$8,800 (£6,069)

11
**A pair of George III
painted and cane shield-
back armchairs,** last
quarter 18th cent,
painted with pendant
floral sprays in tones of
red, blue and green on
an ivory ground, each
bearing the stamp RHN,
NY 12-14 Apr,
$5,500 (£3,846)

12
**A George III mahogany
wheel-back armchair,** late
18th cent, the circular
backrest pierced with
stellate rays, the tapered,
scrolled arms and solid
curved seat raised on
curved legs ending in
castors, *NY 12-14 Apr,*
$3,575 (£2,500)

13
**A George III mahogany
small sofa,** *c*1800, 127cm
(50in), *NY 21 Jan,*
$2,860 (£1,972)

14
**A George III needlepoint
upholstered mahogany settee,**
*c*1770, with an arched
backrest and scrolled
armrests, a loose-cushioned
seat, 216cm (85in),
NY 21 Jan,
$8,250 (£5,690)

1 2
3 4 5 6
7 8 9
10 11 12
13 14

1
A George III mahogany tub chair, c.1770, with an open spindled backrest, serpentine-fronted upholstered seat, on square tapered legs joined by an X-stretcher, *NY 21 Jan,* $3,410 (£2,352)

2
A late George III mahogany metamorphic library armchair, in the manner of Morgan and Saunders, Irish, c.1810, the chairback released by a brass catch opening to form a set of four-tread library steps, *L 27 Jan,* £2,200 ($3,190)

3
A George III mahogany settee, c.1765, in the Chinese Chippendale style, with lattice-work back and arms, needlework-covered seat, the square chamfered legs carved with blind fret decoration and with pierced brackets, 165cm (66in), *L 15 June,* £2,860 ($4,033)

4
A set of four early George III chairs, c.1765, *L 16 Nov,* £3,520 ($4,646)

5
An early George III mahogany armchair, c.1760, with acanthus-leaf carved scrolled toprail above a pierced leaf-carved moulded splat within leaf-carved uprights, the upholstered seat covered in modern needlework, *L 16 Nov,* £2,530 ($3,340)

6
A set of four George III mahogany chairs, c.1775, in the Hepplewhite style, each with interlaced heart-shaped back with drapery swagged ribbon-tied Prince-of-Wales plume, *L 14 Dec,* £2,090 ($2,613)

7
A pair of George III carved mahogany shield-back armchairs, last quarter 18th cent, each with a pierced leaf-carved open backrest, *NY 9 June,* $3,190 (£2,294)

8
A set of eight George III mahogany chairs, c.1780, the slightly arched backs each with four leaf-carved and beaded stick splats, *L 27 Jan,* £2,640 ($3,828)

9
A set of eight George III mahogany chairs, c.1780, including two armchairs, the moulded backs with arched cresting rails and vase-shaped splats, *P 16 Oct,* £3,520 ($4,400)

10
A set of eight George III carved mahogany dining chairs, c.1790, including two armchairs with downswept moulded armrests, each with an arched rectangular pierced backrest, *NY 21 Jan,* $15,400 (£10,621)

11
A pair of George III stained walnut armchairs, 3rd quarter 18th cent, *NY 20 Oct,* $5,225 (£4,390)

12
A set of six late George III carved mahogany dining chairs, last quarter 18th cent, each with a serpentine toprail, a pierced baluster splat and a drop-in-seat, *NY 12-14 Apr,* $2,530 (£1,769)

13
A set of six George III mahogany dining chairs, c.1780, the shield-shaped backs with pierced waisted splats headed by wheat-ears, with leather-covered dished stuffed seats and moulded tapering legs, *L 10 Feb,* £2,200 ($3,084)

14
A set of six early George III mahogany chairs, c.1760, each with a serpentine toprail and interlaced vase splat headed by leaves, the drop-in seats on square chamfered legs, *L 16 Nov,* £4,950 ($6,534)

15
A pair of George III mahogany ladder-back side chairs, last quarter 18th cent, each with four pierced serpentine rails, drop-in-seat, *C 4 Oct,* £308 ($397)

1 2 3
4 5 6
7 8 9
10 11
12 13 14 15

1

A set of eight George III dining chairs, last quarter 18th cent, *NY 20 Oct*, $6,325 (£5,315)

2

A set of eight George III mahogany dining chairs, *c*1800, including two armchairs, with curved panelled toprails, reeded X-frame splats, leather-covered drop-in seats, *L 6 Apr*, £3,960 ($5,702)

3

A set of six Regency mahogany dining chairs, *c*1820, the concave toprails inlaid with brass stringing and slightly overscrolled reeded backs, with rope-twist splats, *L 6 Apr*, £2,970 ($4,279)

4

A pair of Regency mahogany armchairs, *c*1810, with curved panelled toprails and X-splats, turned arm supports, stuffed dipped seats and sabre front legs, *L 5 Oct*, £1,705 ($2,217)

5

A set of six Regency parcel-gilt ebonised caned dining chairs, 1st quarter 19th cent, each open backrest with a double transverse splat of slightly concave form, *NY 20 Oct*, $2,200 (£1,849)

6

A set of four Regency gilt decorated green painted cane seated dining chairs, *c*1810, together with fourteen matching chairs of a later date, *NY 21 Jan*, $4,400 (£3,034)

7

A set of four Regency bamboo-turned and grained armchairs, *c*1810, *NY 12-14 Apr*, $7,150 (£5,000)

8

A pair of Regency painted and parcel-gilt ebonised caned armchairs, 1st quarter 19th cent, *NY 20 Oct*, $7,150 ($6,008)

9

A pair of Regency gilt-decorated ebonised arm-chairs, *c*1815, each with a reeded frame, an upholstered rectangular backrest and scrolled padded armrests, a loose-cushioned caned seat, *NY 21 Jan*, $12,650 (£8,724)

10

A set of eight George IV rosewood chairs, *c*1825, with curved toprails, leaf-carved crossbars, stuffed drop-in seats and fluted tapering front legs, *L 14 Dec*, £1,650 ($2,063)

11

A set of six Regency mahogany chairs, *c*1810, including two armchairs, with brass inlaid toprails and rope-twist mid-bars, on ring-turned tapering legs, *P 13 Nov*, £2,750 ($3,685)

12

A set of twelve William IV mahogany dining chairs, *c*1830, including a pair of armchairs, the deep concave toprails carved with stylised lotus, the armchairs with downswept reeded scrolled arms and stuffed seats, *L 14 Dec*, £4,400 ($5,500)

13

A pair of early Victorian rosewood grained beechwood armchairs, *c*1840, each with a loose-cushioned spindled backrest, scrolled padded armrests, loose-cushion seat and ring-turned legs ending in brass casters, *NY 21 Jan*, $3,850 (£2,655)

14

A set of six William IV mahogany chairs and a very similar armchair, *c*1830, with curved rectangular toprails, lotus-capped supports, *L 17 Feb*, £792 ($1,110)

15

A set of four William IV Irish hall chairs, *c*1830, stamped HH, the solid moulded seats carved with anthemions and with turned gad-rooned legs, *L 16 Nov*, £1,100 ($1,452)

1   2   3
4   5   6
7   8
9   10   11
12   13   14   15

1
A William IV mahogany chaise longue, 2nd quarter 19th cent, of small proportions, with a curved padded arm and downswept carved back, padded seat, on octagonal tapering supports, 86 x 152cm (34 x 60in), *C 4 Oct,* £748 ($965)

2
A William IV walnut settee, 2nd quarter 19th cent, with a padded back and scroll sides with roleau cushions, on a conforming rail, gadrooned supports and brass castors, 198cm (78in), *C 27 Mar,* £506 ($754)

3
A set of eight rosewood balloon-back chairs, *c.*1850, with moulded backs and scroll-carved crossbars, the buttoned serpentine-fronted seatrails continuing into the cabriole legs with scroll feet, *L 17 Feb,* £1,078 ($1,511)

4
A carved walnut salon suite, *c.*1850, comprising a large armchair, an upholstered chair, a sofa and a set of six chairs each with rose-carved oval toprails and serpentine seatrails and cabriole legs, sofa 183cm (72in), *L 28 Sept,* £3,520 ($4,576)

5
A Victorian walnut salon armchair, 3rd quarter 19th cent, with a moulded waisted padded back, padded arms and serpentine fronted seat on moulded foliate capped cabriole supports with castors, *C 29 Mar,* £715 ($1,065)

6
A walnut drawing room suite, mid-19th cent, including a double chair-back settee, a gentleman's and lady's armchair and a set of four side chairs, *C 29 Mar,* £2,640 ($3,934)

7
A Victorian carved walnut and button-upholstered settee, *c.*1850, covered in rose-pink dralon, the ornate back with a floral scroll-carved cresting rail and twin pierced scroll splats, 196cm (77in), *P 18-25 Sept,* £1,100 ($1,419)

8
An early Victorian rosewood chaise longue, *c.*1840, with a padded back and scroll end, loose padded seat, on moulded baluster supports, 190.5cm (75in), *C 30 Oct-2 Nov,* £396 ($507)

9
A Victorian carved walnut spoon-back occasional chair, *c.*1850, with a pierced scroll splat, the back and bowed seats covered in floral beadwork, *P 13 Nov,* £385 ($516)

1

2

3

4

5

6

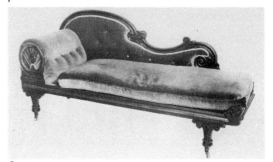

7

8

9

1

A set of twelve George II-style mahogany dining chairs, c.1900, including a pair of armchairs, the serpentine top-rails with pierced vase splats, stuffed drop-in gross point needlework seats, on leaf-carved cabriole legs and claw and ball feet, *L 10 Feb*, £6,160 ($8,636)

2

A set of eight George III-style mahogany chairs, modern, including two carvers, with pierced and interlaced vase-shaped splats, *P 15-18 May*, £1,210 ($1,682)

3

A set of six George III-style mahogany chairs, c.1900, including two carvers, branded WJH, trade plate of James Shoolbred & Co, *P 20-22 Mar*, £1,122 ($1,672)

4

A pair of satinwood armchairs, c.1900, Hepplewhite-style, each moulded shield-back with five carved stick splats, with out-scrolled arms, dipped stuffed seats and square tapering front legs, *L 28 Sept*, £1,375 ($1,788)

5

A set of twelve George II-style carved mahogany dining chairs, c.1920, including a pair of armchairs, with vase splats and shaped uprights, needlework covered drop-in seats on cabriole legs with claw and ball feet, *L 17 Feb*, £8,250 ($11,567)

6

A set of four George II-style carved mahogany library armchairs, scrolling armrests ending in dolphin head terminals, *NY 21 Jan*, $11,550 (£8,250)

7

A set of four George II-style walnut side chairs, each open backrest with bowed cresting rails and vase-shaped splats, *NY 9 June*, $2,090 (£1,504)

8

A Knole settee, c.1900, upholstered in celadon green cord with 18th cent Aubusson tapestry panel fragments, 178cm (82in), *HS 24/25 Oct*, £2,200 ($2,794)

9

A set of four Louis XVI-style parcel-gilt rosewood chairs, stamped Gillow, c.1870, the padded splayed shaped backs with fluted pillars and chapeau gendarme finials, *L 17 Feb*, £462 ($648)

10

A walnut bergère three-piece suite, 20th cent, including a settee and two armchairs, each with a low back with leaf-carved terminals, padded seat above a carved blind fretwork apron, *C 1/2 Feb*, £825 ($1,155)

11

A set of ten William and Mary-style walnut and cane chairs, c.1900, including two armchairs, with scroll cresting rails and turned back supports, the tapestry seat cushion above square and turned legs joined by stretchers, *P 13 Nov*, £1,760 ($2,358)

12

A reclining wing armchair, c.1900, with adjustable back and seat, a footrest and cushion, with a reading and wine table on brass supports, with Foot's Patent brass label, *L 17 Feb*, £1,705 ($2,390)

1 2 3

4 5

6

7 8

9 10

11 12

1

An American carved
walnut side chair,
Newport, Rhode Island,
c.1760, the arched crest
centred by a convex
shell over a vase-form
splat, *NY 8 Dec,*
$13,750 (£11,458)

2

An American carved
maple side chair,
Connecticut, c.1750, the
shaped moulded crest
continuing to moulded
stiles and centred by a
vase-form splat,
NY 30 June,
$2,420 (£1,793)

3

An American carved
walnut side chair,
Pennsylvania, c.1765, the
shaped cresting with
incised edge and volute-
carved terminals centred
by a volute- and foliate-
carved reserve, *NY 30 June,*
$2,750 (£2,037)

4

A pair of American
carved mahogany side
chairs, Philadelphia,
c.1770, each having a
pierced beaker-form
splat and slip seat, on
cabriole legs ending in
claw-and-ball feet,
NY 30 June,
$3,575 (£2,648)

5

An American carved
mahogany armchair,
New York, c.1770, the
shaped crest above a
pierced beaker-form splat
and shaped arms ending
in volute-carved hand
holds, *NY 30 June,*
$3,960 (£2,933)

6

A pair of Federal inlaid
mahogany side chairs,
New York, c.1795, each
having a moulded and
shaped crest above a
flowerhead and plume-
carved splat, *NY 28 Jan,*
$2,200 (£1,517)

7

A set of five American
carved mahogany side
chairs, Massachusetts,
1760-80, each having a
shaped crest above a
pierced vase-form splat
and slip seat on cabriole
legs ending in pad feet,
NY 28 Jan,
$16,500 (£11,379)

8

An American carved
mahogany side chair,
Eastern Massachusetts,
c.1770, the shaped fan-
carved crest above a
pierced volute-carved
splat and slip seat on
angular cabriole legs
ending in pad feet,
NY 28 Jan,
$2,750 (£1,897)

9

A set of six American
maple ladder-back side
chairs, Massachusetts,
c.1790, each having a
pierced serpentine crest
above three similarly
shaped pierced splats,
NY 8 Dec,
$9,075 (£7,563)

10

A set of six Federal carved
and inlaid mahogany side
chairs, Salem, Massachu-
setts, c.1790, each having
a shaped inlaid and
reeded crest centred by
three moulded uprights,
NY 28 Jan,
$9,900 (£6,828)

11

An American carved
mahogany lolling chair,
attributed to Joseph
Short, Newburyport,
Massachusetts, c.1785,
NY 8 Dec,
$12,100 (£10,083)

12

A 'harlequin' set of eight
Federal carved mahogany
side chairs, probably
Rhode Island, c.1800,
NY 26 Jan,
$7,150 (£4,931)

13

A mahogany wing arm-
chair, Massachusetts,
1750-70, on cabriole legs,
joined by stretchers,
NY 28 June,
$22,000 (£16,296)

14

A carved mahogany wing
armchair, Pennsylvania,
c.1775, the seat with
loose cushion, on square
moulded legs joined by
an H-stretcher, *NY 28 June,*
$7,425 (£5,500)

15

A Federal inlaid maple
lolling chair, Massachusetts,
c.1795, the upholstered
back with serpentine
crest above shaped line-
inlaid arm supports,
NY 8 Dec,
$3,300 (£2,750)

1

A Federal carved mahogany sofa, attributed to Duncan Phyfe, New York, c.1805, 223cm (80in), *NY 26 Jan*, $16,500 (£11,379)

2

A Federal carved mahogany armchair, School of Duncan Phyfe, New York, c.1810, the moulded leaf-carved crest above reeded down-curving scrolled arms and upholstered seat, *NY 28 Jan*, $3,080 (£2,124)

3

A Federal carved mahogany small settee, Coastal New England, c.1815, on ring-turned tapering legs ending in castors, 151cm (59½in), *NY 28 June*, $8,250 (£6,111)

4

A set of eight Federal carved curly maple caned-seat side chairs, New York, c.1820, each having a concave crest and backrail, on sabre legs joined by stretchers, *NY 30 June*, $2,750 (£2,037)

5

A set of eight Federal carved tiger maple side chairs, New York or New England, c.1820, *NY 8 Dec*, $5,500 (£4,583)

6

An American painted, decorated and turned Windsor comb-back armchair, branded S Paine, Massachusetts, c.1770, painted overall in grained brown with gold highlights, *NY 8 Dec*, $4,400 (£3,667)

7

A pair of American turned Windsor brace-back bow-back chairs, Rhode Island, c.1780, each having a moulded bowed crest above seven tapered and shaped spindles, *NY 30 June*, $4,290 (£3,178)

8

An American painted and turned Windsor fan-back armchair, c.1785, the turned legs now on rockers, painted black, *NY 28 Jan*, $2,750 (£1,897)

9

A pair of American turned Windsor bow-back side chairs, Rhode Island, c.1790, each having a bowed crestrail above seven turned and tapered spindles, *NY 8 Dec*, $1,980 (£1,650)

10

An American painted, decorated and turned Windsor sack-back writing armchair, New England, possibly Vermont, 1790-1810, *NY 28 Jan*, $6,600 (£4,552)

11

A pair of American laminated rosewood chairs, attributed to Joseph W Meeks, mid-19th cent, *L 9 Mar*, £594 ($886)

12

An American carved oak 'House of Representatives' armchair, c.1857, stencilled Bembe & Kimmel, 928 Broadway, New York, and marked with an inventory number, *NY 24/25 Feb*, $3,300 (£2,276)

13

An American rococo laminated rosewood récamier, attributed to John Henry Belter, New York, c.1855, *NY 16 June*, $2,200 (£1,606)

14

An American rococo laminated rosewood settee and armchair, John Henry Belter, c.1855, both with a triple arched crestrail centred by carved flowers and fruit, *NY 3 Nov*, $7,700 (£6,160)

15

An American rococo rosewood settee, c.1860, *NY 24/25 Feb*, $990 (£683)

American Furniture

LESLIE KENO

Throughout this century, the market for American furniture has been developing and expanding. The results of the 1984 auction season clearly demonstrated that this is now an extremely stable market in which increasingly sophisticated and knowledgeable collectors participate. New publications— Michael Moses's *Master Craftsmen of Newport; New England Furniture* by Brock Jobe and Myrna Kay; the catalogue of the furniture collection at the Maryland Historical Society by Gregory Weidman, and the catalogue of the collection of Mr and Mrs Stanley Stone by Oswald Rodriguez Roque, to name a few—have heightened awareness of American furniture and at the same time given considerable confidence to buyers.

As the scholarship in the field advances, the market becomes subject to increasingly complex factors. The most important factor is always the quality of the piece, where it stands in comparison with others of its style and type. Design and proportions are especially important, as is the nature of the carving. Perhaps the finest example of virtuoso carving that appeared in our saleroom in 1984 was that on a Federal card table made in Massachusetts circa 1798 (p.85, fig.5). The carving, elegant classical motifs on the frieze and legs and an elaborate basket of fruit and flowers, was attributed to the well-known cabinetmaker Samuel McIntire after comparison with two McIntire card tables at the Museum of Fine Arts in Boston. Although the character and grain of the wood itself is often overlooked when assessing the quality of a piece of furniture, brilliantly-figured mahogany and walnut can greatly enhance the desirability of the piece. The richly-figured veneered frieze on the McIntire card table gives a delicate appearance to what would have been an otherwise bulky table.

The condition of a piece of furniture has always been an important factor in determining its value. Replacements or repairs are just as significant as the condition of the surface. The Chippendale mahogany breakfast table sold in December (p.85, fig.4) had no replaced parts, and, in fact, still had its original hinges and pine glue blocks on the underside. The fact that the table retained these original components and

also had the mellow patina of an old finish contributed to the $37,400 (£31,219) price. Obviously major replacement can have the opposite effect on performance at auction.

The rarity of a particular form can influence bidding a great deal. The Federal lady's writing desk attributed to Duncan Phyfe (p.102, fig.1) is extremely rare because it was made almost entirely of satinwood, which is usually seen only in the form of inlay on American furniture. Very few chairs by the Goddard-Townsend School of Newport are known, and the rarity of the pair sold in January (p.85, fig.1) was further enhanced by the stop-fluted petal carving on the knees, a feature usually found only on case pieces by these distinguished cabinet-makers.

The fourth important factor is provenance. Since the history of furniture in the United States is a relatively short three centuries, it is still possible to find pieces that have descended in the families for which they were originally made. In June, the Tunis family chest-on-chest made in Philadelphia circa 1765 (p.85, fig.12) realized $137,500 (£101,852), and the well-documented provenance probably enhanced its value by about ten to fifteen per cent.

Quality, condition, rarity, and provenance are all important factors that influence the auction prices of American furniture. Occasionally, all of these can be applied in evaluating a single piece. Such was the case with the Williams family Queen Anne mahogany tray top tea table made in Boston between 1740-60 (p.85, fig.3). Elegantly proportioned on graceful cabriole legs, the table was in its original state and retained a fine old surface. As the tray top tea table is an exceedingly rare form and one that has been often faked, the appearance of an original mid 18th century example at auction was an extraordinary event. Originally owned by Susanna Shoemaker, the table descended from her daughter Margaret Shoemaker Williams through six generations of the Williams family. The combination of quality, rarity, original condition, and impeccable provenance resulted in an auction record price of $253,000 (£211,185).

1
An American carved walnut corner chair, Newport, Rhode Island, 1740-60, *NY 28 Jan,* $45,100 (£31,103)

2
An American carved walnut side chair, Pennsylvania, c1780, the shaped crest over a pierced gothic splat above a slip seat with cabriole legs ending in claw-and-ball feet, *NY 8 Dec,* $2,200 (£1,833)

3
A Federal inlaid mahogany lolling chair, Eastern Massachusetts, c1790, the upholstered shaped crest above double line-inlaid down-curving arms, *NY 30 June,* $19,800 (£14,667)

1

2

3

1
A pair of carved mahogany side chairs, Goddard-Townsend School, Newport, Rhode Island, c1765, each having an arched crest centring a scroll-carved shell device, a slip seat on cabriole legs, *NY 26 Jan,*
$143,000 (£98,620)

2
An American carved cherrywood lowboy, Connecticut, c1750, the shaped fan-carved skirt continuing to cabriole legs ending in pad feet, 75 x 92 x 60cm (29½ x 36 x 23½ in), *NY 28 Jan,*
$25,300 (£17,448)

3
A mahogany traytop tea table, Boston, Massachusetts, 1740-60, 71¾ x 75½ x 47½cm (28 x 29¾ x 18¾ in), *NY 8 Dec,*
$253,000 (£211,185)

4
A carved mahogany small drop-leaf dining table, Massachusetts, c1770, claw-and-ball feet, 66 x 90 x 91½cm (26 x 35½ x 36in), *NY 8 Dec,*
$37,400 (£31,219)

5
A Federal carved and inlaid mahogany card table, Massachusetts, c1798, inlaid with a radiating fan centring a satinwood-inlaid conch shell, acanthus carved feet, 76 x 123 x 61cm (30 x 48¾ x 24¼ in), *NY 26-28 Jan,*
$308,000 (£212,194)

6
A Federal inlaid mahogany sideboard, New York, c1790, with line-inlaid drawers and cupboard doors, square tapering legs, 109 x 179 x 61cm (43 x 70½ x 24in), *NY 8 Dec,*
$5,500 (£4,583)

7
A carved curly maple slant-front desk, Massachusetts, 1765-80, the interior fitted with valanced pigeon-holes over short drawers, four long drawers below, 105 x 92 x 46cm (41½ x 36 x 18in), *NY 26 Jan,*
$20,900 (£14,413)

8
An American carved mahogany block-front chest of drawers, Boston, Massachusetts, c1750, the oblong top with moulded edge over four graduated long drawers with cockbeaded surrounds, 73.6 x 85 x 55.9cm (29 x 33 x 22in), *NY 8 Dec,*
$28,600 (£23,833)

9
An American carved mahogany block-front kneehole desk, Boston, Massachusetts, c1740, the oblong top with thumb-moulded edge, the recessed cupboard section with panelled door, 79 x 91.5 x 54cm (31 x 36 x 21¼ in), *NY 30 June,*
$40,700 (£30,148)

10
A carved maple flat-top high-boy, New England, 1760-80, the centre drawer fan-carved, the skirt with acorn pendants continuing to cabriole legs, 188 x 99 x 51cm (74 x 38¾ x 20in), *NY 28 June,*
$11,000 (£8,148)

11
A carved cherrywood bonnet-top highboy, Connecticut, c1765, 221 x 97 x 48cm (87 x 38 x 19in), *NY 26 Jan,*
$23,100 (£15,931)

12
A carved walnut bonnet-top chest-on-chest, Philadelphia, c1765, in two parts, 237 x 107 x 58cm (93½ x 42 x 22¾ in), *NY 28-30 June,*
$137,500 (£101,852)

2

3

4

6

1

5

7

8

9

10

11

12

1
A mahogany bonheur du jour, c.1880, surmounted by pierced brass gallery, inlaid with musical trophy decoration, fold-over rexine-lined writing flap, 107 x 76cm (42 x 30in), *HS 25 June,* £715 ($1,008)

2
A Louis XV ormolu-mounted fruitwood, tulip-wood and purplewood marquetry bureau en pente, mid-18th cent, veneered with various stained and natural fruit-woods to represent flower-filled baskets, branches and birds, 86 x 82.5 x 45cm (34 x 32½ x 17½in), *NY 17 Nov,* $66,000 (£52,800)

3
A small Louis XV bureau dos d'âne, decorated in gold and vermilion with chinoiserie landscapes, the interior with purplewood marquetry, stamped 'Latz', 88 x 69 x 44cm (34½ x 27 x 17¼in), *M 25/26 June,* FF 976,800 (£83,845; $114,246)

4
A Régence kingwood and tulipwood parquetry bureau à gradins, c.1720, the superstructure fitted with pigeon holes and two drawers, 93 x 128 x 70cm (36½ x 50½ x 30in), *NY 7 Apr,* $19,800 (£13,846)

5
A Louis XV rosewood marquetry bureau dos d'âne, 80 x 84 x 46cm (31½ x 33 x 18in), *M 24/25 June,* FF 77,700 (£6,670; $9,088)

6
A French tulipwood bombé and gilt-bronze bureau de dame, by Alphonse Giroux & Cie, Paris, mid-19th cent, 87 x 69cm (34 x 27in), *C 5 July,* £2,750 ($3,732)

7
A French marquetry bureau de dame, c.1900, of serpentine form, quarter-veneered with flowers on rosewood with kingwood border, gilt-bronze mounts, w 71cm (28in), *L 9 Mar,* £990 ($1,475)

8
A French bureau à cylindre by Francois-Gaspard Teune, c.1780, veneered and finely inlaid with various fruitwoods with geometric motifs, 127 x 70cm (50 x 27½in), *F 19 Dec,* L 24,000,000 (£10,471; $12,544)

9
A Louis XVI ormolu-mounted mahogany bureau à cylindre, last quarter 18th cent, the rectangular white veined marble top with a three-quarter pierced ormolu gallery, the whole veneered in mahogany outlined in ormolu, 119 x 158 x 71cm (46¾ x 62 x 28in), *NY 17 Nov,* $20,900 (£16,720)

10
A Louis XIV boulle bureau Mazarin, c.1700, inlaid with scenes from the Commedia Del 'Arte in brass on a red tortoise-shell ground, the sides in contre-partie, w 119.5cm (47in), *L 6 July,* £13,750 ($18,975)

1

2

3

4

5

6

7

8

9

10

1
A late Louis XV small
secrétaire stamped J C
Stumpff JME, c.1770, the
moulded grey and white
marble top above a fitted
secrétaire drawer,
veneered with a kingwood
and purpleheart cross-
banded trellis, 94 x 80cm
(37 x 31½in), *L 30 Nov,*
£3,740 ($4,525)

2
A Louis XV/XVI
transitional small tulipwood
secrétaire/chiffonier,
c.1770, the fall-front
disguised as two drawers
and with a fitted
interior, 114 x 53.5cm (45
x 21in), *L 30 Nov,*
£1,650 ($1,997)

3
A Louis XVI tulipwood
and fruitwood marquetry
secrétaire à abbatant,
signed F Schey, last
quarter 18th cent, with a
moulded grey and white
marble top above an
inlaid frieze, ormolu
mounts 144 x 99 x 42cm
(56½ x 39 x 16½in),
NY 7 Apr,
$12,100 (£8,462)

4
A Louis XVI provincial
walnut secrétaire à
abattant, last quarter
18th cent, the top over a
pair of cupboard doors
enclosing a shelf, 178 x
120 x 45cm (70 x 40¼ x
17¾in), *NY 13 Oct,*
$2,530 (£2,074)

5
A Louis XVI kingwood
and fruitwood parquetry
secrétaire à abattant, last
quarter 18th cent, with a
white marble top, 151 x
86.5 x 39.5cm (56½ x 34 x
15½in), *NY 13 Oct,*
$4,125 (£3,381)

6
A Louis XVI mahogany
veneered secrétaire à
abattant, stamped
Ohneberg, the fall-front
opening to reveal six
small drawers and four
pigeon holes, 143 x 97 x
40cm (58¼ x 38 x 15¾in),
M 24/25 June,
FF 49,950 (£4,288; $5,842)

7
An Empire ormolu-
mounted mahogany secré-
taire à abattant, 1st
quarter 19th cent, the
frieze drawer with an
ormolu mask of Mercury,
142 x 100 x 49.5cm (55¾
x 39¼ x 19½in),
NY 17 Nov,
$6,600 (£5,280)

8
An Empire ormolu-
mounted mahogany
secrétaire à abattant, 1st
quarter 19th cent, bearing
a stamp 'Wallaert A
Gand', 144 x 94.5 x
49.5cm (56½ x 37¼ x
19½in), *NY 13 Oct,*
$4,400 (£3,607)

9
An Empire ormolu-
mounted mahogany
secrétaire à abattant, 1st
quarter 19th cent, with a
rectangular grey marble
top, 138 x 96 x 42cm
(54¼ x 37¾ x 16½in),
NY 13 Oct,
$3,025 (£2,480)

10
A Directoire brass-mounted
secrétaire à abattant,
c.1790, with a three-
quarter brass gallery,
138 x 94cm (54½ x 37in),
L 30 Nov,
£1,980 ($2,396)

11
A Charles X ormolu-
mounted walnut secrétaire
à abattant, signed G
Kintz, 149 x 91 x 39cm
(58½ x 36 x 15½in),
NY 7 Apr,
$2,090 (£1,462)

12
A Louis-Phillipe ebonised
and cut-brass secrétaire
semanier, mid-19th cent,
with a shaped marble
top above a fall-front
enclosing a tulip wood
and amboyna interior,
119 x 68.6cm (47 x 27in),
C 15 Aug,
£330 ($429)

13
A French ebony and
boulle secrétaire à
abbatant, 3rd quarter
19th cent, of small
proportions, inlaid
throughout with cut-
brass on tortoiseshell
ground, 124.5 x 65cm
(49 x 25½in), *C 27 Mar,*
£572 (£852)

1   2   3

4   5   6

7   8   9

10   11   12   13

1

A South German walnut
parquetry bureau, c 1740,
inlaid with walnut cross-
banding enclosing burr-
walnut panels, w 128.5cm
(50½ in), L 18 May,
£3,080 ($4,307)

2

A North Italian rococo
walnut slant-front desk,
mid-18th cent, the slant-
front enclosing three
drawers, a recessed well
and rectangular writing
surface, 107 x 120 x 66cm
(42 x 47 x 26¼ in),
NY 16 June,
$5,500 (£4,015)

3

A Dutch East Indies solid
padouk bureau, c 1770,
the fall-front with a
fitted interior, the four
graduated long drawers
with multiple concave
and convex mouldings,
96 x 102cm (38 x 40in),
L 3 Feb,
£3,630 ($5,089)

4

An Italian inlaid walnut
bureau, c 1730, in
crossbanded wood, the
shaped front inlaid
throughout with scroll-
work and flowers,
cherubs and grotesques,
114 x 114cm (45 x 45in),
L 30 Nov,
£9,350 ($11,314)

5

A Dutch burr-walnut
bombé bureau, c 1770, the
flap with a fitted interior
above three graduated
concave and convex
drawers, on ogee bracket
feet, w 102cm (40in),
L 25 May,
£1,760 ($2,461)

6

A Dutch walnut cylinder
bureau, c 1770, in two
parts, the panelled
cylinder burr-veneered,
outlined with bead and
reel moulding and
opening in conjunction
with a slide, L 25 May,
£2,530 ($3,618)

7

An Italian neoclassical
fruitwood marquetry roll-
top desk, late 18th cent,
the whole inlaid with
shells within roundels
and checkered banding,
123 x 101 x 44cm (48½ x
39¾ x 17½ in), NY 13 Oct,
$1,210 (£992)

8

A Dutch marquetry
cylinder bureau, late 18th
cent, the whole now
inlaid with floral
marquetry on a mahogany
ground, 126 x 127cm
(49½ x 50in), L 23 Nov,
£4,620 ($5,590)

9

A German parquetry
cylinder desk, c 1780, the
upper part with a pair of
tambour doors and three
frieze drawers, the inlaid
cylinder above a pull-
out writing slide with a
stepped serpentine
interior, 146 x 114cm
(57½ x 45in), L 18 May,
£2,860 ($4,147)

10

An Italian ivory-inlaid
cylinder bureau, c 1800,
with a concave cresting,
the cylinder enclosing
an elaborately fitted
interior, with three
frieze drawers and two
short drawers in each
pedestal, 121cm (47½ in),
L 30 Nov,
£6,820 ($8,252)

11

A mahogany cylinder
bureau, 19th cent, 115 x
100 x 52cm (45½ x 39½ x
20½ in), A 13-16 Mar,
Dfl 2,668 (£610; $910)

12

A German neoclassical
mahogany and fruitwood
parquetry cylinder top
bureau, late 18th cent,
122 x 117 x 61cm (52 x 46
x 24in), NY 7 Apr,
$2,640 (£1,846)

13

An Italian rococo fruitwood
parquetry bureau, c 1760,
the slant-front opening
to reveal a fitted writing
interior, the frieze with
three drawers, the whole
veneered in light and
dark fruitwood, 99 x 98 x
51cm (39 x 38½ x 20in),
NY 13 Oct,
$2,860 (£2,344)

14

A Continental walnut
marquetry cylinder bureau,
probably Italian, c 1890,
inlaid with scrollwork
and flowers, the cylinder
with an oval of cherubs
drawing Poseidon's chariot,
enclosing a slide and
drawers, 85cm (33½ in),
L 8 June,
£990 ($1,436)

1

2

3   4

5   6   7

8   9   10

11

12   13   14

1
A North Italian inlaid walnut writing table, mid-17th cent, the top with panels inlaid with figures and a coat-of-arms, 92 x 125cm (36 x 49in), *L 23 Nov,* £5,720 ($6,291)

2
A Piedmontese writing table, *c.*1700, inlaid in ivory, the front with five drawers and a fall-front, part of the top hinged, 113 x 57.5cm (44½ x 22½in), *F 19 Dec,* L 9,500,000 (£4,014; $5,018)

3
A Flemish walnut and olivewood writing table, *c.*1700, with hinged divided top opening in conjunction with a fall-front drawer to reveal a writing interior, 80 x 98cm (31½ x 38½in), *L 30 Nov,* £3,740 ($4,525)

4
A North Italian walnut kneehole writing table, mid-18th cent, with leather-lined tray top and five drawers with simple incised rococo mouldings, raised on moulded cabriole legs, w 130cm (51in), *L 18 May,* £6,600 ($9,230)

5
An Italian kneehole writing table, Piedmont, late 18th cent, the top and five drawers inlaid, 80 x 55cm (31½ x 21½in), *F 19 Dec,* L 11,500,000 (£4,858; $6,073)

6
A North Italian kingwood and marquetry kneehole table, *c.*1780, quarter-veneered, 77 x 110cm (30½ x 43½in), *L 18 May,* £3,300 ($4,785)

7
An Austrian neoclassical painted and parcel-gilt ebonised writing table, *c.*1830, the moulded rectangular leather-lined surface within a border of foliate scrolls above a frieze drawer enclosing a fitted interior, 76 x 72 x 47cm (30 x 28½ x 18½in), *NY 16 June,* $825 (£602)

8
A Lombard marquetry desk, 19th cent, the top inlaid with a central oval marquetry panel of a shipwreck, the front with three drawers in the frieze, *L 30 Nov,* £13,200 ($15,972)

9
A Dutch satinwood and japanned secrétaire à abattant, *c.*1785, set with black japanned panels, 141 x 75cm (55½ x 29½in), *L 18 May,* £1,870 ($2,712)

10
A Russian neoclassical ormolu-mounted mahogany secrétaire à abattant, the top with a pierced ormolu gallery above a frieze drawer, the fall-front opening to form a writing surface, re-backed, 141 x 71 x 31cm (55½ x 28 x 12in), *NY 7 Apr,* $2,090 (£1,462)

11
A Biedermeier carved walnut and pewter-inlaid marquetry and painted fall-front secretary, *c.*1830, the fitted interior with a mirrored niche inlaid with cube marquetry 186 x 107 x 56cm (73 x 42 x 21½in), *NY 7 Apr,* $2,750 (£1,923)

12
A Beidermeier inlaid maple two-part fall-front secretary cabinet, the glazed doors flanked by free-standing columns, 193 x 100 x 48cm (76 x 39½ x 19in), *NY 7 Apr,* $2,970 (£2,077)

13
An Italian neoclassical gilt-metal-mounted walnut and fruitwood marquetry fall-front secrétaire, 1st half 19th cent, 155 x 93 x 44cm (61 x 36½ x 17½in), *NY 7 Apr,* $2,420 (£1,692)

14
A marquetry and harewood secrétaire cabinet, 1890s, the serpentine swan's-neck cresting above a pair of glazed doors, the lower part with a fitted serpentine secrétaire drawer, 204.5 x 122cm (80½ x 48in), *L 17 Feb,* £5,940 ($8,328)

1 2 3

4 5 6

7 8

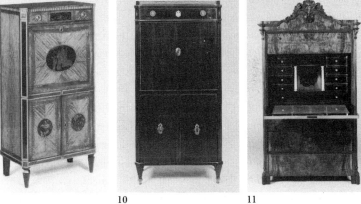

9 10 11

12 13 14

1
A **Danish painted bureau-cabinet,** c 1720, painted with pastoral scenes of figures and views within deep-blue borders decorated in imitation Oriental lacquer, 231 x 135cm (91 x 53in), *L 18 May,* **£6,050 ($8,773)**

2
A **German baroque walnut parquetry bureau chest of drawers,** mid-18th cent, a slant-front opening to form a writing surface and to reveal four small drawers and pigeon holes, 186 x 141 x 66cm (73 x 51½ x 26in), *NY 13 Oct,* **$8,250 (£6,762)**

3
A **South German rococo walnut and fruitwood marquetry three-part bureau cabinet,** mid-18th cent, the upper part with an arched cornice above a pair of doors inlaid with parrots, 221 x 131 x 61cm (87 x 51½ x 24in), *NY 7 Apr,* **$16,500 (£11,538)**

4
A **Venetian walnut bureau cabinet,** with a waved moulded cornice above an arched panelled door containing a bevelled mirror-glass panel, 250 x 160cm (98½ x 63in), *L 30 Nov,* **£35,299 ($42,712)**

5
A **Roman kingwood-veneered bureau cabinet,** mid-18th cent, the serpentine upper part with a pair of doors with crossbanded quarter veneering, 252 x 153cm (99 x 60in), *L 18 May,* **£13,200 ($19,140)**

6
An **Italian walnut bureau cabinet,** Venice-Emiliano, c 1750, inlaid with burr-walnut, the slant-front opening to a fitted interior, 258 x 117cm (101½ x 46in), *F 10 May,* **L 22,600,000 (£9,625; $13,379)**

7
An **Italian walnut bureau cabinet,** mid-18th cent, with a moulded top over a pair of arched panelled doors, inlaid with rococo scrollwork throughout, 226 x 97cm (89 x 38in), *L 30 Nov,* **£13,200 ($15,972)**

8
A **Piedmont veneered walnut bureau cabinet,** 2nd quarter 18th cent, inlaid overall, the upper part with glazed doors, 209 x 99cm (82 x 38in), *F 5 June,* **L 15,000,000 (£6,224; $9,025)**

9
A **Dutch rococo ormolu-mounted slant-front cabinet,** 18th cent, in three parts, inlaid with fruitwood on a burr-walnut ground, 220 x 132 x 70cm (98 x 52 x 27½in), *NY 7 Apr,* **$22,000 (£15,385)**

10
A **Dutch walnut and marquetry bureau cabinet,** mid-18th cent, the marquetry later, 218 x 99cm (84 x 39in), *L 30 Nov,* **£4,730 ($5,723)**

11
A **German mahogany secrétaire bookcase on chest,** c 1850, with cluster pilaster terminals, the ogee-fronted base with a writing drawer above two drawers, 193 x 109cm (76 x 43in), *P 15-18 May,* **£792 ($1,101)**

12
A **Dresden-mounted secrétaire writing cabinet,** c 1866, set with painted panels in the manner of Watteau, 237 x 130 x 60cm (93 x 51 x 24½in), *L 9 Nov,* **£44,000 ($58,520)**

13
A **Florentine walnut and ivory inlaid bureau cabinet,** by F del Soldato, 1880, inlaid throughout with etched ivory figures, birds, foliage and scrolls, 178 x 140cm (70 x 41in), *L 9 Nov,* **£3,300 ($4,389)**

1

2

3

4

5

6

7

8

9

10

11

12

13

1
An American carved mahogany kneehole desk, Maryland, c.1770, on ogee bracket feet, 74 x 92 x 51cm (29¼ x 36 x 20in), *NY 28 Jan,* $6,600 (£4,552)

2
A carved curly maple small slant-front desk, New England, c.1770, the interior fitted with valanced pigeon holes over short drawers, 98 x 90 x 43cm (38¾ x 35¼ x 17in), *NY 28 June,* $5,225 (£3,870)

3
An American carved mahogany slant-front desk, signed Rawson, Providence, Rhode Island, c.1775, 109 x 104 x 56cm (43 x 41 x 22in), *NY 28 Jan,* $15,400 (£10,621)

4
An American carved mahogany oxbow-front slant-front desk, Eastern Massachusetts, c.1775, 113 x 107 x 54cm (44½ x 42 x 21in), *NY 28 Jan,* $3,740 (£2,579)

5
An American carved mahogany slant-front desk, Massachusetts, c.1780, the interior with pigeon holes and a fan-carved drawer, 109 x 104 x 56cm (43 x 41 x 22in), *NY 8 Dec,* $5,225 (£4,354)

6
An American carved tiger maple slant-front desk, New England, c.1780, with a sunburst carved prospect door, 111 x 93 x 49cm (43½ x 36½ x 19in), *NY 8 Dec,* $3,850 (£3,208)

7
An American carved mahogany slant-front desk, signed Mark Pitman, probably Salem, Massachusetts, c.1785, 110 x 103 x 55cm (43½ x 40½ x 21¾in), *NY 28 June,* $11,000 (£7,586)

8
An American carved cherry-wood slant-front desk, Pennsylvania, c.1790, 114 x 102 x 53cm (45 x 40 x 21in), *NY 30 June,* $3,520 (£2,607)

9
An American curly maple slant-front desk, probably New Hampshire, c.1800, stained red, 128 x 104 x 51cm (50½ x 31 x 20in), *NY 28 Jan,* $5,500 (£3,793)

10
A Federal bird's-eye maple and rosewood-inlaid mahogany lady's desk, Massachusetts, c.1805, in two parts, 130 x 85 x 51cm (51 x 33½ x 20in), *NY 28 Jan,* $11,550 (£7,966)

11
An American inlaid mahogany lady's writing desk, Eastern New England, c.1800, in two parts, the upper with a pair of hinged doors, the lower section with a felt-lined writing surface, 123 x 76 x 41cm (48¾ x 30 x 16in), *NY 28 Jan,* $7,700 (£5,310)

12
An American mahogany double pier roll-top rotary desk, William S Wooton, Indianapolis, c.1880, 110 x 147cm (42 x 58in), *NY 24/25 Feb,* $2,750 (£1,897)

13
An American walnut secretary, c.1880, Wooton, Standard Grade, with a carved three-quarter gallery above a pair of convex doors enclosing various compartments and drawers, 193 x 117cm (76 x 46in), *NY 3 Nov,* $6,600 (£5,280)

14
An American walnut double-pier rotary desk, c.1890, labelled 'Wooton's Rotary Desk', the leather-inset rectangular top above three frieze drawers, 81 x 153cm (32 x 60in), *NY 3 Nov,* $1,650 (£1,320)

1   2   3

4   5   6

7   8   9

10   11   12

13   14

1
A George III satinwood marquetry bonheur du jour, last quarter 18th cent, the removable rectangular superstructure with an open compartment flanked by cupboards, hinged writing flap, 95 x 74 x 41cm (37½ x 29 x 18½in), *NY 20 Oct*, $6,600 (£5,546)

2
A George III painted satinwood bonheur du jour, c1780, the upper part with a pair of doors enclosing a mahogany-lined fitted interior, 133.5 x 76.5cm (52½ x 30in), *L 16 Mar*, £3,080 ($4,589)

3
A George III tulipwood-veneered bonheur du jour, c1790, the superstructure with an arched gallery, the projecting lower part with a satinwood-banded baize-lined hinged writing surface, 117 x 76cm (46 x 30in), *L 16 Mar*, £5,060 ($7,539)

4
A Regency gilt-decorated black japanned bonheur du jour, c1815, in the manner of John MacLean, the superstructure with a three-quarter-galleried top above a brass Chinese fretwork-enclosed compartment, 115 x 84 x 51cm (45 x 33 x 20in), *NY 21 Jan*, $12,100 (£8,345)

5
A George III-style mahogany Carlton House desk, 20th cent, with a pull-out leather writing surface, inlaid in satinwood and boxwood, 102 x 120cm (40 x 47in), *C 10 Jan*, £1,540 ($2,233)

6
A George III mahogany serpentine writing and reading table, mid-18th cent, with serpentine moulded top, the false frieze drawer opening to form a writing surface, 107 x 109 x 64cm (42 x 43 x 25in), *NY 20 Oct*, $12,650 (£10,630)

7
A George III oak bureau, c1800, of country manufacture, the front with a frieze drawer above two graduated long drawers, 95 x 84 x 42cm (37½ x 33 x 16½in), *NY 12-14 Apr*, $2,420 (£1,692)

8
A George III mahogany bureau, last quarter 18th cent, the sloping fall-front enclosing a fitted interior, 108 x 98.5cm (42½ x 38¾in), *C 5 July*, £1,485 ($2,015)

9
A George III mahogany bureau, c1800, the fall-front above three short drawers and three long drawers, 112 x 117cm (44 x 46in), *C 11-14 Dec*, £792 ($990)

10
A George I-style bureau on stand, 1910-20, the upper part with concave and convex sides and a fitted interior, w 71cm (28in), *L 17 Feb*, £902 ($1,265)

1

2

3

4

5

6

7

8

9

10

1

A Queen Anne walnut and featherbanded kneehole writing desk, the quarter-veneered crossbanded top above two frieze drawers, 76 x 79cm (30 x 31in), *P 20-22 Mar,* £1,485 ($2,213)

2

A George I inlaid walnut kneehole writing table, 1st quarter 18th cent, with a moulded crossbanded rectangular top, 78 x 83 x 50cm (30½ x 32½ x 19½in), *NY 12-14 Apr,* $3,575 (£2,500)

3

A George I walnut kneehole desk, c 1725, 74 x 71cm (29 x 28in), *L 26 Oct,* £4,840 ($6,195)

4

A late George II mahogany small kneehole desk, c 1755, 76 x 80 x 47cm (30 x 31½ x 18½in), *L 14 Dec,* £935 ($1,169)

5

A George III mahogany kneehole desk, c 1780, with moulded top crossbanded in satinwood, three drawers each side of a kneehole cupboard, w 124cm (49in), *L 15 June,* £2,310 ($3,257)

6

A late George III mahogany pedestal partner's writing table, early 19th cent, with a green leather inset top, 80 x 121 x 77cm (31½ x 47½ x 30½in), *NY 21 Jan,* $7,150 (£4,931)

7

A George IV mahogany partner's desk, c 1825, with tooled leather inset top, w 168cm (66in), *P 15-18 May,* £2,475 ($3,440)

8

A Victorian walnut and burl walnut pedestal desk, c 1860, locks stamped Ohurr's Patent 373 St Paul London, Makers to her Majesty, 109 x 125cm (43 x 49in), *NY 3 Nov,* $2,475 (£1,980)

9

A late George III pollard elm small pedestal writing table, early 19th cent, with leather inset, 75 x 123 x 67cm (29½ x 48½ x 26½in), *NY 21 Jan,* $6,325 (£4,362)

10

A Victorian pedestal writing desk, late 19th cent, with inset leather writing surface, the pedestals with carved panelled door enclosing shelves and drawers, 73.5 x 157.5cm (29 x 62in), *C 19 July,* £627 ($834)

11

A mahogany kneehole writing desk, late 19th cent, the rectangular top with inset leather writing surface and gadrooned border, 76 x 137cm (30 x 54in), *C 16 Oct,* £880 ($1,126)

12

A William IV burr yew-wood kidney-shaped writing table, second quarter 19th cent, the crossbanded top inset with a gilt-tooled leather writing surface, the back with a pair of cupboard doors, opening to adjustable shelves, 77 x 185 x 94cm (31½ x 73 x 37in), *NY 20 Oct,* $33,000 (£27,731)

1   2   3

4   5

6   7

8   9

10

11   12

1
A walnut double-domed
bureau cabinet, c.1710,
with later bevelled
mirror plates, enclosing
a fitted interior, 196 x
91cm (77 x 36in), L·16 Nov,
£18,150 ($23,958)

2
A William and Mary
inlaid burr-walnut bureau
bookcase, c.1690, 198 x 99
x 61cm (78 x 39 x 24in),
NY 21 Jan,
$11,550 (£7,966)

3
A late George II
mahogany bureau
bookcase, mid-18th cent,
with a moulded broken
dentil pediment above a
pair of mirrored doors,
the fall-front opening to
a fitted interior, 247 x
125 x 61cm (97 x 49 x
24in), NY 12-14 Apr,
$6,050 (£4,231)

4
An early George III
mahogany bureau bookcase,
c.1760, the glazed doors
with octagonal panels,
the lower part with fitted
interior, 226 x 97cm (89
x 38in), L 5 Oct,
£3,630 ($4,719)

5
A George III mahogany
bureau bookcase, 3rd
quarter 18th cent, the
moulded cornice above a
pair of panelled doors,
207 x 105 x 53cm (81½ x
41½ x 21in), NY 9 June,
$2,200 (£1,583)

6
A George III oak bureau
bookcase, late 18th cent,
the later upper part with
a pair of twelve-panel
glazed doors, 186 x 92cm
(73½ x 36in), L 21 Sept,
£1,265 ($1,607)

7
A Queen Anne-style
walnut bureau bookcase,
c.1900, the doors enclosing
adjustable shelves, the
crossbanded fall revealing
a fitted interior, 196 x
91.5cm (77 x 36in),
P 13 Nov,
£1,265 ($1,695)

8
An English rosewood
Davenport, 1830s, the
three-quarter gallery
above a writing slope
which slides forward
over the knees, w 52cm
(20½in), L 17 Feb,
£990 ($1,388)

9
A Victorian burr-walnut
Davenport, c.1850, the
sides with a pen drawer
and four real and four
opposing dummy
drawers, w 54cm (33in),
P 13 Nov,
£462 ($619)

10
A Victorian walnut
Davenport, c.1850, the
fitted superstructure
with galleried hinged
lid, the serpentine front
with a leather-lined
moulded writing surface,
w 53cm (21in), L 28 Sept,
£715 ($930)

11
A Victorian walnut
Davenport, mid-19th
cent, with a galleried
superstructure above a
pair of panelled doors
enclosing pigeon holes,
108 x 61cm (42½ x 24in),
C 5 July,
£1,320 ($1,791)

12
A Victorian walnut
harlequin Davenport,
mid-19th cent, the
galleried top with a pop-
up action enclosing a
cedar-lined interior, 92 x
61cm (36 x 24in), C 27 Mar,
£1,375 ($2,049)

1

2

3

4

5

8

9

6

7

10

11

12

1

A George III inlaid mahogany cylinder bureau, late 18th cent, 99 x 83 x 50cm (39 x 32½ x 19½in), *NY 12-14 Apr,* **$9,350 (£6,538)**

2

A George III mahogany tambour desk, the tambour flanked by a pair of brass strips and with a fitted interior, w 101cm (41½in), *L 13 July,* **£3,080 ($4,220)**

3

A Victorian mahogany roll-top desk, c.1880, the top with marble super-structure with brass galleried surround, the roll-top with fitted interior, 107 x 90cm (42 x 35½in), *CT 21 Mar,* **R 1,500 (£829; $1,236)**

4

A Victorian rosewood marquetry cylinder bureau, c.1870, the cylinder front enclosing a fitted interior with pull-out baize-lined writing surface, 104 x 74cm (41 x 29in), *L 28 Sept,* **£792 ($1,030)**

5

A George III satinwood and rosewood crossbanded secrétaire chest, c.1790, with a raised open shelf back, 143 x 86cm (58½ x 32in), *P 21-24 Feb,* **£6,820 ($9,562)**

6

A George III mahogany secrétaire chest of drawers, c.1800, with a fitted secrétaire drawer above two long drawers, 95 x 116 x 54cm (37½ x 45 x 21in), *NY 21 Jan,* **$1,540 (£1,062)**

7

A Regency brass-mounted rosewood secrétaire cabinet, 1st quarter 19th cent, with a later shallow superstructure, the top with a moulded brass rim, the front with a fitted secretary drawer above a pair of panelled doors, 112 x 92 x 38cm (44 x 36 x 15in), *NY 20 Oct,* **$6,600 (£5,546)**

8

A small brass-mounted camphorwood campaign secrétaire, c.1870, in two parts, each with two drawers, the upper one fitted as a secrétaire drawer, 99 x 76cm (39 x 30in), *L 17 Feb,* **£935 ($1,311)**

9

A George III carved and inlaid mahogany secretary bookcase, third quarter 18th cent, with a leaf-carved, swan's-neck pediment above a plain frieze, 246 x 104 x 52cm (97 x 41 x 20½in), *NY 12-14 Apr,* **$6,325 (£4,423)**

10

A George III mahogany bookcase cabinet, c.1800, the pair of doors enclosing shelves, 222 x 80 x 35cm (87½ x 31½ x 13½in), *NY 21 Jan,* **$5,500 (£3,793)**

11

A George III mahogany secrétaire bookcase, c.1770, the pair of doors with ogee and lancet bars, 219 x 113cm (86½ x 44½in), *L 16 Nov,* **£3,740 ($4,937)**

12

A George III inlaid and painted satinwood secretary bookcase, last quarter 18th cent, the frieze painted with flowerheads, 236 x 109 x 47cm (93 x 43 x 18½in), *NY 20 Oct,* **$17,600 (£14,790)**

13

A William IV mahogany secrétaire bookcase, 2nd quarter 19th cent, the sliding fall-front enclosing a fitted interior and leather writing surface adjustable by ratchet, 246.5 x 138cm (97 x 54½in), *C 29 Mar,* **£3,300 ($4,917)**

1 2 3 4 5 6 7 8 9 10 11 12 13

Paris Furniture
of the 19th Century

CHRISTOPHER PAYNE

Guild requirements in Paris in the 18th century stated that the cabinet maker (*ébéniste*) must sign furniture supplied by him to the public. The collector therefore became accustomed to the added cachet of a signature. This was almost always in the form of a *marque au fer,* or cold iron stamp, impressed into the carcass or seatrail of a piece. Sometimes this stamp would be accompanied by a JME—for Jurés-Menuisiers-Ebénistes.

Only royal pieces were exempt from the stamp, though many are, in fact, signed. Some 18th century pieces had their stamp removed or at least partly obliterated by the dealers (Marchands Merciers) to stop the penny-pinching nobility from going behind the retailer's back to the cabinet maker! The strict definition of labour and the requirement to sign was abolished in 1791 under the Directorate. For some twenty to thirty years the practice of signing almost dropped away, to be revived in the middle of the 19th century by the better makers of the Paris *meubles de luxe,* who mainly operated around the Faubourg St Antoine.

Not always were the later signatures hidden. Millet and Sormani often engraved their name and/or address quite clearly on the lockplate. Towards the end of the century François Linke had a neatly engraved script signature on the top right hand *bronze doré* mount of his pieces. Henry Dasson also used this technique, although the salon suite (p.97, fig.2) carries an example of his use of an 18th century style stamp. These were maker/retailers entering into the full spirit of commercialism that dominated the century.

Other fine makers also signed, but more discreetly. Alfred Beurdeley often simply signed the reverse of a major piece of a bronze mount with a BY. Occasionally the back was signed with a hot iron stamp, a *marque au feu.* Linke occasionally stamps, as opposed to casts, an *F.L.* on the reverse of his bronzes. Zweiner used the 18th century cold stamp technique. Rarely, however, did the makers actually hide their names as their forefathers had done (usually under several kilos of heavy marble).

It is difficult to assess the added advantage of a stamp in terms of price. There are not many people who can attribute a piece categorically to an individual maker in terms of its design, as several makers often made similar pieces, especially when copying 18th century models. Better pieces by Linke can often be attributed to him on stylistic grounds because of his individual art nouveau style bronze work, but the confirmation of a signature is always a bonus.

The natural consequence is that there is now a temptation to 'improve' a piece by adding a signature. This is especially so with Linke's name in the United States, where his work is very popular. Often, however, the signatures are extremely crude and shaky and on inferior pieces.

One of the most interesting pieces in this section is possibly fig.8 on p.97. This cries out for the E.H.B. brand mark of Edward Holms Baldock. The desk is English from the 1840s, but Baldock was a supplier of 18th century pieces—a dealer who also sold good quality modern pieces in a quasi-Louis style.

The signed pieces in this section are normally the better pieces, as few would sign an indifferent piece. If you like it, buy it. If it is signed be prepared to pay 10 to 100 per cent more, depending on the quality, the maker and the rarity of the piece in question.

1
A French rosewood and ormolu-mounted small bureau plat, stamped G Durand, 1840s, the square leather-lined top with a gilt-bronze border, 95 x 65cm (37½ x 25½in), *L 9 Mar,*
£4,400 ($6,556)

2
A pair of small mahogany étagères, stamped G Durand, *c*.1850, each with three stepped open shelves clasped in gilt-bronze with a moulded gilt-bronze border above a drawer, 110 x 44.5cm (43¼ x 17½in), *L 8 June,*
£3,300 ($4,785)

3
An ebonised brass and mother-of-pearl-inlaid jardinière, *c*.1850, in the manner of Maison Alfonse Giroux, w 66cm (26in), *L 9 Nov,*
£440 ($585)

4
A parquetry bureau à cylindre by P-G Durand, *c*.1860, after a model by J H Riesener, 107 x 113cm (42 x 44½in), *L 9 Nov,*
£5,500 ($7,315)

5
A small French chinoiserie and kingwood secrétaire cabinet, by Alfred Beurdeley, Paris, *c*.1860, 152cm (56in), *L 9 Nov,*
£19,800 ($26,334)

1 2

3 4

5

1
A tulipwood and kingwood arc en arbalette bureau plat, 1880s, signed Henry Dasson, the crossbanded leather-lined top with a gilt-bronze border, the frieze with three drawers above three dummy drawers, 81 x 216 x 104cm (32 x 85 x 41in), *L 9 Mar,*
£14,300 ($21,321)

2
A French Aubusson upholstered giltwood salon suite, stamped Henry Dasson, 1870s, comprising four fauteuils, a pair of bergères and a canapé, *L 9 Mar,*
£12,100 ($18,029)

3
A set of fifteen caned walnut armchairs, stamped J Sarazin, c 1900, in Louis XV style, each moulded frame with cartouche-back serpentine seat, cabriole legs headed by fan panels, *L 9 Nov,*
£1,980 ($2,633)

4
A Louis XV-style gilt-bronze-mounted inlaid kingwood side table, stamped P Sormani, Paris 10 rue Charlot, late 19th cent, the floral inlaid shaped top above a single frieze drawer raised on cabriole legs, 71 x 56cm (28 x 22in), *NY 3 Nov,*
$2,420 (£1,936)

5
A pair of gilt-bronze and kingwood display cabinets, by François Linke, c 1900, each of bow front form, the glazed door and sides applied with a gilt-bronze rococo cartouche, the bombé lower part inlaid with flowers, 203 x 112cm (78 x 44in), *L 9 Nov,*
£19,800 ($26,334)

6
A Louis XVI-style gilt-bronze-mounted mahogany bedstead and dresser, Linke, 20th cent, the bed surmounted with a gilt-bronze putto amongst bullrush and foliage, the dresser with a mirror superstructure, decorated overall with trophies and foliage, dresser 198 x 176cm (78 x 65in), bed w 183cm (72in), *NY 3 Nov,*
$17,600 (£14,080)

7
A gilt-bronze-mounted tulipwood parquetry bureau plat, F Linke, late 19th cent, in Louis XV style, with an inset leather writing surface surrounded by gilt-bronze banding above three frieze drawers, 82 x 165cm (32 x 65in), *NY 16 June,*
$16,500 (£12,044)

8
An English porcelain-mounted kingwood and tulipwood parquetry bureau plat, mid-19th cent, the serpentine top inset with a leather panel and with moulded brass border, the frieze containing a drawer, 75 x 129.5cm (28½ x 51in), *L 9 Mar,*
£6,380 ($9,506)

1

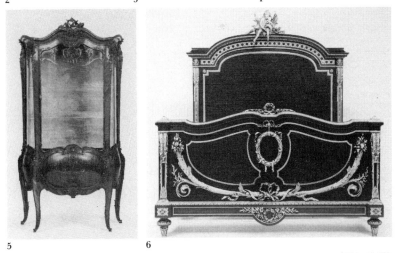

2   3   4

5   6

7   8

1

A **Breton walnut table,** mid-18th cent, the frieze carved with roundels and flowers, on spiral-twist legs, w 170cm (67in), *L 25 May,* £1,870 ($2,615)

2

A **Louis XVI brass-mounted fruitwood drop-leaf supper table,** late 18th cent, the circular top with a brass rim, h 70cm (27½in), d 99cm (39in), *NY 16 Nov,* $2,420 (£1,936)

3

A **Louis XVI mahogany extension dining table,** late 18th cent, with nine additional leaves of later date, 73.5 x 551cm (29in x 18ft 1in), *NY 16 June,* $8,250 (£6,022)

4

A **Directoire walnut drop-leaf extension dining table,** late 18th/19th cent, with four later leaves, 71 x 127 x 128cm (28 x 50 x 50½in), *NY 16 Nov,* $3,850 (£3,080)

5

A **Directoire ormolu-mounted bleached mahogany bouillotte table,** with a circular galleried white mottled marble top, h 76cm (30in), d 80.5cm (31¾in), *NY 16 Nov,* $5,500 (£4,400)

6

An **Empire ormolu-mounted mahogany centre table,** 1st quarter 19th cent, inset with a green leather writing surface, the plain frieze fitted with five drawers, h 76cm (30in), d 76cm (51in), *NY 13 Oct,* $4,950 (£4,057)

7

An **Empire ormolu-mounted mahogany guéridon,** 1st quarter 19th cent, the circular white mottled marble top raised on a baluster-shaped stem with waisted ormolu mount, h 74cm (29in), d 98cm (38½in), *NY 16 Nov,* $5,500 (£4,400)

8

An **Empire ormolu-mounted mahogany guéridon,** early 19th cent, the circular marble top above a frieze with ormolu stars and palmettes, h 75cm (29½in), d 94cm (37½in), *NY 17 Nov,* $17,600 (£14,080)

9

A **Louis XVI-style ormolu guéridon,** 19th cent, with a circular brown mottled marble top raised on incurved supports, h 77cm (30¼in), d 76cm (30in), *NY 13 Oct,* $4,400 (£3,607)

10

A **Régence-style carved stained softwood marble topped centre table,** c1880, the moulded rust and grey top with projecting corners, the frieze richly carved on all sides, 83 x 175cm (33½ x 69in), *L 8 June,* £4,400 ($6,380)

11

A **Louis XV-style marquetry table à Rognon,** last quarter 19th cent, the frieze with a tambour shutter opening to reveal three drawers, the sides quarter-veneered in tulipwood, 74 x 56cm (29 x 22in), *NY 15 Dec,* $4,125 (£3,466)

12

A **French brass-mounted purplewood and satinwood table vide poche,** early 19th cent, 72 x 74 x 33.5cm (28¼ x 29 x 13¼in), *NY 4 May,* $7,150 (£5,107)

1   2

3   4

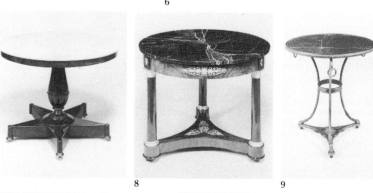

5   6

7   8   9

10   11   12

1
An ormolu-mounted king-wood and tulipwood parquetry centre table, c.1900, in Louis XV style, 73.5 x 93cm (29 x 36½in), L 8 June, £1,265 ($1,834)

2
A French serpentine red boulle centre table, c.1860, inlaid throughout with cut-brasswork on red tortoiseshell, the top with ebonised banding and cast-brass border, w 147cm (58in), L 9 Mar, £1,100 ($1,639)

3
A gilt-bronze mounted rosewood centre table, c.1870, with shaped serpentine top and frieze on scroll legs, 71 x 155cm (28 x 61in), L 9 Nov, £1,925 ($2,560)

4
A Louis XV-style carved giltwood centre table, late 19th cent, with a mottled white marble top with moulded border, 75 x 91.5cm (29½ x 36in), NY 15 Dec, $1,100 (£924)

5
A French ebonised and satinwood marquetry table a volets, c.1870, with ormolu mounts, the top with twin 'D'-shaped drop leaves, w closed 70cm (31in), P 24 July, £500 ($667)

6
A French tulipwood circular table, c.1850, the crossbanded top veneered in segments and centred by a Sèvres-type plaque, 70 x 46cm (27 x 18in), L 8 June, £902 ($1,308)

7
A Louis XVI-style gilt-bronze-mounted mahogany centre table, late 19th cent, based on an eighteenth century model now at the Petit-Trianon, 87 x 82cm (34 x 32in), NY 24/25 Feb, $4,610 (£3,110)

8
A small gilt-bronze-mounted mahogany table, in the style of Riesener, possibly by Edwards and Roberts, c.1880, 76 x 50cm (30 x 20in), L 9 Mar, £1,430 ($2,131)

9
A Louis XVI-style marquetry and parquetry occasional table, 19th cent, the top and stretcher inlaid within kingwood, purpleheart and satinwood reserves, 72.5 x 46.5cm (28½ x 18¼in), NY 15 Dec, $3,575 (£3,004)

10
A small porcelain-mounted kingwood-veneered table, the top inlaid with an oval plate painted with Sèvres marks within a blue-gilt border, 72 x 37cm (28½ x 14½in), L 8 June, £880 ($1,276)

11
A Louis XV-style kingwood and gilt-bronze specimen table, early 20th cent, the shaped rectangular glazed top enclosing a lined interior with glazed sides, 77 x 90cm (30½ x 35½in), C 4 Oct, £715 ($922)

12
A Louis XV-style gilt-bronze-mounted tulipwood vitrine table, late 19th cent, 74 x 61cm (29 x 24in), NY 24/25 Feb, $1,320 (£910)

13
A pair of Louis XVI-style kidney-shaped vitrine tables, 78 x 69cm (30½ x 27in), NY 24/25 Feb, $1,650 (£1,138)

1
A Louis XV marquetry rosewood and satinwood tric-trac table, stamped Denizot, 76 x 70 x 45cm (30 x 27½ x 18in), *M 25/26 June*, **FF 133,200 (£11,433; $15,579)**

2
A Louis XVI ormolu-mounted mahogany tric-trac table, last quarter 18th cent, with a removable leather-inset top lined on the reverse with a green baize playing surface, 71 x 114 x 57cm (28 x 45 x 22½in), *NY 13 Oct*, **$4,950 (£4,057)**

3
A French burr-walnut serpentine-fronted card table, *c*1850, the fold-over top veneered à quatre faces, the scroll frieze centred by a floral motif, the moulded cabriole legs with leaf-carved knees, w 87cm (34in), *P 18 Sept*, **£418 ($539)**

4
A Louis XV/XVI silvered-brass-mounted fruitwood and tulipwood marquetry table en chiffonnière, 3rd quarter 18th cent, attributed to Dusautoy, 77.5 x 56 x 42cm (30¾ x 22¼ x 16½in), *NY 17 Nov*, **$24,200 (£19,360)**

5
A Louis XV tulipwood parquetry table en chiffonnière, mid-18th cent, with a moulded rouge royal marble top, 71 x 41 x 33cm (28 x 16 x 13in), *NY 7 Apr*, **$1,870 (£1,308)**

6
A Louis XV ormolu-mounted kingwood parquetry table en chiffonnière, mid-18th cent, with a shaped rectangular marble top, 74 x 49 x 29cm (29½ x 16¼ x 11¼in), *NY 13 Oct*, **$2,750 (£2,254)**

7
A small Louis XV king-wood table, *c*1750, the rectangular serpentine top inlaid with a diamond banding, 67 x 36cm (26½ x 14in), *L 6 July*, **£1,210 ($1,670)**

8
A Louis XV provincial fruitwood side table, mid-18th cent, the moulded serpentine-fronted white marble top above a shaped apron raised on cabriole legs, 72 x 73 x 46cm (28¼ x 28¾ x 18in), *NY 16 June*, **$1,870 (£1,365)**

9
A Louis XVI marquetry citronnier and satinwood work table, stamped RVLC, Roger Van der Cruse called Lacroix, 73 x 65 x 38cm (28¾ x 25½ x 15in), *M 24/25 June*, **FF 105,450 (£9,052; $12,333)**

1
**A Venetian Lacca Povera
bureau cabinet,** *c.*1740,
the arched cornice sur-
mounted by four
giltwood figures emble-
matic of the Seasons and
a Papal cartouche, the
pair of mirror-glazed
doors enclosing a fitted
interior, the whole decorated with figures within
gilt cartouches on a red
ground, 263 x 115cm
(103½ x 45½in), *L 30 Nov,*
£220,000 ($226,200)

2
**A Viennese parcel-gilt
mahogany secrétaire,**
*c.*1825, of inverted tear-
shaped form, the semi-
circular top outlined
with an egg and dart
moulding enclosing a
pull-out fall-fronted
drawer, above a frieze
drawer and a panelled
flap enclosing a fitted
interior including secret
drawers, 171 x 109cm
(67½ x 43in), *L 30 Nov,*
£24,200 ($29,282)

3
**A Braunschweig inlaid
walnut cabinet on chest,**
*c.*1760, the crossbanded
doors each inlaid with a
rococo alcove centred by
an engraved ivory
woman, 218 x 128cm
(86 x 50½in), *L 18/25 May,*
£16,500 ($23,067)

4
**A Neapolitan kingwood-
veneered vitrine,** *c.*1760,
the cresting with an octafoil roundel centred by a
mother-of-pearl disc, the
sides similarly inlaid,
h 220cm (86in),
L 18/25 May,
£10,450 ($14,609)

1

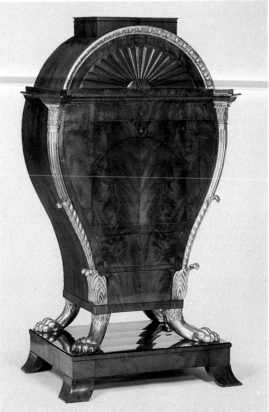

2

3

4

1

A Federal inlaid satinwood and mahogany lady's writing desk, attributed to Duncan Phyfe, New York, *c.*1805, 104 x 62 x 46cm (41 x 24½ x 18in), *NY 26 Jan*, **$66,000 (£45,517)**

2

An American carved mahogany armchair, New York, *c.*1770, with a shaped acanthus-carved crestrail above a tassel- and volute-carved vase-form splat, *NY 28 Jan*, **$71,500 (£49,310)**

3

An American carved mahogany block-front desk, Massachusetts, *c.*1770, the moulded lid opening to an interior with fan-carved drawers and pigeon holes, 114 x 102 x 58cm (45 x 40 x 23in), *NY 8 Dec*, **$40,700 (£33,917)**

4

An American carved mahogany bonnet-top highboy, Boston, Massachusetts, *c.*1755, in two parts, the upper with moulded swan's-neck pediment with three finials above drawers, 224 x 104 x 54cm (88 x 41 x 21in), *NY 28 Jan*, **$68,750 (£47,414)**

1

2

3

4

1
A Louis XV ormolu-mounted kingwood parquetry bureau plat, signed Schlichtig, mid-18th cent, the shaped leather-lined top with an ormolu rim and foliate ormolu clasps at the corners, the shaped front with three drawers, 77 x 144 x 85cm (30¼ x 56¾ x 33½in), *NY 17 Nov*, $57,750 (£46,200)

2
A kingwood bureau plat, in Louis XV-style, *c.*1900, with leather-lined gilt-metal-moulded shaped top above three frieze drawers and on gilt-metal-mounted cabriole legs, 79 x 175cm (31 x 69in), *L 9 Mar*, £3,630 ($5,409)

3
A kingwood and marquetry writing desk, in Louis XV-style, the top of serpentine outline with a leather writing surface and gilt-bronze-moulded border, w 193cm (76in), *L 9 Mar*, £4,620 ($6,884)

4
A kingwood bureau plat, late 19th cent, in Louis XV-style with gilt-bronze mounts, serpentine top, three drawers in the shaped frieze and cabriole legs, 75 x 131cm (29½ x 51½in), *L 9 Mar*, £1,705 ($2,540)

5
A Louis XV ormolu-mounted purplewood, kingwood and bois satiné parquetry writing table, mid-18th cent, the mounts marked with the crowned C, 71 x 99 x 47.5cm (28 x 39 x 18¾in), *NY 4 May*, $38,500 (£27,500)

6
A kingwood and tulipwood parquetry writing table, early 20th cent, with gilt-bronze mounts, surmounted by a clock signed Barthelemy, 131 x 101.5cm (51½ x 40in), *L 8 June*, £3,850 ($5,583)

7
A Louis XV ormolu-mounted tulipwood and bois satiné table à écrire, 3rd quarter 18th cent, 74.5 x 73 x 43cm (29¼ x 28¾ x 16½in), *NY 7 Apr*, $13,200 (£9,231)

8
A Louis XV provincial fruitwood writing table, mid-18th cent, the top with inset leather writing surface and a hinged compartment for writing implements, 70 x 64 x 49cm (27½ x 25 x 19in), *NY 7 Apr*, $2,420 (£1,692)

9
A Louis XV veneered satinwood writing table, with two side drawers, 70 x 85 x 44cm (27½ x 33½ x 17½in), *M 24/25 June*, FF 16,650 (£1,429; $1,947)

10
A Louis XV veneered satinwood writing table, stamped Coulon, 66 x 50 x 36cm (25 x 20 x 14in), *M 24/25 June*, FF 17,760 (£1,524; $2,077)

11
A Louis XVI mahogany table à écrire, last quarter 18th cent, raised on circular tapered legs, 72 x 61 x 41cm (28½ x 24 x 16½in), *NY 13 Oct*, $2,640 (£2,164)

1   2
3   4
5   6

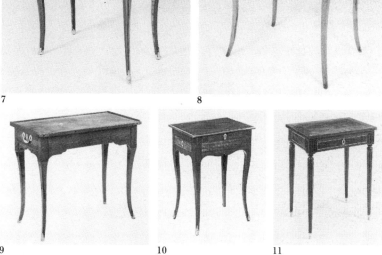

7   8
9   10   11

1
A Dutch oak table, early
17th cent, the double-
plank top with rounded
ends, the shaped frieze
on four baluster legs
joined by flat stretchers,
79 x 213cm (31 x 84in),
HS 28 Mar,
£3,520 ($5,245)

2
A Spanish oak table, 17th
cent, with cleated three-
plank top, the panelled
frieze with a pair of
drawers, the shaped
trestle supports with a
spiral-twist iron
stretcher, 84 x 133cm (33
x 52½in), *L 25 May,*
£935 ($1,337)

3
**An Italian baroque walnut
refectory table,** probably
Roman, 17th cent, the
top with incised trailing
vine decoration, on
massive trestle supports
carved with a coat-of-
arms, 81 x 287 x 98cm
(32 x 113 x 38¾in),
NY 23/24 Nov,
$22,000 (£18,188)

4
**A large North Italian
walnut table,** late 17th
cent, the frieze with five
drawers, the shaped
supports joined by a
stretcher, 307 x 78cm
(121 x 30¾in), *F 10 May,*
**L 10,500,000 (£4,276;
$6,157)**

5
**A Swiss walnut and
marquetry table,** mid-
17th cent, inlaid with
panels of marquetry, the
frieze fitted with a single
drawer, 78 x 103cm (30¾
x 40½in), *L 3 Feb,*
£1,320 ($1,850)

6
**A Swiss walnut draw-leaf
table,** c1670, the
panelled rectangular top
with two rectangular
leaves, raised on bulbous
and spirally turned legs
joined by flat stretchers,
75 x 275cm (29½ x
108½in), *L 18 May,*
£3,960 ($5,742)

7
**A Dutch baroque
marquetry centre table,**
2nd half 17th cent,
raised on later bun feet,
76 x 108 x 90cm (30 x
42½ x 35½in),
NY 23/24 Nov,
$4,125 (£3,409)

8
**A Dutch marquetry and
mahogany side table,**
c1745, the frieze fitted
with a drawer, later
marquetry, 75 x 84cm
(29½ x 33in), *L 23 Nov,*
£1,760 ($2,130)

9
**A Neapolitan kingwood
and tulipwood parquetry
card table,** c1760, the
hinged top inlaid with a
central star motif and
with a drawer in the
shaped frieze, the cabriole
legs ending in gilt-
bronze feet, 84 x 80cm,
(33 x 31½in), *L 18 May,*
£1,760 ($2,461)

10
A marquetry games table,
Spanish or Portuguese,
c1790, the quarter-
veneered rosewood top
with a ribbon border
and a central oval of an
arch, the polished interior
lined in leather and with
four wells, w 99cm
(39in), *L 3 Feb,*
£1,430 ($2,005)

11
**A North Italian neo-
classical tulipwood and
fruitwood marquetry
games table,** in the
manner of Maggiolino,
late 18th cent, 81 x 89 x
44cm (32 x 35 x 17¼in),
NY 13 Oct,
$2,200 (£1,803)

12
**A Dutch walnut and
marquetry games table,**
late 18th cent, the
triangular fold-over top
on slender tapering
cabriole supports, inlaid
with a central urn of
flowers and trailing
flowering foliage, 75.5 x
98cm (29¾ x 39½in),
C 4 Oct,
£550 ($688)

13
**A Dutch oval satinwood
table,** c1795, the top
inlaid with a fan patera
and crossbanded in
tulipwood, 104 x 101.5cm
(29 x 40in), *L 23 Nov,*
£1,100 ($1,331)

1

2

3

4

5

6

7

8

9

10

11

12

13

1
A marquetry and parcel-gilt work table, Italian or Spanish, early 19th cent, with hinged lid, the yew-wood veneered polygonal body inlaid, 75 x 51cm (29½ x 20in), *L 18 May,* £1,980 ($2,769)

2
A round mahogany extending table, 19th cent, on three volute-shaped feet, 75 x 108.5cm (30 x 42¾in), *A 1 Oct,* Dfl 1,740 (£409; $528)

3
An Austrian games table, *c*1840, the maple veneer inlaid with floral and geometric motifs in mahogany, the open top 101 x 100cm (39¾ x 39½in), *F 5 June,* L 2,400,000 (£996; $1,444)

4
A Biedermeier mahogany extending table, *c*1815, the almost circular top made in sections, plinth veneered with diamonds and gilt-bronze appliqués, 79 x 151cm (31 x 59½in), *L 30 Nov,* £11,000 ($13,310)

5
A marquetry satinwood centre table, possibly German, *c*1855, the octagonal top with a wide banding of amboyna inlaid with floral reserves on an ebony ground within satinwood bandings, w 122cm (48in), *L 9 Nov,* £2,750 ($3,658)

6
A marquetry octagonal centre table, probably South German or Lombardy, *c*1840, the top inlaid with an armorial device and a radiating pattern of cartouches filled with devices representing Architecture, Poetry, Painting and Music, w 237cm (50in), *L 9 Mar,* £5,500 ($8,195)

7
A Milan exhibition ivory-inlaid rosewood-veneered centre table, by Pietro Bertinetti, dated 1838, 80 x 148 x 76cm (31½ x 58 x 30in), *L 8 June,* £20,900 ($30,305)

8
A Florentine marble-topped parcel-gilt walnut centre table, *c*1860, the inset black marble top with a central panel in a variety of stones, the border with green leafy scrollwork, 85 x 158 x 104cm (33½ x 62 x 41½in), *L 8 June,* £18,700 ($27,115)

9
An Hispano-Moresque centre table, *c*1880, the whole inlaid in ivory with Moorish devices on a walnut ground, w 124.5cm (49in), *L 9 Mar,* £792 ($1,181)

10
A small Roman mosaic roundel or table top, signed A Trois, Roma, 1850, and with a view of St Peter's and its piazza, 38.5cm (15in), *L 8 June,* £2,640 ($3,828)

11
A pair of Venetian blackamoor small tables, *c*1800, each moulded circular marbled top supported on a crouching blackamoor figure on rock work base, 49.5cm (19½in), *L 9 Nov,* £1,650 ($2,195)

12
An Italian bronze and marble circular tripod table, *c*1860, the black top inlaid in green with a roundel of a hound and a bird, the stem supported on young naked Hercules, 74 x 51cm (29 x 20in), *L 9 Nov,* £792 ($1,053)

13
An inlaid marble and ebonised-wood table, mid-19th cent, the inset black top with a chessboard in black marble and a variety of mottled brown stones within a mosaic border of four different coloured flowers, 65 x 53cm square, (35½ x 21in), *L 9 Nov,* £2,310 ($3,072)

14
A North African table, *c*1900, the octagonal leaf-carved top supported on a fully modelled standing camel, 82.5cm (32½in), *L 9 Nov,* £572 ($761)

1   2   3

4   5   6

7   8

9   10

12   13   14

1
A Charles II oak side table, c.1675, with cleated two-plank top, the frieze with a two-panelled drawer veneered in fruitwood, on turned baluster legs of exaggerated form joined by moulded stretchers, 72 x 90cm (28½ x 35½in), *L 24 Feb,*
£1,100 ($1,540)

2
A William and Mary oak side table, c.1690, the rectangular top with a frieze drawer, on turned double baluster legs joined by stretchers, w 81cm (32in), *L 24 Feb,*
£550 ($770)

3
A Charles II oak large oval gateleg table, c.1680, with a frieze drawer, the square and baluster turned supports joined by stretchers, w 137cm (54in), *P 12-15 June,*
£1,430 ($2,059)

4
A William and Mary oak oval drop-leaf table, late 17th cent, with a hinged oval top, a frieze drawer at one end, 72 x 146 x 121cm (28½ x 57½ x 47½in), *NY 21 Jan,*
$2,310 (£1,650)

5
A William and Mary oak gate-leg table, late 17th cent, with a hinged oval top on turned legs joined by a moulded box stretcher, 74 x 145 x 168cm (29 x 57 x 66in), *NY 9 June,*
$3,630 (£2,612)

6
An oak gateleg table, c.1700, with a circular two-flap top, on turned supports, 74 x 122cm (29¼ x 48in), *C 5 July,*
£396 ($537)

7
An English yew wood gateleg table, c.1720, the oval two-flap top over a shaped frieze containing a single drawer, with turned column legs joined by square stretchers, 71 x 103cm (28 x 40½in), *L 21 Sept,*
£2,860 ($3,632)

8
A George II mahogany spider-leg drop-leaf table, c.1745, with rectangular top and eight slender turned legs with stretchers, 71 x 76cm (28 x 30in), *L 15 June,*
£2,750 ($3,878)

9
A George III mahogany pembroke table, c.1800, with two rectangular drop leaves and two drawers, the cross-frame stretchers centred by a wheel-shaped panel, 69 x 84cm (27 x 33in), *HS 25 June,*
£605 ($853)

10
A George III inlaid mahogany serpentine-shaped pembroke table, c.1780, with a hinged crossbanded top above a frieze drawer, 71 x 47 x 70cm (28 x 18½ x 27½in), *NY 21 Jan,*
$10,450 (£7,207)

11
A George III mahogany pembroke table, c.1790, the oval ebonised moulded top crossbanded in kingwood and above a crossbanded frieze drawer, on square tapered legs with ebonised stringing, 71 x 75cm (28 x 29½in), *L 14 Dec,*
£3,960 ($4,950)

12
A George III inlaid mahogany and burr-yew wood pembroke table, c.1790, with a rectangular drop-leaf at each side, one end containing a drawer, the whole inlaid with yew wood panels, 71 x 49 x 73cm (28 x 19 x 28½in), *NY 12-14 Apr,*
$7,150 (£5,000)

13
A late George III calamander wood pembroke table, c.1800, with a rectangular moulded top with a crossbanded satin-wood border, the plain frieze containing a drawer, 74 x 46 x 71cm (29 x 18 x 27¾in), *NY 12-14 Apr,*
$3,025 (£2,115)

1

3

2

4

5

6

7

8

9

10

11

12

13

1
A George I burr-walnut concertina-action games table, *c.*1715, the cross- and feather-banded top with projecting rounded corners and enclosing a baize-lined interior with money wells, w 81cm (32in), *L 16 Nov,* £7,260 ($9,583)

2
A George II red walnut card table, *c.*1740, with projecting rounded corners and candle-stands and counter wells, a frieze drawer and plain cabriole legs with pad feet, 81cm (32in), *L 13 July,* £1,540 ($2,110)

3
A George I inlaid walnut games table, 1st quarter 18th cent, 75 x 85 x 43cm (29½ x 33½ x 17in), *NY 12-14 Apr,* $12,650 (£8,846)

4
A George II carved mahogany games table, mid-18th cent, the edges carved with flowerheads and twisted ribbon on a finely punched ground opening to an inset velvet-lined gaming surface, 70 x 90 x 41cm (27½ x 35½ x 16in), *NY 20 Oct,* $7,700 (£6,470)

5
A George III carved mahogany serpentine-fronted games table, *c.*1770, 72 x 90 x 42cm (28½ x 35½ x 16½in), *NY 21 Jan,* $3,520 (£2,427)

6
A George II walnut concertina-action games table, the playing surface with money wells, the plain slightly concave frieze raised on cabriole legs carved at the knees, 70 x 84 x 83cm (27½ x 33 x 32½in), *NY 12-14 Apr,* $11,550 (£8,077)

7
A George III mahogany tea and games table, last quarter 18th cent, the fold-over triple top of moulded serpentine outline, 77.5 x 89cm (30½ x 35in), *C 4 Oct,* £748 ($965)

8
A Regency rosewood trestle games table, 1st quarter 19th cent, the rectangular top with a sliding central panel enclosing a back-gammon well, the reversed inlaid to form a chess board, 69 x 117 x 68cm (27 x 43 x 26¾in), *NY 20 Oct,* $5,500 (£4,621)

9
A George III satinwood card table, *c.*1800, the top with a wide rosewood crossbanding outlined in boxwood and holly, the conforming frieze on square tapering legs, with ebonised stringing, w 89cm (35in), *L 5 Oct,* £2,860 ($3,718)

10
A pair of Regency rosewood and cut-brass card tables, *c.*1820, each with rectangular hinged top swivelling to reveal a counter well, the frieze raised on a pair of lyre supports, the whole inlaid with brass foliage and stringing, w 91.5cm (36in), *L 16 Nov,* £11,000 ($14,520)

11
A pair of rosewood serpentine card tables, *c.*1840, each moulded hinged top with a circular baize-lined well, on a jewelled columnar support with acanthus-carved downswept legs, with scalloped feet, w 91.5cm (36in), *L 17 Feb,* £1,540 ($2,159)

1 2 3

4

5 6

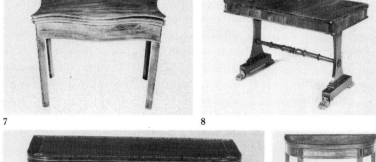

7 8

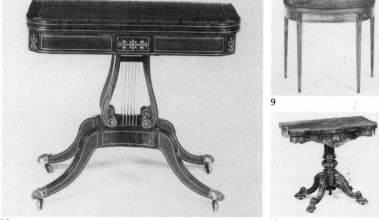

9

10 11

1

A George III satinwood-crossbanded mahogany breakfast table, *c*1790, the downswept legs inlaid with boxwood and ebony stringing, w 142cm (56in), *L 6 Apr,* £3,300 ($4,752)

2

A George IV mahogany breakfast table, *c*1825, the circular hinged top with a rosewood-crossbanded border and two rows of bead and reel moulding, w 122cm (48in), *L 5 Oct,* £990 ($1,287)

3

A Regency circular rosewood breakfast or dining table, *c*1810, the hinged top crossbanded in satinwood and rosewood, on a grained rosewood pillar with four hipped sabre legs, w 120cm (47in), *L 15 June,* £1,980 ($2,792)

4

A walnut breakfast table, *c*1840, the circular quarter-veneered hinged top in well-figured wood of golden colour, the crossbanded moulded edge with a wide banding with stylised foliage in satin-birch within ebony stringing, 132cm (52in), *L 28 Sept,* £2,365 ($3,075)

5

A circular burr-walnut and ebonised centre table, *c*1870, raised on three slender gilt-incised pillars centred by a fourth thicker pillar and hipped sabre legs, d 118cm (40½in), *L 28 Sept,* £825 ($1,073)

6

A walnut and marquetry decagonal centre table, *c*1840, the hinged quarter-veneered burr-wood top with a central ebony medallion inlaid with musical trophies, cast gilt-brass border, 72 x 121cm (28½ x 47½in), *L 8 June,* £3,080 ($4,466)

7

A satinwood marquetry painted and gilt-bronze centre table, probably by Holland, 3rd quarter 19th cent, 74 x 93cm (29 x 36½in), *C 29 Mar,* £2,530 ($3,770)

8

A late George III inlaid mahogany drum table, 1st quarter 19th cent, the frieze containing an arrangement of real and false drawers, 75 x 122cm (29½ x 48in), *NY 12-14 Apr,* $6,710 (£4,692)

9

A Regency satinwood drum-top library table, *c*1810, the revolving top inset with leather, the frieze with four drawers and four hinged compartments, 69 x 104cm (27 x 41in), *L 16 Nov,* £4,400 ($5,808)

10

A Regency rosewood sofa table, in the manner of Gillow of Lancaster, *c*1815, the frieze and sabre legs inlaid with pale wood stringing, the two drawers with star-shaped handles, pad feet, 71 x 150cm (28 x 59in), *L 16 Mar,* £6,050 ($9,021)

11

A Regency brass and satinwood inlaid rosewood pedestal sofa table, *c*1825, 70 x 92 x 61cm (27½ x 36 x 24in), *NY 21 Jan,* $4,400 (£3,034)

12

A Regency rosewood pedestal sofa table, *c*1815, inlaid with brass stringing and foliage, w 150cm (59in), *L 6 Apr,* £1,265 ($1,822)

13

A George IV mahogany sofa table, *c*1820, the rectangular top with rounded flaps inlaid with ebonised stringing, with two real opposing two dummy frieze drawers, w 163cm (64in), *L 10 Feb,* £825 ($1,157)

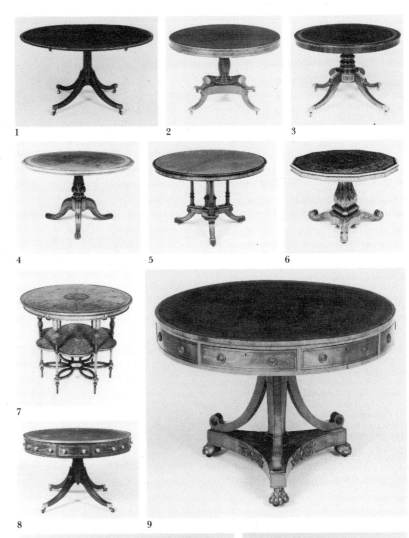

1   2   3

4   5   6

7

8   9

10   11

12   13

1
A late George III mahogany breakfast table, c.1800, the rectangular top with rounded corners crossbanded in rosewood, 71 x 143.5cm (28 x 52½in), L 14 Dec, **£1,540 ($1,925)**

2
A Regency mahogany tripod breakfast table, early 19th cent, the two-flap top above a real drawer and a dummy drawer, 71 x 91 x 104cm (28 x 36 x 41in), C 16 Oct, **£396 ($607)**

3
A George III mahogany three-pedestal dining table, with two extra leaves, 69 x 239 x 116cm (27 x 45½in), NY 20 Oct, **$3,575 (£3,004)**

4
A George III mahogany D-end dining table, c.1790, including a leaf insertion, 243cm (114in), HS 24/25 Oct, **£11,550 ($14,669)**

5
A Regency mahogany and crossbanded dining table, with telescopic action and one leaf, the circular tapering legs ending in brass cappings and castors, 137 x 183cm (54 x 72in), P 15-18 May, **£1,265 ($1,758)**

6
An expanding dining table, stamped Johnstone Jupe & Co, 6-7 Bond Street, London, 1835-8, the circular eight segment top swivelling and with sixteen leaves, with cabinet for the leaves, 73 x 158cm (29 x 62in), L 17 Feb, **£33,000 ($46,266)**

7
A William IV mahogany D-end extending dining table, c.1835, the Hawkins Patent telescopic action with three leaves and a winder, 147 x 302cm (58 x 119in), P 24 July, **£2,750 ($3,671)**

8
A Victorian mahogany extending dining table, c.1850, the moulded top with D-shaped ends and three extra leaves, 73 x 344cm (28½ x 135½in), L 17 Feb, **£880 ($1,234)**

9
A Victorian mahogany extending dining table, 3rd quarter 19th cent, the top of five large fluted tapering supports, including five leaves, the leaves contained in a rectangular chest, 76 x 366 x 488cm (30 x 144 x 192in), C 5 July, **£1,650 ($2,238)**

10
A mahogany extending dining table, 20th cent, the rectangular top carved with a flowerhead border on blind fret and foliate carved supports, including two leaves, 76 x 302 x 130cm (30 x 119 x 51in), C 5 July, **£880 ($1,194)**

1

A late George II mahogany reading table, mid-18th cent, the rectangular adjustable top raised on an adjustable, turned and spirally-fluted pedestal, 72 x 61cm (28½ x 24in), *NY 12-14 Apr,* $2,860 (£2,000)

2

A George III carved mahogany tripod supper table, *c*1760, the shaped tilting top carved with plate recesses, above a birdcage support, on leaf-carved cabriole legs ending in claw and ball feet, top recarved, 69 x 77cm (27 x 30½in), *NY 21 Jan,* $2,970 (£2,048)

3

A George II brass-inlaid mahogany tilt-top tripod table, 2nd quarter 18th cent, with slightly dished top centred by a brass flowerhead, 72 x 69cm (28½ x 27in), *NY 12-14 Apr,* $4,675 (£3,269)

4

A George III carved mahogany tilt-top tripod table, 3rd quarter 18th cent, the fluted pillar with a birdcage top and raised on cabriole legs carved at the knees in high relief with foliage, 74 x 77cm (29 x 30¼in), *NY 20 Oct,* £2,200 ($1,849)

5

An early George III mahogany tripod wine table, *c*1755, 61 x 31cm (24 x 12in), *L 16 Nov,* £5,940 ($7,841)

6

An early George III mahogany dumb waiter, *c*1760, the three graduated revolving circular tiers divided by twist-turned baluster supports, h 114.5cm (57in), *L 10 Feb,* £1,155 ($1,617)

7

A George III mahogany two-tier dumb waiter, early 19th cent, each dished tier with drop flaps, 97 x 64cm (38 x 25in), *C 2-5 Oct,* £858 ($1,107)

8

A late George III small satinwood tripod table, *c*1810, w 54.5cm (21½in), *L 6 Apr,* £682 ($982)

9

A William IV engraved and specimen marble inlaid carved rosewood trestle table, *c*1830, each corner with a Royal coat-of-arms, 73 x 72 x 47cm (28½ x 28 x 18½in), *NY 21 Jan,* $6,050 (£4,172)

10

A Victorian slate centre table, *c*1865, the circular top with Pietra Dura inlaid floral wreath, d 54cm (21in), *P 13 Nov,* £935 ($1,253)

11

A boulle and porcelain-mounted table, *c*1850, the top inset with an oval Sèvres dish surrounded by boulle banding and set with Sèvres panels, the platform stretcher centred by a porcelain panel, 81 x 63.5cm (32 x 25in), *L 9 Nov,* £3,410 ($4,535)

12

A small satinwood-veneered table, English, 2nd quarter 19th cent, the frieze with a Sèvres-style oval plaque at the front and back, 70 x 32cm (27½ x 12½in), *L 9 Mar,* £1,760 ($2,622)

13

An ivory-inlaid rosewood occasional table, *c*1875, designed by Stephen Webb, stamped Collinson & Lock, London, 75 x 56.5cm (29 x 22¼in), *L 28 Sept,* £3,300 ($4,290)

14

A Victorian oval satinwood-veneered centre table, *c*1890, the top inlaid with partridgewood crossbanding, 75 x 103cm (29½ x 40½in), *L 17 Feb,* £2,970 ($4,164)

15

A late Victorian rosewood and inlaid centre table, *c*1900, w 112cm (44in), *P 16 Oct,* £616 ($770)

1
A George III inlaid satin-wood centre table, late 18th cent, inlaid with satinwood panels within crossbanded tulipwood borders, 74 x 53 x 32cm (29 x 21 x 14¼in), *NY 20 Oct,* $1,650 (£1,387)

2
A George III penwork and polychrome decorated parquetry inlaid rosewood worktable, c.1810, 92 x 51 x 39cm (28½ x 20½ x 15½in), *NY 21 Jan,* $4,400 (£3,034)

3
A George III inlaid mahogany work table, late 18th cent, of canted rectangular form with a hinged lid, on square tapered legs joined by an X-stretcher and ending in block toes, 77 x 53 x 39cm (30 x 21 x 15½in), *NY 9 June,* $1,045 (£752)

4
A Regency inlaid rosewood work table, c.1820, rectangular with a frieze drawer, on ring-turned legs joined by a platform stretcher, 74 x 46 x 38cm (29 x 22 x 15in), *NY 21 Jan,* $825 (£569)

5
A Regency rosewood work table, c.1815, with canted corners and a maplewood banding, with two drawers above a U-shaped bag and the U-shaped support on a concave platform and hipped sabre legs, 83cm (32½in), *L 13 July,* £1,375 ($1,884)

6
A rosewood two-tier table, mid-19th cent, each dished tier with a galleried top on a turned stem and concave sided base, 76 x 43cm (30 x 17in), *C 10 Jan,* £462 ($670)

7
An olivewood work table, mid-19th cent, the octagonal moulded top enclosing a fretted lid and yellow moiré silk lined interior, 71 x 48cm (28 x 19in), *C 5 July,* £1,320 ($1,791)

8
A Victorian walnut combined games- and work table, 3rd quarter 19th cent, the fold-over top inlaid in boxwood and ebony, 69 x 68.5cm (27¼ x 27in), *C 10 Jan,* £748 ($1,085)

9
A Victorian papier-mâché work table, c.1850, with gilt borders, the shaped top painted with a floral spray, 48cm (19in), *P 24 July,* £462 ($617)

10
A quartetto of George III-style mahogany tables, late 19th/early 20th cent, each with a rectangular cockbeaded top on slender ring-turned supports and downswept feet, 74 x 53cm (29 x 21in), *C 5 July,* £792 ($1,074)

11
A quartetto of Vernis Martin occasional tables, late 19th/early 20th cent, painted with figures and landscape views, 71 x 56cm (28 x 22in), *C 1-3 May,* £330 ($462)

12
A George II mahogany architect's table, c.1760, of unusual form, the adjustable hinged top with a bookrest and a pair of unusual Chinese fret flaps and with a pair of brass candle-slides, the lower part with a writing surface, 87 x 81cm (34 x 32in), *L 6 Apr,* £6,160 ($8,870)

13
A Victorian gilt-decorated chinoiserie lacquer Sutherland table, 1st half 19th cent, each drop-leaf decorated in tones of red and gilt on a black ground, 69 x 84 x 86cm (27 x 33 x 34in), *NY 20 Oct,* $9,350 (£7,857)

14
A George III mahogany artist's table, c.1790, the adjustable hinged top on twin ratchet supports, the frieze with a drawer and an apron drawer, w 58cm (23in), *HS 25 June,* £1,265 ($1,784)

1 2 3 4

5 6 7 8

9 10 11

13 14 12

1

A George I gilt-gesso side table, c.1720, the moulded top with a foliate strapwork design on a punched ground, with cavetto frieze and the apron with leaves on a punched ground and centred by a cartouche, 71 x 113cm (28 x 44½in), *L 16 Nov,* **£7,700 ($10,164)**

2

A George II oak side table, 2nd quarter 18th cent, the drawer with brass loop handles and backplates, 72 x 74 x 47cm (78¼ x 29 x 18½in), *NY 9 June,* **$1,320 (£950)**

3

An early George III mahogany small serpentine side table, c.1770, with moulded top, three frieze drawers and square tapering legs with block feet, w 92cm (36in), *L 27 Jan,* **£5,720 ($8,294)**

4

A George III mahogany silver table, last quarter 18th cent, the top with a full gallery pierced with a double serpentine ribbon, 76 x 88 x 57cm (29½ x 34½ x 22¼in), *NY 20 Oct,* **$7,150 (£6,008)**

5

A George III carved mahogany serpentine-fronted side table, c.1780, the frieze centred by a swag-carved panel raised on square tapering legs, 93 x 186 x 86cm (36½ x 73 x 34in), *NY 9 June,* **$2,970 (£2,137)**

6

A pair of George III carved mahogany side tables, last quarter 18th cent, with a moulded frieze carved with fret/work, 91 x 159 x 76cm (36 x 62½ x 29¾in), *NY 20 Oct,* **$9,900 (£8,319)**

7

A George III inlaid mahogany side table, last quarter 18th cent, the top with a deep cross-banded border, 37 x 198 x 75cm (34½ x 78 x 29½in), *NY 20 Oct,* **$4,730 (£3,974)**

8

A George III mahogany side table, c.1770, with rectangular top, a plain frieze and fluted square chamfered legs, 91.5 x 152.5 x 73.5cm (36 x 60 x 29in), *L 26 Oct,* **£1,210 ($1,549)**

9

A George III mahogany and satinwood marquetry serpentine-fronted side table, last quarter 18th cent, of country manufacture, 84 x 183 x 75cm (33¼ x 72 x 29½in), *NY 20 Oct,* **$8,800 (£7,394)**

10

A pair of George III mahogany side tables, c.1775, the fluted friezes centred by panels of scrolling foliage and urns, 89 x 183cm (35 x 72in), *L 16 Nov,* **£44,000 ($58,080)**

1
A pair of George III marquetry inlaid satinwood demi-lune side tables, c.1790, each crossbanded top inlaid with ribbon-tied garlands of flowers, 85 x 128 x 66cm (33½ x 50½ x 26in), *NY 21 Jan,* $27,500 (£19,642)

2
A George III giltwood and satinwood D-shaped side table, c.1775, the top with a giant swagged oval wreath enclosing ribbon-tied flowers, the frieze with a band of beaded roundels enclosing paterae, 78 x 152cm (30½ x 60in), *L 15 June,* £5,060 ($7,135)

3
A pair of George III carved and inlaid mahogany D-shaped side tables, last quarter 18th cent, 78 x 123 x 58cm (30½ x 49½ x 23in), *NY 12-14 Apr,* $9,900 (£6,923)

4
A rosewood library table, by Holland & Sons, c.1835, the leather-lined top with two frieze drawers on fluted trestle supports joined by a pole stretcher, with Greek key fret in relief, w 122cm (48in), *L 17 Feb,* £1,760 ($2,468)

5
A Regency inlaid rosewood writing table, c.1815, the top with a hinged flap at the back, the front with two frieze drawers, on lyre form supports, 72 x 128 x 82cm (28 x 50 x 32½in), *NY 21 Jan,* $11,000 (£7,586)

6
A William IV mahogany and elm partner's writing table, c.1830, with a brown leather-inset moulded rectangular top, each side with three frieze drawers, on gad-rooned legs ending in brass castors, 76 x 149 x 96cm (30 x 58½ x 37½in), *NY 21 Jan,* $3,575 (£2,466)

7
A late George III mahogany writing table, c.1810, the frieze with three drawers at the front and back and with a dummy pair at each side, handles replaced, w 145cm (57in), *L 15 June,* £22,000 ($31,020)

8
A George III mahogany writing table, in the manner of Gillow of Lancaster, c.1800, with ebonised strung borders, the inset top with a three-quarter-gallery and three frieze drawers, w 107cm (42in), *P 13 Nov,* £572 ($766)

9
An early Victorian mahogany writing table, 2nd quarter 19th cent, 75 x 149 x 80cm (29½ x 56½ x 31½in), *NY 9 June,* $2,090 (£1,504)

10
A William IV rosewood library or centre table, c.1835, 137cm (54in), *L 26 Oct,* £935 ($1,197)

11
A George III mahogany partner's writing table, c.1790, with a brown leather inset moulded rectangular top, each side with three frieze drawers, 79 x 122 x 90cm (31 x 48 x 35½in), *NY 21 Jan,* $7,700 (£5,310)

12
An ebonised satinwood-veneered writing table, in the manner of Holland, c.1850, with rounded front corners, a pair of drawers and the tapering ringed legs inlaid to resemble fluting and ending in castors, w 107cm (42in), *L 17 Feb,* £1,078 ($1,511)

13
A pollard oak writing table, 1830s, the quarter-veneered rectangular top with a short drawer in the frieze flanked by deep drawers, on circular tapering legs with lotus-carved capitals, 78.5 x 137cm (31 x 54in), *L 28 Sept,* £660 ($858)

1
An American carved mahogany card table, Philadelphia, c.1765, the oblong top with out-set corners and shaped hinged leaf opening to a playing surface with counters, the frieze with a cockbeaded short drawer, 74 x 80 x 39cm (29 x 31½ x 15½in), *NY 28 Jan*, **$19,800 (£13,655)**

2
An American carved walnut tilt-top tea table, Pennsylvania, c.1770, the circular dished top tilting and revolving on a bird-cage support, 71 x 83cm (28 x 32½in), *NY 8 Dec*, **$3,300 (£2,750)**

3
An American carved mahogany tilt-top tea table, Philadelphia, c.1770, on cabriole legs ending in claw-and-ball feet, h 70cm (27½in), d 84cm (33in), *NY 26 Jan*, **$13,750 (£9,482)**

4
A Federal inlaid mahogany tilt-top candlestand, Philadelphia, c.1785, the oval top with line-inlaid edge tilting and revolving above a birdcage support, 70 x 56 x 41cm (27½ x 22 x 16in), *NY 28 Jan*, **$4,125 (£2,845)**

5
A Federal painted and grained candlestand, New England, c.1810, the square top with inset corners, above an urn and ring-turned standard, painted and grained overall in red and black, 66 x 38cm (26 x 15in), *NY 8 Dec*, **$1,320 (£1,100)**

6
An American carved maple tavern table, New England, 1750-80, the oval top above a plain frieze, on circular tapering legs ending in pad feet, 66 x 100 x 77cm (26 x 39½ x 30½in), *NY 28 Jan*, **$5,775 (£3,983)**

7
An American maple and pine tavern table, New England, c.1750, the rectangular top above a plain frieze on turned legs ending in pad feet, 67 x 117 x 79cm (26½ x 46 x 31in), *NY 8 Dec*, **$2,750 (£2,292)**

8
An American painted maple and pine tavern table, New England, c.1780, the rectangular top with breadboard ends over a single drawer frieze, base painted red, 70 x 122 x 74cm (27½ x 48 x 29in), *NY 8 Dec*, **$2,420 (£2,017)**

9
A small American carved walnut drop-leaf dining table, Massachusetts, c.1760, the oblong top with two D-shaped leaves above a shaped skirt, 67 x 87 x 89cm (26½ x 34½ x 35in), *NY 28 Jan*, **$7,425 (£5,121)**

10
An American carved mahogany drop-leaf dining table, Newport, Rhode Island, c.1765, the rectangular top with two hinged leaves above a shaped frieze, 70 x 122 x 120cm (27½ x 48½ x 47½in), *NY 30 June*, **$4,400 (£3,259)**

11
An American carved mahogany drop-leaf dining table, Pennsylvania, c.1770, 73 x 107 x 133cm (28¾ x 42 x 52½in), *NY 28 June*, **$2,530 (£1,874)**

12
A Federal painted and decorated drop-leaf table, New England, 1800-20, painted and grained all over in shades of brown, 69 x 102 x 105cm (27 x 40 x 41½in), *NY 8 Dec*, **$1,430 (£1,201)**

13
An American carved mahogany three-pedestal dining table, probably Philadelphia, c.1820, in three sections, 71 x 140 x 305cm (28 x 55 x 120in), *NY 30 June*, **$12,100 (£8,963)**

1
A Federal carved curly maple pembroke table, New England, c.1800, 73 x 90 x 89cm (28¾ x 35½ x 35in), *NY 28 June,* $4,125 (£3,055)

2
A Federal inlaid mahogany pembroke table, New York, c.1790, the rectangular top with two hinged shaped leaves with line-inlaid edge, above a single line-inlaid drawer and one mock drawer, 75 x 76 x 96cm (29½ x 30 x 38in), *NY 30 June,* $2,970 (£2,200)

3
A Federal satinwood-inlaid mahogany card table, New York, c.1800, inlaid with a radiating fan centred by a carved rosette, original baize-lined playing surface, 74 x 96 x 49cm (29 x 37¾ x 19in), *NY 26 Jan,* $20,900 (£14,413)

4
A Federal inlaid mahogany card table, Baltimore, Maryland, c.1795, with D-shaped hinged leaf above a frieze, inlaid legs, 75 x 91 x 46cm (29½ x 36 x 18in), *NY 26 Jan,* $5,775 (£3,982)

5
A Federal inlaid mahogany card table, Baltimore, Maryland, c.1800, with felt-lined playing surface, flower-inlaid dies, 74 x 91 x 43cm (29 x 35¾ x 17in), *NY 26 Jan,* $7,150 (£4,931)

6
A Federal inlaid mahogany card table, Philadelphia, c.1805, the oblong top with serpentine front and hinged leaf above a line- and diamond-inlaid frieze, 76 x 90 x 45cm (30 x 35½ x 17¾in), *NY 8 Dec,* $5,775 (£4,813)

7
A Federal inlaid mahogany card table, New England, c.1805, 76 x 92 x 46cm (30 x 36 x 18in), *NY 28 Jan,* $1,870 (£1,290)

8
A Federal mahogany and flame-birch card table, Eastern New England, c.1810, the serpentine-shaped top with hinged leaf over a veneered frieze, 75 x 98 x 45cm (29½ x 38½ x 17½in), *NY 8 Dec,* $6,875 (£5,729)

9
A Federal carved mahogany card table, Massachusetts, c.1810, the oblong top with outset corners, with a hinged leaf, the apron centred by a veneered mahogany oval reserve, 75 x 92 x 45cm (29½ x 36 x 17½in), *NY 8 Dec,* $2,310 (£1,925)

10
A Federal carved and inlaid mahogany sewing table, Eastern Massachusetts, c.1805, 76 x 52 x 37cm (30 x 20¾ x 14¾in), *NY 26 Jan,* $1,925 (£1,327)

11
A Federal carved mahogany work table, New York, c.1810, the oblong top with reeded edge above two small crossbanded cockbeaded drawers, 75 x 53 x 48cm (29¾ x 21 x 18¾in), *NY 28 June,* $2,420 (£1,792)

12
An American gilt-bronze mounted marquetry centre table, H B Herts & Son, New York, c.1885, the floral marquetry top with a gilt-bronze swag banding above a gilt-bronze mounted baluster standard, 74 x 81cm (29 x 32in), *NY 24/25 Feb,* $1,870 (£1,290)

13
An American rococo rosewood pierced-carved centre table, John Henry Belter, New York, c.1855, the shaped white marble top above a pierced frieze, 74 x 100cm (29 x 39in), *NY 3 Nov,* $20,900 (£16,720)

1

2

3

4

5

6

7

8

9

10

11

12

13

1
A pair of Louis XIV giltwood console tables, late 17th cent, each with a Levanto marble top, 85 x 159 x 71cm (33½ x 60½ x 28in), *NY 17 Nov,* $82,500 (£66,000)

2
A Louis XV giltwood console table, mid-18th cent, with a serpentine-fronted brèche d'Alep marble top, 78 x 117 x 57cm (34½ x 46 x 20in), *NY 4 May,* $11,000 (£7,857)

3
A Louis XVI ormolu and brass-mounted mahogany console desserte, last quarter 18th cent, with white mottled marble top, 89 x 131 x 32.5cm (35 x 51½ x 12¾in), *NY 16 Nov,* $3,850 (£3,080)

4
An Empire gilt-bronze mounted mahogany side table, c.1840, 90 x 181cm (35½ x 83in), *NY 24/25 Feb,* $3,410 (£2,352)

5
A Charles X mahogany and walnut console, 2nd quarter 19th cent, with serpentine grey and white veined marble top, 108 x 93 x 35cm (42½ x 36¾ x 13¾in), *NY 16 June,* $825 (£602)

6
A pair of carved giltwood console tables, in Louis XVI-style, each with a shaped marble top above carved frieze with floral swags, 81 x 107cm (32 x 42½in), *NY 24/25 Feb,* $4,730 (£3,262)

7
A serpentine marble-topped giltwood side table, c.1880, in Louis XV-style, with moulded brèche violette top, 89 x 142cm (35 x 56in), *L 9 Nov,* £1,870 ($2,487)

8
A Milanese carved giltwood side table, c.1730, with later top, originally the stand for a cabinet, 85 x 102cm (33¼ x 40in), *L 18 May,* £1,210 ($1,692)

9
A Roman giltwood side table, early 18th cent, the moulded serpentine faux marbre top supported on an elaborately carved frame, the four legs in the form of winged griffins, 91.5 x 150cm (36 x 59in), *L 30 Nov,* £7,700 ($9,317)

10
An Italian pinewood serpentine side table, c.1730, with moulded brèche violette marble top, formerly painted or gilded, 87 x 163cm (34 x 64in), *L 18 May,* £3,520 ($4,923)

11
A pair of Italian neoclassical painted and parcel-gilt consoles, late 18th cent, each with a D-shaped white marble top, 84 x 118 x 43cm (34 x 46½ x 17in), *NY 13 Oct,* $4,290 (£3,516)

12
A pair of Italian neoclassical consoles, late 18th cent, each with a D-shaped ochre mottled marble top, 94 x 132 x 68.5cm (37 x 52 x 27in), *NY 13 Oct,* $4,675 (£3,832)

13
An Italian giltwood serpentine side table, late 19th cent, with moulded Sienna marble top, 102 x 205cm (40 x 80½in), *L 8 June,* £1,980 ($2,871)

1
A Federal inlaid mahogany sideboard, Baltimore, c.1790, the serpentine front with one long drawer flanked by two cupboard doors, 102 x 184 x 66cm (40 x 72 x 26in), *NY 30 June,* **$9,625 (£7,130)**

2
A Federal inlaid mahogany sideboard, New York, c.1790, with two fan- and line-inlaid convex cupboard doors, bookend inlaid dies flanking, 103 x 192 x 77cm (40½ x 87½ x 30½in), *NY 30 June,* **$4,125 (£3,056)**

3
A George III inlaid mahogany sideboard, last quarter 18th cent, formerly with a splash rail, 93 x 212 x 76cm (36¾ x 83½ x 30in), *NY 20 Oct,* **$2,860 (£2,403)**

4
A George III mahogany sideboard, c.1780, the bow-fronted tulipwood crossbanded top with a drawer above a shaped apron and flanked by deep drawers, 168 x 74cm (66 x 29in), *L 26 Oct,* **£5,060 ($6,477)**

5
A George III marquetry inlaid mahogany serpentine-fronted sideboard, c.1790, 97 x 168 x 64cm (38 x 66 x 25in), *NY 21 Jan,* **$6,600 (£4,552)**

6
A George III inlaid mahogany bow-fronted sideboard, c.1800, the crossbanded top fitted with a brass splash rail, 84 x 184 x 72cm (33 x 72½ x 28½in), *NY 20 Oct,* **$8,250 (£6,933)**

7
A Regency mahogany sideboard, early 19th cent, of concave form with two central drawers flanked by a cellaret and a cupboard, now fitted with an elaborate brass rail, 94 x 213 x 87cm (37 x 84 x 34in), *C 5 July,* **£1,320 ($1,791)**

8
A Regency mahogany sideboard, in the manner of Thomas Hope, early 19th cent, on mask-carved supports and a concave plinth base, inlaid throughout with ebony lines, 99 x 214 x 84cm (39 x 84 x 33in), *C 29 Mar,* **£1,760 ($2,622)**

9
A William IV mahogany sideboard, 2nd quarter 19th cent, of serpentine outline, crossbanded throughout in rosewood, 95 x 227cm (37½ x 89¼in), *C 4 Oct,* **£1,210 ($1,561)**

10
A mahogany sideboard, 2nd quarter 19th cent, with two pedestals each fitted with a drawer and a cupboard, later inlaid with boxwood lines and satinwood designs, 115 x 239cm (45 x 94in), *C 27 Mar,* **£550 ($820)**

11
A George III-style inlaid mahogany sideboard, c.1870, with a bowed centre section, 112 x 255cm (44 x 96in), *NY 24/25 Feb,* **$4,400 (£3,034)**

12
A George III-style mahogany sideboard, late 19th cent, of serpentine outline, the moulded rectangular top above a drawer flanked by a cellaret and cupboard, crossbanded throughout, 89 x 152cm (35 x 60in), *C 1 Mar,* **£858 ($1,278)**

1

2

3

4

5

6

7

8

9

10

11

12

1
A pair of George III inlaid mahogany knife urns, last quarter 18th cent, the urns inlaid inside and out with feathered geometric bands, h 62cm (24½in), *NY 20 Oct,* $3,410 (£2,865)

2
A George III mahogany knife box, *c.*1780, outlined with boxwood stringing, later fitted for stationery, 23cm (9in), *HS 24/25 Oct,* £440 ($559)

3
A George III mahogany knife box, *c.*1790, inlaid with satinwood leaf sprays and chevron stringing, now converted for stationery, 22cm (8¾in), *P 20-22 Mar,* £230 ($342)

4
A pair of George III silver-plate-mounted inlaid mahogany knife boxes, *c.*1790, *NY 21 Jan,* $1,320 (£910)

5
A Japanese export lacquer knife urn, *c.*1800, gilt-decorated and inlaid with mother-of-pearl, h 70cm (27½in), *NY 20 Oct,* $3,190 (£2,681)

6
A George II mahogany plate bucket, *c.*1755, with brass liner, h 34cm (13½in), *L 6 Apr,* £748 ($1,077)

7
A George II mahogany brass-bound pail, *c.*1750, the slightly tapering body with fluting, two pairs of brass bands and a brass loop handle, h 37cm (14½in), *L 16 Nov,* £1,375 ($1,815)

8
A George III brass-bound mahogany peat bucket and plate bucket, last quarter 18th cent, 38cm (15in) and 40cm (15¾in), *NY 9 June,* $2,200 (£1,583)

9
A Victorian brass and copper oval coal bucket, 19th cent, open body composed of brass rod spindles interrupted by cushion-form copper mouldings, h 47cm (14½in), *NY 20 Oct,* $4,400 (£3,697)

10
A George III brass-bound hexagonal wine cooler, *c.*1780, with fitted zinc interior, 47cm (18½in), *HS 24/25 Oct,* £2,420 ($3,073)

11
A George III mahogany cellaret, *c.*1810, baize-lined interior, inlaid throughout with boxwood lines, *C 11-14 Dec,* £396 ($495)

12
A Regency mahogany cellaret, *c.*1820, the tapering panelled body raised on lion-paw feet, h 61cm (24in), *L 26 Oct,* £550 ($704)

13
A Regency mahogany wine cooler in the manner of Thomas Hope, *c.*1820, with fitted interior, 90cm (35½in), *L 15 June,* £2,420 ($3,412)

14
A George III mahogany wine cooler or jardinière, *c.*1770, the shallow coopered body with two brass bands and a pair of loop handles, h 56cm (22in), *L 6 Apr,* £1,485 ($2,138)

15
A mahogany decanter box, 18th cent, 22cm (8⅝in), *A 21 Sept,* **Dfl 1,624** (£377; $487)

16
A Victorian coromandel decanter box, *c.*1890, with four cut-glass decanters above a spring-loaded drawer containing six glasses, 23cm (9in), *HS 24/25 Oct,* £770 ($978)

1   2   3   4   5

6   7   8   9

10   11

12   13

14   15   16

1
A Louis XIV giltwood rectangular mirror, the glass in red and gold eglomise decorated with chinoiserie figures and arabesques, 116 x 101cm (45½ x 39¾in), *M 24/25 June,* FF 222,000 (£19,055; $26,401)

2
A Louis XV giltwood mirror, 2nd quarter 18th cent, the plate contained within a voluted frame carved with a shell at the cresting and scrolls, flowers and foliage all around, 147 x 82.5cm (58 x 32½in), *NY 17 Nov,* $7,700 (£6,160)

3
A Louis XV large giltwood mirror, mid-18th cent, the plate surmounted by a basket of flowers, the frame carved with foliate scrolls and trailing roses, 267 x 152cm (105 x 60in), *NY 13 Oct,* $8,250 (£6,762)

4
A Louis XVI giltwood mirror, 3rd quarter 18th cent, the rectangular mirror plate within a conforming frame with carved leaf tips and beading, surmounted by a basket of fruits and flowers, 165 x 100cm (65 x 39½in), *NY 16 Nov,* $5,225 (£4,180)

5
A Flemish carved giltwood mirror, late 17th cent, enclosed by a narrow border of leaves and grapes surrounded by a boldly swirling foliate border, possibly originally a picture frame, 167 x 117cm (66 x 46in), *L 18 May,* £1,650 ($2,393)

6
A Flemish carved giltwood mirror, late 17th cent, the rectangular plate contained within a laurel-carved frame, surmounted by a cherub, flowers and foliage, 152.5 x 99cm (60 x 39in), *L 18 May,* £3,300 ($4,615)

7
A Flemish giltwood frame, late 17th cent, the rectangular plate enclosed by a leafy border, surmounted by a pair of winged cherub heads, 117 x 92cm (46 x 36in), *L 18 May,* £990 ($1,385)

8
An Italian rococo giltwood mirror, 1st half 18th cent, contained within a frame carved with floral sprays at each side, the pierced cresting with a mask and scrolls, 165 x 117cm (65 x 46in), *NY 16 June,* $2,860 (£2,088)

9
A set of three Venetian engraved glass and giltwood girandoles, c.1740, the shaped plates engraved with allegorical figures of a hunter and a warrior, 130 x 79cm (51 x 31in), *L 30 Nov,* £19,800 ($23,958)

10
An Italian rococo giltwood mirror, mid-18th cent, the mirrored cresting surmounted by a pierced shell-shaped motif, 145 x 112cm (57 x 40in), *NY 17 Nov,* $3,410 (£2,728)

11
A pair of Italian giltwood mirrors, c.1775, in bead-decorated frames carved with acanthus leaves, the cresting with a flower-filled urn hung with swags, 66 x 36cm (26 x 14in), *L 3 Feb,* £825 ($1,157)

12
A Swedish giltwood mirror, late 18th cent, the rectangular plate below a helmet and feather cresting and ribbon-tied swags of laurel divided by lion masks, 157.5 x 81.5cm (62 x 32in), *L 3 Feb,* £2,310 ($3,239)

13
A large Venetian engraved mirror-glass, c.1880, the border and shaped cresting richly engraved with flowers, with ebonised trestle-shaped stand, 218 x 106cm (86 x 41½in), *L 9 Mar,* £1,815 ($2,704)

1 2 3
4 5 6
7
8 9 10
11 12 13

1
A William and Mary
walnut cushion-framed
mirror, c.1700, h 51cm
(20in), P 16 Oct,
£550 ($687)

2
An early George II carved
giltwood and gesso mirror,
c.1730, the swan's-neck
pediment centred by a
lambrequin cartouche,
the sides with pendant
oak-leaves and acorns,
h 147cm (58in), L 16 Nov,
£9,900 ($13,068)

3
A George II parcel-gilt
walnut mirror, c.1740,
with C-scroll and
flowering swag-hung
sides, h 123cm (48½in),
NY 21 Jan,
$4,125 (£2,845)

4
A George II parcel-gilt
walnut mirror, mid-18th
cent, the swan's-neck
cresting centred by a
foliate cartouche, the
sides hung with fruited
vines, h 153cm (60in),
NY 20 Oct,
$6,050 (£5,084)

5
A George II parcel-gilt red
walnut mirror, c.1735,
with an outer egg and
dart moulding and
corbel-shaped lower
cornice, h 109cm (43in),
L 27 Jan,
£1,265 ($1,834)

6
A pair of George III
giltwood mirrors, 3rd
quarter 18th cent, each
glass within a pierced
carved frame, asym-
metrical fan-shaped
cresting, h 102cm (40in),
NY 20 Oct,
$13,750 (£11,555)

7
A George II mahogany
mirror, mid-18th cent,
the moulded frame sur-
mounted by a ho-ho bird,
h 99cm (39in), C 3-6 July,
£550 ($742)

8
An American walnut and
giltwood wall mirror,
c.1755, the shaped
cresting with a central
pierced gilt shell
reserve, 97 x 48cm (38 x
19in), NY 28 Jan,
$4,950 (£3,414)

9
An American carved
mahogany and giltwood
mirror, c.1765, 152 x
74cm (60 x 29in),
NY 26 Jan,
$24,200 (£16,689)

10
A Federal giltwood and
eglomisé wall mirror, New
York, c.1815, an eglomisé
panel depicting a
harbour scene, 117 x
84cm (46 x 33in), NY 8 Dec,
$4,290 (£3,575)

11
A Federal giltwood convex
wall mirror, c.1830, the
frame with black-painted
inner liner, surmounted
by an eagle, 112 x 62cm
(44 x 24in), NY 8 Dec,
$4,070 (£3,392)

12
A Regency carved
giltwood convex mirror,
1st quarter 19th cent, the
circular plate sur-
rounded by a reeded,
ebonised and moulded
giltwood frame fitted
with giltwood balls,
h 112cm (44in),
NY 12-14 Apr,
$4,950 (£3,461)

13
A pair of George III-style
painted and parcel-gilt
mirrors, late 19th/early
20th cent, the painted
panel above depicting a
court scene, the pagoda
top painted black,
highlighted with gilding,
h 94cm (37in), NY 9 June,
$4,400 (£3,165)

1

2

3

4

5

6

7

8

9

10

11

12

13

1
A pair of George II-style giltwood oval mirrors, with shell and scroll apron and similar cresting headed by leafy plumes, h 112cm (44in), L 27 Jan, £3,080 ($4,466)

2
A giltwood mirror, in George III style, early 20th cent, with an acanthus-carved cresting, h 112cm (44in), L 9 Nov, £880 ($1,170)

3
An ormolu- and porcelain-mounted mirror, c 1840, bordered by porcelain plaques, 120 x 84cm (47 x 33in), L 9 Mar, £14,850 ($22,127)

4
A Louis XVI-style carved and giltwood mirror, late 19th cent, the oval mirror enclosed by a moulded and beaded frame surmounted by cherubs, scrolling foliage and flowerheads, 147cm (58in), NY 15 Dec, $880 (£739)

5
A gilt-bronze girandole, late 19th cent, the cartouche-shaped plate enclosed by rococo scrollwork, each side with a cherub holding a pair of candle-arms, 60 x 53cm (23½ x 21in), L 9 Nov, £715 ($951)

6
A George III inlaid mahogany toilet mirror, last quarter 18th cent, the serpentine cross-banded base with three drawers, h 58cm (23in), NY 9 June, $440 (£316)

7
A George II walnut toilet mirror, 2nd quarter 18th cent, with a later bevelled mirror plate, above a three-drawer base, 59 x 38cm (23 x 15in), C 3-6 July, £550 ($742)

8
A George III mahogany swing toilet mirror, 1st quarter 19th cent, 66 x 75cm (26 x 29½in), C 3-6 July, £132 ($178)

9
A William IV mahogany gentleman's toilet mirror, 2nd quarter 19th cent, 61cm (24in), C 2-5 Oct, £165 ($213)

10
A Regency oval cut-glass dressing mirror, Irish, 1st quarter 19th cent, the frame of alternating blue glass and reverse-gilt glass studs, h 81cm (32in), NY 20 Oct, £4,675 (£3,928)

11
A George III-style painted mahogany dressing table mirror, late 19th cent, with oval plate above a three-drawer bow-front base, 71 x 92cm (28 x 36in), C 2-5 Oct, £264 ($340)

12
A Victorian walnut cheval mirror, 3rd quarter 19th cent, 165cm (65in), C 3-6 July, £231 ($312)

13
A George III-style mahogany cheval mirror, late 19th cent, on down-swept supports and brass claw feet and castors, 179 x 71.1cm (70½ x 28in), C 1 Mar, £297 ($442)

1
A Régence ormolu twelve-light chandelier, c.1715, the central section decorated with putti and children, the scrolling branches with bearded masks and acanthus leaves, NY 4 May, $198,000 (£141,429)

2
A Swedish gilt-metal and cut-glass chandelier, late 18th/early 19th cent, the central baluster stem surmounted by a pierced ring with chains of drops leading to a larger ring supporting eight candle-branches, 117cm (46in), L 18 May, £4,180 ($6,061)

3
A Swedish ormolu and cut-glass six-light chandelier, 19th cent, hung with faceted diamond-shaped and tear drop pendants and prisms, 101cm (40in), NY 17 Nov, $7,700 (£6,160)

4
A Regency ten-light chandelier, c.1810, rising in chains of faceted beads to the pendant-hung corona, 122 x 96cm (50 x 34in), L 16 Mar, £3,850 ($5,736)

5
A Russian ormolu and cut-glass eight-light chandelier, 19th cent, with a blue-glass plate and ormolu stylised petals, the whole hung with cut-glass prisms and tear drop pendants, h 93cm (36½in), d 84cm (33in), NY 17 Nov, $53,900 (£43,120)

6
A Russian ormolu, cut-glass and crystal eighteen-light chandelier, early 19th cent, 105cm (41¼in), M 24/25 June, FF 333,000 (£28,584; $38,947)

7
A Louis XV-style ormolu, cut-glass and rock crystal sixteen-light chandelier, 19th cent, with rock crystal and glass pendants, 132cm (52in), NY 15 Dec, $6,600 (£5,546)

8
An ormolu rock crystal and cut-glass twelve-light chandelier, in Louis XV style, 19th cent, hung with moulded and faceted cut-glass and rock crystal pendants, 108cm (42½in), NY 15 Dec, $7,975 (£6,701)

9
A French faceted glass and gilt-bronze twelve-light chandelier, late 19th cent, in Empire style, the upper tier formed as eight upright acanthus palmettes, 112cm (44in), NY 16 June, $2,310 (£1,686)

10
An Empire-style cut-glass chandelier, 19th cent, the cut-glass corona in the form of fans, enclosing five lights fitted for electricity, 102cm (40in), NY 3 Nov, $1,210 (£968)

11
A French rock crystal cage-frame chandelier, 19th cent, of twelve lights, hung with chains and beads and large faceted and pear-shaped drops, h 102cm (40in), w 68cm (27in), L 9 Nov, £2,860 ($3,804)

12
A champlève polychrome enamel chandelier, c.1880, in the Moorish manner, with ten lights supported by the cinquefoil enamel ring inlaid with arabic writing, 49.5cm (19½in), L 9 Mar, £1,980 ($2,952)

1
A Regency gilt-metal mounted glass hall lantern, early 19th cent, now electrified, h 49cm (19½in), *NY 21 Jan,* $1,100 (£759)

2
A George III brass hanging lantern, stamped Hanbury, Dublin, 2nd half 18th cent, h 71cm (28in), *C 10 Jan,* £1,540 ($2,233)

3
An American hanging hurricane lamp, early 19th cent, of blown colourless glass and cast metal, the domed lid supported by two chased metal bands, 41cm (16in), *NY 8 Dec,* $880 (£733)

4
A pair of painted and parcel-gilt wall brackets, mid-18th cent, each with mirrored backplate supporting eight shelves, seven with supports of Gothic-style heads, *L 18 May,* £2,310 ($3,231)

5
A pair of Louis XV gilt-bronze wall-lights, mid-18th cent, each with a leaf-scroll backplate supporting two similar candle-branches and nozzles, 39cm (15½in), *L 6 July,* £2,310 ($3,188)

6
An Italian brass lantern, c.1880, with faceted glazed body surmounted by a crown, 127cm (50in), *L 9 Mar,* £4,950 ($7,380)

7
A pair of Louis XVI ormolu three-branch wall-lights, last quarter 18th cent, each with a circular fluted backplate in the form of a flaming torch, 66cm (26in), *NY 17 Nov,* $16,500 (£13,200)

8
A pair of Louis XVI ormolu three-branch wall-lights, last quarter 18th cent, 61cm (24in), *NY 4 May,* $16,500 (£11,786)

9
A pair of Louis XVI ormolu three-branch wall-lights, last quarter 18th cent, decorated with foliate rinceaux and linked by floral garlands, headed by satyr's and female masks, 80cm (31½in), *NY 17 Nov,* $27,500 (£22,000)

10
A large Louis XV-style gilt-bronze five-light sconce, French, late 19th cent, each arm cast with rococo scrollwork, fitted for electricity, 74cm (29in), *NY 24/25 Feb,* $990 (£683)

11
A set of six Régence-style three-light appliques, late 19th cent, each oval backplate cast with a central coat-of-arms, 43cm (17in), *NY 15 Dec,* $8,250 (£6,933)

12
A set of four Régence ormolu two-light bras de lumière, c.1720, each with a backplate centred by a head of a putto and decorated with acanthus leaves, 42.5cm (16¾in), *NY 7 Apr,* $19,800 (£13,846)

13
A set of four gilt-bronze wall-lights, c.1880, each with three leaf-cast arms, the backplates headed by a swagged two-handled urn, 65cm (25½in), *L 9 Nov,* £2,640 ($3,511)

14
A pair of French bronze and cold-painted alabaster five-light sconces, c.1900, each inset with an alabaster plaque painted with neoclassical figures, 76cm (30in), *NY 3 Nov,* $1,760 (£1,408)

15
A pair of gilt-bronze and glass wall appliques, late 19th cent, each with a pair of U-shaped arms, the leafy backplates hung with festoons of faceted beaded drops, 33cm (25in), *L 9 Nov,* £682 ($907)

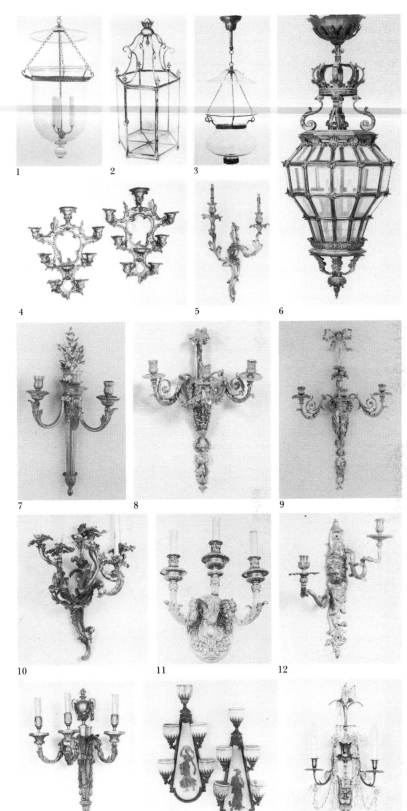

1 2 3

4 5 6

7 8 9

10 11 12

13 14 15

1
A pair of **Russian ormolu and patinated bronze five-light candelabra**, late 18th/early 19th cent, raised on a circular white marble pedestal, 116cm (45½in), *NY 17 Nov*, $7,700 (£6,160)

2
An early **Louis XVI bronze and gilt-bronze candelabrum**, c.1775, the six nozzles hidden within sprays of flowers issuing from a cornucopia held aloft by a cherub, 130cm (51in), *L 6 July*, £3,300 ($4,554)

3
A pair of **Louis XVI ormolu two-light candelabra**, last quarter 18th cent, one representing a little girl, the other an infant satyr, the whole elaborately cast and chiselled with foliage and berries, 37.5cm (14¾in), *NY 17 Nov*, $17,600 (£14,080)

4
A set of four **Louis XVI girandoles**, of six lights, gilt bronze with cut-glass pendants, on triangular bases, 60cm (23½in), *M 25/26 June*, **FF 199,800 (£17,150; $23,368)**

5
A pair of **Louis XVI ormolu-mounted cobalt-blue glass candelabra**, last quarter 18th cent, on shaped grey mottled base and ormolu feet, 57cm (22½in), *NY 16 Nov*, $6,600 (£5,280)

6
A pair of **Empire ormolu five-light candelabra**, 1st quarter 19th cent, each with a circular fluted stem decorated at the top and base with foliate motifs, 58cm (23in), *NY 4 May*, $3,850 (£2,750)

7
A pair of **Louis XVI ormolu patinated bronze and marble three-light candelabra**, last quarter 18th cent, raised on a bow-fronted marble base, 103cm (40½in), *NY 4 May*, $16,500 (£11,786)

8
A pair of **large bronze and gilt-bronze candelabra**, c.1825, each with six arms with engine-turned nozzles and divided by a fruit-cast panache finial, 107cm (42in), *L 25 May*, £2,310 ($3,231)

9
A pair of **Regency cut-glass and gilt-metal three-light candelabra**, c.1810, hung with prisms, with three scrolled candle-branches, h72cm (28½in), *NY 21 Jan*, $2,640 (£1,821)

10
A pair of **gilt-bronze mounted Imari porcelain vases**, c.1860, forming candelabra, the nozzles supported in sprays of lilies, 79cm (31in), *L 9 Nov*, £1,078 ($1,434)

11
A pair of **French parcel-gilt bronze candelabra**, late 19th cent, mounted with the figure of a young boy or a young girl, 44.5cm (17½in), *NY 24/25 Feb*, $770 (£531)

12
A pair of **French gilt-bronze three-arm candelabra**, late 19th cent, in the manner of Meissonnier, signed 'Eug. Bazart', Paris 61cm (24in), *NY 3 Nov*, $3,850 (£3,080)

13
A pair of **French gilt-bronze and marble candelabra**, late 19th cent, each classically draped female raising three candle sockets, white marble bases, 58cm (22¾in), *NY 24/25 Feb*, $990 (£683)

14
A pair of **rock crystal and gilt-bronze candelabra**, c.1900, each with the body in the form of a flattened faceted pear-shaped drop supporting two branches hung with chains of drops, 71cm (28in), *L 9 Nov*, £3,410 ($4,535)

1 2 3 4
5 6 7 8
9 10 11
12 13 14

1
A pair of Franco-Flemish giltwood torchères, late 17th cent, each circular top supported on a pile of fruit held by a female figure, tops and bases 19th cent, 158cm (62in), *L 23-30 Nov,*
£3,300 ($3,993)

2
A pair of Louis XVI-style six-light figural torchères, Carrara marble, ormolu and mottled black marble, by Emile-Joseph-Nastor Carlier, 1880-1, 310cm (122in), *NY 15 Dec,*
$42,900 (£36,050)

3
A pair of Empire-style bronze and ormolu torchères, after Armand Toussaint, *c.*1850, each inscribed and with foundry seal enclosing 'Collas'; together with a pair of red-veined white marble pedestals, total height 254cm (101in), *NY 15 Dec,*
$37,400 (£31,429)

4
A pair of Regence-style giltwood torchères, 19th cent, h 117cm (46in), d 46cm (18in), *NY 24/25 Feb,*
$2,200 (£1,517)

5
A pair of Louis XV gilt—bronze candlesticks, mid-18th cent, 16.5cm (6½in), *L 6 July,*
£770 ($1,063)

6
A pair of Louis XVI ormolu candlesticks, last quarter 18th cent, 28cm (11in), *NY 17 Nov,*
$4,125 (£3,300)

7
A pair of Directoire ormolu candlesticks, late 18th cent, the rims initialled 'LP' (the inventory marks for the collection of King Louis-Philippe), 30cm (11¾in), *NY 17 Nov,*
$2,970 (£2,376)

8
A large pair of Italian ebonised torchères, Florentine, *c.*1880, each of standing Visigoths, 208cm (82in), *L 9 Mar,*
£3,850 ($5,737)

9
A French gilt-bronze and faceted glass sixteen-light torchère, late 19th cent, 164cm (64½in), *NY 16 June,*
$9,350 (£6,825)

10
A pair of gilt-bronze candlesticks, 19th cent, after Dugourc, each with a triple female term stem above a leaf-cast socle, 32.5cm (12¼in), *L 9 Mar,*
£770 ($1,148)

11
A pair of gilt-bronze candlesticks, 19th cent, after a design by Meissonnier, 31cm (12in), · *L 6 July,*
£3,960 ($5,465)

12
A pair of Empire ormolu and patinated bronze candelabra, 1st quarter 19th cent, mounted as lamps, 74cm (29in), *NY 16 Nov,*
$6,875 (£5,500)

13
A Louis XVI ormolu bouillotte lamp, late 18th cent, the stop-fluted pedestal support on a dished base incised with vitruvian scrolls and with three foliate scrolled candle branches, 66cm (26in), *NY 7 Apr,*
$5,390 (£3,769)

14
A Louis XVI-style ormolu and tôle peinte bouillotte lamp, 19th cent, 64cm (25¼in), *NY 17 Nov,*
$2,750 (£2,200)

15
An English bronze student's lamp, by Miller & Sons, 79 Piccadilly, 2nd quarter 19th cent, with adjustable candle-nozzles, shades, h 51cm (20in), *L 15 June,*
£2,035 ($2,869)

1   2   3   5

4

6   7

8   9   10   11

12   13   14   15

1
A French historical tapestry, Felletin, c.1690, from the Alexander the Great series, in triumphal procession entering the city of Babylon, after Le Brun, 285 x 435cm (9ft 4in x 14ft 3in), *NY 2/3 Mar,*
$7,700 (£5,168)

2
A Franco-Flemish verdure tapestry, late 17th cent, 280 x 310cm (9ft 2in x 10ft 3in), *NY 23/24 Nov,*
$2,530 (£2,091)

3
A French tapestry, 'Les Mois Lucas', Gobelins c.1723-30, representing the month of October, (Scorpion) with all the symbols of the wine harvest, the arms of the Comte de Toulouse and his wife at the top corners, 352 x 305cm (11ft 6½in x 8ft 4in), *M 24/25 June,*
FF 444,000 (£38,112; $51,930)

4
A French garden tapestry panel, signed G. Werniers L F, Lille, c.1720, with numerous birds in and around the pond, 240 x 300cm (7ft 11in x 9ft 10in), *NY 2/3 Mar,*
$8,250 (£5,537)

5
A Flemish allegorical tapestry, early 16th cent, probably Tournai, with named figures enclosed in a narrow border of fruiting vines, extensive repairs, reduced in size and the right hand edge of the panel and outer border rewoven, 330 x 220cm (10ft 10in x 7ft 3in), *L 23/30 Nov,*
£12,100 ($14,641)

6
A Brussels late Gothic romance tapestry, c.1515, the centre with a seated prince and his lady, all in shades of blue-green, red oatmeal and yellow, lower border replaced, 335 x 269cm (11ft x 8ft 10in), *NY 2/3 Mar,*
$57,750 (£38,758)

7
A Flemish armorial tapestry, late 17th/early 18th cent, probably Antwerp, a coat of arms in a scrolled cartouche with a motto, in a three-sided frame pattern border, bottom cut, 385 x 245cm (12ft 7in x 8ft) *L 18 May,*
£990 ($1,435)

8
A Flemish mythological tapestry, Brussels, c.1620-30, 'Ulysses taking leave from Nausicaa and King Alcinous', the border with garlands of fruit, animals and masks, 325 x 447cm (10ft 8in x 14ft 8in), *NY 2/3 Mar,*
$11,000 (£7,383)

1

2

3

4

5

6

7

8

1
A Flemish historical
tapestry panel, mid-17th
cent, 292 x 292cm (9ft 7in
x 9ft 7in), *NY 2/3 Mar*,
$4,675 (£3,138)

2
A Franco-Flemish verdure
tapestry, early 18th cent,
a spaniel and birds by a
pond before a moun-
tainous landscape, the
border incorporating an
armorial, 275 x 470cm
(9ft x 15ft 6in),
NY 23/24 Nov,
$13,200 (£10,909)

3
A Brussels historical
tapestry, late 17th cent,
from 'The Wars of
Vespasian', surrounded
by floral borders inhabited
by birds, 347 x 514cm
(12ft 5in x 16ft 10in),
NY 2/3 Mar,
$55,000 (£36,913)

4
An English tapestry,
Royal Windsor, 1884,
'The Royal Residences',
after T. W. Hay, of
Balmoral Castle, seen
from across the river
Dee, acanthus leaf border,
267 x 160cm
(8ft 9in x 5ft 3in), *L 17 Feb*,
£1,100 ($1,542)

5
A Brussels allegorical
garden tapestry, from the
workshop of Jans Frans
van den Hecke, late 17th
cent, allegorical for
Summer, 335 x 340cm
(11ft 2in x 11ft 11in),
NY 23/24 Nov,
$34,100 (£28,182)

6
A Florentine tapestry,
'The Last Supper', by
Guasparri Papini, after
Alessandro Allori,
c.1600, all on a red
ground, the border with
instruments of the Passion,
top border presently
folded under, 420 x 380cm
(13ft 10in x 12ft 5in),
L 18 May,
£6,050 ($8,772)

7
A Brussels' 'Teniers' tapestry, of a milking scene,
attributed to Jerome Le
Clerc, late 17th cent,
four-sided acanthus leaf
frame-pattern border,
with Brussels town and
weaver's mark I.C.,
reduced in height, cut
and joined, 190 x 380cm
(6ft 3in x 12ft 4in),
L 18 May,
£3,960 ($5,742)

8
A rare English Teniers
tapestry, 1st half 18th
cent, Boers merry-
making at a country inn,
within flower and
acanthus border, 231 x
381cm (7ft 7in x 12ft 6in),
NY 2/3 Mar,
$5,775 (£3,876)

9
A Flemish Teniers
tapestry, *c*.1730, probably
Oudenarde, of a milking
scene, frame pattern
border, some splits,
270 x 210cm (8ft 9in x
6ft 10in), *L 23/30 Nov*,
£5,060 ($6,123)

1

2

3

4

5

6

7

8

9

1
A pair of Louis XV
ormolu chenets, mid-18th
cent, representing two
partially-clad children,
raised on asymmetrical
foliate bases, 38cm (15in),
NY 4 May,
$15,400 (£11,000)

2
A pair of Louis XV
ormolu chenets, mid-18th
cent, each with a scrolling
base supporting a seated
lion, 34cm (13½in),
NY 17 Nov,
$11,000 (£8,800)

3
A pair of Louis XV
ormolu chenets, mid-18th
cent, each decorated with
a chinoiserie figure, one
male the other female,
33.5cm (13¼in), *NY 17 Nov,*
$6,600 (£5,280)

4
A pair of gilt-bronze
chenets, in Louis XVI
style, late 19th cent, each
with a flaming garlanded
urn at one end, the
lower end with a winged
fabulous beast, 42cm
(16½in), *L 9 Mar,*
£660 ($984)

5
A pair of American brass
and wrought-iron
andirons, stamped Davis,
Boston, *c*1800, 33cm (13in),
NY 8 Dec,
$1,100 (£917)

6
A pair of Federal brass
and wrought-iron
andirons, probably
Boston, Massachusetts,
*c*1795, 76cm (30in),
NY 28 Jan,
$1,430 (£986)

7
A pair of Federal brass
and wrought-iron
andirons, stamped R
Wittingham, New York,
*c*1800, 48cm (19in),
NY 28 Jan,
$2,750 (£1,897)

8
Two similar Venetian
blackamoor stools or
stands, *c*1870, each
moulded circular top
supported by a seated
blackamoor child, h 51cm
(20in), d 28cm (11in),
L 9 Mar,
£1,705 ($2,542)

9
A pair of Venetian figures
of blackamoors, 19th cent,
each with the figure of a
kneeling boy in a
plumed hat with poly-
chrome decoration, raised
on a separate rectangular
plinth, 140cm (55in),
NY 16 Nov,
$8,525 (£6,820)

10
A pair of Florentine
carved and stained pine
figures, *c*1880, in the
form of medieval page-
boys, each with flowing
hair and wearing a cap
and heraldic tunic,
104cm (41in), *L 9 Nov,*
£3,630 ($4,828)

11
An American gilt-incised
bronze-mounted inlaid
rosewood pedestal, New
York, *c*1865, 114cm (45in),
NY 24/25 Feb,
$1,100 (£759)

12
A large carved and
varnished pine umbrella
and coat stand, German
or Austrian, *c*1880,
226cm (89in), *L 9 Nov,*
£2,420 ($3,219)

13
A carved oak coat and
umbrella stand, Austrian
or German, *c*1880, in the
form of a bear holding a
pine branch on which
two small bear cubs
climb, 185cm (73in),
L 9 Mar,
£1,705 ($2,540)

2

1

3

4

5

6

7

8

9

10

11

12

13

1

A pair of Empire ormolu-mounted patinated bronze urns, 1st quarter 19th cent, applied with female figures, sphinx heads supporting the handles, 50cm (19¾in), *NY 4 May*, $13,200 (£9,429)

2

A French ormolu-mounted Limoges enamelled urn, 19th cent, enamelled with a maiden in a chariot attended by cherubs, the bowl inlaid with stylised birds and foliage, 48cm (19in), *L 9 Nov*, £3,190 ($4,243)

3

A pair of gilt-bronze-mounted vases and covers, *c*1860, each bleu-de-roi body with a pair of satyr mask handles joined by berried laurel swags, 39cm (15½in), *L 9 Mar*, £2,420 ($3,608)

4

A French gilt-bronze-mounted 'Sèvres' cassolet, late 19th cent, the bleu-de-roi vessel with domed cover with three applied ram's heads, 57cm (25½in), *NY 16 June*, $660 (£482)

5

A pair of French parcel-gilt-bronze jardinières, late 19th cent, covers lacking 30cm (11¾in), *NY 24/25 Feb*, $1,760 (£1,214)

6

A pair of French gilt-bronze-mounted marble urns and covers, late 19th cent, each cover surmounted by a putto, on a gilt-bronze square base, 74cm (29in), *NY 16 June*, $2,750 (£2,007)

7

A gilt-bronze and gilt-metal-mounted double-nautilus shell centrepiece, the mounts French, late 19th cent, 30.5cm (12in), *NY 24/25 Feb*, $880 (£587)

8

A gilt-bronze-mounted rouge de flandres marble figural urn, F Barbedienne, late 19th cent, 76cm (30in), *NY 16 June*, $4,950 (£3,613)

9

A George III blue-john vase, *c*1800, with red-, purple- and honey-coloured markings, h 40cm (15¾in), *L 15 June*, £2,035 ($2,869)

10

A pair of George III blue-john obelisks, late 18th/early 19th cent, the rectangular plinths with slate and white marble mouldings, 43cm (17in), *L 15 June*, £2,750 ($3,877)

11

A pair of Roman bronze, gilt-bronze and marble tazze, 2nd quarter 19th cent, 24cm (9½in), *L 18 May*, £8,250 ($11,538)

12

A gilt-bronze-mounted verde antico marble tazza, early 19th cent, the dished top with leaf-cast border with slender socle and square base, 28cm (11in), *L 18 May*, £2,640 ($3,828)

13

A French gilt-bronze-mounted rouge-royal marble pedestal, late 19th cent, formed as a column with gilt-bronze Corinthian capital and bronze-mounted base, 118cm (46½in), *NY 16 June*, $1,320 (£964)

14

A malachite veneered and gilt-metal column, *c*1860, the moulded top supported on a malachite column with a Corinthian gilt-metal capital, 119cm (47in), *L 9 Nov*, £5,940 ($7,900)

15

A Netherlandish carved marble fountain basin, *c*1740, 130cm (51in), *L 18 May*, £5,280 ($7,656)

16

An Italian model of a circular temple, late 18th cent, in white marble and red veined marble, an ormolu figure of Minerva in the centre, the cupola surmounted by an eagle, *F 19 Dec*, **L 4,000,000 (£1,690; $2,112)**

1
A pair of Empire ormolu
and patinated bronze
ewers, 1st quarter 19th
cent, each fitted with a
flared ormolu spout
decorated with a mask,
the handle formed by a
winged female figure,
61cm (24in), *NY 17 Nov,*
$7,700 (£6,160)

2
A pair of gilt-bronze ewers,
after Nicolas Delaunay,
with leopard handles,
the bodies cast with
fluting, masks and
portrait medallions,
30cm (11¾in), *L 6 July,*
£1,265 ($1,746)

3
A Louix XV ormolu,
porcelain and lacquer
inkstand, mid-18th cent,
the base decorated with
chinoiserie lacquer in
gold on a black ground,
fitted with three
Mennecy porcelain pots,
13.5 x 28 x 21cm (5¼ x 11
x 8¼in), *NY 4 May,*
$3,300 (£2,357)

4
A pair of gilt-bronze and
cut-glass ewers, c.1880, the
baluster bodies with
hob-nail faceting, the
handle cast with
acanthus and bulrushes,
30cm (12in), *L 9 Mar,*
£1,265 ($1,886)

5
A pair of Louis XIV gilt-
bronze-mounted boulle
inkstands, early 18th cent,
with fitted pierced lids,
the sides decorated with
strapwork in red shell
and brass, 9 x 14cm (3½
x 5¾in), *L 23-30 Nov,*
£6,600 ($7,986)

6
A Louis XVI gilt-bronze
and lacquered wood
inkstand, c.1775, the base
mounted with lion and
female masks and hung
with swags, w 37cm
(14½in), *L 6 July,*
£1,980 ($2,732)

7
A Regency inkstand in
brass and ebonised wood
with a pair of glass
reservoirs, c.1814, 30.5cm
(12in), *L 16 Mar,*
£5,940 ($8,850)

8
A Regency boulle encrier,
c.1820, with two hobnail-
cut glass inkwells with
lotus lids, cedar-lined
drawer, 38cm (15in),
L 16 Nov,
£572 ($755)

9
A French boulle writing
box, Paris, c.1850, inlaid
with cut-brass foliage on
a red tortoiseshell
ground, w 33cm (13in),
L 9 Mar,
£1,430 ($2,132)

10
A French gilt-bronze-
mounted boulle marquetry
double-inkstand, late 19th
cent, the footed trap with
concave pen trays
flanking a handle and
two cut-glass bottles,
41cm (16in), *NY 24/25 Feb,*
$990 (£683)

11
A Lombard silver-inlaid
ebony casket, c.1700, the
lid with a central panel
of two parakeets within a
border of scrollwork and
flowers and the cypher
'CSA', h 165.cm (6½in),
w 38cm (15in), *L 23-30 Nov,*
£1,870 ($2,263)

12
A gilt-bronze-mounted
inlaid tortoiseshell casket,
French or German, early
18th cent, with scenes of
cherubs in brass, pewter
and coloured shell on a
dark tortoiseshell ground,
h 11cm (4½in), w 19.5cm
(7¾in), *L 6 July,*
£14,300 ($19,734)

13
A French parcel-gilt
bronze casket, c.1875, cast
with a classical female
above a shaped hinged
top, the sides with panels
enclosing classical
figures, 30.5cm (12in),
NY 3 Nov,
$559 (£447)

14
A decorative glass and
metal casket, c.1880, the
lid, front and sides with
glass panels lined with
engraved pierced silvered
metal, 18cm (7in), *L 8 June,*
£715 ($1,037)

1   2   3   4   5   6   7   8   9   10   11   12   13   14

1
An American painted and decorated dressing box, New England, early 19th cent, lined with blue paper and having four compartments, 23 x 46 x 27cm (9 x 18 x 10½in), *NY 8 Dec,* $1,320 (£1,100)

2
A Federal inlaid mahogany miniature chest, Massachusetts, *c.*1810, the top with rope- and line-inlay 13 x 25 x 13cm (5 x 10 x 5in), *NY 8 Dec,* $1,320 (£1,100)

3
A late Victorian burr walnut combined writing and stationery cabinet, *c.*1900 with brass carrying handles, 41cm (16in), *P 18-25 Sept,* £407 ($525)

4
An Anglo-Indian ivory-veneered work box, late 18th cent, 18.5cm (7½in), *L 14 Dec,* £1,980 ($2,475)

5
An English papier-mâché writing box, *c.*1850, enclosing a fitted stationery rack, the whole richly inlaid in mother-of-pearl, h 42cm (16½in), *L 17 Feb,* £550 ($770)

6
A George III satinwood and kingwood crossbanded combined writing box and dressing case, *c.*1790, the front with an arrangement of five dummy drawers and one real drawer, 46cm (18in), *P 11-18 Dec,* £638 ($759)

7
A Victorian rosewood writing cabinet, *c.*1900, inlaid with satinwood and ivory arabesques, 39cm (15½in), *P 14 Nov,* £352 ($472)

8
A George III mahogany table encrier, late 18th cent, with three alphabetically-labelled frieze drawers above a long drawer, 27 x 38cm (10½ x 15in), *C 2-5 Oct,* £462 ($596)

9
An Anglo-Indian ivory-veneered tea caddy, late 18th cent, 27cm (12⅓in), *L 15 June,* £1,265 ($1,784)

10
An Anglo-Indian ivory-veneered sandalwood box, mid-18th cent, 30cm (12in), *L 15 June,* £528 ($744)

11
A George III tortoiseshell-veneered tea caddy, *c.*1780, 15cm (6in), *L 26 Oct,* £770 ($986)

12
A George III inlaid satinwood marquetry tea caddy, late 18th cent, fitted with a pair of removable compartments, flanking a cut-glass mixing bowl, 34cm (13½in), *NY 12-14 Apr,* $1,100 (£769)

13
A George III rectangular inlaid mahogany tea caddy, *c.*1790, 32cm (12½in), *NY 12-14 Apr,* $935 (£653)

14
A Regency paper scroll tea caddy, *c.*1810, 18cm (7in), *P 21-24 Feb,* £275 ($385)

15
A Regency silver-mounted and inlaid brass and tortoiseshell tea caddy, 1st quarter 19th cent, h 12cm (4¾in), *NY 12-14 Apr,* $880 (£615)

16
A Regency tortoiseshell-veneered tea caddy, *c.*1820, h 18.5cm (7¼in), *L 27 Jan,* £418 ($606)

17
A pair of Victorian decorated tea canisters, 19th cent, fitted for electricity, h 65cm (25½in), *NY 20 Oct,* $4,290 (£3,605)

18
A pair of English chinoiserie and gilt-decorated tea canisters, 19th cent, fitted for electricity, h 66cm (26in), *NY 9 June,* $3,300 (£2,374)

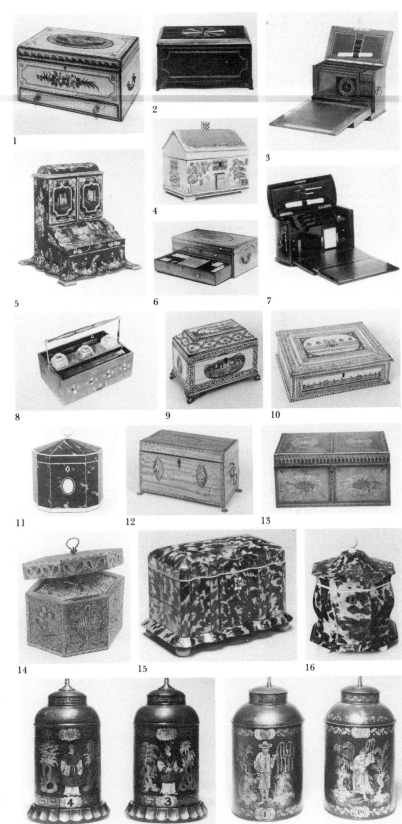

1
An oak and beechwood
sand glass, late 17th/early
18th cent, h 18cm (7¼in),
P 13 Nov,
£242 ($324)

2
A walnut and beechwood
½-hour sand glass,
17th/18th cent, with
canted fret-carved sup-
ports, h 20cm (8in),
P 13 Nov,
£242 ($324)

3
A lignum vitae Wassail or
loving cup, 17th cent,
with a ring-turned body,
h 14cm (5½in), *P 13 Nov,*
£528 ($707)

4
A mahogany caster, 18th
cent, h 13cm (5in),
P 13 Nov,
£207 ($280)

5
A yew wood pepper caster,
18th cent, of typical
turned form, h 12cm
(5in), *P 13 Nov,*
£121 ($162)

6
A fruitwood apothecary
bowl, 18th cent, with a
fret-carved rim above a
turned foot, d 10cm (4in),
P 13 Nov,
£88 ($118)

7
A lignum vitae coffee mill,
18th cent, the turned
body in two graduated
tiers, h 19cm (7½in),
P 13 Nov,
£297 ($398)

8
A walnut beer coaster,
18th cent, the base with
brass gallery, on castors,
69cm (27in), *P 13 Nov,*
£506 ($678)

9
A Scottish amboyna and
tortoiseshell-lined snuff
box, 19th cent, w 10cm
(4in), *P 13 Nov,*
£143 ($192)

10
A rosewood shoe snuff
box, 19th cent, with
studded brass decoration
and sliding lid, 10cm
(4in), *P 13 Nov,*
£110 ($147)

11
A Welsh mahogany
miniature hand mirror,
18th cent, sliding cover
with stylised gouged
decoration, inscribed 'S
heart B 1791' 12cm (4¾in),
P 13 Nov,
£66 ($88)

12
A Welsh sycamore and
mahogany snuff or trinket
box, 18th cent, in the
form of a heart, 7cm
(2½in), *P 13 Nov,*
£77 ($103)

13
A mahogany trinket box,
19th cent, with brass-
nailed decoration, 14cm
(5½in) *P 13 Nov,*
£275 ($368)

14
An English tea caddy,
early 19th cent, shaped
as an apple, h 15cm
(6in), *L 16 Nov,*
£770 ($1,016)

15
A fruitwood compo mould,
18th cent, 42cm (16½in),
P 13 Nov,
£99 ($133)

16
A Tyrolean yew wood nut
cracker, mid-19th cent, in
the form of a double-
sided ogre's face with an
open mouth forming the
aperture, 15cm (6in),
P 13 Nov,
£176 ($236)

17
An ebony gavel, early
19th cent, 15cm (6in),
P 13 Nov,
£55 ($74)

18
A miniature gavel, 19th
cent, with a turned cedar-
wood head, 13cm (5in),
P 13 Nov,
£39 ($52)

1

A Victorian rosewood pole screen, mid-19th cent, with circular wool-worked panel, 150cm (59in), *C 2-5 Oct*, £176 ($227)

2

A Regency ebonised pole screen, early 19th cent, painted with chinoiserie figures, h 145cm (57in), *C 2-5 Oct*, £275 ($355)

3

A mid-Georgian mahogany pole screen, mid-18th cent, with petit-point panel worked with animals and buildings, 155cm (61in), *C 2-5 Oct*, £275 ($355)

4

A George II mahogany pole screen, c.1750, embroidered in gros and petit point, with a lady dancing while a man plays a guitar, h 155cm (61in), *L 15 June*, £1,100 ($1,551)

5

A George III mahogany pole screen, 3rd quarter 18th cent, the adjustable needleworked panel woven with a woman and young boy in a landscape, h 141cm (55½in), *C 27-30 Mar*, £462 ($688)

6

A Louis XV walnut firescreen, carved with rococo scrollwork and foliage, mounted with a tapestry, *M 25/26 June*, FF 21,090 (£1,810; $2,467)

7

A firescreen, 19th cent, h 124cm (48⅞in), w 72.5cm (28½in), *A 13-16 Mar*, Dfl 986 (£225; $335)

8

A Victorian walnut pole screen, c.1860, the bright needleworked panel on a swing frame 129.5cm (51in), *C 11-14 Dec*, £176 ($220)

9

A Victorian decorated papier-maché sporting tea tray, 19th cent, now on a conforming bamboo-turned stand, 81cm (32in), *NY 12-14 Apr*, $3,080 (£2,154)

10

A Victorian decorated papier-maché tea tray now on a stand, 19th cent, depicting a horse and rider before an inn, in the manner of George Morland, 80cm (31½in), *NY 20 Oct*, $2,860 (£2,403)

11

An English papier-maché tea tray, early 19th cent, painted with sprays of summer flowers on a deep red ground, 77 x 59cm (30½ x 23in), *C 2-5 Oct*, £748 ($965)

12

An English black papier-maché tray, 3rd quarter 19th cent, painted with a spray of flowers within a scrolling gilt border, 77.5cm (30½in), *C 2-5 Oct*, £231 ($298)

13

An Edwardian mahogany and satinwood crossbanded tray, c.1910, inlaid with a floral spray, brass handles, 66cm (26in), *P 16 Oct*, £242 ($302)

1 2 3 4 5

6 7

8 9

10 11

12 13

1
A giltwood and Vernis Martin three-fold screen, c.1900, each fold with a glazed panel above a panel painted with young girls in an arcadian landscape, h 174cm (68½in), each fold w 57cm (22½in), *L 8 June,* £858 ($1,244)

2
A late George III mahogany duet stand, c.1800, h 122cm (48in), *L 13 July,* £990 ($1,356)

3
A Victorian walnut music stand, c.1860, with adjustable column, *HS 25 June,* £605 ($853)

4
A George II mahogany reading stand, c.1750, with a hinged, ratcheted, adjustable, rectangular top, 72cm (28½in), *NY 21 Jan,* $1,760 (£1,214)

5
A William IV terrestrial globe by C Smith & Son, 172 Strand, containing 'The Latest Discoveries and Geographical Improvements to 1830', h 90cm (35½in), *L 1 June,* £1,760 ($2,429)

6
A pair of Regency mahogany library globes, C Smith & Co, 172 Strand, London, c.1815, celestial and terrestrial globe, h 112cm (44in), *NY 21 Jan,* $8,800 (£6,069)

7
A pair of George IV mahogany terrestrial and celestial library globes, signed Cary's, and dated 1812 and 1818, h 101.5cm (40in), *L 16 Nov,* £13,200 ($17,424)

8
A Victorian beechwood easel, late 19th cent, h 152.5cm (60in), *C 27/30 Mar,* £396 ($590)

9
A late 18th cent fruitwood spinning wheel, possibly Austrian or Swiss, h 71cm (28in), *L 12 Oct,* £660 ($845)

10
A Flemish linen press, mid-17th cent, in oak and walnut, the upper part set with ebony panels and the screw press above a drawer, the lower part set with ebony, 163 x 73cm (64 x 28in), *L 25 May,* £1,430 ($2,045)

11
An Italian sedan chair, Genoa, mid-18th cent, the wooden frame inlaid with gilt rococo motifs, the cover in leather, the interior upholstered in red velvet damask, *F 10 May,* L 2,034,000 (£828; $1,192)

12
A North Italian carved and painted wood carriage or sleigh body, mid-18th cent, in the form of an hippocamp, decorated in red, 259 x 122cm (102 x 48in), *L 23-30 Nov,* £3,850 ($4,569)

13
A parcel-gilt and polychrome child's sledge, Dutch, 18th cent, carved with rococo ornaments and flowers and decorated with a variety of birds in a landscape, 103cm (40.5in), *A 16 May,* Dfl 10,672 (£2,490; $3,561)

1

2

3

4

5

6

7

8

9.

10

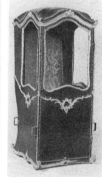

11

12

13

1

A small James I oak buffet, c.1620, with three open shelves, the stepped moulded frieze inlaid with diamond banding on gadrooned and leaf-carved cup and cover supports, 111 x 118.5cm (43¾ x 46½in), *L 24 Feb,*
£8,580 ($12,012)

2

A pair of early George III carved giltwood pier-glasses, c.1770, each with a central arched rectangular plate contained within a frame of similar plates, h 183cm (72in), *L 16 Mar,*
£17,600 ($26,224)

3

A George III mahogany breakfront cabinet, c.1765, in the manner of William Vile, the upper part with central broken pediment with a dentil moulding above a pair of fielded panel doors, flanked by a smaller door surmounted by a fretwork cornice, the projecting lower part with gadrooned and leaf-carved border over drawers, 246 x 171cm (97 x 67in), *L 16 Nov,*
£25,300 ($33,396)

4

A George III giltwood console table, last quarter 18th cent, with a *verde antico* marble top, 85 x 152 x 61cm (34¼ x 59¾ x 61in), *NY 20 Oct,*
$47,300 (£39,747)

1

2

3

4

1
A pair of George III carved mahogany armchairs, c.1770, each with an arched moulded backrest carved and pierced with an urn above leafy scrolls, on ribbon-carved fluted legs, *NY 21 Jan,* **$8,800 (£6,069)**

2
A George III mahogany serpentine chest, c.1780, with a brushing slide above three graduated long drawers, 119.5cm (47in), *L 15 June,* **£2,640 ($3,722)**

3
A George III mahogany sofa table, c.1790 cross-banded in satinwood, the frieze with four drawers, 73 x 152.5cm (29 x 60in), *NY 16 Mar,* **$8,250 (£5,533)**

4
A pair of George III serpentine tables, in the manner of *John Cobb* and in burr-elm with tulip-wood crossbanding, 75 x 76cm (29½ x 30in), *NY 16 Mar,* **$20,900 (£14,017)**

5
A George III inlaid mahogany and satinwood roll-top desk, last quarter 18th cent, the sloping roll-top opening to a leather-lined writing surface and an arrangement of satinwood drawers, 105 x 107 x 71cm (41½ x 42 x 28in), *NY 20 Oct,* **$11,000 (£9,243)**

1

2

3

4

5

1
A walnut month longcase clock, *c*1705, the dial signed 'Dan Quare London', a brass border framing the dial, the cross- and feather-banded waist door veneered in richly figured burr-wood, 254cm (8ft 4in), *L 7 June,*
£18,700 ($27,115)

2
A walnut longcase clock, *c*1725, George Graham No. 657, veneered in burr-wood of restrained figure and warm colouring, the cross- and feather-banded sides in straight-grained wood, 229cm (7ft 6in), *L 1 Nov,*
£19,800 ($25,344)

3
A Swiss rococo ormolu-mounted polychrome decorated bracket clock, mid-18th cent, with white enamel dial, the two-train movement inscribed 'Robert Et Freres du Commun A La Chaux de Fond', 103cm (40½in), *NY 13 Oct,*
$12,100 (£9,918)

4
An early George III red-japanned musical bracket clock, signed 'Step: Rimbault London', the three-train movement with verge escapement and bob pendulum, the case decorated in gilt heightened with black on a vermilion ground, 70cm (27½in), *L 23 Feb,*
£7,150 ($10,024)

5
An olivewood longcase clock, *c*1675, the 9½inch dial signed 'Joseph Knibb Londoni fecit', six pillar movement formerly with maintaining power, plinth restored, *L 7 June,*
£19,800 ($28,710)

6
A veneered ebony quarter-repeating bracket clock, Thomas Tompion No. 99, *c*1690, the dial signed, the movement with latched dial and plates, verge escapement, the backplate signed and engraved with tulips, the moulded case with gilt-metal dome mounts, 32cm (12½in), *L 7 June,*
£34,100 ($49,445)

1

5

2

3

4

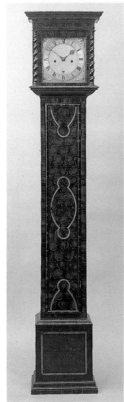
6

1
A gold perpetual calendar wristwatch, Patek Philippe, 1948, the movement with micrometer adjustment, the dial with day and month apertures, moon phase aperture and date dial, signed, d 3.3cm (1¼in), *L 26 July,*
£8,910 ($11,895)

2
A gold double time wristwatch, Piaget, retailed by Asprey, with separate movements for both dials, engine-turned bezel, plain case, d 3.3cm (1¼in), *G 13 Nov,*
SF 2,420 (£751; $1,007)

3
A gold Prince wristwatch, Rolex, *c*1930, the movement signed 'Rolex Extra Prima', set in a two-colour rectangular case, import mark 'Glasgow 1930', 2.4 x 4.2cm (¾ x 1⅝in), *L 26 July,*
£2,200 ($2,937)

4
A gold and enamel tank wristwatch, The European Watch and Clock Co, retailed by Cartier, *c*1930, in a rectangular case with the sides inlaid with black enamel, 2.3 x 3cm (⅞ x 1¼in), *L 26 July,*
£2,860 ($3,818)

5
A rare eight-day fusee keyless pocket chronometer, No. 09587 by Charles Frodsham, the gilt movement fully jewelled, silvered dial, the case engine-turned, casemaker's initials, 'HMF' hallmarked 1915, d 7.2cm (2¾in), *L 23 Feb,*
£20,900 ($29,302)

6
A silver pair cased wandering hour verge watch, by S Bastien Mestral, early 18th cent, the silver dial with two polychrome enamel miniatures, d 6.5cm (2½in), *G 13 Nov,*
SF 24,200 (£7,515; $10,071)

7
A bronze, ormolu and marble clock, *c*.1800, the enamel dial set in a drum-shaped case, surmounted by a figure of a female Indian, 47cm (18½in), *NY 16 Nov,*
$8,800 (£7,040)

8
A Louis XV ormolu and bronze rhinoceros mantel clock, mid-18th cent, the white enamel dial inscribed 'Lepaute H. Du Roy A Paris', the movement with outside count wheel, in a drum-shaped case raised on a bronze rhinoceros, 49.5cm (19½in), *NY 4 May,*
$26,400 (£18,857)

1

2

3

4

5

6

7

8

Clocks and Watches

JOHN VAUGHAN • TINA MILLAR • KEVIN TIERNEY

As a collecting field, clocks and watches are an unusual marriage between antique precision instruments, items of furniture and personal jewellery, but usually only one of these aspects is of prime interest to the collector.

Horological expertise has vastly increased during the last few decades, owing to the researches of such experts as George Daniels, and there are now many collectors worldwide who are rightly fascinated by the development of time-keeping mechanisms and the complex refinements of alarums, repeating features and calendar work that can go with them.

As with all collecting fields, the condition of a watch or clock has a great bearing on its value. With early timepieces—those made before 1700—it is important that the movement be complete, but not necessarily keeping time. Damage or restoration to the dial or the case will, of course, influence value. For those clock collectors who are more interested in clocks as furniture the quality of the dial and case are of paramount importance. Nowhere is this more noticeable than with the longcase (tallcase) or grandfather clock. This evolved with the need to enclose the pendulum and heavy weights, which, together with the anchor escapement, were found to allow greater accuracy and at least an eight-day running period. Ebony or ebonized cases are relatively unpopular compared with walnut or mahogany. Some English clocks and many of the more flamboyant continental examples are classed as furniture for saleroom purposes. French clocks, in particular, are often highly decorative, being designed by craftsmen working in contemporary 18th and 19th century styles. Skeleton clocks, in which all the mechanism is visible, are popular, as are the finer English and French carriage clocks. There is a feature article about these on page 148.

Among English clock collectors, the great early makers, such as Thomas Tompion, Joseph and John Knibb and George Graham, are especially respected. Similarly, the clocks of the Willard family of Boston and other early 19th century American makers are highly regarded by the American market.

When the watch was first invented in the 16th century, it was an object of great wonder, highly prized by the aristocracy. Since the technology of watchmaking advanced slowly—more than 100 years passed before the invention of the hairspring allowed sufficient accuracy to add a minute hand to the movement—watchmakers concentrated on the decorative potential of the watches, making them in intriguing shapes and embellishing them with jewels and painted enamels. They also added complications, such as striking, alarum and astronomical work, to the movements.

Expansion of trade in the 18th century brought new demands for accuracy, which resulted in the invention of the chronometer. It was the first really accurate measurer of time and essential for navigation at sea. At about the same time the development of the cylinder escapement permitted a new, slimmer watch design. Thus the stage was set for the innovations of Breguet, acknowledged in his own time and today as the greatest watchmaker of all time.

The late 19th century saw increasingly complex technical advances, culminating in such choice watches as the perpetual calendar, minute repeating, split-second chronograph. The leader in this field was the Geneva firm of Patek Philippe. The wristwatch is an invention of the early 20th century and it is still developing as a collectors' market. At present, only those with some age, special form or complication by a top maker, such as Patek Philippe, Vacheron & Constantin or Rolex, are in demand at auction. As they are intended to be worn at least occasionally, fashion has a strong part to play in this field.

1
A William and Mary
arabesque marquetry inlaid
walnut longcase clock,
Corn Manley, Norwich,
c1690, with brass dial
and silvered chapter ring,
restorations, 220cm
(7ft 2½in), *NY 21 Jan,*
$2,970 (£2,048)

2
A walnut and marquetry
longcase clock, late
17th/early 18th cent,
inscribed 'Jos. Jackeman,
London Bridge', eight-
day movement
(including pendulum
and weights), 198cm
(6ft 6in), *P 21-24 Feb,*
£5,280 ($7,403)

3
A George I chinoiserie
gilt-decorated black-
japanned longcase clock,
Ge. Voyce Dean, with a
silvered dial with matted
centre, 226cm (7ft 5in),
NY 9 June,
$1,760 (£1,266)

4
A walnut longcase clock,
early 18th cent, inscribed
'John Tickell, Crediton',
with glazed side panels
in the square hood, brass
dial, 217cm (7ft 1½in),
P 21-24 Feb,
£770 ($1,080)

5
A Louis XV ormolu-
mounted marquetry
longcase clock, mid-18th
cent, the dial with a
silvered chapter ring,
231cm (7ft 7in), *NY 15 Dec,*
$20,900 (£17,563)

6
A Dutch walnut longcase
clock, Pieter and Jan
Morijn, Amsterdam, late
18th cent, *A 13-18 June,*
Dfl 14,500 (£3,396;
$4,890)

7
A Dutch burr-walnut
month calendar longcase
clock, the dial signed
'Fromanteel & Clarke',
the five-pillar movement
with Dutch striking
controlled by a rack,
234cm (7ft 8in), *L 7 June,*
£4,290 ($6,221)

8
A Dutch walnut striking
alarum longcase clock,
18th cent, the dial signed
'Thomas Thomsen
Amsterdam', the centre
and base painted with
classical scenes, 292cm
(9ft 7in), *L 12 Apr,*
£4,070 ($5,873)

9
A Federal inlaid
mahogany longcase clock,
c1800, the dial inscribed
'David Williams, Newport',
with brass stop-fluted
columns, minor
restoration to one foot,
239cm (7ft 10in)
NY 30 June,
$9,625 (£7,129)

10
A carved oak longcase
clock, Tiffany & Co, New
York, c1900, in
Renaissance style, the
glazed door enclosing a
brass and silvered dial,
quarter striking West-
minster chimes, 264cm
(8ft 9in), *NY 24/25 Feb,*
$7,700 (£5,310)

11
A Federal carved mahogany
longcase clock, Issac
Brokaw, Bridgetown, NJ,
c1820, white-painted
dial, 245cm (8ft ½in),
NY 28 Jan,
$4,125 (£2,845)

12
A French mahogany month
regulator, early 19th cent,
the silvered dial signed
'R. Revel', mercury
pendulum suspended
from the backboard,
196cm (6ft 5in), *L 23 Feb,*
£2,035 ($2,853)

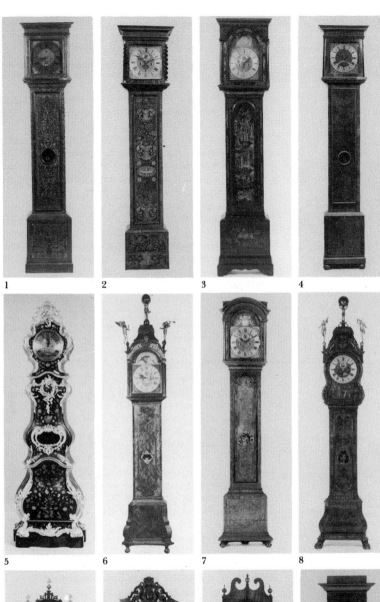

1   2   3   4

5   6   7   8

9   10   11   12

1
**A George II black-
japanned longcase clock,**
the dial signed 'Saml.
Guy London', the
case decorated with
chinoiserie landscapes in
red and gold, 211cm
(6ft 11in), *L 23 Feb,*
£880 ($1,234)

2
**A George II walnut
longcase clock,** the
dial signed 'Thomas Gardner
London', with rack-striking
movement, the front
richly veneered, 224cm
(7ft 4in), *L 1 Nov,*
£2,860 ($3,661)

3
A mahogany longcase clock,
late 18th cent, the
painted dial signed
'Buxton Bp Auckland',
232.5cm (7ft 7½in),
C 3-6 July,
£396 ($537)

4
**A George II inlaid and
carved mahogany longcase
clock,** Cha^S Stokes,
Bewdley, with brass dial,
silvered chapter ring,
restorations to case,
244cm (8ft), *NY 21 Jan,*
$4,400 (£3,034)

5
An oak longcase clock, the
dial signed 'Ra. Sherrat,
Wem', the movement early
18th cent, restored, the
case reconstructed,
196cm (6ft 5in), *C 5 July,*
£660 ($895)

6
An oak longcase clock, last
quarter 18th cent, signed
'G. Young, Sockerby',
brass dial with applied
chapter ring, the move-
ment with anchor escape-
ment with rack striking
on a bell, 221cm (7ft 3in),
C 4 Oct,
£605 ($780)

7
**A George III mahogany
longcase clock,** the
silvered dial inscribed
'Edward Clarke, London',
the eight-day movement
with rack striking on a
bell, 244cm (8ft),
P 16-23 Oct,
£1,870 ($2,338)

8
**A George III mahogany
chiming longcase clock,**
the dial signed 'Eardley
Norton', the three-train
five-pillar movement
chiming on eight bells,
46.5cm (8ft 1in), excluding
top finial, *L 7 June,*
£3,520 ($5,104)

9
An oak longcase clock,
late 18th cent, the dial
signed 'Jno. Webster,
Salop', the movement
with anchor escapement
and rack striking, the
case with mahogany
crossbanding, 232.5cm
(7ft 6½in), *C 29 Mar,*
£528 ($787)

10
**A mahogany longcase
clock,** 3rd quarter 18th
cent, silvered dial signed
'Jno. Legg, Bletchingly',
eight-day movement
with rack striking on a
bell, 237cm (7ft 9½in),
P 11-18 Dec,
£1,375 ($1,647)

11
**A walnut month longcase
clock,** *c* 1750, the dial
signed 'Hines
Needham', strike/silent
at III and a lunar dial,
the five-pillar movement
with two five-wheel trains
and half-hour striking,
cresting reduced, 239cm,
(7ft 10in), *L 26 July,*
£5,060 ($6,755)

1　　2　　3　　4

5　　6　　7

8　　9　　10　　11

1
A George III carved and inlaid mahogany longcase clock, last quarter 18th cent, the painted dial with floral spandrels, 234cm (7ft 8in), *NY 20 Oct,* $4,400 (£3,697)

2
A George III Scottish mahogany longcase clock, the dial signed 'John Peatt Crieff', with rack-striking movement, 208cm (6ft 10in), *L 7 June,* £1,650 ($2,393)

3
A mahogany longcase clock, early 19th cent, the painted dial signed 'Jno. Chivers, Maesteg', 211cm (6ft 11in), *P 16-23 Oct,* £660 ($825)

4
A mahogany regulator, *c.*1840, the silvered dial inscribed 'James Ritchie & Son, Edinburgh', brass cylindrical pendulum bob and weight, 199cm (6ft 6in), *P 16-23 Oct,* £1,815 ($2,269)

5
A mahogany longcase regulator, 2nd quarter 19th cent, the silvered dial signed 'Charles & Co., Liverpool', the movement with deadbeat escapement, 200cm (6ft 7in), *C 29 Mar,* £2,200 ($3,278)

6
A mahogany regulator clock, signed 'James McCabe Royal Exchange London', deadbeat move-ment, the pendulum with roller suspension and wood rod, 190cm (6ft 3in), *L 23 Feb,* £2,420 ($3,392)

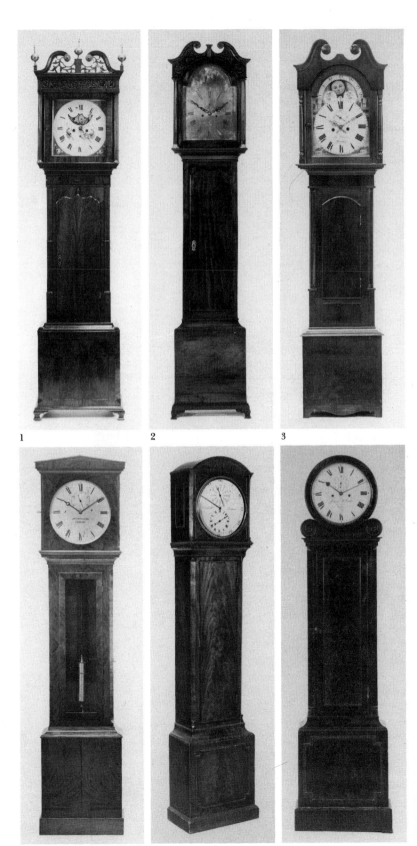

1   2   3

4   5   6

1
A George III mahogany
longcase clock, T
Bradford, London, 3rd
quarter 18th cent, 246cm
(8ft 1in), *NY 12-14 Apr,*
$3,080 (£2,154)

2
An oak and mahogany
longcase clock, with white
enamel dial, the case
with a verre eglomisé
panelled frieze, 229cm
(7ft 6in), *C 12 Jan,*
£748 ($1,085)

3
An oak and mahogany
longcase clock, early 19th
cent, the enamelled dial
signed 'Graham Cocker-
mouth', 220cm (7ft 2½in),
C 5 July,
£308 ($418)

4
A mahogany longcase clock,
2nd quarter 19th cent,
with enamel dial, the
movement with rack
striking, 231cm (7ft 7in),
C 12 Jan,
£770 ($1,117)

5
A Victorian mahogany
longcase clock, mid-19th
cent, with white enamel
dial signed 'Jn. Todd,
Dumfries', the movement
with deadbeat escapement,
rack striking on a bell,
C 4 Oct,
£506 ($653)

6
A mahogany longcase clock,
the dial with rococo
spandrels, a plaque
inscribed 'Tempus Fugit'
in the arch, 229cm
(7ft 6in), *L 1 Nov,*
£825 ($1,056)

7
A mahogany longcase
chiming regulator, 2nd
quarter 19th cent, the
enamel dial signed 'C. &
T. Hammond,
Manchester', the
movement with deadbeat
escapement, the pendulum
with wooden rod, 210cm
(6ft 10½in), *C 5 July,*
£990 ($1,343)

8
A mahogany regulator,
the silvered dial signed
'Brockbank & Atkins
London', the movement
with inner mahogany
case, the deadbeat
escapement with jewelled
pallets, mercury pen-
dulum with steel rod,
193cm (6ft 4in), *L 1 Nov,*
£9,900 ($12,672)

9
An Edwardian rosewood
and inlaid longcase clock,
the brass dial signed
'William Flint, Charing',
254cm (8ft 4in),
P 17-19 Apr,
£1,760 ($2,540)

10
A mahogany chiming
longcase clock, early 20th
cent, the brass dial
signed 'Russell's Ltd., 10
Exchange Street, Man-
chester', the massive
movement with deadbeat
escapement, 254cm
(8ft 4in), *C 12 Jan,*
£3,300 ($4,785)

11
A George III style
mahogany longcase clock,
20th cent, the three-train
movement with anchor
escapement and striking
on eight rods, 205cm
(6ft 10in), *C 30 Oct-2nd Nov,*
£352 ($450)

12
A late Victorian
mahogany chiming
longcase clock, *c* 1900, the
brass dial with a silvered
ring, 280cm (9ft 2in),
C 5 July,
£3,080 ($4,178)

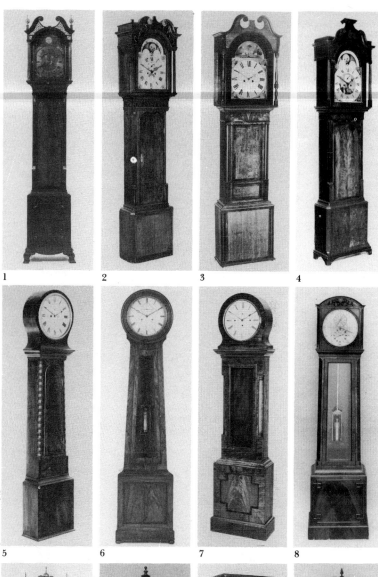

1 2 3 4

5 6 7 8

9 10 11 12

1

An ebony bracket clock,
last quarter 17th cent,
the square dial signed
'Charles Loundes Pall
Mall London', verge
movement with fitted
engraved backplate, the
moulded case mounted
with gilt-metal escutcheons,
33cm (13in), *NY 12-14 Apr,*
$9,900 (£6,923)

2

**An ebony-veneered
bracket clock,** *c* 1680, the
dial signed 'Joseph
Knibb Londini Fecit',
the movement with latched
dial and plates, with
restoration, 37cm (14½in),
L 26 July,
£4,950 ($6,608)

3

**An ebony quarter-striking
bracket clock,** the dial
signed 'Wm. Speakman
London', with later anchor
escapement, the case
with a gilt-metal basket
top pierced with figures
and scrollwork, 35.5cm
(14in), *L 7 June,*
£2,310 ($3,350)

4

**A small George I brass-
inlaid ebonised bracket
clock case,** the whole
outlined with gilt-brass
mouldings, with later
German silvered dial and
movement, 38cm (15in),
L 26 July,
£572 ($764)

5

**An ebony-veneered grande
sonnerie bracket clock,** the
dial signed 'Joseph
Knibb London', the
three-train movement
with latched dial, ten
vase-shaped pillars, and
outside count wheels,
with restoration, 33cm
(13in), *L 1 Nov,*
£12,100 ($15,488)

6

An ebonised bracket clock,
the dial signed 'Josiah
Emery London', the
movement with verge
escapement and engraved
backplate, the case
inlaid with gilt-brass
mouldings, 37cm
(14½in), *L 12 Apr,*
£3,300 ($4,762)

7

**A George I red lacquer
and gilt-decorated bracket
clock,** the silver dial
signed 'William Smith,
London', verge move-
ment, inverted bell-top,
48cm (19in), *NY 9 June,*
$3,080 (£2,216)

8

**A mahogany bracket
clock,** *c* 1790, signed
'John Johnson London',
the movement with later
anchor escapement, the
case veneered in richly
figured wood, 34.5cm
(13½in), *L 1 Nov,*
£2,200 ($2,816)

9

**A George III mahogany
bracket clock,** the
silvered dial inscribed
'R. Clarke, London', the
fusee movement with
verge escapement, bell-
top case, 59cm (23in),
P 17-19 Apr,
£1,430 ($2,063)

10

**A George III ebonised
bracket clock,** *c* 1780, the
dial signed 'Jno.
Waldron, Cornhill,
London', the movement
converted to anchor
escapement, 51cm (20in),
P 16-23 Oct,
£858 ($1,073)

11

**A George III fruitwood
bracket clock,** the fusee
movement with anchor
escapement, in an
inverted bell-top case,
signed William Gibbs,
47cm (18½in), *P 24-27 July,*
£528 ($705)

1

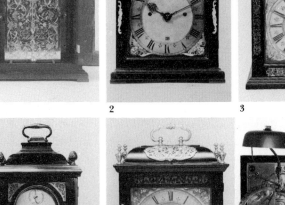

2

3

4

5

6

7

8

9

10

11

1
A George III ebonised
musical bracket clock, the
enamel dial signed
'Ranger London', gilt
hands, three-train move-
ment with twelve bells
and deadbeat escapement,
the arch painted with
automaton figures, the
case with elaborate gilt-
metal mounts, 66cm (26in),
L 12 Apr,
£7,700 ($11,111)

2
A George III mahogany
bracket clock, early 19th
cent, the brass dial
signed 'Richd. Gilkes,
Devizes', the two-train
movement with verge
escapement, the door
with spandrels below the
dial, 41cm (16in),
C 5 July,
£935 ($1,268)

3
A George III mahogany
bracket clock, late 18th
cent, the enamel dial
signed 'Tomlin Royal
Exchange London', the
repeating movement
with verge escapement,
33cm (13in), L 7 June,
£1,540 ($2,233)

4
An early George III
ebonised chiming bracket
clock, the dial signed
'Joseph Smith, Bristol',
the three-train movement
with verge escapement
and lenticular bob, the
case with urn finials and
brass frets, 61cm (24in),
L 1 Nov,
£2,310 ($2,957)

5
An Italian bracket clock,
c.1760, signed 'Gio.
Battista Alberici', verge
escapement, dial decorated
in gilt-metal with a
silver coat of arms, the
walnut case mounted in
gilt-brass, 51.5cm (20¼in),
F 10 May,
L 6,780,000 (£2,761;
$3,975)

6
A George III ebony
balloon mantel clock,
c.1800, the silvered dial
signed 'J. Leroux, London',
the fusee movement with
anchor escapement,
56cm (22in), P 16-23 Oct,
£1,430 ($1,788)

7
A Regency brass-mounted
mahogany mantel clock,
Row, Alton, 1st quarter
19th cent, painted dial,
with pendulum, key and
crank, 41cm (16¼in),
NY 20 Oct,
$825 (£693)

8
A late George III
mahogany bracket clock,
the white enamel dial
signed 'Grignon, London',
the fusee movement with
maintaining power, half
deadbeat escapement and
rise and fall regulation,
the case veneered and
inlaid with ebony stringing,
gilt-brass columns, 25cm
(10in), L 1 Nov,
£1,540 ($1,971)

9
A William IV bracket
clock, c.1830, the silvered
dial inscribed 'Wm.
Wilson, Southampton
Street, Strand', the fusee
movement with anchor
escapement and bell
strike, 30cm (12in),
P 11-18 Dec,
£935 ($1,120)

10
A mahogany wall clock,
the dial inscribed 'James
McCabe, London', the fusee
movement with bell
striking, the case with
brass scale frets on doors
and base, 58cm (23in),
P 21-24 Feb,
£484 ($679)

1

2

3

6

7

4   5

8   9   10

1
A mahogany hanging wall clock, 1st quarter 19th cent, the white enamel dial signed 'Smith & Son, Walton', the movement with anchor escapement and rack striking, lacking bell and weights, 163cm (5ft 4¾in), *C 29 Mar*, **£396 ($590)**

2
A japanned tavern clock, mid-18th cent, with black-painted wooden dial, the weight-driven movement with bell striking, the case signed 'Just Vulliamy', and with chinoiserie decoration, 145cm (57in), *P11-18 Dec*, **£1,045 ($1,252)**

3
A William IV mahogany bracket clock, 2nd quarter 19th cent, with white enamel dial, the movement with anchor escapement and bell striking, 42.5cm (16¾in), *C 4 Oct*, **£187 ($241)**

4
A Federal carved mahogany and verre eglomisé shelf clock, *c*1815, inscribed 'Aaron Willard Boston', with a dished white-painted dial, the panels painted in polychrome, the lower section with mirrorplate, lower panel cracked, 94cm (37in), *NY 30 June*, **$11,000 (£8,148)**

5
A brass-inlaid mahogany travelling or mantel clock, 1802, the engine-turned gilt dial with the repainted signature 'James McCabe Royal Exchange London 1802', a serpent framing the bezel, 24cm (9½in), *L 23 Feb*, **£2,200 ($3,084)**

6
A travelling clock, Vulliamy No. 887, *c*1880, with an arched dial chased with leaf scrolls and flowers, the movement with chain fusees, in a kingwood case, 19cm (7½in), *L 23 Feb*, **£5,720 ($8,019)**

7
A tortoiseshell and silver-mounted carriage clock, London, 1912, with white enamel dial, lever escapement and gong striking 22cm (8½in), *P 24-27 July*, **£798 ($1,065)**

8
A late Victorian ebonised chiming bracket clock, the silvered chapter ring inscribed 'Thompson, Ashford', the repeating three-train fusee movement chiming on eight bells and striking on a gong, 61cm (24in), *P 24-27 July*, **£792 ($1,057)**

9
A Federal bird's-eye maple inlaid cherrywood shelf clock, *c*1815, the dial inscribed 'Benjamin Morrill, Boscowen', 114cm (45in), *NY 30 June*, **$11,000 (£8,148)**

10
A walnut bracket clock, John Moore & Sons, Clerkenwell, London, *c*1840, the movement with quarter striking on nine bells, 61cm (24in), *L 26 July*, **£858 ($1,145)**

11
An ormolu Pendule d'Officier with grande sonnerie and alarum, the enamel dial signed 'Musy Pere et Fils Hgers. de S. A. Sme. A Turin', the case with a leaf-clasp handle, musical trophies at the sides, 21cm (8¼in), *L 12 Apr*, **£2,750 ($3,968)**

12
A silver and enamel quarter-repeating desk timepiece, the enamel dial with an inscribed surround, the case inlaid with guilloché purple enamel bordered in white and with an amethyst repeating button and onyx base, 8.5cm (3¼in), *L 23 Feb*, **£660 ($925)**

13
A gilt and silvered bronze Gothic cathedral clock, signed 'F. L. Hausburg A Paris', with Brocot escapement, 47cm (18½in), *L 1 Nov*, **£715 ($915)**

1   2   3   4

5   6   7

8   9   10

11   12   13

1

A George III silvered metal quarter-striking musical automaton clock for the Oriental market, signed 'Willm. Carpenter London', 96.5cm (38in), *G 13 Nov*, **SF 154,000 (£47,826; $64,087)**

2

A capucine, early 19th cent, the repeating movement with pull alarum, 27cm (10½in), *G 13 Nov*, **SF 4,400 (£1,366; $1,831)**

3

A silvered eight-day timepiece, in the form of a lighthouse, c1900, with double wheel duplex escapement, the movement mounted at the top of the tower, 25cm (9⅞in), *L 1 Nov*, **£495 ($634)**

4

A Comtoise clock, 18th cent, signed 'C. Noury A Quite Beuf, the movement with an anchor escapement, in a posted frame with turned finials, 41cm (16in), *G 13 Nov*, **SF 2,420 (£752; $1,008)**

5

A very small gold and enamel clock, London, 1953, the dial set in a diamond-shaped case inlaid with enamel, 2.4 x 3.9cm (⅞ x 1½in), *L 26 July*, **£605 ($808)**

6

A German alarum timepiece, 18th cent, the silvered brass dial chased with shellwork and scrolls, the movement with verge escapement and visible pendulum, 18cm (7in), *G 13 Nov*, **SF 2,860 (£888; $1,190)**

7

An English brass skeleton clock, late 19th cent, 29.5cm (11⅝in), *F 19 Dec*, **L 1,300,000 (£549; $687)**

8

A Swiss steel-framed wheel cutting engine, 19th cent, stamped on the hand counter wheel 'Paul Odobey A Morez (Jura)', with brass dividing disk, *L 12 Apr*, **£2,310 ($3,333)**

9

A skeleton clock, c1850, signed 'Litherland Davies & Co. Liverpool', 44.5cm (17½in), *L 7 June*, **£2,640 ($3,828)**

10

A gilt-brass timepiece, c1860-4, the backplate signed 'Thos. Cole, London', the silvered dial inscribed 'London & Ryder, 17 New Bond St.', the engraved base with Fahrenheit thermometer and aneroid barometer, 51cm (20in), *P 17-19 Apr*, **£3,080 ($4,444)**

11

A lantern clock, the dial signed 'W. Rayment Stow Markett' and engraved with acanthus scrolls, 41cm (17in), *L 1 Nov*, **£1,760 ($2,253)**

12

A brass lantern clock, c1860, 46.5cm (18¼in), *L 26 July*, **£682 ($910)**

13

An alarum lantern timepiece, late 17 cent, 23.5cm (9¼in), *L 1 Nov*, **£1,320 ($1,690)**

14

A French gilt-metal hexagonal clock case, 1st half 16th cent, the sides engraved with the planets, an engraved allegorical figure of the moon below the fixed dial, removable bell cover, 14.5cm (5¾in), *L 26 July*, **£2,860 ($3,818)**

15

A skeleton clock, with a silvered chapter ring, the movement with chain fusees, anchor escapement, 48cm (19in), *L 26 July*, **£1,100 ($1,469)**

16

A gilt-metal hexagonal rack-striking table clock, c1730, signed 'Christian Minepott, Dorpat', d of chapter ring 11.1cm (4⅜in), *L 23 Feb*, **£2,420 ($3,393)**

17

A gilt-metal striking automaton clock, c1620, some restoration, 33.8cm (13⅜in), *L 12 Apr*, **£12,100 ($17,424)**

1 2 3 4

5 6 7

8 9 10

11 12 13 14

15 16 17

Carriage Clocks

JOHN VAUGHAN

For a clock to work while being moved it must be spring-driven, not weight-driven. Similarly it must be controlled by a balance and not a pendulum. The story of the travelling clock as we know it begins soon after the invention of the balance spring in about 1680, some 20 years behind the pendulum. But early examples are extremely rare; travelling clocks were not made in any numbers before the late 18th century and then mainly in France and Germany. A distinctive French type is known as the *pendule d'officier,* though such clocks were no doubt also used by civilians. They have gilt-metal cases applied with leaves and flowerheads, and enamel dials. German ones are usually in rectangular cases with arched tops, often engraved with leaves and flowers.

In the early 19th century Abraham Louis Breguet, the greatest horologist the world has known, made a few carriage clocks, from which the standard type with glazed rectangular cases evolved. But Breguet's were normally in silver, and fitted with complicated striking, repeating and calendar work.

In the great age of the carriage clock, from about 1830 to the First World War, France was the main centre. The movements, or *ébauches,* were made in a few factories, and then finished to varying standards by different makers. Paul Garnier was the best known early maker; Drocourt, Jacot, Margaine and Richard are famous later names. These manufacturers normally stamped the movements of their clocks (frequently hidden in Jacot's case) and the dials are usually signed by the retailer or not at all. Thus many French clocks bear English names, and they were exported all over the world including Russia, South America and China.

Most carriage clocks strike the hours and half hours, and can repeat the last hour at will. Quarter-striking and grande sonnerie clocks are much rarer. With grande sonnerie clocks the quarters and the last hour are sounded every quarter; such clocks usually have a control in the base for full striking, quarters only or silence. At the other end of the scale some non-repeating clocks were made, and numerous timepieces, as non-striking clocks are termed. Alarums are frequently fitted to all types, but calendar work is seldom found. Gongs replaced bells in about 1860. Most French carriage clocks are between 4½in and 6in high; a fair number of much smaller timepieces, about 3in in height were made and are much more valuable than their normal-sized brethren. Larger clocks, up to 9in high, are very much rarer.

The standard rectangular case comes in various styles, of which the best is the gorge, recognized by the more elaborate mouldings; fluted corner columns found, and occasionally triangular pediments. Examples with chased cases, often in rococo style, were probably made more as portable than travelling clocks. In better examples the cases may be engraved or inlaid with enamel. Enamel or porcelain in place of the normal glazed panels is a sign of high quality, and such clocks are prized, especially when the movement has unusual features. In such clocks it is particularly unusual to find the back and top panels, as well as the dial and sides, in porcelain or enamel. In plainer examples, the normal rectangular white enamel dial is often replaced by a circular dial within an engine-turned or sanded metal surround; this in turn may be overlaid by decorative filigree panels.

While French carriage clocks were mass produced—to an extremely high standard—English ones were made in very small numbers, mainly by first class makers such as Dent, Frodsham and McCabe. Their rarity ensures high prices.

1
A small oval carriage timepiece, late 19th cent, 9.5cm (3¾in), *C 5 July,* £253 ($343)

2
A French carriage clock, mid-19th cent, the dial signed 'E, Dent, Paris', 14.5cm (5¾in), *C 29 Mar,* £770 ($1,147)

3
A repeating carriage clock, the dial signed 'Edward Bright, Brighton', *P 11-18 Dec,* £528 ($633)

4
A repeating alarm carriage clock, Soldano, the platform stamped 'J.S.', in a lacquered brass case, *P 11-18 Dec,* £385 ($461)

5
A five-minute repeating alarm carriage clock, by Margaine, 19cm (7½in), *P 24-27 July,* £770 ($1,028)

6
A grand sonnerie carriage clock, Drocourt, the dial signed 'Elkington, London', 18cm (7in), *P 16-23 Oct,* £968 ($1,210)

7
A brass repeating carriage clock, 3rd quarter 19th cent, the escapement later, 18.5cm (7¼in), *C 12 Jan,* £308 ($447)

8
A small English carriage clock, c.1840, 15cm (6in), *L 1 Nov,* £3,080 ($3,942)

1   2   3   4

5   6   7   8

1
An alarum carriage clock, the dial signed 'Musy Pere & Fils à Turin', within an engraved gilt surround, 13.5cm (5½in), *L 1 Nov,* £825 ($1,056)

2
An English carriage clock, Dent, No. 17904, *c* 1855-60, the dial signed 'Dent 33 Cockspur St. London', 21cm (8¼in), *L 1 Nov,* £4,620 ($5,914)

3
An English quarter-striking carriage clock, signed 'James McCabe Royal Exchange London', 23.5cm (9¼in) *L 23 Feb,* £11,550 ($16,193)

4
An alarum carriage clock, the dial signed 'Bolviller A Paris', with sprays of pink roses in the corners, 18cm (7in), *L 23 Feb,* £770 ($1,080)

5
An English carriage clock, the dial signed 'E. White 20 Cockspur St. London', 21.5cm (8½in), *L 26 July,* £2,870 ($3,832)

6
A grande sonnerie carriage clock, the repeating lever movement with the stamp of Henri Jacot, 17.5cm (7in), *L 7 June,* £990 ($1,436)

7
A grande sonnerie alarum carriage clock, the dial signed 'Le Roy & Fils Pals. Royal Gie. Montpensier 13-15 Paris' and '296 Regent St. London', 14.5cm (5¾in), *L 7 June,* £1,100 ($1,595)

8
A grande sonnerie carriage clock, the backplate and base plate with the stamp of Achille Brocot, 14.5cm (5¾in), *L 7 June,* £990 ($1,436)

9
A silver calendar carriage clock, signed 'Jump London', the case by Anthony Charles Jones, 1886, the engine-turned silver dial with gold Breguet hands, 16cm (6¼in), *L 12 Apr,* £18,700 ($26,984)

10
An enamel-mounted carriage clock, the dial signed 'J. Aitchison Paris', lever movement with gong striking, the backplate with the stamp of Maurice et Cie, 16.5cm (6½in), *SF 2,420 (£752; $1,007)*

11
A small enamel-mounted oval carriage clock, the dial, sides and back with polychrome enamel decoration, later lever platform, the moulded oval case signed 'Gve. Sandoz 147 Palais Royal', 9.5cm (3¾in), *G 13 Nov,* SF 3,080 (£957; $1,282)

12
An enamel-mounted carriage clock, 20th cent, the carrying handle and frame enamelled with red, green and yellow blossoms against a lapis-coloured ground, with key, 20cm (8in), *NY 16 June,* $1,540 (£1,124)

13
A porcelain-mounted repeating carriage clock, late 19th cent, the front and sides mounted with bleu céleste and gilt porcelain panels painted with scenes after Watteau, 15cm (5⅞in), *NY 4 June,* $3,025 (£2,257)

14
An enamel-mounted petite sonnerie repeating carriage clock with alarum, *c* 1900, with white enamel dial, decorated overall with multi-colour champlevé enamel, 15.2cm (6in), *NY 4 June,* $3,850 (£2,873)

15
A small gilt-metal repeating grande sonnerie carriage clock with alarum, Jacot, *c* 1900, retailed by Klaftenberger, 57 Regent St & Paris, 10.4cm (4⅛in), *NY 4 June,* $1,870 (£1,396)

1
A late Louis XIV ormolu-mounted marquetry bracket clock, with engraved gilt-bronze dial, the movement signed 'André Hory à Paris', 81cm (32in), *M 24/25 June*, **FF 66,600 (£5,717; $7,789)**

2
A Louis XV ormolu-mounted green horn bracket clock, mid-18th cent, the case and bracket stamped 'Marchand, JME', the dial signed 'Le Pers A Paris', 133cm (4ft 4½in), *NY 17 Nov*, **$11,000 (£8,800)**

3
A Louis XV ormolu cartel clock, mid-18th cent, with a white enamel dial, two-train movement, 81.5cm (32in), *NY 13 Oct*, **$6,325 (£5,184)**

4
A Louis XV ormolu and patinated bronze musical mantel clock, the dial and movement signed 'Gille Laîné à Paris', within an ormolu case raised on a bronze rhinoceros, 92cm (36¼in), *M 25/26 June*, **FF 1,110,000 (£95,279; $129,825)**

5
A Louis XV ormolu and bronze elephant mantel clock, mid-18th cent, with white enamel dial and two-train movement, 53cm (20¾in), *NY 4 May*, **$13,200 (£9,429)**

6
A Louis XV boulle bracket clock and bracket, *c*1750, the enamel dial signed 'François Béliard A Paris', the movement with verge escapement and outside count wheel, 127cm (4ft 2in), *L 6 July*, **£4,950 ($6,831)**

7
A French boulle bracket clock, 2nd quarter 18th cent, with gilt dial, the movement with anchor escapement signed 'Gaudron, Paris', distressed, *C 29 Mar*, **£1,375 ($2,049)**

8
An early Louis XV quarter-repeating boulle bracket clock and bracket, *c*1730, the dial signed 'Art. Baillon A Paris', the movement with altered anchor escapement and outside numbered count wheel, 63.5cm (25in), *L 6 July*, **£1,210 ($1,670)**

9
A late Louis XV gilt-bronze wall clock, *c*1770, the enamel dial signed 'Coeur A Paris', with outside count wheel and altered anchor escapement, 137cm (54in), *L 6 July*, **£13,200 ($18,216)**

10
A Louis XVI ormolu-mounted red lacquer mantel clock, decorated in chinoiserie, the case stamped 'J. Jollain', 80cm (31½in), *M 24/25 June*, **FF 233,100 (£20,009; $27,263)**

11
A Louis XVI ormolu and marble mantel clock, last quarter 18th cent, the movement striking the hour and half hour, within a drum-shaped case beneath a veined grey and white marble cornice, 42cm (16½in), *NY 17 Nov*, **$3,300 (£2,640)**

12
A Louis XVI ormolu cartel clock, with enamel dial, the movement with square plates, anchor escapement and outside count wheel, 84cm (33in), *L 23-30 Nov*, **£1,375 ($1,660)**

1
A Louis XVI ormolu-mounted Sèvres porcelain lyre clock, last quarter 18th cent, with white enamel chapter ring, the movement framed by a gros bleu Sèvres porcelain frame, 61cm (24in), *NY 17 Nov*, $11,000 (£8,800)

2
A Louis XV/XVI ormolu and bronze mantel clock, 3rd quarter 18th cent, the white enamel dial inscribed 'Julien Le Roy', the movement with outside count wheel, flanked by the seated bronze figure of Urania, Muse of Astronomy, 36cm (14¼in), *NY 17 Nov*, $3,300 (£2,640)

3
A French gilt-bronze and mahogany portico mantel clock, c 1830, 61cm (24in), *NY 24/25 Feb*, $770 (£531)

4
A Restauration white marble and gilt-bronze mantel clock, c 1820, the enamel dial with gilt hands and a border of dark blue stars, the movement signed 'Dubois A Paris', 43cm (17in), *L 6 July*, £825 ($1,139)

5
A Restauration gilt-bronze mantel clock, c 1825, the enamel dial signed 'Lepine Hr. du Roi', the movement with outside count wheel, the case surmounted by a bust of Henri IV, pendulum lacking, 79cm (31in), *L 23-30 Nov*, £990 ($1,195)

6
A gilt and patinated bronze mantel clock, c 1830, with silvered dial, the movement with outside count wheel, set in a rock surmounted by a woman on horseback, 58cm (23in), *L 12 Apr*, £440 ($635)

7
A small bronze and gilt-bronze mantel timepiece, early 19th cent, the enamel dial signed 'Louis Habram À Montbrison', contained in a basket of fruit held in the mouth of a bronze mastiff, watch replaced, 9.5cm (3¾in), *L 6 July*, £2,640 ($3,643)

8
A Restauration bronze and gilt-bronze clock garniture, c 1825, with enamel dial and gilt hands, the movement with silk suspension and outside count wheel, the case supported by a blackamoor girl; with a pair of two-light candelabra, all 43cm (17in), *L 6 July*, £8,250 ($11,385)

9
A Second Empire bronze and ormolu mantel clock, with silvered dial, the movement with 'cherub on a swing' pendulum and outside count wheel, 35cm (14in), *L 1 Nov*, £682 ($873)

10
A Charles X gilt-bronze mantel clock, c 1825, the movement with silk suspension, 47cm (18½in), *C 5 July*, £682 ($925)

11
An Austrian neoclassical painted and parcel-gilt wall clock, 1st quarter 19th cent, with white enamel dial, the movement surmounted by a spread-winged gilt-wood eagle holding green-painted drapery highlighted with gilding, 96.5cm (38in), *NY 7 Apr*, $5,500 (£3,846)

1   2   3

4   5   6

7   8

9   10   11

1
A Napoleon III bronze
and marble mantel clock,
3rd quarter 19th cent,
the clock with gilt dial,
the group representing
Cupid and Psyche, 71cm
(28in), *NY 16 June,*
$1,760 (£1,285)

2
An Empire clock
garniture, *c*1815, in bronze,
gilt-bronze and griotte
marble, the clock with
engine-turned dial
signed 'Chale & Cie, rue
du Richelieu No 89', the
case with figures of
Cupid and Psyche, 67cm
(2ft 2½in), the candelabra
78cm (2ft 6in), *L 23-30 Nov,*
£3,300 ($3,985)

3
A 'Vienna' mantel clock,
late 19th cent, the
rectangular case painted
by various artists, signed,
minor chips to the
enamel dial, 45.7cm (18in),
NY 24/25 Feb,
$2,750 (£1,896)

4
A gilt-bronze mantel clock,
*c*1880, the dial signed 'F.
Barbedienne Paris',
72cm (28½in), *L 8 June,*
£1,650 ($2,393)

5
A gilt-bronze mantel clock,
*c*1880, the dial signed
'Barbedienne Paris', with
pendulum, 58cm (23in),
L 9 Nov,
£968 ($1,287)

6
A Louis XVI-style gilt-
bronze cartel clock,
French, late 19th cent,
the enamel dial signed
'Bouquet/A Paris', 72cm
(28½in), *NY 24/25 Feb,*
$990 (£683)

7
A French earthenware
mantel clock, late 19th
cent, with porcelain dial,
the movement with
anchor escapement, within
a cobalt-blue and gilt
enamelled case, painted
with a bust of a woman,
signed 'Cotti', 35.5cm
(13in), *C 2-5 Oct,*
£264 ($341)

8
A gilt-brass and porcelain-
mounted mantel clock,
3rd quarter 19th cent,
the dial signed 'John
Hall, Paris', the movement
with anchor escapement,
the case applied with
cobalt-blue porcelain
painted panels, 34cm
(13½in), *C 2-5 Oct,*
£374 ($482)

9
A French enamel-mounted
gilt-bronze mantel clock,
*c*1900, retailed by
Tiffany & Co, with
bevelled curved glass
panels, the enamel in
bright colours on a blue
ground, mercury
pendulum, 47cm (18½in),
NY 24/25 Feb,
$1,650 (£1,138)

10
A French onyx mantel
clock, late 19th cent, the
green onyx case sur-
mounted by the figure of
a putto and applied with
gilt mounts, worn, 62.5cm
(24½in), *NY 24/25 Feb,*
$1,320 (£910)

11
A Louis XVI-style parcel-
gilt bronze and marble
mantel clock, late 19th
cent, formed as a figure
of Cupid, the dial
inscribed 'Robin Hger
du Roy/a Paris', the
movement impressed
'Etienne Maxant/
Breveté/Paris', 57cm
(22½in), *NY 16 June,*
$2,750 (£2,007)

1

2

3

4

5

6

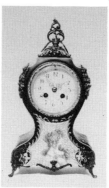

7

8

9

10

11

1

An ormolu, bronze and marble mantel clock, 3rd quarter 19th cent, the enamel dial inscribed 'Lepaute Hger, Du Roy, a Paris', the movement with outside count wheel, 46cm (18in), *C 27-30 Mar,* £462 ($688)

2

A gilt-bronze mantel clock, *c* 1860, with white enamel dial, the Japy movement with outside count wheel, 41cm (16in), *C 2-5 Oct,* £396 ($511)

3

A French gilt-bronze mantel clock, *c* 1850, the movement with silk suspension and outside count wheel, signed 'Japy Freres', 60cm (23½in), *L 8 June,* £1,650 ($2,393)

4

A Louis XVI-style gilt-bronze and marble mantel clock, French, late 19th cent, the white marble case set with two putti, 50cm (19½in), *NY 24/25 Feb,* $1,100 (£758)

5

A French gilt-bronze mantel clock, by Raingo Frères, *c* 1870 with signed enamel dial and a drum case surmounted and flanked by cherubs, 50cm (19¾in), *L 12 Apr,* £1,045 ($1,508)

6

A French bronze mantel clock, *c* 1860, the dial signed 'Victor Paillard F. Cant de Bronzes Paris', the case flanked by a figure of a cupid holding a hammer, 75cm (29½in), *L 9 Nov,* £1,210 ($1,609)

7

A gilt-bronze and porcelain mantel clock, *c* 1860, the dial painted with a cherub and signed 'Deniere Rue Vivienne 15 Paris', the case with 'jewelled Sèvres' porcelain decoration, 51cm (20in), *L 9 Mar,* £3,520 ($5,248)

8

A cloisonné enamel and gilt-bronze XV-style clock garniture, French, late 19th cent, retailed by Overstrijd, Rotterdam, the clock with a cloisonné enamel dial, the candelabra with cloisonné enamelled candle holders, candelabra 57cm (22½in), *NY 16 June,* $1,540 (£1,124)

9

A bronze mystérieuse mantel clock, 1873, cast with a figure by Jules Lafrance, the dial above an adjustable pendulum, and leaf-cast bob, the base signed 'J. Lafrance, Roma', 67cm (26¼in), *L 9 Mar,* £1,155 ($1,722)

10

A gilt-bronze and 'Sèvres' porcelain mantel clock, *c* 1860, the dial painted with flowers, the case surmounted by a 'jewelled urn, 41cm (16in), *L 8 June,* £902 ($1,308)

11

A Louis XIV-style boulle marquetry barometer, mid-19th cent, the ormolu dial with white enamel reserves centred by an ormolu head, surmounted by a figure of Vanity, the pedestal veneered with brass on blue tortoiseshell ground, 115cm (45in), *NY 16 June,* $2,200 (£1,606)

1

2

3

4

5

6

7

8

9

10

11

1
A Louis XVI-style gilt-bronze and marble three-piece clock garniture, French, late 19th cent, the enamel dial signed 'Susse Frères Paris', clock 44.5cm (17½in), *NY 16 June*, $1,760 (£1,285)

2
A gilt-bronze and porcelain clock garniture, c1870, the dial painted with two cherubs on a dark blue ground above a group of a woman and a cupid, the pair of candelabra each with an urn supporting five nozzles, clock 51cm (20in), *L 9 Nov*, £3,740 ($4,974)

3
A French 'Sèvres' and gilt-bronze clock garniture, late 19th cent, the dial signed 'Monbro Fils Aine/A Paris/Jacquier H.ER.', the vases with portraits on a bleu-céleste ground, clock 48cm (19in), *NY 24/25 Feb*, $3,300 (£2,276)

4
A French gilt-bronze and red marble clock garniture, late 19th cent, the clock and two urns of red marble mounted with elaborate neoclassical motifs, 79cm (31in), *NY 24/25 Feb*, $3,300 (£2,276)

5
A French gilt-bronze and marble clock garniture, late 19th cent, retailed by Tiffany & Co, the drum case delicately painted with floral festoons, one nozzle lacking, candelabra 49cm (19¼in), *NY 24/25 Feb*, $3,080 (£2,124)

6
A gilt and patinated bronze clock garniture, c1860, the dial with indistinct signature, in a fluted case with two doves and a cupid, clock 51cm (20in), *L 8 June*, £2,090 ($3,031)

7
A bronze, gilt-bronze and marble clock garniture, late 19th cent, the clock dial inscribed 'Robin H.ger du Roy', the whole mounted on white marble, clock 54cm (21¼in), *F 10 May*, **L 13,560,000 (£5,523; $7,953)**

8
A French gilt-brass clock garniture, late 19th cent, with two three-light candelabra, clock 38cm (15in), *C 4 Oct*, £396 ($511)

9
An ebonised wood and gilt-bronze bracket clock, by Winterhalder and Hoffmeir, c1880, with silvered dial, the movement chiming on five gongs, 69cm (27¼in), *L 12 Apr*, £396 ($571)

10
A French boulle bracket clock, c1870, the movement with outside count wheel, stamped 'Japy Frères', the case inlaid with cut brass on a red tortoiseshell ground, 75cm (29½in), *L 9 Nov*, £770 ($1,024)

11
A neoclassical gilt-bronze and marble mantel clock, c1900, the white dial set within a lyre case supporting a pendulum studded with brilliants, 58cm (23in), *NY 3 Nov*, $1,430 (£1,144)

12
A French two-dialled display regulator, the clock forming the pendulum bob, the enamel dials with Breguet hands and moulded concave brass bezels, the whole suspended from a brass bracket fixed to the top of the later glazed oak case, 145cm (4ft 9in), *L 23 Feb*, £3,190 ($4,472)

1

2

3

4

5

6

7

8

9

10

11

12

1
A silver verge oignon, by
Martinot, Paris, early
18th cent, the balance
bridge with a poly-
chrome enamel of
Cleopatra and the asp,
silver case, restored,
d 5.7cm (2¼in),
SF 12,100 (£3,758; $5,035)

2
A gilt-metal and enamel
watch, by Baltazar
Martinot, Paris, 18th
cent, gilt dial, the case
enamelled with a poly-
chrome miniature, signed
'Mussard pinxit',
d 5.6cm (2¼in), G 13 Nov,
SF 7,150 (£2,220; $2,975)

3
A gold cylinder watch,
George Graham, the
gold champlevé dial
signed 'Graham,
London', casemaker's
initials 'WS', hallmarked
1728, d 4.6cm (1¾in),
L 26 July,
£2,640 ($3,524)

4
A silver pair cased verge
watch, early 18th cent,
signed on the backplate
'T. Tompion E. Banger,
London', silver
champlevé dial, the
inner case lacking the
winding shutter, the
outer slightly bruised,
d 5.5cm (2⅛in), L 23 Feb,
£1,210 ($1,696)

5
A silver cased sun and
moon verge watch, by Jan
Gobels, Amsterdam,
18th cent, silver
champlevé dial, d 5.8cm
(2½in), L 26 July,
£2,640 ($3,524)

6
A repoussé gold pair cased
verge watch, by Harry
Potter, London, the
inner case plain,
hallmarked 1780, the
repoussé outer overlaid
in high relief, 5.3cm
(2in), L 12 Apr,
£1,430 ($2,063)

7
A repoussé gold pair cased
verge watch, by Ellicott,
1762, the outer case
repoussé with a scene of
Diana and Endymion,
both cases initialled
'HT', the outer signed
'G. M. Moser F.', d 4.9cm
(2in), L 1 Nov,
£2,860 ($3,661)

8
A repoussé gold pair case
quarter-repeating verge
watch, by Charles Clay
of London, 1734, later
white dial, the outer case
pierced and repoussé,
signed 'Parbury', both
cases with casemaker's
stamp 'IB', d 5cm (2in),
L 26 July,
£1,870 ($2,496)

9
A silver-gilt pair cased
verge watch, signed
'Willm. Downham,
London', outer case
hallmarked 1778, d 5cm
(2in), C 12 Jan,
£143 ($207)

10
An English silver-gilt pair
cased verge watch, signed
'Wm. Howard, London',
d 4.7cm (1⅞in),
P 17-19 Apr,
£154 ($222)

11
A gold and enamel verge
watch, by Les Frères
Armand of Nismes, mid-
18th cent, signed, d 4.7cm
(1⅞in), G 13 Nov,
SF 12,100 (£3,758; $5,035)

12
A gold and enamel verge
watch, c 1770, d 4.3cm
(1⅝in), G 13 Nov,
SF 7,150 (£2,220; $2,975)

13
A gold and enamel verge
watch, by Charles Le
Roy, Paris, c 1770, d 4.7cm
(1⅞in), G 13 Nov,
SF 12,100 (£3,758; $5,035)

14
A gold and enamel dumb
quarter-repeating verge
watch, by Champion,
Paris, hallmarked 1777,
the back of translucent
blue enamel over
guilloché, d 4cm (1½in),
L 12 Apr,
£1,760 ($2,540)

15
A gold, enamel and split-
pearl set verge watch, by
Thomas Gray of
Sackville Street, c 1780,
the covers set with split
pearls, the back of dark
blue enamel over
guilloché, d 4.7cm
(1¾in), L 12 Apr,
£3,080 ($4,444)

1
A gold and enamel verge
watch, c.1800, signed
'Breguet a Paris', the
back cover with a poly-
chrome enamel miniature,
chipped, overall 8.6cm
(3¼in), L 23 Feb,
£4,620 ($6,477)

2
A silver-gilt cartouche-
shaped snuff box, c.1740,
containing a verge
movement signed 'Pere
Bion, London', silver
champlevé dial, 7.9cm
(3⅛in), L 1 Nov,
£1,320 ($1,689)

3
A gilt-metal pair cased
striking cylinder chaise
watch, by Marriott,
London, late 18th cent,
the back with a
polychrome enamel
pastoral scene,
cracked, d 13.2cm (5⅛in),
L 7 June,
£2,420 ($3,509)

4
A gilt-metal quarter-
repeating verge
movement, by Masmejan
& Sandoz, Lausanne,
mid-18th cent, possibly
for a table clock, white
enamel dial, signed on
the reverse 'Foltier a
Geneve', in circular
brass case, the band
fishskin, d 9.5cm (3¾in),
L 1 Nov,
£1,210 ($1,549)

5
A silver-gilt, enamel and
pearl-set centre seconds
Chinese duplex watch,
early 19th cent, some
restoration, d 5.6cm
(2¼in), L 1 Nov,
£2,090 ($2,675)

6
A gold, enamel and pearl
open faced jump seconds
Chinese duplex watch, by
Vaucher of Fleurier,
c.1820, for the Oriental
market, NY 24 Oct,
$7,975 (£6,537)

7
A silver-gilt pocket
chronometer, No. 1760 by
J R Arnold, originally
with amplitude limiting
device, case hallmarked
1800, d 5.4cm (2⅛in),
L 12 Apr,
£2,310 ($3,333)

8
A gold open faced pocket
chronometer, Murray &
Strachan, Royal
Exchange, London, the
movement with
Earnshaw spring detent
escapement, case hall-
marked 1861, d 5.7cm
(2¼in), L 23 Feb,
£1,430 ($2,005)

9
A silver pocket
chronometer, No. 1692 by
John Roger Arnold,
1797, signed on the
backplate, d 5.3cm (2in),
L 1 Nov,
£4,620 ($5,914)

10
A Lepine calibre quarter-
repeating ruby cylinder
watch, No. 1004 by
Breguet, with early form
of parachute suspension,
the reverse of the dial
signed 'Borel', casemaker's
punch 'PBT, d 5.6cm
(2¼in), G 13 Nov,
SF 15,400 (£4,783; $6,409)

11
Breguet et Fils, a gold
oval ring thermometer,
gold engine-turned dial,
2.9cm (1⅛in), G 13 Nov,
SF 10,450 (£3,245; $4,349)

12
A silver-gilt quarter-
repeating automaton
watch, c.1830, signed
'Piguet & Meyland a
Geneve', d 5.4cm (2⅛in),
L 23 Feb,
£1,540 ($2,159)

13
A gold quarter-repeating
automaton watch, c.1820,
the centre with two putti
in three-colour gold
d 5.5cm (2⅛in), L 7 June,
£3,080 ($4,466)

14
A gold quarter-repeating
automaton watch, by
Frederick Perret, c.1800,
ruby endstone, the white
enamel chapter ring
with multi-coloured gold
figures of Father Time
and History against a
skeletonized plate,
signed, d 6cm (2¼in),
NY 4 June,
$4,400 (£3,284)

15
A gold quarter-repeating
musical watch, c.1820,
6cm (2⅜in), L 23 Feb,
£2,420 ($3,393)

1

2

3

4

5

6

7

8

9

10

11

12

13

14

15

1
A gold cased bras-en-l'air, by Frères Veigneur, Geneva, c.1800, with verge escapement, white enamel dial with arabic numerals in two sectors indicated by the raised arms of a gilt figure, his left arm restored, d 5.4cm (2⅛in), L 26 July, £5,720 ($7,636)

2
A quarter-repeating silver cased pocket watch, No. 1461 by James Tregent, the case hallmarked 1781, P 24-27 July, £319 ($426)

3
A gold open faced pocket watch, by Bracebridge's of London, the case hallmarked 1825, d 4.8cm (1⅞in), P 17-19 Apr, £242 ($349)

4
A gold and enamel duplex watch, B L Vulliamy, 1853, the case decorated with blue, red and black champlevé enamel, d 4.1cm (1½in), L 12 Apr, £1,980 ($2,857)

5
A gold hunting cased duplex watch, by Tolkien & Gravell, hallmarked 1813, P 24-27 July, £462 ($617)

6
A cast gold cylinder watch, by Rundell, Bridge & Rundell, Ludgate Hill, London, later hands, the case decorated with three-colour gold heightened with turquoise and garnets, hallmarked 1817, d 4.4cm (1¾in), L 12 Apr, £1,760 ($2,540)

7
A gold hunting cased half-quarter repeating watch, No. 7186 by James McCabe, Royal Exchange, the movement now with lever escapement, the case hallmarked 1811, d 6.3cm (2½in), L 7 June, £1,320 ($1,914)

8
A gold and enamel open faced watch with eccentric dial, by Leroy & Fils of Paris, c.1840, full plate gilt movement, engine-turned silvered dial, d 4.2cm (1⅝in), NY 4 June, $660 (£493)

9
A small gold cylinder watch, by Charles Oudin et Fils of Palais Royal, 19th cent, signed, silver dial, the centre with engraved decoration, the case engraved overall, d 2.1cm (⅞in), L 23 Feb, £396 ($555)

10
A gold Massey crank roller lever watch, by Lewis Owen of Montgomery, c.1830, the movement with Liverpool jewelling, the dial surrounded by three-colour gold cast decoration, back engine-turned, d 5.1cm (2in), L 26 July, £550 ($734)

11
A gold Massey crank roller lever watch, by S I Tobias & Co, Liverpool, c.1820, d 5.1cm (2in), L 23 Feb, £550 ($771)

12
A gold half-hunting cased lever watch, No. 1269 by W G Hallet, Hastings, the case hallmarked 1867, subsidiary seconds dial and up-and-down below XII, d 4.3cm (1⅝in), L 12 Apr, £495 ($713)

13
A gold hunting cased lever watch with divided lift, 1842, probably by J F Cole, the movement with reversed fusee, the cuvette signed 'Mortimer & Hunt, New Bond Street, London', casemaker's intials 'IJ' for John Jackson of Clerkenwell, d 4.1cm (1½in), L 1 Nov, £825 ($1,056)

14
An early gold hunting cased watch, No. 4755, by A. Lange of Dresden, c.1870, case with maker's mark 'EL&Co,' d 5.5cm (2⅛in), NY 4 June, $1,980 (£1,478)

1
A gold hunting case
keyless lever chronograph,
by Vacheron &
Constantin, Geneva,
c 1900, d 5.3cm (2⅛ in),
NY 14 Feb,
$1,650 (£1,162)

2
A yellow gold half-hunting
cased keyless lever
chronograph, No. 07635
by Charles Frodsham,
the case hallmarked
London, 1889 *P 24-27 July*,
£418 ($558)

3
A gold hunting cased
quarter-repeating
automaton watch, c 1900,
d 5.3cm (2⅛ in),
NY 4 June,
$2,750 (£2,052)

4
A gold hunting cased
minute-repeating watch,
No. 14617 Jules
Jurgensen of
Copenhagen, c 1886,
d 5.1cm (2in),
NY 4 June,
$7,425 (£5,541)

5
A gold hunting cased
minute-repeating keyless
lever watch, by S J Rood &
Co, London, the case
hallmarked 1889, d 5.3cm
(2in), *L 7 June*,
£1,980 ($2,871)

6
A gold hunting case
minute-repeating
chronograph, by
Longines, c 1910, d 5.3cm
(2⅛ in), *NY 4 June*,
$3,575 (£2,668)

7
A gold open faced two-
train five-minute repeating
watch, No. 97802 by
Patek Philippe & Co,
retailed by Tiffany &
Co, c 1900, d 4.7cm
(1¾ in), *NY 24 Oct*,
$4,070 (£3,336)

8
A gold open faced minute-
repeating split-second
chronograph by H R
Ekegrin of Geneva,
c 1890, made for J E
Caldwell, Philadelphia,
Pa, the movement
signed and inscribed
'made by E. Koehn,
Geneva', d 5.3cm (2in),
NY 4 June,
$6,050 (£4,515)

9
A large keyless lever
perpetual calendar
chronograph, c 1880, the
gold cuvette signed
'B. Hass Jne. & Cie de
Genève', d 7cm (2¾ in),
G 13 Nov,
SF 16,500 (£5,124; $6,866)

10
A gold keyless lever
perpetual calendar watch,
by Patek Philippe of
Geneva, d 4.6cm (1¾ in),
L 26 July,
£4,400 ($5,874)

11
A white gold open faced
art deco minute-repeating
perpetual calendar watch
with moon phases, by
Audemars Piguet of
Geneva, c 1925, d 4.9cm
(1⅞ in), *NY 4 June*,
$17,050 (£12,724)

12
A gold hunting cased
quarter-repeating
perpetual calendar
clockwatch, with grande
and petite sonnerie, No.
12126 by Louis
Audemars, Brassus &
Geneva, 1911, d 5.7cm
(2¼ in), *G 13 Nov*,
SF 55,000 (£17,081;
$22,889)

13
A gold hunting cased
minute-repeating
chronograph with
perpetual calendar and
moon phases, by Le
Coultre, c 1890, d 5.9cm
(2¼ in), *NY 24 Oct*,
$13,200 (£10,820)

14
A gold open faced keyless
lever one-minute
tourbillon, No. 09364 by
Charles Frodsham, 1910,
the three-quarter plate
glazed movement by
North & Son, casemaker's
stamp 'HMF (Harrison
Mills Frodsham), d 6.5cm
(2½ in), *G 13 Nov*,
SF 66,000 (£20,497;
$27,465)

15
A heavy gold hunting
cased keyless one-minute
tourbillon with
chronometer escapement,
signed Rodolphe Heger,
Chaux-de-Fonds, d 5.4cm
(2⅛ in), *G 13 Nov*,
SF 68,200 (£21,180;
$28,381)

1
A gold open faced lever centre seconds watch, by J & J Hargreaves of Liverpool, the case hallmarked Chester 1872, d 5.1cm (2in), *C 3-6 July,* £275 ($367)

2
A gold three-quarter plate keyless lever watch, No. 5803 by Parkinson & Frodsham, gold cuvette, *P 24-27 July,* £264 ($352)

3
A silver-gilt open faced world time watch, by J Ullman & Co, *c* 1900, white enamel face with subsidiary dials indicating the time in Bombay, Singapore, Shanghai, Peking and Tientsin, d 5.2cm (2in), *NY 24 Oct,* $880 (£721)

4
A gold coin watch, in the form of a United States $20 piece, containing a keyless lever movement by Golay, the coin dated 1904, almost mint, 3.4cm (1⅜in), *G 13 Nov,* SF 6,050 (£1,879; $2,518)

5
A silver keyless sector watch, by the Record Watch Co, Tramelan, *c* 1900, 7.7cm (3in), *NY 14 Feb,* $1,430 (£1,007)

6
A gold open faced fusee keyless lever watch, No. 2945, by Arnold & Lewis Late Simmons, 7 St Anns Square, Manchester, the case hallmarked 1931, pallet staff broken, d 5.1cm (2in), *L 23 Feb,* £572 ($802)

7
A gold hunting cased keyless lever watch, the case hallmarked Chester, 1900, d 5.1cm (2in), *C 3-6 July,* £297 ($403)

8
A four-colour gold box hinge hunting cased watch, Am Watch Co, P S Bartlett, Waltham, Mass, *c* 1887, full plate gilt lever movement, d 5.5cm (2⅛in) *NY 4 June,* $2,090 (£1,560)

9
A gold open faced keyless lever dress watch, Longines, with damascened nickel movement, silvered dial, the case with reeded bezels and cast gold band, d 4.4cm (1¾in), *L 12 Apr,* £495 ($714)

10
A gold and enamel keyless lever watch, No. 819194 Patek Philippe, 1925-30, the case decorated in coloured mother-of-pearl, the back with blue, pink and black enamel, the case signed 'Janesich', closed 3.6cm (1⅜in), open 5.4cm (2⅛in), *G 13 Nov,* SF 17,600 (£5,466; $7,324)

11
A gold and rock crystal keyless lever dress watch, by Patek Philippe, silvered dial inscribed 'A. Georges-Aron, Nice', pearl winding crown, d 4.6cm (1¾in), *L 23 Feb,* £1,430 ($2,005)

12
A gold hexagonal cased skeleton keyless lever watch, by Audemars Piguet, the gold bezels with satin finish, d 5cm (2in), *L 7 June,* £1,870 ($2,711)

13
A skeleton keyless lever watch, by Audemars Piguet & Cie, the movement with gold train, the bezel of rock crystal, d 4.5cm (1¾in), *L 12 Apr,* £1,650 ($2,381)

14
A gold open faced watch with twenty-four-hour dial, Chronometro Gondolo Patek Philippe & Cie, *c* 1905, the white enamel dial with some numerals in red, signed, d 5.8cm (2¼in), *NY 14 Feb,* $3,850 (£2,711)

15
A gold open faced chronograph, No. 24961, Dent, London, 1887, three-quarter gilt lever movement, Nicole Nielsen winding, d 5.1cm (2in), *NY 10 Apr,* $990 (£692)

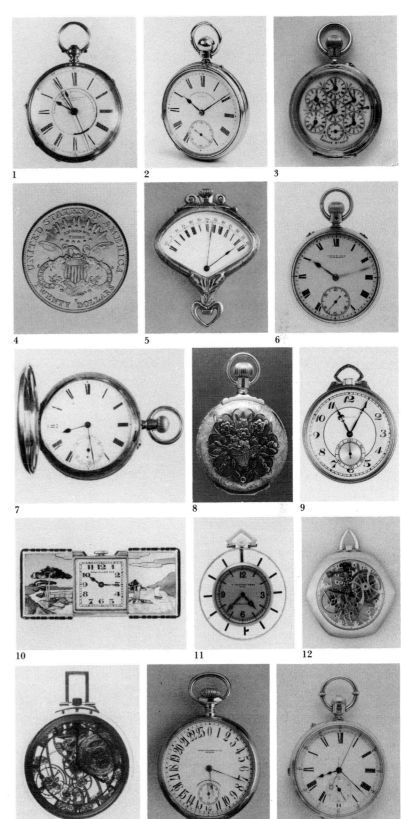

1
A gold wristwatch,
Cartier, c 1975, 3.2cm
(1¼ in), *L 26 July,*
£902 ($1,204)

2
**A gold mysterieuse
wristwatch,** Le Coultre,
c 1945, the dial with
baton numerals inlaid
with diamonds, d 3.2cm
(1¼ in), *L 26 July,*
£770 ($1,028)

3
**A stainless steel reverso
wristwatch,** Jaeger Le
Coultre, c 1935, silvered
dial with sweep seconds,
3.9cm (1½ in), *NY 14 Feb,*
$495 (£349)

4
A gold wristwatch, Jaeger
Le Coultre, retailed by
Cartier, London import
mark 1968, d 3.3cm
(1¼ in), *G 13 Nov,*
SF 3,300 (£1,025; $1,373)

5
**A square gold self-winding
calendar wristwatch** with
moon phases and sweep
seconds, Gubelin, c 1945,
rotor winding in either
direction, silvered matt
dial, signed, 3.3cm
(1¼ in), *NY 24 Oct,*
$3,300 (£2,705)

6
**A stainless steel and gold
self-winding Tonneau
sweep seconds calendar
wristwatch** with moon
phases, Gubelin, c 1955,
d 3.5cm (1⅜ in),
NY 10 Apr,
$605 (£423)

7
**A gold chronograph
wristwatch,** Longines,
c 1950, with start/stop
and return buttons in
the band, d 3.7cm
(1½ in), *L 1 Nov,*
£770 ($986)

8
**A gold calendar
wristwatch,** Omega,
c 1950, the dial with bar
numerals, repeat
signature, day, month
and moonphase
apertures and subsidiary
seconds, enclosed by an
outer date dial, d 3.4cm
(1½ in), *L 26 July,*
£1,320 ($1,762)

9
A gold wristwatch, Patek
Philippe & Co, Geneva,
c 1940 d 3.5cm (1⅜ in),
NY 10 Apr,
$990 (£692)

10
**A white gold square
wristwatch,** Patek
Philippe & Co, Geneva,
c 1963, d 2.5cm (1 in),
NY 4 June,
$825 (£616)

11
**A gold self-winding oval
wristwatch with date,**
Patek Philippe & Co,
Geneva, 3.9cm (1½ in),
NY 24 Oct,
$2,860 (£2,344)

12
**A gold sweep seconds
wristwatch,** Patek
Philippe & Co, Geneva,
c 1955, mono-metallic
compensation balance,
silvered matt dial
applied with gold baton
numerals, signed, d 3.5cm
(1⅜ in), *NY 10 Apr,*
$880 (£615)

13
A gold wristwatch, Patek
Philippe & Co, Geneva,
c 1947, nickel lever movement, mono-metallic
compensation balance,
silvered matt dial, d 3.2cm
(1¼ in), *NY 4 June,*
$1,210 (£903)

14
**A gold rectangular
wristwatch,** Patek
Philippe & Co, Geneva,
c 1928, made for Bailey
Banks & Biddle Co,
circular nickel lever
movement, gilt matt
dial, signed, 3.9cm
(1½ in), *NY 4 June,*
$1,980 (£1,478)

15
**A two-colour gold
wristwatch,** Patek
Philippe & Co, Geneva,
c 1930, 3.1cm (1¼ in),
L 1 Nov,
£1,155 ($1,478)

16
**A pink gold square
wristwatch,** Patek
Philippe & Co, Geneva,
retailed by Hausman,
c 1953 2.5cm (1 in),
NY 14 Feb,
$1,320 (£929)

1
A gold chronograph wristwatch, Patek Philippe & Co, Geneva, c.1945, d 3.2cm (1¼in), *NY 4 June,* $3,850 (£2,873)

2
A pink gold wristwatch, Patek Philippe & Co., Geneva, c.1925, bimetallic compensation balance, silvered gold matt dial applied with gold numerals, signed, d 3.9cm (1½in), *NY 24 Oct,* $715 (£586)

3
A gold rectangular wristwatch, Patek Philippe & Co., Geneva, retailed by Tiffany & Co., c.1920, circular nickel lever movement, silvered matt dial, signed, 4cm (1½in), *NY 24 Oct,* $1,760 (£1,443)

4
A pink gold chronograph wristwatch Patek Philippe & Co., Geneva, c.1945, d 3.9cm (1½in), *NY 4 June,* $4,070 (£3,037)

5
A gold perpetual calendar chronograph wristwatch with tachometer and registers, Patek Philippe & Co., Geneva, c.1955, 3.9cm (1½in), *NY 24 Oct,* $19,800 (£16,229)

6
A slim gold automatic wristwatch, Audemars Piguet, 1967, import mark London, d 3.2cm (1¼in), *L 26 July,* £990 ($1,321)

7
A pink gold wristwatch with calendar and moon phases, Record Watch Co, c.1945, d 3.4cm (1½in), *NY 4 June,* $715 (£534)

8
A stainless steel and gold Prince wristwatch, Rolex Prince, c.1930, 4.2cm (1⅝in), *NY 4 June,* $1,870 (£1,396)

9
A gold Tonneau sweep seconds water resistant wristwatch, Rolex, c.1950, silvered engine-turned dial applied with gold numerals, d 3.5cm (1⅜in), *NY 24 Oct,* $770 (£631)

10
A gold and steel oyster wristwatch, Rolex, the black dial signed 'Rolex Oyster Perpetual Datejust', 3.6cm (1½in), *L 1 Nov,* £990 ($1,267)

11
A gold Tri-Compax calendar chronograph wristwatch, Universal, Geneva, black dial with gilt numerals, d 3.6cm (1⅜in), *L 1 Nov,* £990 ($1,267)

12
A lady's gold self-winding Tonneau waterproof wristwatch, Rolex Oyster Perpetual, c.1945, d 2.5cm (1in), *NY 4 June,* $660 (£493)

13
A gold self-winding waterproof wristwatch with sweep seconds, Rolex Oyster Perpetual, c.1935, Rolex auto rotor chronometer, silvered matt dial with applied gold numerals, d 3.3cm (1¼in), *NY 4 June,* $1,100 (£821)

14
A gold chronograph wristwatch with calendar, moon phases, registers and tachometer, Universal Geneva, Tri Compax, c.1960, d 3.9cm (1½in), *NY 10 Apr,* $1,430 (£1,000)

15
A pink gold wristwatch with sweep seconds, Vacheron & Constantin, c.1945, d 3.8cm (1½in), *NY 24 Oct,* $715 (£586)

16
A gold calendar wristwatch with moon phases, Villereuse, c.1945, d 3.2cm (1¼in), *NY 10 Apr,* $880 (£615)

1
A mahogany clock-cum-barometer with a hygrometer and thermometer, signed 'Willm. Terry London No. 285', 129.5cm (49in), *L 7 June*, £1,210 ($1,755)

2
A Victorian satinwood marine barometer, mid-19th cent, inset with an alcohol thermometer, engraved 'H. Hughes, London', 94cm (37in), *L 6 June*, £4,400 ($6,380)

3
A mahogany wheel barometer/timepiece, with 12in silvered scales, mercury thermometer, hygrometer and spirit-level, inscribed 'V. Zanetti, Manchester', 128cm (50½in), *P 11-18 Dec*, £2,035 ($2,442)

4
A rosewood wheel barometer/timepiece, early 19th cent, mercury thermometer, hygrometer, spirit-level and timepiece, inscribed 'D. Gagioli & Son', 130cm (51in), *P 11-18 Dec*, £1,375 ($1,650)

5
A Partridge wood marine stick barometer, early 19th cent, inscribed 'Geo. Stebbing, Portsmouth', 99cm (39in), *P 11-18 Dec*, £880 ($1,056)

6
A Victorian walnut stick barometer, 3rd quarter 19th cent, the ivory register inscribed 'Garorey, 41 Bull Street, Birmingham', 94cm 37in), *C 27-30 Mar*, £352 ($524)

7
A George III mahogany stick barometer, early 19th cent, the silvered register signed 'Torre & Co., London', applied with a thermometer, 98cm (38½in), *C 27-30 Mar*, £352 ($524)

8
A Victorian walnut wheel barometer, 3rd quarter 19th cent, signed 'Abraham & Co., Liverpool', 103cm (40½in), *C 27-30 Mar*, £176 ($262)

9
A George II red walnut stick barometer, 2nd quarter 18th cent, 98cm (38½in), *C 27-30 Mar*, £1,705 ($2,540)

10
A George III inlaid satinwood barometer/thermometer, I. Vecchio, Nottingham, last quarter 18th cent, 97cm (38in), *NY 20 Oct*, $3,410 (£2,865)

11
A late George III inlaid mahogany cistern barometer/thermometer, Dolland, London, 1st quarter 19th cent, glazed top enclosing engraved brass register, 101cm (39¾in), *NY 20 Oct*, $2,090 (£1,756)

12
A George III inlaid mahogany cistern barometer/thermometer, Charles Ciuaiti, London, late 18th/early 19th cent, the cistern with a hemispherical disc casement, 92cm (36in), *NY 20 Oct*, $1,320 (£1,109)

13
A rosewood and cut mother-of-pearl wheel barometer, Griffin & Hyams, London, mid-19th cent, applied with a hygrometer, thermometer and level, 114cm (45in), *C 3-6 July*, £418 ($567)

14
A George III mahogany angle barometer, signed Whitehurst, Derby', 3rd quarter 18th cent, h 97cm (38in), *C 3-6 July*, £4,510 ($6,118)

15
A rosewood ship's barometer, the ivory register inscribed 'I. & A. Walker, Liverpool', 2nd quarter 19th cent, applied with a thermometer, brass reservoir cover and gimballed wall fitting, 99cm (39in), *C 10 Jan*, £935 ($1,356)

16
An early George III mahogany stick barometer, mid-18th cent, the painted register signed 'Rabalio Fecit', 92cm (36in), *C 10 Jan*, £297 ($431)

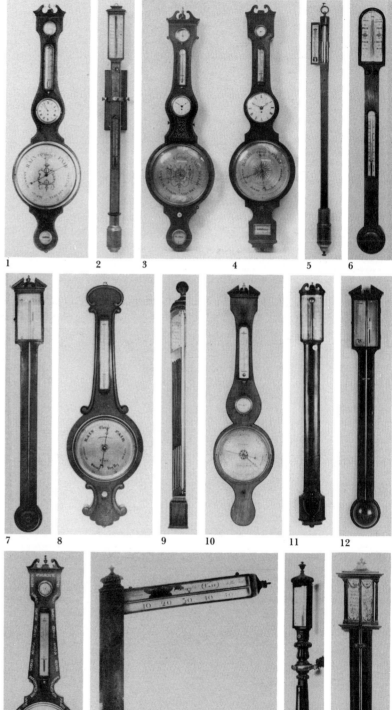

1 2 3 4 5 6

7 8 9 10 11 12

13 14 15 16

1
A marine chronometer,
J R Arnold No. 578, the
movement with Arnold
spring detent escape-
ment, U-type balance
with additional small
circular balance with
poising weights, blued
steel helical spring,
undersprung, in brass
box gimballed in later
calamander wood
carrying case, distressed,
10.5cm (4⅛in), *L 7 June*,
£2,640 ($3,828)

2
An eight-day marine
chronometer, Hatton &
Harris No. 570, the
movement with
Earnshaw spring detent
escapement, 13.3cm
(5¼in), *L 7 June*,
£5,500 ($7,975)

3
A two-day marine
chronometer, Parkinson
& Frodsham No. 3771,
with Earnshaw spring
detent escapement,
restored detent, in
rosewood box with brass
banding, 11.4cm (4½in),
L 23 Feb,
£1,320 ($1,848)

4
A two-day marine
chronometer, Arnold &
Dent No. 1174,
Earnshaw spring detent
escapement, 10.6cm
(4⅛in), *L 1 Nov*,
£1,045 ($1,338)

5
A two-day marine
chronometer, Ulysse
Nardin, Locle, Suisse,
No. 2631, spring detent,
bi-metallic two arm
balance, gimballed in
two tiered brass bound
mahogany box, 19cm
(7½in), *NY 4 June*,
$1,760 (£1,313)

6
A two-day marine
chronometer, Thomas
Roberts, retailed by A
De Casseres,
Amsterdam, blond
mahogany box, 18.5cm
(7¼in), *NY 4 June*,
$1,760 (£1,313)

7
A two-day marine
chronometer, Joseph
Sewell, No. 2931, with
Earnshaw spring detent
escapement, brass bound
ebony box with flush
carrying handles, in
baize lined deck box (2),
13cm (5⅛in), *L 1 Nov*,
£1,375 ($1,760)

8
A two-day marine
chronometer, Hamilton
Watch Co, Lancaster Pa,
No. 2E11222, Model 21
retailed by C B Brown
Co, two tier brass bound
mahogany case with
matching outer deck
box, 19.4cm (7⅝in),
NY 4 June
$1,760 (£1,313)

9
A two-day marine
chronometer, Bliss and
Creighton, New York,
No. 2045, mahogany
box, 17.1cm (6¾in),
NY 4 June,
$1,100 (£820)

10
A two-day marine
chronometer, Morris
Tobias No. 794, spotted
movement with
Earnshaw spring detent
escapement, 11.5cm
(4½in), *L 7 June*,
£1,320 ($1,914)

11
A two-day marine
chronometer, John Bruce
No. 786, Earnshaw
spring detent
escapement, signed
'John Bruce, 26
Wapping, Liverpool,
brass inlaid ebony case
with flush carrying
handles, 12.5cm (5in),
L 7 June,
£1,760 ($2,552)

12
A two-day marine
chronometer, James Poole
No. 5818, Earnshaw
spring detent
escapement, in brass box
gimballed in rosewood
brass bound carrying
case, 12.5cm (5in),
L 7 June,
£1,155 ($1,674)

1   2   3

4   5   6

7   8   9

10   11   12

Collectors' Items

HILARY KAY • DANA HAWKES

Whereas musical boxes, scientific instruments and American folk art (see page 200) have long been collectors' items, some of the fields covered here are relatively new. Their subjects are not well documented and there are few saleroom records. With buyer, seller, dealer and saleroom expert all equally unsure these fields are especially exciting, if more risky, for the collector.

Sotheby's held the first sale specializing in rock and roll memorabilia in London in December 1981. Since then the firm has held annual auctions of the personal effects of pop stars including original handwritten song lyrics, letters, instruments, gold discs, unusual records, signatures and photographs dating from 1956 almost to the present day. The Beatles feature most prominently but many other stars are represented from the Rolling Stones and Elvis Presley to Marc Bolan and Abba. Erstwhile fans usually send the items for sale, where they tend to be bought by the next generation. A number of museums, and institutions are now also buying.

Toy and doll auctions are both expanding very fast. The dolls of interest internationally come in the following categories: automata, early wooden dolls, French fashion dolls and *bébés*; character moulds by Kestner, Kämmer and Reinhardt and Simon and Halbig; large dolls over 30 inches in height; poured wax and waxed composition, unusual china and all-bisque dolls in their original clothes; composition 'Shirley Temple' and early cloth dolls of Lenci and Kathe Kruse, and early Teddy Bears by the firm of Steiff. Toys of international interest are those tin and cast-iron vehicles, trains and aeroplanes by the most highly respected toy makers of the 1900-1920 period, such as Marklin, Bing, Carette, Gunthermann, Ives, Bergman and Brown. Familiar names from the 1930s—Dinky, Hornby, Meccano and Basset-Lowke—also feature, along with toy soldiers by Britains, Heyde and Mignot. Such toys are most valuable if in almost pristine condition in their original box. Disneyana has a growing international market and includes character toys and celluloids from films such as *Pinocchio* and *Fantasia*.

Among nautical works of art sextants, octants and chronometers have always been popular and can be given fairly accurate price estimates. The more decorative ship's fittings have only recently come into their own, but there is now a great demand for ship's figureheads, ship's wheels, engine room telegraphs and navigational lamps. The latter can be bought for £80-150 ($90-170). Finely detailed ship's models, especially those built as presentation pieces, can fetch as much as £5,000 ($5,700). The star items tend to be those models made by French prisoners-of-war during the Napoleonic Wars. They used bones from their meals, straw and human hair to construct superb models of ships from the French and English naval fleets.

Many of the scientific instruments made between the 16th and 19th centuries combined the skills of precision engineering and practical design with scientific theory. They were used in astronomy, surveying, navigation, microscopy and the measurement of time. There are also those used in early scientific experiments such as attractively housed vacuum pumps. Medical and dental instruments, although apparently macabre, are increasingly appreciated, especially by doctors and dentists in the United States. Here can be found dental keys, bullet extractors, large bone saws and sets of naval surgeons' instruments. Finally instruments of technology—typewriters, sewing machines, telephones and early televisions—are rapidly acquiring collectors status.

Mechanical musical instruments have always interested collectors. In the early 19th century Swiss craftsmen began using their watchmaking skills to make small cylinder musical boxes. Over the years percussion and organ accompaniment was added to the standard comb and cylinder movement. German manufacturers introduced the disc playing musical box and so allowed a choice of several hundred popular tunes. Later came the phonograph and later still the gramophone (playing a disc rather than a cylinder). They can fetch £150-1,000 ($170-1,140).

Golf, fishing and cars are hobbies round which specialist collectors can form interesting collections. Early clubs and golf balls are always in demand, but there is increasing interest in other items relating to or illustrating golfers or golf courses and fish and fishermen. Similarly, accessories such as car mascots, lamps, badges, driving coats and spare parts, always feature in automobolia sales.

1
An English 12in terrestrial
globe on stand, Bate
published 1802, the
sphere within a horizontal
ring applied with coloured
print of the Zodiac,
h 48cm (19in), *L 28 Feb,*
£605 ($847)

2
An English 2¾in pocket
terrestrial globe, R.
Cushee, c 1730, contained
in fishskin case, *L 28 Feb,*
£550 ($770)

3
A German Albrecht
orrery, c 1900, on cast-
iron base, w 30.5cm
(12in), *L 12 June,*
£550 ($792)

4
An English brass, ivory
and wood orrery, William
Jones, 1780s, *L 12 June,*
£2,860 ($4,118)

5
An English 18in terrestrial
globe on stand, signed in
Latin 'John Senex
F.R.S.', mid-18th cent,
mounted within brass
meridian engraved with
four quadrant degree
scales, h 112cm (42in),
L 12 June,
£3,300 ($4,752)

6
An English 12in terrestrial
library globe, J. & W.
Cary, c 1800, the sphere
applied with hand-
coloured gores and
mounted within brass
meridia, h 91.5cm (36in),
L 25 Sept,
£2,420 ($3,146)

7
An 18in Malby's celestial
globe, published by
Edward Stanford, on
stand, the sphere
applied with coloured
gores, h 114.5cm (45in),
P 17/19 Apr,
£1,012 ($1,417)

8
A brass sand clock, late
18th cent, for quarter,
half, three-quarters and
full hour, one glass
lacking sand, w 21.5cm
(8½in), *L 25 Sept,*
£935 ($1,216)

9
An English 3in terrestrial
globe, the sphere applied
with coloured gores and
label 'Newton's New &
Improved Terrestrial
Globe', 7.6cm (3in),
P 24/27 July,
£594 ($796)

10
A sand clock, late 18th
cent, mounted in brass
frame, h 14cm (5½in),
L 6 June,
£440 ($638)

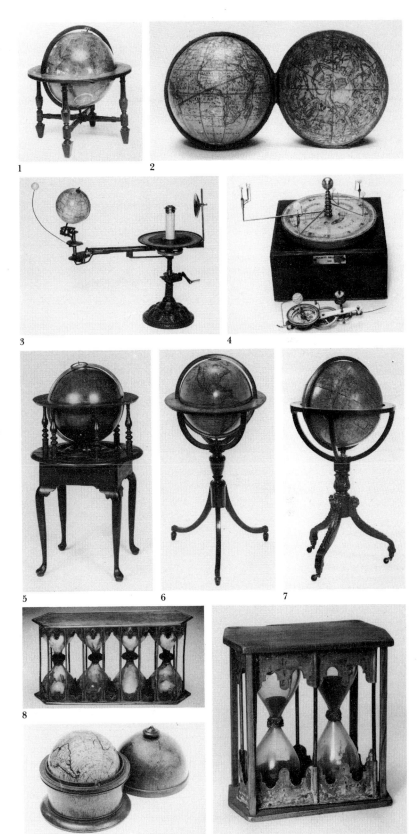

1
A brass gunner's caliper,
English, mid-18th cent,
signed 'Gilbert London'
and engraved with various
linear and non-linear
scales, radius 56cm
(22in), *L 12 June,*
£825 ($1,188)

2
**Five brass imperial standard
measures,** English, mid-
19th cent, for the County
of Kent (deleted) and
engraved 'London County
Council', *L 28 Feb,*
£1,100 ($1,540)

3
**A set of ten brass
cylindrical metric weights,**
de Grave & Co, English,
c 1899, engraved 'London
County Council', corres-
ponding weights from
20kg to 100 kg, the
largest h 21.5cm (8½in),
L 28 Feb,
£1,760 ($2,464)

4
**A George I cast brass wool
weight,** *c* 1720, cast with
the Royal coat of arms,
16.5cm (6½in), *L 12 June,*
£1,100 ($1,584)

5
**A set of English coin
scales,** John Smart, *c* 1720,
with delicate steel beam,
suspension ring and
indicator, complete with
two silver hanging pans
and brass coin wieghts,
case w 27.5cm (10¾in),
L 12 June,
£715 ($1,030)

6
**An early set of English
coin scales,** *c* 1620, with
nineteen brass coin
weights cast with various
denominations, the lid
housing a number of
grain weights, w 21.5cm
(8½in), *L 12 June,*
£1,100 ($1,584)

7
**A set of eleven brass Bate
imperial standard measures**
for the County of
Middlesex, the bushel,
half-bushel, peck and
gallon with handles, the
bushel d 48cm (19in),
L 28 Feb,
£3,850 ($5,390)

8
**A set of English gun metal
imperial bell weights,**
Sewell and Young, dated
1795, ranging in weight
from 56 to 21lb, the
largest h 29cm (11½in),
L 12 June,
£1,980 ($2,851)

9
**A set of ten brass conical
imperial measures,** English,
dated 1890, for the
County of Gloucester,
ranging in capacity from
4 gallons to a quarter
gill, h 38cm (15in),
L 25 Sept,
£1,045 ($1,359)

10
**A set of twelve bronze bell
weights,** dated 1826,
ranging in size from 56lb
to 40oz, *L 25 Sept,*
£1,320 ($1,716)

11
**An English Roberval-type
scale,** S Mordan, *c* 1860,
brass and tortoiseshell
boulle, with four brass
stack weights, ½oz to 4oz,
23cm (9in), *L 25 Sept,*
£748 ($972)

12
**A brass imperial bushel
measure,** de Grave & Co,
London, inscribed 'Govt.
of Good Hope', d 49cm
(19¼in), *JHB 10 May,*
R 5,250 (£2,900; $4,056)

1

2   3

4   5   6

7   8

9   10

11   12

1
An English ivory and brass compound screw-barrel microscope, Edward Scarlett, early 18th cent, signed, the compound tube in stained ivory with sprung stage and screw focusing, in turned ivory slip case, the case 21 x 12cm (8¼ x 4¾in), *L 25 Sept,*
£15,400 ($20,020)

2
An English, Ellis aquatic microscope, mid-19th cent, watchglass stage and forceps and concave reflector screwing into the lid of a fishskin-covered case, h 18cm (7in), *L 25 Sept,*
£418 ($543)

3
An English patent projecting microscope, Wright & Newton, mid-19th cent, for use with standard magic lantern, in fitted pine case with five lenses and other accessories, 41cm (16in), *L 25 Sept,*
£396 ($515)

4
An English brass simple microscope, W & S Jones, *c*1800, on oval ebony base, h 10cm (4in), *L 25 Sept,*
£242 ($315)

5
A Scottish silver simple microscope, John Clark, *c*1750, the folding pillar engraved with five focusing points, h 12cm (4¾in), *L 12 June,*
£12,100 ($17,424)

6
An English brass flea-glass, early 19th cent, with horn-mounted simple lens and steel pin, h 4cm (1⅝in), *L 25 Sept,*
£132 ($172)

7
An English brass reflecting microscope, *c*1827, signed 'John Cuthbert, London', adaptable for use either by reflection or refraction, the case 25.5 x 20cm (10 x 8in), *L 12 June,*
£8,800 ($12,672)

8
An English third form monocular microscope, Edmund Culpeper, *c*1730, the tube with shagreen cover and turned lignum vitae eyepiece, three turned brass supports, 35.5cm (14in), *L 12 June,*
£2,860 ($4,118)

9
An English brass monocular microscope, Powell & Lealand, *c*1850, signed, with rack-and-pinion and long lever and screw focusing, h 37cm (14½in), *L 28 Feb,*
£1,925 ($2,695)

10
An English brass Culpeper-type microscope, late 18th cent, signed 'Shuttleworth London', h 38cm (15in), *L 28 Feb,*
£1,045 ($1,463)

11
An English brass binocular microscope, J. Swift, *c*1870, signed, with dual adjustment with rack-and-pinion and long lever-screw focusing, h 40.5cm (16in), *L 28 Feb,*
£935 ($1,309)

12
An English pocket microscope, early 19th cent, signed 'Cary London', screwing into the lid of a mahogany case with compound tube, w 9.5cm (3¾in), *L 28 Feb,*
£275 ($385)

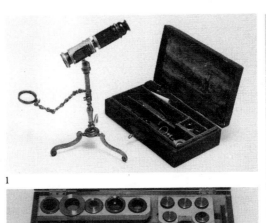

1

2

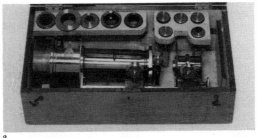

3

4

6

5

7

8

9

10

11

12

1
An English brass surveyor's folding rule, signed and dated 'Humfrey Cole 1574', the upper side engraved with scales of timber measure and borde measure for estimating volume and area; also a vertical sundial for use with a horizontal pin gnomon, now missing, 30.5cm (12in), *L 12 June,* £17,600 ($25,344)

2
A Dutch brass Holland circle or circumferentor, mid-17th cent, signed 'Henricus Sneewins', mounted with four fixed sights, centred by silver compass rose, engraved with four cardinal points and with horizontal sundial above, d 33cm (13in), *L 12 June,* £18,700 ($26,928)

3
An English brass architectonic sector, 3rd quarter 18th cent, radius 30.5cm (12in), *L 28 Feb,* £3,300 ($4,620)

4
An English brass circumferentor, mid-18th cent, signed 'T. Heath London', the 5in diameter compass rose inset with spirit level and engraved with four quadrants and outer silvered circle of degrees, d 30.5cm (12in), *L 12 June,* £990 ($1,426)

5
A pair of brass dividers, probably German, late 17th cent, radius 17cm (6¾in), *L 12 June,* £550 ($792)

6
An English brass combined pedometer and watch, Ralph Gout, late 18th cent, with dials for hours, individual and tens of double paces, d 6cm (2¼in), *L 28 Feb,* £715 ($1,001)

7
A French brass graphometer, signed and dated, Lennel a La Sphere a Paris 1776', the alidade mounted with open sights and vernier scales, inset with compass well, w 35.5cm (14in), *L 25 Sept,* £1,650 ($2,145)

8
A French brass graphometer, Nicholas Bion, late 17th cent, signed, the arc engraved with scale reading to one-tenth of a degree, w 29cm (11½in), *L 25 Sept,* £3,520 ($4,576)

9
A miniature brass graphometer, early 18th cent, the semi-circular plate mounted with three open sights, d 10cm (4in), *L 25 Sept,* £1,485 ($1,931)

10
An English brass perpetual calendar, dated 1753, signed T. W. Fecit 1753', probably by Thomas Wright, d 4.5cm (1¾in), *L 12 June,* £462 ($665)

11
An English mahogany waywiser, Thomas Harris, early 19th cent, the 7in diameter dial engraved with scales for miles, furlongs and poles, h 137cm (54in), *L 28 Feb,* £352 ($493)

12
A Russian brass compass and sundial, 18th cent, recessed compass, folding plumb frame, degree arc and deep chapter ring, w 12cm (4¾in) *NY 4 June,* $1,320 (£985)

13
An English magnetic compass, John Coggs, early 18th cent, the 4¼in diameter printed compass rose signed, contained in beechwood case, 15cm (6in) square, *L 25 Sept,* £550 ($715)

1

A French brass horizontal dial, Jacques Le Maire, mid-18th cent, signed, set for the latitude of Paris at 48 degrees 51 minutes, 20 x 27cm (8 x 10½in), *L 25 Sept,* £1,760 ($2,288)

2

A French silver and gilt brass universal equinoctial dial, Julien Le Roy, *c*1730, the base mounted with magnetic compass and with facility for adjusting for magnetic north, 8.3 x 6.5cm (3¼ x 2½in), *L 25 Sept,* £3,520 ($4,576)

3

A horizontal brass sundial, dated 1596, initialled 'T. H.', the square dial with roman numerals, 11cm (4¼in) square, *L 25 Sept,* £550 ($715)

4

A French brass universal equinoctial ring dial, late 18th cent, signed 'Pre. le Maire a Paris', the outer ring with 13 towns with their corresponding latitudes, equinoctial ring engraved with hour scale, 12.5cm (5in), *L 25 Sept,* £1,540 ($2,002)

5

A German gilt brass sun and moon dial, signed 'Johann Willebrand Augusta 48', *c*1700, the underside listing 39 European cities and their latitudes, w 7.5cm (3in), *L 12 June,* £4,070 ($5,861)

6

A gilt and silvered brass nocturnal, probably by Josua Habermal, Prague, *c*1575-90, the reverse with vertical sundial with sliding index and hinged gnomon, d 12.5cm (4⅝in), *L 12 June,* £19,800 ($28,512)

7

An English brass Butterfield dial, early 18th cent, engraved with acanthus leaves and hour scales for latitudes 51 and 55, 8.2cm (3¼in), *L 12 June,* £825 ($1,188)

8

A French silver Butterfield dial, early 18th cent, signed 'Chapotot a Paris', the oval dial inset, engraved with three hour scales for latitudes 40°, 45° and 50°, 8.2cm (3¼in), *L 12 June,* £1,320 ($1,901)

9

A German polyhedral dial, late 18th cent, the wooden cube applied with five printed dial scales, one printed 'D. Beringer', h 18cm (7in), *L 12 June,* £660 ($950)

10

An English brass universal equinoctial ring dial, mid-18th cent, *L 28 Feb,* £1,012 ($1,417)

11

A French brass Butterfield dial, early 18th cent, signed 'Chapotot à Paris', the octagonal dial with three hour scales, spring loaded folding gnomon, w 6cm (2⅜in), *L 28 Feb,* £572 ($801)

12

A small brass universal equinoctial dial, late 18th cent, with 1½in diameter compass rose, engraved ring of degrees, *L 28 Feb,* £660 ($924)

13

A French ivory diptych dial, Gabriel Bloud, *c*1660, signed, inset with lunar volvelle and latitude scale, with magnetic compass, 8.3 x 7cm (3¼ x 2¾in), *L 28 Feb,* £1,320 ($1,848)

14

A German universal double-crescent altitude dial, signed 'Johann Willebrand in Augsburg', 1st quarter 18th cent, in gilt-brass, silver and steel, the base engraved with 69 European cities with their latitudes, 9.25cm (3⅜in), *L 28 Feb,* £12,100 ($16,940)

15

A French silver Butterfield dial, *c*1680, signed 'Pierre Sevin à Paris', in original velvet-lined brass case, 5.2cm (2¹/₁₆in), *L 28 Feb,* £1,760 ($2,464)

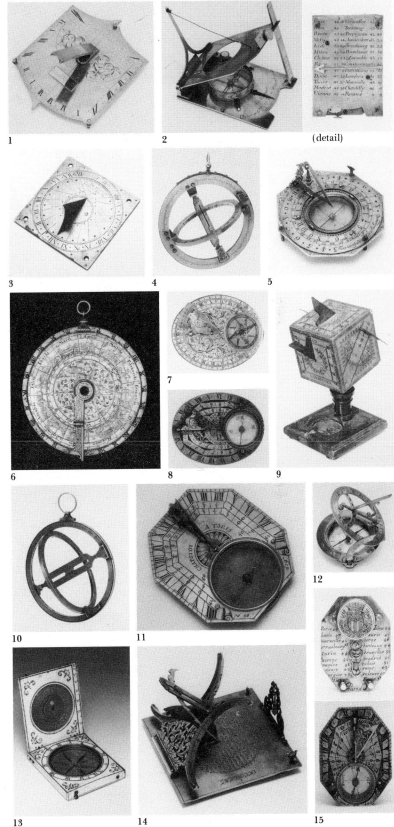

1   2   (detail)

3   4   5

6   7   8   9

10   11   12

13   14   15

1
An English ½in refracting telescope, Christopher Stedman, 3rd quarter 18th cent, with three green leather draws, stamped C. Stedman, London, 59cm (23in), *L 12 June,* £550 ($792)

2
A 2½in English brass Gregorian reflecting telescope on stand, Thomas Blunt, late 18th cent, signed, focusing to the secondary reflector by long shank and screw, 35.5cm (14in), *C 11 July,* £682 ($927)

3
A French 4in Gregorian reflecting telescope, Claude Passemant, mid-18th cent, signed 'Passemant Ingenieur Du Roi Au Louvre', 70cm (27½in), *L 25 Sept,* £715 ($930)

4
An English 4½in brass Gregorian reflecting telescope, Nairne & Blunt, *c*1800, signed, lacking sighting telescope, 66cm (26in), *L 28 Feb,* £935 ($1,309)

5
A French 3in brass Gregorian reflecting telescope, mid-18th century, signed 'Gonichon Rue des Postes a Paris', focusing to the secondary mirror by shank and screw, 36cm (14¼in), *L 25 Sept,* £440 ($572)

6
An English 3in refracting telescope on stand, Dollond, the tube with rack and pinion focusing and sighting telescope mounted at the side, 109cm (43in), *P 24/27 July,* £726 ($962)

7
An English 4in brass reflecting telescope on stand, Peter Dollond, *c*1760, signed, complete with scale and vernier, supported by a bracket above alti-azimuth mount with slow motion adjustment, 69cm (27in), *L 25 Sept,* £2,640 ($3,432)

8
An English brass transit theodolite, T. Cooke & Sons, the sighting telescope focusing by rack and pinion, mounted on a staff head with three levelling screws, h 39cm (15½in), *P 24/27 July,* £352 ($472)

9
An English theodolite, Jesse Ramsden, late 18th cent, signed, the circular base engraved 'Tangent in 100ths of the Radius', h 28cm (11in), *L 25 Sept,* £1,320 ($1,716)

10
A brass simple theodolite or circumferentor, probably Italian, 18th cent, the circle divided 0-45° reading 1° in eight sections, d 19.5cm (7¾in), *L 25 Sept,* £1,155 ($1,502)

11
An English 6in transit theodolite, Troughton & Simms, *c*1890, with rack and pinion focusing, in mahogany case with accessories, h 34cm (13½in), *L 28 Feb,* £528 ($739)

12
An English brass transit theodolite, Cooke, Troughton & Simms Ltd, *c*1940, complete with sighting telescope, spirit level, silver degree scales with magnifiers and verniers, h 30.5cm (12in), *L 25 Sept,* £308 ($400)

13
A Spanish brass theodolite, Rosell, *c*1880, with three levelling screws, h 32cm (12½in), *L 12 June,* £385 ($554)

14
A German brass theodolite, Lingke, mid-19th cent, surmounted by 5in diameter magnetic compass, h 32cm (12½in), *L 12 June,* £495 ($713)

15
An English brass transit theodolite, Troughton & Simms, late 19th cent, the 5in diameter compass rose engraved with cardinal points, circle of degrees and vernier, h 23cm (9in), *L 28 Feb,* £880 ($1,232)

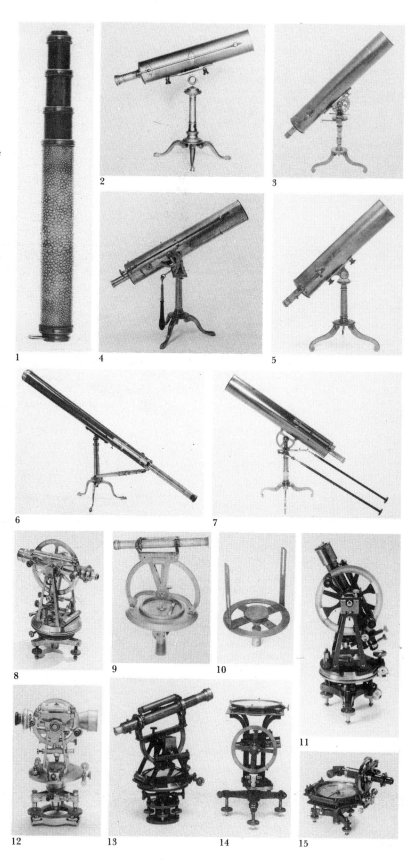

1
A carved and painted wood cigar store Indian, probably the Samuel Robb Shop, New York, c.1886, h 224cm (88in), *NY 30 June*, $25,300 (£18,741)

2
An appliqued cotton crib quilt, Pennsylvania, c.1870, arranged in a heart and leaf pattern, 107 x 94cm (42 x 37in), *NY 28 Jan*, $2,200 (£1,516)

3
A prisoner-of-war boxwood model of the 48-gun ship of the line 'Glory', early 19th cent, 51 x 71cm (20 x 28in), *L 6 June*, £13,200 ($19,140)

4
A brass astronomical ring dial, probably Low Countries, late 16th cent, d 12cm (4¾in), *L 12 June*, £9,900 ($14,256)

5
A moulded copper and zinc pig weathervane, W. Cushing and Sons, Waltham, Massachusetts, 3rd quarter 19th cent, *NY 28 Jan*, $6,875 (£4,736)

1

2

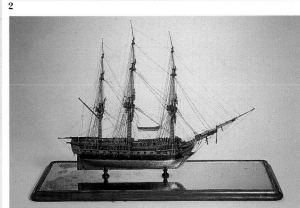

3

4

5

1
A George I wooden doll,
*c.*1725, with gesso-
covered head, the hips
and knees peg-jointed,
41cm (16in), *L 29 May,*
£12,100 ($17,424)

2
**A Vichy 'Pierrot Serenading
the Moon' Musical Auto-
maton, French,** *c.*1870,
h 53cm (21in), *L 3 Oct,*
£10,120 ($13,156)

3
**An American cast-iron
'girl skipping rope'
mechanical bank,**
designed by James H.
Bowen and manufactured
by J. & E. Stevens Co,
late 19th cent, h 21cm
(8¼in), *L 29 May,*
£8,250 ($11,880)

4
**A William and Mary
wooden doll,** *c.*1690, with
painted face and peg-
jointed body, 42.5cm
(16¾in), *L 29 May,*
£17,600 ($25,344)

5
A German tinplate tonneau,
Bing, *c.*1903, finished in
hand-painted cream, the
clockwork mechanism
driving the rear axle,
28cm (11⅜in), *L 3 Oct,*
£7,150 ($9,295)

1

An English brass ship's binnacle, J. W. Ray & Co, Liverpool, early 20th cent, fitted to a brass column, h 1.36m (53½in), *NY 27 Jan*, £303 ($440)

2

A brass ship's binnacle, A. Leitz, San Francisco, the floating magnetic compass in a glazed brass dome flanked by two painted cast iron magnetic compensators, h 1.31m (51½in), *NY 27 Jan*, £455 ($660)

3

An English brass repeating and reflecting circle, *c*1800, signed Troughton, London, the lattice frame inset with silver scale, three index arms, d 53.6cm (21in), *L 6 June*, £2,200 ($3,190)

4

An English ebony octant, *c*1800, signed 'T. Hemsley, Tower Hill, London', brass index arm with vernier, clamping and tangent screws, sighting vane and one set of coloured filters, radius 26.7cm (10½in), *P 11/18 Dec*, £308 ($370)

5

An ebony octant, Continental, mid-19th cent, the 'T' frame inscribed 'C. Johansson', radius 25.5cm (10in), *L 6 June*, £495 ($718)

6

An English brass double-framed sextant, Troughton & Simms, *c*1830, with −5° to 154° platinum scale, two sets of coloured filters and ebony handle, radius 20cm (8in), *L 25 Sept*, £770 ($1,001)

7

An English ebony octant, Charles Jones, Liverpool, early 19th cent, with bone degree scale, three coloured filters, 35.6cm (14in), *NY 10 Apr*, $660 (£462)

8

An English ebony and brass octant, John Hall, Hull, 1791, the frame inset with three bone lozenges, one missing, the vernier with fine adjustment, 43cm (15¾in), *NY 10 Apr*, $880 (£615)

9

An English brass sextant, Norie & Co, *c*1830, the lattice frame with silver scale and vernier, radius 20cm (8in), *L 6 June*, £220 ($319)

10

A French brass aero-nautical fleurais-type sextant, Hurlimann, Ponthus & Therrode, *c*1915, inset with silver scale, index arm with tangent and clamping screws, vernier and magnifier, radius 15.2cm (6in), *L 6 June*, £825 ($1,196)

11

An English brass sextant, Henry Hughes, early 20th cent, inset with platina and gold scale, two sets of coloured filters and walnut handle; with five telescopes and other accessories, radius 20cm (8in), *L 6 June*, £440 ($638)

12

An English bridge-framed sextant, early 19th cent, signed 'Berge London late Ramsden', two sets of coloured filters and mahogany handle, radius 20cm (8in), *L 28 Feb*, £1,210 ($1,694)

13

An English brass sextant, McMillan & Tallis, mid-19th cent, inset with 0°-130° silver arc, with two sets of coloured filters, radius 19cm (7½in), *L 28 Feb*, £264 ($370)

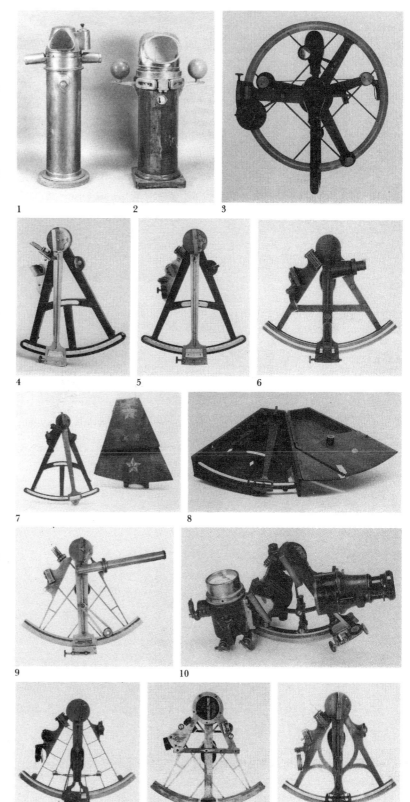

1   2   3

4   5   6

7   8

9   10

11   12   13

1
The speaking trumpet of
HMS Victory, 19th cent,
56.6cm (22¼in), *L 6 June,*
£1,595 ($2,313)

2
A presentation oak casket
for the launching of HMS
Espiegle, English, *c*1900,
containing a mallet and
chisel from the launching
ceremony, w 38cm (15in),
L 6 June,
£825 ($1,196)

3
A diver's brass and copper
helmet, English, early
20th cent, complete with
air intake valve, h 53cm
(21in), *L 25 Sept,*
£715 ($930)

4
Two flare guns, an
English and an American
example, length of the
first 51cm (20in), *NY 27 Jan,*
$137 (£94)

5
A large ship's wheel,
Brown Brothers,
Scottish, mid-19th cent,
d 184cm (6ft), *L 6 June,*
£495 ($718)

6
A prisoner-of-war bone
dominoes casket, French,
early 19th cent, the pine
case with two arched
sliding panels, containing
a set of double nines
bone dominoes, *L 6 June,*
£880 ($1,276)

7
A carved oak ship's
figurehead, English, 19th
cent, h 109cm (43in),
L 6 June,
£572 ($829)

8
A sailor-work wool picture,
English, mid-19th cent,
stitched in eight colours
with a portrait of HMS
Victoria, 55 x 56cm
(20½ x 22in), *L 6 June,*
£528 ($766)

9
A pair of woolwork
pictures, English, mid-
19th cent, portraying the
ships HMS Duncan and
HMS Cambrian, 27 x
37cm (10½ x 14½in),
L 6 June,
£605 ($877)

10
A burr walnut nautical
writing box, English,
c 1880, w 34.5cm (13½in),
L 6 June,
£297 ($430)

11
A decorative prisoner-of-
war straw-work sewing
case, early 19th cent, lid
applied with a watercolour
of Beaufort Castle,
w 33cm (13in), *L 6 June,*
£385 ($558)

1
A polychromed whale-bone stay busk, probably Scottish, *c* 1830, 36cm (14in), *L 6 June,*
£294 ($426)

2
A whalebone stay busk, mid-16th cent, decorated with geometric designs, birds, flowers, trees and a pierced heart, 38cm (15in), *L 6 June,*
£242 ($351)

3
A pair of scrimshawed whale's teeth, English, 1830-50, well engraved with portrait of a sailor sending his sweetheart a love letter by pigeon post, 18cm (7in), *L 6 June,*
£1,650 ($2,393)

4
A scrimshawed whale's tooth, mid-19th cent, inlaid with a small tortoiseshell heart, with well-engraved portrait of a whaling ship, h 18cm (7in), *L 6 June,*
£990 ($1,436)

5
An engraved sperm whale tooth, 19th cent, engraved with an American eagle perched above crossed flags, h 13cm (5in), *NY 27 Jan,*
$880 (£606)

6
A pair of polychromed and scrimshawed whale's teeth, mid-19th cent, decorated by J. Robinson, portraying two whalers, h 16.5cm (6½in), *L 25 Sept,*
£825 ($1,073)

7
An engraved sperm whale tooth, initialled EW, American, *c* 1835, engraved with a sailor and his sweetheart, h 15cm (6in), *NY 30 June,*
$1,980 (£1,467)

8
A pair of sailor's shell-work Valentines, Barbadian, mid-19th cent, w 36cm (14in), *L 25 Sept,*
£770 ($1,001)

9
A whale ivory jagging wheel, American, *c* 1870, old repairs, 21cm (8¼in), *NY 30 June,*
$2,750 (£2,037)

10
A carved sperm whale ivory crochet needle, American, 19th cent, the finial in the form of a lady's hand, 20cm (8in), *NY 30 June,*
$605 (£448)

11
A carved bone prisoner-of-war watch holder, probably French, Dartmoor Prison, *c* 1800, an arched architectural canopy supported by two American Indian figures, minor imperfections, h 25cm (9¾in), *NY 30 June,*
$1,980 (£1,467)

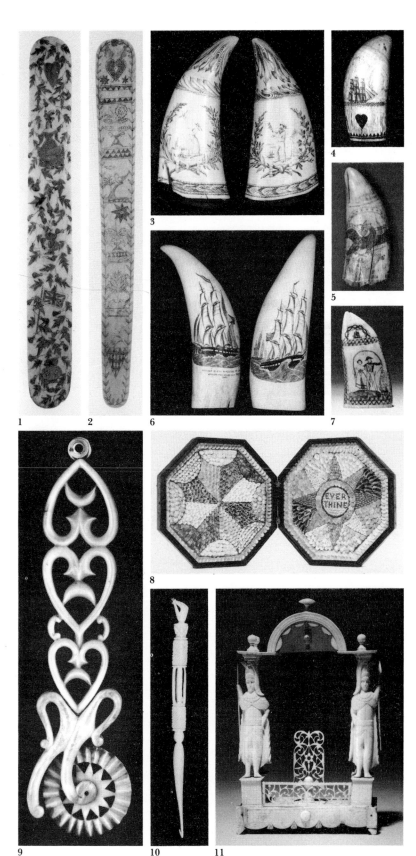

1
A shipbuilder's well-detailed model of Lord Ashburton's steam yacht 'Venetia', Scottish, 1893, ship 142cm (56in), base 171cm (67½in), *L 6 June*, £7,150 ($10,368)

2
A bone model of the 'Royal George', early 19th cent, furnished with 86 cannon, 64cm (25in), *NY 2/3 Mar*, $1,100 (£738)

3
A French prisoner-of-war bone ship's model, early 19th cent, inlaid with plaques of horn and fastened with brass pins, 37cm (14½in), *NY 2/3 Mar*, $4,675 (£3,138)

4
A prisoner-of-war bone model of an 88-gun ship-of-the-line, early 19th cent, 25.5 x 30.5cm (10 x 21in), *L 25 Sept*, £5,500 ($7,150)

5
A shipbuilder's model of the turret deck steamer, 'Duffryn Manor', English, early 20th cent, 112cm (44in), *L 6 June*, £2,200 ($3,190)

6
A model of a paddle steamer 'Caledonian', English, c.1900, 143cm (56in), *L 6 June*, £550 ($798)

7
A half block model of a merchantman, English, mid-19th cent, with painted wooden sails on simulated sea against painted sky background, 46.5 x 67cm (18¼ x 26½in), *L 25 Sept*, £1,100 ($1,430)

8
A sailor-made half-block model of a clipper, English, mid-19th cent, w 86cm (34in), *L 6 June*, £308 ($447)

9
A contemporary model of a Bristol slaver, English, c.1810, with two masts and rigged as a snow-brig, 114cm (45in), *L 6 June*, £1,540 ($2,233)

10
An American scale model of the two-boat brig 'Warrior', Warren Nicholson, contemporary, with all necessary gear and brass cannon, 71 x 97cm (28 x 31in), *NY 8 Dec*, $1,870 (£1,558)

11
An American mahogany and polychrome ship model of the frigate 'Raleigh', early 20th cent; a model of an authentic frigate built in New England and commissioned in 1775, sunk by the British Navy, 104 x 145cm (41 x 57in), *NY 27 Jan*, $2,200 (£1,516)

12
An American scale model of the whaling brig 'Viola', Warren Nicholson, 20th cent, fully rigged with whaleboats, tryworks and all necessary gear, 84cm (33in), *NY 8 Dec*, $4,180 (£3,483)

1

2

3

4

5

6

7

8

9

10

11

12

1
An American portable sewing machine, Wheeler & Wilson type, *c* 1860, 33cm (13in), *L 12 June,* **£396 ($570)**

2
A telegraph, probably French, late 19th cent, with circular indexes for sending and receiving messages, 9.5cm (7¾in), *L 12 June,* **£110 ($158)**

3
A spelter figure of a telephone girl, French, *c* 1905, h 43cm (17in), *L 12 June,* **£286 ($412)**

4
An Ader system wall telephone, French, late 19th cent, mounted with brass and steel speaking trumpet, bell and two bakelite and wood hand sets, h 43cm (17in), *L 12 June,* **£374 ($539)**

5
A 'butterstamp' table telephone, *c* 1880, Continental, h 20cm (8in), *L 12 June,* **£165 ($238)**

6
A German typewriter, Edelmann, *c* 1897, on cast-iron base, w 26.5cm (10½in), *L 28 Feb,* **£242 ($339)**

7
A German typewriter, Helio, *c* 1908, *L 12 June,* **£880 ($1,267)**

8
An American typewriter, Merritt, *c* 1900, *L 28 Feb,* **£264 ($370)**

9
An American typewriter, Hall, *c* 1885, *L 28 Feb,* **£209 ($293)**

10
An English Cuthbertson-pattern electrostatic friction generator, *c* 1810, with 12in diameter glass plate, mounted in mahogany frame, h 47cm (18½in), *L 28 Feb,* **£880 ($1,232)**

11
An English studio easel, Windsor & Newton Ltd, *c* 1880, h 214cm (7ft), *L 28 Feb,* **£715 ($1,001)**

12
An English televisor, John Logie Baird, *c* 1930, complete with screen and two bakelite control knobs, w 69cm (27in), *L 12 June,* **£1,760 ($2,534)**

13
An English barograph, *c* 1900, in mahogany case with graph drawer, w 36cm (14in), *L 28 Feb,* **£440 ($616)**

14
An arithomometer, mid-19th cent, engraved 'Thomas de Colmar a Paris', the brass mechanism with capacity of 6 by 7 by 12 figures, with ivory mounted operating handles, w 46cm (18in), *L 25 Sept,* **£1,210 ($1,573)**

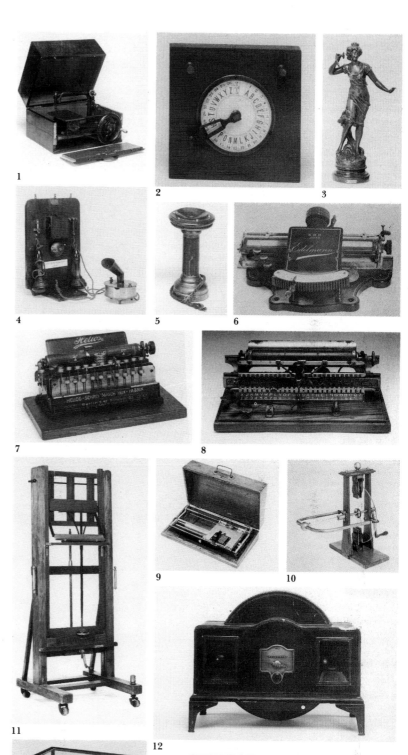

1
A set of dental hygiene instruments, Continental, late 18th cent, nine steel instruments contained in leather-covered card case, 7.5 x 6.5cm (3 x 2½in), *L 25 Sept,*
£440 ($572)

2
A folding iron tooth key, mid-18th cent, pitted overall with corrosion, 15cm (6in), *L 25 Sept,*
£770 ($1,001)

3
A set of dental scaling instruments, *c*.1800, four silver-gilt coloured metal instruments in original case, 7.5cm (3in), *L 25 Sept,*
£495 ($644)

4
A tooth key, late 18th cent, together with three interchangeable claws for differing tooth sizes, 13.3cm (5¼in), *L 12 June,*
£495 ($713)

5
A dental 'Pelican' tooth extractor, late 18th cent, 14cm (5½in), *L 28 Feb,*
£1,760 ($2,464)

6
A dental 'Pelican' tooth extractor, 18th cent, 11cm (4½in), *L 28 Feb,*
£990 ($1,386)

7
A set of dental instruments, Ash, English, 3rd quarter 19th cent, stamped 'Down London', 25.5 x 20cm (10 x 8in), *L 25 Sept,*
£880 ($1,144)

8
An adjustable dental chair, probably English, *c*.1900, h 112cm (44in), *C 7 Nov,*
£220 ($293)

9
A medical or jockey scale, W. & T. Avery Ltd, English, *c*.1900, steelyard for 24 stone to one side (lacking 1lb slide), w 64cm (25in), *C 7 Nov,*
£484 ($644)

10
A ceramic phrenology head, English, mid-19th cent, the front titled 'Phrenology by L. N. Fowler', h 29cm (11½in), *L 12 June,*
£605 ($871)

11
An apothecary's drug jar, English, mid-19th cent, transfer decorated with label 'Rhubarb', lacking lid, h 68.5cm (27in), *C 11 July,*
£550 ($748)

12
An apothecary's drug jar, English, mid-19th cent, painted and transfer decorated with label, 'Sulphur', h 65cm (25½in), *C 11 July,*
£550 ($748)

1

2

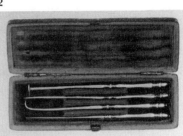

3

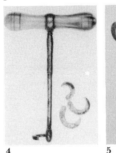

4

5   6

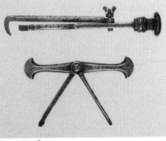

7

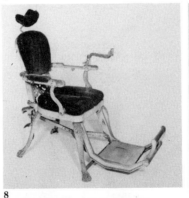

8

9

10

11   12

1
A set of field surgeon's instruments, William Smith, English, early 19th cent, including amputation knives, saws, tourniquet, etc., 48 x 15cm (19 x 6in), *L 25 Sept,* £880 ($1,144)

2
A surgeon's instrument set, English, mid 19th cent, including two Weiss Liston knives, w 46cm (18in), *L 28 Feb,* £715 ($1,001)

3
A set of amputation instruments, Charriere, French, mid-19th cent, 40.5 x 15cm (16 x 6in), *L 25 Sept,* £660 ($858)

4
An American surgeon's kit, G. Tiemann, New York, *c* 1900, 64 pieces, a number missing, 42.5cm (16¾in), *NY 10 Apr,* $1,870 (£1,308)

5
An amputation set, French, Charriere, mid-19th cent, comprising two Liston-type knives, a tourniquet and a bone saw, 40.5 x 24cm (16 x 9½in), *L 28 Feb,* £605 ($847)

6
A cupping and bleeding set, late 19th cent, stamped 'Read & Coy, Makers, 4 Parliament St., Dublin, 21 x 14.5cm (8¼ x 5¾in), *L 25 Sept,* £440 ($572)

7
A 'Junkers' anaesthetic apparatus, Down Brothers, English, late 19th cent, for the inhalation of Bichloride of Methylene, 21.5 x 23cm (8½ x 9in), *L 25 Sept,* £220 ($286)

8
An enema or stomach pump, late 19th cent, w 33cm (13in); and a Traube Stalagnometer, w 30.5cm (12in), *L 25 Sept,* £143 ($186)

9
A mahogany medicine chest, English, *c* 1830, fitted with five racks of medicine bottles, spatula, ointment bottles, beam scales, brass weights and prescriptions, w 23cm (9in), *L 12 June,* £748 ($1,077)

10
A mahogany medicine chest, English, 2nd quarter 19th cent, with 13 compound bottles (three missing), glass mortar and pestle and other accessories, w 22cm (8¾in), *L 28 Feb,* £462 ($647)

11
A cupping and bleeding set, Savigny and Company, English, mid-19th cent, 16 x 16.5cm (6¼ x 6½in), *L 28 Feb,* £660 ($925)

12
A mahogany medicine chest, English, late 18th cent, fitted with 23 glass and compound bottles and various accessories, the back with 'secret' compartment, w 25.5cm (10in), *L 28 Feb,* £935 ($1,309)

13
A medicine chest, English, *c* 1840, with 14 bottles (two missing), scales and mortar and pestle, w 30.5cm (12in), *L 28 Feb,* £418 ($586)

1

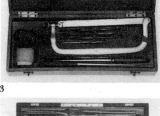

3

2

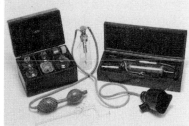

4

5

6 7 8

9

10

11 12 13

1
A large scioptic ball, English, early 19th cent, with two 2½in diameter lenses mounted in mahogany ball, d 12cm (4¾in), *L 12 June*, £935 ($1,346)

2
A scioptic ball, probably English, late 18th cent, the two lenses mounted in lignum vitae socket, 14.5cm (5¾in) square, *L 28 Feb*, £2,860 ($4,004)

3
A Japanese novelty cigarette lighter, Lumix, *c*1948, in the form of a Leica-type camera, w 6.5cm (2½in), *L 25 Sept*, £82 ($107)

4
A 'Luzo' camera, Redding & Gyles, English, 1896-9, together with simple sector shutter, film key and brilliant viewfinder, case 16.5 x 12.7cm (6½ x 5in), *L 12 June*, £550 ($792)

5
A sliding box dry-plate camera, Horne & Thornthwaite, English, 1880s, mahogany body, 12 x 18.4cm (4¾ x 7¼in), *L 28 Feb*, £396 ($555)

6
A 'Kafilmca' microscope camera, Leitz, *c*1932, shutter speeds 1 to 1/125 sec, *L 12 June*, £638 ($919)

7
A tropical hand-and-stand camera, English, Sanderson, *c*1920, with Tessar 13.5cm f/4.5 lens, 8.3 x 10.8cm (3¼ x 4¼in), *L 28 Feb*, £319 ($447)

8
A Nettel Camerawerke 'Argus' monocular detective camera, German, *c*1912, with Holos f/6 lens, 4.5 x 6cm (1½ x 2⅞in), *L 25 Sept*, £352 ($458)

9
A Brins patent miniature detective camera, English, *c*1891, for 25mm diameter circular exposures, 30mm f/3.5 lens, h 15cm (6in), *L 25 Sept*, £1,430 ($1,859)

10
A Marion tropical reflex camera, early 20th cent, with Series II Cooke lens, 7.3in f/4.5, teak body with inset brass reinforcements, 7.6 x 10.2cm (3 x 4in), *L 25 Sept*, £1,430 ($1,859)

11
A Soho tropical reflex camera, English, *c*1920, with Dallmeyer Press 5in f/3.5 lens, teak body with brass fittings, 6.4 x 8.8cm (2½ x 3½in), *L 12 June*, £748 ($1,077)

12
A compass miniature camera, Le Coultre, Swiss, *c*1937, shutter speeds 4.5 to 1/500 sec, 2.4 x 3.6cm (⅞ x 1⅜in), *L 12 June*, £462 ($665)

13
A tropical plate camera, Zeiss Ikon, German, *c*1928, with Tessar 13.5cm f/4.5 lens, 7.6 x 10.2cm (3 x 4in), *L 12 June*, £220 ($317)

1   2   3

4   5

6   7

8

9

10

11   12   13

1

An East European ivory chess set, early 19th cent, the rooks as squat barrels, lacks white knight, the king h 8cm (3⅛in), *L 3 Oct,* £286 ($372)

2

A Chinese ivory chess set, late 19th cent, each piece representing a member of the court, 14cm (5½in), to 6.5cm (2½in), *L 29 May,* £462 ($665)

3

An Indian carved ivory chess set, probably Delhi, *c*1820, the rooks as towers, one side stained green, the king h 14cm (5½in), *L 3 Oct,* £770 ($1,001)

4

An Indian delicately carved ivory chess set, 3rd quarter 19th cent, the king h 11cm (4¼in), *L 3 Oct,* £330 ($429)

5

An English ivory chess set, Jaques Staunton, *c*1880, h 10cm (4in) to 4.5cm (1¾in), *L 29 May,* £605 ($871)

6

A Chinese carved ivory, chess set, early 20th cent, the rooks as castellated elephants, the king h 11cm (4¼in), *L 3 Oct,* £286 ($372)

7

An English games compendium, CS & Co, early 20th cent, w 23cm (13in), *C 7 Nov,* £220 ($293)

8

An ivory chess set and box/board, Delhi, first half 19th cent, richly carved with formal foliage and floral motifs, h 7.5-12.3cm (3-4¾in), *L 29 May,* £880 ($1,267)

9

A French tinplate toy magic lantern, Lapierre, *c*1900, with candle illuminant, h 30.5cm (12in), *L 25 Sept,* £154 ($200)

10

An English triple focusing magic lantern, late 19th cent, in mahogany body, w 66cm (26in), *L 25 Sept,* £330 ($429)

11

A French praxinoscope, Emil Reynaud, late 19th cent, containing coloured lithographic cartoons and centred by a twelve-sided mirror, h 20cm (8in), *L 25 Sept,* £440 ($572)

12

An English stereoscopic viewer on stand, *c*1860-80, with six stereoscopic glass plates, h 43cm (17in), *L 12 June,* £132 ($190)

13

An English 'magic' stereo-scope, Negretti & Zambra, *c*1870, two photograph insertion slots at the side and two sets of lenses, raised on telescopic brass column; with a collection of photographs and plates, h 51cm (20in), *L 25 Sept,* £550 ($715)

14

An English phenakisto-scope, SW Fores, published 1833, with twelve hand-coloured discs, largest disc d 25cm (9¾in), *L 28 Feb,* £495 ($693)

1
A wooden doll, South
German or North
Italian, mid-18th cent, in
limewood, the hands
with long jointed fingers
and separated thumb,
68.5cm (27 in), *L 29 May,*
£1,100 ($1,584)

2
A German wooden doll,
Grodnertal, *c* 1825, with
finely painted features,
brush-stroked black hair,
peg-jointed wooden body
in original dress, 39.5cm
(15½ in), *L 3 Oct,*
£462 ($600)

3
An English wooden doll,
c 1750, with finely painted
rouged cheeks, blonde
real hair nailed-on wig,
the hips and knees peg-
jointed, original clothes,
41cm (16in), *L 29 May,*
£11,000 ($15,840)

4
An English wooden doll,
c 1810, the head and
torso carved from one
piece of wood, replacement
arms and lower legs,
wearing original linen
dress, 41cm (16in),
P 30 Oct/2 Nov,
£858 ($1,098)

5
An English wooden doll,
c 1735, with painted
gesso-covered face,
nailed wig of high-piled
real auburn hair, the
arms peg- and pivot-
jointed at shoulders and
elbows, original under-
clothing and robe, 43cm
(17in), *L 17 Jan,*
£12,100 ($17,545)

6
An English wooden doll,
early 18th cent, with
painted face, the straight
wooden legs string-tied
to the hips, in original
panelled silk dress, wig
missing, 25.5cm (10in),
L 3 Oct,
£935 ($1,216)

7
An English wooden doll,
early 19th cent, the torso
carved from one piece of
wood, later cloth arms,
missing legs, 37cm (14½in),
L 29 May,
£330 ($475)

8
An English wooden doll,
c 1800, the head covered
in gesso, kid arms,
wooden legs peg-jointed
at hips, in original
clothes, 37cm (14½ in),
L 17 Jan,
£1,155 ($1,675)

9
An early wooden doll,
probably Dutch, *c* 1790,
with painted head, straight
legs peg-jointed at hips,
cloth arms, slight cracking,
24cm (9½ in), *L 3 Oct,*
£396 ($515)

10
An English wooden doll in
original box, *c* 1680,
unusually painted brown
eyes, contemporary dress,
28cm (11in), *L 3 Oct,*
£3,190 ($4,147)

11
An English wooden doll,
late 18th cent, in heavy
wood, extra large and
bulbous black eyes, pink
kid forearms with
separately stitched fingers,
long fabric legs, legs
replaced, 72cm (28½ in),
L 29 May,
£1,650 ($2,376)

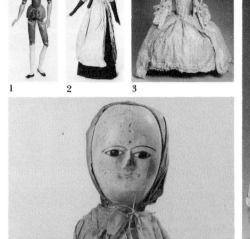

1   2   3

4   5

6   7   8

9   10   11

1
A German girl doll, Kathe Kruse, *c*1914, with articulated hip joints, painted brown eyes and hair; with a quantity of original clothes, 40.5cm (16in), *C 21 Mar,*
£418 ($623)

2
A German boy doll, Kathe Kruse, *c*1914, with moulded fabric head, painted eyes and hair; with a quantity of original clothes, 48cm (19in), *C 21 Mar,*
£1,485 ($2,213)

3
A German cloth doll, Kathe Kruse, *c*1911, seam-stitch articulation at shoulders, swivel joints at hips, in original clothes, 43cm (17in), *L 29 May,*
£935 ($1,346)

4
An Italian glass-eyed felt doll, Lenci, the brown eyes glancing from side to side, 47cm (18½in), *NY 13 Dec,*
$2,970 (£2,496)

5
An Italian felt girl doll, Lenci, with painted brown eyes, 43.2cm (17in), *NY 7 Apr,*
$495 (£346)

6
An Italian felt child doll, Lenci, with painted brown eyes, 43.2cm (17in), *NY 7 Apr,*
$522 (£365)

7
An Italian felt child doll, Lenci, with painted brown eyes, 42cm (16½in), *NY 7 Apr,*
$522 (£365)

8
A poured wax doll, Charles Marsh, London, with brown human-hair wig, the cloth body with wax arms, 50.8cm (20in), *NY 7 Apr,*
$2,750 (£1,923)

9
A German pink-tinted china-head doll, mid-19th cent, with cloth body and china arms, 63.5cm (25in), *NY 7 Apr,*
$467 (£327)

10
A shoulder china doll, German, *c*1860, with painted features, auburn real hair, the stuffed body with china lower limbs and moulded boots, 39.5cm (15½in), *L 29 May,*
£396 ($570)

11
An English waxed shoulder-composition doll, late 19th cent, fixed blue glass eyes, stuffed body, leg broken, 40.5cm (16in), *L 3 Oct,*
£110 ($143)

12
A German shoulder-waxed-composition doll, *c*1880, with fixed blue glass paperweight eyes, blond mohair plaited wig, the stuffed body with squeaker and waxed-composition lower limbs, right arm loose, 41cm (16in), *L 29 May,*
£121 ($174)

13
A German shoulder-waxed-composition doll, *c*1880, with fixed blue glass eyes, blond mohair plaited wig, in original clothes, 46cm (18in), *L 29 May,*
£308 ($444)

14
A waxed shoulder-composition doll, *c*1880, blond mohair wig, stuffed body, original dress, 36cm (14in), *L 3 Oct,*
£330 ($429)

15
An English poured shoulder-wax doll, *c*1880, with fixed blue glass eyes, fair real hair, stuffed body, leg broken, 60cm (23½in), *L 3 Oct,*
£330 ($429)

1   2   3

4

5   6   7

8

9   10

11

12   13   14   15

1

A poured shoulder-wax portrait lady doll, probably by Pierotti, *c* 1900, the cloth lady body with wax limbs in the original 18th century style, broken and repaired on shoulders, 52cm (20½in), *L 17 Jan*, £308 ($447)

2

A set of 'The Dionne Quintuplet' dolls, American, Madame Alexander, *c* 1935, with cot, 19.1cm (7½in), *C 7 Nov*, £495 ($658)

3

A Continental papier-mâché milliner's model, *c*1835, the torso cloth over wood with jointed wood legs, minor repainting, 56cm (22in), *NY 7 Apr*, $3,410 (£2,385)

4

A Japanese doll, late 19th cent, the gofum head with open/closed mouth, 76cm (30in), *L 3 Oct*, £242 ($315)

5

Two Italian crèche figures of an elderly man and woman, mid-19th cent, each terra cotta shoulder-head with inset glass eyes, in original clothes, 29.2 and 30.5cm (11½ and 12in), *NY 23 June*, $495 (£364)

6

A German papier-mâché male milliner's model, *c*1850, with kid body, wood limbs, partial original clothing; with a second papier-mâché doll, 1840s, in original clothing, 51 and 44.5cm (20 and 17½in), *NY 7 Apr*, $1,650 (£1,154)

7

A South German wooden crèche figure, 18th cent, of a workman with up-tilted head, 37cm (14½in), *L 3 Oct*, £187 ($243)

8

A German bisque googly doll, *c* 1911, impressed 241.1, blond mohair wig, composition body, in original outfit, 28cm (11in), *L 17 Jan*, £1,870 ($2,712)

9

A composition boy doll, probably German, late 19th cent, with fixed blue glass eyes, blond fur skin wig, jointed composition body, right lower leg missing, 41cm (16in), *L 3 Oct*, £352 ($458)

10

A German bisque-head googly-eyed doll, J D Kestner, wood and composition ball-jointed body, 29.2cm (11½in), *NY 7 Apr*, $1,650 (£1,154)

11

A German composition mask-faced doll, *c* 1915, stitched five-piece felt-covered body with swivel joints, 38cm (15in), *L 3 Oct*, £550 ($715)

12

A German composition mask-faced doll, *c*1915, with bulbous blue glass eyes, brown plush wig, stitched felt-covered body with swivel joints at shoulders and hips, 38cm (15in), *L 3 Oct*, £495 ($643)

13

A German bisque doll, Kämmer & Reinhardt/ Simon & Halbig, *c* 1910, impressed 117/A53, jointed wood and composition body, 52cm (20½in), *L 3 Oct*, £2,530 ($3,289)

14

A German bisque doll, Kämmer & Reinhardt/ Simon & Halbig, *c* 1910, impressed 12646, 48cm (19in), *L 3 Oct*, £220 ($286)

15

A German bisque Oriental baby doll, *c* 1925, impressed 3½, with weighted brown glass eyes, cloth body, with squeaker, 41cm (16in), *L 3 Oct*, £550 ($715)

16

A German bisque Oriental doll, Armand Marseille, *c*1925, impressed 353 2½K, composition body, 33cm (13in), *L 17 Jan*, £660 ($957)

1
A German mulatto bisque
doll, Simon & Halbig,
impressed 1039 S & H 7,
jointed wood and compo-
sition body, c. 1890,
unclothed, 46cm (18in),
L 29 May,
£462 ($665)

2
A German bisque doll, S.
& C/Simon & Halbig,
c 1890, impressed 73,
with weighted blue glass
eyes, ball-jointed com-
position body, unclothed,
76cm (30in), L 29 May,
£352 ($507)

3
A German shoulder-bisque
swivel-head doll, Simon &
Halbig, c 1880,
impressed S3H 939, with
dimple in chin, gusseted
kid body with bisque
forearms, unclothed, 29cm
(11½in), L 29 May,
£286 ($412)

4
A German bisque doll,
Simon & Halbig/Kämmer
& Reinhardt, c 1900,
impressed 58, with open
mouth and moulded
upper teeth, 61cm (24in),
L 17 Jan,
£352 ($510)

5
A German bisque doll,
Simon & Halbig, c 1890,
impressed S & H WSK
4½, fair long real hair
wig, ball-jointed wood
and composition body,
63.5cm (25in), L 17 Jan,
£352 ($510)

6
A German bisque 'Princess
Elizabeth' doll, Schoenau
& Hoffmeister Porzellan-
fabrik Burggrub, c 1930,
impressed 5, 51cm (20in),
L 3 Oct,
£1,265 ($1,644)

7
A German black bisque
laughing baby doll,
Heuback Köppelsdorf,
c 1928, impressed 463.9/0,
with open smiling
mouth and moulded
upper teeth, pierced ears
with original brass ear-
rings, curved limb com-
position body, 35.5cm
(14in), L 17 Jan,
£550 ($798)

8
A German black bisque
doll, Heuback Köppels-
dorf, c 1910, impressed
418 11/0, five-piece
chunky composition
body, 25.5cm (10in),
L 3 Oct,
£495 ($643)

9
A German black bisque
doll, Heuback Köppels-
dorf, c 1910, impressed
399.3 DRGM with
weighted brown glass
eyes, five-piece
composition body,
unclothed, 46cm (18in),
L 3 Oct,
£352 ($458)

10
A German bisque-head
doll, Kestner, incised 13,
with cork pate and
original mohair hair,
composition ball-jointed
body with straight wrists,
45.7cm (18in), NY 23 June,
$1,320 (£971)

11
A German bisque doll,
probably by J D Kestner,
c 1890, impressed 289
Dep 11, with fixed blue
glass eyes, jointed wood
and composition body,
in original dress, 53cm
(21in), L 3 Oct,
£660 ($858)

12
A German bisque-head
doll, Kestner, incised 16,
with cork pate, blue
threaded glass eyes,
composition ball-jointed
body with straight wrists,
64.8cm (25½in), NY 13 Dec,
$2,530 (£2,126)

13
A German bisque-head
character child, Armand
Marseille, incised 42M
345, with blue painted
intaglio eyes and a
closed mouth, on a wood
and composition ball-
jointed body, 30.4cm
(12in) NY 13 Dec,
$825 (£693)

14
A German bisque-head
character baby, Armand
Marseille, on a five-
piece composition body,
(chipping at the base of
the neck), 30.4cm (12in),
NY 13 Dec,
$2,860 (£2,403)

1
A German bisque-head
doll, Simon & Halbig,
incised S175 H939, with
blue paperweight eyes,
wood and composition
ball-jointed body, 83.8cm
(33in), *NY 13 Dec*,
$2,090 (£1,756)

2
A German bisque doll,
Simon & Halbig, *c* 1910,
impressed 1294 65, with
with open mouth,
trembling tongue, auburn
mohair wig, curved limb
composition body, 71cm
(28in), *L 3 Oct*,
£495 ($644)

3
A German bisque
character doll, Bruno
Schmidt, *c* 1910,
impressed 2048 5, with
open/closed mouth,
weighted brown glass
eyes, curved limb com-
position body, 47cm
(18½in), *L 3 Oct*,
£990 ($1,287)

4
A German bisque-head
doll, incised Queen
Louise/Germany/15,
with blue fixed eyes,
ball-jointed composition
body; with accessories
76.2cm (30in), *NY 23 June*,
$715 (£526)

5
Two German dolls, *c* 1900,
one impressed with a
clover leaf 5, the other
WD 5, both with open
mouth and upper teeth,
fixed brown glass paper-
weight eyes, red mohair
wigs and five-piece
composition bodies, the
girl's legs cracked, 34cm
(13½in), *L 29 May*,
£880 ($1,267)

6
A German bisque doll,
c 1890, impressed C2½,
with open mouth and
upper teeth, weighted
blue glass eyes, blond
mohair wig, jointed
wood and composition
body, 46cm (18in),
L 3 Oct,
£330 ($429)

7
A German Parian-bisque
shoulder-head doll, *c*1870,
stuffed body with bisque
lower limbs, left arm
torn, 53cm (21in), *L 3 Oct*,
£286 ($372)

8
A pair of German all-
bisque dolls, *c* 1880,
impressed 1, one with
blue, the other with
brown weighted glass
eyes, blond mohair wigs,
the bodies jointed at
neck, shoulders and
hips, the girl broken at
shoulders, 15cm (6in),
L 3 Oct,
£308 ($400)

9
A French bisque-head
bébé, shoulder plate
incised 4, the swivel head
with outlined,
open/closed mouth,
35.6cm (14in), *NY 7 Apr*,
$660 (£462)

10
A French bisque-head
fashion doll, on a kid
body, individually stitched
fingers, 40cm (15¾in),
NY 7 Apr,
$1,320 (£923)

11
A 'Belton' bisque-head
doll, probably French,
jointed composition
body, 30.5cm (12in)
NY 7 Apr,
$577 (£403)

12
A French bisque-head
fashion doll, F. Gauthier,
incised FG, the swivel
head with light blue glass
eyes, gusseted kid body,
43.9cm (17¼in), *NY 7 Apr*,
$715 (£500)

13
A French bisque doll,
DEP, *c* 1890, impressed
DEP 7½, with open
mouth and moulded
upper teeth, black real
hair wig, two fingers
broken, 46cm (18in),
L 3 Oct,
£308 ($400)

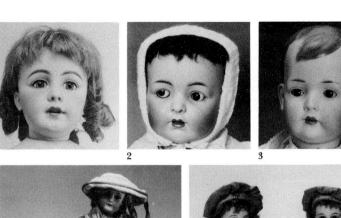

1 2 3

4 5

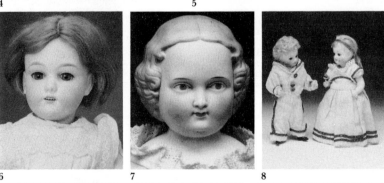

6 7 8

9 10 11 12 13

1
A French bisque swivel-neck fashion doll, F. Gaultier, c 1875, impressed FG, with pale blue paperweight eyes, original blond wig, dressed in original satin bodice and skirt, 58cm (23in), *C 7 Nov,*
£1,760 ($2,341)

2
A French bisque doll, DEP, c 1900, impressed DEP 10½, with fixed brown glass eyes, brown real long hair wig, jointed wood and composition body, 66cm (26in), *L 3 Oct,*
£209 ($272)

3
A French bisque doll, DEP, c 1900, impressed DEP 6, red real hair wig, jointed wood and composition body, distressed, 43cm (17in), *L 3 Oct,*
£440 ($572)

4
A French swivel-head shoulder-bisque fashion doll, c 1860, unmarked, unclothed, 29cm (11½in), *L 3 Oct,*
£286 ($372)

5
A French bisque swivel-head fashion doll, c 1880, impressed 6 on head and both shoulders, the Gesland body with bisque hands and lower legs, in original cream silk and satin dress, 56cm (22in), *L 3 Oct,*
£1,540 ($2,002)

6
A French bisque-head fashion doll, incised 3, with cork pate, blond mohair wig, gusseted kid body, and a fur-covered Afghan hound, 39.5cm (15½in), *NY 7 Apr,*
$1,430 (£1,000)

7
A French bisque shoulder-head fashion doll, incised T, gusseted kid body, individually stitched fingers, 45.8cm (18in), *NY 23 June,*
$880 (£647)

8
A French bisque-head fashion doll, incised 3, the swivel head with cork pate, blue glass eyes, gusseted kid body, 40.6cm (16in), *NY 23 June,*
$825 (£607)

9
A French swivel-head two-faced doll, probably by Bru Jeune et Cie, c 1870, impressed 3, one face gently smiling, the other with closed eyes finely painted, fully gusseted kid body filled with saw-dust, 35.5cm (14in), *L 17 Jan,*
£1,650 ($2,393)

10
A French bisque bébé-head and shoulder-plate, Casimir Bru, with cork pate, blond wig, blue paperweight eyes, 26cm (10¼in), *NY 7 Apr,*
$3,410 (£2,385)

11
A bisque head, probably French, c 1895, impressed 86 12, with open mouth and moulded round hole for teat, 12.5cm (5in), *L 17 Jan,*
£187 ($271)

12
A French bisque-head bébé, incised, Bru Jne B, with brown paperweight eyes, 57.2cm (22½in), *NY 7 Apr,*
$6,600 (£4,615)

13
A French bisque-head bébé, Bru, the swivel head with cork pate, brown paperweight eyes, 40.6cm (16in), *NY 23 June,*
$7,425 (£5,460)

14
A French bisque-head bébé, incised Bru Jne//2, kid-over-wood jointed body with wood legs and bisque arms, original clothes, 31.8cm (12½in), *NY 23 June,*
$3,520 (£2,588)

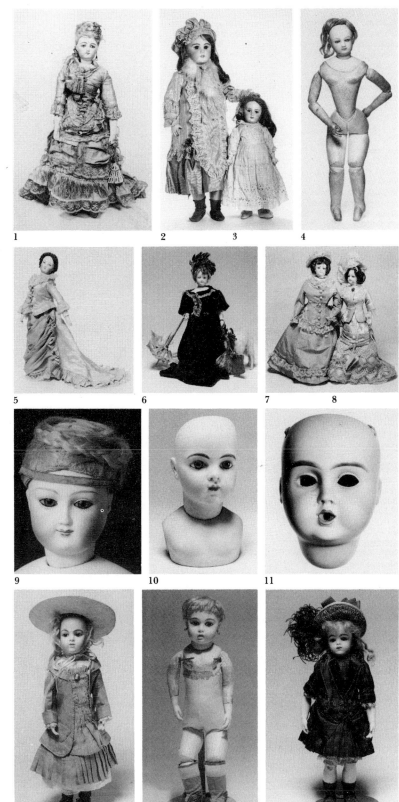

1 2 3 4
5 6 7 8
9 10 11
12 13 14

1
An Emile Jumeau bisque
'talking' doll, French,
c 1880, pull string for
voice box activating her
cry, impressed Depose
E 8 J, with red check
mark, one string broken,
two tiny chips neck
socket, *L 17 Jan*,
£3,850 ($5,583)

2
A French bisque doll,
c 1900, impressed 1902 2,
blond rear hair wig,
jointed wood and
composition body with
blue stamp on buttocks,
51cm (20in), *L 3 Oct*,
£264 ($343)

3
A French bisque-head
bébé, stamped in red
Depose//Tete Jumeau//4,
brown paperweight eyes,
83.8cm (33in), *NY 13 Dec*,
$2,090 (£1,756)

4
A French bisque-head
bébé, probably Jumeau,
incised 1907//14, with
blue threaded glass eyes,
moulded teeth, composi-
tion ball-jointed body,
73.7cm (29in), *NY 13 Dec*,
$1,650 (£1,387)

5
A French bisque doll,
Jumeau, c 1880, with real
auburn hair wig over
cork pate, jointed com-
position lady body, 52cm
(20½in), *L 29 May*,
£1,320 ($1,901)

6
A French bisque-head
bébé, Emile Jumeau, late
19th cent, with blue
paperweight eyes, deli-
cately painted facial
details, in original dress,
50.8cm (20in), *NY 23 June*,
$6,875 (£5,055)

7
A French bisque-head
bébé, Emile Jumeau, late
19th cent, in original
clothing, 50.8cm (20in),
NY 23 June,
$4,125 (£3,033)

8
A French bisque doll,
Jumeau, c 1885, impressed
15, weighted blue glass
eyes, eyes loose, 84cm
(33in), *L 3 Oct*,
£935 ($1,216)

9
A French bisque-head
bébé, Schmitt & Fils,
incised 1/SCH ball-
jointed wood and
composition body,
38.1cm (15in), *NY 7 Apr*,
$4,400 (£3,077)

10
A French bisque doll,
SFBJ, c 1900, impressed
SFBJ 12, with open
mouth and upper teeth,
jointed wood and com-
position body, 69cm
(27in), *L 3 Oct*,
£396 ($515)

11
A French bisque character
doll, SFBJ, c 1910,
impressed 226, with
open/closed mouth,
fixed blue glass eyes,
53cm (21in), *L 3 Oct*,
£528 ($686)

12
A French bisque doll,
SFBJ, c 1922, stamped in
red Tete Jumeau 8,
jointed wood and com-
position body with voice
box, inoperative, 51cm
(20in), *L 17 Jan*,
£209 ($303)

13
A French bisque character
doll, SFBJ, c 1910,
impressed 236-11,
weighted black glass
eyes, blond mohair wig
and curved limb com-
position body, 61cm (24in),
L 29 May,
£396 ($570)

14
A French bisque doll,
Jules Steiner 'C' series,
c 1880, impressed Cie
C3, with fixed hazel
paperweight eyes, jointed
wood and papier-mâché
body, dressed in original
clothes, together with a
trunk carrying further
clothing, 53cm (21in),
C 11 July,
£3,300 ($4,488)

15
A French bisque-head
mechanical walking doll,
Jules Steiner, late 19th
cent, 36.9cm (14½in)
NY 7 Apr,
$1,100 (£769)

16
A French bisque doll,
Jules Steiner, c 1890, face
cracked, 84cm (33in),
L 3 Oct,
£935 ($1,216)

1   2

3   4   5   6   7

8   9   10

11   12   13

14   15   16

1
A **French bisque doll**,
Jules Steiner, *c* 1890,
impressed A 15, with
closed mouth, weighted
blue glass eyes, red real
hair wig, jointed
composition body, 57.5cm
(22½in), *L 3 Oct*,
£2,310 ($3,003)

2
A **French Bourgoin bisque
doll**, Jules Steiner, *c* 1880,
impressed Sie C 2/0,
with closed mouth, white
blond mohair wig, 33cm
(13in), *L 3 Oct*,
£880 ($1,144)

3
A **French bisque-head
doll**, Jules Steiner, jointed
composition body,
operative voicebox, 50.8cm
(20in), *NY 23 June*,
£2,310 (£1,699)

4
A **French bisque-head
fashion doll**, the swivel
head incised 8, with
blond human-hair wig,
cloth body with bisque
lower arms, 63.5cm (25in),
NY 23 June,
$1,650 (£1,213)

5
A **French bisque-head
bébé**, François Gauthier,
incised F 9G., composition
body, with straight wrists,
50.8cm (20in), *NY 23 June*,
$2,860 (£2,103)

6
A **French bisque doll**,
Jules Steiner 'C' series,
c 1880, impressed Sie C
3/0, long real red hair
wig, jointed papier-
mâché body, 27cm (10½in),
L 17 Jan,
£660 ($957)

7
A **French bisque bébé**, F.
Gaultier, *c* 1878,
impressed F4G., original
blond mohair wig over
cork pate, 35.5cm (14in),
L 3 Oct,
£1,760 ($2,288)

8
A **French bisque-head
bébé**, Jumeau, wood and
composition body, 28cm
(11in), *NY 7 Apr*,
$1,540 (£1,077)

9
A **French bisque-head
bébé**, François Gauthier,
incised F7G., wood and
composition ball-jointed
body, with straight
wrists, 40.6cm (16in),
NY 13 Dec,
$1,870 (£1,571)

10
A **French bisque-head
bébé**, stamped in red
Depose//Tete Jumeau,
composition ball-jointed
body, 48.3cm (19in),
NY 13 Dec,
$2,200 (£1,849)

11
A **French bisque-head
fashion doll**, Jumeau,
incised 10, gusseted kid
body, 72.4cm (28½in),
NY 7 Apr,
$2,860 (£2,000)

12
A **French bisque-head
bébé**, E Denamur,
incised E12D, blond
human hair wig,
open/closed mouth,
66cm (26in), *NY 23 June*,
$3,630 (£2,669)

13
A **French bisque-head
bébé**, Jumeau, with cork
pate, blue paperweight
eyes, a closed mouth and
pierced ears, 66cm (26in),
NY 23 June,
$3,520 (£2,669)

14
A **French bisque-head
'Long Face' doll**, Jumeau,
incised 11, 63.5cm (25in),
NY 13 Dec,
$8,800 (£7,395)

15
A **French bisque-head
bébé**, stamped in red
Depose/Tete Jumeau
Bte S.G.D.G//6, composi-
tion ball-jointed body,
38.1cm (15in), *NY 23 June*,
$2,420 (£1,779)

16
A **French bisque doll**,
Jumeau, *c* 1880, 61cm
(24in), *L 29 May*,
£2,090 ($3,010)

1
A child's early pushchair,
English, mid-19th cent,
slight wear, h 71cm (28in),
L 3 Oct,
£286 ($372)

2
An oval doll's pram, 19th
cent, painted with gilt
decoration, *A 26 June,*
Dfl 899 (£211; $298)

3
**A rectangular wooden
doll's bed,** 43c, (17in),
A 26 June,
Dfl 185 (£43; $61)

4
A German tinplate stove,
Marklin, *c*1910, together
with accessories, w 43cm
(17in), *L 3 Oct,*
£550 ($715)

5
A model butcher's shop,
English, late 19th cent,
63.5 x 48.5cm (28 x 19in),
P 30 Oct/2 Nov,
£682 ($873)

6
A doll's house, English,
*c*1880, in the form of a
gothic villa; together
with a quantity of furni-
ture, *c*1930, *C 21 Mar,*
£506 ($754)

7
A doll's house, English,
20th cent, in the form of
a three-storey town
house, together with a
large quantity of furniture,
h 100cm (39½in), *L 3 Oct,*
£462 ($600)

8
A doll's house, English,
*c*1890, in the form of a
two-storey villa, with tall
gabled roof, h 127cm
(50in), *C 7 Nov,*
£308 ($410)

9
A doll's house, English,
*c*1830, storage drawer
below, h 110cm (43in),
C 21 Mar,
£473 ($705)

10
**A late Victorian doll's
house,** English, late 19th
cent, in three storeys,
with papered red brick
exterior, the roof lifting
off, together with a fine
collection of furniture
contemporary with the
house, h 82.5cm (32½in),
L 29 May,
£1,640 ($2,362)

2

1

3

4

5

6

7

8

9

10

1
An early black curly plush teddy bear, German, c1903, probably by Steiff, pads and plush well worn, 34cm (13½in), L 3 Oct, £154 ($200)

2
Teddy bear, c1910, with black button eyes, swivelling head, straw-filled white plush body, h 57cm (22½in), C 27/30 Nov, £187 ($226)

3
A brown plush teddy bear pull toy, Steiff, with marked button in ear, set on cast-iron wheels, (one ear missing), h 45.7cm (18in), NY 13 Dec, £416 ($495)

4
An orange curly plush teddy bear, c1935, with black-stitched snout, linen pads, with growler, h 61cm (24in), L 3 Oct, £66 ($86)

5
A pink-brown plush teddy bear, c1920, the arms each containing a growler when raised, plush worn, h 104cm (41in), L 3 Oct, £286 ($372)

6
A fat blond plush teddy bear, English, c1935, straw-filled stitched body with swivelling joints, cotton pads, growler inoperative, h 81cm (32in), L 3 Oct, £132 ($172)

7
A blond long plush teddy bear, probably Steiff, c1930, with rounded straw-stuffed body with back hump, swivel joints and large feet, h 56cm (22in), L 3 Oct, £176 ($229)

8
A blond plush teddy bear, the head stitched in three sections, black and white glass button eyes, plush worn, h 71cm (28in), L 3 Oct, £93 ($121)

9
A gold plush teddy bear, English, c1955, by Chad Valley Co. Ltd, h 102cm (40in), L 3 Oct, £275 ($358)

10
A white painted rocking horse, English, c1925, with flared nostrils and teeth, real hair mane and tail, chipped, mane cut, 132cm (52in), L 3 Oct, £242 ($315)

11
A rocking horse, late 19th cent, with tooled and studded leather saddle, stirrup irons, on green painted rockers, repainting and repair, 208cm (82in), L 3 Oct, £462 ($601)

12
A white plush donkey on wheels, Steiff, German, c1915, the straw-filled body with dark horsehair mane, pull-string 'voice' on the withers, tail missing, 84cm (33in), L 3 Oct, £165 ($215)

13
A pull-along cow, Steiff, German, c1930, with brown and white fabric hide, pull-cord 'moo', 51cm (20in), C 17/23 May, £231 ($335)

14
A rocking elephant, Steiff, German, c1925, with marked button in ear, 114cm (45in), L 29 May, £440 ($634)

15
A nodding tiger, c1910, the moulded papier-mâché body covered in simulated fur, articulated jaw which opens and shuts as the head nods, clockwork motor within, 58.5cm (23in), L 3 Oct, £352 ($458)

16
A mechanical walking crocodile, possibly by Decamps, French, c1915, the articulated papier-mâché and wooden beast with clockwork mechanism within, 86.5cm (34in), L 29 May, £550 ($792)

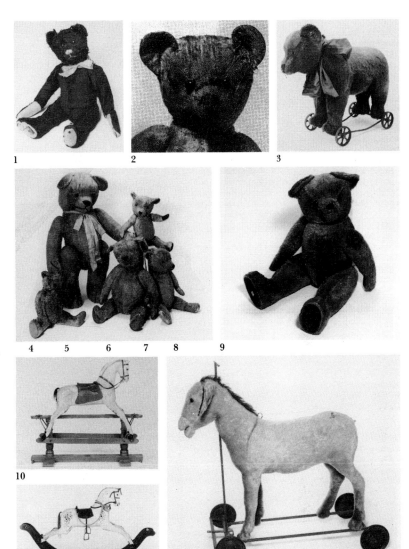

1   2   3

4   5   6   7   8   9

10

11   12

13   14

15   16

1
A singing bird automaton, Bontems, French, late 19th cent, the square base inset with 'Sevres' panels, the bird moving its tail, head and beak, 44.4cm (17½in), *NY 23 June*, $3,300 (£2,426)

2
A singing bird automaton, French, late 19th cent, two feathered birds, with stop, sing and delay-sing control, h 53.3cm (21in), *NY 23 June*, $1,320 (£971)

3
A singing bird automaton, French, c1900, the domed brass cage with hinged door, the bird with tail, head and beak movements, h 55cm (21½in), *L 29 May*, £880 ($1,267)

4
A singing bird automaton, French, c1880, the coin-operated mechanism with tail, head and beak movements, h 51cm (20in), *L 3 Oct*, £880 ($1,144)

5
A musical automaton of a dancing couple, Vichy, French, c1860, keywind mechanism, both redressed, h 34cm (13½in), *L 17 Jan*, £1,320 ($1,914)

6
A musical automaton pierrot playing a mandoline, probably Decamps, French, late 19th cent, the head turning and nodding as the right hand strums, h 43.2cm (17in), *NY 23 June*, $1,320 (£971)

7
A musical automaton of a woman knitting, probably Decamps, French, late 19th cent, h 41.9cm (16½in), *NY 13 Dec*, $3,025 (£2,542)

8
A musical automaton of an Oriental tea server, French, 19th cent, the head turning and nodding, the left hand moving the tray into position while the right hand raises the pot and pours, h 48.2cm (19in), *NY 23 June*, $3,575 (£2,629)

9
A musical automaton of a black banjo player, Vichy or Decamps, French, late 19th cent, the head turning and nodding while the right hand strums, the right leg crossing and uncrossing, h 57.1cm (22½in), *NY 23 June*, $5,500 (£4,044)

10
A musical automaton of a performer with a doll balancing on a standard, probably Decamps, French, late 19th cent, h 109.2cm (43in), *NY 13 Dec*, $11,000 (£9,244)

11
A musical automaton of a flower seller, Leopold Lambert, French, c1880, with Jumeau bisque head, her bisque hands holding in one the ribbon of a basket of flowers, in the other a posy which she raises alternately, her head nodding, 47cm (18½in), *L 3 Oct*, £2,860 ($3,718)

12
A bisque-headed cymbal player, probably French, c1890, the wood body with press squeaker activating the arms to clash the cymbals, h 38cm (15in), *L 29 May*, £220 ($317)

13
A musical automaton of a conjuror, probably by Leopold Lambert, French, c1880, movement in need of attention, h 41cm (16in), *L 29 May*, £1,430 ($2,059)

14
An advertising display automaton, c1930, the electrically operated and articulated figure with movements for mouth, eyebrows and head, 64cm (25in) *L 29 May*, £880 ($1,267)

15
A picture automaton, probably French, driven by a series of wheels and pulleys, 89cm (35in), *L 29 May* £770 ($1,109)

1

A display automaton, German, c1900, wired for electricity, h 91.5cm (36in), *L 3 Oct,* **£1,650 ($2,145)**

2

A musical automaton guitar player, Vichy, French, c1870, her head turning and her right hand playing the guitar, h 36cm (14in), *L 3 Oct,* **£1,100 ($1,430)**

3

A clockwork novelty display of the 'Persil' babies, one grimacing and one laughing, h 49cm (19¼in), *P 21/24 Feb,* **£550 ($771)**

4

A bisque-headed Punchinello puppet, French, c1870, the stiffened cloth body with kid hands, h 61cm (24in), *L 29 May,* **£1,210 ($1,742)**

5

A bisque-headed Marotte doll, German, c1890, with open/closed mouth, and bulbous cardboard body containing the musical movement, h 32cm (12½in), *L 29 May,* **£264 ($380)**

6

A shoulder-bisque Marotte doll, German, c1900, with fixed blue glass eyes, red-blond mohair wig, playing a tune when twirled, h 33cm (13in), *L 17 Jan,* **£253 ($367)**

7

Two Victorian ventriloquist's dummies, by H. Ridehalgh, in the form of an old man and an old woman, dated 1896, with articulated jaws, h 71cm (28in), *C 11 July,* **£352 ($479)**

8

An unusual magician's lamp, English, late 19th cent, wizard's head with grimacing expression, h 18cm (7in), *C 11 July,* **£132 ($179)**

9

A group of articulated wooden hand puppets, all probably French, late 19th cent, *L 3 Oct,* **£286 ($372)**

10

A collection of ten wooden hand puppets, probably all French, late 19th cent, Punch, Judy, policeman, judge, beadle, Joey the Clown, Ally Sloper, hangman, baby, the crocodile, *L 3 Oct,* **£880 ($1,144)**

11

A group of animal skittles, c1910, the felt-covered beasts supported by turned wooden base, two felt-covered balls, the largest h 28cm (11in), *L 17 Jan,* **£330 ($479)**

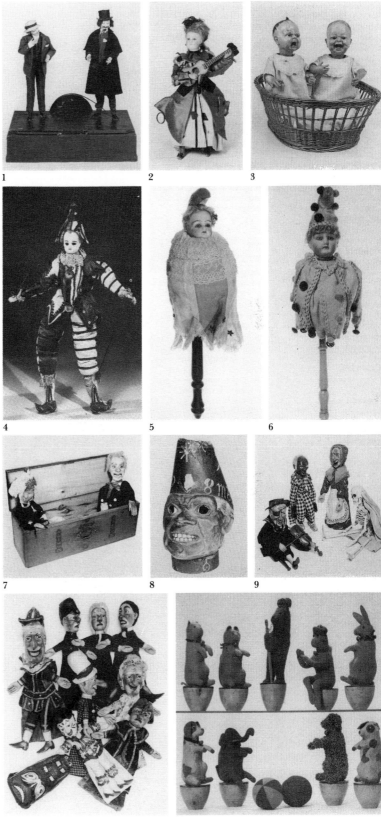

1

2

3

4

5

6

7

8

9

10

11

1
'Walking Down Broadway',
Lehmann, German,
c 1895, dog missing,
NY 13 Dec,
$770 (£647)

2
A painted tin clockwork
carrousel, German, late
19th cent, h 45.7cm (18in),
NY 13 Dec,
$1,870 (£1,655)

3
A negro drummer, Ernst
Plank, German, c 1890,
dressed in original cos-
tume, h 37cm (14½in),
L 3 Oct,
£1,650 ($2,145)

4
A tinplate 'Oh-my',
Lehmann, German,
c 1920, no. 690, h 27cm
(10½in), *L 29 May,*
£209 ($301)

5
A 'Le Gai Violiniste', F.
Martin, French, c 1910,
in original clothes,
h 19.5cm (7¾in), *L 29 May,*
£242 ($348)

6
A tinplate pianist, F.
Martin, French, c 1910,
clockwork, h 15cm (6in),
L 29 May,
£385 ($554)

7
Jolly Nigger and Uncle
Sam, two lithographic
labels, American, late
19th cent, the larger
8.3 x 13.3cm (3¼ x 5¼in),
L 17 Jan,
£209 ($303)

8
A cast-iron Paddy and the
Pig mechanical bank, J. &
E. Stevens, Co, American,
late 19th cent, h 20.5cm
(8in), *L 29 May,*
£385 ($554)

9
A cast-iron Punch and
Judy mechanical bank,
Shepard Hardware Co,
American, late 19th cent,
h 19cm (7½in), *L 29 May,*
£462 ($665)

10
A cast-iron Uncle Sam
mechanical bank,
Shepard Hardware Co,
American, late 19th cent,
h 29cm (11½in),
L 29 May,
£220 ($317)

11
A cast-iron Dinah
mechanical bank, John
Harper & Co, Ltd, English,
20th cent, h 16.5cm
(6½in), *L 29 May,*
£104 ($150)

12
A Stump Speaker cast-iron
mechanical bank,
American, late 19th cent,
h 25cm (9¾in), *L 17 Jan,*
£1,265 ($1,834)

13
A Speaking Dog cast-iron
mechanical bank, Shepard
Hardware and J. & E.
Stevens Co, American,
late 19th cent, 18cm
(7in), *L 17 Jan,*
£286 ($415)

14
An Artillery Bank cast-
iron mechanical bank,
American, late 19th cent,
20.2cm (8in), *L 17 Jan,*
£187 ($271)

15
A Giant in the Tower cast-
iron mechanical bank,
English, late 19th cent,
the giant moving forward
as a coin is deposited,
h 24cm (9½in), *L 3 Oct,*
£2,090 ($2,717)

1   2   3   4

5   6   7

8   9   10   11   12

13

14   15

1
**Meccano Dinky aeroplanes
set 60,** containing
Imperial Airways low
wing monoplane, DH
Leopard Moth, and others,
L 17 Jan,
£330 ($479)

2
**An R100 tinplate
Zeppelin,** Tipp, German,
c 1930, with rear propeller
operated by clockwork
mechanism, 65cm (25½in),
L 17 Jan,
£825 ($1,196)

3
A tinplate model liner,
probably German,
c 1930, 'Queen Mary',
clockwork mechanism
driving the three-bladed
propeller at the rear,
73.7cm (29in), *L 17 Jan,*
£495 ($718)

4
**A painted tin clockwork
battleship the "Maine",**
Marklin, German,
c 1905, the key-wound
clockwork mechanism con-
cealed within the hull,
anchor chain and one
lifeboat lacking, 74cm
(29in), *NY 23 June,*
$15,400 (£11,324)

5
**A painted tin clockwork
battleship,** Bing, German,
c 1900, with deck details
and a four-blade pro-
peller below, lifeboats
missing, partially
restored, 73.7cm (29in),
NY 13 Dec,
$4,125 (£3,466)

6
**A hand-painted tinplate
passenger and vehicle
ferry,** Bing, German,
c 1925, 'Union', the side-
wheeler with clockwork
mechanism concealed
within, lacking rudder,
52cm (20½in), *L 3 Oct,*
£1,045 ($1,358)

7
A battleship, Bing,
German, *c* 1912, 'HMS
Powerful', finished in
two-tone grey with brick
decking, one lifeboat
and one funnel missing,
74cm (29in), *L 29 May,*
£935 ($1,346)

8
A tinplate gun boat, Bing,
German, *c* 1915, with
twin funnels, mast with
crow's nest, clockwork
powered, slight damage,
50cm (19¾in), *L 3 Oct,*
£418 ($543)

9
Britain's Salvation Army,
from sets 10 and 14,
c 1906, *L 29 May,*
£990 ($1,426)

10
Britain's 21st Lancers,
Royal Scots Greys (2nd
Dragoons), and Ninth
Queen's Royal Lancers
(illustrated), 14 figures,
L 29 May,
£93 ($134)

11
**Britain's King's Troop
Royal Horse Artillery,**
with gun limber, six-
horse team with pos-
tillions and five-man
galloping escort, *L 29 May,*
£154 ($222)

12
**Britain's Coronation 'Sove-
reign's Escort' set,** 1953,
containing State Coach,
Life Guards, Horse
Guards, outriders,
footmen, Yeomen of the
Guard, Guardsmen and
many others, w 60cm
(23½in), *L 17 Jan,*
£825 ($1,196)

13
A Noah's Ark, German,
late 19th cent, the
wooden vessel containing
47 pairs of animals and 8
figures of Noah and his
family, 58.5cm (23in),
L 17 Jan,
£1,650 ($2,393)

1

A 2½in gauge engineered model of 4-6-2 LMS locomotive 'Princess Elizabeth', no. 6201, finished in LMS maroon and black lined gold, with matching six-wheeled tender, 113cm (44½in), *L 3 Oct,*
£825 ($1,072)

2

A brass 2-2-2 locomotive, Newton & Co, English, *c* 1860, with non-original tender, 32cm (12½in), *L 3 Oct,*
£770 ($1,001)

3

A gauge 0 20-volt electric Southern 4-4-0 'Eton' locomotive, Hornby, English, *c* 1938, no. 900, together with its no. 2 Special Southern, no. 900, *P 30 Oct/2 Nov,*
£418 ($535)

4

A gauge 0 4-volt electric 4-4-0 locomotive, Marklin, *c* 1930, finished in Midland maroon livery, together with its six-wheeled tender, *P 15/18 May,*
£209 ($291)

5

A gauge 1 spirit-fired live steam LNWR 4-4-0 locomotive, Bing, German, *c* 1905, no. 1902, 51cm (20in), *P 15/18 May,*
£308 ($428)

6

A gauge 2 clockwork 4-4-0 locomotive, Bing, German, *c* 1902, no. 2361, finished in Midland Railway colours, with matching six-wheeled tender and three matching fitted bogie coaches, contained in original box, *L 3 Oct,*
£3,960 ($5,148)

7

A passenger coach, GC & GN, Nüremberg, with four coupés, 41cm (16⅛in), *A 26 June,*
Dfl 348 (£81; $115)

8

A gauge 0 clockwork 4-6-2 locomotive 'Flying Scotsman', Bassett-Lowke, no. 4472, finished in LNER colours, with matching eight-wheeled tender, *L 29 May,*
£352 ($507)

9

A 3½in gauge copper and brass spirit-fired 2-4-0 locomotive, English, *c* 1880s, No. 715, 43.5cm (17¼in), *L 29 May,*
£1,100 ($1,584)

10

A gauge 1 clockwork 4-4-0 locomotive, 'Jupiter', Bing, German, *c* 1910, no. 1975, with matching LNER six-wheeled tender, *L 29 May,*
£462 ($665)

11

A gauge 1 clockwork 4-4-0 locomotive 'Sydney', German, *c* 1910, no. 3410, finished in GWR colours, with matching six-wheeled tender, *L 29 May,*
£715 ($1,030)

12

A tinplate pull-along train, S M J, French, *c* 1905, contained in original cardboard box, w 28cm (11in), *L 29 May,*
£242 ($348)

13

A tinplate 'Rocket' gauge 1 trainset, Marklin, German, *c* 1909, comprising 2-0-2 locomotive no. 1829, open passenger coaches and luggage car, *L 29 May,*
£28,050 ($40,392)

14

A gauge 1 tinplate bogie Kaiserwagen, Marklin, German, *c* 1901, hand-painted, with fitted interior, 28cm (11in), *L 29 May,*
£605 ($871)

15

A gauge 2 'King Edward' 4-4-0 tinplate live steam locomotive and tender, Bing, German, *c* 1908, with original livery, paintwork chipped, some rust, lacking front bogie and spirit burner, *C 21 Mar,*
£935 ($1,393)

16

A tinplate polychrome 'Central Station', 38cm (15in), *A 26 June,*
Dfl 6,960 (£1,630; $2,298)

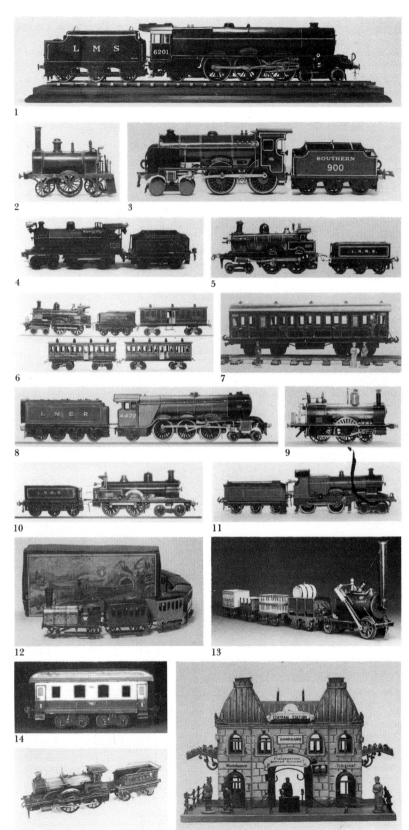

1

A tinplate **Royal Mail van**, Tipp & Co, German, late 1930s, clockwork mechanism powering rear axle, 24cm (9½in), *C 11 July*, £715 ($972)

2

A tinplate **brougham**, probably German, *c* 1905, clockwork mechanism powering rear axle, 18cm (7in), *C 21 Mar*, £88 ($131)

3

A polychrome tinplate **'Bijenkorf' transport van**, Distler, Nüremberg, *c* 1930, with driver, *A 17 Dec*, Dfl 2,436 (£582; $728)

4

A **'Midlands' cast-iron bus**, Wallwork, English, *c* 1900, with rubber tyres, 30.5cm (12in), *NY 13 Dec*, $1,430 (£1,202)

5

Manoil die-cast vehicles, three futuristically styled cars, *L 29 May*, £82 ($118)

6

Dinky 22G and 22H vehicles, good original condition, *L 29 May*, £286 ($412)

7

Three vehicles, **Dinky 24 Series**, 24C town sedan, 24 ambulance, 24 streamlined tourer, *L 29 May*, £330 ($475)

8

A tinplate and clockwork **tipping lorry**, Tipp & Co, German, *c* 1930, with tinplate driver, 26.5cm (10⅜in), *P 15/18 May*, £630 ($887)

9

A tinplate and clockwork **chauffeur-driven limousine**, Distler, finished in blue and black, 20.5cm (8in), *P 15/18 May*, £253 ($352)

10

A tinplate and clockwork **'101' single-seat car**, German, with seated driver, 28cm (11in), *P 15/18 May*, £154 ($214)

11

Three Dinky toys, comprising 33R mechanical horse and Southern Railway box van, 29 Series centre entrance bus and 26 Series railcar, *L 29 May*, £187 ($269)

12

A **lorry and trailer**, Distler, German, *c* 1935, clockwork mechanism, with matching four-wheeled open trailer, 50cm (19¾in), *L 17 Jan*, £418 ($606)

13

Four Spot-on vehicles, comprising Jones Crane, AEC Mammoth Major 8, 4000 gallon auto petrol tanker, and car, dinghy and trailer set, *L 29 May*, £440 ($634)

14

A **non-constructional car**, Meccano, *c* 1935, finished in red and blue, in original box, 22cm (8¾in), *L 29 May*, £528 ($760)

15

A tinplate **racing car**, English, 33cm (13in), *A 26 June*, Dfl 150 (£35; $50)

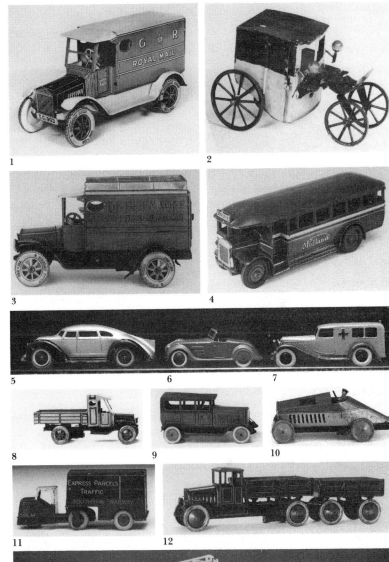

1

2

3

4

5

6

7

8

9

10

11

12

13

14

15

1
A lithographed limousine, Carette, German, c.1910, with opening rear doors, glazed windscreen, 21.5cm (8½in), *L 29 May,* £1,430 ($2,059)

2
A lithographed limousine, Carette, German, c.1912, driver with steering wheel, opening rear doors, gear and hand brake levers, 32cm (12½in), *L 3 Oct,* £1,320 ($1,716)

3
A tinplate open tourer, Carette 50, German, c.1906, steering wheel and clockwork mechanism, containing driver and three passengers, original box, 20cm (8in), *L 17 Jan,* £3,520 ($5,104)

4
A hand-painted four-seat open tourer, Carette, German, c.1910, with rubber-tyred spoked wheels, original box, 32.5cm (12½in), *L 17 Jan,* £6,710 ($9,730)

5
A tinplate landaulette, Carette, German, c.1912, with hinged doors, the rear section with folding oilcloth canopy, *C 7 Nov,* £1,210 ($1,609)

6
A Pickford's removal van (first pattern), Dinky 28 Series, issued c.1934-5, *P 10/13 July,* £396 ($539)

7
A painted tin clockwork Aston Martin, Meccano, English, 1934, finished in red with an off-white running board, with driver, 33cm (13in), *NY 13 Dec,* $550 (£462)

8
A constructor car set, Marklin, German, c.1930, the clockwork motor driving the front axle with differential gears, 35.6cm (14in), *NY 13 Dec,* $825 (£693)

9
A painted tin clockwork racing car, Delage 1500C, JEP, French, c.1928, the mechanism driving the rear axle, with spoked rubber tyres, 45.7cm (18in), *NY 13 Dec,* $660 (£555)

10
A lithographed tin 'Vineta' tram car, Lehmann, early 1900s, finished in black with red doors and trim, 22.9cm (9in), *NY 13 Dec,* $660 (£555)

11
A lithographed tin clockwork limousine, Distler, German, early 1900s, with driver, 25.4cm (10in), *NY 13 Dec,* $715 (£601)

12
A painted tin wind-up Citroen C4 sedan, French, c.1928, painted red with blue roof, with steering mechanism, inoperative, 30.5cm (12in), *NY 13 Dec,* $715 (£601)

13
A tinplate and clockwork Alfa Romeo P2 racing car, CIJ, c.1927, rack and pinion steering, external brake to clockwork mechanism, 52.5cm (20⅝in), *P 30 Oct/2 Nov,* £594 ($760)

14
A tinplate Panhard, CIJ, French, c.1955, finished in light green, battery-powered rear wheels and headlamps, 26cm (10¼in), *L 17 Jan,* £55 ($80)

15
A tinplate Paris bus, JEP, French, c.1925, lithographed 'Madeleine', including driver, 26cm (10¼in), *L 17 Jan,* £330 ($479)

16
A spirit-fired live steam agricultural tractor, Marklin, German, , c.1920, single cylinder, red wheels with black metal tyres, 26.7cm (10½in), *P 30 Oct/2 Nov,* £1,485 ($1,901)

1

2

3

4

5

6

7   8   9   10   11   12

13

14

15

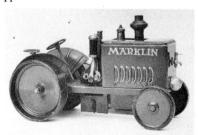
16

1

A hand-painted open-cab limousine, Bing, German, c 1908, with bevelled glass windows, opening doors, 27 cm (10½ in), *L 17 Jan,*
£2,310 ($3,350)

2

A tinplate four-seat open tourer and passengers, Gunthermann, German, c 1910, lithographed in cream lined gold, with rubber-tyred spoked wheels, 19 cm (7½ in), *L 29 May,*
£2,420 ($3,485)

3

A tinplate and clockwork roll-back roof coupé, Gunthermann, German, driver missing, *P 10/13 July,*
£396 ($539)

4

A tinplate vis-à-vis motorcar, Gunthermann, German, c 1899, with driver and rubber-tyred wheels, the vehicle repainted, 24 cm (9½ in), *L 3 Oct,*
£825 ($1,072)

5

A tinplate and clockwork fire engine with pump, Gunthermann, German, c 1912, with pressed tin crew of three, 24 cm (9½ in), *P 30 Oct/2 Nov,*
£715 ($915)

6

A red, blue and yellow lithographed fire engine, Distler, Nüremberg, c 1930, with firemen, *A 17 Dec,*
Dfl 556 (£133; $166)

7

A tinplate hand-painted fire pumper, Gunthermann, German, c 1910, complete with three composition crewmen, hose replaced, 33 cm (13 in), *L 3 Oct,*
£1,650 ($2,145)

8

A tinplate fire engine, Gunthermann, German, c 1910, complete with four crew members, 40 cm (15¾ in), *L 3 Oct,*
£1,430 ($1,859)

9

A tinplate hoop toy, Hull & Stafford type, American, c 1871, the horses' saddles stencilled with patent details, d 22.5 cm (9 in), *L 17 Jan,*
£880 ($1,276)

10

A Zig Zag tinplate vehicle, Lehmann, German, c 1910, no. 640, h 12 cm, *L 17 Jan,*
£660 ($958)

11

A tinplate trotter, G & K, German, c 1920, no. 524, 21 cm (8¼ in), *L 3 Oct,*
£330 ($429)

12

A 'Halloh' gyroscopic motor cycle, Lehmann, German, c 1920, no. 683, clockwork, 21.5 cm (8½ in), *L 29 May,*
£880 ($1,267)

13

A Nu-Nu, Lehmann, German, c 1915, no. 773, clockwork, h 14 cm (5½ in), *L 3 Oct,*
£418 ($543)

14

A tinplate Adam, Lehmann, German, c 1920, no. 689, clockwork, excellent condition, h 20 cm (8 in), *C 7 Nov,*
£605 ($805)

15

A tinplate clockwork tram, Gunthermann, German, c 1925, defective clockwork mechanism, 24 cm (9¼ in), *C 7 Nov,*
£286 ($380)

16

An early mechanical tricyclist, French, c 1890, the figure dressed in original clothes, 21 cm (8¼ in), *L 29 May,*
£770 ($1,109)

17

A tinplate Paddy and the Pig, German, c 1930, the clockwork mechanism causing pig and rider to rock back and forth, h 13 cm (5 in), *C 7 Nov,*
£154 ($205)

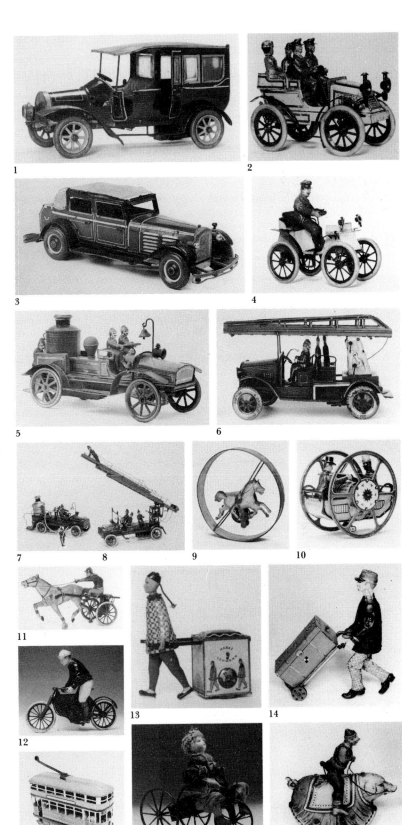

1   2
3   4
5   6
7   8   9   10
11
12   13   14
15   16   17

American Folk Art

NANCY DRUCKMAN

Folk art can be defined as the art of the common man. It has often been created by craftsmen as a means of supplementing their frequently meagre incomes. Coach and sign painters executed family portraits; wood-workers built ships and also carved figureheads and other sculptures; schoolmasters penned ornamental pieces; women and young girls wove material and sewed clothing for everyday use as well as turning out embroideries and decorative fancy pieces. While folk artists have often been ignorant of academic principles and techniques, there is in their best work an intuitive and instinctive emphasis on colour, line, rhythm, pattern and texture which is often unique and quite compelling. These elements are at the core of the similarities between folk and modern art.

The history of collecting American folk art is even shorter than the hundred years in which it flourished. As recently as fifty years ago, most of it enjoyed the dubious status of family junk. Hidden in dusty attics, folded away in trunks and shoe-boxes, it was considered, at best, old-fashioned and quaint. Those people who did seek it—a few social historians and stalwart enthusiasts for modern art with a penchant for championing unpopular artistic causes—were considered hopelessly eccentric. This lack of interest reflected the Americans' generally deprecatory view of their native art as a whole. The notion that American art was inferior to European had existed for two centuries and was reflected in the fact that major museums and private collections contained almost nothing but European works.

Gradually, however, attitudes began to change. Among many reasons, the most significant was the surge of national pride and patriotism following the Second Word War. This rekindled an interest in the American past and brought a reassessement of all aspects of culture. The establishment of public collections reflected a developing concern with the preservation and study of all aspects of American decorative arts, including folk art. This new enthusiasm was also reflected in the auction market. In March 1944, the George H. Lorimer collection of fine American furniture and decorations was sold at Parke-Bernet and folk art achieved notably high prices for the first time.

The field of American folk art as it is known today includes several distinct categories. Folk painting is the most highly sought after and expensive, but there are also highly inventive, imaginative and compelling examples of sculpture, weather-vanes, decoys and cigar store figures. Originally conceived for utilitiarian purposes, these boldly-designed pieces, which represented the work of individual carvers and metal workers in the early days, now fetch tens of thousands of dollars.

Another category is textiles—including quilts, coverlets, samplers and embroideries. Again, each one of these had a function. The quilts and coverlets were used as bed coverings while the samplers and embroideries were teaching tools and evidence of education and social refinement. Within these constraints, the folk artist produced stunningly graphic work and the young schoolgirl stitcher made charming and evocative records of her growing skill with needle and thread.

Finally, there is the historic and artistic work of the sailing artist-artisan—the scrimshander. These men whiled away the long tiresome hours at sea by engraving beautiful depictions of sailing ships or scenes of the whale hunt on polished whale teeth, or fashioned gifts from ivory in the form of jagging wheels, crimpers, walking sticks, boxes and other small objects (see p.175). These pieces are not only artistic treasures in their own right, but provide the collector with a tangible record of an all-but vanished period in American cultural history.

1
A carved wood whirligig, American, 19th cent, h 43cm (17in), *NY 30 June,* $550 (£407)

2
A carved and painted wood Indian whirligig, American, late 19th cent, h 29cm (11½in), *NY 30 June,* $1,760 (£1,304)

3
A carved pine whirligig, American, late 19th/early 20th cent, h 33cm (13in), *NY 30 June,* $990 (£733)

4
A cast-iron butcher's trade sign, American, 19th cent, h 51cm (20in), *NY 27 Jan,* $770 (£530)

5
A carved and painted wood cigar store Indian, probably New England, 19th cent, lacks one arm and one foot, h 166cm (5ft 5in), *NY 30 June,* $2,420 (£1,793)

6
A carved and painted wood cigar store Indian princess, probably Samuel Robb, New York, c 1880, h 155cm (5ft 1in), *NY 30 June,* $4,950 (£3,667)

1

3

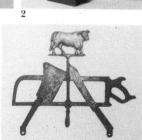

4

5

6

1

A carved and moulded
cement American eagle,
American, late 19th cent,
covered in an old white
polychrome, h 69cm (27in),
NY 8 Dec,
$1,320 (£1,102)

2

A moulded copper and
zinc rearing horse weathervane, A L Jewell & Co,
Waltham, Mass, 3rd
quarter 19th cent, h
43.5cm (17¼in), *NY 28 Jan,*
$4,950 (£3,410)

3

A cast-iron rooster
weathervane, American,
3rd quarter 19th cent,
h 61cm (24in), *NY 28 Jan,*
$2,310 (£1,591)

4

A prancing horse and
rider copper and zinc
weathervane, A L Jewell
& Co, Waltham, Mass,
3rd quarter 19th cent,
retaining some old
yellow paint and
verdigris, h 69cm (27in),
NY 28 Jan,
$7,700 (£5,305)

5

A sheet-copper and zinc
jumping horse weathervane,
A L Jewell & Co, Waltham,
Mass, 3rd quarter 19th
cent, retaining much
original gilding and
verdigris, h 79cm (31in),
NY 28 Jan,
$37,400 (£25,766)

6

A moulded and
hammered copper cow
weathervane, L W Cushing
and Sons, Waltham, Mass,
3rd quarter 19th cent,
h 42cm (16½in), *NY 28 Jan,*
$5,500 (£3,789)

7

A moulded copper and
zinc trotting horse weathervane, L W Cushing and
Sons, Waltham, Mass,
3rd quarter 19th cent,
from a tavern in Trenton,
NJ, h 39cm (15¼in),
NY 28 Jan,
$3,850 (£2,652)

8

A moulded copper horse
and rider weathervane,
American, 3rd quarter
19th cent, found in
Sunapee NH, h 52cm
(20½in), *NY 28 Jan,*
$5,500 (£3,789)

9

A moulded copper ram
weathervane, American,
3rd quarter 19th cent,
h 36.5cm (14¼in), *NY 28 Jan,*
$6,050 (£4,168)

10

A cast-zinc and sheet-
copper rooster weathervane,
Howard & Co, West
Bridgewater, Mass, 3rd
quarter 19th cent, retains
yellow polychrome and
verdigris, 30.5cm (12in),
NY 8 Dec,
$4,400 (£3,667)

11

A moulded and gilded
copper and zinc cow
weathervane, J W Fiske,
New York, late 19th
cent, now covered in
gold paint, h 84cm
(33¼in), *NY 27 Jan,*
$2,640 (£1,819)

12

A moulded copper Goddess
of Liberty weathervane,
Thomas W Jones, New
York, c1884, the figure
holding an American
flag of sheet copper with
pierced stars, h 91.5cm
(36in), *NY 28 Jan,*
$28,600 (£19,704)

13

A carved and polychrome
fish weathervane, American,
19th cent, retaining
much old green and
white paint, 89cm (35in),
NY 30 June,
$1,100 (£815)

1

2

3

4

5

6

7

8

9

10

11

12

13

1
A group of miscellaneous
tin cookie cutters, American,
19th cent, approx 12
pieces, *NY 8 Dec*,
$1,045 (£872)

2
A group of miscellaneous
tin cookie cutters,
American, 19th cent,
approx 10 pieces,
NY 8 Dec,
$825 (£689)

3
A carved ebony and whale
ivory coconut shell dipper,
*c*1900, elaborately carved
in relief with exotic
flowers, berries and leaves,
41cm (16in), *NY 27 Jan*,
$412 (£284)

4
A painted wood 'Bucher'
dome-top box, attributed
to Heinrich Bucher,
Berks County, late 18th
cent, painted with sprays
of tulip blossoms on a
black ground, 24cm (9½in),
NY 30 June,
$660 (£487)

5
A painted and decorated
toleware coffee pot,
American, 19th cent,
painted with large red
flowers on a dark brown
ground, minor restoration,
h 21cm (8¼in), *NY 30 June*,
$935 (£693)

6
A painted and decorated
pine miniature lift-top
blanket chest, signed Miss
H. Taylor, New Scotland,
Albany Co, New York,
19th cent, 48cm (19in),
NY 30 June,
$1,210 (£896)

7
A painted bentwood
'Bucher' bride's box,
attributed to Heinrich
Bucher, Berks County,
Pa, late 18th cent, the lid
painted with tulip
blossoms on a black
ground, 40cm (15½in),
NY 30 June,
$2,090 (£1,548)

8
A sponge-painted pine
miniature blanket chest,
New England, *c*1830,
painted with dark brown
sponge decoration over
an ochre ground, 61cm
(24in), *NY 28 Jan*,
$880 (£606)

9
A tramp art chest,
American, *c*1930, with
deep concentric and
graduated circles, stars
and reel devices in the
characteristic chip-carved
motif, h 38.3cm (15¼in),
NY 8 Dec,
$990 (£825)

10
A painted dome-top small
trunk, probably New
England, 19th cent,
domed lid, painted with
a large open fan, 57cm
(22½in), *NY 8 Dec*,
$440 (£367)

11
Four Shaker bentwood
utility boxes, American,
2nd half 19th cent, in
graduated oval sizes,
17.5cm (7in) to 38cm
(15in), *NY 8 Dec*,
$880 (£733)

12
A carved mahogany cake
board, stamped 'J.
Conger, New York',
early 19th cent, 33 x
58.4cm (13⅜ x 23½in),
NY 8 Dec,
$935 (£779)

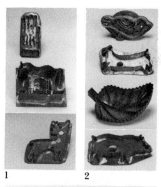

1

2

3

4

5

6

7

8

9

10

11

12

1
An American floral hooked rug, 19th cent, of red, pink, grey, beige and brown fabric, approx 132 x 152cm (52 x 60in), *NY 8 Dec,* $660 (£551)

2
Two American hooked rugs, 19th/20th cent, one worked with the figure of a unicorn, the other with a central thistle, 61 x 87cm (24 x 34in) and 84 x 58cm (33¼ x 23in), *NY 8 Dec,* $330 (£275)

3
A cutwork mourning picture, to the memory of Miss Emeline Wonson, Boston, April 10, 1827, 25 x 20cm (10 x 8in), *NY 8 Dec,* $1,320 (£1,102)

4
A needlework sampler, Mary Snowden, Philadelphia, dated 1806, executed on a linen ground, some holes and discolouration, 61 x 58.5cm (24 x 23in), *NY 27 Jan,* $1,430 (£985)

5
A needlework sampler, Miss Mary S Little, probably Rhode Island, dated Sept 1833, executed on a linen ground, 43 x 42.5cm (17 x 16¾in), *NY 27 Jan,* $1,100 (£758)

6
A needlework sampler, Sarah G Hallar, probably Pennsylvania, dated June 3, 1829, 52 x 43cm (20½ x 17in), *NY 30 June,* $1,210 (£896)

7
A needlework sampler, Dinah Cameron, Central Pennsylvania, dated 1829, on a loosely woven linen ground, some discolouration, 45 x 38cm (17¾ x 15in), *NY 8 Dec,* $1,650 (£1,375)

8
A fabric mammy doll, American, with black leather hands, h 54cm (21¼in), *NY 27 Jan,* $357 (£246)

9
A watercolour Fraktur, Taufschein for Maria Margaretha Scherner, Northampton County, dated 1821, inscribed in ornamental German calligraphy, 17.5 x 30.5cm (7¾ x 12in), *NY 30 June,* $440 (£326)

10
A set of eight carved whalebone clothes pegs, 19th cent, 12cm (5in), *NY 27 Jan,* $357 (£246)

11
Two cast-iron stove plates, Pennsylvania, mid-18th cent, the first dated 1749, the second dated 1763, 62 x 66cm (24½ x 26in) and 50 x 54.5cm (19¾ x 21½in), *NY 27 Jan,* $990 (£682)

1

2

3

4

5

6

7

8

9

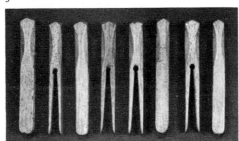

10

11

1

A pieced, appliqued and trapunto Baltimore album quilt, *c* 1840, centred by a depiction of the Baltimore Monument, approx 274 x 264cm (108 x 104in), *NY 8 Dec*, $17,600 (£14,691)

2

A pieced calico 'Star of Bethlehem' quilt, probably Pennsylvania 19th cent, patches arranged in a Star of Bethlehem with Stars of Le Moyne, approx 275 x 254cm (9 x 8ft 4in), *NY 30 June*, $1,210 (£896)

3

A pieced calico crib quilt, American, 19th cent, composed of patches arranged in the Le Moyne Star pattern, approx 102 x 91.5cm (40 x 36in), *NY 27 Jan*, $2,475 (£1,705)

4

A pieced and appliqued calico album quilt, probably Pennsylvania, *c* 1850, composed of brightly coloured red, green, yellow and blue calico and cotton patches, approx 284cm (9ft 4in) square, *NY 30 June*, $3,520 (£2,607)

5

A pieced cotton quilt, Pennsylvania, late 19th cent, composed of jade green, yellow and maroon patches arranged in a Double Star pattern, approx 193cm (6ft 4in) square, *NY 30 June*, $880 (£652)

6

A pieced red, yellow and green cotton quilt, Pennsylvania, late 19th cent, in a Star and Circle pattern, approx 203 x 193cm (6ft 8in x 6ft 4in), *NY 30 June*, $1,650 (£1,222)

7

A pieced and appliqued cotton quilt, probably Pennsylvania, 19th cent, composed of red and green patches arranged in a President's Wreath pattern, approx 203 x 193cm (6ft 8in x 6ft 4in), *NY 30 June*, $715 (£530)

8

A pieced calico 'Diamond Patch' quilt, American, 19th cent, the field heightened with diagonal line quilting, approx 193 x 224cm (6ft 4in x 7ft 4in), *NY 30 June*, $660 (£489)

9

A pieced and appliqued calico quilt, probably Pennsylvania, 19th cent, patches arranged in a Blossom and Bud pattern, the white cotton field heightened with elaborate feather and wreath quilting, approx 214 x 221cm (7 x 7ft 3in), *NY 30 June*, $605 (£448)

10

A pieced red and green cotton quilt, probably Pennsylvania, 19th cent, on a white cotton ground with wreath and vine quilting, approx 193 x 203cm (6ft 4in x 6ft 8in), *NY 8 Dec*, $715 (£596)

1
A rare George II stump-work coat of arms, mid-18th cent, in faded colours on a red silk damask ground, 114.5 x 122cm (45 x 48in), *L 16 Mar,* £770 ($1,147)

2
A Charles II stump-work picture, centred by a pair of figures surrounded by a building, a leopard, a stag, a bird and flowers, heightened in seed pearls, 33.5 x 45cm (13¼ x 17¾in), *L 15 June,* £2,420 ($3,412)

3
A Charles II silk and stump-work casket, late 17th cent, the lid enclosing a mirrored and painted-paper-lined interior, applied with stump work figures, 38 x 29cm (15 x 11½in), *C 3/6 July,* £1,375 ($1,856)

4
A Charles II stump-work picture, *c*1660, depicting the Judgement of Paris, with a variety of stitches in silk with some wire-work, 50 x 43cm (19½ x 17in), *L 16 Nov,* £3,960 ($5,227)

5
A linen sampler, English, dated 1833, worked by Emma Nield in her twelfth year, three figures unfinished, 56 x 46cm (22 x 18in), *C 27/30 Nov,* £165 ($200)

6
An early George III needlework sampler, by Isabella Huticheson, worked with platitudes, country house and park, 51 x 48cm (20 x 19in), *HS 25 June,* £1,320 ($1,861)

7
An English needlework picture, late 17th cent, worked in petit point with figures beside Moses in the bullrushes, 53 x 44cm (21 x 17½in), *C 3/6 July,* £1,540 ($2,079)

8
An English early 19th cent needlework sampler, by Harriot Farrow, aged 12, 1837, 47 x 47cm (18½ x 18½in), *P 18/25 Sept,* £396 ($511)

9
An English early 19th cent needlework sampler, worked with text, plants, figures and alphabet, signed Barbara Watney, her work in the 11th year of her age, Feb 1802, 39 x 31cm (15½ x 12¼in), *P 18/25th Sept,* £440 ($568)

10
A William IV needlework sampler, signed Mary Belt, died June 25th, 1828, aged 23, Frances Eliott finished this work, aged eight years, 1833, 60 x 53cm (23½ x 21in), *HS 25 June,* £935 ($1,318)

1

2

3

4

5

6

7

8

9

10

1
An organ celeste cylinder musical box, Swiss, c.1880, the 49cm cylinder playing twelve airs, w 79cm (31in), *L 29 May*, £1,210 ($1,742)

2
An organ celeste cylinder musical box, Swiss, c.1880, the 15.5cm cylinder playing eight airs, 43cm (17in), *L 17 Jan*, £418 ($606)

3
A cylinder musical box, Nicole Frères, Swiss, c.1880, the 31cm cylinder playing ten airs, w 52cm (20½in), *L 17 Jan*, £429 ($622)

4
A large cylinder musical box, Nicole Frères, Swiss, 1870s, the 60cm cylinder playing twelve popular airs on two combs, w 89cm (35in), *L 17 Jan*, £2,310 ($3,350)

5
A 'bells-drum and castanets-in-sight' cylinder musical box, Charles Ullmann, Swiss, c.1880, 33.5cm cylinder, playing eight popular airs, w 71cm (28in), *L 29 May*, £2,090 ($3,010)

6
A key-wound musical box, Nicole Frères, Swiss, mid-19th cent, the 47cm cylinder musical box playing twelve airs, 66cm (26in), *L 29 May*, £825 ($1,188)

7
A 'two-per-turn' cylinder musical box, Nicole Frères, Geneva, 3rd quarter 19th cent, the 'fat' 22.2cm cylinder playing eight airs, w 38.8cm (15¼in), *NY 23 June*, $2,200 (£1,618)

8
A 'bells-drum-and-castanets-in-sight' cylinder musical box, George Bendon, Swiss, c.1880, the 44cm brass cylinder playing twelve airs accompanied by seven bells, w 71cm (28in), *L 29 May*, £1,045 ($1,505)

9
A key-wound overture cylinder musical box, Nicole Frères, Swiss, c.1845, the 23.5cm cylinder playing three overtures by Rossini, Weber and Meyerbeer, w 44.5cm (17½in), *L 29 May*, £2,200 ($3,168)

10
A 'bells-in-sight' interchangeable cylinder musical box, Swiss, late 19th cent, made by the Societe Anonyme de l'Ancienne Maison Billon et Isaac, 43cm (17in), *L 3 Oct*, £880 ($1,144)

11
A Swiss 'piano forte' cylinder musical box, Nicole Frères, Geneva, the 33.5cm cylinder playing six airs, 51.43cm (20¼in), *NY 23 June*, £1,860 ($2,530)

12
A 'bells-in-sight' cylinder musical box, Bremond, Swiss, c.1880, the 33cm cylinder playing eight popular airs, w 59cm (23in), *C 7 Nov*, £1,430 ($1,902)

13
A 'bells-in-sight' cylinder musical box, Swiss, c.1890, the 28cm cylinder playing eight airs, w 59cm (23in), *C 21 Mar*, £825 ($1,229)

14
A mandoline sublime harmony cylinder musical box, Swiss, c.1880, the 33cm cylinder playing six airs, w 61cm (24in), *L 29 May*, £825 ($1,188)

15
A key-wound cylinder musical box, François Alibert, French, c.1840, the 18cm cylinder playing four airs and arranged with tremolo effect, w 30cm (11¾in), *L 3 Oct*, £550 ($715)

16
A 'bells-and-drun in-view' cylinder musical box, Swiss, late 19th cent, the 27.3cm (10¾in) cylinder playing eight airs, 53.3cm (21in), *NY 23 June*, $2,200 (£1,618)

1
A 15½in polyphon
disc musical box and disc
cabinet, German, c.1900,
with 48 discs stored in
matching cabinet below,
overall h 95cm (37½in),
C 7 Nov,
£1,210 ($1,609)

2
A 20in disc musical box,
Criterion, American,
1900, crank-wound at the
side, with 33 discs,
68.6cm (27in), NY 13 Dec,
$1,650 (£1,387)

3
A 14¾in Symphonium
disc musical box,
German, 1900, the lid
interior with printed
satin vignette, winding
handle and start/stop
button to the sides, w 55cm
(21in), L 29 May,
£1,078 ($1,552)

4
A 16in Orphenion disc
musical box, German,
late 19th cent, together
with 27 metal discs,
65cm (25½in), L 17 Jan,
£550 ($798)

5
An 11in polyphon disc
musical box, German,
c.1900, with 12 metal
discs, w 41cm (16in),
L 29 May,
£396 ($570)

6
An 11⅞in disc polyphon
long case clock, German,
late 19th cent, the case of
turned and carved oak,
with 17 discs, 203cm
(6ft 8in), L 3 Oct,
£2,640 ($3,432)

7
An 11¾in Symphonium
disc musical box,
German, c.1900, with
winding handle and coin
shute at the side, h 90cm
(35½in), L 3 Oct,
£1,210 ($1,573)

8
A 15in disc musical box,
Regina, American,
c.1910, w 63.5cm (25in),
NY 23 June,
$3,080 (£2,265)

9
A 24½in polyphon
autochange disc musical
box, German, c.1900, the
coin-operated movement
with mechanism for
making a selection from
the twelve metal discs,
223cm (7ft 4in), L 17 Jan,
£7,150 ($10,368)

10
A 24½in polyphon disc
coin-operated musical
box, c.1900, crank-wound
from the interior,
213.4cm (7ft), NY 23 June,
$7,425 (£5,460)

11
An Orpheus mechanical
zither, German, c.1904,
with 13in diameter
Ariston cardboard discs,
89cm (35in), C 11 July,
£1,100 ($1,496)

1
A phonograph, probably French, c.1900, with key-wound open motor mechanism, 36cm (14in), *C 21 Mar,* **£176 ($262)**

2
A phonograph, Edison Standard, American, c.1905, with model C reproducer, brass horn 135cm (53in), *L 3 Oct,* **£440 ($572)**

3
A table gramophone, HMV, English, c.1925, model 460 with 30.5cm (12in) turntable, *L 3 Oct,* **£495 ($644)**

4
A table gramophone, HMV model 460, English, c.1924, with 30.5cm (12in), turntable, *JHB 12 June,* **R 400 (£219; $315)**

5
A horn gramophone, Pathé, French, c.1910, with 30.5cm (12in) turntable, Asaphir sound-box, oak petal horn, *L 3 Oct,* **£286 ($372)**

6
A horn gramophone, J. Navarro, Continental, c.1905, 58.4cm (23in) diameter mouth, *L 29 May,* **£550 ($792)**

7
A horn gramophone, Continental, 1905, with 29.2cm (11½in) turntable, Hispano Suiza soundbox, HMV laminated mahogany horn, 56cm (22in) diameter mouth, *L 29 May,* **£660 ($950)**

8
A horn gramophone, French, c.1905, with 29.2cm (11½in) diameter turntable, Imperator soundbox, laminated mahogany horn, 57.2cm (22½in) diameter mouth, *L 29 May,* **£484 ($697)**

9
A chamber barrel organ, Clementi, English, c.1810, h 180cm (5ft 11in), *L 29 May,* **£1,870 ($2,693)**

10
An organette, Ariston, German, c.1900, for discs and cardboard strip, w 46cm (18in), *L 29 May,* **£550 ($792)**

11
A barrel piano, Imhof & Mukle, English, late 19th cent, the three 98cm (38½in) barrels each playing seven tunes. *C 11 July,* **£715 ($972)**

12
A chamber barrel organ, Southwell & White, English, early 19th cent, the three 50cm (19½in) pinned barrels each playing twelve tunes, h 180cm (71in), *C 7 Nov,* **£2,200 ($2,926)**

13
A barrel organ, Wilhelm Bruder Sohne, Orgelbauer in Waldkirch, Baden, mid-19th cent, playing ten tunes, in a walnut case with fruitwood banding, h 53.3cm (21in), *NY 23 June,* **$2,860 (£2,103)**

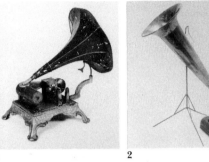
1

2

3

4

5

6

7

8

10

11

9

12

13

1
'Yellow Submarine' celluloid, c.1967, depicting Paul McCartney, image h 19.5cm (7¾in), *L 30 Aug,* £242 ($332)

2
'Yellow Submarine' celluloid, c.1967, depicting John Lennon, image h 22cm (8¾in), *L 30 Aug,* £880 ($1,206)

3
The Beatles 'Yesterday and Today' Butchers sleeve, c.1966, *L 30 Aug,* £330 ($452)

4
Apple Records 'Our First Four' cardboard pack, 1968, containing folders with details of the groups and copies of their singles, *L 30 Aug,* £220 ($301)

5
John Lennon's green corduroy jacket, sold with an affidavit confirming its authenticity, *L 31 Aug,* £2,090 ($2,863)

6
A letter from George Harrison to Stuart Sutcliffe, dated 16th Dec 1960, concerning Harrison's journey back to Liverpool, informing Stuart of bookings for the Beatles, *L 31 Aug,* £550 ($754)

7
The Beatles "gold" album for "Hey Jude", the KIAA award presented to the Beatles, commemorating the sale of more than 500,000 copies of the Apple LP, framed 53.34 by 40.64cm (21 x 16in), *NY 23 June,* £5,257 ($7,150)

8
A Presentation 'Gold' disc for 'The Ballad of John and Yoko', *L 30 Aug,* £6,050 ($8,289)

9
A letter from John Lennon and Yoko Ono concerning war, dated '71, which accompanied a book relating to the US/Japanese war, signed, *L 31 Aug,* £198 ($271)

10
Ringo Starr's Ludwig snare drum, c.1964, finished in pearled grey, with on/off snare and damper mechanisms, d 36.5cm (14½in), *L 30 Aug,* £1,100 ($1,507)

11
Yoko Ono's Rolls Royce Phantom V, 1965, coach builder H. J. Malliner/Park Ward, painted sable brown, *NY 23 June,* $184,250 (£135,478)

12
Bill Wyman's Framus 'Star-Bass' bass guitar, c.1964, with treble/bass control and volume control, *L 30 Aug,* £3,080 ($4,220)

13
The Who, five autographed items, comprising a promotional photograph, three magazine pages and a colour photograph, *NY 23 June,* $825 (£607)

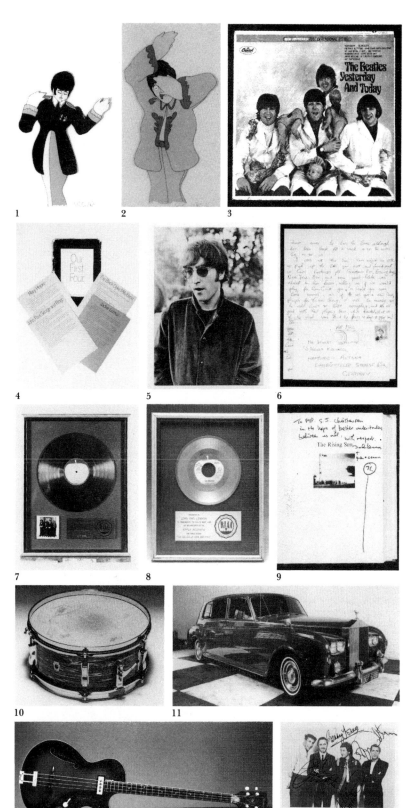

1   2   3

4   5   6

7   8   9

10   11

12   13

1
Charlton Heston, two costumes from 'Planet of the Apes', 20th Century Fox, 1968, and 'Ben Hur', MGM, 1959, costume designer Elizabeth Haffenden, *NY 13 Dec,* $1,210 (£1,017)

2
Lauren Bacall, black satin cocktail dress from 'Written on the Wind', Universal, 1950, costume designer Bill Thomas, *NY 13 Dec,* $192 (£161)

3
Vivien Leigh, black velvet gown from 'That Hamilton Woman', United Artists, 1941, clothing designer Rene Hubert, *NY 13 Dec,* $247 (£208)

4
Jack Lemmon, black chiffon beaded dress from 'Some Like It Hot', United Artists, 1959, costume designer Orry Kelly, *NY 13 Dec,* $1,320 (£1,109)

5
Julie Andrews, orange silk satin flapper dress from 'Star', 20th Century Fox, 1968, costume designer Donald Brooks, *NY 13 Dec,* $1,430 (£1,202)

6
Julie Andrews, gown from 'Star', 20th Century Fox, 1968, costume designer Donald Brooks, *NY 13 Dec,* $1,210 (£1,017)

7
Mae West, black velvet evening gown from "Every Day's a Holiday", Paramount, 1938, Schiaparelli, together with velvet hat, *NY 13 Dec,* $10,175 (£8,550)

8
A 'Chicago Ridge' automatic payout colour wheel slot machine, Paul E Berger Manufacturing Company, Chicago, late 1890s, h 142.2cm (56in), *NY 23 June,* $4,400 (£3,235)

9
A Wurlitzer model 1015 jukebox, *c.*1947, with bubble tubes framing a glazed front revealing 24 selections, restored, h 147cm (58in), *NY 13 Dec,* $7,425 (£6,239)

10
A Wurlitzer model 81 countertop jukebox, *c.*1940, restored, h 58.4cm (23in), *NY 23 June,* $3,300 (£2,426)

11
A Rockola 'Roberts' three-reel slot machine, *c.*1928, with jackpot, repainted, h 63.5cm (25in), *NY 13 Dec,* $1,210 (£1,017)

12
A Bryan's 'Clock' amuse-ment machine, *c.*1930, with original instruction card, and pay-out slot, h 79cm (31in), *C 11 July,* £242 ($329)

13
A Pace 50¢ 'Comet' three-reel slot machine, *c.*1935, restored, h 61cm (24in), *NY 23 June,* $1,100 (£809)

1

2

3

4

5   6

7

8

9   10

11

12

13

1
Walt Disney celluloid from 'Snow White', 1937, depicting Doc, Sneezy, Bashful and Dopey, 22.9 x 19cm (9 x 7½in), *NY 13 Dec,*
$4,400 (£3,697)

2
Dopey and friends, an original Disney celluloid, *L 17 Jan,*
£429 ($622)

3
Walt Disney celluloid from 'Snow White', 1937, depicting Grumpy, 17.8 x 11.4cm (7 x 4½in), *NY 13 Dec,*
$605 (£508)

4
Walt Disney celluloid from 'Pinocchio', 1939, depicting Jiminy Cricket wishing upon a star, 17.8 x 17.8cm (7 x 7in), *NY 13 Dec,*
$1,760 (£1,479)

5
Walt Disney signed Mickey Mouse, in black ink, signed, dated 1946, 19 x 15cm (7½ x 6in), *L 17 Jan,*
£473 ($686)

6
Walt Disney celluloid from 'Dumbo', 1941, depicting Dumbo with Timothy Mouse, 35.6 x 29.2cm (14 x 11½in), *NY 13 Dec,*
$1,430 (£1,202)

7
Walt Disney celluloid from 'The Pointer', 1939, depicting Mickey Mouse and Pluto, 26.7 x 21.6cm (10½ x 8½in), *NY 23 June,*
$880 (£633)

8
Twelve Mickey Mouse stick pins, *c.*1930, pins h 2.3cm (⅞in), *L 29 May,*
£605 ($871)

9
A Wells Minnie and Mickey handcar, English, *c.*1935, lithographed red and yellow, complete with a length of track, 19cm (7½in), *C 21 Mar,*
£308 ($459)

10
Seven stuffed felt dwarfs, Chad Valley type, *c.*1940, based on characters from the Walt Disney cartoon, h 16.5cm (6½in), *L 29 May,*
£220 ($317)

11
A plush Felix the Cat, *c.*1930, the striding beast with wide toothy grin and big eyes, h 43cm (17in), *L 29 May,*
£242 ($348)

12
A plush velvet covered Mickey Mouse, Deans Rag Book, English, *c.*1930s, with plastic moving eyes, slight damage, h 43cm (17in), *P 30 Oct/2 Nov,*
£176 ($225)

13
A large plush Mickey Mouse soft toy, English, *c.*1930, wearing yellow gloves and boots, ears replaced, h 47cm (18½in); with smaller Mickey Mouse, *L 3 Oct,*
£330 ($429)

14
A Mickey Mouse hurdy-gurdy lithographed tin clockwork toy, Distler, German, 1930s, complete with Minnie dancing, h 22cm (8½in), *NY 13 Dec,*
$770 (£647)

1

2

3

4

5

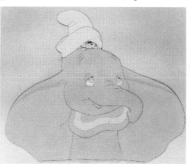
6

7

8

9

10

11

12

13

14

1
A mint condition golf ball, Haskell, c.1912, bramble pattern, original wrapping, *L 24 July,* £132 ($176)

2
A hexagonal-faced gutta percha golf ball, c.1849, the multi-faceted ball painted white, d 4.1cm (1⅝in), *L 24 July,* £308 ($411)

3
A mint condition feathery golf ball, Tom Morris, c.1840, the stitched leather ball numbered '28' in black ink, d 4.1cm (1⅝in), *L 24 July,* £2,200 ($2,937)

4
An early play club, Johnston's, c.1850s, with slim lead weight inset at rear, original whipping and binding, head 14.5cm (5¾in), *L 24 July,* £1,045 ($1,395)

5
A long-nosed putter, R. Forgan, Scottish, c.1880s, horn soled with Prince-of-Wales feathers, lacks leather grip, *L 24 July,* £385 ($514)

6
A long-nosed play club, Tom Morris, Scottish, c.1860, horn soled, slight crack, whipping missing, *L 24 July,* £660 ($881)

7
An early golfing iron, late 18th cent, the long heavy hose with deep nicking around the top, crudely cross-pinned, the wooden handle lacking grip, head 11cm (4¼in), *L 24 July,* £4,620 ($6,168)

8
An adjustable iron, Urquhart, Scottish, c.1895, the variable pitch iron on wooden shaft, re-gripped, head, 9.5cm (3¾in), *L 24 July,* £462 ($616)

9
A Copeland golfing tankard, English, c.1915, the pale green body with raised white decorative panels, 17cm (6¾in), *L 24 July,* £176 ($235)

10
A chrome and bakelite golfing belt buckle, French, c.1930, 7.5cm (3in), *L 24 July,* £82 ($109)

11
A silvered and enamel golfing medal, St. Nicholas Golf Club, Prestwick, 1907, second prize, on length of blue ribbon, enamelled golfer on one side, the whole 9cm (3¾in), *L 24 July,* £605 ($808)

12
A silvered golfing medal, Warrender Park, 1901, 15cm (6in), *L 24 July,* £352 ($470)

13
A silvered and enamel golfing medal, Freshwater Golf Club, 1900, 12cm (4¾in), *L 24 July,* £462 ($617)

14
A Baccarat glass golfing ashtray, w 12.5cm (5in), *L 24 July,* £220 ($294)

15
A composition advertising figure, Penfold, c.1935, dressed in plus fours and cap, with pipe between his lips, on wooden base inscribed 'He Played a Penfold', h 48cm (19in), *L 24 July,* £308 ($411)

16
A toy golfer, Schoenhut, American, c.1930, the figure articulated at the shoulder and head, attached to a shaft with handle to operate the toy club, 35.5cm (14in), *L 24 July,* £165 ($220)

17
A golfing poster, entitled 'Le Touquet Paris Plage', c.1930, mounted on linen, signature indistinct, 104 x 75.5cm (41 x 29¾in), *L 24 July,* £330 ($441)

18
The Golf Courses of the British Isles, by Bernard Darwin, 1910, illustrated by Harry Roumtree, cloth bound, *L 24 July,* £276 ($368)

1
A crank-handled reel, Chevalier Bowness & Son, of brass, the folding ivory knob with spring lock, fixed check in raised casing on backplate, 6.9cm (2¾in), *L 24 July,* £165 ($220)

2
A spike-footed pole wynch, Kelly of Dublin, *c*1800, handle lacking, 4.4cm (1¾in), *L 24 July,* £132 ($176)

3
A 14-0 multiplying big game reel, Edward Vom Hofe, d 18.4cm (7¼in), w 18.1cm (7⅛in), *L 24 July,* £528 ($705)

4
A rare billiken multi-plying reel, C. Farlow, of alloy with bronzed brass foot, counter-balanced handle with ivory knob, retaining most leaded and bronzed finish, 5.7cm (2¼in), *L 24 July,* £385 ($514)

5
A raised-pillar salmon reel, H. L. Leonard, the foot, frame, drum, roller pillars and counter-balanced winding arm of nickel silver, the plates of ebonite, with 1890-patent sliding brake regulator, d 9.5cm (3¾in), *L 2 May,* £308 ($434)

6
A Chippindale patent casting reel, J. E. Miller, of bronzed brass with walnut spool, retaining most lacquered bronzed finish, spool 6cm (2⅜in), *L 2 May,* £165 ($233)

7
A 4½-inch extra wide auxiliary brake 'Silex Major' spinning reel, with brass foot, white regulator dial, black handles, jewelled bearing and button latch, stamped 'R.M.S.' inside, 11.4cm (4½in), *L 2 May,* £143 ($202)

8
A 3-inch 'Bouglé' lightweight reel, 7.6cm (3in), *Glen 27 Aug,* £638 ($874)

9
An iron and brass trolling wynch, the foot, pillars, drum and curved winding arm of forged iron, the endplates of brass, 6.3 x 7.6cm (2½ x 3in), *L 2 May,* £308 ($434)

10
A 2½-inch pattern brass and nickel silver 'Perfect' reel, 1896, bronzing worn on plate, 6.3cm (2½in), *L 24 July,* £1,870 ($2,496)

11
A 3-inch 'Hercules' reel, bronzed brass with ivory handle, fixed check and raised front plate with oval logo and Rod-in-Hand mark, bronzing worn, 7.6cm, *Glen 27 Aug,* £88 ($121)

12
A Scottish trolling wynch or pirn, early 19th cent, turned and carved from hardwood with moulded endplates, beechwood (?) pillars and large bridge foot, the wooden drum with iron crank handle, d 6.4cm (2½in), w 11.7cm (4⅝in), *Glen 27 Aug,* £418 ($573)

13
A trotting reel with unusual level wind device, alloy reel, 3-inch copper wire oscillating line guided, the drum with bone knob and brass counter weights, stamped 'The Homer reel patent appd for', brass foot adaptable for left or right hand wind, 9.2cm (3⅝in), *Glen 27 Aug,* £121 ($166)

14
A modelled and painted life-size sea-trout trophy, Hardy's, of a 37-inch 19lb fish caught on the Laerdal, Norway, August 1927, plaster and wood on dark oak board, 108 x 36.8cm (42½ x 14½in), *Glen 27 Aug,* £748 ($1,025)

15
A carved wood life-size salmon trophy, Farlows, the 39½-inch fish mounted on mahogany board, inscribed 'upper Glen Tana, April 12th 19*7', 116.2 x 38.1cm (45¾ x 15in), *Glen 27 Aug,* £528 ($723)

1   2   3

4   5   6

7   8   9

10   11   12 (above) 13 (below)

14

15

1
A Rolls-Royce silver desk set, with silver pieces hall-marked London, 1924, *HS 30 June,* £2,200 ($3,047)

2
A bronze Mors mascot, signed 'Et. Mercier', cast in the form of a lemon, on radiator cap, h 14cm (5½in), *L 10 Dec,* £1,155 ($1,455)

3
A triplet bicycle, *c*1920-30 with tubular triangulated frame, tangential spokes and pneumatic tyres, *HS 30 June,* £352 ($488)

4
Matchless 8hp motorcycle combination, 1922, original sidecar, three speed gearbox, *HS 30 June,* £1,540 ($2,133)

5
A 'Velocipede', *c*1870, with iron tyred and wooden spoked wheels, restored, wheels d 102cm (40in) and 81.3cm (32in), *HS 30 June,* £638 ($884)

6
BSA 'Round Tank' B26 De Luxe 249cc solo motorcycle, 1926, single vertical cylinder engine, in excellent restored condition, *HS 30 June,* £1,045 ($1,447)

7
Rolls-Royce series L2 Phantom II 40/50hp open tourer, 1930, replica coachwork by Dick Brockman of South Stoke, six cylinder engine, 7668cc, four speed gearbox, *HS 30 June,* £14,300 ($19,805)

8
Bentley Silent Speed Six two-door coupé, 1930, coachwork by J Gurney Nutting, six cylinder engine, 6597cc, four speed gearbox, *L 10 Dec,* £270,600 ($340,956)

1

2

3

4

5

6

7

8

1
**Rolls-Royce 40/50hp
Silver Ghost two-seater
'Balloon Car'**, 1911, six
cylinder engine, 7428cc,
four speed gearbox,
replica coachwork in the
style of Barker, *L 10 Dec,*
£77,000 ($97,020)

2
**Bentley 4½ litre
supercharged drophead
coupé**, 1931, coachwork
by Vanden Plas, super-
charged four cylinder
engine, 4398cc, four
speed gearbox, *L 10 Dec,*
£121,000 ($152,460)

3
**Rolls-Royce Phantom II
series P2 40/50hp three
position drop coupé**, 1934,
coachwork by J Gurney
Nutting, six cylinder
engine cast in threes,
7668cc, four speed
syncromesh gearbox,
L 10 Dec,
£74,800 ($94,248)

4
**Sunbeam 3 litre twin cam
Sportsman's saloon**, 1926,
Weymann-type
coachwork, six cylinder
twin overhead camshaft
water-cooled monobloc
engine, 2920cc,
HS 30 June,
£15,950 ($22,090)

5
**Invicta high chassis 4½
litre coupé**, *c* 1931,
bodywork by the Lance-
field Coachworks,
London W10, Meadows
six cylinder engine,
4467cm, *L 10 Dec,*
£15,180 ($19,126)

6
**Sunbeam Talbot Ten
drophead coupé**, 1947,
four cylinder engine,
1184cc, four speed gear-
box, *HS 30 June,*
£3,300 ($4,571)

7
**Squire 1½ litre drophead
coupé**, 1937, bodywork
by Corsica, supercharged
Anzani four cylinder
engine, 1496cc, *L 10 Dec,*
£27,500 ($34,650)

8
**Alvis Speed Twenty 2½
litre drophead coupé**,
1934, coachwork by
Brainsby Woollard, Ealing,
six cylinder engine,
2511cc, four speed
manual synchromesh
gearbox, *L 10 Dec,*
£23,100 ($29,106)

9
**Morris Minor four door
saloon**, 1964, four cylinder
engine, 1098cc, four
speed gearbox, *L 10 Dec,*
£2,145 ($2,702)

1   2

3

4   5

6

7

8   9

1
A silver travelling corkscrew, Dutch, *c.*1750, disc probe, fine wire helix, *L 26 Sept*, £520 ($671)

2
A silver travelling corkscrew, Joseph Taylor, Birmingham, *c.*1800, with finely turned ivory handle, *L 28 Mar*, £240 ($358)

3
A single-finger steel picnic corkscrew, probably French, tapered steel sheath, fine wire helix, 9.5cm (3¾in), *L 26 Sept*, £320 ($413)

4
A silver champagne tap, French, early 19th cent, large gimlet screw with side steel pumping lever, marked 'Deleuze, Paris and Brevete', *L 26 Sept*, £1,250 ($1,613)

5
A steel folding bow with faceted decoration and sprung screw, probably English, 12.7cm (5in), *L 26 Sept*, £360 ($464)

6
A corkscrew registered by Edwin Cotterill in 1842, with turned ebony handle, bearing Royal coat-of-arms and words 'Edwin Cotterill's Patent Self-Adjusting', 22.5cm (8¾in), *L 26 Sept*, £1,900 ($2,451)

7
A miniature corkscrew, mid-19th cent, turned bone handle impressed mark of a bell and word 'S. Patt', 4cm (1⅝in), *L 26 Sept*, £160 ($206)

8
An 'Empire' corkscrew, James Heeley's 1890 patent double lever, marked 'The Empire and J. Heeley & Sons Patent', *L 26 Sept*, £220 ($283)

9
A steel eyebrow-handled corkscrew, English, *c.*1890, with baluster shank, *L 28 Mar*, £68 ($101)

10
A combination picnic set, Sheffield, late 19th cent, fork plated silver, knife marked 'Underwood 56 Haymarket', *L 28 Mar*, £60 ($89)

11
A variation of Thomason's corkscrew, mid-19th cent, with bone handle, a simple steel shaft passing through long narrow brass barrel, *L 5 Dec*, £440 ($559)

12
A Thomason 1802 patent-type corkscrew with central hermaphrodite raising screw, brass outer barrel, *L 5 Dec*, £360 ($457)

13
A corkscrew, J. Mabson, patented in 1869, number 527, with turned ebony handle, brass barrel, *L 5 Dec*, £680 ($864)

14
A decanting cradle, *c.*1860, of painted tin, attached at the rear to a sliding brass bracket with a wooden raising handle, tablet marked 'Ellis & Adams', 21cm (8¼in), *L 26 Sept*, £560 ($722)

15
A decanting cradle, *c.*1880, with brass spindle, turning handle and carrying handle, wire cradle, *L 28 Mar*, £400 ($596)

16
A teakwood brass bound campaign or travelling cellarette, early 19th cent, now on bun feet, 22 x 32 x 38cm (8½ x 12½ x 15in), *L 28 Mar*, £240 ($309)

Arms and Sporting Guns

FRED WILKINSON • JAMES BOOTH • DAVID WILLE

In 1983 Sotheby's held a sale of arms and armour from Hever Castle which generated worldwide interest and established a record price of £1,925,000 ($3,000,000) for a suit of armour. However, it must be recognized that the pieces sold were of top quality and that the many record prices may have given a rather misleading idea as to the value of arms and armour. In fact under the heading of arms, armour and militaria can be found any number of items to suit the pockets of all collectors. They include European and Asiatic armour, edged weapons of all kinds and all nations, long arms such as muskets, pistols and items with a military association. Interest in all these fields has grown steadily since the Second World War — an interest which has been self-perpetuating in that it has engendered a number of reliable reference books and these in turn have further stimulated demand.

Whilst the early collectors rather concentrated on armour and edged weapons, antique pistols have become the most popular field of collecting since they are more readily available. Gunmakers such as Boutet, the top French gunmaker of the Napoleonic era, and London gunmakers such as Mortimer, Nock, Parker and Wogden signed their names on the barrels of their guns, in effect giving a guarantee of quality. Whilst decoration, style and mechanical features are the usual guides as to date, silver-mounted guns which are hallmarked can often be specifically dated. Cased examples of pistols are particularly prized especially if they retain all their accessories. Presentation swords and weapons with a known history will always carry a higher premium. Condition is very important, but dirt or minor damage from use is normally acceptable and this is preferable to the harm which can be done if the weapon is over-cleaned and restored.

The definition of a 'modern' firearm is very confused, varying from country to country, and largely determined by firearms legislation. For example, in Great Britain, ownership of most breechloading cartridge firing firearms is strictly controlled, whereas in America most of those dating prior to 1897 can be possessed without licence. Wherever the would-be collector lives he should ask local police *and* firearms experts about ownership of *any* breechloading arm built around 1850 and later.

The market for post 1850 breech-loading cartridge arms can be divided roughly into two areas: the first historical, the second functional. The market for historical weapons (often described as 'vintage') tends to fall into the same parameters as that for antique firearms as far as quality, condition and refinishing are concerned. In the field of sporting weapons the English breech-loading double-barrelled gun and rifle are widely regarded as the epitome of the sporting weapon and the period from 1850 to 1900 as being the heyday of the gunmaker-inventor; increasing interest is shown in the early patent actions which illustrate their development.

'London Best' has become a catch phrase and guns by Holland & Holland, Purdey and Boss are regarded as the finest, with 1920-40 as the golden age of British guns. The factors which determine their value are primarily concerned with their mechanical condition because buyers are seeking guns for regular use. It is important that barrels are not worn or pitted, the gun balances properly, and the action and lockwork are not seriously worn. Assuming all this to be good the quality of the engraving and the decorative merits of the stock will add premium to the value.

The most valuable game guns are usually the self-opening sidelock ejector actions, but boxlocks and hammer guns also have an appreciable value; single-trigger actions and 2¾-inch chambers are added bonuses. 28-inch barrels are currently the most popular and guns with long straight stocks appeal to the greater part of the market (stock extensions and pistol grips are regarded as unsightly). Value is seriously affected if a gun or rifle requires major work such as rebarrelling or restocking. Big game rifles are now much in demand because of recently revived interest in Safari hunting.

1
A German two-handed sword, the blade possibly 2nd half 16th cent, the fuller inlaid in copper with the orb, struck on the cusps with maker's mark, the hilt of later date, 164cm (64½in), *NY 24 Nov,* $1,870 (£1,545)

2
A Spanish two-handed sword, possibly mid-16th cent, mounted with flattened diamond section blade, leather covered wood grip and flattened spherical pommel retaining traces of gilding, 178cm (70in), *NY 24 Nov,* $2,420 (£2,000)

3
A Northern European swept hilt rapier, early 17th cent, long double-edged blade, single fuller, one side with running wolf mark, ricasso struck with crown over OT, wire-bound grip, 133.7cm (52⅝in), *L 15 May,* £858 ($1,227)

4
A Scandinavian basket hilted back sword, early 17th cent, straight single-edged blade with twin fullers, 114cm (45in), *L 15 May,* £605 ($865)

5
A German riding sword, *c.*1600, straight double-edged blade, inscribed central fuller, blade maker's mark, wire bound grip, 102.8cm (40½in), *L 15 May,* £770 ($1,101)

6
A Spanish cup hilt rapier, second half 17th cent, mounted with German hexagonal blade, with short fuller on either side and inscribed 'Iohannis Hartcop', 120cm (47in), *NY 24 Nov,* $1,320 (£1,091)

7
An English rapier, early 17th cent, straight double-edged blade, forte with mark of Solingen and forte inscribed 'Hans Hans' and blade smith's mark, some wear, 105.4cm (41½in), *L 15 May,* £3,740 ($5,348)

8
A hunting sword, 17th cent, broad slightly curved single edged blade, some pitting to blade, 76.8cm (30¼in), *L 31 Jan,* £242 ($351)

9
An English combination pistol hanger, third quarter 18th cent, the grip of antler, the turn-off barrel marked P, 74cm (29¼in), *NY 2/3 Mar,* $660 (£443)

10
A Scottish broadsword, 18th cent, with a straight double-edged tri-fullered blade 87.5cm (34½in), fish-skin covered grip, bulbous pommel, *P 20/22 Mar,* £176 ($262)

11
A Russian silver mounted sword, Tula factories, dated 1744, with turquoise stones-centering cartouches applied with silver and silver-gilt wires, 90cm (35½in), *NY 2/3 Mar,* $2,200 (£1,477)

12
A silver hilted dress sword, *c.*1810, mother-of-pearl grips, struck on knuckle bow with mark of Jean Francois Rabin, Paris, 95.2cm (37½in), *L 15 May,* £330 ($472)

13
A naval sword, *c.*1840, straight narrow single-edged blade, engraved 'Rear Admiral Sir Philip Broke ob. 2 Jan 1841', some pitting to blade and wear to gilding, 82.5cm (32½in), *L 2 Oct,* £352 ($454)

14
A George III presentation sword, by John Read, College Green, Dublin, 75cm (29½in), etched with GR cypher, *P 20/22 Mar,* £440 ($656)

15
An Infantry Officer's sword, 1803 pattern, 71cm (27⅞in) pierced brass guard with GR cypher, wirebound fish-skin covered grip, *P 20/22 Mar,* £94 ($140)

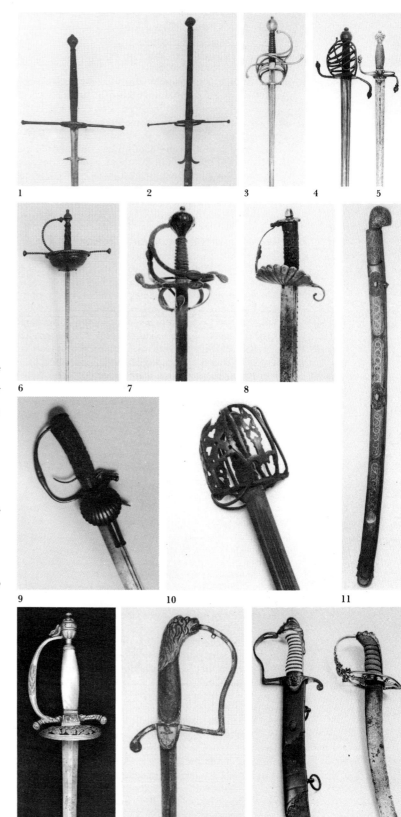

1

A naval officer's sword, c.1820, forte engraved 'Salter, Sword Cutler', 93.3cm (36¾in), L 15 May, £220 ($314)

2

A Light Cavalry Officer's sword, c.1800, curved single-edged blade with broad fuller, engraved, back edge signed 'J. Runkel, Solingen', the hilt of gilt brass, ivory grip, 86.3cm (34in), L 15 May, £110 ($157)

3

A Georgian presentation sabre, by Benjamin Reddell, curved single-edged blade 73cm (28¾in), retaining some blue and gilt finish, copper gilt hilt, a matching brass scabbard engraved 'Clarke & Sons', with pierced panels over fish-skin covering, P 3 Oct, £1,595 ($2,057)

4

A backsword for officer of 1st Troop of Horse Guards, c.1760, straight single-edged blade, broad fuller engraved with orb and cross mark and 'Andrea Ferara', 101.6cm (40in), L 2 Oct, £396 ($511)

5

A dress sword of Royal Bavarian Order of St. George, 19th cent, 83.2cm (32¾in), L 15 May, £1,430 ($2,045)

6

A Swiss dagger, c.1570, original blade of flattened diamond section, gilt brass hilt with yew wood grip, gilt brass sheath with the story of William Tell, 41.3cm (16¼in), L 15 May, £28,600 ($40,898)

7

A presentation Mameluke sword, 19th cent, inscribed 'Presented by the Emir of Afghanistan to Colonel Eales 1311 (1893)', the blade is marked as from a Kabul workshop, 96.5cm (38in), L 2 Oct, £550 ($709)

8

A Polish horseman's hammer, head 16th cent, shaft later, decorated with inlaid silver and ivory, tip with iron cap, 53.4cm (21in), L 15 May, £1,320 ($1,888)

9

A partisan, early 17th cent, the head with strengthened tapering spike, punched with an entwined foliate design, on later turned wood haft, the head 74cm (29¼in), C 4 Oct, £363 ($468)

10

A halberd, German, late 16th cent, the head with tapering spike and pierced blade and fluke, with long straps and later wood haft, the head 54.5cm (21½in), C 4 Oct, £330 ($426)

11

An Italian corseque, late 16th cent, the head with 18in spike flanked by flattened curved fluke on later turned wood haft, the head 60cm (23½in), C 4 Oct, £88 ($113)

12

A German pair of spurs, second half 17th cent, pierced and chiselled and with brass inlay, eight pointed rowel, L 15 May, £715 ($1,022)

13

A South German powder flask, last quarter 16th cent, the front and back covered by gilt copper panels, on velvet covered wooden body, h 14.2cm (5⅝in), L 15 May, £5,500 ($7,865)

14

A German powder flask, early 17th cent, 5¾in (14.5cm), F 10 May, L 960,500 (£391; $563)

15

A staghorn powder flask, early 19th cent, with carved panel, both ends with horn plugs and a turned horn charger, 14.2cm (5⅝in), L 31 Jan, £77 ($112)

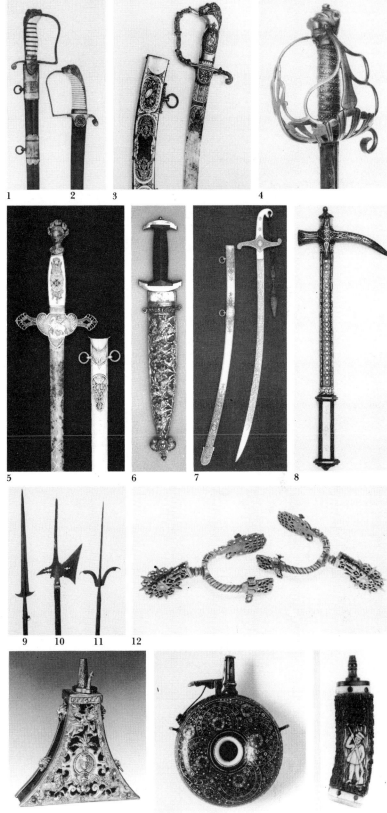

1
A Bohemian wheellock rifle, Caspar Neureiter, Prague, c 1700, the full-length stock inlaid with bone and antler plaques, barrel 87cm (34¼in), *NY 2/3 Mar,* $2,970 (£1,993)

2
Caucasian miquelet lock long gun, late 18th cent, the 45½in round barrel engraved and signed, the action with gilt decoration, the full-length stock with brass barrel bands, 150cm (59in), *C 4 Oct,* £682 ($880)

3
A Caucasian miquelet rifle, 18th cent, octagonal barrel with eight-groove rifling, inset brass front sight and integral back sight, ball trigger, iron ramrod, 133.9cm (52¾in), *L 2 Oct,* £660 ($851)

4
A silver mounted flintlock sporting gun, late 18th cent, engraved 'Bunney London', silver furniture with Birmingham assay marks for 1780/1, wooden horn tipped ramrod, 139cm (53¾in), *L 15 May,* £13,200 ($18,876)

5
A Spanish miquelet sporting gun, c 1800, plain lock signed in gold 'Zarandona', two-stage barrel with silver decorated front sight, wooden ramrod with worm, some minor wear, 127cm (50in), *L 2 Oct,* £572 ($738)

6
A double barrel flintlock sporting gun, c 1825, struck below breech with St. Etienne proof marks, signed 'Vigouroux', wooden ramrod, 130.2cm (51¼in), *L 15 May,* £1,210 ($1,730)

7
A heavy barrelled flintlock Pennsylvania rifle, 1st quarter 19th cent, polygonal barrel signed 'Russ Hamm', lock signed 'M. M. Marlin', stock with brass inlays, some possibly modern, 132.1cm (52in), *H 15 Nov,* $1,045 (£829)

8
An Indian flintlock blunderbuss, 19th cent, iron barrel with octagonal breech, lock dated 1816, lacking inset plaques, side plate and screws, 91cm (36in), *L 31 Jan,* £341 ($494)

9
A knee blunderbuss, 19th cent, full stock, iron furniture, including slide for saddle ring, 49.5cm (19½in), *L 31 Jan,* £264 ($383)

10
A flintlock blunderbuss pistol, late 18th cent, the top flat and sliding bolt safety catch signed 'H. Mortimer', London, full walnut stock, iron furniture, wooden ramrod, 36.2cm (14¼in), *L 15 May,* £1,430 ($2,045)

11
A French eprouvette, 18th cent, the toothed wheel graduated 1 to 13 plain stock, iron pillar trigger guard, 22.8cm (9in), *L 15 May,* £396 ($556)

12
A wheellock pistol, French, 1st quarter 17th cent, stock inlaid with ivory and mother-of-pearl, some minor pits and slight wear to stock, 60.5cm (23⅞in), *L 15 May,* £7,700 ($11,011)

13
A mail coach flintlock brass barrel pistol, late 18th cent, signed 'H. W. Mortimer', full walnut stock, brass furniture, wooden ramrod, horn tip and worm, 38.1cm (15in), *L 2 Oct,* £748 ($965)

14
A Spanish miquelet lock pistol, 1714, and 'Urquiola', barrel and tang blued, wooden horn tipped ramrod, retaining some original colour, 26.8cm (10½in), *L 2 Oct,* £660 ($851)

15
A pair of Swiss gilt flintlock pistols, by Felix Werder, Zurich, c 1630, barrels 32.5cm (12⅞in), *NY 2/3 Mar,* $46,200 (£31,007)

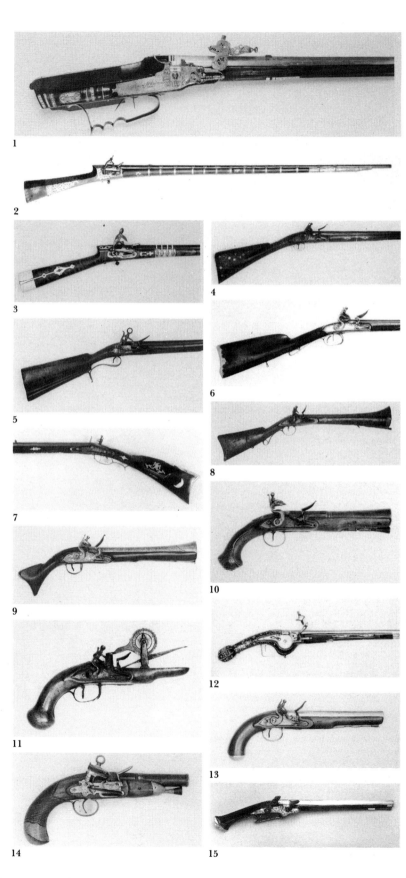

1
A pair of **Belgian** all steel flintlock pistols, late 18th cent, the lockplates inscribed 'Jean Stas, London,' barrels 3.2cm (1¼in), *NY 2/3 Mar*, $1,430 (£959)

2
A tap action four barrel flintlock pistol, *c* 1800, four circular barrels, breech struck with London proof marks and OH, frame signed 'Archer London', two position tap, wooden butt, 24.1cm (9½in), *L 2 Oct*, £770 ($993)

3
A flintlock boxlock pocket pistol, by W. Parker, Holborn, 2in turn-off barrel, decorated with overlaid gold trophies of arms and foliage, section of top strap missing, 16cm (6⅜in), *P 20/22 Mar*, £2,310 ($3,442)

4
A rifled percussion cap pistol, *c* 1840, octagonal damascus barrel signed in gold 'Al Neumann in Aachen', iron furniture, horn tipped ramrod, set trigger, stock repaired, some gold lacking, 31.7cm (12½in), *L 2 Oct*, £308 ($397)

5
A brass spring bayonet boxlock flintlock pocket pistol, *c* 1800, frame signed 'Fisher London', 19.4cm (7⅝in), *L 2 Oct*, £297 ($383)

6
A pair of 24-bore side-cock boxlock Queen Anne-style flintlock holster pistols, by Freeman, London, 5¼in turn-off cannon barrels, one swan-neck cock an old replacement, some wire inlay missing, 30.5cm (12in), *P 20/22 Mar*, £1,100 ($1,639)

7
A pair of flintlock boxlock pocket pistols, 1st quarter 19th cent, each with 1½in round turn-off barrel, signed 'Andertons and Auster London', walnut slab butt, 15cm (6in), *C 3-6 July*, £352 ($477)

8
A flintlock all brass box-lock pistol, early 19th cent, the round belling barrel engraved 'CJ 355', 17.5cm (7in), *C 3-6 July*, £253 ($343)

9
A pair of percussion cap boxlock pocket pistols, 2nd quarter 19th cent, with 1¾in round turn-off barrel, signed 'Boston Wakefield', 14cm (5½in), *C 3-6 July*, £341 ($463)

10
A flintlock boxlock over-and-under double barrelled pistol, early 19th cent, with 3in barrels, signed 'Hobday Biddle & Co, London', 20.3cm (8in), *C 3-6 July*, £264 ($358)

11
A pair of all brass flintlock boxlock pistols, 1st quarter 19th cent, each with 6¾in two-stage barrel, signed 'Nicholson, Corn Hill London', 33.5cm (13¼in), *C 3-6 July*, £462 ($627)

12
A pair of percussion cap muff pistols, *c* 1840, barrels with Birmingham proof marks, boxlocks signed 'Adkin Bedford', 9.8cm (3⅞in), *L 31 Jan*, £374 ($523)

13
An all metal percussion cap pistol, 2nd quarter 19th cent, the 8in two-stage round barrel octagonal at the breech, 33cm (13in), *C 3-6 July*, £330 ($448)

14
A percussion cap knife pistol, *c* 1850, breech with Birmingham proof marks, blades 'Unwin & Rodgers Sheffield', 15.8cm (6¼in), *L 31 Jan*, £286 ($415)

15
A knife pistol, by Samuel Wraggs, third quarter 19th cent, with carved mother of pearl grips, plain 3¾in barrel, 4½in blade, bradawl and boot-hook, signed 'Samuel C. Wraggs, 25, Furnace Hill, Sheffield', 24cm (9½in), *C 2-5 Oct*, £242 ($312)

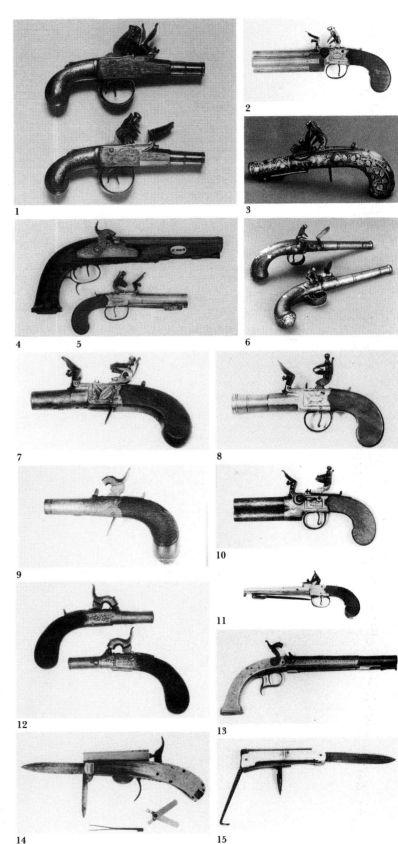

1 2 3 4 5 6 7 8 9 10 11 12 13 14 15

1

A pair of French underhammer percussion pistols, Louis Marin Gosset, 1st quarter 19th cent, with rifled octagonal barrels, gold inlaid inscription 'Invention Gosset', in case including bullet mould and other accessories, barrels 32cm (8¾in), *NY 2/3 Mar*, £9,900 ($6,644)

2

A pair of percussion cap boxlock muff pistols, mid-19th cent, with 1⅜in fluted round barrel folding triggers the butts inlaid with metal studs and escutcheon, contained in case with brass powder flask and bullet mould, retaining some original blueing, 12cm (4¾in), *C 3-6 July*, £451 ($612)

3

A cased pair of ivory mounted pocket pistols, c.1840, Liège proof marks, one butt with small section lacking, 12cm (4¾in); with accessories, ivory powder flask 'Thomas Arquebusier 6 Rue de Rivoli A Paris', case inscribed 'Ax Ax Son Uggla', *L 15 May*, £935 ($1,337)

4

A cased pair of rifled percussion cap target pistols, mid-19th cent, barrels inset in gold 'Contriner', one lock engraved 'Heinr. Kraus' the other 'Ingollersdorf', with all accessories, minor wear, 39.3cm (15½in), *L 2 Oct*, £3,520 ($4,541)

5

A pair of French percussion target pistols, lockplate signed F. Chapouen, Avignon, c.1850, barrels 27cm (10½in), *NY 2/3 Mar*, £3,575 ($2,399)

6

A pair of presentation percussion pistols, Barteolomaeus Joseph Kuchenreuter III, c.1860-70, octagonal steel barrels, silver engraved furniture, in red velvet case with accessories, 27cm (10⅝in), *NY 2/3 Mar*, £4,950 ($3,322)

7

A small bore percussion revolver, mid-19th cent, 2¾in octagonal barrel with front and rear sights, impressed 'David Hn Brevette 6', six chamber cylinder with Liège proof mark, approx .23 calibre, 17.7cm (7in), *L 15 May*, £418 ($598)

8

A 54-bore Adam's patent five-shot percussion double-action revolver, by London Armoury, with accessories, 30.5cm (12in), *P 27 June*, £407 ($573)

9

A Joslyn percussion cap revolver, c.1860, the octagonal barrel 15cm (5⅞in), normally 20.3cm (8in), five-groove rifling, five-chambered cylinder, retaining some colour, 30.4cm (12in), *L 15 May*, £495 ($708)

10

A cased model 1862 .36 police model Colt revolver, 1863/64, retaining most colouring, some wear to plating, 29.2cm (11½in), with accessories, powder flask by James Dixon & Sons, Sheffield, *H 15 Nov*, $2,310 (£1,833)

11

A pair of Colt model 1855 side hammer presentation revolvers, c.1860-61, barrels 9cm (3¼in), *NY 2/3 Mar*, $10,450 (£7,013)

12

A Remington percussion cap revolver, mid-19th cent, the 6¼in octagonal barrel signed 'Remington', worn condition, 34cm (13½in), *C 3-6 July*, £176 ($239)

13

A .44 Whitneyville Walker dragoon Colt revolver, 39.4cm (15½in), *H 15 Nov*, $27,500 (£21,825)

14

A presentation percussion cap .31 1849 Colt pocket revolver, 1861/62, with maker's stamp, 22.2cm (8¾in), *H 15 Nov*, $1,430 (£1,135)

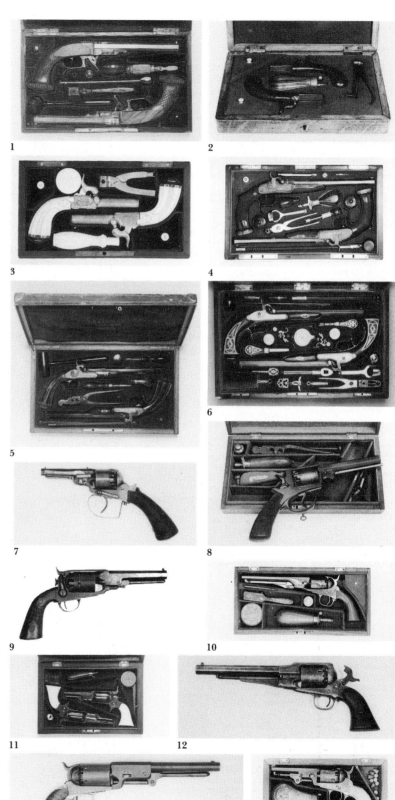

1

2

3

4

5

6

7

8

9

10

11

12

13

14

1
A swivel mounted brass cannon, c.1831, bore approx 3.2cm (1¼in), trunnions stamped 'Montrose 1831' and 'D. Barclay', iron swivel, 53.3cm (21in), mounted on gold and brown painted wooden box, *L 15 May,* £440 ($629)

2
An Irish Volunteer colour and staff, c.1798, the colour was presented to the Kenry Volunteer Pallaskenry, Co. Limerick, pole 272cm (107in), banner 56 x 43.2cm (22 x 17in), *L 2 Oct,* £1,540 ($1,987)

3
An English military cap, c.1690, front flap of blue velvet, front of red embroidered with crown above a WM cypher; possibly worn by a Scottish regiment serving with the Dutch forces, *L 2 Oct,* £7,150 ($9,224)

4
A Persian gold damascened helmet, 19th cent, with adjustable nasal, h 25.5cm (10in), *NY 2/3 Mar,* $990 (£664)

5
A Persian silver and gold damascend helmet and arm guard, 18th/19th cent, mounted with steel and brass mail, h 33cm (13in), *NY 2/3 Mar,* $1,540 (£1,034)

6
A Persian helmet, first half 19th cent, with adjustable nasal, underlaid with red painted metal, with brass studs around the rim; together with an arm guard, h 24cm (9½in), *NY 2/3 Mar,* $935 (£628)

7
A Persian devil helmet, 19th cent, with adjustable nasal, applied with horns, decorated with brass nail heads; together with shield en suite, d 47cm (18½in), *NY 2/3 Mar,* $1,980 (£1,329)

8
A Royal Horse Guards O R helmet, c.1930, white metal skull with brass edging, top spike with red horse hair plume, original leather liner, some minor dents, minor wear to skull, *L 15 May,* £418 ($598)

9
A French Sapeurs Pompiers helmet, mid-19th cent, brass skull, embossed pivoted visor, side plume holder, with liner, fur crest detached, *L 30 Jan,* £385 ($559)

10
A Russian helmet, mid-19th cent, black leather body, large brass badge, brass skin scales, internal liner, *L 2 Oct,* £352 ($454)

11
A Duke of Lancaster's Own Yeomanry helmet, c.1865, black japanned skull, brass edging, gilt band of wreath and plume holder, white horse hair plume, some damage to plume holder, minor dents, *L 2 Oct,* £374 ($482)

12
A close helmet, in style of late 16th cent, the quality of this copy is such as to suggest that it could have been made for a specific purpose such as the Eglington Tournament, *L 2 Oct,* £1,210 ($1,561)

13
A morion, late 16th cent decorative brass headed rivets, brass plume holder, some holes in comb, contemporary repair, plume holder deformed, line of punched holes around base, *L 15 May,* £1,430 ($2,045)

14
A cabasset, late 16th cent, decorative brass headed rivets, brass plume holder, retaining some traces of gilding, small hole in skull and two in brim, *L 15 May,* £880 ($1,258)

1   2
3
4   5   6   7   8
9   10   11
12   13   14

1
Browning. An 'American Mallard' 12-bore superposed single-trigger boxlock ejector sporting gun, no 340 of 500, 28in barrels, approx 7lb, stock 36.8cm (14½in), probably unused, *H 15 Nov*, $5,775 (£4,583)

2
Boss & Co. A 12-bore assisted-opening single-trigger sidelock ejector sporting gun, 28-inch chopper lump barrels, with bouquet and scroll engraving and some hardening colour, approx 6lb 2oz, fitted with extra 28in barrels, stock 36.8cm (14½in), *H 15 Nov*, $15,400 (£12,222)

3
Boss & Co. A composed pair of 12-bore assisted-opening sidelock ejector sporting guns, with 29in barrels, with bouquet and scroll engraving and traces of hardening colour, 6lb 11oz, stocks 38.2cm (15in), *Glen 27 Aug*, £9,900 ($13,563)

4
Boss & Co. A 12-bore single-trigger round-bodied sidelock ejector sporting gun, 29in barrels, right barrel wall below minimum recommended thickness, 6lb 8oz, stock 37.4cm (14¾in), *Glen 27 Aug*, £4,180 ($5,726)

5
Charles Boswell. A 12-bore sidelock ejector sporting gun, 28in barrels, locks with gold-lined cocking indicators, top-lever with bouquet and scroll engraving and traces of colour, 6lb 8oz, stock 36.5cm (14⅜in), *L 2 May*, £2,640 ($3,722)

6
E J Churchill. A pair of 12-bore 'Premier XXV' assisted-opening sidelock ejector sporting guns, 25in barrels with Churchill ribs, locks with gold-lined cocking indicators and gold-numbered top-levers, 6lb 4oz, stocks 38.1cm (15in), *Glen 27 Aug*, £10,450 ($14,317)

7
John Dickson & Son. A 12-bore boxlock ejector sporting gun, 28in barrels, bores slightly pitted, 6lb 8oz, stock 35.5cm (14in), *Glen 27 Aug*, £1,045 ($1,432)

8
John Dickson & Son. A pair of lightweight 12-bore assisted-opening round-action ejector sporting guns, 27in Vickers A steel barrels, 5lb 14oz, stocks 38.1cm (15in), no 2 required rebarrelling, *Glen 27 Aug*, £6,600 ($9,042)

9
John Dickson & Son. A 12-bore assisted-opening round-action ejector sporting gun, 28in sleeved barrels, left bore dented, 6lb 10oz, stock 36.4cm (14⅜in), *L 21 July*, £1,155 ($1,571)

10
Stephen Grant & Sons. A lightweight 12-bore sidelock ejector sporting gun, 26in barrels, retaining most original finish, right bore with slight dent, 6lb 2oz, stock 37.8cm (14⅞in), *Glen 27 Aug*, £4,840 ($6,631)

11
Charles Hellis & Sons. A 12-bore boxlock ejector sporting gun, 26in barrels, 6lb 7oz, stock 35.9cm (14⅛in), *L 2 May*, £1,265 ($1,784)

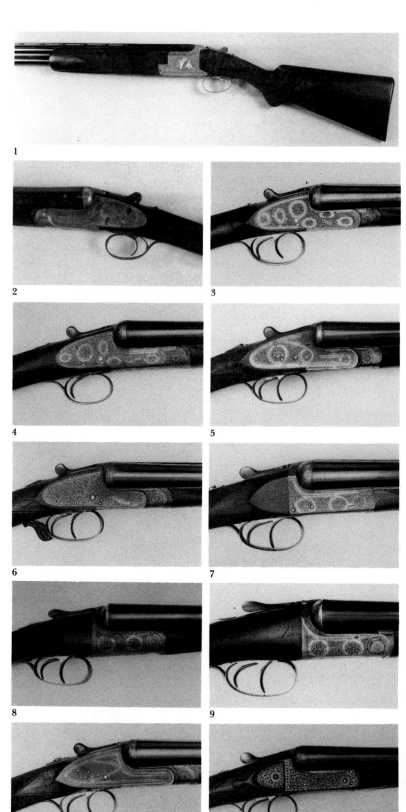

1

2   3

4   5

6   7

8   9

10   11

1
J Purdey & Sons. A lightweight 12-bore self-opening sidelock ejector sporting gun, 28in chopper lump barrels, fore-end restocked with a beavertail, stock 37cm (14½in), also fitted with extra 25in barrels, *H 15 Nov,* $12,100 (£9,603)

2
J Purdey & Sons. A pair of 12-gauge self-opening sidelock ejector sporting guns, *c* 1979, 28in chopper lump barrels, approx 6lb 8oz, stocks 38.1cm (15in), *H 15 Nov,* $35,750 (£28,600)

3
Simson, Suhl. A presentation 16-bore over-and-under ejector sporting gun, 27½in monobloc barrels, Suhl nitro proof for March 1964, *H 15 Nov,* $12,100 (£9,603)

4
Holland & Holland. A composed pair of 12-bore 'Royal' self-opening detachable sidelock ejector sporting guns, 28in barrels, case-hardened frames, with foliate scroll engraving, 6lb 7oz, stocks 35.5cm (14in), *Glen 27 Aug,* £14,300 ($19,591)

5
Holland & Holland. A 16-bore 'Royal Brevis' self-opening sidelock ejector sporting gun, 28in barrels, bores marginal, wall thicknesses low, 6lb, stock 37.4cm (14¾in), *Glen 27 Aug,* £4,400 ($6,028)

6
Holland & Holland. A 12-bore 'Badminton' sidelock ejector sporting gun, 28½in barrels, case-hardened frame, figured walnut stock and fore-end, retaining virtually all original colour, 7lb 8oz, stock, 38.1cm (15in), *L 2 May,* £3,850 ($5,429)

7
J Purdey & Sons. A 12-bore self-opening sidelock ejector sporting gun, 28in chopper lump barrels with Churchill rib, highly coloured frame, retaining virtually all colour, approx 6lb 8oz, walnut stock 37.8cm (14⅞in), *H 15 Nov,* $17,050 (£13,532)

8
J Purdey & Sons. A lightweight 12-bore self-opening sidelock ejector sporting gun, 28in barrels, 6lb 1oz, stock 37.7cm (14¾in), *Glen 27 Aug,* £5,610 ($7,686)

9
Westley Richards & Co. A lightweight 12-bore boxlock ejector sporting gun, 28in barrels, 5lb 14oz, stock 35.5cm (14in), *Glen 27 Aug,* £1,155 ($1,582)

10
John Robertson. A .410 boxlock ejector sporting gun, 26in barrels, 4lb 2oz, shortened stock 35cm (13¾in), *H 15 Nov,* $2,640 (£2,095)

11
T Wild. A 12-bore boxlock ejector wildfowling gun, 30in barrels with 3in chambers, 7lb 15oz, stock 37cm (14⅝in), stock repaired at hand, *L 2 May,* £660 ($930)

1

2

3

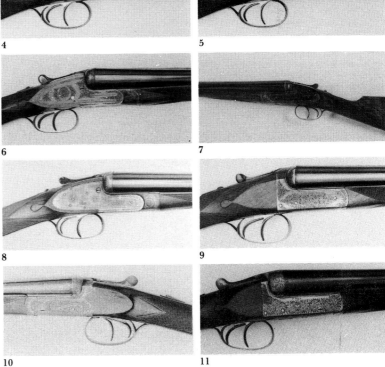

4 5

6 7

8 9

10 11

1
Winchester. A model 21
'Grand American' 20-
bore boxlock ejector sporting
gun with interchangeable
sets of barrels, both sets of
barrels 28in, about 7lb,
stock 35.5cm (14in),
H 15 Nov,
$14,300 (£11,349)

2
Winchester. A 30-30 Win.
lever-action rifle, 20in
barrel, engraved with
scenes of Indians with
buffalo and horses over
a black stippled ground,
signed 'F. E. Hendricks',
walnut stock, *H 15 Nov,*
$3,300 (£2,619)

3
An exhibition game gun,
built by John Wilkes for
the engraver Malcolm
Appleby, engraved
overall with the theme
of woodcock plumage,
12-bore sidelock ejector
action, 28in barrels,
H 15 Nov,
$17,600 (£13,968)

4
Trulock Bros. An
'Improved Lockfast'
patent slide-and-drop
action 12-bore pinfire
sporting gun, 30in
damascus barrels, unsuit-
able for use, in oak case
with accessories by James
Dixon & Sons, *L 2 May,*
£1,210 ($1,706)

5
A Spencer patent slide-
action repeater prototype
.45-70 service rifle, the
29½in barrel with ramp
and ladder sight to 1200
yards, retaining cleaning
rod, 122cm (48in),
L 2 May,
£1,980 ($2,792)

6
Parker Bros. An 8-bore
grade G boxlock non-ejector
gun, 36in damascus barrels,
case-hardened frame
and top-lever, retaining
some colour, approx
12lb 12oz, walnut stock
37cm (14½in), *H 15 Nov,*
$3,300 (£2,619)

7
Parker Field & Sons. A
Field's patent snap-action
12-bore bar-in-wood
pinfire sporting gun, 28in
damascus barrels, 7lb 1oz,
stock 36.4cm (14⅜in),
Glen 27 Aug,
£715 ($979)

8
George Gibbs. A .303 sidelock
ejector sporting rifle, 26in
barrels with leaf sights to
500 yards, bores worn,
8lb 14oz, stock 37.2cm
(14⅝in), *L 31 July,*
£2,530 ($3,441)

9
Watson Bros. A .450/400
express bar-in-wood boxlock
ejector big game rifle,
26¼in Krupp steel barrels
with leaf sights to 300
yards, 10lb 4oz, stock
37.5cm (14¾in), left ejector
defective, *L 2 May,*
£935 ($1,318)

1

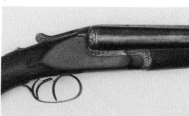

2

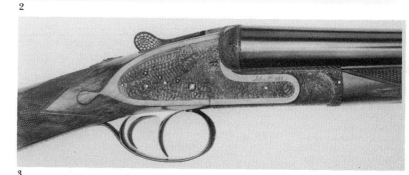

3

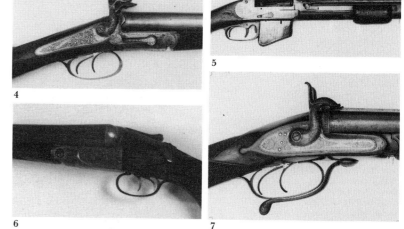

4

5

6

7

8

9

Medals

MICHAEL NAXTON

Medals sought by collectors fall into three categories: medals issued for general service or merely for being present; decorations awarded for a particular act of bravery; and Orders of Chivalry in the gift of the sovereign. The largest market in medals lies in English-speaking and Commonwealth countries where there is closest involvement with the British system of awards. Most British awards up to the Second World War were named personally to the recipient and this is a great attraction for collectors. Because of this and as Americans are forbidden by Act of Congress to sell US medals in the United States, major sales of medals are almost always held in London.

The first true 'campaign' medals started with the award for Waterloo (1815) and, though medal collecting flourished thereafter, it is only in the last ten to fifteen years that medals have come into their own in the commercial sense. As a result, prices are probably now steadying and in the immediate future there may well not be the spectacular increases—proportionately far greater than those in many other collecting fields—which resulted from historically low market values.

For campaign medals the battle commemorated is the key factor. The medal itself may be quite common, for example for the Crimean War (£50-150, $55-170), but those awarded to the cavalry participating in the Charge of the Light Brigade can realize up to £1,500 ($1,700). It is possible to determine if the recipient served in a particular battle by knowing his regiment and checking that the campaign medal bears the relevant clasp—in this case, Balaclava. The same is true for the Boer War, where a commonly awarded medal will fetch £15-30 ($20-35), whereas one awarded to someone present at the Defence of Mafeking will fetch about £750 ($850). Another example concerns the medals awarded to men present at the Defence of Rorke's Drift which can fetch up to £3,500 ($4,000). The identical medal which was issued to all those who served in the Zulu War, 1877-79, will only fetch perhaps £100-150 ($110-170). Thus, a major factor with military medals is the number issued. Medals issued to only a few people are always commercially more desirable than those issued in large numbers, even when the latter are considerably older.

British decorations for gallantry are among the most sought after as they normally bear the name of the recipient. The Victoria Cross and the George Cross are the highest awards. The former is awarded, regardless of rank, for an action of supreme bravery in the face of the enemy. Other bravery awards are only made within certain ranks and within a particular service. The higher the award the rarer and more valuable it tends to be and of the three British services the Royal Air Force, being the youngest, is the least keenly collected at present.

It is the principal Orders of Chivalry, whether British or awarded by other sovereign states, which tend to fetch the highest prices. Few of these reach the market because they are returnable to the sovereign on the recipient's death. However, on occasion, the sovereign may permit the insignia to be kept by the family of the recipient, and it is these that are most highly prized. Sometimes the recipients may have had replicas made more suitable for wearing with contemporary dress than the original and when these pieces are of fine quality they too are very desirable.

Recently there seems to have been increased interest in life-saving medals, especially those which carry a citation. These 19th-century medals issued to lifeboatmen or mercantile seamen of whatever country, now frequently fetch £150-200 ($170-220) or more, whereas they used only to command £50-100 ($55-110).

Any medal that has been either excessively cleaned or damaged from contact wear will be considerably reduced in value and all the medals illustrated here are in good condition. Market value is enhanced if the complete set of individual medals awarded to one recipient is sold together. Much more significantly, *any* alteration to the original naming is very damaging to price, even where the recipient has had the wording changed according to his subsequent rise in rank.

The only medals which remain as unpredictable as ever are those awarded to legendary figures. Thus Captain Oates' Polar medals for Captain Scott's famous last expedition (p.229 fig.16) reached an unprecedented £55,000 ($75,000)—a world auction record price for any service medal.

1
The Most Ancient and Most Noble Order of the Thistle (KT), breast star, by R & S Garrard, London, c.1864, made for Francis Napier, 10th Lord Napier and 1st Baron Ettrick (1819-1898) in 1864. *L 1 Mar,* £3,740 ($5,572)

2
The Most Illustrious Order of St Patrick (KP), breast star, by West & Son of Dublin, 1883, *L 28 June,* £1,980 ($2,703)

3
A Peninsular War Group of Orders awarded to Major General Sir William Williams, KCB, including the Peninsular Gold Cross for the actions of Corunna, Fuentes d'Onor, Ciudad Rodrigo and Badajoz, with one clasp for Salamanca, *L 1 Nov,* £16,500 ($21,120)

4
The Imperial Service Order (ISO), Geo. V, ladies' breast badge, in silver, with gold and enamel centre, *L 1 Mar,* £253 ($377)

5
Argentina, Order of San Martin, Grand Cross set, c.1960, hallmarked but no maker's name, comprising sash badge and breast star, in different coloured golds, with enamel centres, extremely rare, *L 28 June,* £3,630 ($4,955)

6
Bhutan, Royal Order of Bhutan, Grand Cross 'sash set', by Spink of London, in 9ct gold and enamels, excessively rare; only ten such sets were made in 1966-7, *L 28 June,* £3,520 ($4,805)

7
A pair of medals awarded to Lieut George Cull, RM, comprising Naval General Service medal, 1793, 1 clasp, Egypt, Sultan's gold medal (Order of the Crescent); *L 1 Mar,* £990 ($1,475)

8
The three clasp Naval General Service medal, 1793, awarded to Lieut P W P Wallis, RN (later Admiral of the Fleet Sir Provo Wallis, GCB), with clasps for the actions of Anse La Barque 18 Dec. 1809, Guadaloupe and Shannon with Chesapeake. Admiral Sir Provo Wallis held the longest continuous commission in the history of the Royal Navy; 97 years, 1795-1892. *L 28 June,* £7,150 ($9,760)

9
Military General Service medal, 1793, 1 clasp, Martinique (W B Bigland, Lieut RN), excessively rare; only 19 of these medals were awarded to Naval recipients—6 of them with the clasp for Martinique. *L 1 Nov,* £1,815 ($2,323)

10
Military General Service medal, 1793, 1 clasp, Corunna (David Whittan, 42nd Foot), *L 1 Mar,* £220 ($328)

11
Army of India medal, 1799, 2 clasps, Capture of Deig, Laswarree (John Anderson, 8th Lt Dragns), *L 1 Mar,* £1,870 ($2,786)

12
Matthew Boulton's medal for the Battle of Trafalgar, 1805, in white metal. In the absence of an official award to the men who fought at Trafalgar, Matthew Boulton had this medal struck at his own expense, *L 1 Mar,* £374 ($557)

13
Waterloo medal, 1815 (John Parry, 7th Regiment Hussars), with original steel clip and ring suspension. *L 1 Mar,* £286 ($426)

14
Field Officer's small gold medal for the Pyrenees, with clasp for Toulouse, (Major Martin Leggatt, 1st Btn 36th Foot). *L 1 Mar,* £2,860 ($4,261)

1
Waterloo medal, 1815, Hanover issue, *L 1 Nov,* £110 ($141)

2
Ghuznee medal, 1839, (Private William Smith, 16th Lancers). One of the first of the medals for the various campaigns in India leading up to the Mutiny in 1857, *L 1 Mar,* £165 ($246)

3
Cabul medal, 1842, (Cornelius Foster, Pt, HM's 31st Regimt), *L 1 Nov,* £187 ($239)

4
Gwalior Campaign, 1843, Maharajpoor star (Gunner Henry Abbott, 2d Troop 3d Brigade Horse Artillery), *L 1 Nov,* £154 ($197)

5
New Zealand, 1845-66, dated medal for 1845-1847 (C. Yarnold, Private, RM, HMS Racehorse), only 36 medals to this ship, *L 1 Mar,* £407 ($606)

6
Crimea medal, 1854, 4 clasps, Alma, Balaklava, Inkermann, Sebastopol (J Lowdon, Grenadier Gds). *L 1 Mar,* £242 ($361)

7
Canada General Service, 1866, 1 clasp, Fenian Raid 1866 (Gr. T. Biven, RA). These medals were issued for the suppression of the Fenian rebellions in Canada, 1866-70, *L 1 Nov,* £99 ($127)

8
Canadian Indian Peace Medal, 1874, silver medal for Treaty No 4. These medals were presented to the chiefs as gifts of friendship from Queen Victoria, *L 1 Mar,* £1,540 ($2,222)

9
Hong Kong Plague medal, 1894, struck in gold (Emma G. Ireland), only 9 gold medals issued to nurses, *L 1 Nov,* £2,200 ($2,816)

10
Edward VII's Delhi Durbar medal, 1903, in gold, ladies' issue on bow, *L 28 June,* £858 ($1,171)

11
'An Albert Medal (2nd Class), in bronze, 'Presented to Nurse Florence Alice Allen, for gallantry in saving life at Quetta on the 31st May 1935', *L 1 Nov,* £2,640 ($3,379)

12
A 'Railway' George Cross group of 4, awarded to Driver Benjamin Gimbert, LNER, including a George Cross for 25th July, 1944; the recipient saved the destruction of the town of Soham (Cambridgeshire) from a burning ammunition train, *L 28 June,* £7,700 ($10,510)

13
A George Cross (*exchanged* Edward medal), awarded to Walter Lee for the Wombell Colliery disaster on 11 Nov, 1947, *L 1 Nov,* £1,540 ($1,971)

14
A Boy Scout's Silver Cross awarded to Bombardier L. Ryden, RA, for rescuing a drowning boy at Colwyn Bay in 1934, *L 28 June,* £440 ($600)

15
USA, Presidential Gold medal for Lifesaving, awarded to Frederick Hicks, for rescuing men of the American schooner Thomas W. Lawson, wrecked off the Scilly Islands on 14 Dec, 1907, *L 1 Nov,* £770 ($985)

16
The Polar medal, 1904, 1 clasp, Antarctic 1910-13 (Captain L. E. G. Oates, 6th Dragoons, Terra Nova). *L 28 June,* £55,000 ($75,075)

17
The Royal Geographical Society's bronze medal, for Scott's second Antarctic Expedition of 1910-13, awarded to W. H Neale; *L 28 June,* £550 ($751)

Musical Instruments

GRAHAM WELLS • CHARLES RUDIG

The ultimate buyers of fine musical instruments are either amateur or professional players. They buy their instruments in order to play them and the all-important consideration is therefore the sound the instrument makes. Violins by eminent makers that are in good condition can be expected to produce fine tone as that is how these makers achieved their reputations. Their names therefore carry a kind of guarantee; a fact which has led to every manner of fake and forgery—one should never trust a violin label. But as long as orchestral playing remains popular there will always be a steady market for violins. The instruments are the tools of the trade and the players are prepared to make at least one big initial investment in their careers.

There are an enormous number of fine violins in the United States but London is traditionally the worldwide centre of the violin market. Many continental and American players go there as do the Japanese who are very strong buyers of violins. The 17th, 18th and 19th century Italian violin makers are by far the most popular, and deservedly so. But the final price depends very much on condition. A revarnished instrument will be greatly reduced (better virtually no varnish at all), but the worst faults are structural ones. A crack in the back by the soundpost can halve the value. Modern restoration can be extremely good and the surest way to ascertain repairs would be to open the body, though this is not usually practical. A player should ask the advice of an expert before making a purchase. Grafts in bows are another common restoration. Modern fittings are perfectly acceptable on string instruments. Some idea of the difference that condition can make is given by the price of one of the violins sold in November. It was a French instrument of 1887 for which the expected price would be about £1,500 ($1,700). This particular one had no scratches or blemishes and went for £2,400. The Stradivari 'Cathédrale' (page 237, fig. 4) was a violin which had miraculously survived intact. It was largely because it was so well preserved that it fetched a staggering £396,000. An instrument that is known to have belonged to a famous player will also have its value much enhanced. Nowadays 19th and 20th century violins are increasingly sought after, no doubt because of the scarcity of earlier models in equivalent condition. Violins by Josef Rocca, George Craske and Charles J. B. Colin-Mezin have all seen huge increases in prices.

Woodwind players are particularly discerning about condition. Cracks can be a major problem and restored instruments may be hard to sell. Many players prefer to buy a reproduction instrument specially commissioned. However good continental instruments (which are rarer than English ones) sell well and wide-holed 19th century flutes have recently gone up from around £200 ($230) to £600-800 ($680-910). They are often bought by Irish traditional musicians. Pitch also has a bearing on the sale of woodwind instruments. In the 18th century it was much flatter and at the end of the 19th/beginning of the 20th much sharper than it is now. Some players need different instruments of the correct pitch for the period of music that they are playing. Missing keys can also be a problem, but dents in brass instruments are not as they can always be removed. An article on drawing room woodwind instruments can be found on page 241.

On the whole auction houses sell early pianos (prior to 1850) but not later examples for simple reasons of size and weight, though Sotheby's do sometimes include ornate later examples in their furniture sales. Many early keyboard instruments have a tendency to be made from more than one instrument, so the more original the piece the better. Antique harpsichords are highly prized and spinets are popular with amateur musicians as they are also good pieces of furniture. They sell for about £5,000 ($6,300). Square pianos (the predecessors of the modern upright) are now relatively cheap and are often found at less than £1,000 ($1,140). They need a great deal of maintenance and are expensive to restore, but they can be pleasing pieces of 18th century furniture.

Early plucked-string instruments are collectors' pieces. Sotheby's sold a magnificent Italian guitar (page 240, fig. 3) for £7,400. The back of the body was the only part that was original, had the whole been totally authentic it would have made up to £20,000 ($22,800).

1

An Italian violin, by
Nicolo Amati, Cremona,
c.1630, the table by
Antonio and
Hieronymus Amati, Cre-
mona, c.1600, the varnish
of a golden-brown
colour, 35.3cm (13¹⁵/₁₆in),
L 5 Apr,
£18,700 ($26,928)

2

An Italian violin, by
Franceso Ruggieri, Cre-
mona, c.1700, the varnish
of a red-brown colour,
35.2cm (13⅞in),
NY 29 June,
$28,600 (£21,185)

3

An Italian violin, (The
'Lyall' Stradivari), by
Antonio Stradivari, Cremona, 1702, the varnish
of an orange-brown
colour, 35.6cm (14in),
NY 18 Jan,
$231,000 (£159,146)

4

An Italian violin, by
Tommaso Balestrieri,
Mantua, the varnish of a
golden-orange colour,
35.2cm (13⅞in), *L 21 June,*
£30,800 ($43,736)
with a silver-mounted
bow, l of back 35.2cm
(13⅞in), *L 21 June,*
£30,800 ($43,736)

5

An Italian violin, by
Giovanni Grancino,
Milan, c.1708, the varnish
of an orange-brown
colour, 35.5cm (14in),
NY 18 Jan,
$34,100 (£23,493)

6

An Italian violin, by
Carlo and Michelangelo
Bergonzi, Cremona, 1733,
the varnish of an orange-
brown colour, 35.3cm
(14in), *L 21 June,*
£36,300 ($51,546)

7

An Italian violin, by
Gaspare Lorenzini,
Piacenza, 2nd half 18th
cent, the varnish of a
red-brown colour, 35.9cm
(14⅛in), *NY 18 Jan,*
$7,700 (£5,305)

8

An Italian violin, by
Joseph filius Andrea
Guarneri, Cremona,
1714, the varnish of a
golden-red colour,
35.3cm (13¹⁵/₁₆in), *L 5 Apr,*
£88,000 ($126,720)

9

An Italian violin, by
Giulio Degani, Venice,
1897, the varnish of a
dark golden-brown
colour, 35.5cm (14in),
L 22 Nov,
£2,750 ($3,575)

10

An Italian violin, by
Enrico Clodoveo
Melegari, Turin, 1884,
the varnish of a golden-
brown colour, 35.4cm
(13¹⁵/₁₆in), *L 5 Apr,*
£5,740 ($8,266)

11

An Italian violin, by
Enrico Rossi, Pavia, last
quarter 19th cent, the
varnish of a red-orange
colour, 35.9cm (14⅛in),
NY 29 June,
$3,575 (£2,648)

12

An Italian violin, by
Joannes Franciscus
Pressenda, Turin, c.1840,
the varnish of an
orange-red colour,
35.6cm (14in),
NY 29 June,
$38,500 (£28,519)

13

An Italian violin, by
Giovanni Maria Ceruti,
Cremona, 1923, the
varnish of an orange
colour, 35.8cm (14⅛in),
L 20 Sept,
£1,375 ($1,788)

14

An Italian violin, by
Romeo Antoniazzi, Cre-
mona, c.1922, the varnish
of an orange-brown
colour, 35.7cm (14¹/₁₆in),
NY 29 June,
$4,125 (£3,056)

The measurement
given for violins,
violas and violon-
cellos is the length of
the back.

1 2 3 4

5 6 7

8 9 10

11 12 13 14

1
An Italian violin, by
Vincenzo Sannino,
Naples, early 20th cent,
the varnish of an orange
red-brown colour,
35.3cm (13⅞in),
NY 29 June,
$6,600 (£4,889)

2
An Italian violin, by
Giulio Degani, Venice,
1909, the varnish of a
red-orange colour,
35.3cm (13⅞in),
NY 29 June,
$6,600 (£4,889)

3
An Italian violin, by
Alfredo Contino,
Naples, c.1930, the
varnish of a reddish
golden-brown colour,
35.6cm (14in),
NY 18 Dec,
$6,600 (£5,593)

4
An English violin, by
John Johnson, London,
mid-18th cent,
the varnish of a dark
golden-brown colour,
35.7cm (14¹/₁₆in),
NY 18 Dec,
$2,750 (£2,330)

5
An English violin, by
George Craske (1795-
1888), Stockport, the
varnish of a red-brown
colour, 35.2cm (13⅞in),
L 5 Apr,
£2,200 ($3,168)

6
An Irish violin, by
Thomas Perry and
William Wilkinson,
Dublin, c1800, the
varnish of a golden-
orange colour, 35.3cm
(13⅞in), *L 22 Nov,*
£1,320 ($1,716)

7
A Scottish violin, by
Thomas Hardie,
Edinburgh, 1852, the
varnish of a golden-
brown colour, 35.9cm
(14⅛in), *L 5 Apr,*
£1,980 ($2,851)

8
An English violin, by W E
Hill & Sons, London,
1913, the varnish of a
red-brown colour, a copy
of The 'Messie'
Stradivari, 35.8cm
(14¹/₁₆in), *L 21 June,*
£2,640 ($3,749)

9
A French violin, by a
member of the Bernardel
family, Paris, 1720, the
varnish of a red-brown
colour, 35.7cm (14¹/₁₆in),
L 5 Apr,
£6,270 ($9,029)

10
A French violin, by
Nicolas Augustin
Chappuy, Paris, 1775,
the varnish of a golden
colour, 35.3cm (13⅞in),
L 21 June,
£770 ($1,093)

11
A French violin, by
Joseph Bassot, Paris, the
varnish of a toast-brown
colour, 35.7cm (14¹/₁₆in),
NY 18 Jan,
$5,500 (£3,789)

12
A French violin, by
François Louis Pique,
Paris, 1810, sold with a
silver and tortoiseshell-
mounted bow, by W. E.
Hill & Sons, and a chased
silver-mounted bow, by
Charles Bazin, 36.4cm
(14⁵/₁₆in), *L 5 Apr,*
£5,720 ($8,237)

13
A French violin, by
Charles Jean Baptiste
Collin-Mézin, Paris, 1895,
the varnish of a golden-
brown colour, 35.8cm
(14¹/₁₆in), *L 5 Apr,*
£1,100 ($1,584)

14
A French violin, by Gustave
Bernardel, Paris, 1896,
the varnish of an orange-
brown colour, 35.9cm
(14⅛in), *L 21 June,*
£3,740 ($5,311)

1   2   3   4

5   6   7

8   9   10

11   12   13   14

1
A French violin, by Paul
Bailly, Paris, c.1900, the
varnish of a red-brown
colour, 35.6cm (14in),
NY 18 Jan,
$2,750 (£1,895)

2
A French violin, by
Emile Blondelet, Paris,
1923, the varnish of a
red-brown colour,
35.8cm (14¹/₁₆in), *L 5 Apr,*
£990 ($1,426)

3
A Dutch violin, by
Johannes Cuypers, The
Hague, 1793, the varnish
of a golden colour,
35.3cm (13⁷/₈in), *L 5 Apr,*
£7,260 ($10,454)

4
A Belgian violin, by
Nicholas François
Vuillaume, Brussels,
1844, the varnish of an
orange-brown colour,
36.7cm (14⁷/₁₆in), *L 22 Nov,*
£1,980 ($2,574)

5
A small German violin, by
Bruno Bolte, Bremen,
1671, retaining its
original neck, 31.1cm
(12¹/₄in), *L 21 June,*
£1,540 ($2,187)

6
A German violin, by
Sebastian Kloz,
Mittenwald, 1756, the
varnish of a rich orange-
brown colour, 35.5cm
(14in), *L 22 Nov,*
£7,700 ($10,010)

7
A Viennese violin, by
Franz Geissenhof, 1799,
the varnish of a red-
brown colour, 35.7cm
(14¹/₁₆in), *L 21 June,*
£3,630 ($5,155)

8
A Bohemian violin, by
Caspar Strnad, Prague,
c.1812, 35.6cm (14in),
NY 29 June,
$3,850 (£2,852)

9
A Bohemian violin, by
Emmanuel Homolka, 1st
half 19th cent, the
varnish of an orange-
yellow colour, 35.6cm
(14in), *NY 18 Jan,*
$2,310 (£1,591)

10
A Hungarian violin, by
Samuel Felix Nemessányi,
Pesth, 1876, the varnish
of a golden-orange colour,
35.8cm (14¹/₈in), *L 5 Apr,*
£5,500 ($7,920)

11
An American violin, by
Karl August Berger,
New York, 1922, the
varnish of an orange
colour, 35.9cm (14¹/₈in),
NY 29 June,
$1,540 (£1,141)

12
An American violin, by
Alberto Ferdinando
Moglie, Washington DC,
1938, the varnish of a
golden colour, 35.9cm
(14¹/₈in), *L 21 June,*
£1,650 ($2,343)

13
A Portuguese violin, by
Antonio Capela,
Espinho, 1971, the
varnish of a golden-
yellow colour, 35.3cm
(13⁷/₈in), *NY 18 Jan,*
$2,200 (£1,516)

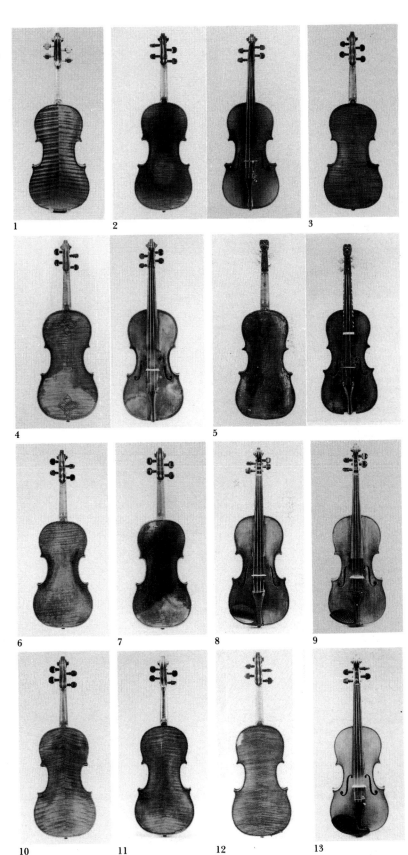

1 2 3
4 5
6 7 8 9
10 11 12 13

1
An English violin case, by W E Hill & Sons, London, the satinwood case inlaid with fruitwood, mahogany and boxwood, *L 5 Apr,* £5,940 ($8,571)

2
An English silver-mounted violin bow, by James Tubbs, London, very worn, 57 grams, *L 5 Apr,* £594 ($857)

3
An English silver-mounted violin bow, by James Tubbs, London, 64 grams, *L 22 Nov,* £1,540 ($2,002)

4
An English chased gold-mounted violin bow, by James Tubbs, London, 60 grams, *NY 18 Jan,* $4,400 (£3,031)

5
An English silver-mounted violin bow, by W E Hill & Sons, London, 56 grams, *L 22 Nov,* £880 ($1,144)

6
An English gold and tortoiseshell-mounted violin bow, by W E Hill & Sons, London, 62 grams, *NY 29 June,* $4,400 (£3,259)

7
An English gold and tortoiseshell-mounted violin bow, by W E Hill & Sons, London, *c.1900,* the head blemished, 61 grams, *L 22 Nov,* £1,540 ($2,002)

8
A gold and tortoiseshell-mounted violin bow, by H Kaston, New York, 62 grams, *NY 18 Jan,* $2,750 (£1,895)

9
A French silver-mounted violin bow, by J B Vuillaume, Paris, *c.1860,* 59 grams, *NY 29 June,* $2,750 (£2,037)

10
A French silver-mounted violin bow, by François Nicolas Voirin, Paris, 56 grams, *L 5 Apr,* £1,760 ($2,540)

11
A French silver-mounted violin bow, by Guillaume Maline, Paris, 2nd quarter 19th cent, unstamped, 57 grams, *NY 29 June,* $3,300 (£2,444)

12
A French silver-mounted violin bow, by Eugène Sartory, Paris, 59 grams, *L 22 Nov,* £2,310 ($3,003)

13
A French gold and ivory-mounted violin bow, by Louis Bazin, Mirecourt, 66 grams, *L 22 Nov,* £990 ($1,287)

14
A French silver-mounted violin bow, by Nicholas Maire, Paris, *c.1850,* 62 grams, *L 22 Nov,* £4,510 ($5,863)

15
A French silver-mounted violin bow, by Joseph Arthur Vigneron, Paris, 55 grams, *L 5 Apr,* £1,870 ($2,698)

16
A French gold and ivory-mounted bow, by Marcel Lapierre, Mirecourt, 62 grams, *NY 29 June,* $990 (£733)

17
A French silver-mounted violin bow, by Paul Simon, Paris, mid-19th cent, 60 grams, *NY 18 Jan,* $4,400 (£3,031)

18
A French silver-mounted violin bow, by Dominique Peccatte, Paris, some wear, 64 grams, *NY 18 Jan,* $9,900 (£6,821)

19
A silver-mounted violin bow, by Gaulard, *c.1850,* 60 grams, *NY 18 Jan,* $1,650 (£1,137)

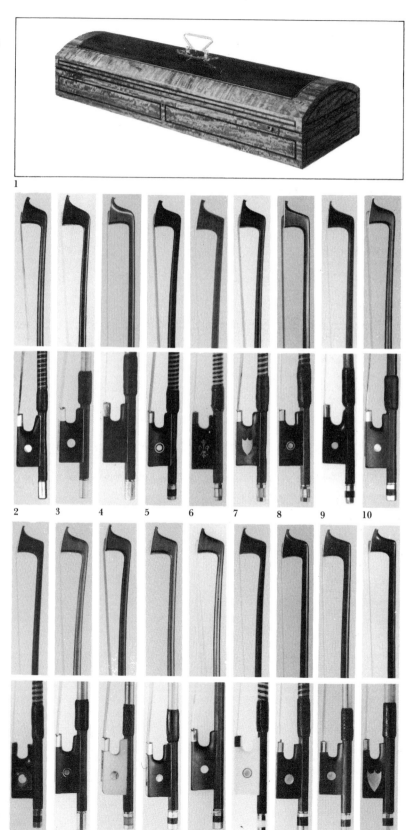

1

2 3 4 5 6 7 8 9 10

11 12 13 14 15 16 17 18 19

1

A Bohemian viola d'amore, mid-18th cent, labelled 'Joannes Florenus Guidantus Fecit Bononiae 1740', remarkable for the fact that most of its fittings are original, 40cm (15¾in), *NY 29 June*, $8,800 (£6,519)

2

An Italian viola, by Giulio Cesare Gigli, Rome, mid-18th cent, the varnish of a golden-brown colour, 38.1cm (15in), *NY 29 June*, $8,800 (£6,519)

3

An Italian viola, by Tommaso Balestrieri, Mantua, *c*1760, the varnish of a golden-red colour, cut down from a larger instrument, 39.8cm (15⅝in), *L 21 June*, £22,000 ($31,240)

4

An English viola, by Georges Adolphe Chanot, Manchester, 1895, the varnish of a golden-brown colour, 40.1cm (16¹/₁₆in), *L 21 June*, £1,430 ($2,031)

5

An Italian viola, by Carlo Bisiach, Florence, *c*1925, the varnish of an orange-brown colour, 40.8cm (16in), *NY 18 Dec*, $12,650 (£10,720)

6

An Italian viola, by Umberto Lanaro, Padua, 1967, the varnish of a yellow colour, 41.9cm (16½in), *NY 29 June*, $1,760 (£1,304)

7

An American silver-mounted viola bow, by Emile A. Ouchard, New York, 74 grams, *NY 18 Dec*, $1,980 (£1,678)

8

A gold and ivory-mounted viola bow, by Johann S Finkel, 68 grams, *NY 18 Dec*, $1,980 (£1,678)

9

A French gold and tortoiseshell-mounted viola bow, by Nicholas Maire, Paris, 19th cent. The frog and adjuster are not original but are French. 72 grams, *NY 18 Jan*, $5,500 (£3,789)

10

An English gold and tortoiseshell-mounted viola bow, by W E Hill & Sons, London, 76 grams, *L 5 Apr*, £1,430 ($2,063)

11

An English silver-mounted viola bow, by Thomas Tubbs, London *c*1800, 65 grams, *NY 29 June*, $3,300, (£2,444)

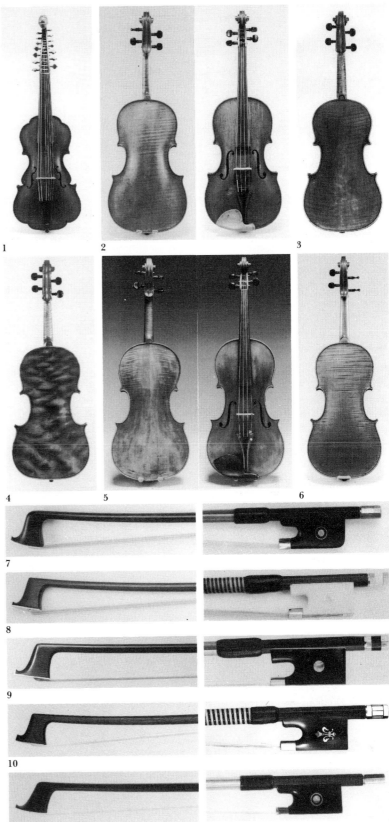

1
An Italian violoncello, by
Francesco Ruggieri,
Cremona, c.1670,
the varnish of a golden-
orange colour, cut down
and later re-enlarged by
W E Hill & Sons,
London, 1926, 75.8cm
(29⅞in), *L 21 June,*
£34,100 ($48,422)

2
A violoncello, converted
in England c.1800 from a
viola da gamba by
Joachim Tielke,
Hamburg, c.1700,
74.5cm (29⁵/₁₆in), *L 5 Apr,*
£5,720 ($8,237)

3
A Bavarian violoncello, by
Sebastian Kloz,
Mittenwald, 1729, the
varnish of a red-brown
colour, 74.1cm (29³/₁₆in),
L 5 Apr,
£5,720 ($8,237)

4
**A rare ornamented Italian
violoncello,** by Nicolo
Gagliano, Naples, mid-
18th cent, the varnish of
an orange-brown colour,
74.1cm (29³/₁₆in),
NY 29 June,
$44,000 (£32,593)

5
An English violoncello, by
William Forster,
London, late 18th cent,
the varnish of red-brown
colour, 73.5cm (28¹⁵/₁₆in),
NY 18 Dec,
$8,800 (£7,458)

6
An English violincello, by
Thomas Dodd, London,
c.1800, the varnish of
light orange-brown
colour, 75.4cm (29⅝in),
L 5 Apr,
£14,300 ($20,592)

7
An English violoncello, by
Joseph Panormo, London,
1st half 19th cent, the
varnish of a red-brown
colour, 74.2cm (29³/₁₆in),
NY 18 Jan,
$19,800 (£13,641)

8
A French violoncello, by
Charles Jean Baptiste
Collin-Mézin, Paris,
1897, the varnish of a
golden-brown colour,
75.7cm (29¹³/₁₆in),
L 21 June,
£2,310 ($3,280)

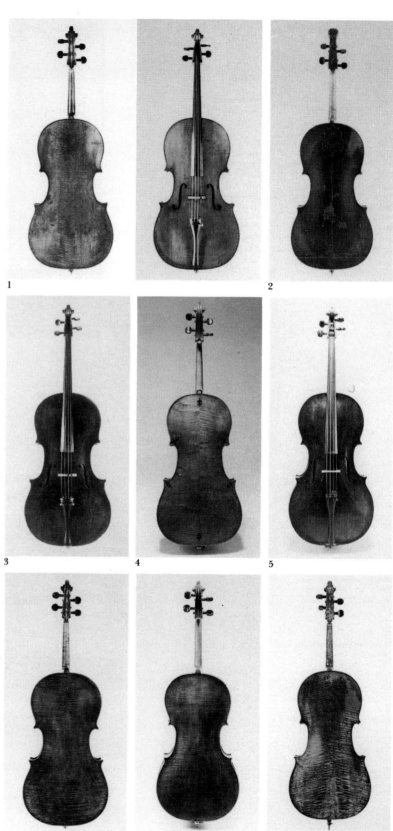

1   2

3   4   5

6   7   8

1

An important Scottish presentation set of union pipes, by Robert Reid, North Shields, 1830, six drones, two regulators, two silver levers controlling the G/D drone change, original mahogany bellows, sold with a manuscript book of tunes, *L 5 Apr,* **£3,960 ($5,702)**

2

An English spinet by John Harrison, London, 1781, the five octave keyboard, GG to g³, with ivory naturals and ebony accidentals, on later trestle stand, 186.5cm (6ft 1½in), *L 21 June,* **£6,050 ($8,591)**

3

A Viennese grand pianoforte by Mathias Müller, Vienna, *c*1820, the six octave keyboard, FF to f⁴, with ivory naturals and ebony accidentals, seven pedals, 233.7cm (7ft 8in), w 124.5cm (4ft 1in), *L 22 Nov,* **£12,100 ($15,730)**

4

A highly important Italian violin, (The 'Cathédrale' Stradivari), by Antonio Stradivari, Cremona, 1707, the varnish of a rich orange-red colour on a golden ground. This is reputed to have belonged to an officer in the army of Napoleon I from whom it was purchased by the French violinist Jean Baptiste Cartier (1765-1841), Accompanist to Queen Marie-Antoinette, who also served under both the Napoleonic and Bourbon regimes. He named the violin 'La Cathédrale'. 35.6cm (14in), *L 22 Nov,* **£396,000 ($514,800)**

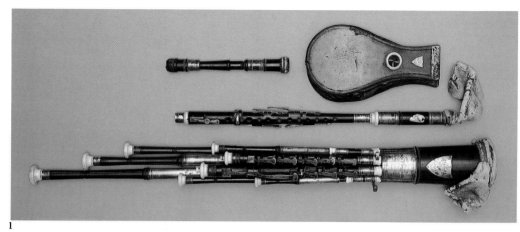

1

2

3

4

1
A French violoncello, by
Jean François Aldric,
Paris, 1825, the varnish
of a red-brown colour,
74.9cm (29½in), *L 22 Nov,*
£18,700 ($24,310)

2
An Italian violoncello,
The 'Bonjour'
violoncello, by Antonio
Stradivari, Cremona,
*c.*1690, varnish of a rich
golden-brown colour,
76.2cm (30in), *L 5 Apr,*
£275,000 ($396,000)

3
An Italian violin, by
Joseph Rocca, Turin,
1842, the varnish of an
orange-brown colour,
35.5cm (14in), *L 22 Nov,*
£33,000 ($42,900)

4
An Italian violin, The
'Rosenheim' violin, by
Antonio Stradivari,
Cremona, 1686, the
varnish of a golden-
brown colour, 35.7cm
(14¹/₁₆in), *L 22 Nov,*
£165,000 ($214,500)

5
A German viola, by Ernst
Busch, Nuremberg,
1641, the varnish of a
red-brown colour,
43.2cm (17in), *L 22 Nov,*
£6,820 ($8,866)

1

2

3

4

5

1
An English gold and
tortoiseshell-mounted
violoncello bow, by W E
Hill & Sons, London,
1931, 78 grams, *L 22 Nov,*
£2,420 ($3,146)

2
A French silver-mounted
violoncello bow, by Gand
Frères, Paris, 2nd half
19th cent, 75 grams,
NY 18 Dec,
$1,980 (£1,678)

3
A French silver-mounted
violoncello bow, by Gand,
Paris, 77 grams,
NY 18 Dec,
$2,200 (£1,864)

4
A French gold-mounted
violoncello bow, François
Nicolas Voirin, Paris,
the frog and adjuster are
not original, 82 grams,
NY 18 Jan,
$2,750 (£1,895)

5
A French silver-mounted
violoncello bow, by André
Vigneron, Paris,
78 grams, *NY 29 June,*
$1,980 (£1,467)

6
A French silver-mounted
violoncello bow, by
Eugène Sartory, Paris,
84 grams, *NY 18 Jan,*
$3,520 (£2,425)

7
An Alsatian double bass,
by the Schwartz
brothers, Strasburg,
1845, the head of plain
beech, brass machine
heads, 109.9cm (43¼in),
L 21 June,
£1,210 ($1,718)

8
A French silver-mounted
double bass bow, by
Victor Fétique, Paris,
L 5 Apr,
£2,310 ($3,333)

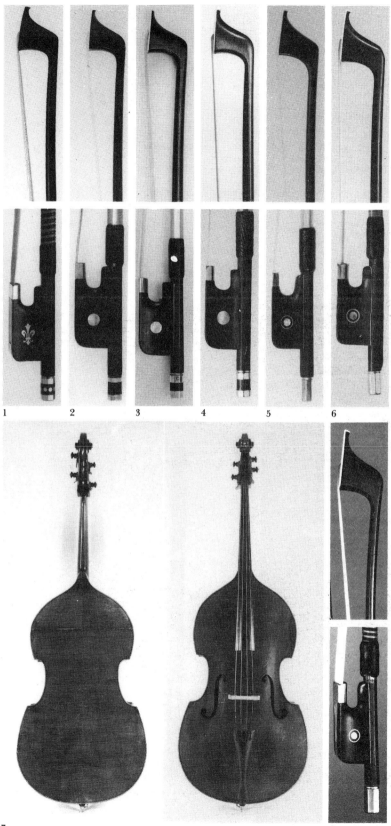

1
An English bass viola da gamba, by Barak Norman, London, c.1710, varnish of a golden-brown colour, extensive but well-restored worm damage, the head later, 68.8cm (27⅛in),
NY 18 Dec,
$14,300 (£12,119)

2
A treble viol converted from a pardessus de viole, 34.3cm (13⁹/₁₆in), string 35.3cm (13⅞in), *L 5 Apr,*
£770 ($1,109)

3
An Italian guitar, the back and ribs by Giovanni Hanggele, Milan, 1639, veneered with ivory and kingwood, engraved with scenes after Hans Bol, the remainder French, mid-19th cent, 46.8cm (18⁷/₁₆in),
L 21 June,
£8,140 ($11,559)

4
A Venetian guitar, school of Sellas, mid-17th cent, repaired by Johann Stoss, 1829. It was traditionally believed to have been the property of Mary Queen of Scots, though this is impossible as the guitar was made at least fifty years after her execution in 1587. It was, however, purchased in the 19th century by Prince George William of Schaumburg-Lippe for his wife Princess Ida, a descendant of Mary Stuart, 46.6cm (18⅜in), string 66.7cm (26¼in),
L 5 Apr,
£5,500 ($7,937)

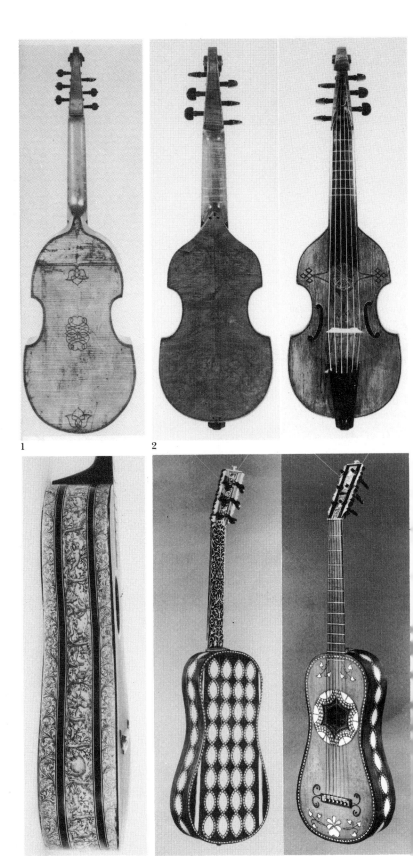

1

2

3

4

Drawing Room Instruments

GRAHAM WELLS

In the 16th century the ability to play a musical instrument was considered a necessary social skill; in the 18th century it had become much less vital a part of one's education, but nevertheless still a desirable attribute, much as it is today. It takes time and application to play any instrument acceptably, and makers were quick to realize that there was a market for any instrument which the slightly less than musical would find relatively simple to learn. This led to the manufacture of what might be termed 'drawing room' instruments.

The first requirement of such an instrument was that it should take little effort to produce the sound in the first place. Keyboard instruments certainly satisfied this need, but anyone who has picked out tunes on the piano with one finger will know that the results are not satisfying. Stringed instruments are an improvement. Indeed, a whole family of hybrid instruments based on a principle somewhere between the harp and the guitar were produced from the mid-18th to mid-19th centuries. The most successful of these were the so-called 'dital harps' made by Edward Light, London.

Producing an acceptable noise from a wind instrument is notoriously difficult for the beginner. The only exception is the recorder, which does not require long practice in lip control. However, for serious music making the recorder had been superseded by the transverse flute in the early 18th century. The soft voiced recorder known as the flageolet was, however, resurrected in the early 19th century to become one of the most popular of all drawing room instruments. In the 17th and early 18th century the flageolet had been used, among other things, for teaching singing birds. Examples are now very rare indeed. By far the leading maker of the new 19th-century version was William Bainbridge,

who worked in Holborn Hill, London, between 1808 and 1831. His earliest instruments consisted of a single tube of boxwood with ivory mounts and small ivory studs between the fingerholes to help locate the fingers. It was soon realized that any such wind instrument has the socially unacceptable habit of collecting the moisture from the breath which then drips out into one's lap. For an instrument possibly intended largely for the amusement of ladies this had to be prevented, so a chamber was turned in the top of the pipe which contained a sponge to absorb the moisture.

Bainbridge indulged in a whole series of developments. His extensive range of instruments are invariably stamped 'New Patent', although relatively few of his inventions actually reached the Patent Office. One major innovation was the addition of a second tube to produce the 'double flageolet' on which one could play simple harmonies. He even produced a 'triple flageolet'; examples are very rare as they rather defeated their own objective of simplicity in performance.

Because it was considered a greater achievement to play the true transverse flute Bainbridge also produced flageolets in this form, replacing the flute head-joint with a flageolet-type head-joint, but with the small ivory mouthpiece projecting from the side instead of the top. Occasionally a double version of the type can also be found. The popularity of Bainbridge's flageolets, together with those of his successor, Hastrick, and the few other makers such as John Simpson, is quite apparent from the relatively large number of surviving instruments. They are well made, attractive instruments, and rewarding to anyone prepared to devote a little time to playing them.

1
An English side-blown boxwood single flageolet, by William Bainbridge, London 1st quarter 19th cent, pitched and fingered as a one-keyed flute, 60cm (23⅜in), *L 22 Nov,* £880 ($1,144)

2
A rare English side-blown boxwood double flageolet, by William Bainbridge, London, *c*1820, nine silver keys, and one lip-operated shut-off key, 59.7cm (23½in), *L 22 Nov,* £1,540 ($2,002)

3
An English six-keyed boxwood flute-flageolet, by William Bainbridge, London, *c*1810, flute head-joint with adjustable stopper, sounding 59.5cm (23⁷⁄₁₆in), with flageolet head-joint 67cm (26⅜in), *L 22 Nov,* £880 ($1,144)

4
An English boxwood double flageolet, by John Simpson, London, *c*1850, eight silver keys, and two silver cut-off keys, 48.9cm (19¼in), *L 22 Nov,* £506 ($658)

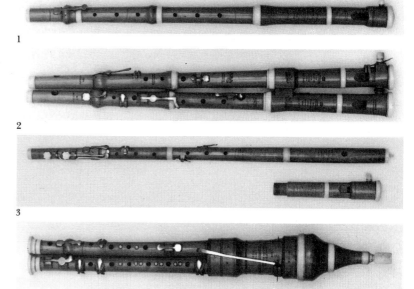

1

2

3

4

1
A Dutch stained boxwood flute d'accord, c1700, two later brass mounts, 35.5cm (14in), *L 22 Nov,* £935 ($1,215)

2
An English one-keyed ivory flute, by Thomas Cahusac the Elder, London, 3rd quarter 18th cent, unmounted, later single key of brass, sounding 53.9cm (21¼in), *L 22 Nov,* £1,760 ($2,288)

3
An English cased pair of five-keyed cocuswood flutes, by Monzani & Co, London, c1815, a bass flute in B♭ and a flute in F, ivory mounts and silver keys, sounding 67.6cm (26⅝in); 44.7cm (17⅞in), *L 5 Apr,* £1,155 ($1,663)

4
A German five-keyed ebony flute, by Johann Heinrich Grenser, Dresden, early 19th cent, the end cap absent, the F key with duplicate touchpiece, sounding 55.2cm (21¾in), *L 22 Nov,* £3,740 ($4,862)

5
An English seven-keyed ebony flute, by James Wood, London, c1814, graduated stopper, sounding l 57.6cm (22⅝in), *L 22 Nov,* £1,100 ($1,430)

6
An English eight-keyed ivory flute, by Louis Drouet, London, c1825, silver mounts (one nickel replacement), the E♭ shaft damaged, tuning slide and graduated stopper, sounding 60.2cm (23¹¹⁄₁₆in), *L 22 Nov,* £1,100 ($1,430)

7
An English ivory flute, by Thomas Stanesby Junior, London, 2nd quarter 18th cent, reduced in length, silver mounts (two replaced), silver key with square cover (also replaced), sounding 55.1cm (21¹¹⁄₁₆in), *NY 29 June,* $5,225 (£3,870)

8
A French nine-keyed glass flute, by Claude Laurent, Paris, 1838, silver mounts and keys, two of the touches with rollers, sounding 62.2cm (24½in), *NY 29 June,* $4,400 (£3,529)

9
An English two-keyed stained boxwood oboe, by William Milhouse, Newark, 3rd quarter 18th cent, twin G holes, bell joint damaged, 58.5cm (23in), *L 22 Nov,* £770 ($1,001)

10
An English two-keyed boxwood oboe, by Thomas Cahusac, London, c1800, the square cover of the silver C key a later brass replacement, the brass E♭ key also a later replacement, twin G and F holes, 56.8cm (22⅜in), *L 22 Nov,* £2,310 ($3,003)

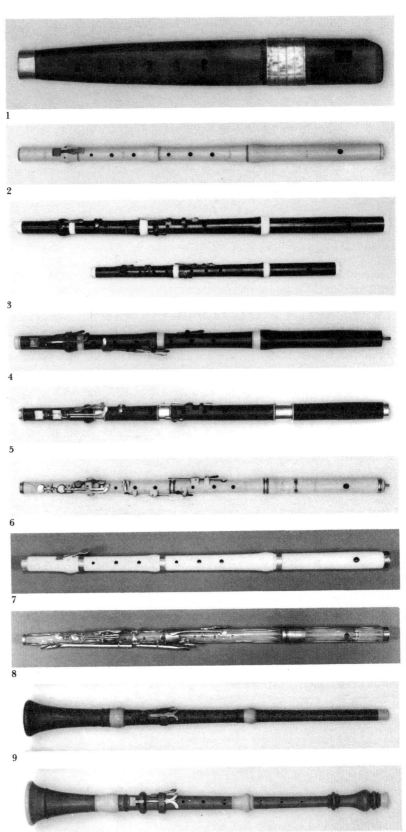

1
A German eight-keyed boxwood oboe, by Gottfried Schuster, Markneukirchen, 1st quarter 19th cent, ivory mounts, brass keys, twin G holes, 55.8cm (21¹⁵/₁₆in), *L 22 Nov,* **£2,090 ($2,717)**

2
A two-keyed boxwood oboe, mid-18th cent, stamped 'Vinc. Panorm: a Marseille'. It is possible that this oboe is English and was marketed by Panormo during his stay in Marseilles. 59.7cm (23½in), *L 21 June,* **£1,430 ($2,031)**

3
A French thirteen-keyed boxwood oboe, by Guillaume Triébert, Paris, c1835. This instrument predates 'Système 3': it lacks an octave key for left index knuckle and uses levers instead of axles for the keys operated by the right little finger; the bell has an inner flange. 58.5cm (23in), *L 22 Nov,* **£2,310 ($3,003)**

4
An English eight-keyed stained pearwood bassoon, by William Milhouse, London, 1st quarter 19th cent, the F key with fishtail touchpiece, crook absent, additional modern bell-joint, 122.7cm (48⅜in), *L 22 Nov,* **£946 ($1,230)**

5
An English eight-keyed stained pearwood bassoon, late 18th cent, unstamped, brass mounts and keys, brass crook, 124.2cm (48⅞in), *L 22 Nov,* **£715 ($929)**

6
An English eight-keyed stained maple bassoon, by William Milhouse, London, c1810, the B key cover absent, the brass crook stamped I K, possibly John Köhler, 123.2cm (48½in), *L 21 June,* **£715 ($1,015)**

7
An English eight-keyed stained pearwood bassoon, by Richard Bilton, London, c1840, brass crook stamped I K, possibly John Köhler, poor condition, 124.5cm (49in), *L 21 June,* **£396 ($563)**

8
An English six-keyed boxwood clarinet in B♭, by Metzler, London, 1st quarter 19th cent, ivory mounts, brass keys, ebony mouthpiece, 66.1cm (26in), *L 5 Apr,* **£165 ($238)**

9
An English eight-keyed boxwood clarinet in C, by George Wood, London, c1830, including Wood's patent B♮ and C# keys, original ebony mouthpiece, 58.5cm (23in), *L 5 Apr,* **£165 ($238)**

10
A German carved boxwood treble recorder, by J W Oberlender, Nuremberg, mid-18th cent, 52.7cm (20¾in), *L 22 Nov,* **£2,090 ($2,717)**

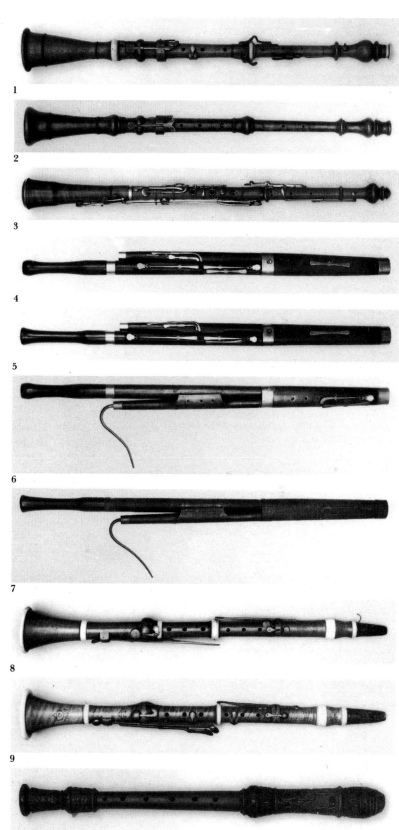

1

2

3

4

5

6

7

8

9

10

1
A French serpent, by C
Baudouin, Paris, c1825,
the keyless body of
leather-bound wood,
brass crook and mount,
later rosewood
mouthpiece, 230cm
(90½in), *L 22 Nov,*
£1,045 ($1,358)

2
**An eleven-keyed English
serpent**, by John Roe,
Liverpool, 2nd quarter
19th cent, the body of
leather-bound wood, brass
mounts and keys, ivory
mouthpiece, 209cm
(6ft 10¼in), *L 21 June,*
£715 ($1,015)

3
**An English brass slide
trumpet**, by John
Augustus Köhler,
London, c.1850, the slide
designed for watch-
spring operation, with
three crooks and three
shanks for C, D, and E♭,
L 5 Apr,
£825 ($1,188)

4
**An English contrebasse à
anche**, by Boosey & Co,
London, c.1875, seventeen
keys, fourteen closed, the
first open and two octave
keys (one absent), crook
fitted with a water key,
99.7cm (39¼in), *L 22 Nov,*
£880 ($1,144)

5
A German brass ophicleide,
by G A Pfretzschner,
Markneukirchen, c.1900,
ten brass keys, brass
crook, with mouthpiece,
115.5cm (45½in), *L 22 Nov,*
£990 ($1,287)

6
**A French single-action
pedal harp**, by
Cousineau, Paris, last
quarter 18th cent, the
table painted in silvered
and gilded birds and
flowers, the pillar
gilded, h 164.5cm
(64¾in) *NY 29 June,*
$2,200 (£1,630)

7
**An unusual English
double-action pedal harp**,
by Frederick Dizi,
London, c.1820, eight
pedals including louvre
pedal, forty-three
strings, needing fairly
extensive restoration,
h 168.3cm (5ft 6¼in),
L 5 Apr,
£506 ($730)

8
An Irish harp, by John
Egan, Dublin, c.1825,
lacquered black with gilt
decoration, the column
with seven ivory ditals
actuating the fourchette
action, thirty strings,
h 88.3cm (34¾in),
L 5 Apr,
£1,100 ($1,587)

9
**An English Gothic double-
action pedal harp**, by
Sebastian and Pierre
Erard, London, c.1829,
forty-six strings, seven
pedals and a louvre
pedal, h 177.1cm (5ft 9¾in),
L 5 Apr,
£1,650 ($2,381)

10
**An English double-action
pedal harp**, by Sebastian
and Pierre Erard, 19th
cent, h 183cm (6ft),
NY 24/25 Feb,
$4,290 (£2,958)

11
**A French single-action
pedal harp**, c.1780,
elaborately painted with
chinoiserie decorations,
h 170cm (5ft 7in),
NY 24/25 Feb,
$2,860 (£1,972)

12
**An American double-action
pedal harp**, by P I Browne
& Co, New York, late
19th cent, h 175cm
(5ft 9in), *NY 16 June,*
$2,200 (£1,606)

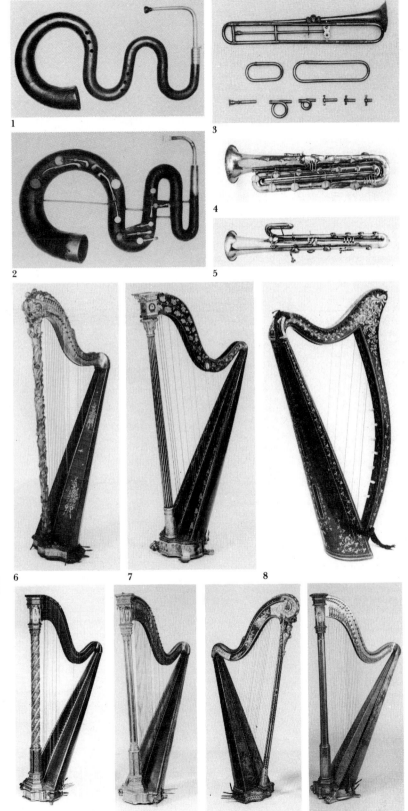

1

2

3

4

5

6

7

8

9

10

11

12

1

An English two-manual harpsichord, by Jacob and Abraham Kirckman, London, 1772, the five and a half octave keyboard, FF to c⁴ (FF omitted), six hand levers controlling 8ft, 8ft lute and 8ft buff stops on the upper manual and 8ft and 4ft on the lower manual, a foot pedal controlling machine stop, original music desk. The upper extension of the keyboard to c⁴ is evidently unique. 241.4cm (7ft 11in), w 101.4cm (3ft 4in), *L 5 Apr,*
£16,500 ($23,760)

2

An English single-manual harpsichord, by Jacob and Abraham Kirckman, London, 1787, the five octave keyboard, FF to f³, three hand levers controlling two 8ft stops and one 4ft stop, and one pedal controlling one of the 8ft stops, frame stand with later upper stretchers 222.3cm (7ft 3½in), w 95.3cm (3ft 1½in), *L 22 Nov,*
£13,750 ($17,875)

3

An English spinet, by Longman and Broderip, London, last quarter 18th cent, with ivory naturals and ebony accidentals, the compass FF to f³ excluding FF#, 188.5cm (6ft 2¼in), *NY 18 Jan,*
$2,475 (£1,706)

4

An English square piano, by Longman & Broderip, London, 1796, the five and a half octave keyboard, FF to c⁴, double action with mopstick overdampers, 161.8cm (5ft 3¾in), w 59.7cm (1ft 11½in), *L 22 Nov,*
£1,430 ($1,859)

5

An English square piano, by Johannes Pohlman, London, 1769, the five octave keyboard, FF to f³, single action with overdampers, three hand levers controlling the forte stops and the harp stop, 145cm (4ft 9in), w 49cm (1ft 7¼in), *L 22 Nov,*
£1,650 ($2,145)

6

An important English chamber organ, by England & Son, London, 1790, the five octave keyboard, GG to f³ with GG omitted, with ivory naturals and ebony accidentals. The organ is in totally original condition except that the original diagonal reservoir was converted in 1836 to a single rise reservoir. It is in full playing order. h 313.5cm (10ft 3in), w 152.5cm (5ft), depth 109cm (3ft 7in), *L 22 Nov,*
£20,900 ($27,171)

1

2

3

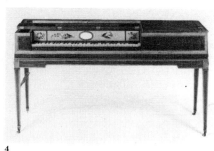

4

5

6

Judaica

JAY WEINSTEIN

Judaica as a field for collectors encompasses those items of special importance to the Jewish people. These include objects of particular artistic, social or historic interest, but works of art used in the practice of religion predominate. In style they may reflect any country where there has been a significant Jewish population and they include textiles as well as metals, ceramics, paintings and books. Jewish ritual inspires works of art covering many themes in life from birth to death, but as certain items appear more frequently than others it seems worth concentrating on these in this short introduction.

The Torah is a handwritten parchment scroll on rollers containing the Pentateuch or first five books of the Bible. It is the holiest of religious objects, used predominantly in the synagogue and in the home for purpose of study. The various ornaments associated with it often appear in the saleroom and are always subject to strong demand. Apart from its textile binding, mantle and curtain, it is hung with a silver shield which is often inscribed in Hebrew with the Decalogue and surmounted by a crown or fitted with detachable finials (known as rimmonim, or 'pomegranates') on the staves. Because it is so holy, it is read with the aid of a tapering shaft, usually of precious metal or ivory, which often ends in a pointing finger known as a yad.

The sabbath is preceded by a blessing which is said over wine and is known as Kiddush (sanctification)—hence the Kiddush cup. It is concluded by the Havdalah (separation) ceremony which divides that day from the rest of the week. The spice box used in this ceremony is very often, though not exclusively, in the form of a tower. Often equally architectural in design are the eight-day lamps used to celebrate the festival of Hanukah (dedication). This festival commemorates the rededication of the Holy Temple in 165 BCE (Before the Christian Era), following armed resistance to the Syrians who had desecrated it three years earlier.

Although some very high prices have recently been paid for the work of particular artists of the modern period, notably for the silver of Ilya Schor and the rarer pieces from Bezalel, the Jewish art school founded in Palestine in 1906, the age of the piece remains an important factor in its value. European silver of the 18th century and earlier is especially favoured. Some criteria, such as hallmarks and condition, are important, but not so much so as in other fields. However, the presence of a contemporary Hebrew inscription on an old piece or a reliable provenance will add greatly to value, while later additions will have the opposite effect.

Non-European works of art and materials other than silver may be areas of increasing interest in the future. It is also likely that there will be greater interest in Judaic antiquities as a whole as this is a subject to which the commercial world has so far paid little attention. New collectors are advised to be wary of the numerous copies, particularly in silver, that exist and to enlist help from a reliable expert when they first begin collecting.

New York is undoubtedly the centre of the market, and seems certain to remain so, although regular sales of entirely Jewish material have recently been successfully started in London. It is significant that in 1985 Jerusalem was for the first time the venue for a sale of this type. It should be noted that items in this field sell more successfully when included in sales specializing in Judaica.

1
A silver Hanukah lamp, Polish, c.1760, eight oil holders in the form of sliding drawers, later servant light, h 22.8cm (9in), *NY 27 June,* $35,200 (£26,074)

2
A Hanukah lamp, German, Frankfurt, c.1780, embossed with lions supporting a Hanukah lamp, fronted by eight oil fonts below the hinged lid, h 13.3cm (5¼in), *L 3 July,* £4,180 ($5,685)

3
A silver Hanukah lamp, probably Vienna, mid-19th cent, pierced and chased with lions flanking the Decalogue, fronted by eight removable candle-holders and servant light, h 20.2cm (8in), *NY 27 June,* $1,430 (£1,059)

4
A parcel-gilt silver Hanukah lamp, Austro-Hungarian, c.1870, decorated with latticework and chased with lions flanking the Decalogue, fitted with silver-plated oil pans, h 28cm (11in), *NY 27 June,* $1,430 (£1,059)

5
A brass Hanukah lamp, Polish, late 18th cent, pierced and cast, fronted by eight oil pans (one slightly damaged), h 28cm (11in), *NY 27 June,* $1,100 (£815)

6
A silver Hanukah lamp, Austro-Hungarian, late 19th cent, embossed and chased with lions flanking a crowned heart, servant light lacking, h 20.2cm (8in), *NY 6/7 Dec,* $1,320 (£1,109)

7
A silver and filigree Hanukah lamp, Polish, c.1830, two servant lights, h 15.2cm (6in), *NY 27 June,* $4,400 (£3,259)

8
A silver Hanukah lamp, Posen, German, c.1890, fitted with eight spoon-form oil receptacles, the sides applied with bell-flower borders, 24cm (9½in), *NY 6/7 Dec,* $7,150 (£6,008)

9
A silver Hanukah lamp, c.1879, embossed with flowering foliage support-ing tulip-shaped sconces, a servant light below the swan finial, h 54.9cm (21⅞in), *L 12 Mar,* £2,420 ($3,606)

10
A silver Hanukah lamp, maker's mark KA, Austro-Hungarian, late 19th cent, the base of stepped crescent form, with eight stemmed candleholders flanking a central servant light, 24cm (9½in), *NY 6/7 Dec,* $3,575 (£3,004)

11
A cast brass Hanukah lamp, Polish, 18th cent, h 26.6cm (10½in), *NY 27 June,* $5,500 (£4,074)

12
A pressed tin Hanukah lamp, possibly American, mid-19th cent, fitted with eight oil pans with crenellated rims, detachable servant light, h 18.5cm (7¼in), *NY 27 June,* $1,870 (£1,385)

13
A bronze Menorah, probably Polish, c.1850, h 38cm (14⅞in), *L 3 July,* £495 ($673)

14
A brass Menorah, Bezalel, Jerusalem, the triangular-shaped back stamped with Solomonic columns beneath Hebrew inscription lacking servant light, h 27cm, (7⅞in), *NY 27 June,* $550 (£407)

15
A brass hanging Sabbath lamp, German, 18th cent, in the form of an eight-point star with knopped stem, h 50.8cm (20in), *NY 27 June,* $440 (£326)

1

2

3

4

5

6

7

8

9

10

11

12

13

14

15

1

A pair of silver Sabbath candlesticks, S. Szkarlat, Warsaw, 1887, chased with foliage, h 33cm (13in), *NY 27 June*, $1,870 (£1,385)

2

A pair of silver Sabbath candlesticks, Labeck, Warsaw, 1887, chased with flowers and scrolls, h 35.5cm (14in), *NY 27 June*, $1,870 (£1,385)

3

A pair of brass Sabbath candelabra, Polish, 18th cent with 19th cent additions, h 47cm (18½in), *L 3 July*, £880 ($1,197)

4

A pair of brass Sabbath candelabra, Polish, 19th cent, foliate arms centred by rampant lions, eagle finials, h 49cm (19¼in), *L 12 Mar*, £1,210 ($1,803)

5

A pair of parcel-gilt Torah finials, maker's mark AK, London, 1897, girdled by bands of miniature eagles, h 34.5cm (13⅝in), *L 3 July*, £1,100 ($1,496)

6

A pair of parcel-gilt Torah finials, Samuel Zyweig, London, 1923, embossed with flowerheads, surmounted by a crown, orb and Star of David finial, h 40cm (15¾in), *L 3 July*, £440 ($598)

7

A pair of parcel-gilt Torah finials, Jacob Rosenzweig, London, 1915, the scrolling brackets hung with bells, h 39.5cm (15½in), *L 3 July*, £495 ($673)

8

A silver Torah shield, Austro-Hungarian, late 19th cent, embossed and chased with lions flanking the Decalogue, h 38cm (15in), *NY 27 June*, $1,320 (£978)

9

A parcel-gilt Torah breast plate, Austro-Hungarian, maker's mark MS, late 18th cent, h 18cm (7⅛in), *L 3 July*, £2,860 ($3,890)

10

A silver Torah shield, Klost (?), Breslau, *c.*1800, embossed and chased figures of Moses and Aaron flanking the Decalogue, h 22.8cm (9in), *NY 27 June*, $8,800 (£6,519)

11

A parcel-gilt Torah breast plate, Jacob Rosenzweig, London, 1915, h 25.5cm (10in), *L 3 July*, £462 ($628)

12

A parcel-gilt Torah breast plate, Jacob Rosenzweig, London, 1923, the engraved compartment containing one festival plaque, h 25.5cm (10in), *L 3 July*, £469 ($638)

13

A parcel-gilt Torah breast plate, maker's mark JL, London, 1898, the plaques maker's mark of Morris Salkind, 1914, h 34.5cm (17⅝in), *L 3 July*, £858 ($1,167)

14

A parcel-gilt silver filigree, and 'gem' set Torah crown, Polish, with niello inscription recording the makers, Moshe ben Reb Yosef SGL and Gedalya ben Reb Yitzchak, dated 1796, h 26.7cm (10½in), *NY 27 June*, $88,000 (£65,185)

15

A pair of parcel-gilt silver Torah finials, Rangoon, dated 1868, struck with Indo-Chinese marks, minor damages, h 19cm (7⅞in), *NY 27 June*, $4,675 (£3,463)

16

A silver Torah pointer, Polish, mid-18th cent, 22.8cm (9in), *NY 27 June*, $3,410 (£2,526)

17

A silver Torah pointer, Italian, early 18th cent, later suspension chain, 18.5cm (7¼in), *NY 27 June*, $1,870 (£1,385)

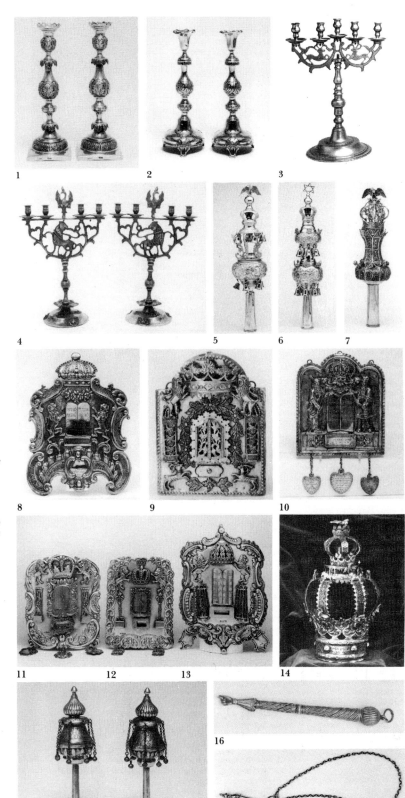

1   2   3

4   5   6   7

8   9   10

11   12   13   14

15   16   17

1
A silver-cased Esther scroll, possibly Czech, c.1800, the columnar case with bright-cut decoration 11.5cm (4½in), *NY 27 June,* $2,475 (£1,833)

2
A parcel-gilt silver-cased Esther scroll, Polish, early 19th cent, the case pierced and chased on a gilt ground, some damage, h 43.2cm (17in), *NY 27 June,* $8,800 (£6,519)

3
A parcel-gilt silver-cased Esther scroll, Austro-Hungarian, maker's mark JZ., c.1870, the cylindrical case embossed and chased, 22.8cm (9in), *NY 27 June,* $3,410 (£2,528)

4
A silver Esther scroll case, designed by Gerald Leslie Brockhurst, executed by Herman Garfield at the Cranbrook Academy, USA, 1946, 26.7cm (10½in), *NY 6/7 Dec,* $6,600 (£5,546)

5
A silver-cased Mezuzah, Palestinian, Bezalel, c.1920, 9cm (3½in), *NY 6/7 Dec,* $660 (£555)

6
A silver spice tower, maker's mark JR, Nuremberg, late 18th cent, the spice section square, chased with brickwork, pierced with rosettes and windows, incomplete, h 26cm (10¼in), *NY 27 June,* $15,400 (£11,407)

7
A silver spice tower, Polish, late 18th cent, h 23.1cm (9¼in), *NY 27 June,* $19,800 (£14,667)

8
A silver spice tower, East German, maker's mark AR, early 19th cent, with square filigree spice section, h 24.8cm (9¾in), *NY 27 June,* $3,850 (£2,852)

9
A silver filigree spice tower, Austro-Hungarian, maker's mark EE, late 19th cent, h 25.5cm (10in), *NY 6/7 Dec,* $1,045 (£878)

10
A silver spice tower, maker's mark HA, London, 1895, composed of filigree in Polish style, h 26.3cm (10⅜in), *NY 6/7 Dec,* $1,540 (£1,294)

11
A silver spice tower presentation, Ilya Schor, 1948, eight-sided, pierced and chased with human, animal and bird figures, h 21.5cm (8½in), *NY 6/7 Dec,* $93,500 (£78,571)

12
A silver fish-form spice container, probably German, c.1860, chased and articulated to represent a carp, with glass bead eyes, 25.5cm (10in), *NY 27 June,* $1,100 (£815)

13
A silver double Circumcision cup, Hieronymus Mittnacht, Augsburg, 1763-65, h 13.2cm (5¼in), *NY 27 June,* $24,200 (£17,926)

14
A George III silver-gilt Etrog container, Allen Dominy, London, 1802, *NY 27 June,* $11,000 (£8,148)

15
A silver Etrog container, with later Palestinian decoration, the box Vienna, 1818, the decoration c.1900, minor damage, 15.2cm (6in), *NY 27 June,* $1,540 (£1,541)

16
A silver Etrog container, German, late 19th cent, in the form of the fruit set on a leafy stem base, h 14cm (5½in), *NY 6/7 Dec,* $1,650 (£1,386)

17
A circumcision knife, Continental, 18th cent, 16.2cm (6⅜in), *NY 27 June,* $1,100 (£815)

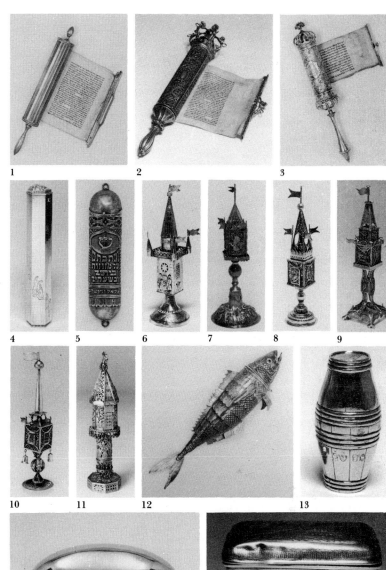

1   2   3

4   5   6   7   8   9

10   11   12   13

14   15

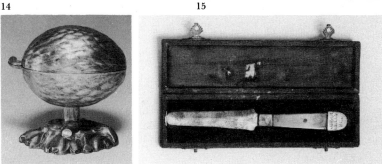

16   17

1
Four matching silver
Kiddush cups,
Lithuanian, Vilna, 1875-
93, comprising one large
and three smaller
examples, each with
engraved tulip-form
bowl, h 17.8 and 12.6cm
(7 and 5in), *NY 27 June*,
$3,850 (£2,852)

2
A glass Kiddush beaker,
Bohemian, *c.*1850, the
central section flashed
with ruby red and
engraved, h 14cm (5½in),
NY 6/7 Dec,
$1,320 (£1,109)

3
A silver covered Havdalah
cup, Moscow, 1756,
maker's mark MB in
Cyrillic, the beaker of
tapering cylindrical
form, embossed and
chased with rococo scrollwork and symbols,
h 16.5cm (6½in),
NY 27 June,
$18,700 (£13,852)

4
A ceramic Passover plate,
East European, mid-19th
cent, with scalloped rim
decorated in blue on a
white ground, minor
wear d 24cm (9½in),
NY 27 June,
$880 (£652)

5
A ceramic Rosh Hashana
plate, Alice and Celia
Silverberg, Elmira New
York, early 20th cent,
signed, one small chip,
d 24cm (9½in),
NY 27 June,
$1,210 (£895)

6
A pewter Passover plate,
German, *c.*1775, the
border with Hebrew
words and flowers, the
centre with a six-pointed
star, d 24cm (9½in),
NY 27 June,
$660 (£489)

7
A pewter Purim plate,
central European, late
18th cent, the rim
engraved in wriggle-
work, the centre
engraved with three fish
entwined, d 29.1cm
(11½in), *NY 6/7 Dec*,
$1,045 (£878)

8
A pewter ceremonial plate,
probably German,
*c.*1800, possibly a Purim
plate, the wavy rim
engraved with
inscription interspersed
with birds and beasts,
d 23cm (9¼in),
NY 27 June,
$495 (£366)

9
A silver alms bowl,
Budapest, 1792-6, dated
in the inscription 1798,
the bowl chased with a
flowerhead in the centre,
d 12.7cm (5in) *NY 6/7 Dec*,
$9,350 (£7,857)

10
A pewter Passover plate,
the plate Dutch, 18th
cent, the decoration
Prague, dated 1770,
finely chased and
engraved with the
Hebrew order of the
Passover and vignettes
relating to those found
in Bohemian manuscript,
Haggadot of the period,
d 43.2cm (17in),
NY 6/7 Dec,
$12,000 (£10,168)

11
A silver festival bowl,
Persian, late 19th cent,
finely chased and engraved
with roundels depicting
the symbols of the
twelve tribes of Israel,
d 16.5cm (6½in),
NY 6/7 Dec,
$1,980 (£1,664)

12
An inlaid brass charity box,
Syrian, late 19th cent,
inlaid with silver and
copper decoration,
h 16.5cm (6½in),
NY 27 June,
$6,050 (£4,481)

13
A brass and wood Jewish
community seal, German,
early 19th cent, the
centre with laurel and
palm wreaths enclosing
the crowned Decalogue,
d 3cm (1¼in), *NY 6/7 Dec*,
$935 (£786)

14
A silver-gilt tankard,
Marx Schaller II, Augs-
burg, *c.*1685, the cylindrical
body matted, h 13.5cm
(5⅜in), *L 12 Mar*,
£18,150 ($27,044)

Glass

DAVID BATTIE

The glass illustrated on the following pages is European and was all made between about 1450 and 1900. Generally speaking, Continental glass is the more widely collected, English glass being mainly of interest to the somewhat conservative English market.

The earliest, and often the most expensive pieces, which appear in the saleroom are the early Venetian wares made on the island of Murano from the middle ages onwards, though few pieces survive from before 1500. From the early 16th century Venice exported pieces made in the new 'crystal' glass all over Europe, but as the century progressed the Netherlands also became a centre for a flourishing glass industry based on Venetian principles of manufacture. It was not until the Venetian *cristalla* was superseded by the lead or flint glass developed in England and Bavaria during the second half of the 17th century that Venice finally lost its supreme position. An elaborate piece of 17th century enamelled Venetian glass can realize up to £40,000 ($45,600).

The Biemann collection, which was sold by Sotheby's in June 1984, included some splendid pieces of early German green or forest glass (see p.252). Most glass collectors concentrate on fine engraving or unusual and rare shapes. The Dutch perfected the art of stipple engraving and a great deal of English glass was exported to Holland for decoration from the mid 17th century to the end of the 18th century. The stipple engraving of David Wolff (1732-98) and Frans Greenwood (1680-1761) is particularly admired.

Somewhat surprisingly English lead glass of the second half of the 17th century and of the baluster period (1690-1720/30) has not really appreciated in value over the last 80 years. More sought after are the late 18th century pieces with enamel decoration by Beilby or wine glasses with the rarer forms of colour twists. Commemorative pieces are also fashionable, but Waterford cut glass, unless of the very highest quality, is still not very expensive. Pairs of decanters remain popular.

German manufacturers produced a vast output of very varying quality. Some of the Nuremberg 17th century glass is especially fine, as there was a link with the court of Rudolf II at Prague, where wheel-engraving had been first mastered. Much of this glass is semi-ceremonial, and as it was made for toasts the pieces can be very large, with elaborate decoration. At the other end of the scale a number of charming 'peasant' pieces, such as an attractive small jar, can be bought for as little as £300-£400 ($340-450).

One field which is attracting an increasing number of collectors is Biedermeier glass of the early 19th century. Prices for this decorative and eminently displayable ware have soared. (A fuller description can be found on page 261).

At the end of the Biedermeier period there was a growing interest in Bohemia in chemical experiments, and colour in glass became increasingly important during the 19th century. The international exhibitions encouraged glass makers to indulge in displays of virtuosity made possible by recent technical advances.

A few words should be said about condition. Cracked or chipped pieces should be avoided; any crack renders the item virtually unsaleable unless it is extremely rare. Likewise trimming—the ground out edge of a bowl or foot— will bring down the price considerably. Collectors must also be on their guard against a 'marriage'— the bowl from one glass, the stem and foot from another. Despite its transparency glass does have 'colour' and recognizing the slight differences is vital in avoiding the occasional forgery.

Within the last 30 years glass paperweights have become an important field for collectors. The most desirable are those made between about 1845 and 1860 at three factories in France: Baccarat, St Louis and Clichy. They were made either with canes (short lengths of extruded glass) or by using heat-softened glass to create flowers, insects and reptiles. The millefiori type were very occasionally signed and dated by the factories and this adds to their value. Some of these paperweights fetch around £50,000 ($60,000), depending on the rarity of the design, but there are still examples to be bought for £80-100 ($90-115). Nowadays there are factories in the United States, Great Britain and France producing excellent limited editions and one offs, and some of these are now avidly collected.

1
A German Gothic beaker 'Krautstrunk', 2nd half 15th cent, the green-tinted body with convex sides decorated with applied prunts, 9.6cm (3¾in), *L 16 June*, **£4,180 ($5,893)**

2
A German Gothic beaker, 'Krautstrunk', c1500, the low smoky-green tinted body applied with a single row of watery prunts, the everted lip emphasized with an applied ring, 5cm (1⅞in), *L 16 June*, **£4,840 ($6,824)**

3
An early German 'Forest-Glass', 'Krautstrunk', possibly Rhine area, 2nd half 16th cent, the pale-green tinted body with wide flared rim, bowl repaired, 8.1cm (3⅛in), *L 12/13 Nov*, **£352 ($464)**

4
A German beaker, 'Bandwurmglas', 17th cent, of olive-green tint, the body decorated with an applied milled spiral trail, everted double-walled foot and sharp kicked-in base, 19.5cm (7¾in), *L 16 June*, **£5,500 ($7,755)**

5
A German green-tinted 'roemer', 17th cent, the large swelling bowl incurving to the rim, the hollow stem decorated with applied smooth prunts, high conical spun foot, 23cm (9in), *L 12-13 Nov*, **£1,100 ($1,452)**

6
A German green-tinted 'roemer', 17th cent, 18cm (7in), *A 16 May*, **Dfl 3,480 (£809; $1,157)**

7
A German or Netherlandish 'roemer', 17th cent, of green-tinted metal, the stem applied with trail above regularly-spaced prunts, 26.5cm (10½in), *L 16 June*, **£2,970 ($4,187)**

8
A Netherlandish diamond-engraved 'roemer', 17th cent, of light smoky-green tinted metal, the cylindrical stem with applied pointed prunts beneath an applied trail, stress crack on kick-in base, 22cm (8⅝in), *L 16 June*, **£25,300 ($35,673)**

9
A Venetian bowl, 1st half 16th cent, the upturned sides with folded rim decorated with two applied translucent-blue trails, traces of gilding around the rim, h 14cm (5½in), d 27.5cm (10⅞in), *L 16 June*, **£2,090 ($2,946)**

10
A Venetian goblet, 16th cent, of greyish metal, the whole decorated 'a retortoli' with twisted white threads, 15cm (5⅞in), *L 6 Mar*, **£2,310 ($3,442)**

11
A Venetian filigree ewer, 2nd half 16th cent, the whole in 'vetro a reticello' the flared neck decorated with a clear applied vermicular ring, auricular folded rim and pinched spout, 37.6cm (14⅞in), *L 6 Mar*, **£4,180 ($6,228)**

12
A Venetian ring beaker, 1st half 17th cent, of slightly grey-tinted metal, round the base two applied loops and two pendent rings, the hollow inverted baluster stem flanked by collars, 12.8cm (5in), *L 16 June*, **£1,430 ($2,016)**

13
A Venetian goblet, 1st half 17th cent, in slightly greyish metal, the exaggerated thistle bowl over a collar above opposed hollow balusters separated by a hollow flattened knop, 19.5cm (7⅞in), *L 6 Mar*, **£1,320 ($1,967)**

1   2   3
4   5   6   7
8   9   10
11   12   13

1
A Façon de Venise filigree goblet, 16th/17th cent, the bowl with swelling base running into five further decreasing rings, the whole in spaced alternate *vetro a fili* and *a retorti* threads, 17.6cm (6⅞ in), *L 16 June,* £2,530 ($3,567)

2
A 'Façon de Venise' enamelled wine glass, 16th/17 cent, the pointed funnel bowl decorated in white enamel, the bowl set on a stem with moulded lion masks and florettes, 15.7cm (6¼ in), *L 16 June,* £3,410 ($4,808)

3
A Dutch 'Façon de Venise' engraved armorial wine glass, 17th cent, decorated in diamond point with the arms of Orange under a crown flanked by olive branches, 14.7cm (5¾ in), *L 12 Nov,* £1,760 ($2,323)

4
A Dutch engraved 'Façon de Venise' serpent-stem goblet, decorated by Willem Mooleyser, c.1690, the coiled stem enclosing blue and opaque-white threads, the stem rejoined at neck, 23.5cm (9⅛ in), *L 16 June,* £2,750 ($3,877)

5
A 'Façon de Venise' serpent-stem goblet, 17th cent, the coiled stem enclosing translucent-turquoise corkscrew threads, 23.2cm (9⅛ in), *L 6 Mar,* £1,760 ($2,624)

6
A 'Façon de Venise' wine glass, possibly Nether-lands, the flared bowl with solid base set on a collar over a filigree stem with double knop and filigree conical foot, 12.9cm (5in), *L 16 June,* £660 ($930)

7
A 'Façon de Venise' 'Kuttrolf', 17th cent, the body decorated with alternate opaque-white threads in *vetro a fili* and *vetro a retorti,* 25cm (9⅞ in), *L 16 June,* £2,640 ($3,722)

8
A 'Façon de Venise' ice glass goblet, possibly Spanish, of straw coloured metal, embellished with 'crackled' decoration, 18.6cm (7⅜ in), *L 12 Nov,* £1,485 ($1,960)

9
A 'Façon de Venise' two-handled cup and cover, 16th/17th cent, of straw-tinted metal, the cup of depressed globular form with everted rim embel-lished with applied prunts and masks, 11cm (4½ in), *L 6 Mar,* £880 ($1,311)

10
A 'Façon de Venise' bucket, probably 1st half 17th cent, the body decorated with evenly-spaced radiating ribbons in alternate plain and multiple strands, handle chipped, 14.3cm (5¾ in), *L 6 Mar,* £1,760 ($2,624)

11
A 'Façon de Venise' cruet, probably Spanish, 17th cent, the body in marked straw-coloured metal, decorated in layers of combed opaque-white threads, 15.5cm (6⅛ in), *L 6 Mar,* £330 ($492)

12
An Italian ormulu-mounted amethyst-tinted vase, possibly Naples, 17th cent, with trumpet neck embellished with gilt-metal mounts, 34.5cm (13½ in), *L 6 Mar,* £990 ($1,476)

13
A Dutch flute, 17th cent, 36.5cm (14¼ in), *A 16 May,* **Dfl 10,440 (£2,426; $3,469)**

1   2   3

4   5   6

7   8   9

10   11   12   13

1
An early English sealed
wine bottle, before 1666,
perhaps, c.1650, of 'globe
and shaft' form, an
applied water seal
bearing the arms of
Carey, for John Carey,
Viscount Rochford
(1608-77), 19.5cm (7¾in),
L 6 Mar,
£2,860 ($4,264)

2
An early sealed 'onion'
wine bottle, c.1720, of
dark-green tint, the rim
fixed with an applied
seal bearing a crest,
18cm (7⅛in), *L 12-13 Nov,*
£396 ($522)

3
A pair of English sealed
wine bottles, dated 1764,
of green metal, each
moulded with the initials
'IH/1764', 24cm (9½in),
P 10-13 July,
£363 ($493)

4
An English green wine
bottle, dated 1770, the
circular seal moulded
'1770/Iames/Oakes/Bury',
25.5cm (10in),
P 10-13 July,
£209 ($284)

5
A pair of green bottles,
18th cent, with later
decoration in poly-
chrome and gilt, 30cm,
(11¾in), *A 12 Mar,*
Dfl 1,218 (£285; $424)

6
A Netherlandish serving
bottle, 17th cent, of
amethyst tint, 17cm
(6¾in), *L 6 Mar,*
£1,760 ($2,624)

7
A South German engraved
ruby-glass silver-mounted
flask, 17th/18th cent, the
everted foot ring with
silver mount, the silver
screw cap with gadroon
and finial, marked EA
(Elias Adam 1704-45),
18.7cm (7⅜in), *L 16 June,*
£2,310 ($3,257)

8
A Netherlands turquoise-
tinted flask, 2nd half 17th
cent, the neck with
lappet-edged band with
chain attachment to the
silver-mounted cork
stopper, 23cm (9in),
L 16 June,
£3,080 ($4,342)

9
A Bohemian enamelled
blue-glass tankard, dated
1608, the neck decorated
in yellow, centred on
rust, white and green
dots, 16cm (6¼in),
L 16 June,
£8,800 ($12,408)

10
A Netherlandish Potsdam
cut 'Goldrubinglas' beaker
and cover, c.1700, 17.5cm
(6⅞in), *L 16 June,*
£770 ($1,085)

11
A German enamelled
'Blacksmith-guild
Humpen', possibly
Franconia, dated 1707,
painted predominantly
in white enamel
embellished with blue
and rust red, 25cm
(9⅞in), *L 16 June,*
£4,180 ($5,893)

12
A Saxon enamelled
apothecary flask, dated
1719, one side painted in
colours with the arms of
Saxony and Poland and
an inscription, 12.7cm
(5in), *L 16 June,*
£1,870 ($2,636)

13
A German enamelled
armorial tumbler, Dresden,
c.1720, painted in
colours with the arms of
Augustus I, King of
Poland, stress crack on
base, 8.9cm (3½in),
L 12-13 Nov,
£550 ($726)

14
A pair of German
engraved amber beakers,
possibly Nuremberg,
c.1720, engraved with
fanciful landscapes
inhabited by a hunter,
angler and unicorn,
9.3-9.8cm (3⅝-3⅞in),
L 16 June,
£1,980 ($2,791)

15
A North German
engraved 'roemer', 1st
quarter 18th cent,
A 16 May,
Dfl 3,480 (£809; $1,156)

16
A German enamelled
beaker, 1738, painted in
colours with the
Sacrificial Lamb, 16.5cm
(6½in), *L 12/13 Nov,*
£638 ($842)

1
An engraved goblet,
17th/18th cent, probably
Bohemian, engraved
with women at their
toilet, 30.5cm (12in),
L 12 Nov,
£2,090 ($2,552)

2
A Nuremberg topo-
graphical goblet, by
Georg Friedrich
Killinger, *c*.1720,
engraved with a view of
Nuremberg beneath a
rainbow on one side and
the triple coats of arms
of the Free Imperial
City of Nuremberg on
the other, 21.4cm (8½in),
L 16 June,
£17,600 ($24,816)

3
A German engraved
goblet, by the Master HI,
c.1710-20, decorated with
a classical scene with
Mercury and Venus
drawing up the ground
plans of a city, 25cm
(9⅞in), *L 12-13 Nov,*
£1,980 ($2,613)

4
A German armorial
goblet, by Anton Wilhelm
Mäuerl, dated 1723,
signed in diamond point
on the base 'Mäuerl' 19cm
(7½in), *L 16 June,*
£8,250 ($11,632)

5
A baluster goblet and
cover, probably German,
c.1720-40, the rounded
funnel bowl set on a
stem with inverted
teared baluster flanked
by collars, 31cm (12⅛in),
L 6 Mar,
£352 ($524)

6
An engraved goblet,
Potsdam/Berlin, *c*.1730-
40 of drawn conical
form, decorated on one
side with the arms of
von Rochow, minor
crizzeling, 20cm (7⅞in),
L 16 June,
£660 ($930)

7
An engraved flute,
German, in English
style, *c*.1760, the
extended funnel bowl
decorated with the
initials AR within an
elaborate crowned
cartouche, opaque-twist
stem, conical foot,
19.5cm (7¾in), *L 16 June,*
£264 ($372)

8
A Silesian engraved and
gilt goblet and cover,
c.1740-50, decorated with
David and Jonathan
holding shields, flanked
by scrolls and a shell
motif initialled DLK,
20.5cm (8⅛in), *L 6 Mar,*
£880 ($1,312)

9
A Silesian engraved footed
beaker, attributed to
Christian Gottfried
Schneider, Warmbrunn,
c.1735-40, divided by
vertical grooves into six
decorated panels, foot
chipped, 15cm (5⅞in),
L 16 June,
£2,420 ($3,412)

10
A Silesian engraved
armorial sweetmeat glass,
'Konfektschale', 2nd
quarter 18th cent, the
twelve-sided bowl
decorated on one side
with a profile bust
portrait, the reverse with
coat-of-arms and
coronet, 19cm (7½in),
L 16 June,
£968 ($1,364)

11
A Silesian engraved and
gilt footed beaker, *c*.1750,
decorated with a music-
making couple seated
out-of-doors, 11.5cm
(4½in), *L 16 June,*
£770 ($1,085)

12
A Silesian mercantile
goblet, mid-18th cent,
the faceted bowl
decorated with a
shipping scene, 17.8cm
(7in), *L 16 June,*
£1,870 ($2,636)

13
A German engraved
goblet, 18th cent, 18cm
(7⅛in), *A 16 May,*
Dfl 462 (£107; $154)

1 2 3
4 5 6 7
8 9 10
11 12 13

1
A Thuringian goblet, mid-18th cent, engraved with a scrollwork cartouche and inscribed, 18.8cm (7⅜in), *L 16 June,* **£352 ($496)**

2
A Thuringian commemorative goblet, dated 1789, inscribed, the bowl supported on a collar over inverted baluster, conical foot, 17.3cm (6¾in), *L 16 June,* **£1,760 ($2,481)**

3
A Saxon crystal goblet, *c*1745, engraved with medallions containing the Empress Maria-Theresa and a monogram, 25.2cm (10in), *M 28 June,* **FF 28,860 (£2,477; $3,375)**

4
An English baluster goblet, *c*1700, the pointed bowl with solid teared base over cyst, set on a large teared acorn over small baluster, folded conical foot, 17.7cm (7in), *L 12-13 Nov,* **£1,760 ($2,323)**

5
An English baluster wine glass, *c*1700, the funnel bowl with solid base set on a teared inverted heavy baluster, folded conical foot, 16.8cm (6⅝in), *L 12-13 Nov,* **£264 ($348)**

6
An English baluster-period wine glass, *c*1710, the rounded funnel bowl with solid teared base set on a stem with annulated shoulder knop, teared section and base knop, domed and folded foot, 16.8cm (6⅝in), *L 12/13 Nov,* **£220 ($290)**

7
An English baluster goblet, *c*1720, the funnel bowl set on a cushion knop above an inverted baluster knop enclosing a bubble of air, 23.8cm (9⅜in), *P 20-22 Mar,* **£330 ($491)**

8
An English Ale, *c*1730-40 the extended funnel bowl with solid base set on a teared stem with swelling, conical foot, 20cm (7⅞in), *L 12-13 Nov,* **£297 ($392)**

9
An English wine glass, *c*1730, the funnel bowl set on a moulded pedestal stem with moulded diamonds at the shoulders, folded conical foot, 20.6cm (8⅛in), *L 12-13 Nov,* **£132 ($174)**

10
An English Jacobite firing glass or syllabub glass, *c*1750, the engraved bowl set on a hollow knop and everted foot, 10cm (4in), *L 6 Mar,* **£495 ($738)**

11
An English Jacobite portrait glass, *c*1750, engraved with a profile portrait of the Young Pretender in Highland dress, the bowl supported on a multi-spiral air-twist stem, conical foot, 16cm (6¼in), *L 12-13 Nov,* **£825 ($1,089)**

12
An English Jacobite wine glass, *c*1750, engraved rounded funnel bowl, teared plain stem, folded conical foot, 16.6cm (6½in), *L 12-13 Nov,* **£275 ($363)**

13
An English Jacobite wine glass, *c*1750, the engraved drawn-trumpet bowl supported on a multi-spiral air-twist stem, conical foot, 15.7cm (6in), *L 12-13 Nov,* **£462 ($609)**

14
An English Jacobite wine glass, *c*1750, the decorated bell bowl supported on a multi-spiral airtwist stem with two knops, conical foot, 17.5cm (6⅞in), *L 12-13 Nov,* **£374 ($493)**

1

An English composite-stemmed wine glass, c.1750, 18cm (7⅛in), *L 6 Mar,* £209 ($311)

2

An English wine glass, c.1750, the ogee bowl with honeycomb moulded base set on a double-series air-twist stem, conical foot, 14.7cm (5¾in), *L 12-13 Nov,* £132 ($174)

3

A Beilby-enamelled wine glass, c.1770, painted in opaque-white enamel with fruiting vine, foot rim chipped, 16cm (6¼in), *L 12 Nov,* £528 ($645)

4

A Beilby-enamelled wine glass, c.1770, painted in white with arched ruins, traces of gilding on the rim, foot chipped, 15.7cm (6⅛in), *L 12 Nov,* £1,430 ($1,746)

5

An English Beilby-enamelled wine glass, c.1770, the bowl decorated, round the rim in white enamel diaper zones edged in scrolls, double series opaque-twist stem, conical foot, 14.7cm (5⅞in), *L 12-13 Nov,* £550 ($726)

6

An English engraved goblet, c.1760, the stem enclosing an opaque-white gauze corkscrew, conical foot, 19.2cm (7⅝in), *L 6 Mar,* £165 ($246)

7

An Irish volunteer glass, c.1779, inscribed 'Newry Rangers 1779', the reverse with ears of corn, mercury-twist stem, conical foot, chip on foot rim, 20.3cm (8in), *L 12-13 Nov,* £1,540 ($2,032)

8

A pair of English engraved goblets, c.1760, set on a double-series opaque-twist stem, conical foot, 18.5cm (7¼in), *L 6 Mar,* £440 ($656)

9

An English mixed-twist flute, c.1760, the drawn-trumpet bowl set on a stem enclosing a central opaque gauze core with entwined air threads, conical foot, 18.5cm (7¼in), *L 6 Mar,* £187 ($278)

10

An English coin wine glass, c.1761, the bell bowl set on a hollow ball knop enclosing a Dutch silver coin dated 1761, the knop flanked by a collar over opaque-white corkscrew stem, conical foot, 15.7cm (6⅛in), *L 12-13 Nov,* £308 ($406)

11

An English 'Newcastle' Royal Armorial wine glass, c.1745, engraved with the arms of Princess Anne, daughter of George II, 17cm (6¾in) *L 12-13 Nov,* £2,200 ($2,904)

12

An English colour-twist wine glass, c.1770, the waisted bucket bowl set on a stem enclosing an opaque-white corkscrew entwined with a pair of translucent amethyst threads, conical foot, 17cm (6¾in), *L 12-13 Nov,* £1,320 ($1,742)

13

An English colour-twist wine glass, c.1770, the rounded funnel bowl set on a stem enclosing a pair of royal-blue corkscrew threads within a pair of opaque-white gauze corkscrews, conical foot, 15cm (5⅞in), *L 12-13 Nov,* £715 ($943)

14

An English wine glass, c.1770, the large ogee bowl faceted round the base, double-series, opaque-twist stem, conical foot, 18cm (7⅛in), *L 12-13 Nov,* £176 ($232)

1
A Dutch-engraved armorial goblet, c.1740-50, the bowl engraved with the arms of the City of Amsterdam, light baluster stem, conical foot, 23cm (9in),
L 12-13 Nov,
£605 ($798)

2
A Dutch engraved 'Newcastle' goblet, c.1740-50, decorated with a 'friendship' device of clasped hands issuing from clouds, above the Eye of God, light baluster stem, conical foot, 18.9cm (7½in),
L 12-13 Nov,
£462 ($609)

3
A Dutch engraved 'West Indian Company' goblet, mid-18th cent, *A 16 May,*
Dfl 6,960 (£1,617; $2,313)

4
A Dutch stipple-engraved glass, signed F. Greenwood fecit 1745, 25cm (9⅞in), *A 1 Oct,*
Dfl 129,920 (£30,569; $39,435)

5
A Dutch goblet, 18th cent, engraved with the arms of the seven provinces, 21.5cm (8½in), *A 1 Oct,*
Dfl 928 (£454; $585)

6
A Dutch engraved wine glass, attributed to Jacob Sang, c.1750-60, the funnel bowl finely-engraved with foliate swags attached to rings, from which hang two shields, supported on a stem with cut knop and faceted inverted baluster sections, 18.5cm (7¼in),
L 12-13 Nov,
£2,640 ($3,484)

7
A Dutch engraved wine glass, by Hendrick Scholting, 1778, the flared bowl with rounded base inscribed with a diamond in cursive script, on a double-series opaque-twist stem, conical foot, 19cm (7½in), *L 16 June,*
£1,650 ($2,326)

8
A Dutch stipple-engraved goblet, c.1770, the glass of 'Newcastle' type, possibly by David Wolff, 18.5cm (7¼in),
L 12-13 Nov,
£2,420 ($3,194)

9
A Dutch stipple-engraved glass, by David Wolff, the Hague, c.1790-5, the bowl stippled with a double portrait of William V of Orange and his wife Sophie Wilhelmine of Prussia, 15.4cm (6⅛in), *L 16 June,*
£7,700 ($10,857)

10
An English candlestick, c.1745, the ribbed cylindrical nozzle with everted rim set on a diamond-shouldered moulded pedestal stem, 20cm (7⅞in), *L 6 Mar,*
£308 ($459)

11
An English baluster candlestick, c.1730-50, the cylindrical nozzle set on collars over a teared true baluster and large beaded ball knop flanked by collars, 21cm (8¼in), *L 6 Mar,*
£528 ($787)

12
A pair of English air-twist tapersticks, c.1750, with cylindrical nozzle over a stem enclosing an air corkscrew flanked by collars, ribbed domed foot, 14.7cm (5¾in),
L 12-13 Nov,
£1,980 ($2,613)

13
A set of five English cut-glass candlesticks, c.1780, each with a faceted stem and domed lobed foot, 26cm (10in), *NY 21 Jan,*
$4,070 (£2,807)

1 2 3 4

5 6 7 8

9 10 11 12

13

1
An English opaque glass mug, 1st half 18th cent, of stoneware form, the handle with pincered terminal and on an applied ring foot, 9.2cm (3⅝in), *P 20-22 Mar,* £462 ($688)

2
An Hungarian 'Milchglas' tankard, Siebenburgen, 18th cent, decorated on body and neck with combed decoration in iron-red, applied scroll handle, 14.5cm (5¾in), *L 12-13 Nov,* £264 ($348)

3
A Bohemian enamelled 'Milchglas' decanter and stopper, c1770, the body painted in colours with ribbon and floral garlands, gilt rim, ball stopper painted with flower head, 29.5cm (11⅝in), *L 6 Mar,* £231 ($344)

4
A Bohemian 'Milchglas' enamelled decanter, c1750, the body painted in colours with a fortified town within an oval cartouche, gilt rim, 23cm (9in), *L 12-13 Nov,* £385 ($508)

5
A Central European enamelled 'Milchglas' vase, mid-18th cent, each side painted in blue, ochre and iron-red, 13.6cm (5⅜in), *L 16 June,* £242 ($341)

6
A Central European enamelled 'Milchglas' tankard, 18th cent, the cylindrical body in colours, with a scene probably of Abraham sacrificing Isaac on a greensward dotted with trees, 21cm (8¼in), *L 12-13 Nov,* £308 ($406)

7
A Bohemian enamelled 'Milchglas' desk set, 2nd half 18th cent, fitted drawer and pounce and sand pots, all enamelled with swags of flowers, gilt line borders, 16.5cm (6½in), h 14cm (5½in), *L 12-13 Nov,* £297 ($392)

8
A South German/Swiss schnapps bottle, mid-18th cent, painted with a red coated gentleman flanking an inscription, all in red, yellow, green, blue and white enamels, 14.5cm (5¾in), *P 10-13 July,* £198 ($269)

9
A Bohemian enamelled 'Milchglas' flask, mid-18th cent, in the form of a pistol, the barrel decorated in colours with spiral flower trails, small chips, 28.5cm (11¼in), *L 12 Nov,* £770 ($1,016)

10
A German enamelled 'Milchglas' flask, 10cm (4in); sold with a similar bottle, 5cm (2in); both mid-18th cent, *P 8-10 July,* £110 ($149)

11
A set of four Bohemian cut-crystal goblets, 18th cent, engraved in gold with pastoral scenes, 24.3cm (9½in), *M 28 June,* FF 22,200 (£1,905; $2,596)

12
A German engraved tankard, possibly Winbach, late 18th cent, decorated with a house and butcher's stall, flanked with initials, with domed pewter cover, 24.5cm (9⅝in), *L 12 Nov,* £770 ($1,016)

13
A pair of goblets, late 18th cent, probably French, c1800, 12cm (4¾in), *A 12 Mar,* Dfl 696 (£163; $243)

14
A Bohemian cut and coloured sweetmeat bowl and cover, c1830, the ruby glass bowl with turnover shaped rim with gilt palisade flutes round the base, 19cm (7½in), *L 12 Nov,* £319 ($421)

   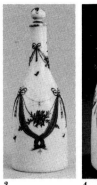      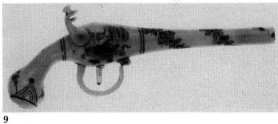    

1

A pair of decanters and stoppers, probably Irish, *c.*1790, the neck applied with three moulded cogged rings, the bull's-eye stoppers moulded with radiating ribs, 26cm (10¼in), *P 20-22 Mar,* **£440 ($655)**

2

An engraved decanter, *c.*1770, of mallet form, the base decorated with a row of flutes, the body inscribed 'Calcavella' between bands of polished ovals, the neck facet-cut 24cm (9½in), *L 6 Mar,* **£572 ($852)**

3

An Irish engraved whisky decanter and stopper, probably by Pugh Glasshouse, Dublin, the body cut with flute and engraved with a label inscribed 'whiskey', hollow engraved stopper, star-cut base, 28.5cm (11¼in), *L 12-13 Nov,* **£242 ($319)**

4

A pair of cut glass decanters and stoppers, 28.5cm (11¼in), *C 27-30 Nov,* **£242 ($295)**

5

A pair of English green-tinted and gilt scent bottles and stoppers, *c.*1770, decorated in the manner of James Giles, cut spire stopper, one stopper chipped, 10.5cm (4⅛in), *L 12-13 Nov,* **£660 ($871)**

6

An Irish wine glass rinser, *c.*1790, engraved with emblems and motto from the insignia of the Ancient and Most Benevolent Order of the Friendly Brothers of St. Patrick, opposed spouts, 9.8cm (3⅞in), *L 6 Mar,* **£495 ($738)**

7

An Irish 'canoe' salad bowl, *c.*1790-1800 with cut arch-and-angle rim and shallow polished diamonds, 28cm (11in), *L 6 March,* **£825 ($1,230)**

8

A Irish salad bowl, *c.*1800, of oval form with turnover rim, the body cut with shallow diamonds, thick knopped stem, oval scalloped foot, 33cm (13in), *L 6 Mar,* **£715 ($1,066)**

9

A pair of English sulphide candlesticks, probably by Apsley Pellatt, *c.*1820, with diamond-cut thistle-shaped nozzle supported on octagonal diamond-panelled stem enclosing a sulphide statuette of 'La Frileuse' after Houdon, one foot chipped, 20.3cm (8in), *L 12-13 Nov,* **£660 ($871)**

10

Three cut candelabra, *c.*1845, each with two opposed branches having vase-shaped nozzle, scalloped drip pan with pendent 'icicle' drops, central spike finial, 50cm (19⅞in), *L 6 Mar,* **£1,045 ($1,557)**

11

A pair of cut crystal bowls with covers, 19th cent, 28.5cm (11⅛in), *A 1 Oct,* **Dfl 870 (£205; $264)**

1

2

3

4

5

6

7

8

9

10

11

Biedermeier Glass

PERRAN WOOD

The term Biedermeier (coined from a comic bourgeois figure in a satirical review) is usually used of the furniture and decorative arts produced in Germany and Austria from the 1820s to the 1840s. When Biedermeier refers to glass, it is the 'cabinet' glass made during the 1820s and 1830s which springs to mind as the most typical product of this period of experiment and new development following the Congress of Vienna in 1815.

Engraving and cutting in the Anglo-Irish tradition continued to be popular among Bohemian glass makers and simple tumblers and glasses were finely cut and engraved with classical subjects. Although the names of a few of these engravers have come down to us, it is the work of Dominik Biemann (1800-57) at the international spa of Franzensbad in the 1830s that stands out above all others. He catered for the well-heeled tourists, producing medallion portraits on beakers or plaques, which, at their best, are marvels of crisp virtuosity.

Other developments centred around the Vienna porcelain factory where Anton Kothgasser (1769-1851) worked as a painter for many years. In about 1816 he set himself up as an enameller on glass and produced a great many glasses — usually tumblers and almost always of the same type of 'cabinet' beaker with flared body and cut everted base — decorated with topographical views of Vienna and its environs for tourists. Other themes tend to be somewhat sugary and simplistic allegorical subjects symbolic of love, loyalty,

friendship, happiness and so on, with suitable inscriptions. Kothgasser had been encouraged by Gottlob Mohn (1789-1825), who had learnt to decorate glasses in transparent enamels, following a technique perfected by his father Samuel Mohn (1761-1815) in Dresden.

The early part of the 19th century saw Bohemia once again taking the lead as an international centre of glass-making. Encouraged by scientific bodies in Prague and Vienna, glasshouses, such as those owned by the Bouquoy family, stepped up their experiments in the chemistry of glass. Recipes were worked out for producing opalescent glass *(beinglas)*, ruby glass *(goldrubin)*, 'vaseline' glass *(uraniumglas)* and glass to imitate semi-precious stone *(edelstein* or *marmorietesglas)*. The Bouquoy glasshouses produced a glass called 'hyalith' in a dense black and red, much influenced by the basalt pottery of Wedgwood. Egermann of Blottendorf near Haida is the most renowned producer of 'lithyalin' glass. The effect was of semi-precious stone and it was created by a secret process using acids and lacquers.

The market and the demand for fine Biedermeier 'cabinet' pieces has accelerated considerably over the last twenty years and high prices are paid for glasses decorated by Kothgasser and Mohn. One example is a beaker signed by Kothgasser showing a dog guarding his master's uniform and inscribed 'Fidelité'. In 1964 it made £420 when it was sold by Sotheby's as part of the Beck Collection. When it was sold again as part of the Krug Collection in 1982 it made £6,500.

1
A South Bohemian gilt 'lithyalin' beaker, probably Bouquoy Glasshouse, c.1830, 14.5cm (5¾in), *L 12 Nov,* **£2,860 ($3,492)**

2
A Bohemian gilt 'hyalith' beaker, Bouquoy Glass-house, c.1830-40, decorated with a chinoiserie frieze of a figure and fanciful birds, 10.5cm (4in), *L 12 Nov,* **£374 ($457)**

3
A 'hyalith' gilt tankard and cover, Bouquoy Glasshouse, South Bohemia, c.1830, with gilt wax-red body, body cracked, 15cm (6in), *L 16 June,* **£605 ($853)**

1   2   3

1
A North Bohemian gilt
'lithyalin' beaker, *atelier*
Friedrich Egermann,
Blottendorf, *c*1830-40,
10.9cm (4¼in), *L 16 June*,
£2,090 ($2,946)

2
A Bohemian engraved
portrait plaque, by
Dominik Biemann (1800-
57) Franzensbad, *c*1840,
engraved in *tiefschnitt*
with a portrait, possibly
Alma von Goethe, signed
on the edge of the frame
'D Biman', 11cm (4⅜in),
L 16 June,
£16,500 ($23,265)

3
A Viennese cut and silver-
mounted tankard, silver
marked Vienna, maker's
mark rubbed, *c*1830, the
baluster body cut with
facets and diamond-
embellished flutes, 13cm
(5⅛in), *L 12 Nov*,
£781 ($1,031)

4
A North Bohemian cut
and engraved 'lithyalin'
beaker, *atelier* Friedrich
Egermann, Blottendorf,
*c*1830-40, in translucent
emerald-green glass, the
bowl cut through with
symbols, 12.1cm (4¾in),
L 16 June,
£3,190 ($4,497)

5
A Bohemian 'lithyalin'
scent bottle, Egermann
atelier, *c*1840, the
shouldered body cut with
facets, matching stopper,
all in tones of brick-red
and brown, lip chipped,
12.5cm (5in), *L 6 Mar*,
£209 ($312)

6
A Bohemian 'goldrubinglas'
beaker, *c*1830-40, the sides
cut with facets beneath a
band of arches over
sunbursts, 11.6cm (4½in),
L 16 June,
£1,210 ($1,706)

7
A Viennese transparent-
enamelled beaker, Anton
Kothgasser, *c*1820,
decorated with a scene of
Cupid arranging flowers
in an urn within an
amber-stained and gilt
frame, inscription in
black, 11cm (4⅜in),
L 12 Nov,
£5,720 ($7,550)

8
A Bohemian 'lithyalin'
beaker, Egermann *atelier*,
Blottendorf, *c*1830-40, in
shaded tones of olive
green, the ovoid body
cut with flutes and
embellished with gilt
foliate scrolls, 12.2cm
(4¾in), *L 12 Nov*,
£1,210 ($1,597)

9
A Viennese transparent-
enamelled beaker, attri-
buted to Anton
Kothgasser, *c*1820-30,
painted with a figure
holding a sword flanked
by a stone bearing the
arms of Austria,
inscribed 'Immorior Fideli-
ter', 11cm (4¼in), *L 6 Mar*,
£3,520 ($5,248)

10
A Viennese transparent-
enamelled beaker, attributed
to Anton Kothgasser,
*c*1820-30, painted with a
dog beside an altar of
friendship with eternal
flame, 11.2cm (4⅜in),
L 6 Mar,
£3,410 ($5,084)

11
A Viennese transparent-
enamelled beaker,
attributed to Anton
Kothgasser, *c*1820-30,
painted with a gilt
amber-stained
rectangular frame,
inscribed beneath 'Gage
de l'inseperabilite', 11cm
(4¼in), *L 6 Mar*,
£1,650 ($2,460)

1   2

3   4   5

6   7   8

9   10   11

1
A Viennese enamelled and gilt beaker, by Anton Kothgasser, c.1820, decorated in 'Etruscan' style round the rim, the remainder of the body gilt overall, *L 12 Nov*, £2,860 ($3,492)

2
A transparent-enamelled Viennese beaker, Kothgasser school, c.1830-50, decorated with a bunch of pansies and inscribed 'Jeden morgen denke mein', 11cm (4¼in), *L 6 Mar*, £2,090 ($3,116)

3
A Viennese transparent-enamelled beaker, Kothgasser school, c.1830-50, the flared bowl painted with a bunch of roses within an amber and gilt serpent oval frame, gilt rim, 10.5cm (4⅛in), *L 6 Mar*, £4,730 ($7,048)

4
A Viennese transparent-enamelled beaker, by Gottlob Samuel Mohn, dated 1815, the cylindrical body with flared rim, 10.6cm (4⅛in), *L 16 June*, £5,500 ($7,755)

5
A North Bohemian cut and engraved beaker, possibly Harrach Glass-house, Neuwelt, c.1825-30, engraved with the goddess of Health, Hygieia, 12.3cm (4⅞in), *L 16 June*, £1,540 ($2,171)

6
A Bohemian stained and engraved goblet, c.1830, cut with faceted and raised ovals, one amethyst stained and engraved with a Turk schooling a stallion, 19cm (7⅛in), *L 12 Nov*, £462 ($564)

7
A North Bohemian com-memorative goblet, probably Neuwelt, c.1835, painted in *schwartzlot* with figures holding standards bearing the Eagles of Russia and Prussia respectively, 25cm (9⅞in), *L 6 March*, £3,190 ($4,756)

8
A Bohemian engraved beaker, circle of Anton Simm, c.1834, the slightly flared bowl decorated with an interior scene showing the murder of the Duke of Friedland, inscribed on the reverse, 11.5cm (4⅝in), *L 16 June*, £715 ($1,008)

9
A Bohemian ruby-stained topographical goblet, after 1844, the ovoid bowl cut with facets round a central panel with a named view of Offenburg, 16cm (6¼in), *L 16 June*, £495 ($698)

10
A North Bohemian pink-stained engraved goblet, c.1835-40, cut with facets around a central ovoid panel engraved with a shooting party, 12.7cm (5in), *L 12 Nov*, £352 ($430)

1
A Bohemian enamelled and gilt tankard and cover, c.1840-60, in opaque-pink glass, the body embellished with enamelled bunches of flowers and gilt scrolls, 20cm (7⅞in), L 6 Mar, £660 ($983)

2
A Bohemian engraved amber-flashed hunting goblet, c.1840-50, the bowl with polygonal everted base decorated with a hunting scene, 24.2cm (9½in), L 12-13 Nov, £660 ($871)

3
A Bohemian goblet and cover, c.1840-50, engraved with Bremserburg Castle, 32cm (12⅝in), A 18-26 Sept, Dfl 580 (£134; $179)

4
A Bohemian enamelled and gilt overlay jar and cover, c.1840-50, the sides painted in colours with flowers and birds, the opaque-white overlay cut through round the base to form a row of double printies outlined in gilt, rims gilt, 15cm (5⅞in), L 6 Mar, £594 ($885)

5
A North Bohemian overlay beaker, possibly Karl Pfohl, Steinschönau, c.1860-5, the clear glass overlaid with ruby red, one side decorated with a horse, the reverse engraved with a coat-of-arms, 15cm (5⅞in), L 16 June, £1,870 ($2,637)

6
A cup and saucer in glass overlay, c.1840, decorated in white and violet with polychrome flowers, M 11 Dec, FF 2,775 (£244; $295)

7
A North Bohemian equestrian overlay beaker, in the manner of Karl Pfohl (1826-94), possibly Steinschönau, c.1840-50, the flared body in clear glass overlaid in translucent ruby, L 16 June, £2,750 ($3,878)

8
A pair of Bohemian cups and covers, 19th cent, the blue ground decorated in polychrome with circular medallions, 25cm (9⅞in), M 11 Dec, FF 6,600 (£581; $702)

9
A Bohemian glass service, c.1850; comprising a jug, one plate and ten beakers, overlaid in polychrome with garlands of flowers, jug 29.3cm (11½in), M 11 Dec, FF 72,150 (£6,357; $7,676)

10
A North Bohemian overlay goblet, Zach, probably Harrach glasshouse, Neuwelt, c.1850-60, the clear glass overlaid in royal blue and cut through to reveal an amazon struggling with a panther, 31cm (12⅛in), L 16 June, £4,180 ($5,894)

1

2

3

4

5

6

7

8

9

10

pair of Bohemian
ngraved goblets,
ngraved and signed by
. J. Boam, 19th cent,
6.5cm (6½in), C 11 Jan,
429 ($622)

North Bohemian
ngraved beaker, in the
anner of Karl Pfohl
1826-94), Steinschönau
r Haida, c1860-70, the
all flared bowl
ecorated with a central
anel in *tiefschnitt* with
scene of mounted arabs
unting lion, 19cm
7½in), L 16 June,
440 ($620)

North Bohemian
overlay goblet, in the
anner of Karl Pfohl
1860, the funnel bowl
ut through in an oval
anel depicting a stag
nd hind in a forest
lade, 27.6cm (10⅞in),
6 Mar,
880 ($1,312)

A Bohemian overlay
oblet, by Franz Zach,
1850, the clear glass
overlaid in translucent
oyal-blue decoration,
he reverse bearing the
rms of Bavaria and
Prussia, signed 'F Zach';
27.6cm (10⅞in), L 6 Mar,
5,170 ($7,708)

A pair of French opaline
cent bottles, c1840, the
globular body in opaque
blue, the shoulder
decorated in silver and
gilt, short gilt neck, gilt
stopper, one stopper
missing, 12cm (4¾in),
L 6 Mar,
£550 ($820)

A pair of French
enamelled opaline vases,
c1840, in opaque white
painted in colours and
gilt rim and border, the
base with gilt and blue-
enamel borders, 42cm
(16½in), L 12-13 Nov,
£572 ($755)

7
An enamelled Bohemian
decanter, c1860, the body
painted in tones of puce
and white with a couple
dancing, a couple
playing raquettes and a
seated lady being
serenaded by her beau,
30cm (11¾in), L 6 Mar,
£319 ($475)

8
A pair of opal vases,
c1840, decorated in
polychrome with floral
scrolling and with gilt
overlay, 49.2cm (19⅜in),
M 11 Dec,
FF 55,500 (£4,890; $5,904)

9
A Bohemian enamelled
and gilt bowl, c1860, the
wide shallow bowl with
convex sides and everted
gilt rim decorated with
evenly-spaced roundels
of enamelled summer
flowers on opaque-white
ground, the foot with an
oval female portrait,
36cm (14in), L 6 Mar,
£462 ($688)

10
A pair of opaline two-
handled vases-on-stands,
probably French,
2nd half 19th cent,
the baluster vases in
robin's egg blue with
applied black handles,
the obverse painted with
rural scene, the whole
decorated in white and
gilt foliage, 49cm
(19¼in), NY 16 June,
$1,980 (£1,445)

11
A pair of gilt portrait
lustres, Turkish or
Bohemian for the
Turkish market, late
19th cent, with thistle-
shaped shade enamelled
with portraits of Middle
Eastern potentates,
70.5cm (27¾in), L 6 Mar,
£572 ($852)

1   2   3

4   5   6

7   8

9   10   11

1
A pair of Bohemian gilt and enamelled vases, c.1860-80, richly decorated overall in pseudo-Islamic style with gilt rosettes outlined in silver, 29.5cm (11⅞in), *L 6 Mar,* £1,210 ($1,803)

2
An English overlay carved decanter and stopper, probably Webb, c.1880, the baluster body overlaid in translucent amethyst and carved in polished engraving, 32cm (12½in), *L 6 Mar,* £297 ($443)

3
A French Clichy filigree jug, mid-19th cent, all in alternate wide opaque-pink and white stripes, 35.6cm (14in), *L 6 Mar,* £319 ($475)

4
A pair of Bohemian blue glass vases, c.1860, overlaid in white and with gilt vermiculation, slight wear, 38cm (15in), *L 8 Nov,* £550 ($731)

5
A Bohemian enamelled and gilt overlay glass vase, c.1860, the cranberry-coloured goblet-form body overlaid with white panels and trelliswork, on a solid gilt ground between gilt foliage, 31cm (12¼in), *P 14 Nov,* £440 ($589)

6
A pair of Bohemian ruby glass vases, c.1860, of exaggerated Chinese *ku* form, the ruby body overlaid in white, the whole gilt with scrolling foliage, gilding rubbed, 48cm (18⅞in), *L 7 June,* £638 ($925)

7
A pair of Bohemian enamelled and gilt overlay glass lustres, c.1860, each trumpet stem with a rim bearing white portrait medallions enamelled with gilt-ground children and flowers against the emerald-green body picked out with gilt foliage, 31.5cm (12¼in), *P 14 Nov,* £660 ($884)

8
A pair of green glass lustres, possibly French, c.1880, the overhanging petalled mouth overlaid in white and painted with flowers and gilt leaves, worn, 32cm (12⅝in), *L 8 Nov,* £550 ($731)

9
A pair of Continental overlay-glass covered vases, late 19th cent, the clear glass overlaid in bright blue and cut with trefoils and cartouches, 58cm (23in), *NY 24-25 Feb,* $1,650 (£1,137)

10
A French enamelled bottle, signed on the base 'IP Imberton', 1882, in Islamic style, painted in enamels and gilt with elaborate scrolls and birds, repaired, 43cm (16⅞in), *L 12-13 Nov,* £1,045 ($1,379)

11
A Bohemian silver and gilt cranberry and clear glass goblet and a cut glass goblet, late 19th cent, the first decorated with rustic scenes of hikers, the second flashed in cobalt-blue and gilt with forest animals, the ground gilt with foliage, both with nicks, 15.2 and 16.5cm (6 and 6⅜in), *NY 16 June,* $715 (£521)

12
An amethyst-overlay part table service and a pair of lustres, probably Bohemian, late 19th/early 20th cent, lustre, 59cm (23in), *NY 18 July,* $2,475 (£1,889)

1
An English cameo glass
vase, Stevens and
Williams, the base
marked 'Stevens &
Williams Stourbridge',
c.1880-90, in frosted mid-
blue overlaid in opaque
white and carved with
honeysuckle, 12.8cm (5in),
L 12-13 Nov,
£660 ($871)

2
An English silver-mounted
cameo-glass claret jug,
Webb, silver marked 'James
Dixon & Sons, 1881', the
body in white over blue,
decorated in cameo
technique, the rim
mounted in silver with
hinged lid with thumbpiece
and inscribed, applied
clear-blue loop handle,
25cm (9⅞in), L 6 Mar,
£374 ($557)

3
A cameo glass scent bottle
base, c.1880, carved with
a whitish convolvulus
spray over a lemon-yellow
ground, 5.4cm (2⅛in),
C 3 Oct,
£253 ($326)

4
An English Webb cameo
glass lamp, c.1880-1900,
the yellow body of
compressed form overlaid
in opaque white and
carved with sprays of
blossom, h 7.5cm (3in),
d 12.5cm (5in), L 12 Nov,
£825 ($1,089)

5
A cameo glass oil lamp,
Stevens & Williams, late
19th cent, turquoise glass
overlaid in white, chips
to feet, 38cm (15in),
NY 24-25 Feb,
$2,200 (£1,517)

6
An English engraved
claret jug, probably
Stourbridge, c.1870-80
the flattened piriform body
engraved in intaglio,
27.5cm (10⅞in), L 12 Nov,
£825 ($1,089)

7
A set of twelve enamelled
and gilt overlay plates,
Continental, late 19th cent,
26cm (10¼in),
NY 24-25 Feb,
$2,090 (£1,441)

8
An English engraved
claret jug, possibly
Stourbridge for Phillips
& Pierce, c.1880,
engraved with Phoebus
Apollo driving chariot
and horse, the base with
florette and geometric
borders, 32cm (12½in),
L 6 Mar,
£1,100 ($1,640)

9
An enamelled-glass handled
vase, probably French,
late 19th cent, in pale
topaz glass, enamelled
with bands of pink
foliage and with a
pheasant, heightened in
gilt, 53cm (20¾in),
NY 24-25 Feb,
$1,210 (£834)

10
A North Bohemian
miniature engraved bowl
and cover, possibly by
Franz Knöchel, for
Lobmeyr, Vienna, dated
1905, engraved with a
coat-of-arms and
pastoral couples, foot
marked with Lobmeyr
logo, L 16 June,
£528 ($744)

11
A suite of glass,
comprising a pair of
decanters and 59 glasses
in six sizes, C 30 Oct,
£396 ($506)

12
A pair of cut crystal bowls
with covers, 19th cent,
34cm (13⅜in), A 1 Oct,
Dfl 1,160 (£273; $352)

1   2

3

4

5   6   7

8   9   10

11   12

1
An extensive yellow glass part table service, probably Venetian, early 20th cent, most with ribbed bowls on knopped blown standards, approx 185 pieces, water goblet 18cm (7in), *NY 18 July,* **$1,320 (£1,007)**

2
A cut glass lamp, 1st half 20th cent, the domical shape enclosing three lights, overall cut with cross-hatch, hobstar and single star motifs, chips, 102cm (40in), *NY 3 Nov,* **$35,200 (£28,160)**

3
A cut glass trumpet-form vase, probably American, *c* 1880-1920, in two parts, the vase with scallop lip and cut with cross-hatched fan devices and hobstars fitting into a flaring foot, chips, 79cm (31in), *NY 3 Nov,* **$2,750 (£2,200)**

4
A pair of cut glass five-light candelabra, probably Continental, 1st half 20th cent, overall cut with cross-hatched panels, chips and losses, lacking one candle holder, 81cm (32in), *NY 3 Nov,* **$1,870 (£1,496)**

5
A North Bohemian cut and gilt goblet, Gebrüder Lorenz Steinschönau, *c* 1920, of amethyst tint, 21.5cm (8½in), *L 16 June,* **£132 ($186)**

6
A Dutch baluster pot, Rozenburg factory, the Hague, 19th cent, with brown, yellow and lilac 'tulip' decoration, 44.5cm (17⅞in), *A 12 Mar,* **Dfl 1,798 (£421; $627)**

7
A German sweetmeat glass, 27cm (10⅝in), *A 12 Mar,* **Dfl 783 (£183; $273)**

8
An American cut glass punch bowl-on-stand, 1880-1920, the sawtooth-cut irregular lip above stellate, diamond cross-hatched and diamond panels, h 32.5cm (13¼in), d 35cm (13¾in), *NY 16 June,* **$825 (£602)**

9
A pair of cranberry glass decanters, each in the form of a swan, brass hinged covers forming their heads 28.5cm (11¼in), *C 30 Oct,* **£682 ($872)**

1

2

3   4

5   6   7

8   9

1
A French Baccarat flower weight, 6.5cm (2½in), L 12-13 Nov, £1,650 ($2,178)

2
A French Baccarat miniature pink and white primrose weight, 5.1cm (2in), NY 17 May, $880 (£607)

3
A French Baccarat garlanded butterfly weight, with deep-purple translucent body, 8cm (3⅛in), NY 17 May, $2,750 (£1,897)

4
A French Baccarat faceted red tanslucent overlay weight, with millefiori canes in claret, green, blue, white and pale salmon pink, 7.6cm (3in), NY 17 May, $3,190 (£2,200)

5
A French St Louis crown weight, set with spirally twisted ribbons of lime green and cobalt blue edged in white, 7 cm (2¾in), NY 17 May, $4,070 (£2,806)

6
A French Baccarat sulphide weight, of a hunter and his dog in a woodland scene, set on a translucent ruby-red ground, 8.9cm (3½in), NY 17 May, $1,870 (£1,290)

7
A French Baccarat close millefiori weight, dated on a single cane 1847, 7.6cm (3in), NY 17 May, $1,430 (£986)

8
A French Baccarat flat bouquet weight, 7.6cm (3in), NY 17 May, $7,700 (£5,310)

9
A French Baccarat patterned millefiori weight, with canes in green, white, blue, red and yellow set on a red translucent ground, 6.6cm (2⅝in), NY 17 May, $1,540 (£1,062)

10
A French Baccarat pink and white dogrose weight, star-cut base, 6.7cm (2⅝in), NY 17 May, $1,045 (£721)

11
A French Baccarat patterned millefiori weight, the centre in white, green, turquoise, salmon-pink and cobalt blue with canes in claret, cobalt-blue and white, 8cm (3⅛in), NY 17 May, $3,850 (£2,655)

12
A French Baccarat blue and white dogrose weight, 7.3cm (2⅞in), NY 17 May, $1,210 (£834)

13
A French Baccarat close millefiori mushroom weight, 7.3cm (2⅞in), NY 17 May, $770 (£531)

14
A French Baccarat butterfly over white pompon weight, the butterfly with a purple body, pale-blue eyes with marbled wings, 7.6cm (3in), NY 1 Nov, $3,575 (£2,793)

15
A French Baccarat upright bouquet weight, set with a central red and white flower, within a torsade of cobalt-blue and white spiral with mercury bands, 7.6cm (3in), NY 1 Nov, $1,430 (£1,117)

16
A French Baccarat scattered millefiori weight, dated B 1847, bruises, 8cm (3⅛in), NY 1 Nov, $935 (£730)

17
A French St Louis miniature crown weight, the spiral twisted ribbons of green, red and white alternating with white latticinio, 4.8cm (1⅞in), NY 17 May, $1,650 (£1,138)

18
A French St Louis pompon weight, the flower set on a swirling salmon-pink latticinio ground, 7.6cm (3in), NY 17 May, $3,520 (£2,428)

1
A French St Louis crown weight, with spirally twisted ribbons of cobalt blue and red divided by white latticinio threads, 7.3cm (2⅞in), *NY 17 May*, $2,860 (£1,972)

2
A French St Louis fruit weight, 7.3cm (2⅞in), *NY 17 May*, $880 (£607)

3
A French St Louis miniature pelargonium weight, 4.5cm (1¾in), *NY 17 may*, $1,210 (£834)

4
A French St Louis dahlia weight, 8cm (3⅛in), *NY 1 Nov*, $2,640 (£2,063)

5
A French St Louis upright bouquet weight, 7cm (2¾in), *NY 1 Nov*, $1,760 (£1,375)

6
A French Clichy swirl weight, the central green-and-white rose within radiating alternate royal-blue and white tapes, 5.8cm (2¼in), *L 6 Mar*, £715 ($1,065)

7
A French Clichy morning glory weight, in shades of variegated blue and white with green markings, set on a swirling latticinio ground, 7.6cm (3in), *NY 17 May*, $17,050 (£11,759)

8
A French Clichy three-colour swirl weight, set with alternating cobalt-blue, opaque-white and lime-green threads, 8cm (3⅛in), *NY 17 May*, $2,970 (£2,048)

9
A French Clichy patterned millefiori weight, set with canes in turquoise, pink, white, claret, green and pale blue, the ground of white latticinio tubing on a bed of horizontal cable, 8.6cm (3⅜in), *NY 17 May*, $1,980 (£1,366)

10
A French Clichy turquoise and white swirl weight, 7.3cm (2⅞in), *NY 17 May*, $935 (£645)

11
A French Clichy concentric millefiori weight, the clear glass set with brighly-coloured canes with a central pink and green rose, divided by assorted latticinio, 8cm (3⅛in), *NY 17 May*, $1,430 (£986)

12
A French Clichy swirl weight, set with alternating opaque white and turquoise threads radiating from a central pink and green rose, 5.4cm (2⅛in), *NY 1 Nov*, $1,320 (£1,031)

13
An American, Sandwich poinsettia weight, 7.6cm (3in), *NY 1 Nov*, $825 (£645)

14
A strawberry plant weight, 7cm (2¾in), *NY 17 May*, $3,575 (£2,466)

15
A painted weight of Queen Victoria, possibly English, painted in enamel, 8cm (3⅛in) *NY 17 May*, $935 (£645)

16
A New England pear weight, the fruit in shades of orange and yellow, base 6.7cm (2⅝in), *NY 17 May*, $935 (£645)

17
An American, Mount Washington Glass Company rose weight, the flower of shaded blue and white mottled petals with a yellow, white and aventurine centre, with yellow and white buds, 10.5cm (4⅛in), *NY 17 May*, $19,800 (£13,655)

18
A rare flower weight, factory unknown, 8.2cm (3¼in), *L 12-13 Nov*, £1,870 ($2,468)

1

2

3

4

5

6

7

8

9

10

11

12

13

14

15

16

17

18

1
A French Clichy miniature swirl weight, the alternating opaque white and pink threads radiating from a large deep-purple and white florette, 4.8cm (1⅞in), *NY 17 May,* $770 (£531)

2
A French Baccarat miniature pansy weight, the petals purple and yellow with dark-amber and black markings with a central white and red honeycomb centre, 4.8cm (1⅞in), *NY 1 Nov,* $412 (£322)

3
A French St Louis miniature pink dahlia weight, the ridged pink petals with a green, pink and white central florette set in clear glass, sunburst base, 5.1cm (2in), *NY 17 May,* $2,200 (£1,517)

4
A French Clichy moss-ground patterned-millefiori weight, set with central green-and-pink rose within a circlet of white starlets and interlaced garlands in pink and blue canes, 6.8cm (2⅝in), *L 6 Mar,* £4,840 ($7,212)

5
A French St Louis faceted concentric millefiori mushroom weight, the canes in salmon pink, white and lime green, within a torsade of white cable entwined with dark salmon-pink thread with a mercury band, cut with top and side circular printies, star-cut base, slight surface wear to base, 7.6cm (3in), *NY 17 May,* $3,410 (£2,352)

6
A French St Louis upright bouquet weight, the clear glass set with a central cobalt-blue flower with yellow centre and salmon-pink, yellow and white buds, the green leaf tips within a torsade of white latticinio spiral, the top cut with seven circular windows, 7.6cm (3in), *NY 1 Nov,* $1,650 (£1,289)

7
A French Baccarat faceted garlanded clematis weight, the flower with white overlapping petals with a green, white and red arrowhead cane growing from a green stalk, cut with top and side printies, star-cut base, minute surface wear, 7.3cm (2⅞in), *NY 1 Nov,* $1,540 (£1,203)

8
A French Clichy flat bouquet weight, the clear glass with a pink double clematis, a double white-and-blue flower, a pansy and three buds bound with a royal-blue ribbon, 8.5cm (3⅜in), *L 6 Mar,* £10,450 ($15,571)

9
A French Baccarat faceted flat bouquet weight, with a central white pompon flower with pale-yellow stamen centre, surrounded by flowers in red and white, cut with side and oval printies, sunburst base, some minute chips, 9.2cm (3⅝in), *NY 17 May,* $12,100 (£8,345)

1
A very rare Beilby
enamelled commemorative
bowl, *c*1765, painted in
coloured enamels on one
side, the interior painted
with a white swan, the
rim gilt, d 24cm (9⅜in),
L 12 Nov,
£19,800 ($24,176)

2
A Venetian 'Calcedonio'
bowl, *c*1500, the brownish-
red translucent body
decorated with marbled
yellow, blue and green
striations, h 12.5cm (4⅞in),
d 19.6cm (7¾in), *L 16 June,*
£25,300 ($35,673)

3
A scent flask and stopper,
Hyalith, South Bohemian,
probably Bouquoy glass-
house, *c*1830-40, of
unusual opaque violet-
pink marbled tone,
globular body cut overall
with vertical flutes, short
neck, fluted mushroom
stopper, stopper repaired,
9.5cm (3¾in), *L 16 June,*
£880 ($1,240)

4
An English cameo glass
vase, signed 'Geo Woodall',
*c*1885, the body in deep
amethyst-tinted glass
overlaid in opaque-white
and carved with the
kneeling Psyche, 19cm
(7½in), *L 12-13 Nov,*
£16,500 ($21,780)

5
A Viennese beaker,
Glasperlen, dated 1830,
the body of typical form,
the rim with band of fine
diamonds, the
remainder overlaid with
a band of woven glass
beads, 12.3cm (4⅞in),
L 16 June,
£715 ($1,008)

6
A gilt beaker North
Bohemian lithyalin *atelier*
Friedrich Egermann,
Blottendorf, *c* 1830-40, of
waisted form in
translucent green glass,
the outer surface faceted,
each facet with gilt letter
spelling AMITIE, gilt
rim, 10.5cm (4⅛in),
L 16 June,
£3,960 ($5,583)

1

3

4

5   6

Jewellery

DAVID BENNETT · JACQUELINE FAY

Auctions of jewels for the collector—pieces valued more for the quality of the workmanship and design than for their gem content—were introduced by Sotheby's in both New York and London during the 1980-81 season. Dating from the 18th century to the present, many of these jewels are attributed to famous and skilful craftsmen and often the exact date and provenance are known. These sales have become extremely popular, and the jewels illustrated here give a tempting glimpse of this vast and exciting subject.

A jewel is a form of self-adornment which is created and bought to be worn. The popularity of certain forms of jewellery is, therefore, to a great extent dependent on fashion. At present rings, necklaces, earrings and double clip brooches are very much in vogue. The latter were first popularized in the 1920s and 1930s and are usually in very attractive architectural designs pave-set with baguette- and brilliant-cut diamonds. They can be worn together as a single piece or separately, usually at either side of the neckline. These stylish clips also come in the form of a single clip or a triple clip and similar designs are often found as earrings. An equally popular decoration for the ear at present is the pendent earring. The typical Edwardian examples are perhaps the most feminine with their skilful use of delicate ribbon bow and floral motifs set with diamonds and frequently embellished with a pearl. The Art Deco period produced some very stylish designs with a penchant towards primary colours in the form of calibré-cut rubies, sapphires and emeralds to define the designs in diamond jewels. Onyx was used for a more forceful black outline. These stunning and often dramatic designs are also seen in brooches, bracelets and rings.

In the 19th century all forms of flora and fauna found their way into the jewellers' designs. In the early 1830s bejewelled serpents, the symbol of eternity, were coiled round arms and necks. Towards the end of the century birds and insects not only adorned the body but were also found alighting in the coiffure. Diamond birds, bees and butterflies transformed the hair into a fantastical garden. These hair ornaments nearly always had fittings to convert them into brooches or pendants. The floral motif has always been popular in jewellery and the jeweller's bench provided some particularly exquisite examples during the naturalistic period of the mid 19th century.

In the late 19th century and early 20th century jewellers let their imaginations run wild. Diamond rabbits were depicted playing ball or nonchalantly chewing carrots and enamelled chicks burst from their shells. It was fun and craftsmanship combined. This craze was not solely the domain of women. Men could secure their cravats with a tiepin sporting a whimsical design such as an enamelled 'frog he went a-wooing'! On both sides of the Atlantic these pieces with an amusing motif and anything that is out of the ordinary usually find very keen bidding.

Among the more famous jewellers who are currently the most sought after (and commanding correspondingly high prices) are the Giulianos, John Brogden, Castellani, Melillo and Fouquet from the 19th and early 20th centuries. Lacloche, Cartier, van Cleef and Arpels, Boucheron and Tiffany are very highly prized—and priced—20th century jewellers. They all believed that design and fine craftsmanship were paramount and the high quality of their work certainly reflects this.

One of the interesting things about collecting jewels from the 19th century in particular is that not only were many new styles created but also a number of styles were revived, including Classical, Gothic and Renaissance. Often it is either impossible or extremely expensive to find jewels from these periods, but the 19th century provides a wealth of pieces in similar styles and sometimes at more reasonable prices.

In any number of ways collecting jewellery can prove both fascinating and rewarding and there is always the additional pleasure in the wearing. There is an article about Edwardian diamond jewellery on page 283.

1
A diamond pendant,
2nd half 17th cent, with
fitted cuir bouillé case. It
is understood that this
was a wedding gift to
Marie Louise de
Bourbon, Princesse de
Bulgarie, in 1665 on her
marriage to Jean III
Sobieski, King of Poland
(1624-96), *L 12 July,*
£2,970 ($4,039)

2
A diamond miniature
brooch, *c.*1775, the oval
miniature of a senior
army officer, *L 12 July,*
£1,540 ($2,094)

3
A rose-diamond and
enamel brooch, mid-18th
cent, set with several full
Dutch rose-cut diamonds,
one missing, applied
with deep blue and
white enamel, imperfect,
brooch pin of later date,
NY 5 June,
$3,300 (£2,463)

4
A silver, gold and
diamond brooch, 18th
cent, with pendant loop,
NY 5 June,
$1,320 (£985)

5
A silver and rose-diamond
Sévigné brooch, late 18th
cent, later fitting,
L 6 Dec,
£3,960 ($4,990)

6
A silver, gold and
diamond brooch, 18th
cent, brooch pin
detachable; *NY 5 June,*
$1,540 (£1,149)

7
A pair of silver, gold and
diamond pendent earrings,
18th cent, set with
two pear-shaped and two old
European-cut diamonds
and 92 smaller old
European-cut diamonds,
with screw backs of later
date, *NY 6 Dec,*
$11,550 (£9,625)

8
A gold, half-pearl and
diamond pendant, 1st
half 19th cent, the
reverse inscribed,
L 24 May,
£440 ($634)

9
A gold, silver and rose-
diamond brooch, early
19th cent. It is a family
tradition that this brooch
was presented by
Napolean to Marshall
Ney. *L 6 Dec,*
£1,100 ($1,386)

10
A diamond brooch in
Brandebourg style,
*c.*1820, *L 6 Dec,*
£4,400 ($5,544)

11
A gold, seed pearl and
enamel pendant, *c.*1820,
the blue enamel centre
decorated with a seed
pearl motif; sold with a
seed pearl and peridot
necklet, *c.*1890, *L 6 Dec,*
£550 ($693)

12
A gold and enamel buckle,
*c.*1830, applied with red,
white, green and blue
enamel, *L 6 Dec,*
£528 ($665)

13
An Italian gold and
mosaic bracelet, 1st half
19th cent, the roman
mosaics representing
views of Rome, mounts
imperfect, *L 6 Dec,*
£1,155 ($1,455)

14
A gold and enamelled
miniature brooch, *c.*1830,
signed on the back
'L'Aurore,' 'H. Capt.,
Geneva', the reverse
with a locket compartment,
NY 6 Dec,
$770 (£642)

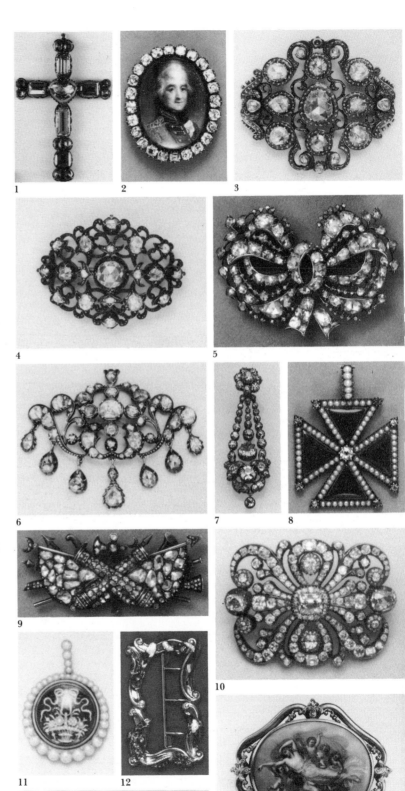

1

2

3

4

5

6

7

8

9

10

11

12

13

14

1

A Swiss two-colour gold, enamelled and jewelled bracelet, c.1830, reversible, enamelled on both sides with 22 portraits of peasant girls in the costumes of the Swiss cantons, two miniatures slightly damaged, also set with rubies, emeralds and turquoise, one stone missing. *NY 5 June,* $4,950 (£3,694)

2

A diamond brooch, c.1830, with three pear-shaped drops surmounted by a cushion-shaped diamond, adapted from an earring, *L 6 Dec,* £5,720 ($7,207)

3

A gold and gem-set Maltese cross, c.1835, the centre set with an emerald and half-pearl cluster, subsequently adapted as a brooch, *Glen 27 Aug,* £385 ($527)

4

A pearl and diamond pendant, 19th cent, mounted in gold and silver, the top centred by a small black button pearl encircled by 7 old-mine diamonds, *NY 17 Oct,* $1,045 (£878)

5

A gold ring, c.1830, the oval bezel with concealed miniature compartment containing the portrait of a young man, the cover set with a faceted garnet applied with a diamond motif, *L 6 Dec,* £1,155 ($1,455)

6

A gold, enamel and half-pearl snake bangle, c.1845, the articulated body decorated with royal blue enamel, garnet eyes, enamel slightly imperfect; sold with a gold bangle, c.1880, *L 6 Dec,* £1,045 ($1,317)

7

A pink topaz and half-pearl demi-parure, c.1830, comprising a pair of pendent earrings and a brooch, en suite, fitted case, *Glen 27 Aug,* £682 ($934)

8

A pair of natural pearl and diamond pendent earrings, early 19th cent, of gold and silver, the pearl drop pendants approx 11.0 and 12.0mm, suspended from leaves set with old-mine diamonds, *NY 6 Dec,* $4,400 (£3,667)

9

An emerald and diamond brooch/pendant, 1st half 19th cent, one small diamond deficient, *L 6 Dec,* £1,760 ($2,218)

10

A gold, enamel and gem-set brooch, c.1840, decorated with green guilloché enamel and a rose-diamond, with pearl and cabochon amethyst drops, slightly imperfect, *L 6 Dec,* £396 ($499)

11

A gold, enamel, ruby and diamond hinged serpent bangle, c.1845, decorated throughout with royal blue enamel scroll motifs, *L 6 Dec,* £6,820 ($8,593)

12

A gold, enamel, pearl and diamond articulated bracelet, c.1850, the back decorated with white enamel motifs, *L 6 Dec,* £3,080 ($3,881)

13

A gold, carbuncle and diamond hinged bangle, c.1860, *L 6 Dec,* £660 ($832)

14

An enamel and diamond brooch, c.1850, decorated with royal blue enamel and rose-diamond foliage, *L 6 Dec,* £2,420 ($3,049)

15

A gold and enamelled miniature bangle-bracelet, 19th cent, with three enamelled miniature plaques depicting shepherdesses and a flower seller, one chipped, framed by split pearls, *NY 5 June,* $1,210 (£903)

1
A gold, enamel and diamond presentation ring, c.1855, the blue enamel centre set with a rose-diamond cypher of Prince Albert, the reverse of the bezel inscribed 'C. L. Eastlake', adapted from a brooch, *L 24 May,* £2,490 ($3,586)

2
An Austro-Hungarian gold, enamel and garnet blackamoor bracelet, mid-19th cent, applied with opaque black and white enamel, *NY 17 Oct,* $1,320 (£1,109)

3
A gold, enamel and gem-set bracelet, c.1860, set with cabochon turquoise and half pearls, the clasp set with half pearls, turquoise and rose-diamonds and decorated with white and blue enamel, *L 6 Dec,* £2,530 ($3,188)

4
A gold and Geneva enamel brooch, the oval enamel after 'La Confidence' by Boucher, signed C. Glardon, c.1860, *L 24 May,* £1,047 ($1,508)

5
A pendant designed as a gold dove with outspread wings, c.1840, pavé-set with turquoises and with ruby eyes, similarly set heart-shaped slide, on gold Brazilian neckchain, *C 10 Jan,* £440 ($638)

6
A diamond brooch, c.1850, pavé-set with cushion-shaped stones with a larger diamond collet-set at the centre, *L 6 Dec,* £1,870 ($2,356)

7
A gold, turquoise and diamond St Esprit brooch, mid-19th cent, *L 6 Dec,* £264 ($333)

8
A gold, enamel and diamond brooch, c.1850, of blue enamelled ribbons, enamel slightly imperfect, *L 6 Dec,* £880 ($1,109)

9
A gold, silver and diamond Maltese cross pendant, mid-19th cent, centred with one old-mine diamond quartered by four old-mine diamonds totalling approx 3.00 carats, completed by 99 old-mine diamonds of approx 16.00 carats, brooch fitting missing, *NY 13 Apr,* $4,950 (£3,462)

10
A gold, lapis lazuli and diamond hinged bangle, c.1880, *L 6 Dec,* £990 ($1,247)

11
A garnet and diamond pendant, c.1850; also sold with a gold carbuncle quatrefoil brooch, c.1860, and a pair of carbuncle and diamond pendent earrings, c.1860, *L 6 Dec,* £2,090 ($2,633)

12
A gold, ruby and diamond bracelet, 3rd quarter 19th cent, on a bracelet of ruched linking, *L 4 Oct,* £5,060 ($6,578)

13
A diamond flower brooch, mid-19th cent, mounted in gold and silver, with two old-mine diamonds of approx 2.00 carats, *NY 13 Apr,* $3,850 (£2,692)

14
A gold and aquamarine brooch, c.1850, leaf and berry design, with a pear-shaped drop, *L 24 May,* £319 ($459)

15
A gold mesh, sapphire and diamond snake bangle-bracelet, 19th cent, the articulated head set with one cushion-shaped sapphire and two ruby eyes, *NY 17 Oct,* $1,760 (£1,479)

1
A gold and diamond
Medusa brooch, 3rd
quarter 19th cent, set
with an old European-cut
diamond, *NY 17 Oct,*
$1,210 (£1,017)

2
A 14-carat gold bracelet,
Dutch, *c*1860, cast and
chased with formal
foliage and set with
seven oval Italian micro-
mosaic plaques repre-
senting bouquets of
flowers, *A 16 Oct,*
Dfl 2,436 (£573; $716)

3
A gold, enamel and
diamond necklace, late
19th cent, the herringbone
chain suspending five
pendants applied with
shaded pink enamel,
NY 5 June,
$1,870 (£1,396)

4
A pair of amethyst and
split-pearl earrings, last
quarter 19th cent, each
with a claw set oval
amethyst embellished with
split-pearl motifs and
tied to a foiled amethyst
surmount by chevron-
shaped buttons,
C 27-30 Mar,
£396 ($590)

5
A gold, enamel and
sapphire brooch/pendant,
unmarked, probably
French, 2nd half 19th
cent, decorated with red
and green enamel, later
pearl and diamond
drop, lacking pendant
loop, *L 24 May,*
£990 ($1,426)

6
An emerald and diamond
ring, by Bailey, Banks &
Biddle, late 19th cent,
gold mount, *NY 5 June,*
$1,210 (£903)

7
A gold, carbuncle and
chrysoberyl Holbeinesque
brooch/pendant, *c*1870,
decorated with crimson,
blue, green and white
champlevé enamel, later
fittings, *L 24 May,*
£880 ($1,267)

8
A gold, enamel, pearl,
emerald and diamond
brooch/pendant, last
quarter 19th cent,
decorated with pink,
white and flame red
enamel, one pearl
deficient, enamel
slightly imperfect,
L 24 May,
£1,540 ($2,218)

9
A gold and Roman mosaic
brooch/pendant, 19th
cent, and a pair of
pendent earrings (not
illustrated), en suite,
fittings missing, *L 18 Oct,*
£660 ($825)

10
A gold and half-pearl
hinged bangle, late 19th
cent, *Glen 27 Aug,*
£286 ($392)

11
A gold, hessonite garnet
and diamond bangle, by
Carlo Giuliano, last
quarter 19th cent, signed
on the hinge and clasp
'C.G.', maker's fitted
case, *L 6 Dec,*
£990 ($1,247)

12
An Italian gold and
micro-mosaic pendent
necklace, *c*1875, with a
gold chain, the whole
weighing approx 22
dwts, *NY 13 Apr,*
$1,210 (£846)

13
A French three-colour
gold and enamelled
miniature brooch/pendant
last quarter 19th cent,
the reverse with glazed
locket compartment,
with fitted box stamped
'La Marche Vinit, Succ.[1],
Paris', *NY 6 Dec,*
$1,320 (£1,100)

14
A diamond
brooch/pendant, last
quarter 19th cent,
lacking brooch fitting,
L 12 July,
£1,320 ($1,795)

15
A peridot and split-pearl
pendant, 19th cent,
centred by an oval
peridot set within a split
pearl border with eight
radiating similarly set
flowers, pearl-set loop,
on gold trace-link
neckchain, *C 27-30 Mar,*
£198 ($295)

1

2

3

4

5

6

7

8

9

10

11

12

13

14

15

1
A pair of half-pearl, emerald and diamond brooches, 19th cent, set with emeralds and rose- and cushion-shaped diamonds, *L 12 July,* £1,320 ($1,795)

2
A pearl and diamond brooch, *c* 1870, set with cushion-shaped diamonds, with a single grey pearl suspended by a diamond chain as a drop, *L 6 Dec,* £1,540 ($1,940)

3
A gold and hardstone cameo brooch, *c* 1830, the cameo greyish-brown and white, cracked, *NY 6 Dec,* $715 (£596)

4
A gold and hardstone cameo pendant, 2nd half half 19th cent, the cameo grey and white hardstone, *NY 6 Dec,* $880 (£733)

5
A gold and sardonyx cameo brooch, *c* 1860, with fitted velvet box stamped 'John Brogden', *NY 6 Dec,* $1,100 (£917)

6
A gold and onyx cameo, by F Tignani, mid-19th cent, the black and white onyx within a silver-gilt frame, with fitted leather box stamped 'Hancocks & Co., 1 Burlington Gardens, London', *NY 6 Dec,* $990 (£825)

7
A gold, shell and coloured hardstone cameo brooch, mid-19th cent, depicting a goddess, probably Camilla, formed of carved malachite, carnelian and various agates, *NY 17 Oct,* $1,100 (£924)

8
An agate cameo, lapis lazuli and split-pearl brooch/pendant, *c* 1860, the cameo grey, reddish-brown and white agate, *NY 5 June,* $935 (£698)

9
A gold and sardonyx cameo pendant, *c* 1860, carved with the profile of Medusa within a simple gold frame, *NY 5 June,* $1,045 (£780)

10
A gold and agate cameo brooch, *c* 1875, the cameo grey and white agate, within a gold frame set with eight pearls, *NY 5 June,* $1,320 (£985)

11
A gold and hardstone cameo brooch, 2nd half 19th cent, the circular black and white agate cameo carved with the three faces of man: a youth, a warrior and an old man, the brooch pin soldered, *NY 13 Apr,* $1,430 (£1,000)

12
A gold, half-pearl and shell-cameo brooch/pendant, *c* 1880, the cameo of Bacchus, *L 10 May,* £495 ($713)

13
A gold and onyx cameo brooch/pendant, by Luigi Rosi, late 19th cent, the black and white onyx cameo carved with a warrior, possibly Mars, slightly loose in mounting, signed on the front 'L. Rosi', the reverse inscribed 'Luigi Rosi, Roma, Piazza d'Espagna, '86', *NY 6 Dec,* $715 (£596)

14
An oval sardonyx cameo, mounted in gold as a brooch within a border of half pearls, *Glen 27 Aug,* £902, ($1,236)

15
A gold, silver, diamond and portrait miniature brooch/pendant, 19th cent, painted in shades of brown and grey, the reverse with a glazed locket compartment, dated 1878, *NY 6 Dec,* $770 (£642)

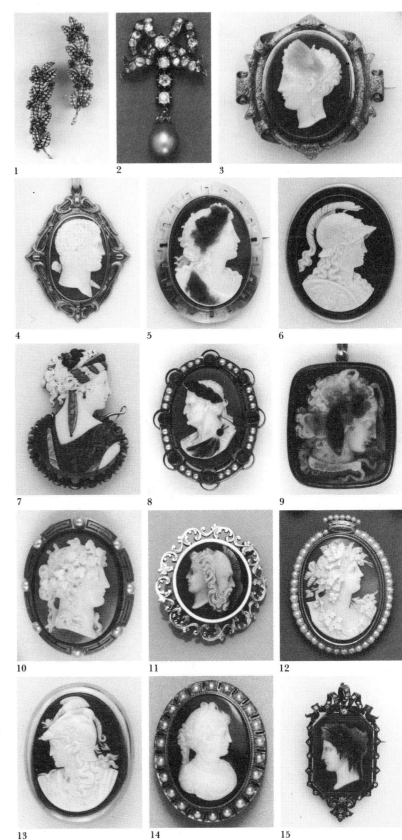

1   2   3

4   5   6

7   8   9

10   11   12

13   14   15

1
An agate cameo pendant, *c* 1860, the stone bordered by black enamel and split pearls, on four-row gold necklace embellished with beads, *C 10 Jan,* £605 ($877)

2
A gold, enamel, agate cameo, diamond and pearl pendant, 3rd quarter 19th cent, in Renaissance style, the scrolls applied with opaque white, pink and black enamel, top segment detachable, *NY 13 Apr,* $3,960 (£2,769)

3
A gold and diamond bangle, 3rd quarter 19th cent, centred by a carved bone plaque tinted in blue, *NY 17 Oct,* $1,540 (£1,294)

4
A diamond and hardstone cameo habille brooch/pendant, 19th cent, gold wire border set with cushion-shaped and rose-cut diamonds, *C 3-6 July,* £616 ($836)

5
A gold, enamel and sardonyx cameo circular brooch, last quarter 19th cent, the cameo set within a border of white and red enamel quatrefoil motifs, *L 6 Dec,* £495 ($393)

6
An Italian gold and lapis lazuli Etruscan-revival bangle-bracelet, *c* 1875, 18-carat gold, approx 28 dwts, *NY 17 Oct,* $1,870 (£1,571)

7
A gold collar in Hellenistic taste, by Phillips of Cockspur St, *c* 1865; and a brooch en suite of girandole design, *L 6 Dec,* £5,060 ($6,376)

8
A gold and Roman mosaic necklace, *c* 1870, on a rope-twist chain with a snap clasp, *P 12 Dec,* £4,180 ($5,008)

9
A gold, emerald, diamond and enamel necklace and pendant, by Giacinto Melillo, Naples, *c* 1900, the arms decorated with black champlevé enamel

10
A gold, enamel, ruby and diamond pendant, by Castellani, *c* 1870, the oval centre concealing a miniature compartment, centre stone replaced, *L 6 Dec,* £3,520 ($4,435)

11
A gold, enamel, ruby, emerald and fresh water pearl pendant, last quarter 19th cent, decorated with blue enamel and set with calibré-cut rubies, *L 24 May,* £770 ($1,109)

12
A gold, enamel, ruby and diamond pendant, *c* 1870, the reverse with hinged miniature compartment, on a gold chain necklet, *L 6 Dec,* £2,860 ($3,604)

13
An Italian gold Etruscan-revival brooch, attributed to Giacinto Melillo, late 19th cent, with fitted box stamped 'Diego D'Estrada', *NY 6 Dec,* $2,200 (£1,833)

14
A gold, chrysoberyl, carbuncle and enamel Holbeinesque pendant, *c* 1870, with a border of crimson, viridian and ultramarine enamel, the reverse of the mount engraved with scrolls, *L 6 Dec,* £1,650 ($2,079)

15
A gold, enamel, coral and seed pearl pendant, *c* 1860, the reverse with a hair compartment, *L 6 Dec,* £880 ($1,109)

16
A gold and turquoise brooch, *c* 1865, centring on a turquoise cluster, similar detachable drop, *C 27-30 Mar,* £220 ($328)

1

An opal and diamond brooch/pendant, last quarter 19th cent, pavé-set with diamonds, *L 24 May,* £935 ($1,346)

2

An amethyst, diamond and seed pearl brooch/pendant, late 19th cent, a buff top amethyst within a gold frame, set with old European-cut diamonds and seed pearls, *NY 5 June,* $1,210 (£903)

3

A gold, seed pearl, enamel and diamond brooch, late 19th cent, the reverse inscribed 'from Rosebery to Louise June 22nd 1897', fitted case by Parkes of Vigo St, *L 6 Dec,* £605 ($762)

4

A peridot, diamond and pearl set pendant, *c.*1900, *P 12-15 June,* £935 ($1,346)

5

A gold, ruby, enamel and diamond presentation brooch, last quarter 19th cent, the blue enamel centre set with Royal Cypher of Queen Victoria, VRI, *L 24 May,* £550 ($792)

6

A diamond brooch, last quarter 19th cent, designed as a heart-shaped cluster of cushion-shaped stones, *L 6 Dec,* £1,650 ($2,079)

7

A diamond memorial padlock, last quarter 19th cent, supporting two charms, one set with a cushion-shaped ruby, *L 6 Dec,* £2,420 ($3,049)

8

A ruby, emerald and diamond brooch, last quarter 19th cent, *L 6 Dec,* £2,200 ($2,772)

9

A ruby and diamond pendant, *c.*1880, set throughout with cushion-shaped rubies and rose- and cushion-shaped diamonds, one drop deficient, one drop unset, *L 24 May,* £1,980 ($2,851)

10

A sapphire, pearl and diamond pendant, last quarter 19th cent, *L 12 July,* £990 ($1,346)

11

An amethyst and diamond pendant, last quarter 19th cent, set throughout with brilliant-cut stones with an oval amethyst at the centre, *L 6 Dec,* £1,100 ($1,386)

12

A pearl, conch pearl and diamond pendant, *c.*1900, on a slender chain necklet, *L 6 Dec,* £715 ($901)

13

A gold, rock crystal, white enamel and diamond pendant, last quarter 19th cent, the white enamel border engraved 'Dieu vous garde', *L 6 Dec,* £418 ($527)

14

A sapphire and diamond brooch, designed as a ribbon pavé-set with cushion-shaped sapphires and with similarly cut diamond tie, *C 3-6 July,* £715 ($970)

15

A diamond, pearl and enamel brooch, *c.*1900, enamelled in white, crimson, green and pink, set with diamonds and pearls and centring on a larger bouton pearl, *C 10 Jan,* £770 ($1,117)

16

A pearl and diamond brooch, *c.*1910, of octagonal outline centred by an openwork ribbon and circlet motif contained within an outer diamond border, millegrain settings, mounted with cushion-shaped stones throughout, *C 3-6 July,* £957 ($1,298)

1
A diamond bow brooch, last quarter 19th cent, pavé-set with cushion-shaped stones, L 26 July, £198 ($265)

2
An opal and diamond brooch, last quarter 19th cent, designed as a cloverleaf, three opals surrounded by rose-diamonds, a circular-cut diamond in the centre, L 24 May, £462 ($665)

3
A diamond brooch, last quarter 19th cent, set throughout with rose- and brilliant-cut stones, L 26 July, £418 ($560)

4
An enamel and diamond brooch, c 1900, designed as a salmon, the tail and fins decorated with enamel, the body pavé-set with rose- and brilliant-cut stones, the eyes set with a cabochon sapphire, enamel slightly imperfect, Glen 27 Aug, £1,100 ($1,507)

5
A French gold, black pearl and sapphire brooch, c 1875, the mount of 18-carat gold, centred by a black pearl, the edges set with three sapphires and three old-mine diamonds, NY 5 June, $1,320 (£985)

6
A rose-diamond brooch, last quarter 19th cent, designed as a bat displayed, one small diamond deficient, L 24 May, £946 ($1,362)

7
A gold and gem-set butterfly brooch, last quarter 19th cent, the body set with rubies and half pearls, the wings pierced and set with rubies, sapphires and rose-diamonds, L 26 July, £715 ($958)

8
An amethyst and rose-diamond brooch, last quarter 19th cent, designed as a dragonfly with sprung wings, the body set with brilliant-cut diamonds, slightly imperfect, L 24 May, £1,375 ($1,980)

9
A diamond brooch, late 19th cent, designed as a humming bird, Glen 27 Aug, £1,210 ($1,658)

10
A sapphire and diamond brooch, last quarter 19th cent, designed as a dragonfly of gold and silver, fitted box stamped 'Debacq & Cie, Paris', containing a concealed hairpin fitting, NY 13 Apr, $2,090 (£1,462)

11
A gold, opal, ruby and rose-diamond plique-à-jour enamel brooch, 1st quarter 20th cent, designed as a dragonfly, the wings with pink and blue iridescent plique-à-jour enamel, later brooch fitting, slightly imperfect, L 24 May, £2,200 ($3,168)

12
A baroque pearl and rose-diamond brooch, late 19th cent, designed as a spray of lily of the valley, L 10 May, £396 ($570)

13
A silver, gold and jewelled bird brooch, 19th cent, studded with rose-cut diamonds, round rubies, one missing, and round sapphires, a seed pearl in its beak, NY 13 Apr, $797 (£557)

14
A baroque pearl and rose-diamond brooch, designed as a butterfly, the wings and antennae set with rose-diamonds, the body set with baroque pearls, L 24 May, £770 ($1,109)

1
A diamond brooch, last quarter 19th cent, set throughout with brilliant-cut stones, *L 6 Dec,* £935 ($1,178)

2
A diamond necklace and a matching bangle bracelet, signed 'Gazdar', French hallmarks, set with lines of circular-cut diamonds, supported by a baguette diamond-set stem, the bangle of similar design, *St M 23-25 Feb,* **SF 121,000 (£38,291; $53,608)**

3
A pearl and diamond brooch, last quarter 19th cent, and a peridot and diamond pendant, *c*1910, the peridot mounted as a swing centre, on a slender chain of fetter and three linking, *L 6 Dec,* £902 ($1,137)

4
A diamond ring, the marquise-shaped bezel pavé-set with cushion-shaped stones, *L 18 Oct,* £495 ($619)

5
A gold and diamond heart brooch/pendant, *c*1900, pavé-set with old European-cut diamonds of approx 2.50 carats, *NY 5 June,* $1,980 (£1,478)

6
A diamond diadem, last quarter 19th cent, set throughout with rose- and brilliant-cut stones, the largest millegrain-set at the centre, *L 12 July,* £4,950 ($6,732)

7
A diamond bracelet, set throughout with rose- and brilliant-cut stones, three stones deficient, *L 24 May,* £2,420 ($3,485)

8
A platinum and diamond lorgnette on chain, *c*1920, the handle set with numerous single-cut diamonds, approx 60cm (24in), *NY 17 Oct,* $6,050 (£5,084)

9
A gold, platinum and diamond pendant, *c*1900, the central old European-cut diamond of approx 1.75 carats, *NY 5 June,* $4,125 (£3,078)

10
A diamond brooch, last quarter 19th cent, designed as a crescent, set throughout with cushion-shaped stones alternating with pairs of smaller diamonds, *L 6 Dec,* £1,155 ($1,455)

11
A gold and diamond bangle, last quarter 19th cent, the front with a cluster of cushion-shaped stones, the sides and back of knife wires, brooch fitting, *L 6 Dec,* £7,700 ($9,702)

12
A golden sapphire and diamond brooch/pendant, *c*1900, the platinum and gold cartouche with a golden sapphire approx 14.00 carats, *NY 13 Apr,* $4,400 (£3,077)

13
Three diamond flower-heads, last quarter 19th cent, en suite, each pavé-set throughout with rose- and cushion-shaped diamonds; tiara, brooch and hair ornament fittings, *L 8 Mar,* £1,870 ($2,788)

14
A ruby and diamond brooch, last quarter 19th cent, pavé-set with cushion-shaped stones, *L 6 Dec,* £495 ($624)

15
A pearl, ruby and diamond brooch, last quarter 19th cent, designed as a winged insect in a spray of leaves, three diamonds deficient, *L 6 Dec,* £550 ($693)

Edwardian Diamond Jewellery

DAVID BENNETT

The golden years between the death of Queen Victoria and the outbreak of the First World War, years of prosperity in England, produced what is arguably some of the finest diamond jewellery ever made. Jewels of this period tend to have a recognizable style and design together with superb workmanship; it is scarcely surprising therefore that such pieces have been fetching very high prices at auction in recent years.

The diamond discoveries in South Africa in the 1870s placed an enormous quantity of stones at the disposal of the cutter, who rapidly improved the appearance of the 'brilliant'; stones were cut to reveal the maximum 'fire' of the material rather than to conserve the greatest weight with the least wastage possible. In order to achieve Total Internal Reflection, where all the light passing through the table of the stone is reflected by the facets at the back of the stone to re-emerge again through the top, greater emphasis was placed on achieving an accuracy of the ideal angle between the table and pavilion facets. In addition, the culet, the extra facet at the tip of a brilliant-cut diamond, was closed up; large culets had been characteristic of earlier versions of the style of cutting.

Platinum was being widely used by the turn of the century. Hitherto, gold-backed silver settings had been employed for most diamond jewellery; the inherent strength of the new metal made it possible for much less of the setting material to be visible while retaining the rigidity required for jewellery.

Delicate saw-piercing of mounts to resemble lace or the ribbon bows and swags of French ormolu furniture mounts of the late 18th century became widespread by 1910—contributing to a general lightening of the impression of the jewel as if the stones were suspended in mid air. The cascades of spectacle-set diamonds worn as longchains, delicate chokers often incorporating rows of seed pearls, bandeaux, brooches, pendants, all demonstrate the fine quality of design and workmanship that have seldom been equalled since.

Due to the manufacturing cost involved, and the high standard of craftsmanship required, fakes of jewels of this period are not common, nevertheless they do exist and there can be little doubt that as prices continue to rise so the temptation will increase. The trained eye will pick up differences in the quality of piercing and finish, and a certain roughness to the setting edges due to lack of wear. The syle of cutting of the stones may also give a clue to the date of manufacture, though one should always allow for stones having been replaced at a later date.

As in other periods, signed jewels are at a premium— particularly those produced by the great jewel houses such as Cartier and Boucheron, both of whom were pioneers of the style.

1
A diamond and fire opal pendant, c 1910, on a chain necklet, cased by Liberty, *L 26 July,* £638 ($852)

2
A diamond pendant, c 1910, designed as a drop of interlinking loops pavé-set with cushion-shaped stones and with three circular-cut diamond swing pendants, on a chain necklet, *L 18 Oct,* £2,035 ($2,544)

3
A seed pearl, emerald and diamond pendant, c 1910, set with rose-diamonds and pearl motifs and bands of calibré-cut emeralds; and a demantoid garnet and diamond pendant, c 1910, *L 6 Dec,* £1,155 ($1,455)

1   2   3

1
A gold and diamond pendant, the rose- and circular-cut stones pavé-set in a pear-shaped design, *L 10 May,*
£825 ($1,188)

2
A diamond clover brooch, *c.*1910, of platinum and gold, set with old European-cut diamonds, *NY 13 Apr,*
$1,210 (£846)

3
A blue enamel, sapphire and diamond brooch, D & Co, *c.*1900, of platinum and gold, with a central sapphire within a guilloché ground applied with translucent blue enamel, *NY 5 June,*
$1,870 (£1,396)

4
A diamond brooch/pendant and chain, by Tiffany & Co, *c.*1910, of gold and platinum set with diamonds, detachable brooch fitting, suspended from a platinum chain decorated with old European- and single-cut diamonds, *NY 17 Oct,*
$6,875 (£5,777)

5
A platinum and diamond brooch/pendant, *c.*1910, set with European-cut diamonds totalling approx 4.00 carats, with later 18-carat white gold brooch fitting, *NY 5 June,*
$2,750 (£2,052)

6
A rose-diamond and seed pearl flèche brooch, *c.*1900, with a flowerhead cluster at the centre, *L 6 Dec,*
£220 ($277)

7
A pearl and diamond stomacher brooch, *c.*1900, decorated in rose- and cushion-shaped diamonds, with small button pearls and with a circular-cut diamond swing centre, *L 6 Dec,*
£2,950 ($3,717)

8
A pair of platinum and diamond pendent earrings, *c.*1915, set with 174 old European-cut and single-cut diamonds of approx 4.00 carats, with fitted box stamped 'Ramond C. Yard Inc.', *NY 5 June,*
$3,575 (£2,668)

9
A diamond brooch, *c.*1900, designed as a butterfly, pavé-set with circular- and cushion-shaped stones and cushion-shaped sapphires as eyes, *L 6 Dec,*
£3,190 ($4,019)

10
A ruby and diamond brooch, *c.*1910, pavé-set with cushion-shaped diamonds, the three larger rubies millegrain-set, *L 6 Dec,*
£2,860 ($3,604)

1   3   4

5   7

6

8   9   10

1
A diamond brooch/pendant, c.1900, in a heart design, with four larger diamonds collet-set as drops, *L 8 Mar*, £1,485 ($2,214)

2
A pearl and diamond brooch/pendant, c.1900, set throughout with rose- and cushion-shaped diamonds and pearls, brooch and pendant fittings, chain necklet, *L 24 May*, £2,640 ($3,802)

3
A sapphire, diamond and seed pearl bracelet, c.1910, the centre decorated with platinum and white gold floral motifs, *NY 13 Apr*, $3,850 (£2,692)

4
A natural pearl and diamond bracelet, c.1915, with five natural button pearls approx 7.5 to 9.2mm, spaced by five collet-set old European-cut diamonds of approx 1.50 carats, *NY 5 June*, $6,050 (£4,515)

5
A diamond bracelet, designed as a row of circular-cut diamonds, claw-set, connected by spindle-shaped links pavé-set with brilliant-cut diamonds, *L 24 May*, £8,800 ($12,672)

6
A seed pearl and diamond bracelet, c.1910, with three pearl and rose-diamond garland motifs flanked by chains of seed pearls, *L 12 July*, £880 ($1,197)

7
A pair of emerald and diamond pendent earrings, c.1905, each with a larger step-cut emerald mounted as a swing centre within a diamond garland, *L 8 Mar*, £11,000 ($16,401)

8
A sapphire and diamond negligée pendant necklace, the pearl-set chain fronted by a diamond-set scroll hung with a pair of bell-shaped drop sets with rose diamonds and a zig-zag band of calibre-cut sapphires, *C 2-5 Oct*, £3,190 ($4,115)

9
A gold, platinum and diamond ring, c.1910, set with three old European-cut diamonds of approx 1.25 carats, *NY 5 June*, $1,210 (£903)

10
A pearl and diamond necklace, signed Cartier, c.1910, mounted in platinum and gold, with two button pearls approx 6.0 and 6.7mm, set with old European-cut and single-cut diamonds, *NY 17 Oct*, $6,600 (£5,546)

11
A diamond necklace, fronted by a band of diamond-set ribbon-work with hanging scroll-shaped cartouche enclosing a swinging flower-shaped pendant centred by a brilliant-cut diamond and with similar diamond drop, one stone deficient, *C 2-5 Oct*, £2,420 ($3,122)

1

2

3   4

5   6

7   8   9

10   11

1
A gold, silver, diamond and seed pearl brooch, late 19th cent, designed as a donkey cart, of 15-carat gold, set with old-mine diamonds, seed pearls and a coral bead, *NY 5 June,*
$825 (£616)

2
A diamond brooch, late 19th cent, designed as a salamander, of rhodium-plated gold and silver, set with old European-cut and rose-cut diamonds, *NY 5 June,*
$1,430 (£1,067)

3
A gold brooch, *c*1900, modelled with the heads of two bloodhounds, each with a chain from its collar, the reverse inscribed 'Boucheron, Paris', *L 24 May,*
£1,320 ($1,901)

4
Two gold brooches, *c*1900, each designed as a chimney sweep, one decorated with enamel, *L 6 Dec,*
£1,045 ($1,317)

5
A gold, silver, ruby and diamond brooch, *c*1880, designed as a hound's head, with a collar of cushion-shaped rubies, *NY 5 June,*
$1,210 (£903)

6
A Russian gold, enamel and blister pearl bar brooch, *c*1900, designed as a line of four mallards, with rose-diamond eyes and blister pearl wings, *L 6 Dec,*
£770 ($970)

7
A diamond brooch, designed as a frog, set throughout with brilliant-cut stones, *L 24 May,*
£715 ($1,030)

8
A rose-diamond and emerald brooch, designed as a hare, the body pavé-set with rose-diamonds, the eye set with a small emerald, *L 24 May,*
£605 ($871)

9
A gold, mother of pearl and enamel brooch, designed as a mallard, *L 10 May,*
£143 ($206)

10
A tourmaline and diamond brooch, *c*1900, designed as a butterfly, set with calibré-cut pink and green tourmaline and rose-diamonds, *L 6 Dec,*
£990 ($1,247)

11
A rose-diamond and enamel tiepin, *c*1900, designed as the head of a cockerel, the comb and beak decorated with red enamel, enamel slightly imperfect, later pin, *L 12 July,*
£220 ($299)

12
A French ruby, emerald and diamond tiepin, by Plisson et Hartz, *c*1900, marked 'PH', *L 12 July,*
£715 ($972)

13
A chalcedony cameo and diamond tiepin, *c*1900, depicting the god Mercury, the winged helmet in 14-carat gold, *NY 13 Apr,*
$770 (£538)

14
A carved labradorite and demantoid garnet tiepin, 19th cent, designed as an owl's head, with two demantoid garnet eyes, *NY 13 Apr,*
$275 (£192)

15
A diamond and enamel tiepin, late 19th cent, designed as a game bird, the head and feet accented with reddish-brown enamel, enamel slightly damaged, *NY 5 June,*
$385 (£287)

16
A diamond and coloured stone tiepin, *c*1920, mounted in platinum, composed of concentric circles which revolve to form various colour combinations, leather box stamped 'Tiffany & Co.', *NY 13 Apr,*
$2,970 (£2,077)

1   2   3

4   5   6

7   8   9   10

11   12   13   14   15   16

1
A platinum and diamond tiepin, c1920, centred by a round diamond approx .40 carat, surrounded by calibré-cut simulated emeralds, *NY 5 June,* $330 (£246)

2
A gold and diamond jewel, c1910, designed as a bicycle, with working pedals, chain and brakes, set with rose-diamonds, and with gem-set headlamp and hubs, *L 6 Dec,* £1,650 ($2,079)

3
A coloured stone and diamond cockerel brooch, c1910, the body pavé-set with small diamonds, the tail feathers formed of rubies, emeralds and diamonds, the comb of small rubies, *G 16 May,* SF 8,250 (£2,625; $3,670)

4
A seed pearl sautoir, c1910, supporting an aquamarine, enamel and diamond pendant with a rose-diamond and black enamel surmount, *L 12 July,* £1,760 ($2,394)

5
A diamond, zircon and pearl pendant, c1900, the cushion-shaped brown zircon mounted at the centre, later chain, *L 12 July,* £605 ($823)

6
A rare gold, diamond and enamel badge brooch, of the First Regiment, The Life Guards, *L 6 Dec,* £495 ($624)

7
A French gold, ruby and diamond brooch, designed as a coiled dragon with a cushion-shaped ruby eye, *L 6 Dec,* £825 ($1,040)

8
A Russian emerald, diamond and pearl serpent brooch, by Igor Cheryatov, Moscow, c1910, the head set with rose-cut diamonds, the mouth bearing a pearl, the body set with emeralds, one missing, *NY 17 Oct,* $4,950 (£4,160)

9
A moonstone, sapphire, diamond and seed pearl pendent watch, c1915, the pendent composed of two miniatures painted on ivory, enamelled in blue and white, the reverse with a watch dial signed 'Paillet and France', suspended from a seed pearl chain, needing repair, *NY 17 Oct,* $11,000 (£9,244)

10
An emerald and diamond ring, *L 18 Oct,* £1,370 ($1,713)

11
A gold, synthetic sapphire and pearl pendent necklace, by J H Shaw, c1915, decorated with three natural pearls and seventeen round diamonds *NY 5 June* $1,540 (£1,149)

12
A pair of cultured pearl and diamond earrings, *L 10 May,* £825 ($1,188)

13
A sapphire and diamond pendent necklace, Black, Starr & Frost, c1920, terminating in two sapphires approx 9.00 carats, the platinum chain set with 49 collet-set diamonds approx 5.00 carats, *NY 13 Apr,* $9,900 (£6,923)

14
A pair of sapphire and diamond pendent earrings, each with a sapphire and diamond drop, *L 12 July,* £2,090 ($2,842)

15
A pearl and diamond bracelet, the centre set with pearls and rose- and brilliant-cut diamonds, *L 26 July,* £1,430 ($1,909)

16
A diamond and black enamel bracelet, by Cartier, c1925, the platinum links set completely with 128 round diamonds of approx 10.25 carats, *NY 5 June,* $11,550 (£8,619)

1
A platinum and diamond jabot, c.1925, the flexible double swag set with 31 baguette and three bullet-shaped diamonds totalling approx 2.50 carats, centred by a triangle-shaped diamond of approx 1.60 carats, *NY 13 Apr*, $5,500 (£3,846)

2
A diamond brooch, c.1920, designed as a giardinetto supporting five chains of cushion-shaped diamonds with a pair of pear-shaped diamonds as drops, *L 8 Mar*, £9,350 ($13,941)

3
A platinum and diamond pendant/brooch, c.1920, with a central diamond of approx .40 carat, *NY 6 Dec*, $11,000 (£9,167)

4
A diamond brooch/pendant, c.1925, set with baguette- and brilliant-cut stones, the tassel subsequently converted as a pendant, *L 24 May*, £2,200 ($3,168)

5
A grey natural button pearl and diamond ring, the pearl 16.3 x 13.5mm, the platinum shank decorated with 20 square-cut diamonds, *NY 17 Oct*, $16,500 (£13,866)

6
A sapphire and diamond ring, by LeBolt, c.1920, of platinum and gold with a square-cut sapphire, *NY 17 Oct*, $2,200 (£1,849)

7
A French art deco diamond and ruby clip, by La Cloche Frères, c.1925, with movable clip mechanism *NY 6 Dec*, $5,225 (£4,354)

8
A pair of carved jade and diamond pendent earrings, c.1920, mounted in platinum, *NY 13 Apr*, $4,950 (£3,462)

9
An onyx and diamond fob watch, c.1925, the onyx bezel set with a marquise-shaped diamond within a border of circular-stones suspended from a similarly set black silk strap, *L 6 Dec*, £1,540 ($1,940)

10
A pair of tanzanite, amethyst and diamond earrings, inscribed 'Cartier', *L 4 Oct*, £935 ($1,216)

11
A seed pearl, emerald and diamond tassel, c.1920, *NY 6 Dec*, $2,750 (£2,292)

12
A jade, diamond and black onyx jabot, by Boucheron, Paris, c.1925, with a black onyx disc flanked by platinum decoration, one small black onyx missing, *NY 13 Apr*, $4,125 (£2,885)

13
A pair of platinum and diamond clips, c.1930, set with two round diamonds of approx .90 carat, eight baguette diamonds of approx .50 carat and 174 round and single-cut diamonds of approx 6.00 carats, *NY 13 Apr*, $4,950 (£3,462)

14
A diamond double-clip brooch of stylised butterfly design, set throughout with circular- and baguette-cut stones, fitted case by Boucheron, *L 6 Dec*, £8,800 ($11,088)

15
A diamond necklace, by Cartier, *L 24 May*, £29,700 ($42,768)

16
An art deco platinum and diamond clip, c.1930, the diamonds totalling 4.00 carats, *NY 17 Oct*, $3,190 (£2,681)

17
A platinum, diamond, black enamel and carnelian clip, c.1925, designed as a Boston terrier, *NY 17 Oct*, $3,575 (£3,004)

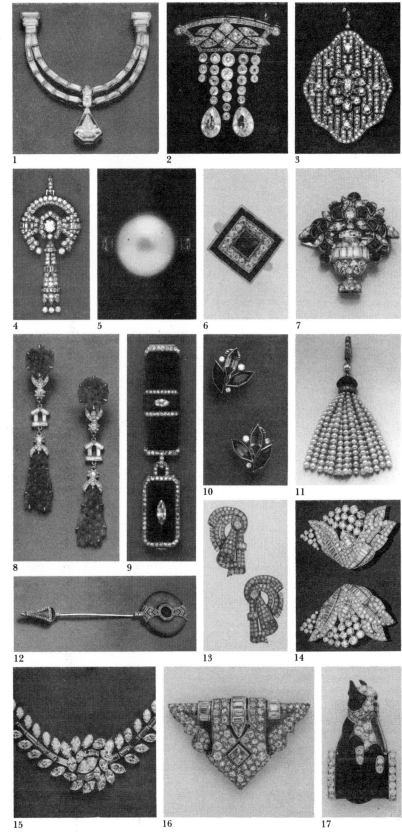

1
A diamond necklace, last
quarter 19th cent, set
with cushion and pear-
shaped stones, *L 24 May,*
£6,820 ($9,821)

2
**A pearl and diamond
stomacher brooch** of
exceptional size, mid-
19th cent, with a large
baroque pearl drop; the
fringe is detachable,
L 24 May,
£9,900 ($14,256)

3
**A pearl and diamond
collar,** c 1910, designed as
five rows of pearls with
rectangular spacers set
with cushion-shaped
stones, the clasp of
similar design, *L 12 July,*
£5,280 ($7,181)

4
**A pair of ruby and
diamond pendent earrings,**
19th cent, the pendants
set with two pear-shaped
rubies approx 2.00
carats, decorated
throughout with 124 old-
mine diamonds of
approx 5.00 carats, screw
earring backs of later
date, mounted in gold
and silver, *NY 5 June,*
$4,950 (£3,694)

1
An emerald and diamond tiara, last quarter 19th cent, the front with cushion-shaped diamonds, with a larger step-cut emerald and diamond cluster at the centre, *L 8 Mar,*
£10,450 ($15,581)

2
A gold and shell cameo diadem, c.1780, the gold frame of filigree and beadwork, c.1800, with fitted leather box stamped 'S. Sheppard, London', *NY 17 Oct,*
$3,850 (£3,235)

3
A gold and enamel brooch/pendant, 3rd quarter 19th cent, the plaque enamelled with matte finish, with two rose-cut diamonds, the reverse with glazed locket compartment, detachable pendant, *NY 6 Dec,*
$1,870 (£1,558)

4
A gold and micro-mosaic brooch, early 19th cent, of a brown and white spaniel; formerly the cover of a snuffbox, now mounted as a brooch, *NY 17 Oct,*
$1,760 (£1,479)

1

2

3

4

1

A gold, enamel, ruby, agate and diamond bracelet, by Carlo Giuliano, c.1865, decorated with white enamel spotted with black enamel, and carved shield-shaped banded agates, signed 'C.G.', *L 24 May,*
£10,450 ($15,048)

2

A gold, enamel and gem-set necklace, by Giuliano, c.1890, decorated with black and white piqué enamel and set with rubies and diamonds, the clasp stamped 'C and A.G.', *L 24 May,*
£4,620 ($6,653)

3

An enamel and pearl pendant, by Carlo Giuliano, last quarter 19th cent, the centre set with a double-sided miniature, the border decorated with blue, white and black piqué enamel, stamped in the loop 'C.G.', enamel slightly imperfect, two seed pearls deficient, *L 24 May,*
£2,200 ($3,168)

4

An enamel and diamond brooch, by Carlo Giuliano, last quarter 19th cent, decorated with black and white piqué enamel and set with a single diamond, signed 'C.G.', *L 24 May,*
£1,430 ($2,059)

5

A zircon, chrysoberyl, pearl and enamel brooch/pendant, by Giuliano, last quarter 19th cent, the reverse inscribed 'to M. E. Gilbert Rhind from Henry Irving, 1902', stamped 'C. & A.G.', Henry Irving (1838-1905), the Shakespearian actor, was knighted in 1895, the first actor to be so honoured. One pearl deficient, clasp imperfect, maker's fitted case, *L 6 Dec,*
£1,045 ($1,317)

6

A gold, enamel, blue spinel and diamond hinged bangle, by Carlo Giuliano, c.1870, the edge of bangle decorated with black and white piqué enamel, the hinge and clasp stamped 'C.G.', maker's fitted case, *L 6 Dec,*
£4,620 ($5,821)

1
A diamond bracelet,
c.1910, designed as a
diamond set band
simulating lace,
G 15-16 Nov,
**SF 71,500 (£23,465;
$28,627)**

2
**A fire opal and diamond
pendant,** c.1905, set with
rose- and cushion-shaped
diamonds, with a larger
fire opal as a swing
centre, *L 6 Dec,*
£2,475 ($3,119)

3
**A diamond and pearl
pendant,** c.1900, the
platinum circular
pendant with a central
button pearl of approx
7.7mm, *NY 5 June,*
$1,870 (£1,396)

4
**A pair of art deco platinum
and diamond clips,** c.1925,
totalling approx 6.00
carats, with mechanism
to convert to a jabot pin
but needing repair,
NY 6 Dec,
$4,950 (£4,125)

5
**A sapphire and diamond
pendant,** c.1905, with a
diamond briolette
mounted as a swing
centre, on a slender
chain necklet and
supporting a pear-shaped
diamond drop, *L 6 Dec,*
£5,060 ($6,376)

6
**A pearl and diamond
circular brooch,** c.1910,
with pearls and
millegrain-set diamonds
within a border of seed
pearls, one pearl
deficient, *L 6 Dec,*
£1,045 ($1,317)

7
**A diamond double-clip
brooch,** each clip
designed as a ram's horn
scroll set with circular-
and baguette-cut stones,
L 6 Dec,
£2,420 ($3,049)

8
**A pair of pearl and diamond
pendent earrings,** by
Lacloche Frères, each
formed of a drop pearl
suspended from a
delicate line of baguette
and carré diamonds,
with a gemmological
report from the SSEF in
Zurich stating that the
pearls are natural,
G 16 May,
SF 8,250 (£2,624; $3,647)

1

2

5

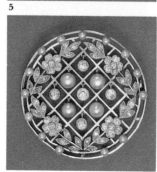

6

3

4

7

8

1
A coral, diamond and black enamel ladybird clip, by Cartier, Paris, c 1930, some chips, mounted in 18-carat white gold, *NY 13 Apr*, $1,320 (£923)

2
An emerald and diamond art deco ring, c 1925, set with a step-cut emerald, the pierced bezel with small round diamonds, *G 15-16 Nov*, SF 6,050 (£1,986; $2,424)

3
An enamel and diamond Indian head clip, by Cartier, Paris, c 1930, enamel slightly worn, *NY 5 June*, $990 (£739)

4
An amethyst and diamond bow brooch, c 1920, mounted in platinum, with gold brooch fitting, *NY 5 June*, $1,870, (£1,396)

5
An emerald, black onyx and diamond bar brooch, by Van Cleef & Arpels, Paris, c 1920, mounted in platinum, *NY 5 June*, $3,190 (£2,381)

6
A ruby and diamond brooch, c 1930, a band of 10 square-cut rubies of approx 8.00 carats, flanked by 22 French-cut diamonds of approx 2.00 carats, *NY 5 June*, $3,190 (£2,381)

7
A diamond brooch, by Cartier, c 1930, pavé-set with circular- and baguette-cut stones, *L 8 Mar*, £3,520 ($5,248)

8
A sapphire and diamond brooch, *L 24 May*, £1,640 ($2,362)

9
A pair of emerald, onyx and diamond ear-pendants, each formed of two larger cabochon emeralds embellished with onyxes, small brilliants and emeralds, *G 15-16 Nov*, SF 44,000 (£14,440; $17,616)

10
A diamond double-clip brooch, pavé-set with circular- and baguette-cut stones, *L 24 May*, £3,960 ($5,702)

11
A pair of black enamel, onyx, emerald, sapphire and diamond cufflinks, *St M 23-25 Feb*, SF 14,300 (£4,525; $6,344)

12
An onyx and diamond bow brooch, c 1925, pierced and pavé-set with brilliant and cushion-shaped diamonds and calibré-cut onyx, six stones deficient, *L 24 May*, £2,310 ($3,326)

13
A lady's sapphire and pearl wrist watch, by Lacloche Frères, *G 16 May*, SF 10,450 (£3,325; $4,648)

14
A pearl, emerald and diamond bracelet, by Lacloche Frères, Paris, c 1930, designed as six larger circular-cut diamonds, alternating with calibré-cut emeralds and pearls, *L 24 May*, £8,250 ($11,880)

15
An art deco aquamarine and diamond pendant on a chain, c 1925, the platinum pendant with central aquamarine, suspended from a white gold chain with diamond clasp, approx 76cm (30in), *NY 17 Oct*, $3,025 (£2,542)

16
An 18-carat gold, coloured stone and diamond brooch, c 1930, the sides decorated with platinum scrolls with calibré-cut rubies and emeralds bordered by diamonds, framed by black enamel, chipped, *NY 13 Apr*, $2,640 (£1,846)

17
A pair of emerald, sapphire and diamond earstuds, *St M 23-25 Feb*, SF 11,000 (£3,481; $4,880)

1

2   3

4

5

6

7

8   9

10

11   12

13

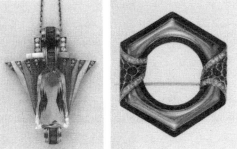

14

15   16   17

1

A gold, sapphire and diamond bracelet-watch, Trabert & Hoeffer, Mauboussin, c 1940, set with a buckle motif concealing a rectangular dial, *NY 5 June*, $2,310 (£1,723)

2

An art deco 18-carat gold bracelet, c 1935, flexible, weighing approx 72 dwts, *NY 13 Apr*, $2,530 (£1,769)

3

A gold, ruby and fancy coloured diamond ring, by Trabert & Hoeffer, Mauboussin, c 1940, the band set with eight diamonds of various natural colours, *NY 13 Apr*, $2,750 (£1,923)

4

A diamond and ruby ring, c 1940, the mount of platinum and gold set with three old European-cut diamonds of approx 1.20, 1.05 and 1.00 carats, and with two cabochon rubies, *NY 6 Dec*, $4,675 (£3,896)

5

A platinum, diamond and ruby ring, c 1940, pavé-set with 48 diamonds of approx 2.00 carats, and 32 calibré-cut rubies, *NY 5 June*, $3,025 (£2,257)

6

A pair of white gold, emerald and diamond earrings, by Trabert & Hoeffer, Mauboussin, c 1940, *NY 5 June*, $1,320 (£985)

7

A white gold and black enamel art deco brooch/ pendant, set with a large coral cabochon and numerous circular diamonds, *A 16 Oct*, Dfl 4,408 (£1,037; $1,296)

8

A two-colour gold and emerald double-clip brooch/bracelet combination by Trabert & Hoeffer, Mauboussin, c 1940, one clip can be fitted to a hinged bangle-bracelet of green gold, slightly damaged, *NY 5 June*, $3,300 (£2,463)

9

An 18-carat gold, sapphire and diamond bangle-bracelet, c 1940, with 21 square-cut and baguette sapphires and 22 single-cut diamonds, *NY 5 June*, $3,575 (£2,668)

10

A beige suede evening bag, art deco, by Janesich, the white gold hoop decorated with rows of circular-cut and cushion-cut diamonds alternated with lapis-lazuli bands, *G 16 May*, SF 10,450 (£3,325; $4,648)

11

A gold and ruby bracelet, by Van Cleef and Arpels, c 1945, the bombé clasp invisibly set with calibré-cut rubies, slightly imperfect, *L 8 Mar*, £6,380 ($9,506)

12

A replica collection of the Crown Jewels of England, in gilt-metal and paste, comprising: The Imperial State crown; St. Edward's crown; the Sovereign's orb; two sceptres; the mace; St. Edward's staff; five swords, including the jewelled Sword of State; the ampulla; the anointing spoon; St. George's spurs; a pair of bracelets; the Coronation ring; several imperfect, *L 24 May*, £9,900 ($14,256)

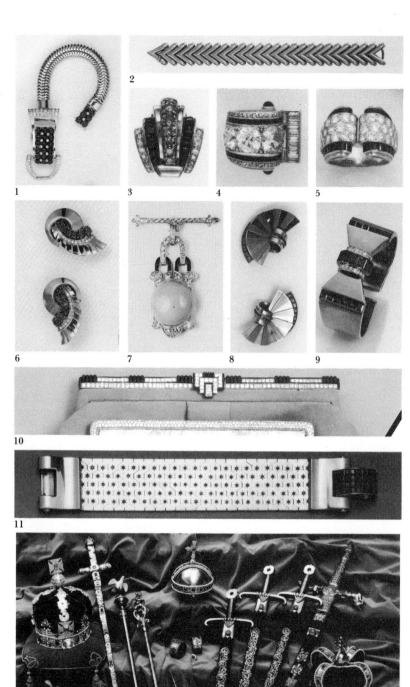

Silver

PETER WALDRON • ELEANOR THOMPSON • KEVIN TIERNEY

In times of stress and war silver has always been at risk of being melted down. However, since the Civil War Britain has been free from the kind of strife that has beset other European nations and it is for this reason that there is a predominance of British silver in the saleroom today. French 17th and 18th century silver was often the model for British goldsmiths and usually of finer quality, but much of it was melted by Louis XIV and again during the Revolution. American 17th and early 18th century silver is equally rare, since only about one in twenty of the early settlers owned silver, and many colonists persisted in buying British and Continental wares until well into the 18th century.

While collectors have long been aware of the basics of the British hallmarking system and most pieces can be fully identified, some of the finer points are still the subject of research. Recent work has concentrated on the retailers and manufacturers rather than on a particular style or period. For example, the firms of Rundell, Bridge & Rundell, Garrard's and George Wickes have proved of special interest. All British silver relating to wining and dining is fetching good prices in the saleroom today; the bargains are to be found on the tea table. Teapots, for example, have always been less expensive than coffee pots, and, whereas an average Georgian coffee pot may today fetch £1,500-2,500 ($1,700-3,000), a teapot of the same period can be bought for under £1,000 ($1,140). Table silver or flatware is ever in demand, but it is not always easy to find a full 18th or 19th century set with matching marks at auction. Later sets or sets that have been made up of pieces of the same pattern are more readily available.

The European silver market still provides many opportunities for the collector, for, although much research has been done in the last ten years, many unidentified and therefore less expensive pieces still appear on the market. There is a greater range of items than is available in British silver and there are also areas that are less sought after than others. One such is 18th century Spanish silver, although the new publication *Enciclopedia de la Plata Espanola* will certainly stimulate interest. Another interesting and quite different field is Chinese export silver, which is mainly 19th century. This is often extremely well made and includes objects which are typically Chinese in design and decoration.

American silver usually only carries a maker's mark, the dating is less precise, and, in the case of common names and initials, there can be uncertainty as to the maker. However, recent scholarship is, again, greatly improving matters for the collector. Just as the market has its favoured English makers, so America singles out Paul Revere the Patriot and Myer Myers, both of whom were capable of original work of high quality. A tablespoon by Revere can reach around $4,000 (£2,750) and one by Myers $2,500 (£2,000), but a spoon by one of their less glamorous contemporaries would fetch only about $150 (£120). Many of the forms popular in 18th century England—wine coasters, tea caddies and cake baskets, for example—are virtually unknown by American makers. The variety increases with the advent of the 19th century, when tea sets become plentiful and the water pitcher emerges as a popular form. It was often used as a presentation piece and was therefore frequently of good quality.

Condition is of primary concern to collectors. A piece that has been lacquered is less desirable than objects which have fine patination. Similarly over-cleaning which has destroyed patination or rubbed away engraving or hallmarks is a serious defect. Contemporary armorials and decoration add significantly to value, whereas later decoration will almost invariably bring down the price, except where the decoration is itself esteemed. In Britain it is illegal to sell a piece of silver which has been altered unless the alteration itself is hallmarked, and even then the value is likely to be much reduced. A christening mug worth some £150 ($170) will only sell for £30-40 ($35-45) if it has been turned into a cream jug by the addition of a spout.

When compared with modern reproduction silver much antique silver seems excellent value. The cost of making something comparable with elaborate 19th century pieces nowadays would be prohibitive for most buyers. This, coupled with fashion, may account for its present favour amongst collectors.

1
A parcel-gift cylindrical
tankard, probably German,
3rd quarter 16th cent,
13.9cm (5½in), 16oz 12 dwt
(518gr), *L 12 Mar*,
£3,300 ($4,920)

2
A German silver-gilt
tankard, *c*1617, the body
embossed and chased with
three strapwork ovals
enclosing portraits of
Diana, a huntsman and
his wife, unmarked, 14.7cm
(5¾in), 9oz (280gr),
G 14 Nov,
SF 9,900 (£3,074; $4,119)

3
A German parcel-gilt
tankard, Danzig, *c*1640,
the cylindrical body later
engraved with a scene
depicting Cupid and
Bacchus, the cover centred
by a portrait, 23.5cm
(9¼in), 36oz 16dwt
(1,146gr), *L 12 Mar*,
£4,180 ($6,232)

4
A Hungarian parcel-gilt
flagon, *c*1639, the tapering
cylindrical body inscribed
in Latin and dated on a
gilt ground, unmarked,
41cm (16⅛in), 44oz 6dwt
(1,380gr), *G 14 Nov*,
**SF 38,500 (£11,956;
$16,021)**

5
A Charles II tankard,
London, 1683, the cylindrical body engraved at
front with armorials within
a foliate mantling,
maker's mark 'FS',
15.5cm (6in), 22oz 14 dwt
(705gr), *L 29 Nov*,
£4,180 ($5,051)

6
A German parcel-gilt
tankard, possibly Marx
Schaller II, Augsburg,
*c*1655, 14.3cm (5⅝in),
14oz 2dwt (440gr),
G 15 May,
SF 8,800 (£2,642; $3,778)

7
A Charles II tankard,
London, 1667, maker's
mark 'TK', 19cm (7½in),
32oz 18 dwt (1,023gr),
L 22 Nov,
£7,150 ($9,295)

8
A Queen Anne tankard,
Richard Green, London,
1713, 17.7cm (7in), 25oz
16dwt (802gr), *L 12 July*,
£1,650 ($2,244)

9
A German parcel-gilt
tankard, Danzig, *c*1650,
the cylindrical barrel
illustrating the three
seasons, Summer, Autumn
and Winter, 19.5cm (7⅝in),
28oz 4dwt (880gr),
G 14 Nov,
SF 13,200 (£4,099; $5,492)

10
A German parcel-gilt
tankard, Philipp
Stenglin, Augsburg, 1708-
10, the barrel flat chased
at the lip with Régence
ornament on a matt
ground, above an
embossed lobed and scale-
work band, 16cm (6¼in),
16oz 10dwt (515gr),
G 14 Nov,
SF 13,200 (£4,099; $5,492)

11
A George II tankard,
Gabriel Sleath, London,
1731, 16.5cm (6½in), 20oz
(622gr), *NY 21 June*,
$1,650 (£1,213)

12
A William and Mary
silver-gilt tankard, London,
1690, engraved with
armorials between crossed
plumes, maker's mark
'I.I', 24.8cm (9¾in), 74oz
10dwt (2,316gr),
NY 13 Dec,
$46,200 (£38,823)

13
A George III tankard, W
& J Priest, London, 1765,
21.6cm (8⅜in), 37oz
(1,150gr), *NY 23 Oct*,
$1,760 (£1,466)

14
A George III tankard,
Walter Brind, London,
1769, engraved with
armorials and mono-
grammed, 24.2cm (9½in),
41oz 10dwt (1,290gr),
NY 21 June,
$2,475 (£1,819)

15
A George III tankard,
John Robins, London,
1782, the baluster body
initialled within an oval
of husks headed by
swags, leaf capped scroll
handle, 20.5cm (8in),
31oz 15dwt (987gr),
L 25 Oct,
£1,155 ($1,466)

1

4

10

7

13

2

5

8

11

14

3

6

9

12

15

1
A George III tapered cylindrical tankard, Sebastian & James Crespell, London, 1767, engraved on the body with a crest within oval surround, bands of applied reeding, 15.5cm (6⅛in), 24oz 10dwt (762gr), *P 17-19 Apr,* £572 ($823)

2
A William IV tankard, John Tapley, London, 1836, the barrel chased with bands of the emblems of the British Isles, the cover chased with a garland of olive, the finial formed as a conch shell, 24.7cm (9¾in), 48oz (1,492gr), *NY 13 Dec,* $2,640 (£2,218)

3
A pair of James II baluster mugs, George Garthorne, London, 1688, flat chased in naive taste with cherubs, birds, monkeys and foliage, below incised reeded rims, 10cm (4in), 19oz 2dwt (594gr), *L 3 May,* £2,420 ($3,436)

4
A German 'Historismus' tankard, late 19th/early 20th cent, the cylindrical body chased in relief with an ancient equestrian battle scene, warrior finial, post-1912 Swedish import mark, 47cm (15¾in), 47oz (1,480gr), *L 8 Nov,* £1,320 ($1,755)

5
A pair of George II baluster mugs, Thomas Cooke & Richard Gurney, London, 1735, 9.3cm (3¾in), 15oz 13dwt (486gr), *L 15 Mar,* £1,155 ($1,722)

6
A thistle cup, John Munro, Inverness, c 1705, of small size with applied reeded girdle below the flared rim, scroll handle, ridged foot, 5cm (2in), 1oz 9dwt (45gr), *HH 27 Mar,* £990 ($1,476)

7
A German silver-gilt tankard, c 1840, 37.5cm (14¾in), 56oz 4dwt (1,748gr), *F 11 May,* L 8,450,000 (£3,441; $4,955)

8
A Queen Anne cylindrical mug, John Rand, London, 1703, 8.7cm (3½in), 4oz 14dwt (146gr), *L 9 Feb,* £286 ($400)

9
A George II baluster mug, William Darker, London, 1732, crested, 11.5cm (4½in), 13oz 4dwt (410gr), *C 3-6 July,* £682 ($920)

10
A George III baluster mug, Whipham & Wright, London, 1766, engraved with a later crest, leaf-capped double-scroll handle, spreading base, 9cm (3½in), 7oz 14dwt (239gr), *L 9 Feb,* £407 ($569)

11
An American mug, Benjamin Burt, Boston, c 1760, 12.4cm (4⅞in), 8oz (248gr), *NY 26 Jan,* $1,210 (£834)

12
A pair of American mugs, Joseph Lownes, Philadelphia, c 1800, 12.1cm (4¾in), 31oz 10dwt (979gr), *NY 26 Jan,* $4,400 (£3,034)

13
A George III tapered cylindrical mug, John Emes, London, 1803, engraved with armorials and foliate mantling between broad bands of reeding, gilt interior and glass bottom, 12cm (4¾in), *L 9 Feb,* £605 ($847)

14
A George IV mug, Rundell, Bridge & Rundell, (John Bridge) London, 1823, embossed and chased with grape-vine on a matted ground, gilt interior, 11.4cm (4½in), 10oz (311gr), *NY 21 June,* $1,540 (£1,132)

15
A Chinese cylindrical mug, Khecheong, Canton, c 1850, the tapering sides embossed with polished bamboo sprays on a matt ground, applied with a crested boss, 13cm (5⅛in), 5oz 14dwt (179gr), *L 9 July,* £462 ($632)

1

2

3

4

5

6

7

8

9

10

11

12

13

14

15

1
**An Iberian silver-gilt
chalice,** probably
Spanish, mid-16th cent,
the polygonal base
embossed with vases of
flowers and formal sprays,
unmarked, 23.4cm (9⅛in),
21oz 16dwt (680gr),
L 12 Mar,
£1,210 ($1,804)

2
**A coconut standing cup
with German gilt metal
mounts,** c.1600, the nut
held by three cast
caryatid straps rising
from Renaissance scroll-
work embellished with
masks, 25.4cm (10in),
G 14 Nov,
SF 8,250 (£2,562; $3,433)

3
**A German parcel-gilt
standing cup and cover,**
Johannes Clauss, Nurem-
berg, c.1630, embossed
with pineapple lobes,
33cm (13in), 11oz (345gr),
G 14 Nov,
SF 8,800 (£2,732; $3,660)

4
**A Victorian silver-gilt cup
and cover,** James Barclay
Hennell, London, 1877,
52cm (20½in), 107oz
18dwt, (3,355gr),
P 16-23 Oct,
£1,695 ($2,118)

5
**A German silver-gilt
standing cup,** Hans Jacob
Baur I, Augsburg,
c.1630, with a plain
tapering sexfoil bowl,
19.3cm (7⅝in), 7oz (220gr),
G 14 Nov,
SF 12,100 (£3,757; $5,034)

6
**A German parcel-gilt
standing cup,** Marx
Merzenbach, Augsburg,
c.1670, the bowl and
cover in the form of a
pear, 14cm (5½in), 2oz
8dwt (75gr), *G 15 May,*
SF 13,200 (£3,963; $5,667)

7
**A German standing cup
and cover,** c.1880, richly
chased in late 16th
cent. style with
allegorical figures, foliate
scrolls, and other motifs
on matted grounds, 58.7cm
(23in), 65oz 13dwt
(2,025gr), *L 7 June,*
£1,265 ($1,834)

8
A silver-gilt cup and cover,
Continental, late 19th
cent, in Gothic style,
32.4cm (12¾in), *NY 18 July,*
$880 (£671)

9
**A Charles II parcel-gilt
cup and cover,** Nicholas
Woolaston, London,
c.1670, of cylindrical
form, the sleeve pierced
and chased with eagles,
reeded rim, 19cm (7½in),
38oz 4dwt (1,194gr),
L 3 May,
£28,600 ($40,612)

10
**A George II cup and
cover,** Paul de Lamerie,
London, 1736, the bell-
shaped bowl engraved
with contemporary
armorials in a rococo
scrolling cartouche,
33cm (13in), 82oz 1dwt
(2,500gr), *M 26 June,*
**FF 444,000 (£38,111;
$51,929)**

11
**A pair of George IV silver-
gilt and ivory cups in sizes,**
Robert Garrard, London,
1825, the ivory South
German, 17th cent,
h 19.4 and 18.5cm (7½
and 7¼in), *L 22 Nov,*
£10,450 ($13,585)

12
**A George II two-handled
cup and cover,** Thomas
Gilpin, London, 1749,
the inverted pear-
shaped body richly
chased with trailing
vines and scalework
ornament, 34.7cm (13¾in),
73oz (2,270gr), *L 14 June,*
£2,860 ($4,118)

13
**A pair of George III two-
handled cups,** George
West, Dublin, 1795, the
inverted bell-shaped
bodies engraved with
floral garlands incor-
porating initialled and
crested cartouches, 18cm
(7in), 28oz 1dwt (872gr),
C 3-6 July,
£682 ($920)

1   2   3   4

5   6   7   8

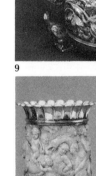

9

10

11

12   13

1
A German parcel-gilt
beaker and cover, Johann
Schuch I, Augsburg,
1680-5, engraved with
three architectural
landscapes, 18.4cm (7¼in),
12oz 4dwt (380gr),
G 14 Nov,
SF 23,100 (£7,173; $9,611)

2
A German beaker,
Nuremburg, late 17th
cent, of roemer type,
chased with flowers, gilt
interior, maker's mark
'HC', 9.5cm (3¾in), 3oz
(93gr), *NY 23 Oct,*
$1,980 (£1,650)

3
A German silver-gilt
monatsbecher, Heinrich
Straub, Nuremberg, c1610,
representing the month
of October, with a chased
band illustrating relevant
scenes including the
Zodiac sign for Libra,
9cm (3½in), 7oz 14dwt
(240gr), *G 15 May,*
**SF 46,200 (£13,873;
$19,838)**

4
A Latvian parcel-gilt
roemer-form beaker, Riga,
early 17th cent,
engraved with a gilt
band of foliate strap-
work, the stem chased
with shells, the rim
slightly distorted, 12cm
(4¾in), 4oz 10dwt (140gr),
NY 21 June,
$5,500 (£4,044)

5
A German parcel-gilt
Hans, in the Cellar cup,
Wolfgang Rossler,
Nuremberg, c1690, the
octafoil bowl and
matching domed foot
with lobes alternately
white and gilt silver,
24.8cm (9¾in), 13oz
(404gr), *NY 13 Dec,*
$3,858 (£3,242)

6
A Swiss silver-gilt **beaker,**
Basle, late 17th cent, of
slightly tapered cylindrical
form with moulded
borders, the body with
granulated finish, maker's
mark 'PB', 8.6cm (3⅜in),
4oz (124gr), *NY 21 June,*
$1,870 (£1,375)

7
A Dutch beaker, Delft,
1631, the tapering
cylindrical body
engraved with scrolling
foliage, 7oz (219gr),
A 7 June,
**Dfl 20,648 (£4,835;
$6,672)**

8
A Dutch parcel-gilt
beaker, probably
Hindrik Muntinck,
Groningen, apparently
1655, the tapering
cylindrical body engraved
with scrolling foliage,
inset with a Saxony
thaler dated 1600,
maker's mark rubbed,
13cm (5⅛in), 7oz 4dwt
(225gr), *L 12 Mar,*
£1,595 ($2,378)

9
A Dutch windmill cup,
probably the Hague,
1646 or 68, the bell-
shaped cup engraved
with scrolling foliate
cartouches, all above a
rhyme, the detachable
superstructure in two
sections, repair to pipe,
25.7cm (10⅛in), 12oz 10dwt
(388gr), *NY 21 June,*
$12,100 (£8,897)

10
A German parcel-gilt
tumbler cup, Daniel
Amende, Augsburg, c1670,
embossed with lobes below
reeded bands, h 5.8cm
(2¼in), 2oz 10dwt (78gr),
L 12 Mar,
£935 ($1,394)

11
A German tumbler cup,
Mainz, c1705, flat chased
with scrolling acanthus
leafage on a matt ground
above lobes and shells,
maker's mark 'IL',
probably Johann
Ledent, h 5.3cm (2⅛in),
2oz 10dwt (80gr),
L 12 Mar,
£880 ($1,312)

12
A Queen Anne tumbler
cup, Ambrose Stevenson,
London, 1710, quite
plain, h 6cm (2¼in), 3oz
5dwt (101gr), *L 22 Nov,*
£638 ($829)

2

5

3

1

8

10

6

12

4

7

11

9

10

11

12

1
A German silver-gilt beaker, Augsburg, 1731-3, of tapered and shaped oval form, chased at the shoulders with winged double shells, maker's mark 'EB', 9.3cm (3⅝in), 5oz (155gr), *NY 13 Dec,* $3,080 (£2,588)

2
An Estonian parcel-gilt beaker, Narva, *c*1740, the trumpet-shaped body monogrammed within foliate sprays below a coronet, possibly Johann Christopher von Haven, 8.6cm (3⅜in), 3oz (93gr), *L 12 Mar,* £792 ($1,180)

3
A German parcel-gilt beaker, Berlin, *c*1760, of tapered cylindrical form, flat-chased below the rim and above the foot with shellwork, foliate scrolls and diaper motif, 9.8cm (3⅞in), 3oz (93gr), *NY 21 June,* $605 (£444)

4
A Louis XV beaker, Paris, 1730, of tulip shape with everted rim and gadroon pedestal foot, 10.8cm (4½in), 5oz 10dwt (171gr), *NY 21 June,* $495 (£363)

5
A French beaker, Jacques Chambert, Versailles, *c*1775, of tulip shape, engraved with flowers and foliage on a matt ground, 12.1cm (4¾in), 5oz 14dwt (180gr), *M 11 Dec,* FF 7,215 (£635; $767)

6
A Swedish parcel-gilt beaker, Kalmar, 1777, the trumpet-shaped body engraved with a coronet above initials, within a foliate and ribbon surround, probably Petter Brandtberg, 19.5cm (7¾in), 14oz 2dwt (440gr), *L 12 Mar,* £880 ($1,312)

7
A Channel Islands christening cup, Pierre Maingy, Guernsey, *c*1763, beaded scroll handles, h 6.1cm (2½in), 2oz 19dwt (91gr), *L 26 Apr,* £429 ($619)

8
A George III beaker, Richard Richardson II, Chester, 1762, the slightly tapered sides engraved with feathered initials within a cartouche, 6.7cm (2⅝in), 2oz 16dwt (87gr), *C 3-6 July,* £363 ($490)

9
A pair of George III wine goblets, William Burch, London, 1791, crested, the pedestal feet with reeded borders, gilt interiors, 15.4cm (6in), 15oz 6dwt (475gr), *L 15 Mar,* £935 ($1,394)

10
An American cup, Louis Buichle, Baltimore, *c*1800, the bell-shaped bowl engraved with a crest, gilt interior, 15.8cm (6¼in), 8oz (248gr), *NY 28 June,* $2,640 (£1,955)

11
A pair of American cups, Joseph Lownes, Philadelphia, *c*1800, the bowls engraved and bright-cut with two vacant cartouches, 16.5cm (6½in), 18oz (560gr), *NY 26 Jan,* $3,520 (£2,427)

12
A pair of George III goblets, London, 1779, each of bell form, embossed and chased with ribbon-tied laurel swags, engraved with an armorial on one side a crest on the other, 18.2cm (7⅛in), 18oz 6dwt (584gr), *NY 18 July,* $2,090 (£1,595)

13
A beaker, Omar Ramsden, London, 1922, of trumpet shape, the moulded girdle decorated with lion masks, in early Norwegian taste, 10.4cm (4⅛in), 3oz (93gr), *NY 23 Oct,* $825 (£687)

1

2

3

4

5

6

7

8

9

10

11

12

13

1
A Spanish ewer, probably
Luis Manso, Valladolid,
early 17th cent, of
cylindrical form, with
moulded rim, 18cm (7¼in),
20oz 10dwt (640gr),
M 11 Dec,
FF 33,300 (£2,934;
$3,515)

2
A Louis XIV silver-
mounted Imari porcelain
ewer, late 17th cent, the
silver, Paris, 1684-7, with
a silver rim and spout
decorated with a bearded
mask, the whole
decorated in blue and
red on a white ground
highlighted with gold,
18cm (7in), *NY 17 Nov*,
$16,500 (£13,200)

3
A German helmet-shaped
ewer, Johann Breckerfelt,
Wesel, 1723-4, armorial
engraved, the harp-shaped
handle capped with a
leaf, 21.9cm (8⅝in), 19oz
18dwt (620gr), *L 12 Mar*,
£3,080 ($5,785)

4
A French silver-gilt ewer
and basin, Jacques Duguay,
Paris, 1765, the baluster
ewer chased with scroll
reserves enclosing
swans, alternating with
flutes and rocaille orna-
ment, scroll handle
moulded with bulrushes,
the oval basin similarly
chased, ewer 23.7cm
(9⅜in), basin w 35.2cm
(13⅞in), 52oz 4dwt
(1,625gr), *G 15 May*,
SF 99,000 (£29,729;
$42,512)

5
A French ewer and basin,
Jean Baptiste-Claude
Odiot, Paris, *c* 1819-38,
the oviform ewer with
reeded borders, scroll
handle with palm and
anthemion terminals, plain
matching basin, ewer
h 27.4cm (10¾in), 69oz
(2,145gr), *NY 23 Oct*,
$2,970 (£2,475)

6
A Swiss vase-shaped ewer,
Elie Papus & Pierre
Henry Dautun, Lausanne,
*c*1790, the body with a
tooled band at the
shoulder, 28.5cm
(11¼in), 17oz 12dwt
(550gr), *G 14 Nov*,
SF 3,850 (£1,195; $1,601)

7
An American water
pitcher, Stephen Richard,
New York, *c* 1826, of
almost hemispherical
form, engraved with
contemporary inscription,
gadroon rim, scroll handle
capped with oak leaves,
21.5cm (8½in), 25oz 10dwt
(793gr), *NY 26 Jan*,
$880 (£607)

8
A William IV claret jug,
E J & W Barnard, London,
1836, the fluted baluster
body chased with matted
leaves and applied with
flowerheads, the rim
applied with bunches of
grapes, 31cm (12¼in),
30oz 10dwt (948gr),
L 26 Apr,
£990 ($1,428)

9
A Victorian Cellini pattern
ewer, London, 1843, the
body cast with portrait
medallions, and floral
motifs, maker's mark
'RWE', 29cm (11½in),
37oz 16dwt (1,175gr),
C 3-6 July,
£825 ($1,119)

10
A Victorian flask-shaped
water jug, London, 1850,
exhibited at the Great
Exhibition, 1851, ribbed
and embossed with six
oval medallions, maker's
mark probably Reily &
Storer overstruck by that
of David Reid for Reid
& Sons of Newcastle,
36.7cm (14½in), 31oz
9dwt (978gr), *L 3 May*,
£1,980 ($2,812)

11
A pair of Victorian wine
jugs, Hunt & Roskell,
London, 1867, the ascos-
shaped bodies textured
to simulate leather, also
stamped Hunt & Roskell
late Storr & Mortimer,
21.5cm (8½in), 65oz
(2,021gr), *C 10 Jan*,
£2,200 ($3,190)

12
A Victorian trophy jug,
Elkington & Co,
London, 1895, the cylindrical body applied with
vacant cartouche below
the satyr's mask spout,
59cm (23¼in), 256oz
(7,961gr), *L 25 Oct*,
£6,380 ($8,103)

1   2   3

4

5   6

7

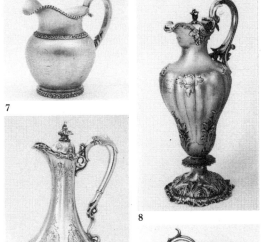

8

10   11

9

12

1

A Portuguese ewer and basin, Oporto, c.1850, the fluted bodies on similar bases, with corded borders, the ewer with a dolphin forming the handle, 25.1cm (9¾in), basin d 33.3cm (13¼in), 83oz 2dwt (2,586gr), *L 9 July,* **£1,100 ($1,507)**

2

A French ewer and basin, C Peret, Paris, c.1860, embossed with scrolling foliage surrounding armorials, ewer 30.6cm (12in), the basin 37cm (14⅝in), 62oz 10dwt (1,944gr), *F 11 May,* **L 3,955,000 (£1,610; ($2,254)**

3

A Danish ewer, Samuel J N Prahl, Copenhagen, 1874, the bulbous body engraved with harvesting cherubs bordered by geometric bands, 31cm (12¼in), 24oz 2dwt (750gr), *L 9 July,* **£264 ($362)**

4

An Oriental-style water pitcher, American, Tiffany and Co, New York, c.1875, h 25.8cm (10⅛in), 40oz 12dwt (1,248gr), *NY 11/12 May,* **$4,950 (£3,587)**

5

An American silver-gilt thermal iced water ewer and stand, William Wilson & Sons, Philadelphia, c.1890, the baluster body with cavity walls, 34cm (13½in), 120oz 10dwt (3,747gr), *NY 28 June,* **$3,300 (£2,444)**

6

An American large ewer, Tiffany & Co, New York, c.1895, of vase form, chased with scrolling foliage and a frieze of dancing putti, 44.7cm (17⅝in), 90oz (2,799gr), *NY 26 Jan,* **$4,125 (£2,844)**

7

A Victorian silver-gilt-mounted glass claret jug, J C Eddington, London, 1862, of baluster form, wheel engraved with roses, shamrocks and thistles, 28.6cm (11¼in), *L 15 Mar,* **£1,485 ($2,214)**

8

A Victorian silver-mounted glass double-necked claret jug, Heath & Middleton, London, 1895, the plain glass body with twin angular side handles, silver bird's head neck mounts and boot button eyes, 30.8cm (12⅛in), *P 17-19 Apr,* **£858 ($1,195)**

9

A Victorian silver-mounted claret jug, W & G Sissons, Sheffield, 1876, the bulbous glass body etched with trailing vines, silver vine chased collar, 28.6cm (11¼in), *P 21-24 Feb,* **£825 ($1,156)**

10

A Victorian silver-mounted claret jug, William Comyns, London, 1899, the bulbous glass body of quatrefoil section, the silver collar embossed with scrolls and amorini, 26.7cm (10½in), *P 21-24 Feb,* **£572 ($802)**

11

A French cut glass and silver mounted baluster claret jug, 1st standard, c.1860, with leaf-capped scroll handle, 28cm (11in), *C 11-14 Dec,* **£440 ($550)**

12

A pair of French silver-mounted glass claret jugs, c.1900, 34cm (13⅜in), *M 11 Dec,* **FF 36,630 (£3,227; $3,866)**

13

A pair of silver-mounted glass claret jugs, 2nd half 19th cent, incised with floral motifs, mounted in silver-gilt, maker's mark 'AL', 28cm (11in), *F 3 Oct,* **L 2,800,000 (£1,151; $1,496)**

14

A pair of French claret jugs, Boulenger, Paris, c.1880, the cut-glass baluster bodies applied at the necks and bases with silver mounts embossed with stiff leafage, 27cm (10⅝in), *L 9 July,* **£1,320 ($1,808)**

1

A pair of Sheffield plated barrel-form wine coolers, c.1800, corded borders and lion masks and ring handles, engraved with crests and monograms in bright-cut surrounds, h 18.4cm (7¼in), *NY 23 Oct,* $2,090 (£1,742)

2

A pair of Sheffield plated wine coolers, c.1810, the campana-shaped bodies engraved with armorials above bands of lobes and below gadroon, shell and foliate borders, h 23.4cm (9¼in), *L 25 Oct,* £2,200 ($2,794)

3

A pair of George III wine coolers, Rundell, Bridge & Rundell, (Paul Storr), London, 1811, engraved on either side with armorials, an applied girdle above and lobing below, h 24cm (9½in), 250oz (7,780gr), *M 26 June,* **FF333,000 (£28,584; $39,603)**

4

Two matching pairs of George III wine coolers, Rundell, Bridge & Rundell, (Paul Storr), London, 1815 and (Philip Rundell), London, 1819, of partly fluted tub shape engraved with armorials below foliate mantles, h 20.4cm (8in), 363oz 10dwt (11,304gr), *NY 12 Apr,* $57,200 (£40,000)

5

A pair of German wine coolers, c.1902, the bodies embossed and chased with a boar hunt, importer's mark Bertold Muller, London, 1902, plated liners, Tiffany & Co, one foot repaired, h 26.8cm (10½in), 79oz (2,456gr), *NY 21 June,* $1,980 (£1,456)

6

A pair of George III wine coolers, Robert Gainsford, Sheffield, 1819, campana shape, chased with rococo ornament and engraved with later monograms, minor splits and repairs, h 23.4cm (9¼in), 137oz 10dwt (4,276gr), *NY 21 June,* $7,425 (£5,460)

7

A German wine cooler, late 19th cent, of pail form, chased with acanthus, the shoulder chased with frieze of drunken putti, h 26cm (10¼in), 60oz (1,866gr), *NY 24 Feb,* $2,860 (£1,972)

8

A pair of Sheffield plated wine coolers, c.1815, of campana shape, partly lobed with gadroon borders, girdles of shells and anthemia, crested, h 26cm (10¼in), *NY 23 Oct,* $2,750 (£2,292)

9

A pair of George IV wine coolers, R Gainsford, Sheffield, 1826, of campana form on pedestal bases, chased all over in rococo style, h 24.1cm (9½in), 167oz (5,193gr), *NY 12 Apr,* $6,600 (£4,615)

10

A Continental wine cooler, late 19th cent, of campana form, chased with the arms of France, above marine panels, mermaid handles, h 24.8 (9¾in), 68oz (2,114gr), *NY 23 Oct,* $3,300 (£2,750)

1

2

3

4

5

6

7

8

9

10

1
A Charles I wine taster,
maker's mark 'WT',
London, 1647, with domed
centre and saucer-
shaped sides engraved
with a name on rim
base; few English wine
tasters of any date
survive and only two of
earlier date are
recorded, d 10cm (4in),
2oz 16dwt (87gr),
L 22 Nov,
£13,750 ($17,875)

2
A French wine taster,
Pierre-Antoine
Viacourt, Paris, 1758, of
circular form, snake
thumbpiece, inscribed with
a name, d 8.4cm (3⅜in),
2oz 16dwt (89gr), *M 11 Dec,*
FF 6,105 (£538; $644)

3
A pair of George IV wine
coasters, Edward Farrell,
London, 1821, the sides
cast and chased with
classical and hunting
scenes, engraved with a
crest, d 19cm (7½in),
NY 13 Dec,
$2,860 (£2,403)

4
A French wine taster,
Provincial, mid-18th
cent, plain with
mushroom-shaped thumb-
piece, the lip later
engraved with a name,
maker's mark 'CD', 8.2cm
(3¼in), 3oz (93gr),
NY 23 Oct,
$935 (£779)

5
A pair of George III wine
coasters, Rundell, Bridge
& Rundell, (Paul Storr),
London, 1813, chased
with lobes below the
gadroon, shell and foliate
rims, the turned wood
bases centred by a crested
roundel, d 17cm (6¾in),
L 15 Mar,
£4,400 ($6,560)

6
A plated double decanter
wagon, mid-19th cent,
the coasters with ribbed
everted bodies applied
with grape-laden vine
border, artillery wheels,
w 48cm (19in), *C 3-6 July,*
£418 ($567)

7
A French wine taster, P
Berard, Angers,
Juridiction de Tours,
1775-81, with snake
handle, the lip inscribed
with a name, d 7cm
(2⅞in), 3oz (93gr),
NY 23 Oct,
$605 (£504)

8
A pair of George III wine
coasters, Christopher
Haines, Dublin, 1792,
pierced and bright-cut
with bands of formal
leafage, wavy rims, turned
wood bases, d 13cm (5in),
L 15 Mar,
£990 ($1,476)

9
A pair of George IV wine
coasters, Benjamin Smith,
London, 1823, cast and
pierced with lozenge
lattice and flowerheads
above moulded bases
and similar rims, d 14.6cm
(5¾in) *P 11-18 Dec,*
£3,300 ($3,927)

10
A George IV four-bottle
decanter stand, William
Barrett, London, 1825,
fitted with two similar
pairs of cut-glass
decanters, each hung
with a label, maker's
mark 'TW', the stand
h 31cm (12¼in), 85oz 12dwt
(2,662gr), *C 3-6 July,*
£2,145 ($2,910)

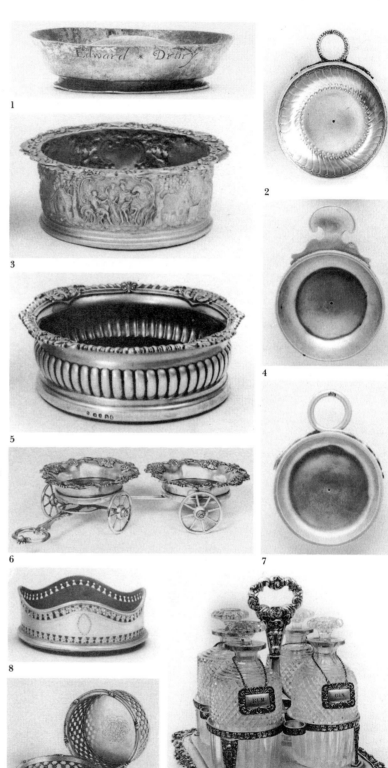

1

2

3

4

5

6

7

8

9   10

1
**A pair of Queen Anne
table candlesticks,** Richard
Syng, London, 1704, the
octagonal bases chased
with a band of lobes
rising to flutes, h 19.1cm
(7½in), 15oz 10dwt
(428gr), *NY 23 Oct,*
$3,850 (£3,208)

2
**A pair of Queen Anne
silver-gilt table candlesticks,**
Jacob Margas, London,
1713, on octagonal bases
with conforming baluster
stems, h 12.7cm (5in),
16oz 10dwt (513gr),
NY 13 Dec,
$7,700 (£6,470)

3
A George I taperstick,
Samuel Margas, London,
1714, the moulded
octagonal base engraved
with a crest, campana-
shaped sconce, h 10.5cm
(4⅛in), 5oz (155gr),
NY 13 Dec,
$1,760 (£1,478)

4
**A set of four French table
candlesticks,** François de
la Pierre, Paris, 1714, of
octagonal baluster form,
chased with borders of
strapwork, shells and
husks on matted grounds,
h 23.5cm (9¼in), 98oz
(3,047gr), *NY 13 Dec,*
$59,400 (£49,915)

5
**A pair of French
candlesticks,** Paris, 1743,
of octagonal baluster
form, the sconces of later
date, h 24cm (9½in), 30oz
14dwt (955gr), *M 6 Mar,*
FF 13,320 (£1,119; $1,665)

6
**A pair of French table
candlesticks,** Lille, 1757,
the octagonal bases
armorial engraved, rising
to knopped tapering
stems and sconces,
maker's mark 'PH',
h 20.4cm (8in), 25oz
14dwt (800gr), *G 15 May,*
SF 11,000 (£3,303; $4,723)

7
**A pair of Swiss table
candlesticks,** Jean-Daniel
Barde, Geneva, c.1750,
the moulded octagonal
bases armorial engraved,
h 22.2cm (8¾in), 26oz
6dwt (820gr), *G 14 Nov,*
SF 2,200 (£683; $915)

8
**A pair of French table
candlesticks,** Antoine
Gaspard Galle, Toulon
Juridiction d'Aix, 1760,
on shaped circular domed
bases, hexagonal baluster
stems, h 28cm (11in),
49oz 10dwt (1,539gr),
NY 13 Dec,
$3,850 (£3,235)

9
**A pair of French table
candlesticks,** Etienne
Moreau, Paris, 1776, on
shaped circular bases
with a border of guilloche,
h 27cm (10⅝in), 41oz
(1,275gr), *NY 13 Dec,*
$6,600 (£5,546)

10
A Maltese table candlestick,
2nd quarter 18th cent,
the octagonal base with a
scalloped rim, the well
engraved with armorials
of a Knight of Malta,
h 14.6cm (5¾in), 9oz
10dwt (295gr), *NY 21 June,*
$1,540 (£1,132)

11
**A pair of German table
candlesticks,** Johann Van
Holten I, Hamburg,
c.1760-70, with shaped
circular domed bases,
baluster stems and urn-
shaped sconces, h 20.3cm
(8in), 25oz (777gr),
NY 21 June,
$3,850 (£2,830)

12
**A pair of German table
candlesticks,** Hans Jakob
Baur IV, Augsburg,
1771-3, all spiral lobed
and fluted, h 21.6cm
(8½in), 24oz (746gr),
NY 21 June,
$2,200 (£1,617)

1   2   3

4   5

6   7   8   9

10   11   12

1
A set of four George II table candlesticks, James Gould, London, 1738, the shaped square bases engraved with armorials, the stems knopped lobed and fluted, h 17.2cm (6¾in), 59oz (1,856gr), L 22 Nov, £8,250 ($10,725)

2
A pair of George II silver-gilt harlequin tapersticks, William Cripps, London, c.1750, the circular bases cast with rocaille and scrolls, h 14cm (5½in), 10oz 3dwt (315gr), L 14 June, £1,705 ($2,455)

3
A pair of George III table candlesticks, John Carter II, London, 1769, the sexfoil bases cast with shells rising to knopped lobed and fluted stems, maker's mark on one only, h 25.5cm (10in), 39oz 10dwt (1,228gr), L 14 June, £1,375 ($1,980)

4
A pair of George III table candlesticks, William Cafe, London, 1771, the hexagonal bases cast with shells and rising to knopped lobed and fluted stems, h 29cm (11½in), 49oz 4dwt (1,530gr), L 25 Oct, £2,750 ($3,492)

5
Four George III table candlesticks, William Gould, London, 1764/8, the shaped square bases cast with a border of shells and engraved with a coat of arms, h 23.5cm (9¼in), 76oz 12dwt (2,382gr), C 3-6 July, £2,970 ($4,009)

6
A George III taperstick, Robert Sharp, London, 1790, the square base engraved with the Prince of Wales feathers, gadroon borders, h 15cm (6in), 6oz 5dwt (194gr), L 9 Feb, £572 ($800)

7
A set of four George III table candlesticks, William Cafe, London, 1758 (3) and 1759 (1), with square bases, gadroon borders, one nozzle another maker, c.1760, h 27.9cm (11in), 105oz (3,265gr), NY 23 Oct, $7,700 (£6,416)

8
A pair of George II table candlesticks, Philips Garden, London, 1756, with triform bases engraved with armorials, the upper stem supported by a chinaman in a flowered coat, h 31cm (12¼in), 81oz 15dwt (2,542gr), L 22 Nov, £24,200 ($31,460)

9
A pair of George III table candlesticks, William Cafe, London, 1760, the stepped square bases supporting twisted column stems and corinthian capital sconces, h 28cm (11in), 52oz (1,617gr), L 15 Mar, £2,530 ($3,772)

10
A George III taperstick, Nicholas Dumee, London, 1776, the circular base rising to a baluster stem and sconce, with alternate matted bands and plain lobes, h 14.5cm (5¾in), 4oz 1dwt (125gr), L 9 Feb, £770 ($1,078)

11
A pair of George III table candlesticks, Carter, Smith & Sharp, London, 1778, sunk centres engraved with the Royal Arms and supporters, fluted column stems, h 29cm (11⅜in), 42oz 10dwt (1,321gr), NY 13 Dec, $4,400 (£3,697)

12
A pair of George III table candlesticks, John Parker & Edward Wakelin, London, 1764, the square bases engraved with armorials, crested detachable nozzles, h 32.3cm (12¾in), 41oz 7dwt (1,285gr), L 25 Oct, £1,210 ($1,536)

1

2

3

4

5

6

7

8

9

10

11

12

1
A set of four George III table candlesticks, William Hall, London, 1770, with square bases wih gadroon borders, cluster column stems, papyrus sconces and detachable nozzles, h 31cm (12¼in), *NY 12 Apr,* $4,950 (£3,461)

2
A pair of Swiss table candlesticks, Elie Papus & Pierre Henry Dautun, Lausanne, c 1770, the trumpet-shaped stems and sconces lobed and fluted above and below the knops, h 22.2cm (8¾in), 19oz 4dwt (600gr), *G 14 Nov,* **SF 14,300 (£4,440; $5,949)**

3
A pair of Italian table candlesticks, Lorenzo Petroncelli, Rome, c 1765, the bases engraved with armorials, h 27.5cm (10¾in), 30oz 10dwt (950gr), *F 20 Dec,* **L 5,650,000 (£2,301; $3,313)**

4
A pair of Italian table candlesticks, Turin, c 1825, h 29cm (11½in), 17oz 18dwt (558gr), *F 11 May,* **L 1,100,000 (£448; $645)**

5
A set of four Italian table candlesticks, Naples, c 1778, baluster stems with chased foliage, h 23cm (9in), 38oz (1,184gr), *F 20 Dec,* **L 10,170,000 (£4,142; $5,964)**

6
A pair of Dutch table candlesticks, Johannes Petrus van Straatsburg, Utrecht, 1785, the square bases applied with festoons, column stems, 46oz (1,433gr), *A 7 June,* **Dfl 8,120 (£1,901; $2,623)**

7
A set of four George III table candlesticks, John Parsons & Co, Sheffield, 1786, the circular bases swirl fluted below V-shaped stems, beaded borders, h 30cm (11¾in), *L 20 Sept,* £3,960 ($5,148)

8
A pair of silver-gilt jewel-set table candlesticks, Austrian or Hungarian, mid-19th cent, shaped square bases and baluster stems, stamped and chased with flowers and foliage, h 24.2cm (9½in), *NY 23 Oct,* $2,200 (£1,833)

9
Two matching pairs of Georgian table candlesticks S C Younge & Co, Sheffield, 1814/22, the shaped bases and baluster stems decorated with shellwork and swirled scrolls, 31.7cm (12½in), *NY 13 Dec,* $3,850 (£3,235)

10
A pair of George III candlesticks, John Roberts & Co, Sheffield, 1809, with gadroon and reeded borders, the tulip-form sconces with detachable nozzles, 20.3cm (8in), *NY 18 July,* $605 (£461)

11
A pair of Corinthian column candlesticks, Birmingham, 1956, stepped square bases, beaded borders, h 30.5cm (12in), *C 19 June,* £275 ($382)

12
A pair of Victorian figure candlesticks, J S Beresford, London, 1878, drilled for electricity, h 35cm (13¾in), 150oz (4,665gr), *C 3-6 July,* £5,060 ($6,831)

13
Four Victorian table candlesticks, Hawksworth, Eyre & Co, Sheffield, 1891, with square bases, draped and stop-fluted column stems with corinthian capitals, h 29.2cm (11½in), *NY 23 Oct,* $1,980 (£1,650)

14
A pair of Australian table candlesticks, J M Wendt, Adelaide, c 1875, the stems in the form of a male and female aboriginal, h 20.5cm (8⅛in), 42oz 14dwt (1,330gr), *L 12 Mar,* £8,250 ($12,300)

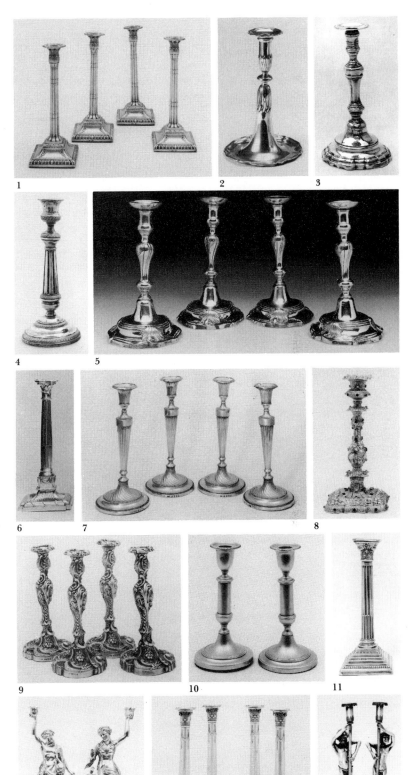

1

2

3

4

5

6

7

8

9

10

11

12

13

14

1
A pair of plated French three-light candelabra, c.1760, the branches possibly of later date, decorated with formal leafage, the curving arms with foliate centre, h 37cm (14½in), *M 26 June,* **FF 13,320 (£1,143; $1,557)**

2
A pair of Italian three-light candelabra, Emanuele Caber, Milan, c.1810, the stem in the form of an Egyptian figure, h 37cm (14½in), 86oz 2dwt (2,678gr) *F 10 May,* **L 8,814,000 (£3,590; $5,169)**

3
A pair of German five-light candelabra, Johann Georg Wilhelm Heinicke, Berlin, c.1825, the square bases rising to a cylindrical section applied with four classical figures, h 70.5cm (27¾in), 178oz (5,535gr), *NY 23 Oct,* **$5,500 (£4,583)**

4
A pair of Italian five-light candelabra, Milan, c.1815, with fluted and gadroon stem, h 58.3cm (23in), *F 11 May,* **L 5,876,000 (£2,393; $3,445)**

5
A pair of George III candelabra, William Pitts, London, 1811, each for four lights, cast and chased with eagles', lions', dragons' and dolphins' heads, h 53cm (23¾in), 405oz (12,620gr), *M 26 June,* **FF 199,800 (£17,150; $23,368)**

6
A plated three-light candelabrum and a pair of table candlesticks, c.1840, h 47cm (18½in), the candlesticks 28cm (11in), *C 1-3 May,* **£143 ($200)**

7
An early Victorian four-light candelabrum, Joseph & John Angell, London, 1837, the triform base with foliate and scroll decorated supports, three detachable leaf-wrapped scroll branches, h 49cm (19¼in), 81oz 6dwt (2,528gr), *L 9 Feb,* **£1,210 ($1,694)**

8
A pair of Victorian candelabra, William Moulson for Lambert & Rawlings, London, 1851, each four lights, h 65.4cm (25¾in), 293oz (9,110gr), *L 3 May,* **£10,450 ($14,839)**

9
A pair of French candelabra, Odiot, Paris, c.1870, each for seven lights, flame finials, h 55.8cm (22in), 368oz 2dwt (11,450gr), *G 15 May,* **SF 18,700 (£5,615; $8,029)**

10
A pair of French silver-gilt candelabra, Keller, Paris, c.1900, each for six lights, on shaped circular mirror plateaux, the stems with grinning satyr masks, h 53cm (20⅞in), plateaux d 43cm (17in), 450oz (14,000gr), *M 26 June,* **FF 94,350 (£8,098; $11,035)**

11
A Victorian six-light candelabrum, Mortimer & Hunt, London, c.1840, drip-pans Paul Storr, h 69.2cm (27¼in), 359oz (11,164gr), *NY 12 Apr,* **$6,600 (£4,615)**

12
A pair of Austrian seven-light candelabra, Backruch, Vienna, late 19th cent, triform bases with paw feet headed by acanthus and ram's masks, h 55.3cm (21¾in), 206oz (6,406gr), *NY 24 Feb,* **$5,060 (£3,489)**

13
A Victorian centrepiece, Mortimer & Hunt, London, 1840, h 61cm (24in), 172oz (5,349gr), *L 9 Feb,* **£2,090 ($2,926)**

14
An electroplated seven-light candelabrum-cum-centrepiece, Elkington & Co, 1847, h 73cm (28¾in), *L 12 July,* **£1,650 ($2,244)**

15
A German dessert dish stand, Koch & Bergfeld, Bremen, c.1905, silver coloured metal, stamped 'Schurmann', h 43cm (17in), dish d 36.5cm (14¼in), 39oz (1,213gr), *L 8 Mar,* **£550 ($820)**

1   2   3
4   5   6
7   8   9
10   11   12
13   14   15

1
An electroplated six-light candelabrum-cum-table centrepiece, c1840, the central column supporting a cut-glass dish, including an alternative glass bowl and fitting for each branch and with six blanking plates for arms not in use, h 76cm (30in), C 2-5 Oct,
£1,155 ($1,489)

2
An electroplated centrepiece, c1870, the stem modelled as a winged cherub supporting a dish holder above his head, complete with cut-glass dish, h 52.8cm (20¾in), L 29 Nov,
£660 ($798)

3
An electroplated table centrepiece, c1870, fitted with three parian figures of kneeling maidens, the centre in the form of a palm tree rising to a cut-glass dish and trumpet-shaped glass holder, glass dish repaired, h 62cm (24½in), C 3-6 July,
£242 ($326)

4
A Continental silvered-metal and glass figural tazza, c1900, formed as a female water carrier, the colourless tazza with scalloped edge, h 46cm (18in), NY 18 July,
$990 (£755)

5
A George II épergne, Benjamin Gignac, London, 1758, with contemporary cut-glass dishes mounted with shell and gadroon borders, the central extension unmarked and possibly later, w 59.5cm (23½in), 114oz 12dwt (3,564gr), C 3-6 July,
£7,150 ($9,652)

6
An electroplated table centrepiece and mirror plateau, Elkington & Co, 1854, the naturalistic base applied with plants and animals supporting a cut-glass bowl, h 76cm (30in), C 2-5 Oct,
£1,155 ($1,489).

7
A George III épergne, Thomas Pitts I, London, 1769, engraved with a crest, h 42cm (16½in), 96oz 18dwt (3,013gr), L 22 Nov,
£7,480 ($9,724)

1

2

3

4

5

6

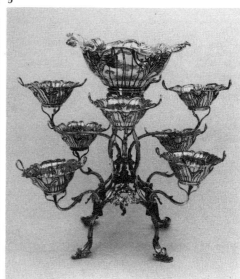
7

1

A George III shaped oblong snuffers tray, John Berthellot, London, 1765, engraved with a crest, gadroon border, w 19cm (7½in), 8oz 13dwt (269gr), *L 9 Feb,* **£396 ($554)**

2

A French shaped oblong snuffers trays and a pair of snuffers, *c* 1725, monogrammed, possibly I Navier, Perpignan, w 20cm (7⅞in), 13oz (405gr), *M 11 Dec,* **FF 73,260 (£6,455; $7,794)**

3

A French snuffers tray and a pair of snuffers, Guillaume Cardon, Dunkerque, jurisdiction of Lille, *c* 1745, the tray with a shaped moulded rim, flying scroll handle, w 22cm (8⅝in), 12oz 18dwt (403gr), *G 15 May,* **SF 6,600 (£1,981; $2,832)**

4

An Italian taper box, Bologna, *c* 1790, h 9.5cm (3¾in), 4oz 2dwt (128gr), *F 20 Dec,* **L 542,400 (£236; $280)**

5

A Sicilian oil lamp, Catania, 1811, hung with a probe, an extinguisher, a pair of tweezers, a pair of snuffers and a cartouche-shaped shade, h 71.6cm (28¼in), 53oz 6dwt (1,658gr), *L 12 Mar,* **£2,090 ($3,116)**

6

An Italian oil lamp, Vincenzo Bugarini, Rome, *c* 1825, hung with an extinguisher, tweezers (broken), and a pair of snuffers, by another maker; together with four later cylindrical sconces with drip-pans fitting into the spouts, h 91.4cm (36in), *NY 13 Dec,* **$4,125 (£3,466)**

7

A pair of Flemish wall sconces, Antwerp, 1689, maker's mark an orb and cross, the cartouche-shaped backplates embossed with the Annunciation surrounded by lobate ornament, h 51.7cm (20⅜in), *G 14 Nov,* **SF 41,800 (£12,981; $17,394)**

8

An Italian table lamp, Pietro Paulo Spagna, Rome, mid-19th cent, in the form of Mercury, hung with tweezers, helmet-form extinguisher and pick, h 61.5cm (23¾in), *NY 21 June,* **$1,100 (£808)**

9

A James II hand candlestick, London, 1686, the circular pan with moulded rim and domed centre, cylindrical stem pierced with a trefoil, the handle applied with a beaded rat-tail, d 14cm (5½in), 7oz 10dwt (233gr), *NY 13 Dec,* **$6,600 (£5,546)**

10

A set of four George III circular chamber candlesticks, William Sharp, London, 1817, one nozzle 1799, with beaded borders, detachable nozzles and extinguishers, engraved with armorials, 14cm (5½in), 38oz 17dwt (1,208gr), *L 3 May,* **£2,530 ($3,592)**

11

A Belgian travelling chamber candlestick, Namur, 1773, with detachable stem, 4oz 18dwt (154gr), *A 7 June,* **Dfl 4,640 (£1,086; $1,498)**

12

A pair of George III chambersticks, William Cafe, London, 1762, plain circular above shell supports, spool shaped sconces, gadroon borders, d 16cm (6¼in), 28oz 14dwt (829gr), *P 11-18 Dec,* **£1,100 ($1,309)**

13

A pair of American chamber candlesticks, Dominick & Haff, Newark & New York, 1879, of square form, chased all over with flowers and foliage on a matted ground, w 12.7cm (5in), 16oz 10dwt (513gr), *NY 26 Jan,* **$770 (£531)**

14

A pair of George III chamber candlesticks, Rundell, Bridge & Rundell, (Paul Storr), London, 1815, d 16.8cm (6⅝in), 28oz (870gr), *NY 12 Apr,* **$4,675 (£3,269)**

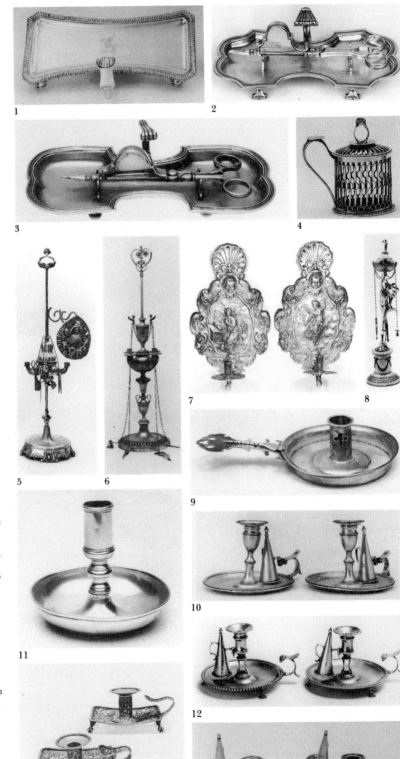

1

2

3

4

5

6

7

8

9

10

11

12

13

14

Silversmiths' Reproductions

JOHN CULME

Eighty years ago the manufacturing silversmiths and platers, Thomas Bradbury & Sons Ltd of Sheffield, issued an illustrated price list, in which they proudly announced that 'Reproductions of Antique Silver' were one of their specialities. They were just one of the many firms then catering for the huge Home and Colonial market through a network of retailers, whose customers, chary of buying something avowedly 'modern', felt more comfortable with the daintiness of older forms.

Bradbury's and their contemporaries cannot wholly be blamed for the frankly trivial nature of the wares which poured from their factories, because, by popular demand, 'reproduction' silver had become the support of many a business. Late Victorians and Edwardians were smitten with the more acceptable aspects of the 18th century; their houses, their furniture and furnishings, even the clothes they wore reflected this preoccupation, but it does not completely explain away the silversmiths' 'Tudor' salt cellars (p.311, fig.3) or 'Reprodutions of Elizabethan Apostle Spoons'.

Long before, in the middle of the 18th century, there had been the stirrings of interest in old silver, particularly in Apostle spoons. Retail silversmiths, seeing interest develop and prices rise, began to take second-hand silver seriously. It was only a matter of time before silversmiths began to supplement the supply with new wares in restrospective patterns. Rundell, Bridge & Rundell, the Crown jewellers, and Garrard's, both retail establishments with substantial workshops of their own but also employing outworkers such as John Houle and Emes & Barnard, were probably the first in the field producing dishes and cups in rich 17th and early 18th century styles as early as 1809.

Collectors as yet were more or less dilettanti, acquiring haphazardly; the 'stamp collecting' mentality of more recent times was almost unheard of. But, as far as old silver was concerned, this was about to change with the publication in 1851 of the London date letters from the end of the 15th century down to 1835. Well-known retailers of the 1850s and 1860s, R. & S. Garrard & Co. and Lambert & Co. among them, with important stocks of old plate, encouraged by example both the collector and those looking for alternatives to the over-decorated modern wares then widely available.

Lambert's, employing on a more or less permanent basis for fifty years and more the manufacturing silversmiths C.T. & G. Fox (p.312, fig.12), were also forced, through the sheer magnitude of their business, to order work from other manufacturing firms. These in turn were often general suppliers to the trade and several, like Hawksworth, Eyre & Co. Ltd of Sheffield, owners of an impressive collection of late 18th century steel dies and actual makers of silver and plated candlesticks, came to rely heavily on the sale of 'reproductions'. Edward Barnard & Sons did a brisk business in bright-cut tea services of the Hester Bateman type, while the biggest silver factory in London in 1900, Charles Stuart Harris & Sons Ltd (p.312, fig.10), specialized in uniformly diluted antique styles which owed much to English design of the Queen Anne and George I period. More authentic copies of old plate, were sold by Crichton Brothers, the Edwardian antique silver dealers in Bond Street.

Antiquarian interest in Apostle spoons during the 18th century and 20th century mass-production of antique-style silver would seem, at first glance, to be worlds apart. But the revelations of 1851 about London date letters, which actually sprang from an examination of Apostle spoons and suchlike, eventually created two markets: one for serious collectors of genuine old silver, the other for quiet conservatives simply drawn towards the sobriety of antique patterns.

1
A pilgrim bottle, London, 1921, maker's mark 'EJG', h 54.6cm (21½in), 169oz 10dwt (5,271gr), *NY 21 June,* **$6,600 (£4,853)**

2
A set of four table candlesticks, Crichton Bros, London, 1900/10, h 28cm (11in), 149oz 4dwt (4,640gr), *L 20 Sept,* **£2,200 ($2,860)**

3
A steeple salt, Crichton Bros, London, 1910, h 49cm (19¼in), 69oz 14dwt (2,167gr), *L 20 Sept,* **£1,210 ($1,573)**

4
A set of four table candlesticks, in the manner of Paul de Lamerie, London, 1957, h 35.5cm (14in), 242oz (7,540gr), *M 26 June,* **FF 44,400 (£3,811; $5,193)**

5
A George IV inkstand, Matthew Boulton & Co, Birmingham, 1827, 27.6cm (10⅞in), 32oz (995gr), *NY 12 Apr,* **$3,410 (£2,385)**

6
A two-bottle oblong inkstand, Carrington & Co, London, 1912, w 30.5cm (12in), 47oz 10dwt (1,477gr), *P 21-24 Feb,* **£902 ($1,265)**

1   2   3   4

5   6

1
A George III tea set, Peter & Ann Bateman, London, 1796, of shaped oval form, the ribbed upper bodies bright-cut with foliate swags, 41oz 6dwt (1,284gr), *L 14 June,* £4,620 ($6,653)

2
A Victorian tea set, Frederick Elkington, London and Birmingham, 1872/3/4, comprising a tea pot, coffee pot, milk jug, sugar basket, four teaspoons and a pair of sugar tongs, maker's mark struck over that of E Barnard & Sons on the larger pieces, 40oz 15dwt (1,267gr), *L 29 Nov,* £990 ($1,198)

3
A pair of four-light candelabra, Goldsmiths & Silversmiths Co Ltd, London, 1937, the octagonal bases rising to knopped flared stems and attenuated campana-shaped sconces, h 34.5cm (13½in), 129oz 9dwt (4,025gr), *L 14 June,* £1,760 ($2,534)

4
A George I taperstick, Hugh Arnett & Edward Pocock, London, 1724, of hexagonal form with conforming knopped stem, engraved with a crest, h 11.4cm (4½in), 3oz 12dwt (111gr), *NY 12 Apr,* $1,430 (£1,000)

5
A set of four George III table candlesticks, Sheffield, 1779, the square bases with beaded rims rising to panels chased with urns, possibly John Smith, h 30.5cm (12in), *NY 12 Apr,* $3,850 (£2,692)

6
A pair of table candlesticks, Sheffield, 1909, the square bases stamped with classical figures within husk borders h 22.2cm (8¾in), *C 16 Oct,* £418 ($535)

7
A set of three Queen Anne casters, Charles Adam London, 1710, the baluster bodies crested above applied girdles, the covers pierced with scrolls below ball finials, one blind, h 16.3cm (6¼in), 20oz 3dwt (642gr), *L 9 Feb,* £2,530 ($3,547)

8
A caster, Tessiers Ltd, London, 1934, with bayonette lock cover, the cylindrical body applied with a girdle below the pierced detachable cover, h 18.4cm (7¼in), 11oz 6dwt (351gr), *C 13-16 Mar,* £110 ($164)

9
A William III Monteith bowl, Anthony Nelme, London, 1696, the almost hemispherical body fluted and with matted panels below the drop handles, engraved with a contemporary coat of arms, d 27cm (10⅝in), 59oz (1,224gr), *M 26 June,* FF 355,200 (£30,489; $41,544)

10
A punch bowl, Charles Stuart Harris, London, 1894, chased with alternate swirl lobes and beading below a band of foliate scrolls, d 26cm (10¼in), 39oz 15dwt (1,236gr), *L 9 Feb,* £770 ($1,080)

11
A set of six George II salt cellars, Paul Crespin, London, 1734, the compressed circular bodies applied with floral swags between lion mask and paw supports, d 9.2cm (3⅝in), 60oz (1,866gr), *P 16-23 Oct,* £7,150 ($8,938)

12
A set of four Victorian salt cellars, George Fox, London, 1866, with applied floral swags between lion mask and paw feet, gilt interiors, d 8.3cm (3¼in), 35oz 12dwt (1,107gr), *L 25 Oct,* £1,210 ($1,537)

1   2

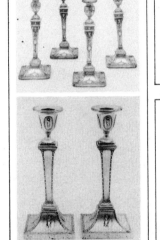

3   4

5 (*above*), 6 (*below*)   7   8

9   10

11 (*above*), 12 (*below*)

1
A George III bowl and cover, Rundell, Bridge & Rundell, (Digby Scott & Benjamin Smith II), London, 1803, the circular bowl applied with a band of arabesques on a matted ground, h 17.5cm (7in), 37oz 5dwt (1,158gr), *L 29 Nov,*
£1,595 ($1,930)

2
A soup tureen, cover and liner with a stand, probably Italian, *c*1880, the circular body raised on paw supports, with lion mask and drop ring handles, h 37.5cm (14¾in), 188oz 14dwt (5,870gr), *G 14 Nov,*
SF 27,500 (£2,313; $2,824)

3
A George II cup and cover, George Boothby, London, 1729, the bell-shaped body applied with strapwork below the reeded girdle engraved with armorials, h 30.5cm (12in), 80oz 13dwt (2,508gr), *L 14 June,*
£2,310 ($3,326)

4
A large two-handled cup and cover, E Barnard & Sons, London 1887, the inverted bell-shaped body engraved with a presentation inscription and a coat of arms, h 44cm (17¼in), 124oz 15dwt (3,879gr), *C 3-6 July,*
£1,815 ($2,450)

5
A George III mug, Emes & Barnard, London, 1817, of bombé circular form with a cast girdle of roses, thistles and shamrocks, twin-headed serpent handle, gilt interior, h 7.6cm (3in), 6oz (186gr), *NY 23 Oct,*
$302 (£251)

6
A child's mug, Carrington & Co, London, 1914, the tapered sides cast with floral scrolls centred by putti supporting a basket of fruit, h 11cm (4¼in), 12oz (373gr), *C 10 Jan,*
£253 ($366)

7
A pair of plated French ewers, *c*1710, the bodies with two applied girdles and with reeded lips, the lower parts with applied matted strapwork decoration, h 26cm (10¼in), *M 26 June,*
FF 44,400 (£3,811; $5,280)

8
A French ewer, Puiforcat, Paris, modern, of helmet shape, applied with strapwork and shell-headed mask, eagle-head handle, h 33cm (13in), 71oz (2,208gr), *NY 21 June,*
$2,750 (£2,022)

9
A pair of James II lighthouse casters, London, 1686, the cylindrical bodies with reeded girdles above cording, 15cm (6in), 10oz 11dwt (328gr), *L 12 July,*
£2,530 ($3,441)

10
A baluster caster, Tessiers Ltd, London, 1928, with slip lock cover, the body applied with a girdle below the similar pierced domed cover, h 18.4cm (7¼in), 8oz 8dwt (261gr), *C 13-16 Mar,*
£143 ($213)

11
Set of forty-nine George III dinner plates, Wakelin & Taylor, London, 1784, with moulded gadroon rims, the borders engraved with contemporary armorials, d 24.3cm (9½in), 776oz (24,133gr), *NY 13 Dec,*
$39,600 (£33,277)

12
A set of twelve Victorian dinner plates, Garrards', London, 1894, circular with beaded rims, the borders engraved with armorials below a baron's coronet, d 25.1cm (9⅞in), 226oz (7,028gr), *NY 13 Dec,*
$6,325 (£5,315)

13
A set of twelve dinner plates, Henry & Arthur Vander for C J Vander Ltd, London, 1930, with gadroon rims, d 24cm (9½in), 231oz 10dwt (7,200gr), *JHB 3 July,*
R 3,200 (£1,702; $2,297)

1 (*above*), 2 (*below*)

3   4

5   6

7

8

9 (*above*), 10 (*below*),   11 (*above*), 12 (*left*), 13 (*right*)

1
A George II silver-gilt table bell, Charles Hatfield, London, 1731, h 13.5cm (5¼ in), 7oz 6dwt (227gr), *L 3 May*, £2,970 ($4,217)

2
A George III table bell, Abstainando King, London, 1811, h 11.4cm (4¼ in), 4oz 10dwt (139gr), *P 21-24 Feb*, £484 ($679)

3
A Dutch table bell, Hendrik Nieuwenhuys, Amsterdam, 1766, lacks clapper, h 13cm (5⅛ in), 8oz 10dwt (264gr), *NY 13 Dec*, $1,650 (£1,386)

4
A table bell, unmarked, probably French, c 1840, h 14.5cm (5¾ in), 10oz 14dwt (335gr), *L 12 Mar*, £385 ($539)

5
A Dutch table bell, Godert van Ysseldijk, the Hague, 1767, later crested and monogrammed, h 14.5cm (5¾ in), 9oz 16dwt (306gr), *L 12 Mar*, £495 ($738)

6
A French table bell, Paris, 1761, armorial engraved below a coronet, maker's mark 'JD', h 10.2cm (4in), 4oz 8dwt (138gr), *SF 12,000 (£3,604; $5,153)*

7
A George I oblong inkstand, Paul de Lamerie, London, 1725, w 25.8cm (10in), 45oz 5dwt (1,407gr), *L 3 May*, £72,600 ($103,092)

8
A George III globe-form inkstand with perpetual calendar, John Robins, London, 1793, fitted interior with silver-mounted inkwell and sander, lacking other fittings, h 15.2cm (6in), 7oz 10dwt, (233gr), *NY 23 Oct*, $2,640 (£2,200)

9
An Italian inkstand, Genoa, 1771, 28.6cm (11¼ in), 42oz (1,306gr), *NY 13 Dec*, $5,500 (£4,622)

10
A George III three-bottle inkstand, Aldridge & Green, London, 1772, w 28.5cm (11¼ in), 20oz 18dwt (649gr), *P 17-19 Apr*, £1,155 ($1,667)

11
A George III inkstand, Rundell, Bridge & Rundell, (Paul Storr), London, 1811, 33.7cm (13¼ in), 35oz 10dwt (1,104gr), *NY 13 Dec*, $7,425 (£6,239)

12
An American inkstand after an original by John Coney, Currier & Roby, New York, c 1936, retailed by Ensko, of triangular form, 19.3cm (7⅝ in), 18oz 10dwt (575gr), *NY 26 Jan*, $1,100 (£759)

13
An Austrian inkstand, late 19th cent, of rococo form, mounted with two urn-shaped covered inkwells, 29.2cm (11½ in), 51oz 10dwt (1,601gr), *NY 21 June*, $880 (£647)

14
An Australian desk set, c 1880, fitted with two bottles with plated mounts, the candlestick, Wm Farmer & Co, Sydney, w 47.5cm (14¾ in), *C 3-6 July*, £902 ($1,223)

15
An Australian plate-mounted emu egg inkstand, c 1870, apparently unmarked, w 27.9cm (11in), *P 17-19 Apr*, £352 ($508)

16
An Australian silver-mounted emu egg inkwell, Jochim Matthias Wendt, Adelaide, c 1870, with a scene of kangaroos inserted in the shell, h 21cm (8⅛ in), *G 15 May*, SF 13,000 (£3,903; $5,581)

17
A desk set, probably Australian, c late 19th cent, centred by a clock, also fitted with three carved and painted emu's eggs, w 37cm (14½ in), *C 10 Jan*, £1,540 ($2,233)

1 2 3 4 5

6 7 8

9 10

11 12

13 14

15 16 17

1
A Queen Anne chocolate pot, John Leach, London, 1707, engraved with armorials, h 25cm (9⅞in), 26oz (808gr), *NY 13 Dec*, $7,700 (£6,471)

2
A George I tapered cylindrical coffee pot, Thomas Farren, London, 1720, engraved with later initials, Britannia Standard, h 25cm (9¾in), 29oz 18dwt (929gr), *L 15 Mar*, £1,870 ($2,786)

3
A George II coffee pot, Thomas Whipham, London, c 1748, chased with scrolling foliage and a coat of arms, h 25.2cm (10in), 27oz 14dwt (864gr), *F 3 Oct*, L 4,500,000 (£1,850; $2,405)

4
An Irish baluster coffee pot, William Townsend, Dublin, c 1755, repoussé in chinoiserie taste with figures and pagoda-like buildings, also engraved with armorials, h 28cm (11in), 35oz 10dwt (1,104gr), *L 9 Feb*, £1,540 ($2,156)

5
A George II baluster coffee pot, Whipham & Wright, London, 1759, engraved with armorials within a rococo cartouche, a crest and a motto, 27.2cm (10¾in), 29oz 18dwt (929gr), *L 9 Feb*, £2,310 ($3,234)

6
A George II rococo chocolate pot, Samuel Courtauld, London, 1750, richly chased with shell and scrollwork, engraved with contemporary armorials and crest, 26cm (10¼in), 36oz (1,119gr), *NY 13 Dec*, $6,600 (£5,546)

7
A George III baluster coffee pot, Smith & Sharp, London 1762, chased with Chinese figures amidst rocaille scrolls and incorporating armorials, 29.2cm (11½in), 38oz 18dwt (1,209gr), *P 24-27 July*, £1,870 ($2,506)

8
A George III coffee pot, London, 1769, the inverted pear-shaped body chased at the base with waved spiral lobes and flutes, 29.2cm (11½in), 33oz 2dwt (1,029gr), *C 3-6 July*, £1,650 ($2,244)

9
A George III coffee jug, Thomas Heming, London, 1764, the baluster body and finial spirally fluted, on a circular gadrooned base, 25.5cm (10in), 23oz 12dwt (734gr), *L 25 Oct*, £1,650 ($2,096)

10
A George III coffee pot, Whipham & Wright, London, 1760, with contemporary chasing of trailing flowers, repair at upper handle terminal, 30cm (11¾in), 38oz (1,181gr), *NY 12 Apr*, $1,650 (£1,154)

11
A George III coffee pot, London, 1765, the baluster body engraved with an armorial, maker's mark 'SW', probably that of Samuel Whitford or Samuel White, 24.8cm (9¾in), 25oz 16dwt (802gr), *P 16-23 Oct*, £1,705 ($2,131)

12
A George III coffee pot, Daniel Smith & Robert Sharp, London, 1771, baluster, with fluted carved spout, the foot and cover with gadrooned borders, 26.6cm (10½in), 26oz 17dwt (835gr), *L 25 Oct*, £1,925 ($2,445)

1

2

3

4

5

6

7

8

9

10

11

12

1
A George III hot water jug on lampstand, Rundell, Bridge & Rundell, (Paul Storr), London, 1816, the fluted-vase shaped body with ribbon-tied reeded shoulder, 30.1cm (11⅞in), 61oz 10dwt (1,912gr), *NY 13 Dec,*
$13,750 (£11,555)

2
A George III vase-shaped hot water jug, London, 1785, quite plain above a stepped spreading base, maker's mark 'BM', 29.2cm (11½in), 17oz 12dwt (547gr), *P 17-19 Apr,*
£572 ($824)

3
A George IV baluster coffee pot, London, 1822, crested and moulded with lobes in chevron formation above a spreading foot, gadroon borders, maker's mark 'IW', the handle Hayne & Cater, 24.1cm (9½in), 28oz 12dwt, (889gr), *P 21-24 Feb,*
£396 ($554)

4
A George III vase-shaped hot water jug, apparently John Schofield, London, 1784, engraved with initials within a husk oval, 30.5cm (12in), 23oz (715gr), *L 14 June,*
£1,210 ($1,742)

5
An American coffee pot, S Kirk, Baltimore, 1828, the pear-shaped body chased with flowers between spiral flutes, the duck head spout rising from a bacchante mask, 28cm (11in), 51oz 10dwt (1,601gr), *NY 28 June,*
$1,980 (£1,467)

6
An American coffee pot, John Ewan, Charleston, SC, *c*1825, the baluster form chased with stylized sprays of leaves and flowerheads, 29.4cm (11½in), 38oz 10dwt (1,197gr), *NY 28 June,*
$1,430 (£1,059)

7
A Louis XV coffee pot, Roch-Louis Dany, Paris, 1787, the plain pear shape with fluted covered spout, engraved with a monogram in cartouche, 22cm (8⅝in), 21oz (653gr), *NY 21 June,*
$2,750 (£2,022)

8
A French baluster chocolate pot, Pierre-Bernard Durand, Marseille, 1763, 25.5cm (10in), 36oz (1,120gr), *M 11 Dec,*
FF 44,400 (£3,912; $4,723)

9
A Sicilian coffee pot, Messina, *c*1780, 20cm (7⅞in), 20oz 6dwt (634gr), *F 11 May,*
L 2,938,000 (£1,196; $3,982)

10
A Maltese baluster coffee pot, Aloisio Troisi, *c*1780, 21.2cm (8⅜in), 14oz 6dwt (446gr), *F 3 Oct,*
L 2,800,000 (£1,151; $1,497)

11
An Italian baluster coffee pot, *c*1760, the body and cover spirally fluted, maker's mark 'BR', 25cm (9⅞in), 19oz 6dwt (1,760gr), *F 10 May,*
L 3,500,000 (£1,426); $2,053)

12
An Italian coffee pot, Genoa, 1768, the baluster body and domed foot spirally lobed and ribbed, with a similar spout rising to an animal's head terminal, 31.3cm (12⅜in), 35oz 12dwt (1,110gr), *G 15 May,*
SF 20,900 (£6,276; $8,974)

13
An Italian coffee pot, Genoa, 1768, the baluster body spirally ribbed and fluted, the spout rising to an animal's head terminal, 29.7cm (11¾in), 46oz 6dwt (1,440gr), *L 12 Mar,*
£8,580 ($12,784)

14
An Italian coffee pot, Genoa, 1777, the baluster body spirally fluted, with a matching spout terminating in a bird's head, 27.2cm (10¾in), 30oz 16dwt (960gr), *L 12 Mar,*
£5,720 ($8,523)

15
A Swiss coffee pot, Jean Redart, Neuchatel, *c*1765, 21.5cm (8½in), 17oz (528gr), *NY 13 Dec,*
$3,300 (£2,773)

1   2   3

4   5   6

7   8   9

10   11   12

13   14   15

1

A Swiss ovoid coffee pot, Antoine Charrier, Nyon, c1765, the body on three hoof supports, engraved with armorials at the hinge of the cover, 16.7cm (6⅝in), 14oz 2dwt (440gr), *G 14 Nov*, **SF 19,800 (£6,513; $7,945)**

2

A Portuguese coffee pot, maker's mark 'ALB', Lisbon, c1780, the baluster body with engraved armorial, 30cm (11⅞in), 47oz 10dwt (1,480gr), *G 14 Nov*, **SF 9,900 (£3,075; $4,120)**

3

A German chocolate pot, Esaias Busch III, Augsburg, c1730, the fluted baluster body flat chased with panels of Régence ornament surrounding applied medallions, also armorial engraved, 28cm (11in), 29oz 4dwt (910gr), *G 14 Nov*, **SF 26,400 (£8,199; $10,986)**

4

A German coffee pot, Johan Wilhelm Bode(n), Brunswick, 1769, the compressed pear-shaped body embossed with rocaille cartouches enclosing flowers, 22.3cm (8¾in), 16oz (500gr), *G 14 Nov*, **SF 13,200 (£4,099; $5,493)**

5

A Hungarian coffee pot, Tirnau, c1770, the baluster body of oval outline, monogrammed below a count's coronet, maker's mark possibly that of Mathias Szaczlauer, 20.8cm (8¼in), 14oz 2dwt (440gr), *G 14 Nov*, **SF 6,050 (£1,879; $2,518)**

6

A German baluster coffee pot, Franz Theodor Baltzer, Münster, c1785, the body spirally fluted, flower and fruit finial and moulded covered spout, 20cm (7⅞in), 10oz 4dwt (320gr), *G 15 May*, **SF 5,500 (£1,651; $2,360)**

7

A German matching coffee pot and hot milk jug, Jacob Wilhelm Kolb, Augsburg, 1771-3, together with a matching teapot, c1900, 25.4 and 20.4cm (10 and 8in), 51oz (1,586gr), *NY 13 Dec*, **$3,300 (£2,773)**

8

A Continental hot water jug and hot milk jug, probably Austrian, late 18th cent, of vase form with beaded shoulders and rims, partly engraved with vertical straps, maker's mark 'WN', 31.1 and 25.7cm (12¼ and 10⅛in), 45oz (1,399gr), *NY 23 Oct*, **$880 (£733)**

9

A French coffee pot, Marc-Augustin Lebrun, Paris, c1820, the vase-shaped body on three paw supports headed by anthemions, the spout terminating in a horse's head, 23cm (9in), 14oz 16dwt (463gr), *L 12 Mar*, **£715 ($1,065)**

10

An Italian coffee pot, Turin, c1825, the vase-shaped body on three paw supports, the finial in the form of a bird, 34.4cm (13½in), 33oz 10dwt (1,044gr), *F 11 May*, **L 2,700,000 (£1,100; $1,584)**

11

A German coffee pot, late 19th cent, modelled in the form of a cockerel, 23.2cm (9⅛in), 39oz (1,212gr), *NY 23 Oct*, **$1,760 (£1,467)**

12

A copper and silver 'Turkish-style' coffee pot, American, The Gorham Co, Providence, RI, 1882, of gourd form with elongated neck, silver pellet finial, 32.4cm (12¾in), *NY 17 Nov*, **$357 (£286)**

13

An Italian coffee pot, Milan, c1815, the ovoid body with gadroon borders and griffin finial, the spout terminating in an animal's head applied with a female figure, 31.7cm (12½in), 23oz 2dwt (720gr), *G 14 Nov*, **SF 3,960 (£1,230; $1,648)**

1

2

3

4

5

6

7

8

9

10

11

12

13

1
A George I teapot,
William Gamble, London,
1715, of plain baluster
form on ring foot, with
curved faceted spout and
domed lid, h 16cm (6¼in),
13oz 12dwt (422gr),
L 25 Oct,
£1,980 ($2,515)

2
A George I octagonal
teapot, Thomas Parr I,
London, 1719, engraved
with armorials within a
formal foliate scroll cartouche surmounted by a
shell, 15.8cm (6¼in), 16oz
8dwt (510gr), *L 3 May,*
£7,150 ($10,153)

3
A Maltese teapot, 2nd
quarter 18th cent, the
pear-shaped body ribbed
at intervals, the cover
armorial engraved with
ribbon-bound reeded rim,
maker's mark of Pierre
Brun, h 14.9cm (5⅞in),
19oz 8dwt (605gr), *L 12 Mar,*
£3,080 ($4,589)

4
A George II silver 'Bullet'
teapot, Abraham Buteux,
London, 1729, with
moulded base and partly
faceted leaf-capped spout,
12.1cm (4¾in), 14oz
(435gr), *NY 12 Apr,*
$2,530 (£1,769)

5
A German teapot, Johann
Christian Girschner,
Augsburg, 1763-5, the
pear-shaped body spirally
fluted at intervals,
h 12cm (4¾in), 9oz 12dwt
(300gr), *G 15 May,*
SF 8,250 (£2,477; $3,542)

6
A George II compressed
circular teapot, Aymé
Videau, London, 1747,
the upper and lower
body engraved with rococo
shells, scrolls and flowers
on a linear ground,
h 12cm (4¾in), 26oz 9dwt
(822gr), *L 3 May,*
£1,980 ($2,812)

7
A George II teapot, James
McKenzie, Edinburgh,
1755, of inverted pear-
shape form, the underside
inscribed 'To Sir Harry
and Lady Lauder from
Lord and Lady Forteviot,
a remembrance of a
happy evening, June
3rd 1927', Assay Master
Hugh Gordon, 18oz
7dwt (570gr), *HH 27 Mar,*
£1,430 ($2,131)

8
A George III teapot and
stand, Robert Hennell,
London, the pot 1790,
the stand 1789, engraved
with crests and initials
within cartouches and
formal leaf and wriggle-
work borders, 18oz 10dwt
(575gr), *P 24-27 July,*
£770 ($1,032)

9
An American teapot,
Samuel Williamson, Phila-
delphia, c.1800, engraved
at the base, shoulder and
cover rim with a band of
wrigglework and a band
of bright-cut leaf-tips,
h 16cm (6¼in), 20oz 10dwt
(637gr), *NY 26 Jan,*
$1,320 (£910)

10
A George III teapot,
Frances Purton, London,
1788, bright-cut engraved
with ovals containing
initials, the domed lid
with green-stained ivory
pineapple finial, h 15cm
(6in), 12oz 16dwt (398gr),
L 25 Oct,
£880 ($1,118)

11
A George III drum-
shaped teapot, Louisa
Courtauld & George
Cowles, London, 1772,
engraved with armorials
below an Earl's coronet
added c.1800, 12.6cm (5in),
18oz 2dwt (562gr),
L 12 July,
£1,485 ($2,020)

12
A Danish oval teapot,
Carol Christiaan Hansen,
Aarhus, c.1820, an open-
work gallery around the
domed cover, h 20cm
(7⅞in), 27oz 14dwt (864gr),
A 17 Dec,
Dfl 4,176 (£998; $1,247)

1

2

3

4

5

6

7

8

9

10

11

12

1

A Dutch teapot, A Bonebakker & Zn, Amsterdam, 1872, 8oz 4dwt (256gr), *A 8 Mar,* **Dfl 667 (£153; $227)**

2

A George III rounded oblong teapot and coffee pot en suite, Urquhart & Hart, London, 1806-8, h 14.7 and 23cm (5¾ and 9in), 48oz 9dwt (1,498gr), *C 10 Jan,* **£1,100 ($1,595)**

3

A Dutch 'bullet' teapot, A Bonebakker & Zn, Amsterdam, 1871, with ivory handle, 10oz 14dwt (333gr), *A 8 Mar,* **Dfl 841 (£192; $286)**

4

A George III teapot and stand, Paul Storr, London, 1799, excluding stand h 14.4cm (5⅝in), 18oz (559gr), *NY 23 Oct,* **$2,310 (£1,925)**

5

A teapot and milk jug, John Greville of Norwich, London, 1968, both with hammer finish, 26oz 11dwt (825gr), *L 25 Oct,* **£198 ($252)**

6

A George I tea kettle on lampstand, Thomas Gladwin, London, 1719, engraved with later armorials, h 38.7cm (15¼in), 91oz (2,830gr), *NY 13 Dec,* **$7,700 (£6,471)**

7

A George II rococo tea kettle on lampstand, Eliza Godfrey, London, 1739, the support for the lamp altered at a later date, h 43.2cm (17in), 99oz 10dwt (3,094gr), *NY 13 Dec,* **$7,150 (£6,008)**

8

A George I kettle on lampstand, Humphrey Payne, London, 1730, engraved around the shoulder with strapwork and foliage on a brickwork and diaper ground, detachable burner, h 32.4cm (12¾in), 65oz 10dwt (2,037gr), *NY 12 Apr,* **$3,300 (£2,308)**

9

A George III tea urn, Rundell, Bridge & Rundell (Paul Storr), London, 1809/10, engraved with two sets of armorials, h 38cm (15in), 211oz (6,562gr), *L 22 Nov,* **£23,100 ($30,030)**

10

A German kettle on lampstand, Elimeyer, mid-19th cent, in high rococo revival style, matching lamp, with separate filling plug, h 38cm (15in), 131oz (4,074gr), *NY 23 Oct,* **$2,640 (£2,200)**

11

A George III tea kettle on lampstand, Edward Cornelius Farrell, London, 1817, the kettle Britannia Standard, h 44cm (17¼in), 149oz 17dwt, (4,635gr), *L 22 Nov,* **£4,400 ($3,384)**

12

A George IV tea urn, Rundell, Bridge & Rundell, (John Bridge), London, 1827, detachable heating rod holder with cap, h 38cm (15in), 146oz (4,540gr), *NY 12 Apr,* **$4,950 (£3,462)**

13

A George III tea urn, London, 1768, engraved with armorials surrounded by trailing flowers, the foot now soldered to the body, h 52cm (20½in), 85oz 10dwt (2,659gr), *NY 24 Feb,* **$2,530 (£1,745)**

14

An Austrian coffee urn and stand, Kruntauer, Vienna, 1818, with an animal's head at the terminal of the spigot, the stand with a winged lion mask and paw brackets; and a burner, Vienna, 1819, h 28.7cm (11¼in), 59oz 2dwt (1,840gr), *G 14 Nov,* **SF 6,600 (£2,050; $2,747)**

15

A tea kettle on lampstand, Austrian, c1910, maker's mark crossed hammer and chasing tool over an anvil, h 32.4cm (12¾in), *NY 17-18 Feb,* **$1,760 (£1,239)**

1
A George III four-piece tea set, John Emes, London, 1805, comprising pot, stand, basin and jug, crested and initialled above ring feet, 34oz 10dwt (1,072gr), *P 16-23 Oct*, £1,045 ($1,306)

2
A William IV three-piece tea set, E Barnard & Sons, 1832, the melon pattern bodies ribbed into panels by leafy fronds and chased and applied with trailing blooms, 62oz 9dwt (1,942gr), *C 2-5 Oct*, £715 ($922)

3
An American three-piece tea set with tongs, John Sayre, New York, c 1805, comprising teapot, covered sugar bowl, creamer and tongs, of shaped oval form, engraved with a monogram, teapot 19cm (7½in), 44oz (1,368gr), *NY 26 Jan*, $3,300 (£2,276)

4
A George IV tea urn and teapot, Joseph Angell, London, 1827, and a matching sugar bowl and cover, probably Continental, 19th cent, chased with matted panels of pendent flowers and fruit, 194oz 17dwt, (6,059gr), *L 9 Feb*, £2,860 ($4,010)

5
A George IV three-piece circular tea set, Joseph Angell, London, 1828, the pot 1826, the compressed inverted pear-shaped bodies crested and fluted at intervals, 42oz (1,306gr), *P 21-24 Feb*, £572 ($802)

6
A Victorian silver-gilt bachelor's tea set, John Figg, London, 1865, chased after Teniers with tavern and village scenes, the shell supports and spouts decorated with masks, 25oz 10dwt (793gr), *L 20 Sept*, £990 ($1,287)

7
A William IV four-piece tea set, Charles Fox, London, 1830, the inverted pear-shaped bodies formed from swirling leafage and rocaille motifs overlaid with floral trails, 86oz 14dwt (2,696gr), *C 3-6 July*, £2,365 ($3,193)

8
A Victorian five-piece tea and coffee set, T Wilkinson & Sons, Birmingham, 1864, the coffee pot Martin, Hall & Co Ltd, Sheffield, 1856, 135oz 18dwt (4,226gr), *L 26 Apr*, £2,530 ($3,643)

9
A four-piece tea and coffee set, Edward Barnard & Sons, London, 1865/6, the tapering circular bodies engraved and decorated with stars, honeysuckle and other motifs, the teapot crested, 64oz 2dwt (1,993gr), *L 25 Oct*, £902 ($1,146)

10
A Victorian four-piece tea and coffee set, E Barnard & Sons, London, 1860, of baluster form engraved and wriggle-worked with leafy strap-work motifs, also engraved with crest, initials and motto, the undersides engraved 'Widdowson & Veale/Strand', 74oz 12dwt (2,320gr), *L 15 Mar*, £1,760 ($2,622)

1

2

3

4

5

6

7

8

9

10

1
A French tea set with plated tray, Odiot, Paris, mid-19th cent, the baluster bodies fluted into panels, chased with strapwork cartouches enclosing rocco ornament; the kettle 43.5cm (28in), 196oz 2dwt (6,100gr), *L 9 July*, £2,420 ($3,315)

2
A Victorian baluster four-piece tea and coffee set, D & C Houle, London, 1857, chased with flowers, foliage and vacant scroll cartouches, eagle finials, the milk jug and sugar basin with gilt interiors, 84oz 6dwt (2,621gr), *L 12 July*, £1,595 ($2,169)

3
A Victorian tea and coffee set, Samuel Smily, London, 1865/7/8, the circular bodies with crested scroll cartouches, chased with matted lozenges, the coffee pot stamped 'AB Savory & Sons London', the teapot and sugar basin 'Goldsmiths Alliance Limited Cornhill', 76oz (2,363gr), *L 25 Oct*, £1,595 ($2,026)

4
A French three-piece coffee set with plated tray, Froment-Meurice, Paris, c.1875, in Moorish taste, chased with bands of raffia and vertical pales, tray 68cm (26¾in), 49oz (1,523gr), *NY 18 July*, $1,100 (£839)

5
A Belgian four-piece tea and coffee set, Brussels, c.1868, engraved with bands of scrolling foliage, 66oz 4dwt (2,060gr), *A 16 Oct*, Dfl 5,104 (£1,201; $1,501)

6
An American three-piece tea set, Gale & Stickler, New York, c.1820, of lobed bombé form, with bands of trailing foliage, raised on four ball and claw supports, 22.8cm (9in), 73oz (2,270gr), *NY 24 Feb*, $935 (£645)

7
An American five-piece tea and coffee set, Lows, Ball & Co, Boston, 1846, of tapered octagonal form with moulded borders, the panels engraved with rococo decoration, coffee pot 31.7cm (12½in), 114oz 8dwt (3,557gr), *NY 23 Oct*, $2,640 (£2,200)

8
An American six-piece tea and coffee set, Gorham Mfg Co, Providence, RI, 1906/8, with lobed and fluted bombé bodies, foliate scroll feet; kettle 32.4cm (12¾in), 207oz 10dwt (6,453gr), *NY 24 Feb*, $3,410 (£2,352)

9
An American six-piece tea and coffee set with matching two-handled tray, Gorham Mfg Co, Providence, RI, c.1905, of pear form on domed base, chased with rococo cartouches, tray 76.8cm (30¼in), 309oz (9,610gr), *NY 28 June*, $6,050 (£4,482)

1

2

3

4

5

6

7

8

9

1
An American five-piece tea set and tray, Whiting Manufacturing Co, Providence, RI, c1895, engraved with initials below applied foliate borders; kettle 31.5cm (12½in), 276oz 3dwt (8,580gr), *L 8 Mar*, £2,420 ($3,606)

2
An American six-piece tea and coffee set with matching two-handled tea tray, Tiffany & Co, New York, early 20th cent, chrysanthemum pattern, tray 76.7cm (30¼in), 498oz (15,487gr), *NY 28 June*, $17,600 (£13,037)

3
An American five-piece tea and coffee service, Tiffany & Co, New York, c1875, of Indo-Persian design, embossed and chased with flowers on a matted ground, ivory supports; coffee pot 25.4cm (10in), 86oz 4dwt (2,680gr), *NY 18 July*, $2,420 (£1,847)

4
An American six-piece tea and coffee set with matching two-handled tray, Gorham Mfg Co, Providence, RI, 1916, retailed by Bigelow, Kennard & Co, coffee pot 23.5cm (9¼in), tray 76cm (29⅞in), 288oz 10dwt (8,972gr), *NY 26 Jan*, $5,170 (£3,566)

5
A three-piece tea set, American, Tiffany & Co, 1902-7, each piece incorporating the same monogram, overlaid with vines, leaves and insects, *C 3-6 July*, £2,200 ($2,984)

6
An oblong tea tray, American, Tiffany & Co, 1902-7, with hammered finish, initialled centre in relief with a foliate monogram, 70.3cm (27¾in), *C 3-6 July*, £2,640 ($3,581)

7
An American six-piece tea and coffee set and two-handled tea tray, Tiffany & Co, New York, 20th cent, of rectangular form with incurved angles and faceted spouts, coffee pot 21.6cm (8½in), tray 77.5cm (30½in), 305oz 10dwt (9,501gr), *NY 26 Jan*, $6,710 (£4,628)

8
An Art Noveau six-piece tea and coffee service, American, The Gorham Co, Providence, RI, Martelé, c1905, all embossed and chased with flowers and leaves against hammered surface, ivory supports, *NY 11/12 May*, $8,250 (£5,978)

1

2

3

5 (*tea set*), 6 (*tray*)
7

8

1
A George I milk jug,
Samuel Margas, London,
1716, pear form with
moulded rim and
spreading base, repairs
to foot and at rim,
12.3cm (4⅞in), 4oz 10dwt
(140gr), *NY 13 Dec,*
$1,100 (£924)

2
A George II octagonal
cream jug, William
Garrard, London, 1737,
baluster shaped with
protruding lip, 10cm
(4in), 2oz 10dwt (78gr),
L 3 May,
£3,520 ($4,998)

3
A George II inverted pear-
shaped milk jug, John
Jacob, London, 1744,
chased with flowers,
foliage and a vacant
rococo cartouche, 12.5cm
(4¾in), 5oz 17dwt (181gr),
L 14 June,
£528 ($760)

4
A George III milk jug,
Henry Chawner, London,
1788, of fluted and
panelled oval vase form
on matching pedestal
base, 13.6cm (5⅜in), 5oz
6dwt (164gr), *NY 13 Dec,*
$550 (£462)

5
An American milk jug,
Lewis Buichle, Baltimore,
*c.*1800, of helmet form on
square pedestal base,
engraved with mono-
grams, 17.2cm (6¾in),
5oz (155gr), *NY 26 Jan,*
$1,100 (£759)

6
An American milk jug,
Lancaster, Pa, *c.*1800, of
baluster form with
spreading foot, shaped
rim, maker's mark 'LH'
possibly Lewis Heck,
14cm (5½in), 4oz 10dwt
(140gr), *NY 26 Jan,*
$550 (£379)

7
A George III helmet-
shaped cream jug, Henry
Chawner, London, 1787,
the panelled body
engraved with a cartouche
and floral swags, 14.5cm
(5¾in), 4oz 6dwt (135gr),
JHB 2 May,
R 550 (£309; $433)

8
An American milk jug,
Bartholomew Le-Roux,
New York, *c.*1760, of
pear form with wavy
rim, raised on three hoof
feet headed by shells,
two rim splits, 11.1cm
(4⅜in), 5oz 8dwt (168gr),
NY 26 Jan,
$2,530 (£1,745)

9
An American milk jug,
Nicholas Roosevelt, New
York, *c.*1760, of pear
form with wavy rim,
raised on three shell feet
repairs to two feet and
minor rim splits, 11.1cm
(4⅜in), 4oz 15dwt
(147gr), *NY 26 Jan,*
$1,760 (£1,214)

10
A George III milk jug,
Abstainando King,
London, 1818, the oblong
baluster body engraved
with a crest, gilt interior,
11cm (4¼in), 6oz 14dwt
(208gr), *L 29 Nov,*
£231 ($280)

11
A George IV milk jug,
Charles Fox, London,
1825, of urn shape chased
with swags of flowers,
16cm (6¼in), 10oz 10dwt
(326gr), *NY 21 June,*
$605 (£445)

12
A George IV silver-gilt
milk jug, Storr &
Mortimer, (Paul Storr),
London, 1820, partly fluted
pear form, the body
chased with trailing
flowers and foliage and
scrollwork, engraved with
a Royal Ducal Badge,
12.7cm (5in), 10oz (311gr),
NY 23 Oct,
$2,750 (£2,292)

2

3

1

4

5   6

9 (hidden)

5 (hidden)

7

8   9

10

11   12

1

A Cape tea caddy, Johan Anton Bünning, c 1760, the body of bombé outline with chamfered corners, h 6.5cm (2⅝in), 4oz 16dwt (150gr), *JHB 2 May,* **R 4,800 (£2,697; $3,771)**

2

A pair of George II tea caddies and a sugar vase and cover, Edward Aldridge & John Stamper, London, 1756, the fitted fishskin case with plated mounts, handle and feet, 16.5 and 15.2cm (6½ and 6in), 27oz 1dwt (841gr), *L 14 June,* **£2,145 ($3,089)**

3

A pair of octagonal tea caddies and a circular sugar bowl and cover, the caddies, John Farnell, 1725, the bowl William Justis, 1749, the caddies 13cm (5in), the bowl 9.5cm (3¾in), 24oz 14dwt (768gr), *L 14 June,* **£3,410 ($4,910)**

4

A pair of George III silver-gilt tea caddies, London, 1770-2, in a wood-lined tortoiseshell and ivory case with silver-gilt keyhole mount, possibly Edward Darvill, w 9.4cm (3¾in), 19oz (590gr), *L 3 May,* **£2,420 ($3,184)**

5

A pair of George I oblong caddies, Edward Gibbon, London, 1720, the sliding shoulder plates with detachable bun covers, 12cm (4¾in), 13oz 18dwt (432gr), *L 20 Sept,* **£1,760 ($2,288)**

6

A Flemish tea caddy, c 1725, flat-chased with Régence ornament, maker's mark only rubbed, 6oz (189gr), *A 7 June,* **Dfl 3,200 (£749; $973)**

7

A pair of George III tea caddies, William Vincent, London, 1772, the bodies of shaped square section chased with trailing blooms, incorporating engraved armorials, 13.5cm (5¼in), 22oz 14dwt (706gr), *P 16-23 Oct,* **£1,320 ($1,650)**

8

A set of three George III vase-shaped tea caddies, Thomas Heming, London, 1772, decorated with plain reserves bordered by matted bands, goat's mask handles, 20.7 and 17.5cm (8¼ and 6⅞in), 29oz 6dwt (911gr), *L 9 Feb,* **£1,540 ($2,159)**

9

A George III tea caddy, Robert Hennell, London, 1781, of oval straight-sided form, bright-cut with borders of formal foliage, 11.4cm (4½in), 12oz 10dwt (388gr), *NY 12 Apr,* **$2,530 (£1,769)**

10

A George III tea caddy, William Plummer, London, 1789, rectangular form with incurved fluted angles, bright-cut borders, 14.3cm (5⅝in), 15oz (466gr), *NY 23 Oct,* **$2,090 (£1,742)**

11

A George III tea caddy, Henry Chawner, London, 1791, 15cm (6in), 12oz 4dwt (379gr), *L 29 Nov,* **£1,265 ($1,531)**

12

A George III oblong two-compartment tea caddy, John Emes, London, 1806, pricked and bright-cut with a band of quatrefoils and scrolling foliage, 19cm (7½in), 21oz 4dwt (659gr), *L 20 Sept,* **£825 ($1,072)**

13

A William IV oblong tea caddy, Edinburgh, 1835, flat chased with flowers, foliage and scrolls on a matted ground, maker's mark TAF, 20.2cm (8in), 29oz 14dwt (923gr), *L 12 July,* **£770 ($1,047)**

14

A Victorian parcel-gilt tea caddy, Joseph Angell, London, 1860, and a die-stamped shell-shaped caddy spoon, George Unite, Birmingham, 1860, engraved with rich scroll and strapwork cartouches applied with cast vignettes, 19.8cm (7¾in), 33oz 9dwt (1,040gr), *L 3 May,* **£2,310 ($3,280)**

1   2
3   4
5   6   7   8
9   10   11
12   13   14

1
A George III sweatmeat basket, Peter and Ann Bateman, London, 1794, the boat-shaped body initialled and bright-cut engraved with scrolls and foliage, gilt interior, w 16cm (6¼in), 7oz (220gr), *JHB 2 May*, *R* 650 (£365; $511)

2
A George III sugar basket and milk jug, Hester Bateman, London, 1784/9, the jug of helmet form on square pedestal base, basket 14.6cm (5¾in), jug h 17.8cm (7in), 9oz 10dwt (295gr), *NY 21 June*, $1,210 (£890)

3
A George III cream pail, London, 1767, the tapering cylindrical body pierced with panels of scrolls below the rope rim, blue glass liner, 7cm (2¾in), 2oz (65gr), *JHB 2 May*, *R* 650 (£365; $511)

4
A Victorian sweetmeat basket, E C Brown, London, 1866, of inverted pear-shaped form, the openwork body pierced with tracery, 11.5cm (4½in), 5oz 8dwt (167gr), *C 13-16 Mar*, £165 ($246)

5
A Jamaican circular sugar bowl and cover, Anthony Danvers, Kingston, c1765, embossed with flowers and scrolls, crested and initialled, 14.5cm (5¾in), 12oz (375gr), *L 9 July*, £858 ($1,175)

6
An Italian covered sugar bowl, Turin, c 1760, control marks of Giovannia Battista Carron and Carlo Micha, w 10cm (4in), 5oz 2dwt (160gr), *L 12 Mar*, £2,970 ($4,425)

7
A French covered sugar bowl, Charles-Denis Bellon, Marseille, 1777, the baluster form decorated with foliage and cartouches, with a strawberry finial, 13.8cm (5½in), 15oz 8dwt (480gr), *M 11 Dec*, FF 24,420 (£2,152; $2,598)

8
An American sugar bowl and cover, c1765, of inverted pear shape, the wide everted rim scalloped and engraved with running tendrils, maker's mark 'JH', 11.7cm (4⅝in), 13oz 6dwt (413gr), *NY 26 Jan*, $4,070 (£2,807)

9
An American sugar bowl and cover, Joseph & Nathaniel Richardson, Philadelphia, c1780, of inverted pear form on a pedestal base, monogrammed, 15.8cm (6½in), 11oz (342gr), *NY 28 June*, $6,600 (£4,890)

10
An American sugar urn and cover, Joseph Richardson Jr, Philadelphia, c1795, with beaded borders and engraved with contemporary monogram, 26cm (10¼in), 14oz (435gr), *NY 28 June*, $1,760 (£1,304)

11
An American sugar vase and cover, Robert Swan, Philadelphia, c1795, with beaded borders, engraved with foliate monogram, pierced gallery at the shoulder, 28cm (11in), 17oz 8dwt (541gr), *NY 26 Jan*, $3,575 (£2,465)

12
A French silver-gilt bowl and cover on stand, Jean-Baptiste-Claude Odiot, Paris, 1819-38, the incurved neck applied with medusa heads, paterae and tendrils, w 23.2cm (9⅛in), 38oz (1,181gr), *NY 21 June*, $5,225 (£3,842)

13
A Swedish sugar box, Zethelius, Stockholm, 1829, of oval form partly chased with lobes and with gadroon and leaf-tip borders, 19cm (7½in), 23oz (715gr), *NY 13 Dec*, $1,320 (£1,109)

14
A Victorian silver-gilt sugar basket and cover, Edward Barnard & Sons, London, 1844; and a sugar spoon, CT & G Fox, London, 1843, 19.5cm (7¾in), 24oz 6dwt (755gr), *L 22 Nov*, £2,310 ($3,003)

1
A Norwegian circular two-handled bowl and cover, probably Christian Madsen of Hisoy, c.1760, spirally ribbed and fluted on three hoof supports, maker's mark 'CM', h 14.8cm (5⅞in), 18oz (560gr), *G 15 May*, **SF 9,900 (£2,972; $4,249)**

2
A German oval bowl, Johann George Blanckert, Konigsberg, 1728, stamped with armorials and monogrammed, the bowl fluted at intervals, with a Swedish stand, Gustaf Möllenborg, Stockholm, 1832, the bowl w 19.3cm (7⅝in), the stand w 23cm (9in), 27oz 2dwt (845gr), *L 12 Mar*, **£2,035 ($3,034)**

3
A French spice box, Jacques-Louis Bouillette, Paris, 1723, with three compartments, with gadrooned border, the cover engraved with armorials, w 12cm (4¾in), 12oz 4dwt (380gr), *M 11 Dec*, **FF 99,900 (£8,802; $10,628)**

4
A Latvian spice box and spoon, Otto Friedrich Brinck, Goldingen, c.1774, with three compartments and centrally hinged lids, with monogram, the spoon unmarked, w 12.7cm (5in), 7oz (220gr), *G 14 Nov*, **SF 4,400 (£1,366; $1,831)**

5
A German spice box and cover, Johann Heinrich Bahlsen (Sr), Hildesheim, 1785, of oblong form, ribbed and fluted at the angles, w 6.2cm (2½in), 2oz (63gr), *G 14 Nov*, **SF 3,740 (£1,161; $1,556)**

6
A Swiss circular toilet box, Carl Jenner, Bern, c.1760, the plain body with detachable lid, armorial engraved within a rococo cartouche, 7.4cm (2⅞in), 7oz 6dwt (230gr), *G 14 Nov*, **SF 8,250 (£2,562; $3,433)**

7
A George II chamber pot, David Willaume, London, 1744, with rolled rim and scroll handle, engraved with the arms of George Booth, 2nd Earl of Warrington, d 18cm (7in), 33oz 18dwt (1,054gr), *L 14 June*, **£10,450 ($15,048)**

8
A French shaped circular toilet box, François-Thomas Germain, Paris, 1750, the moulded body embossed and tooled with floral festoons, d 9cm (3⅝in), 8oz 16dwt (275gr), *G 15 May*, **SF 25,300 (£7,597; $10,863)**

9
Two Dutch biscuit boxes, Jacob Hendrik Stellingwerf, Amsterdam, 1802, one round the other rectangular, both with beaded borders, d 13cm (5⅛in) & 15cm (5⅞in), 28oz 12dwt (890gr), *A 16 Oct*, **Dfl 5,800 (£1,365; $1,706)**

10
A Dutch tobacco box, Wijnand Warneke, Amsterdam, 1776, the oval ogee body embossed with foliate festoons supporting portrait medallions, w 16cm (6⅜in), 17oz (531gr), *L 9 July*, **£2,530 ($3,466)**

11
A Dutch tobacco box and matching brazier, Rotterdam, 1835/6, the lobed bodies on rectangular bases, the brazier with copper liner, 30oz 10dwt (950gr), *A 16 Oct*, **Dfl 3,480 (£820; $1,024)**

1

2

3

4

5

6

7

8

9

10

11

1
An American bowl,
Henricus Boelen II,
New York, c.1730, of
plain hemispherical form
with slightly everted lip,
d 16.5cm (6½in), 12oz
(373gr), *NY 26 Jan,*
$12,100 (£8,345)

2
An American bowl,
Samuel Casey, South
Kingston, RI, c.1760,
circular with flaring
sides, d 14.5cm (5¾in),
8oz 4dwt (255gr),
NY 28 June,
$15,400 (£11,407)

3
A George III bowl, John
Robins, London, 1785, of
hemispherical form,
engraved with a con-
temporary foliate car-
touche enclosing a
monogram, d 14.6cm
(5¾in), 12oz (373gr),
NY 23 Oct,
$660 (£550)

4
A George III punch bowl,
John Robins, London,
1786, the circular partly
fluted bowl raised on a
pedestal foot, bright-cut
with swags of flowers,
d 30.5cm (12in), 87oz
(2,721gr), *NY 13 Dec,*
$7,700 (£6,471)

5
A Swiss circular bowl,
Ludwig Friedrich
Brugger, (Bern), c.1805,
the body engraved at the
lip, on a ribbed spreading
base, d 20.4cm (8in), 18oz
8dwt (575gr), *G 14 Nov,*
SF 4,400 (£1,366; $1,831)

6
A French two-handled
small bowl, Marie-
Joseph-Gabriel Genu,
Paris, 1798-1809, applied
at the shoulder with a
band of flowerheads, gilt
interior, d 9.8cm (3⅞in),
8oz 15dwt (272gr),
NY 21 June,
$550 (£404)

7
An American centrepiece
bowl, S Kirk & Son,
Baltimore Md, c.1900,
circular, with broad
everted scalloped rim,
embossed and chased
with flowers on a matted
ground, d 42cm (16½in),
98oz 10dwt (3,063gr),
NY 26 Jan,
$1,980 (£1,366)

8
An American centrepiece
bowl, the Gorham Co,
Providence RI, Martelé,
1898-1904, 59.1cm
(23¼in), 126oz (3,918gr),
NY 11-12 May,
$12,100 (£8,768)

9
A pair of American tazze,
Tiffany & Co, New York,
1907-47, gilt centres,
25.4cm (10in), 48oz 16dwt
(1,517gr), *NY 18 July,*
$1,210 (£924)

10
An American bowl,
Tiffany & Co, New York,
c.1915, of shallow
circular form with
moulded rim, the centre
etched with a fantastic
bird and stylised foliage,
d 34cm (13⅜in), 35oz
(1,088gr), *NY 18 July,*
$770 (£588)

11
A punch bowl, George
Fox, London, 1893,
d 26.7cm (10½in), 53oz
4dwt (1,654gr), *L 9 Feb,*
£858 ($1,203)

12
A boat-shaped fruit bowl,
Joseph Rodgers & Son,
Sheffield, 1897, w 51.5cm
(20¼in), 104oz 19dwt
(3,263gr), *L 12 July,*
£2,310 ($3,142)

13
An American bowl, J E
Caldwell & Co,
Philadelphia, c.1901,
d 25.8cm (10⅛in), 28oz
10dwt (886gr), *NY 28 June,*
$1,760 (£1,304)

14
A circular rose bowl,
marks for London, 1983,
d 30.5cm (12in), 50oz
16dwt (1,579gr), *C 1-3 May,*
£539 ($755)

15
A replica of the Warwick
vase, West & Son,
London, 1903, 46.5cm
(18¼in), 230oz 2dwt
(7,156gr), *C 10 Jan,*
£4,400 ($6,380)

1
Two identical George II cake baskets, Paul de Lamerie, London, 1737/40, of shaped oval design, the rims and bases cast, pierced and chased with sprays of flowers, w 37cm (14⅝in), 204oz (6,360gr), *M 26 June,* **FF 2,331,000 (£200,086; $272,632)**

2
A George II silver cake basket, Richard Williams, Dublin, c 1750, the shaped swing handle rising from the mouths of scaly monsters, engraved with crest, 38.2cm (15in), 62oz (1,928gr), *NY 13 Dec,* **$6,875 (£5,777)**

3
A George III cake basket, Alexander Johnston, London, 1760, oval with gadroon, shell and foliate open scrollwork rim, the sides pierced, 35.5cm (14in), 39oz 10dwt (1,228gr), *NY 23 Oct,* **$2,750 (£2,292)**

4
A George III cake basket, William Plummer, London, 1791, oval with gadroon rim and reeded swing handle, 39.7cm (15⅝in), 43oz (1,337gr), *NY 13 Dec,* **$1,760 (£1,479)**

5
A George III oblong cake basket, Dorothy Langlands, Newcastle, 1811, with swing handle, engraved with bright-cut bands and foliage, w 33cm (13in), 33oz 2dwt (1,029gr), *C 16 Oct,* **£396 ($507)**

6
A George IV cake basket, James McKay, Edinburgh, 1826, the gadroon rim with spiral and scallop shells, swing handle, 36.2cm (14¼in), 39oz (1,213gr), *NY 24 Feb,* **$1,320 (£910)**

7
A George III oval basket, John Houle, London, 1814, the centre engraved with contemporary armorials, the swing handle with aquatic monster terminals, w 39cm (15¼in), 85oz 9dwt (2,657gr), *L 3 May,* **£7,480 ($10,622)**

8
A George IV silver-gilt oval cake basket, Rundell Bridge & Rundell, (Philip Rundell) London, 1822, the centre engraved with the Percy badge within the Garter motto and below a ducal coronet, w 35.5cm (13¾in), 39oz 10dwt (1,228gr), *L 3 May,* **£7,480 ($10,622)**

9
An American cake basket, Fletcher & Gardiner, Philadelphia, c 1820, cornucopia handles capped by acanthus and centred by a flowerhead, 38.4cm (15⅛in), 47oz (1,461gr), *NY 28 June,* **$6,325 (£4,685)**

10
A pair of oval sweetmeat baskets, S J Philips, London, 1909/11, the slightly baluster sides pierced and engraved with entwined ovals overlaid with swags, w 22.5cm (8¾in), 19oz 15dwt (614gr), *C 10 Jan,* **£605 ($877)**

11
An oval fruit basket, Mappin & Webb, Sheffield, 1898, with swing handle and pierced and stamped floral decoration, w 31.2cm (12¼in), 24oz 7dwt (757gr), *C 17-23 May,* **£264 ($383)**

12
A pair of Austro-Hungarian boat-shaped baskets, Prague, late 19th/early 20th cent, silver-coloured metal, one unmarked, the other maker's mark 'SB', some breaks in castings, 30.3cm (12in), 52oz 13dwt (1,637gr), *L 8 Mar,* **£550 ($820)**

1
A German sweetmeat dish, Augsburg, c1700, of shaped oval form, the centre embossed with a family in an open carriage, 16.2cm (6⅜in), 4oz (124gr), *NY 13 Dec,* $1,760 (£1,479)

2
A Commonwealth circular sweetmeat dish, London, 1654, punched with flowerheads and other beaded motifs, shell grips, maker's mark indecipherable, d 15.2cm (6in), 4oz 1dwt (125gr), *L 14 June,* £1,650 ($2,376)

3
A Charles II porringer, William Ramsay, Newcastle, c1678, the lower body flat chased with blooms, scroll handles, h 6cm (2¼in), 2oz 9dwt (76gr), *L 20 Sept,* £418 ($543)

4
An American porringer, Benjamin Burt, Boston, c1760, the keyhold handle engraved with initials, d 13cm (5⅛in), 7oz 10dwt (233gr), *NY 26 Jan,* $1,870 (£1,289)

5
An American porringer, Daniel Henchman, Boston, c1760, with keyhold handle, d 12.7cm (5in), 8oz (248gr), *NY 26 Jan,* $2,420 (£1,669)

6
An American two-handled porringer, Simeon Soumaine, New York, c1720, the flat shaped handles pierced with a scroll pattern, 27cm (10⅝in), 12oz (373gr), *NY 26 Jan,* $27,500 (£18,966)

7
A French ecuelle and cover, I A Durand, Bayonne, c1730, d 17.5cm (6⅞in), 22oz 10dwt (700gr), *M 11 Dec,* FF 22,200 (£1,956; $2,362)

8
A Louis XV ecuelle and cover, André Tudier, Béziers, Jurisdiction of Montpellier, 1744-50, each handle cast and chased with a winged full face mask, d 18cm (7⅛in), 27oz (840gr), *M 26 June,* FF 38,850 (£3,335; $4,544)

9
A German silver-gilt circular ecuelle, cover and stand, FriedrichSchwester-müller II, the stand, Johann Lotter II, Augsburg, 1745-7, d 19.7cm (7¾in), 17oz (530gr), *G 15 May,* SF 17,600 (£5,333; $7,626)

10
An Italian circular ecuelle and cover, Turin, c1775, the cast openwork handles decorated with scrolls and rocaille ornament, control marks of Bartolomeo Pagliani and Bartolomeo Bernardi, w 28.7cm (11¼in), 20oz 10dwt (638gr), *L 12 Mar,* £3,850 ($5,741)

11
A French silver-gilt christening set, Sixte-Simon Rion, Paris, c1815, comprising a christening cup and cover, a fork and spoon, h 27cm (10⅝in), 39oz 14dwt (1,235gr), *M 11 Dec,* FF 46,620 (£4,107; $4,959)

1

2

3

4

5

6

7

8

9

10

11

1
A French sauce-boat, Marc Bazille, Montpellier, c.1756, with moulded rim, engraved with armorials, w 22.5cm (8⅞in), 14oz 6dwt (445gr), *M 11 Dec,*
FF 53,280 (£4,694; $5,626)

2
A French sauce-boat, Jacques Favre, Paris, 1774, oval, engraved with armorials, the base and rim with foliate scroll borders, w 21.2cm (8¼in), 20oz (625gr), *M 11 Dec,*
FF 38,850 (£3,423; $4,073)

3
A pair of Belgian double-lipped sauce-boats, Mons, 1754, of lobed and ribbed bombé form, moulded rims, maker's mark 'DI', 20.2cm (8in), 25oz 10dwt (793gr), *NY 21 June,*
$4,950 (£3,640)

4
An English oval sauce-boat, c.1740, chased with foliage on a matted ground flanking two crested rococo cartouches, the handle formed by a mythological winged beast, unmarked, 18cm (7in), 15oz 11dwt (483gr), *L 3 May,*
£3,410 ($4,842)

5
A pair of George II oval sauce-boats, Frederick Kandler, London, 1747, helmet shaped, engraved with armorials within a rococo cartouche, 21cm (8¼in), 48oz (1,500gr), *M 26 June,*
FF 31,080 (£2,668; $3,682)

6
A pair of George III sauce-boats, possibly John Swift, London, 1760, the oval bodies chased with trailing flowers, retailer's mark of Gale, Wood & Hughes, New York, c.1845, 18.7cm (7⅜in), 27oz 5dwt (847gr), *NY 28 June,*
$1,980 (£1,467)

7
A pair of George III sauce-boats, Alexander Johnston, London, 1764, of oval bombé form on pedestal bases, small crack in one stem, 20.3cm (8in), 28oz (870gr), *NY 12 Apr,*
$2,200 (£1,538)

8
A pair of George II sauce-boats, George Methuen, London, 1748, with shaped borders, engraved with armorials, 21.3cm (8⅜in), 27oz (839gr), *NY 13 Dec,*
$4,400 (£3,697)

9
Four George III oval sauce-boats, Thomas Heming, London, 1780, the bodies engraved with a widow's coat of arms below beaded borders, w 17.4cm (7in), 39oz 15dwt (1,236gr), *C 2-5 Oct,*
£2,200 ($2,838)

10
A pair of American sauce-boats, Joseph & Nathaniel Richardson, Philadelphia, c.1780, raised on three shell and hoof feet, the sides engraved c.1840, one with lead solder repair at handle, 16.5cm (6½in), 18oz (559gr), *NY 28 June,*
$6,325 (£4,685)

11
A pair of George III sauce-boats, William Abdy, London, 1819, decorated with slight wrigglework borders, 22.3cm (8¾in), 31oz 4dwt (970gr), *P 24-27 July,*
£968 ($1,292)

12
A pair of early Victorian oval sauce-boats, Storr & Mortimer, (Paul Storr), London, 1838, one stamped Storr & Mortimer, the bodies crested below reeded foliate borders, w 21cm (8¼in), 38oz 12dwt (1,200gr), *C 2-5 Oct,*
£7,700 ($9,933)

1   2

3   4   5

6   7

8   9

10   11

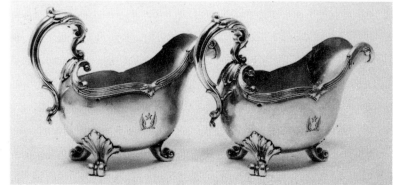

12

1

A pair of George III sauce tureens and covers, Paul Storr, London, 1799, ropework borders centred on each side with an acanthus leaf, 23.2cm (9⅛in), 40oz 8dwt (1,256gr), *NY 13 Dec,* $6,600 (£5,546)

2

A pair of George III oval sauce tureens, covers and stands, Sebastian & James Crespell, London, 1774, each engraved twice with armorials, w 23.6cm (9¼in), 57oz 10dwt (1,788gr), *L 15 Mar,* £4,180 ($6,232)

3

A pair of George III oval sauce-boats, Wakelin & Garrard, London, 1800, the detachable domed covers, crested below urn finials, w 22.3cm (8¾in), 43oz 14dwt (1,359gr), *P 17-19 Apr,* £2,420 ($3,492)

4

A pair of Sheffield Plate sauce tureens and covers, c.1810, oval, gadroon rims and leafy handles, the domed covers also crested, w 20cm (8in), *L 29 Nov,* £528 ($639)

5

A pair of Sheffield Plate shaped oval sauce tureens, c.1830, the melon pattern bodies engraved with a coat of arms and motto, 22.2cm (8¾in), *C 2-5 Oct,* £792 ($1,022)

6

A set of four George III sauce tureens and covers, Benjamin Smith II, London, 1807, the circular bodies with reeded loop handles, h 17.5cm (7in), 126oz 10dwt (3,934gr), *L 22 Nov,* £6,600 ($8,580)

7

A set of four George III sauce tureens and covers, Benjamin & James Smith, London, 1810, the oblong bodies engraved with a crest within baroque scalework and foliate cartouche, the finials Phillip Cornman, 19.7cm (7¾in), 127oz 18dwt (3,977gr), *L 25 Oct,* £5,060 ($6,426)

8

A pair of George III sauce tureens and covers, London, 1809, maker's mark 'SH', 18.5cm (7¼in), 29oz (902gr), *NY 23 Oct,* $1,650 (£1,375)

9

A George II oval soup tureen and cover, George Wickes, London, 1741, engraved on each side with contemporary armorials within a scrolling foliate cartouche, 43cm (16½in), 109oz 8dwt (3,402gr), *L 9 Feb,* £18,150 ($25,414)

10

A George II soup tureen and cover, William Cripps, London, 1750/1, w 36cm (18in), 160oz (5,000gr), *L 22 Nov,* £8,800 ($11,440)

11

A pair of French silver tureen stands, Paris, 1762-8, the high reeded rim wrapped with matted leaves, the centre engraved with armorials, 57.5cm (22⅝in), 206oz 10dwt (6,422gr), *NY 13 Dec,* $5,500 (£4,622)

12

A George III soup tureen, cover and stand, Daniel Smith & Robert Sharp, London, 1763, stand 37.8cm (14¾in), 111oz (3,452gr), *NY 13 Dec,* $8,250 (£6,933)

13

A George III oval soup tureen and cover, Parker & Wakelin, London, 1772, w 39.5cm (15½in), 87oz 10dwt (2,721gr), *L 15 Mar,* £3,850 ($5,740)

14

A German oval soup tureen and cover, Johann Jacob Muller, Berlin, c.1790, gilt interior, 34.3cm (13½in), 75oz (2,332gr), *NY 23 Oct,* $1,650 (£1,375)

15

A French soup tureen, cover and liner, Roch-Louis Dany, Paris, 1786, and a stand, Puiforcat, Paris, c.1880, w 46cm (18⅛in), 152oz 14dwt (4,750gr), *G 14 Nov,* **SF 19,800 (£6,149; $8,240)**

1

A George III soup tureen and cover, William Burwash & Richard Sibley, London, 1805, gadroon borders, engraved on one side with a crest, 45.7cm (18in), 121oz 10dwt (3,778gr), *NY 12 Apr,* $3,960 (£2,769)

2

A George IV soup tureen and cover, Paul Storr, London, 1820, engraved on one side with armorials, gadroon rim with acanthus-flanked shells at intervals, 40.6cm (16in), 129oz (4,011gr), *NY 12 Apr,* $18,700 (£13,077)

3

A Victorian soup tureen, cover and liner, John Samuel Hunt, London, 1851, the ribbed oval body with shell and foliate rim, also stamped Hunt & Roskell, late Storr, Mortimer & Hunt, w 41.5cm (16¼in), 131oz 10dwt (4,089gr), *L 25 Oct,* £4,620 ($5,867)

4

A William IV soup tureen and cover, Robert Hennell II, London, 1835, in the form of the Warwick vase, h 37.5cm (14¾in), 191oz (5,940gr), *NY 21 June,* $6,050 (£4,449)

5

A Sicilian soup tureen and cover, Catania, 1812, of shaped oval bombé form with moulded rim, maker's mark 'SC, 38.7cm (15¼in), 134oz (4,167gr), *NY 21 June,* $9,900 (£7,279)

6

An Italian soup tureen and cover, Pietro Paolo Spagna, Rome, *c* 1825, of circular form with ribbed body and fluted cover, the finial in the form of a cabbage, gilt interior, d 28cm (11in), 115oz 8dwt (3,592gr), *F 11 May,* L 8,800,000 (£3,584; $5,162)

7

An American soup tureen and cover, Tiffany & Co, New York, *c*.1865, of oval form, decorated with paterae, 39.4cm (15½in), 69oz (2,145gr), *NY 26 Jan,* $1,760 (£1,214)

8

An American soup tureen and cover, J E Caldwell & Co, Philadelphia, *c* 1875, of boat shape with scroll-chased ring handles, raised stag finial, lacking one antler, 39.4cm (15½in), 91oz (2,830gr), *NY 28 June,* $1,980 (£1,466)

9

An American soup tureen and cover, Dominick & Haff, Newark and New York, 1888, of oval bombé form on four scrolled supports, embossed and chased overall, 31.8cm (12½in), 52oz (1,617gr), *NY 23 Oct,* $1,320 (£1,100)

10

A Spanish soup tureen, cover, liner and mirror plateau, *c*1970, oval, with cast cherub handles, the sides decorated with foliage and stylised flowers, silver coloured metal, the plateau 57cm (22½in), the tureen 179oz 19dwt (5,596gr), *L 8 Nov,* £2,310 ($3,072)

1

2

3

4

5

6

7

8

9

10

1

A pair of Swiss cushion-shaped entrée dishes, Jean Daniel Barde, Geneva, c.1760, the sides ribbed at intervals below the shaped moulded borders, w 25cm (9⅞in), 51oz 2dwt (1,590gr), *G 14 Nov,* **SF 14,300 (£4,440; $5,950)**

2

A pair of George III entrée dishes and covers, Thomas Heming, London, 1779, 28.9cm (11⅜in), 65oz (2,021gr) *NY 12 Apr,* **$3,740 (£2,615)**

3

A pair of George III entrée dishes, Thomas Jones, Dublin, 1775, engraved with a crest below earl's coronet, one with rim split, 27.6cm (10⅞in), 43oz (1,337gr), *NY 13 Dec,* **$2,200 (£1,849)**

4

Four George III rectangular entrée dishes and covers, Paul Storr, London, 1805, w 31cm (12¼in), 244oz (7,588gr), *C 2-5 Oct,* **£9,900 ($12,771)**

5

A pair of George IV covered entrée dishes on Sheffield plated warming stands, Richard Sibley, London, 1820, the stands, Matthew Boulton & Co, 29.8cm (11¾in), 33oz (1,026gr), *NY 13 Apr,* **$3,960 (£2,769)**

6

A set of four George IV circular vegetable dishes and covers, William Elliott, London, 1823, the handles with maker's mark 'WM', d 26.5cm (10½in), 194oz 17dwt (6,059gr), *L 15 Mar,* **£4,290 ($6,396)**

7

A set of four George III entrée dishes and covers with Sheffield Plate warming stands, Rundell, Bridge & Rundell, (Paul Storr), London, 1813, one patera by James Barber & William Whitwell, York, c.1815, detachable liners by Matthew Boulton & Co, 32cm (12½in), 310oz (9,614gr), *NY 13 Dec,* **$46,200 (£38,824)**

8

A pair of George IV shaped oblong entrée dishes and covers, Thomas James & Nathaniel Creswick Sheffield, 1827, w 34cm (13½in), 122oz 17dwt (3,820gr), *L 14 June,* **£2,200 ($3,168)**

9

A pair of William IV melon pattern entrée dishes and covers, W K Reid, London, 1830, the shaped oblong bases applied with massive gadroon borders, w 33cm (13in), 124oz (3,856gr), *C 3-6 July,* **£2,310 ($3,118)**

10

A set of four Sheffield Plate entrée dishes, covers and heater bases, c.1820, the covers engraved with armorials, w 35cm (13¾in), *L 14 June,* **£1,375 ($1,980)**

11

A pair of French Art Deco entrée dishes and covers, Paris, c.1935, 950 standard, of rectangular octagonal shape with moulded borders, scroll and faceted handles, 35.6cm (14in), 183oz 16dwt (5,716gr), *NY 11/12 May,* **$3,300 (£2,391)**

12

A George III toasted cheese dish, William Burwash & Richard Sibley, London, 1810, engraved with a crest and baron's coronet, ivory end handles, w 32.3cm (12¾in), 55oz 19dwt (1,740gr), *L 29 Nov,* **£1,705 ($2,063)**

13

A set of four electroplated dish covers in sizes, Mappin & Webb, late 19th cent, flower-chased panels and crest finials, 35 to 51cm (14 to 20in), *C 19 June,* **£418 ($581)**

14

A plated set of four meat dish covers, four entrée dishes and a soup tureen on stand en suite, late 19th cent, the oval bodies engraved with a band of foliage within beaded borders, *C 4-6 Sept,* **£990 ($1,287)**

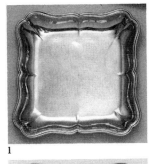
1

2

3

4

5

6

7

8

9

10

11

12

13   14

1
A French mustard pot, Paris, 1742, of fluted baluster form, with armorial, h 10cm (4in), 6oz 4dwt (195gr), *M 11 Dec,* **FF 22,200 (£1,956; $2,362)**

2
A Belgian mustard pot, Mons, 1760, of baluster form, spirally fluted, scroll handle, maker's mark 'IF', h 19cm (7½in), 9oz (279gr), *NY 21 June,* **$1,540 (£1,132)**

3
A Victorian cylindrical mustard pot, George Fox, London, 1867, of quatrefoil outline, scroll pierced and applied with four lion masks, with mustard spoon, George Adams, London, 1867, Old English pattern, h 7.6cm (3in), 4oz 18dwt, (152gr), *P 21-24 Feb,* **£396 ($555)**

4
A George III oval mustard pot, Hester Bateman, London, 1787, festoon engraved, leaf and roundel pierced, plain domed cover, h 7.6cm (3in), *HS 24/25 Oct,* **£506 ($643)**

5
A George III shaped oblong mustard pot, Edward Capper, London, 1797, wriggle-worked with vacant panels below an engraved foliate band, bird finial, h 9.5cm (3¾in), *HS 24/25 Oct,* **£308 ($391)**

6
A George III oval mustard pot, Joseph Scammell, London, 1793, plain between reeded borders, initialled, the domed cover with urn finial, h 14cm (5½in), *HS 24/25 Oct,* **£198 ($251)**

7
A French oil and vinegar cruet, Claude-Nicolas Delanoy, Paris, 1772, of shaped oblong outline, with openwork twining ribbon rim, grapevine holders for the glass bottles and silver stoppers, w 30cm (11⅞in), 23oz (740gr), *M 26 June,* **FF 17,760 (£1,524; $2,077)**

8
A French oil and vinegar cruet, Paris, c1810, maker's mark 'RB', h 30cm (11¾in), 22oz 14dwt (706gr), *F 11 May,* **L 1,900,000 (£774; $1,114)**

9
An Italian oil and vinegar cruet, Guiseppe Mazzini, Rome, c1810, the cut-glass bottles with gilt decoration, h 28cm (11in), 18oz (562gr), *F 20 Dec,* **L 3,200,000 (£1,396; $1,745)**

10
An Italian oil and vinegar cruet, Milan, c1820, with glass bottles and oval galleried base, h 31.5cm (12⅜in), 17oz 4dwt (538gr), *F 20 Dec,* **L 1,400,000 (£611; $764)**

11
An electroplated six-bottle cruet set, c1900, the oval galleried base pierced with tracery and supported on four shell and scroll feet, h 35.5cm (14in), *C 16 Oct,* **£176 ($225)**

12
A strawberry set, Martin Hall & Co, Sheffield, 1865, the shaped oval base with ribbon-tied paterae and husk garland sides, fitted with two engraved and faceted glass dishes and a sifter spoon and cream ladle, w 20.3cm (8in), 16oz 11dwt (514gr), *C 10 Jan,* **£682 ($989)**

13
A French sugar vase with lid, Paris, c1815, the finial in the form of a bee, 22.5cm (8⅞in), 16oz 14dwt (520gr), *F 20 Dec,* **L 1,700,000 (£742; $889)**

14
An Italian sugar vase, with cover, Emanuele Caber, Milan, c1820, decorated with classical figures, lacking liner, 26.5cm (10½in), 18oz 16dwt (587gr), *F 20 Dec,* **L 1,900,000 (£829; $993)**

15
A pair of parcel-gilt vases, probably Turkish, mid-19th cent, the vase-shaped bodies supported on bifurcated scrolled legs, 20.3cm (8in), 28oz 12dwt (889gr), *L 8 Mar,* **£682 ($1,017)**

1 2 3

4 5 6

7 8 9

10 11 12

13 14 15

1
A George I caster, Glover Johnson, London, 1718, of octagonal baluster form, engraved with armorials, h 17.5cm (7in), 6oz 10dwt (202gr), *L 3 May*, £1,925 ($2,734)

2
A George I octagonal caster, probably Richard Watts, London, 1716, engraved with a crest within a foliate scroll, h 16.5cm (6½in), 6oz 16dwt (211gr), *L 22 Nov*, £1,485 ($1,931)

3
A George II vase-shaped caster, Edinburgh, 1739, engraved with a crest and motto, Assay Master Archibald Ure, h 14.6cm (5¾in), 5oz 2dwt (158gr), *HH 27 Mar*, £418 ($623)

4
An American baluster caster, William Burt, Boston, *c*1740-50, with moulded borders, the cover pierced and engraved with panels of trellis, h 13.5cm (5⅜in), 4oz (124gr), *NY 28 June*, $5,775 (£4,278)

5
A pair of Dutch silver-gilt casters, Hendrik Nieuwenhuys, Amsterdam, 1775, of pear shape, spirally fluted and partly chased with panels of trailing flowers, h 23.5cm (9¼in), 28oz 10dwt (886gr), *NY 13 Dec*, $7,700 (£6,471)

6
A Belgian baluster caster, Peeter (Jr) Alio, Brussels, 1717-22, flat-chased with Régence ornament, 8oz 2dwt (254gr), *A 7 June*, **Dfl 6,264** (£1,467; $2,127)

7
A German baluster caster, Johan Jobst Soehlcke (Sen), Hanover, *c*1765, spirally ribbed and fluted, the matching pierced cover centred by an urn finial, h 23.1cm (9⅛in), 10oz 4dwt (320gr), *G 14 Nov*, **SF 8,250** (£2,562; $3,433)

8
A George II Warwick cruet, Samuel Wood, London, 1755-6, the cinquefoil frame on four double-scroll legs with shell feet, h 22.5cm (8⅞in), 38oz 4dwt (1,190gr), *JHB 2 May*, **R 6,000** (£3,370; $4,714)

9
A pair of Dutch baluster casters, Reynier de Haan, The Hague, 1781, the spirally ribbed bodies on cast bases, h 24.2cm (9½in), 28oz 10dwt (888gr), *G 15 May*, **SF 11,000** (£3,303; $4,723)

10
A pair of casters, American, *c*1901, embossed and chased with stylized plants, pellet finials, h 14cm (5⅜in), 11oz 12dwt (346gr), *NY 17/18 Feb*, $2,090 (£1,472)

11
A George III Warwick cruet frame, probably Robert Peaston, London, 1767, the cut-glass bottles with unmarked mounts, the cinquefoil base raised on scroll and shell supports, h 26.5cm (10½in), 55oz 5dwt (1,718gr), *L 29 Nov*, £2,035 ($2,462)

1

2

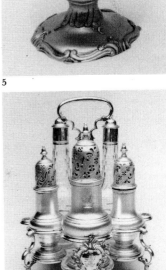
5

3

4

8

6

7

9

10

11

1

A set of four George I
octagonal trencher salts,
James Rood, London,
1720, engraved with a
crest, w 8.3cm (3¼in), 9oz
(279gr), L 20 Sept,
£3,300 ($4,290)

2

A set of four George II
salts, Edward Wakelin,
London, 1742, of circular
bombé form engraved
with a crest, gadroon
rim, raised on four hoof
supports, one beginning
to split at one foot,
d 8.5cm (3⅜in), 21oz
(653gr), NY 12 Apr,
$1,430 (£1,000)

3

A pair of French trencher
salts, Edmé-Pierre Balzac,
Paris, 1776, w 8.5cm
(3½in), 5oz (180gr),
M 26 June,
FF 16,650 (£1,429; $1,947)

4

A set of eight George III
salt cellars, John Wakelin
& Robert Garrard,
London, 1793, the oval
bodies chased with flat
lobes and engraved with
crests above, gilt interiors,
w 14cm (5½in), 38oz
18dwt (1,210gr),
JHB 29 Feb,
R 4,400 (£2,418; $3,605)

5

A set of four George III
salt cellars, David &
Robert Hennell I, London,
1766, the oval bodies
with pierced scrolling
sides below the waved
gadroon rims, 9cm (3⅝in),
11oz 14dwt (365gr),
JHB 6 Nov,
R 1,400 (£606; $739)

6

A pair of American salts,
David Hall, Lancaster,
Pa, c.1810, of elliptical
form, initialled in script,
on four panel feet,
repairs to feet and to one
seam, 9.5cm (3¾in), 4oz
10dwt (139gr), NY 26 Jan,
$1,100 (£759)

7

A set of six George III
oblong salt cellars, Emes
& Barnard, London,
1810, engraved with a
crest within a floral and
foliate wreath, w 9.2cm
(3⅝in), 26oz 12dwt (827gr),
L 14 June,
£660 ($950)

8

A set of six George IV
escallop salt cellars, two
Joseph Cradock &
William Ker Reid, for
Joseph Cradock, London,
1825, cast with rocaille
motifs at the rims,
w 10.2cm (4in), 40oz 9dwt
(1,285gr), L 3 May,
£3,740 ($5,311)

9

Four Victorian figure salts,
John Samuel Hunt for
Hunt & Roskell, London,
two 1856, two 1865, the
baskets with gilt
interiors, the bases
stamped 'Hunt & Roskell
late Storr & Mortimer',
h 16.5 to 18.3cm (6½ to
7¼in), 57oz (1,772gr),
L 3 May,
£16,500 ($23,430)

10

A German cruet set,
Johan Jacob Adam,
Augsburg, 1785-7, with
silver-mounted cut-glass
bottles, 28cm (11in), 53oz
10dwt (1,663gr), NY 21 June,
$1,650 (£1,213)

11

A pair of French double
salts, Paris, 1789, each
vessel in the form of a
sarcophagus with lion
masks, the holders in the
form of sea monsters,
maker's mark 'LC', 15cm
(5⅞in), 30oz 12dwt
(952gr), F 3-4 Oct,
L 3,200,000 (£1,263; $1,642)

12

A George III egg cruet,
William Elliott, London,
1816, with six cups (two
not illustrated), the
rectangular frame with
gadroon rims, shell and
paw feet, central acanthus-
leaf-and-shell carrying
handle, w 22.2cm (8¾in),
36oz 6dwt (1,130gr),
JHB 2 May,
R 1,500 (£843; $1,179)

13

A Victorian cinquefoil egg
cruet, Edward Barnard &
Sons, London, 1871,
the base with no maker's
mark, h 15cm (6in), 20oz
3dwt (631gr), L 25 Oct,
£550 ($699)

14

A Victorian egg frame for
six, Joseph Angell,
London, 1854, the central
handle rising to a model
hen finial, h 21cm (8¼in),
30oz (933gr), C 2-5 Oct,
£880 ($1,135)

1

A pair of lozenge-shaped novelty toast racks, London, 1897, of wire-work construction forming the word 'toast', each supported on four ball feet, 7oz 4dwt (223gr), *C 13-16 Mar*, £110 ($164)

2

A pair of Victorian silver-gilt toast racks, R & S Garrard, London, 1845/6, engraved with initials, crest and ducal coronet, w 15.8cm (6¼in), 22oz 5dwt (691gr), *L 22 Nov*, £1,650 ($2,145)

3

A George III dish ring, Richard Williams, Dublin, c 1770, engraved with form, engraved with armorials within a rocaille cartouche, d 21cm (8¼in), 14oz 12dwt (465gr), *JHB 2 May*, R 1,400 (£786; $1,093)

4

A George III dish ring, Joseph Jackson or John Laughlin, Dublin, 1789, pierced and bright-cut with paterae and floral swags between bands of foliate scrolls, d 20.5cm (8in), 9oz 18dwt (307gr), *L 9 Feb*, £1,265 ($1,771)

5

An early George III dish ring, Samuel Walker, Dublin, c1760, the concave sides pierced and chased, the assymetric cartouche engraved with a coat of arms, d 23.5cm (9¼in), 17oz 3dwt (533gr), *C 2-5 Oct*, £1,760 ($2,270)

6

A George III dish cross, Robert & David Hennell, London, 1795, with revolving arms and sliding feet, detachable cover engraved with a crest, 33.7cm (13¼in), 17oz 10dwt (544gr), *NY 23 Oct*, £660 (£550)

7

A pair of Dutch braziers, Diderick Wilhelm Rethmeijer, Amsterdam, 1792, of circular basket form, beaded borders and pierced rim, d 14.6cm (5¾in), 17oz (528gr), *NY 21 June*, $1,100 (£809)

8

A George III lemon strainer, London, 1767, the circular bowl with gadroon rim pierced with a flowerhead, crested, ribbed clip, stylised foliate scroll handles, 24.1cm (9½in), 4oz (124gr), *NY 23 Oct*, $440 (£366)

9

A George III lemon strainer, probably S Herbert & Co, London, 1765, the circular bowl pierced with radiating flowerheads and with gadroon rim, scroll and shellwork handles, 24.8cm (9¾in), 4oz 10dwt (139gr), *NY 23 Oct*, $825 (£687)

10

A George II saucepan, possibly George Wickes, London, 1728, pear form with moulded rim and short spout, engraved with a crest, repair at spout, h 12.7cm (5in), 28oz (870gr), *NY 21 June*, $1,870 (£1,375)

11

A George I lemon strainer, London, 1722, pierced with flowerheads and geometric motifs, engraved with initials and a crest, scroll pierced handles, w 16.5cm (6½in), 2oz 13dwt (82gr), *L 26 Apr*, £462 ($665)

12

A George III Argyle, Henry Tudor & Thomas Leader, Sheffield, 1779, with circular cylindrical body with beaded rims, engraved with armorials, h 12.3cm (4⅞in), 11oz (342gr), *NY 23 Oct*, $880 (£733)

13

A George III Argyle, Aaron Lestourgeon, London, 1772, of cylindrical form engraved with a crest between moulded borders, the lid with bud finial and gadroon rim, h 12.3cm (4¾in), 12oz 15dwt (396gr), *L 14 June*, £682 ($982)

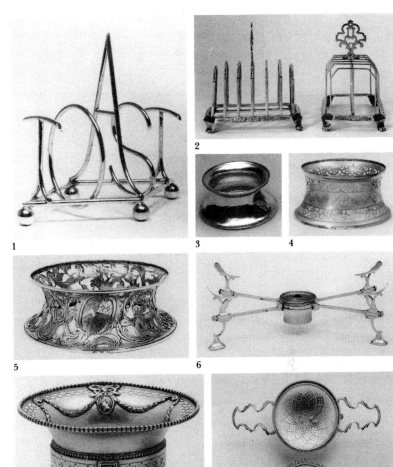

2

1

3

4

5

6

7

8 (*above*), 9 (*below*)

10

11

12

13

1
A William and Mary salver on foot, London, 1691, engraved with armorials with a stylized leafy roundel, trumpet foot, gadrooned borders, maker's mark 'D', d 20.5cm (8in), 11oz 5dwt (349gr), *L 25 Oct,*
£1,210 ($1,536)

2
A pair of Dutch square salvers, the Hague, 1750, the moulded borders with incurved angles decorated with stepped scroll, the centre engraved with English armorials, w 37.6cm (10⅞in), 50oz 10dwt (1,570gr), *NY 21 June,*
$5,500 (£4,044)

3
A Dutch square salver, the Hague, 1746, engraved with contemporary arms of Schepers of Rotterdam impaling Prins, the border with incurved angles, 24oz 10dwt (763gr), *A 7 June,*
Dfl 6,264 (£1,466; $2,023)

4
A Dutch salver, Joannes Christoffel Scholtz, Amsterdam, 1730, engraved with a contemporary monogram, on circular foot, 26oz 8dwt (823gr), *A 7 June,*
Dfl 5,800 (£1,358; $1,874)

5
A Flemish circular salver, Malines, c.1735, the centre monogrammed within a roundel of husks and strapwork on a matt ground, similarly flat chased between fluting at the border, maker's mark 'AR', d 31.2cm (12¼in), 21oz 10dwt (670gr), *G 14 Nov,*
SF 4,950 (£1,537; $2,059)

6
A George II square waiter, Paul de Lamerie, London, 1728, Britannia Standard, with moulded rim and incurved angles, engraved with armorials within a baroque cartouche, raised on four paw feet, w 14cm (5½in), 10oz 4dwt (317gr), *NY 13 Dec,*
$10,450 (£8,781)

7
A George I shaped square waiter, Peter Archambo, London, 1721, engraved with a monogram below a marquess' coronet, moulded border and hoof supports, 14.3cm (5⅝in), 7oz 17dwt (224gr), *L 3 May,*
£935 ($1,327)

8
A Portuguese shaped circular salver on detachable foot, Oporto, c.1770, embossed and chased with shells, flowers and scrolls, maker's mark 'RC', d 32.5cm (12¾in), 38oz 2dwt (1,185gr), *L 12 Mar,*
£1,210 ($1,804)

9
A George II shaped circular salver, William Peaston, London, 1754, the centre quite plain within a shell and scroll border, on three hoof feet, d 17.8cm (7in), 8oz 8dwt (261gr), *C 4-6 Sept,*
£275 ($357)

10
A George II shaped circular salver, R Rew or Rugg, London, 1756, engraved with armorials within a floral rococo cartouche, shell and scroll border, on three hoof feet, d 34.5cm (13½in), 35oz 1dwt (1,049gr), *L 20 Sept,*
£1,210 ($1,573)

11
An early George II shaped circular salver, R Rew or Rugg, London, 1762, engraved with armorials within a rococo cartouche, also later flat chased with a matted band of diaper, three hoof feet, d 26cm (10¼in), 20oz 17dwt (648gr), *L 26 Apr,*
£440 ($633)

12
A George II salver, Robert Abercromby, London, 1743, engraved with armorials within an elaborate rococo cartouche, raised on four chased lion's feet, d 54cm (21¼in), 116oz 10dwt (3,623gr), *NY 13 Dec,*
$7,700 (£6,470)

1
A George III silver
circular chinoiserie salver,
Ebenezer Coker,
London, 1763, the border
cast and chased with a
lozengework fence,
d 71.7cm (28¼in), 225oz
10dwt (7,013gr),
NY 13 Dec,
$13,750 (£11,554)

2
A George III oval salver,
John Crouch & Thomas
Hannam, London, 1788,
with reeded rim and
four panel feet, bright-
cut with formal foliage
and decoration, 54.3cm
(21⅜in), 80oz 10dwt
(2,503gr), *NY 13 Dec,*
$4,950 (£4,159)

3
A pair of George III
shaped circular salvers,
Crouch & Hannam,
London 1775, d 20.7cm
(8in), 26oz 14dwt (830gr),
L 14 June,
£1,485 ($2,138)

4
A pair of George III
salvers, John Crouch &
Thomas Hannam,
London, 1781, beaded
rim and panel feet,
d 23cm (9in), 28oz 1dwt
(872gr), *L 29 Nov,*
£1,210 ($1,464)

5
A George III salver,
Hannam & Crouch,
London, 1805, with
gadrooned border,
d 44.7cm (17⅝in), 77oz
10dwt (2,410gr),
NY 23 Oct,
$2,640 (£2,200)

6
A George III shaped
circular salver, Story &
Elliott, London, 1810,
engraved with a crest
and initial within a band
of flat chased matted
scrolls, panel supports,
d 30.5cm (12in), 27oz
(839gr), *P 21-24 Feb,*
£396 ($554)

7
A George IV salver,
William Eley II, London,
1824, d 73cm (28¾in),
327oz (10,185gr), *L 22 Nov,*
£6,820 ($8,866)

8
A Victorian silver-gilt
salver, John Edward
Terry, London, 1840,
chased with a band of
scrolling foliage, the rim
cast, pierced and chased,
raised on three shell
feet, gilding later,
d 61cm (24in), 197oz
(6,126gr), *NY 13 Dec,*
$5,500 (£4,621)

9
A Sicilian tray, Messina,
1756, engraved with
armorials, with moulded
fluted border, w 64.5cm
(25⅜in), 78oz 18dwt
(2,456gr), *F 20 Dec,*
L 9,400,000 (£4,101; $5,127)

10
A George III oblong salver,
Samuel Hennell & John
Terrey, London, 1813,
engraved with armorials
within a rococo car-
touche, applied with a
cast and chased border,
w 62.5cm (24½in), 226oz
10dwt (7,044gr), *L 15 Mar,*
£5,170 ($7,708)

11
A George I octagonal tray,
Thomas Bolton, Dublin,
1715, with raised
moulded border, the
centre engraved in the
manner of Simon Gribelin
with contemporary
armorials in a scrolling
foliate cartouche, 65.2cm
(25⅝in), 143oz 10dwt
(4,462gr) *NY 13 Dec,*
$55,000 (£46,218)

12
A French two-handled
tray, late 19th cent, in
rococo taste, maker's
mark 'AD', 75cm (29½in),
131oz (4,074gr), *NY 24 Feb,*
$3,410 (£2,351)

13
A Victorian shaped oval
tray, C F Hancock,
London, 1855, engraved
with naturalistic flowers
and leaves, the centre
with a crest and
inscription, on four
foliate supports, w 78cm
(30¾in), 158oz (4,913gr),
L 12 July,
£2,860 ($3,889)

14
A George III two-handled
tea tray, Emes &
Barnard, London, 1815,
w 65.7cm (25⅞in), 107oz
(3,327gr), *NY 23 Oct,*
$5,225 (£4,354)

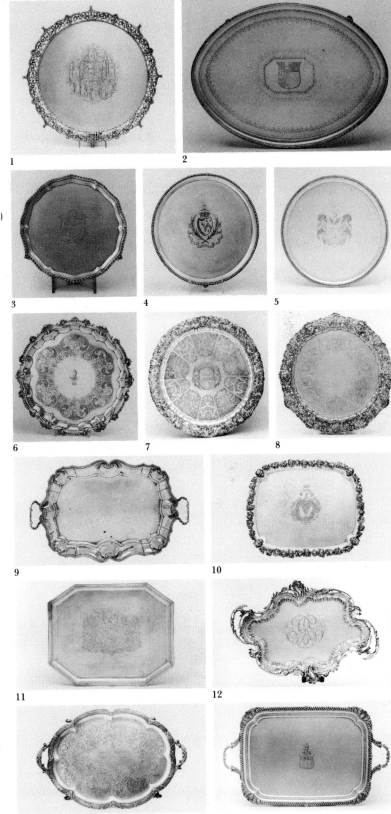

1   2
3   4   5
6   7   8
9   10
11   12
13   14

1

A Dutch dish, Amsterdam, 1651, embossed with lobate ornament surrounding five vignettes of figures, d 48.5cm (19⅛in), 19oz 14dwt (615gr), *G 14 Nov,* **SF 44,000 (£13,664; $18,309)**

2

Two Hungarian parcelgilt hexagonal dishes, *c*.1696, the raised centres engraved with two coats of arms, the borders decorated with embossed tulips and anemones, w 24.5cm (9⅝in), 17oz 6dwt (540gr), *G 14 Nov,* **SF 24,200 (£7,515; $10,070)**

3

A set of four George II dessert dishes, Edward Wakelin, London, 1754, the centres engraved with armorials, 25.1cm (9⅞in), 71oz 4dwt (2,214gr), *NY 12 Apr,* **$23,100 (£16,153)**

4

A George II salver, Paul de Lamerie, London, 1743, flat-chased with foliate shellwork and scrolls, the centre engraved with armorials, raised on four panel feet, d 25.1cm (9⅞in), 21oz 10dwt (668gr), *NY 12 Apr,* **$22,000 (£15,384)**

5

A George III silver-gilt sideboard dish, William Pitts, London, 1816, in 17th cent taste, w 67.5cm (26½in), 106oz 18dwt (3,324gr), *L 22 Nov,* **£2,530 ($3,289)**

6

A Queen Anne strawberry dish, Thomas Bolton, Dublin, 1710-12, engraved with a coat of arms within a leafy strapwork cartouche, d 19.7cm (7¾in), 12oz 14dwt (394gr), *C 2-5 Oct,* **£2,860 ($3,689)**

7

A George III silver-gilt fluted circular dish, Edward Cornelius Farrell London, 1818, Britannia Standard, engraved with armorials within a band of chased fruit and foliage, d 25.5cm (10in), 17oz 3dwt (533gr), *L 3 May,* **£3,080 ($4,373)**

8

An Italian circular dish, Novara, *c*.1820, the border chased with scrolling foliage and shell motifs, maker's mark 'FC', d 39cm (15⅜in), 18oz (560gr), *F 20 Dec,* **L 1,900,000 (£829; $1,036)**

9

Two George IV oval meat dishes in sizes, William Eaton, London, 1820, the gadroon rims with shells and leafage, the borders engraved with a contemporary coat of arms, w 48 and 51cm (18⅞ and 20⅛in), 140oz (4,360gr), *M 26 June,* **FF 35,520 (£3,048; $4,154)**

10

A pair of William IV shaped oval dessert dishes, Harrison Brothers & Howson, Sheffield, 1830, formed as two overlapping leaves, four supports, w 32.6cm (12½in), 49oz 15dwt (1,547gr), *L 12 July,* **£2,200 ($2,992)**

11

A pair of French circular dishes, Pierre-François Grandguillaume, Besançon, *c*.1760, with gadrooned borders, the centre with armorials, d 26.3cm (10⅜in), 36oz (1,120gr), *M 11 Dec,* **FF 51,060 (£4,498; $5,431)**

12

A Louis XV shaped circular sideboard dish, Lille, *c*.1770, with moulded rim, the border engraved with a coat of arms, maker's mark 'ELDV', d 29.5cm (11⅝in), 21oz (680gr), *M 26 June,* **FF 11,100 (£952; $1,298)**

13

A set of twelve German Royal dinner plates, Hossauer, Berlin, 1854-60, engraved with armorials, d 26cm (10¼in), 240oz 10dwt (7,497gr), *NY 13 Dec,* **$5,500 (£4,621)**

14

A set of ten American silver-gilt dinner plates, Tiffany & Co, New York, 1891-1902, in early 19th cent style, engraved with armorials, d 24.8cm (9¾in), 169oz 15dwt (5,279gr), *NY 26 Jan,* **$6,050 (£4,172)**

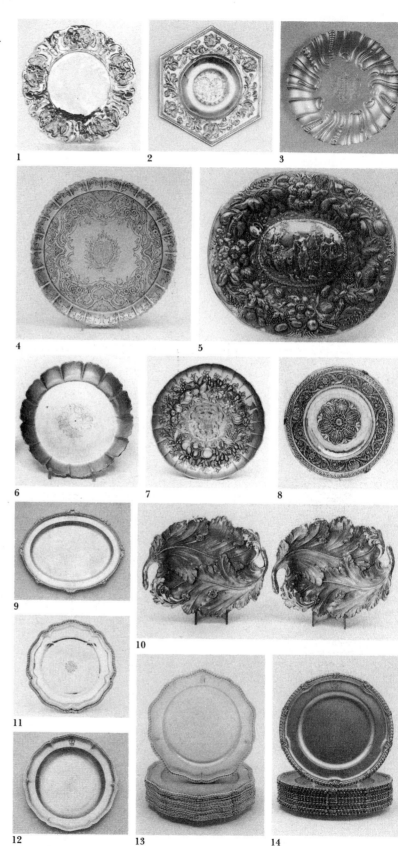

1

A set of four Charles II table candlesticks, Jacob Bodendick, London, 1677, the quadrangular baluster stems mounted on a cushion-shaped knop, all chased with gadroon borders, the bases engraved *c.*1760 with armorials, h 26cm (10¼in), 128oz (3,980gr), *NY 13 Dec,*
$203,500 (£171,008)

2

A George I octagonal caster, Paul de Lamerie, London, 1724, Britannia Standard, engraved with armorials in a baroque cartouche, h 22.7cm (9in), 25oz 10dwt (793gr), *NY 13 Dec,*
$85,800 (£72,101)

3

A pair of George IV silver-gilt double wine coaster wagons, E. E. J. & W. Barnard for Edward Barnard & Sons, London, 1829, complete with two pairs of wine coasters, the wagons 50.5cm (20¼in), the coasters d 18.5cm (7¼in), *L 3 May,*
£121,000 ($171,820)

4

A pair of George I double-lipped sauce-boats in French taste, René Hudell, London, Britannia Standard, 22.3cm (8¾in), 38oz (1,181gr), *NY 13 Dec,*
$79,200 (£66,555)

5

A two-handled silver-gilt cup and cover, Paul de Lamerie, London, 1745, engraved with a contemporary coat of arms and crest, decorated with profuse flower festoons and putti, 36cm (14¼in), 124oz (3,880gr), *M 26 June,*
FF 1,221,000 (£104,806; $142,807)

6

A pair of George III silver-gilt dishes and covers, Rundell, Bridge & Rundell (Paul Storr), London, 1812, with chased and cast borders of vine motifs on a matted ground, d 24cm (9½in), 69oz 12dwt (2,164gr), *L 3 May,*
£30,250 ($42,955)

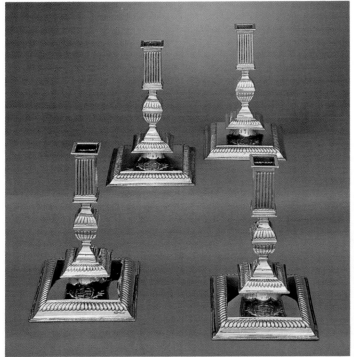
1

2

3

4

5

6

1
A pair of Italian silver-gilt table candlesticks, Turin, c.1760, engraved with the arms of Savoy, pierced for electricity, unmarked, h 23.4cm (9¼in), 34oz (1,060gr), *G 14 Nov,*
SF 18,700 (£5,807; $7,781)

2
A pair of Italian silver-gilt bowls and covers, Turin, c.1760, engraved with the arms of Savoy, the circular bodies on rim bases, the covers spirally ribbed, unmarked, d 9.4cm (3¾in), 17oz (530gr), *G 14 Nov,*
SF 20,900 (£6,491; $8,698)

3
An Italian silver-gilt bowl and cover, Genoa, c.1760, applied with cast open-work scroll and rocaille decorated handles, the cover spirally ribbed and chased, d 14.8cm (5⅞in), 20oz (620gr), *G 14 Nov,*
SF 28,600 (£8,882; $11,902)

4
An Italian silver-gilt chamber candlestick, Turin, c.1760, engraved with the arms of Savoy, the circular pan with a shaped leaf moulded border, unmarked, w 20cm (7⅞in), 7oz 16dwt (245gr), *G 14 Nov,*
SF 9,900 (£3,074; $4,119)

5
Two silver-gilt models of stags, Johann Ludwig Biller I, Augsburg, c.1700, h 62.5cm (24⅝in), *G 15 May,*
SF 605,000 (£181,681; $259,803)

6
A Dutch tapering cylindrical beaker, Antoni Magnus, Deventer, ?1664, with engravings after Abraham Bosse and Jacques Callot, armorial on the underside, 18.4cm (7¼in), 11oz 12dwt (362gr), *G 15 May,*
SF 132,000 (£39,639; $56,683)

1   2   3   4   1

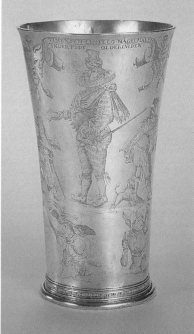

5   6

1
Two Victorian parcel gilt allegorical figures, C T & G Fox, London, 1845, representing summer and autumn, h 37cm (14½in), 122oz 4dwt (3,800gr), L 3 May, £4,840 ($6,873)

2
A German model of a stork, Ludwig Neresheimer & Co, Hanau, importer's mark of Berthold Muller for B Muller & Son of London, Chester, 1901, flat-chased or cast with feathers, hinged wings and detachable head, h 46.5cm (18¼in), 72oz 8dwt (2,251gr), L 8 Nov, £1,980 ($2,633)

3
A German figure of a hare, B Neresheimer of Hanau imported Berthold Muller, Chester, 1907, h 27cm (10⅝in), 18oz 19dwt (589gr), C 10 Jan, £605 ($877)

4
A German model of a stag, late 19th cent, the head detachable, with 1891-1901 Vienna import mark, 46cm (18in), 67oz (2,083gr), L 8 Nov, £1,100 ($1,463)

5
A pair of Spanish parcel-gilt and jewelled figures of equestrian knights in armour, c.1970, chased with foliage and applied with coats of arms, with ivory faces, h 29.5cm (11¾in), 119oz 1dwt (3,816gr), L 8 Dec, £2,090 ($2,780)

6
A German group of St George and the Dragon, Simon Rosenau, Bad Kissingen, c.1900, h 39cm (15½in), 75oz 3dwt (2,337gr), L 8 Mar, £1,650 ($2,460)

7
A German figure of a grape picker of 'Büttenmann', c.1880, detachable head, the basket detached, with a pseudo-Augsburg mark, h 26.6cm (10½in), 30oz 19dwt (964gr), L 8 Nov, £935 ($1,244)

8
A German jewelled figure of a town crier, early 20th cent, set with multi-coloured cabochons, silver-coloured metal, h 15.7cm (6⅛in), L 7 June, £550 ($798)

9
A gilt metal and cloisonné enamel vase, Elkington & Co, of Birmingham, c.1873-9, probably from a design by Auguste Adolphe Willms, decorated in Chinese style, h 35.5cm (14in), L 8 Nov, £396 ($527)

10
A pair of German figures of knights in armour, probably Dr. Herbert Bauer of Hanau, successors to Ludwig Neresheimer & Co, importer's mark I Freeman & Son Ltd, London, 1964, each with carved ivory face, h 28.7 and 30.4cm (11¼ and 12in), 47oz 8dwt (1,474gr), L 8 Nov, £1,650 ($2,195)

11
A German nef, Ludwig Neresheimer & Co, Hanau, late 19th cent, three-masted on four revolving wheels, pseudo-hallmarks of Berthold Muller for B Muller & Son, London, h 82cm (23½in), 174oz 16dwt (5,436gr), L 8 Nov, £3,520 ($4,682)

12
A German parcel-gilt nef, mid-20th cent, on a chased sea-girt oval base sprouting dolphins below a figure of Neptune, silver-coloured metal, h 76.5cm (30in), 159oz 8dwt (4,920gr), L 7 June, £5,500 ($7,975)

1   2   3

4   5

6   7   8   9

10   11   12

1
An Elizabeth I apostle spoon, London, 1596, St Bartholomew with open-work rayed nimbus, the bowl back later pricked '1650/ E.D', *L 19 Nov*, £1,320 ($1,729)

2
A Charles I apostle spoon, possibly Thomas Hodges, London, 1641, *L 3 May*, £2,750 ($3,905)

3
A Charles I slip top spoon, Jeremy Johnson, London, 1641, the terminal initialled 'NRC', *L 3 May*, £1,045 ($1,484)

4
A Hungarian silver-gilt spoon, mid-17th cent, with lobate mouldings decorating the stem, rising to a mask finial, maker's mark indecipherable, probably Pozsony, *L 12 Mar*, £440 ($656)

5
A Norwegian spoon, c.1612, the bowl engraved 'Hindrich Michelsen anno 1612' and with a spray within strapwork, the floral terminal also engraved, maker's mark only 'SMB', *L 12 Mar*, £385 ($574)

6
A trefid spoon, Edward Mangy, Hull, c.1670, with rat-tail bowl, the terminal reverse initialled 'ADM IM', 1oz 10dwt (46gr), *L 9 Feb*, £594 ($833)

7
A German spoon and fork, Johann Martin Schmid(t), Augsburg, c.1700, finely engraved with fruit and foliage, the terminals with landscapes within ovals, 2oz 8dwt (75gr), *A 7 June*, Dfl 5,104 (£1,195; $1,733)

8
A set of six silver-gilt knives, spoons and forks, English, c.1685, the spoons and forks with trefid terminals, all engraved, the knives with steel blades, maker's mark only 'DS', *L 3 May*, £5,720 ($8,122)

9
A German silver-gilt spoon, Michael Hafner, Augsburg, c.1695, with trefid terminal and rat-tail bowl, the stem engraved with scrolling foliage on a linear ground and two portrait medallions of Roman emperors, *L 12 Mar*, £550 ($820)

10
A set of six William III three-prong dognose table forks, William Scarlet, London, 1698, with plain terminals, 15oz 10dwt (482gr), *NY 13 Dec*, $4,400 (£3,697)

11
A French olive spoon, Salins, c.1767, the terminal with a coat of arms, the pierced bowl with trellis and foliage, maker's mark 'CT', 3oz (95gr), *M 11 Dec*, FF 6,660 (£587; $709)

12
A pair of American tablespoons, Paul Revere Jr, Boston, c.1805, with coffin handle tips, 22.2cm (8¾in), 3oz 10dwt (108gr), *NY 26 Jan*, $3,630 (£2,503)

13
An American tablespoon, Paul Revere Jr, Boston, c.1800, Old English pattern, 21cm (8¼in), 2oz (62gr), *NY 26 Jan*, $3,740 (£2,579)

1

An American tablespoon, Paul Revere Jr, Boston, c.1785, the handle bright-cut with wriggle-work borders, long moulded drop on reverse of bowl, in unused condition, 21cm (8¼in), 1oz 12dwt (79gr), *NY 28 June,* $4,950 (£3,667)

2

A Swiss tart server, Charles-Louis Duciel, Lausanne, c.1760, the blade pierced with foliage, the terminal Hanoverian pattern; sold with two other items, 7oz 14dwt (240gr), *G 14 Nov,* SF 2,200 (£683; $916)

3

A Swiss tart server, c.1775, the blade pierced with foliage within notched borders, the wood handle rising from a shell and scroll brackets, unmarked, *G 14 Nov,* SF 2,530 (£786; $1,053)

4

A presentation trowel, Mappin & Webb, Sheffield, 1898, the spear-shaped blade bright-cut engraved with foliage and later inscription, the ivory handle carved with sprays of orchids, 37cm (14½in), *C 3-6 July,* £396 ($537)

5

A George III fiddle pattern fish slice, William & Samuel Knight, London, 1811, the blade outlined with wrigglework decoration and pierced and engraved with a coach and four, 4oz 12dwt (143gr), *C 3-6 July,* £286 ($388)

6

A pair of Victorian fish servers, William Theobalds & Robert Atkinson, London, 1838, the handles formed as dolphins and seaweed, the blades with scolling foliage and floral openwork, 28cm (11in), 15oz (466gr), *NY 18 July,* $2,090 (£1,595)

7

A Cape dessert service, John Townsend, c.1830, in silver and agate comprising twelve forks, twelve knives and a butter knife, *L 9 July,* £2,310 ($3,165)

8

A George III cheese scoop, Paul Storr, London, 1816, bacchanalian pattern, 22.8cm (9in), 3oz (93gr), *NY 13 Dec,* $1,210 (£1,017)

9

A George III ice spade, Paul Storr, London, 1819, fiddle, thread and shell pattern, engraved with a crest, 24.2cm (9½in), 4oz 10dwt (139gr), *NY 13 Dec,* $770 (£647)

10

A set of eight George III salt spoons, Paul Storr, London, 1815, 'Stag Hunt' pattern, the handles decorated with a huntsman and hounds at the kill, gilt bowls, 10.8cm (4¼in), 6oz (186gr), *NY 13 Dec,* $1,980 (£1,664)

11

A Victorian portrait caddy spoon, W R Smily, London, 1852, fluted gilt bowl and foliate stem headed by a portrait bust of the Duke of Wellington, 9.5cm (3¾in), *L 22 Nov,* £495 ($644)

12

A pair of George III silver-gilt caddy spoons, Matthew Linwood, Birmingham, 1815, the bowl of each die-stamped with a wickerwork basket containing flowers, 7.2cm (3in), *L 22 Nov,* £968 ($1,258)

13

A George III caddy spoon, Joseph Willmore, Birmingham, 1814, struck in the form of an eagle's head and wing, 7.7cm (3in), *L 19 Nov,* £495 ($648)

14

A George III caddy spoon, Joseph Taylor, Birmingham, 1799, in the form of a jockey's cap, chased with stars and husks, *L 13 Mar,* £253 ($377)

1   2   3   4

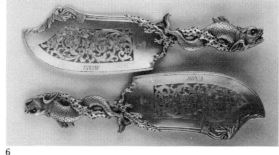

5

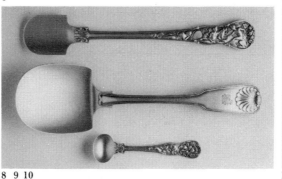

6   7

8 9 10   11

12   13   14

1
A George IV and William IV silver-gilt Coburg pattern dessert service, Chawner & Co, London, 1827-34, the terminals engraved with a crest and garter motto, 126 pieces, 203oz 8dwt (6,325gr), *L 22 Nov,* **£8,800 ($11,440)**

2
A German silver-gilt dessert service, Abraham Warnberger IV, Augsburg, 1775-9, fiddle thread pattern, 69 pieces, 100oz (3,110gr), *NY 13 Dec,* **$3,300 (£2,773)**

3
A George III silver-gilt dessert set, Rundell, Bridge and Rundell, (Paul Storr), London, 1817, the ice spades probably Eley, Fearn & Chawner, London, 1809, hour-glass pattern, 91oz (2,830gr), *NY 13 Dec,* **$15,400 (£12,941)**

4
A French silver-gilt dessert service, Touron, Paris, *c*1865, the foliate terminals applied within reeded borders, 72 pieces, 58oz 16dwt (1,830gr), *L 9 July,* **£1,210 ($1,658)**

5
Fiddle thread pattern table silver, Eley & Fearn, London, 1820, the knives, Moses Brent, 1813, engraved with crests, together with a mustard spoon, 1813, two dessert forks, 1809, and two spoons, 1828; 80 pieces, 132oz (4,105gr), *NY 24 Feb,* **$5,500 (£3,793)**

6
George IV table silver, mostly William Chawner & Thomas Barker, London, 1821/3/4, the handles bright-cut with wrigglework borders and engraved with an eagle, 102 pieces, 163oz (5,069gr), *NY 12 Apr,* **$3,960 (£2,769)**

7
French table silver, Gustave Keller, Paris, *c*1880, with shaped handles with ribbon-tied reeded rims, engraved with armorials, 216 pieces, 206oz (6,406gr), *NY 12 Apr,* **$8,250 (£5,769)**

8
A Victorian silver-gilt bacchanalian pattern dessert service, H & H Lias, London, 1876-7, 64 pieces, 108oz 12dwt (3,377gr), *L 20 Sept,* **£3,300 ($4,290)**

5

2

3

6

1

7

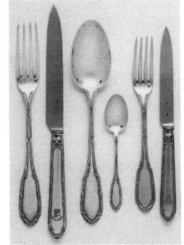
4

8

1
American table silver,
Tiffany & Co, New York,
c.1890, chrysanthemum
pattern, engraved with
monogram, 104 pieces,
129oz (4,012gr), *NY 23 Oct,*
$4,950 (£4,125)

2
American table silver,
Tiffany & Co, New York,
c.1880, chrysanthemum
pattern, 215 pieces, 311oz
6dwt (9,696gr), *NY 26 Jan,*
$9,900 (£6,828)

3
English table silver,
Crichton Bros, London,
1928, feather edge pattern,
173 pieces, 206oz
(6,406gr), *NY 24 Feb,*
$5,500 (£3,793)

4
French table silver,
Puiforcat, Paris, early
20th cent, rat-tail, the
knives with cannon
handles, monogrammed,
238 pieces, 361oz
(11,227gr), *NY 13 Dec,*
$14,300 (£12,017)

5
**A French silver dinner
service and silver-gilt
dessert service,** Puiforcat,
Paris, 20th cent, in
Regency style, the handles
flat-chased with scrolling
strapwork, mono-
grammed, 474 pieces,
749oz (23,293gr),
NY 12 Apr,
$68,200 (£47,692)

6
**Victorian shell and scale
pattern table silver,**
mostly George Adams,
London, 1843, retailed
by Hunt & Roskell Ltd,
late Storr & Mortimer,
butter knife, Holland,
Aldwinkle & Slater,
1910, 143 pieces, 351oz
(10,928gr), *C 10 Jan,*
£10,450 ($15,153)

7
English table silver, C J
Vander, London, 1958,
early English pattern
with three-pronged forks
and pistol-handled
knives, 133 pieces, 160oz
(4,976gr), *NY 23 Oct,*
$8,800 (£7,333)

8
Danish table silver, W &
S Soerensen, 20th cent,
the flat plain handles
applied at the neck with
three horizontal bands,
111 pieces, 121oz 16dwt
(3,787gr), *NY 18 July,*
$2,530 (£1,931)

9
American table silver,
Tiffany & Co, New York,
c.1925, St Dunstan pattern,
engraved with art deco
monogram, 464 pieces,
453oz (14,088gr),
NY 28 June,
$10,450 (£7,741)

1

2

3

4

5

6

7

8

9

1
A **Dutch tobacco box**,
Amsterdam, apparently
1755, w 16.4cm (6½in),
7oz 4dwt (225gr), *L 9 July*,
£462 ($632)

2
A **Dutch wedding heart**,
*c.*1640, engraved on
either side with amatory
scenes, each surrounded
by reserves illustrating
gentlemen, unmarked,
7.6cm (3in), *L 12 Mar*,
£2,420 ($3,608)

3
A **George I 22-carat gold
freedom box with
freedom paper**, The City
of Dublin, Thomas
Bolton, Dublin, 1714,
d 8.2cm (3¼in), 5oz
15dwt (178gr), *L 3 May*,
£26,400 ($37,488)

4
A **George III freedom
box**, The Corporation of
Sadlers, Upholders,
Coachmakers, Dublin,
*c.*1767, maker's mark IL,
d 8cm (3in), 4oz 4dwt
(130gr), *L 3 May*,
£5,720 ($8,122)

5
A **pair of crown-shaped
ceremonial thimbles**, The
Freedom of the
Corporation of Taylors,
*c.*1768, unmarked, 8dwt
(25gr), *L 3 May*,
£5,500 ($7,810)

6
A **William IV snuff box**,
Nathaniel Mills,
Birmingham, 1833,
w 8.3cm (3¼in), *L 13 Mar*,
£407 ($606)

7
A **George III silver-gilt
presentation snuff box**,
Phipps & Robinson,
London, 1808, 8.9cm
(3½in), *L 19 Nov*,
£660 ($864)

8
A **George III parcel-gilt
book-shaped freedom box
with freedom paper**, The
Guild of St Luke,
Benjamin Stokes,
Dublin, *c.*1770, w 8.5cm
(3¼in), *L 3 May*,
£9,900 ($14,058)

9
A **George IV silver-gilt
snuff box**, James
Williams Garland,
London, 1826, w 6.5cm
(2½in), *L 13 Mar*,
£308 ($459)

10
A **George III snuff box**,
John Shaw, Birmingham,
1812, w 7.3cm (2¾in),
L 13 Mar,
£181 ($269)

11
A **George III table snuff
box**, perhaps William
Warwick or William
Whitfield, 18.3cm (3¼in),
L 13 Mar,
£1,430 ($2,132)

12
A **George IV silver-gilt
snuff box**, Thomas Shaw,
Birmingham, 1829,
w 9cm (3½in), *L 13 Mar*,
£638 ($951)

13
A **vesta case**, Sheffield,
1895, the back inscribed
'from Charley's Aunt'
the front stamped with a
portrait of the aunt,
h 4.4cm (1¾in),
C 13-16 Mar,
£71 ($105)

14
An **early Victorian
vinaigrette**, Nathaniel
Mills, Birmingham, 1838,
with a view of Windsor
Castle, w 3.7cm (1½in),
L 13 Mar,
£440 ($656)

15
A **William IV silver-gilt
vinaigrette**, Nathaniel
Mills, Birmingham, 1829,
w 3.8cm (1½in), *L 13 Mar*,
£176 ($262)

16
A **William IV tobacco
rasp**, Sebastian Crespel
II, London, 1834, 11.5cm
(4½in), *L 19 Nov*,
£352 ($461)

17
A **George IV hanging
nutmeg grater**, Charles
Rawlings, London, 1825,
h 10.5cm (4⅛in),
C 3-6 July,
£440 ($594)

18
A **Victorian novelty scent
flask in the form of an owl**,
Charles & George Fox,
London, 1846, h 9.5cm
(3¾in), 5oz 6dwt (164gr),
C 10 Jan,
£572 ($829)

19
A **Victorian vinaigrette**,
Joseph Willmore, Bir-
mingham, 1842, h 4.3cm
(1¾in), *L 13 Mar*,
£132 ($196)

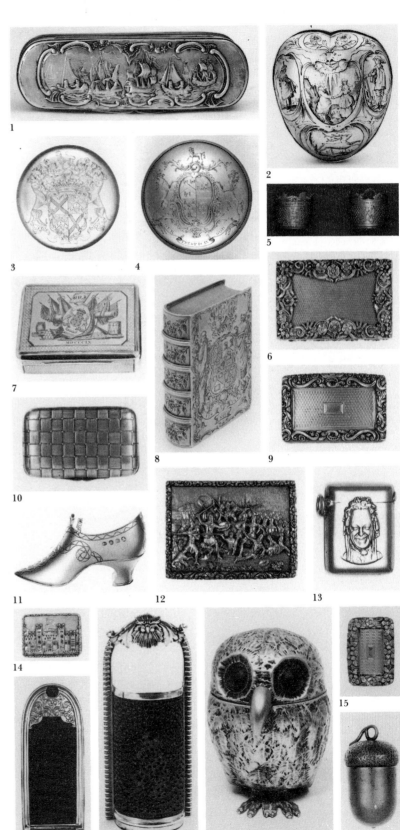

1
A Victorian shaped oblong card case, Nathaniel Mills, Birmingham, 1846, die-stamped with a view of Scott's Memorial, otherwise decorated with a profusion of leafy scrolls, 10.2cm (4in), *L 13 Mar,* **£242 ($360)**

2
A Victorian parcel-gilt silver electrotype card case from a design by George Stanton, Elkington & Co, Birmingham, 1864, both sides decorated with Venus and Cupid, h 9.6cm (3¾in), *L 13 Mar,* **£528 ($787)**

3
A Victorian vinaigrette, E H Stockwell, London, 1876, in the form of a thistle head with two leaves, in original fitted case, probably Carl Kitz, retailer's label J & G Beasley/Jewellers & Silversmiths, London, 10.2cm (4in), *L 19 Nov,* **£660 ($864)**

4
A Victorian dressing case, London, 1863, with four glass boxes and seven jars with silver-gilt mounts, the lid fitted with a mirror, six further implements and a propelling pencil, the majority with mother-of-pearl handles, the box with two secret drawers, maker's mark 'WN', *L 3 May,* **£2,640 ($3,748)**

5
An ovoid spirit flask, *c*1865, the upper body engraved with a shooting scene on one side and a golfer on the other, the lower body with garter crests and mottoes, the detachable beaker base engraved with a fisherman and a curling scene, unmarked, 18.4cm (7¼in), *HH 27 Mar,* **£506 ($754)**

6
A cut-glass and silver mounted inkwell, London, 1889, the hinged cover and collar engraved with reeded bands and inscribed about a crest and motto, h 22.9cm (9in), *C 16 Feb,* **£440 ($616)**

7
A Victorian egg-shaped spoon warmer, Fenton Bros, Sheffield, *c*1870, crested, supported on a cast rocky base, h 10.8cm (4¼in), 14oz 12dwt (454gr), *C 1/2 Feb,* **£176 ($246)**

8
A Dutch miniature longcase clock, late 19th cent, chased with figures and scrolls, h 12.7cm (5in), *C 27-30 Nov,* **£148 ($181)**

9
A Victorian 'champagne bottle' lady's companion with sewing kit, Sampson Mordan for S Mordan & Co, London, 1874, complete with pendant chain and finger-ring, h 10.4cm (4¼in), *L 13 Mar,* **£506 ($754)**

10
A hanging paper clip, London, 1893, with engine-turned base, the spring-loaded clip designed as the figure of a jester playing a lute, maker's mark 'SJ', 11.5cm (4½in), 2oz 1dwt (63gr), *C 10 Jan,* **£187 ($271)**

11
A cut-glass and silver-mounted scent bottle with hinged cover, Henry Matthews, Birmingham, 1906, pierced and stamped with foliate scrolls, h 14cm (5½in), *C 1-3 May,* **£115 ($161)**

12
A pair of table lighters, Goldsmiths and Silver Company, London, 1907/9, designed as two ship's lights, inscribed and fitted with green and red glass windows, h 8.3cm (3½in), *C 11-14 Dec,* **£330 ($412)**

1 2 3

4 5 6

7 8

9 10 11 12

1
A Victorian silver-gilt posy holder, Thomas William Dee for T W Dee & Son, London, 1866, monogrammed, h 10.5cm (4¼in), 3oz 14dwt (114gr), in fitted morocco case with gilt stamped label 'Frazer & Haws/from Garrards'/31 Regent St/Piccadilly', maker's mark probably Joseph Lief & Co, *L 9 July,* £352 ($482)

2
A pair of Victorian cast and chased 'leaping monkey' sugar tongs, London, 1887, maker's mark 'AWB', 14cm (5½in), 2oz 11dwt (79gr), *L 13 Mar,* £264 ($393)

3
A pair of George III silver-gilt boot jacks, Edward Cornelius Farrell, London, 1814, the cast reeded handles terminating at either end with hound masks and applied with entwined serpent, 11.5cm (4½in), 21oz 7dwt (663gr), *L 22 Nov,* £5,500 ($7,150)

4
A set of twelve George III buttons, possibly John Orme, London, *c*.1780, engraved with fishing scenes and motifs, d 2.5cm (1in), 1oz 19dwt (60gr), *L 3 May,* £2,310 ($3,280)

5
A George III silver-gilt eye bath, Joseph Taconet, London, 1801, engraved with a monogram below an Earl's coronet, on spreading base with reeded border, w 4.1cm (1⅝in), *P 21-24 Feb,* £858 ($1,201)

6
An apple corer, *c*.1740, the handle terminal incised with reeding, maker's mark 'TH', 15.8cm (6¼in), *L 9 July,* £352 ($482)

7
A George II bosun's whistle, London, 1743, the curved gun applied with five bands, the keel with wrigglework ornament and a wirework scroll terminal, 17cm (6¾in), *L 9 July,* £1,100 ($1,507)

8
A pair of stirrups, American, A Dugué, early 19th cent, with bevelled serpentine sides and horizontal rowels, complete with silver buckles, 16cm (6¼in), 8oz (248gr), *NY 26 Jan,* $880 (£606) **R 830 (£359; $437)**

9
A George III wine funnel, Charles Fox I, 1816, with lobed shoulder, the detachable strainer with gadroon rim and shell thumbpiece, both parts initialled, h 15.5cm (6¼in), 6oz 4dwt (195gr), *JHB 6 Nov,* **R 830 (£359; $437)**

10
A pair of George IV wine labels, Robert Gray & Son, Glasgow, 1828, each of reeded rectangular form with cut corners, matted and applied with initials in corded wirework, w 5cm (2in), *L 19 Nov,* £264 ($345)

11
Six George III wine labels, three Benjamin Smith and three Benjamin & James Smith, London, 1808/9 and *c*. cast in the form of grape-laden vine wreaths, w 7.9cm (3in), *L 22 Nov,* £1,595 ($2,073)

12
A George IV silver-gilt wine label, Rundell, Bridge & Rundell, (Philip Rundell), London, 1822, of cast cartouche form, w 7.5cm (3in), *L 22 Nov,* £825 ($1,072)

13
A George III shaped oval wine label, Joseph Angell, London, 1815, pierced for Madeira within a cast border of scrolled foliage, w 8.1cm (3¼in), *L 22 Nov,* £121 ($157)

14
A pair of George III cast oval wine labels, George Pearson, London, 1817, pierced for Sherry and Port, w 6.6cm (2½in), *L 22 Nov,* £220 ($286)

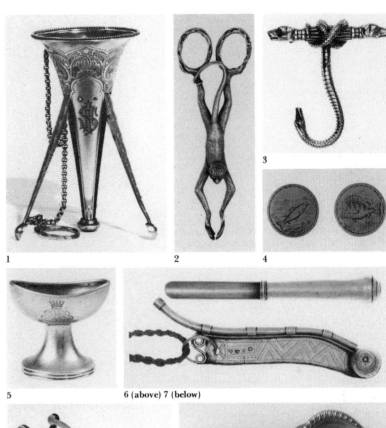

1   2   4

3

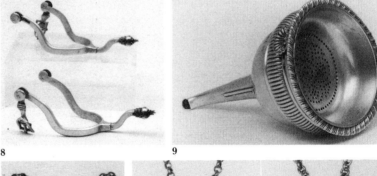

5   6 (above) 7 (below)

8   9

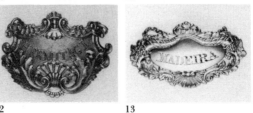

10   11

12   13   14

Objects of Vertu

RICHARD ALLEN • JULIA CLARKE • GERARD HILL

The term 'objects of vertu' derives in a roundabout way from the 17th century 'man of vertu'—a man with a special interest in the fine arts. Now the term is used to describe those exquisite small items once also referred to as *bibelots* or *objets de vitrine*. They signal taste and luxury, having nowadays little or no practical purpose but being eminently displayable in refined and elegant surroundings.

Snuff boxes are the prime examples of such objects and those in gold, sometimes jewelled or enamelled, are the most highly prized of all. They were mainly made in Paris, Germany and Switzerland between 1740 and 1815. Such gold boxes (a very fine late one by the interesting French maker Vachette, who successfully worked from the 1780s through the Revolution into the 19th century, is illustrated on page 376, fig.2) represent the very top, or investment end of the market. But the boxes have also been made in any manner of other materials: tortoiseshell, ivory, mother-of-pearl, lacquer and papier mâché. There are also other containers for small implements: étuis, often carried from the belt on a chatelaine, and nécessaires, more likely to be found on the dressing table. They contained items for sewing or writing, but the skill and delicacy of their craftsmanship far outweigh any practical purpose that might supposedly underlie their creation. Of rather later date, but now of equal appeal, are those vesta cases that are enamelled with pictures of glamorous, even erotic ladies.

On the whole, collectors of vertu tend to specialize in one particular area, whether it be boxes, walking sticks, scent bottles, late 19th century Viennese enamels, seals (usually of the late 18th to early 19th century), pipes or fans. English and Continental enamelled objects also feature here; there is a separate article on English enamels on page 363.

The heyday of the more expensive objects of vertu lasted until about 1830, though they were to reappear in Russia when Fabergé virtually recreated the market. His work and that of his contemporaries is dealt with in the section on Russian works of art on pages 377-88.

Sometimes a particularly lovely frame from a portrait miniature can itself be sold as an object of vertu and such enamelled and jewelled frames may well be decorated on the back with intricate hairwork—a snippet of hair entwined and embellished with jewels.

The portrait miniatures themselves—'pictures in little', whose origins lay in the need for intimate portable likenesses—tend to be collected either because of the identity of the sitter or of the artist. In the earlier periods (from the 16th to the early 19th century) the individual artists take precedence, but the interest in 19th-century works tend to depend on the sitter. Miniatures were originally painted on vellum or card and occasionally on metal; at the beginning of the 18th century ivory became the preferred base. Unfortunately a cracked ivory is just about irreparable; indeed repair or restoration of any miniature is very expensive as there are few restorers capable of such work.

In many respects silhouettes, or 'shades', are the poor relation of the portrait miniature. Serving much the same purpose, they were quicker and cheaper to produce. At their best, they can be superb examples of a skilful craft and fascinating as historical curiosities from the years 1760 to 1860. Either form of portraiture requires the committed collector to have a considerable knowledge of the history of costume—in profile in the case of silhouettes. Less than half the surviving original miniatures were signed, and so date can often only be established from details of clothing. It is less easy to distinguish copies. Many copies exist simply because families wanted to distribute them among themselves, but it is important to be able to differentiate between later copies and those that were contemporary with the original. In any case there are few original examples dating from much later than 1860, when the advent of photography brought these forms of portraiture to an abrupt stop.

1
Designs for two elaborate scent flasks, P. Moreau, Paris, 1765-75, single sheet numbered 21, painted with creamy-grey borders on pink, red and dusky-blue grounds, *G 14 Nov,*
SF 1,760 (£547; $732)

2
Designs for two chatelaines, P. Moreau, Paris, 1765-75, two sheets numbered 32 and 33, the first with a fob watch the second with an etui, *G 14 Nov,*
SF 2,640 (£820; $1,099)

3
A design for a rectangular snuff box lid, French, *c.*1742, watercolour, 6.4 x 8.2cm (2½ x 3¼in), *G 14 Nov,*
SF 7,700 (£2,391; $3,204)

4
An English rectangular ivory snuff box, early 18th cent, the hinged lid carved with a coat-of-arms, small cracks and repairs, 8.6cm (3¼in), *L 9 July,*
£110 ($151)

5
Designs for two bodkin cases and two scent flasks, P. Moreau, Paris, 1765-75, two sheets numbered 26 and 31, *G 14 Nov,*
SF 1,870 (£581; ($778)

6
A French tortoishell and ivory powder box, late 18th cent, the lid inset with a glazed Dieppe ivory plaque, 8.5cm (3⅜in), *L 13 Mar,*
£605 ($901)

7
An ivory snuff box of cartouche form, possibly French, early 18th cent, with Bérainesque decoration, lacking metal hinges, 9cm (3½in), *L 13 Mar,*
£495 ($737)

8
An oval silver and tortoiseshell piqué snuff box, early 18th cent, with a Commedia dell' Arte figure, slight damage, 8.5cm (3¼in), *L 9 July.*
£330 ($452)

9
A German mother-of-pearl snuff box, *c.*1760, carved with a portrait of Frederick the Great and military trophies, gilt-metal mounts, 7.7cm (3in), *NY 21 June,*
$1,210 (£890)

10
An oval mother-of-pearl and silver snuff box, possibly South American or Batavian, 1st half 18th cent, the pearl lid with a naked Venus surrounded by symbols, 8cm (3⅛in), *L 13 Mar,*
£242 ($361)

11
A silver and tortoiseshell snuff box, John Obrisset, *c.*1710, the lid inset with an oval tortoiseshell plaque with a profile portrait of Charles I, after a medal by John Roettiers, 1670, signed OB, silver sides and hinges, 9cm (3½in), *L 9 July,*
£660 ($904)

12
A Neapolitan tortoiseshell piqué snuff box, *c.*1730, the lid inlaid in finely engraved silver with Delilah and Samson, the base with a hound chasing a stag in piqué point, mount, damaged, 8cm (3⅛in), *L 13 Mar,*
£418 ($622)

13
A large German hardstone snuff box, *c.*1740-50, carved in high relief with whorling auricular scrolls, after the manner of the designs of Martin Engelbrecht of Augsburg, silver-gilt mounts, 12cm (4¾in), *G 16 May,*
SF 5,800 (£1,742; $2,491)

14
An oval silver and tortoiseshell snuff box, probably English, *c.*1730, the lid inlaid with a silver piqué posé basket of flowers, 7cm (2¾in), *L 13 Mar,*
£231 ($344)

15
A French mother-of-pearl and stained ivory counter box, Mariaval Le Jeune, Paris, early 18th cent, containing nineteen counters, one small chip, 8cm (3⅛in), *L 13 Mar,*
£462 ($665))

1
A blond tortoiseshell and gold piqué snuff box, probably French, c.1720, the lid inlaid in gold piqué posé et point, later gilt-metal mounts, some damage and restoration, 7.5cm (3in), *L 9 July,* £495 ($678)

2
A circular gold and tortoiseshell piqué snuff box, probably French, c.1740, the lid and bombé sides inlaid overall in gold piqué posé et point 6.5cm (2½in), *L 9 July,* £2,640 ($3,617)

3
A Neapolitan tortoiseshell piqué casket, c.1730, decorated in gold piqué posé et point and carved mother-of-pearl, gold thumbpiece and hinges, some loss of piqué, w 22cm (8⅝in), *G 14 Nov,* **SF 26,400 (£8,199; $10,986)**

4
A tortoiseshell and silver piqué tobacco rasp case, c.1730, the lid inlaid in engraved silver piqué posé, reeded silver mounts, 13cm (5in), *L 9 July,* £495 ($678)

5
A French horn snuff box, c.1790, decorated in gold piqué posé with mullets within borders of scallops and pellets, some piqué lacking, d 6cm (2¼in), *L 9 July,* £187 ($256)

6
A Neapolitan gold and tortoiseshell piqué bonbonnière of egg form, 3rd quarter 18th cent, inlaid in piqué posé et point with nesting fowl within garlands of vine, gold mounts, cracked, 6.5cm (2½in), *L 13 Mar,* £605 ($902)

7
A Neapolitan gold and tortoiseshell piqué snuff box, c.1765-70, decorated in gold piqué posé with temples and ruins, the lid with key pattern, gold shell thumbpiece and mounts, 8.5cm (3¼in), *L 9 July,* £880 ($1,206)

8
A Neapolitan tortoiseshell piqué spyglass, c.1760, the barrel inlaid in gold piqué posé et point with scrollwork enclosing panels of scaling and diaper, some damage and restoration, 6cm (2½in), *L 9 July,* £605 ($829)

9
A tortoiseshell and gold piqué boîte à ballon, probably French, c.1750, decorated with scrollwork enclosing scaled panels, plain gold lip-mount and hinge, a small crack near hinge, d 7.2cm (2⅞in), *G 14 Nov,* **SF 7,700 (£2,391; $3,204)**

10
An inlaid tortoiseshell necessaire, probably French, c.1770, gilt-metal mounts, the interior with folding knife, ivory slips, steel tweezers, pencil holder, bodkin and scissors, 9cm (3½in), *L 13 Mar,* £396 ($590)

11
A continental oval red lacquer snuff box, mid-19th cent, decorated with sprays of flowers on a red ground and with gilded borders, gilt-metal mounts, 9.2cm (3⅝in), *NY 13 Dec,* $715 (£572)

12
A French circular lacquer powder box, c.1860, painted in honey and sepia on tooled or engraved gilt grounds with pastoral scenes, gold mounts and interior, maker's mark A?, the lacquer slightly flawed, d 9.2cm (3⅝in), *G 14 Nov,* **SF 3,300 (£1,025; $1,374)**

13
An English gilt-metal snuff box, Birmingham, c.1750, the lid chased with Hercules and the Cretan bull, w 4.2cm (1½in), *L 9 July,* £396 ($543)

14
An English gold and agate egg bonbonnière, c.1780, the gold mounts chased with rocaille and floral motifs, gold suspension loop, h 3.8cm (1½in), *G 14 Nov,* **SF 3,300 (£1,025; $1,373)**

1   2

3   4   5

6   7   8

9   10   11

12   13   14

1
A French oval boîte à
pomponne, c.1770, the lid
struck with two swans
within leafy interlaced
decoration, the sides
fluted and hung with
swags, some wear, 7.5cm
(3in), *L 13 Mar*,
£187 ($278)

2
An English gold and
hardstone snuff box, mid-
18th cent, the brown
agate lid, body and base
with gold mounts,
chased with rocaille scrolls,
5.5cm (2⅛in), *G 14 Nov*,
SF 11,000 (£3,416; $4,578)

3
A Swedish gold spice box,
Frantz Bergs, Stockholm,
1753 or 1758, enamelled
in translucent dark blue
basse-taille with trailing
flowers on a vannerie
ground, repaired and
slight damage, h 6cm
(2⅜in), *G 14 Nov*,
SF 16,500 (£5,124; $6,866)

4
A Swiss three-colour gold
snuff box, c.1765, chased
with hunting scenes,
unmarked, 8cm (3⅛in),
G 17 May,
SF 16,500 (£5,229; $7,268)

5
A French gold-mounted
Indian jade betel nut box,
Adrien-Jean-Maximilien
Vachette, Paris, c.1797,
the lid and base carved
as three nuts pendent
from a frond, engraved
on the rim 'Vachette
Bijoutier à Paris',
w 10.5cm (4⅛in), *G 13 Nov*,
SF 82,500 (£25,581;
$34,279)

6
An English gold and
hardstone cartouche-
shaped snuff box, c.1760,
w 7cm (2¾in), *G 13 Nov*,
SF 3,300 (£1,083; $1,451)

7
A French silver and
mother-of-pearl snuff box,
maker's mark AD, Paris,
1743, inlaid with flowers
in coloured mother-of-
pearl, 7.5cm (3in),
NY 13 Dec,
$935 (£786)

8
A Swiss four-colour gold
snuff box, c.1760, w 6.4cm
(2½in), *G 14 Nov*,
SF 8,250 (£2,562; $3,433)

9
A French oval two-colour
gold and rock crystal snuff
box, maker's mark E?
over A with a device
between, Paris, 1769,
charge mark of Julien
Alaterre, w 5.5cm (2⅛in),
G 14 Nov,
SF 3,300 (£1,025; $1,373)

10
A French gold-mounted
vernis martin boîte à
portrait, Paris, c.1770, the
lid set with a miniature
of the Comte de Provence
attributed to Drouais,
d 6.3cm (2½in), *G 14 Nov*,
SF 3,740 (£1,161; $1,556)

11
A French circular gold
and enamel snuff box,
Joseph-Etienne Blerzy,
Paris, 1775, 7.1cm (2¾in),
G 16 May,
SF 12,000 (£3,604; $5,153)

12
A Swiss oval three-colour
gold snuff box, c.1780, the
lid set with a glazed
relief of the Three
Graces, pseudo-French
marks, 8.5cm (3⅜in),
G 17 May,
SF 13,750 (£4,358; $6,057)

13
A Swiss oval gold and
enamel bonbonnière,
c.1790, painted with
translucent amber and
opaque white enamel
borders, pseudo-French
marks, 5.5cm (2⅛in),
G 17 May,
SF 9,900 (£3,137; $4,366)

14
A Swiss gold and enamel
snuff box, c.1790, decor-
ated with panels of
translucent dark blue
enamel over engine-
turning within white
decorated borders,
French prestige marks,
enamelled '171', 9.6cm
(3¾in), *G 17 May*,
SF 6,600 (£2,092; $2,907)

15
A French rectangular two-
colour gold snuff box,
Paris, 1786, w 8.9cm
(3½in), *G 14 Nov*,
SF 4,950 (£1,537; $2,050)

1

A Swiss gold and enamel snuff box, J F Bautte, c.1830, enamelled with multi-coloured flowers on a black ground, 6.8cm (2⅝in), NY 21 June, $1,650 (£1,213)

2

A French gold and enamel boîte à portrait Jean-Baptiste Fossin & Fils, Paris, c.1840, inset with a painted oval enamel miniature of Antoine Vitré by Jacques Bordier, signed and dated 1651, 8.4cm (3¼in), G 16 May, SF 85,000 (£25,526; $36,502)

3

An English opaline scent bottle, c.1870, with silver-gilt cap and collar set with corals, stamped 'Leuchars', lip chipped, 8.5cm (3⅜in), L 13 Mar, £242 ($361)

4

An Italian mosaic and hardstone snuff box, Giovanni Andrea Mascelli, Rome, 1828, with silver-gilt mounts, 8.5cm (3⅜in), L 13 Mar, £1,320 ($1,967)

5

An Italian snuff box, Rome, c.1820-30, with silver mounts, 5cm (2in), L 13 Mar, £440 ($484)

6

A Continental circular tortoiseshell snuff box, c.1810, with slightly incurved sides, the cover mounted with a mosaic of a landscape, within a gold border, 9.7cm (3¾in), NY 21 June, $1,650 (£1,213)

7

A micro-mosaic plaque, early 19th cent, 7.5cm (3in), L 13 Mar, £660 ($984)

8

A French gold and enamel pill box, c.1930, w 3.3cm (1¼in), G 13 Nov, SF 2,200 (£722; $967)

9

An English silver-gilt and hardstone casket, London, 1847, the grey-and-white striated agate panels with coffee-coloured or rust-red spotty inclusions, maker's mark WN probably for William Nettleship, w 11.6cm (4½in), L 9 July, £1,265 ($1,733)

10

A circular gold-mounted tortoiseshell and Roman mosaic snuff box, early 19th cent, d 7.4cm (2⅞in), G 13 Nov, SF 3,300 (£1,083; $1,451)

11

A Roman micro-mosaic plaque, early 19th cent, cast gilt-metal frame, 7cm (2¾in), L 13 Mar, £1,980 ($2,950)

12

A Victorian silver-gilt mounted porcelain smelling salts/scent flask/vinaigrette, Henry Williams Dee for HW & L Dee, London, 1870, 11.3cm (4½in), L 13 Mar, £935 ($1,393)

13

A gold and tortoiseshell boîte à miniature, late 18th/early 19th cent, the lid inset with a miniature, watercolour on card, by A Chaplin, signed, after the manner of Hubert Robert, d 10cm (4in), L 9 July, £605 ($829)

14

An Italian pietra dura-mounted wood covered box, early 20th cent, the interior fitted with compartments, 33cm (13in), NY 24/25 Feb, $660 (£471)

15

A French trois-couleurs gilt-metal etui, dated 1838, cast in high relief on a grained ground, the interior with glass scent bottle with gilt decoration, 12cm (4¾in), L 9 July, £242 ($332)

1
A Swedish two-colour gold portrait snuff box, Friedrich Fyrwald, Stockholm, 1794, the lid inset with a glazed oval miniature of King Gustav III of Sweden by Pierre Adolphe Hall, 6.1cm (2⅜in), *G 16 May*, **SF 23,000 (£6,907; $9,877)**

2
A Swedish gold portrait snuff box, Frans Wilhelmsson, Stockholm, 1785, the hinged lid inset with a glazed oval miniature of King Gustav III of Sweden, in the manner of Hall, 7.7cm (3in), *G 16 May*, **SF 22,000 (£6,607; $9,447)**

3
A Swiss gold and enamel snuff box, late 18th cent, with a painted medallion of Venus and Cupid, pseudo-French marks the underside chipped, w 6.5cm (2½in), *L 9 July*, **£2,310 ($3,165)**

4
A German gold and hardstone snuff box, Dresden, late 18th cent, in the manner of Johann Christian Neuber, the lid inset with an oval Swiss enamel plaque painted with Priam and Hector, w 8.5cm (3¼in), *NY 21 June*, **$18,700 (£13,750)**

5
A Swiss oval gold and enamel snuff box, *c* 1800, the lid set with an enamel plaque initialled CA, the spandrels enamelled in blue basse-taille, maker's mark M & P, w 6cm (2⅜in), *G 13 Nov*, **SF 4,400 (£1,444; $1,934)**

6
A Swiss jewelled gold and enamel musical singing bird box with watch, Jean-Georges Rémond & Cie, *c* 1820, the lid painted with Helen and Paris, the front set with a circular gold watch, 9.5cm (3¾in), *G 16 May*, **SF 75,000 (£22,523; $32,207)**

7
A French two-colour gold and enamel snuff box, Etienne-Lucien Blerzy, Paris, *c* 1800, 8.8cm (3½in), *G 16 May*, **SF 12,500 (£3,754; $5,368)**

8
A gold and agate snuff box, probably English, *c* 1810, 7.7cm (3in), *NY 21 June*, **$770 (£566)**

9
A Swiss gold and enamel snuff box, *c* 1820, 9.7cm (3¾in), *NY 21 June*, **$2,420 (£1,779)**

10
An English gold snuff box, Alexander James Strachan, London, 1815, w 7.5cm (3in), *G 13 Nov*, **SF 3,300 (£1,083; $1,451)**

11
A gold-mounted agate snuff box, probably English, *c* 1820, the cover and base of mottled brown agate, 7.8cm (3in), *NY 21 June*, **$1,045 (£768)**

12
A Swiss three-colour circular powder box, late 18th cent, applied with borders of coloured foliage on sanded grounds, maker's mark apparently HB, struck with pseudo-Paris marks for 1798-1809 and later French control marks, worn, d 5.8cm (2¼in), *G 14 Nov*, **SF 1,980 (£615; $824)**

13
A Swiss jewelled gold and enamel automaton and watch, *c* 1810-20, restoration, 9cm (3½in), *G 16 May*, **SF 80,000 (£24,024; $34,354)**

14
A French Royal presentation gold snuff box, Gabriel-Raoul Morel, Paris, *c* 1820, applied with the crown and monogram of Louis XVIII, some chips, 8.5cm (3⅜in), *G 16 May*, **SF 19,000 (£5,706; $8,159)**

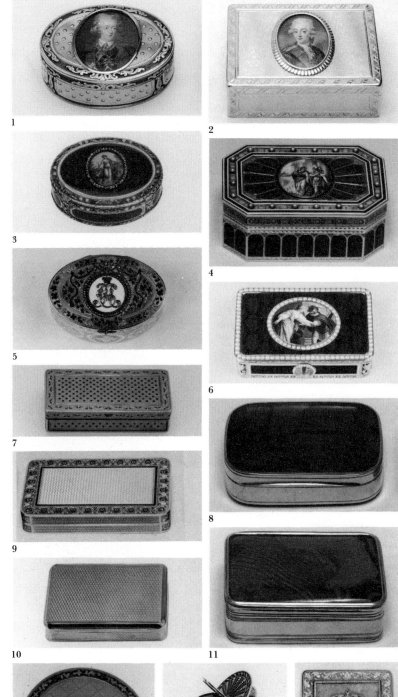

1

A Swiss four-colour gold snuff box, early 19th cent, struck with two pairs of maple leaves incuse and '14' twice, 7.9cm (3⅛in), *G 14 Nov,* SF 4,950 (£1,537; $2,060)

2

A Swiss export gold snuff box, *c*1840, apparently unmarked, 7.2cm (2¾in), *L 9 July,* £682 ($934)

3

A Swiss rectangular gold snuff box, early 19th cent, decorated with chequered panels bordered by engraved scrolling foliage, pseudo-French marks, 8cm (3⅛in), *G 14 Nov,* SF 3,520 (£1,093; $1,465)

4

A Swiss rectangular gold snuff box, Bautte & Moulinié, Geneva, 1815-81, engine-turned, 7.4cm (2⅞in), *G 14 Nov,* SF 2,970 (£922; $1,236)

5

A Swiss rectangular gold and hardstone snuff box, mid-19th cent, the lid inset with a lapis lazuli panel applied with Apollo carved in malachite, maker's mark AM in a horizontal lozenge, 7.3cm (2⅞in), *G 16 May,* SF 2,800 (£841; $1,202)

6

A Swiss gold and enamel oval double-opening snuff box, Jean-Georges Rémond & Cie, *c*1815, the cover enamelled with a mythological scene, lacks music movement, 9cm (3½in), *NY 13 Dec,* $5,280 (£4,437)

7

A Swiss gold and enamel snuff box, 2nd quarter 19th cent, the cover enamelled with a portrait of Napoleon Bonaparte, 9cm (3½in), *NY 13 Dec,* $7,150 (£5,720)

8

An Italian gold table cigar box, 18cm (7⅛in), *G 16 May,* SF 12,000 (£3,604; $5,153)

9

A French gold snuff box, *c*1830, engraved with foliate borders against engine-turned panels, maker's mark possibly LTC, 8.3cm (3¼in), *G 16 May,* SF 3,600 (£1,081; $1,546)

10

A Continental gold and enamel snuff box, mid-19th cent, probably Swiss, the cover and base decorated with foliage on a royal blue ground, 8.8cm (3½in), *NY 13 Dec,* $1,870 (£1,571)

11

An Austrian four-colour gold snuff box, Vienna, 1836, chased in several colour golds on a matt ground, 8.5cm (3⅜in), *G 14 Nov,* SF 5,500 (£1,708; $2,289)

12

A French two-colour gold and mosaic snuff box, Paris, *c*1810, maker's mark LRF, 6.5cm (2½in), *G 14 Nov,* SF 9,900 (£3,075; $4,120)

13

A French three-colour gold snuff box, Paris, *c*1840, inset with earlier ivory miniatures, by Jacques-Joseph de Gault, signed on the lid and base, 8.4cm (3¼in), *G 16 May,* SF 22,000 (£6,607; $9,447)

14

A Swiss gold and enamel snuff box, *c*1830, enamelled overall en grisaille, 8.5cm (3¼in), *NY 13 Dec,* $3,960 (£3,328)

15

An Italian gold and black enamel snuff box, early 19th cent, decorated in black taille d'épargne with vines, 7.5cm (3in), *G 16 May,* SF 5,000 (£1,502; $2,147)

16

A French gold and mosaic snuff box, Paris, 1809-19, the lid inlaid with an oval Roman mosaic plaque, maker's mark SL, possibly for Simon-Achille Léger, 6.5cm (2½in), *G 16 May* SF 5,600 (£1,682; $2,405)

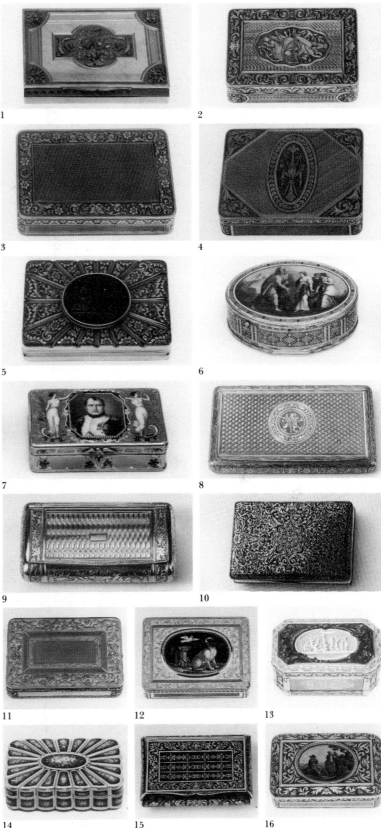

1
An oval shell cameo, by
D Pascoli, c 1860, carved
and undercut with the
profile head of a nymph,
h 6cm (2¾in), L 9 July,
£638 ($874)

2
A shell cameo with an
inscription dated 1848,
5.5cm (2⅛in), L 13 Mar,
£396 ($590)

3
An oval bloodstone
plaque, mid-19th cent,
carved in relief with a
profile of the Emperor
Vespasian, after drawings
by Marcantonio Raimondi,
gilt-metal frame, h 8.5cm
(3¼in), L 9 July,
£770 ($1,055)

4
An English white chalcedony
and gold desk set, Storr &
Mortimer, London,
c 1835, comprising a pen
with chalcedony stem
overlaid with gold and a
desk seal, 15 and 6.5cm
(5⅞ and 2⅞in), L 13 Mar,
£935 ($1,393)

5
A pair of gold and paste
shoe buckles, c 1790, 8cm
(3⅛in), L 13 Mar,
£110 ($164)

6
An English gold and steel
pocket knife, Blofeld, 6
Middle Row, Holborn,
c 1835, with two folding
blades, a pair of scissors
and a detachable awl,
9.2cm (3⅝in), G 17 May,
SF 1,100 (£348; $484)

7
A pair of two-colour gold
and paste shoe buckles,
c 1780, 7.5cm (3in),
L 13 Mar,
£176 ($262)

8
A French gold and enamel
souvenir, late 18th cent,
the interior with pencil
and ivory tablet, worn,
9.5cm (3¾in), G 16 May,
SF 1,800 (£541; $773)

9
A French four-colour gold
chatelaine, c 1875, fitted
with a watch key, a fob
seal and a watch clip,
13.2cm (5⅛in), G 13 Nov,
SF 4,180 (£1,296; $1,737)

10
A French gold-mounted
black leather purse, mid-
18th cent, from the
collection of Mme de
Pompadour, 11cm
(4⅜in), G 16 May,
SF 4,200 (£1,261; $1,804)

11
A Continental vari-
coloured gold-mounted
notebook, probably
Swiss, c 1840, complete
with propelling pencil,
11.8cm (4⅝in), NY 13 Dec,
$605 (£505)

12
An English gold and
enamel bodkin case,
c 1775-80, decorated with
portrait medallions on a
chocolate ground within
translucent green and
opaque white borders,
the banding in
translucent blue and
opaque white, restored,
11cm (4¼in), G 14 Nov,
SF 3,520 (£1,093; $1,465)

13
A Dutch diamond-set
pierced oval silver
miniature frame, late 18th
cent, the borders
mounted with rose-cut
diamonds, h 11cm (4¼in),
L 9 July,
£770 ($1,055)

14
A diamond and emerald
zarf, 19th cent, mounted
in gold and silver, the
bowl and foot decorated
with pavé-set cushion-cut
diamonds on a ground
of step-cut emeralds, the
interior set at the base
with a single diamond,
6.2cm (2½in), G 16 May,
SF 90,000 (£27,027;
$38,649)

15
A gold, enamel and gem-
set vase and cover,
Austrian or French,
c 1885, gilt and painted
on dark blue grounds,
the cover and handles
mounted with pearls, the
foot set with rubies and
emeralds, unmarked,
minor damage, 11.7cm
(4⅝in), G 16 May,
SF 6,000 (£1,802; $2,577)

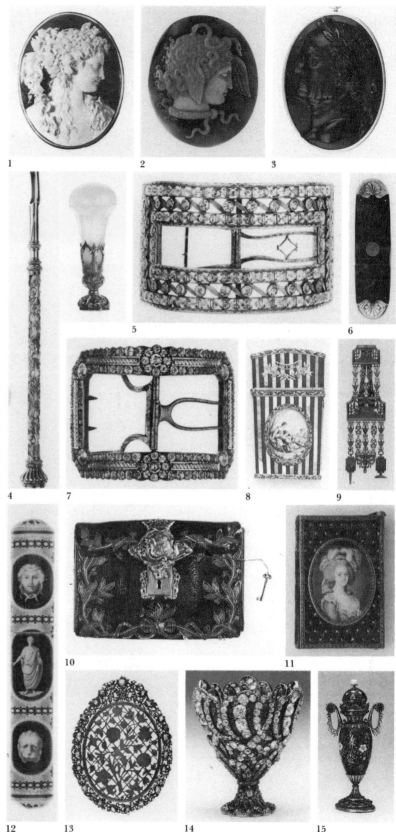

1
An English gold fob chain, c.1835, with four curb-link strands, the mounts further applied with a fox-hunting trophy, a hound and a pendant ring, the slide with a covey of grouse, 24.5cm (9⅝in), *G 17 May,* **SF 825 (£261; $363)**

2
An English gold fob seal, late 18th cent, the carnelian matrix engraved with the Carew/Holdsworth coat-of-arms, 2.5cm (1in), *L 13 Mar,* **£242 ($360)**

3
An English gold-cased fob seal, early 19th cent, the white matrix engraved with the arms of Palk quartering Carew, 3cm (1⅛in), *L 13 Mar,* **£220 ($328)**

4
An English gold fob seal, c.1785, the chalcedony matrix engraved with the initials 'MK', 2.7cm (1in), *G 16 May,* **SF 600 (£180; $258)**

5
An English gold fob double-sided swivel fob seal, late 18th cent, the carnelian matrix engraved on one side with a coat-of-arms, the other a crest, 5.3cm (2⅛in), *G 17 May,* **SF 1,650 (£523; $727)**

6
An English gold double-sided swivel fob seal, c.1770, the chalcedony matrix engraved on one side with armorials, the other with a crest and initials, 4.7cm (1½in), *L 19 Nov,* **£264 ($346)**

7
A gold double-sided swivel fob seal, c.1810, engraved with the arms of Count Esterhazy of Hungary, maker's mark apparently AS incuse, 5cm (2in), *G 16 May,* **SF 3,800 (£1,141; $1,632)**

8
An English gold fob seal, early 19th cent, 4.4cm (1¾in), *G 17 May,* **SF 660 (£209; $291)**

9
A Swiss gold musical fob seal, early 19th cent, h 4.2cm (1⅝in), *G 16 May,* **SF 2,000 (£601; $859)**

10
A gold hunting fob seal, early 19th cent, the carnelian matrix engraved 'D', 3.5cm (1⅜in), *L 13 Mar,* **£682 ($1,016)**

11
An English gold and carved amethyst swivel seal, c.1830, the triangular amethyst seal engraved with the arms of Browne-Lecky, *C 3-6 July,* **£396 ($537)**

12
A Swiss gold and jewelled musical fob seal, c.1820, 4.6cm (1¾in), *NY 21 June,* **$1,100 (£809)**

13
An English gold fob seal, c.1830, the cornelian matrix engraved with the arms of Sir Christopher Cole (1770-1837), 4cm (3½in), *L 19 Nov,* **£286 ($375)**

14
An English three-colour gold fob seal, the carnelian matrix engraved with two crests, a motto and the initials 'TRC'; (of Roper-Curzon, Barons, Teynham,) 5.3cm (2⅛in), *G 16 May,* **SF 1,500 (£450; $644)**

15
An English gold fob seal, late 18th cent, the chalcedony matrix engraved with an intaglio profile of William Shakespeare, 3.3cm (1¼in), *L 19 Nov,* **£187 ($245)**

16
A gold and stained-ivory seal case, perhaps Neapolitan, early 18th cent, carved as the figure of Harlequin with a wobbling head, 9.1cm (3½in), *G 16 May,* **SF 4,200 (£1,261; $1,804)**

17
A gold and hardstone desk seal, 19th cent, 7cm (2¾in), *L 19 Nov,* **£418 ($548)**

1

An Austro-Hungarian portrait meerschaum cheroot holder, c.1875, with amber stem, carved in full relief with 'La Famille Elbin'; the Elbin family were an acrobatic troupe active in the 1870s and 1880s, 20.8cm (8¼in), *L 9 July,* £638 ($874)

2

A meerschaum pipe, probably Austrian c.1875, with curved amber stem, the bowl carved in full relief with a group of the goddess Diana, 39.5cm (15½in), *L 9 July,* £2,750 ($3,768)

3

A pair of Continental jewelled gold and platinum mirrors, the openwork borders set with diamonds, rubies and emeralds, scroll bases and strut supports, 15.3cm (6in), *NY 21 June,* $8,800 (£6,471)

4

An Austrian meerschaum pipe, late 19th cent, carved in full relief with a battle scene, 17cm (6⅝in), *F 3/4 Oct,* L 450,000 (£178; $231)

5

A gold and enamelled thimble/scent bottle case, the thimble enamelled with a green and red foliate rim bordered with white enamel beads, the base inscribed 'The ship E Dartmouth lost on ye island of Carnicobar, June 24th 1782', *P 11/18 Dec,* £2,970 ($3,558)

6

An English gilt silver-mounted metal singing bird box, c.1900, the cover decorated with scenes from Aesop's fables, with hidden key compartment, w 10.2cm (4in), *C 10 Jan,* £715 ($1,037)

7

A pair of ivory, gold and jewelled table candlesticks, the ivory bases and baluster stems with gold cable borders, each base mounted with a bird holding a diamond in its beak, 8.5cm (3⅜in), *NY 21 June,* $2,860 (£2,103)

8

A Continental silver-gilt, enamel and jewelled singing bird box, late 19th cent, enamelled and set with turquoise, pearls and other hardstones, the cover with a jewel-mounted oval reserve opening to reveal a feathered bird, 13.4cm (5¼in), *NY 21 June,* $1,870 (£1,375)

9

A Continental silver and enamel singing bird box, late 19th cent, enamelled in red, green and white and set with blue 'jewels', 10cm (3⅞in), *NY 21 June,* $715 (£526)

10

A German silver singing bird box, c.1900, the sides with doves within oval reserves, the top with a courting couple, the oval centre opening to reveal a brightly feathered bird, 9.7cm (3¾in), *NY 21 June,* $1,430 (£1,051)

11

A singing bird automaton, probably French, 20th cent, the gilded box with raised wirework decoration, 10cm (4in), *C 21 Mar,* £286 ($426)

12

A French silver-gilt and blue enamel desk garniture, Fossin & Fils, Paris, mid-19th cent; *G 14 Nov,* SF 20,900 (£6,491; $8,696)

1
An Austrian enamelled silver cigarette case, maker's mark JF or JP, Vienna, *c*.1890, the hinged lid painted with a cut-out of a siren, enamel with scratched surface, 9cm (3½in), *L 9 July,* £495 ($678)

2
A silver and enamel vesta case, Sampson Mordan for S Mordan & Co, London, 1886, PODR, painted with a guardsman, h 5.7cm (2¼in), *L 19 Nov,* £605 ($793)

3
A French enamelled silver vesta case, *c*.1885, painted on one side with a standing nude, the reverse similar with a nymph weighing Cupid, the interior with a landscape, the surface scratched, 4.7cm (1¾in), *L 9 July,* £275 ($377)

4
A German enamelled vesta case, *c*.1900, struck with the post-1893 French import mark, silver-coloured metal, the secret compartment painted with a nude, 5cm (2in), *L 19 Nov,* £825 ($1,081)

5
A curved rectangular enamelled silver cigarette case, probably German, importer's mark GD, Chester, 1908, painted with a portrait of Una Gitana, 8.5cm (3¼in), *L 13 Mar,* £880 ($1,311)

6
A silver and enamel vesta case, maker's mark of W H Sparrow, apparently struck over that of another, Birmingham, 1902, h 4.7cm (1¾in), *L 19 Nov,* £440 ($576)

7
An enamelled silver vesta case, Sampson Mordan & Co Ltd of London, Chester, 1905, 5.7cm (2¼in), *L 9 July,* £374 ($514)

8
A German enamelled silver cigarette case, importer's mark of George Stockwell for G Stockwell & Co Ltd, London, 1921, also struck 'S&Co/Ld', a little chipped and scratched, 9.4cm (3¾in), *L 19 Nov,* £1,100 ($1,441)

9
A German enamelled curved oblong vesta case, *c*.1910, silver-coloured metal, the secret compartment painted with a wood-nymph, 5cm (2in), *L 13 Mar,* £440 ($656)

10
A German enamelled rectangular cigarette case, *c*.1910, silver-coloured metal, one side engraved and enamelled with translucent gilt-flecked flames consuming a bejewelled Amazon in relief, 9cm (3½in), *L 13 Mar,* £770 ($1,147)

11
An English enamelled silver cigarette case, George Heath for G Heath & Co, London, 1889, the enamel signed in monogram CF and 'H Gray', the surface scratched, 9cm (3½in), *L 9 July,* £572 ($784)

12
A German enamelled curved rectangular cigarette case, *c*.1910, silver-coloured metal, the secret compartment painted with a pink nude, internal cracks to enamel, 8.8cm (3½in), *L 13 Mar,* £1,100 ($1,639)

13
A silver and enamel vesta case, Sampson Mordan & Co Ltd, London, 1908, h 7.5 cm (3in), *L 19 Nov,* £990 ($1,297)

14
A French gold and enamel vesta case, *c*.1885, damage, 5cm (2in), *L 19 Nov,* £660 ($865)

1

An Italian ivory piqué fan, *c*1730, the guards with piqué point et clous decoration and set with pierced foliate mother-of-pearl panels, the leaf painted with Apollo and the Muses, 28cm (11in), *L 9 July,* £220 ($301)

2

An ivory fan, *c*1735, the leaf with painted landscape, animal and bird vignettes outlined in gilt, 27.2cm (10¾in), *L 13 Mar,* £190 ($295)

3

An English ivory fan, *c*1760, the guards carved and decorated with painted panels, the sticks en suite, the leaf painted with a pastoral scene, some damage, 27.8cm (11in), *L 13 Mar,* £297 ($443)

4

An Italian ivory fan, late 18th cent, the sticks pierced and carved, the leaf painted with a view of the Piazza del Popolo, some damage, 25.5cm (10in), *L 9 July,* £264 ($362)

5

A French fan, mid-18th cent, the sticks with pierced foliate mother-of-pearl panels, *F 10 May,* L 791,000 (£322; $463)

6

A North European mother-of-pearl fan, *c*1780, the sticks elaborately carved and three-colour gilt with an allegory of Chastity, the guards pierced over pink shell, the leaf painted with Zephyr and Flora, repaired, 27cm, (10⅝in), *L 9 July,* £880 ($1,206)

7

A French ivory fan, *c*1780, the guards gilt and carved over iridescent mother-of-pearl, 29.9cm (11¾in), *L 13 Mar,* £253 ($377)

8

A North European painted ivory fan, mid-18th cent, the sticks decorated with brightly coloured flowers, the guards pierced over scarlet foil, the leaf painted with vignettes of rustic and romantic subjects, 29.8cm (11¾in), *L 13 Mar,* £176 ($262)

9

A French ballooning fan, 1783, commemorating the ascent of M Robert and Charles in August 1783, the ivory sticks foiled and carved, the guards pierced and carved over gilt foil applied with vari-coloured paste flower centres, some missing, 27cm (10⅝in), *L 9 July,* £308 ($422)

10

A French printed ballooning fan, *c*1783, the bone guards etched and foiled with ballooning emblems, the paper leaf with hand-painted etchings showing the ascent of M Robert and Charles, all reserved against a speckled green and gilt ground, some damage, 27.3cm (10¾in), *L 9 July,* £506 ($693)

11

A French ivory fan, *c*1770, the guards carved and gilt with shepherdesses against a mother-of-pearl ground, the sticks foiled and gilt, the leaf with vignettes with inset stamped and gilt panels of trompe l'oeil decoration, 27cm (10⅝in), *L 13 Mar,* £418 ($623)

12

An Italian fan, late 18th cent, the ivory guards carved over gilt foil, the ivory and sandalwood sticks pierced and carved, the chickenskin leaf painted with Roman views within blue and white borders, gold-mounted half-pearl cluster rivet, sticks with slight damage, 29cm (11½in), *L 9 July,* £352 ($482)

1

2

3

4

5

6

7

8

9

10

11

12

English Enamels 1745-1820

JULIA CLARKE

Recent years have seen a revived interest in English enamels and a consequent sharp rise in prices, particularly at the lower end of the market. 'Trifles', otherwise known as motto or patch boxes, were mass-produced in Staffordshire between 1780 and 1820 for sale as souvenirs in spas and tourist centres, and have trebled in value over five years. Animal bonbonnières, that is small boxes stamped in relief from copper enamelled and painted to resemble beasts from lambs to lions, now command prices in the thousands. Conversely, the larger items, such as caskets or urns, and scholarly objects, such as Battersea portrait plaques, have scarcely changed in value.

The popular fallacy that all the best English enamels were made in Battersea is still current, so it cannot be reiterated too often that this is nonsense. The art of painting and printing on enamels in England flowered from the 1740s, inspired by the influx of objects and artists from abroad. London, the Bilston area, Liverpool and Birmingham, the 'toy' (box) centre of England, have all been credited with initiating the vogue. It is most likely, as with the advent of porcelain in England, that several places were experimenting at the same time.

Technically, the enamelling process consisted of coating copper blanks with powdered glass and arsenic and firing them. The smooth glossy white surface thus produced could then be painted or transfer-printed. Transfer-printing in luminous soft pinks, purples and reds was the speciality of the Battersea factory itself. Opening in late 1753, it closed in early 1756, followed by the bankruptcies of two of the founding partners, Stephen Theodore Janssen, the financial backer (a former Lord Mayor of London among other prestigious positions), and John Brooks, a shiftless but inventive Irish engraver. An advertisement for the sale of Janssen's property lists: 'a quantity of beautiful enamels, colour'd and uncolour'd of the new manufactory carried on at York House at Battersea . . . consisting of Snuff Boxes of all sizes . . . of square & oval pictures of the Royal Family, History & other pleasing subjects . . . Bottle Tickets with chains for all sorts of Liquor.' (*Daily Advertiser,* 28 February 1756). These are the only type of objects that can now be attributed with any certainty to Battersea.

Confusion arises since Battersea copper-plates were bought and used in the Midlands. Generally, however, Staffordshire enamellers preferred to print and brightly colour their boxes with scenes based on earlier French artists such as Watteau. Larger objects like caskets or urns were painted with Italianate scenes and the small étuis, scent bottles and necessaires were decorated with pastoral themes and the ubiquitous pretty sprays of summer flowers. Enamels attributed to so far unidentified London makers are of high quality and are closely related to porcelain, being painted or gilded with birds and flowers against rich blue, turquoise or green grounds. Those from Liverpool were usually transfer-printed in black or brown with portraits of statesmen, soldiers or actors and certain of them are signed by John Sadler of earthenware fame.

The great days of English enamels were over by the 1790s when both the shapes and style of decoration had passed from fashion, leaving only the 'trifles' to remain popular into the early years of the 19th century.

1
A Bilston double-opening nutmeg grater and patch box, *c* 1765-70, some restoration, 5cm (2in), *L 14 Feb,* £2,310 ($3,234)

2
A Bilston snuff box, *c* 1765-70, 8.4cm (3¼in), *L 2 Oct,* £528 ($681)

3
A Bilston snuff box, *c* 1770, slight cracks, 6.5cm (2½in), *L 2 Oct,* £990 ($1,277)

1   2   3

1
A Staffordshire box,
c.1765-70, with corded
gilt-metal mounts, the
white ground, sides and
detachable cover painted
with rural landscapes,
enriched with raised gilt
and yellow scrolls,
minor damage, d 15cm
(6in), *L 2 Oct,*
£3,190 ($4,115)

2
An English enamel snuff
box in the form of a desk,
South Staffordshire,
c.1770, with gilt-metal
mounts, cracks and
chips, 6.4cm (2½in),
NY 21 June,
$1,650 (£1,213)

3
A Staffordshire snuff box,
c.1765, the lid and sides
decorated with pastoral
scenes on a deep purple
ground with raised white
scroll and dot deco-
ration, gilt-metal mounts,
8.5cm, (3¼in), *L 2 Oct,*
£605 ($780)

4
A blue-ground
Staffordshire snuff box,
c.1765 the lid transfer-
printed and painted with
'Les Amours Pastorales'
after Boucher, some
chipping, 8cm (3⅛in),
L 14 Feb,
£660 ($924)

5
A South Staffordshire
enamel shoe-form box,
c.1770, painted with
flowers on a white
ground, the surround
painted sea-green, 9.2cm
(3⅝in), *NY 13 Dec,*
$660 (£555)

6
A double-lidded Stafford-
shire snuff box, c.1790, the
lid coloured with 'The
Fishing Party' on a white
ground within gilded
scrolling, gilt-metal
mounts, snuff spoon,
5cm (2in), *L 14 Feb,*
£935 ($1,309)

7
An early Staffordshire
patch box c.1780, the lid
transfer-printed and
coloured, the interior
with original steel
mirror, some chips,
4.5cm (1¾in), *L 14 Feb,*
£231 ($323)

8
An oval Staffordshire
patch box, c.1800-17, 'A
Trifle from Leicester',
the lid transfer-printed
with the County
Assembly Rooms, restored,
4cm (1½in), *L 14 Feb,*
£176 ($246)

9
A circular Staffordshire
patch box, 1801-05, the
lid transfer-printed and
coloured with a portrait
of Admiral Lord Nelson,
the interior with steel
mirror, restored, 4cm
(1½in), *L 2 Oct,*
£572 ($738)

10
An oval Staffordshire
patch box, early 19th
cent, sold with another
3.5 and 4cm (1⅜ and
1½in), *L 14 Feb,*
£253 ($354)

11
An oval Staffordshire
patch box, late 18th cent,
printed with a view of
Buckingham Palace,
sold with another English
patch box, both 4cm
(1½in), *L 14 Feb,*
£286 ($400)

12
An oval Staffordshire
patch box, early 19th
cent, the lid transfer-
printed in black, 4cm
(1½in), *L 2 Oct,*
£143 ($184)

13
A Staffordshire portrait
patch box, c.1813, the
'Marquis of Wellington',
damaged, 4cm (1½in),
L 14 Feb,
£176 ($246)

14
A Staffordshire patriotic
box, c.1805, the lid
painted with Britannia
gazing at a distant ship,
5.5cm (2⅛in), *L 14 Feb,*
£440 ($616)

15
A Staffordshire patch box
early 19th cent, painted
with a view of Broadlands,
Hampshire, some damage,
5.5cm (2⅛in), *L 14 Feb,*
£297 ($416)

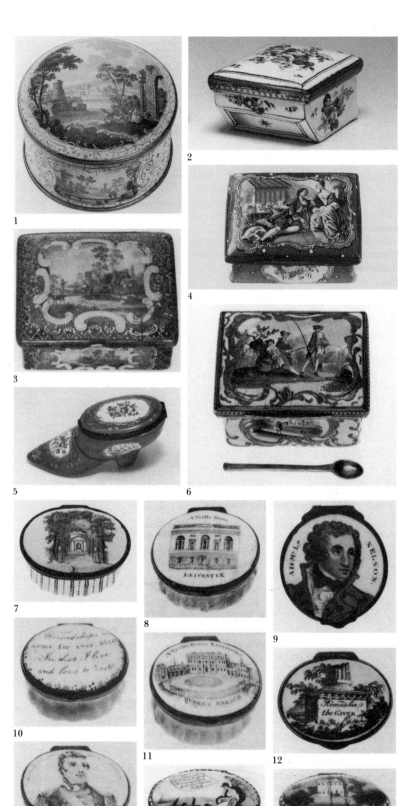

1

A rectangular Birmingham snuff box, c.1750, transfer-printed in black, the lid with a scene after J. E. Nilsson, very slight chipping, 6.2cm (2⅜in), L 14 Feb, £638 ($893)

2

A double-opening commemorative snuff box, probably Birmingham 1761-2, the two lids painted with profile portraits of George III and Queen Charlotte under purple canopies, damaged, 5.5cm (2⅛in), L 14 Feb, £660 ($924)

3

A Birmingham snuff box, c.1760, the lid transfer-printed in black, the interior printed in black with a lady and King Charles spaniel, incised silver mounts, damaged, 6.5cm (2½in), L 14 Feb, £297 ($416)

4

A Birmingham snuff box, c.1760-5, with floral decoration on white ground, the underside with a robin, gilt metal mounts, cracked and chipped, mount loose, 6.2cm (2¼in), L 2 Oct, £880 ($1,135)

5

An oval Staffordshire patch box, c.1802, with later blue lobed base, some restoration, 4cm (1½in), L 2 Oct, £418 ($539)

6

A Napoleonic patch box of oval form, 1814-15, the lid transfer-printed and coloured with a caricature of Napoleon, canary yellow base, some damage, 4cm (1½in), L 14 Feb, £748 ($1,047)

7

A basket-shaped snuff box, c.1760, with slightly bombé lid, two corded gilt-metal handles, the lid decorated in raised gilding on a deep blue background with white dotted diaper, 5cm (2in), L 14 Feb, £253 ($354)

8

A Bilston parrot bonbonnière of circular form, c.1770-5, the lid moulded and painted with a brilliantly plumaged parrot, on a lavender ground, the white enamelled base painted with flowers, 4cm (1½in), L 14 Feb, £1,100 ($1,540)

9

A Bilston dragon bonbonnière of oval form, c.1770, modelled as a scaly green monster with pink wings, the base painted with a shepherd scene, base slight wear, 7cm (2¾in), L 14 Feb, £1,980 ($2,772)

10

A small canary bonbonnière, late 18th cent, modelled with bright colours, the base with black painted landscape, base restored, 4cm (1½in), L 14 Feb, £605 ($847)

11

A hare bonbonnière, c.1770-5, modelled crouched in its form, the base with a sprig of flowers, reeded metal mounts, 4cm (1½in), L 14 Feb, £1,045 ($1,463)

12

An English bonbonnière, late 18th cent, the yellow bird with grey wings and tail, the hinged cover painted with flowers, 5.7cm (2⅛in), NY 13 Dec, $1,210 (£1,017)

13

A French circular dog bonbonnière, late 19th cent, with gilt-metal mounts, embossed with a white and rust King Charles spaniel, the border very slightly chipped, d 4.5cm (1¾in), L 2 Oct, £308 ($397)

14

A South Staffordshire bonbonnière, late 18th cent, in the form of a finch, the hinged cover painted with a flowering branch, 5cm (2in), NY 13 Dec, $990 (£832)

1
An English enamel etui, c.1760, painted with a portrait of Mrs Brooks, and a harvest scene, all within raised gilt scrolls on a turquoise ground, the interior fitted with scent bottle, scissors and other implements, gilt-metal mounts, 10.8cm (4¼in), *NY 13 Dec,* **$825 (£693)**

2
A South Staffordshire etui, c.1770, the enamelled primrose ground with a white diaper pattern and reserves of mythological subjects, the interior fitted with scissors, nail file and other pieces, 10cm (4in), *NY 13 Dec,* **$770 (£647)**

3
A South Staffordshire etui, c.1775, the surrounds enamelled deep blue, fitted with scissors and eleven other implements, 10cm (4in), *NY 13 Dec,* **$880 (£739)**

4
A South Staffordshire combination spy glass and etui, c.1770, the turquoise green ground with reserves of flowers, fitted with a pair of tweezers and five other implements with gilt-metal mounts, 12.5cm (4⅞in), *NY 13 Dec,* **$1,100 (£924)**

5
A Staffordshire needle and bodkin case, c.1770, capped by a thimble, the powder-blue ground with reserves of figures within gilded scrolls with raised white dotted decoration, gilt-metal mounts, some restoration, 13.5cm (5⅜in), *L 14 Feb,* **£715 ($1,001)**

6
A 'honeysuckle group' travelling pen case, c.1765, gilt-metal mounts, 15cm (6in), *L 2 Oct,* **£858 ($1,107)**

7
A South Staffordshire mustard pot, late 18th cent, 15cm (5⅞in), *NY 13 Dec,* **$495 (£396)**

8
A Staffordshire 'Pheasant's Eye' etui, c.1770-80, painted overall in crimson, brown, green and yellow interspersed with gilded snowflake devices, gilt-metal mounts, with complete associated silver-gilt fittings of eight implements, 8.5cm (3⅜in), *L 14 Feb,* **£495 ($693)**

9
A 'Wednesbury' scent bottle case, c.1780, fitted with a glass scent bottle and stopper, w 5cm (2in), *L 2 Oct,* **£286 ($369)**

10
A Staffordshire combination scent bottle and bonbonnière, c.1765, the green ground with raised gilded decoration, gilt-metal mounts and chained scroll stopper, slight damage, 10cm (4in), *L 2 Oct,* **£638 ($823)**

11
A South Staffordshire scent bottle case, c.1770, the interior fitted with a scent bottle, funnel, ivory slide, spoon and scissors, h 7cm (2¾in), *NY 13 Dec,* **$1,760 (£1,408)**

12
A South Staffordshire egg bonbonnière, c.1775-85, with milled gilt-metal mounts, restored, h 4cm (1½in), *L 2 Oct,* **£330 ($426)**

13
A South Staffordshire writing box, c.1770, painted with pastoral scenes, gilt-metal mounts, fitted with two ink bottles with enamelled covers, 15.9cm (6¼in), *NY 13 Dec,* **$1,045 (£836)**

14
A South Staffordshire enamel magnifying glass, c.1765, housed in a circular container, one side enamelled with a gentleman examining a globe, the other with a gentleman regarding the sea with a spy glass, moulded silver mounts, w 6cm (2⅜in), *NY 13 Dec,* **$1,100 (£924)**

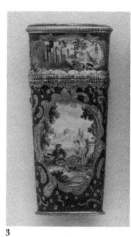

1   2   3

4   5   6   7

8   9   10   11   12

13   14

1

A pair of oval **Bilston enamel plaques**, c.1760, each painted with views of anglers in brilliant colours, wavy gilt-metal frames, 8.2cm (3¼in), *L 14 Feb*, £2,530 ($3,542)

2

A white-ground 'honeysuckle group' snuff box, c.1760-5, the lid painted with a Venetian view, gilt-metal mounts, some damage, 6cm (2⅜in), *L 14 Feb*, £638 ($893)

3

A pair of **English enamel tea caddies and a sugar box**, probably Birmingham, c.1760, painted with vignettes of brightly coloured birds within white scrollwork borders on a salmon ground, gilt-metal mounts, chips, cracks and restoration, caddy 11cm (4¼in), *NY 21 June*, $2,420 (£1,779)

4

A 'honeysuckle group' patch box, c.1760, with engine-turned gilt-metal mounts, painted with three vignettes of ruins and figures on a deep-blue ground, overlaid in raised gilding, the interior with steel mirror, rusted, d 4.2cm (1½in), *L 2 Oct*, £374 ($482)

5

A pair of **South Staffordshire enamel tea caddies and a matching sugar box**, c.1770, the caddies with slip-on covers marked 'Bohea' and 'Green', all painted with shepherds and rustic couples, h of caddies 10.5cm (4⅛in), *NY 13 Dec*, $5,500 (£4,622)

6

A **German enamel snuff box**, c.1756, reeded gilt-metal mounts, surface cracks, 7.1cm (2¾in), *G 14 Nov*, SF 1,430 (£444; $595)

7

A **German enamel snuff box**, mid-18th cent, painted en grisaille, the interior with portrait of Frederick the Great, engraved gold mounts, 8cm (3⅛in), *G 16 May*, SF 2,400 (£721; $1,031)

8

A **French turquoise-ground enamel snuff box**, discharge mark of Antoine Leschaudel, Paris, 1744-50, silver mounts, restored, 8cm (3⅛in), *G 16 May*, SF 1,000 (£300; $429)

9

A **German enamel snuff box**, c.1750-60, celebrating the aims and origins of the Jesuits, with wavy gilt-metal mounts, 9cm (3½in), *G 16 May*, SF 3,800 (£1,141; $1,632)

10

A **German enamel snuff box**, mid-18th cent, of unusually rich and creamy enamel painted with a village scene after the manner of Bechdolff, the interior of the lid by a different hand, gilt-metal mounts, 8cm (3⅛in), *G 16 May*, SF 1,300 (£390; $558)

11

A pair of **South Staffordshire enamel candlesticks**, late 18th cent, painted with figures and bouquets of flowers with gilded flowers and foliage, nozzles restored, 31.2cm (12¼in), *NY 13 Dec*, $1,210 (£1,017)

12

A **Birmingham enamel plaque**, c.1765, probably painted by Penelope Carless of Bilston, the white ground with the arms of Carless (granted to Col William Carlos of Broomhall, Co Stafford, 1685, for his assistance in helping King Charles II to hide in the oak tree in Boscobel Wood), some cracks and corner chips, h 14.5cm (5¾in), *L 2 Oct*, £440 ($568)

13

An **Augsburg enamel snuff box**, c.1750, the lid and sides painted with scenes of Augsburg, engraved silver-gilt mounts, base rubbed, 6.5cm (2½in), *G 16 May*, SF 11,500 (£3,453; $4,938)

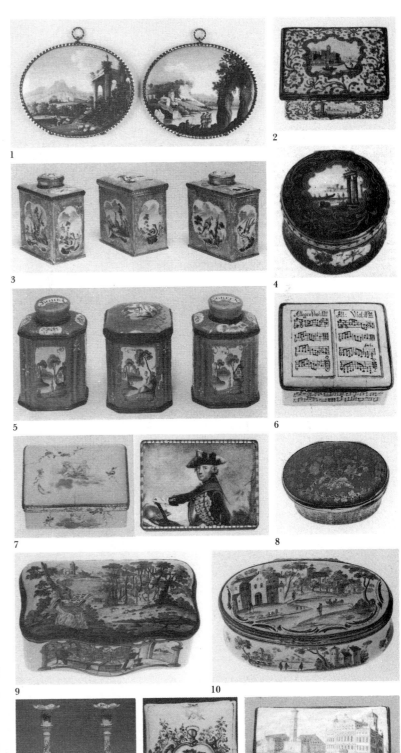

1

A pair of silhouettes of King George III and Queen Charlotte, by William Hamlet the elder, c.1810, painted on convex glass against a plaster ground, papier-mâché frames, oval 6cm (2⅜in), *L 5 July,* £572 ($795)

2

A silhouette of a gentleman, by Mrs Jane Read, c.1800, painted on convex glass, rectangular papier-mâché frame, oval 8cm (3¼in) *L 5 July,* £462 ($642)

3

A bronzed silhouette of an officer, by John Miers, signed c.1810, painted on ivory, gold frame, the reverse with plaited hair, oval 2.8cm (1⅛in), *L 5 July,* £352 ($489)

4

A silhouette of Mrs Francis Miles Robe, by John Miers, c.1805, painted on plaster, papier-mâché frame, oval 8.6cm (3⅜in), *L 5 July,* £121 ($168)

5

Edward Baker Esq, by John Miers, dated 1793, painted on plaster, *verre églomisé* border within papier-mâché frame, oval 11.8cm (4⅝in), *L 5 July,* £297 ($413)

6

A bronzed silhouette of a clergyman, by John Field, c.1810, painted on plaster, rectangular papier-mâché frame, oval 8.9cm (3½in), *L 5 July,* £132 ($183)

7

Elisabeth, Duchess of Teschen, studio of Nicholas Hilliard, c.1605, painted on vellum. Daughter of Princess Anna of Meckleburg and Gotthard, Duke of Curland, she married in 1595 Adam Vensel, Duke of Teschen (1574-1617); she died in 1609. Silver mount, oval 5cm (2in), *L 12 Mar,* £4,180 ($6,228)

8

Judith Norgate, née Lanier (1590-1616/18), by Edward Norgate after Isaac Oliver, c.1613, painted on a playing card, now mounted within a turned fruitwood frame with a gilt slip, oval 5.1cm (2in), *L 5 July,* £27,500 ($38,225)

9

John Harrison Junior (1598-1665), by Edward Norgate, c.1622, painted on a playing card (clubs), oval 5.5cm (2⅛in); also with the arms of John Harrison, by the same hand, dated 1622, oval 6.4cm (2½in), *L 5 July,* £33,000 ($45,870)

10

Mary Harrison, née Buckenham (1610/11-c.1682), by Edward Norgate, c.1630, painted on a playing card now mounted within a turned fruitwood frame with a gilt slip, oval 5.5cm (2⅛in), *L 5 July,* £28,600 ($39,754)

11

King Charles II (1630-85) as a boy, by David Des Granges, signed with initials and dated 1643, mounted within a gold and polychrome enamel locket, oval 3.2cm (1¼in), *L 5 July,* £5,280 ($7,339)

12

A lady, by Samuel Cooper, signed and dated 1649, silver-gilt frame, oval 4.8cm (2⅞in), *L 19 Nov,* £1,870 ($2,450)

13

A nobleman, by Franciscek Smiadecki, c.1650, oil on copper, turned wood frame, oval 5.1cm (2in), *L 12 Mar,* £858 ($1,279)

Measurements are those of the miniature excluding the frame

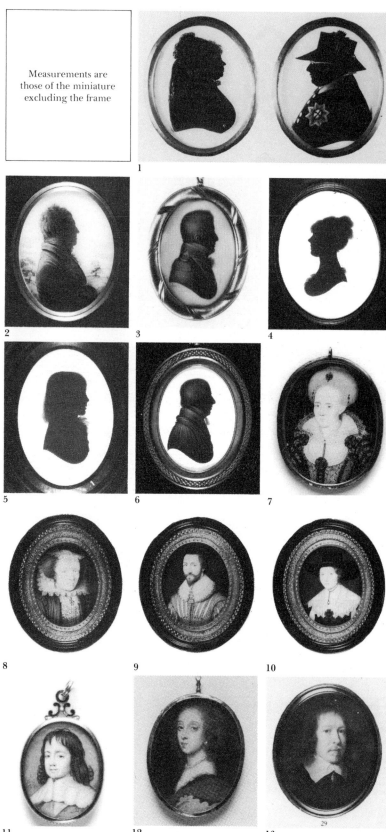

1

2

3

4

5

6

7

8

9

10

11

12

13

1
A gentleman, by Richard Gibson, c.1665, mounted within a brass and enamel frame, oval 4.2cm (1⁹/₁₆in), *L 19 Nov,* £1,430 ($1,873)

2
A plumbago miniature of a gentleman, by Thomas Forster, c.1695, on vellum, mounted within a turned fruitwood frame, oval 9.8cm (2⁷/₈in), *L 19 Nov,* £242 ($317)

3
Vittorio Amedeo II, attributed to L Bourdin, c.1690, mounted within a later silver frame, d 7.5cm (2¹⁵/₁₆in), *G 12 Nov,* SF 27,500 (£8,488; $11,204)

4
A nobleman, possibly Philippe Duke of Orleans, French School, c.1690, oil on copper, mounted within a silver-gilt frame inset with diamonds, oval 2.8cm (1⅛in), £2,860 ($3,747)

5
Queen Anne, by Charles Boit, c.1710, enamel, set within the lid of a gold mounted ivory snuff box, the base with the monogram of Margaret Cavendish, Duchess of Portland (1714/15-85), oval 3.1cm (1¼in), *G 17 May,* SF 3,000 (£898; $1,302)

6
A gentleman, by Christian Friedrich Zincke, c.1720, enamel, mounted within a silver-gilt frame, oval 4.7cm (1⅜in), *L 19 Nov,* £682 ($893)

7
A lady, by Christian Friedrich Zincke, c.1710, her brown hair adorned with a veil, enamel, gold frame with mother-of-pearl reverse, oval 4.7cm (1⅞in), *L 19 Nov,* £858 ($1,123)

8
A young lady, School of Zincke, c.1720, her dark hair upswept, wearing a low-cut dress and blue cloak, enamel, oval 4.4cm (1¾in), *L 12 Mar,* £451 ($671)

9
Anna Cristina Luigia, Princess of Piedmont, (1704-23), fifth and youngest daughter of Theodor, Count Palatine in Sulzbach, Duke of Bavaria, married Carlo Emanuele III in 1722. Slight paint loss, gilt-metal frame, oval 10.6cm (2⅛in), *G 12 Nov,* SF 2,310 (£713; $941)

10
Augustus II of Poland, after a portrait of c.1730. Elector of Saxony, King of Poland (1696-1763), known as 'Augustus the Strong', married Archduchess Maria Josepha, Electress of Austria (1699-1757), gilt-metal frame, oval 9.5cm (3¾in), *G 12 Nov,* SF 3,300 (£1,019; $1,344)

11
Maria Theresa, c.1730. Apostolic Queen of Hungary, Queen of Bohemia, Archduchess of Austria, married Franz Stephan of Lorrain (1708-65), Grand Duke of Tuscany, later Franz I, Holy Roman Emperor, 1736. Gilt-metal frame, oval 6.2cm (2⁷/₁₆in), *G 12 Nov,* SF 1,650 (£509; $672)

12
Louis-Philippe, Duke of Orléans, c.1770. (1725-85) gold frame, oval, 2.8cm (1⅛in), *G 12 Nov,* SF 550 (£170; $224)

13
A young child, attributed to Augustin Dusbourg, c.1785, gilt-metal frame with white enamel border, d 4.5cm (1¾in), *L 19 Nov,* £2,200 ($2,882)

14
Louis XVII, as Dauphin, King of France and Navarre (1785-95), enamel, within a two-colour gold mount, oval 4cm (1⁹/₁₆in), *G 12 Nov,* SF 3,520 (£1,086; $1,434)

15
A lady, French School, c.1790, writing the inscription 'Fidèle à jamais', gilt-metal mount, d 6.4cm (2½in), *G 17 May,* SF 3,000 (£898; $1,302)

1 2 3

4 5 6

7 8 9

10 11 12

13 14 15

1

Madame d'Aigremont, after Nattier, *c*1720, gilt-metal mount, rectangular 7cm (2¾in), *L 12 Mar*, £726 ($1,082)

2

The bath of Venus, by Jacques Charlier, gilt-metal frame, rectangular 7cm (2¾in), *G 17 May*, SF 3,200 (£958; $1,389)

3

A gentleman, by Louis Lié Périn-Salbreux, signed *c*1790, rectangular lemonwood frame, d 6cm (2⅜in), *G 17 May*, SF 3,500 (£1,048; $1,519)

4

A lady, by Jean Baptiste Isabey, signed *c*1795, gilt-metal frame d 7.4cm (2⅞in), *G 17 May*, SF 9,500 (£2,844; $4,124)

5

A young boy, French School, *c*1790, gold frame, the reverse with initials GM on woven hair, d 6.1cm (2⅜in), *L 12 Mar*, £682 ($1,017)

6

Vittorio Amedeo III, *c*1770, gilt-metal frame, oval 4.1cm (1⅝in), *G 12 Nov*, SF 1,320 (£407; $538)

7

Clotilda, Queen of Sardinia, by Jean Laurent Mosnier, signed and dated 1775, gold frame, d 6.3cm (2½in), *G 12 Nov*, SF 4,950 (£1,528; $2,017)

8

Eugenio, Prince of Savoy-Carignan, and his son Guiseppe Marie, by Ignazio Pio Vittoriano Campana, *c*1784. Eugenio (1753-85), Count of Villafranca, married Elisabeth Anne, daughter of François Nicolas Magon de Boisgarin. Gold frame, d 7.7cm (3in), *G 12 Nov*, SF 15,400 (£4,753; $6,274)

9

Charlotte, Queen of Saxony, *c*1785, (1764-82) sixth daughter of Vittorio Amedeo III, King of Sardinia, married in 1781 Prince Anton (1755-1836), later Anton I, King of Saxony. Gilt-metal frame, d 6.1cm (2⅜in), *G 12 Nov*, SF 6,050 (£1,867; $2,465)

10

The Comtesse d'Artois and her children, by Ignazio Pio Vittoriano Campana, *c*1780. Marie-Thérèse de Savoie (1756-1805), daughter of Victor Amadeus III, King of Sardinia, married the Comte d'Artois (later Charles X) in 1773. Mounted within a later gilt-wood frame, rectangular 13.6cm (5⅜in), *G 17 May*, SF 30,000 (£8,982; $13,024)

11

Maria Felicita, Princess of Savoy, by Lorenzo Balbi, *c*1770. Princess Maria Felicita of Savoy (1730-1801), third daughter of Carlo Emanuele III, King of Sardinia. Gilt-metal frame, oval 14.6cm (5¾in), *G 12 Nov*, SF 30,800 (£9,506; $12,548)

12

Joseph II, Holy Roman Emperor, *c*1775. Joseph II (1741-90) married first Donna Isabella di Borbone (1741-63), daughter of Filipo, reigning Duke of Parma, in 1760, and secondly Princess Marie Josephe (1739-67), daughter of Karl VII, Holy Roman Emperor and Elector of Bavaria. Gilt-metal frame, oval 4.1cm (1⅝in), *G 12 Nov*, SF 1,100 (£340; $448)

13

A pair of miniatures of a lady and gentleman, by Henry Spicer, signed and dated 1768 and 1769, enamel, oval 6.3cm (2½in), *L 9 July*, £770 ($1,070)

1

2

3

4

5

6

7

8

9

10

11

12

13

1
A young lady, by
Heinrich Friedrich
Füger, signed c1785,
mounted within a later
rectangular gilt-metal
frame, oval d 6cm
(2⅜in), L 19 Nov,
£9,020 ($11,816)

2
Captain Augustus
Montgomery RN, by
Richard Cosway, c1782.
He commanded the
frigate Inconstant at the
occupation of Toulon in
1793, and the Courageous
74 at Hotham's action off
Genoa in 1795. Gold
frame, the reverse with
woven hair, oval 3.9cm
(1½in), L 12 Mar,
£682 ($1,017)

3
A young lady, by Richard
Cosway, c1795, mounted
within a gold locket
frame, oval 7cm (2¾in),
L 19 Nov,
£1,650 ($2,162)

4
A young boy, by Richard
Cosway, c1800, mounted
within a gold frame, the
reverse with plaited
hair, oval 7cm (2¾in),
L 19 Nov,
£3,520 ($4,611)

5
A grisaille miniature of a
gentleman, school of
Cosway, c1780, gold
frame with brooch
adaptation, oval 3.5cm
(1⅜in), L 13 Mar,
£121 ($180)

6
A young boy, in the
manner of Joseph
Saunders, c1780, gilt-
metal frame, oval 4.1cm
(1⅜in), L 12 Mar,
£242 ($361)

7
A gentleman, by Thomas
Hazlehurst, signed
c1790, gold frame, the
reverse with monogram
J.H.C., oval 7.3cm
(2⅞in), L 5 July,
£550 ($765)

8
A young lady, by Thomas
Hazlehurst, signed
c1790, gold frame, oval
6.3cm (2½in), L 5 July,
£352 ($489)

9
A colour beginning of Mrs
Warren Hastings, by
Ozias Humphry,
inscribed and dated 1789
on the verso. Marian,
née Imhoff, married
Warren Hastings,
Governor-General of
India, in 1777. Gold
frame, oval 11.3cm (4½in),
L 12 Mar,
£1,375 ($2,050)

10
A gentleman, by Ozias
Humphry, c1770, gold
frame, oval 3.8cm
(1½in), L 13 Mar,
£165 ($246)

11
A gentleman, by Joseph
Daniel, c1790, papier-
mâché frame, oval 8cm
(3⅛in), L 12 Mar,
£396 ($590)

12
A lady, by Moses
Griffith, c1785, gold
frame, the reverse with
plaited hair, oval 7.3cm
(2⅞in), L 19 Nov,
£440 ($576)

13
A gentleman, by George
Lawrence, c1790, gold
frame, oval 6.3cm
(2½in), L 13 Mar,
£264 ($394)

14
A gentleman, by Samuel
Shelley, c1785, gold
frame inset with seed
pearls, oval 3.8cm
(1½in), L 5 July,
£990 ($1,376)

15
A gentleman, by
Jeremiah Meyer, c1775,
gold frame inset with
split pearls, the reverse
with coiled hair, oval
6.1cm (1⅜in), L 5 July,
£1,815 ($2,528)

1

2

3

4

5

6

7

8

9

10

11

12

13

14

15

1
A lady, by Jeremiah Meyer, c.1775, fitted fishskin case, oval 5.1cm (2in), *L 12 Mar,*
£682 ($1,017)

2
Mrs 'Perdita' Robinson, by Jeremiah Meyer, c.1780. Mary Robinson (1758-1800) was an actress, author and mistress of George, Prince of Wales. Oval 10cm (3¹⁵⁄₁₆in), *L 12 Mar,*
£2,640 ($3,936)

3
An officer, in the manner of Hone, c.1770, with powdered hair *en queue,* wearing a scarlet uniform with lilac facings and gold braid, oval 3.8cm (1½in), *P 12-15 June,*
£121 ($174)

4
A gentleman, in the manner of Hone, c.1780, with powdered hair, wearing a blue jacket and white cravat, oval 4cm (1½in), *P 12-15 June,*
£143 ($205)

5
Charlotte Porcher, by John Smart, signed and dated India 1788. Second daughter of Admiral Sir William Burnaby Bt, she married in 1787 Josias Dupre Porcher who became Mayor of Madras in 1792. Mounted in a gold frame, oval 5.8cm (2¼in), *L 19 Nov,*
£6,380 ($8,358)

6
John Livesay, by John Smart, signed and dated 1785, set into the lid of a French gold and tortoiseshell snuff box, charge and discharge marks of Henri Clavel, Paris 1780-9, oval 4.1cm (1⅝in), *L 12 Mar,*
£3,850 ($5,740)

7
A lady, by John Smart, c.1777, *enamel,* unframed, slight restoration, oval 4cm (1⅝in), *L 12 Mar,*
£3,520 ($5,248)

8
A colour beginning of a gentleman, by John Smart, c.1780, ormolu frame, oval 4.8cm (1⅞in), *L 12 Mar,*
£528 ($786)

9
The Hon Edward Lygon, by John Smart Junior, signed and dated 1806. The youngest son of the 1st Earl Beauchamp, he was Colonel in 13th Light Dragoons, and Cornet and Sub Lieutenant in the 2nd Life Guards; he died 1860. Watercolour on paper, gilt-metal mount, oval 9.9cm (3⅞in), *L 12 Mar,*
£3,740 ($5,576)

10
An infantry officer, by George Engleheart, c.1775, gold slide frame with split pearl border, oval 4.3cm (1¹¹⁄₁₆in), *L 5 July,*
£1,078 ($1,498)

11
A lady, in the manner of George Engleheart, c.1780, mounted within the lid of an ivory patchbox, oval 3.8cm (1½in), *L 12 Mar,*
£286 ($426)

12
An officer, English School, after George Engleheart, wearing scarlet uniform with white facings, oval 3.5cm (1¼in), *C 3-6 July,*
£132 ($179)

13
A young lady, by Andrew Plimer, c.1790, gilt-metal mount, oval 5.4cm (2⅛in), *L 19 Nov,*
£726 ($951)

14
A young boy called Viscount Bangor, by Nathaniel Plimer, signed and dated 1788, rectangular wood frame, oval 5.6cm (2¼in), *L 5 July,*
£528 ($734)

15
A lady, English School, c.1770, gold slide frame, oval 3.9cm (1½in), *L 13 Mar,*
£176 ($262)

1 2 3

4 5 6

7 8 9

10 11 12

13 14 15

1
A young clansman, English School, c1790, gold frame enamelled in blue and white, the reverse with locks of hair, oval 5.8cm (2¼in), *L 12 Mar,* £2,200 ($3,280)

2
An officer, English School, c1800, gilt-metal mount, oval 9.2cm (3¾in), *L 12 Mar,* £484 ($722)

3
Hercules Ross, by John Thomas Barber Beaumont, signed c1800, gold frame, the reverse decorated with locks of hair, oval 7.9cm (3⅛in), *L 19 Nov,* £902 ($1,182)

4
Edward Austin (1784-1863), by John Wright, signed on the verso c1810, gilt-metal frame, oval 7.2cm (3in), *L 19 Nov,* £220 ($288)

5
A young lady, by William Grimaldi, signed and dated 1809, gold frame, the reverse with hair decoration, oval 7.8cm (2⅛in), *L 19 Nov,* £396 ($519)

6
A mother seated with her two children, by William Grimaldi, signed c1800, gold frame the reverse with hair decoration, rectangular 10.8cm (4¼in), *L 5 July,* £1,265 ($1,758)

7
An elderly lady, by Walter Stephen Lethbridge, c1800, signed in full on the verso, papier-mâché frame, oval 8.9cm (3½in), *L 12 Mar,* £770 ($1,148)

8
Emperor Napolean I, by Jean Francis Hollier, c1810, wearing the uniform of the Foot Grenadiers with white facings, the ribbon and cross of the Legion of Honour and the Iron Cross of Lombardy, oval 7.6cm (3in), *C 3-6 July,* £176 ($239)

9
Carlo Alberto, by Charles Berny d'Ouville, c1810, mounted within a lemonwood frame, rectangular 9.3cm (3⅝in), *G 12 Nov,* **SF 7,150 (£2,207; $2,913)**

10
Carlo Felice, c1810, gilt-metal frame, d 7cm (2¾in), *G 12 Nov,* **SF 7,150 (£2,207; $2,913)**

11
Fernando VII, c1815, chased gilt-metal frame, oval 5cm (2in), *G 12 Nov,* **SF 1,100 (£340; $448)**

12
Maria Carolina, by Adalbert Suchy, signed c1815. Maria Carolina of Austria (1752-1814), Queen of the Two Sicilies, daughter of Franz I, Holy Roman Emperor, married Ferdinando IV. Gilt-metal frame, unglazed, oval 7.2cm (2¹³⁄₁₆in), *G 12 Nov,* **SF 1,760 (£543; $717)**

13
A young boy, German School, c1810, signed with initials F S(?), wearing a blue jacket, white cravat and pink trousers, oval 5.6cm (2¼in), *C 3-6 July,* £264 ($343)

14
A young lady, by Moritz Michael Daffinger, signed c1820, gilt-metal mount, oval 8.6cm (3⅜in), *L 19 Nov,* £5,060 ($6,629)

15
A gentleman, by Claude Jean Besselievre, signed c1820, gilt-metal mount, oval 10.9cm (4¼in), *G 17 May,* **SF 3,000 (£898; $1,302)**

1   2   3

4   5   6

7   8   9

10   11   12

13   14   15

1
A lady, by Maxime David, signed c1830, gilt-metal frame on a plush base, slight paint loss, rectangular 22.3cm (8¾in), *G 17 May,* **SF 11,000 (£3,293; $4,775)**

2
General Jean Andoche Junot, Duc d'Abrantes, by Sophie Liénard, signed c1840. The Duc (1771-1813) commanded the invasion of Portugal in 1807 and was defeated by Wellington at Vimiero in 1808. Porcelain, oval 14.2cm (5⅝in), *G 17 May,* **SF 5,000 (£1,497; $2,171)**

3
Ferdinand Philip Louis Charles Henry, Duke of Orleans, by Madame Aimée Zoé Lizinka de Mirbel, née Rue, signed and dated 1842, gilt-metal mount, oval 10.4cm (4⅛in), *G 17 May,* **SF 6,000 (£1,796; $2,605)**

4
A general, by Louis Marie Sicardi, signed and dated (18)10, gold frame with black enamel border, 7cm (2¾in), *G 17 May,* **SF 48,000 (£14,371; $20,838)**

5
Désirée Clary, Queen of Sweden, by Ferdinando Quaglia, c1810, after Le Fevre. 7.6cm (3in), *G 17 May,* **SF 2,200 (£659; $955)**

6
Maximilian I, King of Bavaria, by Franz Napoleon Heigel, signed c1820, gold-mounted plush frame, rectangular 6.9cm (2¾in), *L 19 Nov,* **£1,155 ($1,513)**

7
A lady, by James Warren Childe, c1820, rectangular 10.2cm (4in), *L 12 Mar,* **£418 ($623)**

8
The 5th Duke of Rutland, by Sir William John Newton, signed c1830. 14cm (5½in), *G 17 May,* **SF 1,900 (£569; $825)**

9
Lady Mary Villiers (1622-85), by Henry Pierce Bone, after Hanneman, signed and dated on the verso 1844, enamel, oval 10.5cm (4⅛in), *L 12 Mar,* **£1,375 ($2,050)**

10
A young lady, by Sir William Charles Ross, c1845, gilt-metal mount, oval 8.9cm (4½in), *L 5 July,* **£528 ($734)**

11
A lady seated with her two children, by Sir William Charles Ross, c1840, gilt-gesso border within glazed rosewood frame, outer case with folding doors, *L 5 July,* **£1,595 ($2,217)**

12
Mary Jane Kelly, by Sir William Charles Ross, signed and dated 1841 on the verso, gilt-metal frame, oval 8.9cm (3½in), *L 5 July,* **£418 ($581)**

13
Lenrose Horne Esq, by Cornelius Durham, c1840, 17.9cm (7in), *L 5 July,* **£330 ($459)**

14
King Edward VII, as Prince of Wales, by William Charles Bell, after Winterhalter, c1850. The original by Winterhalter is in the Royal Collection. Unframed, *enamel,* oval 5.1cm (2in), *L 12 Mar,* **£374 ($558)**

15
Miss Constance Elwes, by William Egley, signed in full on the verso and dated 1862, gilt-metal mount, oval 6cm (2⅜in), *L 12 Mar,* **£330 ($492)**

1
A young lady, French
School, c1830, rectangular
ebonised frame, oval
7.8cm (3¹/₁₆in), *L 19 Nov,*
£286 ($378)

2
A gentleman, by Horace
Hone, signed and dated
1788, chased and
engraved gold frame,
oval 5.1cm (2in),
L 12 Mar,
£440 ($656)

3
Mrs George Aubry, by
John Smart, signed and
dated India 1787. Anna
Aubry, née Botham,
married Capt George
Aubry, officer of the
Indian Army, in 1786.
Gold frame, the reverse
with monogram on woven
hair, oval 6.8cm (2¹¹/₁₆in),
L 19 Nov,
£6,380 ($8,358)

4
A young lady, by Andrew
Plimer, c1795, gold frame,
oval 7.2cm (2⅞in),
L 19 Nov,
£1,375 ($1,801)

5
**A Bilston pug dog
bonbonnière,** c1770,
modelled as a reclining
dog, the hinged lid
painted with a dog in a
classical scene, 5cm (2in),
NY 13 Dec,
$2,970 (£2,496)

6
**A Bilston lion's head
bonbonnière,** c1770, the
embossed box painted to
simulate the coat of a
lion, the hinged cover
painted with a warrior in
combat with a lion,
7.6cm (3in), *NY 13 Dec,*
$3,300 (£2,773)

7
**A Bilston enamel
bonbonnière,** c1770, the
oval box embossed in
the form of a reclining
leopard curled with its
tail to the front on a
grass mound, the hinged
cover painted with a
spray of flowers on a
white ground, restored,
5.4cm (2⅛in), *NY 13 Dec,*
$3,300 (£2,773)

1
A French circular gold and enamel snuff box, Michel-René Bocher, Paris, 1779, with landscapes of bushes in pale lilac bordered by translucent green enamel and white pellets on matt grounds, maker's mark, enamel a little chipped, 5.6cm (2¾in), *G 16 May,* **SF 22,000 (£6,607; $9,447)**

2
A French gold-mounted snuff box, Adrien-Jean-Maximilien Vachette, Paris, 1798-1809, inlaid with *verre eglomisé* panels, w 9.8cm (3¾in), *G 13-14 Nov,* **SF 82,500 (£25,621; $34,332)**

3
A French gold and mother-of-pearl snuff box, François Marteau, Paris, 1738-44, with chinoiserie scenes on carved shell grounds delicately coloured nacreous-green and amethyst, maker's mark, repaired, a few shell panels replaced, w 7.2cm (2⅞in), *G 14 Nov,* **SF 29,700 (£9,224; $12,360)**

4
A French gold boîte à portrait, *c*1810, set with a portrait of Empress Josephine, by J. Guérin, the sides and spandrels chased with military trophies on textured grounds, w 8.3cm (3¼in), *G 13 Nov,* **SF 12,100 (£3,970; $5,320)**

5
A French gold and enamel snuff box, Pierre-François Drais, Paris, 1771-2, enamelled translucent emerald green over a guilloché ground, the cover with an oval enamel miniature, with charge mark and discharge mark of Julien Alaterre, 8.8cm (3½in), *NY 13 Dec,* **$24,200 (£20,336)**

6
A French coloured gold and enamel boîte à portrait, Pierre-François Drais, Paris, 1772, oval, with translucent dark-blue enamel over guilloché grounds, the lid set with a miniature by Pierre-Adolphe Hall, one of the small side miniatures replaced, the glass of another damaged, 1768-75, w 7.5cm (3in), *G 14 Nov,* **SF 41,800 (£12,981; $17,395)**

7
A French gold and tortoiseshell piqué snuff box, Adrien-Jean-Maximilien Vachette, 1783-9, the gold cagework mounts with matted bands enclosing shell panels *c*1720-30, inlaid in coloured gold piqué point, charge and discharge mark of Henri Clavel, Paris, w 8cm (3⅛in), *G 14 Nov,* **SF 77,000 (£23,913; $32,043)**

8
An Italian gold-mounted mosaic snuff box, G Raffaelli, late 18th cent, the lid and base with fine views of the Temple of the Sibyl at Tivoli and an aqueduct scene, the sides with blue and white decoration, signed, d 7.5cm (3in), *G 14 Nov,* **SF 26,400 (£8,199; $10,986)**

1

2

3

4

5

6

7

8

1
A silver-gilt and champlevé enamel tea and coffee service, P Ovchinnikov, Moscow, 1899-1908, the tray 42cm (16½ in), the teapot h 13.5cm (5¼ in), *G 14 Nov,* **SF 308,000 (£95,652; $128,174)**

1

1
A gold-mounted, silver-gilt and translucent enamel cigarette case, Fabergé, workmaster Henrik Wigström, St Petersburg, c.1900, enamelled translucent oyster over a guilloché ground, 10.2cm (4in), *NY 14 Dec,*
$10,450 (£8,782)

2
A gold, enamel and jewelled beetle-form miniature Easter egg, Fabergé, workmaster M Perchin, St Petersburg, c.1900, set with diamonds, 1.7cm (⅜in), *NY 14 Dec,*
$14,850 (£12,479)

3
An agate carving of a seated pug dog, Fabergé, c.1900, the pink stone with scattered grey inclusions, gold mounted ruby eyes, 9cm (3½in), *G 14 Nov,*
SF 9,900 (£3,075; $4,120)

4
Twelve dinner plates, from the Kremlin Service made at the Imperial Porcelain Factory, St. Petersburg, 1837-8, to designs by Th Solntsev, each marked with the cypher of Nicholas I, d 24cm (9½in), *L 15 Feb,*
£5,280 ($7,403)

5
A silver-gilt and shaded cloisonné enamel cigarette case, P Ovchinnikov, Moscow, late 19th cent, the cover painted with a view of the Moscow Kremlin, w 9cm (3½in), *G 14 Nov,*
SF 13,200 (£4,099; $5,493)

6
A silver-gilt and plique-à-jour enamel kovsh, Moscow, c.1880, decorated with arched panels of scroll and leaf ornament encompassing a central rosette, slight restoration, 14.7cm (5¾in), *G 17 May,*
SF 3,800 (£1,138; $1,650)

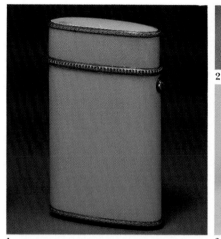

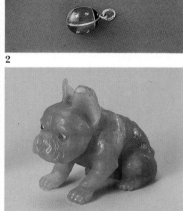

1

3

4

5   6

Russian Works of Art

HEINRICH GRAF VON SPRETI • GERARD HILL

It is not unusual for Russian works of art to be sold with objects of vertu for the simple reason that the same type of item—cigarette cases, small boxes, scent flasks and so on—occurs in both fields. However, Russian works of art are often sold separately because those who collect them are interested, above all, in their historical associations. It is the fact that these are works of art from imperial Russia that gives them their particular cachet.

Carl Fabergé (1846-1920), goldsmith to the Romanovs, is the central figure. Work from the Fabergé workshops has all the attributes a collector might seek. It is exquisitely made of precious and semi-precious materials and there is often an element of fantasy in the design. Fabergé employed more than 500 assistants and set up workshops in Moscow, Kiev and London as well as in St Petersburg. Easter eggs, hardstone carvings of animals and flowers are always favourites and any piece that descends in a direct line from the original buyer, such as the miniature frame which belonged to a member of the German imperial family and is illustrated on page 383 (fig.13), will always find a ready buyer.

The popularity of Fabergé has meant that pieces by him are now less often seen on the market and are very expensive when they are. But several of his contemporaries were goldsmiths whose work can be equally enchanting. Gustav Klingert, Nichols and Plincke, and Ovchinnikov are among them. Items by all three are illustrated here.

It is not only their history that distinguishes Russian works of art: the unique combination of Eastern and Western forms and skills gives them some of their special appeal. The technique of niello engraving was brought from Byzantium to Russia and flourished during the 16th and 17th centuries. The later 19th century cloisonné and plique à jour enamels have long been popular in the West and continue to reflect the Eastern influence. The tea and coffee service shown on page 377 (fig.1) is the kind of elaborately decorative piece which sells very well. Sets of spoons and even single spoons might suit most pockets better. Such items can suffer damage (particularly to the enamel) and it is always wise either to examine the piece very carefully oneself or to ask for a report from the saleroom.

Another Russian speciality which is currently proving popular with collectors is trompe l'oeil silver. The bread baskets complete with napkins and the tea caddy in the form of a packet of tea are good examples (p.386, figs 10 and 11, and p.386, fig. 5). It is rare to find humour and exquisite craftsmanship so skilfully combined.

Russian porcelain is another field where imperial connections have undoubtedly added to the interest. The Imperial Russian Porcelain factory was established in the 18th century on the lines of factories in Western Europe. The Kremlin service of 195 pieces made in 1837-38 (p.378, fig.4 and p.388, fig.4), which was sold during 1984 for about four times its estimated price, was commissioned by Nicholas I for the Grand Kremlin Palace. Its elaborate decoration, inspired by 17th century metalwork, is in a revived Byzantine Slav style.

As the Russian imperial family were in the habit of giving presents throughout the courts of Europe, and as the prestigious Fabergé workshops were much patronized by the wealthier members of Edwardian society, Russian works of art were relatively widespread long before the Russian revolution. It is often possible to trace the provenance of particular items and so to add to the romance of an already fascinating and quietly pleasing subject.

1
A silver-gilt and enamel
presentation punch set,
Ovchinnikov, Moscow,
1872-3, comprising tray,
punch bowl, eight charki
and a kovsh, a wedding
gift to Marie Alexandrovna
daughter of Alexander
II and Alfred, Duke of
Edinburgh, son of
Queen Victoria, 1873,
tray d 50.7cm (20in),
NY 20/21 June,
$44,000 (£32,353)

2
A silver-gilt and enamel
tea set, maker's mark
JFA, Moscow, 1885,
comprising teapot,
covered sugar bowl,
creamer, tea glass holder
and sugar tongs, teapot
h 15.3cm (6in),
NY 20/21 June,
$4,675 (£3,437)

3
A silver-gilt and cloisonné
enamel vodka set,
Sazikov, Moscow, 1893,
comprising a flask with
stopper, six vodka cups
and a shaped circular
tray, the flask 26cm
(10¼in), *G 17 May,*
SF 16,000 (£4,790; $6,946)

4
A silver-gilt and enamel
three-piece coffee set,
Antip Kuzmichev,
Moscow, 1891,
comprising coffee pot,
creamer and sugar bowl,
enamelled with
geometric forms, flowers
and foliage, h 21.7cm
(8½in), *NY 14 Dec,*
$4,400 (£3,697)

5
A silver-gilt and enamel
liqueur set, Pavla
Mishukova, Moscow,
c.1900, comprising
decanter, six cups and a
circular tray, d of tray
22cm (8⅝in), *NY 14 Dec,*
$3,080 (£2,588)

6
A silver and shaded
cloisonné enamel kovsh,
possibly N Alexeyev,
Moscow, 1908-17, with
foliage and flowers on a
cream ground, 9.3cm
(3¾in), sold with a silver
and cloisonné enamel
coffee spoon, c.1900,
L 15 Feb,
£495 ($693)

7
A silver and shaded
enamel tea glass holder,
The Eleventh Artel,
Moscow, c.1910, with
flowers, foliage and
geometric forms on
grounds of lilac, emerald
and sea green, h 12cm
(4¾in), *NY 14 Dec,*
$1,870 (£1,572)

8
A silver-gilt and shaded
enamel bowl, Fyodor
Rückert, Moscow, c.1910,
each handle in the form
of a bear's head, 15.2cm
(6in), *NY 20/21 June,*
$4,675 (£3,437)

9
A silver and shaded
enamel kovsh, Orest
Kurlyukov, Moscow,
c.1900, each side with a
boyar surrounded by
multi-coloured flowers
and foliage, 47cm
(18½in), *NY 14 Dec,*
$11,000 (£9,244)

10
A silver and shaded
enamel tea glass holder,
Vasili Agafonov,
Moscow, c.1900, with
birds inhabiting multi-
coloured flowers and
foliage within borders of
white beads, h 9cm
(3½in), *NY 20/21 June,*
$1,100 (£809)

1

2

3

4

5

6

7

8

9

10

1
A silver-gilt and shaded enamel kovsh, F Agafonov, Moscow, 1899-1908, with multi-coloured flowers against a blue and red ground, white beaded border, 19.5cm (7⅝in), *G 17 May*, **SF 3,800 (£1,138; $1,650)**

2
A silver-gilt and shaded enamel sugar basket, Vasili Agafonov, Moscow, c.1900, 12.2cm (4¾in), *NY 20/21 June*, **$2,750 (£2,022)**

3
A pair of silver-gilt and shaded enamel serving spoons, Nikolai Zverev, Moscow, c.1910, the back of each with an exotic bird within borders of blue beads, 16cm (6¼in), *NY 20/21 June*, **$1,045 (£768)**

4
A silver-gilt and enamel cup and saucer, Gustav Klingert, Moscow, 1889, with multi-coloured foliage and borders of blue beads, d of saucer 12.7cm (5in), *NY 20/21 June*, **$1,210 (£890)**

5
A silver-gilt and shaded enamel kovsh, Marie Semyenova, Moscow, c.1900, the border set with red and green hardstone cabochons, 17.9cm (7in), *NY 14 Dec*, **$3,300 (£2,773)**

6
A set of six silver-gilt and shaded enamel miniature tea glass holders, five by Marie Semyenova and one by Gustav Klingert, Moscow, c.1900, h 5.6cm (2⅛in), *NY 14 Dec*, **$3,080 (£2,588)**

7
A silver-gilt and shaded enamel tea glass holder, Khlebnikov, Moscow, c.1900, with multi-coloured flowers and scrolling foliage, h 8.4cm (3¼in), *NY 14 Dec*, **$935 (£784)**

8
A pair of silver-gilt and enamel sugar shovels, Ivan Khlebnikov, Moscow, c.1900, brightly enamelled with flowers and foliage, 13.7cm (5⅜in), *NY 20/21 June*, **$825 (£607)**

9
A silver-gilt and cloisonné enamel cup and cover, Ovchinnikov, Moscow, probably 1893, painted in blue floral and geometric motifs against a matt and white enamel ground, h 16cm (6¼in), *G 14 Nov*, **SF 4,400 (£1,366; $1,830)**

10
A silver-gilt and plique-à-jour enamel bowl, Khlebnikov, Moscow, c.1910, with multi-coloured flowers and foliage within borders of purple beads, 11cm (4½in), *NY 14 Dec*, **$2,310 (£1,941)**

11
A silver-gilt and shaded enamel covered sugar bowl, probably Fyodor Rückert, Moscow, c.1900, enamelled in the Old Russian style on a sea-green ground, 15cm (5⅞in), *NY 14 Dec*, **$7,700 (£6,471)**

12
A silver-gilt and enamel bowl, Ovchinnikov, Moscow, 1891, with multi-coloured flowers and geometric forms, the ring foot with a border of blue beads, h 8.4cm (3¼in), *NY 20/21 June*, **$1,100 (£809)**

13
A silver-gilt and cloisonné enamel vodka beaker, P Ovchinnikov, Moscow, 1877, with shield-shaped panels of enamelled birds against turquoise and white grounds, 4.8cm (2in), *L 15 Feb*, **£528 ($739)**

14
A silver-gilt and cloisonné enamel serving spoon, Liubavin, Moscow, 1908-17, the back decorated with multi-coloured scrolls enclosing a flowerhead, turquoise beaded border, 20cm (7⅞in), *G 14 Nov*, **SF 1,210 (£376; $504)**

1
A silver-gilt and shaded enamel scent flask, Moscow, c.1900, with flowering plants on grounds of turquoise blue, yellow and olive green, h 13.6cm (5⅜in), *NY 20/21 June,* $2,090 (£1,537)

2
A silver-gilt and shaded enamel covered cup, The Eleventh Artel, Moscow, c.1910, with foliage and geometric forms in blue, green and orange, h 31.9cm (12½in), *NY 20/21 June,* $15,400 (£11,324)

3
A pair of silver-gilt and shaded enamel covered vases, Ovchinnikov, Moscow, c.1900, enamelled with Imperial eagles and foliage, also swans against a Chinese red ground, h 50.7cm (20in), *NY 14 Dec,* $82,500 (£69,328)

4
A silver and enamel cigarette case, NV Alekseyev, Moscow, c.1900, with multi-coloured flowers and foliage bordered by blue beads, 10cm (3⅞in), *NY 20/21 June,* $605 (£445)

5
A silver-gilt and shaded cloisonné enamel serving spoon, Fabergé, Moscow, late 19th cent, painted mainly in tones of blue and grey, 20.5cm (8in), *G 14 Nov,* SF 3,850 (£1,196; $1,603)

6
A silver-gilt and enamel tazza, Gustav Klingert, Moscow, 1895, h 12.7cm (5in), *NY 20/21 June,* $1,980 (£1,456)

7
A silver-gilt and shaded enamel card case, by Fyodor Rückert, retailed by Orest Kurlyukov, Moscow, c.1900, enamelled on one side with the Queen of Hearts, the reverse with the Jack of Clubs, h 10.2cm (4in), *NY 14 Dec,* $12,100 (£10,168)

8
A silver-gilt and shaded enamel oval box, Fyodor Rückert, Moscow, c.1910, the hinged cover enamelled en plein with a young boyarina and her groom, 10.2cm (4in), *NY 14 Dec,* $9,900 (£8,319)

9
A silver-gilt and shaded enamel covered sugar bowl, Nikolai Alekseyev, Moscow, 1894, h 13.4cm (5¼in), *NY 14 Dec,* $1,430 (£1,202)

10
A silver and enamel cigarette case, The Fifteenth Artel, Moscow, c.1910, the cover chased with a falconer in a forest, 10.9cm (4¼in), *NY 20/21 June,* $770 (£566)

11
A silver-gilt and enamel Easter egg, c.1900, apparently unmarked, each end enamelled with a white six-pointed star, 7.2cm (2¾in), *NY 14 Dec,* $1,540 (£1,294)

12
A silver-gilt and shaded enamel scent flask, Ivan Saltykov, Moscow, c.1890, with multi-coloured flowers and foliage on a cream ground, h 6.2cm (2⅜in), *NY 14 Dec,* $1,430 (£1,202)

13
A silver-gilt and enamel circular box, K Fabergé, Moscow, c.1910, enamelled in the Old Russian Style in muted shades of green, brown and purple, d 5.2cm (2in), *NY 20/21 June,* $2,310 (£1,699)

14
A silver-gilt and shaded enamel bowl, Fabergé, by Fyodor Rückert, Moscow, c.1900, with multi-coloured stylized flowers and foliage, 12.2cm (5in), *NY 14 Dec,* $9,900 (£8,319)

1
A gold, diamond and moss-agate brooch, Fabergé, workmaster A Hollming, St Petersburg, c.1900, 3.4cm (1¼in), *G 16 May*, **SF 3,000 (£901; $1,288)**

2
A nephrite and enamel desk clock mounted in silver-gilt, Fabergé, workmaster Henrik Wigström, St Petersburg, c.1910, 11.5cm (4½in), *NY 20/21 June*, **$8,525 (£6,268)**

3
A silver-gilt and translucent enamel cigarette case, Fabergé, workmaster August Fredrik Hollming, St Petersburg, c.1900, royal blue over a guilloché ground, 9.7cm (3¾in), *NY 20/21 June*, **$3,850 (£2,831)**

4
A silver-gilt and translucent enamel small compact case, Fabergé, workmaster Henrik Wigström, St Petersburg, c.1910, powder blue on both sides within white borders, 6.5cm (2½in), *NY 20/21 June*, **$2,420 (£1,779)**

5
A jewelled two-colour gold and ebony cigarette case, Fabergé, St Petersburg, late 19th cent, w 9cm (3½in), *G 14 Nov*, **SF 8,250 (£2,707; $3,305)**

6
A silver-gilt and translucent enamel kovsh, Fabergé, workmaster A Nevalainen, St Petersburg, 1899-1908, enamelled in strawberry-red over engine turning, 8.5cm (3¼in), *L 15 Feb*, **£1,870 ($2,622)**

7
A silver-gilt, translucent enamel and jewelled cigarette case, Fabergé, workmaster August Hollming, St Petersburg, c.1910, 10cm (3⅞in), *NY 20/21 June*, **$13,200 (£9,706)**

8
A silver cigarette case, Fabergé, Moscow, 1908-17, 11cm (4¼in), *G 17 May*, **SF 3,000 (£898; $1,302)**

9
A jewelled gold and enamel nephrite snuff box, Fabergé, workmaster H Wigström, St Petersburg, c.1910, opaque white enamel borders with cabochon rubies, 10cm (4in), *G 17 May*, **SF 24,000 (£7,187; $10,419)**

10
A two-colour gold and hardstone articulated triple desk seal, Fabergé, workmaster H Wigström, St Petersburg, 1908-17, with turquoise matrix handle, 9.1cm (3½in), *G 17 May*, **SF 12,000 (£3,818; $5,338)**

11
A gold-mounted jewelled amethyst miniature egg pendant, Fabergé, workmaster M Perchin, c.1900, set with diamond studs and spirals, h 2.8cm (1⅛in), *G 14 Nov*, **SF 4,620 (£1,435; $1,923)**

12
A silver-gilt and enamel buckle, Fabergé, workmaster M Perchin, St Petersburg, 1899-1903, enamelled in translucent salmon-pink over engine turning, 7cm (2¾in), *G 17 May*, **SF 2,300 (£689; $999)**

13
A silver-gilt, pearl and red enamel miniature frame, Fabergé, workmaster V Aarne, St Petersburg, late 19th cent, enamelled in translucent strawberry-red, 7.2cm (2¾in), *G 17 May*, **SF 7,500 (£2,246; $3,256)**

14
A silver-gilt and translucent enamel desk clock, Fabergé, workmaster M Perchin, St Petersburg, c.1890, enamelled translucent steel grey over a guilloché ground, d 11cm (4¼in), *NY 14 Dec*, **$11,000 (£9,244)**

15
A silver-gilt and translucent enamel circular desk clock, Fabergé, workmaster Henrik Wigström, St Petersburg, c.1900, enamelled powder-blue over a sunray ground, d 11.5cm (4½in), *NY 20/21 June*, **$6,325 (£4,651)**

1
A silver-gilt and translucent enamel miniature tea glass holder, Fabergé, workmaster Anders Nevalainen, St Petersburg, c.1900, the sides enamelled translucent lime green over a guilloché ground, h 5.6cm (2⅛in), *NY 20/21 June*, $2,750 (£2,022)

2
A gold, enamel and smoky quartz 'Historismus' standing cup and cover, Fabergé, workmaster M Perchin, St Petersburg, 1899-1903, 11.7cm (4⅝in), *G 17 May*, SF 45,000 (£13,473; $19,536)

3
A pair of silver ice tongs, K Fabergé, Moscow, c.1900, in the form of eagle's talons rising from acanthus leafage, 22.2cm (8¾in), *NY 14 Dec*, $1,760 (£1,479)

4
A silver-mounted cut-glass claret jug, Fabergé, Moscow, 1893, with shell thumbpiece and scroll handle, h 26.5cm (10⅜in), *NY 20/21 June*, $1,650 (£1,213)

5
A silver smoker's compendium, Fabergé, Moscow, 1894, in the form of a *datcha* surrounded by a meadow, w 37cm (14½in), *G 14 Nov*, SF 60,500 (£18,789; $25,177)

6
A silver inkstand, P Ovchinnikov, Moscow, 1899-1908, cast and chased in the form of a mounted peasant at a trough, 39.5cm (15½in), *G 17 May*, SF 14,000 (£4,192; $6,078)

7
A silver table cigar box mounted with a miniature, Fabergé, Moscow, c.1912, commemorating the Russian victory over Napoleon in 1812, the miniature, signed C Berth, 16cm (6¼in), *NY 14 Dec*, £5,500 (£4,622)

8
A rose quartz carving of a pig, Fabergé, St Petersburg, c.1900, unmarked, cabochon sapphire eyes, h 2cm. (¾in), *G 14 Nov*, SF 4,500 (£1,477; $1,803)

9
A silver and gem-set Imperial presentation casket, Fabergé, Moscow, c.1900, overlaid with silver scrolls and set with precious and semi-precious stones, w 31.5cm (12⅜in), *G 14 Nov*, SF 24,200 (£7,516; $10,071)

10
A silver and marble desk set, maker's mark FK, Moscow, 1899-1908, comprising a pen and inkstand and blotter formed as a rustic scene, base cracked, 28.2cm (11in), *L 15 Feb*, £1,210 ($1,694)

11
A pair of silver table candlesticks, Fabergé, Moscow, c.1900, in rococo style, the base and handles chased with scrolls, the sockets detachable, h 10cm (4in), *M 11 Dec*, FF 53,280 (£4,694; $5,668)

12
A silver service of flatware, Fabergé, Moscow, c.1910, decorated in Louis XVI style, together with twelve similar demi-tasse spoons, by Gratchev, St Petersburg, c.1910, 168 pieces, *NY 14 Dec*, $32,200 (£27,059)

13
A silver teapot, Fabergé, Moscow, c.1910, of slightly bombé form with geometric handle, the slip-on cover with ivory finial, 18.2cm (7⅛in), *NY 14 Dec*, $1,100 (£924)

1

2

3

4

5

6

7

8

9

10

11

12

13

1
A pair of silver
candelabra, Nicholls &
Plincke, workmaster PK,
St Petersburg, late 19th
cent, cast and chased
with three eagles' heads
supporting the nozzles,
20.5cm (8in), *G 16 May*,
SF 3,800 (£1,141; $1,632)

2
A silver tea caddy,
Fabergé, Moscow, late
19th cent, in the form of
a tea packet, engraved
with Imperial warrants
and simulated taxbands,
13cm (5⅛in), *G 17 May*,
SF 26,000 (£7,784; $11,287)

3
A pair of silver nine-light
table lamps, Fabergé,
workmaster Julius
Rappoport, St
Petersburg, *c.*1910,
h 82.5cm (32½in),
NY 14 Dec,
$66,000 (£55,462)

4
A silver cake basket, P.
Sazikov, St Petersburg,
1883, flat-chased with a
strapwork band, the
swing handle pierced
and engraved, 30cm
(11¾in), *G 14 Nov*,
SF 1,760 (£547; $732)

5
A gold cigarette case,
maker's mark AK, St
Petersburg, 1908-1917,
decorated with sunray
reeding, gold thumbpiece
set with a cabochon
sapphire, 10cm (4in),
G 17 May,
SF 3,800 (£1,138; $1,650)

6
An Imperial parcel-gilt
presentation kovsh,
inscribed and dated
17th March 1677,
engraved with double-
headed eagle within a
border of scrolls and
ribbons, 37cm (14½in),
G 17 May,
SF 27,000 (£8,084;
$11,722)

7
An Imperial silver-gilt
presentation kovsh, L.
Artemiev, Moscow,
*c.*1740, embossed with
the Imperial eagle
adorned with a shield,
the front engraved with
a portrait of Empress
Elizabeth, 30cm (11¾in),
G 16 May,
SF 20,000 (£6,006; $8,589)

8
Three vodka cups,
Moscow, *c.*1760, two with
bulbous bases, by
Grigori Lakomkin; the
third with lobed base,
assaymaster Cyrillic
initials VA, 6 to 7.7cm
(2¼ to 3 in), *NY 14 Dec*,
$880 (£739)

9
A silver and parcel-gilt
beaker, possibly G
Lakomkin, Moscow,
1738, the sides chased
with three medallions
enclosing a bird, a horse
and a warrior, 16cm
(6¼in), *G 17 May*,
SF 3,000 (£898; $1,302)

10
A parcel-gilt beaker, F
Petrov, Moscow, 1759-
74, chased with
rocaille ornament
enclosing three panels,
embossed with a stag, a
unicorn and a pelican,
17.5cm (6⅞in), *G 17 May*,
SF 3,200 (£958; $1,389)

11
A silver beaker, Fyodor
Tikhonov Krijev,
Alderman Fyodor
Petrov, Moscow, 1762,
the sides chased with
birds inhabiting rococo
foliage, scrolls and
shellwork, h 15.3cm
(6in), *NY 20/21 June*,
$1,320 (£971)

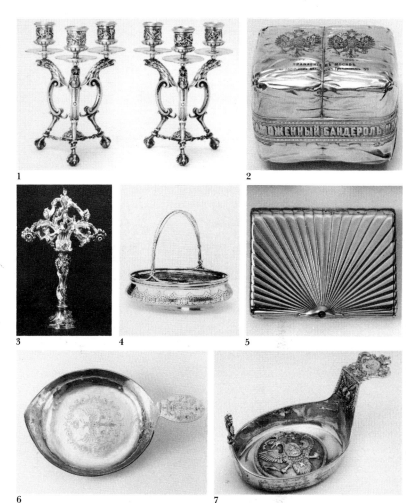

1   2

3   4   5

6   7

8

9   10   11

1
A silver beaker, maker's mark SO, Moscow, 1777, embossed with eagles perched upon rocaille scrollwork, 8cm (3⅛in), *L 15 Feb,* £352 ($494)

2
A set of six silver vodka beakers, maker's mark PED, St Petersburg, late 19th cent, engraved with trompe l'oeil wickerwork, h 4.5cm (1¾in), *G 17 May,* SF 3,200 (£958; $1,389)

3
A silver and glass butter dish, Nicholls & Plincke, workmaster RK, St Petersburg, second half 19th cent, the saucer and bowl formed as a daffodil head, the bowl 7cm (2¾in), *L 15 Feb,* £209 ($293)

4
A pair of silver and glass spirit bottles, St Petersburg, 1880, the trompe l'oeil basketwork covers tied with silver rope, 29cm (11⅜in), *G 17 May,* SF 6,800 (£2,036; $2,952)

5
A trompe l'oeil silver tea caddy, Khlebnikov, Moscow, 1888, engraved to simulate raffia work, 9.5cm (3¾in), *L 9 July,* £330 ($459)

6
A silver tea kettle and stand, Cyrillic maker's mark PED, St Petersburg, 1887, chased to simulate basketweave, the stand in the form of intertwined branches, h 34.3cm (13½in), *NY 14 Dec,* $2,750 (£2,311)

7
A silver water pitcher, Moscow, 1841, h 28.3cm (9½in), *NY 14 Dec,* $495 (£416)

8
A silver-gilt coffee pot, M. Ovchinnikov, Moscow, 1896, in Empire style, the spout and handle in the form of a swan's neck and head, 22cm (8⅝in), *G 17 May,* SF 9,000 (£2,695; $3,907)

9
A silver snuff box, Moscow, 1790, circular, the lid inset with a medallion of Catherine the Great, by Waechter, 9.5cm (3¾in), *L 15 Feb,* £462 ($647)

10
A parcel-gilt trompe-l'oeil bread basket, maker's mark PL, Moscow, 1883, holding a folded cloth with fringes, 37cm (14½in), *G 17 May,* SF 6,500 (£2,070; $2,877)

11
A silver samovar, Gratchev, St Petersburg, 1892, with turned ivory grips set into angular handles, the openwork spigot set with ivory, h 44.2cm (17½in), *NY 14 Dec,* $5,500 (£4,622)

12
A silver samovar, Gratchev, St Petersburg, 1889, h 38.5cm (15⅛in), *NY 14 Dec,* $1,870 (£1,571)

13
A parcel-gilt and enamel bread basket, P. Ovchinnikov, Moscow, 1884, the trompe-l'oeil silver-gilt bowl covered with a lace-trimmed napkin, 38cm (15in), *G 17 May,* SF 10,000 (£3,185; $4,427)

14
A silver and glass fruit-cup jug, Nicholls & Plincke, workmaster RK, *c.*1885, the collar and lid formed as a cast and chased ram's head, 39cm (15⅜in), *L 15 Feb,* £5,280 ($7,403)

15
A lacquered silver-gilt serving spoon, The Ninth Artel, Moscow, 1908-1917, the ground and handle lacquered in red, few slight chips, 19cm (7½in), *G 14 Nov,* SF 990 (£325; $397)

16
A silver-gilt and niello champagne flute, J. Henrikson, St Petersburg, 1832, engraved with two ladies on one side, the other with a building, 17.5cm (6⅞in), *G 17 May,* SF 1,800 (£539; $781)

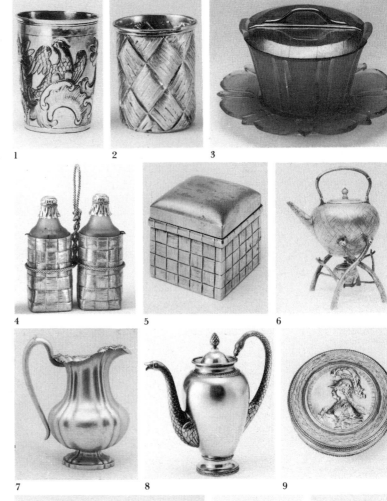

1   2   3

4   5   6

7   8   9

10   11   12

13   14   15   16

1
A silver and cut-glass centrepiece, Morozov, St Petersburg, c.1900, raised on four foliate feet capped by satyrs' masks, 45.8cm (18in), *NY 20/21 June,* $2,200 (£1,618)

2
A pair of silver serving spoons, P Ovchinnikov, Moscow, 1879, the finial formed as a dancing peasant and a man playing an accordion, 23cm (9in), *L 9 July,* £495 ($688)

3
A silver-gilt and niello beaker, maker's mark A Sch, Moscow, 1827, engraved with huntsmen, 6.7cm (2⅝in), *L 9 July,* £382 ($523)

4
A set of three silver-gilt and niello vodka beakers, maker's mark F Ja, Moscow, c.1880, each engraved with a different monument in St Petersburg, h 5.5cm (2⅛in), *G 14 Nov,* SF 2,090 (£650; $870)

5
A parcel-gilt trompe l'oeil tankard, maker's mark IA, St Petersburg, 1860, cast and engraved as an ivy clad bark, the finial in the form of a fox, h 20.5cm (8in), *G 14 Nov,* SF 2,860 (£939; $1,145)

6
A parcel-gilt and niello snuff box, maker's mark A Sch, Moscow, 1824, engraved with men near ruins, reserved against sablé ground, gilt interior, 6.5cm (2½in), *L 9 July,* £495 ($688)

7
A parcel-gilt and niello tankard, V. Semyonov, Moscow, 1862, the sides with views of the Moscow Kremlin and St Basil's Cathedral, h 13.5cm (5¼in), *G 14 Nov,* SF 2,640 (£820; $1,099)

8
A silver and niello snuff box, maker's mark NM, Moscow, mid-19th cent, engraved with rocaille ornaments, silver-gilt thumbpiece, gilt interior, 9.2cm (3⅝in), *G 17 May,* SF 1,300 (£389; $564)

9
A pair of Imperial porcelain vases, St Petersburg, the paintings signed 'Timothy Semyenov' and dated 1836, restoration, h 79.3cm (31¼in), *NY 14 Dec,* $12,100 (£10,168)

10
A silver-gilt and niello snuff box, maker's mark OB, Moscow, 1834, the lid engraved with a battle scene, the base engraved with war trophies, 6.6cm (2⅝in), *G 17 May,* SF 1,200 (£359; $521)

11
A porcelain dinner plate from the service presented by Queen Victoria to Nicholas I, Coalport, c.1845, d 26cm (10¼in), *NY 14 Dec,* $3,740 (£3,143)

1

2

3

4

5

6

7

8

9

10

11

1
Twenty-four Imperial porcelain dinner plates, period of Nicholas II, dated 1905/6, d 25.6cm (10in), *NY 14 Dec,* $4,675 (£3,929)

2
A pair of Imperial porcelain dinner plates, period of Nicholas I (1825-55), d 23.6cm (9¼in), *NY 14 Dec.* $825 (£693)

3
Two Imperial porcelain serving plates, period of Nicholas I (1825-55), d 33cm (13in), sold with a sweetmeat dish dated 1909, *NY 14 Dec,* $935 (£786)

4
Eight dinner plates and eight soup plates, from the Kremlin Service, commissioned by Emperor Nicholas I, Imperial Porcelain Factory, St Petersburg, 1837-8, d 25cm (9¾in), *L 15 Feb,* £7,150 ($10,024)

5
A circular porcelain plate, Lomonosov factory, Petrograd, 1922, painted on undecorated porcelain of the Imperial factory, 25cm (9⅞in), *L 9 July,* £440 ($603)

6
A circular porcelain dish, Lomonosov factory, Petrograd, 1921, painted with flowers on undecorated porcelain of the Imperial factory marked with the cypher of Nicholas II, 1898, 24.5cm (9½in), *L 15 Feb,* £605 ($847)

7
A painted biscuit pastille burner, unmarked, 19th cent, 22cm (8¾in), *L 15 Feb,* £418 ($585)

8
A porcelain figure of a coachman, Gardner, first half 19th cent, h 19cm (7½in), *L 9 July,* £308 ($422)

9
A porcelain figure of a girl, Gardner, first half 19th cent, h 19cm (7½in), *L 9 July,* £418 ($573)

10
A biscuit figure of a chimney sweep, M S Kuznetsov, *c.*1900, h 30cm (11¾in), *L 15 Feb,* £440 ($616)

11
A porcelain figure of a girl, unmarked, 19th cent, restored, h 19.4cm (7¾in), *L 15 Feb,* £330 ($463)

12
A porcelain figure of a sweeper, Popov, 19th cent, h 20.2cm (7⅞in) *NY 14 Dec,* $605 (£508)

13
A porcelain group, Gardner factory, late 19th cent, h 25.6cm (10in), *NY 14 Dec,* $715 (£601)

14
A lacquered papier-mâché caddy, *c.*1860, decorated with Moscow scenes, slightly chipped, 11cm (4½in), *L 15 Feb,* £1,375 ($1,925)

15
A pair of ormolu-mounted cobalt blue glass vases, early 19th cent, mounted on circular marble bases, h 25.7cm (10⅛in), *NY 20/21 June,* $1,100 (£809)

16
A bronze figure of Peter the Great, after Boris Mikhailovich Mikeshin (1873-1937), 1909, h 55cm (21¾in), *NY 20/21 June,* $3,300 (£2,426)

17
A pair of malachite and ormolu candelabra, 19th cent, circular malachite bases, h 16.5cm (10⅜in), *NY 14 Dec,* $5,225 (£4,391)

18
A bronze equestrian group of a falconer, after Evgenie Alexandrovich Lanceray (1848-87), late 19th cent, h 55.4cm (21¾in), *NY 14 Dec,* $4,950 (£4,159)

19
A bronze equestrian group of a mounted soldier, after Evgenie Alexandrovich Lanceray (1848-87), 1885, with Chopin foundry mark, h 75.5cm (29¾in), *NY 14 Dec,* $2,750 (£2,311)

1 2 3
4 5 6
7 8 9 10 11 12
13 14 15 16
17 18 19

European Works of Art

ELIZABETH WILSON • DAVID WILLE

European works of art is the title given to a field ranging in date from Romanesque times through to the early 19th century. It therefore covers the wide area between Antiquities and 19th century sculpture and Decorative arts from 1880, and it is here that the collector can look for a 12th century Spanish wooden crucifix or a 15th century German woodcarving. Here, too, that he can seek to build up his collection of antique iron locks and keys or brass tobacco boxes.

Many of the items included are now considered works of fine art, but they were often first conceived in terms of decoration and, unlike the paintings with which they may be contemporary, were rarely signed and occasioned few documentary records. They were often lumped together in inventories in much the same way as portfolios of drawings used to be and, as a result, provenance and authorship are very difficult to establish with any certainty. Within this field, therefore, authenticity is one of the most important factors in the eyes of collectors. Once this has been established (and Sotheby's aim to be as accurate as possible in their catalogues) the collector feels secure and is prepared to spend very large sums. These days he can put increasing faith in a number of scientific tests which are used to authenticate certain materials. For instance, all purportedly Renaissance terracottas are tested at Sotheby's as a matter of routine.

The heavy reliance on authenticity has tended to mean that the pieces with excellent provenances and ready identification fetch prices far in excess of those paid for pieces whose authorship cannot be confirmed, even though these latter may in many ways be as fine. The Romanesque capital whose origins are well known will be very much more expensive than one without a secure history. The collector who is prepared to trust his eye can acquire some very beautiful pieces—a small medieval ivory, for instance—for less than £1,000 ($1,140).

As has been said, the section covers works in many different media and of many different periods. It includes medieval stone carvings and ivories, Renaissance and Baroque marbles and bronzes, North European woodcarving, Limoges enamels, jewellery, stained glass and metalwork of various dates. (Viennese enamels and 19th century ivories, which are here linked with earlier works of art and illustrated on pages 398-401, are normally included in Objects of Vertu sales or sales of 19th century works of art.)

Of these subjects bronzes currently seem to be back in favour and are collected throughout the world. Woodcarving is regaining its popularity, but prices are still not as high as they were ten years ago. Interest is centred in Belgium and Germany—the homeland of most of the carving—but there are also French, Italian and American collectors. British collectors tend rather to specialize in metalwork. This is illustrated on pages 402-9 and there is an article specifically on iron on page 402.

1
A limestone capital,
French, 12th cent,
carved in the round with
scrolling leaves, h 22cm
(8½in), *NY 23/24 Nov,*
$1,320 (£1,090)

2
**A Romanesque marble
capital,** Southern France,
late 12th cent, carved on
three sides, h 29cm
(11½in), *NY 2/3 Mar,*
$7,150 (£4,798)

3
A Romanesque capital,
French, mid-12th cent,
carved with interlacing
design, supporting two
twin columns of 13th
century type, the capital
h 39.4cm (15½in), the
columns h 117.5cm
(46½in), the bases h 21.5cm
(8½in), *L 3 Apr,*
£20,900 ($30,159)

4
**A North Spanish
Romanesque wood crucifix
figure,** probably Catalan,
*c*1170, crowned, the whole
with later paint over
earlier polychrome, feet
and arms missing, 63.5cm
(25in), *L 13 Dec,*
£26,400 ($33,000)

5
**A Spanish Romanesque
wood group of the
Madonna and Child,**
Leon, 12th cent, traces of
original paint, carved in
the round with parallel
and V-shaped folds, 57cm
(22½in), *NY 23/24 Nov,*
$9,625 (£7,954)

6
A female saint, perhaps
the Magdalene or one of
the Holy Women,
Styria, 2nd half 14th
cent, pine, much
original polychrome and
ground, 107cm (42⅛in),
L 3 Apr,
£33,000 ($47,619)

7
**A Gothic boxwood group
of the Virgin and Child,**
Middle-Rhine, 1st half
15th cent, the Virgin
wearing a cloak, traces of
pigmentation including
Gothic tracery, 38cm
(15in), *NY 2/3 Mar,*
$7,150 (£4,798)

8
**An Alsatian gilt walnut
group of the Madonna
and Child,** late 13th/early
14th cent, some traces
of original paint beneath
later paint, 67cm (26½in),
NY 23/24 Nov,
$1,430 (£1,181)

9
**A Netherlandish polychrome
wood figure of an angel,**
late 15th cent, wearing a
surplice and playing a
lute, much original colour,
47.6cm (18¾in), *L 13 Dec,*
£3,740 ($4,675)

10
**A Gothic oak armorial
panel,** probably North
German, 2nd half 15th
cent, two angels in flight
holding a shield,
w 148cm (58½in),
NY 23/24 Nov,
$4,290 (£3,545)

1
A North Italian polychrome walnut relief, late 15th cent, the Apostle St. Mark seated in his study, the panelling painted in gold and dark blue, h 62cm (24½in), *NY 2/3 Mar,* $5,500 (£3,691)

2
A large Nuremberg polychrome wood group of the Virgin and Child, *c*1490, the Madonna's hands sensitively carved holding the Child to her left, her face restored, 150cm (59in), *L 3 Apr,* £3,740 ($5,397)

3
A painted terracotta figure of Christ, Austrian, 2nd half 16th cent, modelled as 'Ecce Homo', repainted at a later date, bearing initials and the date 1795 on reverse, h 72cm (28¼in), *NY 23/24 Nov,* $1,100 (£909)

4
A Franconian polychrome lindenwood figure of an apostle, early 16th cent, possibly St. John the Evangelist, somewhat repainted, left hand replaced, 66cm (26in). *NY 2/3 Mar,* $4,400 (£2,953)

5
A Flemish polychrome oak relief, *c*1500, perhaps from a retable, showing St. James on horseback and in front of him a kneeling cardinal, perhaps the donor, extensive original gilding and colour, hands defective, 38.5cm (15¼in), *L 13 Dec,* £6,820 ($8,525)

6
A Spanish Gothic wood figure of St. Michael, from the workshop of Gil de Siloe, Burgos, *c*1500, his right arm raised and originally holding a sword, standing on the devil, 77cm (30½in), *NY 23/24 Nov,* $3,850 (£3,181)

7
A South German gilt lindenwood relief, Nuremberg, 1st quarter 16th cent, the Madonna supported by angels, 53cm (23¾in), *NY 23/24 Nov,* $8,525 (£7,045)

8
A limewood relief, St. Anna Selbdritt, Bavarian-Swabian school, *c*1500, presenting the Child to the Madonna who wears a blue-lined cloak over a red dress with traces of embroidered ornament, two hands lacking, the others replaced, w 19cm (7½in), *L 3 Apr,* £8,580 ($12,380)

9
A South German polychrome and giltwood relief of the Virgin and Child, Munich, *c*1500, the Virgin standing on a crescent moon holding a pear in her right hand, 113.4cm (44⅝in), *L 4 July,* £13,750 ($19,113)

10
A South German lindenwood group of St. George and the dragon, Nuremberg, *c*1510-20, retaining traces of gilding, lance replaced. 77cm (30¼in), *NY 23/24 Nov,* $11,000 (£9,090)

11
A South German lindenwood relief of Pieta, lower Franconia, 2nd decade 16th cent, the Virgin with sad expression gently supporting the body of Christ, some restoration, 89cm (35in), *NY 2/3 Mar,* $16,500 (£11,073)

1   2

3   4   5

6   7   8

9   10   11

1
A Franco-Flemish painted
wood group of the
Madonna and Child, 2nd
half 16th cent, repainted,
84cm (33in),
NY 23/24 Nov,
$1,320 (£1,090)

2
An oval boxwood relief,
Italo-Flemish, mid-17th
cent, of St Andrew, 19cm
(7½in), *F 10 May,*
L 2,034,000 (£828; $1,192)

3
An Italian gilt wood group
of the Virgin and Child,
2nd half 16th cent,
enthroned and holding
the Christ Child before
her, 44.5cm (17in),
NY 23/24 Nov,
$1,430 (£1,181)

4
A Baroque boxwood
figure of Christ, 17th cent,
mounted on wooden
cross applied with
original boxwood scroll
inscribed in Hebrew,
Greek and Latin, h of
figure 52cm (20½in),
NY 2/3 Mar,
$22,000 (£14,765)

5
A Netherlandish wood
bozzetto of Venus
Doidelsas, 17th cent,
shown crouching with
arms shielding her body,
slightly worn, 21.5cm
(8½in), *L 13 Dec,*
£1,595 ($1,994)

6
A Spanish giltwood figure
of St Francis, 17th cent,
realistically carved, his
eyes inset in glass,
originally holding a
crucifix in his left hand,
132cm (52in), *NY 2/3 Mar,*
$7,150 (£4,799)

7
A South German linden-
wood bust of St John,
early 18th cent, slightly
over life size, traces of
polychrome, 66cm
(26in), *NY 23/24 Nov,*
$2,200 (£1,818)

8
A pair of Italian giltwood
angels, early 18th cent,
each supporting a
cornucopia fitted with
pricket, 69cm (27¼in),
NY 23/24 Nov,
$2,310 (£1,909)

9
A polychrome wood group
of St John and the Christ
Child, Naples, 2nd half
18th cent, h 69cm (27in),
F 10 May,
L 2,034,000 (£828; $1,192)

10
A pair of terracotta
sphinxes, 18th cent, their
heads apparently portraits
of 18th century ladies,
perhaps Piedmont, 20cm
(8¼in), *L 3 Apr,*
£1,100 ($1,587)

1   2   3

4   5   6

7   8

9   10

1
A Roman marble portrait bust, attributed to Giovanni Antonio Dosio or his circle, last quarter 16th cent, of an elderly statesman, repaired, h 49.5cm (19½in), *NY 23/24 Nov*, $11,000 (£9,090)

2
A pink marble relief of Venus Marina, late 17th cent, against a black marble ground, within a breche violette frame, 23.2cm (9⅛in), *L 17 May*, £1,155 ($1,675)

3
An Italian marble head of Cicero, early 18th cent, slightly weathered, originally fitted into marble shoulders, h 40cm (15½in), *NY 23/24 Nov*, $1,980 (£1,636)

4
A Flemish terracotta group of the Virgin and Child, in the manner of Walter Pompe, early 18th cent, polychrome of later date, h 65cm (25⅝in), *L 3 Apr*, £1,705 ($2,460)

5
A polychrome terracotta group of the Pietà, in the manner of Antonio Maria Maragliano, Genoese, 18th cent, 30cm (12in), *F 10 May*, L 1,695,000 (£690; $993)

6
A wax bust of Voltaire, late 18th cent, shown with receding hair line and deeply wrinkled face, h 29cm (11½in), *L 4 July*, £660 ($917)

7
An Italian white marble bust of a nobleman, 2nd quarter 18th cent, wearing wig and flowing tunic over armour, on grey marble base, h 67cm (26½in), *NY 23/24 Nov*, $1,320 (£1,090)

8
A French marble bust of a young woman, 2nd half 18th cent, her hair tied in plaits, nose repaired, h 36cm (14¼in), *NY 23/24 Nov*, $550 (£454)

9
A wax portrait relief, by Peter Rouw (the Younger), dated 1814, modelled with the bust portrait of Prince Lucien Bonaparte, signed, 16cm (6¼in), *L 21 Nov*, £572 ($749)

10
A Belgian white marble bust of a girl, by Gilles Lambert Godecharle, dated 1801, crisply carved with her wavy hair tied in a bun, chipped, h 51.3cm (20¼in), *NY 23/24 Nov*, $6,600 (£5,454)

11
An Italian white marble bust of a woman, c1830, h 47cm (18½in), *F 10 May*, L 2,486,000 (£1,012; $1,457)

12
An Italian white marble bust of a young woman, c1830, *F 10 May*, L 2,486,000 (£1,012; $1,457)

13
A white marble group, mid-19th cent, of a shepherd boy and his dog, after Berthel Thorwaldsen, h 90cm (35in), *L 3 Apr*, £3,300 ($4,762)

1
A French miniature ivory
casket, late 14th cent,
with silver bindings and
hinges, the lock plate
with secret closing
device, the base later
engraved, 6.5cm (2½in),
L 3 Apr,
£3,080 ($4,444)

2
A Gothic ivory diptych,
14th cent, representing
the Crucifixion and the
Glorification of the
Virgin, h 7cm (2¾in),
M 25/26 June,
FF 22,200 (£1,906; $2,596)

3
A French Gothic ivory
diptych, 2nd half 14th
cent, scenes from the
Passion of Christ,
opened 13 x 10cm (5¼ x
4in), *NY 23/24 Nov,*
$5,500 (£4,545)

4
An ivory figure of Christ
on the cross, Spanish,
19th cent, of exceptionally
large size, the loin cloth
trimmed with gilt edge,
71 x 59cm (28 x 23in),
NY 23/24 Nov,
$3,025 (£2,500)

5
A large Flemish ivory
crucifix figure, mid-17th
cent, mounted on an
ebony veneered cross,
104cm (41in), *L 3 Apr,*
£7,150 ($10,317)

6
A South German ivory
salt, Nuremberg, early
17th cent, the bowl
supported by four
nereids, allegorical for
the four seasons, 13cm
(5in), *NY 2/3 Mar,*
$1,320 (£885)

7
A set of three ivory figures
attributed to Antonio
Leoni, c1710-15, men
dressed in draped togae,
probably representing
St. Matthew, St. John
and the other perhaps
St. Simon, each about
10cm (4in), *L 4 July,*
£4,400 ($6,116)

8
An ivory figure of Perseus,
Dieppe, 18th cent,
leaning on his shield, a
sword in his right hand,
wearing classical armour,
original ivory and wood
socle, blade of sword
missing, h 17.2cm (6¾in),
L 17 May,
£880 ($1,276)

9
An oval ivory portrait
medallion, by Jean
Mancel, early 18th cent,
inscribed 'Henricus de
Laune Aetatis XXVIII',
signed 'IMF', 9.8cm
(3⅞in), *L 17 May,*
£616 ($893)

10
Ivory figures of the Four
Seasons, Dieppe, 18th cent,
each woman wearing con-
temporary costume and
carrying her respective
attributes, some fingers
missing, (two illustrated),
h 19cm(7½in), *NY 2/3 Mar,*
$11,000 (£7,382)

11
A boxwood snuff rasp,
probably German, 18th
cent, carved on both
sides, slight damage,
17cm (6¾in), *L 9 July,*
£605 ($821)

12
A Flemish ivory snuff rasp,
18th cent, carved in
relief with an organ-
grinder, with original
iron grater, 16cm (6¼in),
L 3 Apr,
£605 ($873)

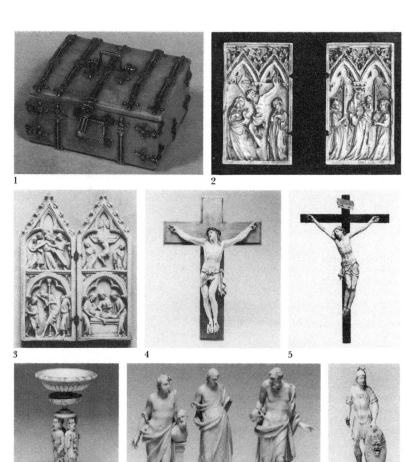

1 2

3 4 5

6 7 8

10 11 12

9

1
A Paduan oil lamp, early 16th cent, attributed to the workshop of Andrea Riccio, in the form of a satyr, his head between his knees, silver eyes, dark brown patina with traces of black lacquer, 14cm (10½in), *L 4 July*, **£42,900 ($59,631)**

2
A Florentine gilt bronze figure of Christ, late 16th cent, after Giambologna, lacking all fingers on his left hand, h 23cm (9in), *NY 23/24 Nov*, **$2,200 (£1,818)**

3
A Florentine bronze group of Samson and the two Philistines, late 16th cent, after the model by Michelangelo, rich brown patina with traces of red-golden lacquer, h 35cm (13¾in), *NY 2/3 Mar*, **$19,800 (£13,288)**

4
A French bronze study of a horse, attributed to the workshop of Antoine Coysevox, *c* 1680, h 84cm (33in), *M 24/25 June*, **FF 2,442,000 (£209,614; $285,614)**

5
A Florentine bronze figure of Morgante, from the workshops of Giambologna, *c* 1600, unusually modelled without a beard, probably formerly holding a cup, the left hand with the hilt of a staff, the remainder missing, lightish brown patina, repaired, 12.8cm (5in), *L 13 Dec*, **£3,300 ($4,125)**

6
An Italian bronze Pieta, probably Roman, 17th cent, after Michelangelo, well cast and chased in red-golden coloured bronze, and dark brown lacquer, h 38cm (15in), *NY 23/24 Nov*, **$5,500 (£4,545)**

7
A bronze figure of Venus Marina, French, 2nd half 17th cent, from the workshops of Michel Anguier, 54.5cm (22½in), *L 3 Apr*, **£8,800 ($12,698)**

8
A Florentine bronze group of children dancing, in the manner of Ferdinando Tacca, mid-17th cent, damaged and repaired, dark brown lacquer over golden patina, h 47cm (18½in), *NY 2/3 Mar*, **$11,000 (£7,382)**

9
A Flemish bronze figure of a boy playing the bagpipes, 17th cent, after Giambologna, 17th cent, on later marble base, h 9.7cm (3¾in), *L 4 July*, **£990 ($1,376)**

1

2

3

4

5

6

7

8

9

1
An Italian bronze figure, after Giambologna, late 17th cent, of a peasant resting on his staff, dressed in a ragged coat and top-boots, dark patina over reddish bronze, h 11.5cm (4½in), *L 4 July*, £1,430 ($1,988)

2
A pair of French bronze figures, from the workshop of Pierre Legros I, late 17th cent, of Thales and a scholar, rich golden-brown lacquer over light golden-coloured bronze, h 16.5cm (6½in), *NY 23/24 Nov*, $8,800 (£7,272)

3
A bronze figure of a proud bull, after Giambologna, Flemish, 17th cent, black lacquer over gold brown patina, on yellow marble base, 25cm (9¾in), *NY 2/3 Mar*, $6,050 (£4,060)

4
A Florentine bronze head of Socrates, 18th cent, after the antique, golden red-brown lacquer, 40cm (15¾in), *L 3 Apr*, £1,705 ($2,460)

5
A French bronze bust, by Guillaume Coustou (Son), c1770, of Madame Lecomte, the young woman with flowers in her dressed hair, h 44.5cm (17½in), *L 4 July*, £2,200 ($3,058)

6
Two French bronze allegorical groups, 18th cent, representing Water and Earth, olive brown patina, h 16 and 18.5cm (6¼ and 7¼in), *NY 23/24 Nov*, $1,650 (£1,363)

7
An Italian bronze figure of Hercules, late 18th/early 19th cent, looking at the apples of the Hesperides in his left hand, separately cast base with integral tree trunk, h 55.5cm (22in), *L 4 July*, £2,310 ($3,211)

8
A French bronze deathmask of Napoleon Bonaparte, c1833, after the plaster taken by Dr Antommarchi on 7 May 1821, rich coloured brown patina, mounted on a wood panel, h 33cm (13in), *NY 23/24 Nov*, $2,200 (£1,818)

9
A pair of French bronze busts, early 19th cent, of a negro and a negress, she is carrying a bow and a quiver with arrows, black lacquer over rich dark brown patination, h 18cm (7in), *L 4 July*, £990 ($1,376)

10
A French bronze figure of a courtier, early 17th cent, dressed in contemporary costume, 21cm (8¼in), *L 4 July*, £5,060 ($7,033)

11
A pair of gilt bronze sphinxes, 1st quarter 19th cent, black marble bases, one inscribed 'Marin Fecit', the other 'Ricourt Fecit', h 23cm (9in), *L 4 July*, £1,540 ($2,141)

1 2 3

4 5 6

7 8 9

10 11

1

A small Italian iron
plaque, 16th cent, chiselled
and damascened in gold,
10.4 x 9.8cm (4⅛ x 3⅞in),
L 21 Nov,
£550 ($721)

2

A rectangular bronze
plaquette, Tuscan, *c*1500,
the Virgin and Child
flanked by two flaming
candelabra, rich brown
patina, 10.8cm (4¼in),
L 5 July,
£4,620 ($6,422)

3

A rectangular bronze
plaquette of the Virgin
and Child with sixteen
angels, Ferrarese, last
quarter 15th cent, 9.3cm
(3¹¹/₁₆in), *L 5 July,*
£462 ($642)

4

Two South German gilt
bronze rectangular
plaques, 3rd quarter 16th
cent, each chased with
triumphal processions,
within carved and gilt
wood frames, 6.7 x 12.7cm
(2⅝ x 5in), *NY 23/24 Nov,*
$1,540 (£1,272)

5

A bronze plaquette of 'Ecce
Homo', Augsburg or
Lombardy, *c*1600,
11 x 8cm (4¼ x 3¼in),
F 19 Dec,
L 850,000 (£359; $449)

6

A Roman bronze relief of
the Holy Family, from the
workshop of Alessandro
Algardi, *c*1640-50, the
rest on the flight into
Egypt, rich red golden-
brown patina, 30 x 35.5cm
(11¾ x 14in), *NY 23/24 Nov,*
$6,600 (£5,454)

7

An Italian bronze plaque,
early 17th cent, centred
by the enthroned Virgin
and Child, Sts Dominic
and Catherine of Siena
kneeling before a group
of bishops, nuns and
emperors, traces of gilding,
h 15cm (6in), *NY 23/24 Nov,*
$605 (£500)

8

An Italian bronze
plaquette, early 17th
cent, of St John
Gualberto of
Passignano, founder of
the Order of Vallombrosa,
signed M.E.M.I.F.,
10.2cm (4in), *L 4 July,*
£396 ($550)

9

An Italian circular gilt
bronze plaquette, 16th
cent, of the Holy
Family, the features
crisply chiselled, 11.3cm
(4⅝in), *L 4 July,*
£990 ($1,376)

10

A bronze medal of Federigo
Montefeltro, Duke of
Urbino, by Sperandio of
Mantua, the reverse with
the Duke on horseback,
rich copper-brown patina,
old cast, 8.9cm (3½in),
L 5 July,
£3,300 ($4,587)

1
A carved ivory table centrepiece, probably French, *c*1870, depicting the triumph of Bacchus, the ebonised wood plinth applied with carved ivory masks and paterae, a little damage, one figure detached, 66cm (26in), *L 8 Mar*, £7,700 ($11,473)

2
An ivory iron maiden, probably French, late 19th cent, wearing a bonnet and ruff, her nail-lined cape opening to reveal a nude victim, slightly damaged ruff, h 18.2cm (7in), *L 13 Mar*, £605 ($902)

3
A Continental carved-ivory figural cup, late 19th cent, carved in medium relief with a mytho-logical scene, raised on a standard carved with figures, tiered circular velvet plinth, h 31cm (12¼in), *NY 24/25 Feb*, $4,950 (£3,531)

4
A pair of Continental Renaissance-style ivory candlesticks, *c*1880, carved in medium relief with young boys huddled together, cracks, 23cm (9in), *NY 3 Nov*, $825 (£660)

5
A Continental carved-ivory and marble equestrian group of Lorenzo de Medici, 2nd half 19th cent, after Verrocchio, brown marble base, 33cm (13in), *NY 24/25 Feb*, $2,310 (£1,593)

6
A carved ivory sweetmeat basket, late 18th/early 19th cent, in the form of menagerie bars behind a parade of wild animals, swing handle with gilt-metal shell mounts, tortoiseshell base, repaired, signed on the rim, 12cm (4¾in), *L 13 Mar*, £495 ($737)

7
A Continental carved-ivory plaque of a Bacchanalian scene, late 19th cent, with young Bacchus cavorting with a goat beneath flowering trees, 14.5 x 12cm (5¾ x 4¾in), *NY 24/25 Feb*, $770 (£549)

8
A set of five French carved ivory character figures, late 19th cent, in workday attire with battered hats, each on a turned ebonised wood plinth, the figures 15cm (6in), *L 7 June*, £1,815 ($2,632)

1

2

3 4

6

5

7

8

1
A pair of ivory ewers,
perhaps German, c 1875,
the body of one carved
in relief with the
Triumph of Neptune, the
other with Bacchus and
his followers, h 51.5cm
(20¼in), *L 7 June,*
£9,350 ($13,558)

2
A German ivory tankard,
late 19th cent, carved in
high relief with the gods
Jupiter and Juno, 51.2cm
(20in), *L 7 June,*
£9,900 ($14,355)

3
**A Viennese enamel and
silver-gilt mounted carved
rock crystal horn and
cover,** c 1880, on an oval
base set with gemstones
below a stag stem,
unmarked, 43cm (17in),
L 8 Mar,
£11,000 ($16,401)

4
**A Viennese carved rock
crystal silver-gilt, enamel
and jewelled horn,** 19th
cent, the rock crystal
body carved with foliage,
birds and animals
supported by a silver
mermaid, the horn with
silver-gilt bands, set with
emeralds, 45.9cm (18in),
NY 12 June,
$4,950 (£3,640)

5
**A German circular ivory
plaque,** late 19th cent,
with applied silver masks
and leaf borders, the
centre with Venus and
Cupid, d 50.4cm (19¾in),
L 7 June,
£8,580 ($12,441)

6
**A pair of ivory vases with
enamelled silver mounts,**
the ivory South German,
the mounts Viennese,
c 1880, carved in high
relief with cherubs, the
foot and lip mounts
decorated in coloured
translucent and opaque
enamels flecked with gilt
paillons, unmarked,
27.5cm (10¾in), *L 8 Mar,*
£5,500 ($8,201)

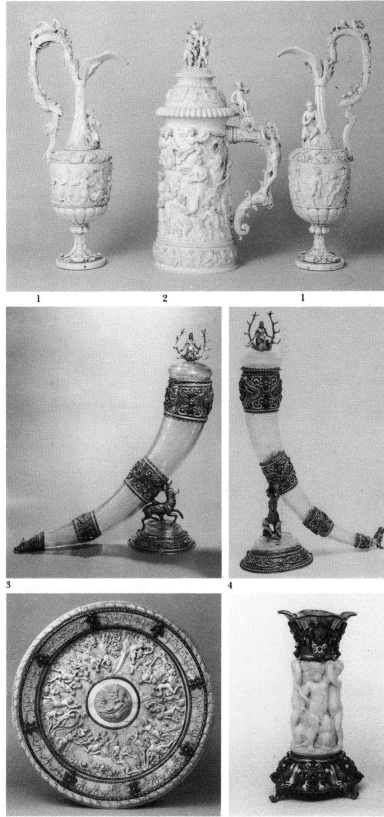

1   2   1

3   4

5   6

1
A Viennese silver-gilt and enamel ewer, late 19th cent, the sides enamelled within oval reserves, the handle surmounted by a bird holding the spout in its mouth, 20.3cm (8in), *NY 20/21 June,* **$3,190 (£2,346)**

2
A Viennese silver-gilt and enamel tazza, late 19th cent, the base enamelled with a lakeside landscape, the stem in the form of a gryphon, the interior of the bowl with an enamelled scene, 15.4cm (6in), *NY 21 June,* **$2,970 (£2,184)**

3
A Viennese lapis-lazuli standing cup with silver and enamel mounts, late 19th cent, the lapis-lazuli bowl in the form of a shell, 17.9cm (7in), *NY 13 Dec,* **$2,750 (£2,311)**

4
A silver and gilt-bronze mounted carved-ivory jewel casket, Continental, mid-19th cent, the sides with panels of allegorical subjects, the hinged cover with gilt-bronze and further set with tortoiseshell, tortoiseshell stringing lacking, 21cm (8¼in), *NY 24/25 Feb,* **$2,640 (£1,821)**

5
A German silver-mounted carved ivory tankard, 19th cent, carved in relief with a battle including Roman soldiers, the cover and base in engraved silver, 35cm (13⅞in), *F 10 May,* **L 7,910,000 (£3,222; $4,640)**

6
A German ivory standing cup and cover, *c*1880, with richly chased silver foot, mounts and detachable cover, the mounts with pseudo-Augsburg marks and ? maker's mark apparently 'JM' or 'TM', the finial group repaired, *L 7 June,* **£8,250 ($11,963)**

7
A Scandinavian silver-gilt and enamel tazza, *c*1900, the stem enamelled in multi-coloured flowers, the base set with four oval miniatures, the surrounds with filigree scrolls on central blue flowerheads, marked 'Bolin' with 84 standard, 33.7cm (13¼in), *NY 13 Dec,* **$3,410 (£2,866)**

8
A German silver-mounted carved ivory tankard, struck with three pseudo-hallmarks including a dagger, *c*1890, the ivory barrel decorated in relief with Bacchanal cherubs, gilt interior, 25cm (9¾in), *L 8 Nov,* **£2,640 ($3,511)**

9
A Continental silver and silver-gilt-mounted carved-ivory mug and footed cup, late 19th cent, the mug carved with a Bacchanalian scene, the interior gilt, the cup with a scene of frolicking nudes, foot restored, 14.5 and 15cm (5¾ and 6in), *NY 18 July,* **$1,320 (£1,008)**

10
A Continental silver-mounted carved-ivory covered tankard, late 19th cent, carved with a medieval battle scene, 32.5cm (12¾in), *NY 18 July,* **$2,090 (£1,595)**

1   2   3

6   7   8

9   10   9

1
A Viennese silver and enamel teapot, Herman Böhm, late 19th cent, enamelled with mythological vignettes, the surrounds with foliage on a pink ground, the silver neck and mid-section enamelled with multi-coloured foliage, 21cm (8½in), *NY 21 June*, $2,970 (£2,184)

2
A Viennese enamel footed vase, late 19th cent, the body painted with three oval panels with rustic scenes, the surrounds with foliage on grounds of cream, olive green and burgundy, gilt-metal foot, 47cm (18½in), *NY 13 Dec*, $5,500 (£4,622)

3
A Viennese silver-gilt cup and cover, c.1860, in the form of a two-headed bird, enamelled overall with mythological scenes, inset with stones and jewels, maker's mark 'RL', some slight damage, *F 3/4 Oct*, L 9,700,000 (£3,829; $4,978)

4
A Viennese enamel ewer and dish, late 19th cent, with silver-gilt mounts, brightly painted on pale blue or buff grounds, the ewer slightly damaged, 13.5cm (5½in), the dish w 16cm (6¼in), *L 19 Nov*, £1,210 ($1,585)

5
A Viennese silver, enamel and rock crystal coffret, Herman Böhm, 2nd half 19th cent, the top and sides with etched rock crystal panels, within a foliate enamel surround, each corner with a lapis-lazuli column, 15.3cm (6in), *NY 13 Dec*, $3,080 (£2,588)

6
A Viennese enamel mantel clock, Jakob Wasserberger, Vienna, c.1895, the engraved silver-gilt body applied with pierced panels decorated in multi-coloured enamels, h 18.4cm (7¼in), *L 13 Mar*, £1,540 ($2,295)

7
A Viennese silver and enamel horn cup, 19th cent, supported on the back of a bearded ancient, enamelled with allegorical and mythological scenes and foliage borders, the horn with bands enamelled to simulate rubies and emeralds, h 38.1cm (15in), *NY 13 Dec*, $6,050 (£5,084)

8
A Viennese enamel and gilt-metal table clock and musical box, late 19th cent, the ebonised wood base applied with gilt-metal allegorical figures, the stem in the form of a dancing fiddler, supporting the timepiece on his head, 25cm (9¾in), *L 7 June*, £2,310 ($3,350)

9
A Viennese enamel jewel box in the form of a cylinder desk, late 19th cent, mounted with enamelled plaques depicting mythological subjects, h 19cm (7½in), *NY 13 Dec*, $2,640 (£2,112)

10
A Viennese rock crystal, silver and enamel tazza, late 19th cent, the border enamelled with satyrs' masks flanked by caryatids, the whole set with etched rock crystal panels, d 24.9cm (9¾in), *NY 13 Dec*, $2,860 (£2,403)

11
A Viennese silver and enamel miniature desk clock, late 19th cent, the central panel decorated with a couple in a landscape, the sides with oval reserves enclosing putti, 10.6cm (4⅛in), *NY 21 June*, $1,760 (£1,294)

12
A Viennese gilt-metal and enamel desk clock, late 19th cent, in the form of a firescreen, the front enamelled with a courting couple in a landscape, the base enamelled with garden vignettes, 15.9cm (6¼in), *NY 21 June*, $715 (£526)

1 2 3

4 5

6 7 8

9 10 11 12

Iron

DAVID WILLE

Iron (found in the form of meteorites) was first used by the people of Egypt and the Near East at the beginning of the 3rd millennium BC. It was worked into ornaments and amulets, and was highly valued because it was so rare. Iron does not occur as a natural metal, and it is not until about 2800 BC that we find evidence of man-made iron. The Hittites are credited with the achievement of producing iron on a large scale and of having the ability to give it a hardness superior to that of bronze around 1400 BC. The collapse of their empire two centuries later marks the beginning of the Iron Age; the eagerly guarded monopoly ceased and production spread both east and west, reaching both China and Europe early in the 1st millennium BC. Bronze, a rare and expensive metal, had been available only to a small élite; with the introduction of iron the nature of warfare, the economy, and class structure changed abruptly, causing a significant growth of the middle classes.

Iron is usually worked into one of three states: wrought iron, steel, or cast iron. It is the amount of carbon present which determines the state. Wrought iron has .01 per cent, steel .5-1.5 per cent, and cast iron 2-5 per cent.

The intrinsic immediacy of wrought iron was most fully realized by the European blacksmiths who were using it from the 11th through to the 13th century. During this time it was worked in a broad exuberant style, such as is found in the great hinges at the main portals of the Cathedral of Notre Dame in Paris. This style was replaced around 1300 by a more restrained and two-dimensional art, strongly influenced by Arab designs. The main centres of production were now France and Spain. During the Renaissance the manufacture of much finer steel tools shifted the emphasis from the large objects to locks, keys, tools, and scientific instruments of almost precious quality. The reign of Louis XIV witnessed a return to the great decorative wrought iron. It was worked into portals, balconies and railings, and the style spread to southern Germany and Austria, where it reached its height during the rococo period.

Cast iron did not come into use in Europe until the late 14th century (though its properties had long been known to the Chinese), when cannons and cast-iron utensils made their first appearance. The decorative use of cast iron, with its premonition of mass production, began with the manufacture of architectural elements in the early 18th century. In 1714 cast-iron balustrades were added to the façade of St Paul's Cathedral in London. The neo-classical period fully adopted cast-iron elements and marked the end of the tradition of wrought iron as produced by the great blacksmiths.

1
A French iron window grille, 16th cent, 59.5cm (23½in), *L 21 Nov,* £492 ($645)

2
A French iron table lectern, late 18th cent, the book support pierced with the instruments of the Passion, the sides with the symbols of a mason, 17.2cm (6¾in), *L 21 Nov,* £1,870 ($2,450)

3
A Spanish wrought-iron lantern, 18th cent, 70cm (15½in), *L 21 Nov,* £462 ($605)

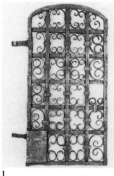

1   2   3

1
A French wrought-iron
lectern, c 1860-70, in
Gothic style, 148cm (58in),
L 21 Nov,
£1,155 ($1,513)

2
A pair of wrought-iron
gates, early 19th cent,
and a pair of faceted
cast-iron posts, h 140cm
(55in), *P 10-13 July,*
£945 ($1,285)

3
A Venetian bronze door-
knocker, from the work-
shop of Tiziano Aspetti,
2nd half 16th cent, rich
dark brown patina,
h 26cm (10¼in),
NY 23/24 Nov,
$2,200 (£1,818)

4
A cast-iron high relief
plaque of the royal coat-of-
arms, 19th cent, 94 x
140cm (37 x 55in),
P 20-22 Mar,
£825 ($1,229)

5
A French iron door-
knocker, 18th cent, the
escutcheon pierced with
scrolling acanthus, 47cm
(18½in), *L 21 Nov,*
£1,100 ($1,441)

6
A French door-knocker,
Bordeaux, c 1750-60,
pierced with Berainesque
ornament, 56cm (22in),
L 21 Nov,
£1,430 ($1,873)

7
A collection of bronze and
iron keys, dating from the
Roman period to the
18th century, overall
h 55cm (21½in),
NY 23/24 Nov,
$4,400 (£3,636)

8
A small German
brass and gilt copper
casket, 17th cent,
stamped MM for Michel
Mann, engraved with
courtly figures in
contemporary costume,
7.3cm (2⅞in), *L 4 July,*
£2,530 ($3,517)

9
A South German gilt
copper and steel miniature
casket, from the work-
shops of Michel Mann,
early 17th cent, the lid
engraved with a view of
a town, the panels with
figures and heraldic
beasts, one foot replaced,
engraving refreshed,
4.8 x 7.3cm (1⅞ x 2⅞in),
L 13 Dec,
£1,650 ($2,063)

10
A brass tobacco box, 2nd
half 18th cent, the lid
signed 'Giese, Iserlohn',
King Frederick II and
Prince Frederick Henry
of Prussia flanking a
medallion depicting the
victory of Rossbach in
1757, w 18.7cm (7½in),
L 24 Feb,
£308 ($431)

11
An English steel tobacco
box, c 1765, stamped
maker's mark T. Shaw,
the lid engraved 'Thos.
Parkin Esq. Mortomly
1765', w 13cm (5⅛in),
L 21 Nov,
£286 ($375)

12
A brass tobacco box, by
Johan Giese, Iserlohn,
mid-18th cent, signed,
the lid with the victory
of Admiral Osbourne at
Carthagena, the base
with the victory at
Merseburg in 1757, 18.5cm
(7¼in), *L 21 Nov,*
£572 ($749)

1 2 3

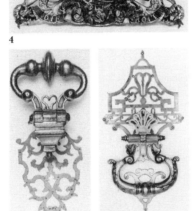

4

5 6 7

8 9

10

11 12

1
An Italian iron locksmith's
sign, 17th cent, in the
centre the arms of the
family Sgaliger of Verona,
57.5cm (22⅝in), *L 21 Nov,*
£682 ($893)

2
Four Venetian keys,
15th/16th cent, one shaft
replaced, the largest
15.2cm (6in), *L 17 May,*
£407 ($590)

3
A French key of silvered
bronze, early 17th cent,
the bow in the form of
two harpies addorsed
framing a grotesque
head, 12cm (4¾in),
L 21 Nov,
£792 ($1,038)

4
A French key, 17th cent,
the whole finely chiselled,
cylindrical shank and
small bit pierced, 9cm
(3½in), *L 21 Nov,*
£242 ($317)

5
A French steel wheel-lock
key, early 17th cent,
pierced and engraved
with the arms of France
surrounded by interlaced
foliage, 22.5cm (8⅞in),
L 21 Nov,
£1,650 ($2,162)

6
A French wrought-iron
padlock, mid-18th cent,
in the shape of a key,
8cm (3⅛in), *NY 23/24 Nov,*
$1,210 (£1,000)

7
A French key, early 19th
cent, in the form of a
pin-fire pistol, the
mechanism operated by
the dog with springs to
the bow, 19cm (7½in),
L 21 Nov,
£1,595 ($2,089)

8
An iron key, Florence,
*c*1880, 12.5cm (4¾in),
F 10 May,
L 1,073,500 (£437; $629)

9
A carriage gateway door-
lock, French, 18th cent, a
counter-lock and two
keys, with fire bolts,
100cm (39⅜in), *L 21 Nov,*
£715 ($937)

10
A French gunsmith's
spoon, 18th cent, of steel,
turned wooden baluster
handle, 27.5cm (10¾in),
L 21 Nov,
£154 ($202)

11
A Nuremberg sugar-
cutter, late 17th cent, of
finely engraved steel
with traces of gilding,
22.5cm (8⅞in), *L 21 Nov,*
£990 ($1,297)

12
A German travelling set of
cutlery, 1st half 18th cent,
the handles chased,
silvered and gilt on
blued steel ground,
19.5cm (7¾in), *NY 2/3 Mar,*
$275 (£185)

13
A French iron scissors case,
18th cent, 10.6cm (4⅛in),
L 21 Nov,
£154 ($201)

1   2   3

4   5   6   7

8   9

10

11

12   13

1
A Gothic mortar, c 1400, of tapering form with square bracket handle, h 20cm (7⅞in), *L 3 Apr,* £3,300 ($4,762)

2
A German Gothic bronze mortar, early 15th cent, four zoomorphic feet, body slightly extended, h 16cm (6¼in), *L 3 Apr,* £990 ($1,429)

3
A bronze holy water bucket, early 16th cent, with mask handle brackets, raised on three feet, h 21.5cm (8½in), *L 3 Apr,* £1,760 ($2,540)

4
A bronze mortar, Netherlandish, dated 1520, with bear head handles, h 15cm (5⅞in), *L 3 Apr,* £2,420 ($3,492)

5
A Flemish bronze mortar, dated 1546, the turned sides centred by a shield, double dolphin handles, h 12.6cm (5in), *L 13 Dec,* £1,265 ($1,581)

6
A French bronze mortar, late 16th cent, cast in relief with a shield with arms, probably of Sadirac of Guyenne, with pestle, dated 1595, h 11.5cm (4½in), *L 13 Dec,* £880 ($1,100)

7
A Dutch bronze mortar, dated 1605, cast with zoomorphic handles, Mannerist strapwork and foliate scrolls, golden brown patina, h 12.3cm (4⅞in), *NY 2/3 Mar,* $495 (£332)

8
A Dutch bronze mortar, by Hendrick Cop, dated 1625, cast with a frieze of dancing putti beneath Gothic arches, dark brown patina over reddish coloured bronze, with pestle, h 13.8cm (5⅜in), *NY 2/3 Mar,* $1,320 (£886)

9
A South German bronze mortar, dated 1642, cast with dolphin handles, golden brown patina, with pestle, h 14.3cm (5¾in), *NY 2/3 Mar,* $1,320 (£886)

10
An Italian bronze mortar, late 16th/early 17th cent, decorated with foliage and winged cherubs, h 14cm (5½in), *F·10 May,* L 904,000 (£368; $529)

11
An Italian bronze mortar, probably Padova, 1st half 16th cent, with a pestle, h 15cm (6in), *F 10 May,* L 2,260,000 (£920; $1,324)

12
A Dutch bronze mortar, inscribed and dated 1751, h 29cm (11½in), on a wooden base, *A 1 Oct,* Dfl 9,048 (£2,129; $2,746)

13
A bronze lavabo, 15th cent, with small handle opening at top, two spouts with dogs heads and handle brackets in form of human heads, swing handle, greenish patination, minor repairs, 18cm (7⅛in), *L 21 Nov,* £715 ($937)

14
A central European bronze cauldron, c 1600, raised on three legs, well cast with grotesque masks of old men, original iron spiralific handle, h 30.5cm (12in), *L 21 Nov,* £660 ($865)

1   2   3   4   5   6   7   8   9

10   11   12   13   14

1

A Gothic dinanderie brass bowl, c 1500, embossed with the Annunciation surrounded by a band of Gothic lettering, 41cm (16in), *NY 2/3 Mar,*
$2,310 (£1,550)

2

A South German brass alms dish, Nuremberg, late 15th cent, the central boss bordered by a frieze of hounds pursuing stags, golden-brown patina, 42cm (16½in), *NY 2/3 Mar,*
$1,980 (£1,329)

3

A brass alms dish, Nuremberg, early 16th cent, chased with St George and the dragon, d 46cm (18in), *F 10 May,*
L 1,073,500 (£437; $629)

4

A brass alms dish, late 17th cent, the centre embossed with a *rosace* contained by a rubbed inscription, the border stamped with rosettes, *C 2-5 Oct,*
£198 ($252)

5

A pair of bronze pricket candlesticks, early 16th cent, the ringed stems each with flattened knops, iron prickets, 39.3cm (15½in), *L 3 Apr,*
£1,430 ($2,063)

6

Two Netherlandish brass pricket candlesticks, c 1500, with deep turned drip pans, 30.5cm (12in), *L 13 Dec,*
£2,530 ($3,163)

7

A pair of German bronze candlesticks, Nuremberg, early 17th cent, maker's mark of L*L, decorated all over with stylised foliage, garlands and strapwork, h 18cm (7⅛in), *L 21 Nov,*
£935 ($1,225)

8

A Flemish brass candlestick, early 16th cent, with ridged trumpet-shaped foot, base drilled for electricity, 21.5cm (8½in), *L 21 Nov,*
£682 ($893)

9

A Flemish brass candlestick, c 1500, the partly ridged stem with ring knops, socket repaired, 15.9cm (6¼in), *L 21 Nov,*
£418 ($548)

10

A Gothic brass candleholder, probably Flemish, c 1500, worn, 35cm (13¾in), *L 21 Nov,*
£2,310 ($3,026)

11

A brass candlestick, German, 16th cent, 27.3cm (10½in), *L 17 May,*
£1,100 ($1,595)

12

Two bronze candlesticks, Spanish, early 17th cent, the turned stems supported on triangular bases, 35cm (13¾in), *NY 23/24 Nov,*
$1,100 (£909)

13

A pair of North Italian bronze pricket candlesticks, c 1600-20, cast and turned, 48cm (19in), *NY 2/3 Mar,*
$2,090 (£1,403)

1
A Charles II brass candlestick, 2nd half 17th cent,
with ribbed cylindrical
stem and trumpet-mouth
foot, 22.8cm (9in),
L 21 Nov,
£2,970 ($3,891)

2
A brass bell-based candlestick, 2nd half 17th cent,
probably German,
socket border trimmed,
23.8cm (9⅜in), *L 21 Nov,*
£330 ($432)

3
A pair of brass candlesticks,
North West Europe, late
17th cent, stamped with
maker's mark ww,
12.7cm (5in), *L 21 Nov,*
£330 ($432)

4
A pair of brass table
candlesticks, c1750,
circular bases with
swirled gadrooned
borders, separate sconces,
22.2cm (8¾in), *L 21 Nov,*
£1,760 ($2,306)

5
A pair of brass table
candlesticks, mid-18th
cent, circular bases with
'wavy' edges, slender
mushroom-knopped
stem and petal-lobed
socket trims, 19.6cm
(7¾in), *L 21 Nov,*
£440 ($576)

6
A pair of brass table
candlesticks, 2nd quarter
18th cent, the square
stepped bases with canted
corners, cylindrical
sockets with narrow
flange, 16.8cm (6⅝in),
L 21 Nov,
£352 ($461)

7
A pair of brass table
candlesticks, c1760,
16.8cm (6⅝in), *L 21 Nov,*
£286 ($375)

8
A pair of brass table
candlesticks, mid-18th cent,
lobed circular bases,
push-rod ejectors,
20.4cm (8in), *L 17 May,*
£242 ($351)

9
A pair of brass table
candlesticks, mid-18th
cent, probably French,
cupped socket flanges,
18.5cm (7¼in), *L 17 May,*
£385 ($558)

10
A pair of paktong candle-
sticks, c1765, engraved
with a crest, one stick
repaired, 26cm (10¼in),
L 21 Nov,
£1,430 ($1,873)

11
A pair of George III
paktong candlesticks,
c1775, with Corinthian
columns rising from
stepped bases, 27.8cm
(11in), *L 21 Nov,*
£462 ($605)

12
A pair of brass table
candlesticks, 18th cent,
18cm (7⅛in), *A 18-26 Sept,*
Dfl 1,725 (£170; $219)

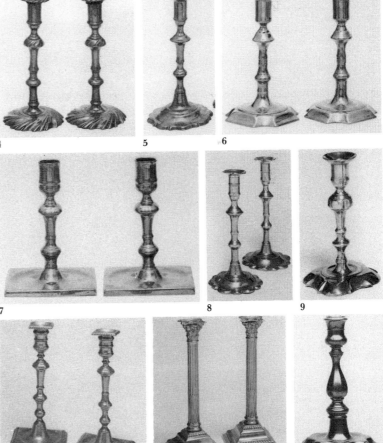

1
An early Hansekanne,
14th/early 15th cent, the
handle cast in relief with
a dragon, the cover cast
on the inside with a
small crucifixion medal-
lion, restored, h overall
21.5cm (8½in), *L 17 May,*
£3,960 ($5,742)

2
**A pair of pricket candle-
sticks,** 16th cent, Central
Europe, probably
Germany, the grease
pans centred by iron
prickets, some repair,
h 44cm (17½in), *L 17 May,*
£1,485 ($2,153)

3
**A South German guild
tankard,** dated 1654,
unidentified maker,
h 17cm (6¾in), *NY 2/3 Mar,*
$880 (£591)

4
**A North German deep
bowl,** 1st half 18th cent,
possibly Hamburg, with
scrolled caryatid
handles, the gadrooned
body outlined in
wriggled-work, w 23.4cm
(9¼in), *L 17 May,*
£418 ($606)

5
**A pair of tureens and
covers,** 18th cent, with
openwork handles,
d 20cm (7⅞in),
A 13/16 Mar,
Dfl 1,334 (£305; $456)

6
A cylindrical flagon,
German, engraved with a
drinking luteplayer and
dated 1823, h 23cm
(9⅛in), *A 17 Dec,*
Dfl 1,160 (£277; $346)

7
**A large North German
guild flagon** by Johann
Hinrich Schlapsy d Ä of
Hamburg, 2nd quarter
18th cent, engraved with
a crowned armorial
device of three wool
shuttles, formerly raised
on three feet, h 39.4cm
(15½in), *L 17 May,*
£506 ($734)

8
**A pair of German candles-
sticks,** *c* 1780, probably
Frankfurt, with ornate
gadrooned borders,
maker's touch dated 1761
inside base, h 18.5cm
(7¼in), *L 21 Nov,*
£715 ($937)

9
A Swiss stegkanne,
Ludwig Roder, Bern,
2nd half 18th cent,
h 26cm (10¼in),
NY 2/3 Mar,
$1,210 (£812)

10
A Dutch 'Rembrandtkan',
17th/18th cent, h 27.5cm
(10in), *A 16 May,*
Dfl 4,176 (£975; $1,394)

11
A pair of covered vases,
19th cent, painted black
with gilt decoration,
h 34.5cm (13½in),
A 13/16 Mar,
Dfl 1,798 (£411; $613)

12
A Dutch coffee urn,
18th/19th cent, painted
in black, on triform
stand, h 46cm (18in),
A 17 Dec,
Dfl 725 (£173; $216)

1

2

3

4

5

6

7

8

9

10

11

12

1
A small saucer or spice
plate, 1st half 17th cent,
the reverse with the
unrecorded touch of SR,
'nature's gilding' patina,
d 10cm (4in), *L 17 May,*
£682 ($989)

2
A pair of Stuart plates,
late 17th cent, narrow
rims with multiple-
reeded borders, d 21cm
(8¼in), *L 21 Nov,*
£440 ($576)

3
A Capstan salt, English,
c 1690-1700, the waist
with a moulded girdle,
faults, h 5cm (2in),
L 21 Nov,
£264 ($346)

4
A trencher salt, English,
c 1700, maker's touch IH,
h 3.5cm (1⅜in); and
another similar, *L 21 Nov,*
£176 ($231)

5
A group of three small
baluster-shaped spice pots,
18th cent, screw-on
covers, h 10cm (4in),
L 17 May,
£165 ($239)

6
Two spice cannisters, late
17th/early 18th cent,
domed slip-on covers,
h 9 and 9.5cm (3½ and
3¾in), *L 17 May,*
£242 ($351)

7
A Stuart tankard, c 1685-
95, the cover with
pierced 'ram's-horn'
billet, denticulations at
front, maker's touch IB,
h 17.7cm (7in), *L 21 Nov,*
£3,960 ($5,188)

8
A group of three Scottish
baluster-shaped measures,
c 1800, with bar-and-ball
thumbpiece, h 10.5 to
7.5cm (4⅛ to 3in),
L 17 May,
£187 ($271)

9
A Queen Anne pint tavern
mug, c 1705-10, inscribed
'John Gose att ye Crown
in Orange Street, in ye
Park', h 11.8cm (4⅝in),
L 21 Nov,
£858 ($1,124)

10
A Scottish crested 'tappit-
hen', 18th cent, of Scots
pint (3 pints imperial)
capacity, 29.5cm (11⅝in),
L 21 Nov,
£528 ($692)

1

**A Gothic miniature silver
buckle,** English, 13th
cent, formed of confront-
ing lions with chiselled
fur, 3.8cm (½in), *L 3 Apr,*
£880 ($1,270)

2

A gold signet ring, 1st
quarter 16th cent, the
oval bezel incised with a
gauntlet within a border
of dots flanked by the
initials TB, *L 4 July,*
£2,640 ($3,670)

3

**A late medieval gold
merchant's ring,** perhaps
English, late 15th cent,
the round bezel con-
taining a swivelling
plaque cut in intaglio,
inscribed, *L 3 Apr,*
£5,280 ($7,619)

4

**A Renaissance gold signet
ring,** German, late 16th
cent, the bezel cut in
intaglio with a boar's
head flanked by the
letters EC, *L 3 Apr,*
£1,430 ($2,063)

5

**An Italian verre églomise
pendant,** 16th cent,
painted in gold, dark
blue and reddish-brown
tones with the Adoration
of the Magi, h 8.6cm
(3⅜in), *NY 2/3 Mar,*
£6,325 (£4,244)

6

**A chalcedony portrait
cameo,** probably Maria
of Austria (1528-1603), in
the manner of Gilles
Légaré, the cameo 2nd
half 16th cent, the frame
3rd quarter 17th cent, set
in a gold cartouche-
shaped frame, h 4.5cm
(1¾in), *L 4 July,*
£3,960 ($5,504)

7

**An agate cameo of
Bacchus,** *c*1600, shown in
portrait profile to
sinister, 3.8cm (1½in),
L 13 Dec,
£528 ($660)

8

A verre églomise pendant,
Italian, 16th cent,
painted in gold, dark
blue and reddish brown
tones, with the
Adoration of the Magi,
the whole set in gilt
metal case, h 8.6cm
(3⅜in), *NY 2/3 Mar,*
$6,325 (£4,244)

9

**A reliquary for relics of St.
Philipp Neri,** Italian, 17th
cent, designed from gilt
and painted paper,
cloth, metal foil and
paste, contemporary gilt
brass oval frame,
h 17.5cm (6⅞in),
L 17 May,
£187 ($271)

10

**A Sicilian gilt copper and
coral holy water stoop,**
mid-17th cent, centred
by a figure of St. John
the Baptist in an archi-
tectural niche flanked by
angels, some losses and
repairs, 46cm (18in),
L 3 Apr,
£11,550 ($16,667)

11

**A composite silver gilt
casket,** applied with fragments of South German
polychrome enamel, set
with numerous intaglios
in hardstones, the enamel
17th cent, the intaglios of
ancient Roman, Renais-
sance and later origin,
the cameos probably
Italian early 16th cent,
11.5cm (4½in), *L 5 July,*
£1,750 ($2,433)

1 2 3 4

5 6 7 8

9 10

11

1
A Florentine bronze stallion,
*c.*1600, from the
Bologna-Susini workshops,
red-brown lacquer over
pale brown patina, 23.8cm
(9⅜in), *L 13 Dec,*
£48,400 ($60,500)

2
**A Paduan bronze figure of
Venus,** attributed to
Severo da Ravenna,
*c.*1500, the cast drapery
lacquered in black, her
body lacquered in choco-
late brown, h 25cm (9¾in),
NY 23/24 Nov,
$26,400 (£21,818)

3
**A Venetian gilt wood
figure of a female saint,** by
the workshop of Tullio
Lombardi, 1st decade 16th
cent, wearing a gold
embroidered cloak, left
hand and feet replaced,
103cm (40½in),
NY 23/24 Nov,
$38,500 (£31,818)

4
**A Franconian limewood
relief of a female saint,**
*c.*1500-05, attributed to
the workshops of
Tilmann Riemensch-
neider, the skirt obscured
by a wide cloak forming
stiff folds, the left hand
replaced, 116.2cm (45¾in),
L 13 Dec,
£44,000 ($55,000)

1

2

3

4

1
A Limoges champlevé enamel book cover, 13th cent, centred by Christ on the cross, on each side the Virgin and St. John, traces of gilding on the well engraved figures, h 23.3cm (8¾in), *L 13 Dec*, £33,000 ($41,250)

2
A gilt bronze Romanesque candlestick, *c*1200, possibly South German, 19cm (7½in), *L 5 July*, £22,000 ($30,580)

3
An iron masterpiece lock and key, French, 18th cent, lock 12.5 x 8cm (4⅞ x 3⅛in), key 9.5cm (3¾in), *L 21 Nov*, £9,020 ($11,816)

4
A Florentine stemma of the Frescobaldi family, from the workshop of Andrea della Robbia, late 15th cent, d 64cm (25¼in), *NY 23/24 Nov*, $7,150 (£5,909)

5
A French iron key, 17th cent, the bow chiselled with two confronting dolphins, reposing on a Corinthian capital, 18cm (7⅛in), *L 21 Nov*, £1,595 ($2,089)

6
A French key, 17th cent, the bow in the form of two confronting dolphins enclosing a pierced monogram, 15.2cm (6in), *L 21 Nov*, £572 ($749)

7
A French key, 17th cent, the bit with pierced cross and 'S' design and eight teeth, 14.2cm (5½in), *L 21 Nov*, £462 ($605)

8
A French key, 17th cent, the bow in the form of confronting dolphins with bared teeth, 17.1cm (6¾in), *L 21 Nov*, £902 ($1,182)

1

2

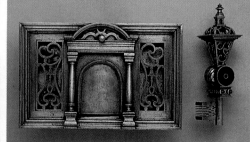

3

4

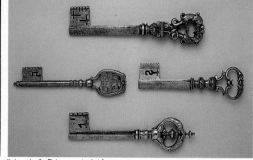

5 (*top*), 6, 7 (*centre*), 8 (*bottom*)

1
**A Limoges figure of Christ
crucified,** 13th cent, the
perizonium with
champlevé enamel in
two shades of blue,
traces of original
gilding, 22.5cm (9in),
L 3 Apr,
£2,090 ($3,016)

2
**A Limoges champlevé
enamel crucifix figure,** 1st
half 13th cent, his eyes
and loin cloth enamelled
in dark blue and white
tones, 17.5cm (7in),
NY 2/3 Mar,
$3,190 (£2,140)

3
**A Limoges grisaille enamel
tazze and cover,** in
Renaissance style, deco-
rated with scenes from
the Life of Diana h 29cm
(11½in), *M 25/26 June,*
FF 14,430 (£1,239; $1,688)

4
A Limoges enamel pyx,
13th cent, decorated with
stylised motifs, h 10.5cm
(4¼in), *M 25/26 June,*
FF 22,200 (£1,906; $2,596)

5
**Four Limoges painted
enamel plaques,** from the
workshop of Couly II
Nouailler, mid-16th
cent, each painted with
one of the apostles
including Sts John,
Thomas, Andrew and
Jacob, within gilt bronze
frames, 16.5 x 14cm (6½
x 5½in), *NY 23/24 Nov,*
$3,080 (£2,545)

6
**A Limoges enamel plaque
depicting Christ seated in
majesty,** 13th cent,
mounted as a book
cover, 21 x 10cm (8¼ x
4in), *M 25/26 June,*
**FF 2,109,000
(£181,030; $246,667)**

7
**Ten Limoges painted
enamel plaques,** from the
workshop of Martin
Didier or M D Pape, 3rd
quarter 16th cent, the
Passion of Christ, several
damaged, 31.5 x 23.5cm
(12⅜ x 9⅜in),
NY 23/24 Nov,
$9,900 (£8,182)

8
A Venetian enamel dish,
15th cent, decorated in
white dashed with green
against a blue ground,
heavily restored, 33cm
(13in), *L 3 Apr,*
£770 ($1,111)

19th Century Sculpture

ROBERT BOWMAN • SARAH HILL

At present there are two sides to the market in 19th century sculpture. The majority of pieces are collected purely for their decorative qualities, but a few individual sculptor's works are sought after by connoisseurs and their sculptures come into the category of fine art. The latter are gradually encroaching on the former as other good works of art become more difficult to find and as interest in the various artistic movements of the 19th century increases.

Patina and quality of finish are universally important and are the two factors which most influence collectors as to whether they will purchase one cast in preference to another. Fine detail is usually thought to indicate an early and good quality casting. In the case of the majority of pieces this is correct. The reason is that initially labour was relatively cheap and the raw materials relatively expensive. Over the years the situation has gradually reversed and today modern casts are easily distinguished from their earlier counterparts by their lack of chiselled detail. The labour required to give this fine finish is now almost prohibitively expensive. Fine patina is also an indication of age in that over the years the polish itself undergoes a chemical reaction with the surface of the metal resulting in a colour change and deep lustre.

Repairs and alterations are critical, but, provided they are of high standard, are of less importance in the decorative market. Of particular strength in the market at present are fine quality animalier bronzes, large continental sculpture of a decorative nature and any object with an oriental flavour. Areas of relative underdevelopment are marble and bronze sculpture of a less obviously attractive nature, such as busts of historical figures. Marble sculpture as a whole is also relatively undervalued in that it realizes less than its equivalent in bronze. This situation is an anomaly when one considers that bronzes are cast in editions taken from an original, whereas a marble sculpture is itself an original. Sculptures in other materials such as terracotta and clay have recently been the subject of increased interest, but as a rule command only a percentage of the price of their bronze and marble equivalents. Similarly, spelter or white metal casts rarely reach a quarter of the price of their bronze equivalents due to the instability of the metal and the fact that it is difficult to repair. It should be borne in mind that in any material size always has a direct bearing on price. Larger casts carry a considerable premium over their smaller brethren.

The market for 19th century sculpture as a whole is a rapidly developing one as interest in this period continues to increase.

1
A terracotta group of a satyr and a young woman, Albert Ernest Carrier Belleuse, c.1870, signed 'A. Carrier Belleuse', 58cm (23in), *L 8 Mar*, £2,310 ($3,444)

2
A terracotta bust of Spring, Albert Ernest Carrier Belleuse, c.1870, the young woman with her head turned and her hair entwined with flowers, signed 'A. Carrier Belleuse', 61cm (24in), *L 8 Mar*, £1,815 ($2,706)

3
A white marble figure of a young Arabian woman, Antonio Rossetti, c.1850, seated naked on a small stool, 61cm (24in), *L 8 Mar*, £572 ($852)

4
A white marble figure of a young Arabian dancer, c.1884, Rudolf Schwenitz, wearing a revealing top and loosely draped skirts, signed 'Rudolf Schwenitz' and dated 1884, 155cm (49in), *L 7 June*, £4,180 ($6,061)

5
A white marble figure of a young girl, after E. Gazzeri, standing nude with a flowing cloth about her thighs, signed 'E. Gazzeri, Roma', 84cm (33in), *C 10 Jan*, £572 ($829)

6
A white marble figure of Venus, after the marble figure by Canova, c.1890, 150cm (59in), *NY 3 Nov*, $2,200 (£1,760)

7
A white marble group of two cupids fighting over a heart, after Pierre Philippe Thomire, 3rd quarter 19th cent, on a moulded base, 44.5cm (17½in), *L 8 Nov*, £1,100 ($1,463)

8
A white marble bust of a woman, late 19th cent, her hair entwined with flowers, wearing a low-cut ruffle-trimmed dress, together with a foliate and spiral-turned marble pedestal, 86cm (34in), *NY 3 Nov*, $1,650 (£1,320)

9
A pair of Carrara marble allegorical figures of Autumn and Winter, Italian, last quarter 19th cent, together with a pair of circular veined dark green and white marble pedestals, 1.76m (5ft 9¼in), *NY 15 Dec*, $5,367 (£4,510)

10
A white marble allegorical group of winged love and a young woman, F Vichi, c.1880, the young man kissing the girl tenderly, signed 'F. Vichi, Firenze', 152cm (60in), *L 7 June*, £7,480 ($10,846)

11
An Italian carved stone group of a maiden and a putto, c.1900, the youthful figure naked but for a scant drape supported by a halter, the cherub tugging at her clothing, 120cm (47in), *NY 24/25 Feb*, $3,630 (£2,503)

1

A bronze group of a horse and jockey, Alfred Barye, last quarter 19th cent, the horse Gladiateur, signed 'Alfred Barye Fils Sculpteur 1865', gilt and brown patination, 45cm (17¾in), *L 7 June,* £4,620 ($6,699)

2

A Barbedienne bronze cast of a running elephant, Antoine Louis Barye, 3rd quarter 19th cent, signed 'Barye' and 'F. Barbedienne Fondeur', rich light and dark brown patination, 14cm (5½in), *L 8 Nov,* £1,650 ($2,194)

3

A pair of Barbedienne bronze figures of a walking tiger and lion, Antoine Louis Barye, *c*1860, each signed 'Barye' and 'F. Barbedienne Fondeur', rich dark green/brown patination, 21.5cm and 22cm (8½ and 8¾in), *L 8 Nov,* £2,420 ($3,218)

4

A small Barbedienne bronze figure of the 'Turkish Horse', Antoine Louis Barye, *c*1870, signed 'Barye' and 'F. Barbedienne Fondeur', rich light and dark brown patination, 11.5cm (4½in), *L 8 Nov,* £2,420 ($3,218)

5

An unusual bronze group of a greyhound, Alfred Barye, *c*1880, signed 'A. Barye F.', rich dark brown patination, 28cm (11in), *L 8 Nov,* £1,650 ($2,194)

6

A spelter group of an Arabian hunter on horseback, Alfred Barye and Emile Guillemin, late 19th cent, signed 'Barye Fils & Ele. Guillemin' and stamped 'Fabrication Francaise', green, brown and light brown patinations, 66cm (26in), *L 8 Mar,* £2,640 ($3,936)

7

A bronze group of a lion and mouse, Isidore Bonheur, *c*1880, signed 'Isidore Bonheur', light brown/red patination, 22cm (8¾in), *L 8 Mar,* £506 ($754)

8

A bronze hunting group, by Edouard Delabrierre, *c*1870, signed 'E. Delabrierre', rich light brown patination, 27cm (10½in), *L 8 Nov,* £1,760 ($2,340)

9

A parcel-gilt-bronze equestrian group, after Alfred Dubucand, late 19th cent, inscribed 'Dubucand', brown-golden patina, 33cm (13in), *NY 24/25 Feb,* $1,540 (£1,062)

10

A bronze figure of a thoroughbred stallion, Alfred Dubucand, *c*1880, signed 'Dubucand' and inscribed 'Kadlin Etalon Pursang Au Haras Du Pin', brown patination, 13cm (5in), *L 8 Nov,* £990 ($1,316)

1   2

3

4   5   6

7   8

9   10

1
A bronze group of two wild horses, Christopher Fratin, c.1850, signed 'Fratin', rich dark green patination, 35.5cm (14in), *L 7 June,* £2,860 ($4,147)

2
A bronze group of a mare and foal, Christopher Fratin, c.1860, signed 'Fratin', slightly rubbed light and dark brown patination, 37cm (14½in), *L 7 June,* £2,530 ($3,668)

3
A French bronze animalier group, mid-19th cent, of two horses, standing side by side on a rocky rectangular base and marble plinth, dark patination, 25.5 x 31cm (10 x 12¼in), *C 27-30 Mar,* £286 ($426)

4
A bronze group of 'Gone Away', attributed to Adrian Jones, c.1880, signed 'Elkington & Co, A.J.A.' 51cm (20in), *L 8 Mar,* £3,740 ($5,576)

5
A bronze figure of a bloodhound, by Ivenovich Lanceray, c.1860, signed in cyrillic, rich brown patination, 18.5cm (7¼in), *L 8 Mar,* £1,430 ($2,132)

6
A bronze group of a mare and foal, Pierre Jules Mêne, c.1868, signed 'P. J. Mêne' and dated 1868, rich light and dark brown patination, 46cm (18in), *L 8 Nov,* £3,960 ($5,266)

7
A bronze group of a horse and jockey, Pierre Jules Mêne, c.1863, signed 'P. J. Mêne' and dated 1863, rich brown patination, 42cm (16½in), *L 8 Mar,* £7,150 ($10,660)

8
A bronze group of a horse and jockey, Pierre Jules Mêne, c.1870, signed 'P. J. Mêne', rich brown patination with golden-brown highlights, 24cm (9½in), *L 7 June,* £1,760 ($2,552)

9
A bronze group of a huntsman with bloodhound, after Pierre-Jules Mêne, late 19th cent, inscribed 'P. J. Mêne', coppery patina, 45cm (19in), *NY 16 June,* $1,760 (£1,284)

10
A bronze group of an Arab falconer on horseback, Pierre Jules Mêne, c.1870, signed 'P. J. Mêne', rich light and dark brown patination, 77.5cm (30½in), *L 8 Mar,* £7,700 ($11,480)

11
A bronze group of a Moroccan horseman, Pierre Jules Mêne, c.1880, signed 'P. J. Mêne', rich gilt and brown patination, 51cm (20in), *L 7 June,* £2,090 ($3,030)

1

2

3

4

5

6

7

8

9

10

11

1
A bronze group, Emile Pinedo, c 1890, entitled 'Depart pour la Mecque' and inscribed 'par Pinedo Expon. des Beaux Art Paris', signed 'Pinedo' and stamped 'Bronze Garanti aux Titre Paris', rich dark and light brown and red patination, 48cm (19in), *L 8 Nov,* £4,180 ($5,559)

2
A bronze group of a soldier on horseback, Mathilde Thomas, c 1870, signed 'Math Thomas', with the Thiebaut Foundry seal, rich brown patination, 58cm (23in), *L 7 June,* £1,870 ($2,711)

3
A bronze equestrian group of Chasse au Kabyle, late 19th/early 20th cent, inscribed 'Waagen Sculptr, France', brown, black and gold patina, 87cm (34in), *NY 3 Nov,* $13,200 (£10,560)

4
A bronze group of a bucking bronco, Walther Winnans, c 1893, signed 'Walter Winnans', dated 1892 and with a seal stamped 'Crystal Palace Exhibition 1893 Awarded to Walter Winnans', rich brown patination, 36cm (14in), *L 7 June,* £3,080 ($4,466)

5
An animalier figure of a whippet, 3rd quarter 19th cent, standing on three legs and looking to dexter, on a cast oval base, unsigned, 13.5 x 21cm (5¼ x 8¼in), *C 3-6 July,* £242 ($328)

6
A large bronze figure of a moose, late 19th cent, signed on a hoof 'Mars', on a grey-black granite plinth, rubbed gold bronze patination, 44 x 51cm (17½ x 20in), *C 27-30 Mar,* £550 ($820)

7
A Barbedienne bronze figure of Mozart, Ernest Barrias, c 1880, signed 'E, Barrias' and 'F. Barbedienne Fondeur' and entitled 'Mozart', rich brown patination, 48cm (19in), *L 8 Nov,* £715 ($950)

8
A cold painted bronze figure of a dancing girl, Franze Bergman, c 1900, the front of her skirt hinged to reveal her naked beneath, signed 'Nam Greb' and with the Bergman seal, 46cm (18in), *L 7 June,* £1,980 ($2,871)

9
A pair of bronze figures of travellers, Emile Blavier, c 1851, one standing with a staff in his hand, the other holding a hat, the former signed 'E. Blavier' and dated 1851, rich brown patination, *L 8 Nov,* £990 ($1,316)

10
A French bronze group of Diana the Huntress, after the Antique, last quarter 19th cent, holding a young doe, stamped with founders 'A Collas Brevete', brown patination, 40cm (15¾in), *C 27-30 Mar,* £264 ($393)

11
A bronze figure of Le Bucheron, mid-19th cent, on a circular base inscribed 'le Bucheron Fable De La Fontaine' and signed 'Chambard', greenish-brown patination, 88cm (34½in), *C 10 Jan,* £770 ($1,117)

12
A bronze figure of Carmen, after Charles-Alphonse Colle, late 19th cent, inscribed 'A Colle' and impressed with circular foundry mark enclosing 'Societie des bronzes de Paris' and impressed 'AP 1868', light brown patina, 71cm (28in), *NY 3 Nov,* $1,045 (£836)

1   2   3

4   5   6

7   8   9

10   11   12

1
A bronze figure of a
mermaid rising from a
wavecrest, after Aimé-
Jules Dalou, late 19th
cent, the figure holding
a lyre as she throws back
her tresses, rich brown
patina, h 35cm (13¾in),
NY 24/25 Feb,
$3,410 (£2,352)

2
A bronze figure of a
classical woman, after
Etienne-Henri Dumaige,
late 19th cent, possibly
representing a water
nymph, golden-brown
patina, h 67.5cm (26½in),
NY 18 July,
$1,100 (£840)

3
A gilt-bronze figure of
Satan, after Jean-Jacques
Feuchère, late 19th cent,
the seated figure
posturing as if thwarted,
h 22.5cm (8¾in),
NY 16 June,
$1,870 (£1,365)

4
A bronze equestrian
group: Bellerphon, after
Emile Herbert, late 19th
cent, rich green-brown
patina, h 76cm (30in),
NY 16 June,
$4,950 (£3,540)

5
A bronze bust of Voltaire,
after Jean-Antoine
Houdon, late 19th cent,
brown patina, h 46cm
(18in), *NY 16 June,*
$715 (£522)

6
A bronze allegorical group
of two men, after Henri
Plé, late 19th cent,
possibly representing the
passage from youth to
maturity, h 60cm
(23½in), *NY 24/25 Feb,*
$1,650 (£1,138)

7
A bronze figure of a
woman harvesting grapes,
after Mathurin Moreau,
late 19th cent, the
peasant woman in mob
cap and barefoot, brown
patina, h 70cm (27½in),
NY 24/25 Feb,
$2,310 (£1,593)

8
A bronze bust of
Napoleon, French, late
19th cent, an eagle
below, brown patina,
h 67cm (22½in),
NY 16 June,
$1,210 (£883)

9
A bronze figure of
Mephistopheles, Jacques
Gautier, c.1890, dark
brown patination, signed
J Gautier, 84cm (33in),
L 8 Mar,
£1,430 ($2,002)

10
A bronze figure of a
female prisoner: Prise de
Corsaire, after Emanuelle
Villanis, in a revealing
knee-length robe, her
wrists manacled, h 85cm
(35½in), *NY 24/25 Feb,*
$2,090 ($1,441)

11
A bronze figure of a
German shepherd dog,
after Louis Riche, early
20th cent, golden-brown
patina, 61cm (24in),
NY 16 June,
$605 (£442)

1   2   3

4   5   6

7

8

9   10   11

1
A large bronze figure of a
North African soldier,
after Jean-Didier Debut,
late 19th cent, inscribed
'D. Debut', with foundry
mark, brown, golden
and reddish patinas,
95cm (37½ in),
NY 16 June,
$5,775 (£4,215)

2
A bronze figure of a
classical woman, after
Etienne-Henri
Dumaige, late 19th cent,
inscribed 'H. Dumaige',
69cm (27 in), *NY 24/25 Feb,*
$1,540 (£1,062)

3
A bronze figure of
Bacchus, after Marcus
Fritzche, last half 19th
cent, inscribed 'M.
Fritzche and Oskar
Gladenbeck G.m.b.H.',
one arm pinned and
loose, 70cm (27½ in),
NY 24/25 Feb,
$1,320 (£910)

4
A bronze figure of Lulli
enfant, after Adrien-
Etienne Gaudez, late
19th cent, inscribed 'A.
Gaudez', titled and
impressed with circular
foundry seal, golden
brown patina, 51cm
(20 in), *NY 3 Nov,*
$2,090 (£1,672)

5
A French silver and gilt
bronze figure of a young
woman, François Mage,
c.1865, inscribed 'Mage,
Société des Bronzes',
48cm (18⅞ in), *F 19 Dec,*
L 1,700,000 (£718; $898)

6
A bronze figure of a
woman harvesting grapes,
after Mathurin Moreau,
late 19th cent, inscribed
'Moreau Math Hors
Concours' and with
circular foundry mark
enclosing 'F.
Gobeau/Fondeur/Paris',
brown patina, 70cm
(27½ in), *NY 24/25 Feb,*
$2,310 (£1,593)

7
A large bronze figure of a
dancing Neapolitan boy,
after Francisque-Joseph
Duret, late 19th cent,
inscribed 'F. Duret and
Delafontaine', brown
patina, 97cm (38 in),
NY 24/25 Feb,
$3,300 (£2,275)

8
A bronze bust of a young
boy, after G. P. Martino,
late 19th/early 20th cent,
wearing a straw hat and
a medallion round his
neck, dark patination,
33cm (13 in), *C 10 Jan,*
£319 ($463)

9
A bronze bust of a young
woman, Georges van der
Straeten, late 19th cent,
signed 'Van Der
Straeten Paris', with
founder's mark 'Bellman
& Ivey', rich dark brown
and red patination, 58cm
(23 in), *L 8 Nov,*
£902 ($1,199)

10
A large bronze figure of a
warrior: Virtutes Civicae
Ense et Labore, after
Emile-Louis Picault, late
19th cent, inscribed 'E.
Picault', titled and with
circular foundry stamp
enclosing 'Vrai/bronze',
mustard and black
patinas, 113cm (44½ in),
NY 16 June,
$3,190 (£2,328)

11
A large bronze group of
Excelsior with a figure of
Victory, after Emile
Louis Picault, c.1900,
standing above a figure
astride a rocky plinth,
blackish patination,
112cm (44 in), *C 27-30 Mar,*
£1,540 ($2,295)

12
A bronze figure of Eve,
late 19th cent, the nubile
young girl standing
naked on a naturalistic
plinth, dark green
patination, 89cm (35 in),
C 3-6 July,
£3,630 ($4,924)

1
A bronze figure of David standing on the head of Goliath, Antonin Mercie, c.1870, signed 'A. Mercie', rich brown patination, 91cm (36in), *L 8 Mar*, £2,530 ($3,772)

2
A bronze figure of an Arab falconer, Emile Guillemain, c.1881, signed 'Ele. Guillemin', rich brown patination, 111cm (43¾in), *L 8 Nov*, £13,200 ($17,556)

3
A bronze figure of 'La Genie de la Danse', Jean Baptiste Carpeaux, c.1872, signed 'B. Carpeaux', dated 1872 and inscribed 'Propriety Carpeaux J.P.', rich light brown patination, 55cm (21½in), *L 7 June*, £2,860 ($4,147)

4
A South African bronze 'The Skapu Player', signed Anton van Wouw' and dated 'Joh-burg 1907', with foundry mark 'G. Massa Rome', dark patination, 33.5cm (13¼in), *JHB 2 May*, R 31,000 (£17,614) ($24,641)

5
A South African bronze 'Bad News', by Anton van Wouw, signed and dated 'SA Joh-burg 1907', with the foundry mark 'G. Massa Roma', the smaller version, 16cm (6¼in), *JHB 10 May*, R 39,000 (£21,788) ($30,481)

6
A South African 'Shangaan' bronze, by Anton van Wouw signed and dated 'S.A. Joh-Burg 1907', with foundry mark 'G. Massa, Roma', dark brown patination, 31cm (12in), *JHB 3 July*, R 16,000 (£8,511) ($11,574)

7
A South African bronze figure, 'The accused', Anton van Wouw, signed and inscribed 'Joh-Burg, SA', foundry G. Nisini, Roma, brown patination, 31cm (12¼in), *JHB 6 Nov*, R 14,000 (£6,061) ($7,394)

1   2   3

4   5

6   7

Decorative Arts from 1880

PHILIPPE GARNER • BARBARA DEISROTH

Some of the principal European stylistic movements since the 1880s have been so consciously dominated by a specific concept of design that interest has since tended to concentrate on the individual periods and styles as exemplified over the whole range of artefacts in whatever medium: jewellery, porcelain, silver, furniture, metalwork, carpets and embroidery. It is because of this interest in specific styles that the illustrations in this section show objects in various different materials which one might have expected to find elsewhere in this book. Here we shall touch briefly on some of the main movements. Twentieth-century studio ceramics, whose roots lie in the Arts and Crafts Movement, are featured on page 450.

The earliest of these movements was the Arts and Crafts Movement of the late 19th and early 20th century. The somewhat idealistic and in many ways unrealistic theory behind it was British in origin, stemming largely from the teachings of William Morris and John Ruskin. In principle the aim was to undo the worst aspects of mass production and the mechanical age and return to a simple aesthetic based on medieval values and the work of the individual craftsman. Hence the vogue for unfussy pegged and dowelled oak furniture and simple, sturdy, hand-made wares; but, apart from the fact that the artefacts were never cheap, their appeal was in any case often to the well-heeled middle classes. The movement spread to the United States and the furniture of Greene and Greene and, more especially, Gustav Stickley, produced around 1900, is very much in the Morris tradition. The architect C. A. Voysey was responsible for Arts and Crafts furniture in Britain, as was Morris himself, and they both also designed metalwork and furnishings.

Art Nouveau also had theorists behind it. In its purest form the movement was French, Belgian and German and can be roughly dated from 1895 to 1905. The idea was to create a style without historical references and antecedents. The guiding light should be Nature. The arts of Japan, which had become known in Europe during the 1860s and 1870s, provided a source of inspiration, and, in particular, their stylization of graphic design was widely admired. Some Gallé glass (though not all of it is strictly Art Nouveau) and Lalique jewellery are typical of the style. Majorelle translated it into furniture and the German factory WMF produced a commercial version of Art Nouveau metalwork. Tiffany glass represents an American manifestation of the style.

Art Deco, which can be dated from about 1910 to about 1925, grew naturally out of Art Nouveau, but was to some extent a reaction to it. It was very much a decorator's style and did not seek justification in aesthetic theory. The sinuous curves typical of Art Nouveau were straightened out and this strictly French style (though it had an influence in the United States and Great Britain) had many affinities with late 18th century France and Neoclassicism. In furniture, E. J. Ruhlmann and Süe et Mare were its main exponents, while some of the lacquer-work of Jean Dunand and the metalwork of Edgar Brandt is also true Art Deco.

The latest of the movements covered here is known as Modernism and can be dated from about 1925 to 1935. Unlike Art Deco this was again a movement founded on theory— a theory that ran quite counter to that of the Arts and Crafts Movement. This time the idea was to come to terms with the machine age and to find an aesthetic that was right for it. Clean lines, unadorned, uncluttered industrial materials were to be the order of the day and in theory the articles could be made mechanically. In practice, however, many of them were not and the hand-burnished steel of Mies van der Rohe's Barcelona chair confirms it as a luxury object. The prototype furniture of Rietveld and the costly limited editions of Pierre Chareau are superbly styled. The series production of PEL reached a wider audience but is equally stylish. Lamps and other objects by Desny and, in America, furniture by Donald Deskey are also truly Modernist.

The wide interest that has been shown in these various movements signifies the importance now generally attached to the story of modern to design. The recent marked increase in interest in post Second World War design, especially of Italian, Scandinavian and American objects, stems from this and seems to indicate that the various artefacts will continue to be usefully grouped on stylistic grounds.

1
A cameo glass vase, Daum, c 1900, engraved mark, 49.5cm (19½in), *M 7 Oct*, **FF 24,420 (£2,111; $2,620)**

2
A cameo peacock feather vase, Daum, c 1900, the blue glass shading to purple near the base, overlaid in green, cameo mark, 29.2cm (11½in), *M 7 Oct*, **FF 6,660 (£576; $715)**

3
A cameo glass landscape lamp, Daum c 1900, in mottled yellow and orange glass overlaid in claret, the shade cut with a bay scene, signed, h 38cm (15in), d 15cm (6in), *NY 11/12 May*, **$2,750 (£1,993)**

4
A cameo glass landscape vase, Daum, c 1910, the grey sides mottled with rose and apricot, overlaid in emerald green and reddish-brown, cameo signature, 53cm (21in), *NY 17 Nov*, **$2,750 (£2,200)**

5
An enamelled glass landscape vase, Daum, c 1910, signed in enamel, 41cm (16¼in), *NY 17/18 Feb*, **$1,100 (£775)**

6
A gilded and enamelled miniature goblet, Daum, c 1900, signed, 5cm (2in), *M 11 Mar*, **FF 3,330 (£280; $416)**

7
An enamelled cameo glass bowl, Daum, c 1900, the grey glass shading to pale blue, overlaid in white, pale blue and green, cut with edelweiss, heightened in enamel, cameo mark, 17.2cm (6¾in), *M 7 Oct*, **FF 7,215 (£624; $774)**

8
An etched and enamelled cameo glass vase, Daum, c 1900, in mottled grey-amber glass, cameo mark, 43cm (17in), *L 29/30 Nov*, **£990 ($1,198)**

9
An etched, gilded and enamelled cameo glass vase, Daum, c 1900, in frosted glass overlaid in clear green, gilt mark, 20.5cm (8⅛in), *L 29/30 Nov*, **£770 ($932)**

10
A massive acid-etched table lamp, marked 'Daum Nancy France', c 1925, 41cm (16in), *M 11 Mar*, **FF 44,400 (£3,731; $5,550)**

11
A cameo glass vase, Daum, c 1900, grey-yellow tinted glass streaked with patches of deeper yellow and specks of brown, overlaid in pink and grey green, engraved mark, 21cm (8¼in), *L 16 Feb*, **£770 ($1,080)**

12
An etched and gilded glass vase, Daum, c 1900, the grey glass tinted with deep pink purple towards the top, gilt mark, 34.5cm (13⅝in), *L 28 Sept*, **£605 ($787)**

13
A massive acid-etched table lamp, marked 'Daum Nancy France', 1920s, in frosted grey glass mottled with pale yellow, 40.5cm (16in), *L 29/30 Nov*, **£5,500 ($6,655)**

14
An etched glass vase, Daum, 1920s, marked, 15.2cm (6in), *L 6 July*, **£143 ($197)**

15
An etched-glass and bronze two-armed lamp, Daum and Edgar Brandt, c 1925, 49cm (19⅜in), *NY 11/12 May*, **$3,575 (£2,591)**

16
An acid-etched glass centre bowl, Daum, c 1930, *NY 11/12 May*, **$2,970 (£2,152)**

17
An etched glass vase, Daum, c 1930, 37.5cm (14¾in), *NY 17/18 Feb*, **$880 (£620)**

1
A glass lamp, Gallé,
*c*1900, the grey glass
overlaid in blue and
mauve and cut with
stylised flowers, signed,
26.5cm (10½in), *M 11 Mar*,
FF 42,180 (£3,545; $5,273)

2
A cameo glass lamp,
Gallé, *c*1900, the yellow
glass overlaid in red and
cut with magnolias,
signed, 58cm (22⅞in),
M 11 Mar,
FF 88,800 (£7,462; $11,100)

3
A cameo glass ewer,
Gallé, *c*1900, with silver
mounts, the opal glass
with green inclusions,
overlaid with pink,
decorated with flowers
and foliage, cameo
signature, 33.5cm (13⅛in),
M 7 Oct,
FF 42,180 (£3,646; $4,526)

4
A glass landscape vase,
Gallé, *c*1900, in shades
of grey and yellow over-
laid in deep blue,
cameo signature, 35.7cm
(11in), *M 11 Mar*,
FF 47,730 (£4,011; $5,966)

5
A mould-blown cameo
glass vase, Gallé, *c*1900,
the yellow glass overlaid
in purple blue and
decorated in high relief
with branches ripe with
plums, cameo mark, 32cm
(12⅝in), *M 7 Oct*,
FF 56,610 (£4,893; $6,074)

6
A glass landscape vase,
Gallé, *c*1900, in shades
of grey and pink overlaid
in brown, cameo mark,
52cm (20½in), *M 7 Oct*,
FF 34,410 (£2,974; $3,692)

7
A glass waterlily vase,
Gallé, *c*1900, of half-
moon shape, in shades of
grey and yellow overlaid
in deep mauve deco-
rated in cameo with water
lilies, signed, *M 11 Mar*,
FF 6,105 (£513; $763)

8
A cameo glass vase, Gallé,
*c*1900, decorated with
lilies, the yellow glass
overlaid with amber,
cameo signature, 47.5cm
(18¾in), *M 11 Mar*,
FF 11,100 (£933; $1,388)

9
A bottle vase, Gallé,
*c*1900, cameo signature,
24cm (9½in), *P 15-18 May*,
£396 ($550)

10
A glass vase, Gallé,
*c*1900, the rich green
glass with inserted pockets
of bright blue, deep
blue, red and yellow,
cameo signature in light
relief, 68.2cm (26⅞in),
M 11 Mar,
FF 72,150 (£6,063; $9,019)

11
An enamelled glass vase,
Gallé, *c*1900, of smoked
glass, the flowers
enamelled in red and
green, the stems and
leaves heightened in
gilt, cameo signature,
59cm (23¼in), *M 11 Mar*,
FF 11,100 (£933; $1,387)

12
An enamelled glass vase,
Gallé, *c*1900, green
tinted glass with acid
texturing, enamelled
with daisies and poppies
in white, yellow, red and
green enamel, detailed
with gilding, 19cm (7½in),
L 29/30 Nov,
£990 ($1,198)

13
An enamelled glass cup
and cover, Gallé, 1890s,
in green glass with
dappled internal orange
and light surface
opalescence, etched,
gilded and enamelled
with lilies in shades of
white, purple and green,
26.5cm (10½in), *L 6 July*,
£2,970 ($4,099)

14
An internally decorated
and wheel-carved 'Marine'
vase, Gallé, *c*1900,
carved signature, 13.5cm
(5⅜in), *L 13 Apr*,
£6,050 ($8,730)

15
A 'Rose de France' glass
vase, Gallé, *c*1900, the
very pale green glass
etched with silhouettes
of branches, the stem,
three leaves and rose
applied in several tones
of pink, the rose in
relief, signed, 18.7cm
(7⅜in), *M 7 Oct*,
**FF 200,355 (£17,317;
$21,497)**

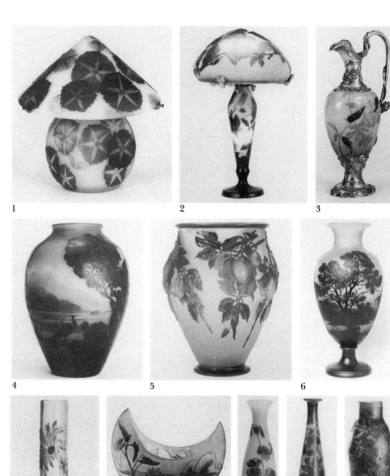

1   2   3

4   5   6

7

8   9   10

11   12

13   14   15

1

A cameo glass stoppered bottle, Gallé, c.1900 the grey body streaked with pale lavender, the whole fire-polished, cameo signature, 13.5cm (5¼in), *NY 17/18 Feb,* $880 (£620)

2

A cameo glass covered box, Gallé, 1904-10, the pale grey sides shaded with peach, overlaid in shades of green and white and cut with maple buds and leafage, cameo signature, 17cm (6¾in), *NY 17/18 Feb,* $550 (£387)

3

A cameo glass vase, Gallé, c.1900, in milky grey-yellow glass, overlaid with pink-brown and etched with sprays of Chinese lanterns, cameo mark, 18.5cm (7¼in), *L 13 Apr,* £770 ($1,111)

4

A cameo glass landscape vase, Gallé, c.1900, the grey glass sides shading to aquamarine at the neck and base, overlaid in ochre, partially fire-polished, cameo signature, 45.4cm (17⅞in), *NY 17/18 Feb,* $3,300 (£2,324)

5

A cameo glass vase, Gallé, c.1900, the pale grey sides shaded with amber and lavender with lavender foil inclusions, overlaid in amber, grey, lavender and dusty rose, signed, 33cm (13in), *NY 11/12 May,* $4,290 (£3,109)

6

A cameo glass vase, Gallé, c.1900, in grey glass shaded with salmon, overlaid in deeper salmon, the whole fire-polished, cameo signature, 19cm (7½in), *NY 11/12 May,* $770 (£558)

7

A cameo glass vase, Daum Nancy, c.1900, the mottled orange and dusty rose sides overlaid in burnt orange and brown, 59cm (23¼in), *NY 11/12 May,* $1,320 (£957)

8

A cameo glass vase, Gallé, c.1900, peach tinted, overlaid in deep red/brown and etched with maiden-hair fern, cameo mark, 17cm (6¾in), *L 29/30 Nov,* £418 ($506)

9

A cameo glass vase, Gallé, c.1920, the lemon-yellow sides overlaid in deep orange, cameo signature, 42.5cm (16¾in), *NY 17/18 Feb,* $4,400 (£3,099)

10

A mould-blown cameo glass bowl, Gallé, c.1920, the slightly opalescent olive-green walls overlaid in rust and sea green, cameo signature, 32cm (12½in), *NY 17/18 Feb,* $6,600 (£4,648)

11

A mould-blown cameo glass clematis vase, Gallé, c.1925, in citron-yellow glass overlaid in citron, green and brown, cameo signature, 25cm (9¾in), *NY 17 Nov,* $3,190 (£2,552)

12

A mould-blown cameo glass plum vase, Gallé, c.1925, the yellow glass overlaid in medium red, cameo signature, 33cm (13in), *NY 17 Nov,* $6,875 (£5,500)

13

A mould-blown cameo glass plum vase, Gallé, c.1925, the deep amber glass overlaid in Sienna-red, cameo signature, 32cm (12½in), *NY 11/12 May,* $5,500 (£3,986)

14

A mould-blown cameo glass rose-hip vase, Gallé, c.1925, in yellow glass overlaid in shades of violet, the sides moulded with branches of rose-hips, raised on a pale violet foot, cameo signature, 25cm (9¾in), *NY 11/12 May,* $1,980 (£1,435)

15

A mould-blown cameo glass elephant vase, Gallé, c.1925, cameo signature, 39cm (15¼in), *NY 17/18 Feb,* $11,000 (£7,746)

1 2 3
4 5 6 7
8 9 10
11 12
13 14 15

1
A glass brooch, Lalique, 1920s, circular moulded with the head of a grotesque beast, metal moulded, backed with orange foil, heightened with staining, 4.2cm (1⅝in), *L 29/30 Nov,* £374 ($453)

2
An opalescent glass vase, Lalique, 1920s, milky white, moulded with formalised leaves, 17cm (6¾in), *L 6 July,* £352 ($486)

3
A frost glass vase, Lalique, 1920s, moulded in the form of a sea urchin, stencilled mark, 18.5cm (7¼in), *L 28 Sept,* £275 ($358)

4
A glass bowl, Lalique, 1920s, squat globular moulded with flowers, black enamel centres, impressed mark, 12.5cm (5in), *L 28 Sept,* £308 ($400)

5
An opalescent glass figure of a mermaid 'Sirènes', engraved 'R Lalique France', 1920s, moulded mark, 10cm (4in), *L 29/30 Nov,* £528 ($639)

6
A glass vase, Lalique, 1920s, moulded in low relief with sprays of honesty, heightened with blue-grey staining, impressed mark, 23.5cm (9¼in), *L 29/30 Nov,* £550 ($666)

7
An opalescent glass thistle vase, Lalique *c*1930, engraved signature, 21cm (8¼in), *M 11 Mar,* FF 5,500 (£466; $694)

8
A moulded yellow glass chandelier, Lalique, *c*1925, pendant from a silken cord and silken ceiling cap, d 30cm (12in), *NY 11/12 May,* $1,540 (£1,116)

9
A moulded yellow glass vase, Lalique, *c*1932 of bullet form, the pale yellow walls moulded in medium relief with intertwining thorny branches, 24cm (9½in), *NY 11/12 May,* $880 (£638)

10
A moulded blue glass coupe 'Flora Bella' Lalique, *c*1932, with flattened cavetto and short sides, the sapphire-blue body moulded on the exterior in medium relief with bands of overlapping leafage, d 39.5cm (15½in), *NY 17 Nov,* $2,200 (£1,760)

11
A glass perfume bottle and stopper, Lalique, *c*1925, of gently swollen conical form, moulded with concave flowers, detailed with brown staining, flat stopper with flower, engraved mark, 13.2cm (5¼in), *L 29/30 Nov,* £198 ($240)

12
A glass perfume bottle, Lalique, *c*1925, moulded with satyr masks and garlands of flowers, stopper moulded with rosebuds, surface grey staining, 12.5cm (5in), *L 13 Apr,* £308 ($444)

13
A glass perfume bottle and stopper, Lalique, *c*1925, frosted stopper moulded as a cluster of fruit with leaves trailing to frame the faceted bottle, 13.5cm (5⅜in), *L 29/30 Nov,* £638 ($772)

14
A glass perfume bottle, Lalique, 1930s, the body moulded as a spiral shell, the stopper as a crouching naked woman, moulded mark, 9.7cm (3⅞in), *L 6 July,* £242 ($334)

15
A blue glass bottle, stencilled 'R Lalique France', for Worth, 1930s, ribbed cylindrical, stepped neck, opaque turquoise glass stopper, 27.5cm (10⅞in), *L 13 Apr,* £286 ($413)

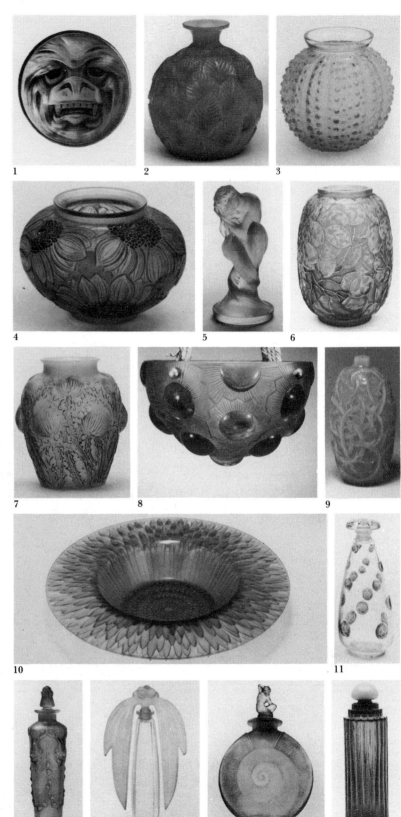

A smoked glass cockerel mascot, Lalique, 1920s, 20.75cm (8in), *L 6 July,* £484 ($667)

A glass cockerel head mascot, Lalique, 18cm (7in), *L 6 July,* £198 ($273)

A smoked glass car mascot of a cock, moulded signature 'R Lalique', *c*1930, sculpted in full relief, 20cm (7⅞in), *M 11 Mar,* FF 12,210 (£1,026; $1,526)

4
A glass car mascot, 'The Spirit of the Wind', moulded mark 'R Lalique' *c*1925, original chromed metal mount with credit for Breves Gallery, Knightsbridge, 26cm (10¼in), *L 29/30 Nov,* £1,650 ($1,997)

5
A glass car mascot, 'The Spirit of the Wind', moulded mark 'R Lalique France', *c*1930, light lilac tint, h 15cm (5⅞in), *L 6 July,* £3,080 ($4,250)

6
A pair of frosted glass mascots, 'Epsom', both moulded 'R Lalique' *c*1932, each realistically modelled as the head of a horse with stylised moulded mane, chrome mounts, black onyx base, minor chips to lower edge, 15cm (6in), *NY 11/12 May,* $2,530 (£1,833)

7
A glass St Christopher mascot, intaglio mark 'Lalique France', 1930s, 11.5cm (4½in), *L 6 July,* £187 ($258)

8
A glass cordial set, stencilled mark 'R Lalique France', 1930s, decanter and stopper and eight glasses, moulded with scrolls on neck and stem, pink-tinted, 19.5cm (7¾in), *L 13 Apr,* £352 ($508)

9
A set of glass, comprising 56 glasses and three decanters, Lalique, *c*1925, the feet and stopper decorated in black enamel, engraved marks, *M 7 Oct,* FF 24,420 (£2,111; $2,620)

10
A set of glass, Lalique, *c*1925, comprising 67 glasses, 22 finger-bowls, three decanters, engraved marks, *M 7 Oct,* FF 18,870 (£1,631; $2,025)

11
A set of glass, Lalique, *c*1930, comprising 7 champagne glasses, 6 large wine glasses, stems moulded with two naked figures and 6 small bowls, moulded with rectangular panel of matching figures, 11, 15.5 and 5.7cm (4⅜, 6⅛ and 2¼in), *L 29/30 Nov,* £715 ($865)

12
A Bacchus vase, engraved 'R Lalique France', *c*1930, moulded with two masks of Bacchus, their horns forming handles, octagonal foot, clear glass, 30.7cm (12in), *M 11 Mar,* FF 8,880 (£746; $1,110)

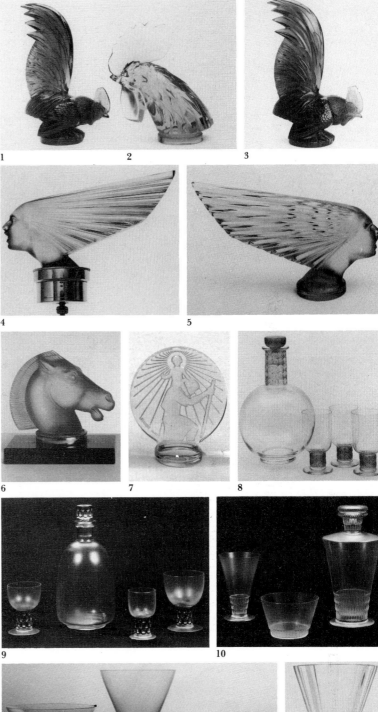

1   2   3

4   5

6   7   8

9   10

11   12

1
An iridescent glass vase, engraved mark 'Loetz Austria', c.1900, with delicate feathered lustre trails of peacock green-purple, pink-gold ground, 23.5cm (9¼in), L 29/30 Nov, £11,550 ($13,976)

2
A silver-overlay iridescent glass vase, Loetz, c.1900, in pale salmon glass, decorated with deep sapphire blue waves and amber iridescent oil spotting, the pierced overlay in the form of iris blossoms, unsigned, 15cm (6in), NY 18 July, $825 (£630)

3
A pair of iridescent glass vases, c.1900, 20cm (7⅞in), P 15-18 May, £572 ($795)

4
A silver-overlay iridescent paperweight glass vase, Loetz, c.1900, the amber walls shading to lime green, decorated with silvery-blue iridescent sprays, unsigned, Lebolt silver mounts, 21.2cm (8¾in), NY 11/12 May, $1,210 (£877)

5
An iridescent glass vase, inscribed 'Loetz Austria', c.1900, the pale-yellow glass with a medial band of apple-green dripping into deep salmon and silvery-iridescent blue, 16.6cm (6⅝in), NY 17 Nov, $4,675 (£3,740)

6
A cameo glass landscape lamp, Muller Frères, c.1900, base and shade in lightly-tinted glass overlaid in deep orange-pink and blue-brown, etched with an alpine landscape, h 67.7cm (26¾in), L 13 Apr, £6,050 ($8,730)

7
A bronze table lamp with Muller Frères glass shade, c.1905, the shade in orange mottled glass, stencilled mark on shade, 44.5cm (17½in), L 16 Feb, £220 ($308)

8
A cameo glass and wrought-iron lamp, Muller Frères, c.1925, the base inscribed Virtz/Luneville, the shade in mottled yellow and grey glass, overlaid in sea blue and cut with wisteria blossoms and leafage, h 66cm (26in), NY 11/12 May, $4,400 (£3,188)

9
A pâte-de-verre and wrought-iron lamp, G Argy-Rousseau, c.1925, signed, h 34.5cm (13½in), NY 11/12 May, $17,050 (£12,355)

10
A pâte-de-verre figural Veilleuse shade, signed 'A Walter/Nancy', c.1925, in the form of a seated dove, shading from pale green to sea green splashed with mustard, 17.5cm (6⅞in), NY 17/18 Feb, $1,320 (£930)

11
A pâte-de-verre vase, A Walter, c.1925, the olive-green walls moulded with leafage in shades of forest green, sienna and lemon, 11.5cm (4½in), NY 11/12 May, $1,650 (£1,195)

12
A pâte-de-verre bowl, G Argy-Rousseau, c.1925, in pale mottled grey glass, moulded in medium relief with pendant grape vines in shades of deep purple, raspberry and Chinese red, signed, 9cm (3½in), NY 11/12 May, $2,750 (£1,993)

13
An enamelled and gilt glass vase, Heilgenstein, c.1928, enamelled in translucent turquoise, aquamarine, lime and emerald green, heightened with gilding, signed, 18.5cm (7¼in), NY 11/12 May, $770 (£558)

14
An enamelled glass bottle, Marcel Goupy, 1920s, enamelled mark, 23.5cm (9¼in), L29/30 Nov, £220 ($266)

1
An embroidered three-fold screen made for the drawing room of Bullerswood, Morris and Co, *c.*1889, the panels probably designed by May Morris, each panel in green and orange silks against a pale-blue ground, h 184cm (72⅝in), *L 29/30 Nov,*
£18,700 ($22,627)

2
An eggshell earthenware vase, Rozenburg, decorated by Samuel Schellinck, with date code for 1902, finely-painted with stylised iris, poppies and a butterfly, shades of green, mauve and ochre on white, 32.5cm (9¼in), *L 13 Apr,*
£9,350 ($13,464)

3
A 'Fantasque' jardinière, Wilkinson Ltd, 1930s, painted with a broad frieze of formalised fruit, printed marks, 21.5cm (8½in), *L 29/30 Nov,*
£770 ($932)

4
A stoneware vase, Hans Coper, *c.*1953-56, glazed in a rich manganese brown with sgraffito radiating lines in cream, minor rim chips, impressed HC seal, 24.2cm (9½in), *L 29/30 Nov*
£10,670 ($12,911)

5
A stoneware 'optical jar', Elizabeth Fritsch, 1976, painted with broad diagonal bands of deep olive and ashen white, the rim and interior terracotta, 25.2cm (10in), *L 13 Apr,*
£2,640 ($3,802)

1

2

3

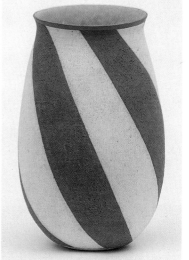

4

5

1
A set of silver tableware, Wiener Werkstatte, designed by Josef Hoffman, 1904, *M 11 Mar*, **FF 177,600 (£14,924; $22,200)**

2
A silver tazza, Gilbert Marks, London, 1898, the knopped stem and raised foot repoussé and finely chased with poppies and leaves, signed, 34.5cm (13½in), *L 29/30 Nov*, **£3,300 ($3,993)**

3
A silver and jade bowl and cover, Jean Puiforcat, c.1925, d 25cm (9⅞in), *M 11 Mar*, **FF 39,960 (£3,358; $4,995)**

4
A bronze and ivory starfish girl, Chiparus, 1930s, in close fitting metallic purple-blue cat suit with studded marine decoration, on shaped brown marble base with applied green and black marble square, 75.7cm (29¾in), *L 29/30 Nov*, **£9,900 ($11,979)**

1

2

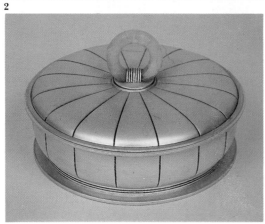
3

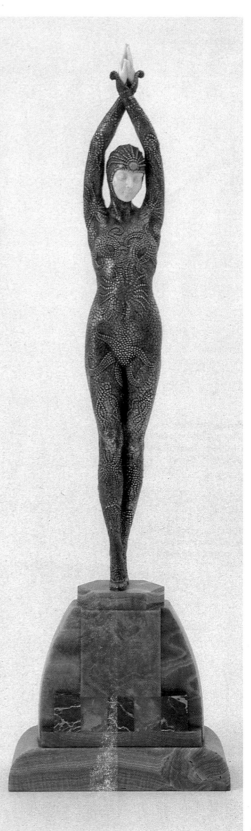
4

1
A Tiffany Favrile glass and bronze wisteria lamp, 1899-1920, with an overall pattern of lavender-blue blossoms and blue-green leafage, shade unsigned, base impressed 'Tiffany Studios, New York', h 68.5cm (27in), d 46cm (18in), *NY 17 Nov,* $40,700 (£32,560)

2
A Tiffany Favrile decorated Cypriote glass vase, *c.*1895, 21cm (8¼in), *NY 17 Nov,* $4,675 (£3,740)

3
A cameo glass lamp, Gallé, *c.*1900, signed, h 62cm (24⅜in), *M 7 Oct,* **FF 366,300 (£31,659; $39,303)**

4
A vase, Gallé, *c.*1900, in the form of a flower, the petals etched in relief, 11.7cm (4⅝in), *M 7 Oct,* **FF 277,500 (£23,984; $29,775)**

5
A large glass 'Handkerchief' vase, etched mark 'Venini Murano Italia', *c.*1955, 28.2cm (11⅛in), *L 29 Nov,* £1,870 ($2,581)

6
A Tiffany Favrile, Tel El Amarna vase, *c.*1910, 25.5cm (10in), *NY 24 Apr,* $64,900 (£44,759)

1

2

3

4

5

6

1
An ivory-inlaid ébène de macassar and shagreen coiffeuse and matching chair, designed by Emile Jacques Ruhlmann, *c.*1932, h 122cm (48in), w 93.5cm (36¾in), *NY 17 Nov,* **$24,200 (£19,360)**

2
A Scottish inlaid mahogany cabinet, probably by Wylie & Lockhead, *c.*1900, set with pierced copper-plated hinge plates and handles, inlaid in various fruit-woods, the top doors inset with enamelled peacock feather panels, h 183cm (72in), *L 29/30 Nov,* **£2,640 ($3,194)**

3
A coffee table in carved wood, glass and metal, designed by Carlo Mollino, *c.*1950, the two shelves in glass, h 43.5cm (17in), *M 7 Oct,* **FF 166,500 (£14,391; $17,865)**

1

2

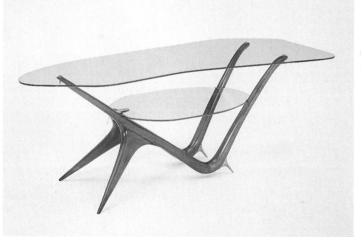

3

1

A decorated Aurene glass vase, Steuben, 1904-30, 32cm (12½ in), *NY 11/12 May,* $2,970 (£2,152)

2

A glass vase, signed 'H Copillet', *c* 1900, the amber glass with iridescent ochre, green and purple, 19.5cm (7¾ in), *M 11 Mar,* FF 9,900 (£839; $1,249)

3

A cameo glass landscape vase, signed in cameo 'deVez', *c* 1900, in pale blue overlaid in salmon and green, 31.5cm (12⅜ in), *NY 11/12 May,* $605 (£438)

4

A cameo glass vase, signed in cameo 'A Delatte/Nancy', *c* 1920, the mottled grey and maroon sides overlaid in purple, 34cm (13¼ in), *NY 17/18 Feb,* $1,320 (£930)

5

A cameo glass landscape vase, cameo mark 'Legras' *c* 1900, grey glass tinted with pink and green, overlaid in white, green and brown, 29.5cm (11⅝ in), *L 16 Feb,* £770 ($1,080)

6

A painted-glass and patinated-metal landscape lamp, Handel, probably decorated by William Runge, early 20th cent, h 61cm (24in), *NY 24 Mar,* $2,310 (£1,593)

7

An iridescent glass lamp, Fostoria, *c* 1912, in opalescent glass decorated with striated green feathering edged in amber iridescence, h 38.5cm 15¼ in), d 17cm (6⅝ in), *NY 11/12 May,* $880 (£638)

8

A blue glass covered compote, *c* 1920, designed by Josef Hoffmann for the Wiener Werkstätte and executed by Moser Karlsbad, 22cm (12½ in), *NY 11/12 May,* $1,320 (£957)

9

An amethyst glass covered compote, *c* 1920, designed by Josef Hoffmann for the Wiener Werkstätte and executed by Moser Karlsbad, 28cm (11in), *NY 11/12 May,* $1,320 (£957)

10

Two black glass perfume bottles, 1920s, designed by Sue et Mare, the smaller with gilt label for 'Le Dandy D'orsay' 11.5 and 9cm (4½ and 3½ in), *L 28 Sept,* £176 ($229)

11

An etched black glass vase, etched mark 'Verart, France', *c* 1925, 34.2cm (13½ in), *L 6 July,* £242 ($334)

12

A glass clock case, moulded mark 'P M Faure France', *c* 1930, 16cm (6⅜ in), *L 16 Feb,* £143 ($200)

13

An engraved glass tazza, Orrefors, designed by Simon Gate, *c* 1925, the panelled smoky grey glass finely engraved with nude female figures, 24.5cm (9⅝ in), *NY 17 Nov,* $550 (£440)

14

A blown glass apple vase, Orrefors, designed by Ingeborg Lundin, *c* 1959, shading from clear to smokey topaz at the applied neck, 33cm (13in), *NY 17 Nov,* $1,430 (£1,144)

15

A Graal glass vase, Orrefors, designed by Ingeborg Lundin, *c* 1970, in colourless glass cased inside in periwinkle and outside in white, the top banded with a yellow and blue coil, 19cm (7½ in), *NY 17/18 Feb,* $275 (£194)

16

Two glass vases, Orrefors, designed by Ingeborg Lundin, *c* 1970, 16 and 19cm (6¼ and 7½ in), *NY 17/18 Feb,* $550 (£387)

1
A glass 'Ariel' bowl,
Orrefors, designed by
Edvin Ohrstrom, c1970,
with stripes of milky
green and white, with
bubbly 'stripes' between,
engraved, d 12.7 (5in),
L 29 Nov,
£99 ($120)

2
An 'Ariel' glass vase,
Orrefors, designed by
Ingeborg Lundin, c1975,
with internal design of
zebra heads in brown
and milky white in Ariel
technique, engraved
mark, 18.5cm (7¼in),
L 29 Nov,
£4,180 ($5,058)

3
Three miniature latticino
glass 'Handkerchief' vases,
each with etched Venini
Murano mark, c1955,
two with opaque green
and white decoration,
the third with clear
green and pink-brown
decoration, 5.7 to 8.5cm
(2⅜ to 3⅜in), *L 29 Nov,*
£374 ($453)

4
A glass vase, etched mark
'Venini Murano Made
in Italy', 1950s, amber
with white trails, 36cm
(14⅛in), *L 6 July,*
£198 ($273)

5
A large pair of glass
hanging lamps, each
stamped 'Venini Murano',
c1950, d 52cm (20½in),
M 11 Mar,
FF 14,430 (£1,213; $1,804)

6
A glass tazza, Venini,
c1960, internally decorated
with concentric stripes of
bright orange, green and
blue, h 18cm (7in),
L 29 Nov,
£1,650 ($1,996)

7
A glass vase, designed by
Flavio Poli, engraved mark
'Seguso Murano, pièce
unique', c1950, in grey-
blue thick glass, 28cm
(11in), *M 11 Mar,*
FF 26,085 (£2,192; $3,261)

8
A glass vase, engraved
mark 'Archimede Seguso
Murano', c1950, 32.5cm
(12¾in), *M 11 Mar,*
FF 17,760 (£1,492; $2,220)

9
A 'Patchwork' glass bowl,
Barovier & Toso,
designed by Ercole
Barovier, c1955, squat
bulbous, amber patchwork
design, 14.5cm (5¾in),
L 29 Nov,
£286 ($346)

10
A glass vase, Iittala,
designed by Tapio
Wirkkala, c1950, in
colourless glass with fine
engraved vertical lines,
24.5cm (9⅝in), *M 7 Oct,*
FF 3,330 (£288; $357)

11
A glass vase, Iittala,
designed by Tapio
Wirkkala, c1955, slender
bud form, with fine
engraved vertical lines,
32cm (12⅝in), *L 29 Nov,*
£352 ($426)

12
A tomato-red glass bottle
vase, Nuutajarvi-Notsjo,
designed by Kaj Franck,
c1955, 19cm (7½in),
L 29 Nov,
£638 ($772)

13
A glass vase, Rosenthal,
designed by Hertha
Bengston, and made by
B Colelli, c1975, onion
form, gently spiralling
variegated brown lines,
stencilled mark, 21cm
(8¼in), *L 29 Nov,*
£242 ($293)

14
An enamelled and etched
glass plaque, designed by
Giancarlo Begotti,
c1958, in pale green
glass cut, enamelled in
brick tones and gilt, with
an African tribe at
worship, signed in enamel,
43cm (17in), *NY 17/18 Feb,*
$880 (£620)

15
A glass standing plaque,
designed by Alfredo
Barbini, c1970, in clear
glass invested with the
figures of four floating
squid, bubbles and blue-
tinged wave formations;
sold with a small Barbini
glass plaque invested
with a jellyfish, h 22cm
(8¾in), *NY 17/18 Feb,*
$550 (£387)

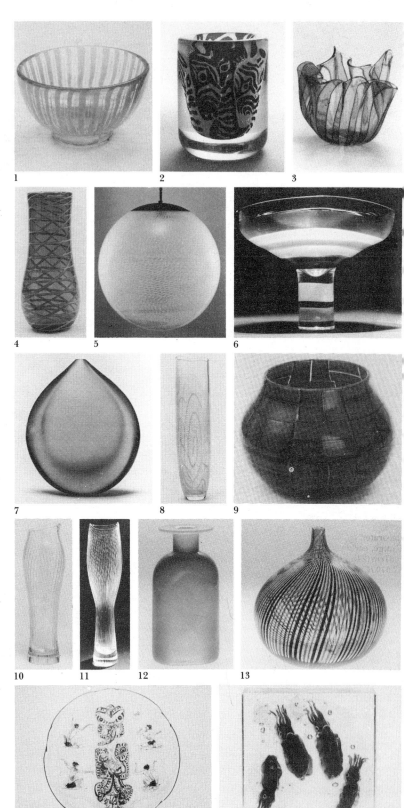

1
**A Tiffany Favrile glass
Tel El Amarna vase,**
c.1919, in brilliant tur-
quoise, the neck in black
glass decorated with
silvery-blue iridescent
and black interlocking
zig-zags, 22.5cm (8¾in),
NY 24 Mar,
$2,750 (£1,897)

2
**A Tiffany Favrile decorated
black glass vase,** 1892-1928,
the body shading from
iridescent black to deep
navy blue, intaglio carved
in silvery-blue iridescence,
deep ochre, mustard and
brown, 9cm (3½in),
NY 11/12 May,
$14,850 (£10,761)

3
**A Tiffany-Favrile intaglio-
carved glass vase,** c.1917,
in amber iridescent glass
decorated in green with
trailing vines and intaglio-
carved leaves, 23cm
(9in), *NY 17/18 Feb,*
$1,760 (£1,239)

4
**A Tiffany Favrile paper-
weight glass finger bowl
and under plate,** 1892-
1928, in clear glass
decorated with stylised
deep dusty-rose, amber
and green lotus blossoms
and leafage, d 18.5cm
(7¼in), *NY 11/12 May,*
$2,200 (£1,594)

5
**A set of twelve Tiffany
Favrile glass intaglio-
carved water goblets,**
1892-1928, inscribed, 18cm
(7in), *NY 17/18 Feb,*
$3,850 (£2,711)

6
**A Tiffany Favrile intaglio-
carved glass cabinet vase,**
1892-1928, in opaque to
clear lime-green glass,
the neck and shoulder
intaglio carved with
lozenge devices enclosing
leafage, inscribed, 10cm
(4in), *NY 24 Mar,*
$1,540 (£1,062)

7
**A silver-mounted glass
perfume vial,** Tiffany,
c.1919, decorated with
chocolate-brown and
lime-green stripes, the
neck with silver lip and
attached cap, inscribed
'LCT', 12cm (4¾in),
NY 24 Mar,
$1,100 (£759)

8
**A Tiffany Favrile cameo
glass vase,** 1892-1928, the
clear glass sides intaglio
carved with sprigs of
wild flowers and overlaid
in lavender, white and
green and cut with crocus
blossoms, 32.5cm (12¾in),
unsigned, *NY 24 Mar,*
$4,400 (£3,034)

9
**A Tiffany Favrile, glass
compote,** c.1905, in amber
iridescence decorated
with green leaves and
trailing vines, raised on
an amber iridescent
square stem, inscribed,
23.5cm (9¼in),
NY 11/12 May,
$1,540 (£1,116)

10
**A Tiffany Favrile, glass
decorated cabinet vase,**
c.1900, in ivory glass
decorated with silvery-
blue lappets and dark
blue scrollwork, inscribed,
9cm (3½in), *NY 11/12 May,*
$880 (£638)

11
**A Tiffany Favrile iridescent
glass vase,** 1918, milky
white glass with gold
lustre interior, finely
decorated with feathered
trails of green,
L 29/30 Nov,
£1,540 ($1,863)

12
**A carved and inlaid
iridescent glass vase,**
engraved 'L C Tiffany
Favrile', c.1905, applied
with patches and trails of
green carved as vine
leaves and trails with
peacock/gold lustre,
19.75cm (7¾in),
L 29/30 Nov,
£495 ($599)

1
A bronze lamp base,
Tiffany, 1899-1920, the
standard in the form of
two tiers of pierced
bulging leafage, raised
on an onion-form
support continuing to a
circular foot, 56cm (22in),
NY 24 Mar,
$2,530 (£1,745)

2
A bamboo lamp, Tiffany
Studios, *c*1900, with rich
streaked green leaves
against an opalescent
ground, the bronze base
in the form of a bamboo
shoot, 78cm (30¾in),
L 13 Apr,
£15,400 ($22,222)

3
A bronze lamp base with
leaded glass shade,
Tiffany Studios, *c*1910,
the shade with panels of
white and green
streaked glass, shade
stamped, 'Elows Studios',
39.5cm (15½in), *L 28 Sept,*
£407 ($529)

4
A Tiffany Favrile glass
and bronze lantern lamp,
1899-1920, the shade
with amber iridescent
turtleback tiles within
amber surrounds, the
cover with mottled amber
to mauve tiles, unsigned,
62cm (24½in),
NY 11/12 May,
$2,200 (£1,594)

5
A Tiffany Favrile glass
and bronze lamp base,
1899-1920, the six
elongated branches
ending in pod-form
cups, supporting opales-
cent glass socket
surrounds decorated in
green feathering, one
socket surround lacking,
one damaged, replaced
switch, 50.5cm (19⅞in),
NY 24 Mar,
$1,210 (£834)

6
A Tiffany Favrile glass
and bronze counter-
balance desk lamp, 1900-
20, the domed green
glass shade intaglio
carved with leafage,
h 42.5cm (16¾in), d 18cm
(7in), *NY 24 Mar,*
$4,180 (£2,883)

7
A Tiffany Favrile glass
and bronze counter-
balance desk lamp, 1900-
20, the lime-green shade
intaglio carved with a
band of leafage, h 37.5cm
(14¾in), d 18cm (7in),
NY 24 Mar,
$2,860 (£1,972)

8
A Tiffany Favrile red glass
cabinet vase, 1892-1928,
gourd form with bulging
neck and tomato-red
sides, the interior in
yellow iridescence,
unsigned, 5cm (1⅞in),
NY 24 Mar,
$2,090 (£1,441)

9
A Tiffany Favrile glass
moth ornament, 1899-
1920, with striated pale-
green and opalescent
body, mottled blue-grey
and pale-green wings set
with cypriote glass spots
and strips and amber
cabochon eyes, 19cm
(7½in), *NY 17 Nov,*
$1,980 (£1,584)

10
A Tiffany Favrile glass
and gilt-bronze humidor,
1892-1928, the caramel
sides decorated with two
bands of silver-blue and
amber iridescent lappets,
gilt-bronze cover,
inscribed, 19.5cm (7¾in),
NY 24 Mar,
$1,980 (£1,366)

11
A Tiffany Favrile glass
and bronze inkwell, 1902-
20, the sides set with
variously coloured mosaics
shading from pale lime
green to deep sapphire
blue, pale amber irides-
cent cover, 7.5cm (4in),
NY 24 Mar,
$4,675 (£3,224)

12
A Tiffany Favrile glass
and bronze two-branch
candlestick, 1892-1928,
with bell-form sockets
decorated with green
striated feather devices
edged in amber irides-
cence, 23cm (9in),
NY 11/12 May,
$2,090 (£1,514)

1   2   3

4   5   6

7   8   9

10   11   12

1
A Tiffany Favrile glass and bronze eighteen-light lily lamp, 1899-1920, each stem raising an amber iridescent floriform shade, one shade lacking, 51cm (20in), *NY 11/12 May*, $23,100 (£16,739)

2
A Tiffany Favrile glass and bronze five-light lamp, 1900-20, the shade supports hung with opalescent strands of tiles and raising green damascene shades, one shade lacking, one shade with upper rim chips, h 84cm (33in), d of shades 20cm (8in), *NY 24 Mar*, $13,750 (£9,483)

3
A Tiffany Favrile glass and bronze cherry blossom lamp, 1899-1920, the shade with an overall pattern of dusty-rose and white blossom and green leafage, base depatinated, h 52cm (20½in), d 39cm (15¼in), *NY 11/12 May*, $4,675 (£3,388)

4
A Tiffany Favrile glass and bronze flowering water lily lamp, 1900-20, with an overall pattern of pale dusty-rose, crimson and white against a blue, green and turquoise ground, h 68.5cm (27in), d 52cm (20½in), *NY 24 Mar*, $27,500 (£18,966)

5
A Tiffany Favrile glass and bronze laburnum lamp, 1900-20, with an overall pattern of golden blossoms pendent from mauve branches, mottled blue-grey ground, h 77.5cm (30½in), d 56cm (22in), *NY 24 Mar*, $44,000 (£30,345)

6
A Tiffany Favrile glass and gilt-bronze geometric lamp, 1900-20, with an overall pattern of lavender, blue and green against a milky-white ground, h 59.5cm (23½in), d 57cm (22½in), *NY 24 Mar*, $31,900 (£22,000)

7
A Tiffany Favrile glass and bronze turtleback tile border lamp, 1899-1920, the shade with bands of mottled green tiles set with a medial band of emerald green turtleback tiles, h 56cm (22in), d 41cm (16in), *NY 11/12 May*, $8,030 (£5,819)

8
A Tiffany Favrile glass and bronze cupola nasturtium lamp, 1900-20, in mottled shades of yellow, amber, crimson and salmon, the white trellis and mottled green leafage reserved against a mottled blue ground, h 58.3cm (23in), d 40.5cm (16in), *NY 24 Mar*, $18,700 (£12,897)

9
A Tiffany Favrile glass and bronze dragonfly lamp, 1899-1920, the shade of ochre dragonflies with red eyes and striated green and pink wings, set against a ground of mottled opalescent mint-green glass, base with replaced upper section, h 63.5cm (25in), d 50cm (20in), *NY 17/18 Feb*, $9,900 (£6,972)

10
A Tiffany Favrile glass and bronze oriental poppy floor lamp, 1900-20, with an overall pattern of golden-yellow and burnished gold blossoms with deep blue and purple centres, reserved against a pale green ground, base unsigned, h 196cm (77in), d 66cm (26in), *NY 24 Mar*, $57,200 (£39,448)

11
A Tiffany Favrile glass and gilt-bronze tulip floor lamp, 1899-1920, composed of a field of golden tulips against a mottled blue-green ground, h 164cm (64in), d 57cm (22½in), *NY 17/18 Feb*, $23,100 (£16,268)

1

2

3

4

5

6

8

7

9

10

11

1
A gold, diamond and ruby brooch, c.1900, the clover motif lightly engraved with the profile of a young woman wearing a headband of seven tiny diamonds and a small round ruby, *NY 5 June*, $770 (£575)

2
A gold and diamond brooch, c.1900, engraved and chased with the profile of a young woman with flowing tresses in whiplash style, studded with old-mine diamonds, *NY 17 Oct*, $1,430 (£1,202)

3
A gold and diamond clip, c.1900, the profile of a young woman framed by foliate scrollwork and decorated with several old European-cut diamonds, *NY 13 Apr*, $880 (£615)

4
A gold and diamond pendant-brooch, c.1900, engraved and chased with the head of a young woman in exotic head-dress, set with eight old-mine and rose-cut diamonds and suspending a pearl pendant, detachable, *NY 17 Oct*, $1,760 (£1,478)

5
A gold pendant, c.1900, of cartouche shape, depicting the profile of a young woman with flowing tresses, signed Zacha, *NY 13 Apr*, $715 (£500)

6
A gold, enamel and diamond flower brooch, c.1900, the stylised heart-shaped frame embellished with diamonds, the central floral spray heightened with translucent green and amber enamels, *NY 13 Apr*, $660 (£462)

7
A gold and plique-à-jour enamel brooch, c.1900, designed as the bust of a winged lady, wearing a rose-cut diamond collar suspending a pearl drop, *NY 13 Apr*, $3,025 (£2,115)

8
A plique-à-jour enamel and jewelled ship pendant-brooch, c.1900, the gold mount engraved at the base with dolphins beneath a diamond and ruby ship sailing on platinum waves, *NY 17 Oct*, $1,870 (£1,571)

9
A gold, pearl and plique-à-jour enamel pendant, c.1900, in the form of a single spray of berries, finely chased gold stem with four delicate leaves in green plique-à-jour enamel, 6.7cm (2⅝in), *L 29/30 Nov*, £880 ($1,065)

10
A gold plique-à-jour enamel brooch, c.1900, profile head of a young woman, headband and choker set with brilliants, background design of flowers in red and green plique-à-jour enamel, 4cm (1⅝in), *L 6 July*, £1,760 ($2,429)

11
A gold, black, opal and enamel necklace, c.1900, the large opal applied on both sides with chased gold irises and leaves, the latter in translucent green and brown enamel, 50.8cm (20in), *NY 17 Oct*, $17,600 (£14,789)

12
A French plique-à-jour enamel and diamond leaf brooch, c.1900, the maple leaf of platinum and gold applied with shaded green to gold plique-à-jour enamel, *NY 17 Oct*, $4,950 (£4,160)

13
A jewelled plique-à-jour enamel bracelet, c.1900, composed of gold shaped-oval serpent links, centring shaded plique-à-jour enamel wings alternately set with round rubies and round diamonds, *NY 13 Apr*, $2,750 (£1,923)

1

2

3

5

6

4

7

8

9

10

11

12

13

1
A gold and turquoise pendant, Theodor Fahrner, c.1910, the large turquoise matrix suspended from an elongated loop hung with a slender gold ring, central diamond chip, 4.2cm (1⅝in), *L 29/30 Nov,* **£220 ($266)**

2
A silver and enamel pendant, J Cromer Watts, c.1920, the central blue stone amulet carved in the form of an Egyptian cat, detailed in blue, turquoise and white enamel, 4.7cm (1⅞in), *L 6 July,* **£308 ($425)**

3
An enamelled pendant, Limoges, c.1920, shield shaped in gold frame, depicting the profile of a young girl, pearl drop, 5cm (2in), *L 6 July,* **£231 ($319)**

4
A silver and mother-of-pearl pendant and chain, attributed to the Guild of Handicraft Ltd, c.1905, the hammered openwork quatrefoil body set with a central mother-of-pearl panel, 3cm (1¼in), *L 13 Apr,* **£209 ($302)**

5
A plique-à-jour enamel, diamond and sapphire-mounted pendant neck-lace, I Gautrait, c.1900, the triangular pendant with the head of a maiden framed by leaves with cream, yellow and green enamel details against a pale yellow and mauve enamel ground, *NY 17/18 Feb,* **$14,300 (£10,070)**

6
A gold and emerald brooch, probably by Henry Wilson, c.1905, the fan-shaped surmount in an openwork design of roses and leaves set with a relief of the head of Mercury, *L 6 Dec,* **£660 ($832)**

7
A gold and moonstone pendant necklace, Bent Gabrielsen, c.1956, the pendant with cabochon moonstone centred by concentric gold rings, stamped Denmark, 23.5cm (9¼in), *NY 17 Nov,* **$2,090 (£1,672)**

8
A cloak clasp, Artificers Guild, c.1920, the two pierced square motifs applied with beading, scrolls and ropework, central milky-green stones, silver-coloured metal, w 13cm (5⅛in), *L 29/30 Nov,* **£572 ($692)**

9
A silver buckle, Chester, 1902, pierced, cast and chased with the profile of a young woman, a border of irises and dragonflies, maker's mark 'AJS', 7.7cm (3in), *L 6 July* **£253 ($349)**

10
A silver and enamel belt buckle, Lawrence Emmanuel, 1909, open strapwork design detailed with blue-green enamel, w 6.5cm (2½in), *L 28 Sept,* **£66 ($86)**

11
A French jewel-mounted jade card case, Cartier, c.1930, the front set with a carved red stone leaf mounted on a diamond-set stand, 9cm (3½in), *NY 21 June,* **$2,970 (£2,184)**

12
A French gold and enamel compact, Cartier, Paris, 1925, enamelled Chinese red on all sides and with gilded scroll borders in the Oriental style, 6.7cm (2⅝in), *NY 21 June,* **$3,300 (£2,426)**

13
An enamel and diamond rectangular compact, c.1925, enamelled black on both sides with gold borders and diamond-set monogram, three diamond-set thumb-pieces, *NY 20/21 June,* **$1,870 (£1,350)**

1   2   3   4

5

6   7

8   9   10

11   12   13

1
A silver dish, Hukin and Heath, London, 1881, designed by Christopher Dresser, w 19cm (7½in), *L 29/30 Nov*, £418 ($506)

2
An electroplated double sugar basket, Hukin and Heath, c1884, the design attributed to Christopher Dresser, with two spoons, 15.5cm (6in), *L 13 Apr*, £165 ($238)

3
An electroplated-mounted glass jug, Hukin and Heath, 1880s, the design attributed to Christopher Dresser, 22.5cm (8¾in), *L 13 Apr*, £82 ($118)

4
A copper-plated silver-mounted jug, Heath and Middleton, London, 1892, the design attributed to Christopher Dresser, 42cm (16.5in), *L 13 Apr*, £660 ($952)

5
A silver-mounted claret jug, Hukin and Heath, London, 1881, designed by Christopher Dresser 22cm (8½in), *L 13 Apr*, £1,045 ($1,504)

6
A silver and turquoise buckle, designed by C R Ashbee and made for his wife Janet, Guild of Handicraft Ltd, c1897, 8.25cm (3¼in), *L 29/30 Nov*, £4,510 ($5,457)

7
Six silver and enamel coffee spoons, Liberty and Co, Birmingham, 1902, each finial detailed in turquoise, green and orange enamels, in fitted box for Edward & Sons, Glasgow, 11cm (4⅜in), *L 6 July*, £374 ($516)

8
A 'Cymric' silver and enamel spoon, Liberty and Co, Birmingham, 1902, designed by Archibald Knox, broad shallow bowl enamelled in blue and green, 12.2cm (4⅞in), *L 16 Feb*, £594 ($833)

9
A 'Cymric' silver and enamel belt buckle, Liberty and Co, Birmingham, 1903, designed by Archibald Knox, 9.2cm (3⅝in), *L 6 July*, £319 ($440)

10
A 'Cymric' silver and enamel vase, Liberty and Co, Birmingham, 1902, the design attributed to Archibald Knox, 19.2cm (7⅝in), *L 13 Apr*, £4,180 ($6,032)

11
A silver and enamel vesta case, Liberty and Co, Birmingham, 1906, designed by Archibald Knox, 4.5cm (1¾in), *L 6 July*, £93 ($128)

12
A 'Cymric' silver and enamel frame, Liberty and Co, Birmingham 1903, h 23cm (9⅛in), *L 16 Feb*, £3,740 ($5,243)

13
A silver and enamel chamberstick, Liberty and Co, Birmingham, cast with delicate entrelac design, richly enamelled in blue-green turquoise and purple with touches of gilt, d 18cm (7⅛in), *L 29/30 Nov*, £7,700 ($9,317)

14
A silver and enamel clock, Liberty and Co, 1902, the design attributed to Archibald Knox, the face enamelled in rich blue-green, h 16.5cm (6½in), *L 29/30 Nov*, £4,400 ($5,324)

15
A silver-coloured-metal mounted copper rose bowl, Liberty and Co, c1905, the design attributed to Oliver Baker, 34.7cm (13¾in), *L 13 Apr*, £990 ($1,429)

16
A silver and copper clock, William Hutton and Sons Ltd, London, 1899, the lower rectangular body inset with a copper panel, 31.2cm (12⅜in), *L 29/30 Nov*, £770 ($932)

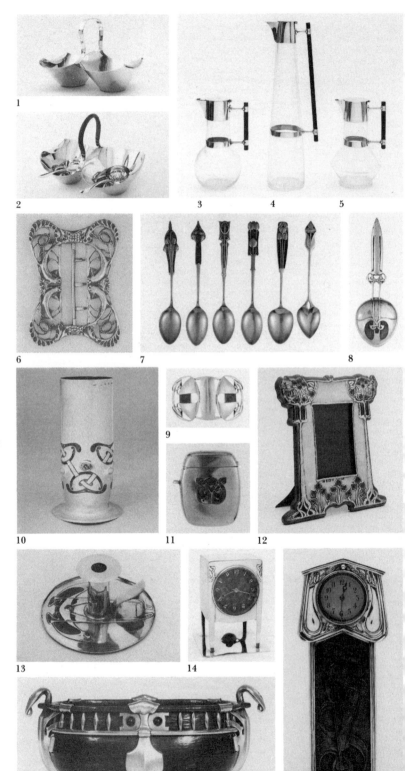

1
A silver sugar caster, William Hutton and Sons, London, 1902, cast with rectangular panelling set with rose-coloured cabochons, stamped 'Mappin and Webb', 19cm (7⅛in), *L 13 Apr,* **£572 ($825)**

2
A silver frame, A & J Zimmerman, Birmingham, 1903, border cast with irises and entwined leaves against a 'wicker' ground, blue velvet back, 20cm (7⅞in), *L 29/30 Nov,* **£264 ($319)**

3
A set of four silver vases, Gilbert Marks, London, 1897, repoussé and hammered with sprays of bluebells, harebells, cornflowers and poppies, 20.7cm (8¼in), *L 13 Apr,* **£2,860 ($4,127)**

4
A silver vase, Gilbert Marks, London, 1901, slender flower form on knopped stem and raised circular foot, the body chased with four tall tudor roses, 28.7cm (11¼in), *L 29/30 Nov,* **£1,760 ($2,130)**

5
A presentation bowl, Omar Ramsden, the body 1920, the cover 1922, in Arts & Crafts style, the shallow circular bowl chased with leaping fish and rose motifs on a textured watery ground, d 45.7cm (18in), *P 17 Oct,* **£3,850 ($4,813)**

6
Six teaspoons, six coffee spoons, a caddy spoon and tongs, Omar Ramsden, London, 1923-4, square section hammered stems, central twist, *L 6 July,* **£440 ($607)**

7
A silver and enamel cigarette box, Omar Ramsden, London 1937, the lid pierced with a galleon in full sail, h 6.25cm (2½in), *L 29/30 Nov,* **£660 ($799)**

8
A hammered silver bowl, Sybil Dunlop, London, 1928, the rim applied with a row of open foliate cartouches, each set with a square blue stone cabochon, d 18cm (7in), *L 13 Apr,* **£550 ($794)**

9
A silver spoon, Sybil Dunlop, London, 1937, the elliptical finial set with elliptical bluestone cabochon, hammered bowl, 13.2cm (5¼in), *L 16 Feb,* **£99 ($138)**

10
An electroplated three-piece 'cube' tea set, Leicester, *c* 1925-30, comprising teapot with integral wicker-covered handle, cream jug and sugar basin, patent details, 12cm (4¾in), *L 16 Feb,* **£462 ($648)**

11
A silver sugar caster, H G Murphy, London, 1928, the beehive-shaped pierced cover with coil finial, the base with a band of beading, 15cm (5⅞in), *L 29/30 Nov,* **£396 ($479)**

12
A Scottish silver sugar caster, Edinburgh, 1934, applied with raised strips in chevron design, hammered ground, stepped base, cog wheel finial, star-cut underside, maker's mark 'WAD', 19cm (7½in), *L 13 Apr,* **£440 ($635)**

13
A set of table silver, Charles Boyton, London, 1936, flared flat sectioned stems, stepped finials, 80 pieces, *L 16 Feb,* **£2,750 ($3,856)**

14
A silver and gilt coffee pot, London, 1973, gently tapered, long tapering spout, gilt at the base and hinged cover, dark wood handle and flat knob, overall light stippled texture, maker's mark 'JMW', 28.2cm (11⅛in), *L 29/30 Nov,* **£363 ($439)**

1
A pair of silver candlesticks,
F Boucheron, Paris,
*c*1890, designed and
signed by F Guillaume,
each in the form a nude
maiden, the bases
weighted with wood,
31.8cm (12½in),
NY 11/12 May,
$6,050 (£4,384)

2
**A silver-plated three-piece
tea service,** designed by
Paul Follot, *c*1900, all
with exaggerated angular
handles and gadrooned
lids, teapot 29cm (11in),
NY 17 Nov,
$2,860 (£2,288)

3
A small beaker, Puiforcat,
*c*1930, 8.5cm (3⅜in),
L 6 July,
£154 ($213)

4
**A bonbon dish in silver
and ebony,** Jean Puiforcat,
*c*1930, 12oz 10dwt (390gr),
12.5cm (4⅞in), *M 7 Oct,*
FF 5,550 (£480; $595)

5
A silver cigarette box,
Puiforcat, *c*1930, 18cm
(7⅛in), *M 11 Mar,*
FF 3,552 (£298; $444)

6
A silver and ebony tea set,
Puiforcat, *c*1935, com-
prising a teapot, a hot
water jug, milk jug and
sugar bowl and cover,
h 18cm (7⅛in), *M 7 Oct,*
FF 22,200 (£1,919; $2,382)

7
**A parcel-gilt four-piece tea
and coffee service with
matching tray,** Puiforcat,
Paris, *c*1937, each of
flared cylindrical form
with recessed and gilt
band near foot, wooden
strap handles, 59oz 16dwt
(1,859gr), h 15.3cm (6in),
NY 11/12 May,
$5,225 (£3,786)

8
**A silver-gilt punch bowl
and ladle,** Jean Després,
*c*1935, the base and
handle with chain decor-
ation, engraved signa-
ture, d 20cm (7⅞in),
M 11 Mar,
FF 2,886 (£243; $361)

9
A silver box and cover,
Jean Després, *c*1935,
applied with geometric
motifs, engraved signa-
ture, 8.5cm (3⅜in),
M 11 Mar,
FF 5,106 (£429; $638)

10
A silver cigarette box,
*c*1930, with an abstract
form of a hockey player,
in enamel, 10.7cm (4¼in),
M 11 Mar,
FF 3,552 (£298; $444)

11
**A gold cigarette case of
reeded rectangular form,**
Cartier, 1927, decorated
with black enamel borders
and engraved with a
monogram, importer's
mark, 11.2cm (4¼in),
L 9 July,
£1,650 ($2,261)

12
**A silvered-metal wine
cooler,** Christofle, *c*1934,
designed by Luc Lanel
for the Compagnie
Générale Transatlan-
tique, commissioned for
the SS Normandie, 21cm
(8¼in), *NY 18 July,*
$1,980 (£1,511)

1

2

3

4

5

6

7

8

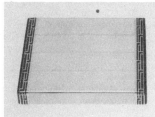
9

10

11

12

1
A silver inkwell, Wiener
Werkstatte, designed by
Josef Hoffmann, c.1904,
of bowed triangular
section, pierced grid
sides, monogram marks
and import mark for
1904, 6.5cm (2⅝in),
L 13 Apr,
£2,640 ($3,810)

2
**A nickel-plated bowl with
handle,** in the style of
Josef Hoffmann, c.1905,
the handle and rim
pierced with squares,
22cm (8⅞in), *M 7 Oct,*
FF 6,660 (£576; $715)

3
An ashtray, Wiener
Werkstatte, designed by
Josef Hoffmann, c.1905,
11cm (4¼in), *M 7 Oct,*
FF 26,640 (£2,302; $2,855)

4
A bottle stopper, Weiner
Werkstatte, designed by
Josef Hoffmann, c.1905,
bulbous, hammered sur-
face, beaded rim, silver-
coloured metal, 3.2cm
(1¼in), *L 16 Feb,*
£275 ($386)

5
**Two silvered metal
candlesticks,** each marked,
Argentor, after a design
by Josef Hoffmann,
c.1910, the tall stems
pierced with chequers,
circular bases, 28cm (11in),
L 16 Feb,
£605 ($848)

6
**A pair of glass flower
baskets,** Wiener
Werkstatte, designed by
Josef Hoffmann, c.1905,
25.2cm (9⅞in), *M 11 Mar,*
FF 9,435 (£793; $1,179)

7
A bottle stopper, designed
by Josef Hoffmann,
c.1910, hammered surface,
monogrammed 'JH' and
'WW', *M 11 Mar,*
FF 3,885 (£326; $486)

8
A silver match box,
Wiener Werkstatte,
designed by Josef Hoff-
mann, c.1905, decorated
and pierced with stylised
flowers, 7.5cm (3in),
M 11 Mar,
FF 9,990 (£839; $1,249)

9
**A five-piece silver coffee
service,** Wiener Werk-
statte, designed by Josef
Hoffmann, c.1925, each of
lobed circular section
with scalloped edge,
d of tray 45.1cm (17¾in),
NY 17/18 Feb,
$21,450 (£15,106)

10
A silver-plate cup, Wiener
Werkstatte, designed by
Josef Hoffman, c.1920,
hammered surface,
18.5cm (7¼in), *M 11 Mar,*
FF 62,160 (£5,224; $7,770)

11
**A silver and enamel
basket,** Wiener Werkstatte,
designed by Josef Hoff-
mann, c.1920, each side
with a cabochon medallion
in white enamel on a
blue background,
w 26.5cm (10½in), *M 7 Oct,*
FF 77,700 (£6,716; $8,337)

12
**A silver-plate and lapis
vase,** designed by
Koloman Moser, c.1905,
of conical winged shape,
monogrammed on base
'KM', 15cm (5⅞in),
M 7 Oct,
FF 18,870 (£1,631; $2,025)

13
A silver-plate vase,
Wiener Werkstatte,
designed by Josef Hoff-
mann, c.1910, hammered
surface, 28.5cm (11¼in),
M 7 Oct,
FF 14,430 (£1,247; $1,548)

14
**A silver sugar bowl and
tongs,** Wiener Werkstatte,
designed by Josef Hoff-
mann, c.1910, hammered
finish, 5.2cm (2⅛in),
M 7 Oct,
FF 18,870 (£1,631; $2,025)

15
**An electroplated electric
kettle,** Cehal, a design by
Peter Behrens, c.1910,
faceted globular body,
wicker-covered handle,
24.5cm (9⅝in),
L 29/30 Nov,
£253 ($306)

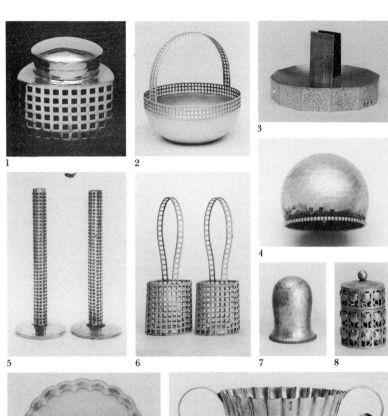

1

2

3

4

5

6

7

8

9

10

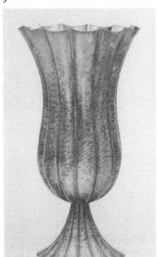

13

14

15

11

12

1
A set of silver tableware, Georg Jensen, Copenhagen, in the 'Acorn' pattern, 84 pieces, 102oz 12dwt (3,190gr), *NY 11/12 May,* $3,850 (£2,790)

2
A set of tableware, Georg Jensen, designed 1930s, silver-coloured metal, stamped, *L 29/30 Nov,* £3,080 ($3,727)

3
A set of silver tableware, Georg Jensen, Copenhagen, in the 'Parallel' pattern, 74 pieces, 81oz 8dwt (2,531gr), *NY 17 Nov,* $7,150 (£5,720)

4
A set of silver tableware, A Dragsted, Copenhagen, 60 pieces, 65oz 4dwt (2,027gr), *NY 17 Nov,* $1,430 (£1,144)

5
A silver centrepiece bowl, Georg Jensen, Copenhagen, 1919, designed by Johan Rohde, 94oz 4dwt (2,929gr), h 22cm (8⅝in), d 34.5cm (13½in), *NY 17 Nov,* $5,280 (£4,224)

6
A circular tureen and cover, Georg Jensen, imported London, 1925, the shallow bowl with lightly hammered finish below a plain border interrupted by beading, 38oz 2dwt (1,184gr), d 24.7cm (9¾in), *C 3 July,* £770 ($1,045)

7
A silver bowl, Georg Jensen, imported London, 1931, designed by Harald Neilsen, manufacturer's and designer's monograms, d 18cm (7⅛in), *L 16 Feb,* £165 ($231)

8
A pair of silver two-light candelabra, Georg Jensen, Copenhagen, with reeded foliate branches terminating in faceted tulip-form sconces, 95oz 12dwt, (2,973gr), 21cm (8¼in), *NY 17 Nov,* $3,960 (£3,168)

9
A silver three-piece coffee service, Georg Jensen, Copenhagen, c1925, h 15.2cm (6in), 16oz (497gr), *NY 17/18 Feb,* $880 (£620)

10
A silver water jug, Georg Jensen, c1925, hammered surface, 26oz 4dwt (814gr), 26.7cm (10½in), *NY 11/12 May,* $1,870 (£1,355)

11
A pair of silver candlesticks, Georg Jensen, 1938-44, designed by Sigvard Bernadotte, fixed nozzles, 24oz (746gr), 24.8cm (9¾in), *NY 18 July,* $1,870 (£1,427)

12
A silver centrepiece bowl, Georg Jensen, Copenhagen, c1950, designed by Henning Koppel, the smooth concave sheet supported by an openwork foot, 102oz 12dwt (3,190gr), 15.9cm (6¼in), *NY 11/12 May,* $4,400 (£3,188)

13
A pair of silver two-light candelabra, Georg Jensen, Copenhagen, c1955, designed by Henning Koppel, 55oz 4dwt (1,716gr), h 8cm (3⅛in), *NY 11/12 May,* $2,750 (£1,993)

14
A coffee pot, Georg Jensen, c1930, designed by Harald Neilsen, fruit finial, dark stained, silver-coloured metal, 24cm (9⅜in), *L 13 Apr,* £374 ($540)

15
A silver teapot, Bulgari, Rome, 1972, of conical form with hinged, domed lid, 33oz 4dwt, (1,032gr), 11.2cm (4⅜in), *NY 11/12 May,* $1,650 (£1,196)

16
An Italian silver vase, 20th cent, sold with twelve Italian silver cups, early 20th cent, 21.6 and 3.8cm (8½ and 1½in), 51oz (1,586gr), *NY 18 July,* $880 (£672)

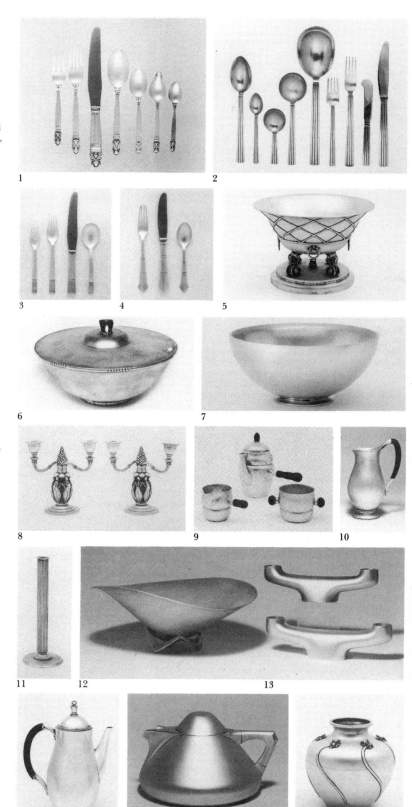

1

A pewter dressing mirror, WMF, c.1900, circular, swivel-mounted in support, cast as a young woman with arms upstretched, 49cm (19¼in), L 6 July, £374 ($516)

2

A pewter centrepiece with blue glass liner, WMF, c.1900, pierced and cast with butterflies and tendrils, w 40.5cm (16in), L 6 July, £396 ($546)

3

An electroplated pewter-mounted green glass decanter and stopper, WMF marks, c.1900, 39cm (15¼in), L 6 July, £220 ($304)

4

An electroplated pewter candlestick, WMF, c.1900, cast as a young woman in clinging robes, two large stems spreading from behind her terminating in 'bud' candle-holders, 25.7cm (10⅛in), L 29/30 Nov, £418 ($506)

5

A pewter candlestick, Kayserzinn, c.1900, possibly designed by Hugo Leven, slender trumpet cast with formalised stems and leaves, shaped undulating drip pan supported in three branches, drilled for electricity, 42cm (16½in), L 28 Sept, £352 ($458)

6

A pewter oil lamp, Kayserzinn, c.1900, on a long trumpet-shaped base, decorated in light relief with flowers, 25.7cm (10⅛in), M 11 Mar, FF 2,664 (£224; $333)

7

A 'Tudric' pewter tea and coffee set, Liberty and Co, c.1905, designed by Archibald Knox, comprising teapot, coffee pot, hot water jug, sugar basin and milk jug, each cast with formalised leaves, L 16 Feb, £572 ($802)

8

A hammered pewter box, Liberty and Co, c.1905, designed by Archibald Knox, stamped, 12.2cm (4¾in), L 6 July, £286 ($395)

9

A pair of 'Tudric' pewter candlesticks, Liberty and Co, c.1905, designed by Rex Silver, 15.5cm (6⅛in), L 6 July, £352 ($486)

10

A pair of brass altar vases, Hardman, c.1900, after a design by A W N Pugin, the flattened ovoid body set with blue and green enamelled panels of stylised foliage, 26.5cm (10⅜in), L 29/30 Nov, £154 ($186)

11

A pair of wrought-iron candlesticks, c.1910, the design attributed to Edward Spencer, each with domed foot supporting a faceted stem with four branches linked by a twisted collar, hammered finish, 42.5cm (16¾in), L 29/30 Nov, £352 ($426)

12

A copper and brass spirit kettle on stand, c.1900, the kettle with angled brass spout and detachable cover with insect finial on hexagonal foliate stem, 87.6cm (34½in), C 2 Nov, £187 ($239)

1
A German chromium-
plated zeppelin shaker,
*c*1935, the compartment
containing four tea-
spoons, 30.5cm (12in),
M 7 Oct,
FF 8,880 (£768; $953)

2
A gilt bronze barometer/
thermometer/clock,
Gustave Keller, *c*1900,
15cm (6in), *M 11 Mar,*
FF 7,770 (£653; $971)

3
A bronze shell-mounted
crab inkwell, Tiffany,
1892-1902, the crab with
hinged back opening to
a small compartment,
his two claws holding a
bucket with hinged
shell-mounted lid,
21.5cm (8½in),
NY 17/18 Feb,
$2,090 (£1,472)

4
A pair of bronze 'bamboo'
candlesticks, Tiffany,
1899-1920, each cast as a
bamboo reed with base
split to eight segments,
26cm (10¼in), *NY 18 July,*
$2,200 (£1,679)

5
An enamel-on-copper
covered circular box,
Tiffany, 1904-14, salmon
orange against a ground
shading from deep purple
to pale pink, inscribed
Louis C Tiffany SC323
and 22469, d 16cm (6¼in),
NY 24 Mar,
$3,080 (£2,124)

6
A large patinated bronze
lamp, Tiffany & Co,
*c*1900, in the form of a
giant single flower, stem
entwined with slender
scrolling leaves, 248cm
(97⅝in), *L 29/30 Nov,*
£12,100 ($14,641)

7
An enamel-on-copper vase,
Tiffany, 1904-14, the
upper section pierced
with green and amber
foliage above green,
lavender and amber
calla lilies, the ground
shading from sapphire
to green and amber,
33.5cm (13¼in),
NY 24 Mar,
$39,600 (£27,310)

8
An enamel-on-copper vase,
Fauré, Limoges, *c*1920,
delicately enamelled
with pendant flowering
trumpet vines and
foliage in shades of green,
ochre and rust reserved
against an emerald-
green, sapphire-blue
and sky-blue ground,
24cm (9½in),
NY 11/12 May,
$1,320 (£957)

9
An enamel-on-copper vase,
Fauré, Limoges, *c*1925,
enamelled in medium
and low relief with
irregular panels of
chevrons in shades of
salmon, yellow, white,
cranberry and ochre,
dent to base, 25cm
(9¾in), *NY 11/12 May,*
$2,200 (£1,594)

10
A patinated metal vase,
inscribed 'Jean Dunand',
*c*1903, the coppery vessel
patinated with geometric
devices and snowy
patterns in silver metal,
worn, 28cm (11in),
NY 11/12 May,
$5,775 (£4,185)

11
A patinated metal vase,
1920s, spherical, geo-
metric decoration, 17cm
(6¾in), *L 6 July,*
£253 ($349)

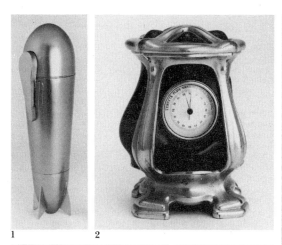

1

2

3

4   5   6

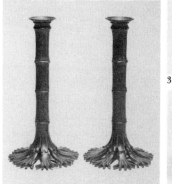

7   8   9

10   11

1
A large bronze inkstand, Raoul Larche, c1900, of a young woman sitting on a covered rock, signed and with foundry mark 'Siot Decauville Fondeur Paris', FF 33,300 (£2,798; $4,163)

2
A gilt-bronze and ivory figural inkstand, French, c1900, the base cast with foliage below two circular inkwells with hinged leaf-moulded covers flanking a young maiden, 34cm (13½in), NY 17 Nov, $1,650 (£1,320)

3
A gilt-bronze figural lamp, Loie Fuller, by Raoul Larche, c1900, representing a dancer, signed and with foundry mark 'Siot Decauville fondeur Paris' 32.5cm (12¾in), M 11 Mar, FF 37,740 (£3,171; $4,718)

4
A gilt-bronze figural lamp, Loie Fuller, after François-Raoul Larche, early 20th cent, the magician of light extending her arms from which billow her draperies, hiding two light sockets, inscribed 'Raoul Larche' and with foundry marks, NY 11/12 May, $19,250 (£13,949)

5
A polychromed bronze and ivory figural lamp, 'Parachute Lady', after R W Lange, c1925, the young woman in short full-skirted costume wearing a flight cap, inscribed, 84cm (33in), NY 17 Nov, $6,875 (£5,560)

6
A silvered and gilt-bronze figure of Nature unveiling herself before Science, after Louis-Ernest Barrias, c1900, inscribed 'E Barrias' and impressed with circular foundry mark 'Susse Frères Editeurs Paris', 59.5cm (23in), NY 17/18 Feb, $4,125 (£2,905)

7
An Austrian polychromed and parcel-gilt bronze figure of a snake dancer, early 20th cent, the young woman wearing a beaded halter and wrap skirt, green onyx base, 40.5cm (16in), NY 17/18 Feb, $825 (£581)

8
A gilt-bronze figure 'Joueuse de flute', chiselled mark 'A Léonard sculp', c1900, foundry mark 'Susse Fondeurs Paris', 50cm (19⅝in), M 7 Oct, FF 66,600 (£5,756; $7,146)

9
'Bacchantes', a bronze dancing girl, Le Faguays, c1925, gilt-bronze, with green cold-painted skirt, dancing with a pole entwined with grapes and vines, coppery cold-painted details, mottled black-brown stepped marble base, 55.7cm (22in), L 13 Apr, £1,980 ($2,857)

10
A bronze, gold and ivory dancer, 'D'Angkor', Colinet, c1920, signed, 65cm (25½in), M 11 Mar, FF 183,150 (£15,391; $22,894)

11
A bronze and ivory dancing girl, Omeath, draped costume with traces of pale blue metallic cold painting, pale green marble base with cluster of three gilt bronze balls at one corner, 27.2cm (10¾in), L 29/30 Nov, £385 ($466)

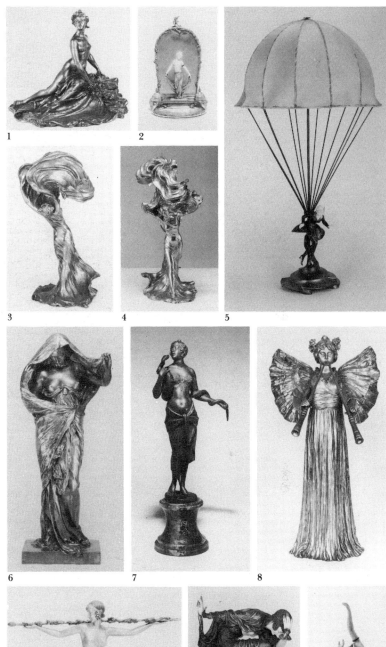

1
'Tamara', a dancer in
bronze and ivory,
Chiparus, c.1925, the
costume decorated in
pearls, the head and
hands in ivory, the base
in red marble, 65cm
(25½ in), *M 11 Mar,*
FF 52,170 (£4,384; $6,521)

2
A bronze and ivory figure,
Chiparus, c.1925, the
young woman kneeling
with one arm above her
head, in gold cold-
painted skirt and
jewelled bodice, red,
silver and coppery-gold
cold-painting, mottled
brown marble base,
56.5cm (22⅛ in), *L 13 Apr,*
£11,000 ($15,873)

3
A bronze and ivory figure
of a dancer, after
Demetre Chiparus,
c.1925, her head and
hands of ivory, green,
silvered and gilt patinas,
red marble base, ivory
with cracks, 50.5cm
(19¾ in), *NY 17/18 Feb,*
$7,700 (£5,423)

4
A silvered-bronze figure of
a woman, 'Egyptian
Dancer', after Demetre
Chiparus, c.1925, on a
truncated ochre and
verde antico marble
plinth, figure rubbed,
56.5cm (22¼ in),
NY 11/12 May,
$2,860 (£2,072)

5
A gilt-bronze figure of a
dancer, after Demetre
Chiparus, c.1925, the
figure of a woman
standing in halter and
long fringed skirt, onyx
plinth, depatinated,
plinth chipped, 40.5cm
(16in), *NY 11/12 May,*
$1,650 (£1,196)

6
A bronze and ivory figure,
Chiparus, 1930s, close
fitting bodice and full
skirt, green cold-painted
with gilt and polished
bronze details, mottled
grey-green marble base,
56.5cm (22¼ in),
L 29/30 Nov,
£3,520 ($4,259)

7
A bronze and ivory figure,
bronze marked 'F Preiss',
c.1910-21, standing semi-
naked, one knee resting
on tree stump, foundry
mark 'PK', 22.5cm
(8⅞ in), *L 28 Sept,*
£550 ($715)

8
A polychromed-bronze and
ivory figure of a dancer,
Con Bric, after Fritz
Preiss, c.1925, green
onyx truncated base with
black onyx bands, h 34cm
(13½ in), *NY 17 Nov,*
$3,300 (£2,640)

9
A cold-painted bronze and
ivory figure, 'Autumn
Dancer' after Fritz Preiss,
c.1930, in short blue-
green waisted tunic with
long sweeping trail and
turbanned cap, green
and black onyx socle and
octagonal base, 37.5cm
(14¾ in), *NY 17 Nov,*
$4,400 (£3,520)

10
A sculpture in bronze and
ivory, 'The Flame
Leaper', marked 'F Preiss',
c.1930, the socle in black
marble, 35.7cm (14in),
M 7 Oct,
FF 61,050 (£5,277; $6,550)

11
A bronze and ivory figure
of a young woman leaning
on a gate, Preiss, 1930s,
cold-painted pink-silver
shirt and silver blue
casual trousers, green
marble base, 25.5cm
(10⅛ in), *L 29/30 Nov,*
£1,870 ($2,263)

12
A carved ivory figure of a
little boy, base carved 'F
Preiss', 1930s, standing
naked with bow drawn,
on brown marble base,
18.2cm (7¼ in), *L 13 Apr,*
£990 ($1,429)

1

2

3

4

5

6

7

8

9

10

11

12

1
A bronze and ivory figure, Philippe, 1930s, a young woman in bobbed hair standing in silver costume studded with green and 'diamond' stones at the neck, on circular mottled green marble base, 42cm (16½in), *L 29/30 Nov*, £4,180 ($5,058)

2
A cold-painted bronze bather, Zach, *c*1930, in casual pose, green costume, rectangular mottled grey marble base, signed in the maquette, 32cm (12⅝in), *L 28 Sept*, £660 ($858)

3
A gilt-bronze figure of an Egyptian dancer, Isis, after Claire Jeanne Roberte Colinet, *c*1925, inscribed 'Cl J F Colinet, black marble base, 56cm (22in), *NY 17 Nov*, $4,950 (£3,960)

4
A parcel-gilt bronze and soapstone figure of a serenading Pierrot, early 20th cent, his head and hands of soapstone, green patina with gilt and silvered highlights, inscribed 'Gazan', impressed foundry marks, 54cm (21¼in), *NY 17/18 Feb*, $2,475 (£1,743)

5
A bronze and ivory figure of a ski jumper, French, *c*1925, the bronze figure with ivory face, the jump in white and mottled black and beige onyx, greenish brown patina, minor chips to base, 35cm (13¾in), *NY 17/18 Feb*, $1,650 (£1,162)

6
A cold-painted bronze figure, Lorenzl, 1930s, nude, in dancing pose, holding a large alabaster dish, triangular striped marble base, marked, 23.5cm (9¼in), *L 16 Feb*, £451 ($632)

7
A parcel-silvered bronze mask, Boris Lovett-Lorski, *c*1930, cast on an angle, inscribed 'Lorski', black onyx base, chipped, 19cm (7½in), *NY 11/12 May*, $6,325 (£4,583)

8
A patinated lamp with glass shade, marked 'Fayral', shade marked 'Daum Nancy France', *c*1930, 51cm (20⅛in), *L 6 July*, £902 ($1,245)

9
A carved ivory nude figure, *c*1930, kneeling to drink from a bowl in her hands, 9.5cm (3¾in), *L 6 July*, £495 ($683)

10
A bronze study of a boatman, Ouline, *c*1903, straining his foot against a rock, marked, stamped 'Bronze', w 56.5cm (22¼in), *L 16 Feb*, £253 ($355)

11
A large bronze study of a youth, Le Faguays, *c*1930, in brief loincloth, bracing against a slender pole, green patinated, black marble base, signed, 75cm (29½in), *L 16 Feb*, £572 ($802)

1   2   3

4   5   6

7

8   9

10   11

British Art Pottery and Studio Ceramics

JANE TAYLOR

This relatively new field in the established auction market comprises two distinct categories of British ceramics. The first—and more widely recognized—is that of late 19th century art pottery. Catering for a public educated in the principles of the Arts and Crafts movement as taught by Ruskin and William Morris, many of the major potteries funded studios which produced individually decorated items rather than mass-produced factory wares. One of the first was established in the early 1870s by Doulton at their Lambeth base. Many major potteries (Wedgwood, Minton and Pilkington among them) followed suit, either by directly financing and establishing a studio or by employing outside artists to decorate their own wares. Smaller factories, operating as studio-workshops run by industrially trained potters, flourished by the end of the century, as did studios run by artists like William de Morgan and the Martin brothers who carried out all the various processes themselves.

The second category, that of 20th-century studio ceramics, is far newer to the saleroom. Although its beginnings are generally ascribed to Bernard Leach in the early 1920s, there were already a few potters working independently in their studios before Leach started his own pottery at St Ives, in Cornwall. Leach, visited Japan in 1909 where he was introduced to the tea ceremony and the traditions of Japanese ceramics. These so fascinated him that he turned his attention to pottery. On his return to England Leach started his own pottery at St Ives in 1920 with the help of his friend and fellow-potter Shoji Hamada. There he produced not only wares which were intended to be within the reach of most pockets, but also 'specials' which were made for exhibition or on commission. Many of Leach's pupils,such as Michael Cardew, went on to start their own potteries. Meanwhile William Staite Murray was producing his forceful brush-decorated pots. These were annually exhibited in London throughout the 1920s and 1930s, and, being considered works of art, were highly priced.

In 1938 Lucie Rie arrived in London from Vienna. Trained in the traditions of the Wiener Werkstätte and initially finding little sympathy for her work in Britain, she made functional wares during the late 1940s and the 1950s, moving on to the fine glazed or sgraffito work which she is still producing today. In 1946 she was joined by Hans Coper, who was beginning to produce his own sculptural forms, for which he is now so well-known, by the early 1950s. It must be remembered that most potters and those interested in ceramics at this time were totally steeped in the orientalism of Bernard Leach and his followers. By 1966 Coper was teaching at the Royal College of Art and was to influence a new generation of potters who were to break away from the traditions of Leach.

Studio potters of the last twenty years have gradually become more concerned with colour, pattern and surface decoration and with their relation to sculpture or form. Styles, techniques and materials are extremely diverse: porcelain, earthenware, stoneware; casting, throwing, laminating lacquer, lustre and raku—all are used.

The markets for art pottery and studio ceramics are very different. Nineteenth century art pottery has held its own place in the market for at least fifteen years. There are several well-established dealers, and although there will always be exceptions, especially for large and unusual pieces, prices remain fairly steady. This is not so with 20th century studio ceramics—especially those of the Coper/Rie era. The work of such potters is now seen, as was intended, as fine art, but there are very few dealers or galleries who stock past work (virtually all auction buyers are private collectors), so the saleroom is the best place to find it. Sotheby's, who pioneered the field with the first major specialized sale in 1980, have seen the price of a Coper pot rise from £105 ($120) in 1975 (today's equivalent price would be £5,000-7,000 ($5,700-8,000) for a similar example) to an auction record of £13,000 ($18,500) in 1983.

1
A pair of vases, Doulton, decorated by Florence Barlow, dated 1879, 47.4cm (18½in), *L 13 Apr,* £418 ($602)

2
A metal-mounted stoneware oil lamp, Doulton, decorated by Florence F Barlow, dated 1882, incised marks, *C 27 Mar,* £682 ($1,016)

3
A silver-mounted biscuit barrel and cover, Doulton, decorated by Florence Barlow, 1881, 20cm (7⅞in), *L 29/30 Nov,* £352 ($426)

4
A stoneware jug, Doulton, decorated by Barlow, 1874, 26cm (10⅛in), *P 18-25 Sept,* £231 ($298)

5
A pair of vases, Doulton, decorated by H Barlow, and F Roberts, 29.2cm (11½in), *L 29/30 Nov,* £385 ($466)

6
A vase, Doulton, decorated by H Barlow, 28.5cm (11⅛in), *L 13 Apr,* £418 ($603)

7
A vase, Doulton, decorated by H Barlow, 29.2cm (11½in), *L 13 Apr,* £110 ($158)

1
A jug, Doulton decorated by Hannah Barlow, dated 1878, incised with a frieze of deer between studded floret borders, the foot and neck glazed in green and tan, impressed Lambeth mark, incised marks, 22.8cm (9in), *L 13 Apr,* £396 ($570)

2
A jug, Doulton, incised by Hannah Barlow, dated 1881, with geese annoying a cat, the neck glazed in blue, ochre and green, impressed Lambeth mark, incised marks, 21.5cm (8½in), *L 13 Apr,* £352 ($507)

3
A vase, Doulton, decorated by Edith Lupton, 1880s, crisply incised with scrolling foliage glazed in shades of blue, green and ochre, impressed Lambeth mark, incised marks, 26.3cm (10⅜in), *L 29/30 Nov,* £308 ($373)

4
A pair of vases, Doulton, decorated by Edith Lupton, dated 1883, painted in coloured slips, carved foliage between, the rim and foot glazed in blue and olive-brown, impressed Lambeth mark, incised marks, 40.2cm (15⅞in), *L 13 Apr,* £352 ($507)

5
A stoneware jardinière and stand, Doulton, 76.2cm (30in), *C 17 July,* £440 ($585)

6
A stoneware 'World's Columbian Exposition 1893' jug, Doulton, 1893 crisply sprigged with portraits of Columbus and Washington flanking the American eagle impressed marks, 18.5cm (7⅞in), *P 18-25 Sept,* £154 ($199)

7
A vase, Doulton, decorated by Eliza Simmance, 1890s, impressed Lambeth mark, incised marks, 27.3cm (10¾in), *L 29/30 Nov,* £176 ($213)

8
A jardinière, Doulton decorated by Mark V Marshall and Francis C Pope, glazed in shades of blue, green and ochre, hair crack to rim, impressed Lambeth mark, incised marks, 34.5cm (13⅝in), *L 29/30 Nov,* £264 ($319)

9
A pair of stoneware vases of squat globular form, Doulton decorated by Eliza Simmance, dated 1887, with incised foliage and applied florettes, picked out in green glazes on a blue ground, impressed Lambeth mark, 16.5cm (6½in), *C 18 Oct,* £220 ($275)

10
A stoneware vase, Doulton, decorated by Frank Butler, early 20th cent, incised marks, 30cm (11⅞in), *P 18-25 Sept,* £143 ($184)

11
A faience charger, Doulton, decorated by Harry Simeon, late 19th cent, 51.5cm (20¼in), *C 3 Oct,* £484 ($624)

12
A set of ten lustre tiles, de Morgan, 1880s, painted in ruby lustre on Wedgwood blanks, five with beasts and birds, and five with flowerheads, two with minor chips, 15.5cm (6in), *L 13 Apr,* £1,430 ($2,063)

13
An 'Isnik' vase, de Morgan, 1890s, painted in pale green, yellow, blue and turquoise within manganese outlines, with winged serpent-like beast amongst branches on an overall blue ground, 35.5cm (14in), *P 15-18 May,* £2,750 ($3,823)

14
A lustre dish, de Morgan, decorated by Charles Passenger, 1890s, in ruby, salmon-pink and gold lustre with two stylised deer, against a ground of leafy stems, painted CP initials, 31cm (12¼in), *L 29/30 Nov,* £440 ($532)

1
A jardinière and stand,
Martin Brothers, 1880s,
carved and incised with
ribbed leaves, all glazed
in shades of blue, brown
and green; and another
matching stand, both
damaged, 77.5 and 40cm
(30½ and 15¾in),
L 29/30 Nov,
£165 ($199)

2
A pair of vases, Martin
Brothers, dated 1893,
incised with lizards and
other reptiles amidst
scrolling leafy stems,
glazed in shades of
brown and olive, both
cracked, incised marks,
23.9cm (9⅜in), *L 13 Apr,*
£330 ($476)

3
A stoneware spoonwarmer,
Martin Brothers, dated
October 1889, modelled
as a grotesque reptilian
creature, glazed in
mottled olive brown
with blue highlights,
incised marks, 14cm
(5½in), *NY 18 July,*
$880 (£672)

4
A pair of vases, Martin
Brothers, dated 1886,
each slender ovoid body
incised with birds amidst
berried branches detailed
in brown glaze, incised
marks, 31.4cm (12⅜in),
L 29/30 Nov,
£440 ($532)

5
A 'face' jug, Martin
Brothers, dated 14
October 1903, modelled
on either face with a
smirking countenance
beneath a shock of hair,
incised mark, 18.5cm
(7¼in), *L 29/30 Nov,*
£1,210 ($1,464)

6
A bird, Martin brothers,
dated February 1898,
standing with wings
drawn into its body and
splayed feet, the
plumage detailed in
shades of brown and
green, incised marks,
27.5cm (10⅞in),
L 29/30 Nov,
£2,200 ($2,662)

7
A charger, Della Robbia,
decorated by Elizabeth
Wilkins and W I W,
dated 1895, with
scrolling stylised
dolphins, enclosed by
scallop shells and scrol-
ling foliage, picked out
in typical palette, incised
marks, 47cm (18½in),
C 10 Jan,
£330 ($479)

8
A vase, Della Robbia,
decorated by Charles
Collis and Lizzie Wilkins,
dated 1900, with stylised
waterlilies in pale shades
of green and yellow,
twin loop handles,
minor glaze flakes, incised
marks, 39.3cm (15½in),
L 29/30 Nov,
£220 ($266)

9
A jardinière and stand,
Minton, decorated in
green and pink glazed
with stylised flowers and
foliage, 101.6cm (40in),
C 4 Sept,
£726 ($944)

10
**A majolica jardinière and
stand,** Staffordshire, decorated in relief and picked
out in brightly coloured
glazes with flowers and
stylised foliage, 114.3cm
(45in), *C 4 Sept,*
£506 ($658)

11
'Water Sprite' a Royal
Doulton figure, 1934,
after a model by Richard
Garbe, 35cm (13¾in),
L 30 Nov,
£1,100 ($1,331)

12
A 'Chang' vase, Royal
Doulton, by Harry
Nixon, 1927, 28.1cm
(11in), *L 30 Nov,*
£1,210 ($1,464)

1
A trumpet-shaped vase, Macintyre, decorated in underglaze blue, iron red and gilding with stylised flowers and foliage, blue-scale borders, 30.5cm (12in), *C 23 May,* £88 ($128)

2
A pair of 'Florian Ware' vases, Moorcroft Macintyre, *c*1900, tube-lined with stylised peacock feathers coloured in shades of blue, printed and painted marks, 27.6cm (10⅞in), *L 29/30 Nov,* £1,100 ($1,331)

3
A 'Florian Ware' vase, Moorcroft Macintyre, *c*1903, tube-lined with panels of flag iris enclosed by scrolling leaves coloured in shades of yellow, blue and green, printed and painted marks, 20cm (7⅞in), *L 13 Apr,* £308 ($444)

4
A pair of 'Florian Ware' vases, Moorcroft Macintyre, *c*1900, each ovoid body tube-lined with stylised tulips surrounded by scrolling leaves, coloured in shades of blue, green and yellow, marks, one rim chipped and cracked, *L 29/30 Nov,* £418 ($506)

5
A 'Florian Ware' vase, Moorcroft Macintyre, *c*1899, tube-lined with panels of stylised iris enclosed by scrolling leaves, coloured in shades of blue, marks, 25.5cm (10in), *L 29/30 Nov,* £418 ($506)

6
A pair of vases, Moorcroft, 1920s, each shouldered ovoid body tube-lined with trails of stylised wisteria coloured in shades of blue, green, crimson and yellow, drilled for electricity, impressed marks, one rim repaired, 36cm (14⅛in), *L 29/30 Nov,* £242 ($293)

7
A 'Claremont' pattern bowl, William Moorcroft, early 20th cent, the compressed sides slip-trailed with red flushed toadstools on a mottled green/blue ground, Liberty mark, 26cm (10⅛in), *P 15-18 May,* £374 ($520)

8
A lustre vase, Elton, *c*1910, modelled with a stylised flowering stem beneath a mottled and crackled gold and silver glaze veined in green, painted mark, minor rim glaze flake, 18.4cm (7¼in), *L 29/30 Nov,* £220 ($266)

9
A jardinière, Moorcroft Macintyre, *c*1903, the bell body tube-lined with stylised poppies coloured in blue and orange against a mustard-yellow ground, marks, 20.7cm (8⅛in), *L 13 Apr,* £319 ($459)

10
A high-fired vase, Ruskin, *c*1910, the bell body with cylindrical neck and flared rim, glazed in mottled shades of mauve and crimson clouded and speckled in turquoise, impressed mark, 21.2cm (8⅜in), *L 29/30 Nov,* £165 ($199)

11
A high-fired vase, Ruskin, 1908, the squat bulbous body with trumpet neck glazed in mottled turquoise shading to mauve at the rim and heavily speckled in green, impressed mark, 31cm (12¼in), *L 29/30 Nov,* £242 ($293)

12
A high-fired vase, Ruskin, 1920s, the cylindrical neck thinly glazed in streaked blood-red and olive thickening to deep crimson at the base, speckled in turquoise and green, impressed mark, base restored, 36cm (14⅛in), *L 13 Apr,* £176 ($253)

1
A porcelain bowl, Lucie Rie, 1950s, glazed in ashen-white, the rim exterior banded in deep brown with sgraffito cross-hatching, impressed LR seal, 10.4cm (4⅛in), *L 13 Apr,*
£495 ($713)

2
A stoneware bowl, *c*1980, incised through a mottled pale turquoise and buff glaze, stained deep brown, the rim banded in a bronze-brown glaze, impressed LR seal, 24cm (5½in), *L 13 Apr,*
£1,210 ($1,742)

3
A stoneware bowl, Lucie Rie, 1950s, glazed in a brown-speckled ashen-white, impressed LR seal, 13.9cm (5½in), *L 13 Apr,*
£330 ($476)

4
A stoneware bowl, Lucie Rie, 1970s, impressed LR seal, 28.2cm (11⅛in), *L 13 Apr,*
£1,650 ($2,367)

5
A stoneware vase, Lucie Rie, 1970s, impressed LR seal, 20.5cm (8in), *L 29/30 Nov,*
£385 ($466)

6
A porcelain vase, Lucie Rie, 1970s, glazed in ashen-white, impressed LR seal, 26cm (10¼in), *L 29/30 Nov,*
£550 ($666)

7
A stoneware vase, Hans Coper, late 1960s, washed in an ashen-white glaze thinning to reveal patches of rough 'sharkskin' texturing stained deep brown, impressed HC seal, 32.5cm (12⅞in), *L 29/30 Nov,*
£1,980 ($2,396)

8
A stoneware 'Tripot', Hans Coper, *c*1958, rubbed and stained with patches of deep brown, beneath a washy ashen-white glaze, the interiors and rims glazed matt, deep brown, impressed HC seal, *L 13 Apr,*
£3,300 ($4,762)

9
A stoneware vase, Hans Coper, *c*1970, the whole tooled with horizontal lines and washed in a thin ashen-white glaze blistered to reveal patches of brown staining, impressed HC seal, *L 13 Apr,*
£4,290 ($6,178)

10
A stoneware vase, Bernard Leach, late 1950s, the body tooled with horseshoe-shaped indentations beneath a dribbled olive glaze thinning to reveal the brown body beneath, impressed BL and St Ives seals, *L 13 Apr,*
£286 ($412)

11
A stoneware bowl, Bernard Leach, *c*1962, glazed overall in a heavily speckled buff, impressed BL and St Ives seals, d 25.5cm (10in), *L 13 Apr,*
£330 ($475)

12
An earthenware jar and cover, probably by Bernard Leach, St Ives, *c*1924, incised through cream slip beneath a translucent amber glaze, 19.5cm (7⅝in), *L 30 Nov,*
£308 ($373)

13
A preserve pot and cover, Bernard Leach, 1950s, with scrolling brush-strokes in brown against a band of washy-blue, impressed St Ives seal, painted BL, 11.2cm (4⅜in), *L 29/30 Nov,*
£143 ($173)

14
A stoneware vase, Bernard Leach, early 1960s, brushed in a creamy-white hakeme thinly speckled in brown, impressed BL and St Ives seals, 29cm (11⅜in), *L 29/30 Nov,*
£550 ($666)

15
A stoneware bottle-vase, Bernard Leach, *c*1960, glazed in a glossy black orange-peel textured tenmoku, shaded to rust at the neck and foot, impressed BL and St Ives seals, 36.2cm (14¼in), *L 29/30 Nov,*
£528 ($639)

1
A stoneware bottle-vase, Hamada Shoji, c1960, glazed in a mottled rust and treacle brown splashed with trails of copper green, 19.5cm (7⅝in), *L 13 Apr,* £1,210 ($1,742)

2
A stoneware bowl, Michael Cardew, Wenford Bridge, 1970s, with notched vertical bands in thick mustard slip against a brown ground, impressed seals, 31.5cm (12⅜in), *L 29/30 Nov,* £440 ($532)

3
A stoneware gwari casserole dish and cover, Michael Cardew, Wenford Bridge, 1970s, impressed seals, d 33cm (13in), *L 13 Apr,* £220 ($317)

4
A matt glaze four-colour pottery plate, Van Briggle, 1902, incised in tones of royal blue, maroon, white and blue green, 21.5cm (8½in), *NY 18 July,* $1,760 (£1,344)

5
A porcelain 'Laminated' bowl, Dorothy Feibleman, early 1970s, inlaid in blue, green and white slips, 11.2cm (4⅜in), *L 29/30 Nov,* £110 ($133)

6
A stoneware jug, Michael Cardew, Wenford Bridge, c1970, the ribbed body combed with stylised grass-stems through a rich treacle-brown glaze, impressed seals, 21cm (8¼in), *L 29/30 Nov,* £104 ($126)

7
A raku stoneware bowl, Robin Welch, c1980, stamped, 34.2cm (13½in), *L 13 Apr,* £209 ($302)

8
A raku bowl, Martin Smith, c1978, glazed with a finely-veined ashen-white with diagonal bands against the black-stained ground, d 31.5cm (12⅜in), *L 13 Apr,* £385 ($551)

9
A raku bowl, Martin Smith, c1978, d 38.2cm (15in), *L 13 Apr,* £330 ($472)

10
A high-glaze pottery Venetian landscape vase, Rookwood, decorated by Charles Schmidt, 1902, painted in shaded tones of ice blue and ochre, 22cm (8¾in), *NY 18 July,* $1,430 (£1,092)

11
A wax-glaze pottery vase, Rookwood, decorated by Edward T Hurley, 1933, 15cm (6in), *NY 18 July,* $605 (£462)

12
A vellum-glaze pottery landscape vase, Rookwood, decorated by Edward T Hurley, 1908, painted in muted tones of grey, green, beige and black, 25.3cm (10in), *NY 18 July,* $770 (£588)

13
A silver-overlay standard glaze pottery jug, Rookwood, decorated by William P McDonald, 1894, in avocado green and gold against a brown and ochre ground, 17.8cm (7in), *NY 18 July,* $2,090 (£1,595)

14
A 'jazz' bowl, Cowan Pottery, designed by Viktor Schreckengost, c1931, d 35.5cm (14in), *NY 18 July,* $2,520 (£2,687)

15
A pottery vase, Natzler, mid-20th cent, glazed in mottled vivid turquoise parting to reveal the reddish underbody, signed 19cm (7½in), *NY 18 July,* $1,100 (£840)

16
A pottery vase, Gertrud and Otto Natzler, 1965, invested with a matt speckled turquoise glaze dripping at the foot, signed, h 24cm (9½in), *NY 18 July,* $1,650 (£1,260)

1
A faience vase, Gallé, c 1880, decorated with a landscape surrounded by honesty, in blue on a white ground, the feet modelled in the form of honesty, signed, 26.5cm (10⅜in), *M 11 Mar,* **FF 4,662 (£392; $582)**

2
A lustre-glazed earthenware jug, Delphin Massier, 1900, the handle modelled in the form of an art nouveau maiden, the neck moulded with a Grecian mask, marked, 38.7cm (15¼in), *L 13 Apr,* **£253 ($365)**

3
A pottery urn, Zsolnay Pecs, c 1900, cylindrical, modelled with a hunt in a wooded landscape and glazed in lustrous tones of green, ochre and brown on a creamy ground, firing crack, marks, 52cm (20½in), *NY 24 Mar,* **$4,510 (£3,110)**

4
A square baluster-shaped 'eggshell' vase, Rozenburg, the Hague, decorated by S Schellink, with polychrome flower decoration, 15.5cm (6in), *A 16 May,* **Dfl 3,712 (£604; $863)**

5
An eggshell porcelain vase, Rozenburg, the Hague, decorated by J Schellink, c 1909, 27cm (10½in), *NY 11/12 May,* **$1,760 (£1,275)**

6
An iridescent pottery bowl, Zsolnay Pecs, early 20th cent, painted in shades of ochre, deep burgundy and gilt, against a deep purple ground, 10cm (4in), *NY 11/12 May,* **$1,320 (£957)**

7
A portrait vase, Amphora Pottery, c 1900, in shades of blue, dusty rose and cream reserved against a muted blue and green ground, gilt sunrise, 24cm (9½in), *NY 11/12 May,* **$1,210 (£877)**

8
A vase, Teplitz Pottery, c 1900, the olive-green body moulded with wisteria in shades of emerald green, olive green, sky blue and dusty rose, 46cm (18in), *NY 11/12 May,* **$660 (£478)**

9
A pottery artichoke vase, Tiffany, 1904-14, the whole invested with a cream matte glaze heightened with avocado green, the interior glazed in mottled blue and green, 28.5cm (11¼in), *NY 24 Mar,* **$1,100 (£759)**

10
A baluster-shaped vase, Gouda, with polychrome decoration of flowers and butterflies, 33.5cm (13⅛in), *A 16 May,* **Dfl 1,392 (£323; $462)**

11
An Austrian ceramic jardinière with secessionniste decoration, c 1905, in a green glaze, the frieze with geometric indentations and with green and blue grey in light relief, 24.5cm (9⅝in), *M 7 Oct,* **FF 3,330 (£288; $357)**

12
A pottery vase, Sèvres, decorated by Taxile Doat, c 1907, the white neck and collar above three gilt lion head masks, reserved on a sea-green and ochre crystalline ground, age cracks to neck, 14cm (5½in), *NY 11/12 May,* **$660 (£478)**

13
A porcelain pot and cover, Fraure Uth, c 1920, decorated with black and gilt scrolled design, blue and white ground, underglazed marks, 20.5cm (8⅛in), *L 6 July,* **£220 ($304)**

14
A dinner service, Meissen, c 1901-2, each piece decorated with abstract celadon-green panels outlined in underglaze blue reserved on a white ground, three pieces with minor imperfections, 79 pieces, *NY 17/18 Feb,* **$12,100 (£8,251)**

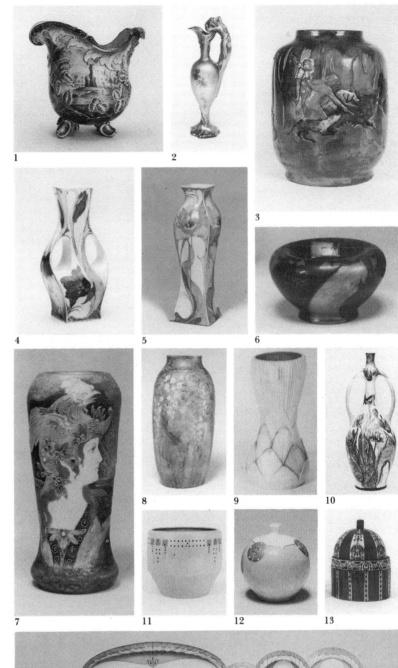

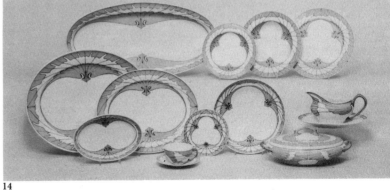

1
Fifteen ceramic tiles, designed by Antonio Gaudi, *c*.1900, each with celadon glaze cast in low relief with shells, scroll-work, foliage and grasses, impressed 'E F Escofet y Ca', some chips, 25.5cm (10in), *NY 17 Nov,* $2,310 (£1,848)

2
A seraphis earthenware clock, Ernst Wahliss, possibly designed by Karl Klaus, 1910-15, 25cm (9⅞in), *L 6 July,* £1,705 ($2,353)

3
A porcelain part tea set, Theodore Haviland, Limoges, designed by Edouard Marcel Sandoz, 1920s, printed factory marks, *L 13 Apr,* £264 ($381)

4
A pair of earthenware table lamps, designed by Walter Rhaue, *c*.1925, cut and applied with a formalised face, decorated with pink, orange and green, pale-pink ground, fluted paper shades, 44cm (17¼in), *L 13 Apr,* £660 ($952)

5
An earthenware dancing figure, Goldscheider, 1920s, bikini top, long split dark red skirt, painted with flowers, impressed mark, 39cm (15¼in), *L 28 Sept,* £418 ($543)

6
A butterfly girl, Goldscheider, after a model by Lorenzl, *c*.1930, striding with arms outstretched in butterfly wing cape, shades of brown and blue, printed factory marks and facsimile signature, 41.5cm (16¼in), *L 29/30 Nov,* £462 ($559)

7
A figure of a naked girl kneeling on a globe, 1930s, in a check beret with a book in her hand and dog beside her, marked 'Lenci Torino Made in Italy', *L 16 Feb,* £1,980 ($2,776)

8
A vase, Longwy Pottery, *c*.1925, moulded in low relief with nude female figures in brilliant tones of cobalt blue, chocolate, yellow, lavender and grey against a turquoise ground, 32.5cm (12¾in), *NY 24 Mar,* $1,870 (£1,290)

9
A vase Lachenal Pottery, *c*.1925, in cream glaze decorated with a medial band of frolicking simians in shades of blue, green and brown, the whole with light craquelure, signed, restored, 41cm (16in), *NY 24 Mar,* $990 (£683)

10
A pottery vase, René Buthaud, *c*.1925, 33cm (13in), *NY 17 Nov,* $1,760 (£1,408)

11
A ceramic crazed vase, Boni Frères, *c*.1935, 33.5cm (13⅛in), *M 7 Oct,* FF 9,900 (£863; $1,072)

12
A ceramic bowl, Jean Mayodon, dated April 1928, decorated with a scene of the hunt and a draught-board, in shades of grey green and mauve on a cream ground, 25cm (9⅞in), *M 11 Mar,* FF 4,995 (£419; $624)

13
A decorated earthenware pitcher, Guido Gambone, 1950s, poly-chrome abstract decoration with predominant red and yellow on crazed white ground, marked, 30cm (11⅞in), *L 16 Feb,* £693 ($972)

14
A ceramic plate, Madoura, decorated after a drawing by Pablo Picasso, *c*.1950, 38.2cm (15in), *M 11 Mar,* FF 2,775 (£233; $347)

15
Five earthenware plates, *c*.1960, each printed with the detail of a face, in half-tone grid form, monochrome, printed 'Fornasetti Milano Made in Italy', *L 16 Feb,* £143 ($200)

1
**A bizarre part dinner
service,** Royal Staffordshire ('The Biarritz'),
1930s, comprising 6
dinner plates, 6 dessert
plates, 6 side plates, 3
serving plates and one
vegetable dish and
cover, orange and green
sprig in one corner,
L 6 July,
£264 ($364)

2
A bizarre part service,
Royal Staffordshire
('The Biarritz'), 1930s,
each item with 'BM'
printed marks, 34 pieces,
L 6 July,
£440 ($607)

3
A bizarre wall plate,
Wilkinson Ltd, 1930s,
painted with formalised
landscape with trees on a
cliff, shades of orange,
yellow, red and brown,
printed marks, 33.2cm
(13⅛in), *L 28 Sept,*
£374 ($486)

4
A black basalt vase,
Wedgwood, designed by
Keith Murray, 1920s,
flared, sharply ribbed
frieze, printed and
impressed marks, 20.2cm
(8in), *L 6 July,*
£165 ($228)

5
A large bizarre jug, 1930s,
the flared cylindrical
body and waisted neck
brightly painted with
diamonds and stylised
leaves, printed marks,
30cm (11⅞in),
P 15-18 May,
£880 ($1,223)

6
A bizarre charger,
Newport Pottery, 1930s,
painted with a single
colourful tree, lightly
ribbed, printed marks,
painted 'Latona', 45cm
(17¾in), *L 29/30 Nov,*
£1,430 ($1,730)

7
A bizarre dinner service,
Newport Pottery, 1930s,
painted with stylised
trees, shades of blue,
green and yellow with
black, printed marks, 26
pieces, *L 29/30 Nov,*
£495 ($599)

8
A bizarre 'Latona' jug,
Newport Pottery, 1930,
painted at the shoulder
with bold formalised
flowers in bright
primary colours, printed
marks, 30cm (11⅞in),
L 28 Sept,
£660 ($858)

9
**A bizarre 'Fantasque' tea
set,** Newport Pottery,
1930s, comprising 4 cups
with saucers, milk jug,
large sugar basin, 4 plates,
cake plate, painted with
cottage landscape in
bright red, orange and
green, printed marks,
L 29/30 Nov,
£550 ($666)

9

1
A bizarre 'Fantasque' 'Gay Day' two-person tea set, Wilkinson Ltd, 1930s, painted with marigolds and summer flowers, various stencilled marks, 9 pieces, *L 28 Sept,*
£352 ($458)

2
A bizarre 'Fantasque' vase, Newport Pottery, 1930s, spherical, painted with highly formalised multi-coloured landscape, printed marks, 14cm (5½in), *L 28 Sept,*
£572 ($744)

3
A bizarre bowl, Wilkinson Ltd, 1930s, shallow, conical four flange legs, painted on the interior with a formalised landscape with trees and houses in red, green and black, printed marks, d 18.7cm (7⅜in), *L 28 Sept,*
£165 ($215)

4
A bizarre 'Fantasque' bowl, Wilkinson Ltd, 1930s, painted with trees and cottages in bright orange, red, blue, green and yellow, printed marks, 19cm (7½in), *L 6 July,*
£209 ($288)

5
A bizarre biscuit barrel and matching small bowl, Newport Pottery, 1930s, stylised sunburst design, orange, purple, blue, black and yellow, barrel with blue wicker-covered handle, printed marks, h 15.5cm (6⅛in), *L 13 Apr,*
£418 ($602)

6
A large 'Fantasque' vase, Wilkinson Ltd, 1930s, baluster, painted with a bold frieze of formalised fruit, printed marks, 36.2cm (14¼in), *L 29/30 Nov,*
£1,540 ($1,863)

7
A bizarre bowl, Wilkinson Ltd, signed Clarice Cliff, 1930s, the bowl in deep mottled inky-blue, feet painted in brilliant red, blue, green and yellow, printed marks, d 19cm (7½in), *L 29/30 Nov,*
£1,210 ($1,464)

8
A bizarre bonbon set, Newport Pottery, six triangular dishes and one larger dish with arch handles, stylised flowers in orange, brown and black, printed marks, 20.5cm (8⅛in), *L 6 July,*
£440 ($607)

9
An 'Archaic' vase, Newport Pottery, 1930s, modelled as an Egyptian column head, painted in shades of yellow, red, blue and green, factory marks, 31.5cm (12¼in), *L 28 Sept,*
£1,650 ($2,145)

10
A bizarre vase, Newport Pottery, 1930s, painted with delicate stylised landscape with trees and flowers, pastel shades of green, pink and blue, printed marks, 24.2cm (9½in), *L 28 Sept,*
£330 ($429)

11
A bizarre box and cover, Newport Pottery, 1930s, cube, flange handles, with a bold formalised design in orange, black, green and blue, printed marks, 12.5cm (5in), *L 6 July,*
£715 ($987)

12
A jar and cover, Clarice Cliff, 1930s, the shouldered ovoid body boldly painted in blue, purple, yellow, pink, grey and black with a vorticist pattern within striped borders, printed marks, 24.5cm (9⅝in), *P 18-25 Sept,*
£374 ($482)

1

2   3

4   5

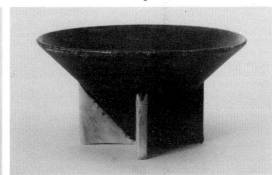

6   7

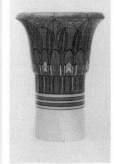

8   9

10   11   12

1
An inlaid walnut sideboard, 1870s, in the style of Charles Bevan, the central doors inlaid with stylised floral and geometric panels, flanked by mirror-backed shelves, 168 x 48.5 x 134.5cm (66⅛ x 19 x 53in), *L 29/30 Nov,*
£1,650 ($1,997)

2
An inlaid and carved oak-cased Erard piano, Gillow and Co, probably designed by Bruce Talbert, 1870s, *L 29/30 Nov,*
£4,620 ($5,590)

3
A gilt-incised and ebonised marquetry walnut side cabinet, *c.*1860, h 226cm (89in), w 122cm (48in), *NY 16 June,*
$4,290 (£3,131)

4
A sideboard, Aesthetic Movement, 1880s, with a pair of doors with painted panels allegorical of Labour and Pleasure, part ebonised and gilt, 158 x 183 x 42.5cm (62¼ x 72 x 16¾in), *L 6 July,*
£275 ($380)

5
A bedroom suite, *c.*1900, comprising a wardrobe, a dressing table and a bedside cupboard, all inlaid with a stylised scrolling foliate design, *C 2 Nov,*
£495 ($634)

6
A light oak bedroom suite, *c.*1876, comprising dressing table, wardrobe and bedside table, each with polychromed birds and stencilled 'Gothic' decoration, wardrobe h 218cm (85⅞in), *L 6 July,*
£495 ($683)

7
An inlaid bedroom suite, Christopher Pratt & Sons, 1880s, comprising a half-tester bed, a dressing table, a chest of drawers and a pair of cane-seated chairs, each piece inlaid in ebony, bone and fruitwoods, bed h 242cm (95in), *L 29/30 Nov,*
£6,380 ($7,720)

8
An inlaid mahogany display cabinet, Christopher Pratt and Sons, *c.*1905, the central glazed door with scrolling floral pewter surmounted by a band inlaid in mother-of-pearl, 194 x 142 x34.5cm (76⅜ x 56 x 13⅝in), *L 29/30 Nov,*
£2,860 ($3,461)

9
A mahogany occasional table, designed by E W Godwin, *c.*1880, 66.5cm (26in), *L 29/30 Nov,*
£198 ($240)

10
A set of three leaded glass windows, Glasgow School, *c.*1905, the three forming a semi-circle, inset with dark blue, green, amber and opalescent glass, h 75.5cm (29¾in), w 145cm (57⅛in), *L 6 July,*
£154 ($213)

11
Two stained beech high back chairs, Glasgow School, *c.*1905, the backs with gesso roundels, seats covered in green velvet, printed with formalised floral design, one roundel replaced, 136cm (53½in), *L 6 July,*
£660 ($911)

12
Three oak chairs, Wylie & Lochhead, probably designed by E A Taylor, *c.*1905; sold with a Scottish oak umbrella stand, 107 and 107.5cm (42⅛ and 42⅜in), *L 13 Apr,*
£220 ($317)

13
An inlaid oak fall-front bureau, designed by M H Baillie Scott, *c.*1900, the front with beaten metal hinge plates in the form of stylised birds, 87 x 23 x 118cm (34¼ x 9 x 46½in), *L 29/30 Nov,*
£2,640 ($3,194)

14
An inlaid oak book-cupboard, designed by M H Baillie Scott, *c.*1905, the door inlaid in pewter and coloured woods with a stylised flowerhead, the whole banded with chequered inlay, 51 x 14.7 x 18.5cm (20 x 5⅞ x 7¼in), *L 13 Apr,*
£308 ($444)

1

2

3

4

5

6

7

8

9

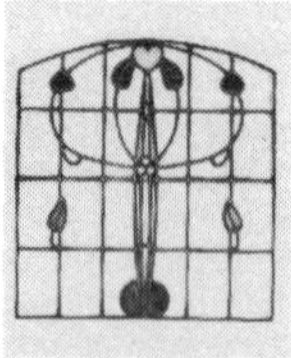
10

11

12

13

14

1
An oak mantel clock, designed by C F A Voysey, c 1895, the face inlaid in pewter with the motto 'Tempus Fugit', 50.5cm (19⅞in), *L 29/30 Nov*, **£9,350 ($11,314)**

2
An oak sideboard, Liberty & Co Ltd, c 1900, the top surmounted with a carved entrelac frieze, hinge with stamped Liberty mark, 137 x 60 x 137.5cm (54 x 23⅝ x 54⅛in), *L 16 Feb*, **£352 ($494)**

3
A set of six oak dining chairs, c 1900, two carvers and four side chairs with curved backs and aprons with pierced floral motifs, armchair h 119cm (46⅞in), *L 6 July*, **£990 ($1,366)**

4
A pair of oak rush-seated armchairs, c 1900, after a design by George Walton, pierced with a heart above flat arms, 81.5cm (32in), *L 29/30 Nov*, **£825 ($998)**

5
A pair of ash 'Gimson Armchairs', designed by Ernest Gimson, 1930s, five arched back splats, turned legs and stretchers, rush seat, 114cm (44⅞in), *L 29/30 Nov*, **£462 ($559)**

6
An oak wardrobe, Gordon Russell, 1930s, panelled door and sides with octagonal section uprights; and an oak bed-head and end, *en suite*, wardrobe h 192cm (75⅝in), *L 16 Feb*, **£506 ($709)**

7
A dining table and six armchairs, Gordon Russell, 1940s, the circular table with slender D-section legs, the armchairs with cane backs and seats, affixed metal labels with facsimile signature, chairs h 93cm (36⅝in), *L 29/30 Nov*, **£418 ($506)**

8
An oak blanket chest, Gordon Russell, the top set with three wrought-iron *fleur de lys* strap hinges, h 165.5 x 32 x 70.5cm (65 x 12½ x 27¾in), *L 30 Nov*, **£495 ($599)**

9
A cherry part bedroom suite, Gordon Russell, 1929, comprising a dressing table with swing-mirror to one side, a pair of single beds with panelled bedheads and ends and a dressing table, all with original paper labels with names of designer and makers, *L 29/30 Nov*, **£495 ($599)**

10
A 'Mouseman' oak table, Robert Thompson of Kilburn, 1930s, the rectangular adzed top on two flared octagonal supports linked by a trestle base, carved with a mouse, 182.5cm (72in), w 84.2cm (33⅛in), h 73cm (28¾in), *L 13 Apr*, **£1,320 ($1,905)**

11
An oak dining suite, 1928, the extending dining table on reeded pedestal legs, two armchairs and six side chairs, affixed label 'Token Handmade Furniture Designed by Betty Joel Made by W R Hamilton at Token Works Portsmouth', *L 16 Feb*, **£1,760 ($2,468)**

12
A pair of armchairs, 1930s, curved back and arms set with a sycamore strip, upholstered in beige leather, on castors, h 87cm (34⅛in), *L 16 Feb*, **£715 ($1,002)**

13
A minipiano and stool, Eavestaff, 1930s, black-painted, chromed metal banding and pedal plate, w 130cm (51⅛in), *L 16 Feb*, **£770 ($1,080)**

14
A white-painted plywood desk, the design attributed to Gerard Summers, c 1930, left-hand bank of four drawers, w 117cm (46⅛in), h 73cm (28¾in), *L 16 Feb*, **£330 ($463)**

1
A burr sycamore dining room suite, designed by Ray Hille, 1930s, comprising dining table, eight chairs, small and large sideboard, table/h 260.5cm (102½in), *L 28 Sept,* £2,750 ($3,575)

2
A deep tuft buttoned sofa, designed by Syrie Maugham for her daughter Lady Glenderon, on turned wooden legs, 237cm (93¾in), *L 13 Apr,* £1,540 ($2,217)

3
A small shagreen and ivory vanity box on stand, *c*1930, the box with mirror within, h 63.5cm (25in), *L 29/30 Nov,* £1,540 ($1,863)

4
A shagreen and ivory vitrine on stand, *c*1930, the triangular cupboard with mirrored interior and central glass shelf, the single lower shelf covered in green stained sharkskin banded with ivory, h 147.5cm (58in), *L 29/30 Nov,* £3,630 ($4,392)

5
A tubular steel settee, PEL S3, 1930s, black rexine upholstery, and a tubular steel cantilevered armchair, 1930s, settee w 118cm (32¾in), *L 28 Sept,* £176 ($229)

6
A chromed tubular steel desk, probably PEL, 1930s, re-upholstered in black simulated leather, h 72cm (28½in), *L 16 Feb,* £352 ($494)

7
A chromed tubular steel and smoked glass coffee table, PEL, HT9, 1930s, later square smoked glass top, 54cm (21¼in), *L 16 Feb,* £99 ($139)

8
A Romney Axminster seamless carpet, Templeton's, 1930s, the ground with overlapping rectangles of toned grey and green, three bands of orange strips with patches of black, 315 x 260cm (124 x 102½in), *L 29/30 Nov,* £1,870 ($2,263)

9
A tufted carpet, 1930s, in shades of beige and lovat green, squiggled design with touches of tomato red, 352 x 267cm (138⅝ x 105in), *L 28 Sept,* £407 ($529)

10
A set of eight tubular steel cantilever armchairs, 1930s, upholstered in red rexine, 80cm (31½in), *L 6 July,* £132 ($182)

11
A Romney Axminster seamless carpet, Templeton's, 1930s, the central beige ground with pale green border, regular rectangular motifs in flecked grey with black and white stripes, 360 x 260cm (141¾ x 102in), *L 6 July,* £605 ($835)

12
A rug, 'S'-shaped motif in shades of brown and beige, 231 x 173cm (90⅞ x 68⅛in), *L 16 Feb,* £297 ($416)

13
Four 'Antelope' chairs, designed by Ernest Race for the South Bank Festival of Britain, 1950/1, white-painted metal wire frames, shaped yellow-painted plywood seats, 77.8cm (30⅝in), *L 16 Feb,* £484 ($679)

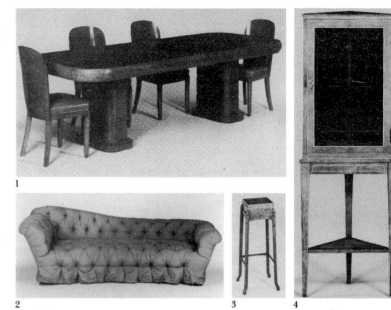

1

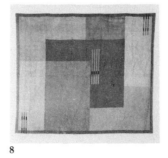

2

3

4

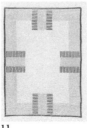

5

6

7

8

9

10

11

12

13

1
An American pewter-inlaid and marquetry stained-oak writing table, designed for Gustav Stickley by Harvey Ellis, c.1903, h 77.5cm (30½in), *NY 18 July,* $9,350 (£7,137)

2
An American stained-oak sideboard, in the manner of Gustav Stickley, early 20th cent, h 122cm (44in), *NY 18 July,* $385 (£294)

3
An American carved-oak settee, probably Prairie School, early 20th cent, carved with openwork sunburst motifs and set with turned spindles, 224cm (88in), *NY 18 July,* $3,300 (£2,519)

4
An American stained-oak tall case clock with leaded-glass decoration, early 20th cent, the coppery face with 'hammered' decoration set above a glass door leaded with long-stemmed tulips, h 170cm (67in), w 61cm (24in), *NY 18 July,* $1,210 (£924)

5
An American stained-oak dressing table with mirror, designed by Gustave Stickley, early 20th cent, together with a stained-oak stool with rush seat, h 142cm (56in), w 92cm (36in), *NY 18 July,* $1,430 (£1,092)

6
An American lucite-mounted walnut dressing table, designed by Gilbert Rohde, for the Herman Miller Furniture Co, mid-1930s, mounted with three gilt mirrors above a demi-lune glass shelf, h 127cm (50in), w 122cm (48in), *NY 11/12 May,* $2,750 (£1,993)

7
A mahogany cabinet-on-stand, designed by Frank Lloyd Wright for Heritage Henredon, c.1955, the doors opening to reveal a single shelf and applied with concentric squares, h 66cm (26in), *NY 18 July,* $715 (£546)

8
A black-painted mesh chair, designed by Charles Eames, c.1951, shaped white vinyl upholstery, 83cm (32¾in), *L 16 Feb,* £264 ($370)

9
A fibreglass dining suite, Knoll International, designed by Eero Saarinen, 1956/7, comprising six '151' 'Tulip' chairs, fibreglass-reinforced polyester with cast-aluminium bases, and matching table, d 136cm (53½in), *L 16 Feb,* £528 ($740)

10
A 'Chicken Wire' relaxing chair, Knoll International, designed by Harry Bertoia, 1950s, black-painted, black vinyl drop-in seat, 65cm (25⅝in), *L 28 Sept,* £77 ($100)

11
A lounge chair '679' and stool, Herman Miller, designed by Charles Eames, 1956, the seat and back in sections of laminated rosewood upholstered in black hide, 81cm (31in), and a '671' stool en suite, *L 28 Sept,* £682 ($887)

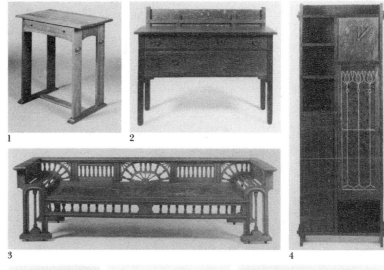

1   2   4

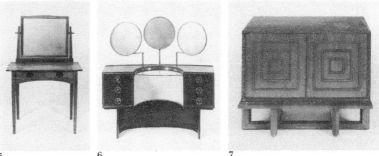

3

5   6   7

8   9

10   11

1

A vitrail, Georges de Feure, c.1900, representing a young woman in a long robe, made in glass of various colours, the details enamelled, in an oak frame with stand, h 254cm (100in), *M 7 Oct*, **FF 222,000** (£19,188; $23,820)

2

A fruitwood marquetry nest of four tables, Gallé, c.1900, the rectangular tops decorated with flowers and butterflies, h 71cm (28in), w 58cm (22¾in), *M 11 Mar*, **FF 14,430** (£1,213; $1,804)

3

A fruitwood marquetry table, Gallé, c.1901, the rectangular top with raised reeded edge inlaid with blossoming prunus branch, signed in marquetry, h 63.5cm (25in), *NY 24 Mar*, $1,320 (£910)

4

A carved walnut and fruitwood étagère, Ecole de Nancy, c.1900, the back set with shirred green silk fabric, alterations, h 121cm (47½in), *NY 24 Mar*, $2,420 (£1,669)

5

A gueridon, Gallé, c.1900, with carved dragonfly legs and decorated in fruitwood marquetry with waterlilies and a dragonfly, signed in marquetry, h 76cm (23in), w 66cm (26in), *M 11 Mar*, **FF 177,600** (£14,924; $22,200)

6

A carved walnut étagère, Majorelle, c.1900, the frieze elaborately carved with fruits and flowers continuing to two twisted square supports framing a central glazed cupboard, h 190cm (74¾in), w 90cm (35½in), *NY 17 Nov*, $7,425 (£5,940)

7

A 'waterlily' suite of bureau furniture in mahogany and gilt bronze, Louis Majorelle, c.1900-5, comprising desk, armchair and bookcase, desk h 78.5cm (31in), w 159cm (63¾in), bookcase h 281cm (110⅝in), *M 7 Oct*, **FF 288,600** (£24,944; $30,966)

8

A carved fruitwood étagère, attributed to Majorelle, c.1900, the square top mounted with rollers to support a rotating plinth, h 101cm (39¼in), w 51cm (20in), *NY 24 Mar*, $1,650 (£1,138)

9

A 'waterlily' gilt-bronze mounted mahogany armchair, Louis Majorelle, c.1900, the seat and back upholstered in velour, 71cm (28in), *M 11 Mar*, **FF 210,900** (£17,723; $26,363)

10

A gilt-bronze mounted cabinet, Majorelle, c.1900, the surround carved with ombellifère blossoms, gilt bronze floriform mounts, h 159cm (62½in), w 70cm (27½in), *NY 24 Mar*, $8,250 (£5,690)

1

2

3

4

5

6

7

8

9

10

1
A suite of six carved
fruitwood side chairs,
designed by Plumet et
Selmersheim, c.1900,
each leg with strapwork
support, *NY 11/12 May*,
$3,300 (£2,391)

2
A mother-of-pearl and
fruitwood marquetry inlaid
bird's eye maple side chair,
designed by Paul Follot,
c.1910, the rectangular
open back with central
splat inlaid in mother-
of-pearl, ebony and
boxwood, *NY 17 Nov*,
$1,100 (£880)

3
A large mirror frame in
wrought iron and copper,
Emile Robert, c.1905-10,
h 185cm (72⅞in),
M 11 Mar,
FF 55,500 (£4,664; $6,938)

4
A shagreen and ivory bed,
André Groult, 1925,
monogrammed and
dated, h 97cm (38⅛in),
w 173cm (68in), *M 7 Oct*,
FF 599,400 (£51,806;
$64,313)

5
A stool in shagreen and
ivory, Jules Leleu, c.1925,
the arched seat supported
by four octagonal legs,
52.8cm (20⅞in), *M 11 Mar*,
FF 244,200 (£20,521;
$30,525)

6
An ebony cabinet inlaid in
mother-of-pearl and silver,
1927, the doors decorated
with an inlaid bouquet
of flowers in mother-of-
pearl of various colours,
the ribbon inlaid in
silver, h 157cm (61⅞in),
M 11 Mar,
FF 1,433,000 (£121,261;
$180,375)

7
An amboyna, shagreen
and gilt bronze gaming
table, Emile Jacques
Ruhlmann, c.1925,
h 75.2cm (29⅝in),
M 11 Mar,
FF 255,300 (£21,454;
$31,913)

8
A silvered-bronze cheval
mirror, designed by
Emile Jacques Ruhlmann,
c.1925, raised on two
everted tapering ribbed
legs and a hinged back
rest, 44cm (17¼in),
NY 17 Nov,
$2,860 (£2,288)

9
A rosewood, silver and
ivory mirror, designed by
Emile Jacques Ruhlmann,
c.1920-25, the columns
inlaid in ivory, 35.6cm
(14in), *M 11 Mar*,
FF 53,280 (£4,477; $6,660)

10
A macassar 'Cla-Cla' table,
Emile Jacques Ruhlmann,
c.1925, stamped, 84.5cm
(33¼in), *M 11 Mar*,
FF 144,300 (£12,126;
$18,037)

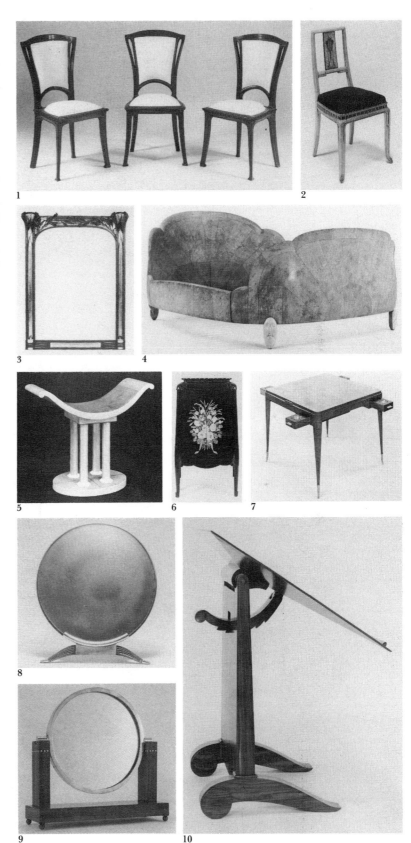

1
A marble and wrought-iron centre table, designed by Paul Kiss, *c*1925, the octagonal red-brown top and stepped foot conjoined with a swag-moulded apron and support, h 81cm (32in), d 120cm (47in), *NY 11/12 May,* $7,975 (£5,779)

2
A French wrought-iron screen, *c*1925, 79 x 79cm (31⅛ x 31⅛in), *L 6 July,* £484 ($668)

3
A wrought-iron and marble circular occasional table, designed by Edgar Brandt, *c*1925, the mottled white, red and greige marble top fitting into four downward-curving supports, h 63.5cm (25½in), d 75cm (29½in), *NY 17 Nov,* $4,400 (£3,520)

4
A wrought-iron console table, attributed to Edgar Brandt, *c*1925, the top with cream marble, w 58cm (22¾in), *M 7 Oct,* FF 9,435 (£815; $1,012)

5
A pair of wrought-iron console tables, attributed to Raymond Subes, *c*1929, h 97cm (38⅛in), *M 7 Oct,* FF 23,310 (£2,015; $2,501)

6
A French side table, *c*1925, the oval top inlaid with sunburst veneer with central satinwood oval, on swollen fluted legs, ribs outlined in black, h 79cm (31in), w 89.5cm (38⅞in), *L 29/30 Nov,* £880 ($1,065)

7
An oak and parchment stool, designed by Jean Michel Frank, *c*1932, the shaped rectangular seat above an X-form support with oval central section flaring to a shaped rectangular base, *NY 17 Nov,* $3,300 (£2,640)

8
A mahogany six-leafed draught screen, by Jean Michel Frank, *c*1930, stamped 'J M Frank Chanaux & Co', each leaf 185 x 50cm (72⅝ x 19⅝in), *M 7 Oct,* FF 77,700 (£6,716; $8,337)

9
A pair of upholstered armchairs, designed by Pierre Chareau, *c*1928, each with curved arched crest and waisted back, the armrests in ébène de macassar and the whole raised on silvered bun feet, *NY 11/12 May,* $34,100 (£24,710)

10
A palissander and burl walnut vitrine cabinet, retailed by Mercier Frères, Paris, *c*1930, the inset chromed vitrine section with glass shelves, h 160cm (63in), w 103cm (40½in), *NY 11/12 May,* $4,125 (£2,989)

11
A pair of pickled-oak tub chairs, Continental, *c*1935, of ten-sided section open on three sides revealing mustard upholstered back and seat cushion, *NY 17 Nov,* $880 (£704)

1
A rosewood, shagreen and brass cabinet, designed by André Domin and Marcel Genevrière for Dominique, c.1935, with inset marble top, the rectangular body with rounded corners centring a pair of shagreen doors inlaid in brass, h 98cm (38½ in), *NY 11/12 May,* **$11,550 (£8,370)**

2
A desk, French c.1930, right-hand upright curving above top to form short shelf, 87 x 162.5 x 86.5cm (34¼ x 63 x 34in), *L 13 Apr,* **£825 ($1,188)**

3
A lacquered metal umbrella stand, French, c.1930, lacquered on three sides in black, the front in light and dark shades of gold with various lozenge devices, h 68cm (26¾ in), *NY 17 Nov,* **$825 (£660)**

4
A burled-wood dining table, French, c.1935, the rectangular top with pull-out extensions, raised on two short tapering supports each continuing to a serpentine drop-crest and two legs terminating in brass sabots, 182cm (71½ in), *NY 17 Nov,* **$1,320 (£1,056)**

5
A set of six burled-wood side chairs, French, c.1935, upholstered in green leather, *NY 17 Nov,* **$1,980 (£1,584)**

6
A blond-wood parquetry extension dining table and eight chairs, designed by Jules Leleu, c.1938, comprising six side chairs and two armchairs, 180cm (71in), *NY 11/12 May,* **$3,300 (£2,391)**

7
A stylish chromed-metal and glass dressing table, designed by Louis Sognot, c.1935, the asymmetrical shallow unit with scrolling side supports enveloping a bar of glass, h 49cm (19½ in), *NY 11/12 May,* **$2,420 (£1,754)**

8
A tubular cheval mirror, attributed to Louis Sognot, c.1930, with a rectangular mirror, 180.5cm (71in), *M 11 Mar,* **FF 4,440 (£373; $555)**

9
A rocking chair, Louis Sognot, c.1930, 92cm (36⅛ in), *M 7 Oct,* **FF 9,990 (£863; $1,072)**

10
A pair of chrome tubular metal stools, Louis Sognot, c.1930, the seats in wood, 77.5cm (30½ in), *M 11 Mar,* **FF 9,435 (£793; $1,179)**

2

1

4 (*table*), 5 (*chairs*)

3

6

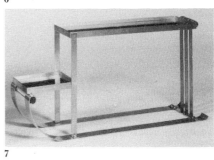

7

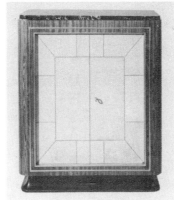

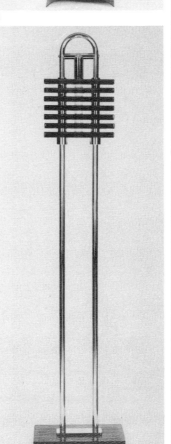

8

9   10

1
A pair of mahogany open armchairs, probably Austrian, c 1900, each with arched backrail above an oval pierced splat, *NY 17 Nov,* $1,100 (£880)

2
A pair of bentwood armchairs, J Kohn, after a design by Otto Wagner, c 1905, plywood seats with sunburst motif, open arched backs, 81.5cm (32in), *L 6 July,* £330 ($445)

3
An oak armchair, in the style of Josef Olbrich, c 1905, with shaped open arms and sides, leather seat, 80cm (31⅜in), *L 29/30 Nov,* £484 ($586)

4
An Austrian bentwood hall stand, c 1905, middle shelf carved with recesses for umbrella etc, h 182cm (71¾in), *L 13 Apr,* £110 ($159)

5
A side cabinet, designed by Josef Urban, c 1904, the upper cabinet glazed with thick bevelled glass and black-painted elliptical brass glazing bars supported on black-stained elliptical wood legs, h 146cm (57½in), *L 13 Apr,* £1,045 ($1,508)

6
A 'Sitzmachine' armchair, by J & J Kohn, designed by Josef Hoffmann, c 1905, with adjustable positions, h 110cm (43¼in), *M 11 Mar,* **FF 166,500** (£13,992; $20,813)

7
A bentwood settee, probably designed by Josef Hoffmann for Thonet, c 1905, the outset scrolling backrail continuing to integral arm rests, above a panelled upholstered back, 124cm (49in), *NY 17 Nov,* $3,575 (£2,860)

8
A small bentwood side table, in the style of Josef Hoffmann, c 1905, with circular top, wood spheres below the rim, h 54cm (21¼in), *L 6 July,* £215 ($297)

1

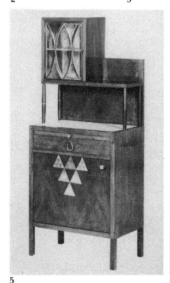

2

3

4

5

6

7

8

1

A rosewood stand, Gustav Serrurier-Bovy, c.1897, 146.5cm (57¾in), *M 7 Oct,* **FF 44,400 (£3,838; $4,764)**

2

A stained-oak centre table, in the manner of Gustav Serrurier-Bovy, early 20th cent, h 79cm (31in), *NY 18 July,* **$715 (£546)**

3

A '1919' armchair, Gerrit Rietveld, after a 1919 model, c.1950, made by van de Groenekan, stamped 'H G M GAvd Groenekan de Bilt Nederland', 91.5cm (36in), *M 7 Oct,* **FF 105,450 (£9,114; $11,314)**

4

A tall oak bookcase/ cabinet, designed by Patriz Huber, c.1901, slender sinuous upright supports rising from lower unit to overhung top, h 208cm (82in), w 77cm (30½in), *L 13 Apr,* **£880 ($1,270)**

5

A tubular steel 'Weissenhof' chair, designed by Mies Van der Rohe, c.1928-30, cantilever, curved arms extending down onto curved supports, slung and upholstered in green canvas, designed 1927, h 77.5cm (30½in), *L 13 Apr,* **£418 ($603)**

6

A circular rosewood table, Edward Colonna, c.1899, h 50cm (19¾in), *M 7 Oct,* **FF 9,990 (£863; $1,072)**

7

A rosewood stand, Edward Colonna, c.1899, h 110cm (43¼in), *M 7 Oct,* **FF 13,320 (£1,151; $1,429)**

8

A pair of carved oak side chairs, Ivan Busquets, Barcelona, c.1900, each shaped back carved with asymmetrical groupings of foliage, upholstered in cut velour, *NY 17 Nov,* **$1,879 (£1,496)**

9

A pair of carved-oak open armchairs, Ivan Busquets, Barcelona, c.1900, the arched back with pierced whiplash moulding carved with asymmetrical foliage, upholstered in white muslin, *NY 17 Nov,* **$4,125 (£3,300)**

10

A 'Lip' sofa, inspired from a design by Salvador Dali, late 1960s, upholstered in red jersey, *L 13 Apr,* **£1,980 ($2,857)**

1
An étagère, Carlo Bugatti, c.1900, in wood, copper and ivory, h 76cm (30in), w 61cm (24in), *M 7 Oct*, **FF 15,540 (£1,343; $1,667)**

2
A high-backed chair, Carlo Bugatti, c.1900, in wood inlaid with copper and covered in vellum, the seat recovered in vellum, the border with embossed leather, signed, 157.5cm (62in), *M 7 Oct*, **FF 35,520 (£3,070; $3,811)**

3
A throne armchair, Bugatti, c.1900, the circular back vellum-covered, painted with bamboo, asymmetric uprights, decorated with inlaid brass and pewter and applied beaten metal, 153cm (60⅛in), *L 6 July*, **£2,860 ($3,947)**

4
A chair, Carlo Bugatti, c.1900, carved wood with leather seat, h 115cm (45¼in), *M 7 Oct*, **FF 31,080 (£2,686; $3,330)**

5
A banquette, Carlo Bugatti, c.1900, in carved wood with leather cover, h 58.5cm (23in), *M 7 Oct*, **FF 11,100 (£959; $1,189)**

6
A side chair, Bugatti, c.1900, with a padded circular slung back with beaten copper, inlaid in ivory and pewter, applied beaten copper strips, 90cm (35½in), *L 16 Feb*, **£935 ($1,311)**

7
A red marble and wood table, Gio Ponti, c.1935, w 300cm (108in), *M 11 Mar*, **FF 155,400 (£13,059; $19,425)**

8
A bar/cabinet in rosewood and vellum, Paolo Buffa, c.1935, h 139.5cm (55in), *M 7 Oct*, **FF 42,180 (£3,646; $4,526)**

9
A pair of oak and rope chairs, Carlo Mollino, 1948, 87cm (34¼in), *M 7 Oct*, **FF 53,280 (£4,605; $5,717)**

10
An Italian umbrella-stand, Rudi Righi, c.1950, the cylindrical container painted in white lines over a blue ground, the base in black, 77cm (30¼in), *M 11 Mar*, **FF 2,220 (£187; $278)**

1

2

3

4

5   6

7

8

9

10

1
An Italian enamelled-steel modular office desk and typing station, 'Spazio' series, Olivetti, c.1959, fitted with an olive green baize top and with a leather band-form blotter, 197cm (77½in), *NY 11/12 May,*
$2,200 (£1,594)

2
An adjustable swivel desk chair, Arflex Milano, c.1960, brown leather arms, green woven upholstery, *L 6 July,*
£165 ($228)

3
A 'Spazio' desk and cabinet, Studio B.B.P.R. Olivetti, designed in 1959, olive green painted metal, green felt tops, the desk with leather writing surface, h 77.8cm (30⅝in), w 197cm (77½in), *L 6 July,*
£660 ($911)

4
An inflatable plastic armchair, Plasteco Milano Senago, 1971, in the form of a tyre, colourless plastic, labelled 'Made in Italy', d 80cm (31⅜in), *M 7 Oct,*
FF 2,997 (£259; $322)

5
A 'Pileo' lamp, designed by Gae Aulenti, 1972, marked S.P.A. Artemide Milano, in white plastic, 140cm (55⅛in), *M 7 Oct,*
FF 4,995 (£432; $536)

6
A chromed metal, glass and perspex dining table, Albrizzi, 1970s, 274 x 107cm (107 x 42in), *L 28 Sept,*
£220 ($286)

7
A spiral chrome tubular metal chair, Staabmobler, designed by Poul Henningsen, c.1930, the seat and back in synthetic black leather, 81cm (31⅞in), *M 7 Oct,*
FF 7,215 (£624; $774)

8
A plywood table, Finmar Ltd, designed by Alvar Aalto, 1930s, circular top, lower shelf, arched legs, d 62.7cm (24⅜in), *L 16 Feb,*
£396 ($555)

9
Two plywood tables, Finmar Ltd, designed by Alvar Aalto, 1930s, one with Finmar label, h 69cm (27¼in), w 99cm (39in), *L 6 July,*
£253 ($349)

10
A prototype plywood stool, attributed to Isokon, c.1935, rounded square top on open framework of cut sheet plywood, h 45cm (17¾in), *L 16 Feb,*
£242 ($339)

11
An upholstered armchair, Finmar Ltd, designed by Alvar Aalto, 1930s, continuous plywood arms/feet, upholstered in striped brown and beige tweed, h 68cm (26⅞in), *L 28 Sept,*
£176 ($229)

12
A plywood chaise longue, designed by Bruno Mathsson, manufactured by Karl Mathsson, 1935/41, curved plywood frame, slung with inter-laced maroon webbing, 75cm (29½in), *L 6 July,*
£275 ($380)

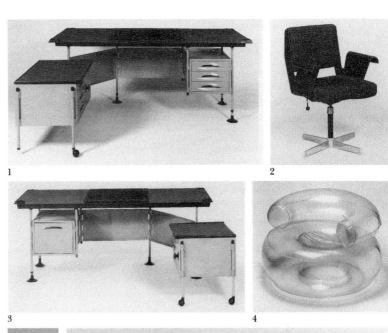

1

2

3

4

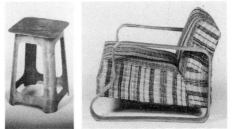

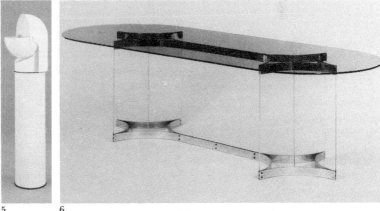

5

6

7

8

9

10

11

12

1
A parcel gilt-bronze and
etched glass chandelier,
French, c.1925, the
reeded standard with
angular light fixture
supporting nine etched
glass panels, 97 cm (38 in),
d 43 cm (17 in),
NY 17/18 Feb,
$1,210 (£852)

2
A silvered bronze and
alabaster sconce, designed
by Albert Cheuret,
c.1925, the flaring three-
sided sconce cast with
overlapping bands,
h 23 cm (9 in), *NY 17 Nov,*
$1,045 (£836)

3
A pair of chromed-metal
lamps, French, c.1925,
h 48 cm (19 in),
NY 17/18 Feb,
$1,870 (£1,317)

4
A chrome-plated bronze
lamp, Edouard-Wilfred
Buquet, c.1930, the
hemispherical shade
pivoting between a U-
form support, h 40.5 cm
(16¼ in), *NY 17 Nov,*
$1,870 (£1,496)

5
A metal and Perzel glass
standard lamp, c.1930,
h 172 cm (67¾ in),
M 11 Mar,
FF 22,200 (£1,866; $2,775)

6
A standard lamp, 1930s,
with a pink frosted
plastic shade, coppery
metal support, stem with
rods of clear glass,
circular base with peach
mirror glass, h 174 cm
(68⅝ in), *L 13 Apr,*
£154 ($222)

7
A set of four wall lights,
1930s, each with
chromed metal shade,
the stem with rods of
amber and clear glass,
h 47.5 cm (18¾ in),
L 16 Feb,
£902 ($1,265)

8
A pair of wall lights,
c.1930, designed for the
Pavilion Hotel Scar-
borough, stepped
scalloped bronze bases,
three rows of overlapping
everted tinted amber
and purple glass panels
slotted into bronze
frame, 57.5 cm (22⅝ in),
L 28 Sept,
£374 ($486)

9
A pair of wall lamps,
c.1930, with flared
chromed metal shades,
with stepped semicircles
of part frosted glass
above stepped chromed
metal base, w 48.5 cm
(19 in), *L 6 July,*
£572 ($789)

10
A chromium-plated metal
and iron 'Topo' adjustable
table lamp, Stilnovo,
designed by Joe Colombo,
1960s, h 48.5 cm (19 in),
L 13 Apr,
£154 ($222)

11
Five lamps, 'Pillola',
designed by Cesare
Casati and Emanuele
Ponzio, 1968, h 55.5 cm
(21¾ in), *M 7 Oct,*
FF 22,200 (£1,918; $2,379)

1

2

3

4

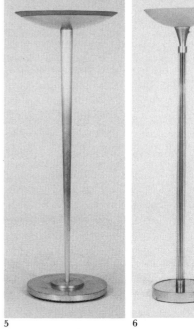

5   6

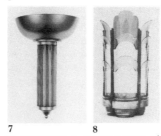

7   8   9

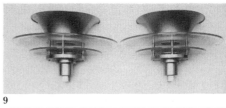

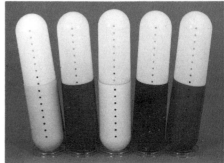

10   11

European Ceramics

DAVID BATTIE • LETITIA ROBERTS

Ceramics have been an important aspect of our lives since the 17th century when they largely superseded pewter and wooden tableware, but they were, of course, produced before that time. The collector is faced with a huge choice ranging from early faience and stoneware, through delftware and early 18th century porcelain, to elaborate 19th-century pieces. Most collectors, and dealers, tend to concentrate on one particular field within the medium. Saleroom catalogues are arranged to reflect this.

There will always be a select group of dedicated collectors who seek only the earliest and rarest examples of a particular ware and until recently their taste has influenced the market. Thus for some time there has been a considerable imbalance between the prices realized for products from the often experimental first ten years of a factory and its later more sophisticated products. This imbalance is beginning to disappear as a new generation of collectors enters the market, seeking pieces which are judged more for their decorative qualities than for their historical significance. Thus the more flamboyant pieces from the end of the 18th century are beginning to increase in popularity and are rising in value in the wake of the already strongly established market for 19th century decorative pieces.

The high price of modern commercial wares also has its effect on auction prices. Mid 19th century services, such as Masons Ironstone, which have sufficient plates for twelve or more settings have been selling well and are bought as much to be used as for decoration. On the other hand mid 18th century tea and coffee sets, such as those from Meissen, which are not generally bought for use, are often divided when sold at auction to maximize the value of the individual pieces.

The condition of all ceramics, particularly porcelain, is significant. As it is not always described in detail in catalogue entries it is essential to view sales thoroughly in advance. Serious damage can reduce the value of a piece dramatically. A piece that has been smashed and reassembled has little commercial value, unless it is exceptionally rare or decorative. It is not difficult to detect restoration, but it does require some expertise and practice. Damaged pieces should not be restored before being offered for sale at auction, since buyers prefer to be responsible for their own restoration and many would rather leave a piece in a slightly damaged state than have it badly repaired. As in every collecting field the top prices are paid for pieces of the highest quality from any period; age is generally of secondary importance.

Marks are, of course, an important factor in the study of ceramics. Not only do marks help to identify the factory, they can also serve to date the majority of pieces and, occasionally, as with Sèvres, they can also give the identity of the painter or enameller. Most factories had several variations to their marks, and throughout the 18th and 19th centuries many factories had no compunctions about copying each other's marks, since no regulations existed. Identification can, therefore, be a problem. While there are handbooks that will help the new collector to a broad attribution, it is necessary to turn to the specialized reference works for detailed identification and up-to-date information on forged marks. Ultimately, it is only from experience that the collector will be able to attribute a piece with certainty.

Continental wares were increasingly popular in 1984. German porcelain lost ground over the previous year, but the market for faience and stoneware strengthened in Europe, though not in the United States because of the strength of the dollar. Sèvres porcelain gained enormously in price, following a period of dormancy. A feature article on Sèvres appears on page 500. Good prices were realized by English porcelain and Staffordshire majolica—Minton and George Jones in particular. English tea and dessert services dating from the first half of the 19th century also sold well when well painted and gilt. English pottery animal and figure groups fetched considerably higher prices than previously, with Walton and Obadiah Sherratt models proving especially popular amongst American buyers.

Those ceramics which are included in decorative arts sales can be found on pages 450ff. Oriental ceramics are to be found on pages 604ff and 633ff.

1
An Hispano-Moresque
dish, 15th cent, painted
with an armorial within a
basket work design applied
with ribs and dots
heightened in blue, broken
once and repaired,
41.5cm (16¼in),
NY 23/24 Nov,
$4,950 (£4,090)

2
An Hispano-Moresque
dish, Catalonia, late 15th
or early 16th cent,
painted in iridescent
gold lustre, the well with
raised central boss,
cracked, 32.5cm (12⅞in),
L 9 Oct,
£682 ($880)

3
An Hispano-Moresque
charger, 16th cent, with
central boss, decorated
in copper lustre with a
stylised flowerhead design,
39cm (15⅜in), *C 28 Mar,*
£550 ($820)

4
An Hispano-Moresque
armorial dish, probably
Valencia, 1st half 16th
cent, painted in copper
lustre, the raised central
boss with a shield
charged with an eagle,
symbolic of Sicily, chipped
and cracked, 39cm
(15⅞in), *L 9 Oct,*
£1,045 ($1,348)

5
An Hispano-Moresque
charger, 16th cent, the
boss decorated in copper
lustre, the rim with
lightly moulded flowers
and buds edged in cobalt
blue, slight crack, 48.5cm
(19⅛in), *C 28 Mar,*
£770 ($1,148)

6
An Hispano-Moresque
dish, 16th/17th cent,
decorated in copper
lustre, the lightly moulded
flowers edged in cobalt
blue, rim chips, 34.9cm
(13¾in), *C 28 Mar,*
£440 ($656)

7
A Deruta double-handled
goblet, *c*1520, decorated
in gold lustre, some
restoration, 21cm (8¼in),
F 19 Dec,
L 2,100,000 (£887; $1,109)

8
An Urbino bowl (scudella)
and cover (tagliere),
probably workshop of
Orazio Fontana, *c*1535-
40, from an accouch-
ment set, 19.7cm (7¾in),
L 5 July,
£7,700 ($10,703)

9
An Urbino flask, 2nd half
16th cent, painted with
scenes from the Old
Testament, the handles
in the form of satyrs'
heads, neck restored,
29.5cm (11⅝in), *F 19 Dec,*
L 2,700,000 (£1,178; $1,411)

10
A Deruta maiolica plate,
*c*1520, the centre
painted with a portrait
of a Turkish Sultan, in
tones of blue, orange,
ochre and emerald green
on white ground, 42cm
(16½in), *NY 23/24 Nov,*
$7,975 (£6,590)

11
A documentary Gubbio
lustred Urbino dish, dated
1534, probably painted
in the workshop of
Guido Durantino, with
Salome receiving the
head of John the Baptist
from Herod, heightened
in the bottega of Maestro
Giorgio Andreoli with
iridescent ruby and
pinkish mushroom lustre,
rim and footring damaged,
26.5cm (10⅜in), *L 12 June,*
£11,000 ($15,840)

1

2

3

4

5

6

7

8

9

10

11

1
An Urbino Istoriato dish,
c 1540-50, of shallow
saucer form with
upturned and flared
rim, painted with
Bacchantes being turned
into trees, repaired, 27.3cm
(10¾in), *L 12 June,*
£1,980 ($2,851)

2
An Urbino Istoriato tazza,
dated 1539, painted with
the story of Cadmus
slaying the dragon,
minor chips to rim,
crack, 27.5cm (10⅞in),
L 9 Oct,
£5,500 ($7,095)

3
**An Urbino Istoriato deep
dish,** *c* 1550-60, painted
with the story of Joseph,
with the Ishmaelites
handing over the silver
to Joseph's brothers, the
rim reduced, 26.5cm
(10⅜in), *L 12 June,*
£880 ($1,267)

4
**An Urbino Istoriato
Crespina,** *c* 1560-70, painted
with the serpent tempting
Adam and Eve, the base
inscribed 'Adam e Eva',
minor chips on rim,
27cm (10⅝in), *L 9 Oct,*
£2,970 ($3,831)

5
A Tuscan dish, probably
Deruta, 3rd quarter 16th
cent, of plain shallow
concave form, boldly
painted in cobalt, ochre,
yellow, green and white,
21.7cm (8½in), *L 5 July,*
£1,430 ($1,987)

6
A Deruta charger, *c* 1520,
the sunken centre painted
with St Francis receiving
the stigmata, the foot-
ring revealing a buff/
brown clay, rim chipping,
41.5cm (16¼in), *L 12 June,*
£14,850 ($21,384)

7
A Faenza Crespina,
c 1540-60, the central
boss painted with a
putto, the fluted well
showing scrolling leaves
on ochre and blue
grounds, one chip and
crack restored, 23cm (9in),
L 9 Oct,
£1,870 ($2,412)

8
A Faenza Crespina, *c* 1550-
60, the centre with a
portrait of a young
woman, 27.5cm (10⅞in),
L 12 June,
£1,485 ($2,138)

9
A Maiolica dish, probably
Faenza, mid-16th cent,
painted with the
triumphal procession of a
Roman Emperor, cracked
and repaired, 48cm
(18¾in), *NY 23/24 Nov,*
$1,100 (£909)

10
**A Castel Durante armorial
charger,** *c* 1500, painted
with the arms of Monte
Feltro and della Rovere,
three hairline cracks
secured by staples on the
reverse, 38.5cm (15⅛in),
NY 23/24 Nov,
$4,950 (£4,090)

11
**A Castel Durante saucer
dish,** *c* 1530, painted in
the manner of Nicola
Pellipario with the
portrait of a young
woman, restored, 23.2cm
(9⅛in), *L 5 July,*
£2,750 ($3,822)

12
A Montelupo dish, early
17th cent, boldly painted
with a foot-soldier in
yellow, cobalt, manganese,
green and ochre, 32cm
(12½in), *L 12 June,*
£935 ($1,346)

13
A Faenza dish, probably
Deruta, dated 1633,
decorated in polychrome
with a central medallion
of the Virgin Mary,
chipped, 41.5cm (16¼in),
M 27 June,
FF 8,880 (£762; $1,039)

14
A Castelli dish, 1st
quarter 18th cent,
painted in the Grue
workshop, decorated in
subdued colours with a
horse grazing, the border
with four putti, 23.8cm
(9¼in), *L 12 June,*
£715 ($1,029)

15
**A Talavera de la Reina
oviform jar,** 2nd half 17th
cent, painted with a
continuous scene of deer
hunters, probably after
Johannes Stradanus, 47cm
(18½in), *L 9 Oct,*
£1,540 ($1,987)

1   2   3

4   5   6

7   8   9

10   11   12

13   14   15

1
A pair of Turin polychrome albarelli, Rossetti's factory, mid-18th cent, the central section bearing the name of the drug, the rims reduced, 18cm (7⅛in), *L 12 June,* £1,210 ($1,742)

2
An albarello, Venice, 17th cent, decorated in bright colours on a blue ground, the base and neck decorated in green and blue, base damaged, 17.5cm (6⅞in), *M 27 June,* FF 12,210 (£1,048; $1,428)

3
A documentary Puglia albarello, 17th/18th cent, painted in a subdued polychrome palette with the figure of a female, inscribed 'Puglia' above the name of the drug 'Oximell. Absinth.', rim chipped, 21cm (8¼in), *L 9 Oct,* £550 ($710)

4
A Trapani albarello, early 18th cent, painted in cobalt outlined in manganese and sparingly heightened in ochre with the sacred monogram IHS, chipped, 26.5cm (10½in), *HS 28 Mar,* £330 ($492)

5
A Caltagirone albarello, late 17th/early 18th cent, glaze flaked, 26cm (10¼in), *HS 28 Mar,* £550 ($820)

6
An albarello, probably Gerace, factory of Giacomo Cefali, 17th cent, painted in Venetian style with the portrait of a young man, reserved on a bright oily cobalt-blue ground, 16.5cm (6½in), *L 12 June,* £418 ($602)

7
A Tuscan albarello, 16th cent, 21.5cm (8½in), *L 12 June,* £550 ($792)

8
An Angarano dish, 1st quarter 18th cent, painted in blue, the centre with a greyhound, 39cm (15⅞in), *F 3/4 Oct,* L 2,600,000 (£1,026; $1,334)

9
A Faenza dish, Ferniani workshops painted by Filippo Comerio, c1775-80, decorated with a figure in green and manganese, the border in pink and purple, cracks, 24cm (9½in), *F 10 May,* L 1,243,000 (£506; $728)

10
A Lodi teapot and cover, Antonio Maria Cappellotti, c1740, painted in polychrome with a Chinese figure, the base and cover monogrammed 'AMC Lodi' cover chipped, light cracks, 14.7cm (5¾in), *F 3/4 Oct,* L 6,000,000 (£2,369; $3,080)

11
A Faenza octagonal teapot and cover, mid-18th cent, with polychrome decoration depicting a chinoiserie scene and a hunting scene, base chipped, 23cm (9in), *F 3/4 Oct,* L 2,500,000 (£987; $1,283)

12
A Faenza coffee pot and cover, mid-18th cent, painted with bouquets of flowers, 22cm (8¾in), *F 3/4 Oct,* L 1,600,000 (£632; $822)

13
A Le Nove dish, Pasquale Antonibon, 3rd quarter 18th cent, 23cm (9in), *F 3 Oct,* L 500,000 (£206; $267)

14
A Le Nove coffee pot and cover, Pasquale Antonibon, c1750-60, decorated in blue, green, yellow and manganese, 24cm (9½in), *F 3 Oct,* L 2,000,000 (£822; $1,069)

15
A Le Nove teapot, Pasquale Antonibon, 1750-60, and a maiolica cover not matching, 11.2cm (4¼in), *F 3 Oct,* L 950,000 (£390; $507)

16
A Faenza tureen and cover, Ferniani period, c1765, modelled after a silver original and painted with various buildings on 'islands', three chips to cover, 35cm (13⅞in), *L 9 Oct,* £682 ($880)

1
A Rhenish stoneware
bellarmine (Bartmann
krug), Frechen or Cologne,
2nd quarter 16th cent,
covered in a pale honey-
coloured salt-glaze, 18cm
(7⅛in), *L 12 June,*
£3,520 ($5,069)

2
A Cologne salt-glazed
stoneware pewter-mounted
mug (Pinte), 2nd quarter
16th cent, with panels
depicting 'The Fall' after
an engraving by Virgil
Solis, the glaze of a pale
honey colour, *L 12 June,*
£1,540 ($2,218)

3
A signed Siegburg
stoneware tankard
(schnelle), *c*1675-85,
applied with plaques of
Athene, Juno and Venus
above armorials, pewter
cover, cracks and chips,
27.5cm (10⅞in), *L 9 Oct,*
£2,200 ($2,838)

4
A Siegburg stoneware
tankard (schnelle), late
16th cent, moulded in
shallow relief with
portraits of Judith,
Lucretia and Faith above
armorials, pewter lid,
21cm (8¼in), *L 12 June,*
£2,310 ($3,326)

5
An Annaberg stoneware
jug, late 17th cent,
handle replaced, 25cm
(9¾in), *NY 2/3 Mar,*
$1,320 (£886)

6
An Annaberg stoneware
'Birnkrug', *c*1660-70, later
pewter cover, 20cm
(7⅞in), *L 12 June,*
£990 ($1,426)

7
A Creussen stoneware
apostle tankard, dated
1685, pewter footrim and
lid, 16cm (6¼in),
NY 2/3 Mar,
$3,300 (£2,215)

8
A Creussen stoneware
apostle tankard, dated
1673, brown glazed and
painted with the Lamb
of God and foliate
scrolls, pewter mounts,
13.5cm (5¼in),
NY 2/3 Mar,
$4,125 (£2,768)

9
A Creussen stoneware
tankard, 2nd quarter
17th cent, turned and
applied with angel's
heads and foliate
ornament, pewter cover,
h 11.5cm (4¾in),
NY 23/24 Nov,
$2,200 (£1,818)

10
A Westerwald stoneware
'Sternkanne', mid-17th
cent, the body covered
in a manganese glaze
and pierced at the front
with a floret within a
star, the foot with silver-
plated mounts, 19.7cm
(7¾in), *L 9 Oct,*
£495 ($639)

11
A Westerwald stoneware
'Sternkanne', 1668,
applied with an oval
medallion incorporating
the arms of Louis XIV,
the initials 'IB' and the
date, pewter lid, 26cm
(10¼in), *L 12 June,*
£880 ($1,267)

12
A Westerwald stoneware
jug, late 17th cent, the
front with portrait
medallion of Queen
Mary, 23cm (9in),
NY 2/3 Mar,
$605 (£406)

13
A Westerwald stoneware
jug, 18th cent, painted in
blue on grey ground,
pewter lid, 27cm (11½in),
NY 2/3 Mar,
$495 (£332)

14
A Westerwald stoneware
jug, 18th cent, decorated
in blue on a grey ground
with a medallion
initialled 'GR', 33cm
(13in), *M 27 June,*
FF 3,330 (£286; $390)

15
A stoneware tankard,
probably Bunzlau,
early 18th cent, the
body brown-glazed,
mounted with a pewter
footrim and cover,
20.6cm (8⅛in), *NY 16 June,*
$385 (£281)

16
A Westerwald stoneware
jug, late 18th cent, four
bead-edged panels incised
with stags or floral
motifs, pewter cover,
25.1cm (9⅞in), *NY 16 June,*
$440 (£321)

1
A Frankfurt/Hanau faïence jug, 1st half 18th cent, the spirally moulded body painted in shades of blue with chinoiserie scenes in landscapes, damage to spout, chips to footrim, 27cm (10¾in), *L 9 Oct,*
£660 ($851)

2
A Frankfurt/Hanau faïence pewter-mounted jug, early 18th cent, the cream-glazed body painted in shades of blue, crack to handle, minor chips, 21cm (8¼in), *L 9 Oct,*
£770 ($993)

3
A Nuremberg faïence pewter-mounted tankard, Kordenbusch workshop, mid-18th cent, decorated in shades of blue with Christ on his way to Emmaus accompanied by two disciples, minor chips, crack to bottom, 21cm (8¼in), *L 9 Oct,*
£1,485 ($1,916)

4
A Hanau faïence pewter-mounted jug, (*Enghalskrug*), 1st half 18th cent, painted in cobalt blue, 26.5cm (10½in), *L 12 June,*
£660 ($950)

5
A Nuremberg faïence pewter-mounted armorial tankard (*Walzenkrug*), 3rd quarter 18th cent, painted in greyish cobalt on a pale blue ground, the lid struck with the mark of Johann Mehlin of Bamberg, 21cm, (8¼in), *L 12 June,*
£1,320 ($1,901)

6
A Thuringian faïence pewter-mounted cylindrical tankard (*Walzenkrug*), probably Erfurt, 2nd half 18th cent, painted in green, manganese, ochrish-yellow and deep cerulean, 23cm (9in), *L 12 June,*
£605 ($871)

7
A Bayreuth faïence pewter-mounted tankard (*Walzenkrug*), Knoller period 1728-44, painted in pale manganese and cobalt, 'BK' mark in blue, minor rim chips, 24cm (9in), *L 12 June,*
£572 ($824)

8
A pair of Mettlach ewers, late 19th cent, each of shell moulded form, the necks applied with satyrs, simulated 'jewelled' borders, printed marks in green, some repair, 40.5cm (16in), *C 3 Oct,*
£385 ($497)

9
A Mettlach pewter-mounted Stein, 1898, the cylindrical body lightly moulded and coloured with views of named villages in a forest of trees, the hinged lid surmounted by a schloss, 40cm (15¾in), *L 8 Mar,*
£1,155 ($1,721)

10
A Mettlach pewter-mounted Stein, 20th cent, incised with three elves seated on barrels, hinged cover decorated with cats, 26.7cm (10½in), *C 5 July,*
£330 ($449)

11
A South German faïence yellow-ground teapot and cover, possibly Göppingen, *c*1770-80, the finely-ribbed pear-shaped body enamelled in manganese, green, cobalt and black, 13.5cm (5⅜in), *L 12 June,*
£220 ($316)

12
A Frankfurt marbled faïence dish, *c*1700, in the form of a chrysanthemum flowerhead, the interior covered in a marbled ochre, manganese and pale cobalt on a white ground, 29cm (11¾in), *L 12 June,*
£2,860 ($4,118)

13
A Mettlach wall plaque, *c*1900, decorated after J Stahl, moulded signature, with a scene of Jason and the Argonauts, hair crack 46.3cm (18⅛in), *L 7 June,*
£286 ($415)

14
A pair of Kellinghusen faïence shoes, *c*1800, coloured yellow with manganese sole incised through the glaze in script GH, both restored, 19.5cm (7⅝in), *L 9 Oct,*
£396 ($512)

1 2 3 4

5 6 7

8

9 10 11

12 13 14

1
A faïence soup tureen and cover, Moustiers, Olerys factory, 2nd half 18th cent, decorated in polychrome with flowers and garlands of flowers, 31cm (12⅛in), *M 27 June,* **FF 11,100 (£953; $1,298)**

2
A faïence set of six plates, Moustiers, Olerys factory, c.1750, decorated in polychrome with mythical figures and exotic animals, 25cm (9⅞in), *M 27 June,* **FF 55,500 (£4,764; $6,491)**

3
A faïence dish, Moustiers, Olerys factory, c.1750, decorated in green and ochre with grotesque figures of musicians, birds and flowers, w 37.2cm (14⅝in), *M 27 June,* **FF 15,540 (£1,334; $1,818)**

4
A faïence dish, Moustiers, Olerys-Laugier factory, mid-18th cent, decorated in blue with armorials within flowers and garlands, w 38.9cm (15¼in), *M 27 June,* **FF 8,880 (£762; $1,039)**

5
A pair of faïence plates, Moustiers, Frères Ferrat factory, 2nd half 18th cent, decorated in polychrome with a large central medallion with scenes of Chinese life, framed by yellow scrolls, the rim in red, d 24cm (9⅜in), *M 27 June,* **FF 14,430 (£1,239; $1,687)**

6
A faïence mustard pot and cover, Moustiers, Frères Ferrat factory, 2nd half 18th cent, decorated with polychrome flowers bordered in red, 13cm (5⅛in), *M 27 June,* **FF 8,325 (£715; $973)**

7
A faïence dish, Moustiers, Clerissy factory, c.1725, decorated in blue in the manner of Berain, w 42cm (16½in), *M 27 June,* **FF 5,550 (£476; $649)**

8
A Marseille faïence cache-pot, Saint-Jean-du-Désert, early 18th cent, the handles in the form of Indian masks, cracks, h 16.8cm (6⅝in), *M 27 June,* **FF 8,880 (£762; $1,039)**

9
A pair of Marseille faïence plates, fauchier Neveu, c.1750-60, the yellow glazed body embellished with sprigs of various flowers in grand feu colours, damage to one, 28cm (11in), *L 9 Oct,* **£990 ($1,277)**

10
A pair of Marseille tureens and covers, 18th cent, the finial in the form of an apple, w 35.5cm (14in), *M 27 June,* **FF 24,420 (£2,096; $2,856)**

11
Two Marseille faïence plates, Gaspard-Joseph Robert, c.1770-80, one flat, the other of bowl form, 24.5cm (9⅝in), *M 27 June,* **FF 33,300 (£2,858; $3,894)**

1
A faïence mustard pot and cover, Niderviller, Beyerle period, c.1765-70, decorated in polychrome with flowers, the green handle in the form of a branch, 10.5cm (4⅛in), *M 27 June*, **FF 4,440 (£381; $519)**

2
A faïence ewer and basin, Montpellier, c.1760, decorated in polychrome, the basin with cracks, ewer h 25cm (9⅞in), *M 27 June*, **FF 3,885 (£334; $454)**

3
A faïence plate, probably Lunéville, c.1770, decorated with an oriental in fancy dress, mark in manganese, 25cm (9⅞in), *L 9 Oct*, **£264 ($340)**

4
A set of twelve Sceaux faïence plates, c.1770, decorated in polychrome with flowers, fruit and insects, the rim with alternate blue and red combing, 24cm (9⅜in), *M 27 June*, **FF 28,860 (£2,477; $3,375)**

5
A Strasbourg tureen and cover, Paul Hannong period, c.1760, decorated with sprays of *fleurs fines* in *petit feu au poncif*, a rose-spring forming the knop, crack to bowl, minor chips, 30cm (11⅞in), *L 9 Oct*, **£825 ($1,064)**

6
A Brussels faïence tureen, 18th cent, in the form of a boar's head, restorations, w 39cm (15⅜in), *M 11 Dec*, **FF 28,860 (£2,543; $3,070)**

7
A French earthenware jardinière, 3rd quarter 19th cent, painted by J Bernard, signed, d 51.4cm (20¼in), *NY 24/25 Feb*, **$825 (£569)**

8
A Sceaux faïence pot-pourri vase and cover, J Chapelle period, c.1755, decorated in polychrome relief with an exotic animal, vine branches in green, blue and red, chips and repairs, 33.5cm (13¼in), *M 27 June*, **FF 72,150 (£6,193; $8,439)**

9
An Eastern European faïence figure, possibly Holitsch, 3rd quarter 18th cent, of a monkey holding a blue, purple and yellow tulip, the blue/green stem outlined in manganese, restoration to left arm and leaves, 13.6cm (5⅜in), *L 9 Oct*, **£385 ($497)**

10
A pair of Delphin Massier faïence aviary ornaments, early 20th cent, each in the form of two parrots with brightly coloured plumage, 40cm (15¾in), *L 8/9 Nov*, **£275 ($366)**

11
An Alcora faïence bust of a Blackamoor, wearing a blue cloak with purple border, white tunic and white hat with yellow cockade, his face in manganese-purple, minor chips, 12.3cm (4⅞in), *L 12 June*, **£1,320 ($1,901)**

12
A continental Majolica pedestal, late 19th cent, in the form of a bear, the whole glazed in tones of brown, green and red, 101cm (39⅞in), *L 7 June*, **£1,100 ($1,595)**

1

2

3

4

5

6

7

8

9

10

11

12

1
An Urbino Istoriato dish,
c.1550-60, painted with
the story of Europa and
the Bull, the background
with tall misty mountains
rising against a cerulean
and saffron sky, the reverse
inscribed 'Europa', 29cm
(11⅜in), L 5 July,
£7,700 ($10,703)

2
An Urbino Istoriato dish,
c.1550-60, with a sunken
centre and wide flat rim,
painted with naked men
and women disporting
themselves in and around
a stone bath, 26.5cm
(10⅜in), L 12 June,
£3,410 ($4,910)

3
**A London Delft polychrome
'blue-dash' tulip charger,**
probably London,
c.1675-85, decorated in
blue, copper-green,
yellow and ochre, within
a yellow-line border and
blue-dashed rim, 43.2cm
(17in), L 24 July,
£8,800 ($11,748)

4
**A Mintons 'Majolica'
blackamoor,** dated 1873,
the whole in typical and
colourful 'majolica' glazes,
102.2cm (40¼in), L 14 Feb,
£6,050 ($8,482)

5
**A Mintons 'Majolica'
peacock,** c.1875, after a
model by P Comolera,
moulded signature, its
plumage naturalistically
textured, the whole
coloured in bright
'majolica' glazes, minor
damage, 152.4cm (60in),
L 14 Feb,
£18,700 ($26,217)

1
**A Berlin pierced dessert
service,** mid-19th cent,
painted with a spray of
colourful summer flowers,
the octagonal rim pierced
with a border of pale-
green trellis below a gilt
bound-red border, minor
restoration, 32 pieces,
L 7 June,
£4,180 ($6,061)

2
**An extensive Meissen
dinner service,** late 19th
cent, each piece painted
with colourful scattered
flower sprigs within a
gilt rim, minor chips,
303 pieces, *L 7 June,*
£13,200 ($19,140)

1

2

1
A square Delft blue and white plaquette, dated 1756, decorated with a view of Amsterdam, 22.5 x 22.5cm (8⅞ x 8⅞ in), *A 1 Oct,*
Dfl 11,368 (£2,675; $3,451)

2
A Dutch Delft polychrome tile, 17th cent, *A 9 Mar,*
Dfl 174 (£40; $60)

3
A Dutch Delft blue and white tile, 17th cent, with decoration of a stumbling horse and horseman, *A 9 Mar,*
Dfl 139 (£32; $48)

4
An early Dutch Delft polychrome dish, 1st quarter 17th cent, painted in ochre, cobalt blue and green on a white ground, 24.3cm (9½ in), *L 9 Oct,*
£6,600 ($8,514)

5
A Delft blue and white tankard, *c* 1690, the pear-shaped body painted on the front with an interior scene, the reverse with birds in flowering branches, hair crack on rim, 19.7cm (7¾ in), *NY 17 Nov,*
$1,210 (£968)

6
A Delft blue and white puzzle jug, De Drye Porceleyne Flesschen, *c* 1710, the pear-shaped body painted with birds amidst flowering shrubbery, 20.3cm (8in), *NY 17 Nov,*
$1,430 (£1,144)

7
A Delft blue and white cuspidor, *c* 1725, the quatrefoil body painted with floral sprigs; sold with a Delft blue and white beaker vase, 7.6cm (3in), *NY 16 June,*
$495 (£361)

8
A Delft polychrome vase and cover, De Drye Clocken Factory, *c* 1690, painted in blue, iron red, yellow and green, the whole heightened in iron-red cold paint, cover chipped and lion knop repaired, small hair cracks on rim, 50.8cm (20in), *NY 17 Nov,*
$880 (£704)

9
A pair of Dutch Delft blue and white marriage-plates, Albertus Kiehl, inscribed 'Iiprom Etoly' '6 April, 1760', the marriage symbolised with joining hands, the border with stylised leaf- and flower-motifs, *A 16 May,*
Dfl 1,430 (£332; $475)

10
A Dutch Delft blue and white tobacco jar, 3rd quarter 18th cent, painted in blue with a scrollwork panel enclosing the name 'Marteniek', slight crack, glaze chips, 29.8cm (11¾ in), *C 5 July,*
£374 ($507)

11
A Friesian Delft blue and white dish, 18th cent, with decoration of a man on horseback, 30.5cm (12in), *A 18/26 Sept,*
Dfl 1,624 (£381; $492)

12
A Dutch Delft blue and white oil and vinegar set, decorated with stylised flowers, 23.5cm (9¼ in), *A 16 May,*
Dfl 4,640 (£1,078; $1,542)

13
A Dutch Delft or Frankfurt faïence bowl and cover, early 18th cent, w 18.3cm (7¼ in), *NY 16 June,*
$935 (£682)

14
A Dutch Delft polychrome shaped plaque, 18th cent, representing the biblical scene Genesis 24, verse 14, 22.5cm (8⅞ in), *A 16 May,*
Dfl 2,784 (£647; $925)

15
A Dutch Delft polychrome birdcage, late 19th cent, the base painted with scenes of rustic lovers and landscape views, a Delftware bird on a perch inside, 47cm (18½ in), *L 7 June,*
£550 ($798)

16
A pair of Dutch Delft polychrome milking groups, 16.5cm (6½ in), *A 17 Dec,*
Dfl 1,044 (£249; $312)

1
A Liverpool Delft blue and white rectangular pill slab, *c*1690, painted in blue with the rhinoceros crest and arms of the Worshipful Society of Apothecaries, some chips and crackled glaze, 27 x 24.4cm (10⅝ x 9⅝in), *NY 13 Apr*, $1,980 (£1,385)

2
A Bristol Delft polychrome rectangular pill slab, 1740-50, painted in blue with the rhinoceros crest and arms of the Worshipful Society of Apothecaries, 29.9 x 24.4cm (11¾ x 9⅝in), *NY 12/14 Apr*, $4,070 (£2,846)

3
A London Delft blue and white octagonal pill slab, early 18th cent, decorated in blue with the arms of the Worshipful Society of Apothecaries, chips, wear, 25.5cm (10in), *L 22 May*, £1,265 ($1,834)

4
A London Delft blue and white dry drug jar, dated 1662, inscribed 'V:Aregon', hair cracks and abrasion on rim, base drilled, 19.2cm (7½in), *NY 13 Apr*, $1,980 (£1,385)

5
An early London Delft blue and white dated wet drug jar, 1666, inscribed 'S:De:Prassio' for a syrup of White horehound on a 'winged-angel' label, 16.5cm (6½in), *L 22 May*, £3,080 ($4,466)

6
A London Delft blue and white pill pot, *c*1725, painted with a label inscribed 'P:Macri', below a basket of flowers, minor imperfections, 9.4cm (3¾in), *NY 13 Apr*, $880 (£1,258)

7
A London Delft blue and white wet drug jar, last quarter 17th cent, inscribed 'S. Ivivbin' for Syrup of Ground Pine on a 'winged-angel' label with claw-like tassles, 18cm (7in), *L 22 May*, £495 ($718)

8
A London Delft drug jar, 3rd quarter 17th cent, inscribed 'Diascordiv', 20.5cm (8in), *L 22 May*, £352 ($510)

9
A London Delft blue and white large dry drug jar, *c*1725, painted on the front with a scroll-edged label inscribed 'C:Cynosb', minor imperfections, 30.8cm (12⅛in), *NY 12-14 Apr*, $880 (£615)

10
A pair of London Delft blue and white pill jars, early 18th cent, each decorated with a 'songbird' label, one inscribed 'P:Hier:Cu:Ag', the other 'P:Cynogl' for Hound's-tongue pills, one chipped on foot, 9cm (3½in), *L 22 May*, £792 ($1,148)

11
A London Delft blue and white dated drug jar, 1738, with a 'cherub and shell' label, inscribed 'E:Lenitiv' above the initials 'W I', cracks, slight glaze flaking, 18cm (7in), *L 22 May*, £1,430 ($2,074)

12
A London Delft blue and white sack bottle, dated 1647, the front inscribed 'Sack', chip on foot at back, 15.7cm (6⅛in), *NY 12-14 Apr*, $5,170 (£3,615)

1   2

3

4   5

6

7   8

9

10   11   12

1
A London white tankard, 2nd half 17th cent, decorated with rows of pushed-out bosses, the white tin-glaze crazed overall and showing a pink hue, minor glaze chips, 21cm (8¼in), *L 2 Oct*, £9,900 ($12,771)

2
A London Delft dish, mid-17th cent, in the white after a metal original, moulded with a border of trefoils around the central boss, crazing to glaze and minor chips, 33.6cm (13¼in), *L 22 May*, £3,300 ($4,785)

3
A Delft polychrome octagonal plate, London or Bristol, dated 1687, painted in blue and manganese with a China-nan amidst shrubbery, the rim with stylised floral border, hair crack to rim, w 20.4cm (8in), *NY 13 Apr*, $1,210 (£846)

4
A London Delft polychrome blue-dash 'Oak Leaf' charger, 1690-1710, painted with five blue leaves surrounded by tan-heightened yellow and blue berries and sprigs, some chips and hair cracks, 29.8cm (11¾in), *NY 13 Apr*, $4,125 (£2,885)

5
An English Delft polychrome 'William and Mary' portrait charger, London or Bristol, 1688-94, painted in blue, yellow and manganese, small hair cracks, 32.4cm (12¾in), *NY 12-14 Apr*, $11,550 (£8,076)

6
A Delft polychrome 'George I' portrait charger, London or Bristol, 1714-27, painted in blue, iron-red and green, riveted star crack, 33.5cm (13¼in), *NY 12-14 Apr*, $1,870 (£1,308)

7
A London Delft polychrome Royal portrait plate, c.1689-90, painted in blue and ochre with half-length portraits of William and Mary, two hair cracks, 21.4cm (8½in), *NY 12-14 Apr*, $3,850 (£2,692)

8
A London Delft blue and white plate, dated 1699, painted in blue edged in black with a Chinaman seated in a fenced garden, the rim with blue scallop border, 21.9cm (8⅝in), *NY 12-14 Apr*, $1,760 (£1,231)

9
A Delft polychrome patriotic plate, London or Bristol, dated 1717, inscribed 'God Save King George', within a blue and green foliate roundel, damaged, 22.3cm (8¾in), *NY 13 Apr*, $1,045 (£731)

10
A Delft blue and white mug, London or Bristol, c.1730, with a blue-dashed strap handle, painted with three arched floral panels, repaired chips and hair crack, 10.3cm (4in), *NY 12-14 Apr*, $825 (£577)

11
A London Delft blue and white mug, early 18th cent, painted in tones of blue with birds, the base decorated with a child in a basket, crack in base, 17.2cm (6¾in), *L 2 Oct*, £935 ($1,206)

12
A London Delft polychrome plate, c.1750, painted in blue, iron red, yellow and green with a Chinaman in a fenced garden, 34.3cm (13½in), *NY 12-14 Apr*, $880 (£615)

1

2

3

4

5

6

7

8

9

10

11 (*above and detail below*)

12

1
A London Delft blue and white sauceboat, c.1760-70, of silver shape, with serpent-entwined handle, painted in strong tones of blue with chinoiserie landscapes, 17.2cm (6¾in), *L 22 May,* £660 ($957)

2
A Bristol Delft powdered manganese bowl, c.1750, the exterior with a powdered manganese ground painted in blue with four fish, white-glazed interior, hair cracks, 22.3cm (8¾in), *NY 13 Apr,* $2,090 (£1,462)

3
A London Delft blue and white sweetmeat dish, 1760-70, with a central star-shaped compartment surrounded by five scalloped fan-shaped compartments, small hair cracks, 19.3cm (7⅝in), *NY 13 Apr,* $770 (£538)

4
A London Delft polychrome bowl, 1760-70, boldly painted in manganese, blue, green and yellow with a chinoiserie landscape, 23.1cm (9⅛in), *NY 12-14 Apr,* $467 (£327)

5
A London Delft blue and white fuddling cup, mid-17th cent, formed as three conjoined baluster-shaped vessels with entwined rope-twist handles heightened with blue dashes, minor imperfections, 7.9cm (3⅛in), *NY 12-14 Apr,* $1,870 (£1,308)

6
A London Delft blue and white teapot stand or salver, probably Lambeth, c.1720-30, after a silver original, chips and wear, 13.5cm (5¼in), *L 24 July,* £352 ($470)

7
A Lambeth or Bristol Delft polychrome posset pot and cover, c.1700, the bulbous body painted with oriental ferns, the loop handles striped in blue and green, hair crack to cover, 23.5cm (9¼in), *P 20-22 Mar,* £462 ($693)

8
A London Delft blue and white posset pot and cover, 1730-40, applied with strap handles, painted in blue with stylised sprays of flowers, 15.2cm (6in), *C 10 Jan,* £935 ($1,356)

9
A Bristol Delft blue and white plate, mid-18th cent, painted in blue with a kiln belching smoke, in a stylised rural setting, typical wear to rim, 22.9cm (9in), *L 22 May,* £286 ($415)

10
A Bristol Delft blue and white plate, 2nd quarter 18th cent, in blue decorated with a ferocious scaly dolphin, wear on rim, 22.9cm (9in), *L 22 May,* £462 ($670)

11
A Bristol Delft polychrome 'Cockerel' plate, c.1720-30, the crowing bird brightly painted in yellow, iron-red and blue, flanked by trees 'sponged' in manganese, minor wear and chips, 20.3cm (8in), *L 24 July,* £825 ($1,103)

12
A Bristol Delft polychrome dish, c.1730-40, painted in blue, grey green, iron red and bright yellow with a parrot perched in an oriental shrub, chipping to rim, 33.1cm (13in), *L 2 Oct,* £330 ($426)

13
A pair of Bristol Delft polychrome 'Tulip' plates, 1730-40, the central tulip and flanking buds painted in blue, yellow, green and iron red, 33.1 and 33.3cm (13 and 13⅛in), *NY 13 Apr,* $2,750 (£1,923)

14
A Bristol Delft powdered purple-ground plate, c.1750, painted in blue with a central floral spray within a 'woolsack' panel reserved on the pale lavender ground, 32cm (12⅝in), *NY 12-14 Apr,* $605 (£423)

1
A pair of Delft blue and white large wall cornucopiae, Bristol or Liverpool, 1750-60, each painted with long floral sprays between dotted scalework panels, one with long hair crack, h 27.8 and 28.6cm (11 and 11¼in), *NY 13 Apr*, $880 (£615)

2
A pair of Liverpool Delft blue and white wall cornucopiae, 1750-60, each with a spirally-fluted body painted with a floral sprig above a curled tip shaded in blue, the rim with a Chinaman, h 23.7 and 22.5cm (9⅜ and 8⅞in), *NY 12-14 Apr*, $1,430 (£1,000)

3
A Bristol Delft blue and white bulb-pot, *c*1760, each side painted in tones of blue with a lady and gallant in a landscape, typical wear on edges, 10.2cm (4in), *L 24 July*, £825 ($1,101)

4
A pair of Liverpool Delft polychrome flower bricks, *c*1760, painted and 'pencilled' in manganese, sage green, bright yellow and iron red with birds amongst shrubs, some damage, 13cm (5in), *L 24 July*, £1,265 ($1,689)

5
A Liverpool Delft polychrome documentary flower brick, dated 1761, the front inscribed 'William, Done, Bricklayer Cheshire, 1761', the reverse and ends painted in 'Fazackerly' flowers, cracked, 12.3cm (4⅞in), *NY 13 Apr*, $3,190 (£2,231)

6
A Liverpool Delft polychrome flower brick, *c*1760, painted in manganese, yellow and olive-green on the front with a rowing scene, repaired chip and crack, 14.1cm (5½in), *NY 13 Apr*, $1,320 (£923)

7
A Liverpool Delft blue and white bottle, *c*1760, painted with two hounds baiting a boar in a landscape, the flaring rim with a trellis diaper border, 23cm (9in), *NY 12-14 Apr*, $550 (£385)

8
Two Liverpool Delft blue and white bottles, 1740-60, each painted with floral sprays beneath stylised ruyi-head borders, 23.3 and 23.1cm (9⅛in), *NY 13 Apr*, $715 (£500)

9
An assembled pair of Liverpool Delft polychrome plates, *c*1760, painted in shades of blue, manganese, green and yellow with a gentleman and his sweetheart, 22.5cm (8⅞in), *NY 12-14 Apr*, $1,100 (£769)

10
A Liverpool Delft blue and white puzzle jug, *c*1760, inscribed with verse, the neck pierced with blue-edged floral motifs, repairs, 19.4cm (7⅝in), *NY 12-14 Apr*, $577 (£403)

11
A Liverpool Delft blue and white puzzle jug, 3rd quarter 18th cent, pencilled in blue with a rhyme, the neck pierced with stylised florettes, chipped, 17.8cm (7in), *C 10 Jan*, £374 ($544)

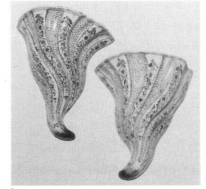

1   2

3   4

5   6

7   8

9   10   11

1

An early earthenware watering-pot, late 16th/17th cent, the reddish-brown body dipped with an apron of galena glaze, 31.8cm (12½in), *L 22 May*, £770 ($1,117)

2

An English earthenware 'aquamanile', 14th cent, modelled as a ram, decorated with translucent yellow stripes over a mottled green ground, damaged and with head repaired, 28cm (11in), *L 22 May*, £1,870 ($2,712)

3

An inscribed and dated North Staffordshire slipware cup, 1711, of thistle form, 'feathered' in cream and chocolate-brown slips, the whole with a translucent yellow-tinted lead-glaze, minor chips, 10.2cm (4in), *L 22 May*, £3,080 ($4,466)

4

A Staffordshire inscribed slipware model of a cradle, last quarter 17th cent, the buff-coloured body slipped in red clay overall and trailed and 'jewelled' with chocolate-brown and cream slips, some damage, 22.9cm (9in), *L 22 May*, £550 ($798)

5

A Staffordshire 'Boar's Head' dish, 18th cent, decorated with slip trails combed into the brown ground beneath a lead glaze, glaze chip, 44.4cm (17½in), *L 14 Feb*, £572 ($802)

6

An inscribed and dated Donyatt fuddling cup, 1762, formed as six conjoined vessels linked by 'rope-twist' handles, mottled in copper green with a translucent yellow lead-glaze, chips and damage, 16.5cm (6½in), *L 24 July*, £638 ($852)

7

A slipware dish, 18th cent, the interior trailed in cream on the chocolate-brown ground, 27.5cm (10⅞in), *P 10-13 July*, £704 ($957)

8

A slipware baking dish, late 18th cent, trailed in cream slip on a dark brown ground, 36.8cm (14½in), *C 3 Oct*, £440 ($568)

9

A dated slipware rectangular dish, 1795, boldly trailed in cream slip on a dark brown ground, notched rim, 33.6cm (13¼in), *L 2 Oct*, £1,650 ($2,128)

10

A Staffordshire slipware baking dish, early 18th cent, the interior trailed in ochre and chocolate coloured slip with a stylised bird, reserved on a rich cream slip, some flaking, 35.3cm (13⅞in), *C 28 Mar*, £7,700 ($11,473)

11

A Nottingham stoneware 'carved jug', c.1700-10, glazed in lustrous brown, small chips, 10.2cm (4in), *L 22 May*, £1,155 ($1,675)

12

A brown-glazed stoneware jug, possibly Nottingham, mid-18th cent, inscribed 'GR' beneath a crown, chips to rim, 17.5cm (6⅞in), *P 10-13 July*, £352 ($479)

13

A giant salt-glazed stoneware hunting jug, early 19th cent, moulded with traditional and patriotic motifs including two central 'Johnson and Boswell' figures, hair cracks, 39cm (15¼in), *P 20-22 Mar*, £330 ($492)

14

A Staffordshire salt-glaze bear jug and cover, c.1740, repaired, chain missing, 18.3cm (7¼in), *NY 13 Apr*, $1,540 (£1,077)

15

A Nottingham brown stoneware bear jug and cover, c.1760, clasping a cub to her chest, the removable head forming a cup and with a chain, 23.3cm (9⅛in), *NY 13 Apr*, $990 (£692)

1

A Staffordshire salt-glaze teapot and cover, c.1760, enamelled with trailing leafy flower-sprays heightened in gilding, chip to spout, minor star-crack in base, 12.2cm (4¾in), L 22 May, £462 ($670)

2

A Staffordshire solid agate small teapot and cover, 1745-50, marbleised in blue and brown on a cream-coloured ground, spout repaired, 9.9cm (3⅞in), NY 13 Apr, $935 (£654)

3

A Staffordshire salt-glaze teapot and cover, c.1745, thinly cast and finely moulded with sprigs of acorns and oak leaves alternating with shells, small hair crack on rim, 14.3cm (5⅝in), NY 13 Apr, $1,760 (£1,231)

4

A Staffordshire solid agate figure of a seated cat, c.1745-50, its body striated in brown and splashed with blue patches, 12.7cm (5in), L 22 May, £352 ($510)

5

A Jackfield-type black-glazed cream jug, mid-18th cent, after a silver shape, 9.3cm (3¾in), P 14 Nov, £99 ($133)

6

A Staffordshire Redware coffee pot and cover, c.1760, 17.3cm (6¾in), L 22 May, £418 ($606)

7

A Staffordshire pink lustre Masonic large jug, 1828, painted in brown, green, ochre, iron red and blue with three named children, the sides transfer printed, 23.9cm (9⅜in), NY 30 June, $770 (£570)

8

A Staffordshire glazed red stoneware coffee pot and cover, c.1770, engine-turned with combed and zig-zag bands, chipped cover interior, 23cm (9in), P 14 Nov, £143 ($192)

9

A Staffordshire salt-glaze 'Scratch-Blue' mug, dated 1759, cracked, slight chip, 15cm (5⅞in), C 28 Mar, £792 ($1,180)

10

A Yorkshire creamware jug and cover, probably Rothwell, c.1770, splashed in manganese brown, chip to cover, 16cm (6¼in), L 22 May, £396 ($574)

11

An American 'Rockingham'-glazed earthenware frog jug, probably from the Southern Porcelain Company, Kaolin, South Carolina, 1856-62, some chips, 27cm (10⅝in), NY 26 Jan, $605 (£417)

12

A Staffordshire copper lustre 'General Jackson' commemorative jug, c.1828, 14.7cm (5¾in), NY 30 June, $1,045 (£774)

13

Two Staffordshire yellow-glazed earthenware jugs, c.1820, decorated in iron-red, green, brown and black, small hair cracks, one spout damaged, 15.8 and 9.6cm (6¼ and 3¾in), NY 30 June, $385 (£285)

14

A Wedgwood/Whieldon 'Pineapple' teapot and cover, c.1765, small hair cracks, 13.8cm (5⅜in), NY 12- 14 Apr, $1,430 (£1,000)

15

A Whieldon teapot and cover, c.1760, picked out in blue, green, ochre and brown against the streaky blue and grey ground, spout repaired, 11.7cm (4⅝in), NY 12-14 Apr, $1,100 (£769)

16

A Whieldon coffee pot and cover, 1760-5, covered in a streaky brown glaze splotched in green and yellow, body repaired, spout restored, 23.5cm (9¼in), NY 12-14 Apr, $1,320 (£923)

1
A pearlware crocus-pot and cover, early 19th cent, of 'D' section, painted with rural scenes in blue, green, brown and ochre between blue-line borders, minor chips, 19cm (7½in), *L 24 July*, £352 ($470)

2
A Liverpool creamware transfer-printed and enamelled jug, dated 1802, printed with portrait medallions and American patriotic motifs, 27.7cm (10⅞in), *NY 30 June*, $990 (£733)

3
A Liverpool creamware transfer-printed and enamelled jug, c1805, printed in black and enamelled with American motifs, spout cracked, discolouration, 26.8cm (10½in), *NY 30 June*, $1,980 (£1,467)

4
A pearlware loving cup, late 18th cent, naively painted in blue, green ochre and brown with a sailing boat before a bridge, discolouration, 12cm (4¾in), *L 22 May*, £132 ($191)

5
A Liverpool creamware transfer-printed jug, c1800, the rim cold gilded with a border of circlets, 20.2cm (8in), *NY 30 June*, $550 (£407)

6
A Whieldon model of a Suffolk Punch, 1770-80, the stocky horse dappled in manganese, its mane and bridle picked out in manganese, the base green-washed with yellow edges, hair crack to base, chipped ear, 20cm (7⅞in), *P 20-22 Mar*, £4,100 ($6,109)

7
A pair of Walton pearlware figures of the Lion and the Unicorn, early 19th cent, each resting on a mound base before a bocage and wearing a crown, chips and repairs, 15.2 and 16cm (6 and 6¼in), *L 2 Oct*, £2,750 ($3,547)

8
A pair of cow-creamers, possibly Ferrybridge, early 19th cent, each with sponged brown and pink bands, one repaired, 16.5cm (6½in), *L 22 May*, £462 ($670)

9
A pottery cow-creamer and cover, c1800, modelled as an ochre and black spotted beast, damaged, 15cm (5⅞in), *P 10-13 July*, £418 ($569)

10
A Staffordshire cow-creamer and stopper, late 18th cent, its pale hide flecked in yellow and iron brown, restored, 12cm (8in), *P 14 Nov*, £352 ($472)

11
An Obadiah Sherratt Group, 'Bull-baiting', c1835, modelled with a tethered bull tossing a terrier, some damage and repair, 32.3cm (12¾in), *L 24 July*, £2,200 ($2,937)

12
A Staffordshire figure of a ferocious lion, early 19th cent, with reddish brown coat and shaggy liver-coloured mane, on a base 'sponged' in brown, yellow, black and blue, minor hair cracks and chips, 32cm (12⅝in), *L 2 Oct*, £1,100 ($1,419)

13
A Staffordshire pearlware lion, early 19th cent, 31.5cm (12¼in), *P 14 Nov*, £1,100 ($1,474)

14
A Staffordshire group of a bitch and puppy, c1825, with brown patched coats, the base raised on moulded feet, minor chips, 18.4cm (7¼in), *L 22 May*, £264 ($383)

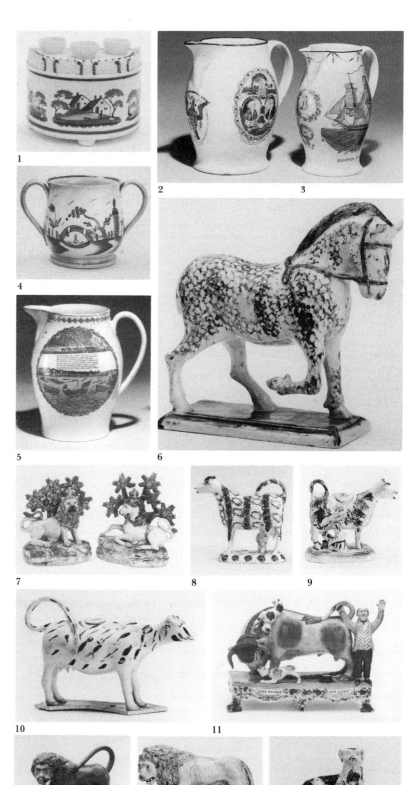

1

2

3

4

5

6

7

8

9

10

11

12

13

14

1

A Staffordshire pearlware 'Collier' Toby jug, possibly Thomas Hollins, 1780-90, wearing a dark brown hat and shoes, teal-blue coat and blue breeches, filled-in chip, 24.8cm (9¾in), *NY 12-14 Apr,* $825 (£577)

2

A North country Toby jug, early 19th cent, the toper in a long puce coat, black wig and tricorn, blue and green sponged base, chip on hat, 24.5cm (9⅝in), *P 20-22 Mar,* £220 ($328)

3

A Staffordshire 'Traditional' Toby jug, *c* 1800, the toper wearing a bright yellow jacket and lilac breeches; sold with a 'Dr Johnson' Toby jug, early 19th cent, 24.2cm (9½in), *L 24 July,* £385 ($513)

4

A Dixon Austin & Co, Sunderland, figure of 'Spring', picked out in bright colours; and another figure allegorical of 'Winter', the figure wearing a brown cloak, 22.2 and 23.6cm (8¾ and 9¼in), *C 4 Sept,* £297 ($386)

5

A set of four Dixon, Austin & Co figures of the Seasons, *c* 1825, after models by Ralph Wood, each modelled as a classical maiden in tones of green, blue, orange and ochre, one repaired, 21.6 to 22.8cm (8½ to 9in), *L 2 Oct,* £990 ($1,277)

6

A Staffordshire figure of Pomona, *c* 1780, Whieldon-type, allegorical of 'Autumn', splashed in a treacle-brown glaze over regularly dotted spots of yellow, green and blue, 31cm (12⅛in), *P 24/25 Jan,* £1,100 ($1,595)

7

A Walton group of a Woman and Child, *c* 1820-5, moulded at the front with a red florette and blue scrollwork, the woman in yellow bonnet, purple dress and a black-flowered skirt, restoration, 22.8cm (9in), *L 22 May,* £308 ($447)

8

A Staffordshire figure of 'The Lost Sheep', early 19th cent, probably Wood and Caldwell, after a Ralph Wood original, the shepherd wearing a brown coat, turquoise waistcoat and yellow breeches, 19.7cm (7¾in), *L 22 May,* £198 ($287)

9

A pair of Staffordshire groups, 'The Sailor's Departure and Return', early 19th cent, probably Wood and Caldwell, showing a sailor and his lass, restored, 22.8 and 24.2cm (9 and 9½in), *L 22 May,* £330 ($479)

10

A Staffordshire figure of Shakespeare, depicted standing resting on three books supported by a marbled column, 47cm (18½in), *C 31 Jan,* £66 ($96)

1

2

3

4

5

6

7

8

9

10

1
A Staffordshire figure of
Benjamin Franklin
mounted as a lamp, mid-
to late 19th cent, wearing
a crimson neckerchief, a
gilt-decorated white
waistcoat, coat and
breeches, glaze crackled,
39.5cm (15½in), NY 26 Jan,
$715 (£493)

2
A Staffordshire portrait
figure of Emily Sandford,
c.1849, wearing a blue
bodice and green skirt;
she was the mistress of
the murderer James
Rush, who was hanged
at Norwich Castle in
April 1849, 24.2cm
(9½in), L 14 Feb,
£374 ($524)

3
A pair of Staffordshire
portrait figures of F G
Manning and Maria
Manning, (they were
executed in 1849 for the
murder of Patrick
O'Connor, Maria's
former lover,) 24.2 and
23.5cm (9½ and 9¼in),
L 14 Feb,
£825 ($1,157)

4
A Staffordshire group of
Mr Van Amburgh,
c.1840, the lion tamer,
dressed in theatrical
Roman costume, with
lions and a leopard,
minor chip and hair
crack, 14.6cm (5¾in),
L 14 Feb,
£2,750 ($3,856)

5
A Leeds creamware
commemorative jug, 1802,
decorated in slate blue,
iron red and grey, with
a butcher at work,
inscriptions, repaired,
16.2cm (6⅜in), C 3 Oct,
£660 ($851)

6
A Phillips & Co
Sunderland jug, early
19th cent, printed black
and picked out in
coloured enamels with a
cartoon entitled 'The
Ascent of the Aerial
Balloon', chip, slight
cracks, 19.7cm (7¾in),
C 27 Mar,
£297 ($443)

7
A Staffordshire pearlware
mug, 1790s, printed with
the execution of Louis
XVI, picked out in
enamels, damaged, 8.5cm
(3⅜in), P 24/25 Jan,
£242 ($351)

8
A Staffordshire canary
yellow pottery jug, 1820s,
printed with two portrait
busts, each titled, 'The
Determined Enemy of
Corruption and the Con-
stitutional Friend of His
Sovereign', 14.5cm (5⅝in),
P 24/25 Jan,
£143 ($207)

9
A Bourne salt-glazed
stoneware spirit flask,
mid-1830s, moulded as
'Daniel O'Connell Esq'
holding an impressed
'Irish Reform Cordial',
20.5cm (8in), P 10-13 July,
£275 ($374)

10
A Stephen Green Lambeth
stoneware character jug in
the form of Napoleon,
17.5cm (7in), C 31 Jan,
£99 ($144)

11
A Staffordshire pottery
mug, c.1838, commemorat-
ing the Coronation of
Queen Victoria, printed
in puce with two
portraits of the young
monarch, 8.5cm (3⅜in),
P 24/25 Jan,
£374 ($544)

1

2   3

4   5

6

7   8

9   10   11

1

A pair of Mason's iron-stone Imari vases and covers, c.1825, decorated with growing peonies divided by blooms and gilt foliage on a rich blue ground, some repair, 48.3cm (19in), *C 5 July,* £1,650 ($2,238)

2

A Davenport ironstone Imari pattern dinner service, c.1840, each piece decorated with peonies and bamboo growing from rockwork, 93 pieces, *C 11 Jan,* £3,300 ($4,785)

3

A Mason's ironstone punch bowl, early 19th cent, printed and painted with 'famille-rose' colours, 35.8cm (14⅛in), *C 5 July,* £605 ($823)

4

An Ashworth Brothers ironstone dinner service, the majority late 19th cent, each piece decorated in underglaze-blue, iron-red and gilding, some wear and damage, 99 pieces, *L 24 July,* £2,200 ($2,937)

5

A Staffordshire ironstone dinner service, the majority mid-19th cent, each piece decorated in oriental taste with a basket of flowers, in underglaze-blue, green and puce, replacements by Ashworth Brothers, some chips, cracks and wear, 60 pieces, *L 2 Oct,* £1,100 ($1,419)

6

A Hicks & Meigh ironstone soup tureen and cover, printed in underglaze-blue and picked out in coloured enamels with flowers and foliage, 40.6cm (16in), *C 30 Oct,* £385 ($493)

7

A Spode 'Pheasant' pattern 'Stone China' dinner service, c.1830, each piece transfer-printed in underglaze-blue and painted in bright enamels, some repairs, chips, 125 pieces, *L 14 Feb,* £5,940 ($8,328)

8

A Spode and Edward Challinor composite part service, the majority c.1815-45, with scenes from the 'Indian Sporting' and 'Oriental Sports' series, chips and cracks, 22 pieces, *L 24 July,* £792 ($1,057)

9

A Staffordshire pearlware blue printed dinner service, c.1820, each piece with a chinoiserie design, some damage, 78 pieces, *C 5 July,* £330 ($449)

1
A Wemyss, Robert Heron & Son carp tureen and cover, c 1900, modelled by Karel Nekola, coloured in tones of bright pink shading to grey-green, heightened in bright yellow, small restoration, 46.9cm (18½in), *L 14 Feb,* £3,630 ($5,089)

2
A Wemyss quaich, Robert Heron & Son, c.1900, the interior painted with an appled bough, in red, yellow and orange below the dark green rim, 26.7cm (10½in), *C 28 Mar,* £341 ($508)

3
A Wemyssware jardinière, c 1900, painted with growing crocus, retailer's mark for T Goode & Co, 27.3cm (10¾in), *C 28 Mar,* £660 ($983)

4
A Wemyssware cylindrical mug, 1920s, painted with irises in bud and in bloom, slight staining, 14.5cm (5¾in), *P 18-25 Sept,* £264 ($341)

5
A Wemyssware cylindrical mug, 1920, painted with plums, slight staining, 14cm (5½in), *P 18-25 Sept,* £121 ($156)

6
A Wemyssware water jug, of globular form, painted with pink roses and foliage, turquoise borders, 24.2cm (9½in), *C 4 Sept,* £88 ($114)

7
A large Weymssware doorstop, modelled as a black and white spotted pig sitting with ears erect, black painted mark, 50cm (19¾in), *P 15-18 May,* £770 ($1,070)

8
A Minton 'Majolica' ewer, dated 1865, moulded in low relief, picked out in brightly coloured translucent glazes, slight damage, 38cm (15in), *C 3 Oct,* £550 ($710)

9
A pair of Minton 'Majolica' vases, c 1870, of lobed baluster form, decorated in relief, all picked out in brightly coloured glazes, one vase restored, 35.5cm (14in), *C 3 Oct,* £770 ($993)

10
A Minton 'Majolica' jardinière, dated 1870, applied with double putti handles divided by lion masks, all picked out in brightly coloured glazes, 27cm (10½in), *C 3 Oct,* £506 ($653)

11
A Minton 'Majolica' figure of a maiden, dated 1863, after an original sculpture by W Calder Marshall, RA, moulded signature, one toe missing, minor chips, 36.2cm (14¼in), *L 22 May,* £2,530 ($3,669)

12
A Minton 'Majolica' beetle box and cover, dated 1871, the insect with protruding yellow eyes, grey and blue body and green elytra, the interior turquoise, 10.7cm (4¼in), *L 22 May,* £1,210 ($1,755)

13
A Minton 'Majolica' game pie dish and cover, dated 1870, the body in the form of a wicker basket, the whole coloured in typical glazes, 33.6cm (13¼in), *L 24 July,* £638 ($852)

14
A Minton 'Majolica' chestnut dish and spoon, dated 1858, the whole glazed in tones of green, brown and ochre, the interior turquoise, rim chip repaired, 28cm (11in), *L 24 July,* £638 ($852)

15
A Minton 'Majolica' game pie dish, cover and liner, dated 1901, the whole glazed in tones of green, brown, ochre and blue, the liner plain, 41.9cm (16½in), *L 22 May,* £1,210 ($1,755)

1   2

3   4   5

6   7   8

9   10   11

12   13

14   15

1
A Wedgwood brown-glazed stoneware toy teapot and cover, *c*1770, the cylindrical body set with a tapering spout and moulded strap handle, the cover with ball finial, chipped cover, 7.4cm (2⅞in), *P 14 Nov*, £121 ($162)

2
A Wedgwood and Bentley black basaltes vase and cover, 1769-80, the shoulder decorated in relief with a border of laurel leaves above cherub heads, the cover married, 17.2cm (6¾in), *NY 12-14 Apr*, $935 (£654)

3
A Wedgwood and Bentley black basaltes mantel ornament, 1769-80, the body engine-turned with vertical flutes beneath a band of moulded drapery swags, the sides with satyr's mask handles, repairs to knop and handles, 20cm (7⅞in), *NY 12-14 Apr*, $990 (£692)

4
A Wedgwood black basaltes jug with encaustic decoration, *c*1800, painted in iron red, black and white on the front with a classical maiden, the reverse with a stylised plant, foot reduced, small chips, 19.2cm (7½in), *NY 12-14 Apr*, $770 (£538)

5
A Wedgwood black-jasper-dip Portland vase, early 19th cent, the body sprigged with reliefs of typical classical figures in an Arcadian setting, the base with a Phrygian head, 28cm (11in), *L 14 Feb*, £660 ($925)

6
A Wedgwood black basaltes Pelike vase with encaustic decoration, late 18th cent, painted *en grisaille* with classical scene between white, iron red and blue borders of flowers and trelliswork, 30.2cm (11⅞in), *NY 12-14 Apr*, $4,290 (£3,000)

7
A Wedgwood blue and white jasper vase, late 18th cent, the shield-shaped body sprigged with white reliefs of 'Venus in her Chariot' and 'Cupid Watering Swans' after Charles Le Brun, chips, 38.9cm (15¼in), *L 22 May*, £2,420 ($3,509)

8
A pair of Wedgwood blue and white jasper square flower pots, late 18th cent, each pale blue body dipped in deeper blue and decorated in white relief with 'The Dipping of Achilles', 'Sacrifice to Aesculapius' and a classical maiden, both with repairs, 15.5cm (6⅛in), *NY 12-14 Apr*, $935 (£654)

9
A pair of Wedgwood black basaltes candlesticks, *c*1900, the moulded reliefs of classical figures, foliate scrolls and formal borders with bronzed gilt details, one stem repaired, 13.3cm (5¼in), *L 2 Oct*, £682 ($879)

10
A Wedgwood blue jasper-ware potpourri vase and cover, 19th cent, in the form of a temple, applied with white reliefs of fluted columns, the cover formed from a domed tiled roof, chips, 17.8cm (7in), *L 22 Mar*, £550 ($798)

11
A Wedgwood blue-jasper-dip potpourri vase and cover, mid-19th cent, of bucket shape, sprigged in white with classical figures divided by trees between flowering foliage and green leaf borders, 36.2cm (14¼in), *C 11 Jan*, £319 ($463)

12
A Wedgwood black-jasper-dip vase and cover, mid-19th cent, the shield-shaped body sprigged with white reliefs of classical maidens between borders of berried branches and yellow-jasper florettes, knop repaired, *L 22 May*, £770 ($1,117)

1

2

3

4

5

6

7

8

9

10

11

12

1
A pair of Wedgwood lilac-jasper-dip vases and covers, 1867, each sprigged with green ground panels of classical figures and white reliefs of vine swags, flanges of covers restored, impressed date code, 26.8cm (10½in), *L 22 May*, £660 ($957)

2
A Wedgwood 'three-colour' jasperware vase and cover, late 19th cent, the white body sprigged in green and lilac with two oval figure medallions enclosed by green foliate swags and lilac ribbons, slight damage, 36.2cm (14¼in), *C 3 Oct*, £792 ($1,022)

3
A Wedgwood black basaltes bronzed and gilt vase and cover, late 19th/early 20th cent, the body decorated in bronzed and gilt relief with flowerheads flanked by garlands pendant from rams' heads, 18.5cm (7¼in), *NY 12-14 Apr*, $990 (£692)

4
A Wedgwood part 'nautilus service', 1872, each piece moulded as a shell including scallop, mussel, oyster and nautilus, shaded in tones of cream to candy-pink, impressed date mark, 21 pieces, *L 22 May*, £2,200 ($3,190)

5
A Wedgwood earthenware part service, early 19th cent, printed in brown with lotus flowers picked out in pink and pale green, comprising eighteen plates, two dishes, two tureens and cover, some damage, *P 24/25 Jan*, £1,430 ($2,074)

6
A Wedgwood dragon lustre 'Chalice Bowl', c 1920, printed in gold, the exterior stained and mottled in blue and painted in tones of green and violet, the interior in green, blue and violet with a 'Wantley Dragon' and clouds on a mother-of-pearl lustre ground, d 27.3cm (10¾in), *NY 12-14 Apr*, £880 (£615)

7
A Wedgwood dinner service, each piece printed and painted in iron red and blue with flowering foliate borders, 110 pieces, *C 18 Oct*, £784 ($934)

8
A Wedgwood fairyland lustre bowl, 1920s, decorated on the interior with the 'Jumping Faun' design and on the exterior with 'Feather Hat' variation of 'Woodland Elves' pattern, in colourful glazes with clear gilt details, 25.3cm (10in), *L 22 May*, £825 ($1,196)

9
A Wedgwood 'Daventry' lustre bowl, 1920s, of octagonal shape, the exterior decorated in oriental style against a ruby-red ground, the interior with a central scene against a yellow ground, 17.2cm (6¾in), *L 2 Oct*, £286 ($369)

10
A Wedgwood fairyland lustre vase, 1920s, of baluster form, decorated with the 'Candlemas' design of panels with candles topped by heads and borders with elves tugging on bell-ropes, 31cm (8¼in), *L 2 Oct*, £638 ($823)

11
A Wedgwood flame fairyland lustre bowl, 1920s, the interior decorated with the 'Woodland Bridge' variation of the 'Woodland Elves' design, the exterior with 'Poplar Trees' pattern, all in brightly coloured glazes against an orange-red background and gilt details, 23.5cm (9¼in), *L 24 July*, £935 ($1,248)

12
A Wedgwood dragon lustre 'Lily Tray', c 1920, printed in gold and painted in tones of iron-red, blue, green and yellow with a dragon within a 'Papillon' border on a mother-of-pearl lustre ground, the exterior in red and blue, d 28cm (11in), *NY 12-14 Apr*, $550 (£385)

1

2

3

4

5

6

7

8

9

10   11

12

1
**A pair of John Rose,
Coalport, parian busts of
The Prince of Wales and
Princess Alexandra,** 1863,
the prince wearing a
buttoned jacket, his wife
with her hair dressed in
a jewelled bow, chips,
34.2 and 33cm (13½ and
13in), *L 22 May,*
£308 ($447)

2
A bust of Enoch Wood, 1st
half 19th cent, modelled
by Enoch Wood, the
potter depicted full face,
wearing a high-collared
coat and cravat, 54.6cm
(21½in), *C 5 July,*
£440 ($597)

3
A small pot lid, Bear,
Lion and Cock, (Ball 19),
C 19/20 June,
£66 ($94)

4
Two small pot lids, Bears
at school, (Ball 9),
C 19/20 June,
£109 ($155)

5
A medium pot lid,
England's pride (Ball
149), *C 19/20 June,*
£90 ($129)

6
A pot lid, The Late
Prince Consort; sold
with another, Garibaldi,
(Ball 153 and 169),
C 19/20 June,
£72 ($103)

7
**A medium pot lid and a
large pot lid,** Royal
Harbour, Ramsgate,
(Ball 42), *C 19/20 June,*
£72 ($103)

8
A medium pot lid, Allied
Generals, (Ball 168),
C 19/20 June,
£85 ($121)

9
A large pot lid, Nelson
Crescent, Ramsgate,
(Ball 43), *C 19/20 June,*
£60 ($86)

10
A medium pot lid,
Stratfieldsaye, (Ball 188),
C 19/20 June,
£48 ($68)

Bibliog:
A. Ball, *The Price Guide
to Pot Lids,* publ. 1980.

1
A Chantilly waste bowl,
c 1740, painted in
Kakiemon style in brilliant
enamels, brown rim, horn
in iron red, 20.5cm
(8⅛in), L 9 Oct,
£2,530 ($3,264)

2
**A Mennecy bouillon cover
and dish,** 2nd half 18th
cent, decorated in poly-
chrome colours with birds,
fruits and foliage, the
handles in the form of
leafy branches, the borders
edged in pink, impressed
mark 'DV', dish
chipped, h 11cm (4⅜in),
M 27 June,
FF 14,430 (£1,239; $1,688)

3
A Chantilly seau à verre,
c 1750, the tin-glazed
body painted in purple,
blue, yellow, iron red
and green, the sides with
brown and lavender twig
handles, the rim edged
in brown, hunting horn
mark in iron red, 10.8cm
(4¼in), NY 16 Nov,
$715 (£572)

4
**A pair of Mennecy seaux à
verre,** mid-18th cent,
each moulded on the
front and reverse with a
scallop shell and rocaille
heightened in rose, one
also in yellow, chipped
handles repaired, h 15cm
(5⅞in), NY 4 May,
$6,875 (£4,911)

5
**A pair of Saint-Cloud cups
and saucers,** mid-18th
cent, in white porcelain
decorated in relief with
branches of plum trees,
h 7.1cm (2¾in),
M 27 June,
FF 14,430 (£1,239; $1,688)

6
**A Tournai part dinner
service,** decorated at the
Hague, 1775-80, painted
in shades of green,
brown, iron red, yellow,
blue, grey and puce, 18
pieces, NY 17 Nov,
$3,850 (£3,080)

7
**A Clignancourt urn and
cover,** c 1790, the body
finely painted with butterflies, moths and bugs
beneath a band of
coloured roses on a
black ground bordered
by gilt lines, gilt knop
repaired, 36.7cm (14.4in),
L 12 June,
£462 ($665)

8
**A Paris Empire style
cabinet cup and saucer,**
c 1815-20, painted with a
view of 'La Place de
L'Opéra', reserved in a
rectangular panel on a
solid gilt ground,
gilding rubbed, L 9 Oct,
£242 ($312)

9
**A set of six Vieux Paris
Palais Royal plates,**
c 1825, each painted with
a scene of peasants
making merry, slight
rubbing to gilding, 24cm
(9½in), L 8 Nov,
£715 ($951)

10
**A Vieux Paris part tea and
coffee service,** Marc
Schoelcher, 1820-8, all
painted with scenes of
animals in their natural
habitat, all within wide
gilt borders, several
repairs and chips, 17
pieces, coffee pot 25.4cm
(10in), NY 16 June,
$1,760 (£1,313)

1   2

3   4   5

6

7   8   9

10

1

A pair of Vieux Paris urns, Duc d'Angouleme Factory, 1800-10, with a periwinkle-blue ground finely gilded with neoclassical devices within foliate borders, the upper section painted *en grisaille,* 47.3cm (17⅝in), *NY 17 Nov,* $6,875 (£5,500)

2

A pair of Paris gilt-ground vases, early 19th cent, painted with a panel of figures fishing on the banks of a river, rim chip restored, gilding a little rubbed, 27.5cm (10⅞in), *L 8 Nov,* £418 ($556)

3

A pair of Paris vases, *c*1820, each painted with a scene of a maiden and a cupid, reserved on a blue ground with tooled gilt swan and lyre motifs, handle restored, 35.5cm (14in), *L 8 Mar,* £682 ($1,016)

4

A pair of Darte Frères vases, *c*1830, each painted with panels of Turkish soldiers against a ruby-red ground with tooled burnished gilt borders, stencilled mark with Palais Royale address, one with small chips, 51cm (20in), *L 8 Mar,* £2,420 ($3,606)

5

A pair of Paris vases, *c*1830, painted with a panel of lovers in gardens, within tooled gilt borders against a bright blue ground, stems chipped or repaired, gilding rubbed, 40cm (15¾in), *L 7 June,* £528 ($766)

6

A pair of feuillet-decorated Paris candlesticks, *c*1830, each painted with vignettes of country life, all within gilt borders against a ruby-red ground, gilt mark, 44cm (17¼in), *L 7 June,* £528 ($766)

7

A Paris tea and coffee service, *c*1830, probably from the workshop of A P Deroche, 30 pieces, coffee pot 21cm (8¼in), *M 11 Dec,* FF 6,105 (£538; $649)

8

A Paris corbeille, *c*1830, in the form of a basket, restoration to one handle, w 38cm (15in), *M 11 Dec,* FF 3,330 (£293; $354)

9

A pair of Paris pâte-sur-pâte cache-pots, *c*1870, each decorated in diaphanous white reliefs with riverscapes against a mushroom ground between blue and gilt-line borders, hair cracks, 16.7cm (6⅝in), *L 7 June,* £462 ($670)

10

A Jacob Petit clock garniture, *c*1830, the clock-case painted with a scene of two ladies, the vases painted within gilt borders, clock 33cm (12⅞in), vases 23.2cm (9⅛in), *L 8 Nov,* £1,540 ($2,048)

1 2 3

4 5

6

7

8

9 10

Vincennes and Sèvres

DAVID BATTIE

The year 1984 witnessed a major reappraisal in the fortunes of porcelain from the famous French factory Sèvres. The revival began in June with the sale of a comprehensive collection formed by Hugh Burton-Jones. Estimates were doubled, trebled or even quadrupled. The world record price for a single lot of European porcelain was achieved for a *rose pompadour* ewer and basin from another collection which sold for £126,500 ($182,160) and is now in the Getty Museum (p. 500, fig. 6). Such extraordinary rises in auction prices are generally followed by a period of reflection when the market readjusts and common pieces which have been dragged up to high levels by the boom fall again in subsequent sales. In the case of Sèvres, where only major pieces had fetched realistic prices particularly in New York, this has not happened, though buyers are now taking greater account of condition.

Throughout its history, beginning at Vincennes in about 1746, the French royal porcelain factory has had mixed fortunes. Plagued from the outset by financial difficulties, the factory came to be reliant on the wits of Madame de Pompadour, Louis XV's mistress, to make up its annual deficit from the king's coffers. None the less during the third quarter of the 18th century the factory was responsible for producing some of the finest soft-paste porcelain. It is a difficult medium and the factory's production was regulated under the most stringent quality controls and with the protection of Louis XV. It was thus always very expensive.

Sèvres porcelain falls roughly into three periods: the first begins with its origins at Vincennes and lasts until 1756 when the factory moved to the site at Sèvres. Date codes were introduced in 1753 and the factory then became the *manufacture royale* with Louis XV as principal shareholder. Hard paste was introduced in 1769.

The coloured grounds on the soft-paste pieces from the middle period were often spectacular, with the enamel melting beautifully into the glaze. The most famous ones were the early *bleu lapis*, dating from 1749, *bleu céleste*, dating from 1752, *jaune jonquille*, dating from 1753, and *rose pompadour*, dating from 1757 used to best effect with green enamel. These and other coloured grounds including complex diapers were offset by immensely rich gilding framing panels of birds, landscapes and figures in the manner of Boucher.

The Republic took over the factory four years after the start of the Revolution. Quantities of original pieces were sold from the collections of landed families—mostly to England—and a great many undecorated pieces were sold from the factory. This was repeated after Napoleon's defeat when yet more pieces arrived. Considerable numbers of blank pieces were decorated in England and sparsely decorated pieces had coloured grounds or figure subjects added. Not surprisingly the large collections that were built up throughout the 19th century included fakes and forgeries and in the 1920s, when this was finally realized, the market collapsed. Over popularity had led to the downfall and there was to be no revival for over fifty years. Expertise has now progressed sufficiently for differentiation to be possible (items not entirely from the Sèvres factory are catalogued today as 'Sèvres' or Sèvres-pattern),—hence the renewed confidence.

1
A large Vincennes tankard and cover (grand gobelet litron couvert), c.1753, 15.3cm (6in), *L 12 June,* **£36,300 ($52,272)**

2
A Vincennes seau à verre (or demi-bouteille), 1753, 13.2cm (5¼in), *L 12 June,* **£2,090 ($3,010)**

3
A rare Vincennes ewer and basin (pot à eau à la Romaine), c.1753, ewer 24.2cm (9½in), basin 36cm (14⅛in), *L 12 June,* **£22,000 ($31,680)**

4
A rare Vincennes watering can (arrosoir), 1754, painted by Bardet 20cm (7⅞in), *L 12 June,* **£31,900 ($45,936)**

5
A pair of Vincennes shell-shaped dishes, dated 1753, sold with four other items, *NY 16 June,* **$1,320 (£963)**

6
A rare Sèvres Rose Pompadour ewer and basin (broc feuille d'eau et jatte), 1757, basin w 29cm (11½in), ewer h 19cm (7½in), *L 12 June,* **£126,500 ($182,160)**

1

2

3

4

5

6

1
A Sèvres tea cup and saucer (Hébert), dated 1757, painted by Jean-Baptiste Tandart, with coloured flowers within a turquoise-green wavy ribbon, very slight scratching, cup 6cm (2⅜in), *L 12 June,*
£1,430 ($2,059)

2
A Sèvres teapot and cover, dated 1758, painted by François-Joseph Aloncle, with exotic birds within a gilt panel reserved on an emerald-green ground, minute chip to knop, gilding on cover worn, 12cm (4¾in), *L 12 June,*
£3,520 ($5,069)

3
A Sèvres cup and saucer (Hébert), dated 1765, painted by Etienne Evans, with birds within a tooled line border reserved in a duck-egg blue ground gilt with laurel, painter's mark, date M, gilding slight wear, cup 6.5cm (2½in), *L 12 June,*
£1,540 ($2,218)

4
A Sèvres milk jug (pot à lait à pieds), dated 1780, painted by Etienne-François Bouillat, with loops of flowers between apple-green and gilt scrolls, 12.5cm (4⅞in), *L 12 June,*
£605 ($871)

5
A Sèvres milk jug (pot à lait à pieds), c.1770, probably painted by Etienne Evans, with a bird within gilt borders reserved on the bright blue ground, 9.5cm (3¾in), *L 12 June,*
£462 ($665)

6
A Sèvres cup and saucer, 1768, painted by François Aloncle, with bird scenes on a yellow ground, cup 8cm (3⅞in), *M 27 June,*
FF 11,100 (£953; $1,298)

7
A Sèvres trembleuse cup and saucer, (enforcée), 1765, probably painted by Thévenet père, with polychrome and gilt garlands of flowers and trellis, cup 9cm (3½in), *M 27 June,*
FF 14,430 (£1,239; $1,688)

8
A Sèvres tea cup and saucer, dated 1767, painted by François Aloncle, with bird landscapes within a reserve of *oeil-de-perdrix* in red, blue and gilt, cup 6cm (2¼in), *M 27 June,*
FF 19,980 (£1,715; $2,337)

9
A Sèvres ewer and basin (pot à l'eau ordinaire et jatte), dated 1763, painted by Thévenet père, with shell and feather roundels within green wreaths and hung with pink ribbons, blue and gilt borders, some wear to gilding, ewer 19cm (7½in), basin 29cm (11½in), *L 12 June,*
£4,950 ($7,128)

10
A pair of Sèvres vases, (Hollandais), 1763, painted by Charles Tandart with polychrome garlands of flowers, 44cm (17¼in), *M 27 June,*
FF 133,200 (£11,433; $15,579)

11
A pair of Sèvres bleu-du-roi vases mounted in ormolu as Brules-Parfums, c.1780, each with a tapering cylindrical body mounted on the rim with an ormolu gallery pierced with vitruvian scrolls, 25cm (9¾in), *NY 17 Nov,*
$5,500 (£4,400)

12
A Sèvres trembleuse cup and saucer (enfoncée), dated 1763, painted by Pierre-Antoine Mereaud, with swags of flowers and feathery leaves within a bleu nouveau border, gilding slight wear, cup 8.6cm (3⅜in), *L 12 June,*
£462 ($665)

13
A pair of Sèvres jardinières, dated 1766, painted by Rosset and Levé with panels of flowers reserved on a probably later gilt caillouté bleu nouveau ground, firing faults, gilding worn, *L 12 June,*
£1,870 ($2,693)

1   2

3   4

5   6   7

8   9

10   11   12   13

1
A Sèvres apple-green vase
'flacon à mouchoir'
mounted in ormolu, 1765-
75, the shield-shaped
body with a rich green
ground interrupted with
moulded drapery swags,
small chip on one end,
flange repaired, 30.2cm
(11⅞in), *NY 4 May*,
$10,450 (£7,464)

2
A Sèvres plate from the
Madame du Barry service,
dated 1772, mono-
grammed DB in gilt and
floral garlands, a gilt
dentil edged blue
border, 24.4cm (9⅝in),
NY 4 May,
$4,070 (£2,907)

3
A Sèvres tankard (tasse
litron), *c*1760, enamelled
by Vincent Taillandier
with sprays of summer
flowers within blue lines,
the mouth with gilt
dentil, 12cm (4¾in),
L 12 June,
£1,100 ($1,584)

4
A Sèvres sucrier and cover,
dated 1764, painted by
Nicquet, the rims with
gilt dentil edges,
together with a Cozzi
fluted sugar bowl
(cracked), h 10.2cm (4in),
NY 17 Nov,
$550 (£440)

5
A Sèvres small plateau,
dated 1759, painted by
Vincent Taillandier, in
shades of rose, yellow,
green, iron red and
blue, the footrim edged
in gilding, 17.6cm (6⅞in),
NY 17 Nov,
$990 (£792)

6
A Sèvres tea caddy and
cover, *c*1780, painted by
Vincent Taillandier,
with swags of summer
flowers pendant from
puce and blue ribbons
on an apple-green
ground gilt with diaper,
7.7cm (3in), *L 12 June*,
£3,300 ($4,752)

7
A Sèvres seau à bouteille,
*c*1765, boldly painted by
Pierre-Joseph Rosset,
the scroll handles, rim
and foot with blue and
gilt details, restored, 20cm
(8⅝in), *L 12 June*,
£242 ($348)

8
Two Sèvres dishes,
triangular, 1756 and 1762,
with polychrome decor-
ation, the borders with
floral decoration in gilt
shaped fields against a
'bleu celeste' ground,
20cm (7⅞in), *A 1 Oct*,
Dfl 4,176 (£983; $1,268)

9
A Sèvres sucrier and cover,
1758, with a green
ground decorated in
polychrome with bouquets
of flowers, 6.9cm (2¾in),
M 27 June,
FF 9,990 (£858; $1,168)

10
A Sèvres cup and saucer,
1756, painted by Charles
Buteux, with vignettes of
cupid surrounded by
deep blue, cup h 7cm
(2⅝in), *M 27 June*,
FF 12,210 (£1,048; $1,428)

11
A Sèvres dish, 1756,
decorated in poly-
chrome by Carrié,
w 29.1cm (11⅜in),
M 27 June,
FF 11,100 (£953; $1,298)

12
A Sèvres bleu-du-roi
teapot and cover, dated
1767, possibly painted by
Antoine-Toussaint
Cornailles, in shades of
rose, purple, iron red,
yellow, blue and green,
12.4cm (4⅞in),
NY 17 Nov,
$880 (£704)

13
A Sèvres teapot and cover,
dated 1761, painted by
Antoine-Toussaint
Cornailles, with groups
of flowers beneath an
apple-green shoulder
bordered by gilt S-
scrolls, minute chip on
spout, 12.3cm (4⅞in),
L 12 June,
£2,750 ($3,960)

1
A pair of 'Sèvres' 'jewelled' cabinet plates, mid-19th cent, each painted with a portrait of Md de Longueville or Louise de Lorraine, with a gros blue round rim, gilt borders with colourful enamel studs, 24.5cm (9⅝in), *L 7 June,* £550 ($798)

2
A pair of 'Sèvres' 'jewelled' vases, 3rd quarter 19th cent, painted by Vernet, signed, with a harbour scene, the reverse with a riverscape, formal bands of green and red enamel 'jewelling', gilding rubbed, 30cm (11⅞in), *L 8 Nov,* £990 ($1,317)

3
A pair of 'Sèvres' bleu-celeste-ground 'jewelled' vases, mid-19th cent, each painted with cherubs, the knopped neck with tooled gilt flowers, the borders with red and white enamel studs, slight wear to enamels and gilding, 25cm (9⅞in), *L 8 Nov,* £880 ($1,170)

4
A pair of 'Sèvres' gilt-bronze-mounted 'jewelled' vases and covers, mid-19th cent, painted with panels of a maiden within gilt borders, 41.5cm (16¼in), *L 7 June,* £880 ($1,276)

5
A pair of 'Sèvres' 'jewelled' potpourri vases and covers, mid-19th cent, each painted by L Malpass, signed, with a panel of children at play, against a gros bleu ground, knops repaired, glaze bloomed, slight damage to enamels, 48.5cm (19in), *L 8 Nov,* £1,045 ($1,390)

6
A 'Sèvres' gilt-bronze-mounted covered case, late 19th cent, painted with a panel depicting two maidens and a gentleman, within gilt borders reserved on a bleu-celeste ground; sold with a gilt-metal-mounted pedestal, vase 83cm (32in), *NY 16 June,* $2,530 (£1,846)

7
A 'Sèvres' gilt-bronze-mounted and 'jewelled' box, mid-19th cent, of spherical form, painted with panels of putti, within ornate gilt borders, some enamels missing, 26cm (10¼in), *L 8 Mar,* £858 ($1,278)

8
A pair of 'Sèvres' bleu-celeste-ground vases and covers, mid-19th cent, each painted by Leber, one signed, with panels within gilt borders, covers repaired, 37cm (14½in), *L 8 Nov,* £2,200 ($2,926)

9
A pair of 'Sèvres' covered vases, late 19th cent, each painted by Chanele (?), signed, with an oval panel depicting a bacchic celebration, reserved on a bleu-du-roi ground, one cover secured, 96.5cm (38in), *NY 16 June,* $7,150 (£5,219)

10
A pair of 'Sèvres' gilt-bronze-mounted covered vases, late 19th cent, each painted by Polyet, signed, with a maiden and her lover, within gilt borders reserved on a bleu-du-roi ground, covers associated, 100.3cm (39½in), *NY 3 Nov,* $8,250 (£6,600)

11
A 'Sèvres' gilt-bronze-mounted vase and cover, late 19th cent, painted with an oval panel, signed, within scrolling gilt borders and reserved on a bleu-du-roi ground, 118.2cm (46½in), *NY 16 June,* $7,425 (£5,420)

1   2   3

4   5   6

7   8

9   10   11

1
A pair of 'Sèvres' gilt-bronze-mounted vases and covers, c.1900, painted by J Pascault, signed, with a continuous scene of rustic lovers in a garden, covers fixed, 91 cm (35⅞in), L 8 Mar, £5,720 ($8,522)

2
A pair of 'Sèvres' gilt-bronze-mounted covered urns, c.1910, each painted in a continuous frieze after Boucher by E Collot, signed, bleu-du-roi borders, heightened in gilding, 78.8cm (31in), NY 3 Nov, $4,620 (£3,696)

3
A 'Sèvres' gilt-bronze-mounted Napoleonic covered vase, late 19th cent, painted by L Vernet, signed, with a continuous frieze depicting the battlefield at Austerlitz, deep-green borders, 100.2cm (39½in), NY 16 June, $5,225 (£3,813)

4
A pair of 'Sèvres' gilt-bronze-mounted covered vases, c.1900, each painted by Collot, signed, with a maiden attended by cupid, reserved on a pale-blue ground, one cover restored, 52.3cm (20⅝in), NY 16 June, $1,430 (£1,044)

5
A pair of 'Sèvres' large bowls mounted in gilt-bronze as potpourri vases, c.1910, each painted by Deach (?), signed, with maidens in a garden, the reverse with landscapes, reserved on a bleu-du-roi ground, 40.7cm (16in), NY 24/25 Feb, $4,125 (£2,845)

6
A pair of 'Sèvres' gilt-bronze-mounted vases and covers, late 19th cent, each painted by Quentin, signed, with panels of rustic lovers, within ornate gilt borders against a gros bleu ground, 71.5cm (28in), L 8 Nov, £5,500 ($7,315)

7
A pair of 'Sèvres' gilt-bronze-mounted oval centre bowls, late 19th cent, each painted with a panel of lovers, the first, after Lancret, the second by Rubb, signed, reserved on a bleu-du-roi ground within gilt borders, NY 3 Nov, $7,700 (£6,160)

8
A 'Sèvres' gilt-bronze-mounted oval centre bowl, late 19th cent, painted with an oval panel depicting two putti, the reverse with flowers, reserved on a bleu-celeste ground, w 48.3cm (19in), NY 16 June, $2,420 (£1,766)

9
A 'Sèvres' gilt-bronze-mounted centre bowl, late 19th cent, of oval shape painted with a panel of rustic figures, gilt borders against a bleu-celeste ground, 46.5cm (18¼in), L 7 June, £770 ($1,117)

10
A 'Sèvres' casket, late 19th cent, of shaped rectangular form, the cover painted by Geyer, signed, within a gilt border against a gros-bleu ground, 25.5cm (10⅛in), L 8 Mar, £935 ($1,393)

11
A 'Sèvres' Napoleonic giltwood table, c.1900, mounted in the centre with a circular charger painted by Zeller (?) signed indistinctly, with a portrait of Napoleon I surrounded by eleven small oval plaques painted with portraits, d 53.3cm (21in), NY 3 Nov, $3,080 (£2,464)

12
A 'Sèvres' bleu-celeste-ground plaque, late 19th cent, painted with a portrait panel of Louis XVI encircled by a ring of smaller portraits, enclosed by tooled gilt borders, slight rubbing to gilding, 50.8cm (20in), L 8 Mar, £550 ($820)

1

2

3

4

5

6

7

8

9

10

11

12

1

A Böttger teabowl and a saucer, the porcelain c.1720, the decoration c.1725, each piece decorated in the manner of J G Horoldt with orientals in ornamental gardens, the borders in iron red and gilding, *L 9 Oct,*
£1,650 ($2,128)

2

A Meissen teapot and cover, 1725-30, decorated in the manner of J E Stadler, with panels of chinoiserie figures and flowers within gilt borders reserved on a powder-blue ground, repairer's mark, chip on rim, 11cm (4⅜in), *L 12 June,*
£1,760 ($2,534)

3

A Meissen plate, c.1735, painted in Kakiemon style with a yellow tiger stalking near a tree trunk, brown rim, slight wear, minor chip, 23.2cm (9⅛in), *L 9 Oct,*
£572 ($738)

4

A pair of Meissen dishes, c.1730-5, probably painted by C F Herold, the centre with four chinoiserie vignettes on lustre and gilt Laub-und-Bandelwerk, workman's mark for Grund Senior, 18.3 and 18.4cm (7⅛in), *L 12 June,*
£11,550 ($16,632)

5

A Meissen plate, c.1745, decorated in underglaze-blue after a contemporary Chinese original, probably by Peter Colmberger, 23.2cm (9¼in), *L 9 Oct,*
£1,430 ($1,845)

6

A Meissen sugar caster and cover, 1730-5, the almost globular body painted with a harbour scene, enclosed by gilt scrollwork borders enriched in purple, restoration to base and cover, 17cm (6⅝in), *L 9 Oct,*
£1,100 ($1,419)

7

A Meissen teapot and cover, c.1735, modelled by Johann Joachim Kaendler, in the form of a cockerel, the plumage picked out in brightly coloured enamels with its tail forming a handle, the cover probably a later replacement, some repair, 15.8cm (6¼in), *C 10 Jan,*
£1,001 ($1,451)

8

A Meissen teapot and cover, 1730-40, the octagonal and turquoise-glazed body with scroll handle and curved spout in gilding, painted with two harbour scenes, knop and handle restored, 13.5cm (5⅜in), *L 9 Oct,*
£1,100 ($1,419)

9

A Meissen cup and saucer, c.1760, of quatrefoil form moulded with feathery panels picked out in pink enclosing studies of birds and flowers, gilt rims, minute chip to rim of cup, gilding with slight wear, *L 12 June,*
£660 ($950)

10

A Meissen ewer and cover, c.1735, the fish spout applied with a satyr's mask, painted in famille verte style with the 'Vogelbaum' pattern showing two birds and indianische Blumen heightened in gilding, chip to handle, 15cm (5⅞in), *L 9 Oct,*
£2,640 ($3,405)

11

A Meissen chocolate pot and cover, c.1745, crisply painted with lovers in gardens, the background in grey monochrome, the short spout and handle picked out in gilding, the knop and handle in green-stained ivory, spout damaged, 18cm (7⅛in), *L 12 June,*
£1,100 ($1,584)

12

A Meissen bullet-shaped teapot and cover, c.1745-50, delicately enamelled with vignettes of Watteauesque figures, the handle and spout detailed in gilding, 10cm (4in), *L 12 June,*
£748 ($1,077)

1

A Meissen part tea and coffee service, mid-18th cent, comprising coffee pot and cover, eight tea cups and saucers, four coffee cups, decorated with scenes of peasants, Altozier border and gilt rims, *L 9 Oct,* **£2,090 ($2,696)**

2

A Meissen urn and cover, *c*1755, painted in iron red, yellow, blue, puce and shades of green and sprigs of deutsche Blumen, drilled and mounted in ivory and French silver-gilt beast-head, marks for A Risler & Carre, Paris, *NY 16 June,* **$660 (£482)**

3

A Meissen dish, *c*1750-60, the centre painted with a bouquet of Manierblumen with a spirally scalloped and osier-moulded neuozier, border decorated with flower sprays, 35cm (13¾in), *L 12 June,* **£429 ($618)**

4

A Meissen circular tureen and cover, *c*1760, of bombé form, painted with Manierblumen within osier-moulded borders, the sides and cover applied with gilt-edged handles, 24cm (9½in), *L 12 June,* **£572 ($824)**

5

A Meissen teapot and cover, *c*1755, the ovoid body with osier moulded rim applied with a scroll-handle and fish spout, painted in bright colours, gilt rims, and two Meissen cups and saucers en suite, 11.5cm (4½in), *L 9 Oct,* **£715 ($922)**

6

A gold-mounted Meissen snuff box, *c*1750, of rectangular form, painted with bouquets and scattered sprigs, the lid painted on the interior with a basket of flowers, 7.7 x 5.7cm (3 x 2¼in), *L 9 Oct,* **£1,650 ($2,129)**

7

A Meissen bonbonnière, *c*1745, painted with Watteauesque figures in bright enamels with greyish-russet background, the interior of the lid painted with a woman and Harlequin, gilt-metal mounts, 6.9cm (2¾in), *L 12 June,* **£3,300 ($4,752)**

8

A gold-mounted Meissen snuff box, *c*1755, the basket-moulded exterior enamelled with scattered flowers, the interior of the lid painted with a basket of summer flowers, 8.5 x 6.5 x 4cm (3⅜ x 2½ x 1⅝in), *L 12 June,* **£2,530 ($3,643)**

9

A Meissen artichoke box and cover, *c*1760-70, naturalistically modelled and coloured, swords mark in blue, some repair, 15.8cm (6¼in), *C 3 Oct,* **£1,265 ($1,632)**

10

An outside-decorated Meissen cabbage tureen and cover, early 19th cent, naturalistically detailed in yellowish green and puce, slight restoration, 15cm (5⅞in), *L 12 June,* **£660 ($950)**

11

A Meissen chocolate pot and cover, mid-18th cent, the globular body moulded with flowers and applied flowering branches, all naturalistically coloured, gilt rims, spout restored, 19.5cm (7⅞in), *L 9 Oct,* **£550 ($709)**

12

A pair of Meissen fruit coolers, 20th cent, with covers and liners, painted on either side in colourful enamels with two birds perched in a tree, the cover with pierced gallery, the purple knop with three green leaves, one chipped, 19.6 and 20cm (7¾ and 7⅞in), *NY 16 Nov,* **$825 (£660)**

13

A pair of Meissen pierced baskets and covers, *c*1780-90, 17cm (6¾in), *L 9 Oct,* **£1,210 ($1,561)**

1
A Meissen teapot and cover, early 19th cent, of octagonal pyramidal form, each side painted with a view of Dresden within gilt line borders, spout glued, 10cm (4in), *P 20-22 Mar,* £825 ($1,299)

2
A pair of Meissen wine coolers, mid-19th cent, each painted with a continuous landscape scene of figures in gardens, divided by tooled gilt borders, one with minor chips to handles, 10.8cm (4¼in), *L 8 Nov,* £1,760 ($2,341)

3
A Meissen part tea and coffee service, *c.*1880, painted with colourful summer flowers, sprigs and insects within an osier-moulded border, a few cracks and minor chips, 47 pieces, coffee pot 17.7cm (6⅞in), *L 8 Nov,* £2,200 ($2,926)

4
A set of four Meissen dishes, *c.*1880, in two sizes, painted with colourful summer flowers and insects within an osier-moulded border and gilt rim, 46 and 36cm (18 and 14in), *L 8 Nov,* £770 ($1,024)

5
A Meissen dinner service, *c.*1880, each piece painted in shades of pink with sprays of stylised flowers within a lattice-pattern border, details and rims gilt, some damage, 75 pieces, largest serving dish 59cm (23⅛in), *L 8 Nov,* £5,720 ($7,608)

6
A pair of Meissen candlesticks, 3rd quarter 19th cent, each painted with a gardener and his companion in a wooded garden, the sconce and base with gilt-lined borders, 13.5cm (5¼in), *L 8 Mar,* £990 ($1,475)

8
A set of twelve Meissen plates, *c.*1880, each moulded in light relief and brightly coloured with fruits and flowers within gilt diaper panels bordered by foliate scrolls, 23cm (9in), *L 7 June,* £770 ($1,117)

7
A pair of Meissen pierced dessert dishes, *c.*1880, each painted with a colourful spray of summer flowers, gilt details, one with hair crack, 23cm (9⅛in), *L 8 Mar,* £396 ($590)

9
A Meissen 'Blue Onion' pattern part dinner service, *c.*1900, each piece decorated in underglaze-blue with fruits and flowers, the rims edged in gilding, several pieces with minor imperfections, 111 pieces, dinner plate d 24.2cm (9½in), *NY 18 July,* $4,950 (£3,779)

1
A Meissen pierced cabinet
plate, c.1860, painted
with the portrait of a
child within a deep-blue-
ground pierced and
shaped rim with gilt
formal borders, 23.9cm
(9⅜in), *L 8 Mar,*
£770 ($1,147)

2
A pair of Meissen bowls,
covers and stands, 3rd
quarter 19th cent, applied
in high relief with sprigs
of fruits and flowers and
painted with various
insects, chips, stand
24cm (9½in), *L 8 Mar,*
£858 ($1,278)

3
A pair of Meissen pierced
vases, mid-19th cent, each
of 'beaker' form, reticu-
lated overall with criss-
cross gilt strands and
applied with leafy trails
of brightly coloured fruits
and flowers, chips, 33.5cm
(13in), *L 8 Nov,*
£682 ($907)

4
A Meissen clock-case,
c.1880, minor damage,
37cm (14½in), *L 8 Nov,*
£770 ($1,024)

5
A Meissen centrepiece and
stand, 3rd quarter 19th
cent, the pierced oval
bowl set above two
lovers playing hide and
seek around a tree-trunk,
applied with flowers, the
whole with puce and gilt
details, minor chips,
56.5cm (22⅛in), *L 8 Mar,*
£1,320 ($1,967)

6
A Meissen clock-case, 1st
quarter 19th cent, sur-
mounted with the figure
of Jupiter, the base with
scrolled feet and foliage
below the figures of
Prometheus chained to a
rock by Zeus, the whole
well coloured, chips,
cracks and repairs,
71.8cm (28⅛in), *L 8 Nov,*
£1,430 ($1,902)

7
A pair of Meissen five-
light candelabra, 3rd
quarter 19th cent, em-
blematic of Autumn and
Winter, each scrolled base
supporting two children,
minor damage, 43cm
(16⅞in), *L 8 Nov,*
£902 ($1,199)

8
A Meissen candelabrum,
late 19th cent, the base
with three putti playing
musical instruments,
small repairs, 56.5cm
(22¼in), *C 11 Jan,*
£715 ($1,037)

9
A large Meissen floral-
encrusted mirror, late
19th cent, surmounted
by a basket of flowers
and a bevelled mirror
flanked by two putti, the
whole applied with
birds, caterpillars and
butterflies amidst
brilliantly coloured
flowers, minor losses
and repairs, h 139.7cm
(55in), *NY 3 Nov,*
$7,700 (£6,160)

10
A pair of Meissen floral-
encrusted covered vases
and stands, late 19th cent,
each ovoid vessel
painted with an oval
panel depicting a maiden
and two gentlemen, the
reverse with summer
blossoms, the whole with
turquoise enamel and
gilt details, losses and
repairs, 87.6cm (34½in),
NY 3 Nov,
$7,700 (£6,160)

11
A Meissen vase and cover,
late 19th cent, the ovoid
vessel painted on each
side with a panel
depicting courting couples,
the cover mounted with
a figure of Ceres, the
whole heightened by
pastel enamels and gilt
details, losses, 134.6cm
(53in), *NY 16 June,*
$5,500 (£4,014)

12
A Meissen vase and cover,
3rd quarter 19th cent,
unusually large and in
three sections, elaborately
moulded with rococo
scrolls and lattice and
applied with flowers,
with coloured and gilt
details, repairs, chips,
130cm (51in), *L 8 Mar,*
£2,530 ($3,769)

13
A Meissen swan tureen
and cover, 3rd quarter
19th cent, the white
plumage naturalistically
modelled, wing
repaired, chips, 37cm
(14⅝in), *L 8 Mar,*
£935 ($1,393)

1
A Berlin vase, c 1820, of
campana form, painted
with two panels emble-
matic of Day and Night,
against an azure or black
ground, the circular foot
with a band of florets
below simulated marble
and gilt handles, rim
chip restored, foot
repaired, d 50.5cm (19⅞in),
L 8 Nov,
£2,860 ($3,804)

2
A Berlin vase, c 1833,
painted with Crown
Prince Friedrich Wilhelm,
later King Friedrich
Wilhelm IV of Prussia
on horseback, the two
panels divided by tooled
gilt military trophies,
52cm (20¾in), *L 9 Oct,*
£19,800 ($25,542)

3
A Berlin vase and cover,
late 19th cent, the
shouldered body painted
with a wide frieze with
two gallants and a
maiden in a landscape,
gilt formal bands and
details against a brown
ground, stem chipped,
50.5cm (19⅞in), *L 8 Mar,*
£1,045 ($1,557)

4
**A Berlin pâte-sur-pâte
wall plate,** c 1890,
decorated in diaphanous
white relief, signed with
the initials HC, with a
maiden against a
celadon-green ground
25.7cm (10⅛in), *L 8 Nov,*
£748 ($995)

5
**A pair of 'Berlin' vases and
covers,** mid to late 19th
cent, each painted with
panels of 18th cent rustic
lovers within moulded
and gilt garlands and
formal borders, 25cm
(9⅞in), *L 8/9 Mar,*
£396 ($590)

6
**A Berlin part tea and
coffee service,** 2nd
quarter 19th cent, each
decorated with gilt
anthemion motifs and
scrolls against a pink
ground, comprising a
teapot and cover, coffee
pot and milk jug, two
cups and a saucer, coffee
pot 21.5cm (8½in), knops
and one spout restored,
L 8 Nov,
£374 ($497)

7
A Berlin plaque, late 19th
cent, painted and signed
with initials with the
scene of a gypsy girl
holding a tambourine,
impressed sceptre and
KPM, 24 x 16.5cm
(9½ x 6½in), *L 8 Nov,*
£1,100 ($1,463)

8
A Berlin oval plaque, 3rd
quarter 19th cent,
painted with the portrait
of a pensive maiden
resting her head and
arms on a green cushion,
wearing a white robe,
framed, 17.5cm (6⅞in),
L 8 Nov,
£935 ($1,243)

9
A Berlin plaque, 1852,
painted by C A
Lippold after Caspar
Netscher, signed, inscribed
and dated with 'The
Harpsichord Player' the
scene of a Dutch
interior, framed, 28.6 x
34cm (11⅛ x 13⅜in),
L 8 Mar,
£3,740 ($5,572)

10
A Berlin plaque, 3rd
quarter 19th cent,
painted with a romantic
scene in the manner of
Bouguereau, of classical
lovers admiring a pink
rose, impressed sceptre
and KPM, framed and
glazed, 41.5 x 31.5cm
(16⅞ x 12⅜in), *L 8 Mar,*
£1,320 ($1,966)

11
A Berlin plaque, c 1880,
painted with the scene of
peasant children playing
around a wheel-barrow,
impressed sceptre and
KPM, framed, 28 x 22.6cm
(11 x 8⅞in), *L 7 June,*
£1,375 ($1,993)

12
A Berlin plaque of Ruth,
3rd quarter 19th cent,
painted after Landelle
with the maiden wearing
a grey gown in a wheat-
field, impressed sceptre
and KPM, 23.5 x 16.2cm
(9¼ x 6⅜in), *NY 16 June,*
$825 (£602)

 1
 2
 3
 5
 4
 6 
 7
 8
 10
 11
 12

1
A Berlin dinner service,
1913, each piece painted
with sprays of colourful
and naturalistic flowers,
sceptre in underglaze
blue and KPM, additional
mark for 150th anniver-
sary of factory, one plate
repaired, minor chips,
108 pieces, *L 8/9 Mar,*
£2,750 ($4,100)

2
**A Nymphenburg 'Holz-
maserdekor' teapot and
cover,** *c*1780, all striated
in russet, brown and
pale yellow to resemble
knotty wood, the body
and cover reserved with
tromp l'oeil 'prints'
painted en grisaille, the
rims edged in worn
gilding, 12cm (4¾in),
NY 17 Nov,
$440 (£352)

3
**A set of five Berlin pierced
dessert plates,** *c*1900, each
painted with a spray of
coloured flowers within
a shaped rim gilt with
scrolls and branches,
sceptre in underglaze
blue, orb and KPM in
red, 26cm (10¼in),
L 8 Nov,
£935 ($1,244)

4
**A Nymphenburg cabinet
cup and saucer,** *c*1835-40,
the cup with bell-shaped
bowl finely painted with
Maximilian Joseph Platz,
the interior and scroll
handle in burnished
gilding, 9.6cm (3¾in),
L 12 June,
£1,320 ($1,900)

5
A Höchst solitaire, *c*1765,
decorated with birds in
landscapes supported by
gilt scrollwork and within
purple band on the
border entwined by
green laurel, gilt rims,
10 pieces, tray 33.5cm
(13⅛in), *L 9 Oct,*
£3,300 ($4,257)

6
A Ludwigsburg plate,
*c*1760, painted in famille
rose style with two
fabulous birds in a land-
scape, encircled by a rim
of iron-red scrolls, two
minute shell chips,
23.6cm (9¼in), *L 9 Oct,*
£2,860 ($3,689)

7
A Frankenthal tea caddy,
*c*1765-70, of arched
rectangular shape,
painted with cartouches
with peasant figures
after Teniers, enclosed
by scattered sprigs and
sprays of flowers, 11.2cm
(4¾in), *C 5 July,*
£550 ($748)

8
**A Fürstenberg neo-
classical vase and cover,**
*c*1790, the cylindrical
body in sepia camaieu
with oval panels of
classical figures, incised
and script F and AB
mark in underglaze
blue, knop cracked,
42.5cm (16¾in), *L 9 Oct,*
£660 ($851)

9
**A pair of Thuringian
vases,** late 18th cent, of
campana shape moulded
with bacchic mask
handles, painted with
profile portrait medallions
within garland borders,
repaired base, *C 28 Mar,*
£231 ($344)

10
**A Frankenthal oval tureen
and cover,** *c*1760, painted
by Andreas Handschuh
with naturalistic bouquets
and sprays of summer
flowers, within osier-
moulded borders, the
cover surmounted by a
sliced lemon knop, 35cm
(13⅞in), *L 12 June,*
£1,210 ($1,742)

1

2   3   4

5

6   7   8

9   10

1
A Plaue centrebasket, of
pierced shell-shape,
painted with a floral
spray and encrusted
with floral garlands,
supported by three
winged putti, 40cm
(15¾in), *C 30 Oct,*
£365 ($467)

2
**A pair of Helena
Wolfsohn yellow-ground
bottle vases and covers,**
late 19th cent, each
globular body painted
with scenes after
Wouverman within gilt
borders, gilding rubbed,
25cm (9⅞in), *L 8 Nov,*
£275 ($366)

3
**A pair of Helena
Wolfsohn yellow-ground
vases and covers,** late 19th
cent, in Meissen taste,
painted in puce camaïeu
with panels of lovers in
gardens, one cover
damaged, 30.5cm (12in),
L 8 Mar,
£330 ($492)

4
**A pair of Dresden vases
and covers,** late 19th cent,
with cylindrical body,
spirally fluted neck and
pedestal base, the body
picked out in turquoise
and gilding, some
chipping, 42cm (16½in),
C 5 July,
£572 ($776)

5
A Dresden mirror frame,
late 19th cent, of circular
shape, the beaded border
applied in high relief
with modelled and
coloured garden flowers
amongst foliage, two
cherubs flanking a
portrait of Marie
Antoinette, some damage,
67.5cm (26½in), *L 8 Mar,*
£770 ($1,147)

6
A Dresden mirror frame,
late 19th cent, of oval
shape, the border applied
with trails of modelled
flowers, surmounted by
an oval panel with the
portrait of a lady flanked
by putti, chips, 74cm
(29⅛in), *L 8 Mar,*
£902 ($1,344)

7
A Dresden clockcase, late
19th cent, in Meissen
style, moulded with
pastel-coloured and gilt
rococo scrolls, applied
round the dial with
flowers, four cherubs
emblematic of the seasons,
chips, 48cm (18⅞in),
L 8 Nov,
£605 ($805)

8
**A pair of Dresden six-light
candelabra,** late 19th
cent, each modelled as
an eighteenth-century
maiden or gallant wearing
floral painted and
pastel-coloured clothes,
some damage, 69.5cm
(27in), *L 7 June,*
£572 ($829)

9
**A pair of Potschappel
covered vases and stands,**
late 19th cent, Dresden
monogram for Carl
Thieme, each ovoid
vessel painted with a
panel of lovers within
thickly encrusted
borders of flowers, 102.9cm
(41½in), *NY 3 Nov,*
$6,325 (£5,060)

10
A Dresden Volkstedt vase,
1890s, the body formed
from swirling leaves and
tendrils trailing to a
large pink flower
enclosing a painted por-
trait of a maid, 46cm
(18in), *L 7 June,*
£495 ($718)

11
**A pair of Potschappel
vases,** each painted by
Bernard, signed, with 'A
Shower of Flowers' or
'Daughters of the
Dance', the deep-blue
ground with gilt formal
borders, 54.5cm (21⅜in),
L 8 Mar,
£770 ($1,147)

1

2 3 4

5 6

7 8

9 10 11

1
A pair of Vienna campanaform urns, dated 1814, allegorical of 'The Four Seasons', each with a dark green ground, chips, one with crack, 34.3cm (13½in), *NY 17 Nov,* $880 (£704)

2
A Vienna vase, signed and dated 1828, painted by Lorenz Herr, with a portrait of the first Emperor of Austria, 34cm (13¼in), *L 9 Oct,* £2,640 ($3,406)

3
A Vienna coffee service, *c.*1765-70, comprising coffee pot and cover, hot-water jug and cover, sugar box and cover and six cups and saucers, each painted en bleu camaieu detailed in black, some flaking of the enamel, coffee pot 24cm (9½in), *L 12 June,* £2,640 ($3,802)

4
A Du Paquier 'Imari' pattern footed bowl, 1730-5, painted in underglaze-blue, iron red and gilding, d 23cm (9in), h 12.2cm (4¾in), *NY 17 Nov,* $1,760 (£1,408)

5
A pair of Vienna plates, early State period, *c.*1749, underglaze blue shield marks, 23.7cm (9⅜in), *L 12 June,* £341 ($491)

6
A Vienna cabinet cup and saucer, dated 1811, the cup painted by Ignaz Obenbigler, h 10.1cm (4in), d 15.5cm (6⅛in), *NY 16 June,* $550 (£401)

7
A Vienna Empire-style cup and saucer, dated 1816 and 1817, the cup painted with 'Vue d'une partie du palais J:R du cote de rempart, a Vienne', the deep cerulean ground decorated in gilding, *L 9 Oct,* £638 ($823)

8
A set of nine Vienna plates, late 19th cent, decorated with mythological scenes, 24.2cm (9½in), *M 11 Dec,* FF 33,300 (£2,934; $3,543)

9
A Vienna gilt-ground cabinet cup and saucer, dated 1816, the double-ogee sides painted with a black ground oval panel of flowers, impressed numeral for date, shield mark, *L 9 Oct,* £352 ($454)

10
A 'Vienna' cabinet plate, late 19th cent, painted by Weigel, signed, blue-ground rim with gilt motifs, factory mark obscured by a gilt rose, 25.3cm (10in), *L 7 June,* £385 ($558)

11
Two 'Vienna' portrait vases, *c.*1910, each painted by Wagner, signed, with 'Mignon' or 'Clematis' with gilt borders and reserved on a lustrous brown or pale-green ground, 14.6cm (5¾in), *NY 16 June,* $1,100 (£803)

12
A 'Vienna' circular plaque of Jupiter and Juno, late 19th cent, painted by Richter (?), signed indistinctly, within a claret border heightened with gilt scrolling devices, d 48.3cm (19in), *NY 18 July,* $605 (£462)

13
A 'Vienna' ewer and stand, late 19th cent, the ewer painted by Jager, signed, slight wear to stand, stand 31.5cm (12⅜in), *L 8 Nov,* £1,595 ($2,121)

14
A 'Vienna' cabinet plate, late 19th cent, painted by Harrass, signed, with 'Unmasked', the deep-blue ground rim with ornate gilt scrolls, diaper panels and vase motifs, 24.2cm (9½in), *L 8 Nov,* £528 ($702)

15
A 'Vienna' covered vase on stand, late 19th cent, painted by H Stadler, signed, with 'The Golden Age' 129.5cm (51in), *NY 16 June,* $10,175 (£7,427)

1

2

3

4

5

6

7

8

9

10

11

12

13

14

15

1

An Amstel tête-à-tête,
c 1800, each piece
painted with scenes of
peasants on the banks of
a river, handle of jug
repaired, one saucer
chipped, 11 pieces, 34cm
(13⅜ in), *L 8 Mar,*
£2,200 ($3,278)

2

**A Cozzi Venice chinoiserie
sugar bowl and cover,**
1765-75, the oval body
and cover each spirally
fluted and painted in
iron red, green, purple
and yellow within a gilt-
heightened iron-red and
green border, knop
chipped, red anchor mark,
h 9.6cm (3¾ in), *NY 16 June,*
$1,650 (£1,204)

3

A coffee cup, possibly
Doccia, *c* 1750, the 'U'-
form body finely painted
with a scene of a Turk
kneeling beside a river,
within a gilt-edged
cartouche incorporating
purple panels, *P 14 Nov,*
£143 ($192)

4

A Doccia charger, 1755-
65, painted in Imari
style in cobalt blue, iron
red and gold with
branches of flowering
prunus and peonies,
within a trellis diaper
and floral panel borders,
40.1cm (15¾ in), *NY 17 Nov,*
$302 (£242)

5

A Doccia dessert service,
c 1760, comprising two
pierced baskets and
stands, two large bowls
and four smaller bowls
of rococo oval form,
three circular bowls and
ten plates, some wear,
one basket and stand,
one bowl and two plates
damaged, L 9 Oct,
£1,320 ($1,703)

6

A porcelain dish, the
Hague, *c* 1780, decorated
in manganese with a
lute-player and girl in a
landscape, the border
with gilt and polychrome
decoration, 29cm (11½ in),
A 1 Oct,
Dfl 1,334 (£314; $405)

7

**A Cozzi coffee cup and
saucer,** *c* 1770, painted in
Imari style in underglaze
blue, iron red and
gilding with stylised
flowers and rockwork,
red anchor mark, *L 9 Oct,*
£286 ($369)

8

**A Swiss oval porcelain
basket,** Nyon, early 19th
cent, with two handles,
decorated in blue with
cornflowers, marked,
w 27cm (10⅝ in), *A 9 Mar,*
Dfl 596 (£159; $237)

9

An Italian porcelain ewer,
Naples, late 19th cent,
with relief decoration
of a bacchic scene in an
orchard, the handle in
the form of a bacchic
female rising from leaf
ornaments, marked,
51cm (19⅞ in), *A 18-26 Sept,*
Dfl 1,160 (£272; $351)

10

**A pair of Cozzi vases and
covers,** *c* 1770, painted in
Imari style with flowers
and foliage in underglaze
blue, iron-red and gilding,
several cracks and chips,
50cm (19¾ in), *F 10 May,*
**L 12,000,000 (£4,888;
$7,039)**

11

A Doccia teabowl, 1770-
80, decorated *alla
Sassonia,* with chinoiserie
figures, 8cm (3¼ in),
L 9 Oct,
£352 ($454)

1
**A Meissen figure of a
Harlequin playing the
bagpipes,** c1745,
probably modelled by
Johann Joachim
Kaendler, in bright-
coloured gilt-edged
clothes, restored, repaired,
13.6cm (5⅜in), *NY 17 Nov,*
$880 (£704)

2
**A Meissen figure of
Harlequin,** c1744,
modelled by Peter
Reinicke and Johann
Joachim Kaendler, repairs,
14.8cm (5⅞in), *NY 17 Nov,*
$2,200 (£1,760)

3
**A Meissen Italian comedy
figure of Mezzetin,** c1750,
from the Duke of
Weissenfels series,
modelled by Peter
Reinicke, wearing gilt-
edged bright-coloured
clothes, hand repaired,
13cm (5⅛in), *L 12 June,*
£221 ($318)

4
**A Meissen group of
Columbine and Pantaloon,**
c1741, modelled by
Johann Joachim Kaendler,
the actress with blue cap
and white dress with
iron-red edge and
yellow bodice, restoration,
16cm (6¼in), *L 9 Oct,*
£2,200 ($2,838)

5
**A Meissen group of
fighting Harlequins,**
c1740, modelled by
Johann Joachim Kaendler,
wearing brightly coloured
clothes, minor repairs,
16cm (6¼in), *L 12 June,*
£27,500 ($39,600)

6
**Two Meissen figures of
Harlequin,** 20th cent,
both wearing colourful
costumes, each on a
scroll-mounted base
applied with flowers and
heightened in gilding,
23.5 and 23.8cm (9¼ and
9⅜in), *NY 16 Nov,*
$660 (£528)

7
**A Meissen group of
Harlequin and Columbine
dancing,** late 19th cent,
after the 1744 model by
Johann Joachim
Kaendler, minor imper-
fections, 22.2cm (8¾in),
NY 24/25 Feb,
$1,045 (£721)

8
**A Meissen figure of a
drunken fisherman,**
c1740, modelled by
Johann Joachim Kaendler,
wearing a green hat,
brown breeches, restor-
ation to both hands,
18.5cm (7¼in), *L 9 Oct,*
£825 ($1,064)

9
**A Meissen figure of a fish-
wife,** c1740, modelled by
Johann Joachim Kaendler,
wearing a brown skirt,
green apron, purple and
black bodice, black bonnet
and white scarf, some
restoration, 19cm (7½in),
L 9 Oct,
£825 ($1,064)

10
**A Meissen figure of a
drunken fisherman,**
c1740, modelled by
Johann Joachim Kaendler,
wearing a russet hat, a
green-lined tan waistcoat
and white shirt, left
elbow and one fish tail
repaired, 17.8cm (7in),
NY 17 Nov,
$825 (£660)

11
**A Meissen figure of a
fishwife,** 1740-50,
modelled by Johann
Joachim Kaendler, wear-
ing a black cap, orange-
dotted white fichu, a
puce-laced blue bodice,
yellow apron and brown
skirt, repaired and cracked,
18.5cm (7¼in), *NY 17 Nov,*
$715 (£572)

1   2

3

4

5

6

7

8   9

10   11

1
**A pair of Meissen figures
of Bolognese hounds
mounted on German
ormolu bases,** c.1770,
modelled by Johann
Joachim Kaendler, seated
with ochre- and brown-
spotted white coats,
some repair and restor-
ation, 21.4 and 22.8cm
(8⅜ and 9in), *NY 17 Nov,*
$26,400 (£21,120)

2
A pair of pots and covers,
Comte d'Artois factory,
Paris, c.1780, decorated
with polychrome
flowers, the handles in
turned wood, d 20.5cm
8⅛in), *M 11 Dec,*
FF 33,300 (£2,934; $3,543)

3
**A Meissen group of
skaters,** c.1755, probably
modelled by Kaendler
and Eberlein, he wearing
a pale pink dress-coat,
lilac waistcoat and pink
breeches, she in yellow
coat over a puce
trimmed green skirt,
repair to female's ankle,
14cm (5½in), *L 12 June,*
£2,420 ($3,484)

4
**A Meissen rectangular
snuff box,** c.1760, the
exterior painted with
bouquets and sprays of
Manierblumen, the
interior of the lid
stippled with a man and
woman seated in an
alcove, 8.3 x 6.5 x 4.2cm
(3¼ x 2½ x 1⅝in), *L 12 June,*
£1,155 ($1,663)

5
**A pair of Spode 'New
Shape Jars',** c.1810-20,
decorated with pattern
no 1166, each with scrolling gilt acanthus-leaf-
moulded handles, gilding
slightly rubbed on foot-
rims, 13.2cm (5¼in),
L 22 May,
£990 ($1,436)

1

2

3

4

5

1
A Sèvres Rose Pompadour
'vase à élèphants', dated
1757, modelled by Jean-
Claude Duplessis,
39.1cm (15⅜in), *NY 17 Nov*,
$115,000 (£92,400)

2
A Vincennes cup and
saucer (gobelet Calabre),
c1753, decorated in tooled
gilding with two birds
within a flower and trellis
border, slight wear, cup
8.2cm (2¼in), *L 12 June*,
£4,400 ($6,336)

3
A Sèvres apple-green cup
and saucer, (tasse or
gobelet feuille de choux),
dated 1759, moulded
with leaf panels edged in
spiky gilding and
painted by Etienne Evans,
cup 7.8cm (3⅛in),
L 12 June,
£9,900 ($14,256)

4
A Vincennes bleu lapis
potpourri jar and cover
and a pair of birds
mounted in ormolu on a
Japanese lacquer stand,
1753-60, painted by
André-Vincent
Vielliard, h 21.5cm (8½in),
26.5cm (10⅜in), *NY 17 Nov*,
$33,000 (£26,400)

5
A pair of Sèvres vases
mounted in silver-gilt,
c1814, reserved on the
front and reverse with
views of palaces, Palais
de St Cloud and Palais
de Schönbrunn on one
and Palais de Windsor
and Palais de Sarskocello
on the other, signed
Robert, h 34.5cm (13⅝in),
d 24cm (9½in), *NY 17 Nov*,
$110,000 (£88,000)

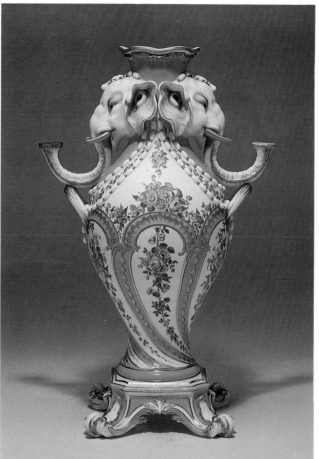

1

A Meissen figure of a
pastry-seller, c.1760,
modelled by Johann
Joachim Kaendler and
Peter Reinicke, wearing
a lilac bodice, yellow
apron and floral-painted
skirt, restored, 19cm (7½in),
L 12 June,
£605 ($871)

2

A Meissen figure of a lady
gardener, c.1770, wearing
a turquoise-beribboned
white hat and blouse,
gilt-laced iron-red
stomacher, white, puce
and turquoise skirt and
yellow overskirt, 13.4cm
(5¼in), *NY 16 Nov,*
$605 (£484)

3

A pair of Meissen figures
of a flower-seller and a
vintager, mid-19th cent,
their eighteenth-century
clothes brightly coloured
and gilt, 16 and 16.8cm
(6¼ and 6⅞in), *L 8 Nov,*
£572 ($761)

4

A Meissen figure of a
Tyrolean musician, c.1745,
modelled by Johann
Joachim Kaendler, playing
a hurdy-gurdy, 12.4cm
(4⅞in), *NY 17 Nov,*
$1,430 (£1,144)

5

A Meissen figure of a
shepherd, 1748-50,
modelled by Johann
Joachim Kaendler and
Peter Reinicke, wearing
a yellow-lined white
jacket above green
breeches, a pale-yellow
hat, minor restoration,
L 9 Oct,
£825 ($1,064)

6

A pair of Meissen figures
of a shepherd and
shepherdess, c.1880, their
clothes coloured in tones
of lilac, green and
brown, chips, 25 and
24cm (9⅞ and 9½in),
L 8 Nov,
£528 ($702)

7

A pair of Meissen figures
of falconers, c.1750,
modelled by J F
Eberlein, the man with
green trimmed coat and
black hat and boots, his
companion in yellow
jacket and black bodice,
both with damage and
restoration, 17.8 and
17.2cm (6¾ and 7in),
L 12 June,
£825 ($1,188)

8

A pair of Meissen figures
of Greek and Levantine
musicians, 1745-50,
modelled by Johann
Joachim Kaendler, both
wearing brightly coloured
clothes edged in gold,
neck repaired, scarf
chipped, 20.2cm (8in),
NY 17 Nov,
$1,320 (£1,056)

9

A Meissen figure of a
bagpiper, c.1741,
modelled by Johann
Joachim Kaendler, after
the engraving 'Le Romain'
by Jaques Dumont,
wearing a blue waistcoat,
pale-yellow stockings
and black hat and shoes,
restoration to hat and
pipe, 23.5cm (9¼in),
L 9 Oct,
£1,100 ($1,419)

10

A Meissen group, 1745-
50, modelled by Johann
Joachim Kaendler, the gallant
with a white coat and
yellow breeches, his
companion with a white
dress with red ribbons
and a black hat,
restored, 13.4cm (5¼in),
L 9 Oct,
£825 ($1,064)

11

A Meissen group of
shepherd lovers, 1740-5,
modelled by Johann
Joachim Kaendler, her
yellow skirt with oriental
flowers, he wearing tur-
quoise breeches, some
restoration, 16cm (6¼in),
L 9 Oct,
£880 ($1,135)

1

2

3

4

5

6

7

8

9

10

11

1
A Meissen sweetmeat figure of a blackamoor, 1745-50, wearing a chartreuse and puce feather headdress and a blue, chartreuse and puce feather skirt, cover missing, both arms repaired, 18.5cm (7¼in), *NY 17 Nov,* $770 (£616)

2
A pair of Meissen sweetmeat dishes, mid-19th cent, each modelled with the figure of a cook, the man with a saucepan and his companion with a goose, bird's head missing, chips, 17cm (6⅝in), *L 7 June,* £440 ($638)

3
A Meissen double-shell sweetmeat dish, 3rd quarter 19th cent, modelled with the figure of a chef in a pink jacket holding a saucepan, minor damage, 24.5cm (9⅝in), *L 8 Mar,* £220 ($329)

4
A pair of Meissen sweetmeat figures, late 19th cent, depicting a lady and a gallant seated behind a shaped oval flower-applied dish, slight chips, 31.7cm (12½in), *C 11 Jan,* £726 ($1,053)

5
A pair of Meissen figures, 3rd quarter 19th cent, decorated in underglaze blue and gilding, man's cane missing, small chips, 15.2 and 16.5cm (6 and 6⅜in), *L 8/9 Nov,* £605 ($805)

6
A Meissen group of lovers, early 19th cent, wearing eighteenth-century clothes painted with flowers, the whole on a pierced gilt scroll base, minor damage, 19cm (7½in), *L 8/9 Nov,* £605 ($805)

7
A Meissen figure of a lady of 'The Order of Pug-Dogs', late 19th cent, the whole with gilt details, 28.6cm (11¼in), *NY 3 Nov,* $1,430 (£1,144)

8
A Meissen allegorical figure of 'Smell', late 19th cent, from a set of the Senses, modelled as a girl seated by a table enjoying the scent of a posy, minor chips, 14cm (5½in), *L 8 Nov,* £440 ($585)

9
A pair of Meissen figures of a lady and gallant, late 19th cent, their clothing picked out in coloured enamels and gilding, some repair, 50.3 and 48.3cm (19⅜ and 19in), *C 5 July,* £478 ($1,014)

10
A Meissen figure of a dancer, *c.*1750, possibly modelled by Kaendler and Meyer, wearing a yellow hat, a puce stomacher and a yellow apron decorated in *indianische Blumen* over a lilac skirt, left arm repaired, 13cm (5in), *L 12 June,* £1,210 ($1,742)

11
A Meissen figure of a gallant, *c.*1755, probably modelled by Kaendler and Reinicke, wearing a puce dress-coat over a gilt-stippled and trimmed waistcoat, repaired, 13cm (5in), *L 12 June,* £990 ($1,426)

1

2

3

4

5

6

7

8

9

10   11

1
Two Meissen figures of children, early 20th cent, their rustic clothes painted with sprigs, each seated on a gilt scroll-edged mound base, minor chips, 12.5cm (4⅞in), *L 8 Mar,* £440 ($656)

2
A Meissen group, 2nd half 19th cent, modelled as five child musicians accompanied by a spotted dog on a circular rock and grass-moulded base, chips, 20cm (7⅞in), *P 10-13 July,* £440 ($598)

3
A Meissen figure of a little girl carrying a doll, 19th cent, dressed in eighteenth-century costume, on a rocaille base, 13cm (5⅛in), *A 9 Mar,* Dfl 301 (£69; $102)

4
A Meissen group of Thespian cherubs, 3rd quarter 19th cent, the boy wearing a blue drape his companion wearing a loosely tied yellow scarf, chips, 11.5cm (4½in), *L 7 June,* £275 ($398)

5
A Meissen group of a girl and a kid, *c*1910, after a model by J Hirt, moulded signature, the whole coloured in a pastel palette, goat's ear repaired, 44cm (17⅞in), *L 7 June,* £715 ($1,037)

6
A Meissen group of Europa and the bull, late 19th cent, the scantily draped maiden seated on a docile beast and attended by two nymphs, chips, 21.5cm (8½in), *L 8 Nov,* £495 ($658)

7
A pair of Meissen figures of Cupids, late 19th cent, each winged cherub wearing a scant green or pink drape, some damage and restoration, 19.5 and 20cm (7⅝ and 7⅞in), *L 8 Nov,* £682 ($907)

8
A Meissen group emblematic of 'Astronomy', 3rd quarter 19th cent, modelled as three putti on a mound base edged with garland and formal borders, the whole well coloured, minor chips, 19.8cm (7⅜in), *L 8 Mar,* £550 ($819)

9
A Meissen figure of Count Bruhl's tailor, 3rd quarter 19th cent, after J J Kaendler, wearing a striped waistcoat and floral painted yellow frock coat, the animal with brown coat, some restorations and chips, 43.2cm (17in), *L 7 June,* £2,200 ($3,190)

10
A Meissen figural candelabrum, mid-18th cent, modelled in the manner of J J Kaendler, with a lady holding her white apron seated under a tree with two branches terminating in the nozzles (modern replacements), restored, 24.7cm (9¾in), *L 9 Oct,* £825 ($1,064)

1   2

3   4   5

6   7

8

9   10

1
A Meissen 'Nodding Pagoda' figure, late 19th cent, modelled in the form of a rotund Chinese woman wearing a robe, 17.8cm (7in), *NY 3 Nov,* $1,650 (£1,320)

2
A Meissen 'Nodding Pagoda' figure, late 19th cent, the corpulent figure seated crosslegged and wearing a floral-painted robe and leaf hat, 15cm (5⅞in), *L 8 Nov,* £605 ($804)

3
A pair of Meissen 'Nodding Pagoda' figures, 3rd quarter 19th cent, after original models by J J Kaendler, each wearing a robe painted with stylised flowers, minor chips, 17.5cm (6⅞in), *L 8 Mar,* £1,320 ($1,967)

4
A Meissen figure of a dog, *c.*1770, the animal with grey and white fur and wide eyes, seated on a purple cushion with yellow braid and tassels, 24.5cm (9⅝in), *L 9 Oct,* £2,530 ($3,264)

5
A pair of Meissen figures of bolognese terriers, 1755-65, probably modelled by Johann Joachim Kaendler, each with brown and black eyes, one with russet spots, the other with coat spotted in sepia, repaired, 12.4 and 12.2cm (4⅞ and 4¾in), *NY 16 Nov,* $1,870 (£1,496)

6
A pair of Meissen figures of pug dogs, *c.*1750, modelled by Johann Joachim Kaendler, both sitting, the female suckling a puppy, the fur in brown and black, restorations, 24.3cm (9½in), *M 27 June,* FF 133,200 (£11,433; $15,578)

7
Two Meissen figures of birds, late 19th cent, one as a parrot, the other as a hoopoe, one wing repaired, chips, 33cm (13in), *L 8/9 Nov,* £528 ($702)

8
A pair of Meissen figures of parrots, *c.*1880, each perched on a tree-stump, their plumage coloured in red, green and blue, some damage, 42cm (16½in), *L 8 Mar,* £682 ($1,016)

9
A Meissen figure of a dove, mid-18th cent, seated on an oval base encrusted with flowers, the plumage of the wings and tail picked out in brown and grey, 15.2cm (6in), *M 27 June,* FF 22,200 (£1,905; $2,596)

10
A Meissen figure of a dove, mid-18th cent, on an oval base, the red eyes with black pupils and the feathers in grey and with white flecking, shading to white on the wing, tail and breast, 15.2cm (6in), *M 27 June,* FF 22,200 (£1,905; $2,596)

11
A Meissen figure of a monkey, mid-19th cent, seated on an ivy-trailed rocky base eating an apple, his fur naturalistically textured and coloured, minor restoration, 72cm (28¼in), *L 8 Nov,* £1,100 ($1,463)

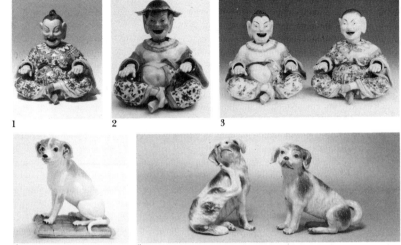

1   2   3

4   5

6

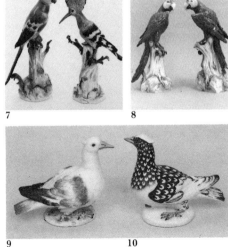

7   8

9   10   11

1
A **Ludwigsburg chinoiserie figure of a child**, c.1765-70, holding a ring on which a parrot (a Meissen replacement) is perched, hat repaired, 10.8cm (4⅛in), *L 12 June*, £330 ($475)

2
A **Ludwigsburg figure of a butcher**, 1768-78, modelled by Pierre François Lejeune, wearing a blue hat, a blue-edged white jacket, an iron red waistcoat and maroon-edged yellow breeches, 13cm (5⅛in), *NY 17 Nov*, $1,100 (£880)

3
A **Fürstenberg figure of Mezzetin**, c.1775, modelled by Johann Christof Rombrich, wearing a brightly coloured costume, 11.8cm (4⅝in), *L 12 June*, £2,310 ($3,326)

4
A **Fürstenberg figure of a lady musician**, c.1775-80, wearing a floral-patterned skirt with pink bodice and white apron, yellow hat and green shoes, the base outlined in pink, 18.2cm (7⅛in), *L 9 Oct*, £550 ($710)

5
A **Frankenthal group of singers**, 1787, after Joh. Peter Melchior, a central figure conducting surrounded by a man, a woman and two children, repaired, 25cm (9⅞in), *L 9 Oct*, £1,045 ($1,348)

6
A **Frankenthal figure of a cupid in disguise**, c.1755-7, modelled by Johann Wilhelm Lanz, shown in the guise of a colour-grinder (Farbenreiber), wings missing and damage overpainted, 11cm (4⅜in), *L 12 June*, £165 ($238)

7
A **Frankenthal figure of a young girl allegorical of 'winter'**, c.1755-6, probably modelled by Johann Wilhelm Lanz, wearing winter attire, a beribboned bonnet, flowered shawl and skirt and yellow clogs, 10.4cm (4in), *L 12 June*, £528 ($760)

8
A **Frankenthal figure of a child fish-seller**, c.1755-60, modelled by Johann Wilhelm Lanz, wearing a puce flowered smock-dress and close-fitting white bonnet, 10.5cm (4⅛in), *L 12 June*, £550 ($792)

9
A **Limbach figure of Harlequin**, c.1775-80, wearing a green hat, chequered jacket and yellow breeches decorated with playing cards, on a base detailed in puce, 13.7cm (5¼in), *L 12 June*, £4,620 ($6,653)

10
A **Kloster-Veilsdorf figure of Jupiter**, 1764-5, from a set of the Seven Planets, modelled by Wenzel Neu, the god naked save for a purple drape, some restoration, 22.2cm (8¾in), *L 9 Oct*, £550 ($709)

11
A **Frankenthal allegorical group of Peace and Harmony**, c.1760, modelled by Johann Wilhelm Lanz, showing two casually-draped putti, one holding a lyre, 14cm (5½in), *L 9 Oct*, £660 ($851)

12
A **Kloster-Veilsdorf equestrian figure** of a Roman warrior, c.1770, detailed in yellow, puce, orange-red, cerulean, pale russet, black and gilding, part baton and reins missing, base cracked, 19cm (7½in), *L 12 June*, £1,320 ($1,901)

13
A **Kloster-Veilsdorf figure of Mars**, 1764-5, from a set of the Seven Planets, modelled by Wenzel Neu, probably repaired by Schubarth, damage to neck, 31.7cm (12½in), *L 9 Oct*, £495 ($639)

1   2   3   4

5   6

7   8   9

11

10   12   13

1
A Zurich figure of a youth,
c.1785, probably by the
'Master of the dancing
groups', leaning against
a tree, 14.6cm (5¾in),
L 9 Oct,
£1,870 ($2,412)

2
A Höchst group of 'Die
Musikantenfamilie', *c*.1777,
modelled by J|P
Melchior, with a gallant
seated on a mound playing
a hurdy-gurdy, his
companion standing
close to him, 28cm
(11in), *L 12 June,*
£1,045 ($1,505)

3
An Ansbach figure of a
rustic youth, *c*.1765-70,
wearing a hat bound
with a puce ribbon, blue
coat, yellow breeches
supported by puce braces
and a red-striped sash,
some restoration, 14.5cm
(5¾in), *L 12 June,*
£660 ($950)

4
A Vienna theatrical group,
c.1770, modelled as an
actor and a child, some
minor repairs and imper-
fections, 26.3cm (10⅜in),
NY 17 Nov,
$990 (£792)

5
A Doccia Italian comedy
figure, *c*.1760-70, wearing
a yellow hat and breeches,
lilac jacket and black
apron, carrying a basket,
hand repaired, 10.5cm
(4in), *L 12 June,*
£2,640 ($3,802)

6
A Doccia figure of
Harlequin, *c*.1760-70,
wearing a diamond-
patterned costume in red,
yellow, blue and mauve,
hat restored, small chip
to stick, 10.4cm (4in),
L 12 June,
£715 ($1,030)

7
A Dresden group of
musicians, late 19th cent,
modelled as a lady playing
a lute and a gallant
playing a pipe, both
wearing pastel-coloured
clothes, minor damage,
22.5cm (8⅞in), *L 8/9 Nov,*
£220 ($293)

8
A pair of Paris bottles and
stoppers, *c*.1840, modelled
by Jacob Petit, each in
the form of carnival
figures, the costume and
base gilded, 22.5cm (8⅞in),
F 11 May,
L 1,600,000 (£651; $938)

9
A 'Sèvres' biscuit bust of
Napoleon I, 19th cent,
wearing a military jacket,
firing cracks, overpainting,
chips, 69cm (27⅛in),
L 7 June,
£880 ($1,276)

10
A pair of Continental
figures of cockerels, *c*.1900,
each perched on a sheaf
of wheat and crowing,
their plumage variously
coloured, chips, 43 and
43.5cm (16⅞ and 17⅛in),
L 8 Nov,
£495 ($658)

11
A pair of Paris 'jewelled'
figures and stands, *c*.1845,
decorated and gilded by
Francisque Rousseau, the
gallant and the young
lady wearing brightly
coloured traditional dress,
34 and 33cm (13⅜ and
12⅞in), *L 8 Nov,*
£605 ($804)

12
A 'Sèvres' biscuit figure of
'La Baigneuse', *c*.1775,
modelled by Étienne-
Maurice Falconet, toes
and thigh repaired, 35cm
(13¾in), *NY 4 May,*
$2,200 (£1,571)

13
A Samson ormolu-
mounted parrot, mid-19th
cent, naturalistically
modelled on a tree stump
and brightly enamelled,
well chased rococo base,
35.6cm (14in), *L 8 Nov,*
£462 ($614)

14
A Samson figure of an
elephant, *c*.1900, the
animal well modelled
and wearing a blanket
decorated in iron red
and gilding in Japanese
style, 48.3cm (19in),
C 5 July,
£660 ($895)

1

2

3

4

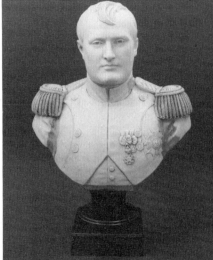
9

5

6

7

8

11

12

10

13

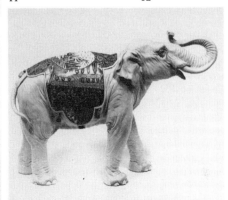
14

1
A pair of Bow 'New Dancers' candlestick figures, *c*1760-5, their clothes brightly coloured and gilt with sprigs and motifs, some damage and some restoration, 24cm (9½in), *L 22 July,* £440 ($587)

2
A pair of Bow candlestick groups, *c*1765, each modelled as a Cupid garlanded in red, blue and yellow flowers, small repairs, 24.1cm (9½in), *L 22 May,* £1,320 ($1,914)

3
A Bow figure of a tawny owl, *c*1760, perched on a tree-stump splashed in two shades of green and applied with a puce flowerhead between its claws, the plumage in shades of brown, firing cracks and repairs, 21cm (8¼in), *L 2 Oct,* £3,960 ($5,108)

4
A Bow figure of a gardener, *c*1765, wearing a gilt-detailed puce jacket, gilt-edged dark underglaze-blue hat, turquoise breeches and black shoes, the base enriched in blue, puce and gilding, restoration, 24.3cm (9½in), *L 24 July,* £550 ($734)

5
A Chelsea pastoral figure of a lady, *c*1765, wearing a turquoise bodice, flowered yellow and white striped skirt and feathered head-dress, restored, 26cm (10¼in), *L 22 May,* £242 ($351)

6
A Chelsea group of the Triumph of Galatea, *c*1755-6, the Nereid wearing a yellow-lined drapery, a child Triton blowing a conch horn, slight damage, 15.2cm (6in), *L 22 May,* £2,200 ($3,190)

7
A pair of Chelsea fable candlestick groups of 'The Fox and Grapes' and 'The Fox and the Cat', *c*1760-5, applied with brightly coloured flowers and foliage, sconces missing, 23.8cm (9⅜in), *L 24 July,* £1,100 ($1,469)

8
Two Chelsea fable candlestick groups of 'The Cock and Jewel' and 'The Vain Jackdaw' *c*1768, applied with brightly coloured flowers and foliage, sconces missing, 20.4cm (8in), *NY 12-14 Apr,* $660 (£462)

9
A pair of Chelsea bocage candlestick groups, *c*1765, emblematic of The Seasons, each modelled as a girl and gallant standing before a flowering bush, some damage and restoration, 27.7cm (11in), *L 24 July,* £1,155 ($1,542)

10
A pair of Chelsea fable candlesticks of 'The Vain Jackdaw' and 'The Cock and Jewel', *c*1770, each with brightly coloured birds on a scrolled base and before a bocage of flowers, some restoration, 27.5cm (10¾in), *L 24 July,* £770 ($1,028)

11
A Chaffers Liverpool bust of George II, *c*1760, in the white; 34.2cm (13½in), *L 2 Oct,* £3,520 ($4,541)

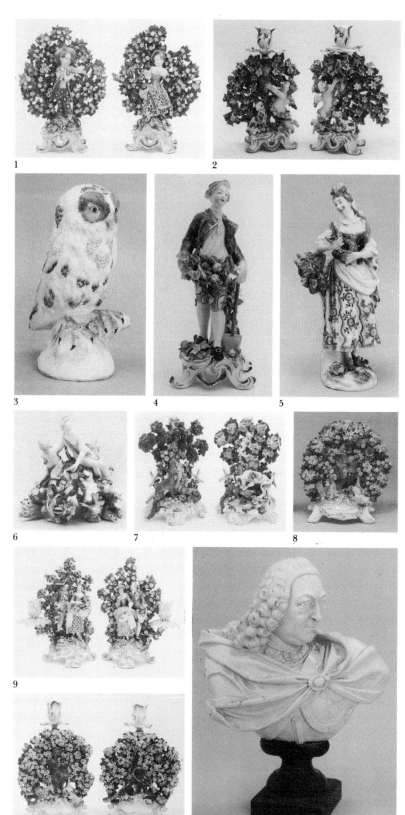

1
A **Derby figure of Harlequin**, c1750-5, in the white, raised on a square base applied with flowers and foliage, restoration, 13.3cm (5¼in), *L 22 May.*
£990 ($1,436)

2
An early **Derby 'dry-edge' figure of Kitty Clive as Mrs Riot (the 'Fine Lady') in David Garrick's farce 'Lethe'**, c1750-2, from an engraving by Charles Mosley after Thomas Worlridge, 23.8cm (9⅜in), *L 22 May.*
£5,280 ($7,656)

3
A **Derby figure of a musician**, c1760-65, wearing an orange-lined white cloak over a purple jacket and turquoise breeches, some restoration, 26.7cm (10½in), *L 22 May,*
£253 ($367)

4
A **Derby 'dancing group'** c1770, inspired by a Meissen original, their clothes pastel-coloured and gilt details, the base edged with pink and pale-blue scrolls, chips, 18.4cm (7¼in), *L 24 July,*
£935 ($1,248)

5
A **pair of Derby biscuit figures of a shepherdess and a shepherd**, c1800, modelled by J J Spangler and W Coffee, the young woman feeding a sheep, the young man with a dog at his feet, some damage, 28 and 33cm (11 and 13in), *L 24 July,*
£990 ($1,322)

6
A **pair of Derby candlestick figures**, c1835, each modelled as a gallant or a maiden, standing on a gilt and pink scroll base, minor damage, 24.1cm (9½in), *L 24 July,*
£638 ($851)

7
A **pair of Derby 'Ranelagh Dancers' candlestick figures**, c1835, each modelled as a gallant or young lady in richly decorated clothes, one branch repaired, chips, 25.5 and 24.7cm (10 and 9¾in), *L 24 July,*
£572 ($764)

8
A **Longton Hall figure of a boy piper**, c1755-6, wearing a black hat, purple jacket and green breeches, gilt-scroll-edged base applied with two flowers, pipe and hand restored, 14.2cm (5⅝in), *L 22 May,*
£792 ($1,148)

9
A **Longton Hall figure of an actor**, c1755, wearing a gilt-trimmed white coat over a puce waistcoat and deep blue breeches, 19.1cm (7½in), *L 22 May,*
£682 ($989)

10
A **Longton Hall figure of Columbine**, c1755, playing the hurdy-gurdy, wearing a yellow-ribboned pink hat, green bodice, yellow skirt and under-skirt decorated with playing cards, minor chips, 12.7cm (5in), *L 22 May,*
£2,090 ($3,031)

11
A **pair of Longton Hall musician figures**, c1758, the lady in yellow and purple, the man in an orange-lined purple jacket and green breeches, the lady restored, the man with minor damage, 28.5cm (11¼in), *L 22 May,*
£3,410 ($4,945)

12
A **pair of Longton Hall figures of gardeners**, c1755-6, each standing on a scroll-moulded base picked out in green, puce and gilding, the man restored, small chips, 12 and 11cm (4¾ and 4¼in), *L 22 May,*
£660 ($957)

13
A **Rockingham figure of a white cat**, c1830, wearing a gilt collar, its features picked out in brown and red, ear chipped, 6.5cm (2½in), *L 2 Oct,*
£418 ($539)

14
Two **Minton candlestick-groups of a gardener and companion**, c1835-40, each brightly coloured and gilt, slight damage and restoration, 23.5cm (9¼in), *L 22 May,*
£1,650 ($2,393)

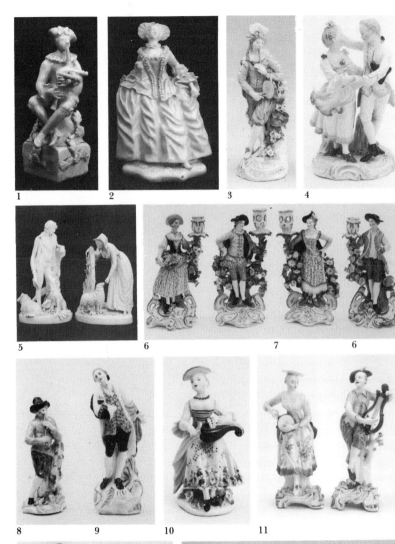

1   2   3   4

5   6   7   6

8   9   10   11

12

13

14

1
A pair of Staffordshire porcelain figures of the **Lion and the Unicorn,** mid-19th cent, each wearing a gilt crown, unicorn damaged, 8.8cm (3½in), *L 24 July,* £275 ($367)

2
A pair of Staffordshire porcelain lion and lamb groups, *c* 1850, each beast lying on a base with gilt borders, the lion's mane formed from shredded clay, 12.1cm (4¾in), *L 22 May,* £1,100 ($1,595)

3
A pair of Minton **candlesticks,** *c* 1830, each modelled as a gallant holding a basket of flowers or a girl with flowers in her apron, their clothes richly coloured and gilt, minor damage, 21.5cm (8½in), *L 24 July,* £1,012 ($1,351)

4
A Robinson and Leadbeater parian bust of **Lord Roberts,** 1900, in full uniform, incised and impressed marks including 'A Hopkins sculpt, July 1900', 53.5cm (21in), *C 11 Jan,* £209 ($303)

5
A Royal Doulton figure of **'Pretty Lady',** 1919, the young woman wearing a white-spotted grey gown, 24.7cm (9¾in), *L 14 Feb,* £440 ($617)

6
A Royal Doulton figure of **'The Bather',** 1920s, the young woman slipping out of a blue-lined and mottled mauve robe, 19.7cm (7¾in), *L 22 May,* £330 ($479)

7
A Royal Doulton figure of **'Pamela',** 1937, wearing a flounced dress and carrying flowers, printed and painted titles, 19cm (7½in), *L 22 May,* £242 ($351)

8
A Royal Doulton figure of **'Pierrette',** 1921, the young girl holding out the hem of her black and white costume, 17.8cm (7in), *L 22 May,* £396 ($574)

9
A Royal Doulton figure of **Mr W S Penley as 'Charley's Aunt',** *c* 1920, designed by Albert Toft, 17.2cm (6¾in), *L 22 May,* £286 ($415)

10
A Royal Doulton figure of **'The Mask',** 1926, 17.2cm (6¾in), *L 22 May,* £550 ($798)

11
A Royal Doulton figure of **'The Sunshine Girl',** 1929, her black and orange swimming suit with polka dots, painted title, 12.7cm (5in), *L 24 July,* £825 ($1,101)

12
A pair of Royal Worcester figures of **'Eastern Water Carriers',** 1877, after models by James Hadley, their clothes coloured in bronze, green and pink with gilt details, pots repaired, chips, 45.7 and 43.2cm (18 and 17in), *L 24 July,* £550 ($734)

13
A pair of Royal Worcester figures of **a boy and a girl with baskets,** 1884, each in Kate Greenaway-style clothes with gilt details, hair crack in one basket, 24cm (9½in), *L 22 May,* £396 ($574)

14
A pair of Royal Worcester figures of **a boy and girl with baskets,** 1895, each wearing Kate Greenaway-style dress, decorated in 'shot enamels', shades of apricot and gilding, 24cm (9½in), *L 24 July,* £462 ($617)

15
A pair of Royal Worcester figures of **a boy and girl,** *c* 1883, after models by James Hadley, each wearing Kate Greenaway-style clothes with gilt details, 21.5cm (8½in), *L 24 July,* £660 ($881)

16
A pair of Royal Worcester **candlestick figures,** *c* 1886, modelled by James Hadley, of a boy and girl each standing before treestumps, toned in pale colours and gilding, 26.3cm (10⅜in), *C 10 Jan,* £572 ($829)

1   2

3   4   5

6   7   8   9   10

11   12   13

14   15   16

1

A Lund's Bristol bowl and
cover, c.1750, painted in
smudgy underglaze blue
with a pavilion amongst
islands, small hair crack
to cover, chip to rim of
bowl, d 11.2cm (4⅜in),
L 2 Oct,
£2,200 ($2,840)

2

A Lund's Bristol/early
Worcester fluted coffee
cup, c.1751-2, painted in
coloured enamels with a
butterfly, insects and scattered sprigs, small chip
repaired, 5.4cm (2⅛in),
L 2 Oct,
£308 ($397)

3

A William Ball Liverpool
bowl, 1760-2, painted in
brilliant underglaze blue
with a girl in a rustic
landscape with a church
and an obelisk to one
side, 15.2cm (6in), *C 3 Oct,*
£1,595 ($2,058)

4

A William Ball Liverpool
saucer dish, c.1758, in
bright underglaze blue,
minor wear, 18.4cm (7¼in),
L 14 Feb,
£2,200 ($3,084)

5

A Chaffer's Liverpool
baluster-shaped mug,
c.1755-6, painted in
underglaze blue after
Pillement's 'Romantic
Rocks' with an Oriental
fishing in a sampan,
13.4cm (5¼in), *L 22 May,*
£792 ($1,148)

6

A Lund's Bristol sauceboat,
c.1750, of silver shape,
painted in underglaze
blue in scroll-moulded
panels with an oriental
scene, the interior with
flower sprays and
ribboned emblems,
small chip on rim, 18cm
(7in), *L 14 Feb,*
£1,320 ($1,851)

7

A William Reid Liverpool
blue and white sauceboat,
1755-60, the rocaille-
moulded polygonal
sides picked out with a
garland around the foot,
the interior with another
floral border about a
central peony, 17.7cm
(6¾in), *P 14 Nov,*
£2,090 ($2,801)

8

A Plymouth blue and
white sauceboat, 1770-2,
the exterior crisply
moulded with foliate
cartouches painted with
oriental islands, flared
foot, foot damaged, 20.6cm
(8⅛in), *C 5 July,*
£363 ($492)

9

A Bow blue and white
sauceboat, c.1760, of
irregular hexagonal out-
line, the sides painted
with the 'Desirable
Residence', 18cm (7in),
P 14 Nov,
£286 ($383)

10

A Bow 'Partridge' or
'Quail' pattern bowl and
cover, c.1758-60, painted
in Kakiemon style with
birds and shrubs within
iron-red and gilt
borders, d 10.7cm (4⅛in),
L 2 Oct,
£2,090 ($2,696)

11

A Bow teapot and cover,
c.1756, painted in
underglaze blue with an
oriental lady seated in a
landscape playing a koto,
below ribboned
emblems, cracked and
chipped, 9cm (3½in),
C 28 Mar,
£429 ($639)

12

A Bow plate, c.1755-8,
vigorously painted with
a Turk's Cap Lily,
attracting a dragon-fly
and moths, slight wear,
two small hair cracks on
rim, 22.9cm (9in),
L 14 Feb,
£605 ($848)

13

A Bow oblong octagonal
dish, c.1755-8, painted
with a spray of bright
yellow flowers, probably
a Dyer's Greenweed,
attracting winged insects,
brown-edged rim, some
wear, small hair crack
on reverse, 26.7cm
(10½in), *L 14 Feb,*
£1,320 ($1,851)

14

A Bow mug, c.1760-5,
painted in 'famille-rose'
palette with birds
amongst flowers by rock-
work, brown-edged rim,
handle repaired, 14.9cm
(5⅞in), *C 5 July,*
£264 ($359)

1
A Chelsea 'fig' box and cover, c.1752-6, small chips, 10.2cm (4in), *L 22 May,* £4,840 ($7,018)

2
A Chelsea 'leveret' tureen and cover, c.1752-6, 9.5cm (3¾in), *L 22 May,* £4,620 ($6,699)

3
A pair of Chelsea plates, 1758-60, each boldly decorated in the manner of James Giles, with exotic birds and branches, brown-edged rims, one with slight chip to foot-rim, 21cm (8¼in), *C 3 Oct,* £440 ($568)

4
A pair of Chelsea cabbage leaf dishes, c.1759, each painted in the centre with a sprig of yellow peaches superimposed on the rose-heightened moulded veins, the rim edged in green shading to yellow, some restoration, 27.8 and 28.5cm (11 and 11¼in), *NY 12-14 Apr,* $1,760 (£1,231)

5
A 'Chelsea ewer' cream-boat, c.1765-70, painted with Orientals in a garden, the interior rim with an iron-red border, 11.4cm (4½in), *L 22 May,* £374 ($542)

6
A pair of Derby sauce-boats, c.1760, slight chips, 12.7cm (5in), *C 3 Oct,* £341 ($440)

7
A pair of Derby leaf-moulded sauceboats, 1758-62, each with overlapping leaves edged in pale green shading to yellow, painted on the exterior and interior in shades of rose, iron-red, yellow, blue and green, 18.4cm (7¼in), *NY 12-14 Apr,* $1,210 (£846)

8
A Chelsea 'Hans Sloane' dish, c.1753-54, painted with a leafy branch bearing exotic fruit, a butterfly and two ladybirds, some wear, 27.6cm (10⅞in), *L 22 May,* £2,530 ($3,669)

9
A Chelsea-Derby dessert dish, 1770-5, painted with a central cluster of fruit within a gilt entwined garland, the periwinkle-blue and gilt border hung with a husk garland, slight chip, 26.7cm (10½in), *C 3 Oct,* £176 ($227)

10
A Derby feeding cup, c.1775-80, printed in dark underglaze blue with a gilliflower and other scattered floral sprigs inhabited by a butterfly, minor chips, 9cm (3½in), *L 24 July,* £605 ($808)

11
A Derby jug, c.1760, the baluster body painted with exotic birds in a landscape and a flower spray enclosed by sprigs, very slight chip to spout, 22.8cm (9in), *C 5 July,* £495 ($673)

12
A Derby 'Mask' jug, c.1762-5, slight wear, small chips to spout, 17.2cm (6¾in), *L 22 May,* £528 ($756)

13
A garniture of three Derby Bough pots, 1825-30, minor imperfections, covers missing, 21.2 and 18.8cm (8⅜ and 7⅞in), *NY 12-14 Apr,* $825 (£577)

14
A Derby coffee pot, cover and stand, early 19th cent, decorated with elaborate scrolls and stylised leaves in gilding, purple, blue and red between purple key-fret borders on an orange ground, 24.3cm (9½in), *L 24 July,* £770 ($1,028)

15
A Derby potpourri vase, lid and cover, c.1830, painted in underglaze blue, iron red, puce, mauve, green, black and gilding, 48cm (19in), *P 14 Nov,* £715 ($958)

16
A Derby breakfast tea and coffee service, c.1820, 81 pieces, *C 5 July,* £1,265 ($1,716)

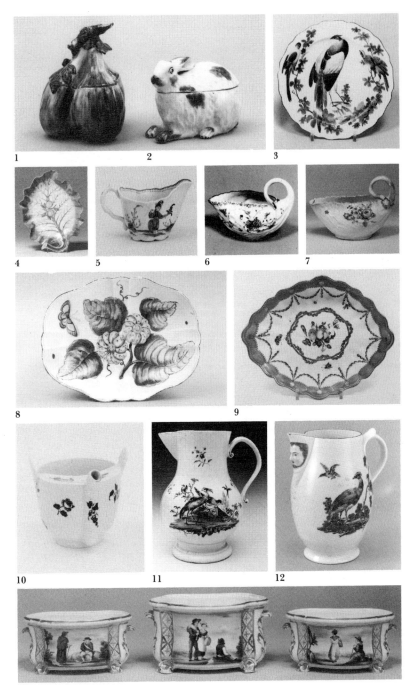

1
A Longton Hall loving cup, c.1755, painted in lime green, bright yellow, greyish-blue and raspberry pink and delineated in black with Chinese 'magician' figures, minor chip and hair crack to rim, d 11.5cm (4½in), *L 2 Oct,*
£1,540 ($1,987)

2
A Lowestoft blue and white bowl, c.1758-9, the interior painted with a panel of waterfowl in an island landscape, the exterior with oriental plants and birds, small chips on rim, slight wear, 21.6cm (8½in), *L 2 Oct,*
£2,640 ($3,406)

3
A Lowestoft milk jug, c.1775, painted in dark underglaze blue with a Chinese river scene below a diaper border, brown-edged rim, 8.3cm (3¼in), *L 24 July,*
£143 ($192)

4
A Lowestoft bell-shaped mug, c.1770-80, printed with naturalistic flower sprays and butterflies, chip on rim, hair crack to foot rim, 14.6cm (5¾in), *L 24 July,*
£253 ($339)

5
A Caughley mug, c.1775-80, printed with the 'Parrot Pecking Fruit' pattern, 11.4cm (4½in), *L 24 July,*
£264 ($354)

6
A Worcester 'King of Prussia' mug, c.1757, transfer-printed in black with a named portrait of Frederick the Great, signed 'RH Worcester' with the anchor rebus of Richard Holdship, 8.9cm (3½in), *L 24 July,*
£550 ($737)

7
An early Worcester pear-shaped bottle, c.1754-5, finely painted with a Chinaman standing before a fence enclosing shrubs and rockwork, the reverse with a flower spray, foot chipped, 12.1cm (4¾in), *L 22 May,*
£1,210 ($1,755)

8
A Worcester waste bowl, c.1765, printed in black and enamelled in soft colours with a Chinese lady and gentleman seated taking coffee, the interior with a figure within a black-line border, 12.1cm (4¾in), *L 22 May,*
£264 ($182)

9
A Longton Hall 'strawberry-moulded' plate, and a soup plate en suite, c.1754-7, painted in the manner of the 'Trembly Rose Painter' slight wear, cracked and chipped, 23 and 23.5cm (9 and 9¼in), *L 14 Feb,*
£506 ($709)

10
A pair of Worcester 'cos lettuce' sauceboats, one with small chip on rim, 18cm (7in), *L 22 May,*
£440 ($368)

11
A pair of Worcester sauce-boats, c.1760, each crisply moulded with overlapping cos lettuce leaves, painted in coloured enamels, brown-edged rims, 17.9cm (7in), *C 3 Oct,*
£715 ($922)

12
A Worcester blue and white 'Pine Cone' pattern circular basket, c.1775, transfer-printed in underglaze blue with a cluster of flowers and fruit, d 28.3cm (11⅛in), *NY 12-14 Apr,*
$880 (£615)

13
A Worcester blue and white sauceboat, mid-1760s, the ribbed silver-form body moulded with cartouches, painted with the 'Little Fisherman' and 'The Fisherman and Billboard Island' patterns, 19.8cm (7¾in), *P 14 Nov,*
£286 ($383)

14
A pair of Worcester double-lipped sauceboats, c.1760, small rim chip on each, 18.7 and 19cm (7⅜ and 7½in), *L 2 Oct,*
£650 ($839)

1
A Worcester 'Beckoning Chinaman' cylindrical mug, c.1755-8, enamelled over 'pencilled' outlines with two oriental figures by an ornamental rock, the reverse with a flowering branch, very slight wear, 14cm (5½in), *L 22 May*, £1,100 ($1,595)

2
A Worcester sifter-spoon, c.1770, painted in underglaze blue with stylised florets and 'comma' foliage, 13.2cm (5¼in), *L 2 Oct*, £770 ($993)

3
A Worcester pear-shaped 'Mask' jug, c.1765, printed in underglaze blue with naturalistic flower sprays, scrolling handle, minor chips on rim, 14cm (5½in), *L 24 July*, £143 ($192)

4
A Worcester 'Mansfield' pattern small teapot and cover, 1765-75, painted in underglaze-blue on either side and on the cover with a stylised floral spray within a 'pineapple', 9.6cm (3¾in), *NY 12-14 Apr*, $550 (£385)

5
A Worcester pear-shaped bottle, c.1770-75, with knopped mouth, printed with the 'Pine Cone' pattern below cell-diaper borders, 23cm (9in), *L 24 July*, £396 ($529)

6
A Worcester cuspidor or 'saffer-pot', c.1770-75, printed with the 'Three Flowers' pattern, flower sprigs and butterflies, some wear, 11.5cm (4½in), *L 24 July*, £253 ($338)

7
A pair of Worcester blue printed salad bowls, c.1770-75, the interiors moulded with scallop shell panels, printed and painted in bright underglaze blue with flower and fruit sprays, 25.2cm (9⅞in), *C 5 July*, £528 ($718)

8
A Worcester 'Trailing Vine' pattern sauce-tureen, cover and stand, c.1775, painted in underglaze-blue with fruiting vines and insects within dentil borders, slight wear on stand, 23.8cm (9⅜in), *L 22 May*, £660 ($957)

9
A pair of Worcester leaf dishes, 1765-70, painted with luxuriant sprays and sprigs of coloured flowers, very slight rubbing, 32.1cm (12⅝in), *C 3 Oct*, £990 ($1,277)

10
A pair of Worcester 'Lord Henry Thynne' plates, c.1770, each decorated with a central landscape medallion within turquoise borders, the rim with blue ground band with gilt edging, slight rubbing, 22.3cm (8¾in), *C 3 Oct*, £671 ($865)

11
A Worcester apple-green-ground cylindrical mug, c.1770, painted in gilt-edged mirror-shaped panels with brightly coloured exotic birds in parkland, 12cm (4¾in), *L 22 May*, £550 ($798)

12
A Worcester blue-scale fluted dish, c.1765-70, painted in gilt-edged panels with exotic birds in parkland, butterflies and moths reserved on a blue-scale ground, very minor wear, 30.2cm (11⅞in), *L 14 Feb*, £506 ($709)

13
A Worcester coffee-cup and saucer, c.1765-70, richly decorated with a 'Japan' pattern of flowering shrubs divided by radiating gros-bleu and gilt bands, *L 22 May*, £165 ($239)

14
A Worcester tea service, c.1770, each fluted piece decorated with 'cabled' turquoise borders outlined in gilding, slight wear to gilding, 23 pieces, *L 14 Feb*, £880 ($1,233)

1 2 3 4 5 6 7 8 9 10 11 12 13 14

1

A pair of Worcester Barr, Flight and Barr sauce-tureens and covers, c.1813, each painted in 'Japan' pattern in iron red, green, turquoise, pink, blue, brown and gold, one knop chipped and one cover chipped, 16.7cm (6⅝in), *NY 16 Nov,* $1,100 (£880)

2

A pair of Chamberlain's Worcester ice pails, covers and liners, c.1800, each painted in blue, yellow, green, maroon and black with cornflower and gilt leaf sprigs, one loop knop repaired, 28 and 28.4cm (11 and 11¼in), *NY 16 Nov,* $1,540 (£1,232)

3

A Chamberlain's Worcester 'Named View' mug, c.1810, the cylindrical body painted with a view of Oxford 'from the London Road', against a lilac ground below a gilt anthemion border, 8.9cm (3½in), *L 14 Feb,* £748 ($1,047)

4

A set of nine Chamberlain's Worcester 'Union' dessert plates, c.1820s, each piece painted with a flower spray within a gilt leaf border encompassed by an olive-ground rim moulded with sprays in white, three damaged, minor rubbing to gilding, 21.2cm (8⅜in), *HS 25 June,* £880 ($1,241)

5

A London-decorated Nantgarw plate, c.1818-22, painted in the centre in the style of the 'MacIntosh' service, the rim finely gilt reserved with panels of fruit and flowers, slight wear, 24.2cm (9½in), *L 14 Feb,* £1,045 ($1,465)

6

A set of three Chamberlain's Worcester armorial dessert dishes, painted by P. Bradley, each pale yellow ground reserved with the crest of a collared hind head surrounded by wild flowers, 32.5 and 34cm (12⅞ and 13⅜in), *HS 25 June,* £1,650 ($2,327)

7

A Nantgarw sucrier and cover, 1813-22, painted with colourful flower sprays between blue line borders, cover chipped, gilding slightly rubbed, 18.5cm (7¼in), *C 11 Jan,* £484 ($702)

8

An A J & W Ridgway tea service, c.1825, decorated in underglaze blue, colourful enamels and gilding with a 'Japan' pattern, cracks and repairs, 34 pieces, *L 24 July,* £396 ($529)

9

A New Hall tea service, c.1790, each piece with a blue and gilt border of oval medallions linked by interwoven ribbon and leaf trails, several pieces repaired, 44 pieces, *L 24 July,* £1,045 ($1,395)

10

An H & R Daniel tea and coffee service, c.1825-30, each piece painted with colourful flower sprays enclosed by rich dark-blue and gilt borders, cracks, 44 pieces, *C 5 July,* £605 ($821)

11

A John Ridgway sweetmeat basket, c.1840, painted with the scene of a sailor-boy in the rigging of a sailing ship, 25.3cm (10in), *L 22 May,* £825 ($1,196)

12

A Davenport botanical part dessert service, 1840s, each Brunswick-green matt border enclosing a finely painted botanical specimen titled on the reverse, some damaged, 24 pieces, *HS 25 June,* £220 ($308)

13

A Davenport dessert service, c.1860, each piece painted with sprays of wild flowers and moths against a blue-ground band between gilt formal borders, one plate repaired, plate 22.9cm (9in), *L 24 July,* £264 ($352)

1
A Coalport vase and cover, painted with mirror-shaped panels of exotic birds and flowering foliage, enclosed by gilt foliage on a dark blue ground, 26cm (10¼in), *C 27 Nov,* £220 ($269)

2
A Coalport vase and cover, c.1910, painted by F H Chivers, signed, with a panel of pink roses lying on a woodland bank, reserved on a royal blue ground with gilt borders, 25.5cm (10in), *L 24 July,* £462 ($617)

3
A Coalport dessert service, c.1830-40, a few cracks, some wear, 22 pieces, *L 24 July,* £352 ($470)

4
A pair of ice pails, covers and liners, of Coalport type, c.1840, painted with sprays and sprigs of colourful summer flowers and foliage, the borders and pine-cone finial with gilt details, some wear, 34.3cm (13½in), *L 22 May,* £1,430 ($2,074)

5
A Coalport fruit-painted tea and coffee service, c.1840, some damage, 38 pieces, *C 3 Oct,* £495 ($639)

6
A set of six Coalport plates, c.1860, each painted in Sèvres style with a central spray of fruit and flowers within a pink and gilt rim, retailer's mark for Daniell, London, 24.1cm (9½in), *L 14 Feb,* £231 ($324)

7
A Rockingham tea and coffee service, 1930-42, decorated in grey and gilding with stylised foliage, 47 pieces, *C 11 Jan,* £308 ($447)

8
A Coalbrookdale basket, c.1820, the exterior with a blue ground, slight chips, 23.5cm (9¼in), *C 28 Mar,* £198 ($295)

9
A Rockingham breakfast and tea service, 1842-6, each piece glazed on the exterior in rich brown, gilt rims, some staining, 82 pieces, *C 11 Jan,* £440 ($638)

10
A Coalbrookdale basket, c.1830, some damage, 31.8cm (12½in), *L 22 May,* £286 ($415)

11
A Spode Copeland china fish service, c.1910, each piece painted by Arthur H Perry, signed, with a different identified fish amidst aquatic weeds, heightened in gilding, platter 57.7cm (22¾in), 15 pieces, *NY 12 Apr,* $550 (£385)

12
A Spode 'Beaded Hoop', c.1810-20, decorated with pattern no 1166, d 9cm (3½in), *L 22 May,* £550 ($798)

13
A Spode 'flanged top, pierced, covered violet pot and stand', c.1810-20, decorated with pattern no 1166, hair crack to cover, 9.5cm (3¾in), *L 22 May,* £495 ($718)

14
A Spode botanical dessert service, 1815-20, each piece with dolphin and foliate moulded borders, painted with a botanical specimen, pattern number 1875 in black, 28 pieces, *C 5 July,* £770 ($1,047)

15
A Spode two-handled vase, c.1820, painted with bouquets of luxuriant flowers against a deep-blue ground scaled in gilding, 25.5cm (10in), *P 14 Nov,* £2,035 ($2,727)

16
A Spode garniture of spill vases, c.1820, each painted with a scallop shell panel filled with coloured flowers, reserved on a rich blue ground enclosed by gilt foliage, very slight damage, 13.3 and 15.8cm (4¼ and 6¼in), *C 5 July,* £1,375 ($1,865)

1
A Minton flower-encrusted potpourri vase and cover, *c*1825-30, painted with a landscape vignette and a floral spray, 26cm (10¼in), *C 5 July*,
£385 ($522)

2
A Minton 'New Dresden' vase and cover, *c*1840, encrusted with sprays and trails of intricately modelled and brightly coloured flowers around painted panels, minor chips, foot cracked, 40.6cm (16in), *L 22 May*,
£550 ($798)

3
A Minton two-handled jar and cover, 1830-40, painted with panels of fruit on a flower-encrusted ground, on similar stand, star crack, 30cm (11⅞in), *P 10-13 July*,
£352 ($479)

4
A set of fifteen Mintons pâte-sur-pâte dinner plates, dated 1916, each decorated by Alboine Birks, signed, depicting classical profiles in white slip on deep teal ground within gilt borders, 26cm (10¼in), *NY 24/25 Feb*,
$1,760 (£1,214)

5
A Mintons 'Vase Vaisseau à Mat', 1879, in imitation of a Sèvres original, retailer's mark for John Mortlock & Co, London, 45.7cm (18in), *L 24 July*,
£3,740 ($4,993)

6
A set of twelve Mintons pâte-sur-pâte cabinet plates, dated 1911, each decorated by Alboine Birks, signed, with a central grey roundel applied with white slip depicting a maiden and cupids, one damaged, 24.1cm (9½in), *NY 16 June*,
$2,530 (£1,847)

7
A Mintons polychromed pâte-sur-pâte vase, dated 1877, the glazed parian body tinted a deep olive green and decorated by Marc Louis Solon, signed, in white slip, the handles, rim and base with gilt and silvered details, 64.4cm (25⅜in), *NY 18 July*,
$1,980 (£1,511)

8
A Mintons pierced cabinet plate, 1883, decorated *c*1890, painted by A Gregory, signed, 24.8cm (9¾in), *L 22 May*,
£825 ($1,196)

9
A Royal Crown Derby vase and cover, dated 1898, painted by Leroy, signed, 24.3cm (9½in), *L 22 May*,
£528 ($766)

10
A pair of Mintons 'Seaux à Bouteille', late 19th cent, decorated with continuous scenes of shipping between pink and gilt borders, 16.7cm (6⅝in), *C 5 July*,
£638 ($868)

11
A Royal Crown Derby dessert service, 1926, decorated in underglaze blue, iron red and gilding with an 'Imari' pattern of stylised floral panels, 18 pieces, plate 22.2cm (8¾in), *L 24 July*,
£660 ($881)

12
A Goss model of the Goss oven, early 20th cent, printed goshawk and title in black, 7.7cm (3in), *C 11 Jan*,
£165 ($239)

13
A Royal Crown Derby dinner, tea and breakfast service, each decorated overall in a rich 'Imari' pattern, 143 pieces, *C 17 July*,
£3,080 ($4,112)

14
A pair of Crown Derby pink-ground vases, 1877-90, with elephant's head handles, decorated with cranes amongst bamboo and grasses on a pale pink ground, 29.5cm (11⅝in), *C 5 July*,
£330 ($448)

1   2   3

4

5   6

7   8

9

10   11

12   13   14

1
A Belleek 'Echinus' pattern part tea set, 1863-91, glazed in creamy white, cup and sugar bowl restored, minor chips, 17 pieces, *L 22 May*,
£385 ($558)

2
A Belleek teapot and cover, *c* 1870, the cover printed 'D McBirney & Co., Belleek, Fermanagh, Ireland', 20cm (7⅜in), *P 18-25 Sept*,
£165 ($213)

3
A Belleek mirror frame, 1863-91, moulded with basket-weave bordered by bands of beads and applied in high relief with sprays of intricately modelled roses, minor chips, 41.2cm (16¼in), *L 24 July*,
£1,210 ($1,615)

4
A Belleek honey pot and cover, *c* 1900, in the form of a beehive, the sides lightly moulded with shamrocks and flying bees, picked out in naturalistic colours, 15.8cm (6¼in), *C 10 Jan*,
£154 ($223)

5
A Belleek 'Croaking Frog' vase, *c* 1900, the crouching amphibian with head raised and mouth open, its eyes delineated in black, the glaze of yellowish tone, 12.7cm (5in), *C 10 Jan*,
£176 ($255)

6
A Belleek 'Naiads Flower Pot', 1863-91, the body moulded in relief with baby tritons at play with dolphins, the rim with coral border, the reliefs and borders with a lustrous glaze, 26cm (10¼in), *L 24 July*,
£880 ($1,175)

7
A Doulton Burslem vase and cover, *c* 1910, painted by G White, signed, with a maiden standing against a shaded ground, the neck and foot with green and gilt borders, cover chipped and repaired, 51.1cm (20¾in), *L 14 Feb*,
£550 ($771)

8
A Belleek circular basket, 1863-91, with a creamy lustrous glaze, 22.8cm (9in), *L 22 May*,
£2,310 ($3,350)

9
A Royal Doulton 'Shakespeare Jug', moulded with a continuous scene of Shakespearian characters, 26.7cm (10½in), *C 30 Oct*,
£220 ($282)

10
A Royal Doulton 'Dickens Jug', moulded and picked out in bright colours with a continuous scene of Dickensian characters, 26.7cm (10½in), *C 30 Oct*,
£341 ($436)

11
A Royal Doulton character jug titled 'The Clown', 1937-42, the leering face picked out in splashes of colour, red hair, coloured handle, *C 5 July*,
£1,320 ($1,791)

12
A set of twelve Royal Doulton fish plates, *c* 1923, each painted by J Birbeck, Sen, signed, 23.8cm (9⅜in), *NY 24/25 Feb*,
$1,100 (£759)

13
A Royal Doulton 'Toby Gillette' Toby jug, 1984, number 2 from a limited edition of 3, modelled by Eric Griffiths, the reverse with moulded inscription 'Toby Gillette, Jim'll Fix It', sold in aid of the Jimmy Savile Charitable Trust, 17.7cm (7in), *L 22 May*,
£15,950 ($23,127)

14
A Royal Doulton 'Hatless Drake' character jug, *c* 1940, Sir Francis with smiling expression, wearing gold earrings and a white ruff, the reverse with Drake's Drum, 14.7cm (5¾in), *L 24 July*,
£3,520 ($4,699)

15
A Royal Doulton character jug of 'The Clown', *c* 1940, the red-haired version, modelled by H Fenton, 16.2cm (6⅜in), *C 5 July*,
£902 ($1,224)

1
A Royal Doulton large character jug 'Smuts', 1946-8, the base inscribed 'Field Marshal the Rt. Hon. J. C. Smuts, KC, CH, DTD Prime Minister of the Union of South Africa and Commander-in-Chief South African Forces', 18cm (7⅛in), *JHB 23 Aug*, **R 1,900 (£872; $1,140)**

2
A Royal Doulton large character jug 'Monty', *c.*1954, still in production, 15.5cm (6⅛in), *JHB 23 Aug*, **R 130 (£60; $78)**

3
A Wilkinson Ltd 'Winston Churchill' Toby jug, *c.*1940, designed by Clarice Cliff, modelled as a caricature of the statesman as First Lord of the Admiralty, seated on a bull-dog draped with the Union Jack, 30.4cm (12in), *L 2 Oct*, **£792 ($1,022)**

4
A Hadley Worcester jug, the quatrelobed body painted with roses between borders moulded with lambrequins, 18.5cm (7¼in), *P 24/25 Jan*, **£105 ($152)**

5
A Royal Worcester potpourri jar and cover, dated 1893, the multi-lobed body printed and enamelled with fuchsia and daisies, 18cm (7⅛in), *P 24/25 Jan*, **£83 ($120)**

6
A Royal Worcester 'Persian Style' vase, dated 1901, decorated in colours and gilding with peacocks in full display above a band of embossed gilt foliage on an ivory-coloured ground, 38.7cm (15¼in), *C 5 July*, **£550 ($746)**

7
A Royal Worcester vase, 1901, painted by Hawkins, signed, with a panel of ripening fruits amongst foliage and flowers, within gilt scroll borders against a royal-blue ground, 26cm (10¼in), *L 2 Oct*, **£495 ($639)**

8
A Royal Worcester potpourri jar and cover, 1902, painted by C Balwyn, signed, with five swans in flight above reeds and gilt grasses against an azure ground, the border and handles with pink, green, brown and gilt details, 21cm (8¼in), *L 2 Oct*, **£1,430 ($1,844)**

9
A Royal Worcester potpourri jar and cover, dated 1904, painted by H Davis, signed, with a continuous highland landscape with a herd of deer, the borders and neck in green with gilt details, 20.3cm (8in), *L 22 May*, **£715 ($1,037)**

10
Two Royal Worcester teacups and saucers, dated 1926 and 1931, painted and signed by Price, Townsend, and Ayrton, with various fruits, *C 5 July*, **£165 ($224)**

11
A set of six Royal Worcester coffee cups and saucers, 1936, each painted by Stinton, signed, with highland cattle grazing in a misty mountainous landscape, and six silver-gilt coffee spoons, 10.9cm (4¼in), *L 2 Oct*, **£880 ($1,135)**

12
A Royal Worcester dessert service, dated 1912, each piece painted by Cole, signed, with fruits amongst leaves and blossom, the rim with a blue and gilt border, some glaze crazing and wear, one dish cracked, plate 24.7cm (9¾in), *L 2 Oct*, **£220 ($284)**

13
A set of six Royal Worcester coffee cups and saucers, dated 1926-9, painted and signed by Price, Hale, Bee and Moseley with various brightly coloured fruits, *C 5 July*, **£440 ($597)**

1   2   3
4   5   6
7   8   9
10
11
12   13

Asian Art

BRENDAN LYNCH

Asian art is intellectually rather inaccessible to those from the West. It nearly always has a religious basis and those religions concerned—Buddhism, Hinduism, Jainism and Islam—still seem strange and unfamiliar to most people in the West. The iconography requires considerable study if it is to be properly understood by those who have not been brought up amongst its beliefs. This is not to say that much of the art cannot be appreciated for its own sake, for example there has long been a strong market in South Indian Chola bronzes. The few serious collectors of Asian art, other than Indians themselves, are predominantly from Germany, Switzerland and Belgium. In the last twenty years Americans have been taking an increasing interest and spending large sums of money on Asian art, but the state of scholarship is still nowhere near as far advanced as it is, for example, in the field of Chinese art.

Although there is a wealth of Indian art in public collections in England, it is not on the whole well displayed and has often been consigned to storage or the darkest corner of a museum basement. This is not to suggest that such collections are entirely inaccessible—admission can usually be gained by applying to the curator. The Victoria and Albert Museum in London has but one Indian gallery devoted to sculpture, miniature painting and the decorative arts including jewellery and textiles. At the British Museum there is one large gallery divided into geographical subsections concentrating on stone and bronze sculpture covering the Himalayan regions, the Indian subcontinent and South-East Asia. These galleries provide an excellent introduction to Indian art in the broadest sense. The many museums in India, as well as those in the United States, have amassed diverse collections of interest to the more specialist collector.

The auction market for Indian and South-East Asian art is at present largely dominated by dealers who buy for clients in America and the Far East. There is ample opportunity in the saleroom for the new collector who decides to concentrate on a particular aspect of Indian art, whether it be religious images from a particular country, or sculpture, textiles or jewellery of a particular style or date. This is one of the few areas where collecting is still not prohibitively expensive: good examples of medieval and later bronze and stone sculpture can be bought for under £1,000 ($1,140) and items of decorative Indian art of the 17th to 19th centuries for considerably less.

Indian art has long held appeal for the European eye, although it has not been collected on anything like as broad a scale as, for instance, Chinese porcelain. The decorative aspect found in the later largely secular objects—textiles and architecture, for instance—which developed under the Mughal emperors (16th-19th centuries), has a spontaneity which is lacking in the more esoteric medieval Hindu and Buddhist art. This strengthened the link with the non-Indian eye and consequently a European visitor to India in the late 18th century would have been more likely to bring back chintzes, ivory or silver boxes and Kashmir shawls as opposed to Hindu bronzes and sculpture. Under the Raj, Indian art in general, and non-secular art in particular, was largely shunned, with the exception of the traditional crafts encouraged by the Great Exhibitions in London of 1851 and 1862 and 1911. This negative attitude was further strengthened by the predominant rigid Victorian ethics, often shocked by the blatant sensuality of Hindu sculptures.

1
A Javanese bronze
enshrined figure of the
Bodhisattva Padmapani,
c.12th cent, the whole
with brownish-black
patination, 24.2cm
(9½in), L 23 July,
£5,500 ($7,370)

2
A large Thai gilt-bronze
standing figure of Buddha,
the face, hands and feet
with traces of black
lacquer, 178cm (70in),
L 23 July,
£3,300 ($4,422)

3
A large Thai gilt-bronze
standing figure of Buddha,
c.18th cent, 124cm
(48¾in), L 9 Apr,
£3,300 ($4,752)

4
A Thai bronze standing
figure of Buddha,
14th/15th cent, Sukothai
style, the dark green
patina with a thin layer
of earthy encrustation,
42.5cm (16¾in), L 26 Nov,
£1,540 ($1,956)

5
A Thai gilt-bronze figure
of a monk, 19th cent, two
bands of red lacquer
round the lotus throne,
his left hand originally
holding a fan, part of the
handle of which
remains, 41cm (16¼in),
L 23 July,
£385 ($516)

6
A Thai bronze figure of
Buddha, 14th/15th cent,
Sukothai, wearing a
closely fitting monastic
robe, a sash of which
falls over his left
shoulder, 58.5cm (23in),
L 23 July,
£6,380 ($8,549)

7
A Thai bronze figure of
Buddha, dated 1531,
Chiengsen, the whole
with traces of red
lacquer, 52cm (20½in),
L 23 July,
£1,650 ($2,211)

8
A large Thai bronze figure
of Buddha, 16th/17th
cent, the finial now
missing, the whole with
intermittent patches of
gold-leaf, 66cm (26in),
L 23 July,
£1,100 ($1,474)

9
A Thai bronze Buddha
head, 15th/16th cent, the
whole with traces of
gilding, 32.5cm (12¾in),
L 26 Nov,
£2,860 ($3,632)

10
A Thai bronze bust of
Buddha, c.15th cent, the
smiling face with
downcast eyes, originally
inlaid, with greenish-
brown patination, 33cm
(13in), L 26 Nov,
£660 ($838)

11
A Mon style bronze figure
of Buddha, c.9th cent, the
top of the forefinger and
thumb of the left hand
now missing, the whole
with lightly encrusted
red-green patination,
25.2cm (9⅞in), L 9 Apr,
£3,300 ($4,752)

12
A Thai bronze Buddha
head, c.16th cent,
Ayudhya style, with
heavily-lidded inlaid
eyes and eyebrows in
relief, the whole with
traces of gilding, 42cm
(16½in), L 26 Nov,
£2,200 ($2,794)

13
A Khmer grey stone male
head, c.10th cent,
Baphuon, the features of
the face in low relief,
24cm (9½in), L 26 Nov,
£4,180 ($5,308)

14
A Thai buff stone Buddha
head, 16th/17th cent, the
tightly-curled hair with
flattened usnisa, 30cm
(11¾in), L 26 Nov,
£715 ($908)

15
A Khmer buff sandstone
Buddha head, c.12th cent,
Lopburi, the full face
with well-defined
features, 26cm (10¼in),
L 26 Nov,
£1,760 ($2,235)

1   2   3   4

5   6   7   8

9   10   11   12

13   14   15

1
A Chola bronze figure of **Parvati**, *c.*12th cent, the whole with green patina tinged with red, 47.5cm (18⅝in), *L 26 Nov,* £5,280 ($6,701)

2
A Nepalese turquoise-inset copper figure of the Saviouress **Syamatara**, *c.*17th cent, the whole with faint traces of gilding, unsealed, 18cm (7⅛in), *L 9 Apr,* £440 ($634)

3
A Nepalese gilt-copper figure of **Indra**, *c.*16th cent, a foliate halo behind the downcast face, the reverse with traces of red paint, 21.5cm (8½in), *L 23 July,* £2,640 ($3,537)

4
A Nepalese copper figure of the Dakini **Vasya-Vajravarahi**, *c.*16th cent, her forehead with the third eye and traces of orange pigment, the whole originally gilded, 16cm (6¼in), *L 23 July,* £1,045 ($1,400)

5
A Tibetan gilt-bronze figure of **Gautama Buddha (Sakya-Muni)**, *c.*16th cent, with traces of blue pigment, unsealed, 14.5cm (5¾in), *L 26 Nov,* £935 ($1,187)

6
A Nepalese gilt-copper figure of the Saviouress **Tara**, *c.*14th cent, insets including rubies, turquoise and lapis-lazuli, 17.5cm (6⅞in), *L 26 Nov,* £7,150 ($9,080)

7
A Tibetan gilt-copper figure of **Padmasambhava (Pad-ma-hbyung-gnas)**, *c.*18th cent, the urna with turquoise inset, sealed, 18cm (7⅛in), *L 26 Nov,* £715 ($908)

8
A large Tibetan gilt-copper repoussé figure of **Tsong-Kha-Pa** (1357-1419), 18th/19th cent, the necklace inset with turquoise, the cold-gilded face with painted details, yellow brocade peaked hat, sealed, 53cm (21in), *L 26 Nov,* £1,980 ($2,515)

9
A Tibetan gilt-copper figure of **Aksobhya Buddha** *(Don-yod grub-pa)*, 16th/17th cent, unsealed, 20.5cm (8in), *L 23 July,* £1,155 ($1,548)

10
A Tibetan gilt-bronze figure of **Amitayus** *(Tshe-dpag-med)*, *c.*16th cent, the hair with traces of blue pigment, unsealed, 25.7cm (10⅛in), *L 26 Nov,* £1,100 ($1,397)

11
A Tibetan bronze figure of the Saviouress **Sitatara**, the White Tara *(sGrol-dkar)*, *c.*18th cent, the chignon with traces of blue pigment, the face with traces of cold-gilding, sealed, 15.5cm (6⅛in), *L 26 Nov,* £660 ($838)

12
A Tibetan gilt-copper figure of the Yi-dam **Samvara** in Yab-Yum with his Sakti *(bDe-mchong)*, with blue and orange pigments, inset with jewels, base re-sealed and weighted with lead, 16cm (6¼in), *L 26 Nov,* £1,320 ($1,676)

13
A Tibetan painted wood seated figure of **a monk**, 17th/18th cent, the face and hands cold-gilded, the former with painted details, sealed, 22.8cm (9in), *L 26 Nov,* £440 ($559)

14
A Tibetan gilt-copper portrait figure of '**Byams-dbyangs dPal-ldan Rin-chen**, 17th/18th cent, the hair with traces of black paint, unsealed, 14.5cm (5¾in), *L 26 Nov,* £1,320 ($1,676)

1

2

3

4

5

6

7

8

9

10

11

12

13

14

1
A Tibetan painted wood
seated figure of the
Lokapala Dhrtarastra
(Yul-hkhor-bsrung),
17th/18th cent, the face
and hands cold-gilded,
the face with painted
details, 23cm (9in),
L 26 Nov,
£660 ($838)

2
A Tibetan brass figure of
Vajrasattva *(rDo-rje sems-
dpah),* 15th/16th cent,
finial missing, sealed,
13.7cm (5⅜in), *L 23 July,*
£1,210 ($1,621)

3
A very large Tibetan
bronze figure of the
Bodhisattva Manjusri
(hJam-dpal-dByangs),
c.16th cent, silver-inlaid
eyes, the whole with
greenish-yellow
patination, unsealed,
53.4cm (21in), *L 23 July,*
£8,250 ($11,055)

4
A Western Tibetan bronze
figure of **Aksobhya
Buddha** *(Don-yod grub-pa),*
c.14th cent, the whole
with blackish patination
and traces of gilding and
red paint, re-sealed,
36cm (14⅛in), *L 9 Apr,*
£2,420 ($3,485)

5
A large Tibetan gilt-copper
figure of **Sarvabuddha-
Dakina** *(Na-ro kha-cho-ma),*
c.16th cent, her face with
the third eye and traces
of polychrome,
unsealed, 27.3cm
(10¾in), *L 23 July,*
£5,280 ($7,075)

6
A Tibetan gilt-bronze
figure of **Gautama
Buddha** *(Sakya-muni),*
c.18th cent, the face with
painted details, blue-
pigmented hair, the
image solid-cast,
unsealed, 31.5cm
(12⅜in), *L 23 July,*
£880 ($1,179)

7
A Tibetan gilt-bronze
repoussé figure of
Amitayus *(Tshe-dpg-med),*
17th/18th cent, inset with
semi-precious stones,
blue-pigmented hair,
sealed, 50cm (19¾in),
L 9 Apr,
£1,650 ($2,376)

8
A Sino-Tibetan gilt-bronze
figure of the **Saviouress
Sitatara** *(sGrol-dkar),* the
White Tara, 18th cent,
with blue-pigmented
hair, the face cold-gilded,
sealed, 17.5cm (6⅞in),
L 26 Nov,
£990 ($1,257)

9
A Tibetan brass figure of
the **Siddha Nag-Po-pa,**
c.16th cent, seal opened,
20cm (7⅞in), *L 23 July,*
£1,870 ($2,506)

10
A Sino-Tibetan gilt-bronze
figure of the **Winged
Dharmapala Krodha-
Hayagriva in Yab-Yum
with his Sakti** *(rTa-mgrin),*
18th/19th cent, flaming
red-pigmented hair, the
hands damaged, base
sealed, 28cm (11in),
L 26 Nov,
£880 ($1,118)

11
A Tibetan ivory figure of
Avalokitesvara *(sPyan-ras-
gzigs),* 18th/19th cent, one
arm missing, the hair
with traces of blue
pigment, the seal at the
back now open, 27.2cm
(10¾in), *L 9 Apr,*
£660 ($950)

12
A Sino-Tibetan gilt-copper
figure of a **Lama,**
probably Tsong-Kha-Pa
(1357-1419), 18th cent,
the face with benevolent
expression, sealed,
18.5cm (7¼in), *L 23 July,*
£715 ($958)

13
A Sino-Tibetan gilt-bronze
figure of **Dharmapala
Yamantaka as
Vajrabhairava, in Yab-Yum
with his Sakti,** *(Rdo-rje-
hjigs-byed),* 18th cent,
orange-pigmented hair,
re-sealed, 17.4cm (6⅞in),
L 26 Nov,
£6,600 ($8,382)

14
A small Sino-Tibetan
silver figure of **Amitayus**
(Tshe-dpag-med), 18th
cent, sealed, 11.5cm
(4½in), *L 26 Nov,*
£1,210 ($1,537)

1

A Sino-Tibetan gilt-bronze figure of Vajrapani (Phyag-rDor gTum-chung), 18th cent, with red-pigmented flaming hair, eyebrows and beard orange-pigmented, image sealed, base unsealed 12cm (4¾in), L 23 July, £1,320 ($1,769)

2

A Sino-Tibetan gilt-bronze figure of the Dharmapala Yamantaka as Bhairava (rTa-mgrin), 18th cent, painted details and red-pigmented flaming hair, base sealed, 16.5cm (6½in), L 26 Nov, £1,760 ($2,235)

3

A Sino-Tibetan miniature gold figure of Amitayus, (Tshe-dpag-med), 18th cent or later, the domed chignon with cintamani finial unsealed, 4.5cm (1¾in), weight 83g approx, L 26 Nov, £1,650 ($2,096)

4

A large Sino-Tibetan gilt-bronze figure of Garuda (Khyun-khra), 18th cent, with red-painted flaming hair, base sealed, 44cm (17¼in), L 23 July, £9,900 ($13,266)

5

A large Sino-Tibetan gilt-bronze repoussé figure of Kubera (rNam-thos-sras), 18th cent, with turquoise insets, green-painted mane and coat, base with wood seal, 39.5cm (15½in), L 23 July, £3,300 ($4,420)

6

A Sino-Tibetan gilt-bronze figure of Buddha, 18/19th cent, made in the Udayana style, traditionally attributed to King Udahana of Kosambi, with traces of polychrome unsealed, 16.5cm (6½in), L 26 Nov, £770 ($978)

7

A large Sino-Tibetan gilt-bronze figure of an Arhat, 17th/18th cent, the head and hands with traces of cold-gilding, the back of the throne painted red, sealed, 34.2cm (13½in), L 26 Nov, £4,400 ($5,588)

8

A Sino-Tibetan gilt-bronze figure of Avalokitesvara, (sPyan-ras-gzigs), 18th cent, the heads with painted details, unsealed, 18.2cm (7⅛in), L 26 Nov, £1,100 ($1,397)

9

A Sino-Tibetan gilt-bronze figure of Amitayus (Tshe-dpad-med), 18th cent, sealed, 14cm (5½in), L 9 Apr, £330 ($475)

10

A Sino-Tibetan gilt-bronze figure, 18th cent, possibly a form of the Adibuddha Vajradhara (rDo-rje-chan), wearing glass-inset jewellery, blue-pigmented chignon with floral finial, sealed, 18cm (7⅛in), L 26 Nov, £550 ($698)

11

A Sino-Tibetan gilt-bronze figure of Dipankara Buddha (Mar-me-mdsad), 18th cent, blue-pigmented hair, sealed, 15cm (5⅞in), L 26 Nov, £825 ($1,048)

12

A Sino-Tibetan gilt-bronze figure of the Dharmapala Sri-Devi (Lha-Mo), 18th cent, with orange-pigmented flaming hair, her mount with black mane and tail, image sealed, base unsealed, 15.5cm (6⅛in) L 26 Nov, £1,210 ($1,537)

13

A Sino-Tibetan gilt-bronze figure of Avalokitesvara-Sadaksari (sPyan-ras-gzigs Yig-drug-pa), 18th cent, blue-pigmented hair, sealed, 17.5cm (7in), L 26 Nov, £1,320 ($1,676)

14

A Sino-Tibetan gilt-bronze figure of the Dharmapala Mahakala (mGon-dkar), 18th cent, the hands and feet with traces of cold gilding, base sealed 11.5cm (4½in), L 26 Nov, £1,540 ($1,956)

15

A Sino-Tibetan gilt-bronze figure of Kuan-ti on horseback, c.18th cent, his face with painted details, unsealed, 19cm (7½in), L 26 Nov, £2,970 ($3,772)

1
A Gupta pink stone relief,
*c.*6th/7th cent, depicting
four standing figures,
one a River Goddess,
40.3 x 42cm (15⅞ x 16½in),
L 23 July,
£935 ($1,253)

2
**A Kushan mottled red
stone Buddha head,**
2nd/3rd cent, 21.5cm
(8½in), *L 26 Nov,*
£2,200 ($2,794)

3
**A large Rajasthan pink
sandstone relief,** *c.*12th
cent, depicting a
Matrika, the whole with
traces of red pigment,
56cm (22in), *L 23 July,*
£2,860 ($3,832)

4
**A Gandhara grey schist
figure of Buddha,** 3rd/4th
cent, 47cm (18½in),
L 26 Nov,
£2,420 ($3,073)

5
**A large Central Indian
pink sandstone female
torso,** 10th/12th cent,
52cm (20½in), *L 26 Nov,*
£2,090 ($2,654)

6
**A Gandhara grey schist
figure of a headless
Bodhisattva,** 3rd/4th cent,
probably from a relief,
53.5cm (21in), *L 9 Apr,*
£3,850 ($5,544)

7
**A Gandhara grey schist
figure of Buddha,** 3rd/4th
cent, the nose and upper
lip defaced, 58cm
(22¾in), *L 23 July,*
£330 ($442)

8
**A Gandhara grey schist
Bodhisattva bust,** 3rd/4th
cent, a small section of
the rayed aureole
remaining, 35cm
(13¾in), *L 26 Nov,*
£5,280 ($6,706)

9
**A Gandhara grey schist
Buddha head,** 3rd/4th
cent, the moustached
face with well-defined
eyes, 19cm (7½in),
L 26 Nov,
£935 ($1,187)

10
**An over-lifesize Gandhara
grey schist Buddha head,**
3rd/4th cent, the hair
swept into a domed
usnisa, the nose restored,
48.5cm (19in), *L 26 Nov,*
£8,250 ($10,478)

11
**A Gandhara grey schist
figure of a Bodhisattva,**
3rd/4th cent, the right
hand missing, 38.5cm
(15¼in), *L 9 Apr,*
£3,520 ($5,069)

12
**A Gandhara grey schist
head of Buddha,** his ears
with elongated pierced
lobes, 3rd/4th cent,
25.5cm (10in), *L 9 Apr,*
£6,600 ($9,504)

1   2   3

4   5   6

7   8   9

10   11   12

1
A Ghandhara grey schist
figure of Maitreya,
3rd/4th cent, his right
hand missing from the
wrist, 45.5cm (17⅞in),
L 9 Apr,
£1,155 ($1,663)

2
A large Gandhara
fragmentary stucco
Buddha head, probably
from Hadda, 4th/5th
cent, the hair and side of
the head with traces of
black paint, the facial
lines outlined in orange,
the lips also painted,
part of the head missing,
21.5cm (8½in), *L 23 July,*
£825 ($1,105)

3
A Gandhara light grey
schist Buddha head,
3rd/4th cent, the surface
with earth coloured tint,
tip of nose restored,
25.5cm (10in), *L 23 July,*
£3,850 ($5,159)

4
A Gandhara grey schist
figure of Maitreya,
3rd/4th cent, his right
arm missing below the
elbow, 120.5cm (47½in),
L 23 July,
£11,000 ($14,740)

5
A Gandhara grey schist
figure of Buddha, 3rd/4th
cent, the remains of a
halo behind, the whole
with traces of gilding,
43cm (17in), *L 23 July,*
£13,200 ($17,688)

6
A large Central Indian
buff sandstone male head,
10th/12th cent, 33.5cm
(13⅛in), *L 26 Nov,*
£880 ($1,117)

7
A Central Indian reddish-
grey sandstone figure of
Ganesha, *c.*10th cent,
originally with sixteen
arms, a dancing
attendant to his right,
61cm (24in), *L 23 July,*
£1,650 ($2,211)

8
A Central Indian buff
sandstone fragment, *c.*10th
cent, depicting a
headless four-armed
female deity, the upper
arms damaged, 44.5cm
(17½in), *L 9 Apr,*
£1,430 ($2,059)

9
A Central Indian buff
sandstone fragment
depicting Siva and
Yamuna, *c.*9th cent,
72.5cm (28½in), *L 9 Apr,*
£8,250 ($11,880)

10
A Nepalese grey schist stele
depicting Vishnu
supported on Garuda,
17th/18th cent, the faces
with traces of puja, 27cm
(10⅝in), *L 23 July,*
£990 ($1,327)

11
A large Indian dark grey
granite figure of Krishna,
18th/19th cent, the face
with painted details,
112cm (44in), *L 26 Nov,*
£2,200 ($2,794)

12
A large Eastern Indian
black stone stele depicting
Vishnu, 10th/11th cent,
standing on a double
lotus throne, 115cm
(45½in), *L 23 July,*
£12,100 ($16,214)

1   2   3

4   5   6

7   8   9

10   11   12

1
An Indian silver parcel-gilt
finial, 19th cent,
depicting a lion
attacking an antelope,
each originally with
inset eyes, possibly a
mount from a piece of
furniture, 20cm (7¾in),
L 26 Nov,
£2,200 ($2,794)

2
An Indian wood panel,
carved on both sides,
51cm (20in), *L 23 July,*
£132 ($177)

3
A large Indian
polychrome-painted wood
elephant, 19th cent, white
with touches of blue, a
red and gold blanket,
122cm (48in), *L 23 July,*
£1,980 ($2,653)

4
An Indian ivory figure of
an elephant, 20th cent,
composed of numerous
small pieces of ivory
applied with small brass
nails, 40cm (15¾in),
L 26 Nov,
£1,045 ($1,327)

5
A pair of Indian silver
elephants, 20th cent, the
turbaned driver with
articulated arms, 54cm
(21¼in), *L 26 Nov,*
£935 ($1,187)

6
A large Indian 'Bidri'
huqqa-bottle, 19th cent,
decorated with silver-inlaid
foliage, the mouth
applied with a brass rim,
22.5cm (8⅞in), *L 26 Nov,*
£330 ($419)

7
An Indian 'Bidri' huqqa-
bottle, c.18th cent, the
shoulder and foot
encircled by leafy foliate
bands, 18.3cm (7¼in),
L 26 Nov,
£385 ($489)

8
Eleven Malaysian silver
bowls *(batil)* and seven
spoons *(sudn),* all late
19th cent, d of bowls,
9cm-4cm (3¾-1⅝in), each
spoon approx 11.5cm
(4½in), *L 9 Apr,*
£495 ($713)

9
A Burmese silver betel-box,
19th cent, the sides with
circular medallions each
depicting a stylised
human or animal figure,
17.1cm (6¾in), *L 26 Nov,*
£440 ($559)

10
An Indian brass-inlaid
'Bidri' huqqa-bottle, 18th
cent, decorated around
the sides with eight
brass-inlaid flowering
plants, 20.5cm (8in),
L 26 Nov,
£2,420 ($3,073)

11
An Indian enamelled
silver huqqa-section and
lid, Lucknow, c.1800, the
enamelling in blue and
green, bottomless, 9cm
(3½in), *L 26 Nov,*
£440 ($559)

12
A pair of Indian 'Bidri'
huqqa-bottles, 18th/19th
cent, decorated with
silver-inlaid poppies,
16.5cm (6½in), *L 26 Nov,*
£880 ($1,117)

13
An Indian 'Bidri' huqqa-
bottle, c.18th cent,
decorated with
reticulated silver-inlaid
flowerheads, 17cm (6¾in),
L 23 July,
£1,320 ($1,769)

14
An Indian gilt-copper
casket, 18th/19th cent,
the body of deep
octagonal form
decorated with flowering
plants, 21.3cm (8¾in),
L 23 July,
£440 ($590)

1
A Kashmir polychrome-lacquered turban-box, decorated with pink and yellow flowers with gold stems and leaves on dark green ground, the borders with red and black, d 26cm (10¼in), *L 23 July*, £440 ($590)

2
A small Indian parcel-gilt glass case-bottle, 18th cent, each cut gilded, repaired, 8.8cm (3½in), *L 26 Nov*, £825 ($1,048)

3
An Indian parcel-gilt glass huqqa-bottle, 18th cent, with moulded gilt-edged floral sprigs, small section damaged, 19cm (7½in), *L 26 Nov*, £605 ($768)

4
A large Indian carved wood sofa, c.1860, 206 x 79 x 87.5cm (81 x 31 x 34½in), *L 26 Nov*, £770 ($978)

5
An Indian ivory-inlaid wood table, 19th cent, the bands of ivory alternating with ebony around the borders, d 61cm (24in), *L 26 Nov*, £495 ($629)

6
A Mughal ivory-inlaid wood cabinet, on stand, 17th cent, Sind or Gujarat, the doors with brass hinges and lock-piece, 40.5 x 30 x 26.5cm (16 x 11¾ x 10½in), *L 26 Nov*, £935 ($1,187)

7
An Indian silver-covered wood stool, 19th cent or later, the top with foliate medallions on a red velvet ground, 48 x 48 x 16cm (19 x 19 x 6¼in), *L 26 Nov*, £1,045 ($1,327)

8
A Burmese carved wood chair, 19th cent, standing on two cross-stretcher legs, the back and seat of plaited cane-work, 1m (39½in), *L 26 Nov*, £396 ($502)

9
An Indian marble chair, 19th cent or later, 61 x 53cm (24 x 21in), *L 9 Apr*, £825 ($1,188)

10
An Indian green jade ink-well, 19th cent, of rectangular form, with six circular wells, the narrow borders with incised chevron motifs, 13 x 9cm (5⅛ x 3½in), *L 9 Apr*, £1,650 ($2,376)

11
Four Indian ivory bed-legs, 18th cent or later, decorated with five gilt foliate bands, now worn, 32.5cm (12¾in), *L 9 Apr*, £935 ($1,346)

12
An Indian mirror-inset gilt-wood Krishna swing, 19th cent, the square ground-framework and swing seat painted with green and white flowers on red ground, 132 x 82.5cm (52 x 32½in), *L 9 Apr*, £550 ($792)

13
An Indian silver model of the Taj Mahal, c.1900, 13.5 x 13.2 x 14cm (5⅜ x 5¼ x 5½in), *L 9 Apr*, £330 ($475)

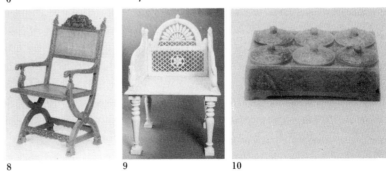

1

A large Indian sheet-silver figure of a horse and rider, the horse wearing extensive knopped and jewelled trappings, the bearded princely rider wearing shoes with pointed toes and extensive jewellery, 94cm (37in), *L 9 Apr*, £1,980 ($2,851)

2

A pair of Goanese gilt-wood angels, 18th/19th cent, with painted facial details and elaborately-curled black hair, 31cm (12⅛in), *L 26 Nov*, £495 ($629)

3

A Balinese painted wood elephant, wearing a red blanket, with short tail, 92cm (36in), *L 23 July*, £1,100 ($1,474)

4

A pair of Balinese polychrome-painted wood sea-horses, the whole decorated in black, beige and dark red, 144cm (56½in), *L 23 July*, £2,200 ($2,948)

5

An Indian embroidered silk torana, Gujarat, 19th cent or later, the pink satin upper section divided into fifteen arched panels with fifteen sections of orange, blue, purple, yellow and green satin below, the whole mounted on a black wool panel, 168 x 32cm (66 x 12½in), *L 9 Apr*, £297 ($428)

6

A large Indian printed cotton floor covering, the white field with small central medallion surrounded by red floral medallions, the borders with dark blue, pale salmon, maroon and black grounds, 439.5 x 251.5cm (14ft 5in x 8ft 3in), *L 9 Apr*, £220 ($317)

7

A South Indian hand-printed cotton shawl *(Kalamkari)*, Masulipatnam, dated 1857, the pink-maroon field with blue and white designs, also red, blue and beige, white ground outer border, 269 x 130cm (8ft 10½in x 4ft 3in), *L 23 July*, £638 ($855)

8

A large Kashmir shawl, *c.*1680, with unworked ivory central medallion, the borders with red, green and muted colours, used as a saddle-cloth, 206 x 203cm (6ft 9in x 6ft 8in), *L 9 Apr*, £880 ($1,267)

9

A Central Indian gold silk sari with Mughal gold thread borders, the end pieces and borders late 18th cent, probably Chandheri, the field 19th cent, 345 x 110cm (11ft 3¾in x 3ft 7¼in), *L 23 July*, £2,860 ($3,832)

10

A Kashmir woven shawl, third quarter of the 18th cent, the ends decorated in green, pink, yellow and blue, the ground of cream, 305 x 134cm (10ft x 4ft 5in), *L 23 July*, £880 ($1,179)

11

A Sinhalese ivory male figure, *c.* 18th cent, his robes with gilt borders, the base with traces of green paint, 27.8cm (10⅞in), *L 9 Apr*, £1,650 ($2,376)

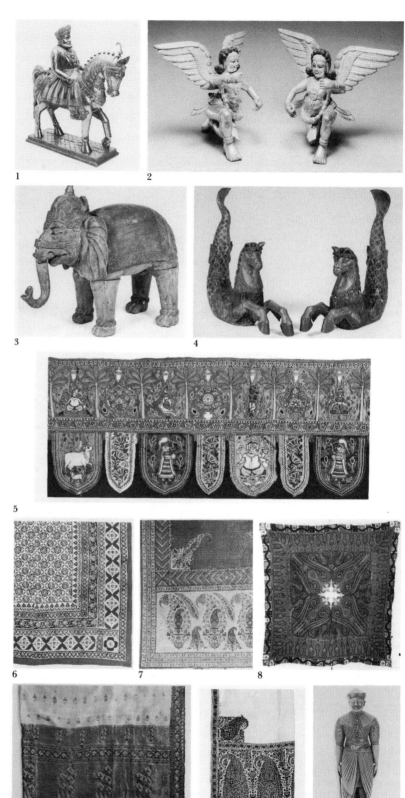

1

A Tibetan skull-cap and stand *(kapala)*, 16th cent or later, the skull-cap inset with three stones, the stand of brass and copper, the latter painted silver, the skulls with red-painted eye sockets, skull-cap d 15cm (6in), stand h 7cm (2¾in), *L 23 July*,
£385 ($516)

2

A Tibetan iron vajra, possibly 14th/16th cent, the whole with brownish-grey patination and traces of gilding, 17cm (6¾in), *L 23 July*,
£550 ($737)

3

A Tibetan parcel-gilt copper box, 18th/19th cent, inset with coral and turquoise pieces, d 36cm (14in), *L 26 Nov*,
£715 ($908)

4

An unusually large Nepalese brass ritual dagger *(kila)*, 18th/19th cent, an inlay originally decorating his forehead and the three eyes, each crown originally extending further, 54cm (21¼in), *L 23 July*,
£605 ($811)

5

A Tibetan bronze ritual vessel, probably 18th cent, in the tradition of an earlier type, d 42.2cm (16⅝in), *L 23 July*,
£3,520 ($4,717)

6

A large Tibetan bronze stupa *(chorten)*, 12th cent or later, inset with coral and turquoise, sealed, 29.2cm (11½in), *L 9 Apr*,
£506 ($729)

7

A Tibetan bronze bell *(ghanta)* **and vajra** *(rdo-rje)*, *c.*17th cent, the handle and the vajra gilded, the bell 21.5cm (8½in) the vajra 18cm (7in), *L 9 Apr*,
£715 ($1,029)

8

A Sino-Tibetan human skull-bowl, with gilt-bronze liner, stand and lid, *(kapala)*, Qianlong, 18th cent, the border inset with red and green glass stones, 25.5cm (10in), *L 26 Nov*,
£2,420 ($3,073)

9

A Tibetan bronze-mounted skull bowl, cover and stand, *(kapala)*, 19th cent, the domed lid decorated with eight sacred emblems in relief around the sides, 24cm (9½in), *L 23 July*,
£462 ($619)

10

A pair of Jaipur gold polychrome-enamelled miniature elephants, rose diamond insets on a navy ground, red trappings, green howdah-seat and white ground base, 7cm (2¾in), *L 9 Apr*,
£2,860 ($4,118)

11

An Indian gold ruby, diamond and emerald-inset necklace, 19th cent, twenty gold botehs inset with a central diamond surrounded by rubies, the reverse plain, 18cm (7in), *L 26 Nov*,
£4,950 ($6,286)

12

A Mughal jade pendant, *c.*18th cent, dark green, decorated on both sides, 9cm (3½in), *L 9 Apr*,
£330 ($475)

13

A Mughal gold-mounted jade pendant, *c.*18th cent, on pale green ground, the reverse plain, 4.5cm (1¾in), *L 26 Nov*,
£715 ($908)

1

2

3   4   5   6

7   8   9

10   10   11

12   13

1
A Tibetan bone
necromancer's apron,
18th/19th cent, with
carved plaques
connected by bone and
polychrome glass beads
and pale green nephrite
plaquettes, 69cm (27in),
L 26 Nov,
£440 ($559)

2
A large Turkoman silver
parcel-gilt heart-pendant,
Tekke, the whole on a
gilt ground with
ungilded motifs, on an
embroidered red cloth,
39.8cm (15⅝in), *L 9 Apr,*
£1,760 ($2,534)

3
A Kazak silver parcel-gilt
bracelet, of wide almost
closed form, with five
oval medallions on a gilt
ground, d 7cm (2¾in),
L 23 July,
£385 ($516)

4
A Nepalese gold amulet-
plaque inset with semi-
precious stones, 19th cent,
with a central coral
medallion depicting
Ganesha, and turquoise
and lapis-lazuli insets,
6.6cm (2⅝in), *L 26 Nov,*
£1,210 ($1,536)

5
A Turkoman silver-
mounted leather box, the
lid with an octagonal
carnelian inset and two
coral-inset bosses, 9.5cm
(3¾in), *L 23 July,*
£330 ($442)

6
A set of Turkoman silver
carnelian-inset jewellery,
mostly Tekke,
comprising headdress
33cm (13in); pendant
21.5cm (8½in); belt
l 71cm (28in); bracelet
with three dentate
projections, one missing,
d 6.7cm (2⅝in); pair of
earrings 14.5cm (5¾in);
and nose-ornament (?)
7.5cm (3in), *L 9 Apr,*
£2,420 ($3,485)

7
A very large signed
Turkoman silver parcel-
gilt heart-pendant, Tekke,
on a gilt ground with
small ungilded motifs,
thirteen carnelian insets,
on a cloth collar
embroidered in
polychrome silk, 37.6cm
(14⅞in), *L 23 July,*
£1,430 ($1,916)

8
A pair of Turkoman silver
parcel-gilt bracelets,
Tekke, divided into
three horizontal bands,
each with three
carnelian insets, 8.2cm
(3¼in), *L 9 Apr,*
£440 ($634)

9
Two Turkoman silver-gilt
bracelets, each decorated
with bands of carnelians,
10.6cm (4⅛in) and 8.5cm
(3⅜in), *L 26 Nov,*
£330 ($419)

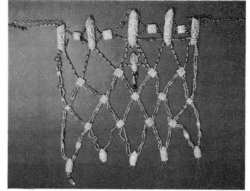

1

2

3

4

5

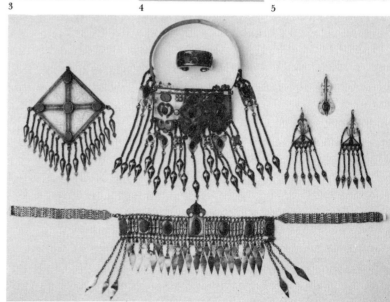

6

7

8

9

Islamic Works of Art

STEPHEN WOLFF • RICHARD KERESEY

Islamic art is the art of a unique civilization, it is not the product of a particular country nor of a particular people. This is the reason why such a surprising degree of unity of style and concept is apparent in all the items in this field, even though they span some ten centuries and may come from countries as far flung as Spain and India. From the start, Islamic art drew heavily on Arab, Turkish and Persian artistic traditions, but the fundamental elements were the message of Islam, the language of the Qur'an, its (Holy Book) and the Arabic form of writing. Calligraphy became the most important single feature in Islamic art. Another essential is the combined concept of infinity on the one hand, and the transience of Man on the other. In making visible part of a pattern which is complete only in infinity, the Islamic artist creates the illusion of eternity. The formulation of complex repeat geometrical patterns or the continuous flow of arabesques are in themselves the perfect application of this principle and can be adapted to any given surface or any size of object. These characteristic patterns are therefore widely used on architecture, ceramics, glass, metalwork (including arms and armour), rugs and textiles, with little distinction between secular and religious objects.

The glazed earthenwares of Islam are outstanding in the history of ceramic development. In the 9th century AD, Mesopotamia contributed two major innovations: the discovery of tin-glazing and the introduction of lustre-painting. Simultaneously, on the eastern side of the Islamic world painters were developing a wide repertoire of slip-painted designs at Nishapur. By the early 13th century the centre had moved to Kashan which produced a huge variety of pieces in techniques ranging from underglaze painted wares to luxury lustre and 'minai' (over glaze painting in enamel colours) pieces. All this was interrupted by the Mongol devastation of Iran in the 1220s, and it was only in the late 13th century that the substantial production of Syrian and Persian blue and white wares began.

Perhaps the best-known of later ceramics are those produced by the Isnik potteries from the 16th century. Under brilliant clear glazes, colours such as cobalt-blue, manganese purple and vivid greens were used in a variety of asymmetrical but balanced floral designs that superseded arabesque decoration. Large flat-rimmed dishes, some decorated with figures or sailing ships and straight tankards, were typical products, but most famous of all are the thousands of painted tiles that sumptuously clad the walls of mosques in Istanbul.

Islamic metalwork is also universally recognized as being of superb quality and intricate workmanship. In this medium, as in ceramics, Islamic craftsmen excelled in the variety of techniques they used and in the decorative effects achieved. The best pieces were of bronze or brass with designs inlaid in gold and silver. On the eastern side of the Islamic world Nishapur was again important in the early period for its metalwork. Later, in the 13th to 14th centuries, there were important metalwork schools in Herat and the province of Fars in western Iran, while at the same time, Syria, Mesopotamia and the Jazira were also producing work of exquisite quality, with the result that it is often difficult to tell in which of these centres a piece was made.

With all Islamic works of art condition is an important factor. Objects dating from the 19th and 20th centuries are expected to be perfect. Early Islamic ceramics, which are made of soft-paste, can be excused some damage. Important factors to look for in ceramics include the quality of potting and drawing and preservation of the glaze surface. With metalwork it is the design and workmanship which are important.

Islamic works have always been valued in the West, but more recently Arabs and Iranians have been taking an increasing interest in their own heritage. It remains a field in which there is much yet to be discovered and in which there are still many exciting opportunities.

1
A highly iridised clear free-form glass ewer, Nishapur, 8th/9th cent, the flattened inverted pear-shaped body standing on six applied flattened feet, restored, with plastic decoration, 20.5cm (8in), *L 17 Oct,* £1,320 ($1,650)

2
A colourless mould-blown glass flask, Nishapur, 9th/10th cent, the body with a frieze of wheel-cut panels interspersed by chevrons, the neck with wheel-cut decoration, 17.3cm (6¾in), *L 17 Oct,* £418 ($523)

3
A Mughal glass huqqa base, 18th cent, of conventional bell-shaped form, with gilt decoration, and an overall design of cinquefoil leaves, 18.5cm (7¼in), *L 18 Apr,* £2,200 ($3,168)

4
A colourless mould-blown glass bottle, Nishapur, 8th/10th cent, of squat barrel-shaped form with broad slightly sloping shoulders, all with iridescence, 8.2cm (3¼in), *L 17 Oct,* £99 ($124)

5
An early Islamic mono-chrome pottery jar, the inverted pear-shaped body standing on a low foot with three curved handles, with a turquoise glaze, 19cm (7½in), *L 18 Apr,* £440 ($635)

6
A glass mosque lamp, 19th cent, with three loop handles, all with blackened etched decoration consisting of inscriptions and conventional arabesques, 27.3cm (10¾in), *L 13 Nov,* £286 ($349)

7
A small 'sari type' slip-painted pottery dish, 10th cent, with a wide sloping rim, decorated in manganese brown, green and red on a cream ground, d 15.2cm (6in), *L 18 Apr,* £1,100 ($1,584)

8
A Mesopotamian tin-glazed pottery bowl, 9th cent, of shallow rounded form with everted lip, decorated in cobalt blue on a greyish-white ground, the rim with a laurel wreath design, d 19.7cm (7¼in), *L 18 Apr,* £1,320 ($1,901)

9
An Ottoman moulded polychome pottery frieze tile, 15th cent, carved in high relief with a *naskhi* inscription in white with turquoise vines and arabesques, some with cobalt-blue centres, 37.5 x 13.5cm (14¾ x 12⅜in), *L 17 Oct,* £4,400 ($5,500)

10
A group of nine Syrian blue-and-white tiles, 15th cent, of hexagonal form, depicting various floral and foliate motifs, average size d 18.5cm (7¼in), *L 18 Apr,* £3,850 ($5,555)

11
An underglaze painted pottery tile, decorated in cobalt blue on a grey ground with four lines of inscription in nastaliq script, 26cm sq (10½in sq), *L 18 July,* £440 ($587)

1

2

4

5

3

6

7

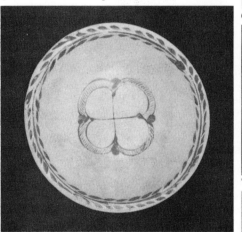

8

9

10

11

1
An early Qajar dagger and sheath, 19th cent, the finely watered steel blade with raised fuller, the hilt enamelled with floral cartouches and surmounted by a cut crystal finial, the sheath with silver rim, 40.5cm (60in), *L 17 Oct,* **£2,200 ($2,750)**

2
A Persian silver-inlaid bronze jug (kuze), Khorassan, early 13th cent, with a slightly concave grooved body, the neck with a continuous line of *naskhi* inscription, the body with two lines of *kufic* inscription, handle missing, 16.5cm (6½in), *L 18 Apr,* **£9,900 ($14,286)**

3
A pale green mould blown glass flask, 12th/ 13th cent, Syria, the tall thin neck with trailed spiralling decoration at the base and top, the spherical body with a frieze of moulded cursive inscription, all with rich peacock blue iridescence and encrustations, 18cm (7in), *L 17 Oct,* **£1,100 ($1,375)**

4
A Fars silver-inlaid brass bowl (tas), 14th cent, with bulbous sides and shallow upright rim, with incised decoration, the fretwork ground filled with black composition, d 17.5cm (6⅞in), *L 17 Oct,* **£7,480 ($9,350)**

5
An Indian sabre (tulwar), Western India, 19th cent, with curving, watered steel blade, the hilt wrought with an elephant's head pommel, the knuckle guard formed from a tiger, all with gold Koftgari decoration and precious stones, 87.6cm (34½in), *L 17 Oct,* **£1,870 ($2,338)**

1

2

3

4

5

1

An Isnik pottery tankard,
17th cent, of tall
cylindrical form with flat
rectangular handle,
decorated in cobalt blue,
green and raised sealing-
wax red, partly outlined
in black, 23.5cm (9¼in),
L 17 Oct,
£1,760 ($2,200)

2

A Kutahya pottery jug,
18th cent, of pear-shaped
form, decorated in black
and yellow staining with
three moulded medallions,
21.6cm (8½in), *L 17 Oct,*
£198 ($247)

3

**A Persian splashed-ware
pottery bowl,** Nishapur,
10th cent, with deep
flaring sides, decorated
with splashes of green,
manganese brown and
yellow, d 28.3cm (11⅛in),
L 17 Oct,
£2,090 ($2,612)

4

An Isnik pottery dish, 2nd
half 16th cent, with
sloping rim, decorated
in cobalt blue, green and
raised sealing-wax red,
with a central saz leaf
surrounded by sprays of
roses, d 30cm (12in),
L 17 Oct,
£4,180 ($5,225)

5

**A Persian lustre pottery
star tile,** Kashan, 13th
cent, decorated in
greenish-brown lustre
on a transparent glaze
with areas of cobalt and
turquoise blue, 20.3cm
(8in), *L 17 Oct,*
£880 ($1,100)

6

**A Persian lustre pottery
star tile,** c mid-13th cent,
decorated in dark
coppery lustre with
arabesque medallions
reserved in white radiat-
ing from a central star,
with a border of cursive
inscription, 30.8cm (12⅛in),
L 18 Apr,
£4,180 ($6,019)

7

**A small Persian slip-painted
pottery bowl,** probably
Nishapur, 10th cent, with
flaring sides, decorated
in manganese brown and
tomato red on a white
ground, d 16cm (6¼in),
L 18 Apr,
£2,090 ($3,009)

8

A Kutahya pottery mug,
18th cent, the body of
rounded form with
gently lobed sides, decorated in cobalt and
turquoise blue, yellow,
black and sealing-wax
red, the rim with a zig-
zag blue line, h 10.2cm
(4in), *L 17 Oct,*
£550 ($687)

1

A Syrian underglaze-painted pottery jar, late 13th/14th cent, decorated in cobalt blue, black and slightly raised brownish-red on a white ground under a transparent greenish-tinged glaze, h 35.8cm (14⅛in), *L 17 Oct,* £52,800 ($66,000)

2

A small Persian slip-painted pottery bowl, probably Nishapur, 10th cent, decorated in manganese brown on a white ground, with a *kufic* inscription, d 13.7cm (5⅜in), *L 18 Apr,* £660 ($950)

3

A Mesopotamian slip-painted pottery bowl, 10th cent, decorated in manganese brown and green, with two lines of *kufic* inscription, d 33.7cm (13¼in), *L 17 Oct,* £715 ($894)

4

A Persian slip-painted pottery bowl, probably Nishapur, 10th cent, decorated in manganese brown and dark green, with bands of decorative script, d 20.5cm (8⅛in), *L 18 Apr,* £660 ($950)

5

A Mesopotamian lustre pottery bowl, 10th cent, decorated in brownish-green lustre on a white glaze, with a *kufic* inscription, d 12.4cm (4⅞in), *L 17 Oct,* £14,850 ($18,563)

6

A Persian buff-ware pottery bowl, probably Nishapur, 10th cent, decorated in black, green and yellow poly-chrome vertical stripes round the sides, d 21.6cm (8in), *L 18 Apr,* £605 ($871)

7

A Persian buff-ware pottery bowl, probably Nishapur, 10th cent, decorated in black, yellow and green, with a trotting horse, a frieze of stylised *kufic* below the rim, d 21cm (8¼in), *L 18 Apr,* £550 ($792)

8

A Persian buff-ware pottery bowl, probably Nishapur, 10th cent, with deep flaring sides, decorated in black and green on a yellow ground, with mytho-logical beasts, d 34cm (13⅜in), *L 18 Apr,* £902 ($1,302)

9

A Persian slip-painted pottery bowl, 10th cent, with slightly convex flaring sides, decorated in greenish-yellow on a cream ground, d 20cm (7⅞in), *L 17 Oct,* £1,760 ($2,200)

10

A Persian splashed-ware pottery bowl, Nishapur, 10th cent, of rounded form with upright rim, decorated with splashes of green, ochre and manganese purple, d 21.5cm (8½in), *L 17 Oct,* £440 ($550)

11

A Persian slip-painted pottery bowl, 10th cent, with flaring sides standing on a low foot, decorated in manganese brown on a white ground, the central stylised flower-head with *kufic* word repeated, d 21cm (8¼in), *L 18 Apr,* £2,310 ($3,326)

12

A Persian slip-painted pottery dish, Nishapur, 10th cent, of shallow rounded form, decorated in manganese brown and tomato red with a central rosette, black rim, d 13cm (5⅛in), *L 17 Oct,* £605 ($756)

13

A Persian slip-painted pottery jug, 10th cent, decorated in greenish-yellow on a cream-coloured ground, h 12cm (4¾in), *L 17 Oct,* £220 ($275)

14

A Persian slip-painted pottery jug, Nishapur, 10th cent, decorated in white slip on a black ground, with *kufic* inscription, h 15cm (5⅞in), *L 17 Oct,* £770 ($962)

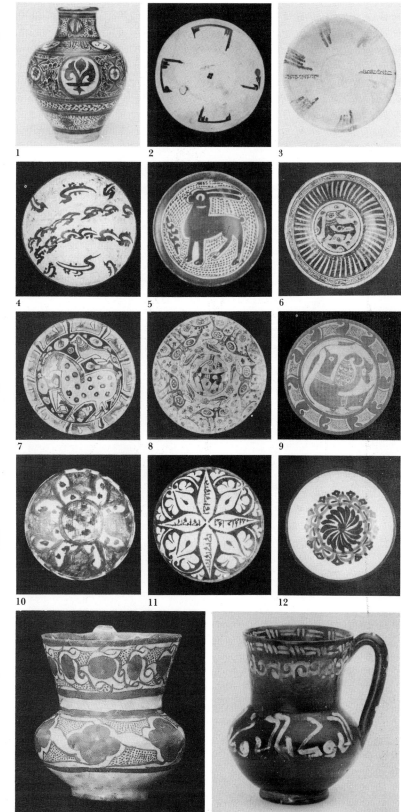

1
A Persian splashed-ware pottery bowl, Nishapur, 10th cent, decorated in manganese brown, green and yellow on a cream ground, embellished with sgraffiato scrolling, d 26.5cm (10½in), *L 17 Oct*, £440 ($550)

2
A Persian slip-painted pottery bowl, Nishapur, 10th cent, decorated in manganese brown on a white ground, the sides with *kufic* inscription, d 36.8cm (14½in), *L 17 Oct*, £1,430 ($1,787)

3
A Persian slip-painted pottery bowl, 10th cent, decorated in manganese brown on a cream ground, d 20.7cm (8⅛in), *L 17 Oct*, £462 ($577)

4
A Persian slip-painted pottery bowl, Nishapur, 10th cent, decorated in manganese brown on a cream ground, the sides with *kufic* word repeated, d 25.8cm (10⅛in), *L 17 Oct*, £825 ($1,031)

5
A Persian slip-painted pottery bowl, Nishapur, 10th cent, decorated in manganese brown, d 14cm (5½in), *L 17 Oct*, £308 ($385)

6
A Persian slip-painted pottery bowl, 10th cent, decorated in greenish-yellow on a cream ground, d 23.5cm (9¼in), *L 17 Oct*, £1,100 ($1,375)

7
A Persian slip-painted pottery bowl, Nishapur, 10th/11th cent, decorated in manganese brown and green on a white ground, with *kufic* inscription, d 18.5cm (7¼in), *L 17 Oct*, £330 ($413)

8
A Persian slip-painted pottery bowl, Nishapur, 10th cent, decorated in manganese brown and tomato red, with areas of yellow staining black, d 18.5cm (7¼in), *L 17 Oct*, £572 ($715)

9
A Persian Minai pottery bottle, 12th/13th cent, decorated in black and red enamelling over turquoise glaze on a white ground, h 22.8cm (9in), *L 17 Oct*, £2,200 ($2,750)

10
A Persian lustre pottery bottle, 12th/13th cent, decorated in brown lustre on a white ground with two bands of cursive inscription scratched through the lustre, 33cm (13in), *L 18 Apr*, £4,950 ($7,128)

11
A Persian underglaze-painted pottery cock's head ewer, 13th cent, decorated in black under a turquoise glaze, 26.1cm (10¼in), *L 18 July*, £1,100 ($1,468)

12
A Persian monochrome pottery albarello, 12th/13th cent, decorated with dribbled cobalt-blue stripes radiating from the neck, under a highly iridised transparent glaze, 17.2cm (6¾in), *L 18 July*, £528 ($704)

13
A Persian monochrome pottery ewer, 12th/13th cent, decorated with a frieze of circular indentations under a turquoise-blue glaze, 19cm (7½in), *L 18 Apr*, £550 ($792)

14
A Persian monochrome pottery bowl, 12th/13th cent, decorated with a frieze of moulded vertical ribs under a smooth lavender-blue glaze with areas of golden iridescence, d 16.2cm (6⅜in), *L 17 Oct*, £825 ($1,031)

15
A Persian silhouette-ware pottery cup-bowl, 12th/13th cent, the exterior decoration carved through black slip under turquoise glaze, the interior decorated in black slip, d 17.2cm (6¾in), *L 17 Oct*, £1,430 ($1,788)

1
A Persian underglaze-painted pottery bowl, 12th/13th cent, with shallow flaring sides and upright rim, decorated in cobalt blue on a white ground, d 10.8cm (4¼in), *L 17 Oct,* £242 ($302)

2
A Persian lustre pottery bowl, Kashan, 12th/13th cent, with flaring sides, standing on a low foot, decorated in brown lustre, the exterior covered with cobalt-blue glaze, d 10.9cm (4¼in), *L 17 Oct,* £2,530 ($3,162)

3
A Persian lustre pottery dish, 12th/13th cent, with shallow lobed sides, standing on a low foot, decorated with a central spotted pigeon, the exterior with vertical lines, d 10.8cm (4¼in), *L 18 Apr,* £770 ($1,108)

4
A Persian Ladjvardina pottery jug, 13th cent, decorated in white and red enamel and leaf gilding on a cobalt-blue ground, 19.7cm (7¾in), *L 18 Apr,* £1,045 ($1,505)

5
A Persian Sultanabad pottery pitcher, 14th cent, with inverted pear-shaped body, decorated in raised white slip, outlined in black, on a greyish-brown ground, 28cm (11in), *L 18 Apr,* £1,210 ($1,742)

6
A Persian underglaze-painted pottery bowl, Kashan, 1200-1220, with deep flaring sides, standing on a high foot, decorated in black and cobalt blue on a white ground, with bands of cursive inscription scratched through the black slip, d 21.3cm (8⅜in), *L 17 Oct,* £1,045 ($1,306)

7
A Persian underglaze-painted pottery bowl, Kashan, 1200-20, decorated in black and cobalt blue on a white ground, d 21.9cm (8⅝in), *L 17 Oct,* £1,320 ($1,650)

8
A Persian lustre pottery star tile, 13th/14th cent, decorated in brown lustre on a transparent cobalt-blue glaze, with a central hare amongst foliage, the border with cursive inscription, 21cm (8¼in), *L 17 Oct,* £550 ($688)

9
A Persian lustre pottery star tile, 13th/14th cent, decorated in brown lustre on a transparent and cobalt-blue glaze, with a spotted stag, the border with geometric strapwork, 20.3cm (8in), *L 17 Oct,* £385 ($481)

10
An Isnik pottery dish, late 16th/early 17th cent, with sloping rim, decorated in cobalt blue, green and raised sealing-wax red, with a central cypress tree surrounded by roses and tulips, 28cm (11in), *L 17 Oct,* £2,640 ($3,300)

11
An Isnik pottery tile, 2nd half 16th cent, decorated in two shades of cobalt blue, dark green and sealing-wax red, 24.5cm sq (9⅝in), *L 18 Apr,* £825 ($1,188)

12
An Isnik pottery dish, 2nd half 16th cent, of rounded form with sloping rim, decorated in cobalt blue, turquoise green and raised sealing-wax red, 30.2cm (11⅞in), *L 17 Oct,* £1,760 ($2,200)

13
A pottery dish in the Isnik 'rosette and saz leaf' style, Cantagalli factory, Florence, late 19th cent, with sloping bracketed rim, decorated in cobalt blue, green and manganese purple, 31.1cm (12¼in), *L 18 July,* £143 ($191)

1   2   3

4   5   6

7   8   9

10   11

12   13

1
A Kutahya pottery ewer, 18th cent, with a conical body, narrow flaring neck and S-shaped spout, decorated in manganese purple and cobalt blue, 24.8cm (9¾in), *L 18 Apr,* £825 ($1,188)

2
A Kutahya pottery jug, 18th cent, of squat pear-shaped form with high cylindrical neck, decorated in yellow, blue, black and sealing-wax red on a white ground, 13.2cm (5¼in), *L 17 Oct,* £495 ($618)

3
A Kutahya pottery mug, 18th cent, with slightly concave sides, decorated in yellow, cobalt blue, manganese purple and sealing-wax red, 10.2cm (4in), *L 17 Oct,* £220 ($275)

4
A Kutahya pottery flat dish, 18th cent, with a lobed rim, decorated in cobalt blue and black, the rim with a band of leaves and rosettes, 27.3cm (10¾in), *L 17 Oct,* £275 ($343)

5
A pottery urn in the Isnik 'rosette and saz leaf' style, Villeroy & Boch, Rhine Valley, *c*1900, of ovoid form with twin lug handles on the shoulder, decorated in the 'Rhodian' palette of sealing-wax red, cobalt blue and green on a clear white ground, 73.7cm (29in), *L 18 Apr,* £2,310 ($3,326)

6
A Safavid blue-and-white pottery dish, 17th cent, of shallow rounded form with sloping bracketed rim, decorated in shades of cobalt blue on a white ground, marked on the base in blue, 47cm (18½in), *L 17 Oct,* £2,420 ($3,025)

7
A Safavid Kubachi pottery dish, 16th/17th cent, of shallow rounded form with wide sloping rim, decorated in shades of cobalt blue and black on a white ground, 35.5cm (14in), *L 18 Apr,* £550 ($792)

8
A Safavid blue-and-white pottery bowl, 17th cent, of deep rounded form, decorated in various tones of cobalt blue, the interior with a stylised dragon, the exterior with Chinese landscapes, 47.7cm (18¾in), *L 18 Apr,* £880 ($1,269)

9
A Safavid Kubachi blue-and-white pottery dish, 16th/17th cent, of shallow rounded form, with narrow sloping rim, decorated in shades of cobalt blue, 33cm (13in), *L 18 Apr,* £550 ($792)

10
A Safavid octagonal polychrome dish, probably Kirman, 17th cent, decorated in raised browny-red and shades of indigo, the exterior with a panel design, 16.2cm (6⅜in), *L 10 Jan,* £176 ($255)

11
A Safavid polychrome Kubachi pottery dish, 17th cent, of shallow rounded form with sloping rim, decorated in raised mustard yellow, green, brown and cobalt blue, 26.7cm (10½in), *L 17 Oct,* £330 ($413)

12
A Safavid polychrome Kubachi pottery dish, *c*1600, of shallow rounded form with narrow sloping rim, standing on a low foot, decorated in raised mustard yellow, cobalt blue, brown and green, 33cm (13in), *L 18 Apr,* £2,420 ($3,492)

1
A Safavid blue-and-white pottery bottle, 17th cent, with squat globular body, decorated in shades of cobalt blue on a white body under a colourless transparent glaze, 9.5cm (4¾in), *L 18 Apr,* **£352 ($506)**

2
A Safavid blue-and-white pottery bowl, 17th/18th cent, of deep rounded form, standing on a shallow foot, the central medallion with a flowerhead surrounded by scrolls, the exterior with sprays of chrysanthemums, 18.5cm (7¼in), *L 18 Apr,* **£385 ($554)**

3
A Safavid blue-and-white pottery vase, 17th cent, with inverted pear-shaped body, three receptacles at the shoulder, decorated in shades of cobalt blue and outlined in black, the neck with an engraved Qajar metal replacement, 25cm (9⅛in), *L 18 Apr,* **£385 ($554)**

4
A Safavid blue-and-white pottery vase, 17th cent, with inverted pear-shaped body, decorated in shades of cobalt blue, the sides with dog of fo medallions and floral sprays, 33.7cm (13¼in), *L 18 July,* **£220 ($293)**

5
A Safavid lustre pottery bottle, 17th cent, of pear-shaped form with slender tapering neck, decorated in brown lustre on a transparent glaze, the mouth with a metal replacement mount, 24cm (9½in), *L 17 Oct,* **£748 ($935)**

6
A Safavid underglaze painted pottery figure of an elephant, 17th cent, on a rectangular base with figures, all decorated in shades of cobalt blue and black on a white ground, the trunk and head with naturalistic detail, h 29.2cm (11½in), *L 17 Oct,* **£3,080 ($3,850)**

7
A Persian underglaze-painted pottery jar, 19th cent, of inverted pear-shaped form, decorated in black under a turquoise glaze, 26.7cm (10½in), *L 13 Nov,* **£110 ($147)**

8
A Persian underglaze-painted pottery jar, 19th cent, of inverted pear-shaped form with short neck and slightly everted rim, decorated in shades of blue outlined in black, 32.5cm (12¾in), *L 17 Oct,* **£990 ($1,237)**

9
A Persian polychrome painted pottery jar, 19th cent, of inverted pear-shaped form, decorated in green, cobalt blue and manganese purple, with a hunting scene, 28.2cm (11⅛in), *L 17 Oct,* **£462 ($577)**

10
A pair of Qajar pottery cats, 19th cent, decorated in black, cobalt blue, green and manganese brown, with sprays of flowers, 14cm (5½in), *L 18 July,* **£110 ($147)**

11
A Qajar enamelled cup, 19th cent, of rounded form, decorated with oval medallions and an alternating design of maidens and decorative bouquets, on a white ground, d 8.8cm (3½in), *L 10 Jan,* **£110 ($159)**

12
A Qajar octagonal moulded polychrome tile, with a central medallion depicting Bahram-e-Gur and two companions, enclosed by an arabesque border, 37cm (14½in), *L 18 July,* **£440 ($587)**

13
A Qajar moulded polychrome pottery tile, with a central pictorial medallion depicting a seated princess and her companion, surrounded by a scroll design, 29.3 x 28.5cm (11½ x 11¼in), *L 18 July,* **£60 ($80)**

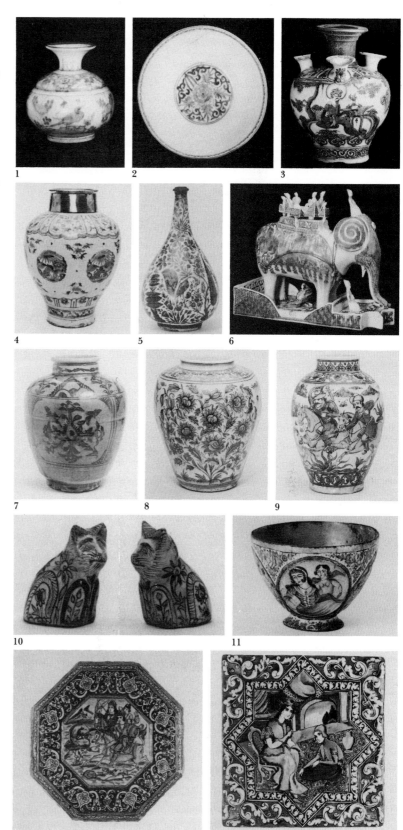

1   2   3

4   5   6

7   8   9

10   11

12   13

1
A Turkish dagger (kard),
18th cent, the jade
handle with inlaid gold
decoration and inset
with turquoises, 36cm
(14in), *L 18 Apr*,
£440 ($634)

2
A Caucasian silver and
niello dagger, 19th cent,
51cm (20in), *NY 24 Nov*,
$605 (£500)

3
A Caucasian dagger
(kindjal), Georgia, 19th
cent, the plain steel
blade with a central
fuller, the hilt with ivory
grips and inlaid gold
foliate decoration, silver
parcel-gilt and niello
sheath, 50.3cm (19¾in),
L 17 Oct,
£1,320 ($1,650)

4
A Turkish kard, 19th
cent, the translucent
stone hilt, probably
agate, with silver filigree
mounts, the silver
scabbard engraved and
set with turquoises bearing
the *tughra* of Mahmud
II (1808-39), 25cm (9¾in),
L 18 Apr,
£308 ($444)

5
A Norther Ottoman
Empire silver yataghan,
18th/19th cent, the
hilt and mounts deeply
embossed and chiselled
in the European style,
69cm (27in), *L 18 Apr*,
£935 ($1,349)

6
A Qajar devil mask
helmet, 18th/19th cent,
overall h 61cm (24in),
L 18 Apr,
£330 ($476)

7
An Indian jade child's
dagger hilt, 18th cent, of
green jade inlaid with
gold set with diamonds
and rubies, 10cm (4in),
L 17 Oct,
£440 ($550)

8
An Indian jade-hilted
dagger (khandar),
17th/18th cent, the
carved jade hilt set with
rubies and emeralds and
inlaid with gold, 35cm
(13¾in), *L 17 Oct*,
£440 ($550)

9
An Indian jade mounted
dagger, 19th cent, the re-
curved damascus steel
blade mounted with grey
coloured jade handle
and scabbard mounts, all
inlaid with emeralds and
rubies, 39.5cm (15½in),
NY 24 Nov,
$8,250 (£6,818)

10
A North Indian dagger
(khanjar), 19th cent, with
a plain double-edged
watered steel blade, the
elephant's head hilt with
gold Koftgari decoration
and later ruby eyes,
36cm (14½in), *L 17 Oct*,
£2,310 ($2,888)

11
An Indian jade-hilted
dagger (khanjar), 19th
cent, the watered steel
Indo-Persian blade
decorated with gold
Koftgari work, 37cm
(14½in), *L 18 July*,
£2,200 ($2,937)

12
An Indian sword, 19th
cent, the forte with gold
Koftgari decoration,
Indo-Muslim hilt with
disc pommel, 76.5cm
(30in), *L 17 Oct*,
£880 ($1,100)

13
An Ottoman silver
mounted yataghan,
Turkey, 19th cent,
overall 79cm (31in),
NY 2/3 Mar,
$1,100 (£738)

14
A Qajar axe, with profuse
gold inlaid decoration
and inscriptions, the
blade of etched watered
steel, 73.5cm (29in),
L 18 Apr,
£1,650 ($2,376)

15
An Indian sabre (tulwar),
18th cent, made for the
Indian Export Market,
probably in Genoa, the
hilt of Indo-Muslim
form, European blade,
85cm (33½in), *L 18 Apr*,
£495 ($713)

16
A Kurdish miquelet
flintlock musket, the 50in
two-stage barrel of Italian
Export manufacture,
165cm (65in), *L 18 Apr*,
£605 ($873)

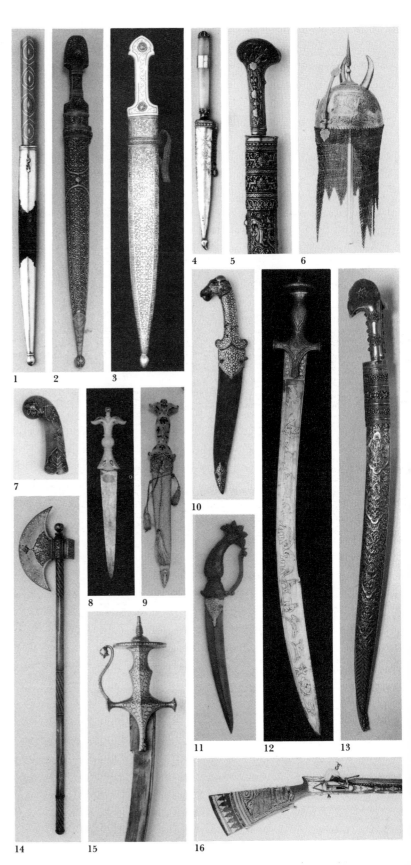

1 2 3

7

8 9

10

11 12 13

14 15 16

1
A North Indian axe,
Hindustan, 18th cent,
with pierced and
chiselled steel blade and
head covered with gold
foil, two panels with
Persian verse, 67cm
(26½in), *L 18 Apr,*
£3,080 ($4,435)

2
A North Indian axe,
probably Lahore, 18th
cent, of Persian form,
the watered steel head
framed by gold Koftgari
arabesques, the haft of
lacquered wood in
colours familiar from
Indian miniatures, 69cm
(27in), *L 18 Apr,*
£440 ($634)

3
**A Veneto-Saracenic silver-
inlaid brass candlestick,**
*c.*1560, with domed base
supporting a wide drip-
pan, the incised
decoration with a strap-
work design, h 17.1cm
(6¾in), *L 17 Oct,*
£2,200 ($2,750)

4
**A Veneto-Saracenic silver-
inlaid brass bowl and
cover,** the bowl of almost
hemispherical form with
flat base, the lid with a
central medallion,
d 14.3cm (5¾in),
L 18 Apr,
£1,760 ($2,534)

5
A Fars brass bowl (tas),
14th cent, with bulbous
sides, with incised
decoration, the sides
with epigraphic cartouches
flanked by pictorial
roundels, d 17.9cm (7in),
L 18 July,
£1,430 ($1,909)

6
An Indian helmet,
18th/19th cent, with
central plume holder, two
lower plume holders and
movable nasal bar,
decorated in gold and
silver, h 28cm (11in),
L 18 Apr,
£220 ($317)

7
**A Mamluk silver-inlaid
bronze cup,** late
13th/early 14th cent, of
rounded form flaring out
to a narrow rim, the
exterior with a band of
cursive inscription,
d 107cm (4¼in), *L 17 Oct,*
£6,600 ($8,250)

8
**A Mamluk brass
candlestick base,** Egypt,
14th cent, of truncated
conical form with bevelled
ridges round the upper
and lower edge, with
incised decoration with
naskhi inscription, now
mounted for electricity,
d 31cm (12¼in), *L 18 Apr,*
£1,540 ($2,218)

9
**A Mamluk silver-inlaid
brass vase,** 14th cent, with
squat pear-shaped body,
with a bevelled ridge
round the shoulder and
a flaring neck, the
incised decoration of
naskhi inscription with
traces of silver inlay,
probably reduced in
size, 17.1cm (6¾in),
L 18 Apr,
£3,850 ($5,544)

1   2

6

8

3

4

5

7

9

1
A Persian bronze jug,
Khorassan, 12th/13th cent,
with squat pear-shaped
body and cylindrical neck,
with incised decoration,
the neck with a wide
frieze of *kufic* inscription,
h 16.5cm (6½in), *L 17 Oct,*
£605 ($756)

2
A Persian bronze bucket,
Khorassan, 12th cent, of
bulbous form with flattened
rim, swing handle and
flaring foot, with incised
decoration, with bands
of *kufic* and cursive
inscriptions, d 15.9cm
(6¼in), *L 17 Oct,*
£6,600 ($8,250)

3
A Persian silver and copper
inlaid brass jug (kuze),
Khorassan, 13th cent, of
squat bulbous form, with
continuous lines of
naskhi and *kufic*
inscriptions, handle missing, 16.8cm (6⅝in),
L 18 Apr,
£8,250 ($11,880)

4
A Mamluk tinned copper
basin, Egypt, 15th cent,
with deep, inward-
sloping sides, the exterior
with an incised frieze of
cartouches and roundels,
d 28cm (11in), *L 10 Jan,*
£352 ($510)

5
A Persian copper basin,
late 15th cent, of squat
rounded form, with slightly
sloping T-shaped rim,
with incised decoration,
on a hatched ground,
d 33cm (13in), *L 17 Oct,*
£4,180 ($5,225)

6
A Persian glass flask, the
body of dimpled triangular
form encased in silver
openwork with a design
of three panels surrounded
by scrolling vines, 26cm
(10¼in), *L 17 Oct,*
£440 ($550)

7
A Persian brass jug
(mashrabe), 16th cent,
with bulbous body, short
cylindrical neck, the entire
surface with engraved
decoration on hatched
ground, the base with
incised decoration, signed,
handle missing, 13.3cm
(5¼in), *L 18 Apr,*
£1,430 ($2,059)

8
A silver-inlaid high-tin
bronze jug, Persia or
Southern Anatolia, 14th
cent, of faceted squat
bulbous form, the body
decorated with seven lobed
medallions, handle
probably not belonging,
20.3cm (8in), *L 18 Apr,*
£13,200 ($19,008)

9
A Persian openwork
tinned copper plaque,
18th cent, of rectangular
form with lobed ends,
decorated with a *nasta'liq*
inscription on an open-
work ground of scroll-
ing sprays, 17.8cm (7in),
L 18 Apr,
£1,430 ($2,063)

10
An Ottoman silver
travelling scribe set, 1808-
39, consisting of an inkpot
and pen case, the
borders and ends of both
chased and stamped with
foliage design, stamped
with the *tughra* marks of
Sultan Mahmud II, signed,
23.5cm (9¼in), *L 17 Oct,*
£2,310 ($2,888)

11
An Ottoman silver mirror
back, 19th cent, of
circular form with a
scalloped edge, the decoration embossed with a
central vase of flowers
with crescent moons and
stars, 25.2cm (10in),
L 18 July,
£352 ($470)

12
An Ottoman gilt copper
(tombak) incense burner,
17th cent, of shallow
rounded form, standing
on a high splayed foot,
curved, faceted handle,
with *talik* inscription,
27.3cm (10¾in), *L 18 Apr,*
£4,400 ($6,336)

1

A silver covered cup and stand, late 19th cent, the faceted circular body engraved with stylised foliage, bird finial, on a similarly engraved moulded stand, unmarked, h 13.5cm (5in), 11oz (343gr), *L 18 July*, £495 ($661)

2

An Ottoman silver bowl, *c*1880, the circular body applied with three scroll handles on a pedestal base, *tughra* mark, h 15cm (6in), 19oz 16dwt (618gr), *L 18 July*, £352 ($469)

3

An Ottoman tulip-shaped silver cup, *c*1890, engraved into strapwork and military symbols, knopped stem and moulded foot, *tughra* mark, h 13.3cm (5in), 5oz 6dwt (165gr), *L 18 July*, £209 ($279)

4

An Ottoman gold pendant, 19th cent, of boteh-shaped form surmounted by a coronet, all with floral decoration chased in relief around a plain heart-shaped cartouche, 10.1cm (4in), *L 17 Oct*, £132 ($165)

5

An Ottoman silver ewer, basin and stand, 19th cent, the baluster ewer lobed beneath the tapering neck, the circular bowl with flared rim similarly chased, *tughra* marks, 47cm (18½in), 94oz 4dwt (2,930gr), *L 18 Apr*, £5,280 ($7,603)

6

An Indian parcel-gilt silver seal, dated 1192AH/AD1775, of bell-shaped form with openwork handle at the top, the base incised with a *nasta'liq* inscription, h 7.6cm (3in), *L 17 Oct*, £1,540 ($1,925)

7

An Indo-Persian steel writing set, 19th cent, comprising an inkwell, candlestick, penholder and knife, with gold and silver damascening with a foliage design, 21.7cm (8½in), *L 18 July*, £330 ($441)

8

An Indian steel writing set, 19th cent, comprising inkwell, candlestick and penholder, decorated with gold damascening with a foliate design, 20cm (8in), *L 13 Nov*, £154 ($188)

9

A Qajar enamelled gold bracelet, 19th cent, decorated in polychrome enamel with five floral medallions interspersed by panels of filigree circles enclosing seed pearls, d 6cm (2⅜in), *L 17 Oct*, £1,100 ($1,375)

10

A Qajar steel mirror case and stand, 2nd half 19th cent, the circular hinged case and domed pedestal foot with lobed edges, the case decorated in gold damascening with a *nasta'liq* inscription 59.7cm (23½in), *L 13 Nov*, £704 ($860)

11

A Qajar steel ewer, 19th cent, with pear-shaped body, standing on a splayed foot, with incised decoration and gold damascening, foliate medallions and scrolling vines, 34.3cm (13½in), *L 17 Oct*, £1,100 ($1,375)

1   2   3

4   5   6

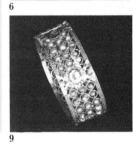

7   8   9

10   11

1
A Qajar steel cockerel,
19th cent, standing on
one leg, decorated in
gold damascening, with
foliate medallions and
naturalistic details on
the head, wings and tail,
37cm (14½in), L 10 Jan,
£1,210 ($1,755)

2
A silver and copper inlaid
brass tray, Syria or
Egypt, c.1900, of circular
form with a design of
epigraphic cartouches
around a triangular
medallion, 31.1cm
(12¼in), L 13 Nov,
£110 ($134)

3
A pair of Qajar steel
pigeons, 19th cent, decorated in gold and silver
damascening with
naturalistic detail, with
attached crest and tail,
h 22.5cm (8⅞in), L 17 Oct,
£2,200 ($2,750)

4
A silver and copper inlaid
brass tray, probably
Egypt, c.1900, of circular
form, with a central
medallion, arabesque
medallions and epi-
graphic cartouches, 29cm
(11½in), L 18 July,
£88 ($117)

5
A silver and copper inlaid
brass jug, probably
Egypt, c.1900, of bell-
shaped form, decorated
with inscription cartouches
within strapwork borders
and trefoil medallions,
19.5cm (7⅝in), L 18 July,
£385 ($514)

6
A silver and copper inlaid
tray, probably Egypt,
c.1900, enclosing
arabesques and inscrip-
tions, 26cm (10¼in),
L 18 July,
£77 ($103)

7
A silver and copper inlaid
brass bowl, probably Egypt,
c.1900, of squat bulbous
form, decorated with a
frieze of inscription
cartouches and
decorative roundels,
d 12cm (4⅝in), L 18 July,
£285 ($380)

8
A silver and copper inlaid
brass bowl, probably Egypt,
c.1900, of squat bulbous
form, decorated with
large botehs, stars and
rosettes on a scrolling
arabesque ground, d 12cm
(4⅝in), L 18 July,
£352 ($470)

9
A silver inlaid brass tray,
probably Egypt, c.1900,
of circular form, with a
geometric design against
a background of scrolls,
d 37.4cm (14⅞in), L 18 July,
£352 ($470)

1

2

3

4

5

6

7

8

9

1
A silver and copper inlaid
brass box, probably
Egypt, c1900, of
rectangular form,
decorated in the Mamluk
style, 12 x 8.2cm
(4¾ x 3¼in), L 18 July,
£121 ($162)

2
A silver and copper inlaid
brass box and cover, Syria
or Egypt, stamped 1914,
of circular form with flat
lid, the top and sides
decorated with inscription
cartouches interspersed
by scrolling arabesques,
h 10.8cm (4¼in), L 13 Nov,
£143 ($175)

3
A silver inlaid brass casket,
Syria or Egypt, c1900, of
square form, with
incised and inlaid
decoration in the Mamluk
style, the wooden
interior with geometric
decoration, h 17.8cm
(7in), L 17 Oct,
£2,090 ($2,613)

4
A silver and copper inlaid
brass scribe set, probably
Egypt, c1900, comprising
a pen box and an inkwell,
decorated with friezes of
inscriptions against a
scrolling background, lid
missing, 31cm (12¼in),
L 18 July,
£275 ($367)

5
A pair of Islamic steel
scissors, 19th cent, decorated
in silver damascening with
a floral design, 34.9cm
(13¾in), L 13 Nov,
£220 ($269)

6
A gilt silver-coloured
metal refreshment set,
c1900, comprising ewer,
tray and six stemmed
cups, decorated in niello
with a panel design
enclosing arabesques, ewer
h 22.8cm (9in), 27oz
(843gr), L 13 Nov,
£220 ($269)

7
A Persian wooden printing
block, decorated with a
nasta'liq inscription carved
in mirrored relief, 33cm
(13in), L 13 Nov,
£88 ($118)

8
An Indian ivory inlaid
wooden chest, Gujarat or
Sind, 18th cent, of
rectangular form with
fall front, the interior
with seven inlaid drawers,
50.8 x 31.1 x 27.3cm
(20 x 12¼ x 10¾in),
L 17 Oct,
£1,430 ($1,788)

9
A silver ewer, 19th cent,
the baluster body fluted
into panels and flat
chased with formal
strapwork and foliage,
with tughra marks, 52cm
(20½in), 204oz (6368gr),
L 18 Apr,
£7,150 ($10,296)

10
A silver and copper inlaid
brass box, 13 x 7.3cm (5 x
3in), L 18 July,
£176 ($235)

11
A Persian coco-de-mer
shell (kashkul), 19th cent,
carved with a frieze of
nasta'liq inscription, the
top with a scene of
dervishes, the base with
lobed medallion with a
date, surrounded by
four fish, 29.2cm (11½in),
L 10 Jan,
£352 ($510)

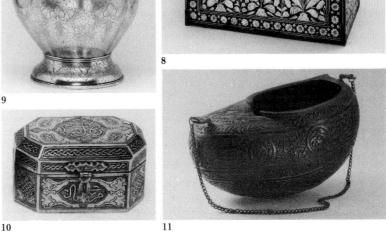

African, Oceanic, American Indian and Pre-Columbian Art

ROBERTO FAINELLO • ELLEN NAPIURA • FATMA TURKKAN-WILLE

For auction purposes the arts of the native civilizations of Africa, the Pacific Islands and the Americas are described by region of origin—African, Polynesian, Pre-Columbian and North American Indian. The market for Pre-Columbian art is largely in New York and South America, whereas African and Polynesian art is sold on both sides of the Atlantic. A feature article on North American Indian art can be found on page 576.

The term 'Pre-Columbian' is used to describe works of art made in Central and South America and in the Caribbean Islands before the arrival of the *conquistadores*. It therefore encompasses an extraordinarily broad range of objects dating from about 1500 BC to the end of the 15th century AD. All of them necessarily reflect the pure aesthetic sense of the native civilizations before there was any question of European influence. Most of the objects offered at auction are ceremonial items or tomb offerings, rather than functional objects whose value would be archeological rather than aesthetic. The materials are almost as diverse as the forms: terracotta, stone, bone, fabric, copper, gold or jade.

A number of important permanent installations of Pre-Columbian material have opened at major museums over the past few years. The Rockefeller Wing at the Metropolitan Museum of Art in New York is one such and Pre-Columbian holdings form the core of the Dallas Museum of Fine Arts. There is also an exceptionally fine selection in Mexico City. This new interest and the accompanying scholarship are contributing to the expansion of the market.

Very few pieces of tribal art can be attributed beyond the tribe of origin to a specific hand. In general, the information which will increase the price of an object at auction is a well-documented provenance—for instance, an established collection date or publication in the relevant literature. As in most areas, the collector of tribal art has to be especially aware of fakes, which are often mass produced for sale to tourists in the country of origin. Oceanic material is rather more scarce than African, the main reason being that fewer items were produced, particularly in sculpture, and, after Cook's visits to the islands, almost everything genuinely tribal had been collected by 1880. Tribal peoples used the natural materials available to them, mainly wood but also ivory, bone, fibre, human and animal hair and bark. As these are comparatively perishable materials, particularly vulnerable to humid climates, pieces in good condition are quite rare. However, the collector of tribal art is appreciative of a certain amount of wear as a sign of age. Evidence of use, such as the wear on suspension loops or holes, or a good patination from years of handling will enhance the object in his eyes.

In 1984 interest in tribal art was spurred by the exhibition, 'Primitivism in 20th-century art', which was held at the Museum of Modern Art in New York. This exhibition and the accompanying catalogue aimed to illustrate the profound influence of tribal art on early 20th century artists, many of whom collected such items and often incorporated techniques used by tribal sculptors into their own works. It is possible that this exhibition will attract new buyers to the market and encourage hitherto wary collectors to be more adventurous in their purchases.

Sotheby's have recently introduced separate sales of tribal furniture, utilitaria and jewellery and these might well be of interest to the more general buyer. Such items as stools, neckrests, bowls, textiles and jewellery have proved extremely popular, especially among interior designers (a profession now having a marked effect on many traditional collectors' fields). Price levels in this previously neglected area are likely to continue to rise. However, items that are useful as well as attractive can still be obtained for very modest sums and could form the basis of an interesting collection from which to expand into the more esoteric forms of masks and sculpture.

1
A Djenne terracotta
equestrian group, 33cm
(13in), *L 25/26 June,*
£2,860 ($4,033)

2
A Dogon female figure,
standing on a cylindrical
base worn away at the
back, the columnar neck
supporting a bearded
helmet head, sacrificial
patina, 63.6cm (25in),
NY 29/30 Nov,
$6,875 (£5,729)

3
A Dogon wood female
figure, the lower part of
the legs missing, weather
eroded patina, 24cm (9½in),
L 25/26 June,
£1,320 ($1,861)

4
A Bambara wood mask,
with square pierced mouth
and eyes, pierced on
either side for attachment,
19.5cm (7¾in), *L 9 Apr,*
£935 ($1,349)

5
A Bambara male antelope
headpiece, *tji wara*, the
downcast helmet head
with pierced nose and
ears decorated with metal
rings, brown patina with
encrustation on the head
and horns, 42.9cm (16⅞in),
NY 29/30 Nov,
$2,200 (£1,833)

6
A Senufo heddle-pulley, in
the form of a figure
combining human and
bird attributes, rich
blackish-brown patina,
21.3cm (8⅜in),
NY 29/30 Nov,
$4,180 (£3,483)

7
A Senufo wood female
figure, the large feet
partly missing, incised
scarification on the body
and forehead, brown
encrusted patina, 47.5cm
(18¾in), *L 25/26 June,*
£880 ($1,241)

8
A Baule wood mask, on a
rectangular frame, the
finely carved head with
small pierced protruding
mouth, scarification on
cheeks and forehead,
38cm (14⅞in), *L 3 Dec,*
£1,430 ($1,716)

9
A Baule face mask, in the
form of a monkey's
head, with pierced close-
set eyeholes, incised
criss-crosses on the cheeks,
encrusted black patina,
24.4cm (9⅝in),
NY 29/30 Nov,
$1,540 (£1,283)

10
A Guro heddle-pulley,
surmounted by a monkey's
head with iron suspen-
sion loop attached at the
top, rich dark brown
patina, h with loop
18.4cm (7¼in),
NY 29/30 Nov,
$1,320 (£1,100)

11
A Guro heddle-pulley, in
the form of a female
standing with legs apart
forming the pulley cage,
rich black patina, 21cm
(8¼in), *NY 29/30 Nov,*
$2,530 (£2,108)

12
A Guro and a Baule
heddle-pulley, the Guro
with the finial in the
form of a bird, the Baule
pulley in the form of a
goli mask, 14 and 18cm
(5½ and 7⅛in), *L 3 Dec,*
£440 ($528)

13
A Baule wood colonial
figure, wearing European
shoes, shorts and short-
sleeved shirt,
scarification on the face
and neck, a string of
white glass beads around
the neck, 43.5cm (17⅛in),
L 25/26 June,
£2,750 ($3,878)

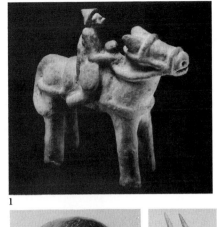
1

2

3

4

5

6

7

8

9

10

11

12

13

1
A **Dan wood mask,** with short flattened nose and narrow pierced slit eyes, pierced around the edge for attachment, 25.5cm (10in), *L 25/26 June,* **£605 ($853)**

2
A **Dan wood mask,** the face with bulging pierced eyes, rectangular holes pierced around the edge for fibre attachments, very fine black patina, 24.5cm (9⅝in), *L 25/26 June,* **£5,500 ($7,755)**

3
A **Mende Bundu helmet mask,** *Sande Society,* a panel of cowrie shell decoration carved at the back, 34.9cm (13¾in), *NY 29/30 Nov,* **$440 (£364)**

4
A **Dan wood maternity group,** the mouth open to reveal bone-inset teeth, the eyes painted white, with two tresses of braided human hair, the baby on the back, 61cm (24in), *L 3 Dec,* **£13,200 ($15,850)**

5
A **Baga drum,** supported by a caryatid resting her hands on a female child, brown, black and white painted details, 92.3cm (36⅜in), *NY 29/30 Nov,* **$2,530 (£2,108)**

6
A **Bijogo female ancestor figure,** standing on a fragmentary cylindrical base, the right foot and left arm broken away, sacrificial patina, traces of red pigment, 53.3cm (21in), *NY 29/30 Nov,* **$2,750 (£2,292)**

7
An **Ashanti clay head,** the ringed neck supporting the slightly upturned head, three keloid marks on the lower forehead and the temples, 27cm (10⅝in), *L 25/26 June,* **£440 ($620)**

8
An **Ashanti clay head,** with a ringed neck, prominent eyes closed, raised scarification on the temples, 18.7cm (7⅜in), *L 25/26 June,* **£374 ($527)**

9
An **Ashanti terracotta head of a princess,** the carved oval face with small protruding lips, a single keloid scarification mark and a small cylindrical attachment on the forehead, 32cm (12⅝in), *L 3 Dec,* **£825 ($990)**

10
An **Akan terracotta head,** the prominent nose with pierced nostrils, incised scarification on the temples, the granulated coiffure partly damaged, 16.5cm (6½in), *L 9 Apr,* **£440 ($635)**

11
An **Ashanti wood comb,** the finial in the form of four stylised human figures, the whole decorated with geometric designs and brass studs, fine brown patina, 20.5cm (8in), *L 3 Dec,* **£1,430 ($1,716)**

12
A **Benin wood reliquary head of an oba,** *uhumwelao,* wearing the typical ridged necklace representing coral beads, the cap-like coiffure with a feather projection, 63cm (24⅞in), *L 3 Dec,* **£1,980 ($2,376)**

13
A **Benin bronze pectoral fragment,** 18th cent, cast in the form of a warrior or king figure, the left arm broken at the elbow, the lower torso also broken away, greenish-brown patina, 12.9cm (5in), *NY 29/30 Nov,* **$3,080 (£2,567)**

1   2

3   4   5   6

7   8   9

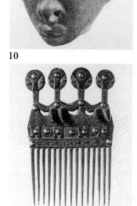

10

11   12   13

1
A pair of Yoruba brass edan staffs, Ogboni Society, *Ijebu Ode,* joined together by a linked chain, greenish-brown patina, h 20.7cm (8⅛in), *NY 29/30 Nov,* $440 (£367)

2
A Yoruba wood figure, wearing a European costume, probably a shrine image for Ogo Elegba 38cm (15in), *L 9 Apr,* £836 ($1,206)

3
A Cameroons doll, *namdji,* wearing beaded strands around the ankles, torso, chest and neck, some with brass ring and cowrie shell suspensions, 25.7cm (10⅛in), *NY 29/30 Nov,* $825 (£682)

4
An Ibibio wood figure, wearing a painted black uniform with the belt, dagger and flask carved in relief, 56cm (22⅛in), *L 9 Apr,* £748 ($1,079)

5
A Chamba wood male figure, the carved head with pierced rectangular ears and incised scarification, 56cm (22in), *L 25/26 June,* £396 ($558)

6
A Mambila dance crest, *suah buah,* in the form of an oval head with truncated beard, orange, black and white pigment, an attachment on the forehead probably missing, 27.9cm (11in), *NY 29/30 Nov,* $11,000 (£9,167)

7
An Urhobo male shrine figure, the right forearm broken away, white pigment overall, traces of indigo, 172.8cm (68in), *NY 29/30 Nov,* $8,250 (£6,875)

8
A Western Grasslands clay pipe bowl, Grasslands area probably Bamum, 15.9cm (6¼in), *NY 29/30 Nov,* $1,430 (£1,192)

9
A Kota wood reliquary figure, the concave oval head covered with copper and brass strips, the side panels and coiffure covered with incised brass sheets, 47.5cm (18¾in), *L 3 Dec,* £4,620 ($5,544)

10
A Kota wood reliquary figure, the head and upper part of the body entirely overlaid with copper and brass, 61cm (24in), *L 3 Dec,* £3,740 ($4,488)

11
A Nbaka wood female figure, raised scarification marks running down the spine, fine brown patina, possibly a representation of the female divinity *Nabo,* 45.5cm (18in), *L 9 Apr,* £1,760 ($2,540)

12
A Punu 'white face' mask, an incised scarification mark in relief on the forehead, remains of kaolin and black pigment, 30.4cm (12in), *NY 29/30 Nov,* $2,310 (£1,925)

13
A Kota wood and brass reliquary figure, *mbulu ngulu,* the front covered with applied incised brass and copper strips, a lozenge carved in relief at the back, rich encrusted brown patina, 58.4cm (23in), *NY 29/30 Nov,* $6,600 (£5,500)

14
A Ngbaka wood axe, the handle covered in brass wire and terminating in a human head, the coiffure painted black, the metal blade projecting from the mouth, 28cm (11in), *L 25/26 June,* £660 ($931)

1 2 3

4 5 6 7

8 9 10 11

12 13 14

1
A Villi wood face mask, the concave face with prominent inverted T-shaped nose, pierced eyes, an old label inscribed 'Masque de Feticheur Loango', the whole painted in white and red, with chin, eyebrows and nose in black, 41cm (16¼in), *L 9 Apr*, £3,575 ($5,159)

2
A Bembe miniature fetish figure, the right forearm missing, with elaborate cicatrice on the torso, glass eye inlays, 11.2cm (4⅜in), *NY 29/30 Nov*, $495 (£409)

3
A Pende ivory pendant mask, very fine honeyed patina darker at the back, 6.5cm (2⅝in), *L 3 Dec*, £4,620 ($5,544)

4
A Pende initiation mask, *mbuya*, decorated with a woven fibre headcovering, encrusted brown patina with traces of white pigment, 29.9cm (11¾in), *NY 29/30 Nov*, $1,760 (£1,467)

5
A Yaka initiation mask, with thick raffia collar and coiffure, surmounted by a tall fibre cap, painted details, 55.2cm (21¾in), *NY 29/30 Nov*, $1,320 (£1,091)

6
A Lwalwa wood mask, a small hole between nose and mouth with a string of cloth inserted, reddish patina with traces of white paint, 31cm, (12¼in), *L 9 Apr*, £715 ($1,032)

7
A Kuba wood box, with a human face carved in relief on the lid, black patina with traces of red cam powder, 29cm (11½in), *L 9 Apr*, £242 ($349)

8
Two Kuba cups, each in the form of a human head, one with openwork base, h 18.1 and 17.1cm (7⅛ and 6¾in), *NY 29/30 Nov*, $495 (£409)

9
A Songe wood Kifwebe mask, of highly abstract form, the forehead and face with incised geometric decorations painted in white, black and red, worn surface, 33cm (13in), *L 9 Apr*, £1,650 (£2,381)

10
A Songe axe, composed of an expanding wood handle decorated with copper sheeting and strips, and expanding openwork iron blade decorated with incised human heads, 40.7cm (16½in), *NY 29/30 Nov*, $935 (£779)

11
A Luba kifwebe mask with prominent triangular nose and square mouth, the whole decorated with deeply cut parallel curving lines, 22.5cm (8⅞in), *L 25/26 June*, £1,320 ($1,861)

12
A Kongo wood male figure, wearing a European style jacket with raised buttons and a carved necklace, black encrusted patina, 57cm (22¼in), *L 9 Apr*, £4,950 ($7,143)

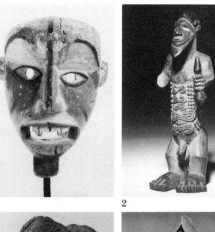
1

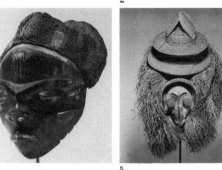

3

4

5

6

7

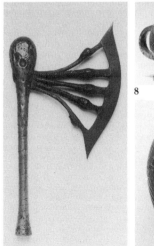
8

9

10   11   12

1
A Lunda comb, the rectangular grip surmounted by a seated male and female figure, wearing brass ornaments, with scarification and incised coiffures, brown patina, 15.8cm (6³⁄₁₆in), *NY 29/30 Nov,* $1,980 (£1,636)

2
A Chokwe wood chief's chair (Ngundja), the backrest comprising horizontal panels with openwork decoration depicting young women, young men and figures wearing the *Cikunza* mask relating to the circumcision rites, the seat in antelope skin, dark patina, 103cm (40⅝in), *L 9 Apr,* £2,200 ($3,175)

3
A Mangbetu pottery vessel, the globular body with strap handle, the neck in the form of a human head, patches of incised decoration, 33.5cm (13¼in), *L 9 Apr,* £2,200 ($3,175)

4
A Chokwe face mask, with pierced ears and incised tripartite coiffure, painted with red enamel, 23.5cm (9¼in), *NY 29/30 Nov,* $1,430 (£1,182)

5
Three Mangbetu pottery vessels, the globular bodies with incised decoration, the spouts formed as heads, 30, 30 and 31cm (11⅞, 11⅞ and 12¼in), *L 3 Dec,* £1,210 ($1,452)

6
An Azande throwing knife, with brass windings on the handle, abstract geometric street blade, incised with linear devices on one side, 36cm (14⅛in), *NY 29/30 Nov,* $385 (£321)

7
An East African carving of a European, dark patina, the brim of the hat, pages of the book and the edge of the base painted in gold, part of the brim of the hat broken, 22cm (8¾in), *L 25/26 June,* £286 ($403)

8
A Makonde helmet mask, stylised head with pronounced curving lips, remains of human hair on the skull, black pigment on the facial surface, 27.3cm (10¾in), *NY 29/30 Nov,* $1,540 (£1,283)

9
A Ndebele beaded apron, *jocolo,* the hide decorated with multi-coloured beads on a white ground, some of the beads translucent, 75 x 54cm (29½ x 21¼in), *L 25/26 June,* £242 ($341)

10
Two Ndebele beaded hide aprons, one with a white beaded panel containing hooked devices in blue and red, the other with circles and wedges beaded against the hide ground and trimmed with tiny brass rings, 52.7 and 56cm (20¾ and 22in), *NY 29/30 Nov,* $495 (£409)

11
A Warega wood mask, the eyes and mouth pierced, the left side of the face painted white, the right side and forehead painted red, some restoration on the left cheek, 32cm (12⅝in), *L 3 Dec,* £880 ($1,056)

12
A Southeast African wood staff, the finial formed by an equestrian group, the rider's left arm missing from the shoulder to above the wrist, the whole of reddish and light wood with polished patina, perhaps Zulu or other Nguni-speaking people, 123cm (48½in), *L 9 Apr,* £1,320 ($1,905)

13
A pair of Ngoni-Tonga wood figures, male and female, both carved of light wood, the feet, neck and coiffure stained dark brown, wearing narrow panels of beadwork, male 87cm (34¼in), female 97cm (38¼in), *L 3 Dec,* £1,980 ($2,376)

1

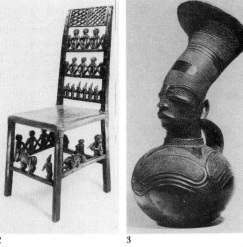

2   3

4   5   6

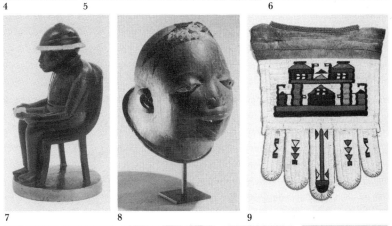

7   8   9

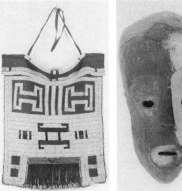

10   11   12   13

1
A Huon Gulf headrest,
the arched structure supported at either end by a seated figure facing outwards, each with a limb missing, old worn patina, 15cm (5⅞in), *L 25/26 June,* £495 ($698)

2
A Huon Gulf headrest, two semicircular arcs projecting from the base and one from below the top, the whole with deeply incised linear decoration, 16.5cm (6½in), *L 25/26 June,* £264 ($372)

3
Two Saramaka stools, each with openwork rectangular base and concave seat carved with a curvilinear pattern, one with metal tack decoration, 49.6 and 42cm (19½ and 17⅜in), *NY 29/30 Nov,* $715 (£591)

4
An Ibo title stool, with incised circular base and concave seat, the mid-section carved with a column of carinated ribs and interlocked upward and downward projections, 31.7cm (12½in), *NY 29/30 Nov,* $660 (£545)

5
A Lobi stool, with a head projecting up from the curving seat, a pair of cylindrical supports below and extended support at the front, 54.6cm (21½in), *NY 29/30 Nov,* $1,870 (£1,545)

6
Two Lozi wood stools, both with circular seats and four flaring legs with small feet, h 18cm and 15cm (7 and 5⅞in), *L 25/26 June,* £66 ($93)

7
A Pokot wood neckrest, the small rectangular rest section supported by two legs with curving 'feet', 18cm (7in), *L 25/26 June,* £46 ($65)

8
A Gurunsi stool, with contoured tapering seat, a pair of diagonal block legs projecting below the back, a rectangular support with flaring foot at the front, 72.1cm (28⅜in), *NY 29/30 Nov,* $660 (£545)

9
A Somalian neckrest, the curving form supported by a column of circular section, richly decorated with incised geometric designs, a skin covering on the base, 20.5cm (8in), *L 3 Dec,* £198 ($238)

10
A Senufo wood bed, carved from a single piece of wood, an angled pillow section carved at one end, highly polished patina, 177cm (69⅝in), *L 25/26 June,* £1,430 ($2,016)

11
A Senufo chair, supported by four male and female caryatids, the curving arms and backrest carved with projecting porpianong bird's heads, painted details, h 88.9cm (35in), *NY 29/30 Nov,* $8,250 (£6,818)

12
An Ashanti wood stool, with incised linear decoration, the support in the form of a standing baboon, light brown patina, h 42cm (16½in), *L 25/26 June,* £825 ($1,163)

13
A French Ashanti style stool, of red lacquered wood, 'rainbow' shape, 59cm (23¼in), *L 3 Dec,* £1,430 ($1,716)

14
An Ashanti wood stool, with pierced circular support, a line of serrated decoration along each edge, reddish patina, and a miniature version of the same, h 45 and 14cm (17⅞ and 5⅞in), *L 25/26 June,* £418 ($589)

15
An Ashanti wood stool, the seat supported by a carved lion with incised mane, h 32.5cm (12¾in), *L 3 Dec,* £1,430 ($1,716)

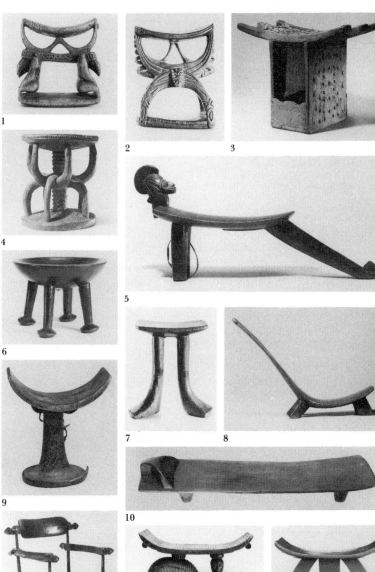

1
An Ashanti wood stool, the arched seat supported by a quadruped of cubistic form, 48.5cm (19in), *L 25/26 June,* £495 ($697)

2
An Ashanti stool, with broad curving seat and bird caryatid, 51.8cm (20⅜in), *NY 29/30 Nov,* $3,300 (£2,727)

3
A Duala wood stool, each side composed of three carved rings, curved seat section with incised decoration around the edge, 21cm (8¼in), *L 25/26 June,* £352 ($496)

4
A Cameroons stool, with ring base surmounted by the opposed forequarters of three leopards, each with deeply carved spots, 47.2cm (18⅝in), *NY 29/30 Nov,* $825 (£682)

5
A Cameroons table, three tiers of carved human heads between undulating bands forming the support, with blackened decoration, h 70cm (27½in), w 66cm (25⅞in), *L 3 Dec,* £825 ($990)

6
A Cameroons wood stool, the sides carved in a lattice pattern with animal (hyena) heads, 43.2cm (17in), *L 25/26 June,* £506 ($713)

7
A Luba neckrest, with oval base, and concave lozenge pillow with a flaring lateral panel carved with a lattice pattern at each side, 14cm (5½in), *NY 29/30 Nov,* $935 (£728)

8
A Chokwe stool, with incised decoration on the legs and supports, rectangular hide seat tightly and finely bound on the underside, 26cm (10¼in), *NY 29/30 Nov,* $660 (£545)

9
A Chokwe stool, the circular seat supported by a caryatid carrying a small child on her back, the coiffure incised, 41.5cm (16⅜in), *NY 29/30 Nov,* $990 (£818)

10
A Zambian (?) stool, with pierced ring base and flattened circular seat, the lattice-work body carved with a pair of opposed oval face masks, h 47cm (18½in), *NY 29/30 Nov,* $1,210 (£1,000)

11
A Kamba wood and metal chair, inlaid with brass and copper decorations, the edges and the pads of the feet covered with aluminium strips, large crack to rear of seat, 97cm (38⅛in), *L 25/26 June,* £1,210 ($1,706)

12
An East African chair, with pierced base ring, the seat surmounted by a flaring backrest carved with two openwork triangles behind the head, 126.4cm (49¾in), *NY 29/30 Nov,* $2,200 (£1,818)

13
Two Shona neckrests, one with pierced support, the other with a ribbed spherical centre to the support, 11.5 and 13cm (4½ and 5⅛in), *L 3 Dec,* £330 ($396)

14
A pair of Zulu wood stools, of light-coloured wood with darkened triangular decoration around the edges, 20 and 22cm (7⅞ and 8⅝in), *L 25/26 June,* £154 ($217)

15
A headrest/stool, Kenya or Ethiopia, with concave lozenge pillow and eccentric tripod supports, 22.2cm (8¾in), *NY 29/30 Nov,* $247 (£204)

1

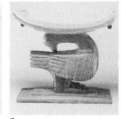

2

3

4

5

6

7

8

9

10

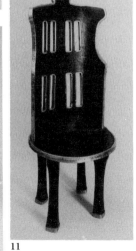

11

12

13

14

15

1
A Sumba turtle shell
comb, h 14.5cm (5¾in),
L 3 Dec,
£121 ($145)

2
**A Saramake winnowing
tray,** d 60.1cm (23⅝in),
NY 29/30 Nov,
$660 (£545)

3
**A Philippine Islands male
figure,** Ifugao, *bulul, the*
head with crescentic ears
in relief, pierced three
times at the top with two
wood plugs, traces of
hair remaining, encrusted
dark brown patina, 50.8cm
(20in), *NY 29/30 Nov,*
$1,100 (£916)

4
**A Philippine Islands
spoon,** Ifugao, the long
handle carved with three
pairs of embracing
human figures, 41.9cm
(16½in), *NY 29/30 Nov,*
$770 (£636)

5
**A New Guinea trophy
head,** overmodelled in
clay, with shells in the
eyes, painted with black
and red over a white
ground, strands of human
hair across the forehead,
16.6cm (6½in),
NY 29/30 Nov,
$1,540 (£1,272)

6
A Toraja wood head,
the eyes inset with bone
and with wood pupils,
darkened coiffure, the
nape of the neck incised
'Pal Jukan', 44cm (17⅜in),
L 3 Dec,
£1,210 ($1,452)

7
**A New Guinea trophy
head,** Iatmul, Middle Sepik
River, cowrie shells in
the eyes and inset
around the facial peri-
meter, painted with black
and red over a white
ground, an opercula shell
inset on the forehead,
human hair attachments,
19cm (7½in), *NY 29/30 Nov,*
$1,980 (£1,650)

8
**A New Guinea canoe
prow,** Middle Sepik area,
decorated with a fringe
of cassowary feathers,
red, black and white
pigment, 43.2cm (17in),
NY 29/30 Nov,
$1,870 (£1,558)

9
**A New Guinea suspension
hook** 73.7cm (29in),
NY 29/30 Nov,
$825 (£682)

10
A New Guinea comb,
Papuan Gulf,
rich brown patina,
remains of red and white
pigment, 32.1cm (12⅝in),
NY 29/30 Nov,
$825 (£688)

11
**A New Guinea female
figure,** Maliwe Village,
Washkuk area, Ambunti
Mountains, *nokwi,* red,
black and cream painted
details, remains of
human hair on the
genital area, 139.7cm
(55in), *NY 29/30 Nov,*
$1,430 (£1,192)

12
A New Guinea yam mask,
Washkuk area, Upper
Sepik River, *numau
ablatak,* used for the
mindja ceremony, red,
yellow, white and black
pigment, 130.2cm
(51¼in), *NY 29/30 Nov,*
$1,870 (£1,558)

13
A New Guinea mask,
Abelam area, red and
white painted details,
49.6cm (19½in),
NY 29/30 Nov,
$990 (£825)

14
**A Solomon Islands feather
currency roll,** Santa Cruz,
composed of a band of
matted fibre coil
decorated with the
scarlet head and breast
feathers of the honey
bird, 81.3cm (32in),
NY 29/30 Nov,
$1,760 (£1,467)

15
A Solomon Islands shield,
in coiled basketry tech-
nique, with plaited bind-
ings on the perimeter
and geometric patterns
in dark brown, 91.1cm
(33⅞in), *NY 29/30 Nov,*
$1,100 (£909)

16
A New Britain mask,
Gazelle Peninsula,
decorated with white
and red pigment, a crest
of human hair at the top,
25.4cm (10in),
NY 29/30 Nov,
$1,980 (£1,650)

1 2 3 4 5 6 7 8 9 10 11 12 13 14 15 16

1
A Fijian Islands cannibal fork, *ai qula ni bokola*, carved of reddish-brown wood with four straight prongs, cylindrical handle and oval grip, 29.5cm (11⅝in), *NY 29/30 Nov*, $660 (£550)

2
A Tongan Islands neckrest, *kali fafapo*, with concave pillow of lozenge section supported by a pair of broad curving arms each flaring at the base, rich brown patina, 31.4cm (12⅜in), *NY 29/30 Nov*, $1,320 (£1,100)

3
A Samoan wood club, the V-shaped handle terminating in a flattened top with a medial ridge at either side and transversal incised geometric decorations, fine patina, 59cm (23⅛in), *L 25/26 June*, £440 ($620)

4
A Marquesas Islands headdress, *peue ei*, composed of pierced porpoise teeth and strands of translucent blue and red glass trade beads bound to a double twisted coir band, looped at both ends, 25.4cm (10in), *NY 29/30 Nov*, $935 (£779)

5
A Maori nephrite pendant, *hei tiki*, carved of pale green stone, one pierced paua shell circlet for suspension, 12cm (4¾in), *NY 29/30 Nov*, $4,400 (£3,666)

6
A Maori nephrite figure pendant, *hei tiki*, hollowed circular eyerims, pierced for suspension, 6.7cm (2⅝in), *L 3 Dec*, £605 ($726)

7
A Maori wood handclub (*wahaika*), with a tiki figure along the back, a mask above the suspension hole, slight damage to the edge of the blade, the whole with a fine old patina, 39cm (15⅝in), *L 9 Apr*, £4,840 ($6,984)

8
A Maori wood figure, with clearly cut eye sockets, open mouth and *moko* scarification around the mouth and on the forehead, dark patina, the feet partly missing, 37.5cm (14¾in), *L 25/26 June*, £1,760 ($2,482)

9
A Maori whalebone handclub, *kotiate* with pinched 'sinus' on each side of the ovoid blade and a tiki head carved on the butt, incised and haliotis shell details, pierced for suspension, 31.5cm (12⅜in), *NY 29/30 Nov*, $1,210 (£1,000)

10
A Hawaiian Islands food bowl, *pakaka*, a rich brown patina on the exterior, d 30.5cm (12in), *NY 29/30 Nov*, $1,100 (£917)

11
A Hawaiian Islands meat bowl, *umeke ipu kai*, in highly polished *koa* wood, one oblong native repair, d 41.4cm (16¼in), *NY 29/30 Nov*, $1,980 (£1,650)

12
An Easter Island gorget, *rei miro*, of highly polished toromiro wood, carved in the form of a curving fish, shell and obsidian inlays in the eye, rich variegated brown patina 43.2cm (17in), *NY 29/30 Nov*, $13,200 (£11,000)

13
An aboriginal pearl shell pendant, Kimberly area, deeply incised with an abstract meander pattern darkened with reddish pigment, h 14.1cm (5⁹⁄₁₆in), *NY 29/30 Nov*, $1,650 (£1,375)

14
A Maori skirt, with woven *taniko* work waist band of varying shades of brown fibre, the skirt of flax leaf, the pattern formed by scorching, 50.5cm (19⅞in), *L 25/26 June*, £418 ($589)

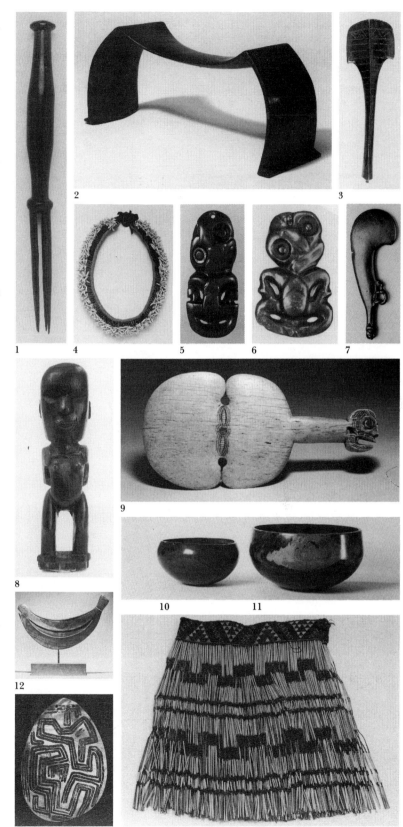

1
A Shipibo bowl, the cream ground decorated with linear patterns painted in orange and brown, h 14cm (5½in), *L 9 Apr,* £990 ($1,426)

2
A Pre-Columbian stone vessel, the stone veined and of hematite hue, with a seated figure at either side. This bowl may originate from the Guerrero/Colima area and date from around 200 BC. w 20cm (7⅞in), h 10.5cm (4⅛in), *L 3 Dec,* £3,080 ($3,696)

3
A Costa Rican stone trophy-head, Las Mercedes type, *c*AD 800-1500, 12cm (4¾in), *NY 27/28 Nov,* $1,100 (£917)

4
A Costa Rican stone metate, *c*AD 800-1500, in grey volcanic stone, the base a standing pelican with openwork pouch, 58.5cm (23in), *NY 27/28 Nov,* $3,575 (£2,979)

5
A Costa Rican lidded vessel, *c*AD 500-1000, similar to an incensario, with areas of black, white and reddish-brown pigment, h 45cm (17¾in), *NY 27/28 Nov,* $1,650 (£1,375)

6
A Costa Rican jade axe-god, *c*300 BC-AD 300, the beaked face with two smaller heads in profile within it, in blue-green stone, 17.1cm (6¾in), *NY 27/28 Nov,* $1,045 (£871)

7
A Paracas embroidered border fragment, Paracas Necropolis style, *c*400-100 BC, woven in cotton and wool, demon felines alternating with demon-masked mythological men, 40.6 x 11.5cm (16 x 4½in), *NY 27/28 Nov,* $1,980 (£1,650)

8
A gold breastplate, Veraguas, Panama, *c*AD 1000-1200. The number and placement of bosses on a breastplate may have been related to the status of the wearer; they were probably worn as pectorals specifically by warriors. d 28.9cm (11⅜in), *NY 27/28 Nov,* $14,300 (£11,917)

9
A Paracas bridge-spout vessel, *c*400-100 BC, incised on one side with a snarling feline's head with details in red pigment, d 15.3cm (6in), *NY 27/28 Nov,* $770 (£642)

10
A Paracas bowl, Callango style, *c*400-100 BC, the interior incised and painted with a stylised grinning puma, in ochre and red on a brownware ground, d 24.1cm (9½in), *NY 27/28 Nov,* $1,980 (£1,650)

11
A Middle Mochica warrior vessel, *c*AD 100-500, wearing a cape, skirt and helmet, painted in reddish-brown over a cream slip, h 22.2cm (8¾in), *NY 27/28 Nov,* $770 (£642)

12
A Middle Mochica monkey whistling vessel, *c*AD 100-500, in the form of a crouching monkey with tail and arms painted in red on the oblate body, the ears with pendent earrings, h 24.4cm (9⅝in), *NY 27/28 Nov,* $880 (£733)

13
A Middle Mochica portrait head vessel, *c*AD 100-500, the face symbolically painted and tattooed, in black, brown and deep red, h 28cm (11in), *NY 27/28 Nov,* $2,860 (£2,383)

14
A Mochica portrait head vessel, *c*AD 200-500, wearing a domed helmet, painted in brown and cream, h 29.5cm (11⅝in), *L 9 Apr,* £440 ($634)

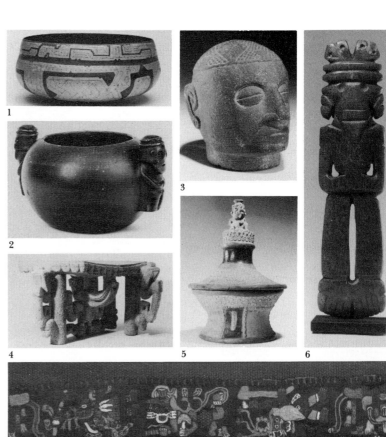

1
2
3
5
6

4
8
9
10

7

11
12
13
14

1

An early Nazca gold headdress ornament, c AD 300-600, the elongated projecting tongue of the repoussé 'bloodsucker' holding a captive figure, now headless, 40.6cm (16in), *NY 27/28 Nov,* $10,175 (£8,479)

2

A Tairona gold toucan pendant, c AD 1000-1500, a loop at the end of the beak for a dangle, now missing. The Tairona Indians, whose name means 'goldmakers', identified the toucan as *huacamaya,* the holy bird, h 12.8cm (5in), *NY 27/28 Nov,* $11,000 (£9,167)

3

An Inca silver beaker, Bolivia, c AD 1400-1532, the finial composed of four miniature llamas, h 17.2cm (6¾in), *NY 27/28 Nov,* $3,190 (£2,658)

4

A Teotihuacan stone figure of a warrior, classic, c. AD 250-650, in dark green stone mottled with black, h 18.5cm (7¼in), *NY 27/28 Nov,* $770 (£641)

5

A Las Bocas gadrooned bowl, middle preclassic, c.1150-550 BC, in thin buffware painted overall with uneven white slip, d 15.2cm (6in), *NY 27/28 Nov,* $5,225 (£4,354)

6

A Chancay wood funerary mask, Central Coast, c AD 1300-1450, clam shell eyes with pupils of twine and hair for the eyelashes, the facial plane painted in red, h 67.3cm (26½in), *NY 27/28 Nov,* $2,200 (£1,833)

7

An Ecuadorean gold bowl, colonial period, AD 1500-1650, various dents and small crack to the rim, h 12.5cm (5in), d 23.5cm (9¼in) *L 25/26 June,* £4,180 ($5,894)

8

A Lambayeque/Chimu gold funerary mask, c AD 900-1400, repoussé, pierced possibly for attachment, w 42.6cm (16¾in), *NY 27/28 Nov,* $3,410 (£2,841)

9

An Olmec carved vase, Las Bocas, middle preclassic, c 1150-550 BC, incised with an open-mouthed profile of the jaguar-dragon, remains of red pigment in all incised areas, h 10.5cm (4⅛in), *NY 27/28 Nov,* $11,000 (£9,167)

10

A pair of Chimu wood idols, Chan Chan area, c AD 1000-1400, one with face covered in red pigment and inlaid with spondyllus shell and turquoise stones, each inlaid on both sides with mother-of-pearl and spondyllus set into the wood with black resin, 52.4 and 50.2cm (20⅝ and 19¾in), *NY 27/28 Nov,* $8,800 (£7,333)

11

Three Tlatilco female figurines, middle preclassic, 1150-550 BC, each with traces of red and pigment, h 8.3 to 10.5cm (3¼-4⅛in), *NY 27/28 Nov,* $880 (£733)

12

A Mihoacán female figure, late preclassic, 300-100 BC, coffee-bean applied eyes, painted in brown, white and red, h 19cm (7½in), *NY 27/28 Nov,* $385 (£320)

13

A Colima duck vessel, protoclassic, 100 BC-AD 250, with a spout emerging from the back, painted overall in reddish-brown, 19.8cm (7¾in), *NY 27/28 Nov,* $880 (£733)

14

A Colima gadrooned vessel, protoclassic, 100 BC-AD 250, standing on three parrot-shaped supports, painted overall in reddish-brown, d 30cm (11¾in), *NY 27/28 Nov,* $770 (£642)

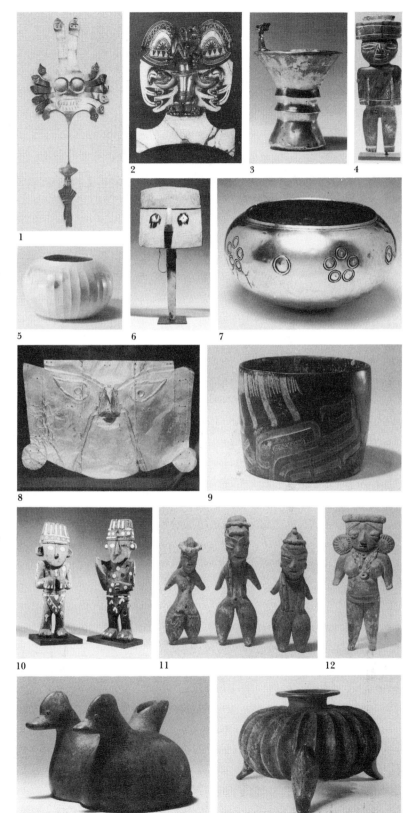

1
An Olmec jade ceremonial sceptre, middle preclassic, c.1150-550 BC, the translucent stone flecked with fine parallel streaks, in rich forest green stone, 11.3cm (4⁷/₁₆in), *NY 27/28 Nov,* **$13,200 (£11,000)**

2
An Olmec serpentine reclining figure, middle preclassic, c.1150-550 BC, the torso depicted frontally with criss-crossed arms and a 'baby' head jutting from the waist, h 9.5cm (3³/₄in), *NY 27/28 Nov,* **$7,975 (£6,646)**

3
A Guerrero stone figure, Mezcala, late preclassic, c.300-100 BC, in greyish-green stone, 12.5cm (4⁷/₈in), *NY 27/28 Nov,* **$660 (£550)**

4
A Huastec female figure, Panuco, late protoclassic, c.AD 100-300, remains of buff pigment overall, 14cm (5¹/₂in), *NY 27/28 Nov,* **$2,310 (£1,925)**

5
A Veracruz dancer, Juachín, late classic, c.AD 550-950, the detachable helmet mask in the form of an aged deity's head, remains of ochre pigment overall, 35.6cm (14in), *NY 27/28 Nov,* **$18,700 (£15,583)**

6
A Veracruz mould-made mother and child, late classic, c.AD 550-950, remains of white pigment overall, 12.3cm (4⁷/₈in), *NY 27/28 Nov,* **$770 (£642)**

7
A Veracruz terracotta pendant, classic/late classic, c.AD 250-950, in the form of the head Xipe-Totec, the face covered with the black of the firing, h 3.5cm (1³/₈in), *NY 27/28 Nov,* **$1,210 (£1,008)**

8
A Chupícuaro standing female figure, late preclassic, c.500-100 BC, the whole painted in reddish-brown with cream and black stepped and curvilinear designs ornamenting the face and body, 36.6cm (14³/₈in), *NY 27/28 Nov,* **$2,200 (£1,833)**

9
A Chupícuaro female figure, late preclassic, c.500-100 BC, the hollow figure painted overall in reddish-brown with cream and brown curvilinear designs, 33.2cm (13¹/₈in), *NY 27/28 Nov,* **$3,740 (£3,117)**

10
A Colima dog, protoclassic, c.100 BC-AD 250, a spout at the back, painted overall in reddish-orange, 22.9cm (9in), *NY 27/28 Nov,* **$880 (£733)**

11
A Colima standing dog, protoclassic, c.100 BC-AD 250, a spout at the back of the head, painted overall in reddish-brown, 36.9cm (14¹/₂in), *NY 27/28 Nov,* **$1,650 (£1,375)**

12
A Colima snake, protoclassic, c.100 BC-AD 250, with incised scales, painted overall in reddish-brown, d 33cm (13in), *NY 27/28 Nov,* **$1,430 (£1,192)**

13
A Colima dog, protoclassic, c.100 BC-AD 250, painted in brownish-black, h 33.6cm (13¹/₄in), *NY 27/28 Nov,* **$7,150 (£5,958)**

14
A Colima dog, protoclassic, c.100 BC-AD 250, painted overall in reddish-brown, 49.5cm (19¹/₂in), *NY 27/28 Nov,* **$5,500 (£4,583)**

1   2   3

4   5   6   7

8   9   10

11   12

13   14

1
A Chinesco female figure,
protoclassic, *c*.100 BC-
AD 250, painted overall
in reddish-brown with
remains of black resist
circular decoration,
some details painted in
buff, 23.5cm (9¼in),
NY 27/28 Nov,
$2,530 (£2,108)

2
**A large Jalisco male
figure,** protoclassic, *c*.100
BC-AD 250, with black
resist decoration
indicating the waist
band, painted in
reddish-brown and buff,
65.3cm (25¾in)
NY 27/28 Nov,
$8,250 (£6,875)

3
A Jalisco face mask,
protoclassic, *c*.100 BC-
AD 250, with extensive
remains of white
pigment, pierced four
times along the crown
for attachments, h 16.9cm
(6⅝in), *NY 27/28 Nov,*
$2,090 (£1,742)

4
A Jalisco musician,
protoclassic, *c*.100 BC-
AD 250, painted overall
in buff, details in red
and white, 32.5cm
(12¾in), *NY 27/28 Nov,*
$1,045 (£871)

5
**A Jalisco seated female
figure,** protoclassic,
100 BC-AD 250, painted
overall in buff, details in
black, 39.5cm (15½in),
NY 27/28 Nov,
$825 (£688)

6
**A preclassic stone mace-
head,** possibly from
Kaminaljuyu, late
preclassic, *c*.300-100 BC,
in brownish-green
opaque stone, d 9.5cm
(3½in), *NY 27/28 Nov,*
$1,430 (£1,192)

7
A Mayan figural vessel,
classic, *c*.AD 250-650, the
torso of the seated
priestess forming the lid,
33cm (13in),
NY 27/28 Nov,
$3,520 (£2,933)

8
A Mayan bowl,
Highlands, early classic,
c.AD 250-550, the
interior painted in a rich
orange slip, d 51.5cm
(20¼in), *NY 27/28 Nov,*
$990 (£825)

9
**A Mayan orangeware
cylinder vessel,** Central
Lowlands, late classic,
c.AD 550-950, finely
incised with an audience
scene showing the Twin
Lords, h 23.9cm (9⅜in),
NY 27/28 Nov,
$15,400 (£12,833)

10
**A Mayan polychrome
tripod dish,** late classic,
c.AD 550-950, painted
with a 'jumping deer'
motif, black and orange
on a pale orange
ground, d 30.5cm
(12½in), *NY 27/28 Nov,*
$2,200 (£1,833)

11
A Mayan tripod dish,
Central Lowlands, late
classic, *c*.AD 550-950, the
tondo painted with the
Water-Lily Jaguar, the
rim decorated in orange
and with black jaguar
spots. The Water-Lily
Jaguar, well known in
the Underworld, is
closely associated with
sacrifice by decapitation.
d 33cm (13in),
NY 27/28 Nov,
$8,800 (£7,333)

12
A Mayan cylinder vessel,
Naranjo style, late
classic, *c*.AD 550-950,
painted in jet black on
pale and dark orange,
23.3cm (9⅛in),
NY 27/28 Nov,
$12,100 (£10,083)

13
A Mayan carved bowl,
Highlands, late classic,
c.AD 550-950, in high
relief with a complex
scene involving pairs of
seated deities, h 12cm
(4¾in), *NY 27/28 Nov,*
$3,300 (£2,750)

14
A Mayan bowl,
Highlands, late classic,
c.AD 550-950, painted in
dark orange and black
on a buff slip, d 22.8cm
(9in), *NY 27/28 Nov,*
$1,430 (£1,192)

American Indian Art

ELLEN NAPIURA

Sales of American Indian art consist of the work of the indigenous inhabitants of North America and of a small area of northern Mexico. The objects are listed in the catalogue according to the geographic location of the various tribal groups—the Woodlands or Eastern and North-eastern United States and Canada, the Great Lakes, the Plains, the South-west, and the Pacific Coast north through British Columbia and Alaska. Of course, the boundaries we know today did not exist when these peoples inhabited and governed these territories.

Excavations in areas such as Mississippi, Arizona and St Lawrence Island off the coast of Alaska have provided evidence of peoples who lived there well before the arrival of Columbus in 1492, and even before AD 1000. There were once more than 1,000 tribes and subgroups of Indians; many did not survive the arrival of the white man and many others did not survive the ultimate conquest of their land.

For most of them it was the environment and their day to day needs that provided the impetus for the art and artefacts they created. They gradually refined their skills, as a matter of prestige and pride, passing them from one generation to the next until the day when the commercially manufactured goods that traders brought to them replaced most of the traditional objects. Some of the rarest items, and today some of the most desirable, are ceremonial. To ensure that all the power should be contained in them these could only be created by the shaman or medicine man.

Certain items were traditionally made by women, such as the blankets woven by the south-western Navajo and the Chilkat Tlingit of Alaska, and the pots that were made at the Rio Grande pueblos and then painted by husbands or sons. Nature supplied the natives with all their own materials, from raw ingredient to finished product. Weavers, for example, cultivated the soil to provide the right fodder for their sheep, so that the wool would be of the correct consistency and curl for carding, spinning, and, ultimately, for weaving.

Looking at the geographical areas one can identify specific types of object that are particular to each. From the eastern areas come porcupine quillwork, moosehair embroidery, some beading on tradecloth, utilitarian wooden objects and ceremonial pieces, including dolls and masks, such as those made by the Iroquois. From the Great Lakes come floral and geometrically beaded bandoleer bags, wooden clubs and pipe stems with red catlinite pipeheads. South-eastern tribes, such as the Seminole, Creek and Delaware Indians, produced profusely beaded bandoleers with complex floral patterns, finger-woven garters and sashes, ceremonial wood sculpture, and some basketry and pottery, most of it prehistoric. The states in the Plains beaded hides with symbolic and geometric patterns or painted them with historical records or buffalo counts, and produced wood and stone weaponry, some of which was combined with items obtained through trade. From the Plateau area come beaded hide ornaments and clothes, often with larger trade beads, storage bags made of cornhusks and embroidered with yarn or dyed grass, and dentalium shell headdresses. In the South-west, in addition to the pottery of ancient cultures, are found historic and contemporary pottery, silverwork, textiles, baskets, ceremonial items, including small Hopi wood kachina dolls and dance regalia, and watercolours. Californian Indians produced some of the finest baskets still in existence, as did those Indians from the Nevada Basin area. Further north one finds the master carvers from British Columbia and Alaska producing great masks, frontlets, fantastic feast dishes and boxes to store these items. The finest use of bone and ivory, copper and steel, and argillite, a stone found only in the Queen Charlotte Islands, is found here. From further north in Alaska come Eskimo ivory sculpture and utilitarian objects, clothing and hunting equipment made from parts of the seal, walrus and whale, while the Tlingit of the Central Alaska finger wove fine ceremonial blankets and tunics, engraved silver, and made objects similar to those created by their British Columbian neighbours.

1
A Zuni polychrome dough bowl, d 43.5cm (17⅛in), *NY 25/26 Oct,* $1,760 (£1,443)

2
A Zuni terracotta jar, h 23cm (9in), *L 3 Dec,* £825 ($990)

3
A Zuni polychrome effigy vessel, in the form of an owl, painted over a white slip in black and red with feather decoration and other details, h 45.1cm (9⅞in), *NY 27/28 Apr,* $2,090 (£1,462)

1

2

3

1
An Acoma polychrome jar, painted over a creamy-white slip in black and two shades of red, d 30.5cm (12in), *NY 27/28 Apr*, $880 (£615)

2
A Qahatika canteen, with three small pierced ring handles, painted over a pale red slip in black, one handle broken away, neck repaired, h 19.1cm (7½in), *NY 27/28 Apr*, $935 (£654)

3
A Casas Grandes polychrome jar, *c* AD 1160-1260, painted over a pinkish-cream slip in black and deep orange, d 26cm (10¼in), *NY 27/28 Apr*, $577 (£403)

4
A Casas Grandes polychrome jar, *c* AD 1160-1260, painted over a cream slip in black and red, h 23.5cm (9¼in), *NY 27/28 Apr*, $440 (£308)

5
A Four Mile polychrome olla, *c* AD 1250-1350, painted over a reddish slip in black and cream, d 19.7cm (7¾in), *NY 25/26 Oct*, $495 (£406)

6
A Mimbres black-on-white picture bowl, *c* AD 950-1150, painted on the interior with a figure combining human and animal attributes, d 14.5cm (5¹¹/₁₆in), *NY 25/26 Oct*, $990 (£811)

7
A Hohokam red-on-buff jar, Santa Cruz Phase, *c* AD 500-900, painted with a fringed and serrated band enclosing rows of 'negative' circles, d 20.3cm (8in), *NY 25/26 Oct*, $330 (£270)

8
A Hopi polychrome jar, painted black and pale red, over a burnished cream slip, an old label remaining on the base, 'made by Nampeyo Hopi', d 26cm (10½in), *NY 27/28 Apr*, $990 (£692)

9
A San Ildefonso blackware jar, the shoulder painted against a highly polished gunmetalware slip with a band containing 'negative' feathers and two double spirals, inscribed 'Adam + Santana', d 14.6cm (5¾in), *NY 25/26 Oct*, $1,485 (£1,217)

10
A San Ildefonso blackware vase, painted over the polished slip in matte, inscribed on the base, 'Marie', h 28.6cm (11¼in), *NY 27/28 Apr*, $2,310 (£1,615)

11
A San Ildefonso blackware plate, finely painted over the polished ground in matte, inscribed on the base 'Marie & Santana', d 27.3cm (10¾in), *NY 27/28 Apr*, $1,760 (£1,231)

12
A Jeddito 'spatter-ware' bowl *c* AD 1300-1600, with rounded body, tapering shoulder and cylindrical rim, the interior decorated with a human hand, restored, d 23.8cm (9⅜in), *NY 27/28 Apr*, $2,475 (£1,731)

1
An Apache coiled storage
jar, olla, woven in willow
and devil's claw, the row
around the base
surmounted by human
figures, horses, dogs and
geometric devices in the
field, h 40cm (15¾in),
NY 27/28 Apr,
$3,960 (£2,769)

2
An Apache coiled tray,
woven in willow and
devil's claw with a
rosette motif on the flat
base, two bands of
'negative' geometric devices
on the flaring sides,
d 44.3cm (17½in),
NY 27/28 Apr,
$1,540 (£1,077)

3
An Apache coiled tray,
tightly woven in willow
and devil's claw with a
double rosette motif, a
row of checkered
triangles at the rim,
d 17.8cm (7in),
NY 27/28 Apr,
$357 (£250)

4
An Apache coiled tray,
woven in willow and
devil's claw with a
radiating meander design,
four standing horses
below the rim, d 45.1cm
(17¾in), *NY 27/28 Apr,*
$990 (£692)

5
A Pomo twined burden
basket, woven in sedge
root and redbud with a
radiating diagonal pattern
of parallelograms bisected
by zigzags, d 34.3cm
(13½in), *NY 25/26 Oct*
$990 (£811)

6
A Pomo twined utility
basket, woven in 'shu-set'
weave in sedge root and
redbud, the warps open
at the rim, d 20.2cm
(8in), *NY 27/28 Apr,*
$605 (£423)

7
A Panamint coiled
polychrome utility basket,
woven in willow,
bulrush and red yucca
root, d 56.4cm (22¼in),
NY 27/28 Apr,
$2,750 (£1,923)

8
A Panamint coiled bowl,
very finely and tightly
woven on a three-rod
willow foundation in
willow and dyed bulrush
root, fine and broad
ticking on the rim,
d 20.3cm (8in),
NY 27/28 Apr,
$5,500 (£3,846)

9
A California Mission coiled
polychrome tray, woven
in pale brown sumac,
variegated yellow and
black-dyed rush with a
'whirling' design, d 41.3cm
(16¼in), *NY 27/28 Apr,*
$1,320 (£923)

10
A Yurok/Karok twined polychrome basket, decorated
in half-twist overlay
technique, in various
colours against a pale
yellow bear grass ground,
d 22.2cm (8¾in),
NY 25/26 Oct,
$550 (£451)

11
A Klikatat coiled basket,
woven from cedar root,
imbricated with two rows
of standing human figures
in dark and reddish
brown against a pale
yellow ground, d 20cm
(7⅞in), *NY 27/28 Apr,*
$1,210 (£846)

12
A Yurok twined utility
basket, woven in pale
yellow with a serrated
zigzag band between rows
of right triangles, h 49.8cm
(19⅝in), *NY 25/26 Oct,*
$1,210 (£992)

13
An Attu twined lidded
basket, woven with open-
work sections on the
base, embroidered in
purple, red and pale
green silk thread,
h 11.4cm (4½in),
NY 27/28 Apr,
$1,540 (£1,077)

14
An Achumawi twined utility
basket, finely woven with
a band of 'negative'
terraced lozenges flanked
by interlocked meanders,
four arrows below the
rim, d 28.2cm (11⅛in),
NY 27/28 Apr,
$990 (£692)

1
A classic Saltillo serape, finely woven in two vertical panels, cochineal purple, red and pink, indigo blue and blue-green, and wood brown detail against a natural ivory ground, 237 x 127cm (93½ x 50in), NY 25/26 Oct, $11,000 (£9,016)

2
A Navajo fringed Germantown blanket, woven with an 'eye dazzler' pattern in black, white, loden and bright green, maroon, purplish-grey and mustard and orange yellow against a red ground, the yarn fringe worn, 136 x 80cm (53½ x 31½in), NY 27/28 Apr, $2,750 (£1,923)

3
A Navajo fringed Germantown blanket, 'Sunday Saddle', woven in white, light green and shaded purple on a pale and bright red ground, 83 x 68cm (32¾ x 26¾in), NY 27/28 Apr, $935 (£654)

4
A classic Navajo chief's blanket, woven in handspun and re-carded yarn with a Third Phase pattern, in red, white and dark indigo blue against linear bands with a brighter indigo, the background stripe in natural ivory and brown, 189 x 136cm (74⅝ x 53½in), NY 25/26 Oct, $5,500 (£4,508)

5
A late classic Navajo serape, woven in white, pale green, pink and shaded bright red three-ply commercial yarn, 183 x 133cm (72 x 52¼in), NY 25/26 Oct, $6,600 (£5,410)

6
A transitional Navajo blanket, woven in a single-ply commercial yarn in black and white over a deep red ground, 215 x 152cm (84¾ x 60in), NY 27/28 Apr, $4,125 (£2,885)

7
A transitional Navajo blanket, woven on natural ivory ground in golden yellow, shades of pale red and bright and dark indigo blue, 200 x 117cm (79 x 46in), NY 25/26 Oct, $3,300 (£2,705)

8
A transitional Navajo wedge blanket, woven on a shaded red handspun ground in beige, black, golden yellow, indigo blue and natural white, 203 x 142cm (80 x 56in), NY 25/26 Oct, $4,675 (£3,832)

9
A classic Navajo child's blanket, woven in natural white and indigo blue dyed handspun and pale maroon and rich red commercial and ravelled yarn, 126 x 60cm (49½ x 29¾in), NY 25/26 Oct, $10,450 (£8,566)

1

2

3

4

5

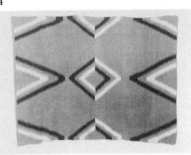
6

7

8

9

1
A Bella Coola wood secret society bird monster mask, to be used by the *Hamatsa,* black and red scalloped and curvilinear painted details, a cotton cord for movement of the hinged lower jaw, 105.7cm (41⅝in), *NY 25/26 Oct,* $7,700 (£6,311)

2
An Iroquois wood mask, carved for the False Face Society representing 'Old Broken Nose', tiny pierced oval eyes and deeply carved wrinkles on the cheeks, h 27.9cm (11in), *NY 27/28 Apr,* $990 (£692)

3
A Plains wood and stone pipe, composed of a red catlinite pipehead and wood stem bound on the grip with red, yellow, purple and faded blue plaited porcupine quill-work, panels of bird's feathers, red horsehair and green silk ribbon, 80.6cm (31¾in), *NY 25/26 Oct,* $1,100 (£902)

4
A Plains wood and stone pipe, composed of a red catlinite pipehead, the wood stem carved in high relief, inscribed in ink 'Purchased from Crazy Horse, Oelrichs S.D. Nov. 24th-92', 89.5cm (35¼in), *NY 25/26 Oct,* $4,675 (£3,832)

5
A Plains wood and stone pipe, decorated with a burnished pattern, brass tacks and red pigment, the black stone pipehead with inlaid lead decoration, inscribed 'From July 4th, 1899, Chief White Cloud', 87.6cm (34½in), *NY 27/28 Apr,* $2,640 (£1,846)

6
A Kwakiutl wood hawk totem, red, green, white, black and yellow painted details, inscribed on the back 'Kwin-Kwin-Qua-Lee-Gee, Khutze Inlet, B.C., 1928, made by Charlie James, Indian of Alert Bay, B.C.', h 76.2cm (30in) *NY 27/28 Apr,* $2,200 (£1,538)

7
A Kwakiutl wood model totem pole, the finial carved as an eagle, polychrome decoration, 105cm (41⅜in), *L 3 Dec,* £2,640 ($3,168)

8
A Northwest Coast wood model totem pole, carved in shallow and sunk relief red, black and green painted details, 74.6cm (29⅜in), *NY 27/28 Apr,* $2,090 (£1,462)

9
A Tlingit fish club, the butt carved as a human figure, the hair in the form of a salmon, 60cm (23⅝in), *L 9 Apr,* £792 ($1,140)

10
A Nootkan whalebone club, the finial carved as an eagle's head, two human faces on either side and a lightning serpent on either side of the blade, pierced for a strap, 57.5cm (22⅝in), *L 9 Apr,* £1,870 ($2,693)

11
A Tlingit steel and bone knife, rich blue-green abalone shell plaques inset in the teeth, cheeks, nostrils and eyes (four missing), yellow patina, inscribed 'Ft. Tongass, Alaska, 1886', 34.2cm (13½in), *NY 25/26 Oct,* $7,150 (£5,861)

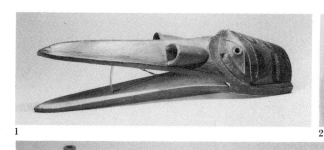
1

2

3

4

5

6

7   8   9   10   11

1
Two Navajo silver and turquoise band bracelets, one set with a large tear-shaped pale blue turquoise stone, the other with a cluster of deep green turquoise stones, w 6.1 and 5.7cm (2⅜ and 2¼in), *NY 25/26 Oct*, $440 (£361)

2
A Haida silver bracelet, engraved with a sea mammal, probably a whale, hatched and filed details, w 5.5cm (2⅛in), *NY 25/26 Oct*, $880 (£721)

3
Two Navajo silver and turquoise wrist ornaments, including an expanding man's bracelet, together with a leather *ketoh* surmounted by a silver plaque set with two deep green turquoise stones, w 7cm (2¾in), 9.2cm (3⅝in), *NY 25/26 Oct*, $660 (£541)

4
A Navajo silver and turquoise bracelet, w 7cm (2¾in), *NY 25/26 Oct*, $396 (£325)

5
A Navajo silver and turquoise band bracelet, set with pale blue oval turquoise stones, w 7.9cm, (3⅛in, *NY 25/26 Oct*, $440 (£361)

6
A Canadian silver cross of Lorraine or Jesuit Cross, bearing the stamp 'CA' (Charles Arnoldi, 1779-1817), h 13.7cm (5⁷/₁₆in), *NY 25/26 Oct*, $1,760 ($1,443)

7
A Navajo silver and turquoise band bracelet, w 8.2cm (3¼in), *NY 25/26 Oct*, $467 (£383)

8
A Navajo silver and turquoise squash blossom necklace, strung on hide, 41.2cm (16¼in), *NY 27/28 Apr*, $1,650 (£1,154)

9
Two Southwest silver and turquoise pins, 10.7cm (4⁹/₁₆in), w 9.6cm (3¾in), *NY 25/26 Oct*, $220 (£180)

10
A Navajo silver and hide belt, 92.1cm (36¼in), *NY 25/26 Oct*, $880 (£721)

11
A Northeastern beaded cloth bandoleer, with opaque and translucent glass seed beads against a red tradecloth ground, trimmed with blue, black and green silk ribbon and opaque white glass beads, 75cm (29½in), *NY 25/26 Oct*, $2,860 (£2,344)

12
A Cree Indian woman's hood, mid-19th cent, of black tradecloth, with suspended strands of multi-coloured beads, the sides applied with red, yellow, blue and green ribbon, 63.5cm (25in), *L 9 Apr*, £3,132 ($4,510)

13
A Plains beaded and fringed hide girl's dress, the yoke decorated with yellow, white, pale green, dark blue and translucent red glass beadwork against a pale blue ground, the hem similar, 58.7cm (23⅛in), *NY 27/28 Apr*, $2,200 (£1,538)

14
A pair of Plains quilled hide moccasins, in yellow and shades of deep purple dyed porcupine quillwork, a narrow strip of pale green quillwork around the front, 23.4cm (9¼in), *NY 27/28 Oct*, $1,320 (£923)

15
A Northern Plains cradle-board, composed of a wood frame overlaid with hide, decorated in yellow and translucent red and green on a white ground, the hood trimmed with red and blue tradecloth, 86.3cm (34in), *NY 25/26 Oct*, $880 (£721)

16
A Sioux beaded hide man's vest, stitched in yellow, light green, pale and dark blue, translucent red and faceted silver against a white beadwork ground, 50.2cm (19¾in), *NY 27/28 Apr*, $660 (£462)

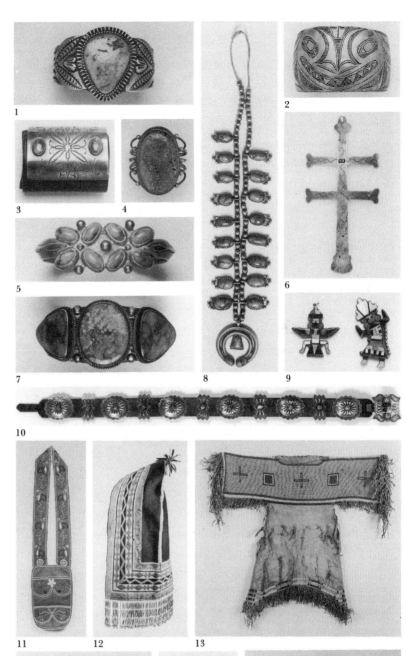
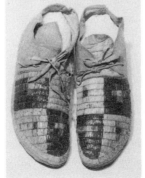

1
A Hopi wood kachina doll,
representing Ho-ó-te or
Ahote, wearing a black
case mask, a star and
crescent moon painted
on the cheeks, feathers
inserted on the top and
back of the head, h 24.1cm
(9½in), *NY 27/28 Apr,*
$880 (£615)

2
A Hopi wood kachina doll,
possibly representing the
Navajo or Tasaf kachina,
with brown painted body
and green case mask, a
single ear decorated with
red horsehair, a red forehead, h 32.3cm (12¾in),
NY 27/28 Apr,
$880 (£615)

3
A Plains hide doll, wearing
a beaded and fringed
hide dress, long necklace,
tiny beaded mouth and
eyes, braided human hair
coiffure, h 53.2cm (21in),
NY 25/26 Oct,
$990 (£811)

4
A Mohave polychrome doll,
enclosed in a cradle of
wood rods, cloth and
vegetables fibres, with
cotton cord and blue
wool yarn wrappings,
the face with red, yellow,
black and white painted
details, horsehair coiffure,
NY 25/26 Oct,
$1,320 (£1,082)

5
**An Eskimo whale baleen
basket,** woven in three
shades of baleen, the
fitted lid surmounted by
an ivory knob in the form
of a polar bear's head,
inlaid nostrils and eyes,
an ivory disc in the base
engraved 'Barrow, Alaska',
d 10.6cm (4⅛in),
NY 25/26 Oct,
$412 (£338)

6
**An Eskimo whale baleen
basket,** woven in pale
yellow baleen, the ivory
handle carved in the form
of a seal pup's head,
engraved mouth and
whiskers, drilled and inlaid
eyes, d 8.3cm (3¼in),
NY 25/26 Oct,
$605 (£496)

7
An Eskimo ivory needlecase,
carved in the form of a
swimming ribbon seal
with engraved coat
darkened with pigment
and 'negative' linear
bands encircling the collar,
side and tail fins, 9.9cm
(3⅞in), *NY 27/28 Apr,*
$1,100 (£769)

8
**An Eskimo ivory bowhead
whale ornament,** Okvik
site, Punuk Island, prob-
ably Old Bering Sea
(Classic) period, *c* AD 300,
yellow patina, 10.9cm
(5¹/₁₆in), *NY 27/28 Apr,*
$770 (£538)

9
**An Eskimo ivory bow drill
mouthpiece,** Papghan Ken-
lenga site, St. Lawrence
Island, Thule or
possibly earlier, *c* AD
1200-1700, with a deeply
drilled cavity below for
attachment of the drill,
yellowed patina, 5.9cm
(2⁵/₁₆in), *NY 27/28 Apr,*
$715 (£500)

10
**A Siberian Eskimo ivory
tusk,** finely engraved
with whale and seal
hunting scenes, darkened
in black and red pigment,
a silver cap on the wider
end, 54cm (21¼in),
NY 27/28 Apr,
$1,650 (£1,154)

11
**An Eskimo ivory harpoon
nest,** from a *umiak* prow,
carved in two sections
joined together by ivory
and baleen plugs, in the
form of polar bears, the
drilled nostrils, eyes and
ears with remains of inlay,
ivory chains suspended
below, w 15.9cm (6¼in),
94.9cm (37⅜in),
NY 25/26 Oct,
$13,200 (£10,819)

12
An Eskimo ivory doll,
Okvik site, Punuk Island,
1st millennium BC, with
engraved angular mark-
ings, incised scarification
on the chin and cheeks
and engraved eyebrows,
black patina, h 7.6cm
(3in), *NY 27/28 Apr,*
$1,430 (£1,000)

1

5

6

7

8

2

3

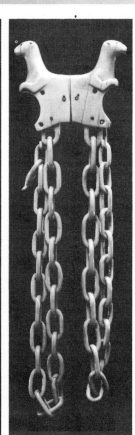

9

4

10

11

12

1
A Veracruz standing priestess, Nopiloa, late classic, c AD 550-950, the mould-made rattle figure with remains of white pigment overall, decorative details in black, 36.9cm (14½in),
NY 27/28 Nov,
$17,600 (£14,667)

2
An Aztec basalt figure of the 'Goddess with Tasselled Headdress', c AD 1440-1520, her recessed throat once inlaid, in grey volcanic stone with traces of red and ochre pigment on the face. This goddess is often identified as Chalchiuhtlicue, the goddess of water, 43.2cm (17in),
NY 27/28 Nov,
$27,500 (£22,917)

3
A Chinesco seated female figure, Type C, protoclassic, c 100 BC-AD 250, painted overall in rich ochre-coloured slip with ornamental details at the waist, arms and face in red pigment, 26cm (10¼in),
NY 27/28 Nov,
$10,725 (£8,938)

4
A Tlatilco bowl, middle preclassic, c 1150-550 BC, in thin orange-buffware with white slip overall, possibly of Veracruz origin, h 14.3cm (5⅝in),
NY 27/28 Nov,
$20,900 (£17,417)

5
A contemporary Pima coiled polychrome tray, Kathryn Josa, c 1975, finely woven on a pale willow ground in black devil's claw and reddish-brown yucca root, d 37.7cm (14⅞in),
NY 25/26 Oct,
$4,610 (£3,787)

6
A Northwest Coast wood wolf headdress, probably Tlingit, in light weathered wood, blue and black painted details, remains of copper sheets on the teeth, remains of hide headstrap at the back, one ear fragmentary, 25.4cm (10in),
NY 25/26 Oct,
$11,000 (£9,016)

7
A Haida wood rattle, carved in two sections and joined together with iron nails and cotton cord, green, black and red painted details, h 31.8cm (12½in),
NY 27/28 Apr,
$22,000 (£15,385)

8
A classic Navajo serape, finely woven on a natural white handspun ground in shades of dark brown and rich indigo blue, 230 x 132cm (90½ x 52in),
NY 25/26 Oct,
$44,000 (£36,066)

1
**A Djenne terracotta
figure,** kneeling in an
attitude of pain, a raised
zigzag line down the
spine and arms, 17cm
(6¾in), *L 25-26 June,*
£1,980 ($2,792)

2
**A Marquesas Islands stone
tiki figure,** powerfully
carved with the
musculature of the squat
body clearly delineated,
a small section of the
right knee restored, 14.3cm
(5¾in), *L 9 Apr,*
£5,060 ($7,302)

3
**A Shankadi wood female
figure,** kneeling and
holding a bowl with a
conical lid, the head with
worn features, the left
arm with native repairs,
wearing a necklace of
white glass beads, dark
worn patina, 33cm (13in),
L 25/26 June,
£4,070 ($5,739)

4
**A Bwiti wood reliquary
figure,** covered with
flattened copper and brass
wire and sheeting, 41cm
(16⅛in), *L 25/26 June,*
£3,520 ($4,963)

5
**A Yombe wood fetish
figure,** the finely carved
head with flattened nose
and mirror-inset eyes,
the fetish material at the
front and on the top of
the head missing, fine
brown patina, 34.5cm
(13⅝in), *L 25/26 June,*
£6,600 ($9,306)

6
**An Easter Island dance
paddle,** carved in the
form of an abstract male
figure, rich reddish-
brown patina with
lighter areas on the grip
and one side of the
blade, 80.7cm (31¾in),
NY 29/30 Nov,
$38,500 (£32,083)

1

2

3

4

5

6

1

An Egyptian turquoise faience seal of Amenhotep II, 18th dynasty, reign of Amenhotep II, 1439-1413 BC, one side moulded in sunk relief with the prenomen of the king 'Acheprure', his nomen on the reverse, 1.8cm (⅝in), *NY 1/2 Mar*, **$660 (£446)**

2

A bronze figure of Bastet, 26th dynasty, 664-525 BC, the cat-headed goddess striding on a rectangular base with two kittens crouching at her feet, the god Nefertum cradled in her left arm, h 12.1cm (4¾in), *NY 1/2 Mar*, **$8,800 (£5,902)**

3

An Egyptian bronze figure of a cat, Late Period, 712-30 BC, with pointed ears, the eyes recessed for inlay, 22.2cm (8¾in), *L 21 May*, **£8,250 ($11,880)**

4

A dark blue sandcore glass alabastron, 4th cent BC, horizontal rim edged with yellow trailing and twin trailed handles, the body decorated with opaque yellow and white trailing, repaired and with minute areas of restoration, 16.5cm (6½in), *L 9/10 July*, **£3,850 ($5,275)**

5

An iridescent pale green glass pilgrim flask, *c*6th cent AD, the base indented with moulded rosette and pontil mark, multi-coloured iridescence and some encrustation, small section of rim missing, 16.5cm (6½in), *L 9/10 July*, **£6,050 ($8,289)**

6

A dark blue mould-blown glass flask, 1st/2nd cent AD, a greenish-blue trailed handle attached to the shoulder and neck, the body with vertical ribbing, some encrustation, 8cm (3⅛in), *L 10 Dec*, **£825 ($1,040)**

1

2

3

4

5

6

1
An Etruscan nenfro sphinx,
Vulci, *c* mid-6th cent
BC, of Ionian inspiration,
with long spiral tresses
over her shoulders,
66cm (26in), *NY 8 June,*
$16,500 (£11,870)

2
A Sicilian terracotta antefix,
*c.*500 BC, in the form of
a gorgoneion mask, with
two rows of snail locks,
snakes in relief on either
side of the face, 33.7cm
(13¼in), *L 9/10 July,*
£3,850 ($5,275)

3
**A Roman bronze figure of
Herakles,** *c.* 2nd/3rd cent
AD, lower part of legs
missing, 17.8cm (7in),
L 21 May,
£3,520 ($5,069)

4
**A Hellenistic terracotta
figure of a young woman,**
Apulia, *c.*330-220 BC,
27.4cm (10¾in), *L 9/10 July,*
£715 ($980)

5
An Ionian pottery amphora,
6th cent BC, decorated
with black-glazed horizontal bands, the handles,
interior and exterior rim
also black-glazed, 31.8cm
(12½in), *L 9/10 July,*
£1,760 ($2,411)

6
**A Roman marble bearded
male head,** *c.* 1st/2nd cent
AD, probably from a
herm, 33.7cm (13¼in),
L 10 Dec,
£7,150 ($9,009)

1

4

2

5

3

6

Antiquities

FELICITY NICHOLSON • RICHARD KERESEY

Antiquities is a vast and complex collecting area, embracing civilizations which rose and fell in successive and overlapping waves from the 6th millennium BC to the 10th century of our own era, and encompasssing territories stretching from Scandinavia to Ethiopia, from Afghanistan to Spain. A love and knowledge of history is a prime motivation of the collector in this field. Antiquities are in themselves a vivid evocation of our past, and are often the only source of information available to us. This strong historical force is not unique to antiquities, of course, but it probably has greater relevance here than in any other field.

The other factors which motivate and influence the collector are common to all fields of art and antiques: aesthetic appeal, quality, rarity, and state of preservation. The number of ancient works of art and utilitarian objects which survive intact is surprising, but fragments, especially of marble sculpture or Greek painted pottery, are much sought after if the quality is high. Restoration and remodelling often have an adverse effect on price. Some collectors concentrate in a specific area, but most eventually develop a collection which includes several: Greek pottery, Egyptian stone sculpture, Roman glass, Near Eastern bronzes and Roman portraits, for example. The fact that the subject is so wide makes it all the more interesting and ensures that there are still plenty of unresearched areas.

The pleasures of collecting in this field are tremendous and far outweigh the well-known problem of authenticity. When a question does arise, it can seldom be answered either by the object's provenance or by reliance on a single expert. And science, at present, can play only a limited role. The body of expertise depends chiefly on recognized specialists in each area, those who combine experience with the proverbial 'good eye', or, in other words, have an informed intutition. Consensus is the key, and the collector should have a keen ear as well as a keen eye. He can, if he is shrewd, still find good pieces for just a few hundred pounds or dollars: a small Roman bronze of the 1st-3rd century AD, for instance, or a small Greek or South Italian vase of the 4th century BC. A pleasing piece of Roman glass can cost as little as £200-300 ($225-350).

The rewards of collecting antiquities are evident from a single visit to a great museum. Objects of merit worth only a few hundreds of pounds or dollars stand close by those worth many millions. It is a field open to people of modest as well as substantial means.

1
A Phoenician glass head pendant, c.6th cent BC, with cobalt blue beard, yellow mouth, white face with cobalt blue eyes, and cobalt blue and white spiral fillet, 2.4cm (1in), *NY 1/2 Mar,* **$1,650 ($1,115)**

2
An opaque black sandcore glass oinochoe, 4th/3rd cent BC, the body decorated with opaque yellow, turquoise and white trailing, the foot, neck and rim edged with yellow trailing, 11.1cm (4⅜in), *L 9/10 July,* **£4,180 ($5,727)**

3
A pale blue mould-blown glass 'lotus-bud' beaker, 1st cent AD, decorated with almond-shaped drops, the base with two concentric circles, some encrustation, 11.7cm (4⅝in), *L 9/10 July,* **£2,860 ($3,918)**

4
A cobalt blue bottle, 1st cent AD, with slightly indented base, twin concave handles, rounded rim turned in, iridescence, 7.5cm (3in), *NY 1/2 Mar,* **$935 (£632)**

5
An aquamarine glass ribbed bowl, 1st cent AD, with flat base and slightly rounded sides encircled by fourteen ribs, d 11.6cm (4½in), *NY 8 June,* **$770 (£554)**

6
A pale manganese purple glass jug, 1st/2nd cent AD, a pale green handle attached to the shoulder and rim, the body decorated with spiral trailing, some iridescence, 15.9cm (6⅛in), *L 9/10 July,* **£1,155 ($1,582)**

7
An iridescent pale green mould-blown glass grape flask, c.2nd AD, the body with small circular bosses representing grapes, fine silvery iridescence, 13.4cm (5¼in), *L 10 Dec,* **£1,430 ($1,802)**

8
A green glass jug, 2nd/3rd cent AD, cylindrical neck and trefoil lip, a strap handle attached to the shoulder and rim, the base with pontil mark, some encrustation, 23.8cm (9⅜in), *L 10 Dec,* **£880 ($1,109)**

9
An amber-coloured glass flask, c.2nd/3rd cent AD, the indented base with pontil mark, some encrustation, 18.3cm (7¼in), *L 21 May,* **£660 ($950)**

10
A yellow glass jug, 3rd/4th cent AD, a green glass handle, a turquoise zigzag thread around the base of the body, the base with pontil mark, some iridescence, 13.3cm (5¼in), *L 10 Dec,* **£715 ($901)**

11
A large green glass jug, c.4th cent AD, a vertically ribbed handle attached to the shoulder and neck, the base with pontil mark, some encrustation, 27.9cm (11in), *L 10 Dec,* **£935 ($1,178)**

12
A green glass ewer, c.4th cent AD, an applied dark green splayed foot, dark green trailed bands round neck and foot, the body decorated with vertical ribbing, 22.8cm (9in), *L 21 May,* **£605 ($871)**

1　　　　　　　　2　　　　　　　　3

4　　　　　　　　5

6　　　　　　　　7　　　　　　　　8

9　　　　　　　　10　　　　　　　11　　　　　　　12

1

An iridescent pale greenish-blue glass jug, 2nd/3rd cent AD, the indented base with pontil mark, fine iridescence, 13.3cm (5¼in), *L 9/10 July,* £1,320 ($1,808)

2

A manganese purple glass jug, 2nd/3rd cent AD, a pale green reinforcement trail round the underside of the rim and a single green thread encircling the neck, pale green trailed handle, some iridescence, 15.9cm (6¼in), *L 9/10 July,* £990 ($1,356)

3

An iridescent pale bluish-green flask, c.3rd/4th cent AD, the base with pontil mark, fine iridescence, 17.5cm (6⅞in), *L 9/10 July,* £1,320 ($1,808)

4

An iridescent pale green glass flask, 2nd/3rd cent AD, with globular body, indented base, cylindrical neck and rolled rim, multi-coloured iridescence, 14.9cm (5⅞in), *L 9/10 July,* £935 ($1,178)

5

An iridescent pale green glass jug, 3rd/4th cent AD, the body decorated with six faint indentations and diagonal ribbing, with milky iridescence, 15.2cm (6in), *L 9/10 July,* £1,870 ($2,562)

6

A green glass flask, 4th/5th cent AD, with twin trailed handles attached to the shoulder and neck, the base indented with pontil mark, 30cm (11¾in), *L 10 Dec,* £835 ($1,178)

7

A green glass flask, c.4th/5th cent AD, with four handles attached to the shoulder and neck and trailed on to the rim, the base indented with pontil mark, 22.2cm (8¾in), *L 21 May,* £440 ($634)

8

A pale greenish-blue mould-blown glass pilgrim flask, c.6th cent AD, the indented base with pontil mark, some encrustation and iridescence, 18.4cm (7¼in), *L 9/10 July,* £1,815 ($2,487)

9

A green glass jar, 4th/5th cent AD, with twelve threads attached to the shoulder and 'collar' and trailed on to the rim, the body with faint indentations, some encrustation, 17.8cm (7in), *L 9/10 July,* £1,980 ($2,713)

10

A pale green mould-blown glass jug, c.4th/5th cent AD, the body decorated with small circular indentations, the base with pontil mark, some iridescence, 18.5cm (7¼in), *L 10 Dec,* £440 ($554)

11

An olive green jar, c.4th/6th cent AD, the handles and zigzag decoration in aquamarine glass, 9.8cm (3⅞in), *NY 1/2 Mar,* $495 (£335)

12

A pale greenish-blue mould-blown glass pilgrim flask, c.6th cent AD, the base with pontil mark, some encrustation, 13cm (5⅛in), *L 10 Dec,* £990 ($1,247)

1   2   3   4   5

6   7   8

9   10

11   12

1
A Sasanian silver bowl, c.6th cent AD, with high splayed foot, fluted exterior, d 17.3cm (6¹³/₁₆in), *NY 1/2 Mar,* $3,300 (£2,213)

2
A Sassanian silver bowl, 5th/6th cent AD, of oval form, the centre with a gilded boar's head in relief, 16.9cm (6⅝in), *L 9/10 July,* £1,045 ($1,432)

3
A Sassanian silver bowl, c.5th/6th cent AD, of oval form, the exterior with a series of graduated lobes filled with scrolling foliage and dots, 19.1cm (7½in), *L 9/10 July,* £935 ($1,281)

4
A Merovingian or Carolingean gold ring, c.6th/7th cent AD, the hoop intersected by two bezels each supported by shoulders formed as heads of ducks, the smaller bezel incised 'Pax', the other with a monogram, *L 9/10 July,* £3,300 ($4,521)

5
A Roman gold ring, c.3rd cent AD, the shoulders inscribed 'Onebe noyo', the small bezel incised with a fantastic animal, d 2.5cm (1in), *L 9/10 July,* £4,400 ($6,028)

6
An Hellenistic gold ring, c.2nd/1st cent BC, the oval bezel with the figure of Athena standing within a punched border, d 1.9cm (¾in), *L 9/10 July,* £2,200 ($3,014)

7
An early Ionic gold ring, 1st half 6th cent BC, the elongated bezel was originally raised and the sides are decorated with filigree scrolls between beaded bands, the bezel decorated with eagles and a stag, d 2cm (¾in), *L 9/10 July,* £2,420 ($3,315)

8
A pair of Roman gold earrings, 2nd/3rd cent AD, with tear-shaped garnets in a beaded setting, 5.4cm (2⅛in), *NY 1/2 Mar,* $1,760 (£1,180)

9
A Parthian silvered bronze bowl, c.1st/2nd cent AD, the sides with large petal, scroll and tongue motifs, an abstract design engraved in the tondo, d 20.7cm (8⅛in), *L 10 Dec,* £2,420 ($3,049)

10
A Parthian bronze support, c.2nd/3rd cent AD, in the form of a rampant panther, h 8.6cm (3⅜in), *NY 1/2 Mar,* $440 (£295)

11
A Luristan bronze whetstone handle, c.900-700 BC, in the form of the foreparts of an ibex, a small figure of an ibex surmounting its back, 9.5cm (3¾in), *L 10 Dec,* £1,980 ($2,495)

12
A Luristan bronze horse's bit, c.800-600 BC, the cheekpieces in the form of horned and winged sphinxes, 17.2cm (6¾in), *L 9/10 July,* £660 ($904)

13
A Luristan bronze bird pendant, c.800-600 BC, of highly stylised form with ram's head projecting from the tail, h 5.9cm (2⁵/₁₆in), *NY 1/2 Mar,* $660 (£443)

14
A Luristan bronze whetstone handle, c.800-600 BC, in the form of the fore-quarters of a couchant ibex, smooth deep brown patina, 10.1cm (4in), *NY 1/2 Mar,* $1,320 (£885)

15
A Luristan bronze axehead, 9th/8th cent BC, the blade held in the mouth of a grotesque animal's head, the ridged cylindrical shaft surmounted by a reclining animal, 12.1cm (4¾in), *L 9/10 July,* £2,090 ($2,863)

1   2   3

4   5   6   7

8   9   10

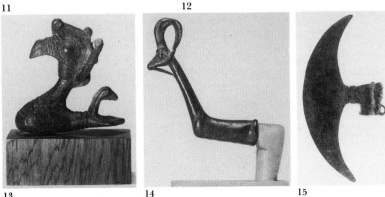

11   12

13   14   15

1
An Achaemenid bronze head of an ibex, c.5th cent BC, with short tapering beard and recessed eyes, h 5.4cm (2⅛in), *NY 1/2 Mar,* $660 (£443)

2
A diorite bowl, Iran, c.6th cent BC, with flat base and deeply recessed centre, d 12.5cm (4¹⁵/₁₆in), *NY 1/2 Mar,* $357 (£239)

3
An Iranian bronze shallow bowl, c.5th cent BC, with central raised omphalos, the exterior with close petal and lozenge-shaped designs, 19.7cm (7¾in), *L 9/10 July,* £440 ($603)

4
An Iranian bronze axehead, 2nd millennium BC, with ridged shaft, lunate at either end, w 17.2cm (6¾in), *L 9/10 July,* £1,320 ($1,808)

5
An Iranian bronze figure of a ram, 2nd millennium BC, 11.4cm (4½in), *L 10 Dec,* £1,320 ($1,663)

6
A Western Asiatic terracotta ovoid jar, Ziwiye, 8th/7th cent BC, with enamel decoration only partially remaining, 12.7cm (5in), *L 9/10 July,* £275 ($377)

7
A Mesopotamian terracotta relief fragment, c.900-700 BC (?), stamped with the figure of a winged bird-headed divinity striding to right and holding a spear, 15.9cm (6¼in), *NY 1/2 Mar,* $1,045 (£706)

8
A Cypro-Geometric pottery single-handled pitcher, c.1050-700 BC, decorated in dark brown and reddish slip with concentric circles and bands, 39.4cm (15½in), *L 9/10 July,* £660 ($904)

9
A Cypriot bichrome amphora, c.5th cent BC, the globular body painted over a cream slip in two shades of brown with encircling bands, lines and concentric circles, 23.2cm (9⅛in), $660 (£917)

10
A Cypriot orange pottery pitcher, c.2000 BC, with a stag in relief on front of spout, three in relief on the shoulder, 63.5cm (25in), *L 21 May,* £1,210 ($1,742)

11
A Cypriot pottery amphora, c.700 BC, the decoration in dark brown and purple slip, 45.7cm (18in), *L 9/10 July,* £660 ($904)

12
A Cypriot limestone female bust, c.5th cent BC, wearing a necklet and holding a tambourine, 13.7cm (5⅜in), *L 9/10 July,* £495 ($678)

13
A Cypriot pottery 'base ring ware' askos, Late Bronze Age, c.1600-1225 BC, in the form of a bull, a hole at the back of the neck and one through the nose for pouring; sold with another similar, 9.5cm and 10.9cm (3¾in and 4¼in), *L 21 May,* £605 ($871)

14
A South Italian Greek black-glazed pottery 'Plastic Vase', 4th cent BC, in the form of a boar, 10.8cm (4¼in), *L 9/10 July,* £638 ($874)

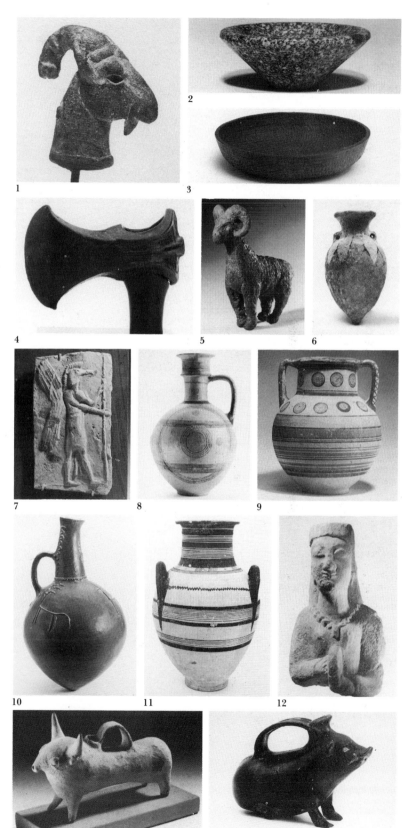

1
An alabaster cosmetic jar,
2nd/3rd dynasty, 2780-
2570 BC, the rounded
rim and disk lid carved
separately, d 12.4cm
(4⅞in), *NY 1/2 Mar*,
$4,070 (£2,730)

2
A basalt bust of a man,
12th dynasty, 1991-1785
BC, wearing a skirt with
fold at the waistline and
a close-fitting cap,
h 10.5cm (4⅛in),
NY 1/2 Mar,
$1,320 (£885)

3
An Egyptian serpentine
vase, 12th dynasty, 1991-
1785 BC of slender flaring
form with spreading base
and flanged rim, 7.6cm
(3in) *NY 8 June*,
$1,210 (£871)

4
Three Egyptian cosmetic
jars, 12th/early 18th
dynasty, 1991-1500 BC,
two in banded alabaster
each with disc foot and
rim, the third in
magnesite marble with
disc rim, 6, 5.1 and
3.5cm (2⅜, 2 and 1⅜in),
NY 8 June,
$605 (£435)

5
A bright blue faience
ring, 18th dynasty, reign
of Tutankhamun, 1347-
1337 BC, the oval bezel
moulded in sunk relief
with the prenomen of
the king, 2.1cm (¾in),
NY 8 June,
$880 (£633)

6
A blue faience ring, 3rd
Intermediate period,
1080-745 BC, the oval
bezel moulded in relief
with the head of
Hathor, 2.4cm (1in),
NY 8 June,
$440 (£317)

7
Five white faience tiles,
20th dynasty, period of
Rameses III, 1193-1162
BC, each in the form of a
marguerite, d 3.5-5.6cm
(1½-2¼in), *NY 8 June*,
$770 (£554)

8
A small Egyptian
limestone male head,
17th/early 18th dynasty,
4.5cm (1¾in), *L 21 May*,
£418 ($602)

9
An Egyptian alabaster
vessel, 18th/19th
dynasty, *c*.1567-1200 BC,
with rounded body and
flaring foot, flanged rim,
12cm (4¾in), *L 21 May*,
£1,320 ($1,901)

10
A mask from a limestone
anthropoid sarcophagus,
21st/22nd dynasty, 1080-
720 BC, of massive
form, the surface
roughened overall,
60.9 x 73.6cm
(24 x 29in), *NY 8 June*,
$4,950 (£3,320)

11
An Egyptian polychrome-
painted wood
sarcophagus, 21st
dynasty, *c*.1000 BC, the
hands originally in
relief (now missing), the
body and sides painted
with numerous divinities
and wings, 180.4cm
(71in), *L 9/10 July*,
£6,820 ($9,343)

1
An Egyptian wood face mask, 22nd/26th dynasty, 946-525 BC, with eyes and eyebrows painted in black, remains of red painted ornament on the wig, 25.4cm (10in), *NY 1/2 Mar,*
$2,090 (£1,412)

2
A brilliant blue winged scarab, Late period, 712-30 BC, in three sections pierced for attachment to the mummy, w 13.6cm (5⅜in), *NY 1/2 Mar,*
$385 (£258)

3
A fragment from the upper part of an Egyptian polychrome-painted wood coffin, Late Period, the bearded head with deep jewelled collar, a figure of a goddess below flanked by udjat eyes, 89cm (35in), *L 21 May,*
£1,760 ($2,534)

4
A granite head of a man, late 25th/early 26th dynasty, *c*670-610 BC, wearing a wide wig rounded at the shoulders, traces of a square-topped back pillar remaining, h 7cm (2¾in), *NY 1/2 Mar,*
$1,650 (£1,107)

5
An Egyptian bronze figure of a king, Late Period, *c.*712-30 BC, wearing a striated royal kilt, with nemes headdress with uraeus, 19.1cm (7¼in), *L 9/10 July,*
£3,300 ($4,521)

6
An Egyptian bronze royal figure, 26th dynasty, wearing a tripartite wig with uraeus and pleated kilt, 14.3cm (5⅝in), *L 21 May,*
£1,320 ($1,901)

7
An Egyptian wood mummy mask, 26th dynasty, *c*664-525 BC, the wig and other details polychrome-painted on a white ground, the face painted white with black eyes, 35.8cm (13⅞in), *L 10 Dec,*
£2,860 ($3,604)

8
An Egyptian bronze figure of a cat, 26th dynasty, *c*664-525 BC, with a neck-cord with udjat eye pendant incised around its neck, 17.8cm (7in), *L 21 May,*
£6,270 ($9,029)

9
An Ancient Egyptian bronze mummy-case for the body of a falcon, 26th dynasty, *c*664-525 BC, surmounted by the figure of a falcon (sacred to Horus), wearing the double-crown, 14cm (5½in), *L 21 May,*
£1,540 ($2,218)

1

2

5

3

4

6

7

8

9

1
A limestone votive relief fragment, 26th dynasty/Ptolemaic period, 664-30 BC, carved in high relief with ram-headed Khnum wearing a beaded necklace, 7.9 x 9.5cm (3⅛ x 3¾in), *NY 1/2 Mar,* $3,300 (£2,213)

2
An Egyptian bronze figure of a fish (Oxyrhynchus), 26th/30th dynasty, 664-342 BC, part of the crown remaining, with engraved details, 5.4cm x13.4cm (2⅛ x 5¼in), *L 21 May,* £385 ($554)

3
A bronze figure of the horus falcon, 26th/30th dynasty, 664-342 BC, the stylised eye markings engraved, h 14.6cm (5¼in), *NY 8 June,* $4,950 (£3,320)

4
An Egyptian faience Ushabti figure, from Hawara, 30th dynasty, c480 BC, with some pale green glaze remaining, with nine lines of hieroglyphic inscription terminating at the plain back pillar, 21.5cm (8½in), *L 21 May,* £1,210 ($1,742)

5
An Egyptian green-glazed composition Ushabti figure, Persian period, c450-400 BC, with nine horizontal bands of hieroglyphic text, 22.9cm (9in), *L 9/10 July,* £715 ($980)

6
A bronze figure of Harpocrates, 30th dynasty/Ptolemaic period, 380-30 BC, wearing the crown of Upper and Lower Egypt with uraeus and side-lock, h 16.8cm (6⅝in), *NY 1/2 Mar,* $990 (£664)

7
A Romano-Egyptian stucco mummy portrait female head, c1st/3rd cent AD, the eyes with black-painted details, wearing small earrings, 28cm (11in), *L 10 Dec,* £1,870 ($2,356)

8
A limestone head of a king, Ptolemaic period, c200-30 BC, wearing a smooth nemes-headdress with fragmentary uraeus blocked out, h 10.6cm (4⁹⁄₁₆in), *NY 1/2 Mar,* $1,650 (£1,107)

9
A limestone sarcophagus mask, Ptolemaic period, 305-30 BC, the broad face painted in a thin yellow wash, remains of red pigment on the eyes, lips and ears, h 46.1cm (18⅛in), *NY 1/2 Mar,* $5,500 (£3,689)

10
An Egyptian black basalt head of a Ptolemaic prince, 2nd/1st cent BC, wearing a fillet around his head, the eyes depressed, from a herm, 20.3cm (8in), *L 10 Dec,* £4,180 ($5,267)

1

2

3

4

5

6

7

8

9

10

1
**An Hellenistic bronze
amphora**, *c*2nd cent BC,
encircling lines engraved
on the shoulder, rim
folded down and in, twin
foliate handles, 18.7cm
(7⅜in), *NY 1/2 Mar*,
$935 (£632)

2
**A Roman bronze figure of
a dog**, *c*2nd cent AD,
seated, with stiffly curled
tail, 5.5cm (2⅛in), *L 21 May*,
£330 ($475)

3
**A Roman bronze figure of
a bull**, *c*1st cent BC/1st
cent AD, its tail curling
over its back, a hole for
attachment between the
horns, 6cm (2⅜in),
L 21 May,
£462 ($665)

4
**A Roman bronze elephant
head lamp**, *c*2nd/3rd
cent AD, 13cm (5⅛in),
NY 1/2 Mar,
$990 (£664)

5
A Roman bronze lamp,
late 1st cent BC/2nd cent
AD, the handle terminat-
ing in a theatrical mask,
a palmette below, 21cm
(8¼in), *L 10 Dec*,
£2,090 ($2,633)

6
**An East Roman bronze
offering tray**, South Asia
Minor/Syria, *c*2nd cent
AD, the lower finial cast
in relief as a lion
crouching over its prey,
a wild boar, the upper
terminal as the foreparts
of a stag, 29.3cm (11½in),
L 10 Dec,
£2,200 ($2,772)

7
A Roman bronze handle,
*c*1st cent AD, probably
from a beaked oinochoe,
the forequarters of a lion
at the rim, h 17.2cm
(6¾in), *NY 1/2 Mar*,
$660 (£443)

8
**A Roman bronze figure of
Herakles**, *c*2nd/3rd cent
AD, in provincial style
with a fragmentary
stippled lion's skin over
his left arm, h 12cm
(4¾in), *NY 1/2 Mar*,
$412 (£276)

9
**A pair of Roman bronze
handles**, *c*3rd cent AD,
from a vessel, the wings
with duck-head terminals,
the bases in the form of
Medusa masks, 27.3cm
(10¾in), *L 21 May*,
£1,980 ($2,851)

10
An Italic bronze helmet,
*c*480 BC, of the so-called
Corinthian type, a ridge
dividing the crown of
the head from the lower,
neckpiece missing, 20.3cm
(8in), *L 21 May*,
£4,620 ($6,653)

11
**An Etruscan bronze
jockey cap helmet**, 3rd
cent BC, with circular
knop, 19.1cm (17½in),
L 21 May,
£660 ($950)

12
**A Gallo-Roman bronze
figure of Herakles**,
1st/2nd cent AD,
advancing with his right
arm raised, club missing,
11.6cm (4⁹⁄₁₆in),
NY 1/2 Mar,
$1,320 ($892)

1   2   3

4   5

6

7   8   9

10   11   12

1
A Cycladic marble lamp, c.2500 BC, 21.6cm (8½in), M 27 June,
FF 13,320 (£1,143; $1,558)

2
A Villanovan black impasto urn, 9th cent BC, with inverted bowl lid, the body incised and hatched with panels of rotating meanders, a band of broken meanders on the handles, total h 42.5cm (16¾in), NY 1/2 Mar,
$2,310 (£1,561)

3
A Campanian pottery oinochoe by the D-V painter, c.340-320 BC, decorated with a figure of a woman and a naked armed warrior, the decoration enriched with white and yellow paint, 22cm (8⅜in), L 10 Dec,
£1,980 ($2,495)

4
An Etruscan black-figure mug, Pontic Class, c.650-625 BC, the body painted with a frieze of four striding panthers and sirens, h 16.8cm (6⅝in), NY 8 June,
$770 (£516)

5
A Roman pottery pitcher, Pergamon Workshop, 4th cent AD, 23.5cm (9¼in), L 10 Dec,
£660 ($832)

6
Two Hellenistic polychrome terracotta funerary vases, Canosa, 3rd cent BC, the place of the spout taken by a standing figure of a woman, 43.4 and 43.1cm (17¼ and 17in), NY 1/2 Mar,
$3,575 (£2,416)

7
A Corinthian pottery squat trefoil oinochoe, Middle Ripe Animal style, 600-575 BC, decorated in dark brown and purple slip, 10.8cm (4¼in), L 10 Dec,
£1,100 ($1,386)

8
A Corinthian pottery conical oinochoe with trefoil lip, 600-575 BC, panthers, a stag and a goose round the body, rosettes in the field, L 10 Dec,
£825 ($1,040)

9
A Corinthian flat-bottom oinochoe, c.late 7th cent BC, the body painted with a frieze of lions, deer, goats, a duck and a siren, details in red and white, 21.6cm (8½in), NY 1/2 Mar,
$4,180 (£2,824)

10
A Corinthian pottery trefoil oinochoe, c.600 BC, with frieze of tongues in dark brown and purple slip, rays in dark brown slip around the foot, horizontal band in purple slip around the body, 21cm (8¼in), L 9/10 July,
£418 ($573)

11
A Sicilian pottery urn and cover, c.3rd cent BC, one side painted chiefly in pink and white with a figural scene, traces of yellow on the handles, the reverse side plain, 53.7cm (23⅛in), L 10 Dec,
£3,850 ($4,851)

12
A Mycenaean terracotta goddess, Mycenaean IIIB, c.1300-1230 BC, of psi type, wearing a two-piece garment painted in red over the buff-coloured clay, 13cm (5⅛in), NY 8 June,
$1,650 (£1,187)

13
Two Etruscan black-figure chalices, Pontic Class, c.650-625 BC, h 16.2 and 15.2cm (6⅜ and 6in), NY 8 June,
$660 (£443)

14
A Daunian pottery funnel krater, Northern Apulia, 4th cent BC, the decoration in dark brown slip, 29.9cm (11¾in), L 9/10 July,
£330 ($452)

15
A Canosan terracotta head of a woman, c.3rd cent BC, 20.3cm (8in), L 10 Dec,
£352 ($444)

16
A Paestan pottery amphora, 4th cent BC, decorated with figures, added white and yellow details, 49.3cm (19⅜in), L 9/10 July,
£1,980 ($2,713)

1   2   3

4   5   6

7   8   9   10

11   12   13

14   15   16

1
A Roman marble
cinerarium, Flavian
period, *c*AD 69-96, the
name-plate inscribed,
31.2 x 28.6cm (12¼ x
11¼in), *L 10 Dec*,
£1,760 ($2,218)

2
A Roman marble
architectural ornament,
*c*1st cent BC, carved in
relief with a head of
Medusa, w 32.4cm (12¾in),
NY 1/2 Mar,
$880 (£590)

3
A Roman marble capital,
*c*2nd cent AD, of
Corinthian type, h 33cm
(13in), *NY 1/2 Mar*,
$2,420 (£1,623)

4
A Roman marble panel,
*c*1st cent AD, engraved
with a Latin funerary
inscription for
Otacillius Ucundus,
aged 16, 61 x 106.7cm
(24 x 42in), *NY 1/2 Mar*,
$2,200 (£1,476)

5
An Hellenistic terracotta
bull, *c* 3rd cent BC,
couchant, the harness
painted red, the horns
yellow, the body ochre,
h 12.1cm (4¾in), *NY 8 June*,
$192 (£129)

6
An Hellenistic terracotta
ram, 3rd cent BC,
couchant, the harness
painted in red, traces of
pink on the body,
10.2cm (4in), *NY 8 June*,
$330 (£221)

7
An Hellenistic terracotta
figure of a winged victory,
Apulia, probably from
Tarentum, 2nd/1st cent
BC, some lilac-painted
decoration, the wings
with blue-painted decora-
tion, with reddish-
painted lobed coiffure,
29.5cm (11⅝in), *L 9/10 July*,
£2,310 ($3,165)

8
An Hellenistic terracotta
female figure, from
Southern Italy,
*c*3rd/2nd cent BC, with
traces of painted decora-
tion, 28.5cm (11¼in),
L 21 May,
£462 ($665)

9
An Hellenistic terracotta
female figure, *c*3rd cent
BC, a himation tightly
around her head, 21cm
(8¼in), *L 21 May*,
£605 ($871)

10
An Hellenistic terracotta
bust of a lady, Apulia,
*c*2nd cent BC, wearing a
chiton, armlets and ear-
ring, remains of white
pigment, h 22.2cm
(8¾in), *NY 1/2 Mar*,
$2,860 (£1,918)

11
A Greek terracotta
bearded mask, 4th cent
BC, a himation worn
over his head, 20.3cm
(8in), *L 21 May*,
£605 ($871)

12
An Hellenistic polychrome
terracotta roundel,
Canosa, 3rd cent BC,
moulded in high relief
with a head of Medusa,
d 14.6cm (5¾in),
NY 1/2 Mar,
$3,300 (£2,213)

13
A terracotta votive head of
a youth, Etruscan or
Campanian, *c*2nd cent
BC, h 26cm (10¼in),
NY 1/2 Mar,
$1,430 (£959)

14
A Canosan terracotta
figure of a sphinx, Apulia,
3rd cent BC, with traces
of polychrome-painted
decoration, the base
pierced with a hole,
L 9/10 July,
£2,640 ($3,617)

1
An Etruscan terracotta
votive head of a young
man, c.4th/3rd cent BC,
21cm (8¼in), L 10 Dec,
£1,540 ($1,940)

2
A marble herm of
Hellenistic ruler, 1st cent
AD, wearing a Mace-
donian helmet with
cheek protectors,
h 19.4cm (7⅝in),
NY 1/2 Mar,
$1,100 (£738)

3
An Etruscan terracotta
bust of a young man,
4th/3rd cent BC, 42cm
(16½in), L 10 Dec,
£2,860 ($3,604)

4
A Greco-Roman marble
head of a satyr, 1st/2nd
cent AD, his head sur-
mounted by a fragmentary
wreath, h 10.2cm (4in),
NY 1/2 Mar,
$1,320 (£885)

5
A Roman marble face-
mask of a woman,
probably from Egypt,
c.1st cent BC/1st cent
AD, possibly a portrait,
the top and sides smoothly
finished for additions in
another material, pre-
sumably stucco, 12.7cm
(5in), L 5 July,
£1,980 ($2,752)

6
A Roman bronze figure of
Herakles, c.1st cent
BC/1st cent AD, nude,
holding the club in his
right hand, the lionskin
over his left arm, 8.9cm
(3½in), L 9/10 July,
£660 ($904)

7
The upper part of a
Roman marble figure of
Aphrodite, c.3rd quarter
2nd cent AD, of Capitoline
type, her hair bound up
in an elaborate top-knot,
h 38.7cm (15¼in),
NY 8 June,
$7,425 (£4,980)

8
A fragmentary Roman
marble head of Aphrodite,
c.1st/2nd cent AD, her
hair originally worn in a
looped top-knot, 35.6cm
(14in), L 10 Dec,
£3,850 ($4,851)

9
A Roman marble head of
Athena, c.1st cent AD,
wearing a Corinthian
helmet, 20.3cm (8in),
M 27 June,
FF 49,950 (£4,288; $5,842)

10
A Roman bronze attach-
ment, c.2nd cent AD,
probably from a piece of
furniture or chariot, in
the form of a bust of
Athena, 19.1cm (7½in),
L 21 May,
£1,760 ($2,534)

11
A Roman marble head of
Apollo Saurok Tonos
(lizard slayer), c.2nd cent
AD, a copy of a 4th cent
BC work attributed to
Praxiteles, 20.3cm (8in),
L 9/10 July,
£5,720 ($7,836)

12
A Roman marble female
funerary bust, c.2nd/3rd
cent AD, set into a
circular niche, 34.9cm
(13¾in), L 21 May,
£1,100 ($1,584)

13
A Roman bronze steelyard
weight, c.2nd/3rd cent
AD, in the form of the
bust of an emperor, his
eyes inlaid with silver,
10.5cm (4⅛in), L 21 May,
£825 ($1,188)

14
A Boeotian terracotta
figure of a young man, 5th
cent BC, nude except for
a himation worn around
his shoulders, carrying a
cock under his left arm,
27.3cm (10¾in),
L 21 May,
£1,155 ($1,663)

Attic Vases of the 6th and 5th Century BC

Athens and its province of Attica (hence the name Attic) was by far the most prominent centre for the manufacture of Greek painted vases during the 6th and 5th century BC. Although pottery was made in Greece from neolithic times onwards, it was during these centuries, when the Greek civilization was at its height and when the greatest works of art in marble and bronze were being produced, that Greek vase-painting, too, reached its peak and the perfection of its form. The industry declined towards the end of the 5th century BC and, although an attempted revival took place after the Peloponnesian Wars, it was only an echo of the past.

In the 4th century BC the Greek colonists in Southern Italy took over from the mainland and produced a highly decorative and imaginative style of vase-painting. A vast industry grew up there which lasted into the 3rd century BC.

Attic vases were not polychrome but were made only in the colour of the clay with a black 'glaze' and some minor red and white painted details. There were two basic techniques involved (described here only in the simplest terms): 'black-figure' in the 6th century BC, when the figures and decorative motifs were painted in a shiny black 'glaze' against the light ground of the clay with the details incised with a sharp tool, and 'red-figure' which replaced it in the 5th century BC. In this the background was now covered in a black 'glaze', the figures reserved in the orange colour of the clay, and details painted with black rather than incised.

Ancient art is very often connected with religion and has funerary overtones. Although a small class of Attic vases was made for funerary purposes most were solely for domestic use. The Greeks were extremely fond of wine, which they drank diluted with water, and many of the vases reflect this predilection. There was the amphora for the storage of wine, as well as for cereals and food, the krater, which was used for mixing the wine and water, the kyathos or ladle, the hydria or water pitcher and the oinochoe or water jug. There were also many different types of drinking cup; some of them were quite large since they were often handed round at the banquets or symposia the Greeks enjoyed so much. Plates of all kinds held foodstuffs, though fish were honoured with their own special dish with a built-in sauce well. The Greeks used oil instead of soap so oil was contained in small vases such as the alabastron, the aryballos and the lekythos. These all had narrow necks so that their contents only escaped drop by drop. They were also used as perfume flasks. Pyxides were boxes used for cosmetics and pomades.

The subjects depicted on these vases were gods and goddesses shown in any number of mythological scenes. Dionysus with his attendant satyrs and maenads was one of the favourite and most appropriate subjects—his popularity stemming mainly from his connections with wine and revelry. Herakles at his various labours was another favourite. There were also many scenes of war and combat, since wars between neighbouring states were frequent. The scenes from everyday life include young men at various athletic activities and women at domestic pursuits.

Attic vases were exported throughout the Mediterranean world to all the Greek colonies. They were very sought after by the Etruscans and thousands have been found on Etruscan sites in Italy.

1
An Attic pottery red-figure trefoil oinochoe, 5th cent BC, 15.8cm (6¼in), *M 27 June,* **FF 7,770 (£667; $909)**

2.
An Attic black-figure flat-mouthed oinochoe, c.500 BC, 24.4cm (9⅝in), *NY 1/2 Mar,* **$6,600 (£4,459)**

3
An Attic black-figure oinochoe belonging to the Guide Line Class (Class of Vatican G47), c.500 BC, decorated with the figures of Dionysus, Ariadne and a satyr, 22.2cm (8¾in), *L 10 Dec,* **£3,520 ($4,435)**

4
An Attic black-figure lekythos, c.530-520 BC, the body painted with figures holding spears, 18.1cm (7⅛in), *NY 1/2 Mar,* **$605 (£409)**

5
An Attic black-figure siana cup, by the Painter of Amsterdam 214B, c.550 BC, d 34.3cm (13½in), *L 10 Dec,* **£1,650 ($2,079)**

6
An Attic black-figure kylix, 6th cent BC, 21.5cm (8½in), *L 9/10 July,* **£2,640 ($3,617)**

1   2   3   4

5   6

1
An Attic black-figure
pottery band cup, 6th cent
BC, decorated on both
sides with the figures of
two swans and two deer,
d 27.9cm (11in), *L 10 Dec,*
£660 ($832)

2
An Attic black-figure
kylix, 6th cent BC, the
exterior decorated with
erotic scenes and birds
and panthers, enriched
with white and purple
paint, d 28.5cm (11¼in),
L 9/10 July,
£3,300 ($4,521)

3
Two Apulian gnathia-
ware oinochoai, *c.*late 4th
cent BC, each with
ribbed body, trefoil
mouth and cylindrical
handle with lion's head
at the rim and woman's
head at the shoulder, the
neck painted in yellow,
22.2 and 21.6cm (8¾ and
8½in), *NY 1/2 Mar,*
$1,045 (£706)

4
An Attic black-figure neck
amphora, *c.*500 BC,
decorated with warriors
in combat, the foot black
to the outer edge, 26.1cm
(10¼in), *L 10 Dec,*
£4,180 ($5,267)

5
An Attic red-figure trefoil
oinochoe, *c.*460 BC,
decorated with the
figure of a flying Nike,
meander ground line,
tongues around base of
neck, 18.2cm (7⅛in),
L 10 Dec,
£550 ($693)

6
An Attic black-figure
lekythos, Class of Athens
581 Group, from the
workshop of the Marathon
Painter, 500-400 BC,
decorated with the
seated figures of Dionysus,
Ariadne and Hermes,
added red concentric
band below scene,
21.9cm (8⅝in), *L 10 Dec,*
£825 ($1,040)

7
An Attic red-figure 'owl'
skyphos of the Johnson
Group IV, *c.*465 BC,
decorated on both sides
with the figure of an owl
standing between laurel
branches, 17.8cm (7in),
L 10 Dec,
£825 ($1,040)

8
An Attic black-figure olpe,
*c.*500 BC, decorated with
the figure of a satyr
approaching a female
figure, added red and
white details, added red
horizontal band below
scene, 23.7cm (9⅜in),
L 10 Dec,
£1,320 ($1,663)

9
A black-glaze mug,
5th/4th cent BC, with
broad base in three
degrees, horizontal
flutes, on the body and
convex ring handle,
8.1cm (3³/₁₆in), *NY 1/2 Mar,*
$605 (£409)

10
Two Apulian black-glaze
vessels, 4th cent BC, a
mug with ribbed ovoid
body, a small dish with
heavy rounded walls, 8.9
and 11.4cm (3½ and
4½in), *NY 1/2 Mar,*
$522 (£353)

11
An Attic black-figure
white ground lekythos by
the Edinburgh Painter,
6th cent BC, decorated
with the figure of
Herakles fighting, Athena
looking on, some added
red details, 35.4cm (13⅝in),
L 10 Dec,
£1,650 ($2,079)

1
An Apulian black-glaze oinochoe, 4th cent BC, the ribbed body and trefoil mouth with everted lip, h 26cm (10¼in), *NY 1/2 Mar,* $880 (£590)

2
An Apulian terracotta incense stand, 3rd cent BC, in the form of a maenad head, the details painted in pink, black and purple, h 18.1cm (7⅛in), *NY 8 June,* $825 (£553)

3
An Apulian buffware sack askos, Messapian *c.*350-300 BC, with cylindrical spout flanked by stirrup handles, d 23.5cm (9¼in), *NY 8 June,* $880 (£633)

4
Two Apulian terracotta fantastic birds, 3rd cent BC, each of highly simplified form with small spatulate tail and dragon-like head, 19 and 21.6cm (7½ and 8½in), *NY 8 June,* $770 (£516)

5
An Apulian pottery thymiaterion (incense burner), from the Group of Bari 5924 (connected with the White Saccos—Kantharos Group), *c.*315 BC, the decoration enriched with white and yellow paint, 23.8cm (9⅜in), *L 10 Dec,* £605 ($762)

6
An Apulian red-figure lekanis, *c.*330-320 BC, painted on one side with Eros and on the other with a seated maened, d 21.9cm (8⅝in), *NY 1/2 Mar,* $605 (£406)

7
An Apulian red-figure dish, *c.*330-320 BC, painted with the head of a woman facing left, the details in yellow and pink, d 25.1cm (9⅞in), *NY 8 June,* $440 (£295)

8
An Apulian red-figure fish plate, *c.*330 BC, with high foot and overhanging rim, d 21.6cm (8½in), *NY 1/2 Mar,* $990 (£664)

9
An Apulian pottery fish dish, 4th cent BC, with two fish and a squid, decoration enriched with white paint, d 22.8cm (9in), *L 21 May,* £1,100 ($1,584)

10
An Apulian pottery fish plate, by the Eyebrow Painter, 4th cent BC, white painted details, 19.7cm (7¾in), *L 21 May,* £550 ($792)

11
An Apulian pottery basin, from the Darius Workshop, *c.*320/310 BC, the decoration enriched with white-painted details, 38.1cm (15in), *L 21 May,* £2,090 ($3,010)

12
An Apulian pottery oinochoe, *c.*310 BC, in the form of a woman's head, yellow painted stripes at the base of the handle, her white-painted neck and face with some pink-painted details, a pink-painted net covering her hair, reddish-painted earrings, 45.1cm (17¾in), *L 21 May,* £1,650 ($2,376)

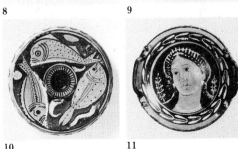

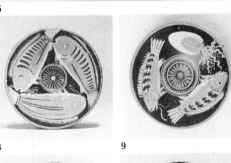

1   2

3

5

4

7

6

8   9

10   11   12

1
An Apulian red-figure
epichysis, 4th cent BC,
the body decorated with
the figure of a satyr,
kneeling and holding a
mirror, 18.4cm (7¼in),
L 9/10 July,
£440 ($603)

2
Two Apulian gnathia-
ware vessels, late 4th cent
BC, an epichysis and a
small skyphos, 17.8 and
7.3cm (7 and 2⅞in),
NY 8 June,
$385 (£277)

3
An Apulian pottery trefoil
oinochoe, *c.*320 BC, the
mouth and handle with
white and blue-painted
decoration, the body
with the figure of a
young woman and of
Eros, decoration in white
and yellow paint, 46.4cm
(18¼in), *L 21 May,*
£935 ($1,346)

4
An Apulian pottery trefoil
oinochoe, *c.*320 BC, the
mouth and handle with
white and blue-painted
decoration, the body
with white and yellow-
painted details, 47cm
(18½in), *L 21 May,*
£990 ($1,426)

5
An Apulian red-figure
mug and cover, *c.*late 4th
cent BC, the body
painted with a doe and a
deer, h 20cm (7⅞in),
NY 8 June,
$495 (£332)

6
An Apulian red-figure
oinochoe, 4th cent BC,
with knotted handle and
lid, the body decorated
with a seated woman
between Eros and a
woman, 22.9cm (9in),
L 9/10 July,
£605 ($829)

7
An Apulian red-figure bell
krater, *c.*340-320 BC,
decorated with Eros seated
on a rocky outcrop, the
details painted in yellow
and white, d 44.8cm
(17⅝in), *NY 8 June,*
$2,420 (£1,741)

8
An Apulian pottery
stamnos, 4th cent BC,
decorated with figures
and Eros, 27cm (10⅝in),
L 10 Dec,
£2,640 ($3,326)

9
An Apulian pottery dinos,
by a late follower of the
Baltimore Painter, *c.*320-
310 BC, decorated with
Eros on both sides,
enriched with white and
yellow paint, 22.9cm (9in),
L 21 May,
£605 ($871)

10
An Apulian pottery
kantharos, 4th cent BC,
decorated with a female
figure, 29.5cm (11⅝in),
L 10 Dec,
£2,090 ($2,633)

11
An Apulian polychrome
volute krater, *c.*late 4th
cent BC, a Medusa mask
in relief on one side of
each volute, one side
painted with a portrait
head, h 30.3cm (11⅞in),
NY 8 June,
$550 (£369)

12
An Apulian pottery volute
krater, from the
workshop of the Patera
Painter, by the Sub-
group of Berkeley 8/61,
*c.*320 BC, the body
decorated on both sides
with Ionic naiskoi,
figures and floral motifs,
the decoration enriched
with white paint, 57.5cm
(22⅝in), *L 10 Dec,*
£1,485 ($1,871)

1

2

3

4

5

6

7

8

9

10

11

12

Japanese Works of Art

NEIL DAVEY • JANE OLIVER

A strong traditional belief in the inevitable and natural connections between form and function, theory and technique, beauty and practicality is the fundamental aesthetic basis of Japanese art. Although largely isolated for centuries, Japan nevertheless borrowed ideas and images from other cultures (first China, then Europe), incorporating them in ways that were uniquely Japanese. An admiring respect for nature, along with a lively sense of humour irreverently poking fun at man and deity alike, is also characteristic.

Collectors of Japanese decorative arts are fast increasing, but once introduced to the elusive Japanese aesthetic they tend to pursue a particular area: netsuke, lacquer and inro, swords and sword fittings, early ceramics and later 19th century works of art are all rich areas for research and enjoyment.

Netsuke are small toggles, usually carved out of ivory or wood, that were used to secure the inro (tiered medicine box) or tobacco pouches on the obi (belt) of the pocketless kimono (robe). They were carved with humour and skill and often represented animals, Buddhist deities in inevitably compromising situations, or stories from Japanese folklore. They were used from the late 17th century until the end of the 19th century and are still produced today by highly respected carvers. The best netsuke have a strong sculptural quality and compact form, with the earlier pieces tending to be well worn and patinated from years of use and handling. Many examples are signed—certain artists are highly regarded and of significant value at auction.

Japanese swords and sword fittings perhaps form the most esoteric field and the one that is most closely allied with social traditions. The sword was the *samurai*'s symbol of rank, power and wealth, and the sword maker was a highly revered master craftsman. For generations, sword masters taught their descendants the difficult craft of making the finely honed and incredibly sharp blades. Sword fittings were almost of equal importance; many were inlaid with precious metals often very skilfully worked in relief. The most able and respected craftsmen often signed their own work, and such pieces, especially in perfect condition, are the most prized.

Lacquerware is perhaps the most luxurious of the Japanese applied arts and most closely exemplifies exquisite craftsmanship and attention to detail. Lacquer involves a painstaking process wherein many layers of lacquer (a rubber-like resin tapped from tree trunks) are applied to a wood and paper box, frame, or inro. Each layer is dried and finely polished to arrive at a hard decorative surface. The lacquer was often sprinkled with tiny particles of precious metals to create delicate designs of flowers, animals and landscapes. Inro were made primarily of lacquer, as were suzuribako (writing boxes), storage boxes of all sizes and dining utensils. Japanese lacquer artists displayed great imagination and innovation and experimented with a wide variety of techniques and styles. Their work brings collectors from all over the globe to compete for the pleasure of owning them.

Japanese ceramics were produced for religious, practical and decorative purposes. Tea ceramics are an essential aesthetic and religious element of the tea ceremony. They were generally of earthenware, simply potted with natural brown or black glazes, and made in particular shapes to complement their function in the ceremony itself. Porcelain, with its more elegant and refined finish, was prized by the wealthy, particularly pieces from the Nabeshima and Kakiemon kilns. Imari and Kutani porcelains were avidly collected in the 19th century after the opening of Japan to the West. They retain their popularity in Europe and America today. Finely enamelled earthenware, most notably represented by the Satsuma kilns, reached its peak in the late 19th century. Artists such as Yabu Meizan and Kinkozan designed delicately painted pieces, gilded with profuse flowers and figural scenes, which are some of the finest products of the Meiji period. (A feature article on this period can be found on page 629.)

The criteria for collecting Japanese decorative arts are much as for any other area. Quality is paramount. Condition is also a major factor and damage can greatly devalue even fine quality pieces. Greater exposure to and understanding of Japanese culture and aesthetics is encouraging ever increasing interest and, since Japanese art represents some of the finest aspects of that culture, collectors worldwide must continue to be fascinated.

1
An Imari garniture, late 17th cent, comprising three ovoid jars and covers and two beaker vases, decorated in underglaze-blue, iron-red and gilding, one beaker vase repaired, *L 24/31 Oct,* **£22,000 ($27,940)**

2
A pair of Imari vases and covers, late 17th cent, decorated in underglaze-blue, iron-red and gilding, the covers surmounted by *shishi* knops, one vase with base crack, h 73.5cm (28⅞ in), *NY 31 Mar,* **$6,325 (£4,383)**

3
A teapot, 19th cent, decorated in the Kakiemon palette, h 14.5cm (5¾ in), *A 10 Sept,* **Dfl 1,740 (£408; $530)**

4
An Imari vase and cover, late 17th cent, decorated in underglaze-blue, iron-red and gilding, the cover surmounted by a European wood knop, the shoulder of the vase with some restoration, 85cm (33½ in), *L 15 Mar,* **£825 ($1,230)**

5
A pair of Imari vases and covers, late 17th cent, decorated in underglaze-blue, iron-red, black enamel and gilding, the covers surmounted by *shishi* knops, 60.7cm (23⅞ in), *L 24/31 Oct,* **£3,080 ($3,912)**

6
A Ko-Imari bottle, of square section, decorated in yellow, green, aubergine and blue enamels and iron-red, the rim with repaired chip, 20.2cm (7⅞ in), *L 24/31 Oct,* **£1,320 ($1,676)**

7
An Imari bowl and cover, late 17th cent, decorated in underglaze-blue, iron-red and gilding, the rim of the cover and the knop chipped, 46.5cm (18¼ in), *L 24/31 Oct,* **£1,100 ($1,397)**

8
A pair of Imari vases, late 17th cent, decorated in underglaze-blue, iron-red and gilding, one with chipped rim, 48.7cm (19¼ in) and 46.4cm (18¼ in), *L 15 Mar,* **£2,310 ($3,444)**

9
An Imari jar and cover, late 17th cent, painted in inky underglaze-blue, green, iron-red, black and gilding, the cover set with a red *shishi* knop, damaged knop, 47cm (18¼ in), *P 14 Nov,* **£605 ($811)**

10
An Imari dish, late 17th cent, decorated in underglaze-blue, iron-red, black enamel and gilding, the reverse with floral sprays, 53.5cm (21 in), *L 24/31 Oct,* **£1,650 ($2,096)**

11
An Imari bowl, late 17th/early 18th cent, decorated in underglaze-blue, iron-red, enamels and gilding, 27.8cm (10⅞ in), *L 15 Mar,* **£550 ($820)**

12
An Imari bowl, late 17th/early 18th cent, decorated in underglaze-blue, iron-red and gilding, 36.7cm (14⅜ in), *L 18 July,* **£2,090 ($2,780)**

1

2

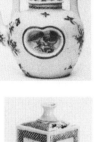

3

4

5

6

7

8

9

10

11

12

1
An enamelled kakiemon
figure of bijin, late 17th
cent, dressed in red
grapevine under-
garment, h 38cm (15in),
A 10 Sept,
Dfl 71,920 (£16,882; $21,946)

2
A pair of Imari models of
carp, late 17th cent,
decorated in underglaze-
blue, iron-red, black
enamel and gilding, one
restored, the other with
small repairs, 31cm
(12⅛in), *L 24/31 Oct,*
£1,320 ($1,676)

3
A Kakiemon model of a
cockerel, late 17th cent,
painted in iron-red and
brilliant blue, green and
yellow enamels, two
claws chipped, one leg
and the comb cracked,
33.9cm (13⅜in),
L 12 Dec,
£5,500 ($6,930)

4
A Kakiemon jar and
cover, late 17th cent,
decorated in iron-red
and blue, green and
reddish-brown enamels,
the cover with one chip,
31.5cm (12⅜in),
L 12 Dec,
£20,900 ($26,334)

5
A Kakiemon dish, late
17th cent, decorated in
iron-red, enamels and
gilding, four spur marks,
21.7cm (8½in), *L 12 Dec,*
£5,500 ($6,930)

6
A Kakiemon dish, late
17th cent, decorated in
iron-red, blue, green
and yellow enamels and
touches of gilding, the
base with five spur
marks, 21.5cm (8½in)
L 12 Dec,
£7,920 ($9,979)

7
A Nabeshima dish, early
18th cent, decorated in
underglaze-blue with a
branch of camellia, the
reverse with three
groups of tasselled cash,
20.4cm (8in), *L 24/31 Oct,*
£4,620 ($5,867)

8
A Nabeshima dish, late
17th/early 18th cent,
covered overall with a
pale celadon glaze and
finely painted in iron-
red, the rim with one
short crack, the foot
chipped, 19.9cm (7⅞in),
L 15 Mar,
£825 ($1,230)

9
An Arita coffee pot, 18th
cent, with gold and red
enamel decoration,
silver lid and tap,
h 26cm (10¼in),
A 10 Sept,
Dfl 3,480 (£816; $1,060)

10
A Nabeshima dish, late
17th/early 18th cent,
decorated in underglaze-
blue, green and yellow
enamels and slight iron-
red, the reverse with
three groups of tasselled
cash, the rim with one
shallow repaired chip
and one crack, d 20.3cm
(8in), h 5.7cm (2¼in),
foot 11cm (4⅜in),
L 12 Dec,
£15,950 ($20,097)

11
An Imari plate, 18th cent,
with accolée armorials of
Ida Maria van Buren
and Joan van Brederode,
d 21cm (8¼in), *A 10 Sept,*
Dfl 3,248 (£762; $990)

12
An Imari barber's bowl,
early 18th cent,
decorated with a bijin in
a pavilion, d 26cm
(10in), *A 10 Sept,*
Dfl 2,784 (£653; $848)

13
Two Imari ewers, late
17th cent, initialled A
and S, h 16cm (6¼in),
A 10 Sept,
Dfl 2,320 (£544; $707)

14
A pair of covered Arita
jars, *c.*1700, decorated
with flowers and clouds,
h 49cm (19¼in), *A 10 Dec,*
Dfl 7,424 (£1,742; $2,264)

1

An unusual Kakiemon bowl, early 18th cent, of rounded *kiku* form decorated in underglaze-blue with an interior circular panel, *Fuku* mark the rim with one small chip, 25.7cm (10⅛in), *L 24/31 Oct,* £1,870 ($2,375)

2

A pair of Arita vases, 2nd half 17th cent, decorated in underglaze-blue with panels of flowers, one with a crack from the rim, h 41.5cm (16⅜in), *NY 31 Mar,* $3,630 (£2,516)

3

An Arita kendi, 3rd quarter 17th cent, decorated in underglaze-blue and enamels, the rim with one repaired chip, 15.8cm (16⅛in), *L 15 Mar,* £242 ($361)

4

A Kakiemon bowl and cover, early 18th cent, in underglaze-blue with decorated panels, *Ka* mark, the rim with slight chip, 20.8cm (8⅛in), *L 15 Mar,* £2,090 ($3,116)

5

A blue and white Arita bottle, late 17th cent, painted in underglaze-blue with panels of landscapes, slight crack, 37.8cm (14⅞in), *L 12 Dec,* £550 ($693)

6

An Arita jar, 2nd half 17th cent, painted in underglaze-blue with pine, prunus and bamboo, the neck with lappet designs, 32cm (12⅝in), *L 18 July,* £462 ($614)

7

An Arita jar, 3rd quarter 17th cent, painted in underglaze-blue, 27.4cm (10¾in), *L 24/31 Oct,* £1,980 ($2,515)

8

A pair of Arita vases and covers, late 17th cent, decorated in underglaze-blue, the covers with some repairs, 63cm (24¾in), *L 24/31 Oct,* £3,520 ($4,470)

9

A blue and white Arita tankard, with 17th cent Dutch pewter cover, *A 10 Sept,* Dfl 1,624 (£381; $495)

10

A pair of Arita apothecary bottles and stoppers, decorated in underglaze-blue, one bottle and cover cracked, the second bottle with a base crack, 53.5cm (21in), *L 24/31 Oct,* £4,400 ($5,588)

11

An Arita covered bowl, 17th cent, decorated with a landscape within chrysanthemums, d 20cm (7¾in), *A 10 Dec,* Dfl 3,828 (£918; $1,092)

12

A pair of Arita vases, 2nd half 17th cent, decorated in underglaze-blue, both drilled with a small hole, 30.2cm (11⅞in), *L 23/31 Oct,* £3,520 ($4,470)

13

A small multi-lobed oval dish, 18th cent, decorated in underglaze-blue, w 15.6cm (6¼in), *A 10 Sept,* Dfl 1,160 (£272; $1,158)

14

A set of five Arita dishes, early 18th cent, in Kakiemon style painted in underglaze-blue, painted *Fuku* mark, 21.3cm (8¾in), *L 24/31 Oct,* £352 ($447)

1   2   3

4   5   6

7   8   9

10   11

12   13   14

1
An Imari lantern, early
18th cent, enamelled in
green, black, aubergine,
rouge-de-fer and gilding,
cover repaired, 20.2cm
(8in), *P 10-13 July,*
£341 ($464)

2
A pair of Imari garden
seats, Meiji period,
painted and gilt with
panels of birds amongst
pomegranate branches,
applied with mask
handles, one restored,
53cm (20⅞in), *L 1 Nov,*
£1,980 ($2,534)

3
An Imari vase, 19th cent,
painted in underglaze-
blue, red and green
enamels, gilt highlight,
h 54.6cm (21½in),
NY 31 Mar,
$1,760 (£1,220)

4
An Imari bowl, late 19th
cent, decorated in
underglaze-blue, iron-
red and gilding with
scrolling *kiku,* 41.4cm
(16¼in), *L 24/31 Oct,*
£2,200 ($2,794)

5
An Imari jardinière, Meiji
period, decorated with
panels of *shishi,* half *kiku*
and *shippo,* the ground
with scrolling foliage and
flowers, 41cm (16⅛in),
L 18 July,
£462 ($614)

6
An Hirado blue and white
vase, Meiji period,
painted in underglaze-
blue, the foot and base of
the neck painted with
bands of plantain leaves,
33.2cm (13⅛in),
NY 31 Mar,
$660 (£457)

7
An Arita vase and cover,
Meiji period, the body
brightly enamelled and
gilt, on a dark blue
ground, cover restored,
54cm (21¼in), *L 1 Nov,*
£352 ($451)

8
An Imari jardinière, late
19th cent, with decorated
panels, between *ho-o*
panels over a blue
lappet foot, repair to
rim, 46.5cm (18½in),
P 20-22 Mar,
£1,210 ($1,803)

9
An Hirado blue and white
censer, Meiji period, h
13cm (5⅛in); together
with a Makuzu Kozan
miniature globular vase,
signed in underglaze-
blue, 8.9cm (3½in),
NY 31 Mar,
$1,320 (£915)

10
A pair of Hirado baluster
vases, *c.*1900, painted in
blue with birds over
waves, the body encoiled
by a dragon in high
relief, small rim cracks,
32cm (12½in),
P 14 Nov,
£385 ($516)

11
A Fukugawa bowl of squat
globular form, *c.*1900,
painted in underglaze-
blue and black with
swimming carp, mark in
underglaze-blue, 39.5cm
(15½in), *C 3/6 July,*
£418 ($567)

12
A Seifu ovoid vase, Meiji
period, with geese
painted in white, yellow
and black on a lavender
ground, signed 'Seifu' in
underglaze-blue,
h 25.5cm (10in), *NY 31 Mar,*
$1,980 (£1,372)

13
A Fukagawa ovoid vase,
Meiji period, decorated
in underglaze-blue with
grey and white carp
swimming within a blue
sea, *Fukagawa* sprig mark
in underglaze-blue,
h 22cm (8¾in), *NY 31 Mar,*
$1,100 (£762)

14
A porcelain vase, Makuzu
Kozan, Meiji period,
decorated in underglaze-
blue, red and green,
signed in white slip
Makuzu Kozan sei, small
hair-line crack on rim,
slight firing cracks, 48cm
(18⅞in), *L 24/31 Oct,*
£1,155 ($1,467)

15
An iris vase, Makuzu
Kozan, Meiji period,
decorated with pale blue
and white flower stands
on a dark blue ground,
signed *Makuzu Kozan* in
underglaze-blue, h 28cm
(11in), *NY 31 Mar,*
$770 (£534)

1
A double gourd vase,
Meiji period, painted
overall in pale red
enamel with a stretched
net pattern against a
cream crackle glaze
ground, the neck red
and blue, impressed
mark *Kinkozan,* 21.6cm
(8½in), *NY 31 Mar,*
$1,100 (£762)

2
**An earthenware Kozan
vase,** Meiji period,
painted and gilt with
flowers and children,
signed *Kozan,* 18cm
(7⅛in), *L 24/31 Oct,*
£1,595 ($2,026)

3
**An earthenware Yozan
flask,** Meiji period,
finely painted and gilt,
signed *Yozan,* 20.5cm
(8⅛in), *L 24/31 Oct,*
£1,210 ($1,537)

4
**A Satsuma hexagonal
vase,** Meiji period,
painted in multi-
coloured enamels
highlighted in gilt, on a
cobalt blue ground, gilt
Satsuma mon and
signature, 32.5cm
(12¾in), *NY 31 Mar,*
$1,100 (£762)

5
**An earthenware Masatani
dish,** Meiji period,
painted with warriors
carrying a Daimyo in a
palanquin, signed
Masatani zokan and
inscribed in *katakana*
script Tomasu B. Guro,
21cm (8¼in), *L 12 Dec,*
£770 ($970)

6
A Yabu Meizan bowl,
Meiji period, painted
and gilt with butterflies
and flowers on a
stippled black ground,
gilt *Yabu Meizan* seal,
d 12.5cm (4⅞in),
NY 31 Mar,
$3,410 (£2,363)

7
A Yabu Meizan bowl,
Meiji period, painted
and gilt with butterflies
and flowers on a
stippled cream ground,
gilt *Yabu Meizan* seal,
d 12.5cm (4⅞in),
NY 31 Mar,
$3,300 (£2,287)

8
**A Kinkozan koro and
cover,** *c.*1900, the deep-
blue ground finely gilt
and enamelled,
impressed, enamelled
and gilt *Kinkozan tsukuru*
mark, 14cm (5½in),
P 14 Nov,
£1,045 ($1,400)

9
A Kinkozan vase, *c.*1900,
finely enamelled and
gilt with two wide
panels, on a dark-blue
ground, signed *Kinkozan
tsukuru,* 31.5cm (12½in),
P 14 Nov,
£880 ($1,179)

10
**A massive Toen, Kanzan
Satsuma jar and cover,**
Meiji period, richly
painted in thick
enamels, the cover
painted Toen ga,
(painted) Ishu in (house)
Kanzan saku, dated
Genroku go nen (fifth
year of Genroku), red
seal painted *Tatsumine
Chikusho* beneath a blue
Satsuma mon, the base
with a large blue
Satsuma mon, 88cm
(34⅝in), *NY 31 Mar,*
$13,750 (£9,529)

11
**A Satsuma hexagonal koro
and cover,** *c.*1880, *Satsuma
mon* in blue enamel, gilt
signature and seal mark
in red, 21cm (8¼in),
P 20/22 Mar,
£330 ($498)

1   2   3   4

5   6   7

8   9

10   11

1
A miniature triangular
vase, Meiji period,
enamelled in orange,
blue and green high-
lighted with black
against a cream crackle
ground, gilt *Kozan*, 7.7cm
(3in), *NY 28 June*,
$660 (£489)

2
A covered Satsuma jar, in
the shape of a lantern,
was rooster finial,
h 15cm (6in), *A 10 Dec*,
Dfl 1,972 (£471; $560)

3
A Satsuma jar and cover,
decorated with figures,
14.5cm (5¾in), *A 10 Dec*,
Dfl 2,552 (£610; $725)

4
A pair of Satsuma jars and
covers, late Edo period,
decorated with enamels
of red, green, blue and
black highlighted in gilt,
soft metal covers,
Satsuma mon and gilt
mark, 22cm and 20cm
(8½in and 8in),
NY 31 Mar,
$2,310 (£1,601)

5
An earthenware ovoid
vase, Meiji period,
painted in richly
coloured enamels and
gilt with the 'Hundred
Antiques' painted in gilt
in a red square
cartouche *Meishido Kizan
tsukuru*, some loss to gilt,
24.9cm (9¾in),
L 24/31 Oct,
£1,540 ($1,956)

6
An earthenware figure of
Fugen Bosatsu astride an
elephant, Meiji period,
the elephant painted
a marbled grey, his
trappings enamelled in
green, brown, purple
and yellow, restoration,
h 62.3cm (24½in),
NY 31 Mar,
$1,650 (£1,143)

7
A Satsuma vase, Hosai,
mid-19th cent, decorated
in enamels and gilding,
the shoulder with
Satsuma mon reserved
on a thick blue enamel
running over the sides,
mark *Satsuma mon*,
Satsuma Hosai, 30.7cm
(12⅛in), *L 24/31 Oct*,
£880 ($1,118)

8
A Satsuma bottle, late
Edo period, raised on a
lobed footrim, decorated
in enamels and gilding,
17.8cm (7in),
L 24/31 Oct,
£748 ($950)

9
A Satsuma earthenware
vase, Ishuin Hozan,
Meiji period, enamelled
and gilt with dragons
and flowers, gilt *dai
Nihon, Satsuma yaki,
Ishuin Hozan*, 15.5cm
(6⅛in), *L 24/31 Oct*,
£660 ($838)

10
A Kyoto stoneware vase,
late 18th/early 19th cent,
painted in blue and
green enamels and gilt
on the crackled glaze,
21.2cm (8¼in), *L 18 July*,
£715 ($951)

11
A pair of Satsuma
earthenware vases, mid-
19th cent, painted in
enamels and gilding,
signed *Satsuma Kuni (no)
yaki* 36.5cm (14⅜in),
L 15 Mar,
£1,320 ($1,968)

12
A Satsuma vase, Meiji
period, of globular form
with tall neck and flared
rim, decorated in iron-
red, enamels and gilding,
26cm (10¼in), *L 24/31 Oct*,
£605 ($768)

13
A large Satsuma
earthenware vase, Seiho,
late Edo period,
enamelled and gilt with
a profusion of flowers,
signed *Seiho ga*, dated
Bunka nensei (1804-17),
61.5cm (24¼in),
L 24/31 Oct,
£4,950 ($6,286)

1

2

3

4

5

6

7

8

9

10

11

12

13

1
A pair of silver presentation boxes, Meiji period, inlaid with gilt, raised on a pierced conforming base, d base 6.4cm (2½in), *NY 10 Nov,*
$1,045 (£829)

2
An inlaid bronze ovoid vase, Meiji period, inlaid in copper, silver and soft metals, seal, 23.3cm (9³⁄₁₆in), *NY 28 June,*
$1,320 (£978)

3
A pair of inlaid iron vases, Meiji period, inlaid in silver, copper, bronze and gilt, gilt metal feet, unsigned, 26cm (10¼in), *NY 10 Nov,*
$825 (£655)

4
A pair of bronze vases, Meiji period, each in the form of a carp dragon (Makatsugyo), the eyes patinated with gilt and *shakudo,* 23cm (9in), *L 24/31 Oct,*
£1,320 ($1,676)

5
A pair of bronze carp vases, Seiun, Meiji period, signed *Seiun chu,* 30.5cm (12in), *L 15 Mar,*
£528 ($787)

6
A silver inlaid bronze vase, Meiji period, dark patina, artist's signature *Kogen,* signed on underside *Yamamoto,* 23cm (9in), *NY 10 Nov,*
$440 (£349)

7
An iron and enamelled silver koro and cover, Yoshizuka, Meiji period, decorated with gold wire enamels on a silver ground, the sides with enamelled handles, finial resoldered, signed *Yoshizuka,* 14.5cm (5¾in), *L 24/31 Oct,*
£1,485 ($1,886)

8
A large bronze censer on dragon-form stand, Meiji period, of tall cylindrical form on a plinth base supporting a swirling dragon stand, h 159cm (62½in), *NY 31 Mar,*
$9,350 (£6,480)

9
A gilt bronze figure of Yoshitsune, Miyao, Meiji period, partly gilt, signed in a gilt reserve *Miyao saku,* on a gold lacquered wood stand, 27.7cm (10⅞in), *L 12 Dec,*
£1,265 ($1,594)

10
A large bronze vase, Toko, Meiji period, cast in high relief with three elephants, signed *Toko no-in* 55cm (21⅝in), *L 24/31 Oct,*
£1,650 ($2,095)

11
A silver wire cloisonné koro and cover, decorated with peacocks and cranes, h 28cm (11in), *A 10 Sept,*
Dfl 22,040 (£5,173; $6,724)

12
An Ota Tameshiro cloisonné vase and cover, Meiji period, decorated in silver wire with swallows and sparrows amongst foliage on grey and green grounds, inlaid stylised *ho-o* mark, slight stress cracks on finial and one on border, 23cm (9⅛in), *L 24/31 Oct,*
£1,155 ($1,467)

13
An Hattori Tadasaburo cloisonné vase, Meiji period, with *moriage* decoration in silver wire, green and yellow on a grey ground, inlaid mark of *Hattori Tadasaburo,* minute crack on neck, 31cm (12¼in), *L 24/31 Oct,*
£1,210 ($1,537)

14
A cloisonné vase, attributed to Hayashi Kodenji, Meiji period, worked in silver wire with colourful flowers, unsigned, 15cm (6in), *L 24/31 Oct,*
£1,430 ($1,816)

1
A pair of Ota Kichisaburo vases, Meiji period, decorated with silver-outlined white and orange chrysanthemums on a pale leaf green ground, inlaid mark *Ota* on underside, 30.5cm (12in), *NY 10 Nov*, $1,760 (£1,397)

2
A cloisonné tray, Meiji period, with silver wire decoration of two pigeons on a blue ground, signed *Kozan* and with *kakihan Kinzan*, 28.2cm (11⅛in), *L 24/31 Oct*, £1,100 ($1,397)

3
A cloisonné vase and cover, Namikawa Yasuyuki, Meiji period, decorated in silver wire on a black ground, signed *Kyoto, Namikawa* on a silver plaque, 13cm (5⅛in), *L 24/31 Oct*, £2,970 ($3,772)

4
A cloisonné koro and cover, Namikawa Yasuyuki, Meiji period, decorated with alternate gold and silver panels of cream, brown and green, base of silver set on three small silver feet, signed on a silver plaque *Kyoto Namikawa*, 8cm (3⅛in), *L 24/31 Oct*, £5,390 ($6,845)

5
A cloisonné kodansu, attributed to Namikawa Yasuyuki, Meiji period, the exterior decorated with silver wire on a black ground, the interior on a blue ground, unsigned, 14cm (5½in), *L 24/31 Oct*, £2,640 ($3,353)

6
A pair of large cloisonné vases, Meiji period, decorated with silver wire on a black ground, both chipped, one repaired, 93.5cm (36¾in), *L 18 July*, £1,760 ($2,341)

7
A pair of large cloisonné vases, Meiji period, decorated with birds and flowers on a black ground, damaged and repaired, 85cm (33½in), *L 18 July*, £1,045 ($1,390)

8
A pair of cloisonné dishes, Meiji period, with silver wire decoration of three white cranes in flight on a pale blue ground, 46cm (18⅛in), *L 1 Nov*, £990 ($1,267)

9
A silver-mounted cloisonné vase, Meiji period, decorated with grey and white on a midnight blue ground, the foot and neck enamelled in lavender and blue, chipped, 25.4cm (10in), *NY 31 Mar*, $550 (£381)

10
A pair of cloisonné vases, Meiji period, hexagonal, enamelled with flowers and birds, chrome mounts, 23.5cm (9¼in), *NY 10 Nov*, $825 (£655)

11
A cloisonné vase and cover, Meiji period, decorated in silver wire on a black ground, 17cm (6¹¹⁄₁₆in), *NY 31 Mar*, $2,750 (£1,906)

12
A pair of cloisonné vases, Meiji period, decorated in *musen-jippo* and silver wire on a pale grey ground, 30.5cm (12in), *L 24/31 Oct*, £605 ($768)

1

2

3

4

5

6

7

8

9

10

11

12

1
A Shibayama vase,
Toshimasa, Meiji period,
decorated in gold *oki-
hirame*, with four *kinji*
panels, the neck with
enamelled silver
mounts, repaired, signed
Toshimasa, 31.5cm (12in),
L 18 July,
£1,540 ($2,048)

2
A pair of silver and
cloisonné mounted
Shibayama vases,
Tomohisa, Meiji period,
inlay losses, signed
Tomohisa on a gilt pad,
25.5cm (10in), *NY 31 Mar*,
$2,530 (£1,753)

3
A Shibayama four-case
inro, Kakosai and
Kyogetsusai, 19th cent,
the *kinji* ground inlaid in
mother-of-pearl, ivory
and coral, signed *Kakosai*
and on a plaque
Kyogetsusai, 9.1cm (3⅝in);
with a Manju netsuke
and an ivory ojime,
signed *Masatami*,
L 24/31 Oct,
£3,300 ($4,191)

4
A Shibayama inro,
Masaaki (Shomei), 19th
cent, inlaid in mother-
of-pearl and horn on a
ground of *kinji*, signed
on a *raden* tablet *Masaaki
(Shomei)*, 11.7cm (4½in),
NY 31 Mar,
$5,280 (£3,659)

5
A Shibayama sheath inro,
Meiji period, inlaid in
mother-of-pearl, ivory
and silver, the ground in
gold *takamakie, togidashi,
kirigane* and *nashiji*,
10.7cm (4¼in); with
silver ojime, *NY 13 Mar*,
$4,675 (£3,240)

6
A Shibayama gold lacquer
inro, 19th cent, inlaid in
mother-of-pearl, horn
and coral, slight *kirigane*
missing, signed on a
raden tablet *Shibayama*,
9.4cm (3¾in), *NY 31 Mar*,
$3,410 (£2,363)

7
A Shibayama three-case
inro, 19th cent, inlaid in
mother-of-pearl, coral
and bone on a ground of
kinji, unsigned, 10.5cm
(4⅝in), *NY 31 Mar*,
$3,850 (£2,668)

8
A Shibayama three-case
inro, 19th cent, inlaid in
mother-of-pearl and
coloured ivory, minute
chip and slight restoration,
10.3cm (4in); with a
Kagamibuta, 4.5cm
(1¾in); and a silver
ojime, *L 24/31 Oct*,
£2,200 ($2,794)

9
A Shibayama tsuba,
Tsuguyasu, Meiji period,
the *kinji* ground with
silver *seppa-dai, hitsu* and
mimi, slight parting of
mimi and ground, signed
Tsuguyasu on a red
lacquer reserve, 10cm
(4in), *NY 31 Mar*,
$2,200 (£1,525)

10
A Shibayama tsuba, Meiji
period, decorated on a
kinji ground, lined in
silver, slight crack at
edge, signed *Shibayama*
on a mother-of-pearl
reserve, 10cm (4in),
NY 31 Mar,
$2,200 (£1,525)

1

2

8

6

7

9

10

1
A four-case inro,
Tsuchida Soetsu, 18th
cent, decorated on the
roiro ground in gold,
pewter and *aogai*, *nashiji*
interior, some small
chips, signed *at the age of
82, Tsuchida Soetsu*, 7.4cm
(2⅞in), *L 15 Mar*,
£352 ($525)

2
A four-case inro,
Kajikawa family, 18th cent,
bearing a *roiro* ground,
decorated in gold
takamakie with details of
gold and silver foil,
slight chips, signed
Kajikawa saku, 7.8cm
(3in), *L 18 July*,
£308 ($410)

3
A four-case inro, Koma
family, 19th cent, decorated
on *nashiji* and *kinji* ground
in gold and coloured
takamakie, slight chips
and wear, signed *Koma*,
9.4cm (3⅝in), *L 15 Mar*,
£385 ($574)

4
A sheath inro, Nemoto
Shibayama, 19th cent,
rimmed with silver,
decorated in shell, horn,
coral and ivory, on a
ground of *kinji*, signed
Nemoto tsukuru with
silvered ojime and wood
and ivory netsuke,
unsigned, *NY 31 Mar*,
$4,840 (£3,354)

5
**A gold lacquer five-case
inro,** Hara Yoyusai, 19th
cent, bearing a *kinji* and
mura-nashiji ground,
decorated in gold and
slight coloured
takamakie, the interior
of *nashiji*, slight chip,
signed *Yoyusai saku*,
9.5cm (3⅞in), *NY 31 Mar*,
$3,190 (£2,211)

6
A four-case inro, Koma
Kansai, 19th cent, bearing
a *fundame* ground deco-
rated in gold and
coloured *takamakie*,
slight wear, signed
Kansai saku; with a gold
ojime and a lacquered
wood netsuke, unsigned,
8.6cm (3⅜in), *NY 31 Mar*,
$2,860 (£1,982)

7
A four-case inro,
Shokasai, 19th cent, the
roiro ground with *hirame*
flakes, and gold
takamakie and gold foil,
slight repairs, signed
Shokasai at the age of 75,
7.3cm (2⅞in), *L 18 July*,
£462 ($614)

8
**A four-case gold lacquer
inro,** Kajikawa family,
19th cent, signed
Kajikawa saku, 8.7cm
(3⅜in), *L 18 July*,
£550 ($732)

9
A four-case inro,
Shokasai, 19th cent, a
fundame ground decorated
in relief, of coloured
metals and gold, small
chip, signed *Shokasai*,
8.9cm (3½in), *NY 31 Mar*,
$2,750 (£1,906)

10
A four-case lacquer inro,
Hasegawa Kyorinsai,
19th cent, decorated in
gold and coloured inlays
on a *kinji* ground, *nashiji*
interiors, cracked, signed
Hasegawa Kyorinsai with
tsubo seal 'Shigeyoshi',
NY 28 June,
$467 (£346)

11
A four-case inro, Hara
Yoyusai, 19th cent, the
roiro ground decorated
in gold, brown and
silver *hiramakie*, *aogai*
and foil, the interior of
nashiji, slight foil flaking,
signed *Yoyusai*, 8.5cm
(3⅜in), *L 15 Mar*,
£550 ($820)

12
A four-case inro, Shinsai,
late 19th cent, decorated
in *roiro*, gold *hiramakie*
and *yamimakie* (black on
black), the interior of
nashiji, signed *Shinsai saku*,
8.5cm (3⅜in); with
staghorn netsuke of
Fukurokuja, unsigned,
L 15 Mar,
£935 ($1,394)

13
A five-case inro, Shiomi
Masanari, 19th cent,
decorated on the *roiro*
ground in gold and
slight coloured *togidashi*,
signed, in seal form,
Shiomi Masanari, 9.4cm
(3¾in), *L 15 Mar*,
£1,320 ($1,968)

1

2

3

4   5   6

7

8

9   10

11

12   13

1

A rare slender two-case inro in the form of a Gyotai, 19th cent, silvered metal on *roiro* ground, 8.5cm (3⅜in), *L 18 July*, £1,760 ($2,341)

2

A lacquered carved-wood two-case inro, 19th cent, the *nashiji* ground lacquered in gold, *nashiji* interiors, unsigned, *NY 28 June*, $990 (£733)

3

A four-case togidashi inro, 19th cent, the *mura-nashiji* ground decorated in gold, silver and red, *nashiji* interior, one corner restored, unsigned, 7.7cm (3in), *L 18 July*, £462 ($614)

4

A wood inro of three cases, 19th cent, decorated in gold *takamakie* and *e-nashiji* with fruiting vine, unsigned, 7.1cm (2⅞in), *L 15 Mar*, £319 ($475)

5

A miniature suzuribako, 19th cent, in the form of an inro, decorated in gold and coloured, *togidashi*, the interior of the box fitted with a *suzuri* and *kiku*-shaped *mizuire*, two brushes, a spike and a knife, unsigned, 9.3cm (3⅝in); with a stag antler Maju netsuke, 19th cent, unsigned, *L 18 July*, £7,150 ($9,510)

6

A gold lacquer five-case inro, 19th cent, the rich *kinji* ground decorated in gold and coloured *takamakie*, the eyes of glass, the interior of *nashiji*, minute chips, unsigned, 10.3cm (4in); with gilt metal ojime and a two-part ivory Manju, unsigned, *L 18 July*, £1,530 ($2,035)

7

A four-case inro, 19th cent, the *mura-kinpun* and *mura-nashiji* ground decorated in gold *hiramakie* and *kirigane*, the interior *nashiji*, the base restored, unsigned, 8.8cm (3½in), *L 15 Mar*, £572 ($853)

8

A pottery inro, netsuke and ojime, Kenya, 19th cent, the inro of two cases painted in coloured enamels with two views from Hiroshige's *Tokaido Road* series, signed *Kenya*, 6.9cm (2¾in), *L 15 Mar*, £572 ($852)

9

A bamboo and staghorn kizeruzutsu, Asakusa school, 19th cent, the top of staghorn, carved with roof-tile ends in low relief, the cord attachment forming the signature *Koku* (sai), 21.3cm (8⅜in), *L 15 Mar*, £352 ($524)

10

A rare wood kizeruzutsu, late 18th/early 19th cent, in the form of a long dragon with hinged body mounted with silver and the eyes of inlaid *aogai* with dark horn pupils, slight damage, unsigned, 22.3cm (8¾in), *L 15 Mar*, £638 ($951)

11

A wood kizeruzutsu, 19th cent, decorated with a snake in applied copper, a silver band and cord attachment at the top, crack, unsigned, 21.4cm (8⅜in), *L 15 Mar*, £374 ($557)

12

An inlaid gold pipe, Shunmei, Meiji period, decorated in *iroe-takazogan* in *shakudo*, *shibuichi*, and gold, signed *Shunmei* with *kakihan*, 22cm (8⅝in), *L 24/31 Oct*, £2,860 ($3,632)

13

A kizeru, 19th cent, bamboo body with *sentoku* and silver mouth-piece and bowl, decorated in *iroe-takazogan*, unsigned, 22.7cm (8⅞in), *L 15 Mar*, £209 ($311)

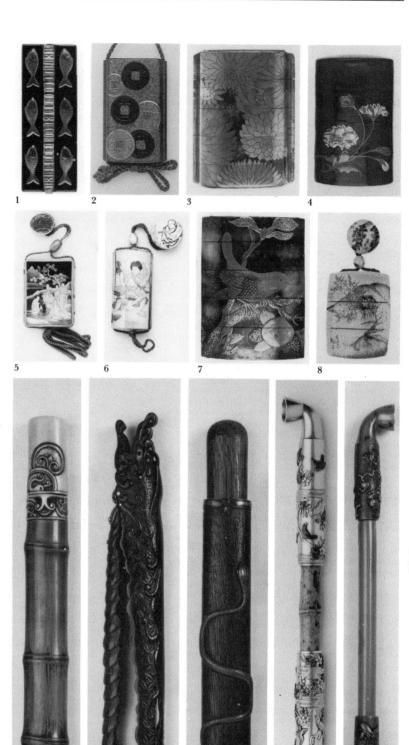

1 2 3 4

5 6 7 8

9 10 11 12 13

1
An ivory kizeruzutsu, Ashi, 19th cent, signed *Ashi* with seal *Yuki (Setsu)*, attached to a leather pouch with *shibuichi*, *shakudo*; with a gold ojime, signed *Ieaki* and an iron and silver pipe, *L 12 Dec*, £242 ($305)

2
An ivory kizeruzutsu, 19th cent, engraved and carved in *shishiaibori*, signed *Kako* (?) with seal 21.4cm (8¼in); containing a pipe of silver and bamboo, signed; with a silver ojime, signed *Issho*(?); and a leather pouch, unsigned, *L 12 Dec*, £1,980 ($2,495)

3
An unusual smoking set, Kosai Shunko, dated *Meiji 13th year (1880) 11th month*, a leather pouch and pipe-case with a silver and gilt *kanemono*, attached to a silver ash-tray netsuke, and a silver ojime, the *kanemono*, and netsuke signed *Kosai Shunko* with seal *Shunko*, the ojime signed *Ittei Shunko*, *L 12 Dec*, £935 ($1,178)

4
A large smoking set, 19th cent, embossed leather pouch and pipe-case with gilded designs, attached by a six-strand chain, to a large *tsuishu* manju applied in silver, a bronze and bamboo pipe, *L 12 Dec*, £1,045 ($1,317)

5
A smoking set, Kansai, Meiji period, embroidered pouch and pipe-case with gilt details, attached by a multi-link chain to a *kagamibuta*, a *shibuichi* ojime, bamboo and silver pipe, the *kanemono* signed *Kansai*, *L 12 Dec*, £682 ($859)

6
A cylindrical black lacquered box with cover, gold *hiramakie* decoration of *tachibana*, h 10.5cm (4in), *A 10 Sept*, Dfl 406 (£95; $123)

7
A large lacquer covered basin, 18th cent, in gold *fundame* on a *nashiji* ground, approx 43 x 33cm (17 x 13in), *NY 31 Mar*, $1,430 (£991)

8
A gold lacquer box and cover containing Cha-no-yu utensils, late Edo period, the box with *fundame* and *nashiji* grounds decorated in gold and silver, 26.5 x 15.5 x 12.5cm (10⅜ x 6⅛ x 4⅞in); a stoneware Chawan; a Chaire; a porcelain napkin holder; a bamboo Cha and woven container; and an ivory Cha, *L 24/31 Oct*, £3,300 ($4,191)

9
A black lacquered bowl with cover, 19th cent, gold *hiramakie*, *nashiji* and *okibirame* decoration of cranes and *minogame*, d 10.5cm (4¼in), *A 10 Sept*, Dfl 1,102, (£258; $335)

10
A lacquer tray, late Edo period, gold decoration on a *nashiji* ground, 30.5 x 21.5cm (12 x 8⅜in), *L 24/31 Oct*, £440 ($559)

11
A part set of lacquered eating utensils, 19th cent, comprising a square table, four covered bowls, three bowls on *tokuri* and a ladle, the table 43cm (17in), *L 15 Mar*, £935 ($1,393)

12
Suzuribako and Bundai, late Edo/Meiji period, decorated in shades of gold and silver, 26.8 x 24.7 x 4.9cm (10½ x 9¾ x 1⅞in); the table (illustrated) 62.4 x 34.4 x 11.9cm (25⅝ x 13½ x 4¾in); both with lacquered wood boxes marked *O Suzuribako* and *Go Bundai*, *NY 31 Mar*, $24,200 (£16,771)

13
A gold lacquer tray, Seishu, Meiji period, decorated on a *kinji* ground, signed *Seishu* with *kakihan*, 27.4 x 16.3cm (10¾ x 6⅜in), *L 24/31 Oct*, £440 ($559)

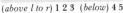

(*above l to r*) 1 2 3 (*below*) 4 5   7

8

9   10   11

12   13

1
A five-tier lacquer picnic-box, 17th cent, decorated in gold on a *roiro* ground, chips and wear throughout, 23.5 x 16 x 12.5cm (9¼ x 6⅜ x 5in), *NY 31 Mar,* $1,430 (£991)

2
A suzuribako/hibachi, 19th cent, one drawer fitted with a *suzuri* and *mizuire,* slight chips, unsigned, 13.5 x 22 x 11.2cm (5¼ x 8⅝ x 4⅜in), *L 18 July,* £935 ($1,244)

3
A suzuribako, late Edo period, decorated in gold on a *roiro* ground, the interior with a fitted tray containing a *suzuri* and silver *mizuire,* 26.2 x 18.9 x 4.6cm (10¼ x 7⅜ x 1¾in), *L 24/31 Oct,* £2,200 ($2,794)

4
A gold lacquer suzuribako, Funabashi Shumin, late Edo/Meiji period, the interior with fitted tray holding a *shakudo-nanako mizuire,* two implements and brushes, small chips, signed *Funabashi Shumin* with seal, 23.8 x 20.8 x 4.6cm (9⅜ x 8⅛ x 1¾in), *L 24/31 Oct,* £4,620 ($5,867)

5
A suzuribako, late Edo/Meiji period, decorated in gold, *mizuire* missing, slight cracks and chips, 24.5 x 18.3 x 3.8cm (9⅝ x 7⅛ x 1½in), *L 24/31 Oct,* £1,980 ($2,515)

6
A lacquer tebako, 18th cent, decorated with flowering plum and pine on a *roiro* ground, engraved gilt brass handles, 38.5 x 30.5 x 25.5cm (15¼ x 12 x 10in), *NY 31 Mar,* $1,870 (£1,296)

7
A gold lacquer kodansu, late Edo period, decorated on a *kinji* ground, interior with three drawers, applied with silver mounts, slight chips around lock, 12.8 x 10.1 x 15.2cm (5 x 4 x 6in), *NY 31 Mar,* $7,370 (£5,107)

8
A lacquer bunko, 19th cent, the *kinji* ground decorated in gold with inlays of rusted pewter and mother-of-pearl, chips and cracks, 46 x 35.5 x 24cm (18 x 14 x 9½in), *NY 31 Mar,* $5,775 (£4,002)

9
A gold lacquer kobako, Meiji period, decorated on a *kinji* ground, silver rims, 15 x 11.5 x 5.5cm (6 x 4½ x 2¼in), *NY 31 Mar,* $880 (£610)

10
A jubako, mid-Edo period, of two tiers, decorated on *fundame* and *nashiji* grounds, small chips, 25.5 x 19 x 14cm (10 x 7½ x 5½in), *L 24/31 Oct,* £2,530 ($3,213)

11
A box and cover, Koma Kansai (after Ritsuo), late Edo period, corners of the cover cracked, signed *Ho Haritsuo, Kansai saku* with *kakihan,* 18.7 x 16.2 x 10.6cm (7¼ x 6⅜ x 4⅛in), *L 24/31 Oct,* £2,200 ($2,794)

12
A gold lacquer tebako, early Meiji period, decorated on a *nashiji* ground, the rims with silver mounts; with silk bag and wood box; 14 x 24 x 18cm (5½ x 9⅜ x 7⅛in), *NY 31 Mar,* $4,675 (£3,240)

13
A lacquer kodansu, 19th cent, decorated in *fundame hiramakie* on a *roiro* ground, the interior with three drawers, silver mounts, some wear and rubbing, chip on front edge, unsigned, 17.2 x 31 x 20.3cm (7 x 12¼ x 8in), *NY 10 Nov,* $990 (£786)

1 2

3 4 5

6 7 8

9 10 11

12 13

1
A **natsume**, 19th cent, decorated in gold on reddish-brown ground with pewter and mother-of-pearl inlays, 6.7cm (2⅝in), *L 15 Mar,* £165 ($246)

2
A **Momoyama export coffer**, *c.*1600, the *roiro* ground decorated in gold *hiramakie* and *aogai* copper mounts, some restoration, 35.6 x 22.4 x 19.2cm (14 x 8⅞ x 7⅝in), *NY 31 Mar,* $3,190 (£2,211)

3
A **lacquer box and cover**, Meiji period, in the form of a *shojo,* worked in gold *togidashi, hiramakie* and *e-nashiji,* two minute chips, 9.5cm (3¾in), *L 24/31 Oct,* £1,320 ($1,676)

4
An **early lacquer box and cover**, 17th cent, decorated on a sparse *nashiji* ground, slight cracks and chips, unsigned, 19 x 10.5 x 11.3cm (7½ x 4⅛ x 4⅜in), *L 18 July,* £495 ($658)

5
A **silver-mounted lacquered wood smoking set**, Meiji period, the plain wood ground decorated in gold *takamakie* and *kirigane,* 15 x 13.5 x 13cm (6 x 5¼ x 5in), *NY 31 Mar,* $1,210 (£839)

6
A **lacquer cabinet**, Meiji/Taisho period, the doors enclosing three drawers, decorated in gold and coloured *takamakie* with cranes, 12.2 x 15cm (4¾ x 6in), *L 24/31 Oct,* £3,960 ($5,029)

7
A **pair of gold lacquer boxes and covers**, Meiji period, in the form of two *oshidori,* the eyes inlaid, some damage and chips, unsigned, 12.5 and 12.3cm (4¹³/15 and 4¹⁵/16in), *L 15 Mar,* £1,210 ($1,803)

8
A **lacquer painting of a miniature landscape**, Shibata Zeshin, signed *Zeshin* with seal, mounted as a *kakemono,* 19 x 16.4cm (7½ x 6½in), *L 15 Mar,* £1,540 ($2,296)

9
A **lacquer box**, Taisho period, decorated in gold *hiramakie* on a ground of *manji*-diaper in matt black on *roiro,* silver-gilt loose ring mounts, some repairs; 21.2 x 19.2 x 4.5cm (7⅞ x 7½ x 1¾in); with a fitted lacquer box; *L 15 Mar,* £440 ($559)

10
A **lacquer box**, 19th cent, the vermilion ground decorated in gold and silver, the rims of silver, 13.3 x 10.2 x 5.5cm (5¼ x 4 x 2⅛in), *L 15 Mar,* £1,210 ($1,803)

1

2

3

4

3

6

5

8

7

9   10

1
A large Miyao clock garniture, Meiji period, the chapter ring with enamel numerals, the hands in form of a dragon, the sides applied with mask and ring handles, on lacquered fruitwood stands, clock h 124cm (48½in), vases h 72.5cm (28½in), *NY 31 Mar,* $60,500 (£42,014)

2
A striking verge bracket clock with alarum, late Edo period, contained in a lacquered fruitwood case on four curved legs, slight losses to case, 45.5cm (17⅞in), *L 24/31 Oct,* £4,400 ($5,588)

3
A pillar clock, 19th cent, the front cover with thirteen hour plaques, the base with fitted drawer for key, 50cm (19¾in), *L 24/31 Oct,* £990 ($1,257)

4
A lacquer cabinet on stand, Taisho period, the *roiro* ground decorated in gold and coloured *hiramakie, takemakie, kirikane, e-nashiji* and mother-of-pearl, slight chips, 64 x 57cm (25¼ x 22¾in), *NY 10 Nov,* $6,600 (£5,238)

5
A shibayama display cabinet, Meiji period, inset with gold lacquer panels inlaid in ivory, bone and mother-of-pearl with birds and flowers, some inlay missing, 240 x 153cm (94½ x 60⅛in), *L 24/31 Oct,* £4,180 ($5,309)

6
An inlaid lacquer tsuitate, Meiji period, worked in ivory, mother-of-pearl and lacquer, stand chipped, crack on reverse panel, 101 x 96cm (39⅜ x 37¾in), *L 24/31 Oct,* £1,870 ($2,374)

7
A lacquer norimono (ceremonial palanquin), Edo period, decorated overall on the *roiro* ground in shades of gold and silver *hiramakie,* gilt copper mounts, the interior lined with Tosa school paintings, 137.5 x 129 x 96.5cm (54 x 50¾ x 38in), *L 24/31 Oct,* £26,400 ($33,528)

1

2

3

5

6

7

1
A Kakiemon dish, late
17th cent, decorated in
iron-red, green, blue
and yellow enamels and
touches of gilding, the
rim with a minute chip,
five spur marks on the
base, 23.1cm (9⅛in),
L 12 Dec,
£13,200 ($16,632)

2
A Kakiemon jar and cover,
late 17th cent, decorated
in iron-red and blue,
green and reddish-brown
enamels, the interior rim
of the cover with one
chip, 31cm (12¼in),
L 12 Dec,
£31,900 ($40,194)

3
A Kakiemon dish, late
17th cent, decorated in
iron-red, blue, green and
yellow enamels and touches
of gilding, the base with
six spur marks, 24.6cm
(9¾in), *L 12 Dec,*
£20,900 ($26,334)

4
A large Namikawa Sosuke,
vase, Meiji period,
decorated in silver, gilt
and wireless techniques
on a pale blue ground,
unsigned, slight stress
cracks on one peony,
55cm (21⅝in),
NY 31 Mar,
$8,800 (£6,098)

5
A fine lacquer cabinet,
Meiji period, applied
throughout with silver
mounts repoussé and chased
with *kiku,* five mounts
missing, 110 x 113 x
51.5cm (43¼ x 44½ x
20¼in), *L 24/31 Oct,*
£71,500 ($90,805)

1

2

3

4

5

1
A Nagamitsu ivory group,
Furukawa Meiji period,
of three hawks, the legs
cast in bronze, the eyes
inlaid, applied with
engraved silver mounts,
signed *Furukawa*,
52.5cm (20⅝in),
NY 31 Mar,
$12,100 (£8,385)

2
A Tonkotsu, Shibata
Zeshin, 19th cent, in the
form of a pouch, the
green ground decorated
in gold and grey, *roiro*
interior, wood cover,
cord loops slightly worn,
signed, in lightly
scratched characters
Zeshin 6.4cm (2½in),
L 15 Mar,
£1,540 ($2,296)

3
A study of a coiled rat,
Masakatsu of Ise
Yamada, 19th cent, the
details finely rendered
in lightly stained wood,
the eyes inlaid with dark
horn, signed in a
polished reserve
Masakatsu with *kakihan*,
3.5cm (1⅜in),
L 24/31 Oct,
£3,410 ($4,331)

4
A study of a toad on a tile
end, Matsuda Sukenaga,
19th cent, the skin and
tile depicted in slightly
worn wood, the eyes
inlaid with ivory and
horn, signed *Matsuda*
Sukenaga tsukuru, 4.5cm
(1¾in), *L 24 Oct*,
£2,640 ($3,353)

5
A four-case Inro, Koma
Koryu, 19th cent, of
ribbed form, the *roiro*
ground with mura-
nashiji and *hirame* flakes,
slight dent, signed *Koma*
Koryu saku with *kakihan*,
7.5cm (3in); with
umimatsu ojime,
unsigned, *L 15 Mar*,
£1,210 ($1,804)

6
A rare wood study of an
oshidori, Masanao of
Kyoto, late 18th cent, the
details finely rendered in
stained boxwood, the
eyes inlaid with dark
horn, signed in an oval
reserve *Masanao*, 5cm
(2in), *L 24 Oct*,
£48,400 ($61,468)

1

2

5

3

4

6

1

A pair of carved wood Koma-inu, Momoyama/early Edo period, traces of polychrome, 67.5cm (26½in), *NY 31 Mar,* $11,000 (£7,623)

2

Part figure of a Haniwa woman, Tumulus period, the arms fragmentary, pierced through at the eyes and mouth, supporting a pot on her head, 58.5cm (23in), *NY 28 June,* $1,320 (£978)

3

A large mask of Hannya, Edo period, the features boldly carved with traces of colour and gesso ground, 49.5cm (19½in), *L 15 Mar,* £462 ($688)

4

A large Jomon jar, Middle period, 3000-2000 BC, with wide mouth and tall loop handles, one broken, restoration, 55.9cm (22in), *NY 28 June,* $1,980 (£1,467)

5

An Oribe bottle, early/mid Edo period, decorated in iron, a thick green glaze running from the shoulder, the rim with lacquer repairs, 13.6cm (5⅜in). *L 15 Mar,* £286 ($426)

6

A pair of wood figures of guardian deities, early Edo period, the details, painted on a gesso ground, the faces lacquered, one gold and one brown, eyes inlaid with glass, some losses and repairs, 55cm and 56cm (21⅞in and 22in), *L 24/31 Oct,* £990 ($1,257)

7

A wood, lacquer and gesso group, Meiji period, depicting two free-standing wrestlers, each grimacing, their eyes and teeth inset, 41.9cm (16½in), *C 2-5 Oct,* £2,530 ($3,264)

8

A group of four chaire, 19th cent, comprising a Seto caddy, an Owari caddy, a Satsuma caddy and an Izumo caddy, *NY 28 June,* $935 (£693)

9

A group of four chaire, 18th/19th cent, comprising a tall cylindrical chaire, a double gourd chaire, a small globular chaire, a globular chaire with cylindrical neck, each glazed in shades of brown, *NY 28 June,* $880 (£652)

10

A group of four chaire, 18th/19th cent, comprising a Kyoto double gourd caddy with pale green glaze, a Takatori caddy with brown-purple glaze, a Karmono caddy with mottled brown glaze and an ovoid Bizen caddy with yellow-brown glaze, *NY 28 June,* $1,045 (£774)

11

A group of four chaire, 18th/19th cent, comprising an Izumo caddy, a Kyoto caddy, a Satsuma caddy and an ovoid caddy, each glazed in shades of brown, *NY 28 June,* $880 (£652)

12

A group of four chaire, 18th/19th cent, comprising Takatori examples, a Shidoro example and Seto examples with brown-yellow glaze, *NY 28 June,* $1,155 (£856)

13

A Karatsu bowl, early/mid Edo period, covered with a crackled glaze and decorated with *hakeme* brushstrokes of white slip, two gold lacquer repairs, 17.1cm (6¾in), *L 15 Mar,* £352 ($525)

14

A Karatsu (or Hagi) Chawan, early Edo period, covered with a crackled cream glaze, some gold and silver lacquer repairs, 14.5cm (5¾in), *L 15 Mar,* £385 ($574)

1

2

3

4

5

6

7

8   9   10   11   12

13   14

1
A composite suit of armour, of Ni Mai Tachi Do Tosei Gusoku type, the helmet by Saotome Iyenari, 17th cent, the rest early 19th cent, *L 24/31 Oct*, £7,700 ($9,779)

2
A composite suit of armour, with helmet by Miochin Munehisa, dated 1534, the rest early 18th cent, *L 24/31 Oct*, £3,150 ($4,00)

3
A shibayama tsuba, Nemoto, Meiji period, slight chip on border, signed *Nemoto tsukuru*, 11.2cm (4⅜in), *L 24/31 Oct*, £1,100 ($1,397)

4
A Diagoro School tsuba, pierced with a waterwheel under a bridge, unsigned, 8.4cm (3¼in), *L 24/31 Oct*, £330 ($419)

5
An oval tsuba, Tadatoki, pierced around the *seppa-dai* with three tattered fans, signed *Bushu ju Akasaka Tadatoki*, 7.6cm (3in), *L 24/31 Oct*, £616 ($782)

6
A Shibuichi tsuba, details in copper, inscribed *Nagatsune* and 'dated' on the bell, first year of Meiwa (1764), 8.5cm (3¼in), *L 24/31 Oct*, £2,750 ($3,492)

7
A Shibuichi tsuba, Riuyeiken Yoshikuni, fashioned around the *seppa-dai* as two *kiku*, signed *Riuyeiken Yoshikuni* with *kakihan*, 6.8cm (2⅝in), *L 24/31 Oct*, £484 ($614)

8
A copper tsuba, Shozui Hogen, applied in silver and *shibuichi* relief, signed *Shozui Hogen*, 8.7cm (3⅜in), *L 15 Mar*, £418 ($623)

9
An oval Shakudo tsuba, Kochiku, *hitsu* plugged in copper, details in gold and silver *nunome*, signed *Kochiku* with *kakihan*, 8.6cm (3⅜in), *L 18 July*, £440 ($585)

10
An oval tsuba, Hashimoto Masanari, pierced around the *seppa-dai* with a wheel of arrows, signed *Bushu ju Masanari* with *kakihan*, 7.3cm (2⅞in), *L 1 Nov*, £660 ($845)

11
A circular tsuba, Tsuneharu, carved in relief, details in copper, *shakudo*, silver and gold, signed *Tsuneharu* with *kakihan*, 8.5cm (3¼in), *L 24/31 Oct*, £800 ($1,118)

12
A tsuba, Seki Yoshinori, fashioned as a crouching rabbit, the eyes inlaid in *shibuichi*, signed *Soriuken Yoshinori*, 6.7cm (2⅝in), *L 18 July*, £385 ($512)

13
A Tanaka-style tsuba, Yukitsugu, applied in relief, plugged in *shakudo*, the outer rim in gold speckles, details in gilt, *shakudo*, gold and silver *nunome*, signed *Yukitsugu*, 7.6cm (3in), *L 18 July*, £330 ($512)

14
A tsuba, early Choshu school, of circular form pierced with an anchor and curling rope, with *udenuki ana*, signed *Choshu hagi ju Kawaji Gonnojo Tomokane saku*, 7.7cm (3in), *L 24/31 Oct*, £165 ($210)

15
A tsuba, applied on the iron plate with soft metal panels, the *hitsu* plugged in cat-scratched gilt, details in silver, gold, *shibuichi*, *shakado* and copper, the outer rim in gold *nunome*, unsigned, 8cm (3⅛in), *L 24/31 Oct*, £1,430 ($1,816)

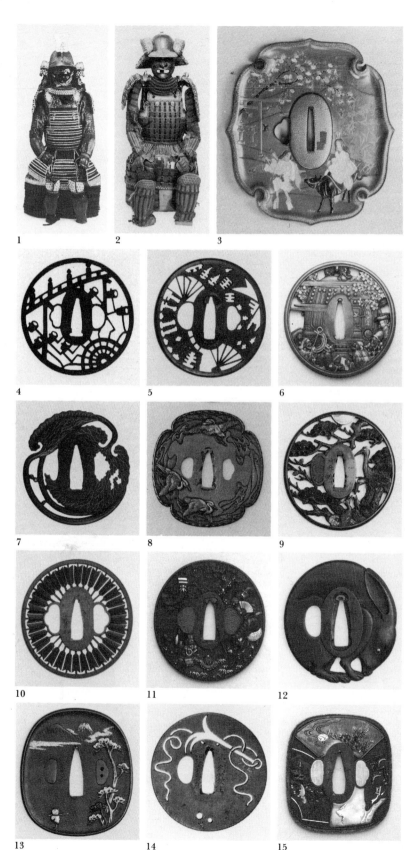

1
A cloisonné mounted
Aikuchi; the blade
22.2cm (8¾in); the Saya
and Tsuka decorated on
the black ground; the
fittings engraved with
kiku, L 24/31 Oct,
£825 ($1,048)

2
A shakudo nanako kozuka,
Goto school, decorated
in relief, details in gilt
and silver, and a *chusho
kozuka* applied in gilt,
L 15 Mar,
£165 ($246)

3
A carved ivory **Wakizashi,**
Meiji period, carved in
relief, the tsuba and
border inscribed with a
key fret pattern, 47cm
(18½in), *NY 28 June,*
$880 (£652)

4
A matchlock gun,
18th/19th cent, the
octagonal barrel
decorated in silver and
gold *nunome,* 28.3cm
(11⅛in), the lacquered
wood stock decorated in
gold, signed *Moriyama
Sukezaemon,* 51.5cm
(20¼in), *L 15 Mar,*
£2,310 ($3,442)

5
A shakudo nanako **Fuchi-
kashira,** Goto Ichijo
(ascribed to), applied in
relief, details in silver,
gilt and *shakudo,* inscribed
Goto Hakuo Ichijo,
L 1 Nov,
£748 ($957)

6
A **Mitokoro-mono,** Goto
Seijo (attributed to),
comprising *kozuka, kogai*
and *menuki,* details in
shakudo and gold
nunome, unsigned,
L 24/31 Oct,
£1,870 ($2,375)

7
A shakudo nanako kozuka,
applied and decorated
in relief, details in
copper and gilt,
unsigned, *L 15 Mar,*
£264 ($393)

8
A **shibuichi set,** Kikuchi
Fusamitsu, decorated in
iroe-honzogan, details in
copper, *shakudo* and gold,
signed *Kikuchi Fusamitsu*
with *kakihan, L 18 July,*
£143 ($190)

9
A **shibuichi set,** Jiriusai
Tomohide, carved in
relief and applied with
Hotei, details in gold
nunome, gilt, copper and
shakudo, signed *Jiriusai
Tomohide* with *kakihan,*
L 18 July,
£275 ($366)

10
A pair of iron **Abumi
(stirrups),** Edo period,
decorated in silver and
copper, the interior of
red lacquer, signed
Nakajima, L 24/31 Oct,
£1,100 ($1,397)

11
A ko-kinko mounted
handachi, ascribed to
Suraga (no) Kami
Morimichi, blade,
koshirae, *L 15 Mar,*
£3,850 ($5,737)

12
A **handachi,** Kaneyoshi,
Koshirae, blade 71.4cm
(28in), *L 24/31 Oct,*
£3,520 ($4,470)

13
A shinshinto **tachi,**
Hanabe Kenryushi
Toshihide, dated Tenpo
3, dragon year (1832)
Spring, ura-mei Jinchu
Hokoku, blade, 72.4cm
(28½in); Saya of sparse
nashiji and gold, silvered
metal mounts, Koshirae,
L 24/31 Oct,
£3,410 ($4,331)

14
A finely mounted koto
Mino **tachi;** blade, 71.1cm
(28in); *Koshirae,* Saya of
nashiji with *kiri-mon* in
gold *hiramakie,* gilt
mounts, *L 24/31 Oct,*
£3,740 ($4,750)

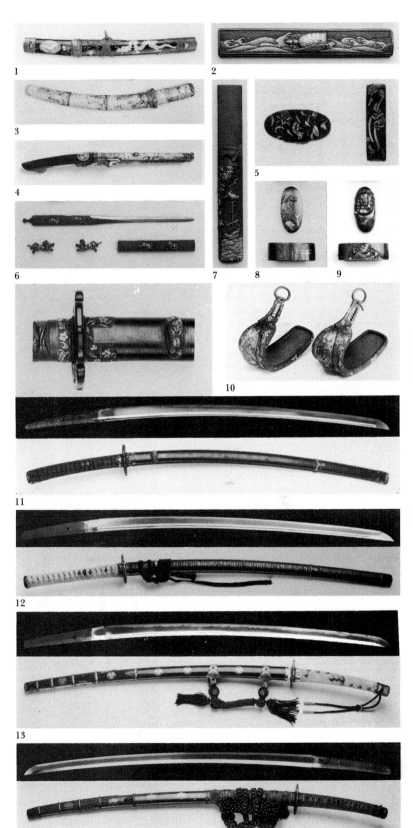

1
An ivory figure of a monkey trainer, Gozan, Meiji period, signed *Gozan*, 43cm (17in), *NY 10 Nov,* $1,045 (£829)

2
A carved figure of a bijin, Doraku, Meiji period, the details carved in pale ivory, signed *Doraku saku,* 28cm (11in), *NY 31 Mar,* $2,200 (£1,525)

3
An ivory okimono, depicting two music-making Tennin, signed *Yoshimasa,* 12.5cm (5in), *A 10 Dec,* Dfl 1,276 (£305; $362)

4
A carved ivory figure of a farmer, Tatake, Meiji period, slight cracks, hat chipped, signed *Tatake,* 29.2cm (11½in), *NY 10 Nov,* $495 (£393)

5
An ivory figure of Kannon, Meido, Meiji period, signed *Meido koku,* 27.9cm (11in), *L 1 Nov,* £308 ($394)

6
Tokyo school figure of a gardener and a boy, Biho (Yoshikuni), Meiji period, the details well rendered in unstained ivory, signed *Biho/(Yoshikuni),* 16.5cm (6½in), *L 15 Mar,* £715 ($1,066)

7
An ivory group, Meiko, Meiji period, depicting four figures, slight chip and loss, signed *Meiko,* 12.8cm (5in), *L 1 Nov,* £880 ($1,126)

8
An ivory carving of a man, Hoko (?), Meiji period, the ivory stained, signed on a red lacquer tablet *Hoko*(?), 10cm (4in), *L 15 Mar,* £660 ($984)

9
An ivory carving, c.1900, of a fisherman accompanied by two boys, signed, 22cm (8⅜in), *P 24-25 Jan,* £198 ($287)

10
An ivory group of a father and son, Masanobu, Meiji period, signed *Masanobu,* 25.5cm (10in), *L 24/31 Oct,* £2,035 ($2,584)

11
An ivory carving, c.1900, in the form of a young dancing maiden holding aloft a basket, 19cm (7½in), *P 24-25 Jan,* £176 ($255)

12
An ivory group of a lady in a palanquin, Meiji period, one handle broken off palanquin, minor cracks, signed *Meishin koku,* 11.4cm (4½in), *NY 10 Nov,* $1,320 (£1,048)

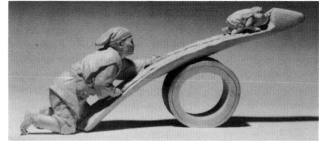

1

2

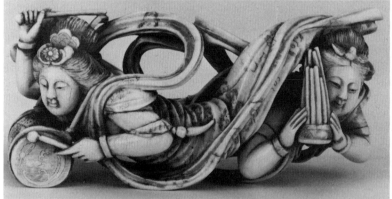

3

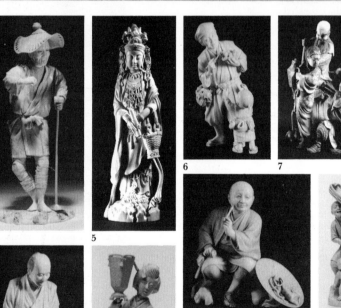

4

5

6

7

8

9

10

11

12

1
An ivory figure of a bijin,
Nobuyuki, Meiji period,
repaired and restored at
the base, signed
Nobuyuki saku, 28.5cm
(11¼in), *NY 10 Nov*,
$1,540 (£1,222)

2
A figure of a man,
Ryushi, Meiji period,
the ivory lightly stained,
sword hilt restored,
signed *Ryushi*, 22.6cm
(8¾in), *L 15 Mar*,
£572 ($853)

3
An ivory figure of a
Yamabushi priest blowing
a conch shell, Togyoku,
Meiji period, signed
Togyoku, 15.2cm (6in),
NY 10 Nov,
$440 (£349)

4
A stained ivory figural
group, Tokumasa, Meiji
period, the robes etched
and stained red, old
break and repair, signed
Tokumasa, 22cm (8⅝in),
NY 10 Nov,
$4,180 (£3,317)

5
An ivory group of the
susuisan-kyo or three *sake*
tasters, Ogawa Soryu (?)
Meiji period, the details
rendered in lightly
stained ivory, signed on
a red lacquer tablet
Ogawa Soryu(?) 12.8cm
(5in), *L 18 July*,
£990 ($1,317)

6
An ivory vase and cover,
Tomioka, Meiji period,
the cover surmounted by
a tiger finial, signed
Tomioka, 34.5cm (13⅝in),
L 18 July,
£715 ($951)

7
An ivory group, Tokyo
school, Meiji period,
signed, 30cm (11¾in),
NY 31 Mar,
$2,530 (£1,753)

8
A sea ivory figure of a
fisherman, signed
Tomeido Tamayuki to,
42.5cm (16⅝in), *L 24/31 Oct*,
£1,045 ($1,327)

9
A wood and ivory figure of
a drum peddlar, Meiji
period, unsigned, 25.8cm
(10⅛in), *L 15 Mar*,
£990 ($1,476)

10
An ivory figure of a bijin,
Tokyo school, Meiji
period, signed, 32cm
(12½in), *NY 31 Mar*,
$4,125 (£2,859)

11
An ivory and wood model
of the Takarabune, Meiji
period, the seven gods
standing or seated on
deck each with their
various attributes, the
hull inlaid with mother-
of-pearl, 53cm (20⅞in),
L 24/31 Oct,
£2,860 ($3,632)

12
An ivory vase and cover,
Meiji period, carved in
relief with immortals,
40cm (15¾in), *NY 31 Mar*,
$2,530 (£1,753)

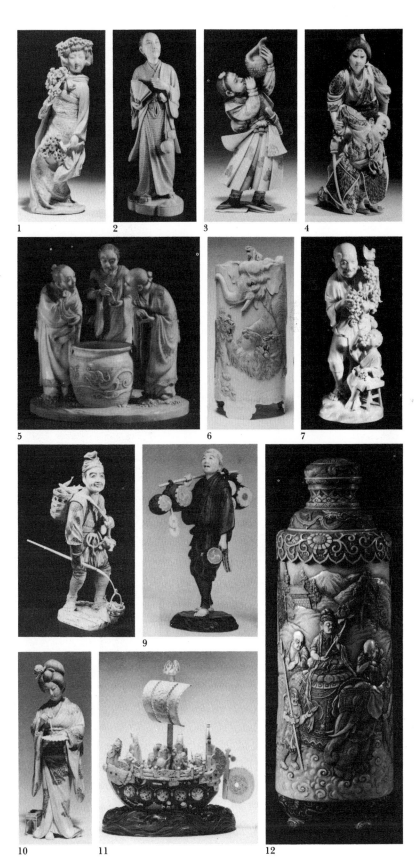

1

2

3

4

5

6

7

9

10

11

12

1

A two-part sentoku and enamel Manju, 18th cent, of *kiku* form, the petals alternately filled with red and green enamel, some enamel missing, unsigned, 3.8cm (1¾in), *L 14 Mar,*
£242 ($361)

2

A model of a mask of a Nio, Fukai Muboku, 19th cent, the eyes inlaid in glass with black, gilt and green pupils, wood lightly worn, signed *Fukai Muboku,* 5.5cm (2⅛in), *L 18 July,*
£319 ($424)

3

A figure of a Karako, early to mid-19th cent, the details well rendered in slightly worn and well-toned wood, unsigned, 4.5cm (1¾in), *L 14 Mar,*
£286 ($426)

4

A group of two mushrooms, early 19th cent, the details slightly worn in the lightly stained wood, unsigned, 5.8cm (2¼in), *L 14 Mar,*
£198 ($295)

5

A model of two Aoi leaves, 18th cent, the details slightly worn, unsigned, 4.3cm (1⅝in), *L 14 Mar,*
£286 ($426)

6

A boxwood study of a chimpanzee, Michael Webb, 1980, the face, ears, hands and feet stained pale brown while the body is black, the eyes inlaid with horn, signed *MJW,* 4cm (1⅝in), *L 24 Oct,*
£1,430 ($1,816)

7

A group of two badgers, Michael Webb, 1978, the boxwood stained black the stripes pale brown, the eyes of dark horn, signed *MJW,* 4.3cm (1¾in), *L 24 Oct,*
£1,650 ($2,096)

8

A study of a crane, late 18th/early 19th cent, the details well rendered in a simple manner, the wood slightly worn, unsigned, 3.2cm (1¼in), *L 14 Mar,*
£825 ($1,230)

9

A wood and ivory figure of a baby boy, Toryo, late 19th cent, applied and inlaid with metal, coloured lacquer and horn, signed on two inlaid tablets *Toryo* with *kakihan,* 3.7cm (1⅜in), *L 14 Mar,*
£594 ($886)

10

A study of a snake, Chokusai, 19th cent, the details rendered in lightly stained ivory, signed on a red lacquer tablet, *Chokusai,* 3.3cm (1¼in), *L 18 July,*
£429 ($571)

11

An ivory study of tortoise and young, Risuke Garaku, 18th cent, repairs to the head and carapace of the smaller, signed horizontally *Garaku,* NY 28 June,
$330 (£244)

12

An ivory study of a cat, Ryugyoku, late 19th cent, signed *Ryugyoku,* 3.4cm (1⁵⁄₁₆in), *L 14 Mar,*
£748 ($1,115)

13

A study of a shishi, Okatori of Kyoto, late 18th cent, the details rendered in slightly worn and well patinated ivory, the eye pupils inlaid, signed *Okatori,* 5.1cm (2in), *L 15 Mar,*
£2,860 ($4,264)

14

A Manju of rectangular form, Doraku, 19th cent, the ivory of good colour, signed *Doraku,* 4.5cm (1¾in), *L 14 Mar,*
£506 ($754)

15

A figure of a Karako, Masakazu of Kyoto, late 18th cent, the details rendered in slightly worn ivory, the hair inlaid with dark horn, signed in an oval reserve *Masakazu,* 6.5cm (2½in), *L 14 Mar,*
£1,100 ($1,640)

16

A model of a pup seated, Gyokuyosai, 19th cent, the ivory stained, signed *Gyokuyosai,* 2.9cm (1⅛in), *L 18 July,*
£396 ($527)

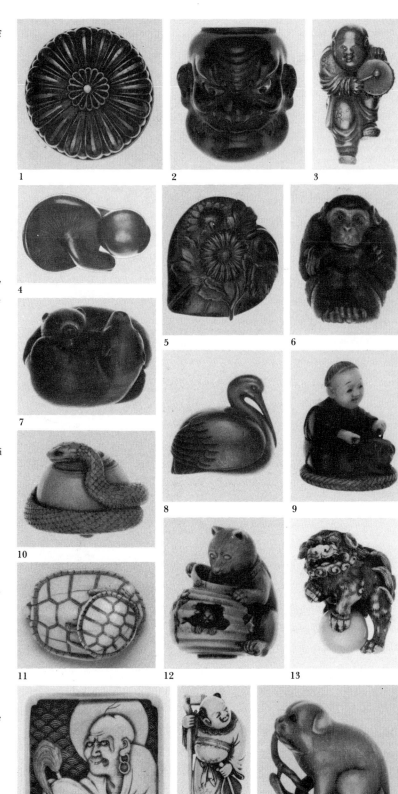

1 2 3
4
5 6
7
8 9
10
11 12 13
14 15 16

1
A group of a tragic actor and boy, Ono Ryomin, mid-19th cent, signed *Ono Ryomin* with *kakihan*, 3.9cm (1½in), *L 24 Oct*, £1,100 ($1,397)

2
A two-part Manju, Tomin, 19th cent, carved in *shishiaibori*, inlaid with coral, pearl and red lacquer, the reverse engraved with a bridge, signed *Tomin*, 4.5cm (1¾in), *L 24/31 Oct*, £638 ($810)

3
A study of a dog, Okatomo (School), late 18th cent, the details rendered in slightly worn ivory, the eye pupils inlaid, one ear chipped, unsigned, 4.1cm (1⅝in), *L 24/31 Oct*, £1,760 ($2,235)

4
An ivory figure of Fuku-rokuju, Yoshinaga style, 18th cent, the ivory worn and showing age cracks and some old chips, unsigned, *NY 28 June*, $550 (£407)

5
A figure of Shoki, Shuyo, early 19th cent, the details rendered in slightly worn ivory, the hat plugged, signed *Shuyo*, with *kakihan*, 4.1cm (1⅝in), *L 18 July*, £286 ($380)

6
A study of a rat on a hat, late 18th cent, the details rendered in slightly worn and well-patinated ivory, the eyes inlaid, unsigned, *L 14 Mar*, £528 ($787)

7
An Okimono-like group of revellers, Tomoyuki, 19th cent, signed *Tomoyuki kore*, 5cm (2in), *L 1 Nov*, £385 ($493)

8
A detailed Manju, Kaigyokusai Masatsugu, 19th cent, carved and pierced with the *Junishi* (the twelve animals of the zodiac), signed *Kaigyokusai*, 4.3cm (1¾in), *L 24/31 Oct*, £13,200 ($16,764)

9
A study of a grazing horse of flat form, 18th cent, the simple details worn and the ivory well patinated, unsigned, 5.5cm (2⅛in), *L 18 July*, £462 ($614)

10
An early study of a rat, 18th cent, the ivory worn, the eyes inlaid, unsigned, 6cm (2⅜in), *L 18 July*, £176 ($234)

11
A study of a hare, Yoshitomo, 18th cent, the details simply rendered in slightly worn ivory which bears age cracks, the eyes inlaid with horn, signed in an oval reserve *Yoshitomo*, 4.6cm (1¾in), *L 24/31 Oct*, £605 ($768)

12
A study of a Tai-fish, late 18th cent, the composition of somewhat flat form, the ivory slightly worn, the eye pupils inlaid with dark horn, unsigned, 6cm (2⅜in), *L 14 Mar*, £1,760 ($2,624)

13
A study of a grazing horse, 18th cent, of unusual proportions, the details simply rendered in a formalised manner, the ivory slightly worn, unsigned, 12.7cm (5in), *L 18 July*, £2,090 ($2,780)

14
A figure of a Chinese woman, 18th cent, the details well rendered in somewhat worn and well patinated ivory, the feet chipped, unsigned, 8.2cm (3¼in), *L 18 July*, £396 ($527)

15
An inlaid ivory study of Ebisu, Yasuhide, 19th cent, the robes stained green and silver and inset with dark horn and mother-of-pearl inlays, signed on an inset red lacquer tablet *Yasuhide*, *NY 28 June*, $1,320 (£978)

1
A figure of a wrestler, 18th cent, the ivory slightly worn, the eye pupils inlaid, unsigned, 9cm (3½in), *L 24 Oct*, £4,400 ($5,588)

2
A small early figure of a Karako, 18th cent, the carved drum containing two loose balls, the ivory slightly worn and dark stained, unsigned, 4.5cm (1¾in), *L 14 Mar*, £418 ($623)

3
A small figure of Momotaro, 18th cent, the details well carved, the ivory slightly worn, unsigned, 3.6cm (1⅜in), *L 14 Mar*, £286 ($426)

4
A figure of a Karako, 18th cent, the details well carved in slightly worn and well-patinated ivory, unsigned, 5.3cm (2⅛in), *L 14 Mar*, £550 ($820)

5
A figure of Okame, late 18th cent, the details rendered in a simple manner, the ivory slightly worn, the hair tinted black, unsigned, 4.8cm (2⅞in), *L 14 Mar*, £660 ($984)

6
An unusual figure of Daruma, early 19th cent, the ivory slightly worn and of a good colour, unsigned, 3.6cm (1⅜in), *L 24 Oct*, £715 ($908)

7
A figure of Sarumwashi, 18th cent, lightly worn and patinated, unsigned, 8.2cm (3¼in), *L 1 Nov*, £176 ($225)

8
An ivory Manju, 19th cent, carved and pierced in Ryusa style, the border stippled, the ivory slightly worn and of a good colour, unsigned, 4.3cm (1⅝in), *L 15 Mar*, £374 ($558)

9
An ivory and silver Manju, 19th cent, forming a kagamibuta, of oval form, the top inlaid with a silver *kiku* bloom, the ivory slightly worn and of a good colour, unsigned, 4.1cm (1⅝in), *L 14 Mar*, £440 ($656)

10
A late ivory two-part Manju, 19th cent, carved in relief, the reverse similarly carved, the ivory slightly stained, unsigned, 4.5cm (1¾in), *L 14 Mar*, £264 ($394)

11
An ivory figure of a penitent Oni, *c*1900, the intricate details well carved in the stained ivory, etched signature *Mitsuharu, NY 28 June*, $550 (£407)

12
A boxwood group of three rats, Ikko, 19th cent, the details crisply carved in lightly stained wood, the eyes inlaid with dark horn, signed *Ikko*, 3.2cm (1¼in), *L 24/31 Oct*, £935 ($1,187)

13
A model of a seated boar, Masanao of Ise, Yamada, early 19th cent, the hairwork and other details well rendered in the patinated wood, the fangs and eyes inlaid, signed in a polished reserve *Masanao*, 4.7cm (1⅞in), *L 24 Oct*, £2,640 (£3,353)

14
A two-part circular Manju, *tsuishu*, early 19th cent, carved in relief with lilies (yama-juri), slightly worn lacquer, the interior of *roiro*, unsigned, 4.6cm (1¾in), *L 14 Mar*, £484 ($722)

15
A study of a Dutchman, 18th cent, standing, holding a struggling crane, unsigned, 11.3cm (4½in), *L 14 Mar*, £4,400 ($6,560)

1   2   3

4   5   6

7   8   9

10   11   12

13   14   15

Works of Art
of the Meiji Period (1868-1912)

MALCOLM FAIRLEY

During the second half of the last century, Japan opened its doors to the West for the first time in over 200 years. This was to lead to a remarkable change in Japanese decorative arts, which were made particularly for the export market. Although a large number of poor quality mass-produced wares were made, there were also craftsmen producing items of the very highest standards and winning awards at the major international exhibitions in Europe and America.

The influence of the West can be seen in the bronze of the two boys playing 'go' (p.630, fig.11) and particularly in the lively bronze camel (p.630, fig. 14) which was made to rival the French 'animalier' school. The ivory group of a young man carrying a girl over a stream (p.631, fig. 14) is almost entirely western in style and could easily be mistaken for a European carving. Both the camel and the ivory group are very fine quality and this is reflected in their value. A rather different style can be seen in the ivory group of a young woman in a kimono with a boy at her feet and another in her arms (p.631, fig. 13). Here great attention is paid to the minute detail of the carving; the group was in fact carved out of one single piece of tusk.

This fascination with detail is apparent time and again in Meiji arts. Perhaps the best examples of all are the cloisonné enamels. Here a number of artists reached a technical peak that was never to be repeated. Those illustrated on pages 630 (fig. 15) and 631 (figs 1,3) show this remarkable work on these jewel-like enamels. The finest pieces are usually signed and have risen dramatically in price in the last few years.

Apart from the bronze groups already mentioned, the *shibuichi* koro and cover and the inlaid iron dish (pp.630,

figs 8,9) show the fine metalwork of the period. From the beginning of the Meiji era, the Samurai class were no longer allowed to wear swords. Thus many of the metalworkers, particularly those previously producing sword fittings, turned their hand to the decorative arts. However, the quality of the metalwork that they produced varies greatly and some mass produced workshop pieces are certainly to be avoided.

The demand for Japanese ceramics was especially strong, but standards were allowed to fall towards the latter part of the period. While many very fine examples of earthenware were made (p.630, figs 2,6,7,10), the majority were gaudy, confused in design and poorly painted. In fact the Kinkozan workshop, which produced the superb example illustrated on page 630 (fig. 2), was also responsible for some of the lowest quality tourist wares. Porcelain production remained on somewhat more traditional lines and many copies of 17th century Imari ware were produced (p.629, fig. 2). However, in figs 1 and 4 on page 630 and 1 and 3 on page 629 a rather more flamboyant style emerges and towards the end of the century some very fine potters producing highly original designs became established. One of the best of these was Makuzu Kozan, who brought porcelain manufacture to a very high degree of perfection.

The finest wares were often made for exhibition in the West. The two superb lacquer boxes (p.631, fig. 5) were shown in the Paris international exhibition of 1900. Although made as functional document and writing boxes their fine quality is greatly admired both in the West and in Japan. Lacquerwork generally reached its technical zenith during the Meiji period and prices today certainly reflect this.

1
A pair of enamelled porcelain vases, Meiji period, enamelled mark, h 29cm (11½in), *NY 31 Mar,* $2,640 (£1,830)

2
An Imari vase and cover, Meiji period, painted in underglaze-blue, iron-red, green and mauve enamels and gilt, h 63.5cm (25in), *NY 10 Nov,* $1,540 (£1,222)

3
An Arita ovoid vase, 19th cent, painted in underglaze-blue and enamels of iron-red, orange, yellow, green and turquoise, h 61.5cm (24¼in), *NY 31 Mar,* $1,100 (£762)

1   2   3

1
A **Kutani porcelain cat,** late 19th cent, the fur patched in pale brown streaked in gilding, with a green bow around his neck, chip to ear, glued paw, 24cm (9½in), *P 14 Nov,* £418 ($560)

2
An **earthenware vase,** Kinkozan, Meiji period, of *zun* form, painted with flowers behind a gilt trellis, painted and impressed *Kinkozan tsukuru,* wood stand, 29.5cm (11⅝in), *L 24/31 Oct,* £4,620 ($5,867)

3
An **Hirado blue and white vase,** the body of disc form, with wide mouth, Meiji period, h 30.5cm (12in), *NY 31 Mar,* $1,650 (£1,143)

4
A **bottle vase,** Fukagawa, Meiji period, painted in underglaze-blue iron-red, enamels and gilt, signed *Fukagawa sei,* 54.3cm (21⅜in), *L 18 July,* £935 ($1,244)

5
An **ovoid vase,** Makuzu Kozan, Meiji period, painted in blue, lavender and dark green on a pale-green ground, signed *Makuzu Kozan* in underglaze-blue, h 35cm (13¾in), *NY 31 Mar,* $1,760 (£1,220)

6
A **Yabu Meizan earthenware vase,** Meiji period, painted and gilt with children preparing for a carnival, gilt *Yabu Meizan,* 12cm (4¾in), *NY 31 Mar,* $2,750 (£1,906)

7
A **Satsuma koro and cover,** late Edo period, painted in multicolour enamels and gilt, gilt *Satsuma* mark, 11.5cm (4½in); together with a similar koro and cover with silvered soft metal cover, 7.5cm (3in), *NY 31 Mar,* $1,210 (£839)

8
A **shibuichi koro and cover,** Masayoshi, Meiji period, details in gold, silver, *shakudo* and copper, one flower from cover missing, signed on a gold tablet *Masayoshi tsukuru,* 11cm (4¼in), overall height 18.5cm (7¼in), *L 24/31 Oct,* £4,400 ($5,588)

9
An **inlaid iron dish,** Komai, Meiji period, 55.3cm (21¾in), *L 24/31 Oct,* £8,250 ($10,477)

10
A **Satsuma vase and cover,** Momo Shuko, 19th cent, decorated in enamels and gilding with roundels of flowers, Buddhist objects and characters, mark *Satsuma-mon, Genroku 13th year (1700) spring, Satsuma (no) Kuni Momo Shuko* 51.8cm (20⅜in), *L 24/31 Oct,* £3,850 ($4,889)

11
A **Tokyo school bronze group of two boys,** Kyoi Masatsune, Meiji period, signed *Kyoi Masatsune saku,* w 53cm (20¾in), *L 24/31 Oct,* £3,740 ($4,750)

12
A **bronze figure of an archer,** Miyao, Meiji period, signed in relief *Miyao* with *kakihan,* overall 38cm (15in), *L 24/31 Oct,* £2,200 ($2,794)

13
A **Kyoto earthenware koro and cover,** Meiji period, painted and gilt, the cover surmounted by a *shishi* finial, chips and repairs to cover, 54cm (21¼in), *L 1 Nov,* £935 ($1,197)

14
A **bronze study of a camel,** Genryusai Seiya, Meiji period, signed *Genryusai Seiya saku,* 34cm (13⅜in) *L 24/31 Oct,* £3,300 ($4,191)

15
A **partial plique-à-jour cloisonné vase,** Ando, Meiji period, inlaid seal of *Ando,* 12.2cm (4⅜in), *L 24/31 Oct,* £2,310 ($2,934)

1
An Hayashi Tanigoro cloisonné tea ceremony set, Meiji period, comprising a fresh water container and cover, a flower vase, a cover stand, a waste water bowl and a pair of silver fire tongs, *NY 31 Mar*, $19,800 (£13,721)

2
A gold lacquer storage box, Meiji period, decorated in gold and silver *fundame* on a *kinji* ground, silver rims, slight chips, 24 x 20 x 13cm (9½ x 8 x 5in), *NY 31 Mar*, $4,070 (£2,821)

3
A cloisonné vase, Namikawa Yasuyuki, Meiji period, decorated in silver wire on a pale blue ground, signed on a silver plaque *Kyoto Namikawa*, 13.5cm (5¼in), *NY 31 Mar*, $7,150 (£4,955)

4
A Shibayama three-case inro, Meiji period, the *kinji* ground inlaid in mother-of-pearl, ivory and coconut shell, unsigned, 9.7cm (3¾in); with an inlaid ivory Manju netsuke, 4.7cm (1¾in), *L 24/31 Oct*, £3,300 ($4,191)

5
A suzuribako and ryoshibako, Uematsu Hobi, Meiji period, the *suzuribako* with a fitted tray containing a *suzuri* and a *shakudo-nanako-mizuire*, both boxes with silver mounted rims, both signed *Hobi* with *kakihan* with original fitted box labelled for the Paris Universal Fair, 1900, the *suzuribako* 23.3 x 17.2 x 4.3cm (9⅛ x 6¾ x 1⅝in), *L 24/31 Oct*, £31,900 ($40,513)

6
A silver and shibayama dish, Meiji period, the central ivory medallion inlaid with mother-of-pearl, stained ivory and coloured hardstones, signed on mother-of-pearl medallion, 31.2cm (12¼in), *C 2-5 Oct*, £1,320 ($1,703)

7
A large pair of cloisonné enamel vases, Meiji period, decorated in silver wire and coloured enamel against a red ground, one chipped, h 153cm (60¼in), *NY 31 Mar*, $26,400 (£18,295)

8
A pair of shibayama vases, Ochiai Tsurufune, Meiji period, the *kinji* ground decorated in *hiramakie*, *takamakie* and *togidashi*, inlaid in mother-of-pearl and ivory, inscribed *dai Nihon, Tokyo. Ochiai Tsurufune tsukuru kore*, 16cm (6¼in), *NY 31 Mar*, $5,060 (£3,507)

9
An inlaid lacquer panel, Itcho Kawanobe (1830-1910), Meiji period, decorated on a *roiro* ground, inlaid with mother-of-pearl and ivory, signed *Itcho* with *kakihan*, 68.5 x 37.5cm (27 x 14¾in), *L 24/31 Oct*, £2,090 ($2,654)

10
An ivory figure of a fisherman, Gyokushu, Meiji period, signed *Gyokushu*, 33.5cm (13⅛in), *L 24/31 Oct*, £1,210 ($1,537)

11
An ivory figure of a basket peddlar, Eisho, Meiji period, some inlay in coloured ivory, signed, 13cm (5⅛in), *L 12 Dec*, £550 ($693)

12
An ivory group of a hairdresser with his client, Kosho (Mitsumasa), Meiji period, signed *Kosho (Mitsumasa)*, 16.5cm (6½in), *L 15 Mar*, £1,210 ($1,804)

13
A Tokyo school ivory group, Ryusai Meigyoku, Meiji period, signed, 31.7cm (12½in), *NY 31 Mar*, $9,075 (£6,289)

14
A Tokyo school ivory Okimono, Ito Yoshiaki, Meiji period, signed *Yoshiaki*, 28.2cm (11⅛in), *L 24/31 Oct*, £4,620 ($5,867)

1

3

2

4

5

6

7

8

9

10

11

12

13

14

Chinese Works of Art

COLIN MACKAY • TIMOTHY SAMMONS

Perhaps the most significant aspect of collecting Chinese art is that, unlike collecting in most other fields, it is a worldwide pursuit. This has long been true, but never more so than at present. With keen interest from such diverse sources it is hardly surprising that collectors in one country may well be in search of things which others elsewhere would scorn. The passion among European and American collectors for the export porcelain of the 18th century is not, for instance, shared by fellow collectors in the Far East; collectors in Japan principally favour early ceramics and notably archaic ritual bronzes among works of art, while those in Hong Kong show a distinct enthusiasm for the mark and period Imperial porcelain of the 18th and 19th centuries. It is to meet this complexity of interest that Sotheby's uniquely holds sales of Chinese ceramics and works of art in four locations: London, New York, Hong Kong and Monte Carlo.

Apart from the prime considerations of quality and rarity, that of condition is of almost universal concern. With ceramics, if a piece is of sufficient rarity imperfect condition will largely be accepted, and in general damage to early wares, such as the pottery of the Tang Dynasty, is also understood, although inevitably prices obtained for those which may have survived intact are noticeably higher. With later porcelain, and especially those pieces whose beauty largely relies on immaculate potting and exquisite decoration, the slightest chip or other flaw will adversely affect their value; the presence of even a hair crack reducing the value by at least two-thirds. But there are times when collectors interested in the same area within the field may well be looking for very different things in the same piece—while some crackling in the glaze on polychrome porcelain of the early Ming reign of the Emperor Chenghua may be regarded as acceptable and even characteristic by connoisseurs in the West, this would not be a view shared by collectors in Japan.

Among non-ceramics the question of condition is usually of lesser consequence —some flaking of the gilding on gilt-bronze figures of the Ming Dynasty is mostly to be expected, slight chipping on pieces of carved lacquer is almost inevitable and virtually no stone sculpture remains in its original pristine state. In some cases deterioration can even be considered an embellishment: the silvery iridescence on the degraded green lead of the Han Dynasty, for instance, or, most conspicuous of all, the patina found on the ritual bronzes of the Shang Dynasty which can result in one piece realizing as much as fifty times more than another vessel of identical form but lacking the preferred texture and colour of the surface.

Although repair may restore the appearance of a piece it will rarely restore its value, and this despite the fact that in some cases the work can be so well done as almost to defy detection. Only with pieces whose principal attraction lies in their decorative appeal will restoration be regarded as acceptable.

In addition to differing tastes and varying criteria on quality and condition among collectors across the globe there also remain outside considerations such as political and economic factors and, most fickle of all, fashion. Fashion is impossible to predict, but a glance at a pre-war sale catalogue will astound the reader by the almost complete reversal of price ratio between, for example, Kangxi biscuit porcelain, then commanding large sums, and early Ming blue and white, which often passed through the salerooms for less than a hundred pounds. The market has, over the past few years, become increasingly particular, resulting in an ever widening divergence in the price obtainable for items of quality and the rest. The recent season saw this further underlined with outstanding pieces often establishing new records.

Nowhere are top prices more likely than with pieces enhanced by having come from a well-known collection, such as the estate of the late Dr Ip Yee dispersed by Sotheby's in Hong Kong in May; a group of early bronzes sold in London in June; the series of Tang Dynasty pottery figures from the Schloss collection sold in New York; or the current world auction record for export porcelain paid for an extremely rare pair of leopards from the late Mrs Florence Gould's estate sold in Monte Carlo. An article on export porcelain figures can be found on page 659.

1
A stone head of Guanyin,
Ming Dynasty, the ears
with pendulous lobes,
the hair piled into a
tight chignon set with a
diadem centred with a
figure of the deity,
42.5cm (16¾ in), *L 4 May,*
£2,090 ($3,072)

2
**A grey limestone head of
Guanyin,** Ming Dynasty,
the hair centred with a
figure of Amitabha
Buddha, 18.4cm (7¼ in),
L 4 May,
£660 ($970)

3
**A carved stone head of
Buddha,** Ming Dynasty,
the full face carved with
arched brows above
heavily lidded eyes, with
extensive traces of brown
and red pigment, 24cm
(9½ in), *NY 4 Dec,*
$2,310 (£1,941)

4
A wood figure of a Lohan,
Ming Dynasty, his robe
with traces of red paint
edged in gold, 57.1cm
(22½ in), *L 4 May,*
£880 ($1,293)

5
A wood figure of Guanyin,
12th/13th cent, the
goddess reclining in
royal ease, overall traces
of gesso and pigmentation,
143cm (56¼ in), *M 27 June,*
**FF 1,110,000
(£95,279; $129,825)**

6
A painted pottery jar,
Neolithic Period, a band
of scallop pattern above
conjoined crosshatched
diamonds, d 22.9cm (9 in),
NY 4 Dec,
$2,640 (£2,218)

7
A painted red pottery jar,
Neolithic Period, Ma
Chang Type, Kansu
Province, h 8.2cm (3¼ in),
NY 4 Dec,
$1,760 (£1,478)

8
A painted red pottery jar,
Neolithic Period, Ma
Changtype, Kansu
Province, of thinly
potted compressed
globular form, the orange
ware painted in red and
reddish-brown, h 8.9cm
(3½ in), *NY 12 June,*
$6,600 (£4,782)

9
A painted Neolithic jug,
Yang Shao Period, in
Pan Shan style, the
upper part boldly painted
in brown and black, with
a band of waisted panels
infilled with geometric
designs, 24.8cm (9¾ in),
L 11 Dec,
£2,860 ($3,604)

10
A Neolithic mortuary urn,
Ma Chang, Kansu
Province, painted in red
and black with four
crosshatched trefoil
clusters, 37.4cm (14¾ in),
NY 4 Dec,
$7,700 (£6,471)

Condition is not stated
in captions to Chinese
Works of Art.

1
A Yueyao lion-form water dropper, Six Dynasties, modelled as a crouching chimera, covered with an olive green glaze, h 12.7cm (5in),
HK 19 Nov,
HK $18,700
(£1,897; $2,485)

2
A grey pottery figure of a drummer, Six Dynasties, the detachable head with a close-fitting cap, the figure with traces of red pigment over a white slip, 16.2cm (6½in),
L 19 June,
£550 ($786)

3
An unglazed grey pottery jar, Zhou Dynasty, of squat shouldered form, standing on a flat base of uneven surface, the sides impressed with a mesh-like pattern, 16.8cm (6⅝in), *L 11 Dec,*
£1,100 ($1,386)

4
A grey pottery tripod vessel (jue), Shang Dynasty, the flared sides with an incised line around the rim, a spout to one side, joined to the compressed body with a thick loop handle, 11.4cm (4½in), *NY 12 June,*
$1,650 (£1,195)

5
A grey pottery figure of a lady, Han Dynasty, the skirt of her robe widely flared at the base, with a double collar, the borders outlined in red pigment, 37cm (14½in), *L 11 Dec,*
£770 ($970)

6
A Proto-Yue jar, 3rd/2nd cent BC, a mesh of stamped crisscross motifs encircling the neck covered with an olive green glaze, above a wide band of basket-weave motifs, left unglazed and burnt a bright reddish-brown in the firing, 22.2cm (8¾in),
NY 4 Dec,
$6,875 (£5,777)

7
A grey pottery figure of a horse, Han Dynasty, the head modelled separately, the body moulded in two parts and horizontally luted together, covered overall in a brick-red pigment largely applied on a white slip, h 16cm (10½in), *L 11 Dec,*
£2,640 ($3,326)

8
A glazed pottery figure of a dog, Han Dynasty, covered overall in a green glaze of even tone, stopping on the legs to reveal the reddish ware, 19cm (7½in), *L 11 Dec,*
£2,090 ($2,633)

9
A green glazed red pottery jar (hu), Han Dynasty, encircled with three raised lines and set with mask and ring handles, covered with a thick green glaze finely crackled, 33.2cm (13in),
HK 19 Nov,
HK $24,200
(£2,454; $3,215)

10
An unglazed grey pottery figure, Wei Dynasty, of a court attendant, traces of white slip and pigments, 22.8cm (9in), *L 11 Dec,*
£660 ($832)

11
A painted grey pottery figure of an official, Northern Wei Dynasty, traces of white slip, red and blue pigmentation, burial dirt encrustation, some restoration, 36.8cm (14½in), *NY 4 Dec,*
$5,060 (£4,252)

12
A painted grey pottery figure of a soldier, Northern Wei Dynasty, shown standing with hands clasping his coat-tails and pierced to hold a standard, extensive traces of red and black pigment, 35.5cm (14in),
NY 4 Dec,
$5,060 (£4,252)

1

2   3

4

5   6

7   8

9   10   11   12

1
A modelled figure of a foreign groom, Tang Dynasty, the topcoat glazed predominantly in green, shading to straw and chestnut, the wide lapels splashed in cream, the head, hands and legs unglazed, 63.5cm (25in), *L 11 Dec,* £30,800 ($38,808)

2
A painted pottery figure of a warrior guardian, Tang Dynasty, standing in a position of warning, extensive traces of white, flesh colour, black and red pigment, 62.2cm (24½in), *NY 12 June,* $2,860 (£2,072)

3
An unglazed pottery figure of a lady, Tang Dynasty, the flared skirt of her robe striped in red pigment, the hair showing traces of black, 29.3cm (11½in), *L 19 June,* £1,430 ($2,045)

4
A pottery figure of an attendant, Tang Dynasty, pierced with a socket to accommodate a banner, the straw glaze largely flaked off, 18.2cm (7⅛in), *L 11 Dec,* £242 ($305)

5
A pair of straw-glazed pottery equestrian figures, Tang Dynasty, covered with a pale yellowish glaze stopping irregularly short on the horses' legs and base, now flaked and degraded to an iridescence, 25.5cm (10in), *NY 4 Dec,* $2,750 (£2,311)

6
An unglazed pottery figure of a prancing horse, Tang Dynasty, traces of red pigment, 37.7cm (14¾in), *L 19 June,* £4,620 ($6,606)

7
A straw-glazed figure of an ox, Tang Dynasty, covered overall with a degraded straw glaze polished to a greenish tint on the head and neck, 13.3cm (5¼in), *HK 19 Nov,* **HK $8,250 (£837; $1,096)**

8
A miniature sancai-glazed pottery figure of a horse, Tang Dynasty, splashed with cream, ochre and green glazes stopping short of the foot to reveal the buff ware, tail off, 6.4cm (2¾in), *NY 4 Dec,* $3,740 (£3,143)

9
A sancai pottery bottle, Tang Dynasty, covered with a bright transparent glaze of green, chestnut and straw falling in even lines down the interior of the mouth and in broad waves down the exterior, an unglazed patch in the centre revealing the pinkish ware, 10.3cm (4in), *HK 21/22 May,* **HK $74,800 (£6,881; $9,909)**

10
A sancai ovoid vase, Tang Dynasty, covered on the exterior in dappled straw, green and chestnut glazes stopping well short of the solid splayed foot to reveal the buff ware, 19.2cm (7½in), *L 19 June,* £2,750 (£3,932)

11
A modelled straw-glazed pottery figure of a camel, early Tang Dynasty, all under a slightly degraded glaze of creamy yellowish colour, 34.9cm (13¾in), *NY 12 June,* $8,525 (£6,177)

12
A two-colour glazed pottery figure of a Bactrian camel, Tang Dynasty, covered in a creamy glaze highlighted in amber on the head, neck, humps and front legs, the base unglazed to show the pinkish-buff ware, 51.7cm (20⅝in), *NY 12 June,* $13,200 (£9,565)

13
A glazed pottery figure of a Bactrian camel, Tang Dynasty, of overall rich chestnut-brown colour, on unglazed flat base, 81.9cm (32¼in), *L 19 June,* £23,100 ($33,033)

1
A Junyao bowl, Song
Dynasty, applied both
inside and out with a
crackled and bubble-
suffused glaze of milky
lavender-blue tone,
draining from the rim
revealing the buff ware
beneath, 11.2cm (4⅜in),
L 11 Dec,
£440 ($554)

2
A Junyao bowl, Song
Dynasty, applied both
inside and out with a
crackled glaze of bright
lavender tone, thinning
on the rim showing the
buff body beneath, 19.1cm
(7½in), *L 11 Dec,*
£3,960 ($4,989)

3
A Junyao lotus bud
waterpot, Song Dynasty,
unglazed and burnt to a
reddish tone in the
firing, the glaze of
lavender-blue colour,
9.8cm (3⅞in), *L 11 Dec,*
£9,900 ($12,474)

4
A Junyao dish, Song
Dynasty, with shallow
flared sides and an
upturned rounded rim,
covered in a pale
lavender glaze draining
from the rim and
coagulating towards the
base, 17.2cm (6¾in),
L 19 June,
£748 ($942)

5
A Jizhou bowl, Song
Dynasty, covered overall
in a crackled reddish-
brown glaze splashed
with ochre droplets,
11cm (4⅜in), *L 19 June,*
£682 ($859)

6
A Henan ribbed black-
glazed jar, Northern
Song Dynasty, the ribs
in white slip showing
through the lustrous
dark brown glaze, the
glaze pooling above the
base, 25.4cm (10in),
NY 4 Dec,
$77,000 (£64,706)

7
A Jizhou meiping, Song
Dynasty, in an olive
glaze over a deep
reddish-brown ground,
22cm (8⅝in), *NY 12 June,*
£20,900 ($15,144)

8
A brown-splashed Henan
jar, Song Dynasty,
covered with a lustrous
bluish-black glaze and
decorated with russet
splashes of five-petalled
flowers, the interior and
base thinning to a
translucent brown
colour, 20.2cm (8in),
NY 4 Dec,
$18,150 (£15,252)

9
A painted Henan
meiping, Song Dynasty,
covered overall with a
dark brownish-black
glaze decorated with two
freely drawn rust-brown
floral sprays, 17.8cm
(7in), *NY 4 Dec,*
$5,500 (£4,622)

10
A Henan ribbed jar and
cover, Song Dynasty, the
vertical ribs in white slip
beneath a dark brown
glaze, 11.3cm (4½in),
L 11 Dec,
£1,540 ($1,940)

11
A Henan vase (yuhuchan
ping), Song/Yuan
Dynasty, covered in a
lustrous dark brown
glaze shading to a paler
tone on the shoulders,
painted on each side
with a russett stylised
bird, 28.3cm (11⅛in),
L 11 Dec,
£3,300 ($4,158)

12
A Henan dark brown
glazed vase (yuhuchun),
Yuan Dynasty, covered
overall with a speckled
olive-brown glaze, the
ring foot showing the
ware burnt orange in the
firing, 26.4cm (10⅜in),
HK 19 Nov,
HK $9,350 (£948; $1,242)

1   2   3

4

5   6

7   8   9

10   11   12

1
A glazed pottery figure of a harnessed horse, Tang Dynasty, of unusually large size, the long mane covered with a straw glaze, the body glazed predominantly in a rich chestnut, the hooves splashed in green, h 72.8cm (28⅝in), *L 11 Dec,* £297,000 ($374,220)

2
An archaic bronze food vessel (gui), Transitional, 11th/10th cent BC, cast on the rounded sides with taotie masks, the smooth patina of marbled green and dark grey colour, w 29.2cm (11½in), *NY 12 June,* $25,500 (£19,927)

3
An archaic bronze wine vessel (zun), 11th/10th cent BC, 21.8cm (8½in), *L 19 June,* £46,200 ($66,066)

4
A moulded celadon glazed vase, Yongzheng seal mark and period, h 52.7cm (20¾in), *NY 12 June,* $20,900 (£15,144)

1

2

3

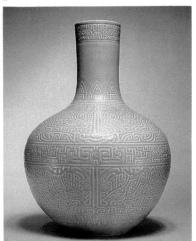

4

1

**A pair of 'famille-rose'
figures of pheasants,**
Qianlong, the clawed
legs picked out in vivid
yellow enamel with
scale markings in rouge-
de-fer, the wings in
different colours with
details in gilding, 32.4cm
(12¾in), *M 27 June*,
FF 577,200
(£49,545; $67,509)

2

**A pair of large biscuit
figures of Maidens Immortal,**
Kangxi, one with an
aubergine-ground jacket
over long green and
ochre robes, the other
with a flower-decorated
stippled green jacket
over yellow and green
robes, 47.6cm (18¾in),
L 3 July,
£30,800 ($41,888)

3

**A pair of 'famille-rose'
Buddhist lions,** early
Qianlong, the mane in
blue ringlets, with a
yellow blaze on the back,
the remainder of the
body green with a
yellow collar around the
neck, 43.1cm (17in),
L 3 July,
£18,700 ($25,432)

4

**A rare 'famille-rose' figure
of a Dutchman,**
Qianlong, said to represent
Governor Duf, coloured
in iron-red and green,
the moustache and curly
beard detailed in grisaille,
45.1cm (17¾in), *M 4 Mar*,
FF 688,200
(£57,831; $86,025)

5

A pair of figures of cranes,
Qianlong, each striding
across an enamelled blue
base, the white bird with
feather markings
moulded beneath the
clear glaze, the neck and
tail picked out in
grisaille, 22.3cm (8¾in),
M 27 June,
FF 88,800 (£7,622; $10,386)

1

2

3

4

5

1
An early Ming blue and white dish, late 14th cent, the underglaze-blue of soft purplish tone with 'heaped and piled' effect, 36.5cm (14⅜in), *HK 21/22 May,* **HK $1,210,000 (£111,316; $160,295)**

2
A 'famille-verte' tureen and cover, Kangxi, 32.3cm (12¾in), *M 27 June,* **FF 77,700 (£6,669; $9,087)**

3
A pair of large 'rose-verte' dishes, Yongzheng, each painted with two *meiren,* reserved on a black stippled green ground, 38.4cm (15⅛in), *NY 12 June,* **$6,050 (£4,384)**

4
A pair of carved cinnabar lacquer vases, Qianlong, with gilt-metal liners, carved with eight different panels depicting scholars and their attendants walking by a lake, 31.8cm (12½in), *L 1/2 Nov,* **£4,400 ($5,632)**

5
A glass overlay snuff bottle, 1780-1850, the body of brilliant dark blue tone overlaid in white on each side with sprays of lily, the blooms in graduated relief, stopper, *NY 15 Mar,* **$6,325 (£4,332)**

6
A cinnabar lacquer snuff bottle, mark of Qianlong, finely carved in three-tiered relief with a continuous design of clustered magnolia, *L 2 July,* **£12,650 ($17,267)**

7
A bamboo snuff bottle, 1780-1850, each side applied with an archaistic *chilong* medallion with incised scrolls, stopper, *NY 15 Mar,* **$2,640 (£1,808)**

8
An enamelled glass snuff bottle, mark and period of Qianlong, Peking Palace Workshops, the milk-white ground decorated in 'famille-rose' enamels with a spray of prunus, *NY 15 Mar,* **$33,000 (£22,603)**

1
A Dehua figure of Guanyin, seal mark He Chaozong, Kangxi, standing on an upturned vase of lotus blossoms, the glaze of creamy white colour pooling to ivory, 50.2cm (19¾in), *NY 4 Dec,* $12,650 (£10,630)

2
A miniature Peking glass vase, Yongzheng mark and period, the glass of brilliant egg yolk colour, 7.8cm (3in), *HK 19 Nov,* **HK $39,600 (£4,016; $5,261)**

3
A bamboo mountain, 17th cent, carved and undercut in deep relief with numerous figures gathered on rocky ledges and within pavilions, 30.7cm (12in), *L 4 May,* £825 ($1,213)

4
A greenish-yellow jade horse, early Qing, the animal lying on its side with head turned sharply back, the pale stone with suffusions of amber, 7.4cm (2⅞in), *HK 19 Nov,* **HK $41,800 (£4,239; $5,553)**

5
A rhinoceros horn libation cup, 17th/18th cent, carved with two small boys on the base, another clambering up a pine tree and a fourth seated on a branch, 10.7cm (4⅛in), *HK 20 Nov,* **HK $26,400 (£2,705; $3,543)**

6
A silver dragon bowl, Tang Dynasty, engraved on the exterior with nine medallions each enclosing a mythical beast or bird, all on a punched ground below a bead border, 10.8cm (4¼in), *NY 4 Dec,* $27,500 (£23,109)

7
A carved ivory plaque, 19th cent, intricately carved showing maidens and attendants conversing in a garden pavilion, the ivory of pale colour, 23 x 14cm (9 x 5½in), *HK 19 Nov,* **HK $49,500 (£5,020; $6,576)**

1

3

2

4

5

6

7

1

A set of six pottery cups and a tray, Tang Dynasty, each splashed with green, chestnut and cream, pooling on the interior, cups 5cm (2in), tray 22cm (8⅞in), *L 19 June,* **£1,650 ($2,359)**

2

A green-glazed pottery jar, Tang Dynasty, covered with a finely crackled leaf-green glaze ending in streaks just above the foot, 18.2cm (7¼in), *HK 19 Nov,* **HK $27,500 (£2,789; $3,654)**

3

A glazed pottery jar, Tang Dynasty, dappled with chestnut, straw and green glazes stopping well short of the flattened base to reveal the buff ware, 21.7cm (8½in), *L 19 June,* **£2,310 ($3,303)**

4

A blue-splashed glazed pottery bowl, Tang Dynasty, the interior splashed in striking tones of blue, cream and chestnut forming a large floral medallion, the chestnut glaze on the exterior showing the buff ware at the base, 19.6cm (7¾in), *NY 12 June,* **$10,725 (£7,771)**

5

A miniature glazed pottery jar, Tang Dynasty, the upper part of the incurved rounded sides applied with a bright green glaze splashed in cream, 4.8cm (1⅞in), *L 11 Dec,* **£440 ($554)**

6

A green-glazed pottery cup, Tang Dynasty, applied both inside and out with a green glaze slightly degraded to a faint iridescence in places, 5.1cm (2in), *L 11 Dec,* **£440 ($504)**

7

A large glazed stoneware jar, Tang Dynasty, the minutely crackled clear glaze of faint greenish tint stopping short of the base, 28.6cm (11¼in), *L 11 Dec,* **£1,430 ($1,802)**

8

A miniature white-glazed pottery ewer, Tang Dynasty, the whole covered with an even cream glaze stopping above the foot showing the buff ware, 7.7cm (3in), *NY 12 June,* **$3,080 (£2,231)**

9

A Dingyao lobed jar and cover, Song Dynasty, covered overall with a transparent ivory-tinted glaze, the rim, footrim and underside of the cover unglazed, 10.8cm (4¼in), *HK 21/22 May,* **HK $137,500 (£12,649; $18,215)**

10

A Dingyao meiping, Liao Dynasty, covered overall with a transparent ivory-tinted glaze gathering in tear drops beneath the rim, 34cm (13⅜in), *HK 19 Nov,* **HK $220,000 (£22,312; $29,229)**

11

A white-glazed ewer, Song Dynasty, of *ding* type, the glaze of creamy colour, with a faintly bluish tint above the foot, the footrim unglazed showing the fine-grained ware, 19.1cm (7½in), *NY 12 June,* **$7,700 (£5,579)**

12

A Yingqing funerary vase, Song Dynasty, applied with a small dog and a baby below a dragon, covered with a crackled translucent bluish-white glaze falling short of the splayed foot, 45.4cm (17⅞in), *NY 4 Dec,* **$3,300 (£2,773)**

1 2 3 4 5 6 7 8 9 10 11 12

1
A Yingqing flower-shaped bowl, Song Dynasty, the interior carved as a single flowerhead, covered overall in a blue-tinted glaze, 19.2cm (7½in), *L 19 June*, £1,210 ($1,524)

2
A Yingqing dish, Song Dynasty, carved on the interior with a stylised floral spray, the pale bluish glaze also covering the exterior, 15.3cm (6in), *L 11 Dec*, £605 ($762)

3
A brown-splashed Yingqing box and cover, Song Dynasty, 5.3cm (2⅛in), *HK 19 Nov*, **HK $33,000** (£3,347; $4,385)

4
A pair of iron-brown painted Yingqing funerary vases and covers, Song Dynasty, each with applied figures around the neck, both vases freely painted in underglaze iron-brown, 31.1cm (12⅛in), *NY 4 Dec*, $7,700 (£6,471)

5
A Cizhou three-colour glazed pottery pillow, Song Dynasty, the top incised with a clematis vine picked out in yellow and green on a white ground, the green glaze stopping above the base showing the white slip, 33.3cm (12in), *NY 12 June*, $4,400 (£3,188)

6
A carved Dingyao dish, Jin Dynasty, incised with a lotus spray, covered overall in a transparent ivory-tinted glaze, the rim unglazed, 11.7cm (4⅝in), *L 11 Dec*, £2,970 ($3,742)

7
A painted Cizhou pillow, Jin Dynasty, Pacun ware, painted in dark chocolate brown on a cream slip ground beneath a transparent glaze, the base unglazed to show the buff ware, 36cm (14in), *NY 12 June*, $12,100 (£8,768)

8
A Dingyao jar and cover, Song Dynasty, with a glaze of ivory tone with tear markings of greenish tint, 13cm (5⅛in), *NY 12 June*, $5,579 (£4,042)

9
A moulded Dingyao dish, Jin Dynasty, the interior with a pair of stags, reserved on a stippled ground, the rim bound in copper, covered overall with a transparent ivory-tinted glaze, 22.3cm (8¾in), *L 11 Dec*, £6,050 ($7,623)

10
A painted Cizhou jar (guan), Yuan Dynasty, painted in brown on a cream-coloured ground, the interior glazed brown, 28.6cm (11¼in), *NY 12 June*, $4,950 (£3,586)

11
A shouldered Cizhou jar, Yuan Dynasty, applied with a white slip on the exterior and painted in ferruginous brown beneath the overall translucent ivory-tinted glaze, 24.8cm (9¾in), *L 11 Dec*, £770 ($970)

12
A carved Cizhou bowl, Jin Dynasty, with deep rounded sides, incised through the white slip with a central medallion, the unglazed foot showing the buff ware, 21.3cm (8⅜in), *NY 12 June*, $2,750 (£1,992)

13
A Cizhou sgraffiato jar, Yuan Dynasty, carved through the brown glaze to the buff ware beneath with a stylised flowering scroll, 31.7cm (12½in), *L 19 June*, £715 ($900)

1
A carved Northern
celadon dish, Northern
Song Dynasty, decorated
with a central peony
spray, covered overall
with a transparent olive
green glaze suffused
with crackle, the footrim
unglazed, 20.5cm (8in),
L 11 Dec,
£15,950 ($20,097)

2
A carved Northern
celadon bowl, Song
Dynasty, decorated with
a large peony, the olive
glaze thinning to a
lighter tone on the
highlights, the short foot
unglazed on the rim to
reveal the greyish ware,
19.6cm (7¾in),
HK 21/22 May,
HK $79,200 (£7,286;
$10,491)

3
A carved Northern
celadon bowl and cover,
Northern Song Dynasty,
the exterior with a
feathery floral meander,
the interior plain, the
translucent crackled
glaze of olive green tone,
15.9cm (6¼in), *L 11 Dec,*
£3,740 ($4,712)

4
A carved Northern
celadon bowl, Song
Dynasty, decorated on
the exterior with petals,
the interior divided into
six lobes, covered
overall with an olive
green glaze pooling on
the details, 11.6cm
(4⅝in), *HK 21/22 May,*
HK $7,150 (£658; $948)

5
A Longquan celadon
bowl, Song Dynasty, the
conical sides moulded
and carved on the
exterior with overlapping
upright petals, covered
overall with a pale
bluish-green glaze thinning
slightly at the rim,
13.1cm (5¼in), *HK 20 Nov,*
HK $41,800 (£4,283; $5,611)

6
A Longquan celadon bowl,
Song/Yuan Dynasty,
decorated in relief,
covered overall with an
olive green glaze, 14.5cm
(5¾in), *A 10 Dec,*
Dfl 812
(£194; $232)

7
A carved Northern
celadon bowl, Jin
Dynasty, the interior
with a central lotus,
covered overall with an
olive green glaze, 13.7cm
(5⅜in), *HK 19 Nov,*
HK $68,200 (£6,917; $9,061)

8
A massive Longquan
celadon dish, early Ming
Dynasty, covered overall
with a translucent olive
green glaze, the base
with an unglazed ring
burnt orange in the
firing, 50.3cm (19⅞in),
HK 21/22 May,
HK $19,800
(£1,816; $2,615)

9
A Longquan celadon dish,
Ming Dynasty, impressed
in the centre with a
medallion enclosing a
diaper pattern, encircled
on the well by a peony
scroll, covered overall
with an olive green
glaze, 43.8cm (17¼in),
HK 20 Nov,
HK $25,300 (£2,592; $3,396)

10
A carved celadon dish,
Ming Dynasty, with
an even olive green
glaze, 33.6cm (13¼in),
NY 12/13 Oct,
$990 (£811)

11
A Longquan celadon bowl,
Ming Dynasty, covered
overall with a thick pale
green glaze, 15.6cm (6⅛in),
L 11 Dec,
£715 ($901)

12
A celadon narcissus bowl,
18th cent, moulded with
lotus florets, 35.6cm
(14in), *NY 12/13 Oct,*
$1,540 (£1,262)

13
A Zhejiang celadon vase,
Ming Dynasty, carved
and combed beneath the
crackled translucent
olive green glaze, 38.7cm
(15¼in), *L 11 Dec,*
£990 ($1,247)

1
An early Ming blue and white cupstand, Yongle Period, the underglaze-blue of purplish tone, the base burnt a deep orange in the firing, 19.7cm (7¾in), *HK 19 Nov*, **HK $159,500 (£16,176; $21,191)**

2
A finely painted early Ming blue and white dish, Yongle Period, the underglaze-blue of soft purplish-blue tone with light 'heaped and piled' effect, the base unglazed, 37.7cm (14¾in), *HK 19 Nov*, **HK $902,000 (£91,481; $119,840)**

3
A blue and white moon flask, (bianhu), early 15th cent, six character mark and period of Xuande, 25.7cm (10in), *L 19 June*, **£48,400 ($69,212)**

4
An early Ming blue and white bowl, Xuande, six character mark of the period, 32cm (11⅞in), *L 11 Dec*, **£38,500 ($48,510)**

5
A Ming blue and white stemcup, late 15th cent, painted on the exterior in 'windswept' style with a sage and attendant in a landscape, h 11.2cm (4½in), w 15.5cm (6¼in), *HK 21/22 May*, **HK $9,350 (£860; $1,238)**

6
A blue and white melon-form bird-feeder, six character mark of Xuande and of the period decorated in purplish blue, the glaze of greenish tint covering the flat base, fitted ivory cover, 7.7cm (3in), *HK 21/22 May*, **HK $37,400 (£3,441; $4,955)**

7
A Ming blue and white bowl, Wanli, six character mark of the period 13.3cm (5¼in), *L 11 Dec*, **£605 ($762)**

8
A Ming blue and white lobed jar, Wanli, four character mark, each lobe decorated with a foliate ruyi motif within a quatrefoil panel, interspersed by florets, metal cover, 16.3cm (6½in), *HK 21/22 May*, **HK $9,900 (£911; $1,312)**

9
A blue and white jar, Jiajing, six character mark of the period, the upper part painted with alternating phoenix and crane medallions between pairs of lingzhi motifs, 8.9cm (3½in), *L 11 Dec*, **£2,420 ($3,049)**

10
A blue and white baluster jar, mark and period of Wanli, decorated with a frieze of the Eight Immortals walking across crested waves, 16.7cm (6¼in), *L 19 June*, **£4,400 ($6,292)**

11
A blue and white saucer dish, mark and period of Wanli, decorated on the interior with a medallion enclosing three ruyi-shaped cloud scrolls, the underglaze-blue of rich purplish tone, 18.5cm (7¼in), *HK 20 Nov*, **HK $17,400 (£1,783; $2,336)**

12
A blue and white vase, Wanli, 30cm (11¾in), *P 10/13 July*, **£440 ($598)**

13
A blue and white 'Kraak Porselein' dish, Wanli, Period, 50.2cm (19¾in), *NY 12/13 Oct*, **$1,980 (£1,623)**

14
A blue and white Swatow jar, 16th cent, freely painted with a sinuous dragon amidst clouds, all beneath a slightly tinted glaze, 35.5cm (14in), *L 11 Dec*, **£572 ($721)**

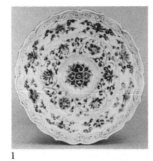

1

2

3

4

5

6

7

8

9

10

12

11

13

14

1
A rare green dragon bowl,
mark and period of
Chenghua, 20.7cm (8⅛in),
HK 20 Nov,
HK $715,000
(£73,258; $95,968)

2
**A blue and white beaker
vase,** Transitional, painted
in shaded tones of
underglaze-blue with a
phoenix in flight above
blossoming peony, pinks
and ruyi, 17.6cm (7⅜in),
NY 12 June,
$550 (£398)

3
**A blue and white
brushpot,** four character
Chenghua mark, Tran-
sitional, painted on the
exterior with a scene of
scholars engaged in
various pursuits, the
underglaze-blue of vivid
tone, 16.5cm (6½in),
HK 21/22 May,
HK $13,200 (£1,214; $1,748)

4
**A blue and white beaker
vase,** Transitional,
painted with butterflies
hovering over numerous
vessels filled with
flowers arranged as a
continuous frieze above
a band of blue-ground
medallions, 45.4cm (17⅞in),
L 3 July,
£660 ($898)

5
**A blue and white double
gourd vase,** Transitional,
decorated with scholars
in a landscape, 31.5cm
(12⅜in), *A 10 Dec,*
Dfl 7,076 (£1,690; $2,011)

6
**A blue and white
brushpot,** Transitional,
painted with two sages
in conversation beneath
a willow tree, 12.7cm
(5⅛in), *HK 21/22 May,*
HK $7,700 (£708; $1,020)

7
A blue and white vase,
Transitional, decorated
in a vivid tone of
underglaze-blue with
scattered sprigs of flowers
and butterflies, 38.1cm
(15in), *NY 4 Dec,*
$1,650 (£1,387)

8
A polychrome beaker vase,
Transitional, of *gu* form,
the upper section
decorated with four
petal-shaped panels each
enclosing a differing
flowering spray, 39.8cm
(15¾in), *HK 20 Nov,*
HK $22,000 (£2,254; $2,952)

9
**A polychrome jar and
cover,** Transitional,
painted in cobalt and
enamels with a group of
children and ladies in a
garden, 39.4cm (15½in),
L 3 July,
£682 ($927)

10
**A pair of polychrome
dishes,** Tianqi, 15cm (6in),
HK 20 Nov,
HK $8,800 (£902; $1,182)

11
**A Ming-style blue and
white pilgrim flask,** seal
mark and period of Qian-
long, decorated in under-
glaze-blue of fine colour
with simulated 'heaped
and piled' effect, 49cm
(19¼in), *HK 20 Nov,*
HK $198,000
(£20,287; $26,576)

12
A blue and white vase, six
character mark of
Qianlong, 19th cent,
66.6cm (26¼in), *L 3 July,*
£1,078 ($1,466)

13
A blue and white bowl, six
character mark and
period of Kangxi, the
interior painted in a
deep tone of blue with a
central medallion enclos-
ing a floral spray, 13cm
(5⅛in), *HK 21/22 May,*
HK $16,500
(£1,518; $2,186)

14
**A Ming-style blue and
white vase, (yuhuchun
ping),** six character mark
and period of Yongzheng,
the underglaze-blue of
vivid purple-blue tone
with pronounced simu-
lated 'heaped and piled'
effect, 28.8cm (11⅜in),
HK 21/22 May,
HK $330,000
(£30,359; $43,717)

1

2

3

4

5

6

7

8

9

10

11

12

13

14

1
A pair of blue and white pitchers, Kangxi, the sides decorated with four quatrefoil panels linked by strapwork, filled with floral scrolls, the loop handle with a dragon's head terminal, 27cm (10½ in), *L 3 July,* £2,090 ($2,842)

2
A pair of blue and white bottle vases, Kangxi, each brightly decorated on the sides with leaping dragons chasing a 'flaming pearl' amidst scattered sprigs and clouds, 26.2cm (10¼ in), *L 3 July,* £792 ($1,072)

3
A pair of blue and white ewers and covers, Kangxi, each vessel of Near Eastern metal shape, with a panel on each side filled with blue-ground scrolls, reserved on a 'fish-net' diaper, 17.7cm (7⅝ in), *L 20 Nov,* £990 ($1,297)

4
A baluster vase and cover, Kangxi, the sides vertically ribbed and painted with a dense feathery floral design between lightly moulded double tiers of petals filled with further stems, 57.2cm (22½ in), *L 20 Nov,* £440 ($576)

5
A blue and white beaker vase, Kangxi, with a central bulb, decorated overall with panels enclosing groups of precious objects and flowering sprays, 51.5cm (20¼ in), *L 20 Nov,* £330 ($432)

6
A moulded blue and white bowl, mark of Chenghua, Kangxi, decorated on the exterior with a deer hunt, the interior with a deer standing near a rock, ruyi decorations at the rim, 15.5cm (6⅛ in), *A 16 May,* **Dfl 1,972,** (£460; $658)

7
A blue and white two-handled vase, Kangxi, painted on the body with interconnecting lobed panels of flowers under a neck of further foliate panels upon a 'cracked-ice' ground, 21cm (8¼ in), *HS 25 June,* £352 ($496)

8
A blue and white covered jar, Kangxi, of deep U-shape, decorated with ancient objects and flowers in a landscape, on a wooden foot, 24cm (9⅜ in), *A 16 May,* **Dfl 3,480 (£812; $1,161)**

9
A blue and white plate, mark of Chenghua, Kangxi, decorated with a dignitary, two musicians and a boy servant in an interior, 27cm (10⅝ in), *A 16 May,* **Dfl 812 (£189; $270)**

10
A blue and white deep dish, mark and period of Kangxi, painted in cobalt of brilliant colour with a pair of song-birds beside ornamental rocks and a flowering tree, 35.6cm (14in), *L 3 July,* £484 ($658)

11
A pair of dishes, Qianlong, painted in underglaze-blue, the centre of each painted with a small craft moored at an islet and buildings along the opposite side of the lake, sold with another similar, 54.5cm (21½ in), *L 20 Nov,* £605 ($793)

12
A blue and white jardinière, Qianlong, the sides painted with a repeated landscape scene between double lion mask handles projecting in bold relief, left in the biscuit and showing traces of gilding, 61cm (24in), *L 20 Nov,* £2,200 ($2,882)

1
A blue and white part service, Qianlong, each piece painted with a view of a lakeside mansion set among trees, a small boat moving across the water beyond, 46 pieces, *L 20 Nov,*
£3,300 ($4,323)

2
A blue and white bidet, Qianlong, of keyhole shape, the interior painted with a view across a lake, the exterior with floral sprays and formal borders, 61cm (24in), *L 20 Nov,*
£990 ($1,297)

3
A blue and white garden seat of conventional barrel shape, with pierced interlocking cash on the sides and top, painted in Ming style, 47.6cm (18¾in), *L 20 Nov,*
£825 ($1,081)

4
A blue and white jar, 18th cent, decorated in Ming style with an overall pattern of lotus meander, the underglaze-blue with 'heaped and piled' effect, 45.7cm (18in), *NY 12/13 Oct,*
$1,210 (£992)

5
A blue and white dish, Kangxi, *aiye* mark, decorated with a cracked-ice ground, reserved with a shaped panel enclosing a flying bird beside a blossoming prunus tree, 27.5cm (10¾in), *A 10 Dec,*
Dfl 1,044 (£249; $298)

6
A Yen-yen vase, Kangxi, decorated overall with boughs of prunus reserved on an underglaze-blue cracked-ice ground between narrow toothed borders around the base and rim, 46.7cm (18½in), *L 3 July,*
£770 ($1,047)

7
A blue and white covered wall cistern, Kangxi, the pear-shaped body with flattened back, painted with a scene of a boy descending a staircase towards other figures, the spout within the jaws of a moulded animal's head, 56cm (22in), *A 10 Dec,*
Dfl 9,512 (£2,272; $2,721)

8
A pair of covered ginger jars, Kangxi, each painted in bright cobalt blue with dragons and phoenix, fungus marks, 23cm (9in), *A 10 Dec,*
Dfl 3,248 (£776; $929)

9
A tureen and cover, Qianlong, of octagonal shape, the finial in the form of a lotus flower, 35cm (13¾in), *A 9 Mar,*
Dfl 1,972 (£460; $657)

10
An 'Imari' baluster vase and cover mounted as a lamp, *c.*1740, painted in underglaze-blue, iron-red, brown and gold with two phoenix perched amidst flowering shrubbery, together with an English porcelain vase, mounted as a lamp, 29.3cm (11½in), *NY 26 Jan,*
$660 (£455)

11
An 'Imari' coffee pot and cover of conical form, Kangxi, decorated in underglaze-blue enhanced in rouge-de-fer and gilding, with flowering plants, 23cm (9in), *A 10 Dec,*
Dfl 3,364 (£803; $961)

12
An 'Imari' dish, Kangxi, decorated with chrysanthemums in iron-red, blue and gold, 43cm (17in), *NY 12/13 Oct,*
$990 (£811)

1
A Ming-style blue and white moon flask, seal mark and period of Yongzheng period, painted with a composite scroll of chrysanthemum, peony and lotus blooms, 37.5cm (14¾in), *L 11 Dec,* £4,400 ($5,544)

2
A Ming-style dish, six character mark and period of Yongzheng, painted with contrived 'heaping and piling' in cobalt of rich colour, 50.8cm (20in), *L 11 Dec,* £6,600 ($8,316)

3
(A blue and white vase, (yuhuchun ping), mark and period of Yongzheng, painted with a bird perched in a spreading prunus tree, 23.2cm (9⅛in), *HK 20 Nov,* HK $22,000 (£2,254; $2,953)

4
A pair of blue and white saucer dishes, marks and period of Yongzheng, the underglaze-blue of soft tone with finely drawn outlines, 15.3cm (6in), *NY 4 Dec,* $4,400 (£3,697)

5
A blue and white dragon and phoenix bowl, mark and period of Kangxi, the interior with a central dragon medallion, all in purplish tones of underglaze-blue, 15.5cm (6⅛in), *NY 12 June,* $3,300 (£2,391)

6
A blue and white bowl, mark and period of Kangxi, the interior with a central medallion of boys at play, 20.1cm (7⅞in), *NY 12 June,* $495 (£358)

7
A pair of blue and white 'Three Friends' dishes, seal mark and period of Daoguang, the interior with a central medallion enclosing the 'Three Friends' of plum, pine and bamboo, the underside with a frieze of children playing, 18.1cm (7⅛in), *NY 4 Dec,* $2,530 (£2,126)

8
A Qing blue and white dragon bowl, seal mark and period of Qianlong, the exterior painted in bright cobalt with two dragons chasing 'flaming pearls', the interior plain, 10.8cm (4¼in), *L 19 June,* £396 ($566)

9
A pair of blue and white bowls, six character mark and period of Tongzhi, each painted on the exterior with a pair of dragons chasing 'flaming pearls', the interior plain, 11.2cm (4⅜in), *L 19 June,* £286 ($409)

10
A pair of early Ming-style blue and white altar sticks, Guangxu, the tapering bodies of square section in the form of a pagoda, painted in rich underglaze-blue, 54.3cm (21⅜in), *C 4 July,* £935 ($1,268)

11
A yellow-ground Ming-style dish, six character mark and period of Yongzheng, the central medallion painted in underglaze-blue of deep tone with lotus and peony blossoms, the border covered with a translucent green enamel, 27.3cm (10¾in), *L 11 Dec,* £16,500 ($20,790)

12
A green and aubergine dragon dish, six character mark and period of Kangxi, the central medallion engraved with a dragon in pursuit of a 'pearl', the cavetto with a similar frieze of two dragons, all on a brilliant emerald ground, 24.7cm (9¾in), *L 11 Dec,* £9,900 ($12,474)

1

A pair of doucai dragon saucer dishes, six character mark and period of Yongzheng, 20.9cm (8¼in), *L 11 Dec*, £9,240 ($11,642)

2

A pair of doucai bowls, marks and period of Kangxi, 16cm (6¼in), *NY 12 June*, $660 (£478)

3

A doucai fishbowl (gang), seal mark and period of Qianlong, decorated in a palette of soft coral-red, tones of green, yellow, aubergine and underglaze-blue, 33cm (13in), *NY 4 Dec*, $11,000 (£9,244)

4

A doucai vase, Qianlong, six character mark and period of Kangxi, 62.2cm (24½in), *NY 12 June*, $4,950 (£3,586)

5

A doucai jar and cover, seal mark and period of Qianlong, decorated with iron-red and yellow chrysanthemum medallions wreathed by bright green leaves between bands of two-tone underglaze-blue wash, h 12.2cm (4⅞in), *HK 21/22 May*, **HK $132,000** (£12,143; $17,500)

6

A doucai bowl, seal mark and period of Jiaqing, 16.2cm (6½in), *L 19 June*, £3,850 ($5,505)

7

A doucai waterpot, 18th cent, 6.5cm (2⅝in), *HK 20 Nov*, **HK $6,380** (£654; $856)

8

A pair of iron-red decorated bowls, seal marks and period of Daoguang, 12.2cm (4¾in), *L 19 June*, £770 ($1,101)

9

A 'famille-verte' month cup, six character mark and period of Kangxi, decorated on the exterior with a crab-apple, emblematic of the fifth month, a couplet and seal in underglaze-blue on the reverse, 6.7cm (2½in), *HK 21/22 May*, **HK $23,100** (£2,125; $3,060)

10

A 'famille-verte' month cup, mark and period of Kangxi, the exterior with sprays of peony, emblematic of the sixth month, a couplet and seal in underglaze-blue on the reverse, 6.4cm (2⅜in), *HK 20 Nov*, **HK $68,200** (£6,987; 9,152)

11

An engraved and enamelled biscuit bowl, six character mark and period of Kangxi, 14.9cm (5⅞in), *L 11 Dec*, £5,060 ($6,376)

12

A 'famille-rose' bowl, six character mark and period of Guangxu, encircled by a frieze of flowering lotus enamelled in 'famille-rose' palette, 17.8cm (7in), *L 11 Dec*, £385 ($485)

13

A pair of turquoise-ground 'famille-rose' bowls, four character mark and period of Guangxu, 14cm (5½in), *HK 22 Nov*, **HK $9,350** (£979; $1,282)

14

A 'famille-rose' bowl, seal mark and period of Daoguang, 13.8cm (5⅜in), *HK 20 Nov*, **HK $15,400** (£1,578; $2,067)

15

A blue-ground 'famille-rose' bowl, seal mark and period of Daoguang, 14.8cm (5¾in), *HK 21/22 May*, **HK $13,750** (£1,265; $1,822)

16

A colour-ground faceted 'famille-rose' vase, underglaze-blue seal mark and period of Qianlong of unusually large size, 68.6cm (27in), *HK 21/22 May*, **HK $418,000** (£38,454; $55,374)

1
A biscuit group, Kangxi, representing a European merchant with a Buddhist lion cub at his side, 13.7cm (5½in), *M 27 June,* **FF 133,200 (£11,433; $15,578)**

2
A biscuit four-tier box and cover, Kangxi, six character mark of Chenghua, of cylindrical form, decorated with phoenix medallions on a green and yellow trellis-pattern ground, 19.7cm (7¾in), *M 27 June,* **FF 15,540 (£1,333; $1,817)**

3
A biscuit winepot and cover, Kangxi, in the form of a *shou* character and of rectangular section, 22.8cm (9in), *M 27 June,* **FF 22,200 (£1,905; $2,596)**

4
A pair of biscuit figures of parrots, Kangxi, in green and aubergine enamels, 21.3cm (8⅜in), *M 27 June,* **FF 33,300 (£2,858; $3,894)**

5
A biscuit figure of a deity, Kangxi, his foot poised above a cat-like animal glazed in yellow, dressed in a green-ground robe with stylised sprigs picked out in yellow and aubergine, 20.7cm (8⅛in), *M 4 Mar,* **FF 14,430 (£1,212; $1,803)**

6
A biscuit 'egg and spinach' bowl, Kangxi, of small size, splashed overall with bright green, amber and straw glazes, 11.3cm (4½in), *HK 20 Nov,* **HK $1,760 (£180; $235)**

7
A turquoise-glazed dish, Kangxi, in the form of a lotus leaf, the incised veining radiating to the frilled upturned edges forming the shallow sides, the overall minutely crackled glaze of intense colour pooling in places, 25.1cm (9⅞in), *M 4 Mar,* **FF 31,080 (£2,612; $3,885)**

8
A pair of biscuit wall vases, Kangxi, decorated in moulded relief with lotus and a *shou* character, 15.2cm (6in), *L 3 July,* **£572 ($777)**

9
A biscuit equestrian figure, Kangxi, the dappled pony applied with a colourless glaze splashed in deep aubergine, the rider dressed in a green jacket over a yellow robe, 14cm (5in), *M 27 June,* **FF 15,540 (£1,333; $1,817)**

10
A biscuit supper set, Kangxi, the thirteen dishes forming the petals of an open lotus flower, 59cm (23¼in), *M 27 June,* **FF 31,080 (£2,668; $3,635)**

11
A turquoise biscuit vase, Kangxi, the tapering neck with an everted rim, covered overall in a brilliant finely crackled glaze applied on the biscuit, 40.3cm (15⅞in), *M 4 Mar,* **FF 23,310 (£1,959; $2,913)**

12
A pair of biscuit vases, Kangxi, of beaker form and hexagonal section, decorated with panels on a green and yellow trellis-pattern ground, moulded bands of lotus petals picked out in aubergine, 22.8cm (9in), *M 27 June,* **FF 9,990 (£857; $1,168)**

13
A biscuit libation cup, 18th cent, in the form of an open peony bloom, glazed inside and out in vivid green enamel, the hollow stem glazed in aubergine springing from the yellow calyx, 14.3cm (5⅝in), *M 4 Mar,* **FF 17,760 (£1,492; $2,220)**

1

2

3

4

5

6

7

8

9

10

11

12

13

1

A Ge-type globular vase,
mark and period of
Qianlong, covered
overall with a thick ash-
grey glaze suffused with
a dark crackle, a
purplish wash on the
footrim, 16.3cm (6⅜in),
HK 21/22 May,
HK $126,500
(£11,637; $16,757)

2

A Ge-type mallet vase,
mark and period of
Qianlong, covered overall
with a thick glaze of pale
ash-grey tone suffused
with a bold black crackle
and scattered lines
continuing over the
countersunk base,
28.6cm (11¼in),
HK 21/22 May,
HK $154,000
(£14,167; $20,400)

3

A blue flambé-glazed vase,
Qianlong, the vivid
deep blue glaze streaked
with milky rivulets and
violet speckles, draining
to a mushroom tone
round the rim of the
galleried mouth, 34.3cm
(13½in), *L 11 Dec,*
£462 ($582)

4

A flambé-glazed vase,
mark and period of
Daoguang, covered
overall with a vivid
reddish-purple glaze
suffused with lilac on the
interior of the mouth
and falling in vertical
rivulets down the
exterior, 18.8cm (7⅜in),
HK 20 Nov,
HK $16,500
(£1,690; $2,215)

5

A blue-glazed stemcup,
mark and period of
Yongzheng, the exterior
covered with a
transparent blue glaze of
rich tone thinning
slightly at the top of the
stem and pooling above
the footrim, 10.8cm
(4¼in), *HK 21/22 May,*
HK $71,500
(£6,580; $9,500)

6

A blue-glazed bowl, mark
and period of Qianlong,
glazed both inside and
out in bright cobalt-blue
draining to white on the
slightly flared rim,
17.8cm (7in), *HK 20 Nov,*
HK $35,200
(£3,607; $4,725)

7

A flambé-glazed meiping,
*c*1800, the well-potted
body covered with a rich
crimson glaze flecked
with milky lavender,
33cm (13in), *NY 12/13 Oct,*
$1,320 (£1,082)

8

**A celadon-glazed ovoid
jar,** mark and period of
Qianlong, supported on
a countersunk base,
covered overall with a
thick sea-green glaze,
19.4cm (7⅝in),
HK 21/22 May,
HK $8,580 (£789; $1,136)

9

**A massive blue-glazed
bottle vase,** 19th cent,
well potted and covered
on the exterior with a
rich blue glaze of bright
tone, with white-glazed
rim and interior, 67.3cm
(26½in), *NY 16/17 Mar,*
$4,950 (£3,322)

1
An eggshell armorial soup plate, Yongzheng, with the arms of van Hardenbroeck of Utrecht, 21.3cm (8⅜in), *M 27 June*, **FF 72,150 (£6,193; $8,438)**

2
A pair of armorial plates, Qianlong, the centre decorated in 'famille-rose' enamels with the arms of Roche, 23.5cm (9¼in), *A 10 Dec*, **Dfl 4,060 (£970; $1,162)**

3
A teapot and cover, Qianlong, decorated in grisaille and gilding with two monograms; sold with a milk jug and cover of the same pattern, 19.1 and 12.5cm (7½ and 4⅞in), *M 27 June*, **FF 4,440 (£381; $519)**

4
A pair of armorial platters, 1775-85, each painted with the arms probably of Jackson, 32.6cm (12⅞in), *NY 26 Jan*, **$1,210 (£834)**

5
A pair of armorial octagonal plates, c.1790, each painted with the arms of John Barnes; sold with a teapot and cover and a Staffordshire punch pot, plates 24cm (9½in), *NY 26 Jan*, **$715 (£493)**

6
An armorial oval soup tureen and cover, c.1795, painted with the arms of a member of the Erskine family, the borders in blue and gilding, 35.3cm (13⅞in), *NY 30 June*, **$1,045 (£774)**

7
A Masonic coffee pot and cover, 1790-1800, painted on either side in gold, black and brown with Masonic devices, 23.7cm (9⅜in), *NY 26 Jan*, **$330 (£227)**

8
A set of three armorial plates, Qianlong, the centre of each decorated in 'famille-rose' enamels with the arms of Ross, 22.8cm (9in), *L 3 July*, **£715 ($972)**

9
A set of three armorial plates, Qianlong, with the arms of Dobree, 20cm (8⅞in), *L 20 Nov*, **£792 ($1,038)**

10
An armorial teacaddy, Qianlong, decorated in 'famille-rose' enamels, decorated on either side with coats-of-arms, 11.2cm (4⅜in), *L 3 July*, **£330 ($449)**

11
An armorial plate, Qianlong, decorated with the arms of Campbell, four sprays of flowers in 'famille-rose' enamels around the rim, 22.9cm (9in), *M 27 June*, **FF 3,108 (£267; $364)**

12
An octagonal plate, Qianlong, 22.9cm (9in), *M 27 June*, **FF 2,775 (£238; $325)**

13
A pair of armorial dishes, Qianlong, richly decorated in 'famille-rose' palette, the arms of Kopersled of Schole in the centre, a gilt border and the rim with rococo scrolls in pink enamel and gilding, 28.6cm (11¼in), *M 27 June*, **FF 15,540 (£1,333; $1,817)**

14
An armorial punch bowl, Qianlong, the exterior with the arms of Amyas of Norfolk, and landscape panels, 28.2cm (11⅛in), *L 20 Nov*, **£1,870 ($2,449)**

15
A ewer and cover, Qianlong, with the arms of Collingwood, 32.4cm (12¾in), *L 20 Nov*, **£1,540 ($2,017)**

1

2

3

4

5

6

7

8

9

10

11

12

13

14

15

1
A 'famille-verte' saucer-shaped dish, c.1710, 24cm (9½in), A 10 Dec,
Dfl 6,844 (£1,635; $1,958)

2
A lighthouse coffee pot and cover, 1800-10, with American eagle decoration, 24cm (9½in), NY 26 Jan,
$2,200 (£1,517)

3
A 'European-subject' dish, c.1725, 35.8cm (14⅛in), L 20 Nov,
£4,400 ($5,764)

4
A pair of 'European subject' plates, Qianlong, richly decorated in 'famille-rose' enamels, 22.8cm (9in), M 4 Mar,
FF 13,320 (£1,119; $1,665)

5
A 'European-subject' plate, Qianlong, decorated in grisaille, 22.8cm (9in), M 27 June,
FF 13,320 (£1,143; $1,557)

6
A set of six 'Italian Comedy' plates, Kangxi, c.1720, for the Dutch market, each painted in underglaze-blue, iron-red, green, yellow, brown and gold, A 16 May,
Dfl 26,680 (£6,226; $8,903)

7
A 'Rotterdam Riot' plate, 1691-95, Chenghua mark, painted in shades of underglaze-blue with a group of rioters attacking the house of Jacob van Zuylen van Nyevelt, 20cm (7⅞in), NY 26 Jan,
$1,760 (£1,213)

8
A 'famille-rose' cup and saucer, Qianlong, decorated after a print by Picart, 'Les Pèlerins de l'Isle de Cythère', A 10 Dec,
Dfl 1,856 (£443; $530)

9
A teapot and cover, Qianlong, decorated in 'famille-rose' enamels with 'Le Printemps' taken from an engraving by Larmessin, after a drawing by Lancret, 19.7cm (7¾in), M 27 June,
FF 8,880 (£762; $1,038)

10
A 'blue Fitzhugh' bottle, 19th cent, 24.9cm (9¾in), NY 30 June,
$660 (£488)

11
A pair of blue and white plates, 1735-40, each painted in underglaze-blue with two caterpillars on an iris sprig and a clematis blossom, within a blue band and gilt strapwork border, 23.3cm (9⅛in), NY 26 Jan,
$2,090 (£1,441)

12
A blue and white large plate, 1738-40, painted after Cornelis Pronk in underglaze-blue with six chinoiserie figures by a pond, the border reserved with panels of flowers, fruit and butterflies, 26.6cm (10½in), NY 26 Jan,
$1,980 (£1,365)

13
A mythological punch bowl, c.1745, enamelled in a full 'famille-rose' palette and heightened in gilding on the exterior with three gilt-edged quatrefoil panels of classical scenes, 38.4cm (15⅛in), NY 26 Jan,
$4,950 (£3,413)

14
An octagonal guglet, c.1745, painted in shades of green, iron-red, blue, brown, grey, puce and yellow edged in gilt, iron-red and rose foliate-scroll bordered panels, 25.7cm (10⅛in), NY 26 Jan,
$1,540 (£1,062)

15
A shipping bowl, c.1785, with a ship and three British flags, 22.9cm (9in), NY 26 Jan,
$1,045 (£720)

16
A teabowl and saucer, c.1795, with American marine decoration, d 9 and 14.3cm (3½ and 5⅝in), NY 26 Jan,
$770 (£531)

1
A pair of 'famille-verte' flasks, Kangxi, well painted in bright enamels with arrangements of Precious Objects alternating with landscapes and birds and insects within bands of underglaze-blue key-fret, 23.2cm (9⅛in), *L 20 Nov,* **£3,190 ($4,178)**

2
A 'famille-verte' jardinière, early Kangxi, 36.8cm (14½in), *NY 12 June,* **$4,950 (£3,586)**

3
A 'famille-verte' covered cistern, Kangxi, enamelled with birds among flowering trees above a seeded green-ground floral frieze, a horned mask projecting in relief and picked out in yellow, 46cm (18in), *A 16 May,* **Dfl 6,960 (£1,624; $2,322)**

4
A pair of 'famille-verte' jugs, Kangxi, of helmet shape, each with a floral frieze between seeded green-ground borders raised in light relief, a band of lotus petals coloured in yellow, green and aubergine rising from the base, 18.4cm (7¼in), *M 27 June,* **FF 17,760 (£1,524; $2,077)**

5
A 'famille-verte' tankard, Kangxi, decorated with flowers and birds in petal-shaped panels, divided with flowers on a light green ground, 18th century gilt bronze mounts decorated with Apollo and Diana, 16cm (6¼in), *A 16 May,* **Dfl 8,816 (£2,057; $2,941)**

6
A fluted 'famille-verte' bowl, Kangxi, the exterior enamelled with mixed sprays of flowers above a band of yellow lappets edged in green around the base, the interior with a stem of poppies, 18.2cm (7⅛in), *M 4 Mar,* **FF 6,660 (£559; $832)**

7
A large 'famille-verte', bowl, Kangxi, 34cm (13½in), *A 9 Mar,* **Dfl 9,744 (£2,328; $2,788)**

8
A 'famille-verte' dish, *aiye* mark, Kangxi, brightly enamelled with an overall scene of two exotic butterflies above flowering peonies, 35.2cm (13⅞in), *L 20 Nov,* **£484 ($634)**

9
A pair of 'famille-verte' dishes, Kangxi, each decorated in the centre with a butterfly above a pheasant amongst flowering peonies, the enamels of bright tones, 26.8cm (10½in), *M 4 Mar,* **FF 17,760 (£1,492; $2,220)**

10
A 'famille-verte' saucer dish, *aiye* mark, Kangxi, with lipped rim, the centre enamelled with a butterfly above inter-mingled flowering peony and magnolia trees, 37.8cm (14⅞in), *M 4 Mar,* **FF 8,880 (£746; $1,110)**

11
A 'famille-verte' dish, Kangxi, decorated in the centre with a pair of birds beside a flowering tree, the rim encircled by a seeded green-ground border, 40.7cm (16in), *M 27 June,* **FF 26,640 (£2,286; $3,115)**

12
A pair of 'famille-verte' dishes, Kangxi, 16.2cm (6⅜in), *M 4 Mar,* **FF 6,660 (£559; $832)**

13
A pair of powder-blue ground vases, Kangxi, the mottled ground of brilliant colour, reserved with shaped panels enamelled in 'famille-verte' palette, 18.4cm (7¼in), *M 4 Mar,* **FF 19,980 (£1,678; $2,497)**

14
A 'famille-verte' rouleau vase, Kangxi, painted with a scene of the Three Star Gods, 44.5cm (17½in), *NY 4 Dec,* **$7,150 (£6,008)**

15
'A 'famille-verte' jar and cover, Kangxi, 59.7cm (23½in), *M 4 Mar,* **FF 155,400 (£13,058; $19,425)**

1

2

3

4

5

6

7

8

9

10

11

12

13

14

15

1
A 'famille-verte' vase, Kangxi, fitted for electricity, 44.2cm (17⅜in), *M 27 June*, **FF 57,720 (£4,954; $6,750)**

2
A pair of 'famille-verte' vases and covers, Kangxi, enamelled with panels of flowers and Precious Objects, 43.2cm (17in), *L 3 July*, **£3,520 ($4,787)**

3
A 'famille-verte' triple-gourd vase, Kangxi, decorated in enamels and underglaze-blue heightened in gilding, with alternating stems of lilies and peonies rising from the base, 36.8cm (14½in), *L 3 July*, **£2,860 ($3,889)**

4
A pair of 'famille-verte' vases of rouleau form, 61.6cm (24½in), *L 20 Nov*, **£935 ($1,224)**

5
A rare Chinoiserie 'famille-rose' basin, Yongzheng/ early Qianlong, richly enamelled probably after a design by Cornelius Pronk, 47.6cm (18¾in), *L 20 Nov*, **£35,000 ($46,112)**

6
A 'famille-rose' Yen-yen vase, Yongzheng, painted with landscape panels on a blue ground enriched with scrolling lotus in 'famille-rose' enamels, 43.2cm (17in), *NY 16/17 Mar*, **$1,100 (£738)**

7
A pair of 'famille-rose' covered vases, Qianlong, each decorated with a pair of phoenix in a fenced garden, their plumage brightly coloured, a pink-edged turquoise lappet border around the base and shoulders, 134.7 and 132.2cm (53 and 52in), *M 4 Mar*, **FF 355,200 (£29,849; $44,400)**

8
A 'famille-rose' vase, Qianlong, the pale green ground reserved with two panels painted with figures, 37.5cm (14¾in), *P 14 Nov*, **£176 ($236)**

9
A 'famille-rose' circular tureen and cover, 1735-45, each piece painted in a full palette heightened in gilding, the rim with a turquoise cell diaper border, 28.9cm (11⅜in), *NY 26 Jan*, **$1,650 (£1,138)**

10
A lotus dish, c.1760, painted in shades of rose, green, turquoise, brown, iron-red, white, yellow and gold, 22.6cm (8⅞in), *NY 26 Jan*, **$1,100 (£758)**

11
A 'famille-rose' punch bowl, c.1740, painted on the exterior with two phoenix amidst flowering branches, the interior with a border of iron-red and gilt tassels pendent from pink and turquoise lappets, 38.8cm (15¼in), *NY 26 Jan*, **$3,960 (£2,731)**

12
A 'famille-rose' plate, Yongzheng, decorated in enamels of brilliant tones, 24.4cm (9⅝in), *M 4 Mar*, **FF 6,105 (£513; $763)**

13
A pear-shaped 'famille-rose' teapot and cover, Yonghzeng, 9.5cm (3¾in), *A 10 Dec*, **Dfl 2,668 (£1,116; $1,336)**

14
A tureen and cover, Qianlong, in European silver-shape, 32cm (12⅝in), *A 10 Dec*, **Dfl 8,120 (£1,940; $2,324)**

15
A 'tobacco leaf' part dinner service, Qianlong, each piece decorated in underglaze-blue and 'famille-rose' enamels, 17 pieces, *L 20 Nov*, **£16,500 ($21,615)**

1   2   3   2   4
5   6   7   8
9   10   11
12   13   14
15

1
A 'tobacco leaf' pattern oval platter, painted with tobacco blossom, chrysanthemum and roses, c.1775, 31.1cm (12¼in), *NY 26 Jan,*
$1,760 (£1,213)

2
A 'Compagnie-des-Indes' tureen, cover and stand, Qianlong, with rabbit head handles and lotus bud knop, decorated predominantly in pink enamel with flowers and sprigs within a puce border, 37.4cm (14¾in), *L 20 Nov,*
£3,520 ($4,611)

3
A pair of silver-shape sauceboats, Qianlong, each decorated in 'famille-rose' enamels with groups of female musicians, a floral border around the splayed foot, 24.3cm (9⅝in), *L 20 Nov,*
£286 (£374)

4
A pair of 'mandarin palette' cylindrical tankards, c.1785, each painted with figures on a terrace within a panel bordered in underglaze-blue flowers, scrolls and diaperwork, 12.8cm (5in), *NY 30 June,*
$880 (£651)

5
A 'mandarin palette' bowl, c.1785, painted with Oriental figures in gardens within cartouches edged in gilt scrolls and purple and turquoise foliage, all reserved on a ground of iron-red and gilt panels, 26.2cm (10¼in), *NY 26 Jan,*
$660 (£455)

6
A reticulated oval basket and stand, c.1765, the centre of each painted in shades of rose, purple, green, blue, yellow, white, iron-red and gilding with a butterfly amidst floral sprays, 22.9 and 26.2cm (9 and 10¼in), *NY 26 Jan,*
$1,980 (£1,365)

7
A 'mandarin palette' vase, c.1785, moulded overall with basketwork painted with floral clusters and insects and reserved with raised panels painted with Oriental figures on terraces, 31.8cm (12½in), *NY 26 Jan,*
$990 (£682)

8
A pair of 'famille-rose' vases and covers, Qianlong, decorated in relief with fruiting vines picked out in pale blue enamel, four tree shrews applied on the shoulders, 30.8cm (12⅛in), *L 20 Nov,*
£770 ($1,008)

9
A 'tobacco leaf' pattern charger, 1760-80, painted in underglaze-blue, yellow, rose, iron-red, green, turquoise, white and gilding with a pair of pheasants and a squirrel, 33.8cm (13¼in), *NY 30 June,*
$1,870 (£1,385)

10
A punch bowl, c.1795, painted in blue enamel, salmon, iron-red and gold on the front and reverse with a basket of flowers within oak boughs, flanked by floral and fruit sprigs, 33.3cm (13⅛in), *NY 26 Jan,*
$1,980 (£1,365)

11
A pair of large leaf dishes, c.1770, probably taken from a Chelsea original, each modelled as a cos lettuce leaf with a green-enamelled fluted rim edged in gilding, 35.7cm (14in), *NY 30 June,*
$2,640 (£1,955)

12
A pair of octagonal 'famille-rose' plates, Qianlong, enamelled with peonies in a leaf-shaped panel, 22.5cm (8⅞in), *A 10 Dec,*
Dfl 2,320 (£554; $663)

13
An oval 'famille-rose' dish, Qianlong, with two handles, decorated with two birds among rocks and flowering trees, a spearhead border around the rim, 54cm (21¼in), *A 10 Dec,*
Dfl 1,392 (£332; $397)

1

A set of six 'famille-rose'
plates, Qianlong, 23cm
(9in), *A 16 May*,
Dfl 4,872 (£1,136; $1,624)

2

A set of four octagonal
'famille-rose' plates,
Qianlong, painted with
figures at a lakeside
21.5cm (8½in),
P 24/25 Jan,
£308 ($447)

3

A set of eight 'famille-rose'
plates, Qianlong, 22cm
(8¾in), *A 10 Dec*,
Dfl 7,192 (£1,718; $2,058)

4

A 'famille-rose' teapot and
cover, Qianlong, applied
with lotus flowers and
leaves on a reticulated
foot, 9.5cm (3⅝in),
A 10 Dec,
Dfl 2,088 (£498; $596)

5

A 'famille-rose' teapot and
cover, Qianlong, applied
at the base with a leafy
stem forming a raised
and pierced foot, the
underside moulded in
the form of a chrysanthe-
mum, 10.1cm (4in),
L 3 July,
£330 ($449)

6

A pair of 'famille-rose'
dishes, Qianlong, the
centre of each enamelled
with a spray of flowers
within a lozenge outlined
in black and green, a
bright pink trellis-
pattern border around
the well and rim, 28.3cm
(11⅛in), *M 4 Mar*,
FF 8,325 (£700; $1,041)

7

A pair of 'famille-rose'
tureens, covers and
stands, Qianlong,
decorated with chrysan-
themums and lotus
flowers in blue, green
and iron-red enamels,
22.5cm (9in), *F 3/4 Oct*,
L 14,000,000
(£5,527; $7,185)

8

A 'famille-rose' tureen and
cover, Qianlong, following
a European silver original,
a Buddhist lion knop
36.3cm (14¼in), *M 4 Mar*,
FF 15,540 (£1,306; $1,943)

9

A pair of 'famille-rose'
vases, Qianlong, each
enamelled with a pair of
pheasants perched on
ornamental blue rockwork,
the base and shoulders
with a yellow-ground
lappet border, one of the
two covers matching,
41.9cm (16½in), *M 27 June*,
FF 46,620 (£4,002; $5,453)

10

A 'famille-rose' seven
bordered eggshell ruby
back saucer dish, Yong-
zheng, enamelled with a
lady and two small boys
in an interior setting,
21cm (8¼in), *NY 4 Dec*,
$1,980 (£1,664)

11

A teapot and cover, Yong-
zheng, 12cm (4⅝in),
A 10 Dec,
Dfl 2,552 (£609; $729)

12

An hexagonal garden seat,
Daoguang, decorated in
'famille-rose' enamels
with a continuous frieze
of figures in a palace
garden, the upper and
lower zones with butterflies
and Precious Objects,
47.3cm (18⅝in), *L 3 July*,
£1,540 ($2,094)

13

A Canton yellow-ground
garden seat, Guangxu, of
hexagonal barrel shape,
the central frieze with
dragons among flowers
painted in white enamel
and sepia enriched in
gilding, 45.4cm (17⅞in),
L 20 Nov,
£1,320 ($1,729)

14

A pair of Canton vases of
ribbed ovoid form,
painted in 'famille-rose'
enamel with panels of
dignitaries enclosed by
birds, flowers and insects
on a celadon ground,
63.5cm (25in), *C 17 July*,
£660 ($878)

1
A pair of 'rose medallion' bough vases, 2nd half 19th cent, decorated with two figural reserves and two floral reserves, 25.4cm (10in), *NY 16/17 Mar,* $2,310 (£1,550)

2
A pair of Canton 'famille-rose' gu-form vases, 19th cent, decorated with scroll-bordered panels, figures conversing in a garden alternating with panels of birds, 40cm (15¾in), *NY 12/13 Oct,* $1,320 (£1,082)

3
A Canton 'famille-rose' bowl, Daoguang, painted with a dignitary surrounded by her attendants in a summer-house, 52.1cm (20½in), *L 3 July,* £2,860 ($3,890)

4
A pair of Canton celadon-ground barrel-form garden seats, Jiaqing/Daoguang, enamelled in 'famille-rose' colours with flower sprigs, butterflies and Precious Objects, 47cm (18½in), *P 24/25 Jan,* £825 ($1,196)

5
A Canton 'famille-rose' vase, 19th cent, painted with panels showing dignitaries holding court, the neck applied with gilt *fu*-lion handles, 90.2cm (35½in), *NY 16/17 Mar,* $30,080 (£2,067)

6
A pair of celadon-ground 'famille-rose' vases, late 19th cent, decorated in slip and enamels with panels of immortals in landscapes reserved on a pale celadon ground, 87.7cm (34½in), *NY 16/17 Mar,* $5,775 (£3,876)

7
A Canton 'famille-rose' vase, mid-19th cent, the gilt ground embellished with a field of green scrolling vines issuing pink blossoms, reserved with panels painted with birds and figures, 62.2cm (24½in), *NY 16/17 Mar,* $1,210 (£812)

8
A pair of 'famille-rose' vases and covers, 19th cent, each decorated in relief with fruiting peach and pomegranate branches, the trellis-pattern ground in turquoise and yellow, 62.9cm (24¾in), *L 20 Nov,* £1,045 ($1,369)

9
A pair of Canton 'famille-rose' double-gourd vases and covers, each brightly decorated with panels enclosing figures and floral sprays, reserved on a scroll-filled ground, 33.4cm (13⅛in), *L 20 Nov,* £715 ($937)

10
A 'famille-rose' enamelled fish bowl, 19th cent, with beribboned brocade medallions suspended below a large lotus leaf and blossom, the interior with iron-red fish, 46cm (18⅛in); *NY 16/17 Mar,* $1,210 (£812)

11
A yellow-ground 'famille-rose' goldfish bowl, 2nd half 19th cent, applied, moulded and enamelled with the Hundred Antiques, the interior with five ornamental carp, 40.8cm (16in), *P 14 Nov,* £462 ($619)

12
A pair of 'famille-rose' garden seats, painted with battle scenes from the Romance of the Three Kingdoms, reserved on a bright *wan*-fret ground between turquoise and rose *ruyi* and gadroon borders, 46.3cm (18¼in), *NY 12/13 Oct,* $3,300 (£2,705)

13
A 'famille-rose' jardinière, Guangxu, the sides enamelled with flowering lotus, a pair of kingfishers perched among leafy stems rising from the water washed in tones of translucent green, 46.7cm (18⅛in), *M 4 Mar,* **FF 25,530 (£2,145; $3,191)**

14
A Canton 'famille-rose' part dinner service, mid-19th cent, 153 pieces, *NY 30 June,* $15,400 (£11,407)

Chinese Export Porcelain Figures

It was through the good offices of the East India Companies that Chinese porcelain was exported in such enormous quantities during the 18th and 19th centuries. Chinese porcelain, long legendary in Europe, was now discovered to be eminently practical as tableware and attractive—so attractive, in fact, that it was not long before a flourishing market developed for figures, animals and birds of a partly or wholly decorative nature.

Porcelain and pottery figures had been part of the Chinese repertoire for many centuries, but these generally served religious purposes. During the Kangxi reign (1662-1722), however, wares started being produced specifically for Europe and were often designed solely as ornaments; in due course European designs and models were even copied on commission. The Kangxi figures are typically decorated in 'famille-verte' enamels, such as the splendid pair of leopards illustrated here (p.660, fig. 5). These figures are exceptionally large—some 40 inches in total length—and must have presented tremendous firing problems at the time, requiring the support of numerous bamboo sticks to prevent their collapse in the kiln: the marks left by these are clearly visible still on the underside.

With the advent of the 'famille-rose' palette towards the end of the reign of the Kangxi Emperor many figures were more flamboyantly enamelled: the goose tureens (p.660, fig. 9) and the pheasants (p. 638, fig. 1) are classic examples. Some figures, however, are more restrained. The hawks (p.661, fig. 1) are in sepia with gilding and the hound (p. 661, fig. 4) is brown with white patches.

The Chinese themselves never held export porcelain in such high esteem as they did Imperial wares, but a few pieces made for the home market were also exported. These include articles for the scholar's desk such as water-droppers, brushpots and brushwashers, as well as ewers, like the one in the form of a chicken (p. 660, fig. 6). There are a few amusing figure groups which would have found a place in the home, but game cocks, leopards and jugglers were really for the European market, as were the specially commissioned figures, like that reputed to be of the Dutch Governor Duf, whose price of £57,831 ($86,025) reflects its rarity (p. 638, fig. 4). Figures of the Governor's wife are more frequently found and bring less than a quarter of that sum.

During the 19th century quality declined, though virtuoso pieces were still attempted. The decoration and modelling became rather over-elaborate and crude, while the enamels lost their brightness and clarity. None the less figures, such as the pair of phoenix (p. 662, fig. 11) which fetched £4,950 ($6,485), indicate that many pieces, especially those made during the early part of the century, still have great decorative appeal.

Since Chinese export porcelain figures have always been highly prized by middle and upper class European customers they have inevitably also been expensive. Whilst very high prices are commanded only by rare pieces of the finest quality, more modest works can be bought for less than £1,000 ($1,140). Political upheavals can upset the market. Historically the Portuguese have been the most fervent collectors of Chinese export porcelain; theirs was, after all, the first East India Company to trade with China, and the change of regime in 1974 caused prices to drop overnight. It is only now, some ten years later, that prices are returning to their former values.

1
A pair of tileworks figures of Buddhist lions, Ming Dynasty, each with a brocade ball between its front paws, predominantly glazed in bright turquoise with details picked out in aubergine and cream, 58.4cm (23in), *M 27 June,* **FF 177,600 (£15,245; $20,772)**

2
A pair of biscuit figures of jugglers, Kangxi, each astride Buddhist lions glazed in yellow and green, the manes, tails and fringing picked out in green and aubergine, 16.5cm (6½in), *M 27 June,* **FF 24,420 (£2,096; $2,856)**

1

2

1
A biscuit figure of a Iohan, Kangxi, dressed in a long yellow skirt and green scarf, the tightly curled hair left unglazed and showing traces of gilding, 17.4cm (6⅞in), *M 27 June,*
FF 9,990 (£858; $1,168)

2
A biscuit figure of a boy, Kangxi, dressed in a seeded green-ground jacket with scattered flowers over yellow-ochre pantaloons, 15.5cm (6⅛in), *M 27 June,*
FF 49,950 (£4,288; $5,842)

3
A 'famille-verte' group of two lovers, Kangxi, the young man dressed in a long green robe, she in a yellow jacket over an aubergine robe, 16.2cm (6⅜in), *M 27 June,*
FF 17,760 (£1,524; $2,077)

4
A pair of rare biscuit figures of Asil game cocks, Kangxi, each standing on yellow legs with black scale markings, the plumage moulded with incised details and glazed in green, mauve, yellow, white and blue, outlined in black, 26.6cm (10½in), *L 3 July,*
£25,300 ($34,408)

5
A rare pair of biscuit figures of leopards, Kangxi, the detachable tail swept up behind, the mouth and tongue washed in rouge-de-fer, the body applied in translucent yellow enamel with spots splashed and pencilled in black, 101.6cm (40in), *M 27 June,*
FF 1,443,000 (£123,863; $168,772)

6
A pair of biscuit chicken ewers and covers, Kangxi, the down and feathers incised, the comb and wattles picked out in aubergine, the wings and body in yellow, green and aubergine, 12.7 and 13.4cm (5 and 5¼in), *M 4 Mar,*
FF 23,310 (£1,959; $2,914)

7
A pair of figures of white cocks, Qianlong, differing slightly, the plumage glazed overall in white, the combs, wattles and legs with traces of original cold-painting in red, 33.7 and 35.3cm (13¼ and 13⅞in), *M 27 June,*
FF 31,080 (£2,668; $3,635)

8
A figure of a cock, Qianlong, the clawed legs washed in café-au-lait, the plumage lightly moulded beneath the white glaze, 34.3cm (13½in), *M 27 June,*
FF 13,320 (£1,143; $1,557)

9
A brilliantly enamelled pair of 'Compagnie-des-Indes' goose tureens and covers, Qianlong, the body painted in rouge-de-fer and detailed in gilding and pale lilac with detailing in a deeper tone, the multi-coloured wings with gilt 'eyes', 40cm (15¾in), *L 3 July,*
£50,600 ($68,816)

10
A pair of 'Compagnie-des-Indes' cock tureens and covers, Qianlong, the eyes picked out in black on a gold ground, the wings enamelled in green, yellow, blue mauve, aubergine and pink outlined in grisaille and embellished with gilding, 38.1cm (15in), *L 3 July,*
£36,300 ($49,368)

11
A pair of figures of cranes, Qianlong, each glazed in white over lightly moulded feather markings, the longer plumes and legs left in the biscuit and painted in cobalt turned greyish-black in the firing, 29.5cm (11⅝in), *M 27 June,*
FF 44,400 (£3,811; $5,193)

12
A pair of 'Compagnie-des-Indes' tureens and covers, Qianlong, in the form of birds with removable upper sections, the wings in green, sepia, yellow and lilac, the webbed feet in tones of rouge-de-fer, 15.3cm (6in), *M 4 Mar,*
FF 55,500 (£4,664; $6,938)

1   2   3

4   5

6   7   8   7

9   10

11   12

1
A pair of figures of hawks, Qianlong, the beaks in gilding, plumage on the head and neck washed in sepia and with details pencilled in a richer tone, the wings with gilt quills, 27.3cm (10¾in), *M 27 June,*
FF 111,000 (£9,528; $12,982)

2
A pair of 'famille-rose' figures of cocks, Qianlong, each on a rock-work base washed in blue enamel and sepia and spotted in green, the body in rich rouge-de-fer pencilled in gilding, the wattles and comb in pink, 24.8cm (9¾in), *M 27 June,*
FF 53,280 (£4,753; $6,232)

3
A pair of 'famille-rose' figures of exotic birds, Qianlong, each on a rock-work base washed in green enamel and splashed in pink and blue, the body in rouge-de-fer with multi-coloured plumage, 27cm (10⅝in), *M 27 June,*
FF 46,620 (£4,002; $5,453)

4
A 'Compagnie-des-Indes' figure of a hound, Qianlong, the body with markings pencilled in fur grisaille on a pale rouge-de-fer wash and dappled markings in white enamel, details in iron-red, 24.4cm (9⅝in), *M 4 Mar,*
FF 36,630 (£3,078; $4,579)

5
A pair of figures of hawks, Qianlong, each with the body washed in pale sepia and flecked in a contrasting richer tone, the wings with details in gilding, bright yellow legs, 16.3cm (6⅜in), *M 27 June,*
FF 46,620 (£4,002; $5,453)

6
A pair of 'Compagnie-des-Indes' figures of hounds, Qianlong, each with the chest washed in pale sepia and the remainder densely pencilled in a richer tone with patches left white, the collar in green enamel, 14.9cm (5⅞in), *M 27 June,*
FF 22,200 (£1,906; $2,596)

7
An exportware figure of a kylin, Qianlong, the curly mane in tones of green, the remainder of the body in iron-red and the backbone highlighted in blue enamel, 19cm (7½in), *L 3 July,*
£1,078 ($1,466)

8
A pair of figures of ladies, Qianlong, each standing on a base decorated with floral panels moulded in relief and picked out in enamels, the figures decorated in underglaze-blue, yellow and iron-red, 30.8cm (12⅛in), *M 4 Mar,*
FF 26,640 (£2,239; $3,330)

9
A pair of 'famille-rose' figures, Qianlong, each depicting a bearded old man, one with pink apron over a yellow-ground robe, the other with a turquoise robe, 16.8cm (6⅝in), *M 4 Mar,*
FF 3,330 (£280; $416)

10
A 'famille-rose' figure of a young boy, Qianlong, in a flowing blue robe pencilled in black with stars and cloud medallions, 24cm (9½in), *HS 25 June,*
£330 ($465)

1

2

3

4

5

6

7

8

9

10

1
A pair of 'famille-rose'
groups, Qianlong, each
of a lady seated on a flat
base, dressed in a tunic
figured in blue tied with
an iron-red sash, long
pink pantaloons, the shoes
in rouge-de-fer and
grisaille, 19.4cm (7⅝in),
M 27 June,
**FF 122,100
(£10,481; $14,281)**

2
A 'famille-rose' figure of a
lady, Qianlong, dressed
in a tunic decorated with
gilt-ground roundels of
butterflies and flowers in
puce enamel and tones
of sepia, 49.5cm (19½in),
M 27 June,
FF 35,520 (£3,049; $4,154)

3
A 'Compagnie-des-Indes'
tureen and cover, Jiaqing,
in the form of a duck,
the down and feather
markings pencilled in
rouge-de-fer on a
washed ground of paler
tone, the feathers picked
out in 'famille-rose'
enamels, 14.9cm (5⅞in),
M 4 Mar,
FF 9,990 (£839; $1,249)

4
A pair of figures of
Buddhist lions, Jiaqing,
for use as joss-stick
holders, enamelled in
pink with long bright
green fur and mane
picked out in aubergine,
the tail in yellow, 15cm
(5⅞in), *L 20 Nov,*
£1,320 ($1,729)

5
A 'famille-rose' group of
the Hoho Erxian,
Qianlong, twin spirits of
Mirth and Harmony,
dressed in pink and
green tunics over
turquoise and yellow
pantaloons respectively,
20.3cm (8in), *M 4 Mar,*
FF 9,990 (£839; $1,249)

6
An iron-red decorated
carp tureen and cover,
Jiaqing, the details of the
scales in relief and the
fins and tail picked out
in iron-red, 25.9cm (10in),
L 3 July,
£1,155 ($1,571)

7
A turquoise-glazed frog
jardinière, mark of
Chenghua, Jiaqing, the
eyes picked out in black,
covered in a translucent
turquoise glaze, the feet
left in the biscuit, 26.6cm
(10½in), *M 4 Mar,*
FF 8,880 (£746; $1,110)

8
A green-glazed biscuit
figure of a frog, 18th cent,
the protruding eyes
picked out in black, with
overall raised stippling
simulating the warty
skin, 10.2cm (4in),
M 4 Mar,
FF 14,430 (£1,213; $1,804)

9
A pair of figures of
pigeons, 18th cent, the
clawed legs and pointed
beak washed in café-au-
lait, the pupils of the
eyes in underglaze-blue,
glazed all in white,
17.8cm (7in), *M 27 June,*
FF 25,530 (£2,191; $2,986)

10
A pair of Guangdong
figures of ducks, 19th cent,
each standing on a
brown-glazed rock base,
the bird glazed in white,
the moulded plumage
showing through, 24.2cm
(9½in), *L 20 Nov,*
£935 ($1,224)

11
A pair of 'famille-rose'
figures of phoenix, 19th
cent, the birds with
yellow down on the
body shading to pink on
the legs, dense multi-
coloured feathers, the
back enamelled in tur-
quoise centred in
gilding, 54.4cm (21in),
L 20 Nov,
£4,950 ($6,485)

12
A pair of figures of phoenix
19th cent, each enamelled
in shades of rose, blue,
turquoise, yellow, black
and iron-red, 23.2 and
23.6cm (9⅛ and 9¼in),
NY 30 June,
$935 (£692)

1

2

5

6

3

4

7

8

9

10

11

12

1
A 'blanc-de-Chine' figure of a sage, 17th cent, standing on a base of crested waves, with well-modelled features, covered in an ivory-tinted glaze, 25.5cm (10in), *L 20 Nov*, £990 ($1,297)

2
A pair of 'blanc-de-Chine' figures of cocks, *c*1700, each standing with head raised, in a crowing attitude, the plumage lightly impressed beneath the overall milk-white glaze, 16.8cm (6⅝in), *M 27 June*, FF 12,210 (£1,048; $1,428)

3
A 'blanc-de-Chine' group, Kangxi, depicting a lady seated on a rock, a flute held in her hands, a small jardinière set at her side, her maid carrying a mandolin, 17.2cm (6¾in), *M 27 June*, FF 8,880 (£762; $1,038)

4
A 'blanc-de-Chine' group, Kangxi, a dignitary seated on a rock ledge, the diminutive figure of an attendant standing at his side, 14cm (5½in), *M 27 June*, FF 11,000 (£944; $1,287)

5
A 'blanc-de-Chine' vase of pear shape, 18th cent, two elephant-head handles projecting in bold relief on the shoulders, 21.6cm (8½in), *M 27 June*, FF 4,995 (£429; $584)

6
A 'blanc-de-Chine' figure of Guanyin, 18th cent, seated with right knee raised in royal ease, dressed in flowing robes and a beaded necklace, 22.7cm (8⅞in), *L 3 July*, £572 ($778)

7
A 'blanc-de-Chine' figure of Guanyin, *c*1700, standing on a base of clouds, the face with well-modelled meditative expression, the glaze of fine ivory tone, 49.5cm (19½in), *M 4 Mar*, FF 10,545 (£886; $1,318)

8
A pair of 'blanc-de-Chine' figures of Buddhist lions, 18th cent, each sitting on a rectangular base with left front paw resting on a brocade ball, the overall glaze of milk-white tone, 26.4cm (10¾in), *M 27 June*, FF 13,320 (£1,143; $1,558)

9
A Dehua figure of Guanyin, Kangxi, the goddess of Mercy wearing a loosely draped robe falling in billowing folds, her face with finely detailed features in a serene expression, 46.5cm (18¼in), *HK 21/22 May*, HK$ 59,400 (£5,464; $7,869)

1

2

3

4

6

7

8

5

9

1
A Ming cloisonné enamel tripod censer, 15th cent, the sides encircled by a band of raised floret-form gilt-bronze bosses reserved on a turquoise-blue ground decorated in red, blue and green, 16.5cm (6½in), *HK 19 Nov*, **HK $231,000** (£23,428; $30,691)

2
A cloisonné enamel brushpot, 17th cent, of hexagonal form, decorated with narrow borders of archaistic dragons, in tones of red, yellow, white, dark blue and green on a turquoise ground, 14.2cm (5½in), *NY 16/17 Mar,* **$1,650 (£1,107)**

3
A cloisonné enamel li ding, 18th cent, decorated with pendent shield panels and a band of eight gilt-bronze whorl appliqués, in blue, yellow, red, pink and green enamels on a turquoise ground, 24.8cm (9¾in), *NY 16/17 Mar,* **$880 (£591)**

4
A pair of cloisonné enamel covered pot-pourri, 18th cent, raised on short tripod legs issuing from gilt-bronze animal masks, the sides decorated on a turquoise ground predominantly in rich lapis blue, 32.4cm (12¾in), *M 4 Mar,* **FF 37,740** (£3,171; $4,717)

5
A pair of Canton enamel candleholders, 18th cent, each lotus-form holder supported on urn-shaped stands brightly painted with lotus blossoms, decorated in pink, green and yellow on an indigo blue ground, 26.7cm (10½in), *NY 16/17 Mar,* **$3,630 (£2,436)**

6
A cloisonné enamel box and cover, Qianlong, of straight-sided hexagonal form, decorated with multi-coloured stylised sprigs in lapis blue on a turquoise ground, 10.8cm (4½in), *M 4 Mar,* **FF 5,328 (£448; $666)**

7
A gilt-bronze and cloisonné enamel altar set, Qianlong, comprising a tripod censer, a vase and a circular covered box, each decorated with shaped gilt-bronze appliqués of birds and deer, reserved on a bright turquoise blue ground, censer 11.7cm (4⅝in), *HK 19 Nov,* **HK $93,500** (£9,483; $12,423)

8
A cloisonné enamel cuspidor and cover, Qianlong, decorated with bats and stylised sprigs in colours on a turquoise ground, the domed cover surmounted by a gilt-bronze conical knop, 14.9cm (5⅞in), *M 4 Mar,* **FF 4,440 (£373; $555)**

9
A cloisonné enamel box and cover, Qianlong, of pentagonal section with panels simulating a flowerhead, the cover with a gilt-metal knop, the sides with blossoms on a turquoise ground, 17.1cm (6¾in), *L 1/2 Nov,* **£1,265 ($1,619)**

10
A cloisonné enamel censer, Jiaqing, the globular body supported on three rams with white hide, the handles modelled as coiled chilong, the knop in the form of two Buddhist lions, 52cm (20½in), *L 4 May,* **£5,280 ($7,762)**

11
A pair of cloisonné enamel vases, Jiaqing, each decorated on a turquoise, ground in red, yellow, aubergine and white amongst numerous dark green foliate motifs, 33.9cm (13⅜in), *M 4 Mar,* **FF 16,650 (£1,399; $2,081)**

1

2

3

4

5

6

7

8

9   10   11

1

A lobed cloisonné vase,
Jiaqing, of quatrefoil
section, decorated with
scrolling exotic blooms
in blue, black, red and
white enamels raised on
a gilt-bronze ground,
27.2cm (10¾in),
NY 16/17 Mar,
$770 (£517)

2

**A pair of cloisonné beaker
vases (gu),** Daoguang, each
turquoise ground finely
inlaid with panels
enclosing a single lotus
flower within interlaced
black key-fret frames,
24.5cm (9⅝in),
P 10/13 July,
£440 ($598)

3

**A cloisonné and champ-
levé enamel tripod censer
and cover,** late 18th/early
19th cent, the turquoise
ground enamelled with
colourful lotus arranged
over three legs in the
form of elephants' heads,
20.5cm (8in),
P 10/13 July,
£308 ($419)

4

A cloisonné enamel basin,
Jiaqing, decorated with
formal lotus scrolls
beneath *ruyi* and key-
fret bands, in red, white
and yellow on a turquoise
ground, 60.9cm (24in),
NY 12/13 Oct,
$2,310 (£1,893)

5

A cloisonné enamel vase,
early 19th cent,
enamelled with a lotus
meander in red and
white, the whole on a
turquoise ground
divided by simple foliate
bands on a dark blue
ground, 38.7cm (15½in),
L 4 May,
£748 ($1,099)

6

**A pair of cloisonné enamel
vases of hu form,** 19th
cent, of the 'Hundred
Deer' pattern, decorated
in colours on a vivid
turquoise ground, the
splayed feet with gilt-
bronze lips, the handles
in gilt-bronze with red
enamel detailing, 48.3cm
(19in), *L 4 May,*
£4,400 ($6,468)

7

**A pair of cloisonné enamel
vases,** 19th cent, each
with a songbird chasing
a butterfly on a
turquoise trellis-pattern
ground, with brass
mounts fitted as a lamp,
45.8cm (18in), *L 1/2 Nov,*
£550 ($704)

8

**A pair of cloisonné enamel
lingzhi trees,** 19th cent,
each tree of gilt-bronze
with gnarled branches
terminating in a lingzhi
cap in red, pink, blue
and green, in turquoise-
ground cloisonné
enamel jardinières,
54.7cm (21½in),
NY 16/17 Mar,
$2,310 (£1,550)

9

A cloisonné enamel vase,
decorated with exotic
butterflies amongst
flowering trees, all on a
pale turquoise ground,
65.7cm (25⅞in), *L 4 May,*
£1,430 ($2,102)

10

A cloisonné sceptre, late
18th/early 19th cent, cast
in the form of a gnarled
peach branch, the head
formed by a peach and
ruyi twig decorated in
shades of pink, red,
turquoise and green
enamels, 31.8cm (12½in),
NY 16/17 Mar,
$1,100 (£738)

11

**A pair of cloisonné enamel
camels,** the detachable
humps forming a cover
enclosing a plain
interior, its back covered
with a rug decorated on
a dark blue and green
ground, the body with
stylised dragons on a
turquoise ground, 40.6cm
(16in), *L 4 May,*
£1,980 ($2,911)

1   2   3

4

6

5

7   8   9

10   11

1
An archaic bronze wine vessel (gu), Shang Dynasty, the central bulb cast with two taotie masks, divided by grooved flanges extending beyond the lip of the rim, the patina with extensive malachite encrustation, 33.7cm (13¼in), *L 19 June*, **£18,700 ($26,741)**

2
An archaic bronze tripod vessel (li), Shang Dynasty, the greyish-green surface with encrustations of brighter green and reddish colours, 16.2cm (6⅜in), *L 11 Dec*, **£2,200 ($2,772)**

3
An archaic bronze vessel (ding), Shang Dynasty, decorated in intaglio, originally inlaid, with a band of cicada blades below a frieze of taotie masks, encrusted green patina, 18.3cm (7¼in), *L 11 Dec*, **£770 ($970)**

4
An archaic bronze ritual vessel (zun), Shang Dynasty, cast on the slightly raised central bulb with a band of deep vertical grooves between borders of crested birds, the patina with bright green encrustation and patches of blue, 24.7cm (9¾in), *NY 4 Dec*, **$15,400 (£12,941)**

5
An archaic bronze bell (zhong), Warring States, cast on either side with a panel of intaglio scrolls forming a loose taotie mask, encrusted bright green patina mottled in yellowish-brown with areas of azurite blue, 25.4cm (10in), *NY 4 Dec*, **$8,800 (£7,395)**

6
An archaic bronze ritual vessel (gu), Shang Dynasty, cast around the central zone with two taotie masks, divided and interspersed by notched vertical flanges, the patina of tones of green with some encrustation, 29.8cm (11¾in), *L 11 Dec*, **£4,950 ($6,237)**

7
A cast archaic bronze tripod vessel (liding) 11th/10th cent BC, 21.3cm (8¾in), *NY 4 Dec*, **$38,500 (£32,353)**

8
A bronze mirror, of shoudai type, Han Dynasty, cast in linear relief with a frieze of animals, silvery-black patina, 17.5cm (6⅞in), *L 19 June*, **£990 (£1,416)**

9
An archaic bronze ritual vessel (gui), Transitional Period, 11th/10th cent BC, the encrusted surface with areas of green and brownish tones, 29.2cm (11½in), *L 11 Dec*, **£2,750 ($3,465)**

10
A shoudai mirror, Eastern Han Dynasty, cast with a band of mythological animals including the Dark Warrior, the greyish patina mottled and with some encrustation, 17.5cm (6⅞in), *L 11 Dec*, **£825 ($1,040)**

11
An archaic bronze sword, 3rd/2nd cent BC, the silvery-grey patina with patches of green encrustation, 54cm (21¼in), *NY 4 Dec*, **$825 (£693)**

12
An inlaid archaic bronze box and cove (fangyi), 11th/10th cent BC, cast in intaglio with a frieze of dissolved taotie masks, inlaid in black, the silver olive-green patina with mottling and malachite encrustations on the interior with traces of azurite, 19.2cm (7½in), *L 19 June*, **£181,500 ($259,545)**

13
An archaic bronze libation vessel (jue), Shang Dynasty, the sides encircled by a frieze of two taotie masks, the patina greyish with pale olive-green encrustations, 19.3cm (7⅝in), *L 11 Dec*, **£3,190 ($4,019)**

1
A parcel-gilt silvered
bronze bowl (pan), Han
Dynasty, 16.5cm (6½in),
NY 4 Dec,
$17,600 (£14,789)

2
An octagonal bronze
mirror, Tang Dynasty,
the field recessed within
a high narrow rim
sloping to a narrow band
of trefoil lappets, the
patina of silver-grey
colour with patches of
green encrustation,
9.8cm (3⅞in), *NY 4 Dec,*
$770 (£647)

3
A barbed and lobed
bronze mirror, Tang
Dynasty, the slightly
recessed centre cast with
four florets, silver patina
with light green
encrustation, 12.4cm
(4⅞in), *NY 12 June,*
$4,070 (£2,949)

4
A bronze vessel, Han
Dynasty, the lower part
of the body encircled by
a band of incised
interlaced scrolls repeated
on the rim, extensive
reddish and green
mottling on the patina,
29.2cm (11½in), *L 19 June,*
£1,650 ($2,359)

5
An inlaid bronze vessel,
Ming Dynasty, the body
encircled by a band of
dragon motifs, raised on
legs in the form of
dragons inlaid in silver
and gold with greenish
encrustations, 16.2cm
(6⅜in), *L 1/2 Nov,*
£407 ($512)

6
A bronze censer and cover,
Ming Dynasty, 33cm (13in),
L 1/2 Nov,
£396 ($507)

7
A gilt-bronze censer, late
Ming Dynasty, mark of
Yunjian Hu Wenming
Zhi, decorated with a
frieze of winged horses
and dragons each centred
on a dragon-fish, 18cm
(7⅛in), *L 1/2 Nov,*
£1,650 ($2,112)

8
A bronze head of a
guardian, Ming Dynasty,
dark blackish-brown
patina, 49.5cm (19½in),
NY 16/17 Mar,
$8,250 (£5,537)

9
A pair of bronze figures of
dignitaries, Ming
Dynasty, the hands pierced
to receive a banner,
32cm (12½in), *L 1/2 Nov,*
£550 ($704)

10
A bronze figure of
Guanyin, Ming Dynasty,
seated on the back of a
fabulous animal, the god-
dess dressed in long robes,
an elaborate necklace and
a diadem on her head,
82.5cm (32½in), *L 1/2 Nov,*
£2,090 ($2,675)

11
A bronze figure of a six-
armed deity, 16th/17th
cent, 62.2cm (24½in),
NY 16/17 Mar,
£2,530 (£1,698)

12
A bronze figure of an
official, Ming Dynasty,
with traces of elaborate
decoration in red, blue,
white, pink and green
pigment with some gilt
highlights, 27.3cm (10¾in),
NY 16/17 Mar,
$1,210 (£812)

13
A gilt-bronze figure of a
bodhisattva, late Ming
Dynasty, the heavily
gilded deity shown seated
in *dhyanasana,*
extensive traces of red
and blue pigment, lotus
throne base, 49.9cm
(19½in), *NY 16/17 Mar,*
$3,300 (£2,215)

14
A bronze figure of
Guanyin, late Ming
Dynasty, traces of orange-
red and pale green
pigment, 114.9cm (46¼in),
NY 16/17 Mar,
$5,500 (£3,691)

1 2 3 4 5 6 7 8 9 10 11 12 13 14

1
A bronze bamboo-form
brush holder, 17th/18th
cent, of 15.8cm (6¼in),
NY 16/17 Mar,
$660 (£443)

2
A bronze incense burner,
mark of Xuande,
Guangxu, in the form of
a peach with a curled
stalk, the whole cast in
low relief with phoenix
flying amongst foliage,
58.4cm (23in), *L 4 May,*
£418 ($614)

3
A large bronze head of
Buddha, 55.9cm (22in),
L 4 May,
£440 ($647)

4
A bronze censer, mark of
Xuande, in the form of a
kylin, the head hinged
at the neck 19.1cm
(7½in), *L 4 May,*
£198 ($291)

5
A splashed gilt-bronze
censer, 17th cent, mark of
Xuande, 21.5cm (8½in),
L 1/2 Nov,
£924 ($1,164)

6
A gold-splashed bronze
kylin censer, 18th cent,
the hinged head with
pierced features and a
horn above the full
mane, with olive brown
patina splashed in gold,
8.3cm (3¼in),
NY 16/17 Mar,
$1,210 (£812)

7
A pair of gold-splashed
bronze vases, 18th cent,
57.2cm (22½in),
NY 12/13 Oct,
$15,400 (£12,623)

8
A gold-splashed bronze
vessel, 17th cent, of
archaic hu form, the
amber-coloured metal
splashed overall with
gold dappling, 30.7cm
(12in), *HK 20 Nov,*
HK $60,500
(£6,199; $8,120)

9
A gold-splashed bronze
censer, 17th cent, Xuande
mark, d 21.5cm (8½in),
NY 12/13 Oct,
$2,970 (£2,434)

10
A gold-splashed bronze
censer, 17th cent,
Xuande mark, cast with
two lion mask handles,
liberally splashed with
gold on the exterior,
19cm (7½in), *NY 12/13 Oct,*
$1,210 (£992)

11
A hunting knife and
scabbard, mark and
period of Qianlong, the
dagger with damascened
black and horn hilt,
bound at the terminals
with gilt-bronze inset
with blue glass beads,
33cm (13in), *HK 19 Nov,*
HK $60,500
(£6,136; $8,038)

12
A hunting knife and
scabbard, 18th cent, the
dagger with a steel blade
and white jade hilt,
bound with a gilt-bronze
band, the scabbard
carved with a flowering
lotus scroll, 32.5cm
(12¾in), *HK 19 Nov,*
HK $46,200
(£4,686; $6,139)

13
An engraved silver
stemcup, Tang Dynasty,
6.7cm (2⅝in), *HK 19 Nov,*
HK $176,000
(£17,850; $23,384)

14
A parcel gilt silver
circular box and cover,
Tang Dynasty, decorated
and gilt in raised relief
with a dove encircled by
three smaller birds
perched on a flowering
scroll, d 4.7cm (2in),
HK 19 Nov,
HK $63,800
(£6,471; $8,477)

15
A parcel-gilt copper hand
warmer and cover, mark
of Hu Wenming Zuo,
late Ming Dynasty,
w 16.1cm (6⅜in),
HK 19 Nov,
HK $20,900
(£2,120; $2,777)

1
A pair of Peking glass overlay vases, overlaid in red with a tiger looking over its shoulder at a bird perched on a tree beneath a dragon, 36.2cm (14¼in), *L 4 May*, £550 ($809)

2
A Peking glass overlay vase, 19th cent, each side carved through the milky white glass overlay with a bottle-form reserve on a mazarine blue ground, 19cm (7½in), *NY 16/17 Mar*, $550 (£369)

3
A glass overlay bowl, the compressed globular body decorated in dark blue with two pairs of dragons confronted on 'flaming pearls' amidst billowing clouds, 15cm (5⅞in), *L 1/2 Nov*, £330 ($415)

4
A glass overlay vase, the bubble-suffused ground decorated in high relief in ruby red with figures representing the four noble professions in a landscape, 29.2cm (11⅝in), *L 1/2 Nov*, £1,870 ($2,394)

5
A blue Peking glass vase, mark and period of Qianlong, with faceted spherical body, the glass of translucent mazarine blue, 23.5cm (9¼in), *NY 16/17 Mar*, $1,430 (£960)

6
A pair of glass overlay bowls, each with a milk-white ground decorated in dark green with a frieze of chrysanthemums and mallow, 16.2cm (6⅜in), *L 1/2 Nov*, £572 ($720)

7
A 'seal type' glass snuff bottle, Yangzhou School, the baluster body with a white ground decorated in red with long-tailed fish amidst clusters of lotus, stopper, *NY 15 Mar*, $4,400 (£3,014)

8
A multi-coloured glass overlay snuff bottle, 18th cent, the opalescent ground overlaid in orange-red on one side with sprays of magnolia, a spray of blue bamboo and a butterfly on the reverse, stopper, *L 2 July*, £330 ($449)

9
A carved glass overlay snuff bottle, 18th cent, decorated on each side, with a cruciform scroll, the terminals decorated in graduated relief, stopper, *L 2 July*, £770 ($1,047)

10
A glass overlay snuff bottle, 1750-1820, the opaque bubble-suffused ground decorated with red, on one side with the stylised character *fu*, the reverse with lu, *LA 31 Oct*, $495 (£387)

11
A glass overlay snuff bottle, 1820-80, the white ground overlaid in deep relief with a tiger looking up at a kylin, the reverse with an eagle attacking a bear, stopper, *NY 15 Mar*, $935 (£640)

12
A glass overlay snuff bottle, 1820-80, the bright blue ground overlaid in cinnabar on one side with a pair of storks, a spotted deer on the other, bats suspending endless knots on the shoulders, *NY 15 Mar*, $770 (£527)

13
A glass overlay snuff bottle, 1800-60, the bubble-suffused ground decorated in green on each side and carved with groups of precious objects, *LA 31 Oct*, $770 (£602)

1
A glass overlay snuff
bottle, 1820-60, stopper,
L 2 July,
£308 ($419)

2
A glass double overlay
snuff bottle, 1800-50, the
pink ground decorated
in green over white with
a pavilion resting on a
rocky outcrop framed by
a pine tree, stopper,
L 2 July,
£660 ($898)

3
A Peking glass snuff
bottle, 18th cent, Peking
Palace Workshops,
LA 31 Oct,
$1,320 (£1,031)

4
A hair crystal snuff bottle,
1820-80, the stone suffused
with slender black
tourmaline needles,
LA 31 Oct,
$440 (£344)

5
A glass inside-painted
snuff bottle, by Ma
Shaoxuan, signed and
dated spring month
1899, painted on front
with a flower seller on a
pale ground, stopper,
L 2 July,
£550 ($748)

6
A rock crystal inside-
painted snuff bottle, by Ye
Zhongsan the Younger,
signed and dated
autumn month 1918,
vividly painted with
small boys dancing and
playing, stopper, *L 2 July,*
£2,750 ($3,740)

7
A rock crystal inside-
painted snuff bottle, by Ye
Zhongsan the Younger,
signed and dated winter
month 1919, painted in
bright colours with the
eighteen lohan, stopper,
NY 15 Mar,
$1,870 (£1,281)

8
A glass inside-painted
snuff bottle, by Ye
Zhongsan the Younger,
signed and dated mid-
autumn 1920, painted
with a scene depicting
Zhouggui the demon-
queller, stopper, *L 2 July,*
£440 ($598)

9
A glass inside-painted
snuff bottle, by Wang
Xisan, signed and dated
winter 1977, one side
painted with a portrait
of Chu Zhuzi, the reverse
with a small pavilion in
a landscape scene,
stopper, *NY 15 Mar,*
$880 (£603)

10
A smoky crystal coin snuff
bottle, carved on the
obverse after a Spanish
eight reales piece with a
bust of Charles III, the
reverse with the arms of
Spain, stopper, *L 2 July,*
£352 ($478)

11
An enamelled snuff bottle,
Jiaqing, modelled as a
Buddhist lion embracing
its young, the mother
enamelled in soft tones
of blue with a green
mane, *LA 31 Oct,*
$1,760 (£1,375)

12
A moulded porcelain snuff
bottle, Jiaqing, decorated
with numerous dragons
passing in and out of
crested waves in pursuit
of 'flaming pearls', covered
overall with a creamy
glaze, stopper, *L 2 July,*
£638 ($868)

13
A porcelain snuff bottle,
Jiaqing, modelled as Liu
Hai standing with one
foot resting on the three-
legged toad, his turquoise
robe scattered with flowers,
stopper, *L 2 July,*
£418 ($568)

14
A moulded porcelain snuff
bottle, mark and period
of Jiaqing, decorated
with an overall design of
Buddhist lions playing,
covered with a creamy
white glaze, original
stopper, *L 2 July,*
£1,045 ($1,421)

15
A porcelain snuff bottle,
Jiaqing, enamelled
in 'famille-rose' colours,
iron-red lotus scroll
borders, an endless knot
on the base, stopper,
NY 15 Mar,
$1,210 (£829)

1   2   3

4   5   6

7   8   9

10   11   12

13   14   15

1
A porcelain snuff bottle,
mark of Qianlong,
Daoguang, imitating glass
overlay, all enamelled in
blue on a white ground,
L 2 July,
£726 ($987)

2
A biscuit porcelain snuff
bottle, by Zhang Guozhou,
signed on the base,
L 2 July,
£1,430 ($1,945)

3
A porcelain snuff bottle,
Daoguang mark and
period, *NY 15 Mar,*
$440 (£301)

4
A slip-decorated Yixing
snuff bottle, Daoguang,
L 2 July,
£1,210 ($1,645)

5
A carved coral snuff
bottle, 1800-50, the stone
of pale pinkish tone,
L 2 July,
£1,650 ($2,244)

6
A carved amber snuff
bottle, sold with two
other amber bottles,
L 2 July,
£396 ($539)

7
A bamboo snuff bottle,
the front carved with a
deer beneath a pine, the
reverse with a phoenix
and magnolia, *L 2 July,*
£330 ($449)

8
A silver snuff bottle,
decorated with a leaping
scaly dragon, *LA 31 Oct,*
$137 (£107)

9
A carved lacquer snuff
bottle, 1800-50, *L 2 July,*
£198 ($269)

10
A black lacquer inlaid
ivory snuff bottle, mark of
Qianlong, the design
picked out on a brownish-
black lacquer ground,
NY 15 Mar,
$1,650 (£1,130)

11
An ivory snuff bottle,
carved as a curled and
flattened lotus leaf,
NY 15 Mar,
£1,045 (£716)

12
A coconut snuff bottle,
with archaic calligraphy,
L 2 July,
£935 ($1,272)

13
A mother-of-pearl snuff
bottle, carved with a
cluster of lotus, the
reverse with two bats,
L 2 July,
£286 ($389)

14
A hornbill snuff bottle,
1800-50, the material of
painted deep orange
colour, *L 2 July,*
£3,300 ($4,488)

15
A 'peanut' agate snuff
bottle, *L 2 July,*
£660 ($898)

16
A silhouette agate snuff
bottle, carved with
figures in a boat,
stopper, *L 2 July,*
£1,595 ($2,169)

17
A chalcedony snuff bottle,
the pale stone with a
translucent ochre skin,
L 2 July,
£1,210 ($1,646)

18
A fossiliferous limestone
snuff bottle, the black
matrix suffused with
minute pale grey shell
markings, *NY 15 Mar,*
$660 (£452)

19
A white jade snuff bottle,
18th cent, with lotus
petals, *L 2 July,*
£440 ($598)

20
A white jade snuff bottle
of ovoid form, sold with
two other white jade
bottles, *L 2 July,*
£374 ($509)

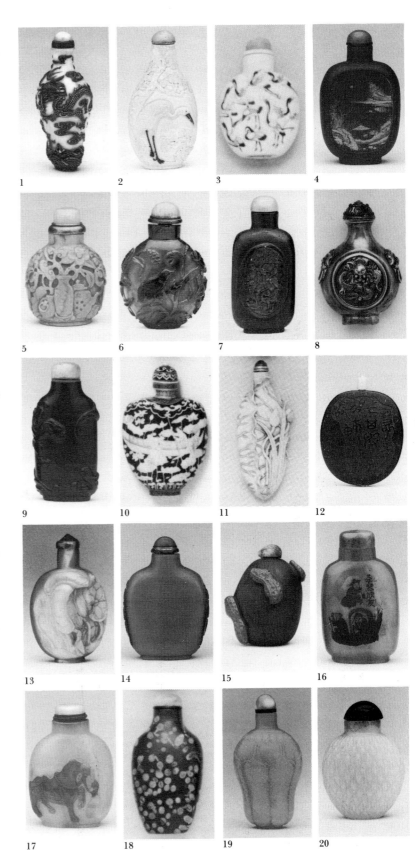

1 2 3 4

5 6 7 8

9 10 11 12

13 14 15 16

17 18 19 20

1
A huali chair-back settee, late 19th cent, each of the chair-backs centred by a marble panel and joined by a moulded shelf, w 159cm (5ft 2½in), *L 1/2 Nov,* £1,705 ($2,182)

2
A pair of huali armchairs, 2nd half 19th cent, with serpentine topped backs and the arms with carved panels, the solid seats on slightly shaped legs with carved front aprons, *L 4 May,* £550 ($809)

3
A carved hongmu horseshoe-back armchair, 19th cent, the shaped top-rail continuing to form the armrests, the seat with woven cane matting, *NY 12/13 Oct,* $990 (£811)

4
A pair of hardwood horseshoe-back armchairs, 18th cent, each with a continuous curved toprail, the seat woven with cane matting, *NY 12/13 Oct,* $18,700 (£15,328)

5
A pair of hongmu spindle-back armchairs, 2nd half 19th cent, each with slightly over-scrolled back, the panelled seat and straight legs with plain open-work apron, *L 4 May,* £748 ($1,100)

6
A set of four spindle-back hardwood armchairs, each with a shaped toprail and armrests above the 'comb' back and sides, *NY 12/13 Oct,* $3,850 ($3,156)

7
A set of six padouk chairs, 19th cent, with turned arched toprails, panelled solid seats and simple legs, joined by stretchers, *L 1/2 Nov,* £1,760 ($2,253)

8
A huali and hardwood centre table, 2nd half 18th cent, with cleated top, the frieze carved with medallions joined by a cord above a pierced apron carved with scrolls, h 87cm (34in), *L 4 May,* £6,600 ($9,702)

9
A carved wood altar table, inset with three burlwood panels, the scroll ends carved with dragon heads flanking a frieze pierced with fretwork, h 85.1cm (33½in), *NY 12/13 Oct,* $1,650 (£1,352)

10
A rosewood altar table, c.1900, the rectangular top with curved ends, above a frieze carved with stylised dragons and pierced latchwork, h 83cm (32¾in), *C 29 Mar,* £715 ($1,065)

11
A Ming-style altar table, the rectangular top with scrolled ends above a beaded apron, the wood of pale colour, h 84cm (33in), *NY 12/13 Oct,* $990 (£811)

1

2

3

4

5

6

7

8

9

10

11

1
A rosewood centre table, early 20th cent, the rectangular top slightly raised at the border and moulded with a Greek key pattern, h 84cm (33in), *C 29 Mar*, £1,210 ($1,803)

2
A burlwood inlaid low table, 19th cent, the rectangular top with a burlwood panel, h 34.3cm (13½in), *NY 12/13 Oct*, $770 (£631)

3
A carved rosewood side table, 19th cent, with beaded borders above a narrow apron pierced with flowering prunus, the splayed feet joined by an arrangement of shelves, h 78.8cm (31in), *NY 12/13 Oct*, $825 (£676)

4
A circular huali table, with panelled top, the five incurved legs divided by aprons and joined by a continuous carved pierced fretwork stretcher, h 53cm (21in), *L 4 May*, £528 ($776)

5
A pair of hongmu square stools, each with inset rattan seat, the rounded legs joined by pierced cloud band stretchers, h 51cm (19in), *L 4 May*, £704 ($1,035)

6
A marble-inlaid carved wood garden seat, of barrel shape, the circular top inset with a marble plaque above openwork *ruyi* motifs, h 41.9cm (16½in), *NY 12/13 Oct*, $357 (£293)

7
Two very similar rosewood and mother-of-pearl inlaid urn stands, early 20th cent, each with a rouge inset marble top, 53 x 51cm (21 x 20in) and 52 x 48 (20½ x 19in), *C 29 Mar*, £825 ($1,229)

8
A marble-inlaid table, the circular top inlaid with a marble panel above an apron carved with kuei dragons, together with a set of six panel-form openwork stools, table h 81.3cm (32in), *NY 12/13 Oct*, $4,400 (£3,607)

9
A six-fold carved screen in hardwood, late 19th cent, with panels of light wood carved with squirrels and grapes and figures, each fold 220 x 43cm (7ft 2½in x 17in), *L 4 May*, £2,970 ($4,366)

10
A carved and inlaid hardwood bed, the aperture for the bedding with three panelled sides, the front and back each in the form of a circle set with carved birds and flowers, the aperture 218 x 132cm (7ft 2in x 4ft 4in), *L 1/2 Nov*, £2,090 ($2,675)

11
A pair of cloisonné mounted parchment (or pigskin) chests, each hinge-lidded rectangular box with turquoise-ground mounts decorated with formal lotus scrolls, 57.2 x 66.1 x 48.2cm (22½ x 26 x 19in), *NY 12/13 Oct*, $4,950 (£4,057)

12
A carved huali dressing chest on stand, mid-19th cent, richly carved, with double hinged mirror-lined top, h 102cm (40in), w 46cm (18in), *L 1/2 Nov*, £990 ($1,247)

1

A carved ivory figure of
Shoulao, Ming Dynasty,
the immortal standing
holding a fan and a
gnarled staff, wearing a
long robe and cap, the
wispy hair and beard
incised, 27cm (10⅝in),
NY 16/17 Mar,
$1,100 (£738)

2

An ivory figure of a man,
Ming Dynasty, wearing
long-sleeved robes tied
at the waist over a long
skirt, the long face
sensitively carved below
incised hair and a court
cap, 13cm (5⅛in),
NY 16/17 Mar,
$1,155 (£775)

3

An ivory figure of
Shoulao, Ming Dynasty,
dressed in long robes
tied with a sash, the
bearded sage with a
benevolent expression,
20.3cm (8in), *NY 12/13 Oct*,
$1,210 (£992)

4

An ivory figure of maternal
Guanyin, Ming Dynasty,
the figure following the
curve of the tusk, holding
a child with a lotus bud
in one hand, traces of
black pigment on the
hair, the patina of rich
honey colour, 17.1cm
(6¾in), *NY 12/13 Oct*,
$990 (£811)

5

A carved ivory figure of
Buddha, 17th cent,
12cm (4¾in), *L 4 May*,
£660 ($970)

6

A carved ivory figure of
Liuhai, 18th cent, seated
astride the back of a
three-legged toad, a
string of cash dangling
from his hands, some
black pigment, 10.2cm
(4in), *NY 16/17 Mar*,
$880 (£591)

7

A pair of ivory figures of
an emperor and empress,
each seated on an
elaborate throne carved
with lotus petals, their
robes decorated with
dragons or phoenix,
details inlaid with hard-
stones, 48.2cm (19in),
NY 16/17 Mar,
$2,640 (£1,772)

8

A set of eight carved ivory
figures of immortals, each
standing holding his or
her attribute, the hair
and robe stained black,
22.8 to 22.3cm (9 to
8¾in), *NY 16/17 Mar*,
$2,200 (£1,477)

9

A pair of carved ivory
wristrests, 18th cent, each
showing scholars on a
footbridge, pavilions
and mountains in the
background, the pale
coloured ivory with
smooth patina, 23.2cm
(9⅛in), *HK 19 Nov*,
HK $49,500 (£5,020; $6,576)

10

An ivory wristrest, 19th
cent, carved in high
relief with immortals
and attendants gathered
below in a pavilion
setting, the reverse
carved in low relief,
29.8cm (11¾in),
NY 16/17 Mar,
$770 (£517)

11

An ivory figure of a lady,
19th cent, 29.8cm (11¾in),
NY 12/13 Oct,
$880 (£721)

12

An ivory card case, 19th
cent, intricately carved
with numerous figures
in garden settings sur-
rounded by trees, 11.2cm
(4⅜in), *NY 16/17 Mar*,
$660 (£443)

13

An ivory brushpot, 19th
cent, intricately carved
and undercut with
numerous squirrels
amidst fruiting grapevines,
the rim and base with
key-fret borders, 13.3cm
(5¼in), *NY 16/17 Mar*,
$1,705 (£1,144)

14

An ivory brushpot, 19th
cent, engraved and
stained in black with
figures in a garden
beside a lake, 16.8cm
(6⅝in), *L 4 May*,
£880 ($1,294)

15

An ivory brushpot, 17.5cm
(6⅞in), *L 4 May*,
£506 ($744)

1
A rhinoceros horn libation cup, 17th cent, pierced and carved in relief with ribbon-tied lotus flowers and leaves, the horn of reddish-brown colour, 20.2cm (8in), *L 4 May*, £572 ($841)

2
A rhinoceros horn libation cup, 17th cent, the interior carved in relief with a three-legged toad standing on a millet spray, the exterior with two rodents eating fruit, of light-brown colour toning dark at the base, 21.6cm (8½in), *L 4 May*, £1,650 ($2,425)

3
A rhinoceros horn libation cup, 18th cent, carved in the form of a large magnolia blossom, supported on a wreath of stems with buds and peach branches, the horn of reddish-brown colour, 9cm (3½in), *HK 19 Nov*, **HK $19,300 (£1,957; $2,564)**

4
A rhinoceros horn libation cup, 18th cent, carved in the form of a lotus leaf with stalk handle which extends into flowers and seed pods at the base, 13.4cm (5¼in), *C 29 Mar*, £784 ($1,115)

5
A rhinoceros horn libation cup, 17th cent, carved on the interior with vine leaves and grapes, the exterior in pierced relief with a family of rodents, of mottled brown tone, 17.3cm (6¾in), *L 4 May*, £1,100 ($1,617)

6
A rhinoceros horn libation cup, 17th cent, carved with a bouquet of fruiting vines and blossoms, the horn of deep brown colour, honey-colour towards the rim, 17.7cm (7in), *L 4 May*, £2,200 ($3,234)

7
A rhinoceros horn flower-form libation cup, 18th cent, the lobed sides carved in shallow relief with a wide band of lotus scroll and a narrow band of the ba jixiang, 8.9cm (3½in), *NY 12/13 Oct*, $1,540 (£1,262)

8
A huang huali brushpot, 17th cent, of plain cylindrical form, the wood of reddish-brown colour with fur-like graining, 16.9cm (6⅝in), *NY 16/17 Mar*, $1,045 (£701)

9
A massive pair of horn libation cups, 19th cent, each with an oval-sectioned bowl carved as a lotus flower supported on a long stem entwined with lotus buds and pods, 83.2cm (32¼in), *L 4 May*, £3,300 ($4,851)

10
A hongmu brushpot, 18th cent, the fine grained wood of reddish-brown colour, applied medallion on the base, 18.3cm (7¼in), *NY 16/17 Mar*, $1,870 (£1,255)

11
Five bamboo wristrests, each delicately carved, depicting different subjects including bamboo trees, a dragon, peony blossoms and a riverscape, 28.3, 22, 14, 11.8 and 8.9cm (11⅛, 8⅝, 5½, 4⅝ and 3½in), *HK 22 Nov*, **HK $9,350 (£979; $1,282)**

12
A Zitan brushpot, 17th cent, carved as a lotus pad cupped to form a cylindrical holder resting on a cluster of buds and leaves, with two chilong on the sides, 17.2cm (6¾in), *NY 12/13 Oct*, $880 (£721)

13
A bamboo brushpot, 17th cent, carved with a lady seated at a writing table overlooking a garden, the bamboo of rich chestnut-brown and smooth patina, 15.2cm (6in), *NY 16/17 Mar*, $3,685 (£2,473)

1
An archaic dark green jade figure of a bear, Shang Dynasty, the dark green jade calcified to a chalky white on the face and paws, *HK 19 Nov,* **HK $165,000** (£16,734; $21,922)

2
An archaic green jade bi, Western Han Dynasty, carved on both sides with wide bands separated by an incised rope-twist border, the translucent stone with fine black speckling, 20.8cm (8⅛in), *NY 12 June,* $22,000 (£15,942)

3
A Moghul green jade bowl, of rich colour with dark flecking, the vessel of oval section with flared fluted sides springing from a foot in the form of an upturned flower, 20cm (7⅞in), *M 27 June,* **FF 27,750 (£2,382; $3,246)**

4
A white jade rectangular bowl, Qianlong, decorated on each side with a panel of confronted archaistic dragons, the stone of pale greenish tone, 18.6cm (7⅜in), *NY 16/17 Mar,* $11,000 (£7,383)

5
A yellowish-green jade brushwasher, Qianlong, carved in high relief with a *chilong* climbing over the rim, the well-polished stone with some brown mottling, 10.2cm(4in), *NY 16/17 Mar,* $5,280 (£3,544)

6
A greenish-white jade cicada, 18th cent, naturalistically carved, the pale stone with russet accentuating the pods and leaf, 9cm (3½in), *HK 19 Nov,* **HK $35,200 (£3,570; $4,677)**

7
A jade tripod censer, 18th cent, the stone of even pale green colour, 10.2cm(4in), *HK 21/22 May,* **HK $11,000 (£1,012; $1,457)**

8
A celadon jade carving, Jiaqing, of a boy on a tree-craft, with his back to the upturned prow, using a stem of lingzhi as a paddle, 15.9cm (6¼in), *L 1/2 Nov,* £1,045 ($1,338)

9
A green jade bowl, late 18th/early 19th cent, raised on a square-cut ring foot, the mottled stone of bright tone, 18.4cm (7¼in), *NY 16/17 Mar,* $935 (£628)

10
A greenish-white Moghul-style jade bowl, 18th/19th cent, carved with stylised flowers encircling the rounded sides, springing from a border of overlapping petals, d 9cm (3½in), *HK 19 Nov,* **HK $52,800 (£5,355; $7,015)**

11
A white jade carving of a purse, 18th cent, incised with lines to simulate the folds, four bats and a small chrysanthemum spray on the sides, 5cm (2in), *HK 20 Nov,* **HK $14,300 (£1,465; $1,919)**

12
A green jade two-handled bowl, late 18th/19th cent, the rounded sides carved on the exterior with continuous lotus scroll, the mottled stone of dark colour with bright green and black mottling throughout, 22.8cm (9in), *NY 16/17 Mar,* $4,400 (£2,953)

13
A mottled greyish-white jade ram group, 19th cent, the ram and kids with long curved horns, the pale stone with grey and pale brown mottling and some russet colouring, 12.1cm (4¾in), *NY 16/17 Mar,* $4,180 (£2,805)

14
A pale greyish-green jade vase, 19th cent, of archaistic bronze form, carved in low relief with deer grazing beneath trees, the stone with opaque white mottling, 27.3cm (10¾in), *NY 16/17 Mar,* $1,650 (£1,107)

1
A greyish-white jade finger citron vase, 19th cent, the upright vase borne on a leafy, gnarled stem which also forms the base, carved to one side with a smaller finger citron and with a beetle, 11.1cm (4⅜in), *NY 16/17 Mar,* $1,430 (£960)

2
A jadeite brushwasher, 19th cent, carved in high pierced relief with two peaches, incorporating the bright-green inclusion, the other side with a bat in flight between the leaves, 7.6cm (3in), *L 4 May,* £550 ($809)

3
A white jade zhadou and cover, 19th cent, carved with a stylised *taotie* band beneath a wide flanged rim, 11.8cm (4⅝in), *NY 12/13 Oct,* $1,760 (£1,443)

4
A pair of spinach jade chrysanthemum bowls, each with deep flared sides carved with concentric rows of petal flutes, the stone of mossy green colour, d 19.7cm (7¾in), *NY 12/13 Oct,* $2,200 (£1,803)

5
A spinach jade bronze-form vase and cover, the vase of flattened *hu* shape carved in low relief with stylised bird motifs, the stone of dark green colour with light green veining, 40cm (15¾in), *NY 12/13 Oct,* $1,650 (£1,352)

6
A spinach green tripod censer and cover, carved in relief with *taotie* masks amidst floral scrolls, the stone of deep green colour with black flecking, 15.2cm (6in), *NY 12/13 Oct,* $1,320 (£1,082)

7
A spinach jade censer and cover, carved with floral scrolls, the jade of dark green colour with paler green mottling, 33cm (13in), *NY 12/13 Oct,* $1,210 (£992)

8
A white jade tripod censer and cover, the handles carved and pierced as ferocious animals' heads, the stone slightly tinted, h 21.7cm (8½in), *L 1/2 Nov,* £5,280 ($6,758)

9
A spinach green jade plaque, of rectangular form, carved in deep undercut relief with a scene of two of the Eight Immortals, the stone of pale green with darker green mottling, 61.6 x 36.8cm (24¼ x 14½in), *NY 12/13 Oct,* $3,960 (£3,246)

10
A jadeite vase and cover, carved in high and pierced relief with two dragons chasing a 'flaming pearl', the stone of mottled pale green and lavender tones with darker suffusions, 27.6cm (10⅞in), *L 1/2 Nov,* £1,650 ($2,112)

11
A spinach green jade vase and phoenix group, elaborately carved as a bronze-form vase and cover, a link chain attached to the cover of the vase, 22.9cm (9in), *NY 16/17 Mar,* $1,430 (£960)

12
A white jade figure of a pony, resting recumbant with limbs tucked into the sides, 11.3cm (4½in), *L 4 May,* £440 ($647)

13
A pair of jadeite carvings, each of two crested water-birds wading through rippling water, the stone of pale crystalline tone suffused with green and lavender markings, 11.4cm (4½in), *L 4 May,* £572 ($841)

14
A dark green jade figure of a water buffalo, with curved horns and long incised tail flicked over the haunches, stone with some opaque buff mottling, 29.2cm (11½in), *NY 12/13 Oct,* $2,420 (£1,984)

1
A pair of jade inset cinnabar lacquer jardinières, carved with panels of lotus on a wan-fret ground enclosing reserves applied with white jade plaques, 27cm (10⅝in), *NY 12/13 Oct*, $660 (£541)

2
A Ming four-tiered cinnabar box and cover, carved with an overall pattern of fruiting lichee branches, each fruit incised with floral wan-fret and diaper motifs, h 8.9cm (3½in), *HK 19 Nov*, **HK $44,000 (£4,462; $5,845)**

3
A Ming cinnabar lacquer dish, 16th cent, carved with a spray of three large peony blossoms, the underside with stylised foliate scrolls, d 18.9cm (7⅜in), *HK 19 Nov*, **HK $66,000 (£6,694; $8,769)**

4
A soapstone figure of Lohan, 17th/18th cent, seated holding an alms bowl in his left hand, the stone of mottled reddish tones, the details finely incised, 6.4cm (2½in), *L 4 May*, **£440 ($647)**

5
A Ming cinnabar lacquer four-tiered box and cover, 16th cent, carved along the side with large peony and plum blossoms, the cover with a team of an immortal and his scholar and attendants, h 16cm (6¼in), *HK 19 Nov*, **HK $28,600 (£2,900; $3,799)**

6
A simulated cinnabar lacquer box and cover, Qianlong, of *ruyi* head section, the cover moulded with two gilt-edged interlaced *ruyi* heads enclosing crested waves, covered overall in a red glaze, 13.3cm (5¼in), *HK 20 Nov*, **HK $17,600 (£1,485; $1,946)**

7
A soapstone figure of Lohan, 18th cent, the immortal holding a *ruyi* sceptre in his hand, the stone of pale yellowish-green with suffusions of amber, 19.5cm (7⅝in), *HK 19 Nov*, **HK $28,600 (£2,901; $3,800)**

8
A soapstone figure of Guanyin, the deity wearing long robes bared at the chest to reveal a lotus necklace, the stone of pale greenish-yellow with grey mottling, 36.9cm (14½in), *NY 12/13 Oct*, $715 (£586)

9
A lapis lazuli spill vase, 19th cent, carved in the form of a finger citron with a pomegranate on one side and a peach on the other, the details lightly engraved, 17.2cm (6¾in), *L 4 May*, £594 ($873)

10
A chalcedony pendant, 19th cent, the stone of varying colour, from brown to grey, pierced and carved as a finger citron attached to a leafy branch, 5.7cm (2¼in), *L 4 May*, £231 ($339)

11
A tourmaline pendant, 19th cent, carved in pierced relief on each side with lingzhi attached to scrolled stems, the metal of burgundy colour, 3.8 (1½in), *L 4 May*, £682 ($1,003)

1

2

3

5

4

8

6 7

9 10 11

Index

Note: page numbers precede illustration numbers